GEOMETRY

About *Geometry*

In *Geometry*, you will develop reasoning and problem solving skills as you study topics such as congruence and similarity, and apply properties of lines, triangles, quadrilaterals, and circles. You will also develop problem solving skills by using length, perimeter, area, circumference, surface area, and volume to solve real-world problems.

In addition to its geometry content, *Geometry* includes numerous examples and exercises involving algebra, data analysis, and probability. These math topics often appear on standardized tests, so maintaining your familiarity with them is important. To help you prepare for standardized tests, *Geometry* provides instruction and practice on standardized test questions in a variety of formats—multiple choice, short response, extended response, and so on. Technology support for both learning geometry and preparing for standardized tests is available at classzone.com.

GEOMETRY

Ron Larson
Laurie Boswell
Timothy D. Kanold
Lee Stiff

McDougal Littell
A DIVISION OF HOUGHTON MIFFLIN COMPANY
Evanston, Illinois • Boston • Dallas

ISBN-13: 978-0-6185-9540-2
ISBN-10: 0-618-59540-6   10 11 12 13 14 0914 13 12 11 10 09

Internet Web Site: http://www.mcdougallittell.com

About the Authors

Ron Larson is a professor of mathematics at Penn State University at Erie, where he has taught since receiving his Ph.D. in mathematics from the University of Colorado. Dr. Larson is well known as the author of a comprehensive program for mathematics that spans middle school, high school, and college courses. Dr. Larson's numerous professional activities keep him in constant touch with the needs of teachers and supervisors. He closely follows developments in mathematics standards and assessment.

Laurie Boswell is a mathematics teacher at The Riverside School in Lyndonville, Vermont, and has taught mathematics at all levels, elementary through college. A recipient of the Presidential Award for Excellence in Mathematics Teaching, she was also a Tandy Technology Scholar. She served on the NCTM Board of Directors (2002–2005), and she speaks frequently at regional and national conferences on topics related to instructional strategies and course content.

Timothy D. Kanold is the superintendent of Adlai E. Stevenson High School District 125 in Lincolnshire, Illinois. Dr. Kanold served as a teacher and director of mathematics for 17 years prior to becoming superintendent. He is the recipient of the Presidential Award for Excellence in Mathematics and Science Teaching, and a past president of the Council for Presidential Awardees in Mathematics. Dr. Kanold is a frequent speaker at national and international mathematics meetings.

Lee Stiff is a professor of mathematics education in the College of Education and Psychology of North Carolina State University at Raleigh and has taught mathematics at the high school and middle school levels. He served on the NCTM Board of Directors and was elected President of NCTM for the years 2000–2002. He is a recipient of the W. W. Rankin Award for Excellence in Mathematics Education presented by the North Carolina Council of Teachers of Mathematics.

Advisers and Reviewers

Curriculum Advisers and Reviewers

Vincent J. Bondi
Mathematics Department Chair
Radnor High School
Radnor, PA

Anne Papakonstantinou
Director, School Mathematics Project
Rice University
Houston, TX

John Fishpaw
Mathematics Department Chair
Austin Academy for Excellence
Garland, TX

Richard Parr
Director of Educational Technology,
  School Mathematics Project
Rice University
Houston, TX

Matthew C. Hill
Mathematics Teacher
Plains High School
Plains, TX

Katherine G. Petersen
Mathematics Teacher
Hammond School
Columbia, SC

Patrick Hopfensperger
Mathematics Specialist
Homestead High School
Mequon, WI

Alice Rau
Mathematics Teacher
Francis Scott Key High School
Union Bridge, MD

Robin Jenkins
Mathematics Teacher
Hillcrest High School
Springfield, MO

Diane Sorrels
Mathematics Department Chair
  and Teacher
Robert E. Lee High School
Tyler, TX

Ohio Panel

Todd Brenn
Mathematics Teacher
Roosevelt High School
Kent, OH

Sinetta Maul
Mathematics Teacher
Ashland High School
Ashland, OH

Cathy J. Miller
Mathematics Teacher
Copley High School
Copley, OH

Jeff Neuman
Mathematics Teacher
Brunswick High School
Brunswick, OH

Bruce Olson
Mathematics Teacher
Canal Winchester High School
Canal Winchester, OH

Julia Pfeil
Mathematics Teacher
Colonel White High School
  for the Arts
Dayton, OH

Carlo T. Trafficante
Mathematics Teacher
Austintown Fitch High School
Austintown, OH

Andrew Tripoulas
Mathematics Teacher
Warren G. Harding
  High School
Warren, OH

Vicki L. White
Mathematics Teacher
Strongsville High School
Strongsville, OH

Texas Panel

Nancy Arroyo
Mathematics Department Chair
Riverside High School
El Paso, TX

Juan A. Cardenas
Mathematics Department Chair
Sam Houston High School
San Antonio, TX

Rita Hines Freeman
Mathematics Teacher
Townview Science and Engineering
  Magnet High School
Dallas, TX

Whitney Hendriex
Mathematics Specialist
Lee High School
Midland, TX

Betsy A. Norris
Mathematics Teacher
Southwest High School
Ft. Worth, TX

Janell O'Loughlin
Mathematics Department Chair
Pasadena High School
Pasadena, TX

Shauna Suggs
Mathematics Teacher
R.L. Turner High School
Carrollton, TX

Richard Treviño
Mathematics Teacher
Martin High School
Laredo, TX

Patricia Winkler
Mathematics Teacher and
  Instructional Technologist
Michael E. DeBakey High School
Houston, TX

Segment Addition Postulate, p. 14
$$AC = AB + BC$$

Essentials of Geometry

Chapter 1 Highlights

PROBLEM SOLVING
- Mixed Review of Problem Solving, 23, 58
- Multiple Representations, 41, 55, 57
- Multi-Step Problems, 8, 14, 23, 46, 54, 55, 58
- Using Alternative Methods, 57
- Real-World Problem Solving Examples, 10, 15, 27, 36, 44, 51, 65

★ ASSESSMENT
- Standardized Test Practice Examples, 18, 50
- Multiple Choice, 6, 13, 20, 29, 39, 44, 46, 53
- Short Response/Extended Response, 7, 12, 14, 20, 22, 23, 30, 32, 40, 47, 54, 55, 58, 66
- Writing/Open-Ended, 5, 12, 19, 23, 28, 38, 44, 52, 58

TECHNOLOGY
At classzone.com:
- Animated Geometry, 1, 3, 14, 21, 25, 43, 52
- @Home Tutor, xxii, 7, 13, 21, 31, 40, 46, 48, 54, 60
- Online Quiz, 8, 14, 22, 32, 41, 47, 56
- Animated Algebra (Algebra Review), 65
- State Test Practice, 23, 58, 69

Properties of Congruence, p. 115
$\overline{AB} \cong \overline{CD}$

Reasoning and Proof

Chapter 2 Highlights

PROBLEM SOLVING

- **Mixed Review of Problem Solving,** 103, 132
- **Multiple Representations,** 77, 111, 120
- **Multi-Step Problems,** 85, 102, 103, 110, 119, 130, 132
- **Using Alternative Methods,** 120
- **Real-World Problem Solving Examples,** 74, 89, 106, 115

★ ASSESSMENT

- **Standardized Test Practice Examples,** 74, 127
- **Multiple Choice,** 75, 76, 83, 90, 99, 100, 109, 116, 128
- **Short Response/Extended Response,** 76, 78, 84, 92, 101, 102, 103, 110, 117, 119, 128, 130, 132, 140
- **Writing/Open-Ended,** 75, 82, 84, 90, 99, 100, 108, 109, 116, 127, 129, 132

⌖ TECHNOLOGY

At *classzone.com*:
- **Animated Geometry,** 71, 72, 81, 88, 97, 106, 119, 125
- **@Home Tutor,** 70, 77, 84, 91, 101, 110, 118, 123, 129, 134
- **Online Quiz,** 78, 85, 93, 102, 111, 119, 131
- **Animated Algebra,** 139
- **State Test Practice,** 103, 132, 143

Applying Slope, p. 174
Slope $= \dfrac{41}{80}$

Parallel and Perpendicular Lines

Chapter 3 Highlights

PROBLEM SOLVING
• **Mixed Review of Problem Solving,** 170, 200
• **Multiple Representations,** 174, 177, 188
• **Multi-Step Problems,** 166, 168, 170, 177, 186, 200
• **Using Alternative Methods,** 188
• **Real-World Problem Solving Examples,** 148, 156, 162, 164, 174, 182, 183, 193, 207

★ **ASSESSMENT**
• **Standardized Test Practice Example,** 173
• **Multiple Choice,** 151, 157, 158, 166, 176, 184, 185, 195, 208
• **Short Response/Extended Response,** 152, 158, 159, 166, 168, 169, 170, 176, 178, 187, 194, 196, 200
• **Writing/Open-Ended,** 150, 151, 157, 165, 170, 175, 184, 195, 200

⌖ **TECHNOLOGY**
At *classzone.com*:
• **Animated Geometry,** 145, 148, 155, 163, 174, 181
• **@Home Tutor,** 144, 151, 153, 159, 167, 176, 179, 186, 196, 202
• **Online Quiz,** 152, 160, 169, 178, 187, 197
• **Animated Algebra,** 207
• **State Test Practice,** 170, 200, 211

Indirect Measurement, p. 257
$\triangle MLK \cong \triangle MPN$

Congruent Triangles

Chapter 4 Highlights

PROBLEM SOLVING

- Mixed Review of Problem Solving, 248, 280
- Multiple Representations, 232
- Multi-Step Problems, 223, 231, 248, 269, 280
- Using Alternative Methods, 232
- Real-World Problem Solving Examples, 220, 226, 236, 242, 251, 257, 266, 274

★ ASSESSMENT

- Standardized Test Practice Examples, 235, 251
- Multiple Choice, 222, 223, 229, 237, 243, 246, 253, 260, 261, 268, 279, 288
- Short Response/Extended Response, 221, 224, 230, 231, 238, 248, 253, 254, 262, 267, 268, 270, 278, 280
- Writing/Open-Ended, 221, 228, 229, 230, 243, 244, 248, 252, 259, 267, 276, 277, 278, 280

🖉 TECHNOLOGY

At classzone.com:
- Animated Geometry, 215, 234, 242, 250, 256, 257, 274
- @Home Tutor, 214, 223, 230, 238, 245, 247, 254, 261, 269, 278, 282
- Online Quiz, 224, 231, 239, 246, 255, 263, 270, 279
- Animated Algebra, 287
- State Test Practice, 248, 280, 291

Inequalities in Triangles, p. 336
$150° > 135°$

Relationships within Triangles

Chapter 5 Highlights

PROBLEM SOLVING
• Mixed Review of Problem Solving, 317, 342
• Multiple Representations, 302
• Multi-Step Problems, 301, 317, 342
• Using Alternative Methods, 302
• Real-World Problem Solving Examples, 295, 305, 311, 329, 336, 349

★ ASSESSMENT
• Standardized Test Practice Examples, 320, 329
• Multiple Choice, 299, 307, 314, 322, 331, 332, 339
• Short Response/Extended Response, 300, 308, 315, 317, 323, 324, 332, 333, 334, 339, 340, 342, 350
• Writing/Open-Ended, 298, 306, 313, 317, 322, 331, 338, 342

⬈ TECHNOLOGY
At classzone.com:
• Animated Geometry, 293, 296, 304, 312, 321, 330, 336
• @Home Tutor, 292, 300, 308, 315, 324, 327, 333, 340, 344
• Online Quiz, 301, 309, 316, 325, 334, 341
• Animated Algebra, 349
• State Test Practice, 317, 342, 353

Applying Similar Triangles, p. 394
$$\frac{66 \text{ in.}}{7 \text{ ft}} = \frac{x \text{ in.}}{102 \text{ ft}}$$

Similarity

Chapter 6 Highlights

PROBLEM SOLVING

- .Mixed Review of Problem Solving, 380, 416
- .Multiple Representations, 363, 378, 404
- .Multi-Step Problems, 362, 378, 380, 385, 394, 402, 414, 416
- .Using Alternative Methods, 404
- .Real-World Problem Solving Examples, 357, 359, 365, 366, 374, 390, 398, 410

★ ASSESSMENT

- .Standardized Test Practice Examples, 383, 411
- .Multiple Choice, 361, 368, 376, 377, 384, 385, 392, 400, 401, 412, 413
- .Short Response/Extended Response, 361, 363, 377, 379, 380, 386, 387, 394, 402, 403, 413, 414, 415, 416, 424
- .Writing/Open-Ended, 360, 367, 376, 380, 384, 385, 391, 394, 400, 412, 414, 416

TECHNOLOGY

At classzone.com:
- .Animated Geometry, 355, 365, 375, 391, 394, 407, 414
- .@Home Tutor, 354, 362, 368, 378, 386, 393, 396, 402, 414, 418
- .Online Quiz, 363, 370, 379, 387, 395, 403, 415
- .Animated Algebra, 423
- .State Test Practice, 380, 416, 427

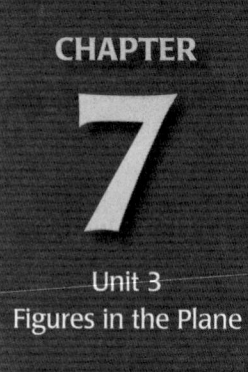

CHAPTER 7

Unit 3
Figures in the Plane

Angle of Elevation, p. 475

$$\sin 21° = \frac{\text{opp.}}{\text{hyp.}}$$

Right Triangles and Trigonometry

Chapter 7 Highlights

PROBLEM SOLVING

- Mixed Review of Problem Solving, 465, 492
- Multiple Representations, 439, 480, 481, 488
- Multi-Step Problems, 438, 445, 456, 463, 465, 471, 479, 488, 492
- Using Alternative Methods, 481
- Real-World Problem Solving Examples, 434, 443, 450, 452, 459, 460, 468, 474, 475, 476, 485

★ ASSESSMENT

- Standardized Test Practice Examples, 434, 458
- Multiple Choice, 437, 438, 444, 454, 461, 462, 470, 478, 486, 487, 500
- Short Response/Extended Response, 438, 439, 446, 447, 455, 456, 463, 464, 465, 471, 472, 479, 487, 488, 492
- Writing/Open-Ended, 436, 444, 445, 453, 461, 462, 469, 477, 478, 485, 487, 488

🧭 TECHNOLOGY

At classzone.com:

- Animated Geometry, 431, 434, 442, 450, 460, 462, 475
- @Home Tutor, 430, 438, 440, 445, 455, 463, 471, 479, 487, 494
- Online Quiz, 439, 447, 456, 464, 472, 480, 489
- Animated Algebra, 499
- State Test Practice, 465, 492, 503

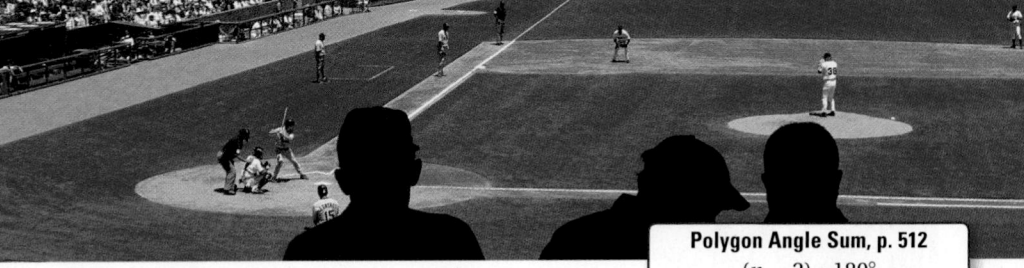

Polygon Angle Sum, p. 512
$(n - 2) \cdot 180°$

Quadrilaterals

Animated Geometry
classzone.com
Activities... 505, 509, 519, 527, 535, 545, 551, 553

Chapter 8 Highlights

PROBLEM SOLVING

- **Mixed Review of Problem Solving,** 532, 558
- **Multiple Representations,** 513, 530
- **Multi-Step Problems,** 512, 532, 539, 556, 558
- **Using Alternative Methods,** 530
- **Real-World Problem Solving Examples,** 510, 517, 523, 524, 536, 543, 545

★ ASSESSMENT

- **Standardized Test Practice Examples,** 509, 517, 553
- **Multiple Choice,** 511, 518, 519, 527, 538, 546, 547, 554, 566
- **Short Response/Extended Response,** 511, 513, 519, 526, 529, 532, 538, 540, 547, 548, 556, 558
- **Writing/Open-Ended,** 510, 518, 520, 526, 537, 546, 554, 558

⊘ TECHNOLOGY

At classzone.com:
- **Animated Geometry,** 505, 509, 519, 527, 535, 545, 551, 553
- **@Home Tutor,** 504, 512, 514, 520, 528, 539, 541, 548, 556, 560
- **Online Quiz,** 513, 521, 529, 540, 549, 557
- **Animated Algebra,** 565
- **State Test Practice,** 532, 558, 569

Identifying Transformations, p. 595
$(a, b) \rightarrow (a, -b)$

Properties of Transformations

Animated Geometry
classzone.com Activities... 571, 582, 590, 599, 602, 611, 619, 626

Chapter 9 Highlights

PROBLEM SOLVING

- Mixed Review of Problem Solving, 597, 634
- Multiple Representations, 606
- Multi-Step Problems, 577, 579, 586, 597, 605, 615, 624, 631, 634
- Using Alternative Methods, 606
- Real-World Problem Solving Examples, 575, 583, 591

★ ASSESSMENT

- Standardized Test Practice Examples, 601, 621
- Multiple Choice, 576, 584, 585, 593, 603, 613, 622, 630
- Short Response/Extended Response, 578, 586, 594, 596, 597, 603, 605, 614, 623, 630, 634, 642
- Writing/Open-Ended, 576, 584, 585, 593, 597, 602, 611, 613, 621, 623, 629, 630, 631, 634

⊘ TECHNOLOGY

At classzone.com:
- Animated Geometry, 571, 582, 590, 599, 602, 611, 617, 619, 626
- @Home Tutor, 570, 578, 586, 595, 604, 607, 613, 623, 631, 633, 636
- Online Quiz, 579, 587, 596, 605, 615, 624, 632
- Animated Algebra, 641
- State Test Practice, 597, 634, 645

CHAPTER

10

Unit 4
Circles and Measurement

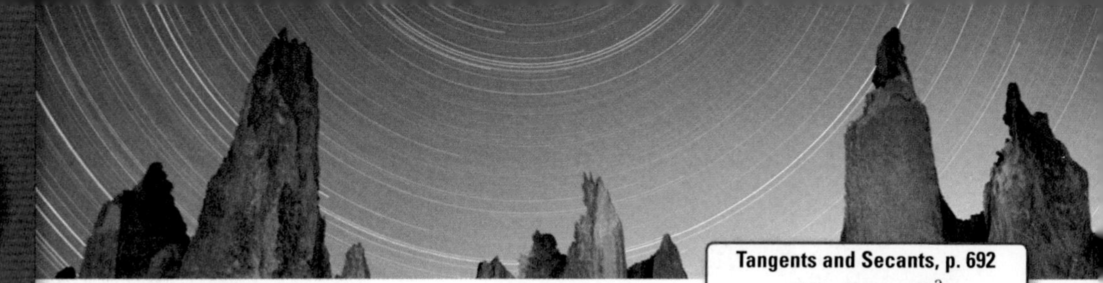

Tangents and Secants, p. 692
$DC \cdot DB = AD^2$

Properties of Circles

Chapter 10 Highlights

PROBLEM SOLVING

- **Mixed Review of Problem Solving,** 687, 706
- **Multiple Representations,** 696
- **Multi-Step Problems,** 669, 687, 706
- **Using Alternative Methods,** 696
- **Real-World Problem Solving Examples,** 660, 665, 674, 682, 692, 701

★ ASSESSMENT

- **Standardized Test Practice Examples,** 673, 690
- **Multiple Choice,** 656, 662, 667, 677, 683, 693, 702, 703, 714
- **Short Response/Extended Response,** 657, 662, 663, 678, 684, 685, 687, 694, 695, 704, 706
- **Writing/Open-Ended,** 655, 661, 667, 668, 669, 676, 678, 683, 684, 687, 692, 702

TECHNOLOGY

At classzone.com:

- **Animated Geometry,** 649, 655, 661, 671, 682, 691, 701
- **@Home Tutor,** 648, 657, 663, 669, 677, 685, 688, 694, 703, 704, 708
- **Online Quiz,** 658, 663, 670, 679, 686, 695, 705
- **Animated Algebra,** 713
- **State Test Practice,** 687, 706, 717

Arc Length, p. 749

$$2(84.39) + 2\left(\frac{1}{2} \cdot 2\pi \cdot 36.8\right)$$

Measuring Length and Area

Animated Geometry
classzone.com

Chapter 11 Highlights

Volume of Cylinders, p. 825
$$V = Bh = \pi r^2 h$$

Surface Area and Volume of Solids

Animated Geometry
classzone.com
Activities... 791, 795, 805, 821, 825, 833, 841, 852

Chapter 12 Highlights

PROBLEM SOLVING

- Mixed Review of Problem Solving, 818, 855
- Multiple Representations, 826, 835, 853
- Multi-Step Problems, 800, 809, 816, 818, 824, 835, 844, 852, 855
- Using Alternative Methods, 826
- Real-World Problem Solving Examples, 796, 805, 813, 822, 831, 840, 848, 849

★ ASSESSMENT

- Standardized Test Practice Examples, 813, 839
- Multiple Choice, 799, 807, 808, 815, 822, 824, 832, 833, 842, 843, 850, 851, 862
- Short Response/Extended Response, 800, 808, 809, 816, 818, 825, 834, 844, 853, 855
- Writing/Open-Ended, 798, 806, 814, 818, 822, 832, 842, 850, 852

🖝 TECHNOLOGY

At classzone.com:

- Animated Geometry, 791, 795, 805, 821, 825, 833, 841, 852
- @Home Tutor, 790, 800, 808, 816, 824, 834, 837, 844, 852, 857
- Online Quiz, 801, 809, 817, 825, 836, 845, 854
- State Test Practice, 818, 855, 865

Contents
of Student Resources

Using Your Textbook

Your textbook contains many resources that you can use for reference when you are studying or doing your homework.

IN EVERY CHAPTER

BIG IDEAS The second page of every chapter includes a list of important ideas developed in the chapter. More information about these ideas appears in the Chapter Summary page at the end of the chapter.

POSTULATES AND THEOREMS The Postulate and Theorem notebook displays present geometric properties you will use in reasoning about figures. You may want to copy these statements into your notes.

KEY CONCEPTS The Key Concept notebook displays present main ideas of the lesson. You may want to copy these ideas into your notes.

VOCABULARY New words and review words are listed in a column on the first page of every lesson. Vocabulary terms appear highlighted and in bold print within the lesson. A list of vocabulary appears in the Chapter Review at the end of each chapter.

MIXED REVIEW Every lesson ends with Mixed Review exercises. These exercises help you review earlier lessons and include exercises to prepare you for the next lesson. Page references with the exercises point you to the lessons being reviewed.

STUDENT RESOURCES AT THE BACK OF THE BOOK

SKILLS REVIEW HANDBOOK Use the Skills Review Handbook topics on pages 869–895 to review material learned in previous courses.

EXTRA PRACTICE Use the Extra Practice on pages 896–919 for more exercises or to review a chapter before a test.

TABLES Refer to the tables on pages 920–925 for information about mathematical symbols, measures, formulas, squares, and trigonometric ratios.

POSTULATES AND THEOREMS Refer to pages 926–931 for a complete list of all postulates and theorems presented in the book.

ADDITIONAL PROOFS Refer to pages 932–938 for longer proofs of some of the theorems presented in the book.

GLOSSARY Use the English-Spanish Glossary on pages 939–980 to see definitions in English and Spanish, as well as examples illustrating vocabulary.

INDEX Look up items in the alphabetical Index on pages 981–1000 to find where a particular math topic is covered in the book.

WORKED-OUT SOLUTIONS In each lesson, exercises identified by a red circle have complete worked-out solutions starting on page WS1. These provide a model for what a full solution should include.

SELECTED ANSWERS Use the Selected Answers starting on page SA1 to check your work.

1 Essentials of Geometry

Before

In previous courses, you learned the following skills, which you'll use in Chapter 1: finding measures, evaluating expressions, and solving equations.

Prerequisite Skills

VOCABULARY CHECK

Copy and complete the statement.

1. The distance around a rectangle is called its __?__, and the distance around a circle is called its __?__.

2. The number of square units covered by a figure is called its __?__.

SKILLS AND ALGEBRA CHECK

Evaluate the expression. *(Review p. 870 for 1.2, 1.3, 1.7.)*

3. $|4 - 6|$ 4. $|3 - 11|$ 5. $|-4 + 5|$ 6. $|-8 - 10|$

Evaluate the expression when $x = 2$. *(Review p. 870 for 1.3–1.6.)*

7. $5x$ 8. $20 - 8x$ 9. $-18 + 3x$ 10. $-5x - 4 + 2x$

Solve the equation. *(Review p. 875 for 1.2–1.7.)*

11. $274 = -2z$ 12. $8x + 12 = 60$ 13. $2y - 5 + 7y = -32$

14. $6p + 11 + 3p = -7$ 15. $8m - 5 = 25 - 2m$ 16. $-2n + 18 = 5n - 24$

@HomeTutor Prerequisite skills practice at classzone.com

In Chapter 1, you will apply the big ideas listed below and reviewed in the Chapter Summary on page 59. You will also use the key vocabulary listed below.

Big Ideas

① Describing geometric figures
② Measuring geometric figures
③ Understanding equality and congruence

KEY VOCABULARY

- undefined terms, *p. 2*
  point, line, plane
- defined terms, *p. 3*
- line segment, endpoints, *p. 3*
- ray, opposite rays, *p. 3*
- postulate, axiom, *p. 9*

- congruent segments, *p. 11*
- midpoint, *p. 15*
- segment bisector, *p. 15*
- acute, right, obtuse, straight angles, *p. 25*
- congruent angles, *p. 26*
- angle bisector, *p. 28*

- linear pair, *p. 37*
- vertical angles, *p. 37*
- polygon, *p. 42*
- convex, concave, *p. 42*
- *n*-gon, *p. 43*
- equilateral, equiangular, regular, *p. 43*

Geometric figures can be used to represent real-world situations. For example, you can show a climber's position along a stretched rope by a point on a line segment.

Animated Geometry

The animation illustrated below for Exercise 35 on page 14 helps you answer this question: How far must a climber descend to reach the bottom of a cliff?

Your goal is to find the distance from a climber's position to the bottom of a cliff.

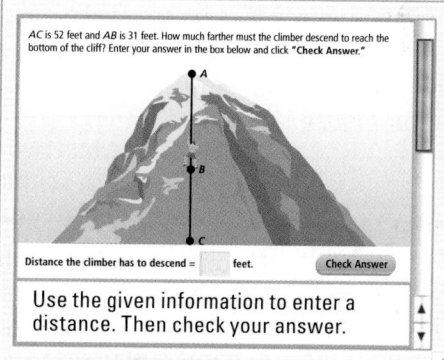

AC is 52 feet and *AB* is 31 feet. How much farther must the climber descend to reach the bottom of the cliff? Enter your answer in the box below and click "Check Answer."

Distance the climber has to descend = ____ feet.   Check Answer

Use the given information to enter a distance. Then check your answer.

Animated **Geometry** at classzone.com

Other animations for Chapter 1: pages 3, 21, 25, 43, and 52

1.1 Identify Points, Lines, and Planes

Before	You studied basic concepts of geometry.
Now	You will name and sketch geometric figures.
Why	So you can use geometry terms in the real world, as in Ex. 13.

Key Vocabulary
• undefined terms
  point, line, plane
• collinear points
• coplanar points
• defined terms
• line segment
• endpoints
• ray
• opposite rays
• intersection

In the diagram of a football field, the positions of players are represented by *points*. The yard lines suggest *lines*, and the flat surface of the playing field can be thought of as a *plane*.

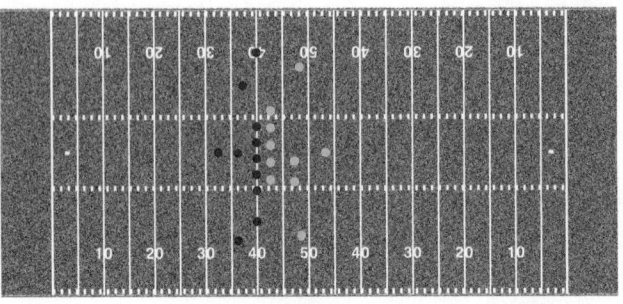

In geometry, the words *point*, *line*, and *plane* are **undefined terms**. These words do not have formal definitions, but there is agreement about what they mean.

KEY CONCEPT   *For Your Notebook*

Undefined Terms

Point A **point** has no dimension. It is represented by a dot.

    A
    •

    point *A*

Line A **line** has one dimension. It is represented by a line with two arrowheads, but it extends without end.

Through any two points, there is exactly one line. You can use any two points on a line to name it.

    line *ℓ*, line *AB* ($\overleftrightarrow{AB}$),
    or line *BA* ($\overleftrightarrow{BA}$)

Plane A **plane** has two dimensions. It is represented by a shape that looks like a floor or a wall, but it extends without end.

Through any three points not on the same line, there is exactly one plane. You can use three points that are not all on the same line to name a plane.

    plane *M* or plane *ABC*

Collinear points are points that lie on the same line. **Coplanar points** are points that lie in the same plane.

EXAMPLE 1   Name points, lines, and planes

a. Give two other names for $\overleftrightarrow{PQ}$ and for plane R.

b. Name three points that are collinear.
Name four points that are coplanar.

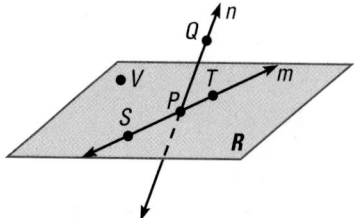

Solution

a. Other names for $\overleftrightarrow{PQ}$ are $\overleftrightarrow{QP}$ and line n.
Other names for plane R are plane SVT and plane PTV.

b. Points S, P, and T lie on the same line, so they are collinear. Points S, P, T, and V lie in the same plane, so they are coplanar.

Animated Geometry at classzone.com

✓ **GUIDED PRACTICE**   for Example 1

1. Use the diagram in Example 1. Give two other names for $\overleftrightarrow{ST}$. Name a point that is *not* coplanar with points Q, S, and T.

DEFINED TERMS In geometry, terms that can be described using known words such as *point* or *line* are called **defined terms**.

KEY CONCEPT   *For Your Notebook*

Defined Terms: Segments and Rays

Line AB (written as $\overleftrightarrow{AB}$) and points A and B are used here to define the terms below.

line

Segment The **line segment** AB, or **segment** AB, (written as $\overline{AB}$) consists of the **endpoints** A and B and all points on $\overleftrightarrow{AB}$ that are between A and B. Note that $\overline{AB}$ can also be named $\overline{BA}$.

segment
endpoint   endpoint
A   B

Ray The **ray** AB (written as $\overrightarrow{AB}$) consists of the endpoint A and all points on $\overleftrightarrow{AB}$ that lie on the same side of A as B.

Note that $\overrightarrow{AB}$ and $\overrightarrow{BA}$ are different rays.

ray
endpoint
A   B

endpoint
A   B

If point C lies on $\overleftrightarrow{AB}$ between A and B, then $\overrightarrow{CA}$ and $\overrightarrow{CB}$ are **opposite rays**.

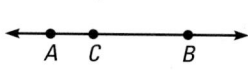

Segments and rays are collinear if they lie on the same line. So, opposite rays are collinear. Lines, segments, and rays are coplanar if they lie in the same plane.

EXAMPLE 2 **Name segments, rays, and opposite rays**

a. Give another name for $\overline{GH}$.

b. Name all rays with endpoint J. Which of these rays are opposite rays?

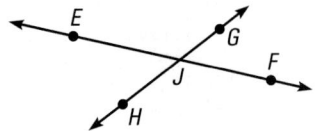

AVOID ERRORS

In Example 2, $\overrightarrow{JG}$ and $\overrightarrow{JF}$ have a common endpoint, but are not collinear. So they are *not* opposite rays.

Solution

a. Another name for $\overline{GH}$ is $\overline{HG}$.

b. The rays with endpoint J are $\overrightarrow{JE}$, $\overrightarrow{JG}$, $\overrightarrow{JF}$, and $\overrightarrow{JH}$. The pairs of opposite rays with endpoint J are $\overrightarrow{JE}$ and $\overrightarrow{JF}$, and $\overrightarrow{JG}$ and $\overrightarrow{JH}$.

✓ **GUIDED PRACTICE** | for Example 2

Use the diagram in Example 2.

2. Give another name for $\overline{EF}$.

3. Are $\overrightarrow{HJ}$ and $\overrightarrow{JH}$ the same ray? Are $\overrightarrow{HJ}$ and $\overrightarrow{HG}$ the same ray? *Explain.*

INTERSECTIONS Two or more geometric figures *intersect* if they have one or more points in common. The **intersection** of the figures is the set of points the figures have in common. Some examples of intersections are shown below.

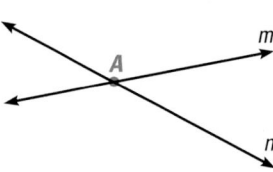

The intersection of two different lines is a point.

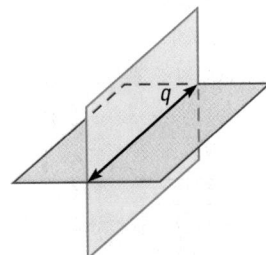

The intersection of two different planes is a line.

EXAMPLE 3 **Sketch intersections of lines and planes**

a. Sketch a plane and a line that is in the plane.

b. Sketch a plane and a line that does not intersect the plane.

c. Sketch a plane and a line that intersects the plane at a point.

Solution

a.
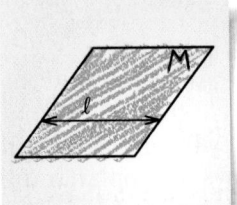

b.
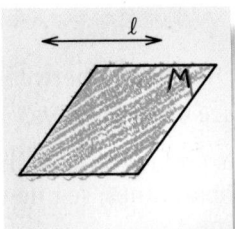

c.
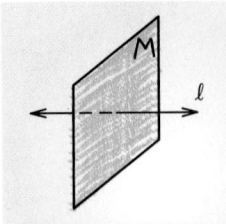

EXAMPLE 4 **Sketch intersections of planes**

Sketch two planes that intersect in a line.

Solution

STEP 1 **Draw** a vertical plane. Shade the plane.

STEP 2 **Draw** a second plane that is horizontal. Shade this plane a different color. Use dashed lines to show where one plane is hidden.

STEP 3 **Draw** the line of intersection.

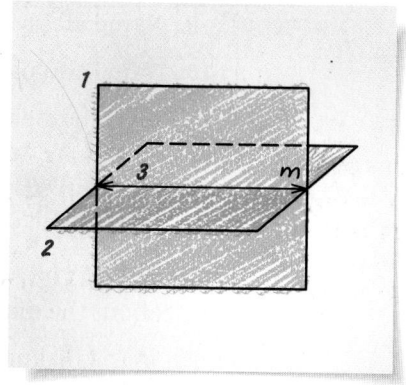

✓ **GUIDED PRACTICE**   for Examples 3 and 4

4. Sketch two different lines that intersect a plane at the same point.

Use the diagram at the right.

5. Name the intersection of $\overleftrightarrow{PQ}$ and line k.

6. Name the intersection of plane A and plane B.

7. Name the intersection of line k and plane A.

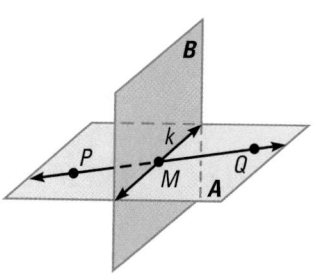

1.1 EXERCISES

HOMEWORK KEY

◯ = **WORKED-OUT SOLUTIONS**
on p. WS1 for Exs. 15, 19, and 43

★ = **STANDARDIZED TEST PRACTICE**
Exs. 2, 7, 13, 16, and 43

SKILL PRACTICE

1. **VOCABULARY** Write in words what each of the following symbols means.

   a. Q **b.** $\overline{MN}$ **c.** $\overrightarrow{ST}$ **d.** $\overleftrightarrow{FG}$

2. ★ **WRITING** *Compare* collinear points and coplanar points. Are collinear points also coplanar? Are coplanar points also collinear? *Explain.*

EXAMPLE 1
on p. 3
for Exs. 3–7

NAMING POINTS, LINES, AND PLANES **In Exercises 3–7, use the diagram.**

3. Give two other names for $\overleftrightarrow{WQ}$.

4. Give another name for plane V.

5. Name three points that are collinear. Then name a fourth point that is *not* collinear with these three points.

6. Name a point that is *not* coplanar with R, S, and T.

7. ★ **WRITING** Is point W coplanar with points Q and R? *Explain.*

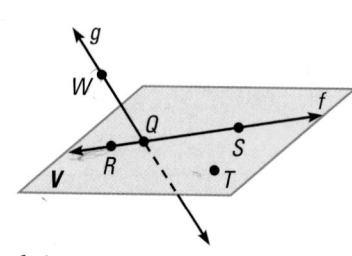

EXAMPLE 2
on p. 4
for Exs. 8–13

NAMING SEGMENTS AND RAYS In Exercises 8–12, use the diagram.

8. What is another name for $\overline{ZY}$?

9. Name all rays with endpoint V.

10. Name two pairs of opposite rays.

11. Give another name for $\overrightarrow{WV}$.

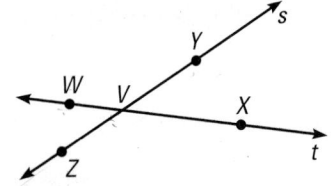

12. **ERROR ANALYSIS** A student says that $\overrightarrow{VW}$ and $\overrightarrow{VZ}$ are opposite rays because they have the same endpoint. *Describe* the error.

13. ★ **MULTIPLE CHOICE** Which statement about the diagram at the right is true?

   Ⓐ A, B, and C are collinear.

   Ⓑ C, D, E, and G are coplanar.

   Ⓒ B lies on $\overleftrightarrow{GE}$.

   Ⓓ $\overrightarrow{EF}$ and $\overrightarrow{ED}$ are opposite rays.

SKETCHING INTERSECTIONS Sketch the figure described.

14. Three lines that lie in a plane and intersect at one point

15. One line that lies in a plane, and one line that does not lie in the plane

16. ★ **MULTIPLE CHOICE** Line AB and line CD intersect at point E. Which of the following are opposite rays?

   Ⓐ $\overrightarrow{EC}$ and $\overrightarrow{ED}$ Ⓑ $\overrightarrow{CE}$ and $\overrightarrow{DE}$ Ⓒ $\overrightarrow{AB}$ and $\overrightarrow{BA}$ Ⓓ $\overrightarrow{AE}$ and $\overrightarrow{BE}$

READING DIAGRAMS In Exercises 17–22, use the diagram at the right.

17. Name the intersection of $\overleftrightarrow{PR}$ and $\overleftrightarrow{HR}$.

18. Name the intersection of plane EFG and plane FGS.

19. Name the intersection of plane PQS and plane HGS.

20. Are points P, Q, and F collinear? Are they coplanar?

21. Are points P and G collinear? Are they coplanar?

22. Name three planes that intersect at point E.

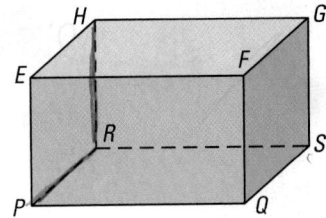

23. **SKETCHING PLANES** Sketch plane J intersecting plane K. Then draw a line ℓ in plane J that intersects plane K at a single point.

24. **NAMING RAYS** Name 10 different rays in the diagram at the right. Then name 2 pairs of opposite rays.

25. **SKETCHING** Draw three noncollinear points J, K, and L. Sketch $\overline{JK}$ and add a point M on $\overline{JK}$. Then sketch $\overrightarrow{ML}$.

26. **SKETCHING** Draw two points P and Q. Then sketch $\overrightarrow{PQ}$. Add a point R on the ray so that Q is between P and R.

◯ = **WORKED-OUT SOLUTIONS**
on p. WS1

★ = **STANDARDIZED TEST PRACTICE**

REVIEW
ALGEBRA
....
For help with
equations of
lines, see
p. 878.

ALGEBRA In Exercises 27–32, you are given an equation of a line and a point. Use substitution to determine whether the point is on the line.

27. $y = x - 4$; $A(5, 1)$

28. $y = x + 1$; $A(1, 0)$

29. $y = 3x + 4$; $A(7, 1)$

30. $y = 4x + 2$; $A(1, 6)$

31. $y = 3x - 2$; $A(-1, -5)$

32. $y = -2x + 8$; $A(-4, 0)$

GRAPHING Graph the inequality on a number line. Tell whether the graph is a *segment*, a *ray* or *rays*, a *point*, or a *line*.

33. $x \leq 3$

34. $x \geq -4$

35. $-7 \leq x \leq 4$

36. $x \geq 5$ or $x \leq -2$

37. $x \geq -1$ or $x \leq 5$

38. $|x| \leq 0$

39. CHALLENGE Tell whether each of the following situations involving three planes is possible. If a situation is possible, make a sketch.

   a. None of the three planes intersect.

   b. The three planes intersect in one line.

   c. The three planes intersect in one point.

   d. Two planes do not intersect. The third plane intersects the other two.

   e. Exactly two planes intersect. The third plane does not intersect the other two.

PROBLEM SOLVING

EXAMPLE 3
....
on p. 4
for Exs. 40–42

EVERYDAY INTERSECTIONS What kind of geometric intersection does the photograph suggest?

40.

41.

42.

43. ★ **SHORT RESPONSE** *Explain* why a four-legged table may rock from side to side even if the floor is level. Would a three-legged table on the same level floor rock from side to side? Why or why not?

   @HomeTutor for problem solving help at classzone.com

44. SURVEYING A surveying instrument is placed on a tripod. The tripod has three legs whose lengths can be adjusted.

   a. When the tripod is sitting on a level surface, are the tips of the legs coplanar?

   b. Suppose the tripod is used on a sloping surface. The length of each leg is adjusted so that the base of the surveying instrument is level with the horizon. Are the tips of the legs coplanar? *Explain.*

   @HomeTutor for problem solving help at classzone.com

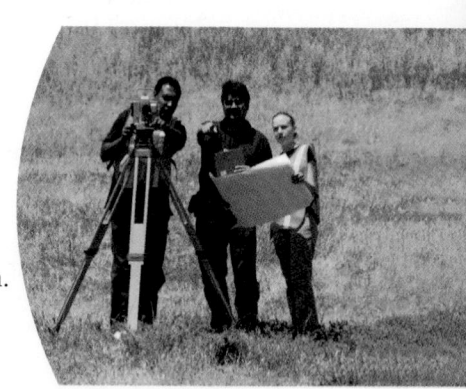

45. MULTI-STEP PROBLEM In a *perspective drawing*, lines that do not intersect in real life are represented by lines that appear to intersect at a point far away on the horizon. This point is called a *vanishing point*. The diagram shows a drawing of a house with two vanishing points.

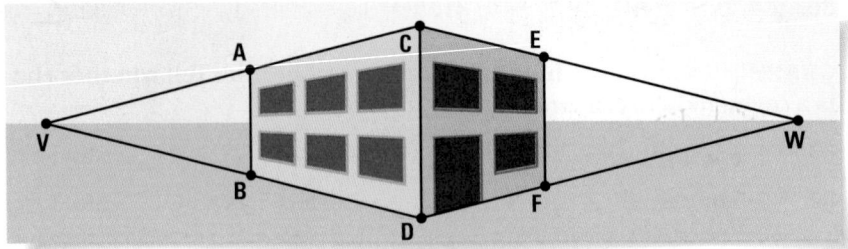

a. Trace the black line segments in the drawing. Using lightly dashed lines, join points A and B to the vanishing point W. Join points E and F to the vanishing point V.

b. Label the intersection of $\overleftrightarrow{EV}$ and $\overleftrightarrow{AW}$ as G. Label the intersection of $\overleftrightarrow{FV}$ and $\overleftrightarrow{BW}$ as H.

c. Using heavy dashed lines, draw the hidden edges of the house: $\overline{AG}, \overline{EG}, \overline{BH}, \overline{FH}$, and $\overline{GH}$.

46. CHALLENGE Each street in a particular town intersects every existing street exactly one time. Only two streets pass through each intersection.

2 streets

3 streets

4 streets

a. A traffic light is needed at each intersection. How many traffic lights are needed if there are 5 streets in the town? 6 streets?

b. *Describe* a pattern you can use to find the number of additional traffic lights that are needed each time a street is added to the town.

MIXED REVIEW

Find the difference. *(p. 869)*

47. $-15 - 9$

48. $6 - 10$

49. $-25 - (-12)$

50. $13 - 20$

51. $16 - (-4)$

52. $-5 - 15$

PREVIEW
Prepare for
Lesson 1.2
in Exs. 53–58.

Evaluate the expression. *(p. 870)*

53. $5 \cdot |-2 + 1|$

54. $|-8 + 7| - 6$

55. $-7 \cdot |8 - 10|$

Plot the point in a coordinate plane. *(p. 878)*

56. $A(2, 4)$

57. $B(-3, 6)$

58. $E(6, 7.5)$

---

8   **EXTRA PRACTICE** for Lesson 1.1, p. 896   🡒 **ONLINE QUIZ** at classzone.com

1.2 Use Segments and Congruence

Before	You learned about points, lines, and planes.
Now	You will use segment postulates to identify congruent segments.
Why?	So you can calculate flight distances, as in Ex. 33.

Key Vocabulary
- **postulate, axiom**
- **coordinate**
- **distance**
- **between**
- **congruent segments**

In Geometry, a rule that is accepted without proof is called a **postulate** or **axiom**. A rule that can be proved is called a *theorem*, as you will see later. Postulate 1 shows how to find the distance between two points on a line.

POSTULATE   *For Your Notebook*

POSTULATE 1   **Ruler Postulate**

The points on a line can be matched one to one with the real numbers. The real number that corresponds to a point is the **coordinate** of the point.

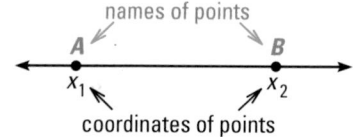

The **distance** between points A and B, written as AB, is the absolute value of the difference of the coordinates of A and B.

$$AB = |x_2 - x_1|$$

In the diagrams above, the small numbers in the coordinates x_1 and x_2 are called *subscripts*. The coordinates are read as "x sub one" and "x sub two."

The distance between points A and B, or AB, is also called the *length* of $\overline{AB}$.

EXAMPLE 1   Apply the Ruler Postulate

Measure the length of $\overline{ST}$ to the nearest tenth of a centimeter.

Solution

Align one mark of a metric ruler with S. Then estimate the coordinate of T. For example, if you align S with 2, T appears to align with 5.4.

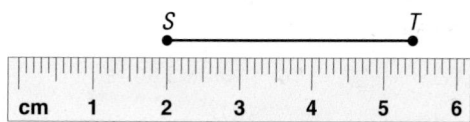

$ST = |5.4 - 2| = 3.4$ **Use Ruler Postulate.**

▶ The length of $\overline{ST}$ is about 3.4 centimeters.

ADDING SEGMENT LENGTHS When three points are collinear, you can say that one point is **between** the other two.

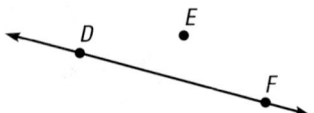

Point *B* is between points *A* and *C*.

Point *E* is not between points *D* and *F*.

POSTULATE   *For Your Notebook*

POSTULATE 2 Segment Addition Postulate

If *B* is between *A* and *C*, then $AB + BC = AC$.

If $AB + BC = AC$, then *B* is between *A* and *C*.

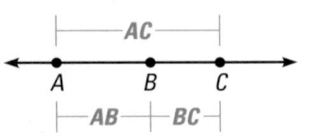

EXAMPLE 2 **Apply the Segment Addition Postulate**

MAPS The cities shown on the map lie approximately in a straight line. Use the given distances to find the distance from Lubbock, Texas, to St. Louis, Missouri.

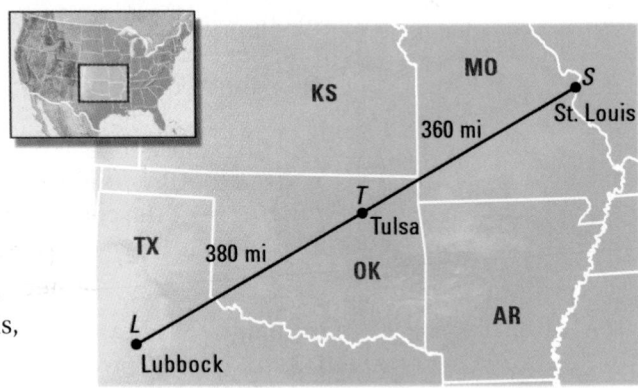

Solution

Because Tulsa, Oklahoma, lies between Lubbock and St. Louis, you can apply the Segment Addition Postulate.

$$LS = LT + TS = 380 + 360 = 740$$

▶ The distance from Lubbock to St. Louis is about 740 miles.

✓ **GUIDED PRACTICE**   for Examples 1 and 2

Use a ruler to measure the length of the segment to the nearest $\frac{1}{8}$ inch.

1. •————————————•
    M   *N*

2. •———————————————•
    P   *Q*

In Exercises 3 and 4, use the diagram shown.

3. Use the Segment Addition Postulate to find *XZ*.

4. In the diagram, *WY* = 30. Can you use the Segment Addition Postulate to find the distance between points *W* and *Z*? *Explain* your reasoning.

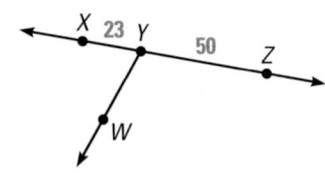

EXAMPLE 3 **Find a length**

Use the diagram to find *GH*.

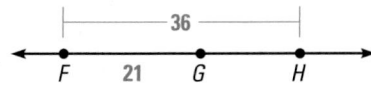

Solution

Use the Segment Addition Postulate to write an equation. Then solve the equation to find *GH*.

$FH = FG + GH$	**Segment Addition Postulate**
$36 = 21 + GH$	**Substitute 36 for *FH* and 21 for *FG*.**
$15 = GH$	**Subtract 21 from each side.**

CONGRUENT SEGMENTS Line segments that have the same length are called **congruent segments**. In the diagram below, you can say "the length of $\overline{AB}$ is equal to the length of $\overline{CD}$," or you can say "$\overline{AB}$ *is congruent to* $\overline{CD}$." The symbol $\cong$ means "is congruent to."

READ DIAGRAMS

In the diagram, the red tick marks indicate that $\overline{AB} \cong \overline{CD}$.

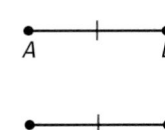

Lengths are equal.	Segments are congruent.
$AB = CD$	$\overline{AB} \cong \overline{CD}$
"is equal to"	"is congruent to"

EXAMPLE 4 **Compare segments for congruence**

Plot *J*(−3, 4), *K*(2, 4), *L*(1, 3), and *M*(1, −2) in a coordinate plane. Then determine whether $\overline{JK}$ and $\overline{LM}$ are congruent.

Solution

To find the length of a horizontal segment, find the absolute value of the difference of the *x*-coordinates of the endpoints.

$JK = \left| 2 - (-3) \right| = 5$ **Use Ruler Postulate.**

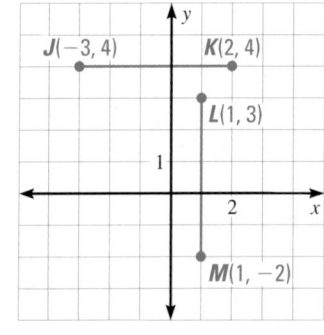

To find the length of a vertical segment, find the absolute value of the difference of the *y*-coordinates of the endpoints.

$LM = \left| -2 - 3 \right| = 5$ **Use Ruler Postulate.**

▶ $\overline{JK}$ and $\overline{LM}$ have the same length. So, $\overline{JK} \cong \overline{LM}$.

REVIEW USING A COORDINATE PLANE

For help with using a coordinate plane, see p. 878.

✓ **GUIDED PRACTICE**   for Examples 3 and 4

5. Use the diagram at the right to find *WX*.

6. Plot the points *A*(−2, 4), *B*(3, 4), *C*(0, 2), and *D*(0, −2) in a coordinate plane. Then determine whether $\overline{AB}$ and $\overline{CD}$ are congruent.

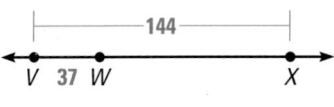

1.2 EXERCISES

SKILL PRACTICE

In Exercises 1 and 2, use the diagram at the right.

1. **VOCABULARY** *Explain* what $\overline{MN}$ means and what *MN* means.

2. ★ **WRITING** *Explain* how you can find *PN* if you know *PQ* and *QN*. How can you find *PN* if you know *MP* and *MN*?

EXAMPLE 1
on p. 9
for Exs. 3–5

MEASUREMENT Measure the length of the segment to the nearest tenth of a centimeter.

3.

4.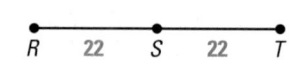

5.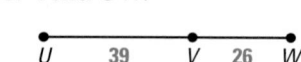

EXAMPLES 2 and 3
on pp. 10–11
for Exs. 6–12

SEGMENT ADDITION POSTULATE Find the indicated length.

6. Find *MP*.

7. Find *RT*.

8. Find *UW*.

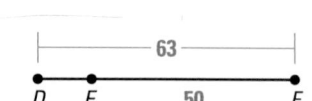

9. Find *XY*.

10. Find *BC*.

11. Find *DE*.

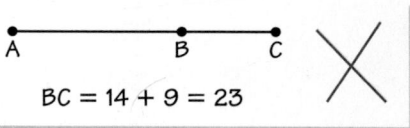

12. **ERROR ANALYSIS** In the figure at the right, *AC* = 14 and *AB* = 9. *Describe* and correct the error made in finding *BC*.

$$BC = 14 + 9 = 23$$

EXAMPLE 4
on p. 11
for Exs. 13–19

CONGRUENCE In Exercises 13–15, plot the given points in a coordinate plane. Then determine whether the line segments named are congruent.

13. $A(0, 1)$, $B(4, 1)$, $C(1, 2)$, $D(1, 6)$; $\overline{AB}$ and $\overline{CD}$

14. $J(-6, -8)$, $K(-6, 2)$, $L(-2, -4)$, $M(-6, -4)$; $\overline{JK}$ and $\overline{LM}$

15. $R(-200, 300)$, $S(200, 300)$, $T(300, -200)$, $U(300, 100)$; $\overline{RS}$ and $\overline{TU}$

ALGEBRA Use the number line to find the indicated distance.

16. *JK*   17. *JL*   18. *JM*   19. *KM*

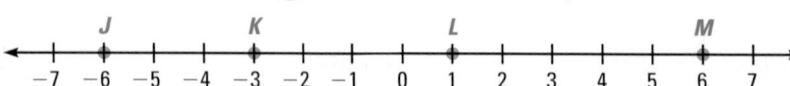

20. ★ **SHORT RESPONSE** Use the diagram. Is it possible to use the Segment Addition Postulate to show that *FB* > *CB* or that *AC* > *DB*? *Explain.*

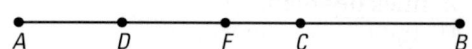

FINDING LENGTHS In the diagram, points *V*, *W*, *X*, *Y*, and *Z* are collinear, *VZ* = 52, *XZ* = 20, and *WX* = *XY* = *YZ*. Find the indicated length.

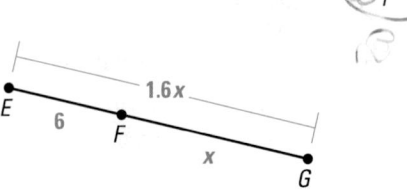

21. *WX*

22. *VW*

23. *WY*

24. *VX*

25. *WZ*

26. *VY*

27. ★ **MULTIPLE CHOICE** Use the diagram.
What is the length of $\overline{EG}$?

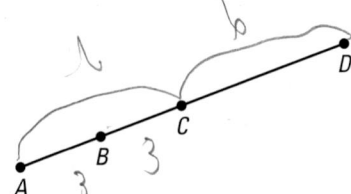

(**A**) 1

(**B**) 4.4

(**C**) 10

(**D**) 16

XY **ALGEBRA** Point *S* is between *R* and *T* on $\overline{RT}$. Use the given information to write an equation in terms of *x*. Solve the equation. Then find *RS* and *ST*.

28. $RS = 2x + 10$
$ST = x - 4$
$RT = 21$

29. $RS = 3x - 16$
$ST = 4x - 8$
$RT = 60$

30. $RS = 2x - 8$
$ST = 3x - 10$
$RT = 17$

31. **CHALLENGE** In the diagram, $\overline{AB} \cong \overline{BC}$, $\overline{AC} \cong \overline{CD}$, and *AD* = 12. Find the lengths of all the segments in the diagram. Suppose you choose one of the segments at random. What is the probability that the measure of the segment is greater than 3? *Explain*.

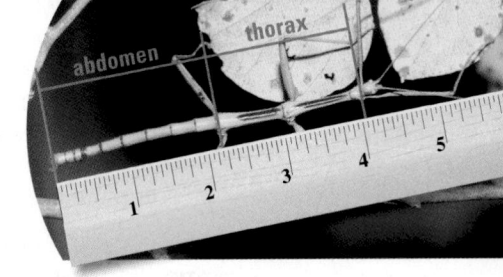

PROBLEM SOLVING

32. **SCIENCE** The photograph shows an insect called a walkingstick. Use the ruler to estimate the length of the abdomen and the length of the thorax to the nearest $\frac{1}{4}$ inch. About how much longer is the walkingstick's abdomen than its thorax?

@HomeTutor for problem solving help at classzone.com

EXAMPLE 2
on p. 10
for Ex. 33

33. **MODEL AIRPLANE** In 2003, a remote-controlled model airplane became the first ever to fly nonstop across the Atlantic Ocean. The map shows the airplane's position at three different points during its flight.

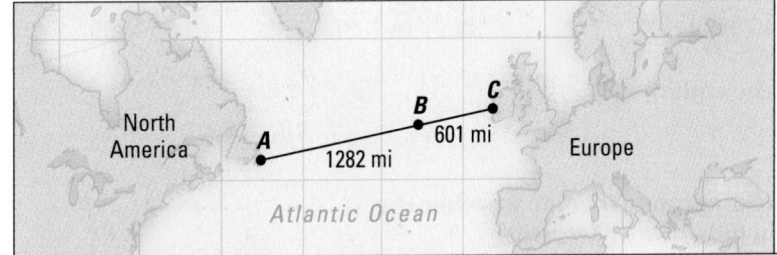

A	Leave Cape Spear, Newfoundland
B	Approximate position after about 1 day
C	Land at Mannin Bay, Ireland, after nearly 38 hours

a. Find the total distance the model airplane flew.

b. The model airplane's flight lasted nearly 38 hours. Estimate the airplane's average speed in miles per hour.

@HomeTutor for problem solving help at classzone.com

34. ★ **SHORT RESPONSE** The bar graph shows the win-loss record for a lacrosse team over a period of three years.

  a. Use the scale to find the length of the yellow bar for each year. What does the length represent?

  b. For each year, find the percent of games lost by the team.

  c. *Explain* how you are applying the Segment Addition Postulate when you find information from a stacked bar graph like the one shown.

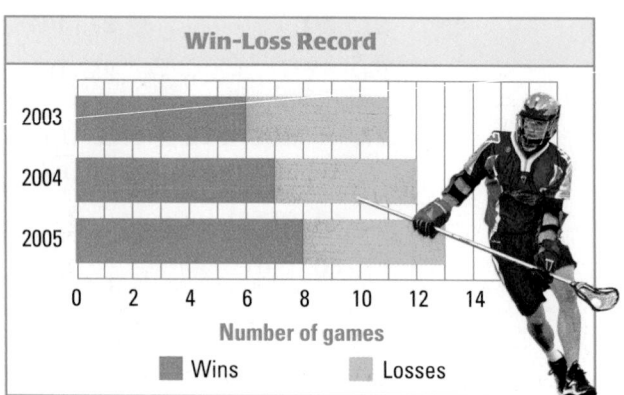

Win-Loss Record

Number of games

■ Wins ■ Losses

35. **MULTI-STEP PROBLEM** A climber uses a rope to descend a vertical cliff. Let *A* represent the point where the rope is secured at the top of the cliff, let *B* represent the climber's position, and let *C* represent the point where the rope is secured at the bottom of the cliff.

  a. **Model** Draw and label a line segment that represents the situation.

  b. **Calculate** If *AC* is 52 feet and *AB* is 31 feet, how much farther must the climber descend to reach the bottom of the cliff?

Animated **Geometry** at classzone.com

36. **CHALLENGE** Four cities lie along a straight highway in this order: City A, City B, City C, and City D. The distance from City A to City B is 5 times the distance from City B to City C. The distance from City A to City D is 2 times the distance from City A to City B. Copy and complete the mileage chart.

	City A	City B	City C	City D
City A		?	?	?
City B	?		?	?
City C	?	?		10 mi
City D	?	?	?	

MIXED REVIEW

PREVIEW

Prepare for Lesson 1.3 in Exs. 37–42.

Simplify the expression. Write your answer in simplest radical form. *(p. 874)*

37. $\sqrt{45 + 99}$

38. $\sqrt{14 + 36}$

39. $\sqrt{42 + (-2)^2}$

Solve the equation. *(p. 875)*

40. $4m + 5 = 7 + 6m$

41. $13 - 4h = 3h - 8$

42. $17 + 3x = 18x - 28$

Use the diagram to decide whether the statement is *true* or *false*. *(p. 2)*

43. Points *A*, *C*, *E*, and *G* are coplanar.

44. $\overleftrightarrow{DF}$ and $\overleftrightarrow{AG}$ intersect at point *E*.

45. $\overrightarrow{AE}$ and $\overrightarrow{EG}$ are opposite rays.

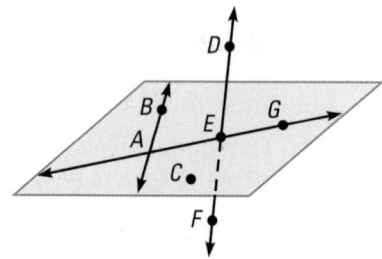

1.3 Use Midpoint and Distance Formulas

Before   You found lengths of segments.

Now   You will find lengths of segments in the coordinate plane.

Why?   So you can find an unknown length, as in Example 1.

Key Vocabulary
• midpoint
• segment bisector

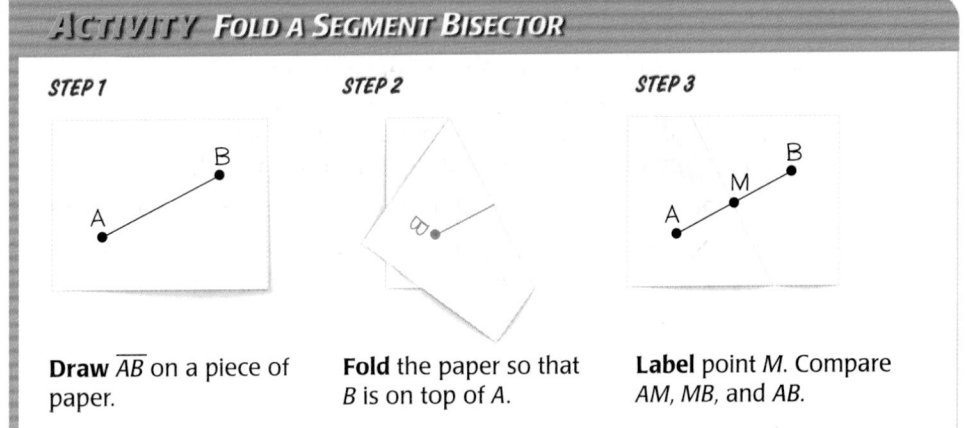

ACTIVITY *FOLD A SEGMENT BISECTOR*

STEP 1   **STEP 2**   **STEP 3**

Draw $\overline{AB}$ on a piece of paper.

Fold the paper so that B is on top of A.

Label point M. Compare AM, MB, and AB.

MIDPOINTS AND BISECTORS The **midpoint** of a segment is the point that divides the segment into two congruent segments. A **segment bisector** is a point, ray, line, line segment, or plane that intersects the segment at its midpoint. A midpoint or a segment bisector *bisects* a segment.

M is the midpoint of $\overline{AB}$.
So, $\overline{AM} \cong \overline{MB}$ and $AM = MB$.

$\overleftrightarrow{CD}$ is a segment bisector of $\overline{AB}$.
So, $\overline{AM} \cong \overline{MB}$ and $AM = MB$.

EXAMPLE 1   **Find segment lengths**

SKATEBOARD In the skateboard design, $\overline{VW}$ bisects $\overline{XY}$ at point *T*, and $XT = 39.9$ cm. Find *XY*.

Solution

Point *T* is the midpoint of $\overline{XY}$. So, $XT = TY = 39.9$ cm.

$XY = XT + TY$ **Segment Addition Postulate**

$ = 39.9 + 39.9$ **Substitute.**

$ = 79.8$ cm   **Add.**

EXAMPLE 2 **Use algebra with segment lengths**

ALGEBRA Point M is the midpoint of $\overline{VW}$. Find the length of $\overline{VM}$.

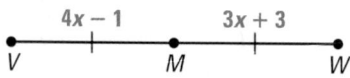

Solution

REVIEW ALGEBRA
For help with solving equations, see p. 875.

STEP 1 **Write** and solve an equation. Use the fact that $VM = MW$.

$$VM = MW \qquad \text{Write equation.}$$
$$4x - 1 = 3x + 3 \qquad \text{Substitute.}$$
$$x - 1 = 3 \qquad \text{Subtract } 3x \text{ from each side.}$$
$$x = 4 \qquad \text{Add 1 to each side.}$$

STEP 2 **Evaluate** the expression for VM when $x = 4$.

$$VM = 4x - 1 = 4(4) - 1 = 15$$

▶ So, the length of $\overline{VM}$ is 15.

CHECK Because $VM = MW$, the length of $\overline{MW}$ should be 15. If you evaluate the expression for MW, you should find that $MW = 15$.

$$MW = 3x + 3 = 3(4) + 3 = 15 ✓$$

✓ **GUIDED PRACTICE** for Examples 1 and 2

READ DIRECTIONS
Always read direction lines carefully. Notice that this direction line has two parts.

In Exercises 1 and 2, identify the segment bisector of $\overline{PQ}$. Then find PQ.

1.

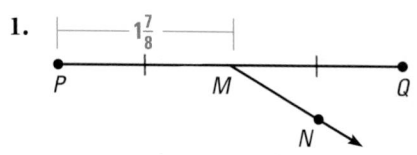

2.

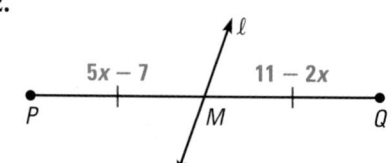

COORDINATE PLANE You can use the coordinates of the endpoints of a segment to find the coordinates of the midpoint.

KEY CONCEPT *For Your Notebook*

The Midpoint Formula

The coordinates of the midpoint of a segment are the averages of the x-coordinates and of the y-coordinates of the endpoints.

If $A(x_1, y_1)$ and $B(x_2, y_2)$ are points in a coordinate plane, then the midpoint M of $\overline{AB}$ has coordinates

$$\left(\frac{x_1 + x_2}{2}, \frac{y_1 + y_2}{2} \right).$$

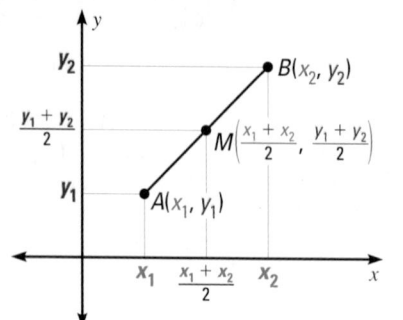

EXAMPLE 3   **Use the Midpoint Formula**

a. **FIND MIDPOINT** The endpoints of $\overline{RS}$ are $R(1, -3)$ and $S(4, 2)$. Find the coordinates of the midpoint M.

b. **FIND ENDPOINT** The midpoint of $\overline{JK}$ is $M(2, 1)$. One endpoint is $J(1, 4)$. Find the coordinates of endpoint K.

Solution

a. **FIND MIDPOINT** Use the Midpoint Formula.

$$M\left(\frac{1 + 4}{2}, \frac{-3 + 2}{2}\right) = M\left(\frac{5}{2}, -\frac{1}{2}\right)$$

▸ The coordinates of the midpoint M are $\left(\frac{5}{2}, -\frac{1}{2}\right)$.

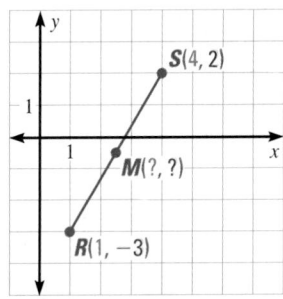

b. **FIND ENDPOINT** Let (x, y) be the coordinates of endpoint K. Use the Midpoint Formula.

STEP 1 Find x.

$$\frac{1 + x}{2} = 2$$

$$1 + x = 4$$

$$x = 3$$

STEP 2 Find y.

$$\frac{4 + y}{2} = 1$$

$$4 + y = 2$$

$$y = -2$$

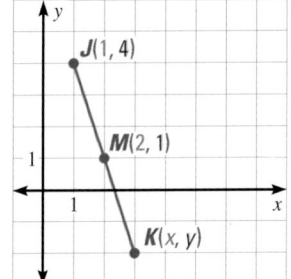

CLEAR FRACTIONS
Multiply each side of the equation by the denominator to clear the fraction.

▸ The coordinates of endpoint K are $(3, -2)$.

✓ **GUIDED PRACTICE**   for Example 3

3. The endpoints of $\overline{AB}$ are $A(1, 2)$ and $B(7, 8)$. Find the coordinates of the midpoint M.

4. The midpoint of $\overline{VW}$ is $M(-1, -2)$. One endpoint is $W(4, 4)$. Find the coordinates of endpoint V.

DISTANCE FORMULA The Distance Formula is a formula for computing the distance between two points in a coordinate plane.

KEY CONCEPT   *For Your Notebook*

The Distance Formula

READ DIAGRAMS
The red mark at one corner of the triangle shown indicates a right triangle.

If $A(x_1, y_1)$ and $B(x_2, y_2)$ are points in a coordinate plane, then the distance between A and B is

$$AB = \sqrt{(x_2 - x_1)^2 + (y_2 - y_1)^2}.$$

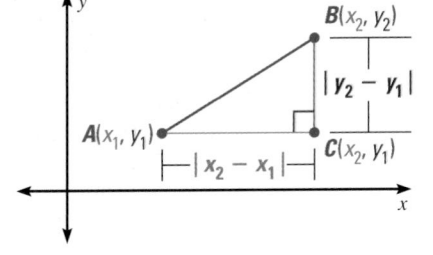

The Distance Formula is based on the *Pythagorean Theorem,* which you will see again when you work with right triangles in Chapter 7.

Distance Formula

$$(AB)^2 = (x_2 - x_1)^2 + (y_2 - y_1)^2$$

Pythagorean Theorem

$$c^2 = a^2 + b^2$$

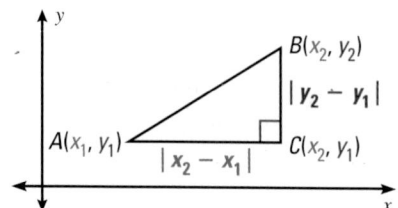

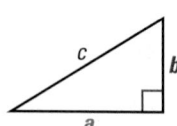

⭐ **EXAMPLE 4** **Standardized Test Practice**

ELIMINATE CHOICES
Drawing a diagram can help you eliminate choices. You can see that choice A is not large enough to be *RS.*

What is the approximate length of $\overline{RS}$ with endpoints $R(2, 3)$ and $S(4, -1)$?

(A) 1.4 units   **(B)** 4.0 units   **(C)** 4.5 units   **(D)** 6 units

Solution

Use the Distance Formula. You may find it helpful to draw a diagram.

$$RS = \sqrt{(x_2 - x_1)^2 + (y_2 - y_1)^2}$$ **Distance Formula**

$$= \sqrt{[(4 - 2)]^2 + [(-1) - 3]^2}$$ **Substitute.**

$$= \sqrt{(2)^2 + (-4)^2}$$ **Subtract.**

$$= \sqrt{4 + 16}$$ **Evaluate powers.**

$$= \sqrt{20}$$ **Add.**

READ SYMBOLS
The symbol ≈ means "is approximately equal to."

$$\approx 4.47$$ **Use a calculator to approximate the square root.**

▶ The correct answer is C. **(A) (B) (C) (D)**

✓ **GUIDED PRACTICE** **for Example 4**

5. In Example 4, does it matter which ordered pair you choose to substitute for (x_1, y_1) and which ordered pair you choose to substitute for (x_2, y_2)? *Explain.*

6. What is the approximate length of $\overline{AB}$, with endpoints $A(-3, 2)$ and $B(1, -4)$?

(A) 6.1 units   **(B)** 7.2 units   **(C)** 8.5 units   **(D)** 10.0 units

1.3 EXERCISES

HOMEWORK KEY

○ = WORKED-OUT SOLUTIONS
on p. WS1 for Exs. 15, 35, and 49

★ = STANDARDIZED TEST PRACTICE
Exs. 2, 23, 34, 41, 42, and 53

SKILL PRACTICE

1. **VOCABULARY** Copy and complete: To find the length of $\overline{AB}$, with endpoints $A(-7, 5)$ and $B(4, -6)$, you can use the __?__.

2. ★ **WRITING** *Explain* what it means to bisect a segment. Why is it impossible to bisect a line?

EXAMPLE 1
on p. 15
for Exs. 3–10

FINDING LENGTHS Line ℓ bisects the segment. Find the indicated length.

3. Find RT if $RS = 5\frac{1}{8}$ in.

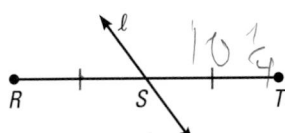

4. Find UW if $VW = \frac{5}{8}$ in.

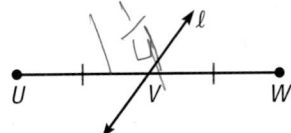

5. Find EG if $EF = 13$ cm.

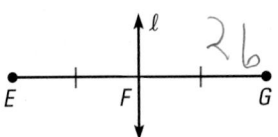

6. Find BC if $AC = 19$ cm.

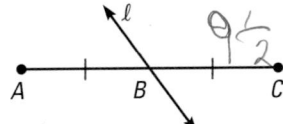

7. Find QR if $PR = 9\frac{1}{2}$ in.

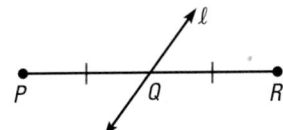

8. Find LM if $LN = 137$ mm.

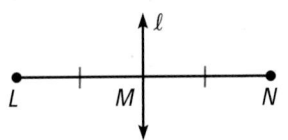

9. **SEGMENT BISECTOR** Line RS bisects $\overline{PQ}$ at point R. Find RQ if $PQ = 4\frac{3}{4}$ inches.

10. **SEGMENT BISECTOR** Point T bisects $\overline{UV}$. Find UV if $UT = 2\frac{7}{8}$ inches.

EXAMPLE 2
on p. 16
for Exs. 11–16

XY ALGEBRA In each diagram, M is the midpoint of the segment. Find the indicated length.

11. Find AM.

12. Find EM.

13. Find JM.

14. Find PR.

15. Find SU.

16. Find XZ.

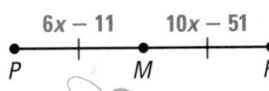

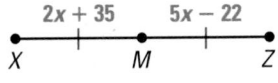

EXAMPLE 3
on p. 17
for Exs. 17–30

FINDING MIDPOINTS Find the coordinates of the midpoint of the segment with the given endpoints.

17. $C(3, 5)$ and $D(7, 5)$

18. $E(0, 4)$ and $F(4, 3)$

19. $G(-4, 4)$ and $H(6, 4)$

20. $J(-7, -5)$ and $K(-3, 7)$

21. $P(-8, -7)$ and $Q(11, 5)$

22. $S(-3, 3)$ and $T(-8, 6)$

23. ★ **WRITING** Develop a formula for finding the midpoint of a segment with endpoints $A(0, 0)$ and $B(m, n)$. *Explain* your thinking.

24. ERROR ANALYSIS *Describe* the error made in finding the coordinates of the midpoint of a segment with endpoints $S(8, 3)$ and $T(2, -1)$.

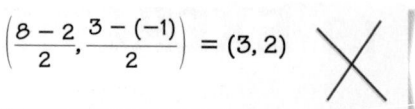

$$\left(\frac{8-2}{2}, \frac{3-(-1)}{2}\right) = (3, 2)$$

FINDING ENDPOINTS Use the given endpoint R and midpoint M of $\overline{RS}$ to find the coordinates of the other endpoint S.

25. $R(3, 0), M(0, 5)$ (-3, 10)

26. $R(5, 1), M(1, 4)$ (-3 7)

27. $R(6, -2), M(5, 3)$

28. $R(-7, 11), M(2, 1)$

29. $R(4, -6), M(-7, 8)$

30. $R(-4, -6), M(3, -4)$

EXAMPLE 4
on p. 18
for Exs. 31–34

DISTANCE FORMULA Find the length of the segment. Round to the nearest tenth of a unit.

31.

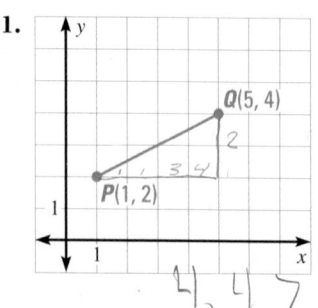

32.

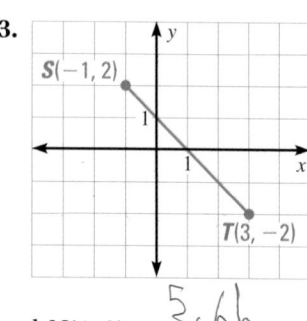

33.

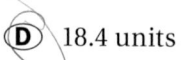

34. ★ MULTIPLE CHOICE The endpoints of $\overline{MN}$ are $M(-3, -9)$ and $N(4, 8)$. What is the approximate length of $\overline{MN}$?

A 1.4 units   **B** 7.2 units   **C** 13 units   **D** 18.4 units

NUMBER LINE Find the length of the segment. Then find the coordinate of the midpoint of the segment.

35.

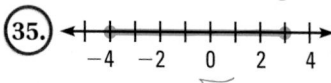

36.

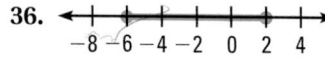

37.

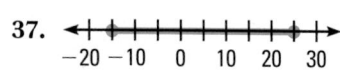

38.

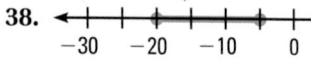

39.

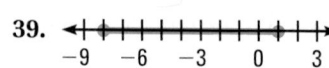

40.

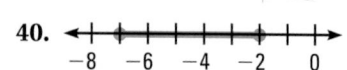

41. ★ MULTIPLE CHOICE The endpoints of $\overline{LF}$ are $L(-2, 2)$ and $F(3, 1)$. The endpoints of $\overline{JR}$ are $J(1, -1)$ and $R(2, -3)$. What is the approximate difference in the lengths of the two segments?

A 2.24   **B** 2.86   **C** 5.10   **D** 7.96

42. ★ SHORT RESPONSE One endpoint of $\overline{PQ}$ is $P(-2, 4)$. The midpoint of $\overline{PQ}$ is $M(1, 0)$. *Explain* how to find PQ.

COMPARING LENGTHS The endpoints of two segments are given. Find each segment length. Tell whether the segments are congruent.

43. $\overline{AB}$: $A(0, 2), B(-3, 8)$
$\overline{CD}$: $C(-2, 2), D(0, -4)$

44. $\overline{EF}$: $E(1, 4), F(5, 1)$
$\overline{GH}$: $G(-3, 1), H(1, 6)$

45. $\overline{JK}$: $J(-4, 0), K(4, 8)$
$\overline{LM}$: $L(-4, 2), M(3, -7)$

46. ✖ ALGEBRA Points S, T, and P lie on a number line. Their coordinates are 0, 1, and x, respectively. Given $SP = PT$, what is the value of x?

47. CHALLENGE M is the midpoint of $\overline{JK}$, $JM = \frac{x}{8}$, and $JK = \frac{3x}{4} - 6$. Find MK.

○ = **WORKED-OUT SOLUTIONS**
on p. WS1

★ = **STANDARDIZED TEST PRACTICE**

EXAMPLE 1
on p. 15
for Ex. 48

48. WINDMILL In the photograph of a windmill, $\overline{ST}$ bisects $\overline{QR}$ at point M. The length of $\overline{QM}$ is $18\frac{1}{2}$ feet. Find QR and MR.

@HomeTutor for problem solving help at classzone.com

(49.) DISTANCES A house and a school are 5.7 kilometers apart on the same straight road. The library is on the same road, halfway between the house and the school. Draw a sketch to represent this situation. Mark the locations of the house, school, and library. How far is the library from the house?

@HomeTutor for problem solving help at classzone.com

ARCHAEOLOGY The points on the diagram show the positions of objects at an underwater archaeological site. Use the diagram for Exercises 50 and 51.

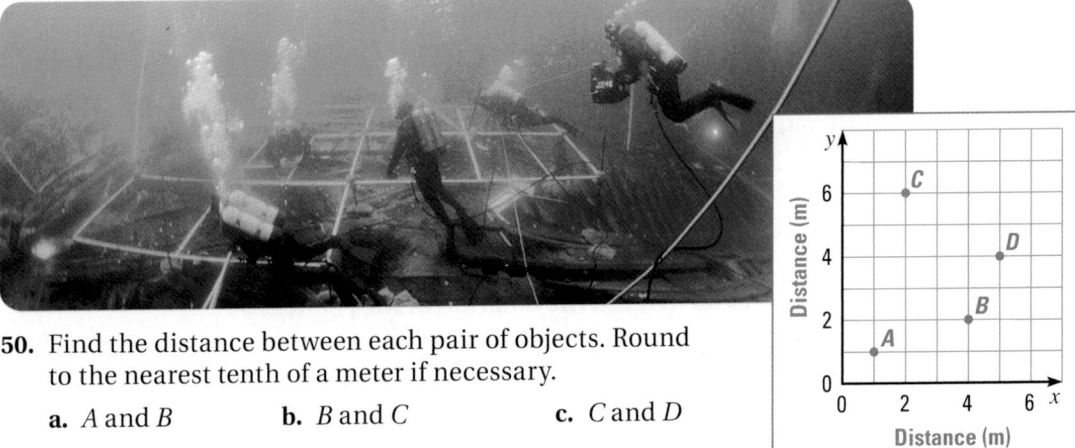

50. Find the distance between each pair of objects. Round to the nearest tenth of a meter if necessary.

   a. A and B **b.** B and C **c.** C and D

   d. A and D **e.** B and D **f.** A and C

51. Which two objects are closest to each other? Which two are farthest apart?

Animated Geometry at classzone.com

52. WATER POLO The diagram shows the positions of three players during part of a water polo match. Player A throws the ball to Player B, who then throws it to Player C. How far did Player A throw the ball? How far did Player B throw the ball? How far would Player A have thrown the ball if he had thrown it directly to Player C? Round all answers to the nearest tenth of a meter.

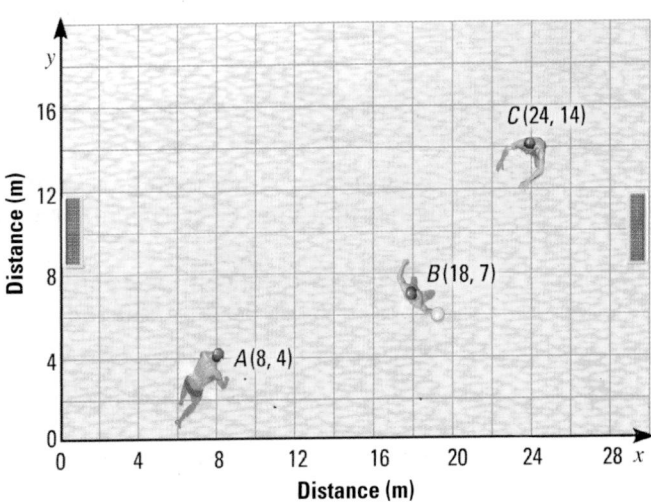

53. ★ **EXTENDED RESPONSE** As shown, a path goes around a triangular park.

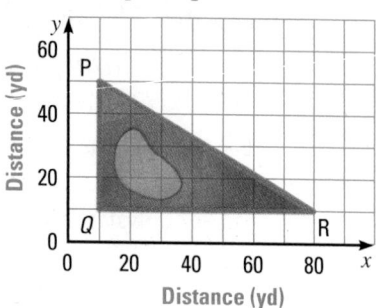

   a. Find the distance around the park to the nearest yard.

   b. A new path and a bridge are constructed from point Q to the midpoint M of $\overline{PR}$. Find QM to the nearest yard.

   c. A man jogs from P to Q to M to R to Q and back to P at an average speed of 150 yards per minute. About how many minutes does it take? *Explain.*

54. **CHALLENGE** $\overline{AB}$ bisects $\overline{CD}$ at point M, $\overline{CD}$ bisects $\overline{AB}$ at point M, and $AB = 4 \cdot CM$. *Describe* the relationship between AM and CD.

MIXED REVIEW

The graph shows data about the number of children in the families of students in a math class. *(p. 888)*

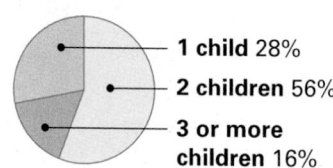

55. What percent of the students in the class belong to families with two or more children?

56. If there are 25 students in the class, how many students belong to families with two children?

PREVIEW
Prepare for Lesson 1.4 in Exs. 57–59.

Solve the equation. *(p. 875)*

57. $3x + 12 + x = 20$ **58.** $9x + 2x + 6 - x = 10$ **59.** $5x - 22 - 7x + 2 = 40$

In Exercises 60–64, use the diagram at the right. *(p. 2)*

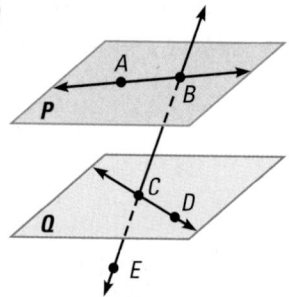

60. Name all rays with endpoint B.

61. Name all the rays that contain point C.

62. Name a pair of opposite rays.

63. Name the intersection of $\overleftrightarrow{AB}$ and $\overleftrightarrow{BC}$.

64. Name the intersection of $\overleftrightarrow{BC}$ and plane P.

QUIZ *for Lessons 1.1–1.3*

1. Sketch two lines that intersect the same plane at two different points. The lines intersect each other at a point not in the plane. *(p. 2)*

In the diagram of collinear points, $AE = 26$, $AD = 15$, and $AB = BC = CD$. Find the indicated length. *(p. 9)*

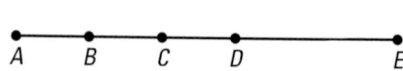

2. DE **3.** AB **4.** AC

5. BD **6.** CE **7.** BE

8. The endpoints of $\overline{RS}$ are $R(-2, -1)$ and $S(2, 3)$. Find the coordinates of the midpoint of $\overline{RS}$. Then find the distance between R and S. *(p. 15)*

Lessons 1.1–1.3

1. **MULTI-STEP PROBLEM** The diagram shows existing roads ($\overleftrightarrow{BD}$ and $\overleftrightarrow{DE}$) and a new road ($\overline{CE}$) under construction.

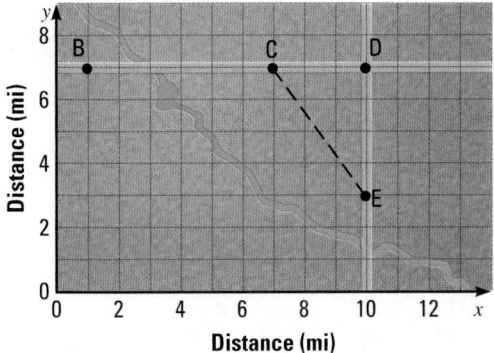

Distance (mi)

Distance (mi)

   a. If you drive from point *B* to point *E* on existing roads, how far do you travel?

   b. If you use the new road as you drive from *B* to *E*, about how far do you travel? Round to the nearest tenth of a mile if necessary.

   c. About how much shorter is the trip from *B* to *E* if you use the new road?

2. **GRIDDED ANSWER** Point *M* is the midpoint of $\overline{PQ}$. If $PM = 23x + 5$ and $MQ = 25x - 4$, find the length of $\overline{PQ}$.

3. **GRIDDED ANSWER** You are hiking on a trail that lies along a straight railroad track. The total length of the trail is 5.4 kilometers. You have been hiking for 45 minutes at an average speed of 2.4 kilometers per hour. How much farther (in kilometers) do you need to hike to reach the end of the trail?

4. **SHORT RESPONSE** The diagram below shows the frame for a wall. $\overline{FH}$ represents a vertical board, and $\overline{EG}$ represents a brace. If $FG = 143$ cm, does the brace bisect $\overline{FH}$? If not, how long should $\overline{FG}$ be so that the brace does bisect $\overline{FH}$? *Explain.*

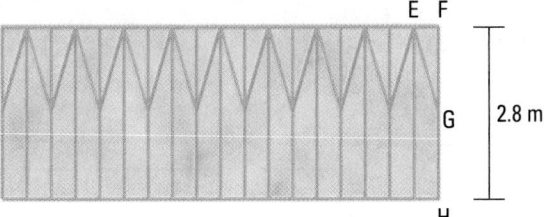

E   F

G   2.8 m

H

5. **SHORT RESPONSE** Point *E* is the midpoint of $\overline{AB}$ and the midpoint of $\overline{CD}$. The endpoints of $\overline{AB}$ are $A(-4, 5)$ and $B(6, -5)$. The coordinates of point *C* are $(2, 8)$. Find the coordinates of point *D*. *Explain* how you got your answer.

6. **OPEN-ENDED** The distance around a figure is its *perimeter*. Choose four points in a coordinate plane that can be connected to form a rectangle with a perimeter of 16 units. Then choose four other points and draw a different rectangle that has a perimeter of 16 units. Show how you determined that each rectangle has a perimeter of 16 units.

7. **SHORT RESPONSE** Use the diagram of a box. What are all the names that can be used to describe the plane that contains points *B*, *F*, and *C*? Name the intersection of planes *ABC* and *BFE*. *Explain.*

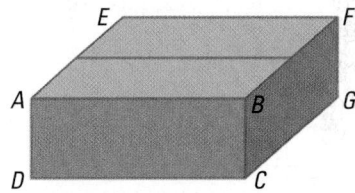

8. **EXTENDED RESPONSE** Jill is a salesperson who needs to visit towns *A*, *B*, and *C*. On the map below, $AB = 18.7$ km and $BC = 2AB$. Assume Jill travels along the road shown.

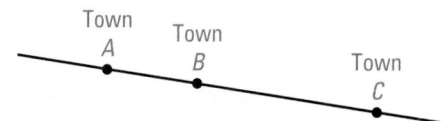

Town A   Town B   Town C

   a. Find the distance Jill travels if she starts at Town *A*, visits Towns *B* and *C*, and then returns to Town *A*.

   b. About how much time does Jill spend driving if her average driving speed is 70 kilometers per hour?

   c. Jill needs to spend 2.5 hours in each town. Can she visit all three towns and return to Town *A* in an 8 hour workday? *Explain.*

1.4 Measure and Classify Angles

Before	You named and measured line segments.
Now	You will name, measure, and classify angles.
Why?	So you can identify congruent angles, as in Example 4.

Key Vocabulary
- **angle**
  acute, right, obtuse, straight
- **sides, vertex of an angle**
- **measure of an angle**
- **congruent angles**
- **angle bisector**

An **angle** consists of two different rays with the same endpoint. The rays are the **sides** of the angle. The endpoint is the **vertex** of the angle.

The angle with sides $\overrightarrow{AB}$ and $\overrightarrow{AC}$ can be named $\angle BAC$, $\angle CAB$, or $\angle A$. Point A is the vertex of the angle.

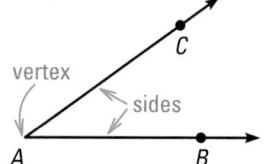

EXAMPLE 1 Name angles

Name the three angles in the diagram.

$\angle WXY$, or $\angle YXW$

$\angle YXZ$, or $\angle ZXY$

$\angle WXZ$, or $\angle ZXW$

You should not name any of these angles $\angle X$ because all three angles have X as their vertex.

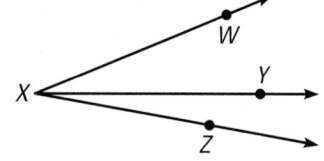

MEASURING ANGLES A protractor can be used to approximate the *measure* of an angle. An angle is measured in units called *degrees* (°). For instance, the measure of $\angle WXZ$ in Example 1 above is 32°. You can write this statement in two ways.

> **Words** The measure of $\angle WXZ$ is 32°.
>
> **Symbols** $m\angle WXZ = 32°$

POSTULATE   *For Your Notebook*

POSTULATE 3 Protractor Postulate

Consider $\overleftrightarrow{OB}$ and a point A on one side of $\overleftrightarrow{OB}$. The rays of the form $\overrightarrow{OA}$ can be matched one to one with the real numbers from 0 to 180.

The **measure** of $\angle AOB$ is equal to the absolute value of the difference between the real numbers for $\overrightarrow{OA}$ and $\overrightarrow{OB}$.

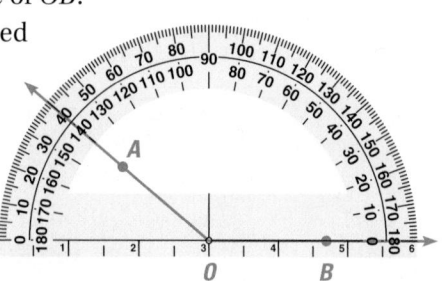

CLASSIFYING ANGLES Angles can be classified as **acute**, **right**, **obtuse**, and **straight**, as shown below.

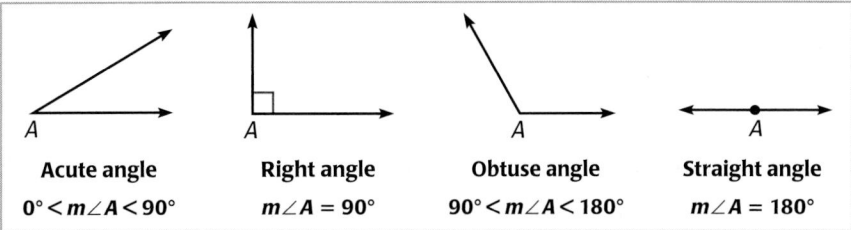

Acute angle	Right angle	Obtuse angle	Straight angle
$0° < m\angle A < 90°$	$m\angle A = 90°$	$90° < m\angle A < 180°$	$m\angle A = 180°$

EXAMPLE 2 **Measure and classify angles**

Use the diagram to find the measure of the indicated angle. Then classify the angle.

  a. $\angle KHJ$ **b.** $\angle GHK$ **c.** $\angle GHJ$ **d.** $\angle GHL$

Solution

A protractor has an inner and an outer scale. When you measure an angle, check to see which scale to use.

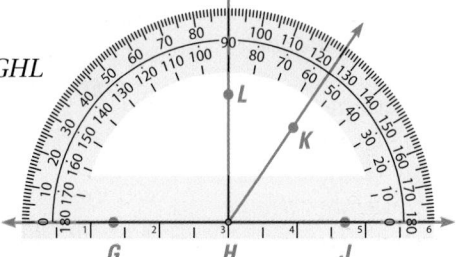

  a. $\overrightarrow{HJ}$ is lined up with the 0° on the inner scale of the protractor. $\overrightarrow{HK}$ passes through 55° on the inner scale. So, $m\angle KHJ = 55°$. It is an acute angle.

  b. $\overrightarrow{HG}$ is lined up with the 0° on the outer scale, and $\overrightarrow{HK}$ passes through 125° on the outer scale. So, $m\angle GHK = 125°$. It is an obtuse angle.

  c. $m\angle GHJ = 180°$. It is a straight angle.

  d. $m\angle GHL = 90°$. It is a right angle.

Animated **Geometry** at classzone.com

✔ **GUIDED PRACTICE**   for Examples 1 and 2

  1. Name all the angles in the diagram at the right. Which angle is a right angle?

  2. Draw a pair of opposite rays. What type of angle do the rays form?

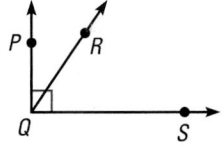

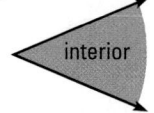

interior

POSTULATE   *For Your Notebook*

POSTULATE 4 Angle Addition Postulate

Words If P is in the interior of $\angle RST$, then the measure of $\angle RST$ is equal to the sum of the measures of $\angle RSP$ and $\angle PST$.

Symbols If P is in the interior of $\angle RST$, then $m\angle RST = m\angle RSP + m\angle PST$.

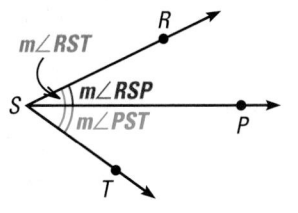

EXAMPLE 3 Find angle measures

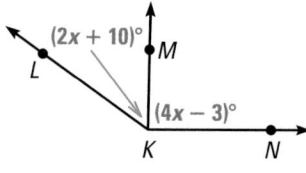

ALGEBRA Given that $m\angle LKN = 145°$, find $m\angle LKM$ and $m\angle MKN$.

Solution

STEP 1 Write and solve an equation to find the value of x.

$m\angle LKN = m\angle LKM + m\angle MKN$	Angle Addition Postulate
$145° = (2x + 10)° + (4x - 3)°$	Substitute angle measures.
$145 = 6x + 7$	Combine like terms.
$138 = 6x$	Subtract 7 from each side.
$23 = x$	Divide each side by 6.

STEP 2 Evaluate the given expressions when $x = 23$.

$m\angle LKM = (2x + 10)° = (2 \cdot 23 + 10)° = 56°$

$m\angle MKN = (4x - 3)° = (4 \cdot 23 - 3)° = 89°$

▶ So, $m\angle LKM = 56°$ and $m\angle MKN = 89°$.

 GUIDED PRACTICE for Example 3

Find the indicated angle measures.

3. Given that $\angle KLM$ is a straight angle, find $m\angle KLN$ and $m\angle NLM$.

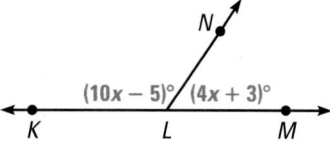

4. Given that $\angle EFG$ is a right angle, find $m\angle EFH$ and $m\angle HFG$.

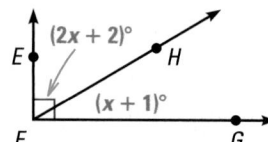

CONGRUENT ANGLES Two angles are **congruent angles** if they have the same measure. In the diagram below, you can say that "the measure of angle A is equal to the measure of angle B," or you can say "angle A is congruent to angle B."

READ DIAGRAMS

Matching arcs are used to show that angles are congruent. If more than one pair of angles are congruent, double arcs are used, as in Example 4 on page 27.

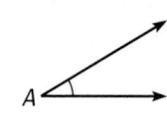

Angle measures are equal.

$m\angle A = m\angle B$

⬆

"is equal to"

Angles are congruent.

$\angle A \cong \angle B$

⬆

"is congruent to"

EXAMPLE 4 **Identify congruent angles**

TRAPEZE The photograph shows some of the angles formed by the ropes in a trapeze apparatus. Identify the congruent angles. If $m\angle DEG = 157°$, what is $m\angle GKL$?

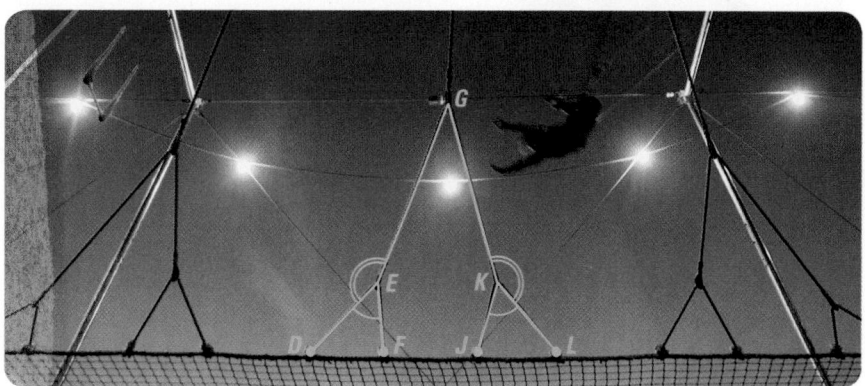

Solution

There are two pairs of congruent angles:

$\angle DEF \cong \angle JKL$ and $\angle DEG \cong \angle GKL$.

Because $\angle DEG \cong \angle GKL$, $m\angle DEG = m\angle GKL$. So, $m\angle GKL = 157°$.

 GUIDED PRACTICE | **for Example 4**

Use the diagram shown at the right.

5. Identify all pairs of congruent angles in the diagram.

6. In the diagram, $m\angle PQR = 130°$, $m\angle QRS = 84°$, and $m\angle TSR = 121°$. Find the other angle measures in the diagram.

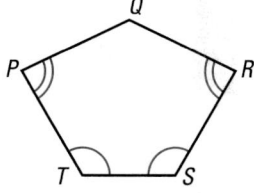

ACTIVITY **FOLD AN ANGLE BISECTOR**

STEP 1

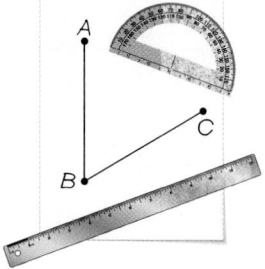

Use a straightedge to draw and label an acute angle, $\angle ABC$.

STEP 2

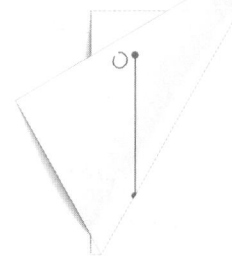

Fold the paper so that $\overrightarrow{BC}$ is on top of $\overrightarrow{BA}$.

STEP 3

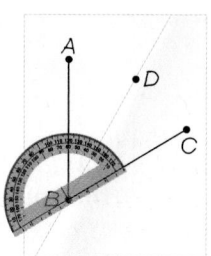

Draw a point D on the fold inside $\angle ABC$. Then measure $\angle ABD$, $\angle DBC$, and $\angle ABC$. What do you observe?

An **angle bisector** is a ray that divides an angle into two angles that are congruent. In the activity on page 27, $\overrightarrow{BD}$ bisects $\angle ABC$. So, $\angle ABD \cong \angle DBC$ and $m\angle ABD = m\angle DBC$.

EXAMPLE 5 **Double an angle measure**

In the diagram at the right, $\overrightarrow{YW}$ bisects $\angle XYZ$, and $m\angle XYW = 18°$. Find $m\angle XYZ$.

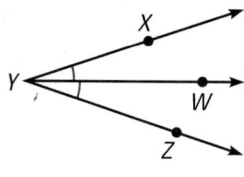

Solution

By the Angle Addition Postulate, $m\angle XYZ = m\angle XYW + m\angle WYZ$. Because $\overrightarrow{YW}$ bisects $\angle XYZ$, you know that $\angle XYW \cong \angle WYZ$.

So, $m\angle XYW = m\angle WYZ$, and you can write

$$m\angle XYZ = m\angle XYW + m\angle WYZ = 18° + 18° = 36°.$$

✓ **GUIDED PRACTICE** for Example 5

7. Angle MNP is a straight angle, and $\overrightarrow{NQ}$ bisects $\angle MNP$. Draw $\angle MNP$ and $\overrightarrow{NQ}$. Use arcs to mark the congruent angles in your diagram, and give the angle measures of these congruent angles.

1.4 EXERCISES

HOMEWORK KEY
○ = **WORKED-OUT SOLUTIONS** on p. WS1 for Exs. 15, 23, and 53
★ = **STANDARDIZED TEST PRACTICE** Exs. 2, 21, 27, 43, and 62

SKILL PRACTICE

1. **VOCABULARY** Sketch an example of each of the following types of angles: acute, obtuse, right, and straight.

2. ★ **WRITING** *Explain* how to find the measure of $\angle PQR$, shown at the right.

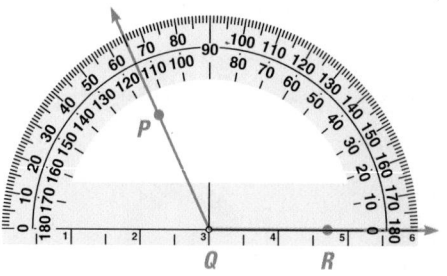

EXAMPLE 1
on p. 24
for Exs. 3–6

NAMING ANGLES AND ANGLE PARTS In Exercises 3–5, write three names for the angle shown. Then name the vertex and sides of the angle.

3.
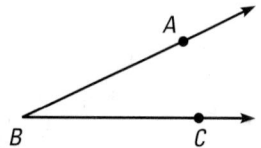

4.
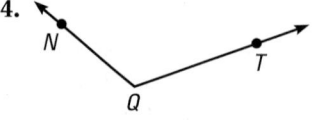

5.
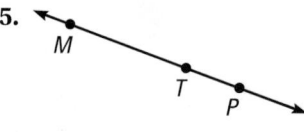

6. NAMING ANGLES Name three different angles in the diagram at the right.

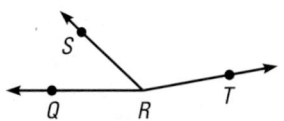

EXAMPLE 2
on p. 25
for Exs. 7–21

CLASSIFYING ANGLES Classify the angle with the given measure as *acute*, *obtuse*, *right*, or *straight*.

7. $m\angle W = 180°$ **8.** $m\angle X = 30°$ **9.** $m\angle Y = 90°$ **10.** $m\angle Z = 95°$

S   Q   r   O

MEASURING ANGLES Trace the diagram and extend the rays. Use a protractor to find the measure of the given angle. Then classify the angle as *acute*, *obtuse*, *right*, or *straight*.

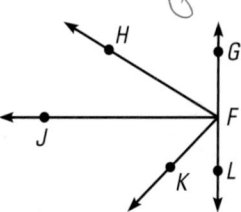

11. $\angle JFL$ R   **12.** $\angle GFH$ a

13. $\angle GFK$ O   **14.** $\angle GFL$ S

NAMING AND CLASSIFYING Give another name for the angle in the diagram below. Tell whether the angle appears to be *acute*, *obtuse*, *right*, or *straight*.

(15.) $\angle ACB$ R   **16.** $\angle ABC$ A

17. $\angle BFD$ S   **18.** $\angle AEC$ O

19. $\angle BDC$ a   **20.** $\angle BEC$ A

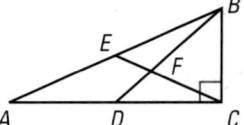

21. ★ **MULTIPLE CHOICE** Which is a correct name for the obtuse angle in the diagram?

(A) $\angle ACB$ (B) $\angle ACD$

(C) $\angle BCD$ (D) $\angle C$

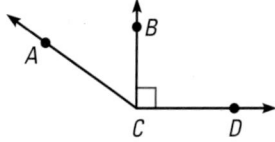

EXAMPLE 3
on p. 26
for Exs. 22–27

ANGLE ADDITION POSTULATE Find the indicated angle measure.

22. $m\angle QST = $ ___?___ 99°   **(23.)** $m\angle ADC = $ ___?___ 65   **24.** $m\angle NPM = $ ___?___ 101

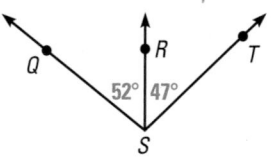

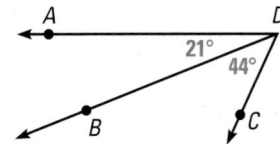

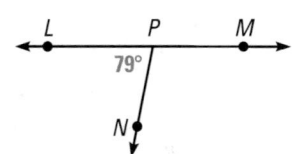

ALGEBRA Use the given information to find the indicated angle measure.

25. Given $m\angle WXZ = 80°$, find $m\angle YXZ$.   **26.** Given $m\angle FJH = 168°$, find $m\angle FJG$.

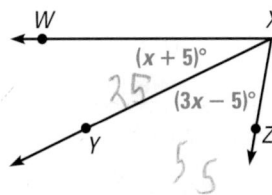

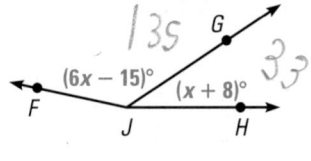

27. ★ **MULTIPLE CHOICE** In the diagram, the measure of $\angle XYZ$ is 140°. What is the value of *x*?

(A) 27   (B) 33

(C) 67   (D) 73

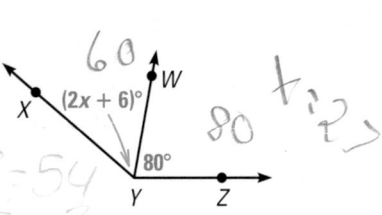

EXAMPLE 4
on p. 27
for Ex. 28

28. CONGRUENT ANGLES In the photograph below, $m\angle AED = 34°$ and $m\angle EAD = 112°$. Identify the congruent angles in the diagram. Then find $m\angle BDC$ and $m\angle ADB$.

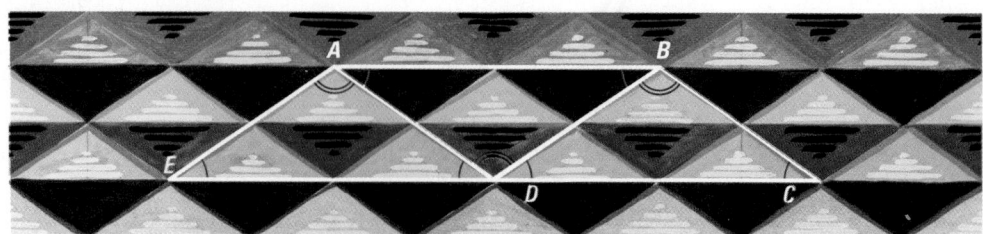

EXAMPLE 5
on p. 28
for Exs. 29–32

ANGLE BISECTORS Given that $\overrightarrow{WZ}$ bisects $\angle XWY$, find the two angle measures not given in the diagram.

29.

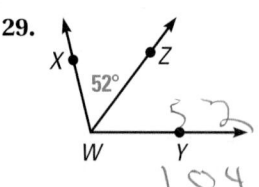

30.

31.

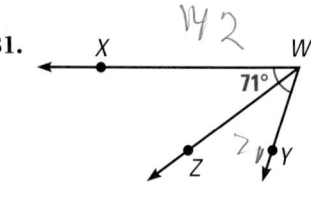

32. ERROR ANALYSIS $\overrightarrow{KM}$ bisects $\angle JKL$ and $m\angle JKM = 30°$. *Describe* and correct the error made in stating that $m\angle JKL = 15°$. Draw a sketch to support your answer.

FINDING ANGLE MEASURES Find the indicated angle measure.

33. $a°$ **34.** $b°$

35. $c°$ **36.** $d°$

37. $e°$ **38.** $f°$

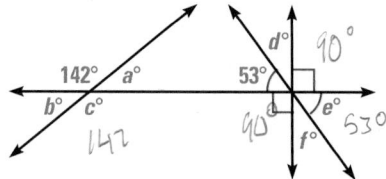

39. ERROR ANALYSIS A student states that $\overrightarrow{AD}$ can bisect $\angle AGC$. *Describe* and correct the student's error. Draw a sketch to support your answer.

xy **ALGEBRA** In each diagram, $\overrightarrow{BD}$ bisects $\angle ABC$. Find $m\angle ABC$.

40.

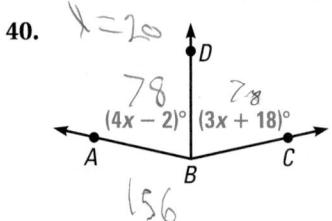

41.

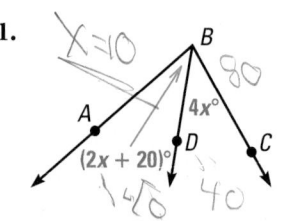

42.

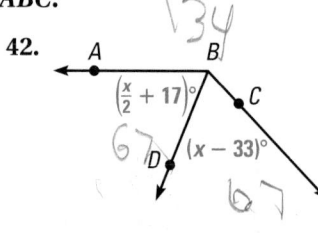

43. ★ SHORT RESPONSE You are measuring $\angle PQR$ with a protractor. When you line up $\overrightarrow{QR}$ with the 20° mark, $\overrightarrow{QP}$ lines up with the 80° mark. Then you move the protractor so that $\overrightarrow{QR}$ lines up with the 15° mark. What mark does $\overrightarrow{QP}$ line up with? *Explain.*

xy **ALGEBRA** Plot the points in a coordinate plane and draw $\angle ABC$. Classify the angle. Then give the coordinates of a point that lies in the interior of the angle.

44. $A(3, 3)$, $B(0, 0)$, $C(3, 0)$ **45.** $A(-5, 4)$, $B(1, 4)$, $C(-2, -2)$

46. $A(-5, 2)$, $B(-2, -2)$, $C(4, -3)$ **47.** $A(-3, -1)$, $B(2, 1)$, $C(6, -2)$

○ = **WORKED-OUT SOLUTIONS**
on p. WS1

★ = **STANDARDIZED TEST PRACTICE**

48. ✖✗ **ALGEBRA** Let $(2x - 12)°$ represent the measure of an acute angle. What are the possible values of x?

49. **CHALLENGE** $\overrightarrow{SQ}$ bisects $\angle RST$, $\overrightarrow{SP}$ bisects $\angle RSQ$, and $\overrightarrow{SV}$ bisects $\angle RSP$. The measure of $\angle VSP$ is 17°. Find $m\angle TSQ$. *Explain.*

50. **FINDING MEASURES** In the diagram, $m\angle AEB = \frac{1}{2} \cdot m\angle CED$, and $\angle AED$ is a straight angle. Find $m\angle AEB$ and $m\angle CED$.

PROBLEM SOLVING

51. **SCULPTURE** In the sculpture shown in the photograph, suppose the measure of $\angle LMN$ is 79° and the measure of $\angle PMN$ is 47°. What is the measure of $\angle LMP$?

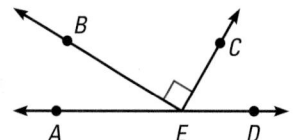

@HomeTutor for problem solving help at classzone.com

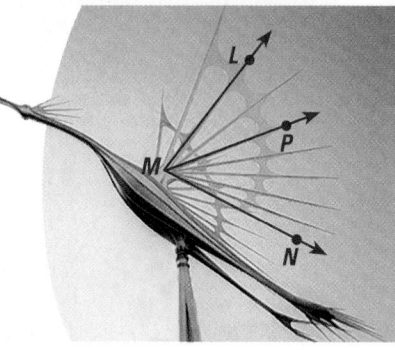

52. **MAP** The map shows the intersection of three roads. Malcom Way intersects Sydney Street at an angle of 162°. Park Road intersects Sydney Street at an angle of 87°. Find the angle at which Malcom Way intersects Park Road.

@HomeTutor for problem solving help at classzone.com

EXAMPLES
4 and 5
on pp. 27–28
for Exs. 53–55

CONSTRUCTION In Exercises 53–55, use the photograph of a roof truss.

53. In the roof truss, $\overrightarrow{BG}$ bisects $\angle ABC$ and $\angle DEF$, $m\angle ABC = 112°$, and $\angle ABC \cong \angle DEF$. Find the measure of the following angles.

    a. $m\angle DEF$ **b.** $m\angle ABG$

    c. $m\angle CBG$ **d.** $m\angle DEG$

54. In the roof truss, $\overrightarrow{GB}$ bisects $\angle DGF$. Find $m\angle DGE$ and $m\angle FGE$.

55. Name an example of each of the following types of angles: *acute, obtuse, right,* and *straight.*

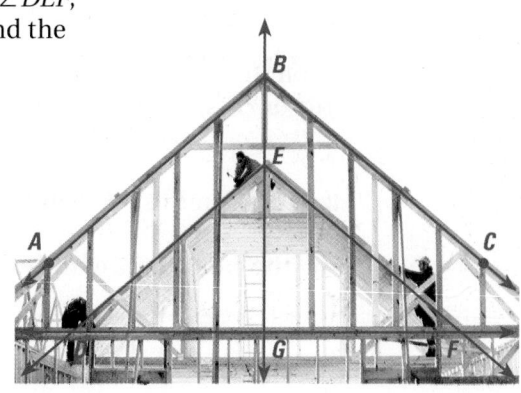

GEOGRAPHY For the given location on the map, estimate the measure of ∠*PSL*, where *P* is on the Prime Meridian (0° longitude), *S* is the South Pole, and *L* is the location of the indicated research station.

56. Macquarie Island   **57.** Dumont d'Urville   **58.** McMurdo

59. Mawson   **60.** Syowa   **61.** Vostok

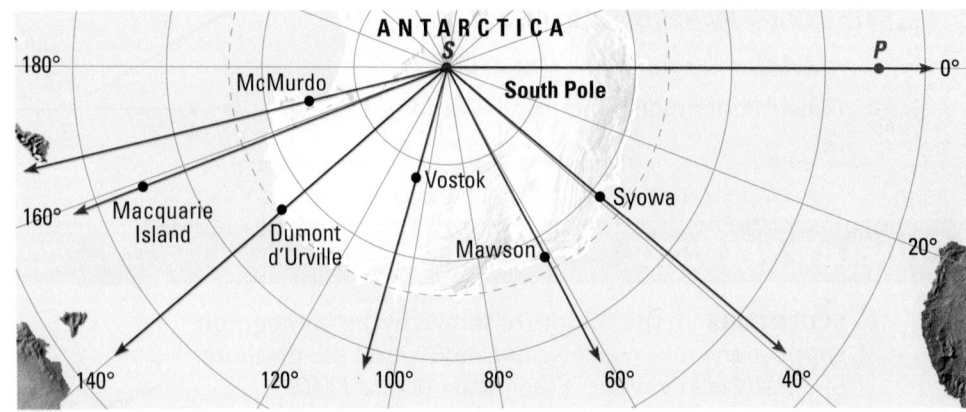

62. ★ **EXTENDED RESPONSE** In the flag shown, ∠*AFE* is a straight angle and $\overrightarrow{FC}$ bisects ∠*AFE* and ∠*BFD*.

   a. Which angles are acute? obtuse? right?

   b. Identify the congruent angles.

   c. If $m\angle AFB = 26°$, find $m\angle DFE$, $m\angle BFC$, $m\angle CFD$, $m\angle AFC$, $m\angle AFD$, and $m\angle BFD$. *Explain*.

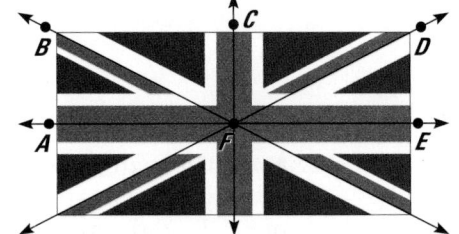

63. **CHALLENGE** Create a set of data that could be represented by the circle graph at the right. *Explain* your reasoning.

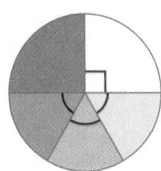

MIXED REVIEW

PREVIEW
Prepare for
Lesson 1.5
in Ex. 64.

64. You and a friend go out to dinner and each pay for your own meal. The total cost of the two meals is $25. Your meal cost $4 more than your friend's meal. How much does each meal cost? *(p. 894)*

Graph the inequality on a number line. Tell whether the graph is a *segment*, a *ray* or *rays*, a *point*, or a *line*. *(p. 2)*

65. $x \le -8$ **66.** $x \ge 6$ **67.** $-3 \le x \le 5$

68. $x \ge -7$ and $x \le -1$ **69.** $x \ge -2$ or $x \le 4$ **70.** $|x| \ge 0$

Find the coordinate of the midpoint of the segment. *(p. 15)*

71. ◄─┼─┼─┼─┼─┼─┼─►
     −6 −4 −2 0

72. ◄─┼─┼─┼─┼─┼─►
     −30 0 30 60

73. ◄─┼─┼─┼─┼─┼─┼─►
     −24 −16 −8 0

1.4 Copy and Bisect Segments and Angles

MATERIALS · compass · straightedge

QUESTION How can you copy and bisect segments and angles?

A **construction** is a geometric drawing that uses a limited set of tools, usually a *compass* and *straightedge*. You can use a compass and straightedge (a ruler without marks) to construct a segment that is congruent to a given segment, and an angle that is congruent to a given angle.

EXPLORE 1 Copy a segment

Use the following steps to construct a segment that is congruent to $\overline{AB}$.

STEP 1

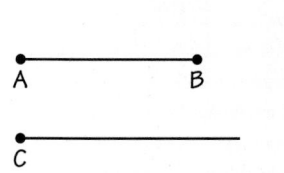

STEP 2

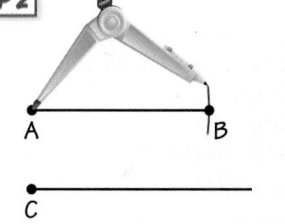

STEP 3

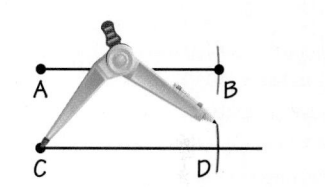

Draw a segment Use a straightedge to draw a segment longer than $\overline{AB}$. Label point C on the new segment.

Measure length Set your compass at the length of $\overline{AB}$.

Copy length Place the compass at C. Mark point D on the new segment. $\overline{CD} \cong \overline{AB}$.

EXPLORE 2 Bisect a segment

Use the following steps to construct a bisector of $\overline{AB}$ and to find the midpoint M of $\overline{AB}$.

STEP 1

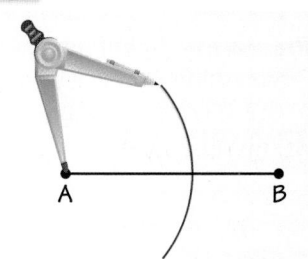

STEP 2

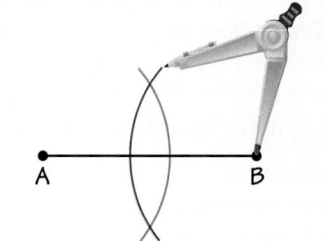

STEP 3

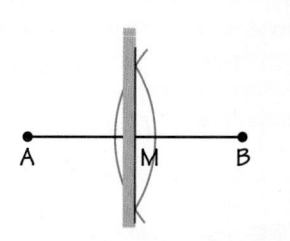

Draw an arc Place the compass at A. Use a compass setting that is greater than half the length of $\overline{AB}$. Draw an arc.

Draw a second arc Keep the same compass setting. Place the compass at B. Draw an arc. It should intersect the other arc at two points.

Bisect segment Draw a segment through the two points of intersection. This segment bisects $\overline{AB}$ at M, the midpoint of $\overline{AB}$.

EXPLORE 3 Copy an angle

Use the following steps to construct an angle that is congruent to ∠A. In this construction, the *radius* of an arc is the distance from the point where the compass point rests (the *center* of the arc) to a point on the arc drawn by the compass.

STEP 1	STEP 2	STEP 3	STEP 4
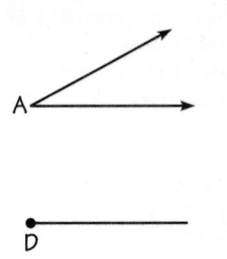	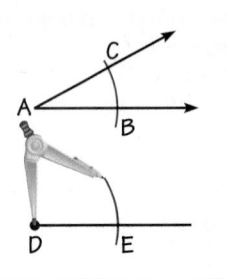	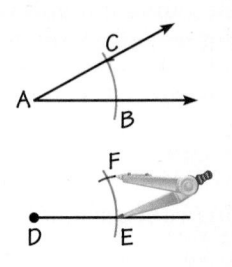	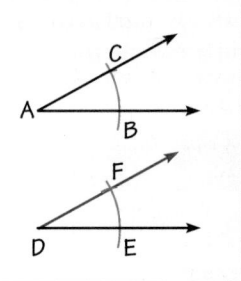

Draw a segment

Draw a segment. Label a point *D* on the segment.

Draw arcs

Draw an arc with center *A*. Using the same radius, draw an arc with center *D*.

Draw arcs

Label *B*, *C*, and *E*. Draw an arc with radius *BC* and center *E*. Label the intersection *F*.

Draw a ray

Draw $\overrightarrow{DF}$.
∠*EDF* ≅ ∠*BAC*.

EXPLORE 4 Bisect an angle

Use the following steps to construct an angle bisector of ∠A.

STEP 1	STEP 2	STEP 3
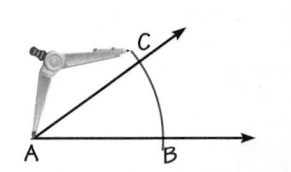	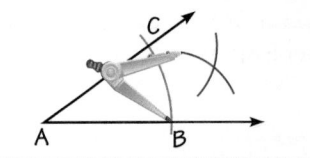	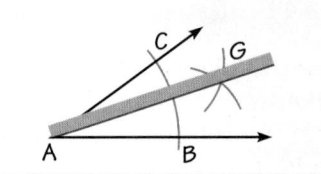

Draw an arc Place the compass at *A*. Draw an arc that intersects both sides of the angle. Label the intersections *C* and *B*.

Draw arcs Place the compass at *C*. Draw an arc. Then place the compass point at *B*. Using the same radius, draw another arc.

Draw a ray Label the intersection *G*. Use a straightedge to draw a ray through *A* and *G*. $\overrightarrow{AG}$ bisects ∠*A*.

DRAW CONCLUSIONS Use your observations to complete these exercises

1. *Describe* how you could use a compass and a straightedge to draw a segment that is twice as long as a given segment.

2. Draw an obtuse angle. Copy the angle using a compass and a straightedge. Then bisect the angle using a compass and straightedge.

1.5 Describe Angle Pair Relationships

Before You used angle postulates to measure and classify angles.

Now You will use special angle relationships to find angle measures.

Why? So you can find measures in a building, as in Ex. 53.

Key Vocabulary
• **complementary angles**
• **supplementary angles**
• **adjacent angles**
• **linear pair**
• **vertical angles**

Two angles are **complementary angles** if the sum of their measures is 90°. Each angle is the *complement* of the other. Two angles are **supplementary angles** if the sum of their measures is 180°. Each angle is the *supplement* of the other.

Complementary angles and supplementary angles can be *adjacent angles* or *nonadjacent angles*. **Adjacent angles** are two angles that share a common vertex and side, but have no common interior points.

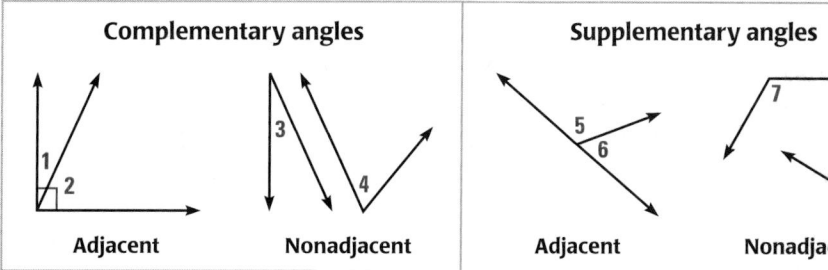

Complementary angles	**Supplementary angles**
Adjacent Nonadjacent	Adjacent Nonadjacent

EXAMPLE 1 Identify complements and supplements

AVOID ERRORS

In Example 1, ∠DAC and ∠DAB share a common vertex. But they share common interior points, so they are *not* adjacent angles.

In the figure, name a pair of complementary angles, a pair of supplementary angles, and a pair of adjacent angles.

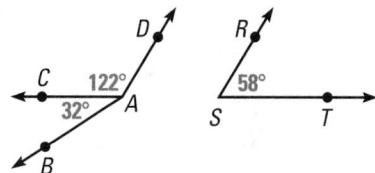

Solution

Because 32° + 58° = 90°, ∠BAC and ∠RST are complementary angles.

Because 122° + 58° = 180°, ∠CAD and ∠RST are supplementary angles.

Because ∠BAC and ∠CAD share a common vertex and side, they are adjacent.

✓ **GUIDED PRACTICE** for Example 1

1. In the figure, name a pair of complementary angles, a pair of supplementary angles, and a pair of adjacent angles.

2. Are ∠KGH and ∠LKG adjacent angles? Are ∠FGK and ∠FGH adjacent angles? *Explain.*

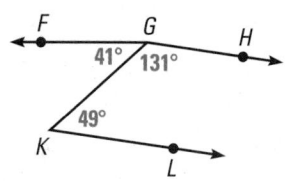

EXAMPLE 2 Find measures of a complement and a supplement

READ DIAGRAMS

Angles are sometimes named with numbers. An angle measure in a diagram has a degree symbol. An angle name does not.

a. Given that $\angle 1$ is a complement of $\angle 2$ and $m\angle 1 = 68°$, find $m\angle 2$.

b. Given that $\angle 3$ is a supplement of $\angle 4$ and $m\angle 4 = 56°$, find $m\angle 3$.

Solution

a. You can draw a diagram with complementary adjacent angles to illustrate the relationship.

$$m\angle 2 = 90° - m\angle 1 = 90° - 68° = 22°$$

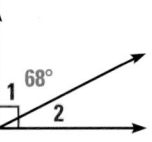

b. You can draw a diagram with supplementary adjacent angles to illustrate the relationship.

$$m\angle 3 = 180° - m\angle 4 = 180° - 56° = 124°$$

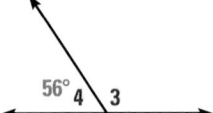

EXAMPLE 3 Find angle measures

READ DIAGRAMS

In a diagram, you can assume that a line that looks straight *is* straight. In Example 3, *B*, *C*, and *D* lie on $\overleftrightarrow{BD}$. So, $\angle BCD$ is a straight angle.

SPORTS When viewed from the side, the frame of a ball-return net forms a pair of supplementary angles with the ground. Find $m\angle BCE$ and $m\angle ECD$.

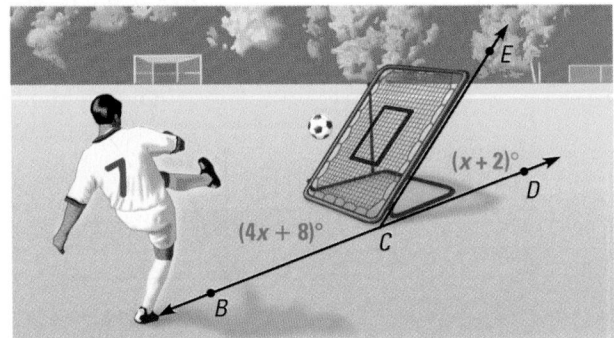

Solution

STEP 1 Use the fact that the sum of the measures of supplementary angles is 180°.

$m\angle BCE + m\angle ECD = 180°$	Write equation.
$(4x + 8)° + (x + 2)° = 180°$	Substitute.
$5x + 10 = 180$	Combine like terms.
$5x = 170$	Subtract 10 from each side.
$x = 34$	Divide each side by 5.

STEP 2 Evaluate the original expressions when $x = 34$.

$$m\angle BCE = (4x + 8)° = (4 \cdot 34 + 8)° = 144°$$

$$m\angle ECD = (x + 2)° = (34 + 2)° = 36°$$

▶ The angle measures are 144° and 36°.

 GUIDED PRACTICE for Examples 2 and 3

3. Given that $\angle 1$ is a complement of $\angle 2$ and $m\angle 2 = 8°$, find $m\angle 1$.

4. Given that $\angle 3$ is a supplement of $\angle 4$ and $m\angle 3 = 117°$, find $m\angle 4$.

5. $\angle LMN$ and $\angle PQR$ are complementary angles. Find the measures of the angles if $m\angle LMN = (4x - 2)°$ and $m\angle PQR = (9x + 1)°$.

ANGLE PAIRS Two adjacent angles are a **linear pair** if their noncommon sides are opposite rays. The angles in a linear pair are supplementary angles.

Two angles are **vertical angles** if their sides form two pairs of opposite rays.

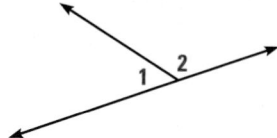

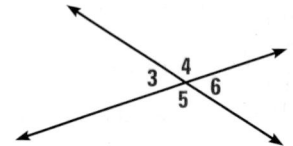

∠1 and ∠2 are a linear pair.

∠3 and ∠6 are vertical angles.
∠4 and ∠5 are vertical angles.

EXAMPLE 4 Identify angle pairs

AVOID ERRORS
In the diagram, one side of ∠1 and one side of ∠3 are opposite rays. But the angles are not a linear pair because they are not adjacent.

Identify all of the linear pairs and all of the vertical angles in the figure at the right.

Solution

To find vertical angles, look for angles formed by intersecting lines.

▸ ∠1 and ∠5 are vertical angles.

To find linear pairs, look for adjacent angles whose noncommon sides are opposite rays.

▸ ∠1 and ∠4 are a linear pair. ∠4 and ∠5 are also a linear pair.

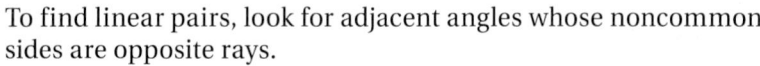

EXAMPLE 5 Find angle measures in a linear pair

⊗ ALGEBRA **Two angles form a linear pair. The measure of one angle is 5 times the measure of the other. Find the measure of each angle.**

Solution

DRAW DIAGRAMS
You may find it useful to draw a diagram to represent a word problem like the one in Example 5.

Let $x°$ be the measure of one angle. The measure of the other angle is $5x°$. Then use the fact that the angles of a linear pair are supplementary to write an equation.

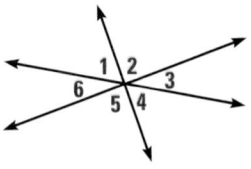

$$x° + 5x° = 180°$$ **Write an equation.**

$$6x = 180$$ **Combine like terms.**

$$x = 30$$ **Divide each side by 6.**

▸ The measures of the angles are 30° and 5(30°) = 150°.

✓ **GUIDED PRACTICE** for Examples 4 and 5

6. Do any of the numbered angles in the diagram at the right form a linear pair? Which angles are vertical angles? *Explain.*

7. The measure of an angle is twice the measure of its complement. Find the measure of each angle.

CONCEPT SUMMARY

For Your Notebook

Interpreting a Diagram

There are some things you can conclude from a diagram, and some you cannot. For example, here are some things that you *can* conclude from the diagram at the right:

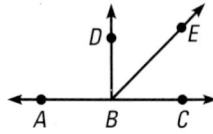

- All points shown are coplanar.
- Points *A*, *B*, and *C* are collinear, and *B* is between *A* and *C*.
- $\overleftrightarrow{AC}$, $\overrightarrow{BD}$, and $\overrightarrow{BE}$ intersect at point *B*.
- ∠*DBE* and ∠*EBC* are adjacent angles, and ∠*ABC* is a straight angle.
- Point *E* lies in the interior of ∠*DBC*.

In the diagram above, you *cannot* conclude that $\overline{AB} \cong \overline{BC}$, that ∠*DBE* ≅ ∠*EBC*, or that ∠*ABD* is a right angle. This information must be indicated, as shown at the right.

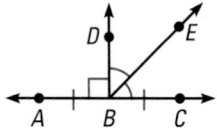

1.5 EXERCISES

HOMEWORK KEY

○ = **WORKED-OUT SOLUTIONS**
on p. WS1 for Exs. 9, 21, and 47

★ = **STANDARDIZED TEST PRACTICE**
Exs. 2, 16, 30, and 53

◆ = **MULTIPLE REPRESENTATIONS**
Ex. 55

SKILL PRACTICE

1. **VOCABULARY** Sketch an example of adjacent angles that are complementary. Are all complementary angles adjacent angles? *Explain.*

2. ★ **WRITING** Are all linear pairs supplementary angles? Are all supplementary angles linear pairs? *Explain.*

EXAMPLE 1
on p. 35
for Exs. 3–7

IDENTIFYING ANGLES Tell whether the indicated angles are adjacent.

3. ∠*ABD* and ∠*DBC*

4. ∠*WXY* and ∠*XYZ*

5. ∠*LQM* and ∠*NQM*

IDENTIFYING ANGLES Name a pair of complementary angles and a pair of supplementary angles.

6.

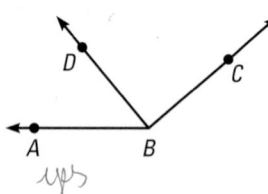
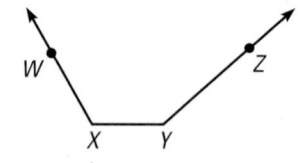

7.

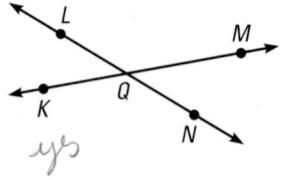

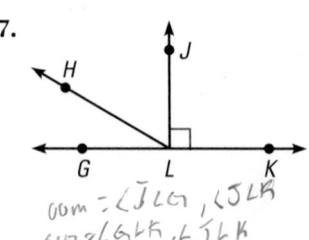

EXAMPLE 2
on p. 36
for Exs. 8–16

COMPLEMENTARY ANGLES ∠1 and ∠2 are complementary angles. Given the measure of ∠1, find m∠2.

8. m∠1 = 43°   9. m∠1 = 21°   10. m∠1 = 89°   11. m∠1 = 5°

SUPPLEMENTARY ANGLES ∠1 and ∠2 are supplementary angles. Given the measure of ∠1, find m∠2.

12. m∠1 = 60°   13. m∠1 = 155°   14. m∠1 = 130°   15. m∠1 = 27°

16. ★ **MULTIPLE CHOICE** The arm of a crossing gate moves 37° from vertical. How many more degrees does the arm have to move so that it is horizontal?

  Ⓐ 37°
  Ⓑ 53°
  Ⓒ 90°
  Ⓓ 143°

EXAMPLE 3
on p. 36
for Exs. 17–19

ⓍⓎ ALGEBRA Find m∠DEG and m∠GEF.

17.
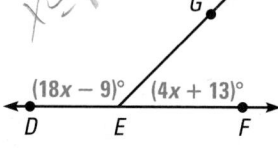

18.
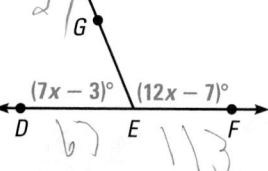

19.
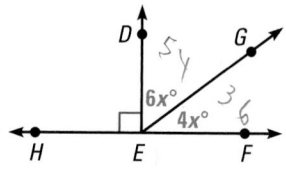

EXAMPLE 4
on p. 37
for Exs. 20–27

IDENTIFYING ANGLE PAIRS Use the diagram below. Tell whether the angles are *vertical angles*, a *linear pair*, or *neither*.

20. ∠1 and ∠4   21. ∠1 and ∠2

22. ∠3 and ∠5   23. ∠2 and ∠3

24. ∠7, ∠8, and ∠9   25. ∠5 and ∠6

26. ∠6 and ∠7   27. ∠5 and ∠9

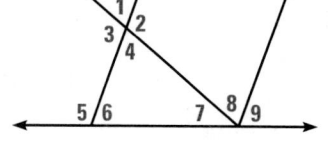

EXAMPLE 5
on p. 37
for Exs. 28–30

28. **ⓍⓎ ALGEBRA** Two angles form a linear pair. The measure of one angle is 4 times the measure of the other angle. Find the measure of each angle.

29. **ERROR ANALYSIS** *Describe* and correct the error made in finding the value of *x*.

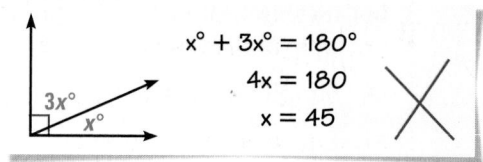

  x° + 3x° = 180°
  4x = 180
  x = 45

30. ★ **MULTIPLE CHOICE** The measure of one angle is 24° greater than the measure of its complement. What are the measures of the angles?

  Ⓐ 24° and 66°   Ⓑ 24° and 156°   Ⓒ 33° and 57°   Ⓓ 78° and 102°

ⓍⓎ ALGEBRA Find the values of *x* and *y*.

31.
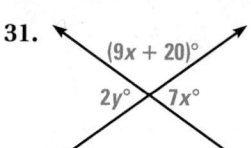

32.
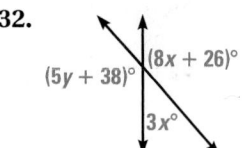

33.
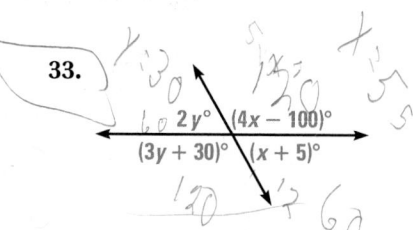

1.5 Describe Angle Pair Relationships   **39**

34. An obtuse angle has a complement.

35. A straight angle has a complement.

36. An angle has a supplement.

37. The complement of an acute angle is an acute angle.

38. The supplement of an acute angle is an obtuse angle.

FINDING ANGLES $\angle A$ and $\angle B$ are complementary. Find $m\angle A$ and $m\angle B$.

39. $m\angle A = (3x + 2)°$
$m\angle B = (x - 4)°$

40. $m\angle A = (15x + 3)°$
$m\angle B = (5x - 13)°$

41. $m\angle A = (11x + 24)°$
$m\angle B = (x + 18)°$

FINDING ANGLES $\angle A$ and $\angle B$ are supplementary. Find $m\angle A$ and $m\angle B$.

42. $m\angle A = (8x + 100)°$
$m\angle B = (2x + 50)°$

43. $m\angle A = (2x - 20)°$
$m\angle B = (3x + 5)°$

44. $m\angle A = (6x + 72)°$
$m\angle B = (2x + 28)°$

45. CHALLENGE You are given that $\angle GHJ$ is a complement of $\angle RST$ and $\angle RST$ is a supplement of $\angle ABC$. Let $m\angle GHJ$ be $x°$. What is the measure of $\angle ABC$? *Explain* your reasoning.

PROBLEM SOLVING

IDENTIFYING ANGLES Tell whether the two angles shown are *complementary*, *supplementary*, or *neither*.

46.

47.

48.

@HomeTutor for problem solving help at classzone.com

ARCHITECTURE The photograph shows the Rock and Roll Hall of Fame in Cleveland, Ohio. Use the photograph to identify an example of the indicated type of angle pair.

49. Supplementary angles

50. Vertical angles

51. Linear pair

52. Adjacent angles

@HomeTutor for problem solving help at classzone.com

53. ★ **SHORT RESPONSE** Use the photograph shown at the right. Given that $\angle FGB$ and $\angle BGC$ are supplementary angles, and $m\angle FGB = 120°$, *explain* how to find the measure of the complement of $\angle BGC$.

○ = **WORKED-OUT SOLUTIONS** on p. WS1

★ = **STANDARDIZED TEST PRACTICE**

◆ = **MULTIPLE REPRESENTATIONS**

54. SHADOWS The length of a shadow changes as the sun rises. In the diagram below, the length of $\overline{CB}$ is the length of a shadow. The end of the shadow is the vertex of $\angle ABC$, which is formed by the ground and the sun's rays. *Describe* how the shadow and angle change as the sun rises.

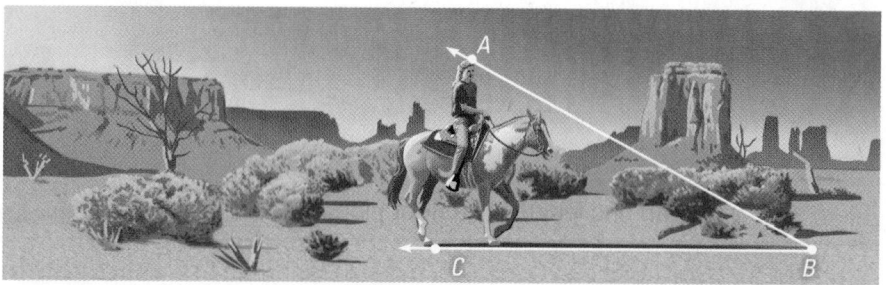

55. ◆ **MULTIPLE REPRESENTATIONS** Let $x°$ be an angle measure. Let $y_1°$ be the measure of a complement of the angle and let $y_2°$ be the measure of a supplement of the angle.

   a. Writing an Equation Write equations for y_1 as a function of x, and for y_2 as a function of x. What is the domain of each function? *Explain.*

   b. Drawing a Graph Graph each function and *describe* its range.

56. CHALLENGE The sum of the measures of two complementary angles exceeds the difference of their measures by 86°. Find the measure of each angle. *Explain* how you found the angle measures.

MIXED REVIEW

Make a table of values and graph the function. *(p. 884)*

57. $y = 5 - x$　　**58.** $y = 3x$　　**59.** $y = x^2 - 1$　　**60.** $y = -2x^2$

PREVIEW
Prepare for
Lesson 1.6 in
Exs. 61–63.

In each figure, name the congruent sides and congruent angles. *(pp. 9, 24)*

61. 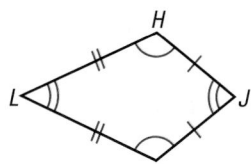　　**62.** 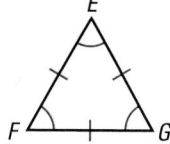　　**63.**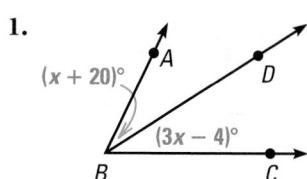

QUIZ *for Lessons 1.4–1.5*

In each diagram, $\overrightarrow{BD}$ bisects $\angle ABC$. Find $m\angle ABD$ and $m\angle DBC$. *(p. 24)*

1. 　　　　　**2.** 　　　　　**3.**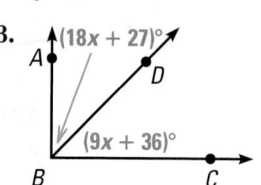

Find the measure of (a) the complement and (b) the supplement of $\angle 1$. *(p. 35)*

4. $m\angle 1 = 47°$　　**5.** $m\angle 1 = 19°$　　**6.** $m\angle 1 = 75°$　　**7.** $m\angle 1 = 2°$

EXTRA PRACTICE for Lesson 1.5, p. 897　　🔁 **ONLINE QUIZ** at classzone.com　　**41**

1.6 Classify Polygons

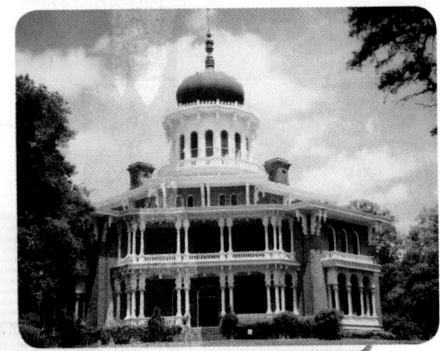

Before	You classified angles.
Now	You will classify polygons.
Why?	So you can find lengths in a floor plan, as in Ex. 32.

Key Vocabulary
- **polygon**
  side, vertex
- **convex**
- **concave**
- *n*-gon
- **equilateral**
- **equiangular**
- **regular**

KEY CONCEPT
For Your Notebook

Identifying Polygons

In geometry, a figure that lies in a plane is called a *plane figure*. A **polygon** is a closed plane figure with the following properties.

1. It is formed by three or more line segments called **sides**.

2. Each side intersects exactly two sides, one at each endpoint, so that no two sides with a common endpoint are collinear.

Each endpoint of a side is a **vertex** of the polygon. The plural of vertex is *vertices*. A polygon can be named by listing the vertices in consecutive order. For example, *ABCDE* and *CDEAB* are both correct names for the polygon at the right.

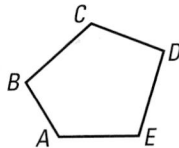

A polygon is **convex** if no line that contains a side of the polygon contains a point in the interior of the polygon. A polygon that is not convex is called *nonconvex* or **concave**.

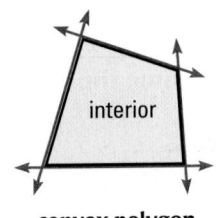

convex polygon

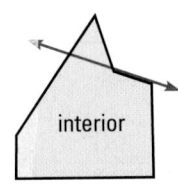

concave polygon

EXAMPLE 1 Identify polygons

Tell whether the figure is a polygon and whether it is *convex* or *concave*.

a.  b.  c.  d.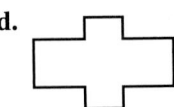

Solution

  a. Some segments intersect more than two segments, so it is not a polygon.

  b. The figure is a convex polygon.

  c. Part of the figure is not a segment, so it is not a polygon.

  d. The figure is a concave polygon.

CLASSIFYING POLYGONS A polygon is named by the number of its sides.

Number of sides	Type of polygon
3	Triangle
4	Quadrilateral
5	Pentagon
6	Hexagon
7	Heptagon

Number of sides	Type of polygon
8	Octagon
9	Nonagon
10	Decagon
12	Dodecagon
n	n-gon

The term **n-gon**, where n is the number of a polygon's sides, can also be used to name a polygon. For example, a polygon with 14 sides is a 14-gon.

In an **equilateral** polygon, all sides are congruent. In an **equiangular** polygon, all angles in the interior of the polygon are congruent. A **regular** polygon is a convex polygon that is both equilateral and equiangular.

regular pentagon

EXAMPLE 2 **Classify polygons**

READ DIAGRAMS
Double marks are used in part (b) of Example 2 to show that more than one pair of sides are congruent and more than one pair of angles are congruent.

Classify the polygon by the number of sides. Tell whether the polygon is equilateral, equiangular, or regular. Explain your reasoning.

a. 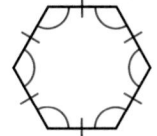   **b.** 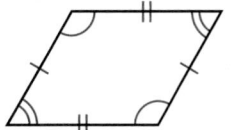   **c.**

Solution

a. The polygon has 6 sides. It is equilateral and equiangular, so it is a regular hexagon.

b. The polygon has 4 sides, so it is a quadrilateral. It is not equilateral or equiangular, so it is not regular.

c. The polygon has 12 sides, so it is a dodecagon. The sides are congruent, so it is equilateral. The polygon is not convex, so it is not regular.

Animated Geometry at classzone.com

✓ **GUIDED PRACTICE**   for Examples 1 and 2

1. Sketch an example of a convex heptagon and an example of a concave heptagon.

2. Classify the polygon shown at the right by the number of sides. *Explain* how you know that the sides of the polygon are congruent and that the angles of the polygon are congruent.

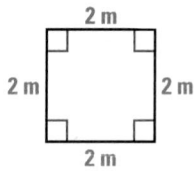

EXAMPLE 3 **Find side lengths**

READ VOCABULARY
Hexagonal means
"shaped like a hexagon."

xy ALGEBRA A table is shaped like a regular hexagon. The expressions shown represent side lengths of the hexagonal table. Find the length of a side.

$(3x + 6)$ in.

$(4x - 2)$ in.

Solution

First, write and solve an equation to find the value of x. Use the fact that the sides of a regular hexagon are congruent.

$3x + 6 = 4x - 2$ **Write equation.**

$6 = x - 2$ **Subtract $3x$ from each side.**

$8 = x$ **Add 2 to each side.**

Then find a side length. Evaluate one of the expressions when $x = 8$.

$3x + 6 = 3(8) + 6 = 30$

▶ The length of a side of the table is 30 inches.

✓ **GUIDED PRACTICE** for Example 3

3. The expressions $8y°$ and $(9y - 15)°$ represent the measures of two of the angles in the table in Example 3. Find the measure of an angle.

1.6 EXERCISES

HOMEWORK KEY

○ = **WORKED-OUT SOLUTIONS**
 on p. WS1 for Exs. 13, 19, and 33

★ = **STANDARDIZED TEST PRACTICE**
 Exs. 2, 7, 37, 39, and 40

SKILL PRACTICE

1. VOCABULARY *Explain* what is meant by the term *n*-gon.

2. ★ WRITING Imagine that you can tie a string tightly around a polygon. If the polygon is convex, will the length of the string be equal to the distance around the polygon? What if the polygon is concave? *Explain*.

EXAMPLE 1
on p. 42
for Exs. 3–7

IDENTIFYING POLYGONS Tell whether the figure is a polygon. If it is not, *explain* why. If it is a polygon, tell whether it is *convex* or *concave*.

3.

4.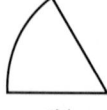

5.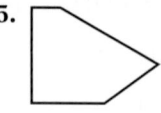

6.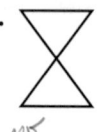

7. ★ MULTIPLE CHOICE Which of the figures is a concave polygon?

Ⓐ    Ⓑ    Ⓒ 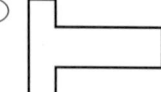   Ⓓ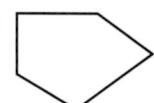

EXAMPLE 2
on p. 43
for Exs. 8–14

CLASSIFYING Classify the polygon by the number of sides. Tell whether the polygon is equilateral, equiangular, or regular. *Explain* your reasoning.

8. 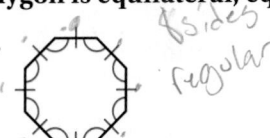 *8 sides regular*

9. 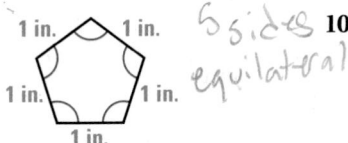 *5 sides equilateral*

10. *3 sides regular*

11.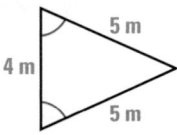

12.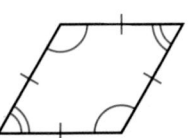

13.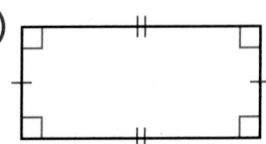

14. **ERROR ANALYSIS** Two students were asked to draw a regular hexagon, as shown below. *Describe* the error made by each student.

Student A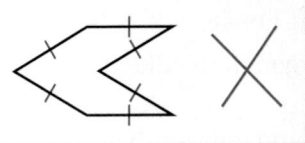

Student B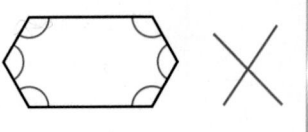

EXAMPLE 3
on p. 44
for Exs. 15–17

15. **ALGEBRA** The lengths (in inches) of two sides of a regular pentagon are represented by the expressions $5x - 27$ and $2x - 6$. Find the length of a side of the pentagon.

16. **ALGEBRA** The expressions $(9x + 5)°$ and $(11x - 25)°$ represent the measures of two angles of a regular nonagon. Find the measure of an angle of the nonagon.

17. **ALGEBRA** The expressions $3x - 9$ and $23 - 5x$ represent the lengths (in feet) of two sides of an equilateral triangle. Find the length of a side.

USING PROPERTIES Tell whether the statement is *always, sometimes,* or *never* true.

18. A triangle is convex.

19. A decagon is regular.

20. A regular polygon is equiangular.

21. A circle is a polygon.

22. A polygon is a plane figure.

23. A concave polygon is regular.

DRAWING Draw a figure that fits the description.

24. A triangle that is not regular

25. A concave quadrilateral

26. A pentagon that is equilateral but not equiangular

27. An octagon that is equiangular but not equilateral

ALGEBRA Each figure is a regular polygon. Expressions are given for two side lengths. Find the value of *x*.

28.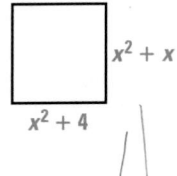
$x^2 + x$
$x^2 + 4$

29.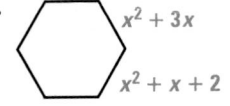
$x^2 + 3x$
$x^2 + x + 2$

30.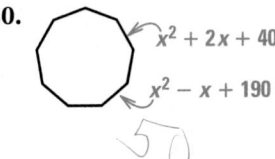
$x^2 + 2x + 40$
$x^2 - x + 190$

31. CHALLENGE Regular pentagonal tiles and triangular tiles are arranged in the pattern shown. The pentagonal tiles are all the same size and shape and the triangular tiles are all the same size and shape. Find the angle measures of the triangular tiles. *Explain* your reasoning.

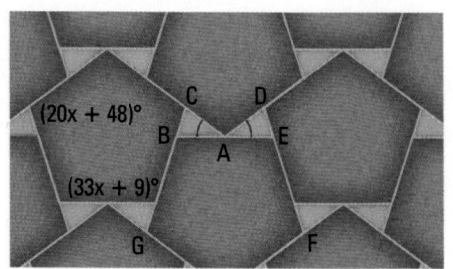

PROBLEM SOLVING

32. ARCHITECTURE Longwood House, shown in the photograph on page 42, is located in Natchez, Mississippi. The diagram at the right shows the floor plan of a part of the house.

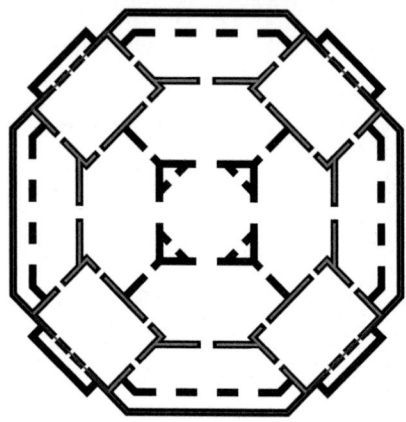

  a. Tell whether the red polygon in the diagram is *convex* or *concave*.

  b. Classify the red polygon and tell whether it appears to be regular.

@**HomeTutor** for problem solving help at classzone.com

EXAMPLE 2
on p. 43
for Exs. 33–36

SIGNS Each sign suggests a polygon. Classify the polygon by the number of sides. Tell whether it appears to be *equilateral*, *equiangular*, or *regular*.

(33.)  **34.**  **35.**  **36.**

@**HomeTutor** for problem solving help at classzone.com

37. ★ MULTIPLE CHOICE Two vertices of a regular quadrilateral are $A(0, 4)$ and $B(0, -4)$. Which of the following could be the other two vertices?

  (A) $C(4, 4)$ and $D(4, -4)$ **(B)** $C(-4, 4)$ and $D(-4, -4)$

  (C) $C(8, -4)$ and $D(8, 4)$ **(D)** $C(0, 8)$ and $D(0, -8)$

38. MULTI-STEP PROBLEM The diagram shows the design of a lattice made in China in 1850.

  a. Sketch five different polygons you see in the diagram. Classify each polygon by the number of sides.

  b. Tell whether each polygon you sketched is concave or convex, and whether the polygon appears to be equilateral, equiangular, or regular.

◯ = **WORKED-OUT SOLUTIONS**
on p. WS1

★ = **STANDARDIZED TEST PRACTICE**

EXAMPLE 3
on p. 44
for Ex. 39

39. ★ **SHORT RESPONSE** The shape of the button shown is a regular polygon. The button has a border made of silver wire. How many millimeters of silver wire are needed for this border? *Explain.*

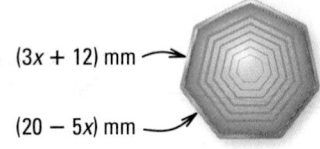

$(3x + 12)$ mm →

$(20 − 5x)$ mm →

40. ★ **EXTENDED RESPONSE** A segment that joins two nonconsecutive vertices of a polygon is called a *diagonal*. For example, a quadrilateral has two diagonals, as shown below.

Type of polygon	Diagram	Number of sides	Number of diagonals
Quadrilateral	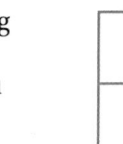	4	2
Pentagon	?	?	?
Hexagon	?	?	?
Heptagon	?	?	?

a. Copy and complete the table. *Describe* any patterns you see.

b. How many diagonals does an octagon have? a nonagon? *Explain.*

c. The expression $\dfrac{n(n − 3)}{2}$ can be used to find the number of diagonals in an *n*-gon. Find the number of diagonals in a 60-gon.

41. **LINE SYMMETRY** A figure has *line symmetry* if it can be folded over exactly onto itself. The fold line is called the *line of symmetry*. A regular quadrilateral has four lines of symmetry, as shown. Find the number of lines of symmetry in each polygon.

a. A regular triangle **b.** A regular pentagon

c. A regular hexagon **d.** A regular octagon

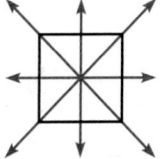

regular quadrilateral
4 lines of symmetry

42. **CHALLENGE** The diagram shows four identical squares lying edge-to-edge. Sketch all the different ways you can arrange four squares edge-to-edge. Sketch all the different ways you can arrange five identical squares edge-to-edge.

MIXED REVIEW

PREVIEW
Prepare for
Lesson 1.7
in Exs. 43–51.

Solve the equation.

43. $\dfrac{1}{2}(35)b = 140$ *(p. 875)*

44. $x^2 = 144$ *(p. 882)*

45. $3.14r^2 = 314$ *(p. 882)*

Copy and complete the statement. *(p. 886)*

46. 500 m = __?__ cm

47. 12 mi = __?__ ft

48. 672 in. = __?__ yd

49. 1200 km = __?__ m

50. $4\dfrac{1}{2}$ ft = __?__ yd

51. 3800 m = __?__ km

Find the distance between the two points. *(p. 15)*

52. $D(−13, 13)$, $E(0, −12)$

53. $F(−9, −8)$, $G(−9, 7)$

54. $H(10, 5)$, $J(−2, −2)$

1.7 Investigate Perimeter and Area

MATERIALS · graph paper · graphing calculator

QUESTION How can you use a graphing calculator to find the smallest possible perimeter for a rectangle with a given area?

You can use the formulas below to find the perimeter P and the area A of a rectangle with length ℓ and width w.

$$P = 2\ell + 2w \qquad A = \ell w$$

EXPLORE Find perimeters of rectangles with fixed areas

STEP 1 *Draw rectangles* Draw different rectangles, each with an area of 36 square units. Use lengths of 2, 4, 6, 8, 10, 12, 14, 16, and 18 units.

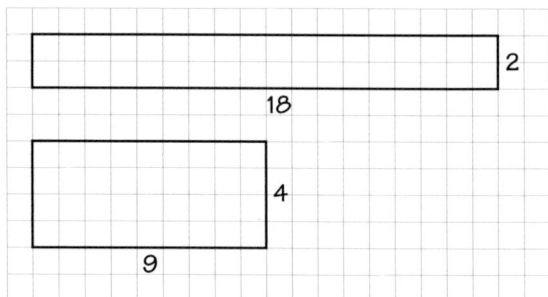

STEP 2 *Enter data* Use the STATISTICS menu on a graphing calculator. Enter the rectangle lengths in List 1. Use the keystrokes below to calculate and enter the rectangle widths and perimeters in Lists 2 and 3.

Keystrokes for entering widths in List 2:

36 ÷ **2nd** [L1] **ENTER**

Keystrokes for entering perimeters in List 3:

2 **×** **2nd** [L1] **+** 2 **×** **2nd** [L2] **ENTER**

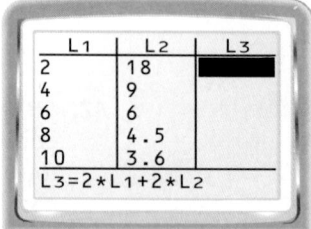

STEP 3 *Make a scatter plot* Make a scatter plot using the lengths from List 1 as the *x*-values and the perimeters from List 3 as the *y*-values. Choose an appropriate viewing window. Then use the *trace* feature to see the coordinates of each point.

How does the graph show which of your rectangles from Step 1 has the smallest perimeter?

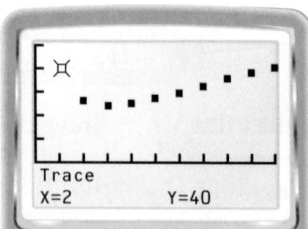

DRAW CONCLUSIONS Use your observations to complete these exercises

1. Repeat the steps above for rectangles with areas of 64 square units.

2. Based on the Explore and your results from Exercise 1, what do you notice about the shape of the rectangle with the smallest perimeter?

1.7 Find Perimeter, Circumference, and Area

Before	You classified polygons.
Now	You will find dimensions of polygons.
Why?	So you can use measures in science, as in Ex. 46.

Key Vocabulary
- **perimeter,** *p. 923*
- **circumference,** *p. 923*
- **area,** *p. 923*
- **diameter,** *p. 923*
- **radius,** *p. 923*

Recall that *perimeter* is the distance around a figure, *circumference* is the distance around a circle, and *area* is the amount of surface covered by a figure. Perimeter and circumference are measured in units of length, such as meters (m) and feet (ft). Area is measured in square units, such as square meters (m^2) and square feet (ft^2).

KEY CONCEPT *For Your Notebook*

Formulas for Perimeter *P*, Area *A*, and Circumference *C*

Square
side length *s*

$P = 4s$

$A = s^2$

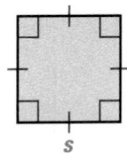

Rectangle
length ℓ and width *w*

$P = 2\ell + 2w$

$A = \ell w$

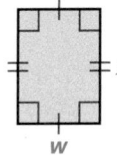

Triangle
side lengths *a*, *b*, and *c*, base *b*, and height *h*

$P = a + b + c$

$A = \frac{1}{2}bh$

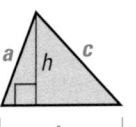

Circle
diameter *d* and radius *r*

$C = \pi d = 2\pi r$

$A = \pi r^2$

Pi (π) is the ratio of a circle's circumference to its diameter.

EXAMPLE 1 **Find the perimeter and area of a rectangle**

BASKETBALL Find the perimeter and area of the rectangular basketball court shown.

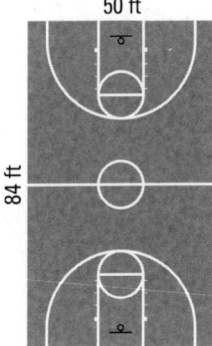

Perimeter	Area
$P = 2\ell + 2w$	$A = \ell w$
$= 2(84) + 2(50)$	$= 84(50)$
$= 268$	$= 4200$

▸ The perimeter is 268 feet and the area is 4200 square feet.

EXAMPLE 2 **Find the circumference and area of a circle**

TEAM PATCH You are ordering circular cloth patches for your soccer team's uniforms. Find the approximate circumference and area of the patch shown.

Solution

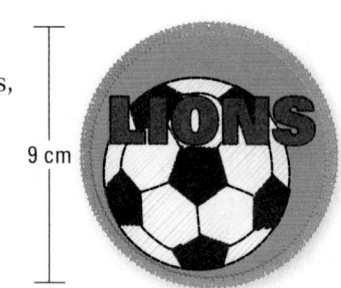

9 cm

APPROXIMATE π
The approximations 3.14 and $\frac{22}{7}$ are commonly used as approximations for the irrational number π. Unless told otherwise, use 3.14 for π.

First find the radius. The diameter is 9 centimeters, so the radius is $\frac{1}{2}(9) = 4.5$ centimeters.

Then find the circumference and area. Use 3.14 to approximate the value of π.

$$C = 2\pi r \approx 2(3.14)(4.5) = 28.26$$

$$A = \pi r^2 \approx 3.14(4.5)^2 = 63.585$$

▶ The circumference is about 28.3 cm. The area is about 63.6 cm^2.

✓ **GUIDED PRACTICE** for Examples 1 and 2

Find the area and perimeter (or circumference) of the figure. If necessary, round to the nearest tenth.

1.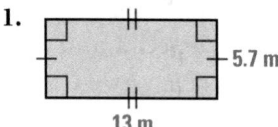
5.7 m
13 m

2.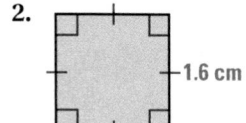
1.6 cm

3.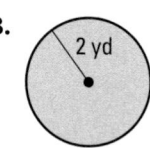
2 yd

★ **EXAMPLE 3** **Standardized Test Practice**

> Triangle *QRS* has vertices *Q*(1, 2), *R*(4, 6), and *S*(5, 2). What is the approximate perimeter of triangle *QRS*?
>
> (A) 8 units   (B) 8.3 units   (C) 13.1 units   (D) 25.4 units

Solution

AVOID ERRORS
Write down your calculations to make sure you do not make a mistake substituting values in the Distance Formula.

First draw triangle *QRS* in a coordinate plane. Find the side lengths. Use the Distance Formula to find *QR* and *RS*.

$$QS = |5 - 1| = 4 \text{ units}$$

$$QR = \sqrt{(4 - 1)^2 + (6 - 2)^2} = \sqrt{25} = 5 \text{ units}$$

$$RS = \sqrt{(5 - 4)^2 + (2 - 6)^2} = \sqrt{17} \approx 4.1 \text{ units}$$

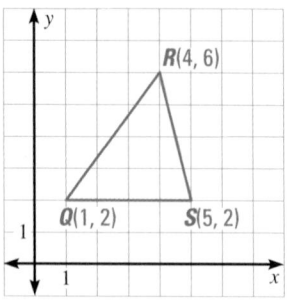

Then find the perimeter.

$$P = QS + QR + RS \approx 4 + 5 + 4.1 = 13.1 \text{ units}$$

▶ The correct answer is C. (A) (B) **(C)** (D)

EXAMPLE 4 Solve a multi-step problem

SKATING RINK An ice-resurfacing machine is used to smooth the surface of the ice at a skating rink. The machine can resurface about 270 square yards of ice in one minute.

About how many minutes does it take the machine to resurface a rectangular skating rink that is 200 feet long and 90 feet wide?

ANOTHER WAY

For an alternative method for solving the problem in Example 4, turn to page 57 for the **Problem Solving Workshop**.

Solution

The machine can resurface the ice at a rate of 270 square yards per minute. So, the amount of time it takes to resurface the skating rink depends on its area.

STEP 1 **Find** the area of the rectangular skating rink.

$$\text{Area} = \ell w = 200(90) = 18{,}000 \text{ ft}^2$$

The resurfacing rate is in square yards per minute. Rewrite the area of the rink in square yards. There are 3 feet in 1 yard, and $3^2 = 9$ square feet in 1 square yard.

$$18{,}000 \text{ ft}^2 \cdot \frac{1 \text{ yd}^2}{9 \text{ ft}^2} = 2000 \text{ yd}^2 \qquad \textbf{Use unit analysis.}$$

STEP 2 **Write** a verbal model to represent the situation. Then write and solve an equation based on the verbal model.

Let t represent the total time (in minutes) needed to resurface the skating rink.

Area of rink (yd²)	=	Resurfacing rate (yd² per min)	×	Total time (min)

$$2000 = 270 \cdot t \qquad \textbf{Substitute.}$$
$$7.4 \approx t \qquad \textbf{Divide each side by 270.}$$

▶ It takes the ice-resurfacing machine about 7 minutes to resurface the skating rink.

✓ **GUIDED PRACTICE** for Examples 3 and 4

4. Describe how to find the height from F to $\overline{EG}$ in the triangle at the right.

5. Find the perimeter and the area of the triangle shown at the right.

6. **WHAT IF?** In Example 4, suppose the skating rink is twice as long and twice as wide. Will it take an ice-resurfacing machine twice as long to resurface the skating rink? *Explain* your reasoning.

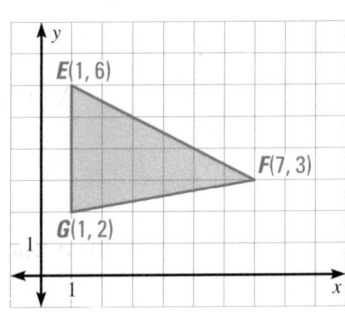

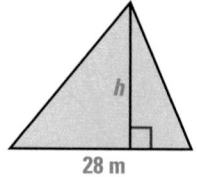

EXAMPLE 5 Find unknown length

The base of a triangle is 28 meters. Its area is
308 square meters. Find the height of the triangle.

Solution

$A = \frac{1}{2}bh$ Write formula for the area of a triangle.

$308 = \frac{1}{2}(28)h$ Substitute 308 for *A* and 28 for *b*.

$22 = h$ Solve for *h*.

▸ The height is 22 meters.

✓ **GUIDED PRACTICE**   for Example 5

7. The area of a triangle is 64 square meters, and its height is 16 meters.
Find the length of its base.

1.7 EXERCISES

HOMEWORK
KEY

○ = **WORKED-OUT SOLUTIONS**
    on p. WS2 for Exs. 7, 21, and 41

★ = **STANDARDIZED TEST PRACTICE**
    Exs. 2, 19, 26, 38, and 45

◆ = **MULTIPLE REPRESENTATIONS**
    Ex. 44

SKILL PRACTICE

1. VOCABULARY How are the diameter and radius of a circle related?

2. ★ WRITING *Describe* a real-world situation in which you would need to
find a perimeter, and a situation in which you would need to find an area.
What measurement units would you use in each situation?

EXAMPLE 1
on p. 49
for Exs. 3–10

3. ERROR ANALYSIS *Describe* and correct the
error made in finding the area of a triangle
with a height of 9 feet and a base of 52 feet.

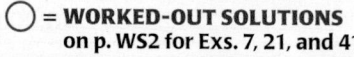

$A = 52(9) = 468 \text{ ft}^2$ ✗

PERIMETER AND AREA Find the perimeter and area of the shaded figure.

4.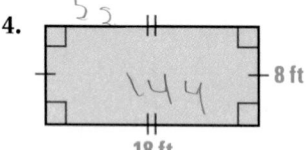
18 ft   8 ft

5.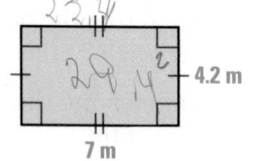
7 m   4.2 m

6.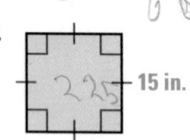
15 in.

7.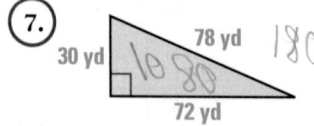
30 yd   78 yd   72 yd

8.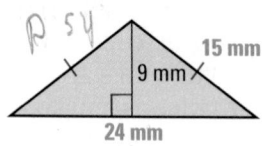
15 mm   9 mm   24 mm

9.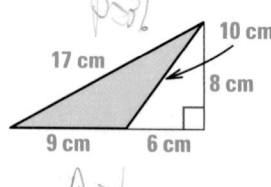
10 cm   17 cm   8 cm   9 cm   6 cm

Animated Geometry at classzone.com

10. DRAWING A DIAGRAM The base of a triangle is 32 feet. Its height is $16\frac{1}{2}$ feet. Sketch the triangle and find its area.

EXAMPLE 2
on p. 50
for Exs. 11–15

CIRCUMFERENCE AND AREA Use the given diameter d or radius r to find the circumference and area of the circle. Round to the nearest tenth.

11. $d = 27$ cm **12.** $d = 5$ in. **13.** $r = 12.1$ cm **14.** $r = 3.9$ cm

 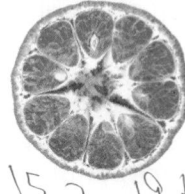  

15. DRAWING A DIAGRAM The diameter of a circle is 18.9 centimeters. Sketch the circle and find its circumference and area. Round your answers to the nearest tenth.

EXAMPLE 3
on p. 50
for Exs. 16–19

DISTANCE FORMULA Find the perimeter of the figure. Round to the nearest tenth of a unit.

16.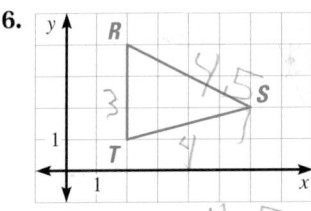

17.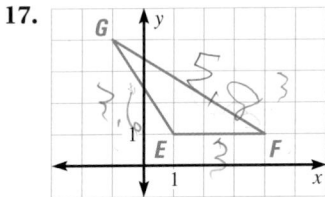

18.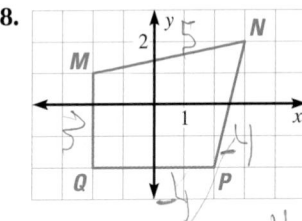

19. ★ MULTIPLE CHOICE What is the approximate area (in square units) of the rectangle shown at the right?

Ⓐ 6.7 Ⓑ 8.0

Ⓒ 9.0 Ⓓ 10.0

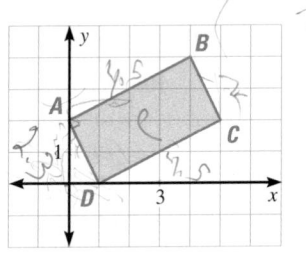

EXAMPLE 4
on p. 51
for Exs. 20–26

CONVERTING UNITS Copy and complete the statement.

20. $187 \text{ cm}^2 = \underline{\ ?\ } \text{ m}^2$ **21.** $13 \text{ ft}^2 = \underline{\ ?\ } \text{ yd}^2$ **22.** $18 \text{ in.}^2 = \underline{\ ?\ } \text{ ft}^2$

23. $8 \text{ km}^2 = \underline{\ ?\ } \text{ m}^2$ **24.** $12 \text{ yd}^2 = \underline{\ ?\ } \text{ ft}^2$ **25.** $24 \text{ ft}^2 = \underline{\ ?\ } \text{ in.}^2$

26. ★ MULTIPLE CHOICE A triangle has an area of 2.25 square feet. What is the area of the triangle in square inches?

Ⓐ 27 in.^2 Ⓑ 54 in.^2 Ⓒ 144 in.^2 Ⓓ 324 in.^2

EXAMPLE 5
on p. 52
for Exs. 27–30

UNKNOWN MEASURES Use the information about the figure to find the indicated measure.

27. Area $= 261 \text{ m}^2$
Find the height h.

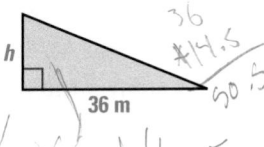

28. Area $= 66 \text{ in.}^2$
Find the base b.

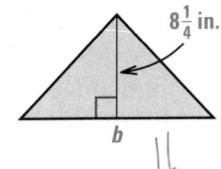

29. Perimeter $= 25$ in.
Find the width w.

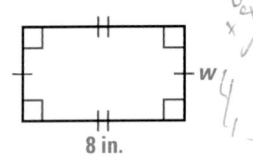

30. UNKNOWN MEASURE The width of a rectangle is 17 inches. Its perimeter is 102 inches. Find the length of the rectangle.

31. 🆇🆈 **ALGEBRA** The area of a rectangle is 18 square inches. The length of the rectangle is twice its width. Find the length and width of the rectangle.

32. 🆇🆈 **ALGEBRA** The area of a triangle is 27 square feet. Its height is three times the length of its base. Find the height and base of the triangle.

33. 🆇🆈 **ALGEBRA** Let x represent the side length of a square. Find a regular polygon with side length x whose perimeter is twice the perimeter of the square. Find a regular polygon with side length x whose perimeter is three times the length of the square. *Explain* your thinking.

FINDING SIDE LENGTHS **Find the side length of the square with the given area. Write your answer as a radical in simplest form.**

34. $A = 184 \text{ cm}^2$ **35.** $A = 346 \text{ in.}^2$ **36.** $A = 1008 \text{ mi}^2$ **37.** $A = 1050 \text{ km}^2$

38. ★ **SHORT RESPONSE** In the diagram, the diameter of the yellow circle is half the diameter of the red circle. What fraction of the area of the red circle is *not* covered by the yellow circle? *Explain*.

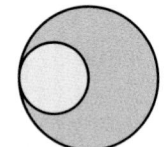

39. CHALLENGE The area of a rectangle is 30 cm^2 and its perimeter is 26 cm. Find the length and width of the rectangle.

PROBLEM SOLVING

EXAMPLES
1 and 2
on pp. 49–50
for Exs. 40–41

40. WATER LILIES The giant Amazon water lily has a lily pad that is shaped like a circle. Find the circumference and area of a lily pad with a diameter of 60 inches. Round your answers to the nearest tenth.

@HomeTutor for problem solving help at classzone.com

41. LAND You are planting grass on a rectangular plot of land. You are also building a fence around the edge of the plot. The plot is 45 yards long and 30 yards wide. How much area do you need to cover with grass seed? How many feet of fencing do you need?

@HomeTutor for problem solving help at classzone.com

EXAMPLE 4
on p. 51
for Ex. 42

42. MULTI-STEP PROBLEM Chris is installing a solar panel. The maximum amount of power the solar panel can generate in a day depends in part on its area. On a sunny day in the city where Chris lives, each square meter of the panel can generate up to 125 watts of power. The flat rectangular panel is 84 centimeters long and 54 centimeters wide.

a. Find the area of the solar panel in square meters.

b. What is the maximum amount of power (in watts) that the panel could generate if its area was 1 square meter? 2 square meters? *Explain*.

c. Estimate the maximum amount of power Chris's solar panel can generate. *Explain* your reasoning.

43. MULTI-STEP PROBLEM The eight spokes of a ship's wheel are joined at the wheel's center and pass through a large wooden circle, forming handles on the outside of the circle. From the wheel's center to the tip of the handle, each spoke is 21 inches long.

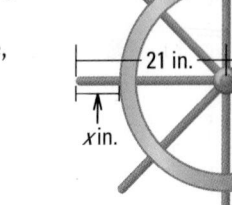

21 in. 21 in.

x in.

a. The circumference of the outer edge of the large wooden circle is 94 inches. Find the radius of the outer edge of the circle to the nearest inch.

b. Find the length *x* of a handle on the wheel. *Explain.*

44. ◆ **MULTIPLE REPRESENTATIONS** Let *x* represent the length of a side of a square. Let y_1 and y_2 represent the perimeter and area of that square.

a. Making a Table Copy and complete the table.

Length, x	1	2	5	10	25
Perimeter, y_1	?	?	?	?	?
Area, y_2	?	?	?	?	?

b. Making a Graph Use the completed table to write two sets of ordered pairs: (x, y_1) and (x, y_2). Graph each set of ordered pairs.

c. Analyzing Data *Describe* any patterns you see in the table from part (a) and in the graphs from part (b).

45. ★ EXTENDED RESPONSE The photograph at the right shows the Crown Fountain in Chicago, Illinois. At this fountain, images of faces appear on a large screen. The images are created by light-emitting diodes (LEDs) that are clustered in groups called modules. The LED modules are arranged in a rectangular grid.

a. The rectangular grid is approximately 7 meters wide and 15.2 meters high. Find the area of the grid.

b. Suppose an LED module is a square with a side length of 4 centimeters. How many rows and how many columns of LED modules would be needed to make the Crown Fountain screen? *Explain* your reasoning.

46. ASTRONOMY The diagram shows a gap in Saturn's circular rings. This gap is known as the *Cassini division*. In the diagram, the red circle represents the ring that borders the inside of the Cassini division. The yellow circle represents the ring that borders the outside of the division.

a. The radius of the red ring is 115,800 kilometers. The radius of the yellow ring is 120,600 kilometers. Find the circumference of the red ring and the circumference of the yellow ring. Round your answers to the nearest hundred kilometers.

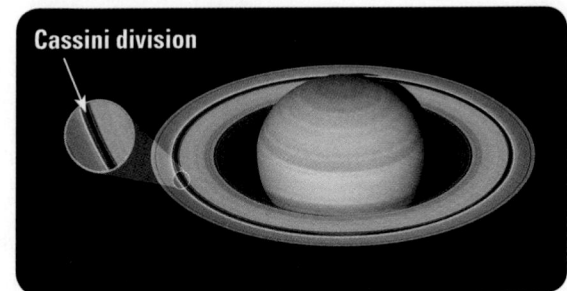

Cassini division

b. Compare the circumferences of the two rings. About how many kilometers greater is the yellow ring's circumference than the red ring's circumference?

47. CHALLENGE In the diagram at the right, how many times as great is the area of the circle as the area of the square? *Explain* your reasoning.

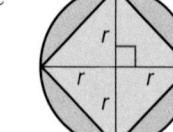

48. *XY* **ALGEBRA** You have 30 yards of fencing with which to make a rectangular pen. Let *x* be the length of the pen.

   a. Write an expression for the width of the pen in terms of *x*. Then write a formula for the area *y* of the pen in terms of *x*.

   b. You want the pen to have the greatest possible area. What length and width should you use? *Explain* your reasoning.

MIXED REVIEW

PREVIEW
Prepare for
Lesson 2.1
in Exs. 49–50.

49. Use the equation $y = 2x + 1$ to copy and complete the table of values. *(p. 884)*

x	1	2	3	4	5
y	?	?	?	?	?

50. Each number in a pattern is 6 less than the previous number. The first number in the pattern is 100. Write the next three numbers. *(p. 894)*

In Exercises 51 and 52, draw a diagram to represent the problem. Then find the indicated measure. *(p. 42)*

51. The lengths (in inches) of two sides of a regular triangle are given by the expressions $5x + 40$ and $8x - 13$. Find the length of a side of the triangle.

52. The measures of two angles of an equiangular hexagon are $12x°$ and $(10x + 20)°$. Find the measure of an angle of the hexagon.

QUIZ *for Lessons 1.6–1.7*

Tell whether the figure is a polygon. If it is not, *explain* why. If it is a polygon, tell whether it is *convex* or *concave*. *(p. 42)*

1. 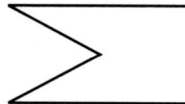   **2.**    **3.**

Find the perimeter and area of the shaded figure. *(p. 49)*

4. 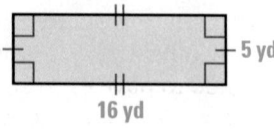   **5.** 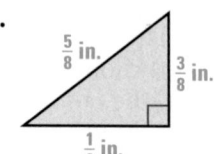   **6.**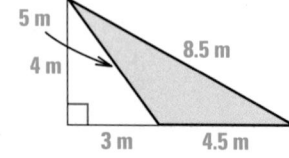

7. GARDENING You are spreading wood chips on a rectangular garden. The garden is $3\frac{1}{2}$ yards long and $2\frac{1}{2}$ yards wide. One bag of wood chips covers 10 square feet. How many bags of wood chips do you need? *(p. 49)*

Using ALTERNATIVE METHODS

Another Way to Solve Example 4, page 51

MULTIPLE REPRESENTATIONS In Example 4 on page 51, you saw how to use an equation to solve a problem about a skating rink. *Looking for a pattern* can help you write an equation.

PROBLEM

SKATING RINK An ice-resurfacing machine is used to smooth the surface of the ice at a skating rink. The machine can resurface about 270 square yards of ice in one minute. About how many minutes does it take the machine to resurface a rectangular skating rink that is 200 feet long and 90 feet wide?

METHOD

Using a Pattern You can use a table to look for a pattern.

STEP 1 **Find** the area of the rink in square yards. In Example 4 on page 51, you found that the area was 2000 square yards.

STEP 2 **Make** a table that shows the relationship between the time spent resurfacing the ice and the area resurfaced. Look for a pattern.

Time (min)	Area resurfaced (yd^2)
1	$1 \cdot 270 = 270$
2	$2 \cdot 270 = 540$
t	$t \cdot 270 = A$

Use the pattern to write an equation for the area A that has been resurfaced after t minutes.

STEP 3 **Use** the equation to find the time t (in minutes) that it takes the machine to resurface 2000 square yards of ice.

$$270t = A$$
$$270t = 2000$$
$$t \approx 7.4$$

▶ It takes about 7 minutes.

PRACTICE

1. **PLOWING** A square field is $\frac{1}{8}$ mile long on each side. A tractor can plow about 180,000 square feet per hour. To the nearest tenth of an hour, about how long does it take to plow the field? (1 mi = 5280 ft.)

2. **ERROR ANALYSIS** To solve Exercise 1 above, a student writes the equation $660 = 180,000t$, where t is the number of hours spent plowing. *Describe* and correct the error in the equation.

3. **PARKING LOT** A rectangular parking lot is 110 yards long and 45 yards wide. It costs about $.60 to pave each square foot of the parking lot with asphalt. About how much will it cost to pave the parking lot?

4. **WALKING** A circular path has a diameter of 120 meters. Your average walking speed is 4 kilometers per hour. About how many minutes will it take you to walk around the path 3 times?

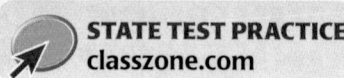
Lessons 1.4–1.7

1. **MULTI-STEP PROBLEM** You are covering the rectangular roof of a shed with shingles. The roof is a rectangle that is 4 yards long and 3 yards wide. Asphalt shingles cost $.75 per square foot and wood shingles cost $1.15 per square foot.

   a. Find the area of the roof in square feet.

   b. Find the cost of using asphalt shingles and the cost of using wood shingles.

   c. About how much more will you pay to use wood shingles for the roof?

2. **OPEN-ENDED** In the window below, name a convex polygon and a concave polygon. Classify each of your polygons by the number of sides.

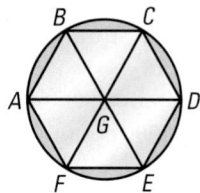

3. **EXTENDED RESPONSE** The diagram shows a decoration on a house. In the diagram, $\angle HGD$ and $\angle HGF$ are right angles, $m\angle DGB = 21°$, $m\angle HBG = 55°$, $\angle DGB \cong \angle FGC$, and $\angle HBG \cong \angle HCG$.

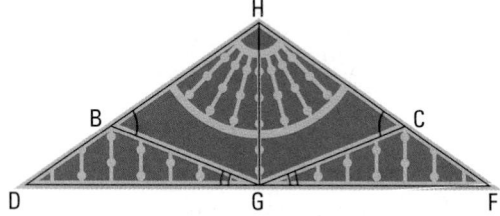

   a. List two pairs of complementary angles and five pairs of supplementary angles.

   b. Find $m\angle FGC$, $m\angle BGH$, and $m\angle HGC$. *Explain* your reasoning.

   c. Find $m\angle HCG$, $m\angle DBG$, and $m\angle FCG$. *Explain* your reasoning.

4. **GRIDDED ANSWER** $\angle 1$ and $\angle 2$ are supplementary angles, and $\angle 1$ and $\angle 3$ are complementary angles. Given $m\angle 1$ is 28° less than $m\angle 2$, find $m\angle 3$ in degrees.

5. **EXTENDED RESPONSE** You use bricks to outline the borders of the two gardens shown below. Each brick is 10 inches long.

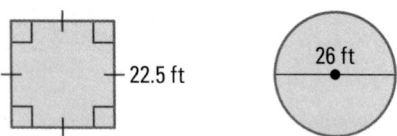

   a. You lay the bricks end-to-end around the border of each garden. How many bricks do you need for each garden? *Explain*.

   b. The bricks are sold in bundles of 100. How many bundles should you buy? *Explain*.

6. **SHORT RESPONSE** The frame of a mirror is a regular pentagon made from pieces of bamboo. Use the diagram to find how many feet of bamboo are used in the frame.

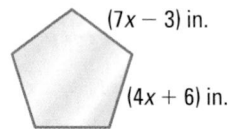

$(7x - 3)$ in.

$(4x + 6)$ in.

7. **GRIDDED ANSWER** As shown in the diagram, a skateboarder tilts one end of a skateboard. Find $m\angle ZWX$ in degrees.

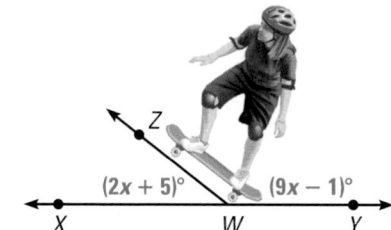

8. **SHORT RESPONSE** Use the diagram below.

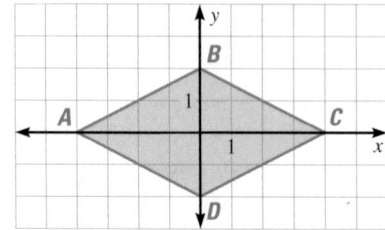

   a. Find the perimeter of quadrilateral $ABCD$.

   b. Find the area of triangle ABC and the area of triangle ADC. What is the area of quadrilateral $ABCD$? *Explain*.

BIG IDEAS *For Your Notebook*

Big Idea 1

Describing Geometric Figures

You learned to identify and classify geometric figures.

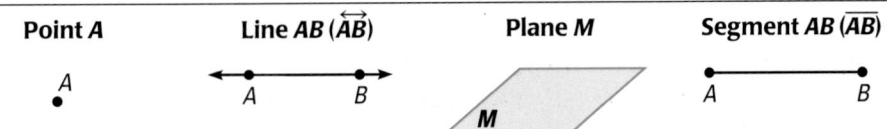

| Point *A* | Line *AB* ($\overleftrightarrow{AB}$) | Plane *M* | Segment *AB* ($\overline{AB}$) |

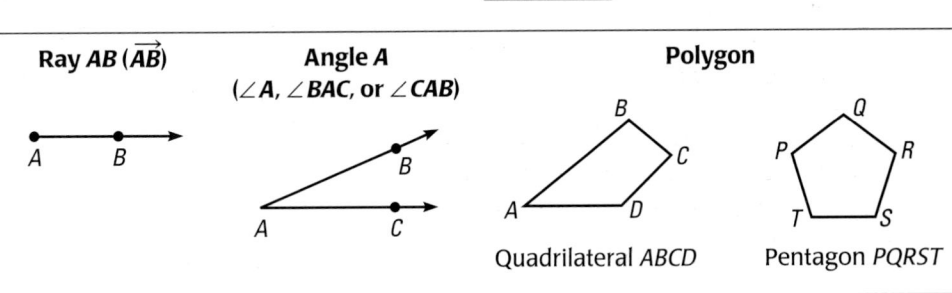

Ray *AB* ($\overrightarrow{AB}$) Angle *A* ($\angle A$, $\angle BAC$, or $\angle CAB$) Polygon

Quadrilateral *ABCD* Pentagon *PQRST*

Big Idea 2

Measuring Geometric Figures

SEGMENTS You measured segments in the coordinate plane.

Distance Formula

Distance between $A(x_1, y_1)$ and $B(x_2, y_2)$:

$$AB = \sqrt{(x_1 - x_2)^2 + (y_1 - y_2)^2}$$

Midpoint Formula

Coordinates of midpoint *M* of $\overline{AB}$, with endpoints $A(x_1, y_1)$ and $B(x_2, y_2)$:

$$M\left(\frac{x_1 + x_2}{2}, \frac{y_1 + y_2}{2}\right)$$

ANGLES You classified angles and found their measures.

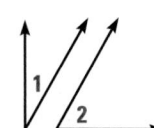

Complementary angles
$m\angle 1 + m\angle 2 = 90°$

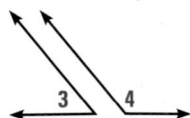

Supplementary angles
$m\angle 3 + m\angle 4 = 180°$

FORMULAS Perimeter and area formulas are reviewed on page 49.

Big Idea 3

Understanding Equality and Congruence

Congruent segments have equal lengths. Congruent angles have equal measures.

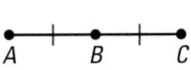

$\overline{AB} \cong \overline{BC}$ and $AB = BC$

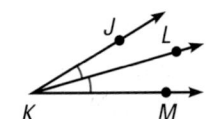

$\angle JKL \cong \angle LKM$ and $m\angle JKL = m\angle LKM$

REVIEW KEY VOCABULARY

For a list of postulates and theorems, see pp. 926–931.

• undefined terms, *p. 2*
  point, line, plane
• collinear, coplanar points, *p. 2*
• defined terms, *p. 3*
• line segment, endpoints, *p. 3*
• ray, opposite rays, *p. 3*
• intersection, *p. 4*
• postulate, axiom, *p. 9*
• coordinate, *p. 9*
• distance, *p. 9*
• between, *p. 10*

• congruent segments, *p. 11*
• midpoint, *p. 15*
• segment bisector, *p. 15*
• angle, *p. 24*
  sides, vertex, measure
• acute, right, obtuse, straight, *p. 25*
• congruent angles, *p. 26*
• angle bisector, *p. 28*
• construction, *p. 33*
• complementary angles, *p. 35*

• supplementary angles, *p. 35*
• adjacent angles, *p. 35*
• linear pair, *p. 37*
• vertical angles, *p. 37*
• polygon, *p. 42*
  side, vertex
• convex, concave, *p. 42*
• *n*-gon, *p. 43*
• equilateral, equiangular, regular, *p. 43*

VOCABULARY EXERCISES

1. Copy and complete: Points *A* and *B* are the __?__ of $\overline{AB}$.

2. Draw an example of a *linear pair*.

3. If *Q* is between points *P* and *R* on $\overleftrightarrow{PR}$, and *PQ* = *QR*, then *Q* is the __?__ of $\overline{PR}$.

REVIEW EXAMPLES AND EXERCISES

Use the review examples and exercises below to check your understanding of the concepts you have learned in each lesson of Chapter 1.

1.1 Identify Points, Lines, and Planes

pp. 2–8

EXAMPLE

Use the diagram shown at the right.

Another name for $\overleftrightarrow{CD}$ is line *m*.

Points *A*, *B*, and *C* are collinear.

Points *A*, *B*, *C*, and *F* are coplanar.

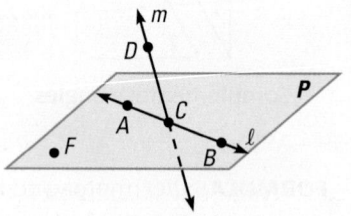

EXERCISES

EXAMPLES
1, 2, and 3
on pp. 3–4
for Exs. 4–8

4. Give another name for line *g*.

5. Name three points that are *not* collinear.

6. Name four points that are coplanar.

7. Name a pair of opposite rays.

8. Name the intersection of line *h* and plane *M*.

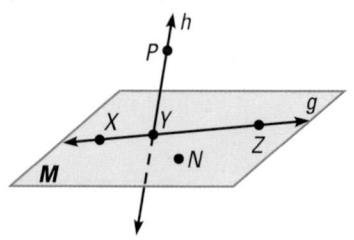

1.2 Use Segments and Congruence
pp. 9–14

EXAMPLE

Find the length of $\overline{HJ}$.

$GJ = GH + HJ$	Segment Addition Postulate
$27 = 18 + HJ$	Substitute 27 for *GJ* and 18 for *GH*.
$9 = HJ$	Subtract 18 from each side.

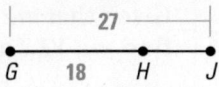

EXERCISES

EXAMPLES
2, 3, and 4
on pp. 10–11
for Exs. 9–12

Find the indicated length.

9. Find *AB*.

10. Find *NP*.

11. Find *XY*.

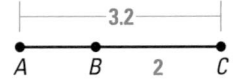

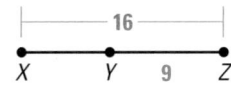

12. The endpoints of $\overline{DE}$ are $D(-4, 11)$ and $E(-4, -13)$. The endpoints of $\overline{GH}$ are $G(-14, 5)$ and $H(-9, 5)$. Are $\overline{DE}$ and $\overline{GH}$ congruent? *Explain.*

1.3 Use Midpoint and Distance Formulas
pp. 15–22

EXAMPLE

$\overline{EF}$ has endpoints $E(1, 4)$ and $F(3, 2)$. Find (a) the length of $\overline{EF}$ rounded to the nearest tenth of a unit, and (b) the coordinates of the midpoint *M* of $\overline{EF}$.

a. Use the Distance Formula.

$$EF = \sqrt{(3 - 1)^2 + (2 - 4)^2} = \sqrt{2^2 + (-2)^2} = \sqrt{8} \approx 2.8 \text{ units}$$

b. Use the Midpoint Formula.

$$M\left(\frac{1 + 3}{2}, \frac{4 + 2}{2}\right) = M(2, 3)$$

EXERCISES

EXAMPLES
2, 3, and 4
on pp. 16–18
for Exs. 13–19

13. Point *M* is the midpoint of $\overline{JK}$. Find *JK* when $JM = 6x - 7$ and $MK = 2x + 3$.

In Exercises 14–17, the endpoints of a segment are given. Find the length of the segment rounded to the nearest tenth. Then find the coordinates of the midpoint of the segment.

14. $A(2, 5)$ and $B(4, 3)$

15. $F(1, 7)$ and $G(6, 0)$

16. $H(-3, 9)$ and $J(5, 4)$

17. $K(10, 6)$ and $L(0, -7)$

18. Point $C(3, 8)$ is the midpoint of $\overline{AB}$. One endpoint is $A(-1, 5)$. Find the coordinates of endpoint *B*.

19. The endpoints of $\overline{EF}$ are $E(2, 3)$ and $F(8, 11)$. The midpoint of $\overline{EF}$ is *M*. Find the length of $\overline{EM}$.

EXAMPLE

Given that $m\angle YXV$ is 60°, find $m\angle YXZ$ and $m\angle ZXV$.

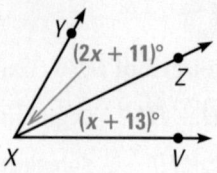

STEP 1 **Find** the value of x.

$m\angle YXV = m\angle YXZ + m\angle ZXV$	**Angle Addition Postulate**
$60° = (2x + 11)° + (x + 13)°$	**Substitute angle measures.**
$x = 12$	**Solve for x.**

STEP 2 **Evaluate** the given expressions when $x = 12$.

$$m\angle YXZ = (2x + 11)° = (2 \cdot 12 + 11)° = 35°$$

$$m\angle ZXV = (x + 13)° = (12 + 13)° = 25°$$

EXERCISES

EXAMPLES
3 and 5
on pp. 26, 28
for Exs. 20–21

20. In the diagram shown at the right, $m\angle LMN = 140°$. Find $m\angle PMN$.

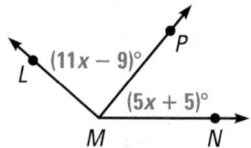

21. $\overrightarrow{VZ}$ bisects $\angle UVW$, and $m\angle UVZ = 81°$. Find $m\angle UVW$. Then classify $\angle UVW$ by its angle measure.

EXAMPLE

a. $\angle 1$ and $\angle 2$ are complementary angles. Given that $m\angle 1 = 37°$, find $m\angle 2$.

$$m\angle 2 = 90° - m\angle 1 = 90° - 37° = 53°$$

b. $\angle 3$ and $\angle 4$ are supplementary angles. Given that $m\angle 3 = 106°$, find $m\angle 4$.

$$m\angle 4 = 180° - m\angle 3 = 180° - 106° = 74°$$

EXERCISES

EXAMPLES
2 and 3
on p. 36
for Exs. 22–31

$\angle 1$ and $\angle 2$ are complementary angles. Given the measure of $\angle 1$, find $m\angle 2$.

22. $m\angle 1 = 12°$ **23.** $m\angle 1 = 83°$ **24.** $m\angle 1 = 46°$ **25.** $m\angle 1 = 2°$

$\angle 3$ and $\angle 4$ are supplementary angles. Given the measure of $\angle 3$, find $m\angle 4$.

26. $m\angle 3 = 116°$ **27.** $m\angle 3 = 56°$ **28.** $m\angle 3 = 89°$ **29.** $m\angle 3 = 12°$

30. $\angle 1$ and $\angle 2$ are complementary angles. Find the measures of the angles when $m\angle 1 = (x - 10)°$ and $m\angle 2 = (2x + 40)°$.

31. $\angle 1$ and $\angle 2$ are supplementary angles. Find the measures of the angles when $m\angle 1 = (3x + 50)°$ and $m\angle 2 = (4x + 32)°$. Then classify $\angle 1$ by its angle measure.

1.6 Classify Polygons

pp. 42–47

EXAMPLE

Classify the polygon by the number of sides. Tell whether it is equilateral, equiangular, or regular. *Explain.*

The polygon has four sides, so it is a quadrilateral. It is not equiangular or equilateral, so it is not regular.

EXERCISES

EXAMPLES
2 and 3
on pp. 43–44
for Exs. 32–35

Classify the polygon by the number of sides. Tell whether it is equilateral, equiangular, or regular. *Explain.*

32.
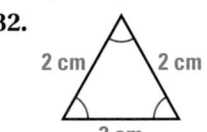
2 cm   2 cm
2 cm

33.
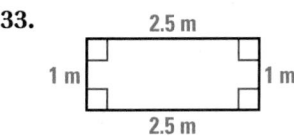
2.5 m
1 m   1 m
2.5 m

34.

35. Pentagon *ABCDE* is a regular polygon. The length of $\overline{BC}$ is represented by the expression $5x - 4$. The length of $\overline{DE}$ is represented by the expression $2x + 11$. Find the length of $\overline{AB}$.

1.7 Find Perimeter, Circumference, and Area

pp. 49–56

EXAMPLE

The diameter of a circle is 10 feet. Find the circumference and area of the circle. Round to the nearest tenth.

The radius is half of the diameter, so $r = \frac{1}{2}(10) = 5$ ft.

Circumference

$C = 2\pi r \approx 2(3.14)(5) = 31.4$ ft

Area

$A = \pi r^2 \approx 3.14(5^2) = 78.5$ ft^2

EXERCISES

EXAMPLES
1, 2, and 3
on pp. 49–50
for Exs. 36–40

In Exercises 36–38, find the perimeter (or circumference) and area of the figure described. If necessary, round to the nearest tenth.

36. Circle with diameter 15.6 meters

37. Rectangle with length $4\frac{1}{2}$ inches and width $2\frac{1}{2}$ inches

38. Triangle with vertices $U(1, 2)$, $V(-8, 2)$, and $W(-4, 6)$

39. The height of a triangle is 18.6 meters. Its area is 46.5 square meters. Find the length of the triangle's base.

40. The area of a circle is 320 square meters. Find the radius of the circle. Then find the circumference. Round your answers to the nearest tenth.

Use the diagram to decide whether the statement is *true* or *false*.

1. Point *A* lies on line *m*.

2. Point *D* lies on line *n*.

3. Points *B*, *C*, *E*, and *Q* are coplanar.

4. Points *C*, *E*, and *B* are collinear.

5. Another name for plane *G* is plane *QEC*.

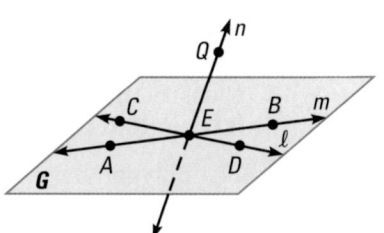

Find the indicated length.

6. Find *HJ*.

7. Find *BC*.

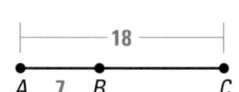

8. Find *XZ*.

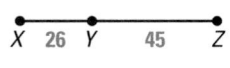

In Exercises 9–11, find the distance between the two points.

9. *T*(3, 4) and *W*(2, 7)

10. *C*(5, 10) and *D*(6, −1)

11. *M*(−8, 0) and *N*(−1, 3)

12. The midpoint of $\overline{AB}$ is *M*(9, 7). One endpoint is *A*(3, 9). Find the coordinates of endpoint *B*.

13. Line *t* bisects $\overline{CD}$ at point *M*, *CM* = 3*x*, and *MD* = 27. Find *CD*.

In Exercises 14 and 15, use the diagram.

14. Trace the diagram and extend the rays. Use a protractor to measure ∠*GHJ*. Classify it as *acute*, *obtuse*, *right*, or *straight*.

15. Given *m*∠*KHJ* = 90°, find *m*∠*LHJ*.

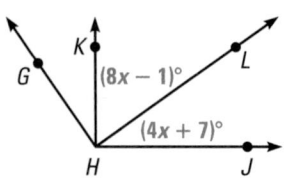

16. The measure of ∠*QRT* is 154°, and $\overrightarrow{RS}$ bisects ∠*QRT*. What are the measures of ∠*QRS* and ∠*SRT*?

In Exercises 17 and 18, use the diagram at the right.

17. Name four linear pairs.

18. Name two pairs of vertical angles.

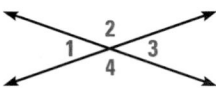

19. The measure of an angle is 64°. What is the measure of its complement? What is the measure of its supplement?

20. A convex polygon has half as many sides as a concave 10-gon. Draw the concave polygon and the convex polygon. Classify the convex polygon by the number of sides it has.

21. Find the perimeter of the regular pentagon shown at the right.

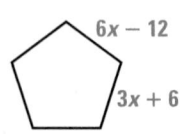

22. **CARPET** You can afford to spend $300 to carpet a room that is 5.5 yards long and 4.5 yards wide. The cost to purchase and install the carpet you like is $1.50 per square foot. Can you afford to buy this carpet? *Explain.*

SOLVE LINEAR EQUATIONS AND WORD PROBLEMS

xy **EXAMPLE 1** *Solve linear equations*

Solve the equation $-3(x + 5) + 4x = 25$.

$-3(x + 5) + 4x = 25$	Write original equation.
$-3x - 15 + 4x = 25$	Use the Distributive Property.
$x - 15 = 25$	Group and combine like terms.
$x = 40$	Add 15 to each side.

xy **EXAMPLE 2** *Solve a real-world problem*

MEMBERSHIP COSTS A health club charges an initiation fee of $50. Members then pay $45 per month. You have $400 to spend on a health club membership. For how many months can you afford to be a member?

Let n represent the number of months you can pay for a membership.

$400 = $ Initiation fee $+$ (Monthly Rate $\times$ Number of Months)

$400 = 50 + 45n$	Substitute.
$350 = 45n$	Subtract 50 from each side.
$7.8 = n$	Divide each side by 45.

▶ You can afford to be a member at the health club for 7 months.

EXERCISES

EXAMPLE 1
for Exs. 1–9

Solve the equation.

1. $9y + 1 - y = 49$

2. $5z + 7 + z = -8$

3. $-4(2 - t) = -16$

4. $7a - 2(a - 1) = 17$

5. $\dfrac{4x}{3} + 2(3 - x) = 5$

6. $\dfrac{2x - 5}{7} = 4$

7. $9c - 11 = -c + 29$

8. $2(0.3r + 1) = 23 - 0.1r$

9. $5(k + 2) = 3(k - 4)$

EXAMPLE 2
for Exs. 10–12

10. **GIFT CERTIFICATE** You have a $50 gift certificate at a store. You want to buy a book that costs $8.99 and boxes of stationery for your friends. Each box costs $4.59. How many boxes can you buy with your gift certificate?

11. **CATERING** It costs $350 to rent a room for a party. You also want to hire a caterer. The caterer charges $8.75 per person. How many people can come to the party if you have $500 to spend on the room and the caterer?

12. **JEWELRY** You are making a necklace out of glass beads. You use one bead that is $1\frac{1}{2}$ inches long and smaller beads that are each $\frac{3}{4}$ inch long. The necklace is 18 inches long. How many smaller beads do you need?

SHORT RESPONSE QUESTIONS

PROBLEM

You want to rent portable flooring to set up a dance floor for a party. The table below shows the cost of renting portable flooring from a local company. You want to have a rectangular dance floor that is 5 yards long and 4 yards wide. How much will it cost to rent flooring? *Explain* your reasoning.

If the floor area is ...	Then the cost is ...
less than 100 square feet	$6.50 per square foot
between 100 and 200 square feet	$6.25 per square foot

Below are sample solutions to the problem. Read each solution and the comments in blue to see why the sample represents full credit, partial credit, or no credit.

SAMPLE 1: Full credit solution

Find the area of the dance floor. Area = $\ell w = 5(4) = 20$ yd^2.

Then convert this area to square feet. There are $3^2 = 9$ ft^2 in 1 yd^2.

$$20 \text{ yd}^2 \cdot \frac{9 \text{ ft}^2}{1 \text{ yd}^2} = 180 \text{ ft}^2$$

Because 180 ft^2 is between 100 ft^2 and 200 ft^2, the price of flooring is $6.25 per square foot. Multiply the price per square foot by the area.

$$\text{Total cost} = \frac{\$6.25}{1 \text{ ft}^2} \cdot 180 \text{ ft}^2 = \$1125$$

It will cost $1125 to rent flooring.

The reasoning is correct, and the computations are accurate.

The answer is correct.

SAMPLE 2: Partial credit solution

The area of the dance floor is 5(4) = 20 square yards. Convert this area to square feet. There are 3 feet in 1 yard.

$$20 \text{ yd}^2 \cdot \frac{3 \text{ ft}^2}{1 \text{ yd}^2} = 60 \text{ ft}^2$$

The flooring will cost $6.50 per square foot because 60 ft^2 is less than 100 ft^2. To find the total cost, multiply the area by the cost per square foot.

$$60 \text{ ft}^2 \cdot \frac{\$6.50}{1 \text{ ft}^2} = \$390$$

It will cost $390 to rent flooring.

The reasoning is correct, but an incorrect conversion leads to an incorrect answer.

SAMPLE 3: Partial credit solution

The computations and the answer are correct, but the reasoning is incomplete.

> The area of the room is 180 ft², so the flooring price is $6.25. The total cost is 180 • 6.25 = $1125.
>
> It will cost $1125 to rent flooring.

SAMPLE 4: No credit solution

The student's reasoning is incorrect, and the answer is incorrect.

> Floor area = 4 × 5 = 20.
>
> Cost = 20 × $650 = $13,000.
>
> It will cost $13,000 to rent flooring.

PRACTICE   Apply the Scoring Rubric

Use the rubric on page 66 to score the solution to the problem below as *full credit*, *partial credit*, or *no credit*. *Explain* your reasoning.

PROBLEM You have 450 daffodil bulbs. You divide a 5 yard by 2 yard rectangular garden into 1 foot by 1 foot squares. You want to plant the same number of bulbs in each square. How many bulbs should you plant in each square? *Explain* your reasoning.

1. First find the area of the plot in square feet. There are 3 feet in 1 yard, so the length is 5(3) = 15 feet, and the width is 2(3) = 6 feet. The area is 15(6) = 90 square feet. The garden plot can be divided into 90 squares with side length 1 foot. Divide 450 by 90 to get 5 bulbs in each square.

2. The area of the garden plot is 5(2) = 10 square yards. There are 3 feet in 1 yard, so you can multiply 10 square yards by 3 to get an area of 30 square feet. You can divide the garden plot into 30 squares. To find how many bulbs per square, divide 450 bulbs by 30 to get 15 bulbs.

3. Divide 450 by the area of the plot: 450 bulbs ÷ 10 yards = 45 bulbs. You should plant 45 bulbs in each square.

4. Multiply the length and width by 3 feet to convert yards to feet. The area is 15 ft × 6 ft = 90 ft². Divide the garden into 90 squares.

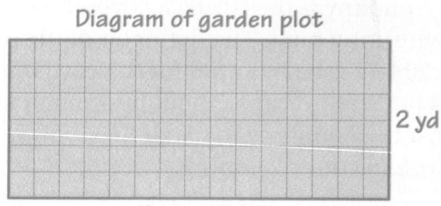

Diagram of garden plot

2 yd = 6 ft

5 yd = 15 ft

SHORT RESPONSE

1. It costs $2 per square foot to refinish a hardwood floor if the area is less than 300 square feet, and $1.75 per square foot if the area is greater than or equal to 300 square feet. How much does it cost to refinish a rectangular floor that is 6 yards long and 4.5 yards wide? *Explain* your reasoning.

2. As shown below, the library (point L) and the Town Hall (point T) are on the same straight road. Your house is on the same road, halfway between the library and the Town Hall. Let point H mark the location of your house. Find the coordinates of H and the approximate distance between the library and your house. *Explain* your reasoning.

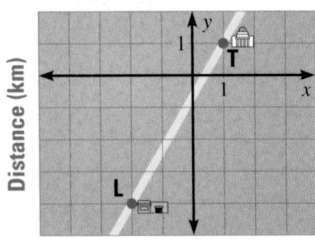

3. The water in a swimming pool evaporates over time if the pool is not covered. In one year, a swimming pool can lose about 17.6 gallons of water for every square foot of water that is exposed to air. About how much water would evaporate in one year from the surface of the water in the pool shown? *Explain* your reasoning.

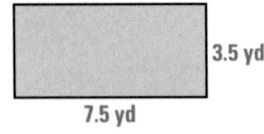

4. A company is designing a cover for a circular swimming pool. The diameter of the pool is 20 feet. The material for the cover costs $4 per square yard. About how much will it cost the company to make the pool cover? *Explain* your reasoning.

5. You are making a mat with a fringed border. The mat is shaped like a regular pentagon, as shown below. Fringe costs $1.50 per yard. How much will the fringe for the mat cost? *Explain* your reasoning.

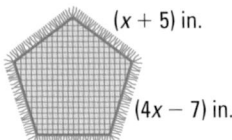

6. Angles A and B are complementary angles, $m\angle A = (2x - 4)°$, and $m\angle B = (4x - 8)°$. Find the measure of the supplement of $\angle B$. *Explain* your reasoning.

7. As shown on the map, you have two ways to drive from Atkins to Canton. You can either drive through Baxton, or you can drive directly from Atkins to Canton. About how much shorter is the trip from Atkins to Canton if you do not go through Baxton? *Explain* your reasoning.

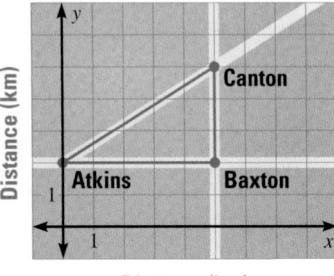

8. A jeweler is making pairs of gold earrings. For each earring, the jeweler will make a circular hoop like the one shown below. The jeweler has 2 meters of gold wire. How many pairs of gold hoops can the jeweler make? *Justify* your reasoning.

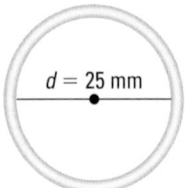

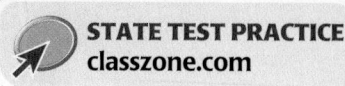
MULTIPLE CHOICE

9. The midpoint of $\overline{AB}$ is $M(4, -2)$. One endpoint is $A(-2, 6)$. What is the length of $\overline{AB}$?

(A) 5 units

(B) 10 units

(C) 20 units

(D) 28 units

10. The perimeter of a rectangle is 85 feet. The length of the rectangle is 4 feet more than its width. Which equation can be used to find the width w of the rectangle?

(A) $85 = 2(w + 4)$

(B) $85 = 2w + 2(w - 4)$

(C) $85 = 2(2w + 4)$

(D) $85 = w(w + 4)$

GRIDDED ANSWER

11. In the diagram, $\overrightarrow{YW}$ bisects $\angle XYZ$. Find $m\angle XYZ$ in degrees.

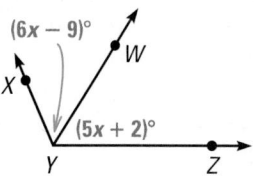

12. Angles A and B are complements, and the measure of $\angle A$ is 8 times the measure of $\angle B$. Find the measure (in degrees) of the supplement of $\angle A$.

13. The perimeter of the triangle shown is 400 feet. Find its area in square feet.

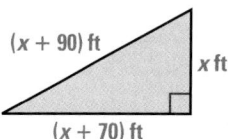

EXTENDED RESPONSE

14. The athletic director at a college wants to build an indoor playing field. The playing field will be twice as long as it is wide. Artificial turf costs $4 per square foot. The director has $50,000 to spend on artificial turf.

   a. What is the largest area that the director can afford to cover with artificial turf? *Explain.*

   b. Find the approximate length and width of the field to the nearest foot.

15. An artist uses black ink to draw the outlines of 30 circles and 25 squares, and red ink to fill in the area of each circle and square. The diameter of each circle is 1 inch, and the side length of each square is 1 inch. Which group of drawings uses more black ink, the *circles* or the *squares*? Which group of drawings uses more red ink? *Explain.*

16. Points A and C represent the positions of two boats in a large lake. Point B represents the position of a fixed buoy.

   a. Find the distance from each boat to the buoy.

   b. The boat at point A travels toward the buoy in a straight line at a rate of 5 kilometers per hour. The boat at point C travels to the buoy at a rate of 5.2 kilometers per hour. Which boat reaches the buoy first? *Explain.*

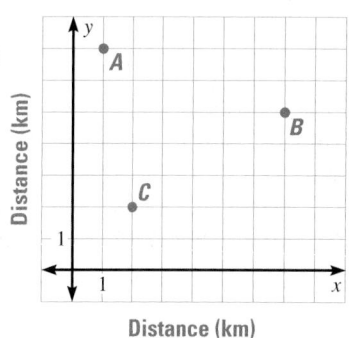

2 Reasoning and Proof

2.1 **Use Inductive Reasoning**

2.2 **Analyze Conditional Statements**

2.3 **Apply Deductive Reasoning**

2.4 **Use Postulates and Diagrams**

2.5 **Reason Using Properties from Algebra**

2.6 **Prove Statements about Segments and Angles**

2.7 **Prove Angle Pair Relationships**

Before

In previous courses and in Chapter 1, you learned the following skills, which you'll use in Chapter 2: naming figures, using notations, drawing diagrams, solving equations, and using postulates.

Prerequisite Skills

VOCABULARY CHECK

Use the diagram to name an example of the described figure.

1. A right angle

2. A pair of vertical angles

3. A pair of supplementary angles

4. A pair of complementary angles

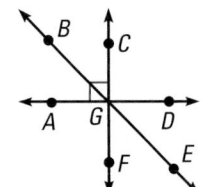

SKILLS AND ALGEBRA CHECK

Describe **what the notation means. Draw the figure.** *(Review p. 2 for 2.4.)*

5. $\overline{AB}$ 6. $\overleftrightarrow{CD}$ 7. EF 8. $\overrightarrow{GH}$

Solve the equation. *(Review p. 875 for 2.5.)*

9. $3x + 5 = 20$ 10. $4(x - 7) = -12$ 11. $5(x + 8) = 4x$

Name the postulate used. Draw the figure. *(Review pp. 9, 24 for 2.5.)*

12. $m\angle ABD + m\angle DBC = m\angle ABC$ 13. $ST + TU = SU$

@HomeTutor Prerequisite skills practice at classzone.com

In Chapter 2, you will apply the big ideas listed below and reviewed in the Chapter Summary on page 133. You will also use the key vocabulary listed below.

Big Ideas

1 Use inductive and deductive reasoning

2 Understanding geometric relationships in diagrams

3 Writing proofs of geometric relationships

KEY VOCABULARY

- conjecture, *p. 73*
- inductive reasoning, *p. 73*
- counterexample, *p. 74*
- conditional statement, *p. 79*
  converse, inverse, contrapositive

- if-then form, *p. 79*
  hypothesis, conclusion
- negation, *p. 79*
- equivalent statements, *p. 80*
- perpendicular lines, *p. 81*

- biconditional statement, *p. 82*
- deductive reasoning, *p. 87*
- proof, *p. 112*
- two-column proof, *p. 112*
- theorem, *p. 113*

Why?

You can use reasoning to draw conclusions. For example, by making logical conclusions from organized information, you can make a layout of a city street.

Animated Geometry

The animation illustrated below for Exercise 29 on page 119 helps you answer this question: Is the distance from the restaurant to the movie theater the same as the distance from the cafe to the dry cleaners?

You are walking down a street and want to find distances between businesses.

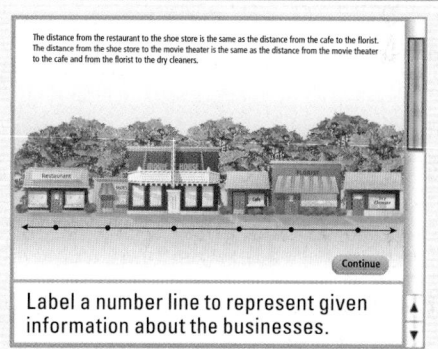

The distance from the restaurant to the shoe store is the same as the distance from the cafe to the florist. The distance from the shoe store to the movie theater is the same as the distance from the movie theater to the cafe and from the florist to the dry cleaners.

Label a number line to represent given information about the businesses.

Animated **Geometry** at classzone.com

Other animations for Chapter 2: pages 72, 81, 88, 97, 106, and 125

2.1 Use Inductive Reasoning

Before	You classified polygons by the number of sides.
Now	You will describe patterns and use inductive reasoning.
Why?	So you can make predictions about baseball, as in Ex. 32.

Key Vocabulary
• conjecture
• inductive reasoning
• counterexample

Geometry, like much of science and mathematics, was developed partly as a result of people recognizing and describing patterns. In this lesson, you will discover patterns yourself and use them to make predictions.

EXAMPLE 1 Describe a visual pattern

Describe how to sketch the fourth figure in the pattern. Then sketch the fourth figure.

Figure 1   Figure 2   Figure 3

Solution

Each circle is divided into twice as many equal regions as the figure number. Sketch the fourth figure by dividing a circle into eighths. Shade the section just above the horizontal segment at the left.

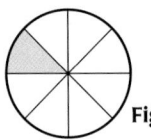

Figure 4

EXAMPLE 2 Describe a number pattern

READ SYMBOLS
The three dots (. . .) tell you that the pattern continues.

Describe the pattern in the numbers −7, −21, −63, −189, . . . and write the next three numbers in the pattern.

Notice that each number in the pattern is three times the previous number.

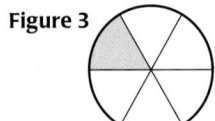

−7,   −21,   −63,   −189, . . .
     × 3   × 3   × 3   × 3

▶ Continue the pattern. The next three numbers are −567, −1701, and −5103.

Animated **Geometry** at classzone.com

✓ GUIDED PRACTICE for Examples 1 and 2

1. Sketch the fifth figure in the pattern in Example 1.

2. *Describe* the pattern in the numbers 5.01, 5.03, 5.05, 5.07, ... Write the next three numbers in the pattern.

INDUCTIVE REASONING A **conjecture** is an unproven statement that is based on observations. You use **inductive reasoning** when you find a pattern in specific cases and then write a conjecture for the general case.

EXAMPLE 3 Make a conjecture

Given five collinear points, make a conjecture about the number of ways to connect different pairs of the points.

Solution

Make a table and look for a pattern. Notice the pattern in how the number of connections increases. You can use the pattern to make a conjecture.

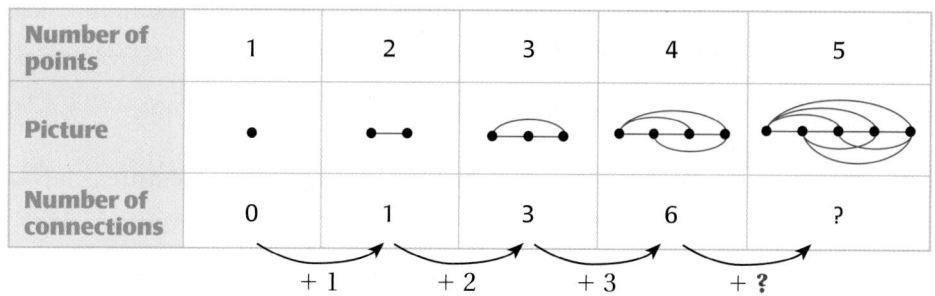

Number of points	1	2	3	4	5
Picture	•	•—•	•—•—•	(4 points)	(5 points)
Number of connections	0	1	3	6	?

+ 1   + 2   + 3   + ?

▶ **Conjecture** You can connect five collinear points $6 + 4$, or 10 different ways.

EXAMPLE 4 Make and test a conjecture

Numbers such as 3, 4, and 5 are called *consecutive integers*. Make and test a conjecture about the sum of any three consecutive integers.

Solution

STEP 1 **Find** a pattern using a few groups of small numbers.

$$3 + 4 + 5 = 12 = 4 \cdot 3 \qquad 7 + 8 + 9 = 24 = 8 \cdot 3$$

$$10 + 11 + 12 = 33 = 11 \cdot 3 \qquad 16 + 17 + 18 = 51 = 17 \cdot 3$$

▶ **Conjecture** The sum of any three consecutive integers is three times the second number.

STEP 2 **Test** your conjecture using other numbers. For example, test that it works with the groups $-1, 0, 1$ and $100, 101, 102$.

$$-1 + 0 + 1 = 0 = 0 \cdot 3 \checkmark \qquad 100 + 101 + 102 = 303 = 101 \cdot 3 \checkmark$$

✓ **GUIDED PRACTICE** for Examples 3 and 4

3. Suppose you are given seven collinear points. Make a conjecture about the number of ways to connect different pairs of the points.

4. Make and test a conjecture about the sign of the product of any three negative integers.

DISPROVING CONJECTURES To show that a conjecture is true, you must show that it is true for all cases. You can show that a conjecture is false, however, by simply finding one *counterexample*. A **counterexample** is a specific case for which the conjecture is false.

EXAMPLE 5 Find a counterexample

A student makes the following conjecture about the sum of two numbers. Find a counterexample to disprove the student's conjecture.

Conjecture The sum of two numbers is always greater than the larger number.

Solution

To find a counterexample, you need to find a sum that is less than the larger number.

$$-2 + -3 = -5$$
$$-5 \not> -2$$

▶ Because a counterexample exists, the conjecture is false.

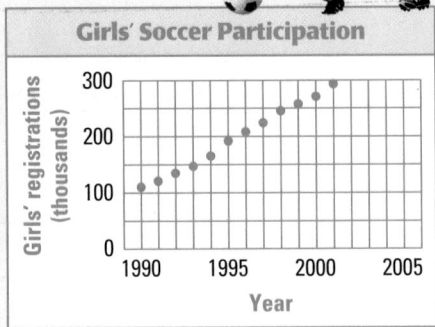

EXAMPLE 6 Standardized Test Practice

Which conjecture could a high school athletic director make based on the graph at the right?

ELIMINATE CHOICES
Because the graph does not show data about boys or the World Cup games, you can eliminate choices A and C.

(A) More boys play soccer than girls.

(B) More girls are playing soccer today than in 1995.

(C) More people are playing soccer today than in the past because the 1994 World Cup games were held in the United States.

(D) The number of girls playing soccer was more in 1995 than in 2001.

Girls' Soccer Participation

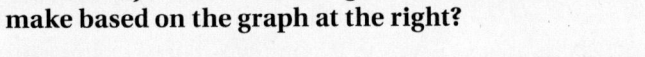

Girls' registrations (thousands) vs. Year (1990, 1995, 2000, 2005)

Solution

Choices A and C can be eliminated because they refer to facts not presented by the graph. Choice B is a reasonable conjecture because the graph shows an increase from 1990–2001, but does not give any reasons for that increase.

▶ The correct answer is B. (A) **(B)** (C) (D)

✓ GUIDED PRACTICE for Examples 5 and 6

5. Find a counterexample to show that the following conjecture is false.
   Conjecture The value of x^2 is always greater than the value of x.

6. Use the graph in Example 6 to make a conjecture that *could* be true. Give an explanation that supports your reasoning.

2.1 EXERCISES

HOMEWORK KEY

○ = WORKED-OUT SOLUTIONS
on p. WS2 for Exs. 7, 15, and 33

★ = STANDARDIZED TEST PRACTICE
Exs. 2, 5, 19, 22, and 36

◆ = MULTIPLE REPRESENTATIONS
Ex. 35

SKILL PRACTICE

1. **VOCABULARY** Write a definition of *conjecture* in your own words.

2. ★ **WRITING** The word *counter* has several meanings. Look up the word in a dictionary. Identify which meaning helps you understand the definition of *counterexample*.

EXAMPLE 1
on p. 72
for Exs. 3–5

SKETCHING VISUAL PATTERNS Sketch the next figure in the pattern.

3.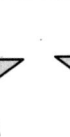

4.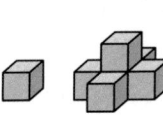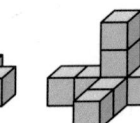

5. ★ **MULTIPLE CHOICE** What is the next figure in the pattern?

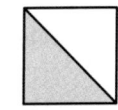 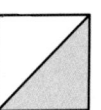 

Ⓐ  Ⓑ  Ⓒ 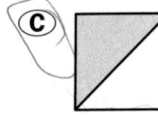 Ⓓ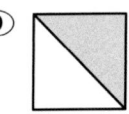

EXAMPLE 2
on p. 72
for Exs. 6–11

DESCRIBING NUMBER PATTERNS *Describe* the pattern in the numbers. Write the next number in the pattern.

6. 1, 5, 9, 13, ?

⑦ 3, 12, 48, 192, ?

8. 10, 5, 2.5, 1.25, . . .

9. 4, 3, 1, −2, ?

10. $1, \frac{2}{3}, \frac{1}{3}, 0, ?$

11. −5, −2, 4, 13, . .

MAKING CONJECTURES In Exercises 12 and 13, copy and complete the conjecture based on the pattern you observe in the specific cases.

EXAMPLE 3
on p. 73
for Ex. 12

12. Given seven noncollinear points, make a conjecture about the number of ways to connect different pairs of the points.

Number of points	3	4	5	6	7
Picture					?
Number of connections	3	6	10	15	?

Conjecture You can connect seven noncollinear points __?__ different ways.

EXAMPLE 4
on p. 73
for Ex. 13

13. Use these sums of odd integers: 3 + 7 = 10, 1 + 7 = 8, 17 + 21 = 38

Conjecture The sum of any two odd integers is __?__

EXAMPLE 5
········
on p. 74
for Exs. 14–17

FINDING COUNTEREXAMPLES In Exercises 14–17, show the conjecture is false by finding a counterexample.

14. If the product of two numbers is positive, then the two numbers must both be positive.

15. The product $(a + b)^2$ is equal to $a^2 + b^2$, for $a \neq 0$ and $b \neq 0$.

16. All prime numbers are odd.

17. If the product of two numbers is even, then the two numbers must both be even.

18. ERROR ANALYSIS Describe and correct the error in the student's reasoning.

True conjecture: All angles are acute.

Example:

19. ★ SHORT RESPONSE Explain why only one counterexample is necessary to show that a conjecture is false.

xy **ALGEBRA** In Exercises 20 and 21, write a function rule relating x and y.

20.

x	1	2	3
y	−3	−2	−1

21.

x	1	2	3
y	2	4	6

22. ★ MULTIPLE CHOICE What is the first number in the pattern?

$$\underline{\ ?\ }, \underline{\ ?\ }, \underline{\ ?\ }, 81, 243, 729$$

(A) 1   **(B)** 3   **(C)** 9   **(D)** 27

MAKING PREDICTIONS Describe a pattern in the numbers. Write the next number in the pattern. Graph the pattern on a number line.

23. $2, \dfrac{3}{2}, \dfrac{4}{3}, \dfrac{5}{4}, \ldots$ **24.** $1, 8, 27, 64, 125, \ldots$ **25.** $0.45, 0.7, 0.95, 1.2, \ldots$

26. $1, 3, 6, 10, 15, \ldots$ **27.** $2, 20, 10, 100, 50, \ldots$ **28.** $0.4(6), 0.4(6)^2, 0.4(6)^3, \ldots$

29. xy ALGEBRA Consider the pattern $5, 5r, 5r^2, 5r^3, \ldots$. For what values of r will the values of the numbers in the pattern be increasing? For what values of r will the values of the numbers be decreasing? Explain.

30. REASONING A student claims that the next number in the pattern $1, 2, 4, \ldots$ is 8, because each number shown is two times the previous number. Is there another description of the pattern that will give the same first three numbers but will lead to a different pattern? Explain.

31. CHALLENGE Consider the pattern $1, 1\dfrac{1}{2}, 1\dfrac{3}{4}, 1\dfrac{7}{8}, \ldots$.

     a. Describe the pattern. Write the next three numbers in the pattern.

     b. What is happening to the values of the numbers?

     c. Make a conjecture about later numbers. Explain your reasoning.

○ = **WORKED-OUT SOLUTIONS** on p. WS1   ★ = **STANDARDIZED TEST PRACTICE**   ◆ = **MULTIPLE REPRESENTATIONS**

32. **BASEBALL** You are watching a pitcher who throws two types of pitches, a fastball (F, in white below) and a curveball (C, in red below). You notice that the order of pitches was F, C, F, F, C, C, F, F, F. Assuming that this pattern continues, predict the next five pitches.

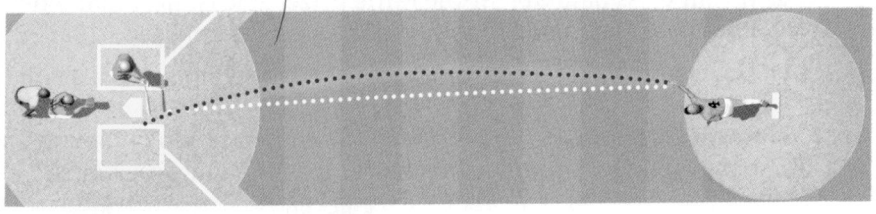

@HomeTutor for problem solving help at classzone.com

EXAMPLE 6
on p. 74
for Ex. 33

(33.) **STATISTICS** The scatter plot shows the number of person-to-person e-mail messages sent each year. Make a conjecture that *could* be true. Give an explanation that supports your reasoning.

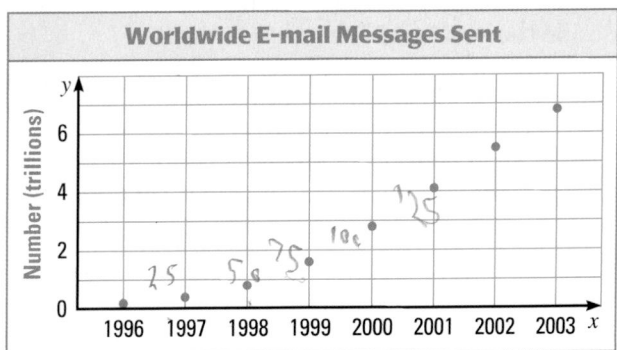

@HomeTutor for problem solving help at classzone.com

34. **VISUAL REASONING** Use the pattern below. Each figure is made of squares that are 1 unit by 1 unit.

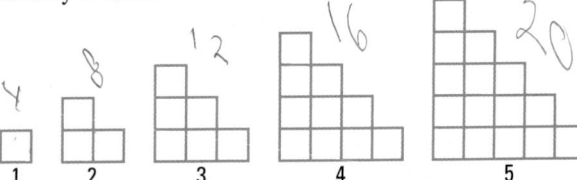

a. Find the distance around each figure. Organize your results in a table.

b. Use your table to *describe* a pattern in the distances.

c. Predict the distance around the 20th figure in this pattern.

35. ◆ **MULTIPLE REPRESENTATIONS** Use the given function table relating *x* and *y*.

a. **Making a Table** Copy and complete the table.

b. **Drawing a Graph** Graph the table of values.

c. **Writing an Equation** *Describe* the pattern in words and then write an equation relating *x* and *y*.

x	y
−3	−5
?	1
5	11
?	15
12	?
15	31

36. ★ **EXTENDED RESPONSE** Your class is selling raffle tickets for $.25 each.

   a. Make a table showing your income if you sold 0, 1, 2, 3, 4, 5, 10, or 20 raffle tickets.

   b. Graph your results. *Describe* any pattern you see.

   c. Write an equation for your income y if you sold x tickets.

   d. If your class paid $14 for the raffle prize, at least how many tickets does your class need to sell to make a profit? *Explain*.

   e. How many tickets does your class need to sell to make a profit of $50?

37. FIBONACCI NUMBERS The *Fibonacci numbers* are shown below. Use the Fibonacci numbers to answer the following questions.

1, 1, 2, 3, 5, 8, 13, 21, 34, 55, 89, . . .

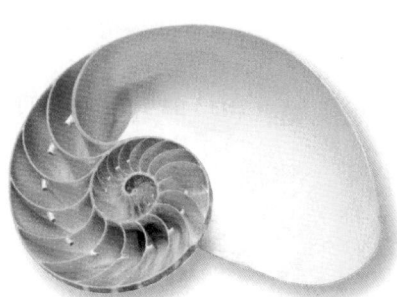

   a. Copy and complete: After the first two numbers, each number is the __?__ of the __?__ previous numbers.

   b. Write the next three numbers in the pattern.

   c. **Research** This pattern has been used to describe the growth of the *nautilus shell*. Use an encyclopedia or the Internet to find another real-world example of this pattern.

38. CHALLENGE Set A consists of all multiples of 5 greater than 10 and less than 100. Set B consists of all multiples of 8 greater than 16 and less than 100. Show that each conjecture is false by finding a counterexample.

   a. Any number in set A is also in set B.

   b. Any number less than 100 is either in set A or in set B.

   c. No number is in both set A and set B.

MIXED REVIEW

Use the Distributive Property to write the expression without parentheses.
(p. 872)

39. $4(x - 5)$ **40.** $-2(x - 7)$ **41.** $(-2n + 5)4$ **42.** $x(x + 8)$

PREVIEW

Prepare for Lesson 2.2 in Exs. 43–46.

You ask your friends how many pets they have. The results are: 1, 5, 1, 0, 3, 6, 4, 2, 10, and 1. Use these data in Exercises 43–46. *(p. 887)*

43. Find the mean.   **44.** Find the median.   **45.** Find the mode(s).

46. Tell whether the *mean, median,* or *mode(s)* best represent(s) the data.

Find the perimeter and area of the figure. *(p. 49)*

47.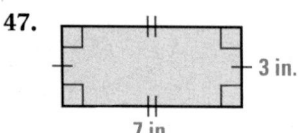
3 in.
7 in.

48.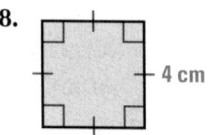
4 cm

49.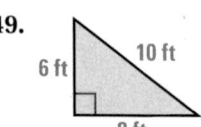
6 ft   10 ft   8 ft

   EXTRA PRACTICE for Lesson 2.1, p. 898   ↗ **ONLINE QUIZ** at classzone.com

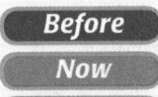

2.2 Analyze Conditional Statements

Before You used definitions.

Now You will write definitions as conditional statements.

Why? So you can verify statements, as in Example 2.

Key Vocabulary
- **conditional statement** converse, inverse, contrapositive
- **if-then form** hypothesis, conclusion
- **negation**
- **equivalent statements**
- **perpendicular lines**
- **biconditional statement**

A **conditional statement** is a logical statement that has two parts, a *hypothesis* and a *conclusion*. When a conditional statement is written in **if-then form**, the "if" part contains the **hypothesis** and the "then" part contains the **conclusion**. Here is an example:

If **it is raining**, then **there are clouds in the sky**.

Hypothesis — Conclusion

EXAMPLE 1 Rewrite a statement in if-then form

Rewrite the conditional statement in if-then form.

a. All birds have feathers.

b. Two angles are supplementary if they are a linear pair.

Solution

First, identify the **hypothesis** and the **conclusion**. When you rewrite the statement in if-then form, you may need to reword the hypothesis or conclusion.

a. **All birds** have **feathers**.

If **an animal is a bird**, then **it has feathers**.

b. Two angles are supplementary if **they are a linear pair**.

If **two angles are a linear pair**, then **they are supplementary**.

✓ **GUIDED PRACTICE** for Example 1

Rewrite the conditional statement in if-then form.

1. All 90° angles are right angles.

2. $2x + 7 = 1$, because $x = -3$.

3. When $n = 9$, $n^2 = 81$.

4. Tourists at the Alamo are in Texas.

NEGATION The **negation** of a statement is the *opposite* of the original statement. Notice that Statement 2 is already negative, so its negation is positive.

Statement 1 The ball is red.

Negation 1 The ball is *not* red.

Statement 2 The cat is *not* black.

Negation 2 The cat is black.

VERIFYING STATEMENTS Conditional statements can be true or false. To show that a conditional statement is true, you must prove that the conclusion is true every time the hypothesis is true. To show that a conditional statement is false, you need to give *only one* counterexample.

RELATED CONDITIONALS To write the **converse** of a conditional statement, exchange the **hypothesis** and conclusion.

READ VOCABULARY
To *negate* part of a conditional statement, you write its negation.

To write the **inverse** of a conditional statement, negate both the hypothesis and the conclusion. To write the **contrapositive**, first write the converse and then negate both the hypothesis and the conclusion.

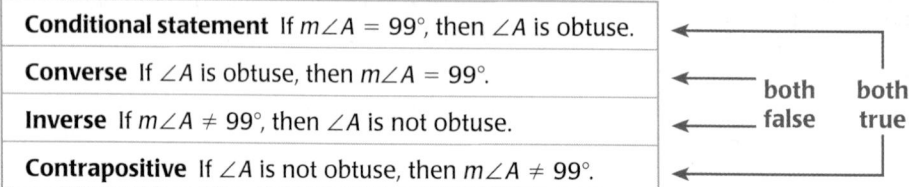

Conditional statement If $m\angle A = 99°$, then $\angle A$ is obtuse.	
Converse If $\angle A$ is obtuse, then $m\angle A = 99°$.	both false
Inverse If $m\angle A \neq 99°$, then $\angle A$ is not obtuse.	
Contrapositive If $\angle A$ is not obtuse, then $m\angle A \neq 99°$.	both true

EXAMPLE 2 Write four related conditional statements

Write the if-then form, the converse, the inverse, and the contrapositive of the conditional statement "Guitar players are musicians." Decide whether each statement is *true* or *false*.

Solution

If-then form If you are a guitar player, then you are a musician. *True*, guitars players are musicians.

Converse If you are a musician, then you are a guitar player. *False*, not all musicians play the guitar.

Inverse If you are not a guitar player, then you are not a musician. *False*, even if you don't play a guitar, you can still be a musician.

Contrapositive If you are not a musician, then you are not a guitar player. *True*, a person who is not a musician cannot be a guitar player.

 GUIDED PRACTICE for Example 2

Write the converse, the inverse, and the contrapositive of the conditional statement. Tell whether each statement is *true* or *false*.

5. If a dog is a Great Dane, then it is large.

6. If a polygon is equilateral, then the polygon is regular.

EQUIVALENT STATEMENTS A conditional statement and its contrapositive are either both true or both false. Similarly, the converse and inverse of a conditional statement are either both true or both false. Pairs of statements such as these are called *equivalent statements*. In general, when two statements are both true or both false, they are called **equivalent statements**.

DEFINITIONS You can write a definition as a conditional statement in if-then form or as its converse. Both the conditional statement and its converse are true. For example, consider the definition of *perpendicular lines*.

KEY CONCEPT   *For Your Notebook*

Perpendicular Lines

Definition If two lines intersect to form a right angle, then they are **perpendicular lines**.

The definition can also be written using the converse: If two lines are perpendicular lines, then they intersect to form a right angle.

You can write "line ℓ is perpendicular to line m" as $\ell \perp m$.

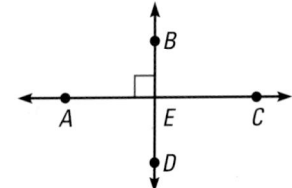

$\ell \perp m$

READ DIAGRAMS
In a diagram, a red square may be used to indicate a right angle or that two intersecting lines are perpendicular.

EXAMPLE 3   **Use definitions**

Decide whether each statement about the diagram is true. Explain your answer using the definitions you have learned.

a. $\overleftrightarrow{AC} \perp \overleftrightarrow{BD}$

b. $\angle AEB$ and $\angle CEB$ are a linear pair.

c. $\overrightarrow{EA}$ and $\overrightarrow{EB}$ are opposite rays.

Solution

a. This statement is *true*. The right angle symbol in the diagram indicates that the lines intersect to form a right angle. So you can say the lines are perpendicular.

b. This statement is *true*. By definition, if the noncommon sides of adjacent angles are opposite rays, then the angles are a linear pair. Because $\overrightarrow{EA}$ and $\overrightarrow{EC}$ are opposite rays, $\angle AEB$ and $\angle CEB$ are a linear pair.

c. This statement is *false*. Point E does not lie on the same line as A and B, so the rays are not opposite rays.

Animated Geometry   at classzone.com

✓   **GUIDED PRACTICE**   for Example 3

Use the diagram shown. Decide whether each statement is true. *Explain* your answer using the definitions you have learned.

7. $\angle JMF$ and $\angle FMG$ are supplementary.

8. Point M is the midpoint of $\overline{FH}$.

9. $\angle JMF$ and $\angle HMG$ are vertical angles.

10. $\overleftrightarrow{FH} \perp \overleftrightarrow{JG}$

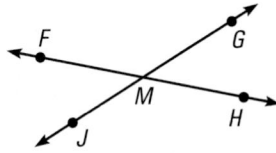

READ DEFINITIONS

All definitions can be interpreted forward and backward in this way.

BICONDITIONAL STATEMENTS When a conditional statement and its converse are both true, you can write them as a single *biconditional statement*. A **biconditional statement** is a statement that contains the phrase "if and only if."

Any valid definition can be written as a biconditional statement.

EXAMPLE 4 Write a biconditional

Write the definition of perpendicular lines as a biconditional.

Solution

Definition If two lines intersect to form a right angle, then they are perpendicular.
Converse If two lines are perpendicular, then they intersect to form a right angle.
Biconditional Two lines are perpendicular if and only if they intersect to form a right angle.

✔ **GUIDED PRACTICE** for Example 4

11. Rewrite the definition of *right angle* as a biconditional statement.

12. Rewrite the statements as a biconditional.

If Mary is in theater class, she will be in the fall play. If Mary is in the fall play, she must be taking theater class.

2.2 EXERCISES

HOMEWORK KEY

○ = **WORKED-OUT SOLUTIONS**
on p. WS2 for Exs. 11, 17, and 33

★ = **STANDARDIZED TEST PRACTICE**
Exs. 2, 25, 29, 33, 34, and 35

SKILL PRACTICE

1. VOCABULARY Copy and complete: The __?__ of a conditional statement is found by switching the hypothesis and the conclusion.

2. ★ WRITING Write a definition for the term *collinear points*, and show how the definition can be interpreted as a biconditional.

EXAMPLE 1
on p. 79
for Exs. 3–6

REWRITING STATEMENTS Rewrite the conditional statement in if-then form.

3. When $x = 6$, $x^2 = 36$.

4. The measure of a straight angle is 180°.

5. Only people who are registered are allowed to vote.

6. ERROR ANALYSIS *Describe* and correct the error in writing the if-then statement.

Given statement: All high school students take four English courses.

If-then statement: If a high school student takes four courses, then all four are English courses.

EXAMPLE 2

on p. 80

for Exs. 7–15

WRITING RELATED STATEMENTS For the given statement, write the if-then form, the converse, the inverse, and the contrapositive.

7. The complementary angles add to 90°.

8. Ants are insects.

9. $3x + 10 = 16$, because $x = 2$.

10. A midpoint bisects a segment.

ANALYZING STATEMENTS Decide whether the statement is *true* or *false*. If false, provide a counterexample.

11. If a polygon has five sides, then it is a regular pentagon.

12. If $m\angle A$ is 85°, then the measure of the complement of $\angle A$ is 5°.

13. Supplementary angles are always linear pairs.

14. If a number is an integer, then it is rational.

15. If a number is a real number, then it is irrational.

EXAMPLE 3

on p. 81

for Exs. 16–18

USING DEFINITIONS Decide whether each statement about the diagram is true. *Explain* your answer using the definitions you have learned.

16. $m\angle ABC = 90°$

17. $\overleftrightarrow{PQ} \perp \overleftrightarrow{ST}$

18. $m\angle 2 + m\angle 3 = 180°$

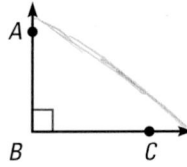
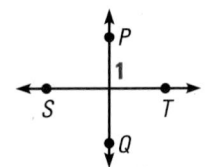
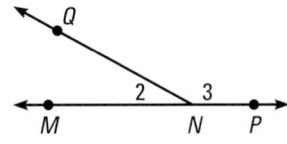

EXAMPLE 4

on p. 82

for Exs. 19–21

REWRITING STATEMENTS In Exercises 19–21, rewrite the definition as a biconditional statement.

19. An angle with a measure between 90° and 180° is called *obtuse*.

20. Two angles are a *linear pair* if they are adjacent angles whose noncommon sides are opposite rays.

21. *Coplanar points* are points that lie in the same plane.

DEFINITIONS Determine whether the statement is a valid definition.

22. If two rays are *opposite rays*, then they have a common endpoint.

23. If the sides of a triangle are all the same length, then the triangle is *equilateral*.

24. If an angle is a *right angle*, then its measure is greater than that of an acute angle.

25. ★ **MULTIPLE CHOICE** Which statement has the same meaning as the given statement?

GIVEN ▶ You can go to the movie after you do your homework.

(A) If you do your homework, then you can go to the movie afterwards.

(B) If you do not do your homework, then you can go to the movie afterwards.

(C) If you cannot go to the movie afterwards, then do your homework.

(D) If you are going to the movie afterwards, then do not do your homework.

xy ALGEBRA Write the converse of each true statement. Tell whether the converse is true. If false, *explain* why.

26. If $x > 4$, then $x > 0$.　　　**27.** If $x < 6$, then $-x > -6$.　　　**28.** If $x \le -x$, then $x \le 0$.

29. ★ **OPEN-ENDED MATH** Write a statement that is true but whose converse is false.

30. **CHALLENGE** Write a series of if-then statements that allow you to find the measure of each angle, given that $m\angle 1 = 90°$. Use the definition of linear pairs.

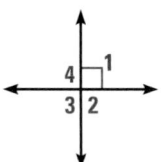

PROBLEM SOLVING

EXAMPLE 4
on p. 82
for Exs. 31–32

In Exercises 31 and 32, use the information about volcanoes to determine whether the biconditional statement is *true* or *false*. If false, provide a counterexample.

VOLCANOES Solid fragments are sometimes ejected from volcanoes during an eruption. The fragments are classified by size, as shown in the table.

31. A fragment is called a *block* or *bomb* if and only if its diameter is greater than 64 millimeters.

　　@HomeTutor for problem solving help at classzone.com

32. A fragment is called a *lapilli* if and only if its diameter is less than 64 millimeters.

　　@HomeTutor for problem solving help at classzone.com

Type of fragment	Diameter d (millimeters)
Ash	$d < 2$
Lapilli	$2 \le d \le 64$
Block or bomb	$d > 64$

(33.) ★ **SHORT RESPONSE** How can you show that the statement, "If you play a sport, then you wear a helmet." is false? *Explain*.

34. ★ **EXTENDED RESPONSE** You measure the heights of your classmates to get a data set.

　a. Tell whether this statement is true: If x and y are the least and greatest values in your data set, then the mean of the data is between x and y. *Explain* your reasoning.

　b. Write the converse of the statement in part (a). Is the converse true? *Explain*.

　c. Copy and complete the statement using *mean*, *median*, or *mode* to make a conditional that is true for any data set. *Explain* your reasoning.

　　Statement If a data set has a mean, a median, and a mode, then the __?__ of the data set will always be one of the measurements.

35. ★ **OPEN-ENDED MATH** The Venn diagram at the right represents all of the musicians at a high school. Write an if-then statement that describes a relationship between the various groups of musicians.

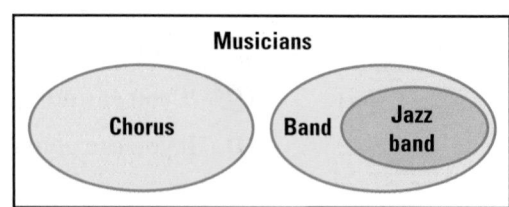

　○ = **WORKED-OUT SOLUTIONS**
　　　on p. WS1　　　　　　　★ = **STANDARDIZED TEST PRACTICE**

36. MULTI-STEP PROBLEM The statements below describe three ways that rocks are formed. Use these statements in parts (a)–(c).

Igneous rock is formed from the cooling of molten rock.

Sedimentary rock is formed from pieces of other rocks.

Metamorphic rock is formed by changing temperature, pressure, or chemistry.

a. Write each statement in if-then form.

b. Write the converse of each of the statements in part (a). Is the converse of each statement true? *Explain* your reasoning.

c. Write a true if-then statement about rocks. Is the converse of your statement *true* or *false*? *Explain* your reasoning.

37. (XY) ALGEBRA Can the statement, "If $x^2 - 10 = x + 2$, then $x = 4$," be combined with its converse to form a true biconditional?

38. REASONING You are given that the contrapositive of a statement is true. Will that help you determine whether the statement can be written as a true biconditional? *Explain*.

39. CHALLENGE Suppose each of the following statements is true. What can you conclude? *Explain* your answer.

If it is Tuesday, then I have art class.

It is Tuesday.

Each school day, I have either an art class or study hall.

If it is Friday, then I have gym class.

Today, I have either music class or study hall.

MIXED REVIEW

PREVIEW
Prepare for Lesson 2.3 in Exs. 40–45.

Find the product of the integers. *(p. 869)*

40. $(-2)(10)$

41. $(15)(-3)$

42. $(-12)(-4)$

43. $(-5)(-4)(10)$

44. $(-3)(6)(-2)$

45. $(-4)(-2)(-5)$

Sketch the figure described. *(p. 2)*

46. $\overleftrightarrow{AB}$ intersects $\overleftrightarrow{CD}$ at point E.

47. $\overleftrightarrow{XY}$ intersects plane P at point Z.

48. $\overleftrightarrow{GH}$ is parallel to $\overleftrightarrow{JK}$.

49. Planes X and Y intersect in $\overleftrightarrow{MN}$.

Find the coordinates of the midpoint of the segment with the given endpoints. *(p. 15)*

50. $A(10, 5)$ and $B(4, 5)$

51. $P(4, -1)$ and $Q(-2, 3)$

52. $L(2, 2)$ and $N(1, -2)$

Tell whether the figure is a polygon. If it is not, *explain* why. If it is a polygon, tell whether it is *convex* or *concave*. *(p. 42)*

53.

54.

55.

2.3 Logic Puzzles

MATERIALS · graph paper · pencils

QUESTION How can reasoning be used to solve a logic puzzle?

EXPLORE Solve a logic puzzle

Using the clues below, you can determine an important mathematical contribution and interesting fact about each of five mathematicians.

Copy the chart onto your graph paper. Use the chart to keep track of the information given in Clues 1–7. Place an X in a box to indicate a definite "no." Place an O in a box to indicate a definite "yes."

Clue 1 Pythagoras had his contribution named after him. He was known to avoid eating beans.

Clue 2 Albert Einstein considered Emmy Noether to be one of the greatest mathematicians and used her work to show the theory of relativity.

Clue 3 Anaxagoras was the first to theorize that the moon's light is actually the sun's light being reflected.

Clue 4 Julio Rey Pastor wrote a book at age 17.

Clue 5 The mathematician who is fluent in Latin contributed to the study of differential calculus.

Clue 6 The mathematician who did work with *n*-dimensional geometry was not the piano player.

Clue 7 The person who first used perspective drawing to make scenery for plays was not Maria Agnesi or Julio Rey Pastor.

	n-dimensional geometry	Differential calculus	Math for theory of relativity	Perspective drawing	Pythagorean Theorem	Did not eat beans	Studied moonlight	Wrote a math book at 17	Fluent in Latin	Played piano
Maria Agnesi				X						
Anaxagoras				X						
Emmy Noether				X						
Julio Rey Pastor				X						
Pythagoras	X	X	X	X	O					
Did not eat beans										
Studied moonlight										
Wrote a math book at 17										
Fluent in Latin										
Played piano										

DRAW CONCLUSIONS Use your observations to complete these exercises

1. Write Clue 4 as a conditional statement in if-then form. Then write the contrapositive of the statement. *Explain* why the contrapositive of this statement is a helpful clue.

2. *Explain* how you can use Clue 6 to figure out who played the piano.

3. *Explain* how you can use Clue 7 to figure out who worked with perspective drawing.

2.3 Apply Deductive Reasoning

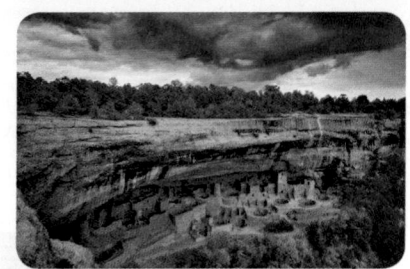

Before	You used inductive reasoning to form a conjecture.
Now	You will use deductive reasoning to form a logical argument.
Why	So you can reach logical conclusions about locations, as in Ex. 18.

Key Vocabulary
• deductive
  reasoning

Deductive reasoning uses facts, definitions, accepted properties, and the laws of logic to form a logical argument. This is different from *inductive reasoning*, which uses specific examples and patterns to form a conjecture.

KEY CONCEPT   *For Your Notebook*

Laws of Logic

READ VOCABULARY

The Law of Detachment is also called a *direct argument*. The Law of Syllogism is sometimes called the *chain rule*.

Law of Detachment

If the hypothesis of a true conditional statement is true, then the conclusion is also true.

Law of Syllogism

If **hypothesis** p, then **conclusion** q.

If hypothesis q, then conclusion r. ⟩→ If these statements are true,

If **hypothesis** p, then **conclusion** r. ←then this statement is true.

EXAMPLE 1   Use the Law of Detachment

Use the Law of Detachment to make a valid conclusion in the true situation.

a. If two segments have the same length, then they are congruent. You know that $BC = XY$.

b. Mary goes to the movies every Friday and Saturday night. Today is Friday.

Solution

a. Because $BC = XY$ satisfies the hypothesis of a true conditional statement, the conclusion is also true. So, $\overline{BC} \cong \overline{XY}$.

b. First, identify the hypothesis and the conclusion of the first statement. The hypothesis is "If it is Friday or Saturday night," and the conclusion is "then Mary goes to the movies."

"Today is Friday" satisfies the hypothesis of the conditional statement, so you can conclude that Mary will go to the movies tonight.

EXAMPLE 2   **Use the Law of Syllogism**

If possible, use the Law of Syllogism to write a new conditional statement that follows from the pair of true statements.

  a. If Rick takes chemistry this year, then Jesse will be Rick's lab partner.

     If Jesse is Rick's lab partner, then Rick will get an A in chemistry.

  b. If $x^2 > 25$, then $x^2 > 20$.

     If $x > 5$, then $x^2 > 25$.

  c. If a polygon is regular, then all angles in the interior of the polygon are congruent.

     If a polygon is regular, then all of its sides are congruent.

Solution

  a. The conclusion of the first statement is the hypothesis of the second statement, so you can write the following new statement.

     If Rick takes chemistry this year, then Rick will get an A in chemistry.

AVOID ERRORS
The order in which the statements are given does not affect whether you can use the Law of Syllogism.

  b. Notice that the conclusion of the second statement is the hypothesis of the first statement, so you can write the following new statement.

     If $x > 5$, then $x^2 > 20$.

  c. Neither statement's conclusion is the same as the other statement's hypothesis. You cannot use the Law of Syllogism to write a new conditional statement.

 Animated Geometry at classzone.com

✓   **GUIDED PRACTICE** | for Examples 1 and 2

  1. If $90° < m\angle R < 180°$, then $\angle R$ is obtuse. The measure of $\angle R$ is 155°. Using the Law of Detachment, what statement can you make?

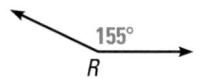

  2. If Jenelle gets a job, then she can afford a car. If Jenelle can afford a car, then she will drive to school. Using the Law of Syllogism, what statement can you make?

State the law of logic that is illustrated.

  3. If you get an A or better on your math test, then you can go to the movies. If you go to the movies, then you can watch your favorite actor.

     If you get an A or better on your math test, then you can watch your favorite actor.

  4. If $x > 12$, then $x + 9 > 20$. The value of x is 14.

     Therefore, $x + 9 > 20$.

ANALYZING REASONING In Geometry, you will frequently use inductive reasoning to make conjectures. You will also be using deductive reasoning to show that conjectures are true or false. You will need to know which type of reasoning is being used.

EXAMPLE 3 Use inductive and deductive reasoning

ALGEBRA What conclusion can you make about the product of an even integer and any other integer?

Solution

STEP 1 **Look** for a pattern in several examples. Use inductive reasoning to make a conjecture.

$(-2)(2) = -4, (-1)(2) = -2, 2(2) = 4, 3(2) = 6,$

$(-2)(-4) = 8, (-1)(-4) = 4, 2(-4) = -8, 3(-4) = -12$

Conjecture Even integer • Any integer = Even integer

STEP 2 **Let** n and m each be any integer. Use deductive reasoning to show the conjecture is true.

$2n$ is an even integer because any integer multiplied by 2 is even.

$2nm$ represents the product of an even integer and any integer m.

$2nm$ is the product of 2 and an integer nm. So, $2nm$ is an even integer.

▶ The product of an even integer and any integer is an even integer.

EXAMPLE 4 Reasoning from a graph

Tell whether the statement is the result of *inductive reasoning* or *deductive reasoning*. Explain your choice.

a. The northern elephant seal requires more strokes to surface the deeper it dives.

b. The northern elephant seal uses more strokes to surface from 250 meters than from 60 meters.

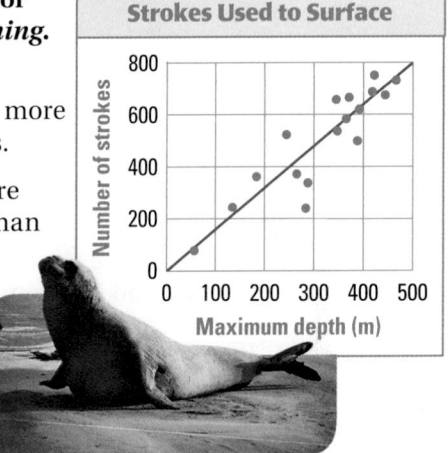

Strokes Used to Surface

Solution

a. Inductive reasoning, because it is based on a pattern in the data

b. Deductive reasoning, because you are comparing values that are given on the graph

---

✓ **GUIDED PRACTICE** for Examples 3 and 4

5. Use inductive reasoning to make a conjecture about the sum of a number and itself. Then use deductive reasoning to show the conjecture is true.

6. Use inductive reasoning to write another statement about the graph in Example 4. Then use deductive reasoning to write another statement.

2.3 EXERCISES

HOMEWORK KEY

○ = WORKED-OUT SOLUTIONS
on p. WS2 for Exs. 7, 17, and 21

★ = STANDARDIZED TEST PRACTICE
Exs. 2, 3, 12, 20, and 23

SKILL PRACTICE

1. **VOCABULARY** Copy and complete: If the hypothesis of a true if-then statement is true, then the conclusion is also true by the Law of __?__.

★ **WRITING** Use deductive reasoning to make a statement about the picture.

2.

3.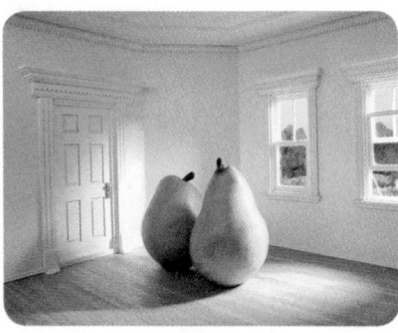

EXAMPLE 1
on p. 87
for Exs. 4–6

LAW OF DETACHMENT Make a valid conclusion in the situation.

4. If the measure of an angle is 90°, then it is a right angle. The measure of ∠A is 90°.

5. If $x > 12$, then $-x < -12$. The value of x is 15.

6. If a book is a biography, then it is nonfiction. You are reading a biography.

EXAMPLE 2
on p. 88
for Exs. 7–10

LAW OF SYLLOGISM In Exercises 7–10, write the statement that follows from the pair of statements that are given.

7. If a rectangle has four equal side lengths, then it is a square. If a polygon is a square, then it is a regular polygon.

8. If $y > 0$, then $2y > 0$. If $2y > 0$, then $2y - 5 \neq -5$.

9. If you play the clarinet, then you play a woodwind instrument. If you play a woodwind instrument, then you are a musician.

10. If $a = 3$, then $5a = 15$. If $\frac{1}{2}a = 1\frac{1}{2}$, then $a = 3$.

EXAMPLE 3
on p. 89
for Ex. 11

11. **REASONING** What can you say about the sum of an even integer and an even integer? Use inductive reasoning to form a conjecture. Then use deductive reasoning to show that the conjecture is true.

12. ★ **MULTIPLE CHOICE** If two angles are vertical angles, then they have the same measure. You know that ∠1 and ∠2 are vertical angles. Using the Law of Detachment, which conclusion could you make?

Ⓐ $m\angle 1 > m\angle 2$ Ⓑ $m\angle 1 = m\angle 2$

Ⓒ $m\angle 1 + m\angle 2 = 90°$ Ⓓ $m\angle 1 + m\angle 2 = 180°$

13. **ERROR ANALYSIS** Describe and correct the error in the argument: "If two angles are a linear pair, then they are supplementary. Angles C and D are supplementary, so the angles are a linear pair."

14. **xy ALGEBRA** Use the segments in the coordinate plane.

a. Use the distance formula to show that the segments are congruent.

b. Make a conjecture about some segments in the coordinate plane that are congruent to the given segments. Test your conjecture, and *explain* your reasoning.

c. Let one endpoint of a segment be (x, y). Use algebra to show that segments drawn using your conjecture will always be congruent.

d. A student states that the segments described below will each be congruent to the ones shown above. Determine whether the student is correct. *Explain* your reasoning.

$\overline{MN}$, with endpoints M(3, 5) and N(5, 2)

$\overline{PQ}$, with endpoints P(1, −1) and Q(4, −3)

$\overline{RS}$, with endpoints R(−2, 2) and S(1, 4)

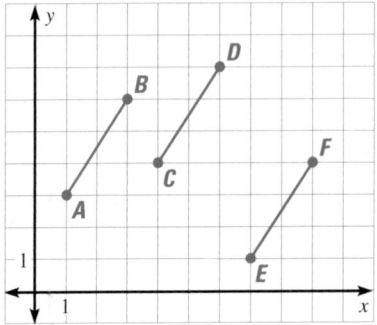

15. **CHALLENGE** Make a conjecture about whether the Law of Syllogism works when used with the contrapositives of a pair of statements. Use this pair of statements to *justify* your conjecture.

If a creature is a wombat, then it is a marsupial.

If a creature is a marsupial, then it has a pouch.

PROBLEM SOLVING

**EXAMPLES
1 and 2**
on pp. 87–88
for Exs. 16–17

USING THE LAWS OF LOGIC In Exercises 16 and 17, what conclusions can you make using the true statement?

16. **CAR COSTS** If you save $2000, then you can buy a car. You have saved $1200.

@HomeTutor for problem solving help at classzone.com

17. **PROFIT** The bakery makes a profit if its revenue is greater than its costs. You will get a raise if the bakery makes a profit.

@HomeTutor for problem solving help at classzone.com

USING DEDUCTIVE REASONING Select the word(s) that make(s) the conclusion true.

18. Mesa Verde National Park is in Colorado. Simone vacationed in Colorado. So, Simone (*must have, may have,* or *never*) visited Mesa Verde National Park.

19. The cliff dwellings in Mesa Verde National Park are accessible to visitors only when accompanied by a park ranger. Billy is at a cliff dwelling in Mesa Verde National Park. So, Billy (*is, may be, is not*) with a park ranger.

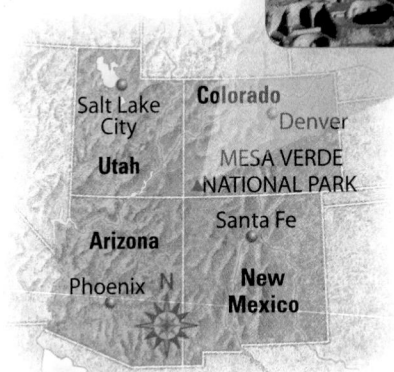

EXAMPLE 4
on p. 89
for Ex. 20

20. ★ **EXTENDED RESPONSE** Geologists use the Mohs scale to determine a mineral's hardness. Using the scale, a mineral with a higher rating will leave a scratch on a mineral with a lower rating. Geologists use scratch tests to help identify an unknown mineral.

Mineral	Talc	Gypsum	Calcite	Fluorite
Mohs rating	1	2	3	4

a. Use the table to write three if-then statements such as "If talc is scratched against gypsum, then a scratch mark is left on the talc."

b. You must identify four minerals labeled *A*, *B*, *C*, and *D*. You know that the minerals are the ones shown in the table. The results of your scratch tests are shown below. What can you conclude? *Explain* your reasoning.

Mineral *A* is scratched by Mineral *B*.

Mineral *C* is scratched by all three of the other minerals.

c. What additional test(s) can you use to identify *all* the minerals in part (b)?

REASONING **In Exercises 21 and 22, decide whether *inductive* or *deductive* reasoning is used to reach the conclusion. *Explain* your reasoning.**

21. The rule at your school is that you must attend all of your classes in order to participate in sports after school. You played in a soccer game after school on Monday. Therefore, you went to all of your classes on Monday.

22. For the past 5 years, your neighbor goes on vacation every July 4th and asks you to feed her hamster. You conclude that you will be asked to feed her hamster on the next July 4th.

23. ★ **SHORT RESPONSE** Let an even integer be $2n$ and an odd integer be $2n + 1$. *Explain* why the sum of an even integer and an odd integer is an odd integer.

24. **LITERATURE** George Herbert wrote a poem, *Jacula Prudentum*, that includes the statements shown. Use the Law of Syllogism to write a new conditional statement. *Explain* your reasoning.

For want of a nail the shoe is lost, for want of a shoe the horse is lost, for want of a horse the rider is lost.

REASONING **In Exercises 25–28, use the true statements below to determine whether you know the conclusion is *true* or *false*. *Explain* your reasoning.**

If Arlo goes to the baseball game, then he will buy a hot dog.

If the baseball game is not sold out, then Arlo and Mia will go to the game.

If Mia goes to the baseball game, then she will buy popcorn.

The baseball game is not sold out.

25. Arlo bought a hot dog.

26. Arlo and Mia went to the game.

27. Mia bought a hot dog.

28. Arlo had some of Mia's popcorn.

○ = **WORKED-OUT SOLUTIONS**
on p. WS1

★ = **STANDARDIZED TEST PRACTICE**

29. CHALLENGE Use these statements to answer parts (a)–(c).

Adam says Bob lies.

Bob says Charlie lies.

Charlie says Adam and Bob both lie.

a. If Adam is telling the truth, then Bob is lying. What can you conclude about Charlie's statement?

b. Assume Adam is telling the truth. *Explain* how this leads to a contradiction.

c. Who is telling the truth? Who is lying? How do you know?

MIXED REVIEW

PREVIEW

Prepare for Lesson 2.4 in Exs. 30–33.

In Exercises 30–33, use the diagram. *(p. 2)*

30. Name two lines.

31. Name four rays.

32. Name three collinear points.

33. Name four coplanar points.

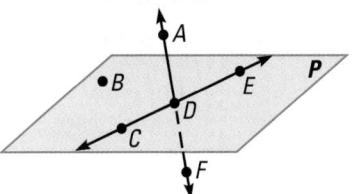

Plot the given points in a coordinate plane. Then determine whether $\overline{AB}$ and $\overline{CD}$ are congruent. *(p. 9)*

34. $A(1, 4)$, $B(5, 4)$, $C(3, -4)$, $D(3, 0)$ **35.** $A(-1, 0)$, $B(-1, -5)$, $C(1, 2)$, $D(-5, 2)$

Rewrite the conditional statement in if-then form. *(p. 79)*

36. When $x = -2$, $x^2 = 4$.

37. The measure of an acute angle is less than 90°.

38. Only people who are members can access the website.

QUIZ *for Lessons 2.1–2.3*

Show the conjecture is false by finding a counterexample. *(p. 72)*

1. If the product of two numbers is positive, then the two numbers must be negative.

2. The sum of two numbers is always greater than the larger number.

In Exercises 3 and 4, write the if-then form and the contrapositive of the statement. *(p. 79)*

3. Points that lie on the same line are called collinear points.

4. $2x - 8 = 2$, because $x = 5$.

5. Make a valid conclusion about the following statements:

If it is above 90°F outside, then I will wear shorts. It is 98°F. *(p. 87)*

6. *Explain* why a number that is divisible by a multiple of 3 is also divisible by 3. *(p. 87)*

Symbolic Notation and Truth Tables

GOAL Use symbolic notation to represent logical statements.

Key Vocabulary
• truth value
• truth table

Conditional statements can be written using *symbolic notation*, where letters are used to represent statements. An arrow ($\rightarrow$), read "implies," connects the hypothesis and conclusion. To write the negation of a statement p you write the symbol for negation ($\sim$) before the letter. So, "not p" is written $\sim p$.

KEY CONCEPT   *For Your Notebook*

Symbolic Notation

Let p be "the angle is a right angle" and let q be "the measure of the angle is 90°."

| **Conditional** | If p, then q. | $p \rightarrow q$ |

Example: If an angle is a right angle, then its measure is 90°.

| **Converse** | If q, then p. | $q \rightarrow p$ |

Example: If the measure of an angle is 90°, then the angle is a right angle.

| **Inverse** | If not p, then not q. | $\sim p \rightarrow \sim q$ |

Example: If an angle is not a right angle, then its measure is not 90°.

| **Contrapositive** | If not q, then not p. | $\sim q \rightarrow \sim p$ |

If the measure of an angle is not 90°, then the angle is not a right angle.

| **Biconditional** | p if and only if q | $p \leftrightarrow q$ |

Example: An angle is a right angle if and only if its measure is 90°.

EXAMPLE 1   **Use symbolic notation**

Let p be "the car is running" and let q be "the key is in the ignition."

   a. Write the conditional statement $p \rightarrow q$ in words.

   b. Write the converse $q \rightarrow p$ in words.

   c. Write the inverse $\sim p \rightarrow \sim q$ in words.

   d. Write the contrapositive $\sim q \rightarrow \sim p$ in words.

Solution

   a. Conditional: If the car is running, then the key is in the ignition.

   b. Converse: If the key is in the ignition, then the car is running.

   c. Inverse: If the car is not running, then the key is not in the ignition.

   d. Contrapositive: If the key is not in the ignition, then the car is not running.

TRUTH TABLES The **truth value** of a statement is either true (T) or false (F). You can determine the conditions under which a conditional statement is true by using a **truth table**. The truth table at the right shows the truth values for hypothesis p and conclusion q. The conditional $p \rightarrow q$ is only false when a true hypothesis produces a false conclusion.

Conditional		
p	q	$p \rightarrow q$
T	T	T
T	F	F
F	T	T
F	F	T

EXAMPLE 2 Make a truth table

Use the truth table above to make truth tables for the converse, inverse, and contrapositive of a conditional statement $p \rightarrow q$.

Solution

READ TRUTH TABLES

A conditional statement and its contrapositive are *equivalent statements* because they have the same truth table. The same is true of the converse and the inverse.

Converse			Inverse					Contrapositive				
p	q	$q \rightarrow p$	p	q	$\sim p$	$\sim q$	$\sim p \rightarrow \sim q$	p	q	$\sim q$	$\sim p$	$\sim q \rightarrow \sim p$
T	T	T	T	T	F	F	T	T	T	F	F	T
T	F	T	T	F	F	T	T	T	F	T	F	F
F	T	F	F	T	T	F	F	F	T	F	T	T
F	F	T	F	F	T	T	T	F	F	T	T	T

PRACTICE

EXAMPLE 1
on p. 94
for Exs. 1–6

1. **WRITING** *Describe* how to use symbolic notation to represent the contrapositive of a conditional statement.

WRITING STATEMENTS Use p and q to write the symbolic statement in words.

    p: Polygon *ABCDE* is equiangular and equilateral.

    q: Polygon *ABCDE* is a regular polygon.

2. $p \rightarrow q$ 3. $\sim p$ 4. $\sim q \rightarrow \sim p$ 5. $p \leftrightarrow q$

6. **LAW OF SYLLOGISM** Use the statements p, q, and r below to write a series of conditionals that would satisfy the Law of Syllogism. How could you write your reasoning using symbolic notation?

    p: $x + 5 = 12$ q: $x = 7$ r: $3x = 21$

EXAMPLE 2
on p. 95
for Exs. 7–8

7. **WRITING** Is the truth value of a statement always true (T)? *Explain.*

8. **TRUTH TABLE** Use the statement "If an animal is a poodle, then it is a dog."

    a. Identify the hypothesis p and the conclusion q in the conditional.

    b. Write the converse, inverse, and contrapositive of the original statement in words. Then tell the truth value of each new statement.

2.4 Use Postulates and Diagrams

Before	You used postulates involving angle and segment measures.
Now	You will use postulates involving points, lines, and planes.
Why?	So you can draw the layout of a neighborhood, as in Ex. 39.

Key Vocabulary
- **line perpendicular to a plane**
- **postulate,** *p. 8*

In geometry, rules that are accepted without proof are called *postulates* or *axioms*. Rules that are proved are called *theorems*. Postulates and theorems are often written in conditional form. Unlike the converse of a definition, the converse of a postulate or theorem cannot be assumed to be true.

You learned four postulates in Chapter 1.

POSTULATE 1	Ruler Postulate	page 9
POSTULATE 2	Segment Addition Postulate	page 10
POSTULATE 3	Protractor Postulate	page 24
POSTULATE 4	Angle Addition Postulate	page 25

Here are seven new postulates involving points, lines, and planes.

POSTULATES   *For Your Notebook*

Point, Line, and Plane Postulates

POSTULATE 5	Through any two points there exists exactly one line.
POSTULATE 6	A line contains at least two points.
POSTULATE 7	If two lines intersect, then their intersection is exactly one point.
POSTULATE 8	Through any three noncollinear points there exists exactly one plane.
POSTULATE 9	A plane contains at least three noncollinear points.
POSTULATE 10	If two points lie in a plane, then the line containing them lies in the plane.
POSTULATE 11	If two planes intersect, then their intersection is a line.

ALGEBRA CONNECTION You have been using many of Postulates 5–11 in previous courses.

One way to graph a linear equation is to plot two points whose coordinates satisfy the equation and then connect them with a line. Postulate 5 guarantees that there is exactly one such line. A familiar way to find a common solution of two linear equations is to graph the lines and find the coordinates of their intersection. This process is guaranteed to work by Postulate 7.

EXAMPLE 1 Identify a postulate illustrated by a diagram

State the postulate illustrated by the diagram.

a.
If 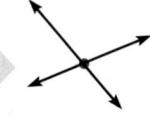 then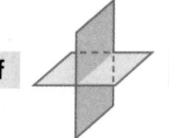

b.
If 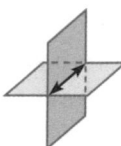 then

Solution

a. **Postulate 7** If two lines intersect, then their intersection is exactly one point.

b. **Postulate 11** If two planes intersect, then their intersection is a line.

EXAMPLE 2 Identify postulates from a diagram

Use the diagram to write examples of Postulates 9 and 10.

Postulate 9 Plane *P* contains at least three noncollinear points, *A*, *B*, and *C*.

Postulate 10 Point *A* and point *B* lie in plane *P*, so line *n* containing *A* and *B* also lies in plane *P*.

Animated **Geometry** at classzone.com

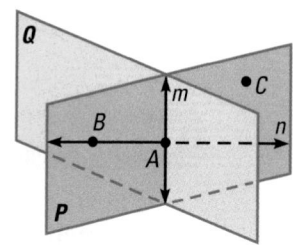

✔ **GUIDED PRACTICE** for Examples 1 and 2

1. Use the diagram in Example 2. Which postulate allows you to say that the intersection of plane *P* and plane *Q* is a line?

2. Use the diagram in Example 2 to write examples of Postulates 5, 6, and 7.

CONCEPT SUMMARY *For Your Notebook*

Interpreting a Diagram

When you interpret a diagram, you can assume information about size or measure only if it is marked.

YOU CAN ASSUME

All points shown are coplanar.

∠*AHB* and ∠*BHD* are a linear pair.

∠*AHF* and ∠*BHD* are vertical angles.

A, *H*, *J*, and *D* are collinear.

$\overleftrightarrow{AD}$ and $\overleftrightarrow{BF}$ intersect at *H*.

YOU CANNOT ASSUME

G, *F*, and *E* are collinear.

$\overleftrightarrow{BF}$ and $\overleftrightarrow{CE}$ intersect.

$\overleftrightarrow{BF}$ and $\overleftrightarrow{CE}$ do not intersect.

∠*BHA* ≅ ∠*CJA*

$\overleftrightarrow{AD} \perp \overleftrightarrow{BF}$ or *m*∠*AHB* = 90°

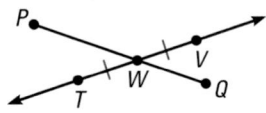

EXAMPLE 3 Use given information to sketch a diagram

Sketch a diagram showing $\overleftrightarrow{TV}$ intersecting $\overline{PQ}$ at point W, so that $\overline{TW} \cong \overline{WV}$.

Solution

AVOID ERRORS
Notice that the picture was drawn so that W does not look like a midpoint of $\overline{PQ}$. Also, it was drawn so that $\overline{PQ}$ is not perpendicular to $\overline{TV}$.

STEP 1 Draw $\overleftrightarrow{TV}$ and label points T and V.

STEP 2 Draw point W at the midpoint of $\overline{TV}$. Mark the congruent segments.

STEP 3 Draw $\overline{PQ}$ through W.

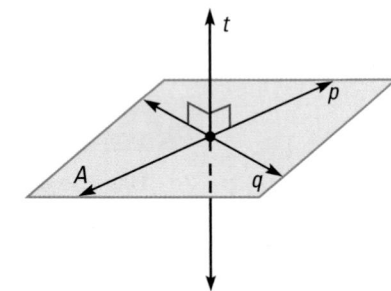

PERPENDICULAR FIGURES A line is a **line perpendicular to a plane** if and only if the line intersects the plane in a point and is perpendicular to every line in the plane that intersects it at that point.

In a diagram, a line perpendicular to a plane must be marked with a right angle symbol.

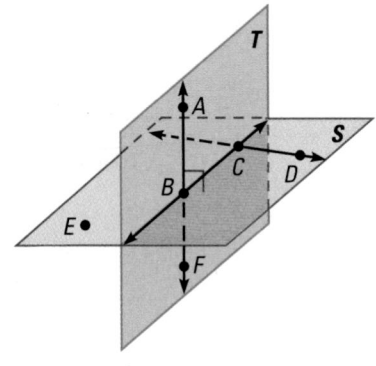

EXAMPLE 4 Interpret a diagram in three dimensions

Which of the following statements *cannot* be assumed from the diagram?

A, B, and F are collinear.

E, B, and D are collinear.

$\overline{AB} \perp$ plane S

$\overline{CD} \perp$ plane T

$\overleftrightarrow{AF}$ intersects $\overleftrightarrow{BC}$ at point B.

Solution

No drawn line connects E, B, and D, so you cannot assume they are collinear. With no right angle marked, you cannot assume $\overline{CD} \perp$ plane T.

✓ **GUIDED PRACTICE** for Examples 3 and 4

In Exercises 3 and 4, refer back to Example 3.

3. If the given information stated $\overline{PW}$ and $\overline{QW}$ are congruent, how would you indicate that in the diagram?

4. Name a pair of supplementary angles in the diagram. *Explain.*

5. In the diagram for Example 4, can you assume plane S intersects plane T at $\overleftrightarrow{BC}$?

6. *Explain* how you know that $\overleftrightarrow{AB} \perp \overleftrightarrow{BC}$ in Example 4.

2.4 EXERCISES

HOMEWORK KEY

○ = WORKED-OUT SOLUTIONS
on p. WS2 for Exs. 7, 13, and 31

★ = STANDARDIZED TEST PRACTICE
Exs. 2, 10, 24, 25, 33, 39, and 41

SKILL PRACTICE

1. **VOCABULARY** Copy and complete: A __?__ is a line that intersects the plane in a point and is perpendicular to every line in the plane that intersects it.

2. ★ **WRITING** *Explain* why you cannot assume ∠*BHA* ≅ ∠*CJA* in the Concept Summary on page 97.

EXAMPLE 1
on p. 97
for Exs. 3–5

IDENTIFYING POSTULATES State the postulate illustrated by the diagram.

3.
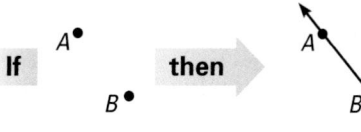
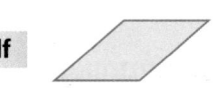

4.
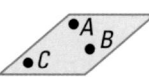

5. **CONDITIONAL STATEMENTS** Postulate 8 states that through any three noncollinear points there exists exactly one plane.

   a. Rewrite Postulate 8 in if-then form.

   b. Write the converse, inverse, and contrapositive of Postulate 8.

   c. Which statements in part (b) are true?

EXAMPLE 2
on p. 97
for Exs. 6–8

USING A DIAGRAM Use the diagram to write an example of each postulate.

6. Postulate 6

7. Postulate 7

8. Postulate 8

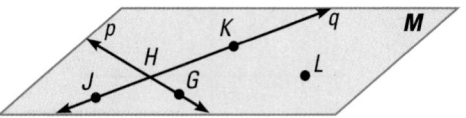

EXAMPLES 3 and 4
on p. 98
for Exs. 9–10

9. **SKETCHING** Sketch a diagram showing $\overleftrightarrow{XY}$ intersecting $\overleftrightarrow{WV}$ at point *T*, so $\overleftrightarrow{XY} \perp \overleftrightarrow{WV}$. In your diagram, does $\overline{WT}$ have to be congruent to $\overline{TV}$? *Explain* your reasoning.

10. ★ **MULTIPLE CHOICE** Which of the following statements *cannot* be assumed from the diagram?

   A Points *A*, *B*, *C*, and *E* are coplanar.

   B Points *F*, *B*, and *G* are collinear.

   C $\overleftrightarrow{HC} \perp \overleftrightarrow{GE}$

   D $\overleftrightarrow{EC}$ intersects plane *M* at point *C*.

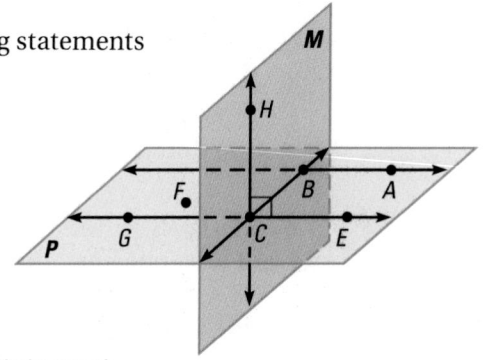

ANALYZING STATEMENTS Decide whether the statement is true or false. If it is false, give a real-world counterexample.

11. Through any three points, there exists exactly one line.

12. A point can be in more than one plane.

13. Any two planes intersect.

USING A DIAGRAM Use the diagram to determine if the statement is *true* or *false*.

14. Planes W and X intersect at $\overleftrightarrow{KL}$.

15. Points Q, J, and M are collinear.

16. Points K, L, M, and R are coplanar.

17. $\overleftrightarrow{MN}$ and $\overleftrightarrow{RP}$ intersect.

18. $\overleftrightarrow{RP} \perp$ plane W

19. $\overleftrightarrow{JK}$ lies in plane X.

20. $\angle PLK$ is a right angle.

21. $\angle NKL$ and $\angle JKM$ are vertical angles.

22. $\angle NKJ$ and $\angle JKM$ are supplementary angles.

23. $\angle JKM$ and $\angle KLP$ are congruent angles.

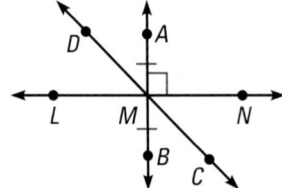

24. ★ **MULTIPLE CHOICE** Choose the diagram showing $\overleftrightarrow{LN}$, $\overleftrightarrow{AB}$, and $\overleftrightarrow{DC}$ intersecting at point M, $\overleftrightarrow{AB}$ bisecting $\overline{LN}$, and $\overleftrightarrow{DC} \perp \overleftrightarrow{LN}$.

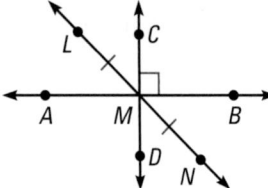

Ⓐ

Ⓑ

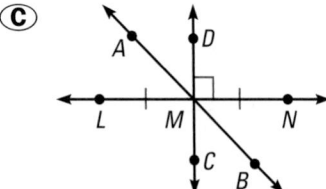

Ⓒ

Ⓓ

25. ★ **OPEN-ENDED MATH** Sketch a diagram of a real-world object illustrating three of the postulates about points, lines, and planes. List the postulates used.

26. **ERROR ANALYSIS** A student made the false statement shown. Change the statement in two different ways to make it true.

Three points are always contained in a line.

27. **REASONING** Use Postulates 5 and 9 to *explain* why every plane contains at least one line.

28. **REASONING** Point X lies in plane M. Use Postulates 5 and 9 to *explain* why there are at least two lines in plane M that contain point X.

29. **CHALLENGE** Sketch a line m and a point C not on line m. Make a conjecture about how many planes can be drawn so that line m and point C lie in the plane. Use postulates to justify your conjecture.

○ = **WORKED-OUT SOLUTIONS** on p. WS1

★ = **STANDARDIZED TEST PRACTICE**

REAL-WORLD SITUATIONS Which postulate is suggested by the photo?

30.

(31.)

32.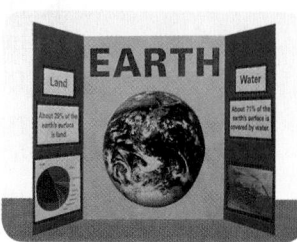

33. ★ **SHORT RESPONSE** Give a real-world example of Postulate 6, which states that a line contains at least two points.

    @HomeTutor for problem solving help at classzone.com

34. **DRAW A DIAGRAM** Sketch two lines that intersect, and another line that does not intersect either one.

    @HomeTutor for problem solving help at classzone.com

USING A DIAGRAM Use the pyramid to write examples of the postulate indicated.

35. Postulate 5

36. Postulate 7

37. Postulate 9

38. Postulate 10

39. ★ **EXTENDED RESPONSE** A friend e-mailed you the following statements about a neighborhood. Use the statements to complete parts (a)–(e).

Subject	Neighborhood
	Building B is due west of Building A.
	Buildings A and B are on Street 1.
	Building D is due north of Building A.
	Buildings A and D are on Street 2.
	Building C is southwest of Building A.
	Buildings A and C are on Street 3.
	Building E is due east of Building B.
	∠CAE formed by Streets 1 and 3 is obtuse.

a. Draw a diagram of the neighborhood.

b. Where do Streets 1 and 2 intersect?

c. Classify the angle formed by Streets 1 and 2.

d. Is Building E between Buildings A and B? *Explain*.

e. What street is Building E on?

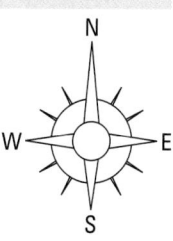

40. MULTI-STEP PROBLEM Copy the figure and label the following points, lines, and planes appropriately.

  a. Label the horizontal plane as *X* and the vertical plane as *Y*.

  b. Draw two points *A* and *B* on your diagram so they lie in plane *Y*, but not in plane *X*.

  c. Illustrate Postulate 5 on your diagram.

  d. If point *C* lies in both plane *X* and plane *Y*, where would it lie? Draw point *C* on your diagram.

  e. Illustrate Postulate 9 for plane *X* on your diagram.

41. ★ **SHORT RESPONSE** Points *E*, *F*, and *G* all lie in plane *P* and in plane *Q*. What must be true about points *E*, *F*, and *G* if *P* and *Q* are different planes? What must be true about points *E*, *F*, and *G* to force *P* and *Q* to be the same plane? Make sketches to support your answers.

DRAWING DIAGRAMS $\overleftrightarrow{AC}$ and $\overleftrightarrow{DB}$ intersect at point *E*. Draw one diagram that meets the additional condition(s) and another diagram that does not.

42. ∠*AED* and ∠*AEB* are right angles.

43. Point *E* is the midpoint of $\overline{AC}$.

44. $\overrightarrow{EA}$ and $\overrightarrow{EC}$ are opposite rays. $\overrightarrow{EB}$ and $\overrightarrow{ED}$ are not opposite rays.

45. CHALLENGE Suppose none of the four legs of a chair are the same length. What is the maximum number of planes determined by the lower ends of the legs? Suppose exactly three of the legs of a second chair have the same length. What is the maximum number of planes determined by the lower ends of the legs of the second chair? *Explain* your reasoning.

MIXED REVIEW

PREVIEW
Prepare for
Lesson 2.5
in Exs. 46–48.

Find the indicated length. *(p. 9)*

46. Find *MP*.

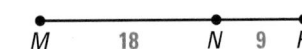

47. Find *AC*.

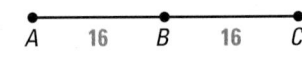

48. Find *RS*.

Line ℓ bisects the segment. Find the indicated length. *(p. 15)*

49. Find *JK*.

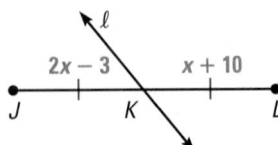

50. Find *XZ*.

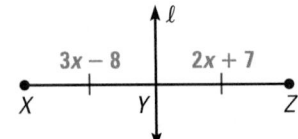

51. Find *BC*.

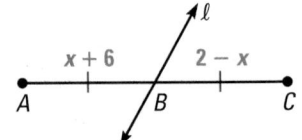

Draw an example of the type of angle described. *(p. 24)*

52. Right angle   **53.** Acute angle   **54.** Obtuse angle   **55.** Straight angle

56. Two angles form a linear pair. The measure of one angle is 9 times the measure of the other angle. Find the measure of each angle. *(p. 35)*

Lessons 2.1–2.4

1. **MULTI-STEP PROBLEM** The table below shows the time of the sunrise on different days in Galveston, Texas.

Date in 2006	Time of sunrise (Central Standard Time)
Jan. 1	7:14 A.M.
Feb. 1	7:08 A.M.
Mar. 1	6:45 A.M.
Apr. 1	6:09 A.M.
May 1	5:37 A.M.
June 1	5:20 A.M.
July 1	5:23 A.M.
Aug. 1	5:40 A.M.

   a. *Describe* the pattern, if any, in the times shown in the table.

   b. Use the times in the table to make a reasonable prediction about the time of the sunrise on September 1, 2006.

2. **SHORT RESPONSE** As shown in the table below, hurricanes are categorized by the speed of the wind in the storm. Use the table to determine whether the statement is *true* or *false*. If false, provide a counterexample.

Hurricane category	Wind speed *w* (mi/h)
1	$74 \leq w \leq 95$
2	$96 \leq w \leq 110$
3	$111 \leq w \leq 130$
4	$131 \leq w \leq 155$
5	$w > 155$

   a. A hurricane is a category 5 hurricane if and only if its wind speed is greater than 155 miles per hour.

   b. A hurricane is a category 3 hurricane if and only if its wind speed is less than 130 miles per hour.

3. **GRIDDED ANSWER** Write the next number in the pattern.

   1, 2, 5, 10, 17, 26, . . .

4. **EXTENDED RESPONSE** The graph shows concession sales at six high school football games. Tell whether each statement is the result of *inductive reasoning* or *deductive reasoning*. *Explain* your thinking.

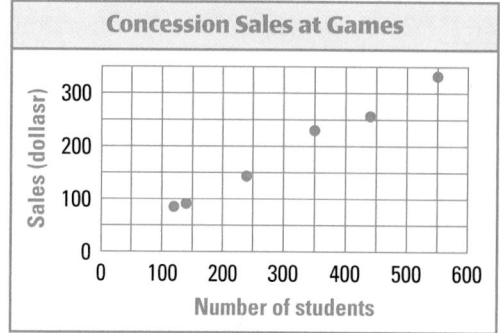

Concession Sales at Games

   a. If 500 students attend a football game, the high school can expect concession sales to reach $300.

   b. Concession sales were highest at the game attended by 550 students.

   c. The average number of students who come to a game is about 300.

5. **SHORT RESPONSE** Select the phrase that makes the conclusion true. *Explain* your reasoning.

   a. A person needs a library card to check out books at the public library. You checked out a book at the public library. You (*must have, may have,* or *do not have*) a library card.

   b. The islands of Hawaii are volcanoes. Bob has never been to the Hawaiian Islands. Bob (*has visited, may have visited,* or *has never visited*) volcanoes.

6. **SHORT RESPONSE** Sketch a diagram showing $\overleftrightarrow{PQ}$ intersecting $\overleftrightarrow{RS}$ at point *N*. In your diagram, ∠*PNS* should be an obtuse angle. Identify two acute angles in your diagram. *Explain* how you know that these angles are acute.

2.5 Justify a Number Trick

MATERIALS · paper · pencil

QUESTION How can you use algebra to justify a number trick?

Number tricks can allow you to guess the result of a series of calculations.

EXPLORE Play the number trick

STEP 1 *Pick a number* Follow the directions below.

a. Pick any number between 11 and 98 that does not end in a zero.   23

b. Double the number. $23 \cdot 2$

c. Add 4 to your answer. $46 + 4$

d. Multiply your answer by 5. $50 \cdot 5$

e. Add 12 to your answer. $250 + 12$

f. Multiply your answer by 10. $262 \cdot 10$

g. Subtract 320 from your answer. $2620 - 320$

h. Cross out the zeros in your answer.   23~~00~~

STEP 2 *Repeat the trick* Repeat the trick three times using three different numbers. What do you notice?

DRAW CONCLUSIONS Use your observations to complete these exercises

1. Let *x* represent the number you chose in the Explore. Write algebraic expressions for each step. Remember to use the Order of Operations.

2. *Justify* each expression you wrote in Exercise 1.

3. Another number trick is as follows:

    Pick any number.
    Multiply your number by 2.
    Add 18 to your answer.
    Divide your answer by 2.
    Subtract your original number from your answer.

    What is your answer? Does your answer depend on the number you chose? How can you change the trick so your answer is always 15? *Explain*.

4. **REASONING** Write your own number trick.

2.5 Reason Using Properties from Algebra

Before	You used deductive reasoning to form logical arguments.
Now	You will use algebraic properties in logical arguments too.
Why	So you can apply a heart rate formula, as in Example 3.

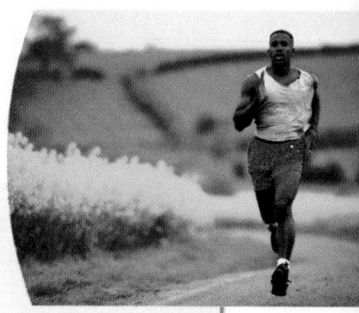

Key Vocabulary
• **equation,** *p. 875*
• **solve an equation,** *p. 875*

When you *solve an equation*, you use properties of real numbers. Segment lengths and angle measures are real numbers, so you can also use these properties to write logical arguments about geometric figures.

KEY CONCEPT   *For Your Notebook*

Algebraic Properties of Equality

Let a, b, and c be real numbers.

Addition Property	If $a = b$, then $a + c = b + c$.
Subtraction Property	If $a = b$, then $a - c = b - c$.
Multiplication Property	If $a = b$, then $ac = bc$.
Division Property	If $a = b$ and $c \neq 0$, then $\dfrac{a}{c} = \dfrac{b}{c}$.
Substitution Property	If $a = b$, then a can be substituted for b in any equation or expression.

EXAMPLE 1   **Write reasons for each step**

Solve $2x + 5 = 20 - 3x$. Write a reason for each step.

Equation	Explanation	Reason
$2x + 5 = 20 - 3x$	Write original equation.	**Given**
$2x + 5 + 3x = 20 - 3x + 3x$	Add $3x$ to each side.	**Addition Property of Equality**
$5x + 5 = 20$	Combine like terms.	**Simplify.**
$5x = 15$	Subtract 5 from each side.	**Subtraction Property of Equality**
$x = 3$	Divide each side by 5.	**Division Property of Equality**

▶ The value of x is 3.

Distributive Property

$a(b + c) = ab + ac$, where a, b, and c are real numbers.

EXAMPLE 2 **Use the Distributive Property**

Solve $-4(11x + 2) = 80$. Write a reason for each step.

Solution

Equation	Explanation	Reason
$-4(11x + 2) = 80$	Write original equation.	Given
$-44x - 8 = 80$	Multiply.	Distributive Property
$-44x = 88$	Add 8 to each side.	Addition Property of Equality
$x = -2$	Divide each side by -44.	Division Property of Equality

Animated **Geometry** at classzone.com

EXAMPLE 3 **Use properties in the real world**

HEART RATE When you exercise, your target heart rate should be between 50% to 70% of your maximum heart rate. Your target heart rate r at 70% can be determined by the formula $r = 0.70(220 - a)$ where a represents your age in years. Solve the formula for a.

Solution

Equation	Explanation	Reason
$r = 0.70(220 - a)$	Write original equation.	Given
$r = 154 - 0.70a$	Multiply.	Distributive Property
$r - 154 = -0.70a$	Subtract 154 from each side.	Subtraction Property of Equality
$\dfrac{r - 154}{-0.70} = a$	Divide each side by -0.70.	Division Property of Equality

✓ **GUIDED PRACTICE** for Examples 1, 2, and 3

In Exercises 1 and 2, solve the equation and write a reason for each step.

1. $4x + 9 = -3x + 2$

2. $14x + 3(7 - x) = -1$

3. Solve the formula $A = \frac{1}{2}bh$ for b.

PROPERTIES The following properties of equality are true for all real numbers. Segment lengths and angle measures are real numbers, so these properties of equality are true for segment lengths and angle measures.

KEY CONCEPT   *For Your Notebook*

Reflexive Property of Equality

Real Numbers   For any real number a, $a = a$.

Segment Length   For any segment AB, $AB = AB$.

Angle Measure   For any angle A, $m\angle A = m\angle A$.

Symmetric Property of Equality

Real Numbers   For any real numbers a and b, if $a = b$, then $b = a$.

Segment Length   For any segments AB and CD, if $AB = CD$, then $CD = AB$.

Angle Measure   For any angles A and B, if $m\angle A = m\angle B$, then $m\angle B = m\angle A$.

Transitive Property of Equality

Real Numbers   For any real numbers a, b, and c, if $a = b$ and $b = c$, then $a = c$.

Segment Length   For any segments AB, CD, and EF, if $AB = CD$ and $CD = EF$, then $AB = EF$.

Angle Measure   For any angles A, B, and C, if $m\angle A = m\angle B$ and $m\angle B = m\angle C$, then $m\angle A = m\angle C$.

EXAMPLE 4   **Use properties of equality**

LOGO You are designing a logo to sell daffodils. Use the information given. Determine whether $m\angle EBA = m\angle DBC$.

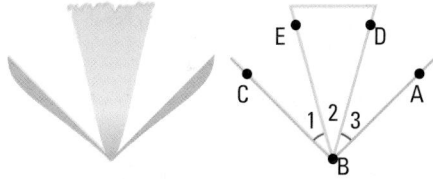

Solution

Equation	Explanation	Reason
$m\angle 1 = m\angle 3$	Marked in diagram.	**Given**
$m\angle EBA = m\angle 3 + m\angle 2$	Add measures of adjacent angles.	**Angle Addition Postulate**
$m\angle EBA = m\angle 1 + m\angle 2$	Substitute $m\angle 1$ for $m\angle 3$.	**Substitution Property of Equality**
$m\angle 1 + m\angle 2 = m\angle DBC$	Add measures of adjacent angles.	**Angle Addition Postulate**
$m\angle EBA = m\angle DBC$	Both measures are equal to the sum of $m\angle 1 + m\angle 2$.	**Transitive Property of Equality**

EXAMPLE 5 **Use properties of equality**

In the diagram, $AB = CD$. Show that $AC = BD$.

Solution

Equation	Explanation	Reason
$AB = CD$	Marked in diagram.	**Given**
$AC = AB + BC$	Add lengths of adjacent segments.	**Segment Addition Postulate**
$BD = BC + CD$	Add lengths of adjacent segments.	**Segment Addition Postulate**
$AB + BC = CD + BC$	Add BC to each side of $AB = CD$.	**Addition Property of Equality**
$AC = BD$	Substitute AC for $AB + BC$ and BD for $BC + CD$.	**Substitution Property of Equality**

✓ **GUIDED PRACTICE** for Examples 4 and 5

Name the property of equality the statement illustrates.

4. If $m\angle 6 = m\angle 7$, then $m\angle 7 = m\angle 6$.

5. If $JK = KL$ and $KL = 12$, then $JK = 12$.

6. $m\angle W = m\angle W$

2.5 EXERCISES

HOMEWORK KEY

◯ = **WORKED-OUT SOLUTIONS**
on p. WS2 for Exs. 9, 21, and 31

★ = **STANDARDIZED TEST PRACTICE**
Exs. 2, 5, 27, and 35

◆ = **MULTIPLE REPRESENTATIONS**
Ex. 36

SKILL PRACTICE

1. **VOCABULARY** The following statement is true because of what property? The measure of an angle is equal to itself.

2. ★ **WRITING** *Explain* how to check the answer to Example 3 on page 106.

EXAMPLES 1 and 2
on pp. 105–106
for Exs. 3–14

WRITING REASONS Copy the logical argument. Write a reason for each step.

3.
$3x - 12 = 7x + 8$	Given
$-4x - 12 = 8$	?
$-4x = 20$	?
$x = -5$	?

4.
$5(x - 1) = 4x + 13$	Given
$5x - 5 = 4x + 13$	?
$x - 5 = 13$	?
$x = 18$	?

5. ★ **MULTIPLE CHOICE** Name the property of equality the statement illustrates: If $XY = AB$ and $AB = GH$, then $XY = GH$.

   (**A**) Substitution   (**B**) Reflexive   (**C**) Symmetric   (**D**) Transitive

WRITING REASONS Solve the equation. Write a reason for each step.

6. $5x - 10 = -40$ 7. $4x + 9 = 16 - 3x$ 8. $5(3x - 20) = -10$

9. $3(2x + 11) = 9$ 10. $2(-x - 5) = 12$ 11. $44 - 2(3x + 4) = -18x$

12. $4(5x - 9) = -2(x + 7)$ 13. $2x - 15 - x = 21 + 10x$ 14. $3(7x - 9) - 19x = -15$

EXAMPLE 3
on p. 106
for Exs. 15–20

ALGEBRA Solve the equation for y. Write a reason for each step.

15. $5x + y = 18$ 16. $-4x + 2y = 8$ 17. $12 - 3y = 30x$

18. $3x + 9y = -7$ 19. $2y + 0.5x = 16$ 20. $\frac{1}{2}x - \frac{3}{4}y = -2$

EXAMPLES 4 and 5
on pp. 107–108
for Exs. 21–25

COMPLETING STATEMENTS In Exercises 21–25, use the property to copy and complete the statement.

21. Substitution Property of Equality: If $AB = 20$, then $AB + CD = \underline{\ ?\ }$.

22. Symmetric Property of Equality: If $m\angle 1 = m\angle 2$, then $\underline{\ ?\ }$.

23. Addition Property of Equality: If $AB = CD$, then $\underline{\ ?\ } + EF = \underline{\ ?\ } + EF$.

24. Distributive Property: If $5(x + 8) = 2$, then $\underline{\ ?\ } x + \underline{\ ?\ } = 2$.

25. Transitive Property of Equality: If $m\angle 1 = m\angle 2$ and $m\angle 2 = m\angle 3$, then $\underline{\ ?\ }$.

26. **ERROR ANALYSIS** *Describe* and correct the error in solving the equation for x.

$7x = x + 24$	Given
$8x = 24$	Addition Property of Equality
$x = 3$	Division Property of Equality

27. ★ **OPEN-ENDED MATH** Write examples from your everyday life that could help you remember the *Reflexive, Symmetric,* and *Transitive* Properties of Equality.

PERIMETER In Exercises 28 and 29, show that the perimeter of triangle ABC is equal to the perimeter of triangle ADC.

28.

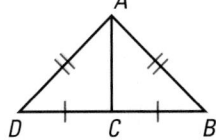

29.

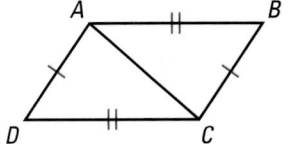

30. **CHALLENGE** In the figure at the right, $\overline{ZY} \cong \overline{XW}$, $ZX = 5x + 17$, $YW = 10 - 2x$, and $YX = 3$. Find ZY and XW.

EXAMPLE 3
on p. 106
for Exs. 31–32

31. **PERIMETER** The formula for the perimeter P of a rectangle is $P = 2\ell + 2w$ where ℓ is the length and w is the width. Solve the formula for ℓ and write a reason for each step. Then find the length of a rectangular lawn whose perimeter is 55 meters and whose width is 11 meters.

@HomeTutor for problem solving help at classzone.com

32. **AREA** The formula for the area A of a triangle is $A = \frac{1}{2}bh$ where b is the base and h is the height. Solve the formula for h and write a reason for each step. Then find the height of a triangle whose area is 1768 square inches and whose base is 52 inches.

@HomeTutor for problem solving help at classzone.com

33. **PROPERTIES OF EQUALITY** Copy and complete the table to show $m\angle 2 = m\angle 3$.

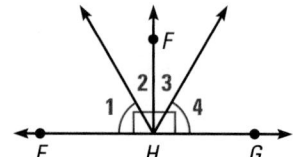

Equation	Explanation	Reason
$m\angle 1 = m\angle 4$, $m\angle EHF = 90°$, $m\angle GHF = 90°$	?	Given
$m\angle EHF = m\angle GHF$	?	Substitution Property of Equality
$m\angle EHF = m\angle 1 + m\angle 2$ $m\angle GHF = m\angle 3 + m\angle 4$	Add measures of adjacent angles.	?
$m\angle 1 + m\angle 2 = m\angle 3 + m\angle 4$	Write expressions equal to the angle measures.	?
?	Substitute $m\angle 1$ for $m\angle 4$.	?
$m\angle 2 = m\angle 3$	?	Subtraction Property of Equality

34. **MULTI-STEP PROBLEM** Points A, B, C, and D represent stops, in order, along a subway route. The distance between Stops A and C is the same as the distance between Stops B and D.

a. Draw a diagram to represent the situation.

b. Use the Segment Addition Postulate to show that the distance between Stops A and B is the same as the distance between Stops C and D.

c. *Justify* part (b) using the Properties of Equality.

EXAMPLE 4
on p. 107
for Ex. 35

35. ★ **SHORT RESPONSE** A flashlight beam is reflected off a mirror lying flat on the ground. Use the information given below to find $m\angle 2$.

$m\angle 1 + m\angle 2 + m\angle 3 = 180°$

$m\angle 1 + m\angle 2 = 148°$

$m\angle 1 = m\angle 3$

○ = **WORKED-OUT SOLUTIONS** on p. WS1　　★ = **STANDARDIZED TEST PRACTICE**　　◆ = **MULTIPLE REPRESENTATIONS**

36. ◆ **MULTIPLE REPRESENTATIONS** The formula to convert a temperature in degrees Fahrenheit (°F) to degrees Celsius (°C) is $C = \frac{5}{9}(F - 32)$.

   a. Writing an Equation Solve the formula for *F*. Write a reason for each step.

   b. Making a Table Make a table that shows the conversion to Fahrenheit for each temperature: 0°C, 20°C, 32°C, and 41°C.

   c. Drawing a Graph Use your table to graph the temperature in degrees Fahrenheit (°F) as a function of the temperature in degrees Celsius (°C). Is this a linear function?

CHALLENGE **In Exercises 37 and 38, decide whether the relationship is** *reflexive, symmetric,* **or** *transitive.*

37. Group: two employees in a grocery store
Relationship: "worked the same hours as"
Example: Yen worked the same hours as Jim.

38. Group: negative numbers on a number line
Relationship: "is less than"
Example: −4 is less than −1.

MIXED REVIEW

PREVIEW
Prepare for Lesson 2.6 in Exs. 39–40.

In the diagram, $m\angle ADC = 124°.$ *(p. 24)*

39. Find $m\angle ADB$.

40. Find $m\angle BDC$.

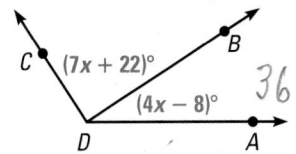

$11x + 14 = 124$
36
$11x = 110$
$x = 11$

41. Find a counterexample to show the conjecture is false.

   Conjecture All polygons have five sides. *(p. 72)*

42. Select the word(s) that make(s) the conclusion true. If $m\angle X = m\angle Y$ and $m\angle Y = m\angle Z$, then $m\angle X$ (*is, may be,* or *is not*) equal to $m\angle Z$. *(p. 87)*

QUIZ *for Lessons 2.4–2.5*

Use the diagram to determine if the statement is *true* **or** *false*. *(p. 96)*

  1. Points *B*, *C*, and *D* are coplanar.

  2. Point *A* is on line ℓ.

  3. Plane *P* and plane *Q* are perpendicular.

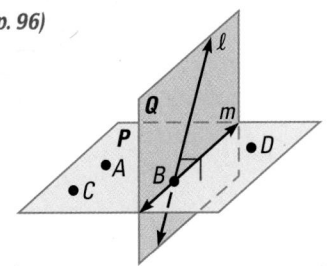

Solve the equation. Write a reason for each step. *(p. 105)*

  4. $x + 20 = 35$

  5. $5x - 14 = 16 + 3x$

Use the property to copy and complete the statement. *(p. 105)*

  6. Subtraction Property of Equality: If $AB = CD$, then $\underline{\ ?\ } - EF = \underline{\ ?\ } - EF$.

  7. Transitive Property of Equality: If $a = b$ and $b = c$, then $\underline{\ ?\ } = \underline{\ ?\ }$.

2.6 Prove Statements about Segments and Angles

Before You used deductive reasoning.

Now You will write proofs using geometric theorems.

Why? So you can prove angles are congruent, as in Ex. 21.

Key Vocabulary
• proof
• two-column proof
• theorem

A **proof** is a logical argument that shows a statement is true. There are several formats for proofs. A **two-column proof** has numbered statements and corresponding reasons that show an argument in a logical order.

In a two-column proof, each statement in the left-hand column is either given information or the result of applying a known property or fact to statements already made. Each reason in the right-hand column is the explanation for the corresponding statement.

EXAMPLE 1 Write a two-column proof

WRITE PROOFS
Writing a two-column proof is a formal way of organizing your reasons to show a statement is true.

Write a two-column proof for the situation in Example 4 on page 107.

GIVEN ▶ $m\angle 1 = m\angle 3$

PROVE ▶ $m\angle EBA = m\angle DBC$

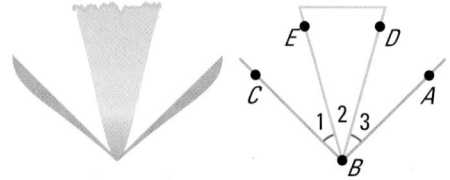

STATEMENTS	REASONS
1. $m\angle 1 = m\angle 3$	1. Given
2. $m\angle EBA = m\angle 3 + m\angle 2$	2. Angle Addition Postulate
3. $m\angle EBA = m\angle 1 + m\angle 2$	3. Substitution Property of Equality
4. $m\angle 1 + m\angle 2 = m\angle DBC$	4. Angle Addition Postulate
5. $m\angle EBA = m\angle DBC$	5. Transitive Property of Equality

---

✓ **GUIDED PRACTICE** for Example 1

1. Four steps of a proof are shown. Give the reasons for the last two steps.

GIVEN ▶ $AC = AB + AB$

PROVE ▶ $AB = BC$

STATEMENTS	REASONS
1. $AC = AB + AB$	1. Given
2. $AB + BC = AC$	2. Segment Addition Postulate
3. $AB + AB = AB + BC$	3. ?
4. $AB = BC$	4. ?

THEOREMS The reasons used in a proof can include definitions, properties, postulates, and *theorems*. A **theorem** is a statement that can be proven. Once you have proven a theorem, you can use the theorem as a reason in other proofs.

TAKE NOTES
Be sure to copy all new theorems in your notebook. Notice that the theorem box tells you where to find the proof(s).

THEOREMS   *For Your Notebook*

THEOREM 2.1 Congruence of Segments

Segment congruence is reflexive, symmetric, and transitive.

Reflexive   For any segment AB, $\overline{AB} \cong \overline{AB}$.

Symmetric   If $\overline{AB} \cong \overline{CD}$, then $\overline{CD} \cong \overline{AB}$.

Transitive   If $\overline{AB} \cong \overline{CD}$ and $\overline{CD} \cong \overline{EF}$, then $\overline{AB} \cong \overline{EF}$.

Proofs: p. 137; Ex. 5, p. 121; Ex. 26, p. 118

THEOREM 2.2 Congruence of Angles

Angle congruence is reflexive, symmetric, and transitive.

Reflexive   For any angle A, $\angle A \cong \angle A$.

Symmetric   If $\angle A \cong \angle B$, then $\angle B \cong \angle A$.

Transitive   If $\angle A \cong \angle B$ and $\angle B \cong \angle C$, then $\angle A \cong \angle C$.

Proofs: Ex. 25, p. 118; Concept Summary, p. 114; Ex. 21, p. 137

EXAMPLE 2   **Name the property shown**

Name the property illustrated by the statement.

a. If $\angle R \cong \angle T$ and $\angle T \cong \angle P$, then $\angle R \cong \angle P$.

b. If $\overline{NK} \cong \overline{BD}$, then $\overline{BD} \cong \overline{NK}$.

Solution

a. Transitive Property of Angle Congruence

b. Symmetric Property of Segment Congruence

✓ **GUIDED PRACTICE**   for Example 2

Name the property illustrated by the statement.

2. $\overline{CD} \cong \overline{CD}$

3. If $\angle Q \cong \angle V$, then $\angle V \cong \angle Q$.

In this lesson, most of the proofs involve showing that congruence and equality are equivalent. You may find that what you are asked to prove seems to be obviously true. It is important to practice writing these proofs so that you will be prepared to write more complicated proofs in later chapters.

EXAMPLE 3 **Use properties of equality**

Prove this property of midpoints: If you know that M is the midpoint of $\overline{AB}$, prove that AB is two times AM and AM is one half of AB.

GIVEN ▶ M is the midpoint of $\overline{AB}$.

PROVE ▶ **a.** $AB = 2 \cdot AM$

   b. $AM = \frac{1}{2}AB$

> **WRITE PROOFS**
> Before writing a proof, organize your reasoning by copying or drawing a diagram for the situation described. Then identify the GIVEN and PROVE statements.

STATEMENTS	REASONS
1. M is the midpoint of $\overline{AB}$.	1. Given
2. $\overline{AM} \cong \overline{MB}$	2. Definition of midpoint
3. $AM = MB$	3. Definition of congruent segments
4. $AM + MB = AB$	4. Segment Addition Postulate
5. $AM + AM = AB$	5. Substitution Property of Equality
a. 6. $2AM = AB$	6. Distributive Property
b. 7. $AM = \frac{1}{2}AB$	7. Division Property of Equality

✓ **GUIDED PRACTICE** for Example 3

4. WHAT IF? Look back at Example 3. What would be different if you were proving that $AB = 2 \cdot MB$ and that $MB = \frac{1}{2}AB$ instead?

CONCEPT SUMMARY *For Your Notebook*

Writing a Two-Column Proof

In a proof, you make one statement at a time, until you reach the conclusion. Because you make statements based on facts, you are using deductive reasoning. Usually the first statement-and-reason pair you write is given information.

Proof of the Symmetric Property of Angle Congruence

GIVEN ▶ $\angle 1 \cong \angle 2$

PROVE ▶ $\angle 2 \cong \angle 1$

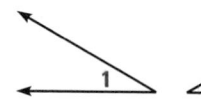

Copy or draw diagrams and label given information to help develop proofs.

Statements based on facts that you know or on conclusions from deductive reasoning →

STATEMENTS	REASONS
1. $\angle 1 \cong \angle 2$	1. Given
2. $m\angle 1 = m\angle 2$	2. Definition of congruent angles
3. $m\angle 2 = m\angle 1$	3. Symmetric Property of Equality
4. $\angle 2 \cong \angle 1$	4. Definition of congruent angles

← Definitions, postulates, or proven theorems that allow you to state the corresponding statement

↑ The number of statements will vary.

↑ Remember to give a reason for the last statement.

EXAMPLE 4 **Solve a multi-step problem**

SHOPPING MALL Walking down a hallway at the mall, you notice the music store is halfway between the food court and the shoe store. The shoe store is halfway between the music store and the bookstore. Prove that the distance between the entrances of the food court and music store is the same as the distance between the entrances of the shoe store and bookstore.

ANOTHER WAY

For an alternative method for solving the problem in Example 4, turn to page 120 for the **Problem Solving Workshop**.

Solution

STEP 1 **Draw** and label a diagram.

food court — *A*   music store — *B*   shoe store — *C*   bookstore — *D*

STEP 2 **Draw** separate diagrams to show mathematical relationships.

A *B* *C* *D*   *A* *B* *C* *D*

STEP 3 **State** what is given and what is to be proved for the situation. Then write a proof.

GIVEN ▶ *B* is the midpoint of $\overline{AC}$.
  C is the midpoint of $\overline{BD}$.

PROVE ▶ *AB* = *CD*

STATEMENTS	REASONS
1. *B* is the midpoint of $\overline{AC}$. *C* is the midpoint of $\overline{BD}$.	1. Given
2. $\overline{AB} \cong \overline{BC}$	2. Definition of midpoint
3. $\overline{BC} \cong \overline{CD}$	3. Definition of midpoint
4. $\overline{AB} \cong \overline{CD}$	4. Transitive Property of Congruence
5. *AB* = *CD*	5. Definition of congruent segments

✓ **GUIDED PRACTICE** | **for Example 4**

5. In Example 4, does it matter what the actual distances are in order to prove the relationship between *AB* and *CD*? *Explain.*

6. In Example 4, there is a clothing store halfway between the music store and the shoe store. What other two store entrances are the same distance from the entrance of the clothing store?

2.6 Prove Statements about Segments and Angles   **115**

2.6 EXERCISES

SKILL PRACTICE

1. **VOCABULARY** What is a *theorem*? How is it different from a *postulate*?

2. ★ **WRITING** You can use theorems as reasons in a two-column proof. What other types of statements can you use as reasons in a two-column proof? Give examples.

EXAMPLE 1
on p. 112
for Exs. 3–4

3. **DEVELOPING PROOF** Copy and complete the proof.

GIVEN ▶ $AB = 5$, $BC = 6$
PROVE ▶ $AC = 11$

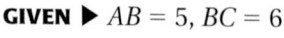

STATEMENTS	REASONS
1. $AB = 5$, $BC = 6$	1. Given
2. $AC = AB + BC$	2. Segment Addition Postulate
3. $AC = 5 + 6$	3. _?_ Addition POE
4. _?_ $AC = 11$	4. Simplify.

4. ★ **MULTIPLE CHOICE** Which property listed is the reason for the last step in the proof?

GIVEN ▶ $m\angle 1 = 59°$, $m\angle 2 = 59°$
PROVE ▶ $m\angle 1 = m\angle 2$

STATEMENTS	REASONS
1. $m\angle 1 = 59°$, $m\angle 2 = 59°$	1. Given
2. $59° = m\angle 2$	2. Symmetric Property of Equality
3. $m\angle 1 = m\angle 2$	3. _?_ Transitive

   Ⓐ Transitive Property of Equality   Ⓑ Reflexive Property of Equality

   Ⓒ Symmetric Property of Equality   Ⓓ Distributive Property

**EXAMPLES
2 and 3**
on pp. 113–114
for Exs. 5–13

USING PROPERTIES Use the property to copy and complete the statement.

5. Reflexive Property of Congruence: _?_ ≅ $\overline{SE}$

6. Symmetric Property of Congruence: If _?_ ≅ _?_ , then $\angle RST \cong \angle JKL$.

7. Transitive Property of Congruence: If $\angle F \cong \angle J$ and _?_ ≅ _?_ , then $\angle F \cong \angle L$.

NAMING PROPERTIES Name the property illustrated by the statement.

8. If $\overline{DG} \cong \overline{CT}$, then $\overline{CT} \cong \overline{DG}$.   9. $\angle VWX \cong \angle VWX$

10. If $\overline{JK} \cong \overline{MN}$ and $\overline{MN} \cong \overline{XY}$, then $\overline{JK} \cong \overline{XY}$. 11. $YZ = ZY$

12. ★ **MULTIPLE CHOICE** Name the property illustrated by the statement "If $\overline{CD} \cong \overline{MN}$, then $\overline{MN} \cong \overline{CD}$."

   Ⓐ Reflexive Property of Equality   Ⓑ Symmetric Property of Equality

   Ⓒ Symmetric Property of Congruence Ⓓ Transitive Property of Congruence

13. ERROR ANALYSIS In the diagram below, $\overline{MN} \cong \overline{LQ}$ and $\overline{LQ} \cong \overline{PN}$. *Describe and correct the error in the reasoning.*

Because $\overline{MN} \cong \overline{LQ}$ and $\overline{LQ} \cong \overline{PN}$, then $\overline{MN} \cong \overline{PN}$ by the Reflexive Property of Segment Congruence.

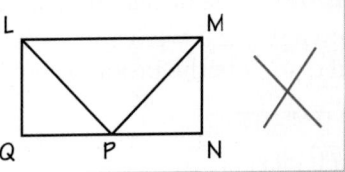

EXAMPLE 4
on p. 115
for Exs. 14–15

MAKING A SKETCH In Exercises 14 and 15, sketch a diagram that represents the given information.

14. CRYSTALS The shape of a crystal can be represented by intersecting lines and planes. Suppose a crystal is *cubic*, which means it can be represented by six planes that intersect at right angles.

15. BEACH VACATION You are on vacation at the beach. Along the boardwalk, the bike rentals are halfway between your cottage and the kite shop. The snack shop is halfway between your cottage and the bike rentals. The arcade is halfway between the bike rentals and the kite shop.

16. DEVELOPING PROOF Copy and complete the proof.

GIVEN ▶ $RT = 5$, $RS = 5$, $\overline{RT} \cong \overline{TS}$
PROVE ▶ $\overline{RS} \cong \overline{TS}$

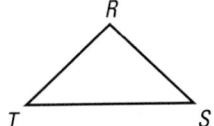

STATEMENTS	REASONS
1. $RT = 5$, $RS = 5$, $\overline{RT} \cong \overline{TS}$	1. __?__ Given
2. $RS = RT$	2. Transitive Property of Equality
3. $RT = TS$	3. Definition of congruent segments
4. $RS = TS$	4. Transitive Property of Equality
5. $\overline{RS} \cong \overline{TS}$	5. __?__

⟨xy⟩ ALGEBRA Solve for *x* using the given information. *Explain* your steps.

17. GIVEN ▶ $\overline{QR} \cong \overline{PQ}$, $\overline{RS} \cong \overline{PQ}$

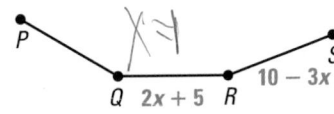

18. GIVEN ▶ $m\angle ABC = 90°$

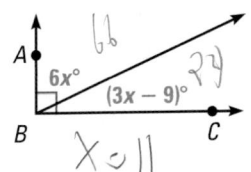

19. ★ SHORT RESPONSE *Explain* why writing a proof is an example of deductive reasoning, not inductive reasoning.

20. CHALLENGE Point *P* is the midpoint of $\overline{MN}$ and point *Q* is the midpoint of $\overline{MP}$. Suppose $\overline{AB}$ is congruent to $\overline{MP}$, and $\overline{PN}$ has length *x*. Write the length of the segments in terms of *x*. *Explain.*

a. $\overline{AB}$ **b.** $\overline{MN}$ **c.** $\overline{MQ}$ **d.** $\overline{NQ}$

21. **BRIDGE** In the bridge in the illustration, it is known that $\angle 2 \cong \angle 3$ and $\overrightarrow{TV}$ bisects $\angle UTW$. Copy and complete the proof to show that $\angle 1 \cong \angle 3$.

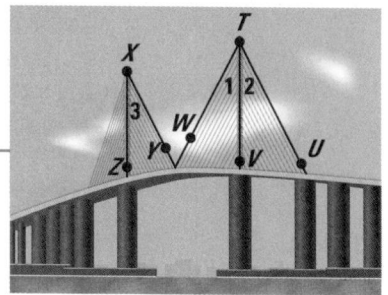

STATEMENTS	REASONS
1. $\overrightarrow{TV}$ bisects $\angle UTW$.	1. Given
2. $\angle 1 \cong \angle 2$	2. _?_
3. $\angle 2 \cong \angle 3$	3. Given
4. $\angle 1 \cong \angle 3$	4. _?_

@HomeTutor for problem solving help at classzone.com

EXAMPLE 3
on p. 114
for Ex. 22

22. **DEVELOPING PROOF** Write a complete proof by matching each statement with its corresponding reason.

GIVEN ▶ $\overrightarrow{QS}$ is an angle bisector of $\angle PQR$.

PROVE ▶ $m\angle PQS = \frac{1}{2} m\angle PQR$

STATEMENTS	REASONS
1. $\overrightarrow{QS}$ is an angle bisector of $\angle PQR$.	A. Definition of angle bisector
2. $\angle PQS \cong \angle SQR$	B. Distributive Property
3. $m\angle PQS = m\angle SQR$	C. Angle Addition Postulate
4. $m\angle PQS + m\angle SQR = m\angle PQR$	D. Given
5. $m\angle PQS + m\angle PQS = m\angle PQR$	E. Division Property of Equality
6. $2 \cdot m\angle PQS = m\angle PQR$	F. Definition of congruent angles
7. $m\angle PQS = \frac{1}{2} m\angle PQR$	G. Substitution Property of Equality

@HomeTutor for problem solving help at classzone.com

PROOF Use the given information and the diagram to prove the statement.

23. **GIVEN** ▶ $2AB = AC$

   PROVE ▶ $AB = BC$

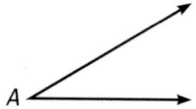

24. **GIVEN** ▶ $m\angle 1 + m\angle 2 = 180°$
   $m\angle 1 = 62°$

   PROVE ▶ $m\angle 2 = 118°$

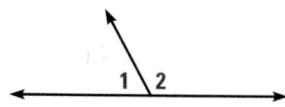

PROVING PROPERTIES Prove the indicated property of congruence.

25. Reflexive Property of Angle Congruence

   GIVEN ▶ A is an angle.

   PROVE ▶ $\angle A \cong \angle A$

26. Transitive Property of Segment Congruence

   GIVEN ▶ $\overline{WX} \cong \overline{XY}$ and $\overline{XY} \cong \overline{YZ}$

   PROVE ▶ $\overline{WX} \cong \overline{YZ}$

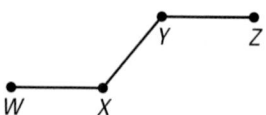

○ = **WORKED-OUT SOLUTIONS** on p. WS1   ★ = **STANDARDIZED TEST PRACTICE**

27. ★ **SHORT RESPONSE** In the sculpture shown, $\angle 1 \cong \angle 2$ and $\angle 2 \cong \angle 3$. Classify the triangle and *justify* your reasoning.

28. ★ **SHORT RESPONSE** You use a computer drawing program to create a line segment. You copy the segment and paste it. You copy the pasted segment and then paste it, and so on. How do you know all the line segments are congruent?

EXAMPLE 4
on p. 115
for Ex. 29

29. **MULTI-STEP PROBLEM** The distance from the restaurant to the shoe store is the same as the distance from the cafe to the florist. The distance from the shoe store to the movie theater is the same as the distance from the movie theater to the cafe, and from the florist to the dry cleaners.

Restaurant   Shoe store   Movie theater   Cafe   Florist   Dry cleaners

Use the steps below to prove that the distance from the restaurant to the movie theater is the same as the distance from the cafe to the dry cleaners.

a. Draw and label a diagram to show the mathematical relationships.

b. State what is given and what is to be proved for the situation.

c. Write a two-column proof.

Animated **Geometry** at classzone.com

30. **CHALLENGE** The distance from Springfield to Lakewood City is equal to the distance from Springfield to Bettsville. Janisburg is 50 miles farther from Springfield than Bettsville is. Moon Valley is 50 miles farther from Springfield than Lakewood City is.

a. Assume all five cities lie in a straight line. Draw a diagram that represents this situation.

b. Suppose you do not know that all five cities lie in a straight line. Draw a diagram that is different from the one in part (a) to represent the situation.

c. *Explain* the differences in the two diagrams.

MIXED REVIEW

PREVIEW
Prepare for
Lesson 2.7
in Exs. 31–33.

Given $m\angle 1$, find the measure of an angle that is complementary to $\angle 1$ and the measure of an angle that is supplementary to $\angle 1$. *(p. 35)*

31. $m\angle 1 = 47°$ **32.** $m\angle 1 = 29°$ **33.** $m\angle 1 = 89°$

Solve the equation. Write a reason for each step. *(p. 105)*

34. $5x + 14 = -16$ **35.** $2x - 9 = 15 - 4x$ **36.** $x + 28 = -11 - 3x - 17$

Another Way to Solve Example 4, page 115

MULTIPLE REPRESENTATIONS The first step in writing any proof is to make a plan. A diagram or *visual organizer* can help you plan your proof. The steps of a proof must be in a logical order, but there may be more than one correct order.

PROBLEM

SHOPPING MALL Walking down a hallway at the mall, you notice the music store is halfway between the food court and the shoe store. The shoe store is halfway between the music store and the bookstore. Prove that the distance between the entrances of the food court and music store is the same as the distance between the entrances of the shoe store and bookstore.

METHOD **Using a Visual Organizer**

STEP 1 **Use** a visual organizer to map out your proof.

The music store is halfway between the food court and the shoe store. The shoe store is halfway between the music store and the bookstore.

Given information	M is halfway between F and S.	S is halfway between M and B.
Deductions from given information	M is the midpoint of $\overline{FS}$. So, $FM = MS$.	S is the midpoint of $\overline{MB}$. So, $MS = SB$.
Statement to prove		$FM = SB$

STEP 2 **Write** a proof using the lengths of the segments.

GIVEN ▶ M is halfway between F and S.
 S is halfway between M and B.

PROVE ▶ $FM = SB$

STATEMENTS	REASONS
1. M is halfway between F and S.	1. Given
2. S is halfway between M and B.	2. Given
3. M is the midpoint of $\overline{FS}$.	3. Definition of midpoint
4. S is the midpoint of $\overline{MB}$.	4. Definition of midpoint
5. $FM = MS$ and $MS = SB$	5. Definition of midpoint
6. $MS = MS$	6. Reflexive Property of Equality
7. $FM = SB$	7. Substitution Property of Equality

1. **COMPARE PROOFS** *Compare* the proof on the previous page and the proof in Example 4 on page 115.

   a. How are the proofs the same? How are they different?

   b. Which proof is easier for you to understand? *Explain.*

2. **REASONING** Below is a proof of the Transitive Property of Angle Congruence. What is another reason you could give for Statement 3? *Explain.*

   GIVEN ▶ $\angle A \cong \angle B$ and $\angle B \cong \angle C$

   PROVE ▶ $\angle A \cong \angle C$

STATEMENTS	REASONS
1. $\angle A \cong \angle B$, $\angle B \cong \angle C$	1. Given
2. $m\angle A = m\angle B$, $m\angle B = m\angle C$	2. Definition of congruent angles
3. $m\angle A = m\angle C$	3. Transitive Property of Equality
4. $\angle A \cong \angle C$	4. Definition of congruent angles

3. **SHOPPING MALL** You are at the same mall as on page 120 and you notice that the bookstore is halfway between the shoe store and the toy store. Draw a diagram or make a visual organizer, then write a proof to show that the distance from the entrances of the food court and music store is the same as the distance from the entrances of the book store and toy store.

4. **WINDOW DESIGN** The entrance to the mall has a decorative window above the main doors as shown. The colored dividers form congruent angles. Draw a diagram or make a visual organizer, then write a proof to show that the angle measure between the red dividers is half the measure of the angle between the blue dividers.

5. **COMPARE PROOFS** Below is a proof of the Symmetric Property of Segment Congruence.

   GIVEN ▶ $\overline{DE} \cong \overline{FG}$

   PROVE ▶ $\overline{FG} \cong \overline{DE}$

   D •——————————• E
   F •——————————• G

STATEMENTS	REASONS
1. $\overline{DE} \cong \overline{FG}$	1. Given
2. $DE = FG$	2. Definition of congruent segments
3. $FG = DE$	3. Symmetric Property of Equality
4. $\overline{FG} \cong \overline{DE}$	4. Definition of congruent segments

   a. *Compare* this proof to the proof of the Symmetric Property of Angle Congruence in the Concept Summary on page 114. What makes the proofs different? *Explain.*

   b. *Explain* why Statement 2 above cannot be $\overline{FG} \cong \overline{DE}$.

2.7 Angles and Intersecting Lines

MATERIALS • graphing calculator or computer

QUESTION What is the relationship between the measures of the angles formed by intersecting lines?

You can use geometry drawing software to investigate the measures of angles formed when lines intersect.

EXPLORE 1 Measure linear pairs formed by intersecting lines

STEP 1 *Draw two intersecting lines* Draw and label $\overleftrightarrow{AB}$. Draw and label $\overleftrightarrow{CD}$ so that it intersects $\overleftrightarrow{AB}$. Draw and label the point of intersection *E*.

STEP 2

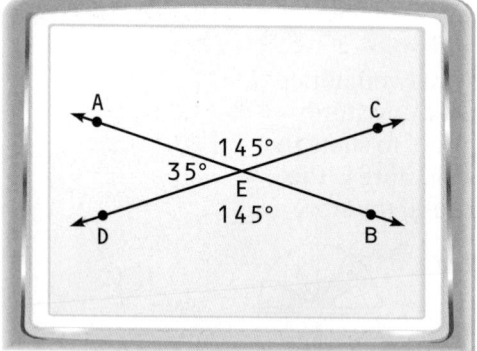

STEP 3

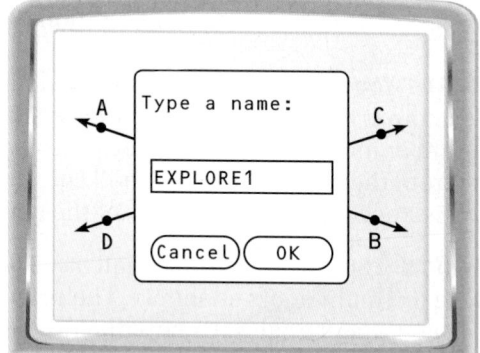

Measure angles Measure $\angle AEC$, $\angle AED$, and $\angle DEB$. Move point *C* to change the angles.

Save Save as "EXPLORE1" by choosing Save from the F1 menu and typing the name.

DRAW CONCLUSIONS Use your observations to complete these exercises

1. *Describe* the relationship between $\angle AEC$ and $\angle AED$.

2. *Describe* the relationship between $\angle AED$ and $\angle DEB$.

3. What do you notice about $\angle AEC$ and $\angle DEB$?

4. In Explore 1, what happens when you move *C* to a different position? Do the angle relationships stay the same? Make a conjecture about two angles supplementary to the same angle.

5. Do you think your conjecture will be true for supplementary angles that are not adjacent? *Explain.*

EXPLORE 2 Measure complementary angles

STEP 1 *Draw two perpendicular lines* Draw and label $\overleftrightarrow{AB}$. Draw point E on $\overleftrightarrow{AB}$. Draw and label $\overleftrightarrow{EC} \perp \overleftrightarrow{AB}$. Draw and label point D on $\overleftrightarrow{EC}$ so that E is between C and D as shown in Step 2.

STEP 2

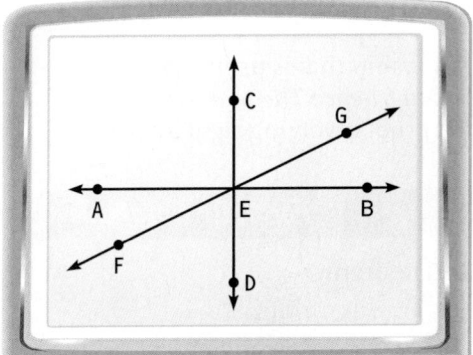

STEP 3

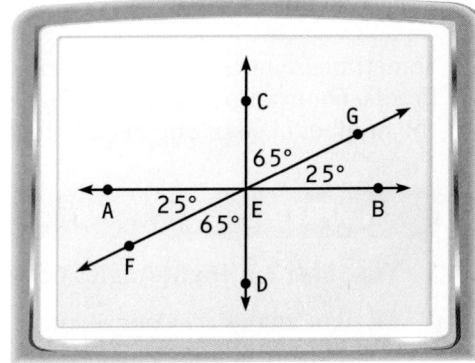

Draw another line Draw and label $\overleftrightarrow{EG}$ so that G is in the interior of $\angle CEB$. Draw point F on $\overleftrightarrow{EG}$ as shown.

Measure angles Measure $\angle AEF$, $\angle FED$, $\angle CEG$, and $\angle GEB$. Save as "EXPLORE2". Move point G to change the angles.

EXPLORE 3 Measure vertical angles formed by intersecting lines

STEP 1 *Draw two intersecting lines* Draw and label $\overleftrightarrow{AB}$. Draw and label $\overleftrightarrow{CD}$ so that it intersects $\overleftrightarrow{AB}$. Draw and label the point of intersection E.

STEP 2 *Measure angles* Measure $\angle AEC$, $\angle AED$, $\angle BEC$, and $\angle DEB$. Move point C to change the angles. Save as "EXPLORE3".

DRAW CONCLUSIONS Use your observations to complete these exercises

6. In Explore 2, does the angle relationship stay the same as you move G?

7. In Explore 2, make a conjecture about the relationship between $\angle CEG$ and $\angle GEB$. Write your conjecture in if-then form.

8. In Explore 3, the intersecting lines form two pairs of vertical angles. Make a conjecture about the relationship between any two vertical angles. Write your conjecture in if-then form.

9. Name the pairs of vertical angles in Explore 2. Use this drawing to test your conjecture from Exercise 8.

2.7 Prove Angle Pair Relationships

Before	You identified relationships between pairs of angles.
Now	You will use properties of special pairs of angles.
Why?	So you can describe angles found in a home, as in Ex. 44.

Key Vocabulary
• **complementary angles,** *p. 35*
• **supplementary angles,** *p. 35*
• **linear pair,** *p. 37*
• **vertical angles,** *p. 37*

Sometimes, a new theorem describes a relationship that is useful in writing proofs. For example, using the *Right Angles Congruence Theorem* will reduce the number of steps you need to include in a proof involving right angles.

THEOREM *For Your Notebook*

THEOREM 2.3 Right Angles Congruence Theorem

All right angles are congruent.

Proof: below

PROOF **Right Angles Congruence Theorem**

WRITE PROOFS
When you prove a theorem, write the hypothesis of the theorem as the GIVEN statement. The conclusion is what you must PROVE.

GIVEN ▶ ∠1 and ∠2 are right angles.
PROVE ▶ ∠1 ≅ ∠2

STATEMENTS	REASONS
1. ∠1 and ∠2 are right angles.	**1.** Given
2. $m\angle 1 = 90°$, $m\angle 2 = 90°$	**2.** Definition of right angle
3. $m\angle 1 = m\angle 2$	**3.** Transitive Property of Equality
4. ∠1 ≅ ∠2	**4.** Definition of congruent angles

EXAMPLE 1 **Use right angle congruence**

Write a proof.

AVOID ERRORS
The given information in Example 1 is about perpendicular lines. You must then use deductive reasoning to show the angles are right angles.

GIVEN ▶ $\overline{AB} \perp \overline{BC}$, $\overline{DC} \perp \overline{BC}$
PROVE ▶ ∠B ≅ ∠C

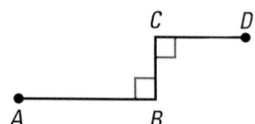

STATEMENTS	REASONS
1. $\overline{AB} \perp \overline{BC}$, $\overline{DC} \perp \overline{BC}$	**1.** Given
2. ∠B and ∠C are right angles.	**2.** Definition of perpendicular lines
3. ∠B ≅ ∠C	**3.** Right Angles Congruence Theorem

2.7

THEOREMS *For Your Notebook*

THEOREM 2.4 **Congruent Supplements Theorem**

If two angles are supplementary to the same angle (or to congruent angles), then they are congruent.

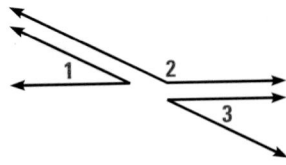

If ∠1 and ∠2 are supplementary and ∠3 and ∠2 are supplementary, then ∠1 ≅ ∠3.

Proof: Example 2, below; Ex. 36, p. 129

THEOREM 2.5 **Congruent Complements Theorem**

If two angles are complementary to the same angle (or to congruent angles), then they are congruent.

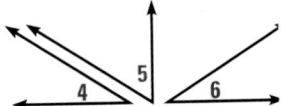

If ∠4 and ∠5 are complementary and ∠6 and ∠5 are complementary, then ∠4 ≅ ∠6.

Proof: Ex. 37, p. 129; Ex. 41, p. 130

To prove Theorem 2.4, you must prove two cases: one with angles supplementary to the same angle and one with angles supplementary to congruent angles. The proof of Theorem 2.5 also requires two cases.

EXAMPLE 2 **Prove a case of Congruent Supplements Theorem**

Prove that two angles supplementary to the same angle are congruent.

GIVEN ▶ ∠1 and ∠2 are supplements.
∠3 and ∠2 are supplements.

PROVE ▶ ∠1 ≅ ∠3

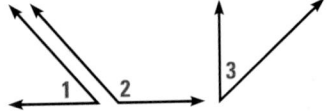

STATEMENTS	REASONS
1. ∠1 and ∠2 are supplements. ∠3 and ∠2 are supplements.	1. Given
2. $m\angle 1 + m\angle 2 = 180°$ $m\angle 3 + m\angle 2 = 180°$	2. Definition of supplementary angles
3. $m\angle 1 + m\angle 2 = m\angle 3 + m\angle 2$	3. Transitive Property of Equality
4. $m\angle 1 = m\angle 3$	4. Subtraction Property of Equality
5. ∠1 ≅ ∠3	5. Definition of congruent angles

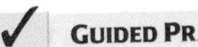 **Geometry** at classzone.com

✓ **GUIDED PRACTICE** for Examples 1 and 2

1. How many steps do you save in the proof in Example 1 by using the *Right Angles Congruence Theorem*?

2. Draw a diagram and write GIVEN and PROVE statements for a proof of each case of the *Congruent Complements Theorem*.

7. ★ **SHORT RESPONSE** The *x*-axis and *y*-axis in a coordinate plane are perpendicular to each other. The axes form four angles. Are the four angles congruent right angles? *Explain.*

EXAMPLE 3
....
on p. 126
for Exs. 8–11

FINDING ANGLE MEASURES **In Exercises 8–11, use the diagram at the right.**

8. If $m\angle 1 = 145°$, find $m\angle 2$, $m\angle 3$, and $m\angle 4$.

9. If $m\angle 3 = 168°$, find $m\angle 1$, $m\angle 2$, and $m\angle 4$.

10. If $m\angle 4 = 37°$, find $m\angle 1$, $m\angle 2$, and $m\angle 3$.

11. If $m\angle 2 = 62°$, find $m\angle 1$, $m\angle 3$, and $m\angle 4$.

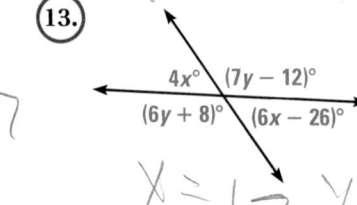
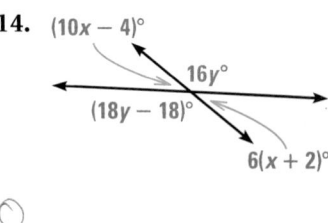

EXAMPLE 4
....
on p. 127
for Exs. 12–14

xy **ALGEBRA** **Find the values of *x* and *y*.**

12.

$(8x + 7)°$
$5y°$ $(7y - 34)°$
$(9x - 4)°$

13.

$4x°$ $(7y - 12)°$
$(6y + 8)°$ $(6x - 26)°$

14. $(10x - 4)°$

$16y°$
$(18y - 18)°$
$6(x + 2)°$

15. **ERROR ANALYSIS** *Describe* the error in stating that $\angle 1 \cong \angle 4$ and $\angle 2 \cong \angle 3$.

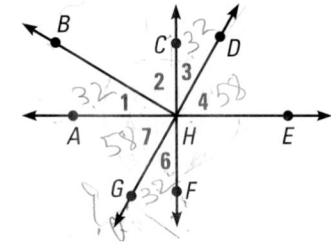

$\angle 1 \cong \angle 4$
$\angle 2 \cong \angle 3$

16. ★ **MULTIPLE CHOICE** In a figure, $\angle A$ and $\angle D$ are complementary angles and $m\angle A = 4x°$. Which expression can be used to find $m\angle D$?

(A) $(4x + 90)°$ **(B)** $(180 - 4x)°$ **(C)** $(180 + 4x)°$ **(D)** $(90 - 4x)°$

FINDING ANGLE MEASURES **In Exercises 17–21, copy and complete the statement given that $m\angle FHE = m\angle BHG = m\angle AHF = 90°$.**

17. If $m\angle 3 = 30°$, then $m\angle 6 = \underline{\ ?\ }$.

18. If $m\angle BHF = 115°$, then $m\angle 3 = \underline{\ ?\ }$.

19. If $m\angle 6 = 27°$, then $m\angle 1 = \underline{\ ?\ }$.

20. If $m\angle DHF = 133°$, then $m\angle CHG = \underline{\ ?\ }$.

21. If $m\angle 3 = 32°$, then $m\angle 2 = \underline{\ ?\ }$.

USE A DIAGRAM
....
You can use inforr
labeled in a diagra
your proof.

ANALYZING STATEMENTS **Two lines that are not perpendicular intersect such that $\angle 1$ and $\angle 2$ are a linear pair, $\angle 1$ and $\angle 4$ are a linear pair, and $\angle 1$ and $\angle 3$ are vertical angles. Tell whether the statement is true or false.**

22. $\angle 1 \cong \angle 2$ **23.** $\angle 1 \cong \angle 3$ **24.** $\angle 1 \cong \angle 4$

25. $\angle 3 \cong \angle 2$ **26.** $\angle 2 \cong \angle 4$ **27.** $m\angle 3 + m\angle 4 = 180°$

xy **ALGEBRA** **Find the measure of each angle in the diagram.**

28.

$10y°$
$(3y + 11)°$ $(4x - 22)°$
$(7x + 4)°$

29.

$2(5x - 5)°$
$(5y + 5)°$ $(7y - 9)°$
$(6x + 50)°$

○ = WORKED-OUT SOLUTIONS
on p. WS1

★ = STANDARDIZED
TEST PRACTICE

126 Chapter 2

128

30. ★ **OPEN-ENDED MATH** In the diagram, $m\angle CBY = 80°$ and $\overleftrightarrow{XY}$ bisects $\angle ABC$. Give two more true statements about the diagram.

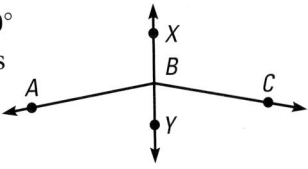

DRAWING CONCLUSIONS In Exercises 31–34, use the given statement to name two congruent angles. Then give a reason that justifies your conclusion.

31. In triangle *GFE*, $\overrightarrow{GH}$ bisects $\angle EGF$.

32. $\angle 1$ is a supplement of $\angle 6$, and $\angle 9$ is a supplement of $\angle 6$.

33. $\overline{AB}$ is perpendicular to $\overline{CD}$, and $\overline{AB}$ and $\overline{CD}$ intersect at *E*.

34. $\angle 5$ is complementary to $\angle 12$, and $\angle 1$ is complementary to $\angle 12$.

35. **CHALLENGE** Sketch two intersecting lines *j* and *k*. Sketch another pair of lines *ℓ* and *m* that intersect at the same point as *j* and *k* and that bisect the angles formed by *j* and *k*. Line *ℓ* is perpendicular to line *m*. *Explain* why this is true.

PROBLEM SOLVING

EXAMPLE 2
on p. 125
for Ex. 36

36. **PROVING THEOREM 2.4** Prove the second case of the Congruent Supplements Theorem where two angles are supplementary to congruent angles.

GIVEN ▶ $\angle 1$ and $\angle 2$ are supplements.
$\angle 3$ and $\angle 4$ are supplements.
$\angle 1 \cong \angle 4$

PROVE ▶ $\angle 2 \cong \angle 3$

@HomeTutor for problem solving help at classzone.com

37. **PROVING THEOREM 2.5** Copy and complete the proof of the first case of the Congruent Complements Theorem where two angles are complementary to the same angle.

GIVEN ▶ $\angle 1$ and $\angle 2$ are complements.
$\angle 1$ and $\angle 3$ are complements.

PROVE ▶ $\angle 2 \cong \angle 3$

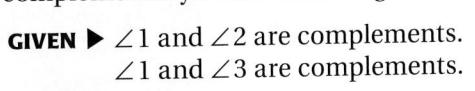
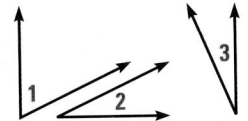

STATEMENTS	REASONS
1. $\angle 1$ and $\angle 2$ are complements. $\angle 1$ and $\angle 3$ are complements.	1. __?__
2. $m\angle 1 + m\angle 2 = 90°$ $m\angle 1 + m\angle 3 = 90°$	2. __?__
3. __?__	3. Transitive Property of Equality
4. __?__	4. Subtraction Property of Equality
5. $\angle 2 \cong \angle 3$	5. __?__

@HomeTutor for problem solving help at classzone.com

PREV
Prepar
Lesson
in Exs.

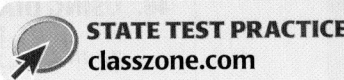
Lessons 2.5–2.7

1. **MULTI-STEP PROBLEM** In the diagram below, $\vec{BD}$ bisects $\angle ABC$ and $\vec{BC}$ bisects $\angle DBE$.

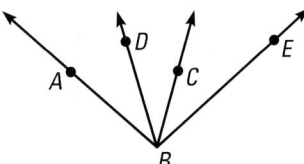

   a. Prove $m\angle ABD = m\angle CBE$.

   b. If $m\angle ABE = 99°$, what is $m\angle DBC$? *Explain*.

2. **SHORT RESPONSE** You are cutting a rectangular piece of fabric into strips that you will weave together to make a placemat. As shown, you cut the fabric in half lengthwise to create two congruent pieces. You then cut each of these pieces in half lengthwise. Do all of the strips have the same width? *Explain* your reasoning.

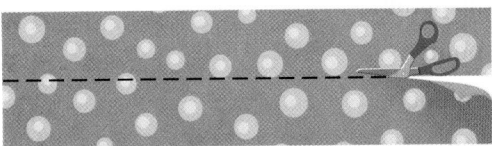

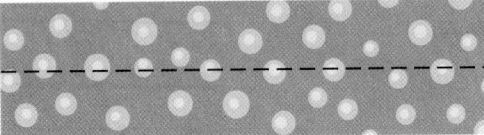

3. **GRIDDED ANSWER** The cross section of a concrete retaining wall is shown below. Use the given information to find the measure of $\angle 1$ in degrees.

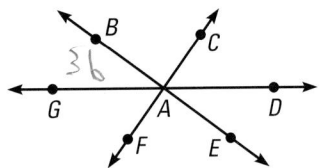

   $m\angle 1 = m\angle 2$

   $m\angle 3 = m\angle 4$

   $m\angle 3 = 80°$

   $m\angle 1 + m\angle 2 + m\angle 3 + m\angle 4 = 360°$

4. **EXTENDED RESPONSE** *Explain* how the Congruent Supplements Theorem and the Transitive Property of Angle Congruence can both be used to show how angles that are supplementary to the same angle are congruent.

5. **EXTENDED RESPONSE** A formula you can use to calculate the total cost of an item including sales tax is $T = c(1 + s)$, where T is the total cost including sales tax, c is the cost not including sales tax, and s is the sales tax rate written as a decimal.

   a. Solve the formula for s. Give a reason for each step.

   b. Use your formula to find the sales tax rate on a purchase that was $26.75 with tax and $25 without tax.

   c. Look back at the steps you used to solve the formula for s. Could you have solved for s in a different way? *Explain*.

6. **OPEN-ENDED** In the diagram below, $m\angle GAB = 36°$. What additional information do you need to find $m\angle BAC$ and $m\angle CAD$? *Explain* your reasoning.

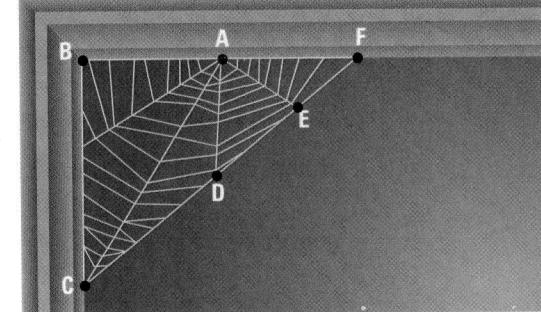

7. **SHORT RESPONSE** Two lines intersect to form $\angle 1$, $\angle 2$, $\angle 3$, and $\angle 4$. The measure of $\angle 3$ is three times the measure of $\angle 1$ and $m\angle 1 = m\angle 2$. Find all four angle measures. *Explain* your reasoning.

8. **SHORT RESPONSE** Part of a spider web is shown below. If you know that $\angle CAD$ and $\angle DAE$ are complements and that $\vec{AB}$ and $\vec{AF}$ are opposite rays, what can you conclude about $\angle BAC$ and $\angle EAF$? *Explain* your reasoning.

Big Idea 1

Using Inductive and Deductive Reasoning

When you make a conjecture based on a pattern, you use inductive reasoning. You use deductive reasoning to show whether the conjecture is true or false by using facts, definitions, postulates, properties, or proven theorems. If you can find one counterexample to the conjecture, then you know the conjecture is false.

Big Idea 2

Understanding Geometric Relationships in Diagrams

The following can be assumed from the diagram:

A, B, and C are coplanar.

$\angle ABH$ and $\angle HBF$ are a linear pair.

Plane T and plane S intersect in $\overleftrightarrow{BC}$.

$\overleftrightarrow{CD}$ lies in plane S.

$\angle ABC$ and $\angle HBF$ are vertical angles.

$\overleftrightarrow{AB} \perp$ plane S.

Diagram assumptions are reviewed on page 97.

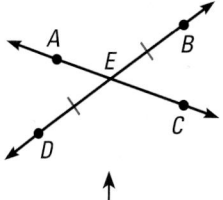

Big Idea 3

Writing Proofs of Geometric Relationships

You can write a logical argument to show a geometric relationship is true. In a two-column proof, you use deductive reasoning to work from GIVEN information to reach a conjecture you want to PROVE.

Diagram of geometric relationship with given information labeled to help you write the proof

GIVEN ▶ The hypothesis of an if-then statement

PROVE ▶ The conclusion of an if-then statement

STATEMENTS	REASONS
1. Hypothesis	1. Given
_____	_____
_____	_____
n. Conclusion	*n.* _____

Statements based on facts that you know or conclusions from deductive reasoning

Use postulates, proven theorems, definitions, and properties of numbers and congruence as reasons.

Proof summary is on page 114.

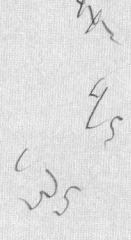

2

REVIEW KEY VOCABULARY

See pp. 926–931 for a list of postulates and theorems.

• conjecture, *p. 73*
• inductive reasoning, *p. 73*
• counterexample, *p. 74*
• conditional statement, *p. 79* converse, inverse, contrapositive

• if-then form, *p. 79* hypothesis, conclusion
• negation, *p. 79*
• equivalent statements, *p. 80*
• perpendicular lines, *p. 81*
• biconditional statement, *p. 82*

• deductive reasoning, *p. 87*
• line perpendicular to a plane, *p. 98*
• proof, *p. 112*
• two-column proof, *p. 112*
• theorem, *p. 113*

VOCABULARY EXERCISES

3–14

17–20

22–24

1. Copy and complete: A statement that can be proven is called a(n) __?__ .

2. **WRITING** *Compare* the inverse of a conditional statement to the converse of the conditional statement.

3. You know $m\angle A = m\angle B$ and $m\angle B = m\angle C$. What does the Transitive Property of Equality tell you about the measures of the angles?

REVIEW EXAMPLES AND EXERCISES

Use the review examples and exercises below to check your understanding of the concepts you have learned in each lesson of Chapter 2.

2.1 Use Inductive Reasoning

pp. 72–78

EXAMPLE

Describe the pattern in the numbers 3, 21, 147, 1029, …, and write the next three numbers in the pattern.

Each number is seven times the previous number.

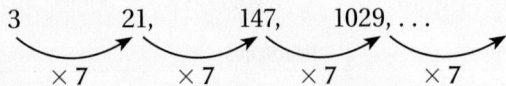

3   21,   147,   1029, . . .

$\times 7$ $\times 7$ $\times 7$ $\times 7$

So, the next three numbers are 7203, 50,421, and 352,947.

EXERCISES

EXAMPLES
2 and 5
on pp. 72–74
for Exs. 4–5

4. *Describe* the pattern in the numbers −20,480, −5120, −1280, −320, ... Write the next three numbers.

5. Find a counterexample to disprove the conjecture:

   If the quotient of two numbers is positive, then the two numbers must both be positive.

2.2 Analyze Conditional Statements
pp. 79–85

EXAMPLE

Write the if-then form, the converse, the inverse, and the contrapositive of the statement "Black bears live in North America."

   a. If-then form: If a bear is a black bear, then it lives in North America.

   b. Converse: If a bear lives in North America, then it is a black bear.

   c. Inverse: If a bear is not a black bear, then it does not live in North America.

   d. Contrapositive: If a bear does not live in North America, then it is not a black bear.

EXERCISES

EXAMPLES 2, 3, and 4 on pp. 80–82 for Exs. 6–8

6. Write the if-then form, the converse, the inverse, and the contrapositive of the statement "An angle whose measure is 34° is an acute angle."

7. Is this a valid definition? *Explain* why or why not.

"If the sum of the measures of two angles is 90°, then the angles are complementary."

8. Write the definition of an *equiangular polygon* as a biconditional statement.

2.3 Apply Deductive Reasoning
pp. 87–93

EXAMPLE

Use the Law of Detachment to make a valid conclusion in the true situation.

If two angles have the same measure, then they are congruent. You know that $m\angle A = m\angle B$.

▶ Because $m\angle A = m\angle B$ satisfies the hypothesis of a true conditional statement, the conclusion is also true. So, $\angle A \cong \angle B$.

EXERCISES

EXAMPLES 1, 2, and 4 on pp. 87–89 for Exs. 9–11

9. Use the Law of Detachment to make a valid conclusion.

If an angle is a right angle, then the angle measures 90°. $\angle B$ is a right angle.

10. Use the Law of Syllogism to write the statement that follows from the pair of true statements.

If $x = 3$, then $2x = 6$.

If $4x = 12$, then $x = 3$.

11. What can you say about the sum of any two odd integers? Use inductive reasoning to form a conjecture. Then use deductive reasoning to show that the conjecture is true.

2.4 Use Postulates and Diagrams
pp. 96–102

EXAMPLE

$\angle ABC$, an acute angle, is bisected by $\vec{BE}$. Sketch a diagram that represents the given information.

1. Draw $\angle ABC$, an acute angle, and label points A, B, and C.

2. Draw angle bisector $\vec{BE}$. Mark congruent angles.

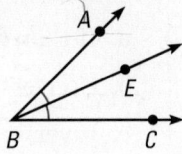

EXERCISES

EXAMPLES
3 and 4
on p. 98
for Exs. 12–13

12. Straight angle CDE is bisected by $\vec{DK}$. Sketch a diagram that represents the given information.

13. Which of the following statements *cannot* be assumed from the diagram?

   Ⓐ A, B, and C are coplanar.

   Ⓑ $\overleftrightarrow{CD} \perp$ plane P.

   Ⓒ A, F, and B are collinear.

   Ⓓ Plane M intersects plane P in $\overleftrightarrow{FH}$.

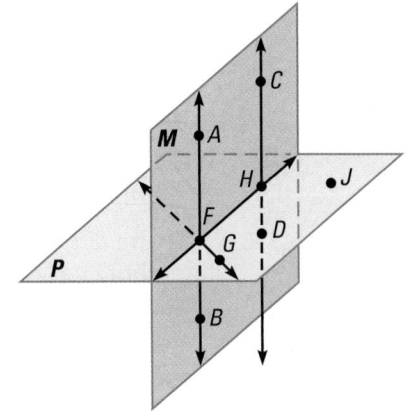

2.5 Reason Using Properties from Algebra
pp. 105–111

EXAMPLE

Solve $3x + 2(2x + 9) = -10$. Write a reason for each step.

$3x + 2(2x + 9) = -10$	**Write original equation.**
$3x + 4x + 18 = -10$	**Distributive Property**
$7x + 18 = -10$	**Simplify.**
$7x = -28$	**Subtraction Property of Equality**
$x = -4$	**Division Property of Equality**

EXERCISES

EXAMPLES
1 and 2
on pp. 105–106
for Exs. 14–17

Solve the equation. Write a reason for each step.

14. $-9x - 21 = -20x - 87$

15. $15x + 22 = 7x + 62$

16. $3(2x + 9) = 30$

17. $5x + 2(2x - 23) = -154$

2.6 Prove Statements about Segments and Angles
pp. 112–119

EXAMPLE

Prove the Reflexive Property of Segment Congruence.

GIVEN ▶ $\overline{AB}$ is a line segment.

PROVE ▶ $\overline{AB} \cong \overline{AB}$

STATEMENTS	REASONS
1. $\overline{AB}$ is a line segment.	1. Given
2. AB is the length of $\overline{AB}$.	2. Ruler Postulate
3. $AB = AB$	3. Reflexive Property of Equality
4. $\overline{AB} \cong \overline{AB}$	4. Definition of congruent segments

EXERCISES

EXAMPLES
2 and 3
on pp. 113–114
for Exs. 18–21

Name the property illustrated by the statement.

18. If $\angle DEF \cong \angle JKL$, then $\angle JKL \cong \angle DEF$.

19. $\angle C \cong \angle C$

20. If $MN = PQ$ and $PQ = RS$, then $MN = RS$.

21. Prove the Transitive Property of Angle Congruence.

2.7 Prove Angle Pair Relationships
pp. 124–131

EXAMPLE

GIVEN ▶ $\angle 5 \cong \angle 6$

PROVE ▶ $\angle 4 \cong \angle 7$

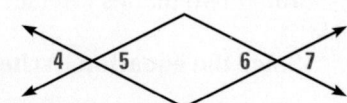

STATEMENTS	REASONS
1. $\angle 5 \cong \angle 6$	1. Given
2. $\angle 4 \cong \angle 5$	2. Vertical Angles Congruence Theorem
3. $\angle 4 \cong \angle 6$	3. Transitive Property of Congruence
4. $\angle 6 \cong \angle 7$	4. Vertical Angles Congruence Theorem
5. $\angle 4 \cong \angle 7$	5. Transitive Property of Congruence

EXERCISES

EXAMPLES
2 and 3
on pp. 125–126
for Exs. 22–24

In Exercises 22 and 23, use the diagram at the right.

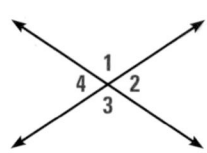

22. If $m\angle 1 = 114°$, find $m\angle 2$, $m\angle 3$, and $m\angle 4$.

23. If $m\angle 4 = 57°$, find $m\angle 1$, $m\angle 2$, and $m\angle 3$.

24. Write a two-column proof.

GIVEN ▶ $\angle 12$ and $\angle 11$ are complementary.
$m\angle 10 + m\angle 11 = 90°$

PROVE ▶ $\angle 12 \cong \angle 10$

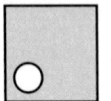

Sketch the next figure in the pattern.

1. 2.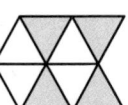

Describe the pattern in the numbers. Write the next number.

3. $-6, -1, 4, 9, \ldots$

4. $100, -50, 25, -12.5, \ldots$

In Exercises 5–8, write the if-then form, the converse, the inverse, and the contrapositive for the given statement.

5. All right angles are congruent.

6. Frogs are amphibians.

7. $5x + 4 = -6$, because $x = -2$.

8. A regular polygon is equilateral.

9. If you decide to go to the football game, then you will miss band practice. Tonight, you are going the football game. Using the Law of Detachment, what statement can you make?

10. If Margot goes to college, then she will major in Chemistry. If Margot majors in Chemistry, then she will need to buy a lab manual. Using the Law of Syllogism, what statement can you make?

Use the diagram to write examples of the stated postulate.

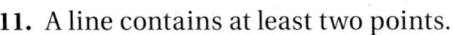

11. A line contains at least two points.

12. A plane contains at least three noncollinear points.

13. If two planes intersect, then their intersection is a line.

Solve the equation. Write a reason for each step.

14. $9x + 31 = -23$

15. $-7(-x + 2) = 42$

16. $26 + 2(3x + 11) = -18x$

In Exercises 17–19, match the statement with the property that it illustrates.

17. If $\angle RST \cong \angle XYZ$, then $\angle XYZ \cong \angle RST$.

18. $\overline{PQ} \cong \overline{PQ}$

19. If $\overline{FG} \cong \overline{JK}$ and $\overline{JK} \cong \overline{LM}$, then $\overline{FG} \cong \overline{LM}$.

A. Reflexive Property of Congruence

B. Symmetric Property of Congruence

C. Transitive Property of Congruence

20. Use the Vertical Angles Congruence Theorem to find the measure of each angle in the diagram at the right.

21. Write a two-column proof.

GIVEN ▶ $\overline{AX} \cong \overline{DX}, \overline{XB} \cong \overline{XC}$
PROVE ▶ $\overline{AC} \cong \overline{BD}$

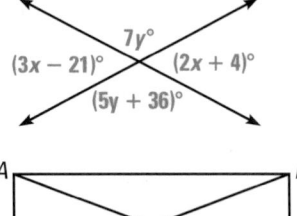

SIMPLIFY RATIONAL AND RADICAL EXPRESSIONS

xy **EXAMPLE 1** *Simplify rational expressions*

a. $\dfrac{2x^2}{4xy}$

b. $\dfrac{3x^2 + 2x}{9x + 6}$

Solution

To simplify a rational expression, factor the numerator and denominator. Then divide out any common factors.

a. $\dfrac{2x^2}{4xy} = \dfrac{\cancel{2} \cdot \cancel{x} \cdot x}{\cancel{2} \cdot 2 \cdot \cancel{x} \cdot y} = \dfrac{x}{2y}$

b. $\dfrac{3x^2 + 2x}{9x + 6} = \dfrac{x(\cancel{3x + 2})}{3(\cancel{3x + 2})} = \dfrac{x}{3}$

xy **EXAMPLE 2** *Simplify radical expressions*

a. $\sqrt{54}$

b. $2\sqrt{5} - 5\sqrt{2} - 3\sqrt{5}$

c. $(3\sqrt{2})(-6\sqrt{6})$

Solution

a. $\sqrt{54} = \sqrt{9} \cdot \sqrt{6}$ Use product property of radicals.

      $= 3\sqrt{6}$ Simplify.

b. $2\sqrt{5} - 5\sqrt{2} - 3\sqrt{5} = -\sqrt{5} - 5\sqrt{2}$ Combine like terms.

c. $(3\sqrt{2})(-6\sqrt{6}) = -18\sqrt{12}$ Use product property and associative property.

      $= -18 \cdot 2\sqrt{3}$ Simplify $\sqrt{12}$.

      $= -36\sqrt{3}$ Simplify.

EXERCISES

EXAMPLE 1
for Exs. 1–9

Simplify the expression, if possible.

1. $\dfrac{5x^4}{20x^2}$

2. $\dfrac{-12ab^3}{9a^2b}$

3. $\dfrac{5m + 35}{5}$

4. $\dfrac{36m - 48m}{6m}$

5. $\dfrac{k + 3}{-2k + 3}$

6. $\dfrac{m + 4}{m^2 + 4m}$

7. $\dfrac{12x + 16}{8 + 6x}$

8. $\dfrac{3x^3}{5x + 8x^2}$

9. $\dfrac{3x^2 - 6x}{6x^2 - 3x}$

EXAMPLE 2
for Exs. 10–24

Simplify the expression, if possible. All variables are positive.

10. $\sqrt{75}$

11. $-\sqrt{180}$

12. $\pm\sqrt{128}$

13. $\sqrt{2} - \sqrt{18} + \sqrt{6}$

14. $\sqrt{28} - \sqrt{63} - \sqrt{35}$

15. $4\sqrt{8} + 3\sqrt{32}$

16. $(6\sqrt{5})(2\sqrt{2})$

17. $(-4\sqrt{10})(-5\sqrt{5})$

18. $(2\sqrt{6})^2$

19. $\sqrt{(25)^2}$

20. $\sqrt{x^2}$

21. $\sqrt{(-a)^2}$

22. $\sqrt{(3y)^2}$

23. $\sqrt{3^2 + 2^2}$

24. $\sqrt{h^2 + k^2}$

EXTENDED RESPONSE QUESTIONS

> **PROBLEM**
>
> Seven members of the student government (Frank, Gina, Henry, Isabelle, Jack, Katie, and Leah) are posing for a picture for the school yearbook. For the picture, the photographer will arrange the students in a row according to the following restrictions:
>
> Henry must stand in the middle spot.
>
> Katie must stand in the right-most spot.
>
> There must be exactly two spots between Gina and Frank.
>
> Isabelle cannot stand next to Henry.
>
> Frank must stand next to Katie.
>
> **a.** *Describe* one possible ordering of the students.
>
> **b.** Which student(s) can stand in the second spot from the left?
>
> **c.** If the condition that Leah must stand in the left-most spot is added, will there be exactly one ordering of the students? *Justify* your answer.

Below are sample solutions to the problem. Read each solution and the comments in blue to see why the sample represents full credit, partial credit, or no credit.

SAMPLE 1: Full credit solution

The method of representation is clearly explained.

a. Using the first letters of the students' names, here is one possible ordering of the students:

I L G H J F K

The conclusion is correct and shows understanding of the problem.

b. The only students without fixed positions are Isabelle, Leah, and Jack. There are no restrictions on placement in the second spot from the left, so any of these three students can occupy that location.

c. Henry, Frank, Katie, and Gina have fixed positions according to the restrictions. If Leah must stand in the left-most spot, the ordering looks like:

L _ G H _ F K

The reasoning behind the answer is explained clearly.

Because Isabelle cannot stand next to Henry, she must occupy the spot next to Leah. Therefore, Jack stands next to Henry and the only possible order would have to be:

L I G H J F K.

Yes, there would be exactly one ordering of the students.

SAMPLE 2: Partial credit solution

The answer to part (a) is correct.

a. One possible ordering of the students is:
Jack, Isabelle, Gina, Henry, Leah, Frank, and Katie.

Part (b) is correct but not explained.

b. There are three students who could stand in the second spot from the left. They are Isabelle, Leah, and Jack.

The student did not recall that Isabelle cannot stand next to Henry; therefore, the conclusion is incorrect.

c. No, there would be two possible orderings of the students. With Leah in the left-most spot, the ordering looks like:

Leah, ____, Gina, Henry, ____, Frank, and Katie

Therefore, the two possible orderings are
Leah, Isabelle, Gina, Henry, Jack, Frank, and Katie
or
Leah, Jack, Gina, Henry, Isabelle, Frank, and Katie.

SAMPLE 3: No credit solution

The answer to part (a) is incorrect because Isabelle is next to Henry.

a. One possible ordering of the students is **L G J H I F K**.

b. There are four students who can stand in the second spot from the left. Those students are Leah, Gina, Isabelle, and Jack.

Parts (b) and (c) are based on the incorrect conclusion in part (a).

c. The two possible orderings are **L G J H I F K** and **L J G H I F K**.

PRACTICE   Apply the Scoring Rubric

1. A student's solution to the problem on the previous page is given below. Score the solution as *full credit*, *partial credit*, or *no credit*. *Explain* your reasoning. If you choose *partial credit* or *no credit*, explain how you would change the solution so that it earns a score of full credit.

a. A possible ordering of the students is I - J - G - H - L - F - K.

b. There are no restrictions on the second spot from the left. Leah, Isabelle, and Jack could all potentially stand in this location.

c. The positions of Gina, Henry, Frank, and Katie are fixed.

_ - _ - G - H - _ - F - K.

Because Isabelle cannot stand next to Henry, she must occupy the left-most spot or the second spot from the left. There are no restrictions on Leah or Jack. That leaves four possible orderings:

I - J - G - H - L - F - K   I - L - G - H - J - F - K
L - I - G - H - J - F - K   J - I - G - H - L - F - K.

If the restriction is added that Leah must occupy the left-most spot, there is exactly one ordering that would satisfy all conditions:

L - I - G - H - J - F - K.

EXTENDED RESPONSE

1. In some bowling leagues, the handicap H of a bowler with an average

   score A is found using the formula $H = \frac{4}{5}(200 - A)$. The handicap is then
   added to the bowler's score.

   a. Solve the formula for A. Write a reason for each step.

   b. Use your formula to find a bowler's average score with a handicap of 12.

   c. Using this formula, is it possible to calculate a handicap for a bowler with an average score above 200? *Explain* your reasoning.

2. A survey was conducted at Porter High School asking students what form of transportation they use to go to school. All students in the high school were surveyed. The results are shown in the bar graph.

   a. Does the statement "About 1500 students attend Porter High School" follow from the data? *Explain*.

   b. Does the statement "About one third of all students at Porter take public transit to school" follow from the data? *Explain*.

   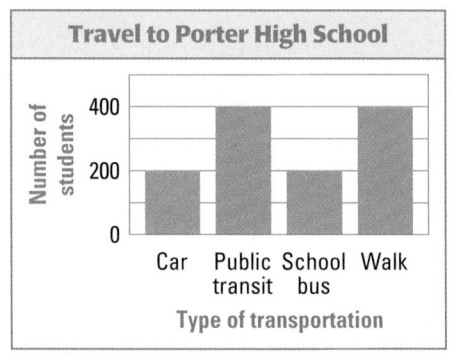

   c. John makes the conclusion that Porter High School is located in a city or a city suburb. *Explain* his reasoning and tell if his conclusion is the result of *inductive reasoning* or *deductive reasoning*.

   d. Betty makes the conclusion that there are twice as many students who walk as take a car to school. *Explain* her reasoning and tell if her conclusion is the result of *inductive reasoning* or *deductive reasoning*.

3. The senior class officers are planning a meeting with the principal and some class officers from the other grades. The senior class president, vice president, treasurer, and secretary will all be present. The junior class president and treasurer will attend. The sophomore class president and vice president, and freshmen treasurer will attend. The secretary makes a seating chart for the meeting using the following conditions.

   > The principal will sit in chair 10. The senior class treasurer will sit at the other end.

   > The senior class president will sit to the left of the principal, next to the junior class president, and across from the sophomore class president.

   > All three treasurers will sit together. The two sophomores will sit next to each other.

   > The two vice presidents and the freshman treasurer will sit on the same side of the table.

   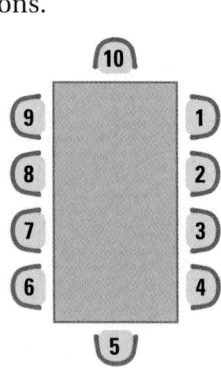

   a. Draw a diagram to show where everyone will sit.

   b. *Explain* why the senior class secretary must sit between the junior class president and junior class treasurer.

   c. Can the senior class vice-president sit across from the junior class president? *Justify* your answer.

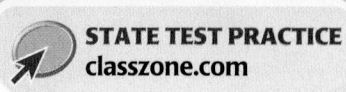
MULTIPLE CHOICE

4. If d represents an odd integer, which of the expressions represents an even integer?

   Ⓐ $d + 2$

   Ⓑ $2d - 1$

   Ⓒ $3d + 1$

   Ⓓ $3d + 2$

5. In the repeating decimal 0.23142314. . . , where the digits 2314 repeat, which digit is in the 300th place to the right of the decimal point?

   Ⓐ 1

   Ⓑ 2

   Ⓒ 3

   Ⓓ 4

GRIDDED ANSWER

6. Use the diagram to find the value of x.

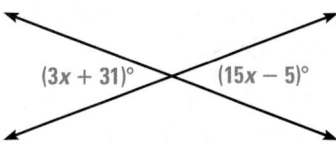

7. Three lines intersect in the figure shown. What is the value of $x + y$?

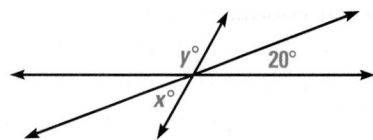

8. R is the midpoint of $\overline{PQ}$, and S and T are the midpoints of $\overline{PR}$ and $\overline{RQ}$, respectively. If $ST = 20$, what is PT?

SHORT RESPONSE

9. Is this a correct conclusion from the given information? If so, *explain* why. If not, *explain* the error in the reasoning.

> If you are a soccer player, then you wear shin guards. Your friend is wearing shin guards. Therefore, she is a soccer player.

10. *Describe* the pattern in the numbers. Write the next number in the pattern.

> 192, −48, 12, −3, . . .

11. Points A, B, C, D, E, and F are coplanar. Points A, B, and F are collinear. The line through A and B is perpendicular to the line through C and D, and the line through C and D is perpendicular to the line through E and F. Which four points must lie on the same line? *Justify* your answer.

12. Westville High School offers after-school tutoring with five student volunteer tutors for this program: Jen, Kim, Lou, Mike, and Nina. On any given weekday, three tutors are scheduled to work. Due to the students' other commitments after school, the tutoring work schedule must meet the following conditions.

> Jen can work any day except every other Monday and Wednesday.
>
> Kim can only work on Thursdays and Fridays.
>
> Lou can work on Tuesdays and Wednesdays.
>
> Mike cannot work on Fridays.
>
> Nina cannot work on Tuesdays.

Name three tutors who can work on *any* Wednesday. *Justify* your answer.

3 Parallel and Perpendicular Lines

Before

In previous chapters, you learned the following skills, which you'll use in Chapter 3: describing angle pairs, using properties and postulates, using angle pair relationships, and sketching a diagram.

Prerequisite Skills

VOCABULARY CHECK

Copy and complete the statement.

1. Adjacent angles share a common __?__ and __?__ .

2. Two angles are __?__ angles if the sum of their measures is 180°.

SKILLS AND ALGEBRA CHECK

The midpoint of $\overline{AB}$ is M. Find AB. *(Review p. 15 for 3.2.)*

3. $AM = 5x - 2$, $MB = 2x + 7$

4. $AM = 4z + 1$, $MB = 6z - 11$

Find the measure of each numbered angle. *(Review p. 124 for 3.2, 3.3.)*

5.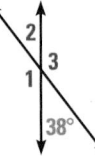

6.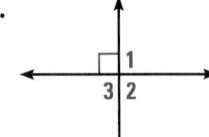

7.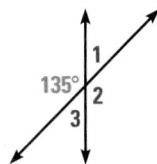

Sketch a diagram for each statement. *(Review pp. 2, 96 for 3.3.)*

8. $\overleftrightarrow{QR}$ is perpendicular to $\overleftrightarrow{WX}$.

9. Lines m and n intersect at point P.

@HomeTutor Prerequisite skills practice at classzone.com

In Chapter 3, you will apply the big ideas listed below and reviewed in the Chapter Summary on page 201. You will also use the key vocabulary listed below.

Big Ideas

1. **Using properties of parallel and perpendicular lines**
2. **Proving relationships using angle measures**
3. **Making connections to lines in algebra**

KEY VOCABULARY

- parallel lines, *p. 147*
- skew lines, *p. 147*
- parallel planes, *p. 147*
- transversal, *p. 149*
- corresponding angles, *p. 149*

- alternate interior angles, *p. 149*
- alternate exterior angles, *p. 149*
- consecutive interior angles, *p. 149*

- paragraph proof, *p. 163*
- slope, *p. 171*
- slope-intercept form, *p. 180*
- standard form, *p. 182*
- distance from a point to a line, *p. 192*

You can use slopes of lines to determine steepness of lines. For example, you can compare the slopes of roller coasters to determine which is steeper.

Animated Geometry

The animation illustrated below for Example 5 on page 174 helps you answer this question: How steep is a roller coaster?

A roller coaster track rises a given distance over a given horizontal distance.

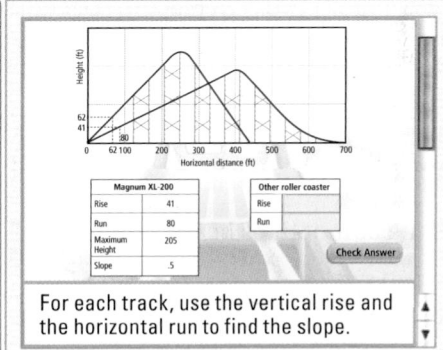

For each track, use the vertical rise and the horizontal run to find the slope.

Animated Geometry at classzone.com

Other animations for Chapter 3: pages 148, 155, 163, and 181

3.1 Draw and Interpret Lines

MATERIALS · pencil · straightedge · lined paper

QUESTION How are lines related in space?

You can use a straightedge to draw a representation of a three-dimensional figure to explore lines in space.

EXPLORE Draw lines in space

STEP 1 *Draw rectangles*	STEP 2 *Connect corners*	STEP 3 *Erase parts*
Use a straightedge to draw two identical rectangles.	Connect the corresponding corners of the rectangles.	Erase parts of "hidden" lines to form dashed lines.

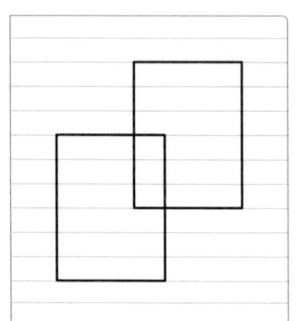 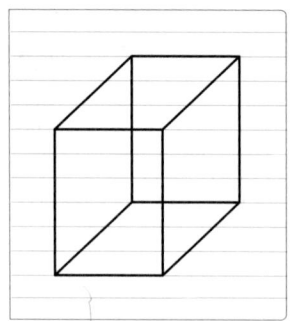 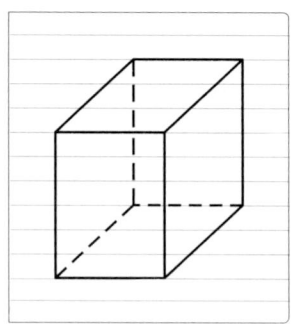

DRAW CONCLUSIONS Use your observations to complete these exercises

Using your sketch from the steps above, label the corners as shown at the right. Then extend $\overline{JM}$ and $\overline{LQ}$. Add lines to the diagram if necessary.

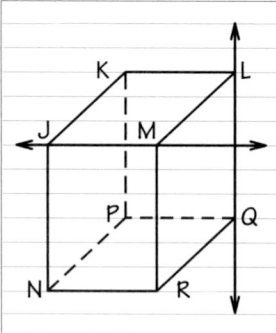

1. Will $\overleftrightarrow{JM}$ and $\overleftrightarrow{LQ}$ ever intersect in space? (Lines that intersect on the page do not necessarily intersect in space.)

2. Will the pair of lines intersect in space?
   a. $\overleftrightarrow{JK}$ and $\overleftrightarrow{NR}$
   b. $\overleftrightarrow{QR}$ and $\overleftrightarrow{MR}$
   c. $\overleftrightarrow{LM}$ and $\overleftrightarrow{MR}$
   d. $\overleftrightarrow{KL}$ and $\overleftrightarrow{NQ}$

3. Does the pair of lines lie in one plane?
   a. $\overleftrightarrow{JK}$ and $\overleftrightarrow{QR}$
   b. $\overleftrightarrow{QR}$ and $\overleftrightarrow{MR}$
   c. $\overleftrightarrow{JN}$ and $\overleftrightarrow{LR}$
   d. $\overleftrightarrow{JL}$ and $\overleftrightarrow{NQ}$

4. Do pairs of lines that intersect in space also lie in the same plane? *Explain* your reasoning.

5. Draw a rectangle that is not the same as the one you used in the Explore. Repeat the three steps of the Explore. Will any of your answers to Exercises 1–3 change?

3.1 Identify Pairs of Lines and Angles

Before	You identified angle pairs formed by two intersecting lines.
Now	You will identify angle pairs formed by three intersecting lines.
Why?	So you can classify lines in a real-world situation, as in Exs. 40–42.

Key Vocabulary
- **parallel lines**
- **skew lines**
- **parallel planes**
- **transversal**
- **corresponding angles**
- **alternate interior angles**
- **alternate exterior angles**
- **consecutive interior angles**

Two lines that do not intersect are either *parallel lines* or *skew lines*. Two lines are **parallel lines** if they do not intersect and are coplanar. Two lines are **skew lines** if they do not intersect and are not coplanar. Also, two planes that do not intersect are **parallel planes**.

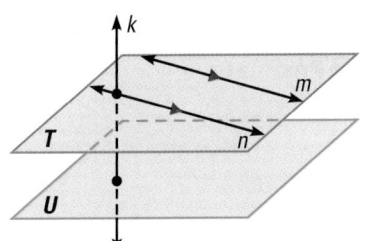

Lines *m* and *n* are parallel lines (*m* ∥ *n*).

Lines *m* and *k* are skew lines.

Planes *T* and *U* are parallel planes (*T* ∥ *U*).

Lines *k* and *n* are intersecting lines, and there is a plane (not shown) containing them.

Small directed triangles, as shown on lines *m* and *n* above, are used to show that lines are parallel. The symbol ∥ means "is parallel to," as in *m* ∥ *n*.

Segments and rays are parallel if they lie in parallel lines. A line is parallel to a plane if the line is in a plane parallel to the given plane. In the diagram above, line *n* is parallel to plane *U*.

EXAMPLE 1 | **Identify relationships in space**

Think of each segment in the figure as part of a line. Which line(s) or plane(s) in the figure appear to fit the description?

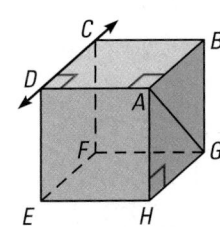

a. Line(s) parallel to $\overleftrightarrow{CD}$ and containing point *A*

b. Line(s) skew to $\overleftrightarrow{CD}$ and containing point *A*

c. Line(s) perpendicular to $\overleftrightarrow{CD}$ and containing point *A*

d. Plane(s) parallel to plane *EFG* and containing point *A*

Solution

a. $\overleftrightarrow{AB}$, $\overleftrightarrow{HG}$, and $\overleftrightarrow{EF}$ all appear parallel to $\overleftrightarrow{CD}$, but only $\overleftrightarrow{AB}$ contains point *A*.

b. Both $\overleftrightarrow{AG}$ and $\overleftrightarrow{AH}$ appear skew to $\overleftrightarrow{CD}$ and contain point *A*.

c. $\overleftrightarrow{BC}$, $\overleftrightarrow{AD}$, $\overleftrightarrow{DE}$, and $\overleftrightarrow{FC}$ all appear perpendicular to $\overleftrightarrow{CD}$, but only $\overleftrightarrow{AD}$ contains point *A*.

d. Plane *ABC* appears parallel to plane *EFG* and contains point *A*.

PARALLEL AND PERPENDICULAR LINES Two lines in the same plane are either parallel or intersect in a point.

Through a point not on a line, there are infinitely many lines. Exactly one of these lines is parallel to the given line, and exactly one of them is perpendicular to the given line.

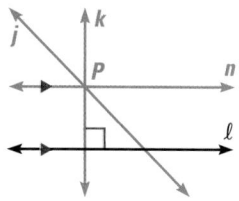

Animated Geometry   at classzone.com

POSTULATES   *For Your Notebook*

POSTULATE 13 Parallel Postulate

If there is a line and a point not on the line, then there is exactly one line through the point parallel to the given line.

There is exactly one line through *P* parallel to ℓ.

POSTULATE 14 Perpendicular Postulate

If there is a line and a point not on the line, then there is exactly one line through the point perpendicular to the given line.

There is exactly one line through *P* perpendicular to ℓ.

EXAMPLE 2   **Identify parallel and perpendicular lines**

PHOTOGRAPHY The given line markings show how the roads are related to one another.

  a. Name a pair of parallel lines.

  b. Name a pair of perpendicular lines.

  c. Is $\overleftrightarrow{FE} \parallel \overleftrightarrow{AC}$? Explain.

Solution

  a. $\overleftrightarrow{MD} \parallel \overleftrightarrow{FE}$ **b.** $\overleftrightarrow{MD} \perp \overleftrightarrow{BF}$

  c. $\overleftrightarrow{FE}$ is not parallel to $\overleftrightarrow{AC}$, because $\overleftrightarrow{MD}$ is parallel to $\overleftrightarrow{FE}$ and by the Parallel Postulate there is exactly one line parallel to $\overleftrightarrow{FE}$ through *M*.

Niagara Falls, New York

✓   **GUIDED PRACTICE**   for Examples 1 and 2

  1. Look at the diagram in Example 1. Name the lines through point *H* that appear skew to $\overleftrightarrow{CD}$.

  2. In Example 2, can you use the Perpendicular Postulate to show that $\overleftrightarrow{AC}$ is *not* perpendicular to $\overleftrightarrow{BF}$? *Explain* why or why not.

ANGLES AND TRANSVERSALS A **transversal** is a line that intersects two or more coplanar lines at different points.

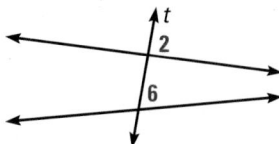
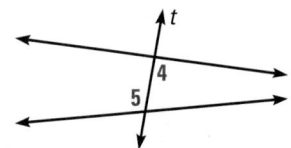
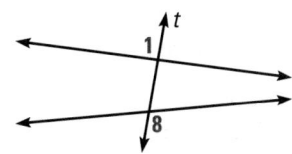
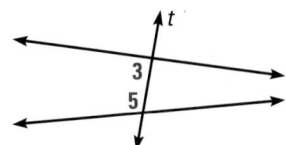
READ VOCABULARY
Another name for consecutive interior angles is **same-side interior angles**.

EXAMPLE 3   **Identify angle relationships**

Identify all pairs of angles of the given type.

a. Corresponding   **b.** Alternate interior
c. Alternate exterior   **d.** Consecutive interior

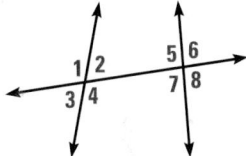

Solution

a. ∠1 and ∠5	**b.** ∠2 and ∠7	**c.** ∠1 and ∠8	**d.** ∠2 and ∠5
∠2 and ∠6	∠4 and ∠5	∠3 and ∠6	∠4 and ∠7
∠3 and ∠7			
∠4 and ∠8			

✓ **GUIDED PRACTICE**   for Example 3

Classify the pair of numbered angles.

3. 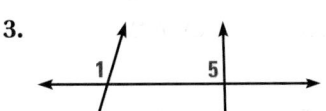   **4.** 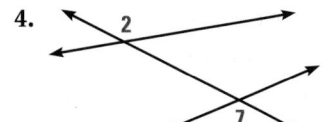   **5.**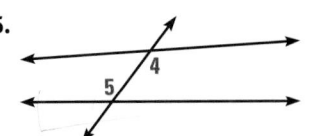

3.1 EXERCISES

HOMEWORK KEY

○ = WORKED-OUT SOLUTIONS
on p. WS3 for Exs. 11, 25, and 35

★ = STANDARDIZED TEST PRACTICE
Exs. 2, 28, 36, 37, and 39

SKILL PRACTICE

1. **VOCABULARY** Copy and complete: A line that intersects two other lines is a _?_.

2. ★ **WRITING** A table is set for dinner. Can the legs of the table and the top of the table lie in parallel planes? *Explain* why or why not.

EXAMPLE 1
on p. 147
for Exs. 3–6

IDENTIFYING RELATIONSHIPS Think of each segment in the diagram as part of a line. Which line(s) or plane(s) contain point *B* and appear to fit the description?

3. Line(s) parallel to $\overleftrightarrow{CD}$

4. Line(s) perpendicular to $\overleftrightarrow{CD}$

5. Line(s) skew to $\overleftrightarrow{CD}$

6. Plane(s) parallel to plane *CDH*

EXAMPLE 2
on p. 148
for Exs. 7–10

PARALLEL AND PERPENDICULAR LINES Use the markings in the diagram.

7. Name a pair of parallel lines.

8. Name a pair of perpendicular lines.

9. Is $\overleftrightarrow{PN} \parallel \overleftrightarrow{KM}$? *Explain.*

10. Is $\overleftrightarrow{PR} \perp \overleftrightarrow{NP}$? *Explain.*

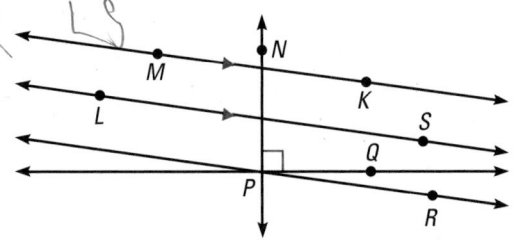

EXAMPLE 3
on p. 149
for Exs. 11–15

ANGLE RELATIONSHIPS Identify all pairs of angles of the given type.

11. Corresponding   12. Alternate interior

13. Alternate exterior   14. Consecutive interior

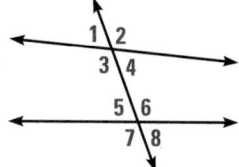

15. **ERROR ANALYSIS** *Describe* and correct the error in saying that ∠1 and ∠8 are corresponding angles in the diagram for Exercises 11–14.

APPLYING POSTULATES How many lines can be drawn that fit each description? Copy the diagram and sketch all the lines.

16. Lines through *B* and parallel to $\overleftrightarrow{AC}$

17. Lines through *A* and perpendicular to $\overleftrightarrow{BC}$

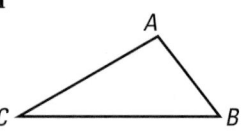

USING A DIAGRAM Classify the angle pair as *corresponding, alternate interior, alternate exterior,* or *consecutive interior* angles.

18. ∠5 and ∠1   19. ∠11 and ∠13

20. ∠6 and ∠13   21. ∠10 and ∠15

22. ∠2 and ∠11   23. ∠8 and ∠4

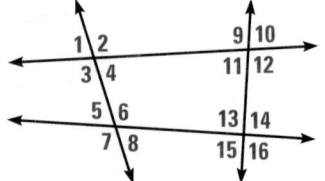

ANALYZING STATEMENTS Copy and complete the statement with *sometimes,* *always,* or *never.* Sketch examples to *justify* your answer.

24. If two lines are parallel, then they are __?__ coplanar.

25. If two lines are not coplanar, then they __?__ intersect.

26. If three lines intersect at one point, then they are __?__ coplanar.

27. If two lines are skew to a third line, then they are __?__ skew to each other.

28. ★ **MULTIPLE CHOICE** ∠*RPQ* and ∠*PRS* are what type of angle pair?

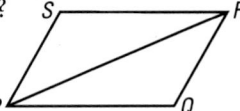

   A Corresponding   **B** Alternate interior

   C Alternate exterior   **D** Consecutive interior

ANGLE RELATIONSHIPS Copy and complete the statement. List all possible correct answers.

29. ∠*BCG* and __?__ are corresponding angles.

30. ∠*BCG* and __?__ are consecutive interior angles.

31. ∠*FCJ* and __?__ are alternate interior angles.

32. ∠*FCA* and __?__ are alternate exterior angles.

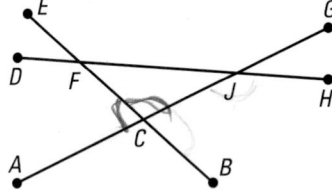

33. **CHALLENGE** Copy the diagram at the right and extend the lines.

   a. Measure ∠1 and ∠2.

   b. Measure ∠3 and ∠4.

   c. Make a conjecture about alternate exterior angles formed when parallel lines are cut by transversals.

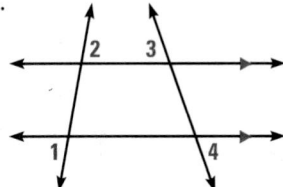

PROBLEM SOLVING

EXAMPLE 2
on p. 148
for Exs. 34–35

CONSTRUCTION Use the picture of the cherry-picker for Exercises 34 and 35.

34. Is the platform *perpendicular, parallel,* or *skew* to the ground?

   @HomeTutor for problem solving help at classzone.com

35. Is the arm *perpendicular, parallel,* or *skew* to a telephone pole?

   @HomeTutor for problem solving help at classzone.com

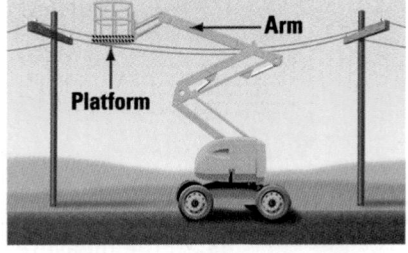

36. ★ **OPEN-ENDED MATH** *Describe* two lines in your classroom that are parallel, and two lines that are skew.

37. ★ **MULTIPLE CHOICE** What is the best description of the horizontal bars in the photo?

   A Parallel   **B** Perpendicular

   C Skew   **D** Intersecting

38. CONSTRUCTION Use these steps to construct a line through a given point *P* that is parallel to a given line *m*.

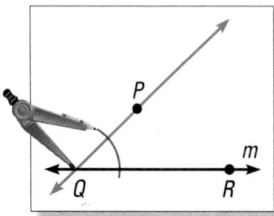 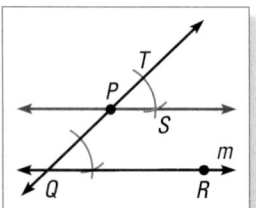

STEP 1 Draw points *Q* and *R* on *m*. Draw $\overleftrightarrow{PQ}$. Draw an arc with the compass point at *Q* so it crosses $\overrightarrow{QP}$ and $\overrightarrow{QR}$.

STEP 2 Copy ∠*PQR* on $\overrightarrow{QP}$. Be sure the two angles are corresponding. Label the new angle ∠*TPS*. Draw $\overleftrightarrow{PS}$. $\overleftrightarrow{PS} \parallel \overleftrightarrow{QR}$.

39. ★ SHORT RESPONSE Two lines are cut by a transversal. Suppose the measure of a pair of alternate interior angles is 90°. *Explain* why the measure of all four interior angles must be 90°.

TREE HOUSE In Exercises 40–42, use the photo to decide whether the statement is *true* or *false*.

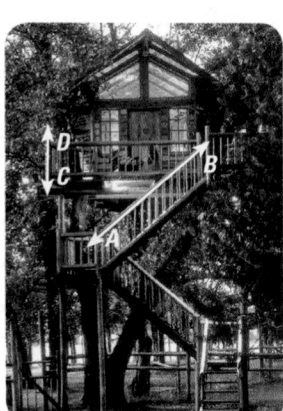

40. The plane containing the floor of the tree house is parallel to the ground.

41. All of the lines containing the railings of the staircase, such as $\overleftrightarrow{AB}$, are skew to the ground.

42. All of the lines containing the *balusters*, such as $\overleftrightarrow{CD}$, are perpendicular to the plane containing the floor of the tree house.

CHALLENGE Draw the figure described.

43. Lines *ℓ* and *m* are skew, lines *ℓ* and *n* are skew, and lines *m* and *n* are parallel.

44. Line *ℓ* is parallel to plane *A*, plane *A* is parallel to plane *B*, and line *ℓ* is not parallel to plane *B*.

MIXED REVIEW

Use the Law of Detachment to make a valid conclusion. *(p. 87)*

45. If the measure of an angle is less than 90°, then the angle is acute. The measure of ∠*A* is 46°.

46. If a food has less than 140 milligrams of sodium per serving, then it is low sodium. A serving of soup has 90 milligrams of sodium per serving.

Find the measure of each numbered angle. *(p. 124)*

PREVIEW
Prepare for
Lesson 3.2
in Exs. 47–49.

47.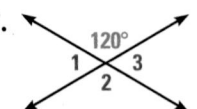

48.

49.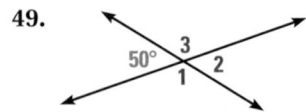

3.2 Parallel Lines and Angles

MATERIALS · graphing calculator or computer

QUESTION What are the relationships among the angles formed by two parallel lines and a transversal?

You can use geometry drawing software to explore parallel lines.

EXPLORE Draw parallel lines and a transversal

STEP 1 *Draw line* Draw and label two points *A* and *B*. Draw $\overleftrightarrow{AB}$.

STEP 2 *Draw parallel line* Draw a point not on $\overleftrightarrow{AB}$. Label it *C*. Choose Parallel from the F3 menu and select $\overleftrightarrow{AB}$. Then select *C* to draw a line through *C* parallel to $\overleftrightarrow{AB}$. Draw a point on the parallel line you constructed. Label it *D*.

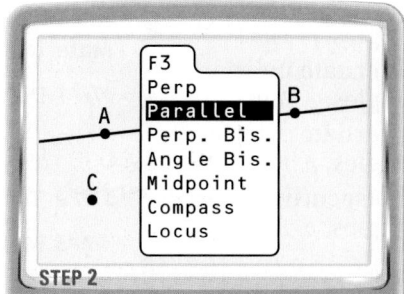

STEP 3 *Draw transversal* Draw two points *E* and *F* outside the parallel lines. Draw transversal $\overleftrightarrow{EF}$. Find the intersection of $\overleftrightarrow{AB}$ and $\overleftrightarrow{EF}$ by choosing Point from the F2 menu. Then choose Intersection. Label the intersection *G*. Find and label the intersection *H* of $\overleftrightarrow{CD}$ and $\overleftrightarrow{EF}$.

STEP 4 *Measure angle* Measure all eight angles formed by the three lines by choosing Measure from the F5 menu, then choosing Angle.

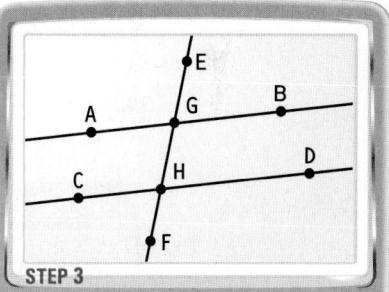

DRAW CONCLUSIONS Use your observations to complete these exercises

1. Record the angle measures from Step 4 in a table like the one shown. Which angles are congruent?

Angle	∠AGE	∠EGB	∠AGH	∠BGH	∠CHG	∠GHD	∠CHF	∠DHF
Measure 1	?	?	?	?	?	?	?	?

2. Drag point *E* or *F* to change the angle the transversal makes with the parallel lines. Be sure *E* and *F* stay outside the parallel lines. Record the new angle measures as row "Measure 2" in your table.

3. Make a conjecture about the measures of the given angles when two parallel lines are cut by a transversal.

   a. Corresponding angles   **b.** Alternate interior angles

4. **REASONING** Make and test a conjecture about the sum of the measures of two consecutive interior angles when two parallel lines are cut by a transversal.

3.2 Use Parallel Lines and Transversals

Before	You identified angle pairs formed by a transversal.
Now	You will use angles formed by parallel lines and transversals.
Why?	So you can understand angles formed by light, as in Example 4.

Key Vocabulary
- **corresponding angles,** *p. 149*
- **alternate interior angles,** *p. 149*
- **alternate exterior angles,** *p. 149*
- **consecutive interior angles,** *p. 149*

ACTIVITY EXPLORE PARALLEL LINES

Materials: lined paper, tracing paper, straightedge

STEP 1 Draw a pair of parallel lines cut by a nonperpendicular transversal on lined paper. Label the angles as shown.

STEP 2 Trace your drawing onto tracing paper.

STEP 3 Move the tracing paper to position ∠1 of the traced figure over ∠5 of the original figure. Compare the angles. Are they congruent?

STEP 4 Compare the eight angles and list all the congruent pairs. What do you notice about the special angle pairs formed by the transversal?

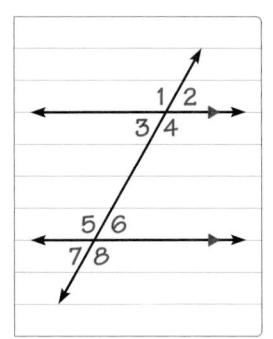

POSTULATE   *For Your Notebook*

POSTULATE 15 Corresponding Angles Postulate

If two parallel lines are cut by a transversal, then the pairs of corresponding angles are congruent.

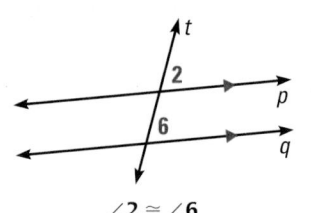

∠**2** ≅ ∠**6**

EXAMPLE 1   Identify congruent angles

The measure of three of the numbered angles is 120°. Identify the angles. Explain your reasoning.

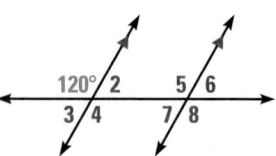

Solution

By the Corresponding Angles Postulate, $m\angle 5 = 120°$.
Using the Vertical Angles Congruence Theorem, $m\angle 4 = 120°$.
Because ∠4 and ∠8 are corresponding angles, by the Corresponding Angles Postulate, you know that $m\angle 8 = 120°$.

THEOREM 3.1 Alternate Interior Angles Theorem

If two parallel lines are cut by a transversal, then
the pairs of alternate interior angles are congruent.

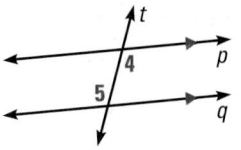

Proof: Example 3, p. 156

$\angle 4 \cong \angle 5$

THEOREM 3.2 Alternate Exterior Angles Theorem

If two parallel lines are cut by a transversal, then
the pairs of alternate exterior angles are congruent.

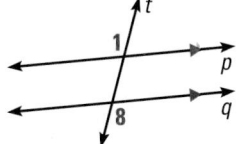

Proof: Ex. 37, p. 159

$\angle 1 \cong \angle 8$

THEOREM 3.3 Consecutive Interior Angles Theorem

If two parallel lines are cut by a transversal,
then the pairs of consecutive interior angles are
supplementary.

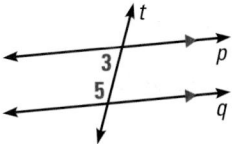

Proof: Ex. 41, p. 159

∠3 and ∠5 are
supplementary.

EXAMPLE 2   **Use properties of parallel lines**

 ALGEBRA **Find the value of *x*.**

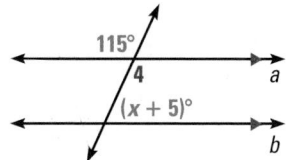

Solution

By the Vertical Angles Congruence Theorem, $m\angle 4 = 115°$. Lines *a* and *b*
are parallel, so you can use the theorems about parallel lines.

$m\angle 4 + (x + 5)° = 180°$	**Consecutive Interior Angles Theorem**
$115° + (x + 5)° = 180°$	**Substitute 115° for $m\angle 4$.**
$x + 120 = 180$	**Combine like terms.**
$x = 60$	**Subtract 120 from each side.**

Animated **Geometry**   at classzone.com

  GUIDED PRACTICE   **for Examples 1 and 2**

Use the diagram at the right.

 1. If $m\angle 1 = 105°$, find $m\angle 4$, $m\angle 5$, and $m\angle 8$. Tell
    which postulate or theorem you use in each case.

 2. If $m\angle 3 = 68°$ and $m\angle 8 = (2x + 4)°$, what is the
    value of *x*? Show your steps.

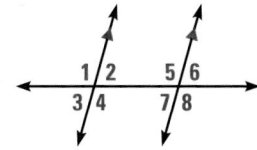

EXAMPLE 3 **Prove the Alternate Interior Angles Theorem**

Prove that if two parallel lines are cut by a transversal, then the pairs of alternate interior angles are congruent.

Solution

Draw a diagram. Label a pair of alternate interior angles as $\angle 1$ and $\angle 2$. You are looking for an angle that is related to both $\angle 1$ and $\angle 2$. Notice that one angle is a vertical angle with $\angle 2$ and a corresponding angle with $\angle 1$. Label it $\angle 3$.

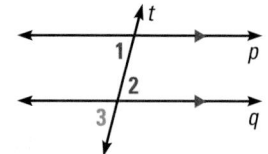

> **WRITE PROOFS**
> You can use the information from the diagram in your proof. Find any special angle pairs. Then decide what you know about those pairs.

GIVEN ▶ $p \parallel q$

PROVE ▶ $\angle 1 \cong \angle 2$

STATEMENTS	REASONS
1. $p \parallel q$	1. Given
2. $\angle 1 \cong \angle 3$	2. Corresponding Angles Postulate
3. $\angle 3 \cong \angle 2$	3. Vertical Angles Congruence Theorem
4. $\angle 1 \cong \angle 2$	4. Transitive Property of Congruence

EXAMPLE 4 **Solve a real-world problem**

SCIENCE When sunlight enters a drop of rain, different colors of light leave the drop at different angles. This process is what makes a rainbow. For violet light, $m\angle 2 = 40°$. What is $m\angle 1$? How do you know?

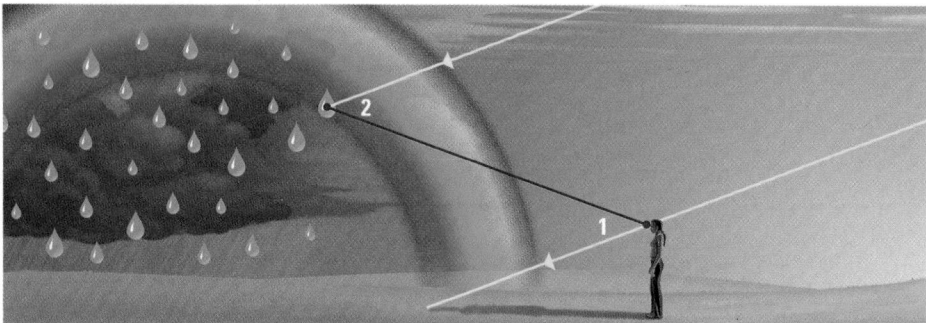

Solution

Because the sun's rays are parallel, $\angle 1$ and $\angle 2$ are alternate interior angles. By the Alternate Interior Angles Theorem, $\angle 1 \cong \angle 2$. By the definition of congruent angles, $m\angle 1 = m\angle 2 = 40°$.

✓ **GUIDED PRACTICE** **for Examples 3 and 4**

3. In the proof in Example 3, if you use the third statement before the second statement, could you still prove the theorem? *Explain.*

4. **WHAT IF?** Suppose the diagram in Example 4 shows yellow light leaving a drop of rain. Yellow light leaves the drop at an angle of 41°. What is $m\angle 1$ in this case? How do you know?

3.2 EXERCISES

SKILL PRACTICE

1. **VOCABULARY** Draw a pair of parallel lines and a transversal. Label a pair of *corresponding* angles.

2. ★ **WRITING** Two parallel lines are cut by a transversal. Which pairs of angles are congruent? Which pairs of angles are supplementary?

EXAMPLES 1 and 2
on pp. 154–155
for Exs. 3–16

3. ★ **MULTIPLE CHOICE** In the figure at the right, which angle has the same measure as ∠1?

   A ∠2   **B** ∠3

   C ∠4   **D** ∠5

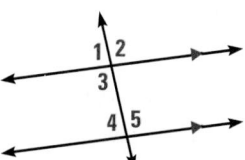

USING PARALLEL LINES Find the angle measure. Tell which postulate or theorem you use.

4. If m∠4 = 65°, then m∠1 = __?__.

5. If m∠7 = 110°, then m∠2 = __?__.

6. If m∠5 = 71°, then m∠4 = __?__.

7. If m∠3 = 117°, then m∠5 = __?__.

8. If m∠8 = 54°, then m∠1 = __?__.

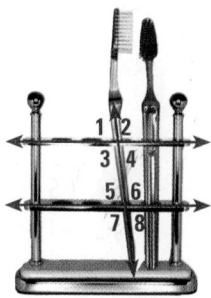

USING POSTULATES AND THEOREMS What postulate or theorem justifies the statement about the diagram?

9. ∠1 ≅ ∠5   10. ∠4 ≅ ∠5

11. ∠2 ≅ ∠7   12. ∠2 and ∠5 are supplementary.

13. ∠3 ≅ ∠6   14. ∠3 ≅ ∠7

15. ∠1 ≅ ∠8   16. ∠4 and ∠7 are supplementary.

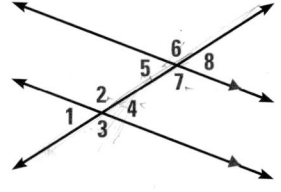

USING PARALLEL LINES Find m∠1 and m∠2. *Explain* your reasoning.

17.

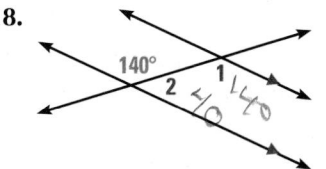

18.

19.

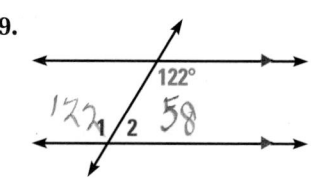

20. **ERROR ANALYSIS** A student concludes that ∠9 ≅ ∠10 by the Corresponding Angles Postulate. Describe and correct the error in this reasoning.

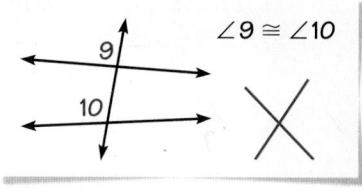

21. ★ SHORT RESPONSE Given $p \parallel q$, *describe* two methods you can use to show that $\angle 1 \cong \angle 4$.

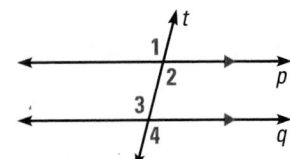

USING PARALLEL LINES Find $m\angle 1$, $m\angle 2$, and $m\angle 3$. *Explain* your reasoning.

22.

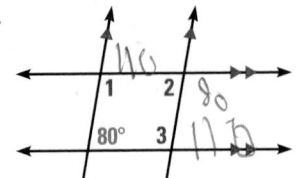

23.

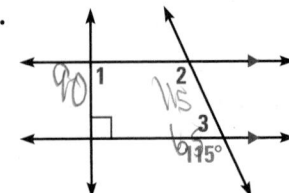

24.

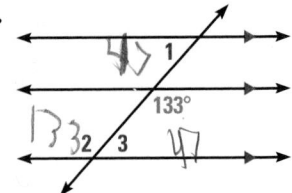

ANGLES Use the diagram at the right.

25. Name two pairs of congruent angles if $\overleftrightarrow{AB}$ and $\overleftrightarrow{DC}$ are parallel.

26. Name two pairs of supplementary angles if $\overleftrightarrow{AD}$ and $\overleftrightarrow{BC}$ are parallel.

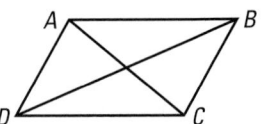

ⓧⓨ ALGEBRA Find the values of x and y.

27.

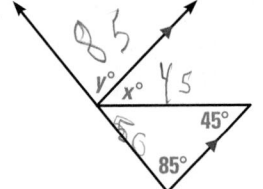

28.

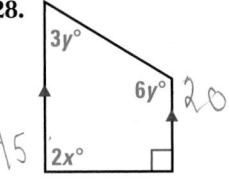

29.

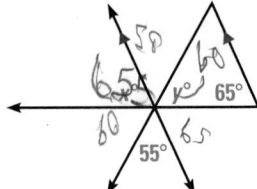

30.

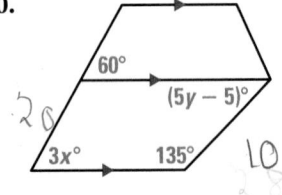

31.

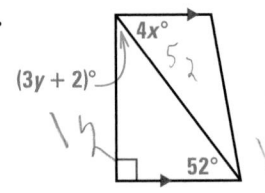

32.

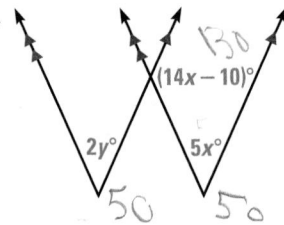

33. ★ MULTIPLE CHOICE What is the value of y in the diagram?

Ⓐ 70 　　Ⓑ 75

Ⓒ 110 　　Ⓓ 115

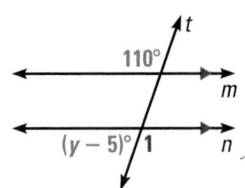

34. DRAWING Draw a four-sided figure with sides $\overline{MN}$ and $\overline{PQ}$, such that $\overline{MN} \parallel \overline{PQ}$, $\overline{MP} \parallel \overline{NQ}$, and $\angle MNQ$ is an acute angle. Which angle pairs formed are congruent? *Explain* your reasoning.

CHALLENGE Find the values of x and y.

35.

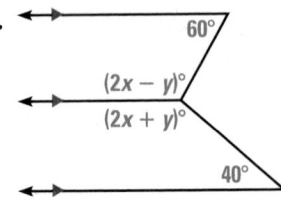

36.

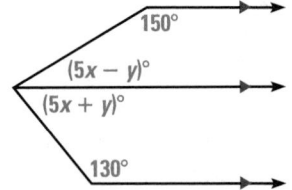

Ⓞ = **WORKED-OUT SOLUTIONS**
on p. WS1

★ = **STANDARDIZED
TEST PRACTICE**

EXAMPLE 3
on p. 156
for Ex. 37

37. PROVING THEOREM 3.2 If two parallel lines are cut by a transversal, then the pairs of alternate exterior angles are congruent. Use the steps below to write a proof of the Alternate Exterior Angles Theorem.

GIVEN ▶ $p \parallel q$

PROVE ▶ $\angle 1 \cong \angle 2$

a. Show that $\angle 1 \cong \angle 3$.

b. Then show that $\angle 1 \cong \angle 2$.

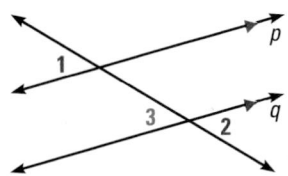

@HomeTutor for problem solving help at classzone.com

EXAMPLE 4
on p. 156
for Exs. 38–40

38. PARKING LOT In the diagram, the lines dividing parking spaces are parallel. The measure of $\angle 1$ is 110°.

a. Identify the angle(s) congruent to $\angle 1$.

b. Find $m\angle 6$.

@HomeTutor for problem solving help at classzone.com

39. ★ SHORT RESPONSE The *Toddler*™ is a walking robot. Each leg of the robot has two parallel bars and a foot. When the robot walks, the leg bars remain parallel as the foot slides along the surface.

a. As the legs move, are there pairs of angles that are always congruent? always supplementary? If so, which angles?

b. *Explain* how having parallel leg bars allows the robot's foot to stay flat on the floor as it moves.

40. ★ EXTENDED RESPONSE You are designing a box like the one below.

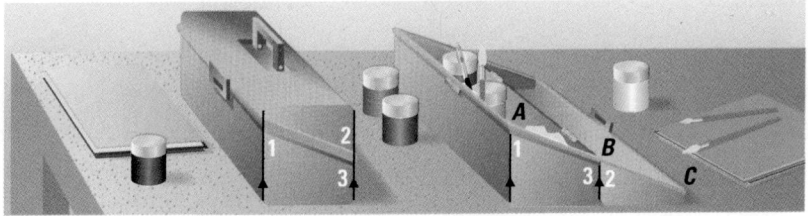

a. The measure of $\angle 1$ is 70°. What is $m\angle 2$? What is $m\angle 3$?

b. *Explain* why $\angle ABC$ is a straight angle.

c. What If? If $m\angle 1$ is 60°, will $\angle ABC$ still be a straight angle? Will the opening of the box be *more steep* or *less steep*? *Explain*.

41. PROVING THEOREM 3.3 If two parallel lines are cut by a transversal, then the pairs of consecutive interior angles are supplementary. Write a proof of the Consecutive Interior Angles Theorem.

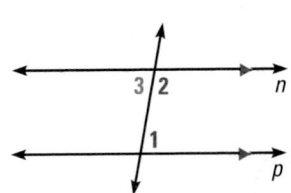

GIVEN ▶ $n \parallel p$

PROVE ▶ $\angle 1$ and $\angle 2$ are supplementary.

42. PROOF The Perpendicular Transversal Theorem (page 192) states that if a transversal is perpendicular to one of two parallel lines, then it is perpendicular to the other. Write a proof of the Perpendicular Transversal Theorem.

GIVEN ▶ $t \perp r$, $r \parallel s$

PROVE ▶ $t \perp s$

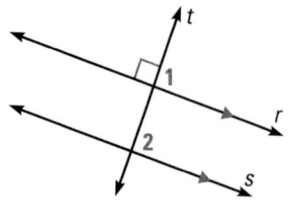

43. CHALLENGE In the diagram, $\angle 4 \cong \angle 5$. $\overline{SE}$ bisects $\angle RSF$. Find $m\angle 1$. *Explain* your reasoning.

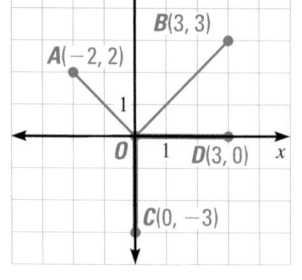

MIXED REVIEW

44. Find the length of each segment in the coordinate plane at the right. Which segments are congruent? *(p. 15)*

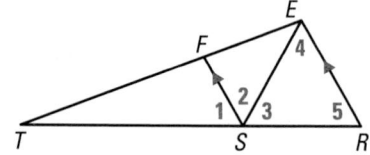

Are angles with the given measures *complementary*, *supplementary*, or *neither*? *(p. 35)*

45. $m\angle 1 = 62°$, $m\angle 2 = 128°$

46. $m\angle 3 = 130°$, $m\angle 4 = 70°$

47. $m\angle 5 = 44°$, $m\angle 6 = 46°$

Find the perimeter of the equilateral figure with the given side length. *(pp. 42, 49)*

48. Pentagon, 20 cm **49.** Octagon, 2.5 ft **50.** Decagon, 33 in.

PREVIEW
Prepare for Lesson 3.3 in Exs. 51–52.

Write the converse of the statement. Is the converse true? *(p. 79)*

51. Three points are collinear if they lie on the same line.

52. If the measure of an angle is 119°, then the angle is obtuse.

QUIZ *for Lessons 3.1–3.2*

Copy and complete the statement. *(p. 147)*

1. $\angle 2$ and __?__ are corresponding angles.

2. $\angle 3$ and __?__ are consecutive interior angles.

3. $\angle 3$ and __?__ are alternate interior angles.

4. $\angle 2$ and __?__ are alternate exterior angles.

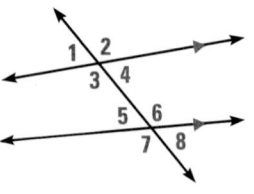

Find the value of *x*. *(p. 154)*

5.

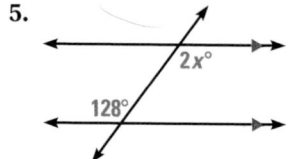

6.

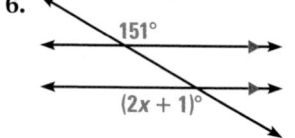

7.

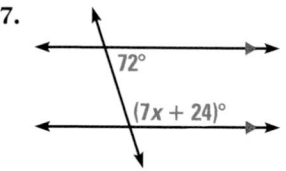

3.3 Prove Lines are Parallel

Before	You used properties of parallel lines to determine angle relationships.
Now	You will use angle relationships to prove that lines are parallel.
Why?	So you can describe how sports equipment is arranged, as in Ex. 32.

Key Vocabulary
• **paragraph proof**
• **converse,** *p. 80*
• **two-column proof,** *p. 112*

Postulate 16 below is the converse of Postulate 15 in Lesson 3.2. Similarly, the theorems in Lesson 3.2 have true converses. Remember that the converse of a true conditional statement is not necessarily true, so each converse of a theorem must be proved, as in Example 3.

POSTULATE
For Your Notebook

POSTULATE 16 Corresponding Angles Converse

If two lines are cut by a transversal so the corresponding angles are congruent, then the lines are parallel.

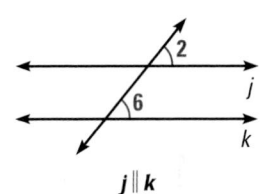

$j \parallel k$

EXAMPLE 1 Apply the Corresponding Angles Converse

ALGEBRA Find the value of x that makes $m \parallel n$.

Solution

Lines m and n are parallel if the marked corresponding angles are congruent.

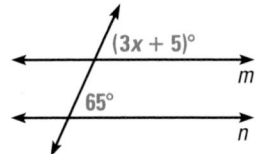

$(3x + 5)° = 65°$	Use Postulate 16 to write an equation.
$3x = 60$	Subtract 5 from each side.
$x = 20$	Divide each side by 3.

▶ The lines m and n are parallel when $x = 20$.

✓ **GUIDED PRACTICE** for Example 1

1. Is there enough information in the diagram to conclude that $m \parallel n$? *Explain.*

2. *Explain* why Postulate 16 is the converse of Postulate 15.

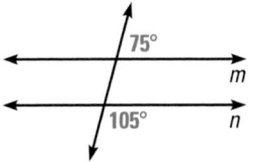

THEOREM 3.4 Alternate Interior Angles Converse

If two lines are cut by a transversal so the
alternate interior angles are congruent,
then the lines are parallel.

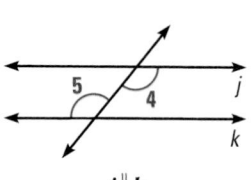

Proof: Example 3, p. 163

$j \parallel k$

THEOREM 3.5 Alternate Exterior Angles Converse

If two lines are cut by a transversal so the
alternate exterior angles are congruent,
then the lines are parallel.

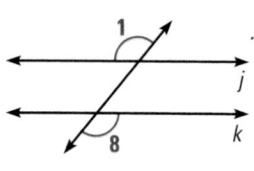

Proof: Ex. 36, p. 168

$j \parallel k$

THEOREM 3.6 Consecutive Interior Angles Converse

If two lines are cut by a transversal
so the consecutive interior angles are
supplementary, then the lines are parallel.

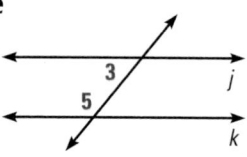

**If ∠3 and ∠5 are
supplementary, then *j* ∥ *k*.**

Proof: Ex. 37, p. 168

EXAMPLE 2   **Solve a real-world problem**

SNAKE PATTERNS How can you tell whether the sides of the pattern are
parallel in the photo of a diamond-back snake?

 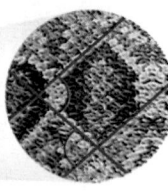

Solution

Because the alternate interior angles are congruent, you know that the sides
of the pattern are parallel.

✓ **GUIDED PRACTICE**   **for Example 2**

Can you prove that lines *a* and *b* are parallel? *Explain* why or why not.

3.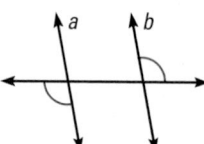

4.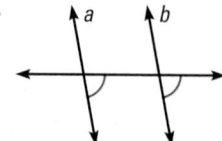

5. $m\angle 1 + m\angle 2 = 180°$

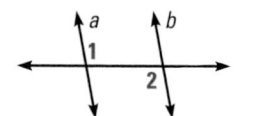

EXAMPLE 3 Prove the Alternate Interior Angles Converse

Prove that if two lines are cut by a transversal so the alternate interior angles are congruent, then the lines are parallel.

Solution

GIVEN ▶ $\angle 4 \cong \angle 5$

PROVE ▶ $g \parallel h$

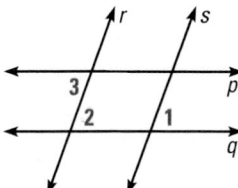

STATEMENTS	REASONS
1. $\angle 4 \cong \angle 5$	**1.** Given
2. $\angle 1 \cong \angle 4$	**2.** Vertical Angles Congruence Theorem
3. $\angle 1 \cong \angle 5$	**3.** Transitive Property of Congruence
4. $g \parallel h$	**4.** Corresponding Angles Converse

Animated Geometry at classzone.com

PARAGRAPH PROOFS A proof can also be written in paragraph form, called a **paragraph proof**. The statements and reasons in a paragraph proof are written in sentences, using words to explain the logical flow of the argument.

EXAMPLE 4 Write a paragraph proof

In the figure, $r \parallel s$ and $\angle 1$ is congruent to $\angle 3$. Prove $p \parallel q$.

Solution

Look at the diagram to make a plan. The diagram suggests that you look at angles 1, 2, and 3. Also, you may find it helpful to focus on one pair of lines and one transversal at a time.

Plan for Proof

a. Look at $\angle 1$ and $\angle 2$.

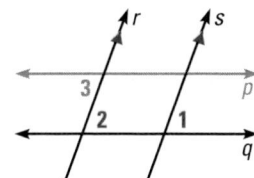

$\angle 1 \cong \angle 2$ because $r \parallel s$.

b. Look at $\angle 2$ and $\angle 3$.

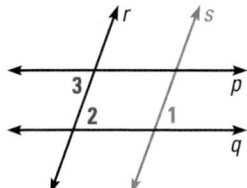

If $\angle 2 \cong \angle 3$, then $p \parallel q$.

Plan in Action

a. It is given that $r \parallel s$, **so** by the Corresponding Angles Postulate, $\angle 1 \cong \angle 2$.

b. It is also given that $\angle 1 \cong \angle 3$. **Then** $\angle 2 \cong \angle 3$ by the Transitive Property of Congruence for angles. **Therefore,** by the Alternate Interior Angles Converse, $p \parallel q$.

THEOREM 3.7 Transitive Property of Parallel Lines

If two lines are parallel to the same line,
then they are parallel to each other.

Proofs: Ex. 38, p. 168; Ex. 38, p. 177

If $p \parallel q$ and $q \parallel r$, then $p \parallel r$.

EXAMPLE 5 **Use the Transitive Property of Parallel Lines**

U.S. FLAG The flag of the United
States has 13 alternating red and
white stripes. Each stripe is parallel
to the stripe immediately below
it. Explain why the top stripe is
parallel to the bottom stripe.

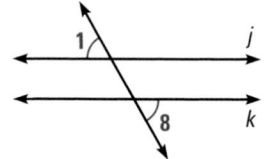

Solution

USE SUBSCRIPTS
When you name several
similar items, you can
use one variable with
subscripts to keep track
of the items.

The stripes from top to bottom can be named s_1, s_2, s_3, . . . , s_{13}. Each stripe
is parallel to the one below it, so $s_1 \parallel s_2$, $s_2 \parallel s_3$, and so on. Then $s_1 \parallel s_3$ by the
Transitive Property of Parallel Lines. Similarly, because $s_3 \parallel s_4$, it follows that
$s_1 \parallel s_4$. By continuing this reasoning, $s_1 \parallel s_{13}$. So, the top stripe is parallel to the
bottom stripe.

✓ **GUIDED PRACTICE** for Examples 3, 4, and 5

6. If you use the diagram at the right to prove
the Alternate Exterior Angles Converse,
what GIVEN and PROVE statements would
you use?

7. Copy and complete the following paragraph proof of the Alternate
Interior Angles Converse using the diagram in Example 3.

It is given that $\angle 4 \cong \angle 5$. By the __?__, $\angle 1 \cong \angle 4$. Then by the Transitive
Property of Congruence, __?__. So, by the __?__, $g \parallel h$.

8. Each step is parallel to the step
immediately above it. The bottom step
is parallel to the ground. *Explain* why
the top step is parallel to the ground.

3.3 EXERCISES

HOMEWORK KEY

○ = WORKED-OUT SOLUTIONS
on p. WS3 for Exs. 11, 29, and 37

★ = STANDARDIZED TEST PRACTICE
Exs. 2, 16, 23, 24, 33, and 39

SKILL PRACTICE

1. **VOCABULARY** Draw a pair of parallel lines with a transversal. Identify all pairs of *alternate exterior angles*.

2. ★ **WRITING** Use the theorems from the previous lesson and the converses of those theorems in this lesson. Write three biconditionals about parallel lines and transversals.

EXAMPLE 1
on p. 161
for Exs. 3–9

(XY) ALGEBRA Find the value of *x* that makes *m* ‖ *n*.

3.
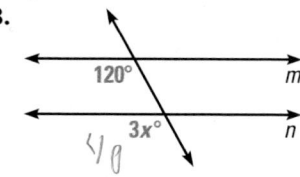
120° *m*
3x° *n*
4 8

4.
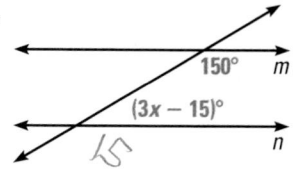
135° *m*
(2x + 15)° *n*
60

5.
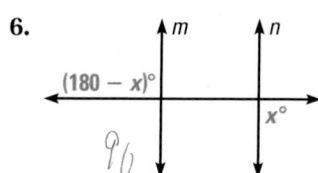
150° *m*
(3x − 15)° *n*
45

6.
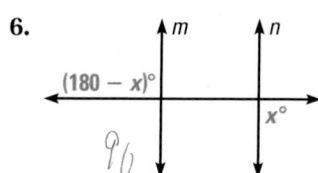
m *n*
(180 − x)°
x°
96

7.
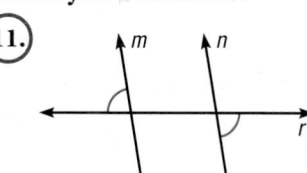
m *n*
2x° x°
60

8.
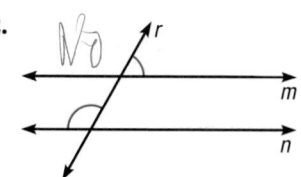
m *n*
(2x + 20)°
3x°
80

9. **ERROR ANALYSIS** A student concluded that lines *a* and *b* are parallel. *Describe* and correct the student's error.

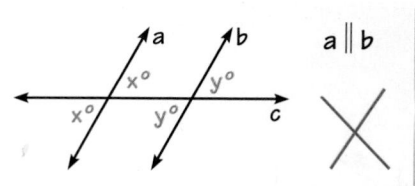
a b
x° y°
x° y° c
a ‖ b

EXAMPLE 2
on p. 162
for Exs. 10–17

IDENTIFYING PARALLEL LINES Is there enough information to prove *m* ‖ *n*? If so, state the postulate or theorem you would use.

10.
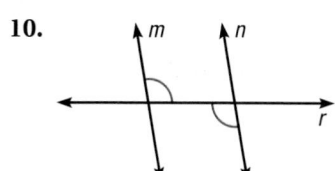
m *n*
r

(11.)
m *n*
r

12.
No
r
m
n

13.
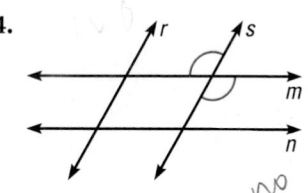
m *n*
r

14.
r *s*
m
n
no

15.
r *s*
m
n

16. ★ **OPEN-ENDED MATH** Use lined paper to draw two parallel lines cut by a transversal. Use a protractor to measure one angle. Find the measures of the other seven angles without using the protractor. Give a theorem or postulate you use to find each angle measure.

17. MULTI-STEP PROBLEM Complete the steps below to determine whether $\overleftrightarrow{DB}$ and $\overleftrightarrow{HF}$ are parallel.

a. Find $m\angle DCG$ and $m\angle CGH$.

b. *Describe* the relationship between $\angle DCG$ and $\angle CGH$.

c. Are $\overleftrightarrow{DB}$ and $\overleftrightarrow{HF}$ parallel? *Explain* your reasoning.

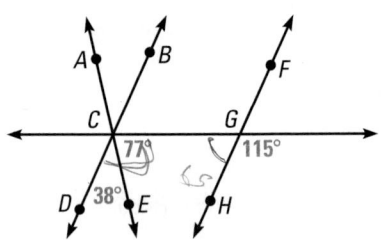

EXAMPLE 3
on p. 163
for Ex. 18

18. PLANNING A PROOF Use these steps to plan a proof of the Consecutive Interior Angles Converse, as stated on page 162.

a. Draw a diagram you can use in a proof of the theorem.

b. Write the GIVEN and PROVE statements.

REASONING **Can you prove that lines *a* and *b* are parallel? If so, *explain* how.**

19.
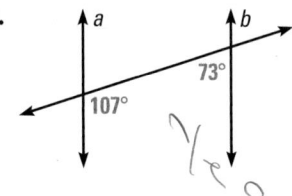

20.
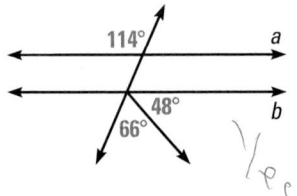

21.
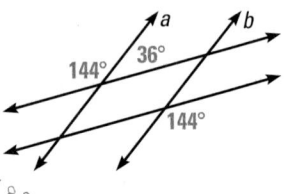

22. ERROR ANALYSIS A student decided that $\overleftrightarrow{AD} \parallel \overleftrightarrow{BC}$ based on the diagram below. *Describe* and correct the student's error.

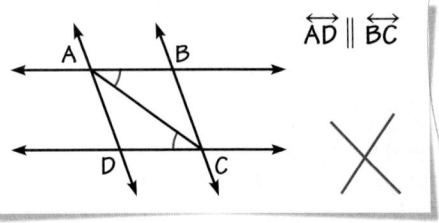

23. ★ MULTIPLE CHOICE Use the diagram at the right. You know that $\angle 1 \cong \angle 4$. What can you conclude?

(A) $p \parallel q$ (B) $r \parallel s$

(C) $\angle 2 \cong \angle 3$ (D) None of the above

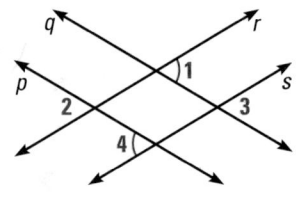

REASONING **Use the diagram at the right for Exercises 24 and 25.**

24. ★ SHORT RESPONSE In the diagram, assume $j \parallel k$. How many angle measures must be given in order to find the measure of every angle? *Explain* your reasoning.

25. PLANNING A PROOF In the diagram, assume $\angle 1$ and $\angle 7$ are supplementary. Write a plan for a proof showing that lines j and k are parallel.

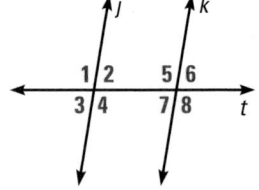

26. REASONING Use the diagram at the right. Which rays are parallel? Which rays are not parallel? *Justify* your conclusions.

27. VISUAL REASONING A point R is not in plane ABC.

    a. How many lines through R are perpendicular to plane ABC?

    b. How many lines through R are parallel to plane ABC?

    c. How many planes through R are parallel to plane ABC?

28. CHALLENGE Use the diagram.

    a. Find x so that $p \parallel q$.

    b. Find y so that $r \parallel s$.

    c. Can r be parallel to s and p be parallel to q at the same time? *Explain.*

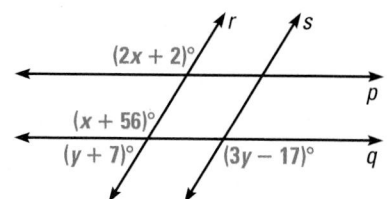

PROBLEM SOLVING

EXAMPLE 2
on p. 162
for Exs. 29–30

(29.) PICNIC TABLE How do you know that the top of the picnic table is parallel to the ground?

@HomeTutor for problem solving help at classzone.com

30. KITEBOARDING The diagram of the control bar of the kite shows the angles formed between the control bar and the kite lines. How do you know that n is parallel to m?

@HomeTutor for problem solving help at classzone.com

31. DEVELOPING PROOF Copy and complete the proof.

    GIVEN ▸ $m\angle 1 = 115°$, $m\angle 2 = 65°$

    PROVE ▸ $m \parallel n$

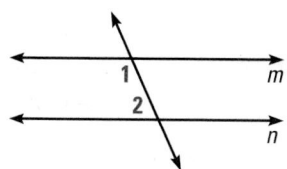

STATEMENTS	REASONS
1. $m\angle 1 = 115°$ and $m\angle 2 = 65°$	**1.** Given
2. $115° + 65° = 180°$	**2.** Addition
3. $m\angle 1 + m\angle 2 = 180°$	**3.** __?__
4. $\angle 1$ and $\angle 2$ are supplementary.	**4.** __?__
5. $m \parallel n$	**5.** __?__

32. BOWLING PINS How do you know that the bowling pins are set up in parallel lines?

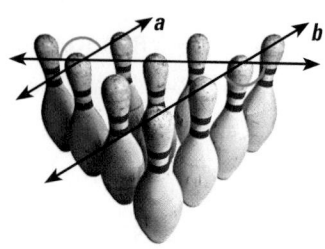

EXAMPLE 5
on p. 164
for Ex. 33

33. ★ **SHORT RESPONSE** The map shows part of Denver, Colorado. Use the markings on the map. Are the numbered streets parallel to one another? *Explain* how you can tell.

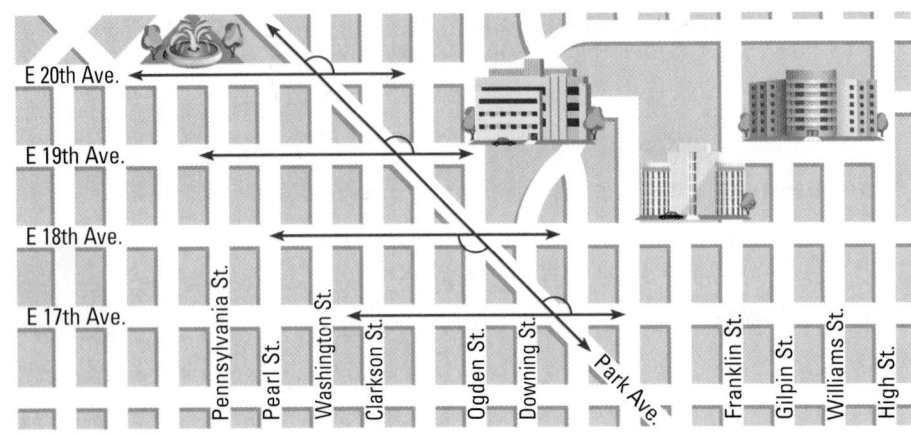

EXAMPLE 3
on p. 163
for Exs. 34–35

PROOF Use the diagram and the given information to write a two-column or paragraph proof.

34. GIVEN ▶ ∠1 ≅ ∠2, ∠3 ≅ ∠4
    PROVE ▶ $\overline{AB} \parallel \overline{CD}$

35. GIVEN ▶ $a \parallel b$, ∠2 ≅ ∠3
    PROVE ▶ $c \parallel d$

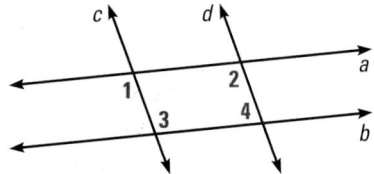

EXAMPLE 4
on p. 163
for Exs. 36–37

PROOF In Exercises 36 and 37, use the diagram to write a paragraph proof.

36. PROVING THEOREM 3.5 Prove the Alternate Exterior Angles Converse.

37. PROVING THEOREM 3.6 Prove the Consecutive Interior Angles Converse.

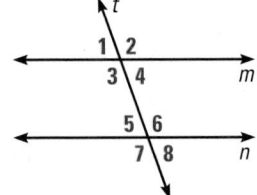

38. MULTI-STEP PROBLEM Use these steps to prove Theorem 3.7, the Transitive Property of Parallel Lines.

    a. Copy the diagram in the Theorem box on page 164. Draw a transversal through all three lines.

    b. Write the GIVEN and PROVE statements.

    c. Use the properties of angles formed by parallel lines and transversals to prove the theorem.

39. ★ **EXTENDED RESPONSE** Architects and engineers make drawings using a plastic triangle with angle measures 30°, 60°, and 90°. The triangle slides along a fixed horizontal edge.

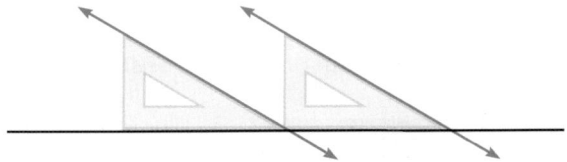

    a. *Explain* why the blue lines shown are parallel.

    b. *Explain* how the triangle can be used to draw vertical parallel lines.

REASONING Use the diagram below in Exercises 40–44. How would you show that the given lines are parallel?

40. *a* and *b*

41. *b* and *c*

42. *d* and *f*

43. *e* and *g*

44. *a* and *c*

45. **CHALLENGE** Use these steps to investigate the angle bisectors of corresponding angles.

    a. **Construction** Use a compass and straightedge or geometry drawing software to construct line ℓ, point P not on ℓ, and line n through P parallel to ℓ. Construct point Q on ℓ and construct $\overline{PQ}$. Choose a pair of alternate interior angles and construct their angle bisectors.

    b. **Write a Proof** Are the angle bisectors parallel? Make a conjecture. Write a proof of your conjecture.

MIXED REVIEW

Solve the equation. *(p. 875)*

46. $\frac{3}{4}x = -1$ **47.** $\frac{-2}{3}x = -1$ **48.** $\frac{1}{5}x = -1$ **49.** $-6x = -1$

50. You can choose one of eight sandwich fillings and one of four kinds of bread. How many different sandwiches are possible? *(p. 891)*

51. Find the value of x if $\overline{AB} \cong \overline{AD}$ and $\overline{CD} \cong \overline{AD}$. *Explain* your steps. *(p. 112)*

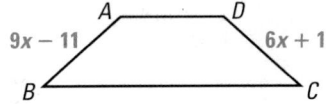

PREVIEW

Prepare for Lesson 3.4 in Exs. 52–54.

Simplify the expression.

52. $\frac{-7-2}{8-(-4)}$ *(p. 870)*   **53.** $\frac{0-(-3)}{1-6}$ *(p. 870)*   **54.** $\frac{3x-x}{-4x+2x}$ *(p. 139)*

MIXED REVIEW *of Problem Solving*

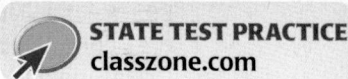

Lessons 3.1–3.3

1. **MULTI-STEP PROBLEM** Use the diagram of the tennis court below.

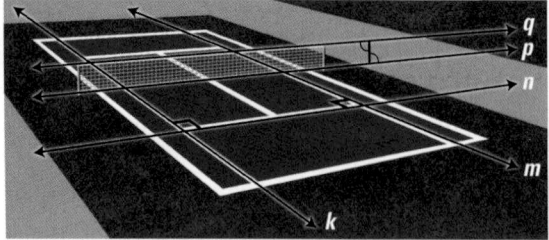

   a. Identify two pairs of parallel lines so each pair is on a different plane.

   b. Identify a pair of skew lines.

   c. Identify two pairs of perpendicular lines.

2. **MULTI-STEP PROBLEM** Use the picture of the tile floor below.

   a. Name the kind of angle pair each angle forms with ∠1.

   b. Lines *r* and *s* are parallel. Name the angles that are congruent to ∠3.

3. **OPEN-ENDED** The flag of Jamaica is shown. Given that $n \parallel p$ and $m\angle 1 = 53°$, determine the measure of ∠2. *Justify* each step in your argument, labeling any angles needed for your justification.

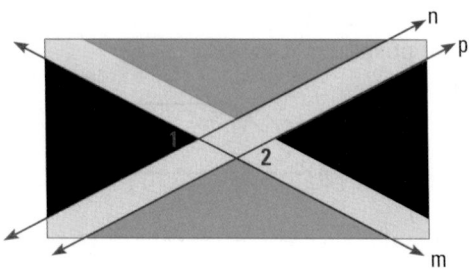

4. **SHORT RESPONSE** A neon sign is shown below. Are the top and the bottom of the Z parallel? *Explain* how you know.

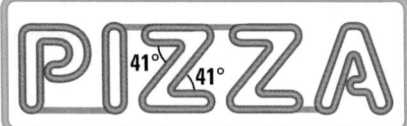

5. **EXTENDED RESPONSE** Use the diagram of the bridge below.

   a. Find the value of *x* that makes lines ℓ and *m* parallel.

   b. Suppose that $\ell \parallel m$ and $\ell \parallel n$. Find $m\angle 1$. *Explain* how you found your answer. Copy the diagram and label any angles you need for your explanation.

6. **GRIDDED ANSWER** In the photo of the picket fence, $m \parallel n$. What is $m\angle 1$ in degrees?

7. **SHORT RESPONSE** Find the values of *x* and *y*. *Explain* your steps.

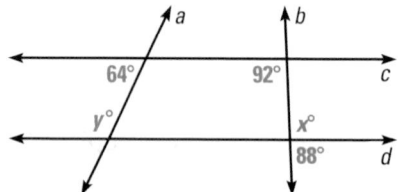

3.4 Find and Use Slopes of Lines

Before	You used properties of parallel lines to find angle measures.
Now	You will find and compare slopes of lines.
Why	So you can compare rates of speed, as in Example 4.

Key Vocabulary
- **slope,** p. 879
- **rise,** p. 879
- **run,** p. 879

The **slope** of a nonvertical line is the ratio of vertical change (*rise*) to horizontal change (*run*) between any two points on the line.

If a line in the coordinate plane passes through points (x_1, y_1) and (x_2, y_2) then the slope m is

$$m = \frac{\text{rise}}{\text{run}} = \frac{\text{change in } y}{\text{change in } x} = \frac{y_2 - y_1}{x_2 - x_1}.$$

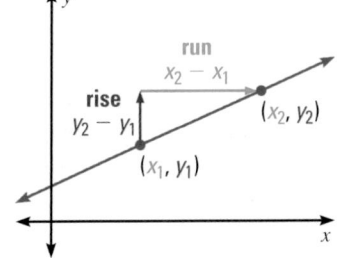

KEY CONCEPT   *For Your Notebook*

Slope of Lines in the Coordinate Plane

Negative slope: falls from left to right, as in line j

Positive slope: rises from left to right, as in line k

Zero slope (slope of 0): horizontal, as in line ℓ

Undefined slope: vertical, as in line n

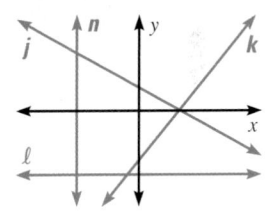

EXAMPLE 1   Find slopes of lines in a coordinate plane

REVIEW SLOPE

For more help with slope, see p. 879.

Find the slopes of line a and line d.

Solution

Slope of line a: $m = \dfrac{y_2 - y_1}{x_2 - x_1} = \dfrac{4 - 2}{6 - 8} = \dfrac{2}{-2} = -1$

Slope of line d: $m = \dfrac{y_2 - y_1}{x_2 - x_1} = \dfrac{4 - 0}{6 - 6} = \dfrac{4}{0}$,

which is undefined.

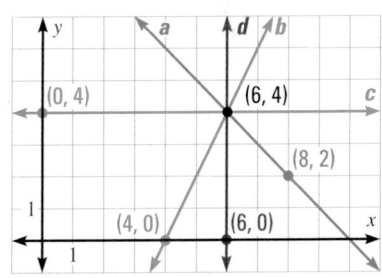

✓ **GUIDED PRACTICE**   for Example 1

Use the graph in Example 1. Find the slope of the line.

1. Line b

2. Line c

COMPARING SLOPES When two lines intersect in a coordinate plane, the steeper line has the slope with greater absolute value. You can also compare slopes to tell whether two lines are parallel or perpendicular.

POSTULATES   *For Your Notebook*

POSTULATE 17   Slopes of Parallel Lines

In a coordinate plane, two nonvertical lines are parallel if and only if they have the same slope.

Any two vertical lines are parallel.

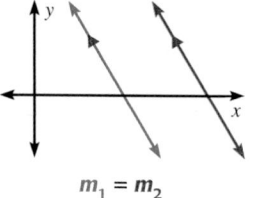

$$m_1 = m_2$$

POSTULATE 18   Slopes of Perpendicular Lines

In a coordinate plane, two nonvertical lines are perpendicular if and only if the product of their slopes is −1.

Horizontal lines are perpendicular to vertical lines.

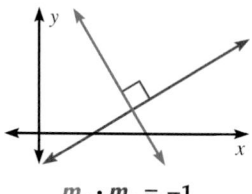

$$m_1 \cdot m_2 = -1$$

READ VOCABULARY

If the product of two numbers is −1, then the numbers are called *negative reciprocals.*

EXAMPLE 2   **Identify parallel lines**

Find the slope of each line. Which lines are parallel?

Solution

Find the slope of k_1 through $(-2, 4)$ and $(-3, 0)$.

$$m_1 = \frac{0 - 4}{-3 - (-2)} = \frac{-4}{-1} = 4$$

Find the slope of k_2 through $(4, 5)$ and $(3, 1)$.

$$m_2 = \frac{1 - 5}{3 - 4} = \frac{-4}{-1} = 4$$

Find the slope of k_3 through $(6, 3)$ and $(5, -2)$.

$$m_3 = \frac{-2 - 3}{5 - 6} = \frac{-5}{-1} = 5$$

▸ Compare the slopes. Because k_1 and k_2 have the same slope, they are parallel. The slope of k_3 is different, so k_3 is not parallel to the other lines.

✓ **GUIDED PRACTICE**   **for Example 2**

3. Line *m* passes through $(-1, 3)$ and $(4, 1)$. Line *t* passes through $(-2, -1)$ and $(3, -3)$. Are the two lines parallel? *Explain* how you know.

EXAMPLE 3 Draw a perpendicular line

Line h passes through (3, 0) and (7, 6). Graph the line perpendicular to h that passes through the point (2, 5).

Solution

STEP 1 Find the slope m_1 of line h through (3, 0) and (7, 6).

$$m_1 = \frac{6-0}{7-3} = \frac{6}{4} = \frac{3}{2}$$

STEP 2 Find the slope m_2 of a line perpendicular to h. Use the fact that the product of the slopes of two perpendicular lines is -1.

$\frac{3}{2} \cdot m_2 = -1$ **Slopes of perpendicular lines**

$m_2 = \frac{-2}{3}$ **Multiply each side by $\frac{2}{3}$.**

STEP 3 Use the rise and run to graph the line.

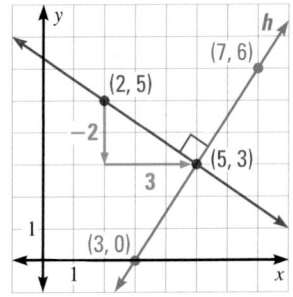

REVIEW GRAPHING

Given a point on a line and the line's slope, you can use the rise and run to find a second point and draw the line.

  EXAMPLE 4   **Standardized Test Practice**

A skydiver made jumps with three parachutes. The graph shows the height of the skydiver from the time the parachute opened to the time of the landing for each jump. Which statement is true?

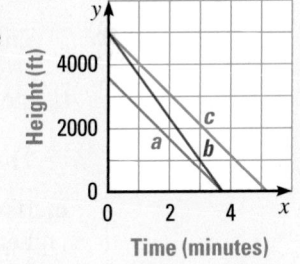

A The parachute opened at the same height in jumps a and b.

B The parachute was open for the same amount of time in jumps b and c.

C The skydiver descended at the same rate in jumps a and b.

D The skydiver descended at the same rate in jumps a and c.

ELIMINATE CHOICES

The y-intercept represents the height when the parachute opened, so the heights in jumps a and b were not the same. So you can eliminate choice A.

Solution

The rate at which the skydiver descended is represented by the slope of the segments. The segments that have the same slope are a and c.

▶ The correct answer is D. (A) (B) (C) (**D**)

✓ **GUIDED PRACTICE**   for Examples 3 and 4

4. Line n passes through (0, 2) and (6, 5). Line m passes through (2, 4) and (4, 0). Is $n \perp m$? *Explain.*

5. In Example 4, which parachute is in the air for the longest time? *Explain.*

6. In Example 4, what do the x-intercepts represent in the situation? How can you use this to eliminate one of the choices?

❖ **EXAMPLE 5** **Solve a real-world problem**

ROLLER COASTERS During the climb on the Magnum XL-200 roller coaster, you move 41 feet upward for every 80 feet you move horizontally. At the crest of the hill, you have moved 400 feet forward.

a. **Making a Table** Make a table showing the height of the Magnum at every 80 feet it moves horizontally. How high is the roller coaster at the top of its climb?

b. **Calculating** Write a fraction that represents the height the Magnum climbs for each foot it moves horizontally. What does the numerator represent?

c. **Using a Graph** Another roller coaster, the Millenium Force, climbs at a slope of 1. At its crest, the horizontal distance from the starting point is 310 feet. Compare this climb to that of the Magnum. Which climb is steeper?

Solution

a.

Horizontal distance (ft)	80	160	240	320	400
Height (ft)	41	82	123	164	205

The Magnum XL-200 is 205 feet high at the top of its climb.

b. Slope of the Magnum $= \dfrac{\text{rise}}{\text{run}} = \dfrac{41}{80} = \dfrac{41 \div 80}{80 \div 80} = \dfrac{0.5125}{1}$

The numerator, 0.5125, represents the slope in decimal form.

c. Use a graph to compare the climbs. Let x be the horizontal distance and let y be the height. Because the slope of the Millenium Force is 1, the rise is equal to the run. So the highest point must be at (310, 310).

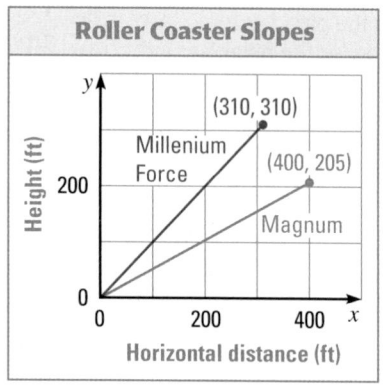

▶ The graph shows that the Millenium Force has a steeper climb, because the slope of its line is greater (1 > 0.5125).

Animated **Geometry** at classzone.com

 GUIDED PRACTICE for Example 5

7. Line q passes through the points (0, 0) and (−4, 5). Line t passes through the points (0, 0) and (−10, 7). Which line is steeper, q or t?

8. **WHAT IF?** Suppose a roller coaster climbed 300 feet upward for every 350 feet it moved horizontally. Is it *more steep* or *less steep* than the Magnum? than the Millenium Force?

3.4 EXERCISES

HOMEWORK KEY
○ = **WORKED-OUT SOLUTIONS**
on p. WS3 for Exs. 7, 13, and 35

★ = **STANDARDIZED TEST PRACTICE**
Exs. 2, 34, 35, and 41

◆ = **MULTIPLE REPRESENTATIONS**
Ex. 37

SKILL PRACTICE

1. **VOCABULARY** *Describe* what is meant by the slope of a nonvertical line.

2. ★ **WRITING** What happens when you apply the slope formula to a horizontal line? What happens when you apply it to a vertical line?

EXAMPLE 1
on p. 171
for Exs. 3–12

MATCHING Match the description of the slope of a line with its graph.

3. *m* is positive.   4. *m* is negative.   5. *m* is zero.   6. *m* is undefined.

A. 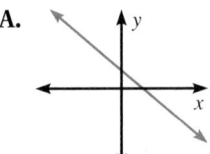   **B.** 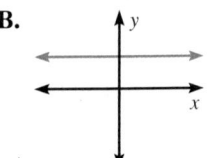   **C.** 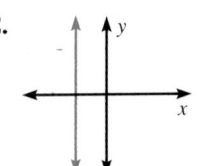   **D.**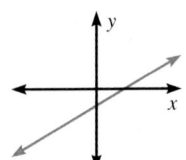

FINDING SLOPE Find the slope of the line that passes through the points.

7. (3, 5), (5, 6)   8. (−2, 2), (2, −6)   9. (−5, −1), (3, −1)   10. (2, 1), (0, 6)

ERROR ANALYSIS *Describe* and correct the error in finding the slope of the line.

11.

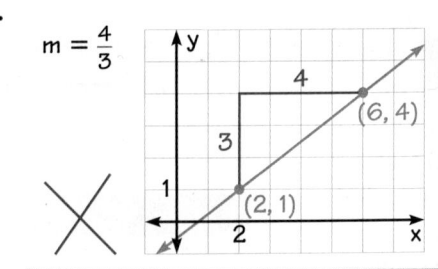

$m = \dfrac{4}{3}$

12.

Slope of the line through (2, 7) and (4, 5)

$m = \dfrac{y_2 - y_1}{x_2 - x_1} = \dfrac{7 - 5}{4 - 2} = \dfrac{2}{2} = 1$

EXAMPLES 2 and 3
on pp. 172–173
for Exs. 13–18

TYPES OF LINES Tell whether the lines through the given points are *parallel*, *perpendicular*, or *neither*. *Justify* your answer.

13. **Line 1:** (1, 0), (7, 4)
    Line 2: (7, 0), (3, 6)

14. **Line 1:** (−3, 1), (−7, −2)
    Line 2: (2, −1), (8, 4)

15. **Line 1:** (−9, 3), (−5, 7)
    Line 2: (−11, 6), (−7, 2)

GRAPHING Graph the line through the given point with the given slope.

16. $P(3, -2)$, slope $-\dfrac{1}{6}$ 17. $P(-4, 0)$, slope $\dfrac{5}{2}$ 18. $P(0, 5)$, slope $\dfrac{2}{3}$

EXAMPLES 4 and 5
on pp. 173–174
for Exs. 19–22

STEEPNESS OF A LINE Tell which line through the given points is steeper.

19. **Line 1:** (−2, 3), (3, 5)
    Line 2: (3, 1), (6, 5)

20. **Line 1:** (−2, −1), (1, −2)
    Line 2: (−5, −3), (−1, −4)

21. **Line 1:** (−4, 2), (−3, 6)
    Line 2: (1, 6), (3, 8)

22. **REASONING** Use your results from Exercises 19–21. *Describe* a way to determine which of two lines is steeper without graphing them.

THEOREMS

THEOREM 3.11 Perpendicular Transversal Theorem

If a transversal is perpendicular to one of two parallel lines, then it is perpendicular to the other.

If $h \parallel k$ and $j \perp h$, then $j \perp k$.

Proof: Ex. 42, p. 160; Ex. 33, p. 196

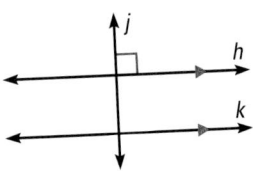

THEOREM 3.12 Lines Perpendicular to a Transversal Theorem

In a plane, if two lines are perpendicular to the same line, then they are parallel to each other.

If $m \perp p$ and $n \perp p$, then $m \parallel n$.

Proof: Ex. 34, p. 196

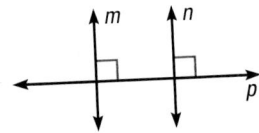

EXAMPLE 3 **Draw conclusions**

Determine which lines, if any, must be parallel in the diagram. Explain your reasoning.

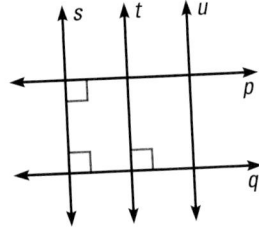

Solution

Lines p and q are both perpendicular to s, so by Theorem 3.12, $p \parallel q$. Also, lines s and t are both perpendicular to q, so by Theorem 3.12, $s \parallel t$.

✔ **GUIDED PRACTICE** **for Example 3**

Use the diagram at the right.

3. Is $b \parallel a$? *Explain* your reasoning.

4. Is $b \perp c$? *Explain* your reasoning.

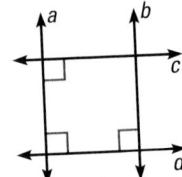

DISTANCE FROM A LINE The **distance from a point to a line** is the length of the perpendicular segment from the point to the line. This perpendicular segment is the shortest distance between the point and the line. For example, the distance between point A and line k is AB. You will prove this in Chapter 5.

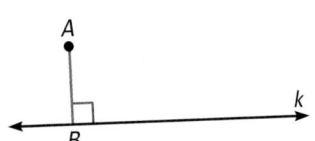

Distance from a point to a line

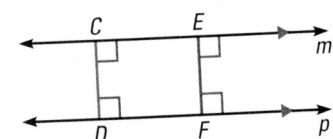

Distance between two parallel lines

The *distance between two parallel lines* is the length of any perpendicular segment joining the two lines. For example, the distance between line p and line m above is CD or EF.

3.4 EXERCISES

HOMEWORK KEY

○ = **WORKED-OUT SOLUTIONS**
on p. WS3 for Exs. 7, 13, and 35

★ = **STANDARDIZED TEST PRACTICE**
Exs. 2, 34, 35, and 41

◆ = **MULTIPLE REPRESENTATIONS**
Ex. 37

SKILL PRACTICE

1. **VOCABULARY** *Describe* what is meant by the slope of a nonvertical line.

2. ★ **WRITING** What happens when you apply the slope formula to a horizontal line? What happens when you apply it to a vertical line?

EXAMPLE 1
on p. 171
for Exs. 3–12

MATCHING **Match the description of the slope of a line with its graph.**

3. *m* is positive.   4. *m* is negative.   5. *m* is zero.   6. *m* is undefined.

A. 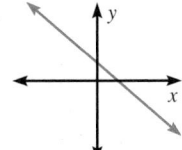   B. 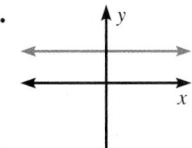   C. 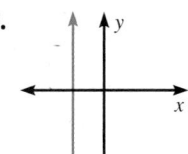   D.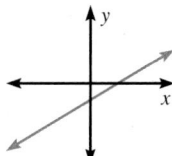

FINDING SLOPE **Find the slope of the line that passes through the points.**

7. (3, 5), (5, 6)   8. (−2, 2), (2, −6)   9. (−5, −1), (3, −1)   10. (2, 1), (0, 6)

ERROR ANALYSIS *Describe* **and correct the error in finding the slope of the line.**

11.

$m = \dfrac{4}{3}$

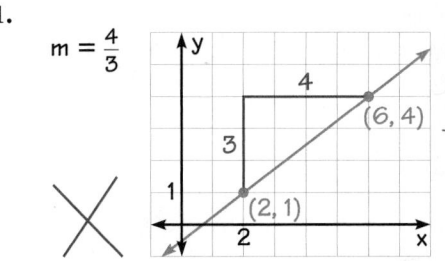

12.

Slope of the line through (2, 7) and (4, 5)

$m = \dfrac{y_2 - y_1}{x_2 - x_1} = \dfrac{7 - 5}{4 - 2} = \dfrac{2}{2} = 1$

EXAMPLES 2 and 3
on pp. 172–173
for Exs. 13–18

TYPES OF LINES **Tell whether the lines through the given points are *parallel*, *perpendicular*, or *neither*. *Justify* your answer.**

13. **Line 1:** (1, 0), (7, 4)
    Line 2: (7, 0), (3, 6)

14. **Line 1:** (−3, 1), (−7, −2)
    Line 2: (2, −1), (8, 4)

15. **Line 1:** (−9, 3), (−5, 7)
    Line 2: (−11, 6), (−7, 2)

GRAPHING **Graph the line through the given point with the given slope.**

16. $P(3, −2)$, slope $−\dfrac{1}{6}$

17. $P(−4, 0)$, slope $\dfrac{5}{2}$

18. $P(0, 5)$, slope $\dfrac{2}{3}$

EXAMPLES 4 and 5
on pp. 173–174
for Exs. 19–22

STEEPNESS OF A LINE **Tell which line through the given points is steeper.**

19. **Line 1:** (−2, 3), (3, 5)
    Line 2: (3, 1), (6, 5)

20. **Line 1:** (−2, −1), (1, −2)
    Line 2: (−5, −3), (−1, −4)

21. **Line 1:** (−4, 2), (−3, 6)
    Line 2: (1, 6), (3, 8)

22. **REASONING** Use your results from Exercises 19–21. *Describe* a way to determine which of two lines is steeper without graphing them.

PERPENDICULAR LINES Find the slope of line *n* perpendicular to line *h* and passing through point *P*. Then copy the graph and graph line *n*.

23.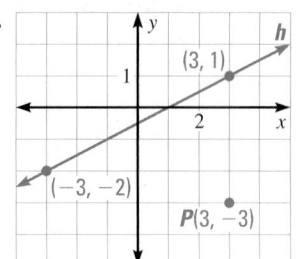

24.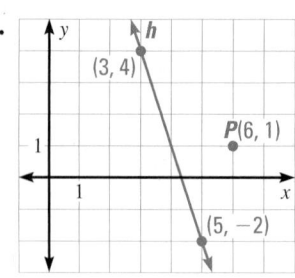

25.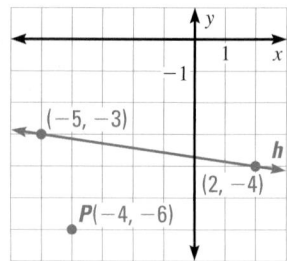

26. REASONING Use the concept of slope to decide whether the points (−3, 3), (1, −2), and (4, 0) lie on the same line. *Explain* your reasoning and include a diagram.

GRAPHING Graph a line with the given description.

27. Through (0, 2) and parallel to the line through (−2, 4) and (−5, 1)

28. Through (1, 3) and perpendicular to the line through (−1, −1) and (2, 0)

29. Through (−2, 1) and parallel to the line through (3, 1) and $(4, -\frac{1}{2})$

CHALLENGE Find the unknown coordinate so the line through the points has the given slope.

30. (−3, 2), (0, *y*); slope −2   **31.** (−7, −4), (*x*, 0); slope $\frac{1}{3}$ **32.** (4, −3), (*x*, 1); slope −4

PROBLEM SOLVING

33. WATER SLIDE The water slide is 6 feet tall, and the end of the slide is 9 feet from the base of the ladder. About what slope does the slide have?

@HomeTutor for problem solving help at classzone.com

EXAMPLE 5
on p. 174
for Exs. 34–37

34. ★ MULTIPLE CHOICE Which car has better gas mileage?

(A) A   **(B)** B

(C) Same rate   **(D)** Cannot be determined

@HomeTutor for problem solving help at classzone.com

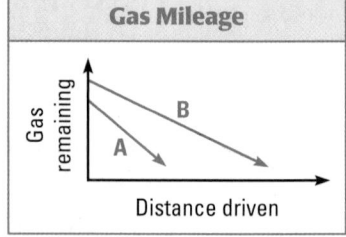

35. ★ SHORT RESPONSE *Compare* the graphs of the three lines described below. Which is most steep? Which is the least steep? Include a sketch in your answer.

Line *a*: through the point (3, 0) with a *y*-intercept of 4
Line *b*: through the point (3, 0) with a *y*-intercept greater than 4
Line *c*: through the point (3, 0) with a *y*-intercept between 0 and 4

○ = **WORKED-OUT SOLUTIONS**
on p. WS1

★ = **STANDARDIZED TEST PRACTICE**

◆ = **MULTIPLE REPRESENTATIONS**

36. MULTI-STEP PROBLEM Ladder safety guidelines include the following recommendation about ladder placement. The horizontal distance h between the base of the ladder and the object the ladder is resting against should be about one quarter of the vertical distance v between the ground and where the ladder rests against the object.

Make sure to place the ladder on a level place. If the ladder is not steady, it is not safe to climb.

Place the base so the distance h to the building is about one quarter of the height v to where the ladder hits the building.

a. Find the recommended slope for a ladder.

b. Suppose the base of a ladder is 6 feet away from a building. The ladder has the recommended slope. Find v.

c. Suppose a ladder is 34 feet from the ground where it touches a building. The ladder has the recommended slope. Find h.

37. ◆ MULTIPLE REPRESENTATIONS The Duquesne (pronounced "du-KAYN") Incline was built in 1888 in Pittsburgh, Pennsylvania, to move people up and down a mountain there. On the incline, you move about 29 feet vertically for every 50 feet you move horizontally. When you reach the top of the hill, you have moved a horizontal distance of about 700 feet.

a. **Making a Table** Make a table showing the vertical distance that the incline moves for each 50 feet of horizontal distance during its climb. How high is the incline at the top?

b. **Drawing a Graph** Write a fraction that represents the slope of the incline's climb path. Draw a graph to show the climb path.

c. **Comparing Slopes** The Burgenstock Incline in Switzerland moves about 144 vertical feet for every 271 horizontal feet. Write a fraction to represent the slope of this incline's path. Which incline is steeper, the *Burgenstock* or the *Duquesne*?

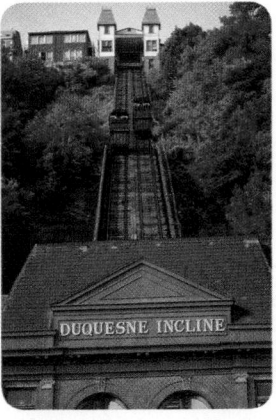

DUQUESNE INCLINE

38. PROVING THEOREM 3.7 Use slopes of lines to write a paragraph proof of the Transitive Property of Parallel Lines on page 164.

AVERAGE RATE OF CHANGE In Exercises 39 and 40, slope can be used to describe an *average rate of change*. To write an average rate of change, rewrite the slope fraction so the denominator is one.

39. BUSINESS In 2000, a business made a profit of $8500. In 2006, the business made a profit of $15,400. Find the average rate of change in dollars per year from 2000 to 2006.

40. ROCK CLIMBING A rock climber begins climbing at a point 400 feet above sea level. It takes the climber 45 minutes to climb to the destination, which is 706 feet above sea level. Find the average rate of change in feet per minute for the climber from start to finish.

41. ★ **EXTENDED RESPONSE** The line graph shows the regular season attendance (in millions) for three professional sports organizations from 1985 to 2000.

a. During which five-year period did the NBA attendance increase the most? Estimate the rate of change for this five-year period in people per year.

b. During which five-year period did the NHL attendance increase the most? Estimate the rate of change for this five-year period in people per year.

c. Interpret The line graph for the NFL seems to be almost linear between 1985 and 2000. Write a sentence about what this means in terms of the real-world situation.

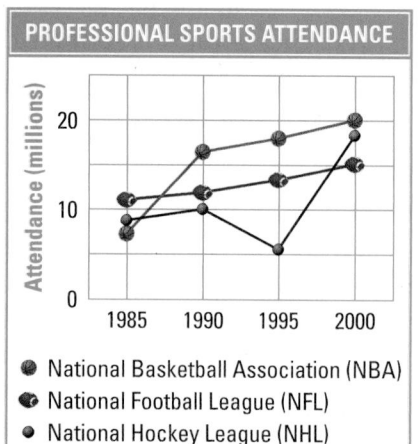

42. CHALLENGE Find two values of k such that the points $(-3, 1)$, $(0, k)$, and $(k, 5)$ are collinear. *Explain* your reasoning.

MIXED REVIEW

43. Is the point $(-1, -7)$ on the line $y = 2x - 5$? *Explain.* **(p. 878)**

44. Find the intercepts of the graph of $y = -3x + 9$. **(p. 879)**

Use the diagram to write two examples of each postulate. (p. 96)

45. Through any two points there exists exactly one line.

46. Through any three noncollinear points there exists exactly one plane.

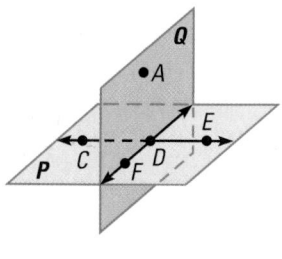

PREVIEW
Prepare for
Lesson 3.5 in
Exs. 47–49.

Solve the equation for y. Write a reason for each step. (p. 105)

47. $6x + 4y = 40$

48. $\frac{1}{2}x - \frac{5}{4}y = -10$

49. $16 - 3y = 24x$

QUIZ *for Lessons 3.3–3.4*

Find the value of x that makes $m \parallel n$. (p. 161)

1.

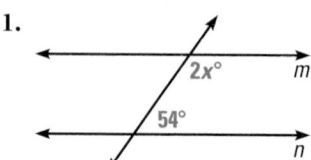

2.

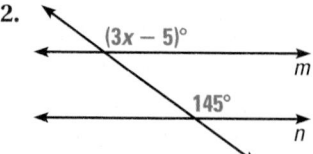

3.

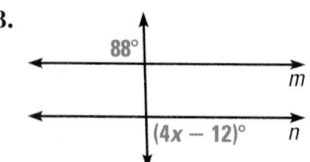

Find the slope of the line that passes through the given points. (p. 171)

4. $(1, -1)$, $(3, 3)$

5. $(1, 2)$, $(4, 5)$

6. $(-3, -2)$, $(-7, -6)$

3.4 Investigate Slopes

MATERIALS • graphing calculator or computer

QUESTION How can you verify the Slopes of Parallel Lines Postulate?

You can verify the postulates you learned in Lesson 3.4 using geometry drawing software.

EXAMPLE Verify the Slopes of Parallel Lines Postulate

STEP 1 *Show axes* Show the *x*-axis and the *y*-axis by choosing Hide/Show Axes from the F5 menu.

STEP 2 *Draw line* Draw a line by choosing Line from the F2 menu. Do not use one of the axes as your line. Choose a point on the line and label it *A*.

STEP 3 *Graph point* Graph a point not on the line by choosing Point from the F2 menu.

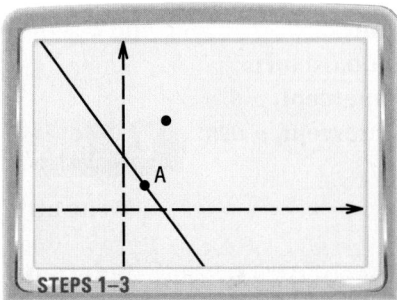

STEPS 1–3

STEP 4 *Draw parallel line* Choose Parallel from the F3 menu and select the line. Then select the point not on the line.

STEP 5 *Measure slopes* Select one line and choose Measure Slope from the F5 menu. Repeat this step for the second line.

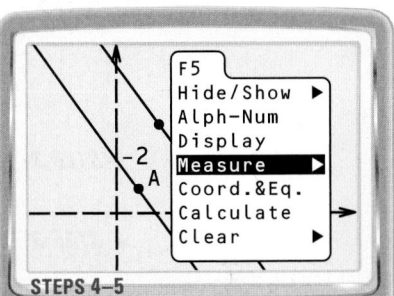

STEPS 4–5

STEP 6 *Move line* Drag point *A* to move the line. What do you expect to happen?

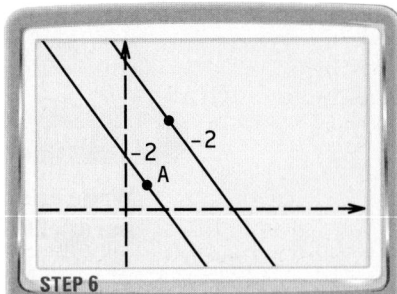

STEP 6

PRACTICE

1. Use geometry drawing software to verify the Slopes of Perpendicular Lines Postulate.

   a. Construct a line and a point not on that line. Use Steps 1–3 from the Example above.

   b. Construct a line that is perpendicular to your original line and passes through the given point.

   c. Measure the slopes of the two lines. Multiply the slopes. What do you expect the product of the slopes to be?

2. **WRITING** Use the arrow keys to move your line from Exercise 1. *Describe* what happens to the product of the slopes when one of the lines is vertical. *Explain* why this happens.

3.5 Write and Graph Equations of Lines

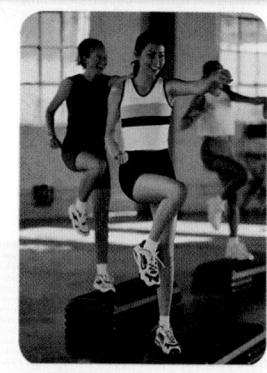

Before You found slopes of lines.

Now You will find equations of lines.

Why? So you can find monthly gym costs, as in Example 4.

Key Vocabulary
- **slope-intercept form**
- **standard form**
- *x*-intercept, *p. 879*
- *y*-intercept, *p. 879*

Linear equations may be written in different forms. The general form of a linear equation in **slope-intercept form** is $y = mx + b$, where m is the slope and b is the *y*-intercept.

EXAMPLE 1 **Write an equation of a line from a graph**

Write an equation of the line in slope-intercept form.

Solution

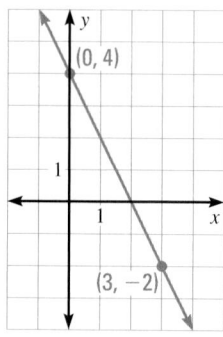

STEP 1 **Find** the slope. Choose two points on the graph of the line, $(0, 4)$ and $(3, -2)$.

$$m = \frac{4 - (-2)}{0 - 3} = \frac{6}{-3} = -2$$

STEP 2 **Find** the *y*-intercept. The line intersects the *y*-axis at the point $(0, 4)$, so the *y*-intercept is **4**.

STEP 3 **Write** the equation.

$y = mx + b$ Use slope-intercept form.

$y = -2x + 4$ Substitute –2 for *m* and 4 for *b*.

EXAMPLE 2 **Write an equation of a parallel line**

Write an equation of the line passing through the point $(-1, 1)$ that is parallel to the line with the equation $y = 2x - 3$.

Solution

STEP 1 **Find** the slope *m*. The slope of a line parallel to $y = 2x - 3$ is the same as the given line, so the slope is 2.

LINEAR EQUATIONS
The graph of a linear equation represents all the solutions of the equation. So, the given point must be a solution of the equation.

STEP 2 **Find** the *y*-intercept *b* by using $m = 2$ and $(x, y) = (-1, 1)$.

$y = mx + b$ Use slope-intercept form.

$1 = 2(-1) + b$ Substitute for *x, y,* and *m*.

$3 = b$ Solve for *b*.

▶ Because $m = 2$ and $b = 3$, an equation of the line is $y = 2x + 3$.

CHECKING BY GRAPHING You can check that equations are correct by graphing. In Example 2, you can use a graph to check that $y = 2x - 3$ is parallel to $y = 2x + 3$.

Animated **Geometry** at classzone.com

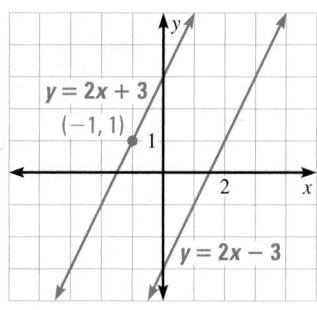

EXAMPLE 3 Write an equation of a perpendicular line

Write an equation of the line j passing through the point $(2, 3)$ that is perpendicular to the line k with the equation $y = -2x + 2$.

Solution

STEP 1 Find the slope m of line j. Line k has a slope of -2.

$-2 \cdot m = -1$ The product of the slopes of $\perp$ lines is -1.

$m = \dfrac{1}{2}$ Divide each side by -2.

STEP 2 Find the y-intercept b by using $m = \dfrac{1}{2}$ and $(x, y) = (2, 3)$.

$y = mx + b$ Use slope-intercept form.

$3 = \dfrac{1}{2}(2) + b$ Substitute for x, y, and m.

$2 = b$ Solve for b.

▶ Because $m = \dfrac{1}{2}$ and $b = 2$, an equation of line j is $y = \dfrac{1}{2}x + 2$. You can check that the lines j and k are perpendicular by graphing, then using a protractor to measure one of the angles formed by the lines.

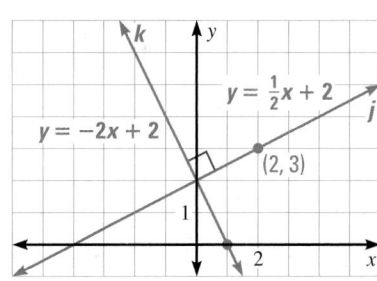

✔ **GUIDED PRACTICE** for Examples 1, 2, and 3

1. Write an equation of the line in the graph at the right.

2. Write an equation of the line that passes through $(-2, 5)$ and $(1, 2)$.

3. Write an equation of the line that passes through the point $(1, 5)$ and is parallel to the line with the equation $y = 3x - 5$. Graph the lines to check that they are parallel.

4. How do you know the lines $x = 4$ and $y = 2$ are perpendicular?

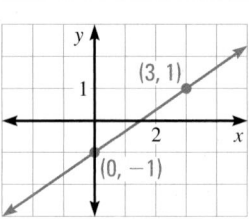

EXAMPLE 4 Write an equation of a line from a graph

GYM MEMBERSHIP The graph models the total cost of joining a gym. Write an equation of the line. Explain the meaning of the slope and the *y*-intercept of the line.

Gym Membership Cost

Solution

STEP 1 **Find** the slope.

$$m = \frac{363 - 231}{5 - 2} = \frac{132}{3} = 44$$

STEP 2 **Find** the *y*-intercept. Use the slope and one of the points on the graph.

$y = mx + b$ **Use slope-intercept form.**

$231 = 44 \cdot 2 + b$ **Substitute for *x, y,* and *m*.**

$143 = b$ **Simplify.**

STEP 3 **Write** the equation. Because $m = 44$ and $b = 143$, an equation of the line is $y = 44x + 143$.

▶ The equation $y = 44x + 143$ models the cost. The slope is the monthly fee, $44, and the *y*-intercept is the initial cost to join the gym, $143.

STANDARD FORM Another form of a linear equation is *standard form*. In **standard form**, the equation is written as $Ax + By = C$, where A and B are not both zero.

EXAMPLE 5 Graph a line with equation in standard form

Graph $3x + 4y = 12$.

Solution

CHOOSE A METHOD
Another way you could graph the equation is to solve the equation for *y*. Then the equation will be in slope-intercept form. Use rise and run from the point where the line crosses the *y*-axis to find a second point. Then graph the line.

The equation is in standard form, so you can use the intercepts.

STEP 1 **Find** the intercepts.

To find the *x*-intercept, let $y = 0$.   To find the *y*-intercept, let $x = 0$.

$3x + 4y = 12$ $3x + 4y = 12$

$3x + 4(0) = 12$ $3(0) + 4y = 12$

$x = 4$ $y = 3$

STEP 2 **Graph** the line.

The line intersects the axes at $(4, 0)$ and $(0, 3)$. Graph these points, then draw a line through the points.

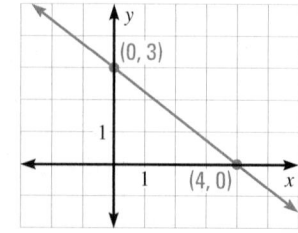

5. The equation $y = 50x + 125$ models the total cost of joining a climbing gym. What are the meaning of the slope and the y-intercept of the line?

Graph the equation.

6. $2x - 3y = 6$ **7.** $y = 4$ **8.** $x = -3$

WRITING EQUATIONS You can write linear equations to model real-world situations, such as comparing costs to find a better buy.

EXAMPLE 6   **Solve a real-world problem**

DVD RENTAL You can rent DVDs at a local store for $4.00 each. An Internet company offers a flat fee of $15.00 per month for as many rentals as you want. How many DVDs do you need to rent to make the online rental a better buy?

ANOTHER WAY

For alternative methods for solving the problem in Example 6, turn to page 188 for the **Problem Solving Workshop**.

Solution

STEP 1   **Model** each rental with an equation.

Cost of one month's rental online: $y = 15$

Cost of one month's rental locally: $y = 4x$, where x represents the number of DVDs rented

STEP 2   **Graph** each equation.

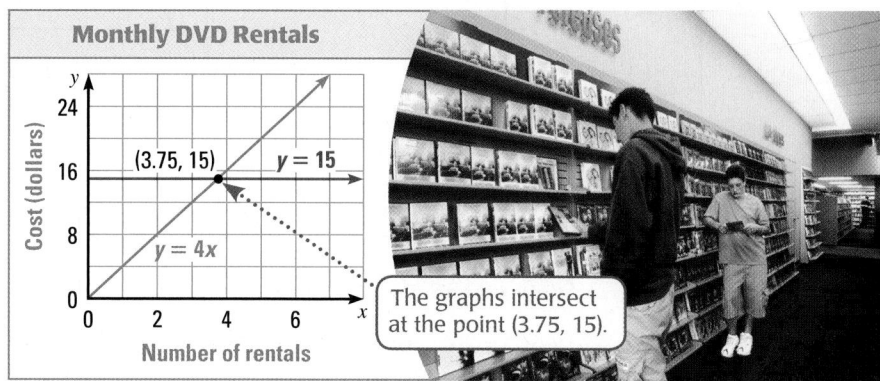

READ VOCABULARY

The point at which the costs are the same is sometimes called the *break-even point*.

▶ The point of intersection is (3.75, 15). Using the graph, you can see that it is cheaper to rent locally if you rent 3 or fewer DVDs per month. If you rent 4 or more DVDs per month, it is cheaper to rent online.

 GUIDED PRACTICE   for Example 6

9. WHAT IF? In Example 6, suppose the online rental is $16.50 per month and the local rental is $4 each. How many DVDs do you need to rent to make the online rental a better buy?

10. How would your answer to Exercise 9 change if you had a 2-for-1 coupon that you could use once at the local store?

3.5 EXERCISES

SKILL PRACTICE

1. **VOCABULARY** What does *intercept* mean in the expression *slope-intercept form*?

2. ★ **WRITING** Explain how you can use the standard form of a linear equation to find the intercepts of a line.

EXAMPLE 1
on p. 180
for Exs. 3–22

WRITING EQUATIONS Write an equation of the line shown.

$y = \frac{4}{3}x - 4$

3.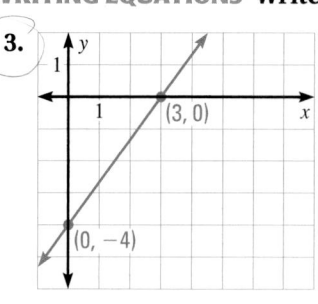

4.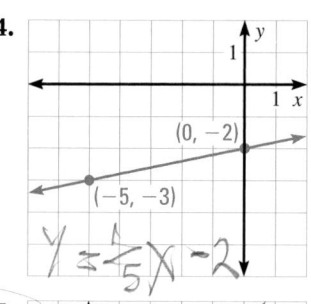

$y = -\frac{1}{5}x - 2$

5.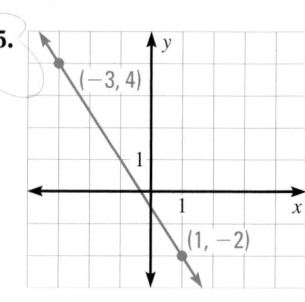

6.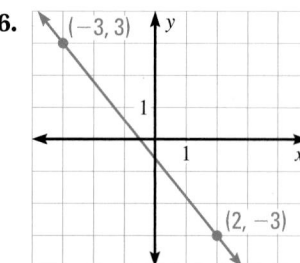

7.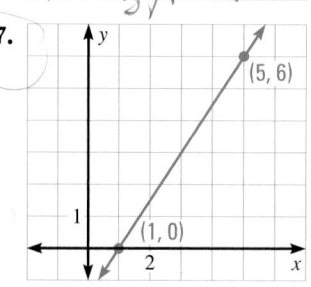

8.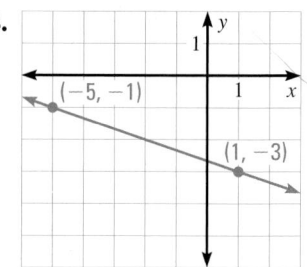

9. ★ **MULTIPLE CHOICE** Which equation is an equation of the line in the graph?

  (A) $y = -\frac{1}{2}x$ **(B)** $y = -\frac{1}{2}x + 1$

  (C) $y = -2x$ **(D)** $y = -2x + 1$

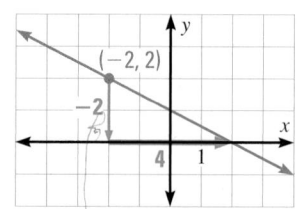

WRITING EQUATIONS Write an equation of the line with the given slope *m* and *y*-intercept *b*.

10. $m = -5, b = -12$ 11. $m = 3, b = 2$ 12. $m = 4, b = -6$

13. $m = -\frac{5}{2}, b = 0$ 14. $m = \frac{4}{9}, b = -\frac{2}{9}$ 15. $m = -\frac{11}{5}, b = -12$

WRITING EQUATIONS Write an equation of the line that passes through the given point *P* and has the given slope *m*.

$y = x + 1$

$y = 4x - 16$ $y = 3x - 20$

16. $P(-1, 0), m = -1$ 17. $P(5, 4), m = 4$ 18. $P(6, -2), m = 3$

19. $P(-8, -2), m = -\frac{2}{3}$ 20. $P(0, -3), m = -\frac{1}{6}$ 21. $P(-13, 7), m = 0$

22. **WRITING EQUATIONS** Write an equation of a line with undefined slope that passes through the point $(3, -2)$.

EXAMPLE 2
on p. 180
for Exs. 23–29

PARALLEL LINES Write an equation of the line that passes through point *P* and is parallel to the line with the given equation.

(23.) $P(0, -1)$, $y = -2x + 3$ **24.** $P(-7, -4)$, $y = 16$ **25.** $P(3, 8)$, $y - 1 = \frac{1}{5}(x + 4)$

26. $P(-2, 6)$, $x = -5$ **27.** $P(-2, 1)$, $10x + 4y = -8$ **28.** $P(4, 0)$, $-x + 2y = 12$

29. ★ **MULTIPLE CHOICE** Line *a* passes through points $(-2, 1)$ and $(2, 9)$. Which equation is an equation of a line parallel to line *a*?

   A $y = -2x + 5$ **B** $y = -\frac{1}{2}x + 5$ **C** $y = \frac{1}{2}x - 5$ **D** $y = 2x - 5$

EXAMPLE 3
on p. 181
for Exs. 30–35

PERPENDICULAR LINES Write an equation of the line that passes through point *P* and is perpendicular to the line with the given equation.

30. $P(0, 0)$, $y = -9x - 1$ **31.** $P(-1, 1)$, $y = \frac{7}{3}x + 10$ **32.** $P(4, -6)$, $y = -3$

33. $P(2, 3)$, $y - 4 = -2(x + 3)$ **34.** $P(0, -5)$, $x = 20$ **35.** $P(-8, 0)$, $3x - 5y = 6$

EXAMPLE 5
on p. 182
for Exs. 36–45

GRAPHING EQUATIONS Graph the equation.

36. $8x + 2y = -10$ **37.** $x + y = 1$ **38.** $4x - y = -8$

39. $-x + 3y = -9$ **40.** $y - 2 = -1$ **41.** $y + 2 = x - 1$

42. $x + 3 = -4$ **43.** $2y - 4 = -x + 1$ **44.** $3(x - 2) = -y - 4$

45. ERROR ANALYSIS *Describe* and correct the error in finding the *x*- and *y*-intercepts of the graph of $5x - 3y = -15$.

> To find the x-intercept,
> let x = 0:
> $$5x - 3y = -15$$
> $$5(0) - 3y = -15$$
> $$y = 5$$
>
> To find the y-intercept,
> let y = 0:
> $$5x - 3y = -15$$
> $$5x - 3(0) = -15$$
> $$x = -3$$

IDENTIFYING PARALLEL LINES Which lines are parallel, if any?

46. $y = 3x - 4$
$x + 3y = 6$
$3(x + 1) = y - 2$

47. $x + 2y = 9$
$y = 0.5x + 7$
$-x + 2y = -5$

48. $x - 6y = 10$
$6x - y = 11$
$x + 6y = 12$

USING INTERCEPTS Identify the *x*- and *y*-intercepts of the line. Use the intercepts to write an equation of the line.

49.

50.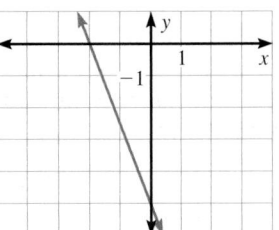

51.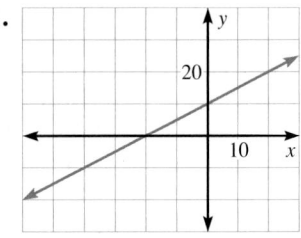

52. INTERCEPTS A line passes through the points $(-10, -3)$ and $(6, 1)$. Where does the line intersect the *x*-axis? Where does the line intersect the *y*-axis?

SOLUTIONS TO EQUATIONS **Graph the linear equations. Then use the graph to estimate how many solutions the equations share.**

53. $y = 4x + 9$
  $4x - y = 1$

54. $3y + 4x = 16$
  $2x - y = 18$

55. $y = -5x + 6$
  $10x + 2y = 12$

56. **xy ALGEBRA** Solve Exercises 53–55 algebraically. (For help, see Skills Review Handbook, p. 880.) Make a conjecture about how the solution(s) can tell you whether the lines intersect, are parallel, or are the same line.

57. **xy ALGEBRA** Find a value for k so that the line through $(-1, k)$ and $(-7, -2)$ is parallel to the line with equation $y = x + 1$.

58. **xy ALGEBRA** Find a value for k so that the line through $(k, 2)$ and $(7, 0)$ is perpendicular to the line with equation $y = x - \dfrac{28}{5}$.

59. **CHALLENGE** Graph the points $R(-7, -3)$, $S(-2, 3)$, and $T(10, -7)$. Connect them to make $\triangle RST$. Write an equation of the line containing each side. *Explain* how you can use slopes to show that $\triangle RST$ has one right angle.

PROBLEM SOLVING

EXAMPLE 4
on p. 182
for Exs. 60–61

60. **WEB HOSTING** The graph models the total cost of using a web hosting service for several months. Write an equation of the line. Tell what the slope and y-intercept mean in this situation. Then find the total cost of using the web hosting service for one year.

@HomeTutor for problem solving help at classzone.com

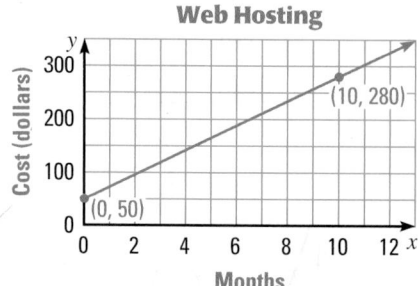

61. **SCIENCE** Scientists believe that a Tyrannosaurus Rex weighed about 2000 kilograms by age 14. It then had a growth spurt for four years, gaining 2.1 kilograms per day. Write an equation to model this situation. What are the slope and y-intercept? Tell what the slope and y-intercept mean in this situation.

@HomeTutor for problem solving help at classzone.com

Field Museum, Chicago, Illinois

EXAMPLE 6
on p. 183
for Exs. 62–65

62. **MULTI-STEP PROBLEM** A national park has two options: a $50 pass for all admissions during the year, or a $4 entrance fee each time you enter.

  a. Model Write an equation to model the cost of going to the park for a year using a pass and another equation for paying a fee each time.

  b. Graph Graph both equations you wrote in part (a).

  c. Interpret How many visits do you need to make for the pass to be cheaper? *Explain.*

○ = **WORKED-OUT SOLUTIONS**
   on p. WS1

★ = **STANDARDIZED**
   TEST PRACTICE

63. PIZZA COSTS You are buying slices of pizza for you and your friends. A small slice costs $2 and a large slice costs $3. You have $24 to spend. Write an equation in standard form $Ax + By = C$ that models this situation. What do the values of A, B, and C mean in this situation?

64. ★ **SHORT RESPONSE** You run at a rate of 4 miles per hour and your friend runs at a rate of 3.5 miles per hour. Your friend starts running 10 minutes before you, and you run for a half hour on the same path. Will you catch up to your friend? Use a graph to support your answer.

65. ★ **EXTENDED RESPONSE** Audrey and Sara are making jewelry. Audrey buys 2 bags of beads and 1 package of clasps for a total of $13. Sara buys 5 bags of beads and 2 packages of clasps for a total of $27.50.

a. Let b be the price of one bag of beads and let c be the price of one package of clasps. Write equations to represent the total cost for Audrey and the total cost for Sara.

b. Graph the equations from part (a).

c. *Explain* the meaning of the intersection of the two lines in terms of the real-world situation.

66. CHALLENGE Michael is deciding which gym membership to buy. Points (2, 112) and (4, 174) give the cost of gym membership at one gym after two and four months. Points (1, 62) and (3, 102) give the cost of gym membership at a second gym after one and three months. Write equations to model the cost of each gym membership. At what point do the graphs intersect, if they intersect? Which gym is cheaper? *Explain*.

MIXED REVIEW

PREVIEW
Prepare for
Lesson 3.6
in Exs. 67–69.

Find the length of each segment. Round to the nearest tenth of a unit. *(p. 15)*

67.
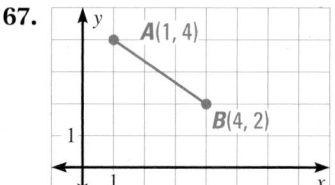

68.
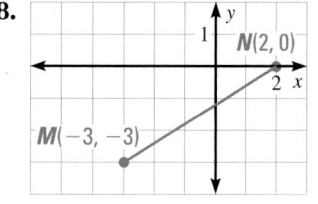

69.
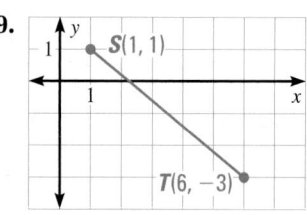

Describe **the pattern in the numbers. Write the next number in the pattern.** *(p. 72)*

70. $-2, -7, -12, -17, \ldots$ **71.** $4, 8, 16, 32, \ldots$ **72.** $101, 98, 95, 92, \ldots$

Find $m\angle 1$ **and** $m\angle 2$. *Explain* **your reasoning.** *(p. 154)*

73.

74.
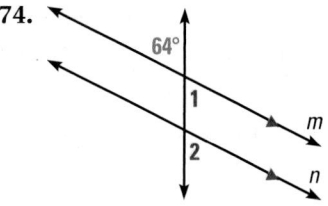

75.
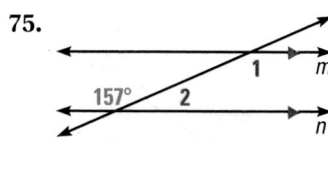

Using **ALTERNATIVE METHODS**

Another Way to Solve Example 6, page 183

MULTIPLE REPRESENTATIONS In Example 6 on page 183, you saw how to graph equations to solve a problem about renting DVDs. Another way you can solve the problem is *using a table*. Alternatively, you can use the equations to solve the problem *algebraically*.

PROBLEM

> **DVD RENTAL** You can rent DVDs at a local store for $4.00 each. An Internet company offers a flat fee of $15.00 per month for as many rentals as you want. How many DVDs do you need to rent to make the online rental a better buy?

METHOD 1   **Using a Table** You can make a table to answer the question.

STEP 1 **Make** a table representing each rental option.

DVDs rented	Renting locally	Renting online
1	$4	$15
2	$8	$15

STEP 2 **Add** rows to your table until you see a pattern.

DVDs rented	Renting locally	Renting online
1	$4	$15
2	$8	$15
3	$12	$15
4	$16	$15
5	$20	$15
6	$24	$15

STEP 3 **Analyze** the table. Notice that the values in the second column (the cost of renting locally) are less than the values in the third column (the cost of renting online) for three or fewer DVDs. However, the values in the second column are greater than those in the third column for four or more DVDs.

▶ It is cheaper to rent locally if you rent 3 or fewer DVDs per month. If you rent 4 or more DVDs per month, it is cheaper to rent online.

METHOD 2 **Using Algebra** You can solve one of the equations for one of its variables. Then substitute that expression for the variable in the other equation.

STEP 1 **Write** an equation for each rental option.

Cost of one month's rental online: $y = 15$

Cost of one month's rental locally: $y = 4x$, where x represents the number of DVDs rented

STEP 2 **Substitute** the value of y from one equation into the other equation.

$y = 4x$

$15 = 4x$ **Substitute 15 for y.**

$3.75 = x$ **Divide each side by 4.**

STEP 3 **Analyze** the solution of the equation. If you could rent 3.75 DVDs, your cost for local and online rentals would be the same. However, you can only rent a whole number of DVDs. Look at what happens when you rent 3 DVDs and when you rent 4 DVDs, the whole numbers just less than and just greater than 3.75.

▶ It is cheaper to rent locally if you rent 3 or fewer DVDs per month. If you rent 4 or more DVDs per month, it is cheaper to rent online.

PRACTICE

1. **IN-LINE SKATES** You can rent in-line skates for $5 per hour, or buy a pair of skates for $130. How many hours do you need to skate for the cost of buying skates to be cheaper than renting them?

2. **WHAT IF?** Suppose the in-line skates in Exercise 1 also rent for $12 per day. How many days do you need to skate for the cost of buying skates to be cheaper than renting them?

3. **BUTTONS** You buy a button machine for $200 and supplies to make one hundred fifty buttons for $30. Suppose you charge $2 for a button. How many buttons do you need to sell to earn back what you spent?

4. **MANUFACTURING** A company buys a new widget machine for $1200. It costs $5 to make each widget. The company sells each widget for $15. How many widgets do they need to sell to earn back the money they spent on the machine?

5. **WRITING** Which method(s) did you use to solve Exercises 1–4? *Explain* your choice(s).

6. **MONEY** You saved $1000. If you put this money in a savings account, it will earn 1.5% annual interest. If you put the $1000 in a certificate of deposit (CD), it will earn 3% annual interest. To earn the most money, does it ever make sense to put your money in the savings account? *Explain.*

3.6 Prove Theorems About Perpendicular Lines

Before You found the distance between points in the coordinate plane.

Now You will find the distance between a point and a line.

Why? So you can determine lengths in art, as in Example 4.

Key Vocabulary
• distance from a point to a line

ACTIVITY FOLD PERPENDICULAR LINES

Materials: paper, protractor

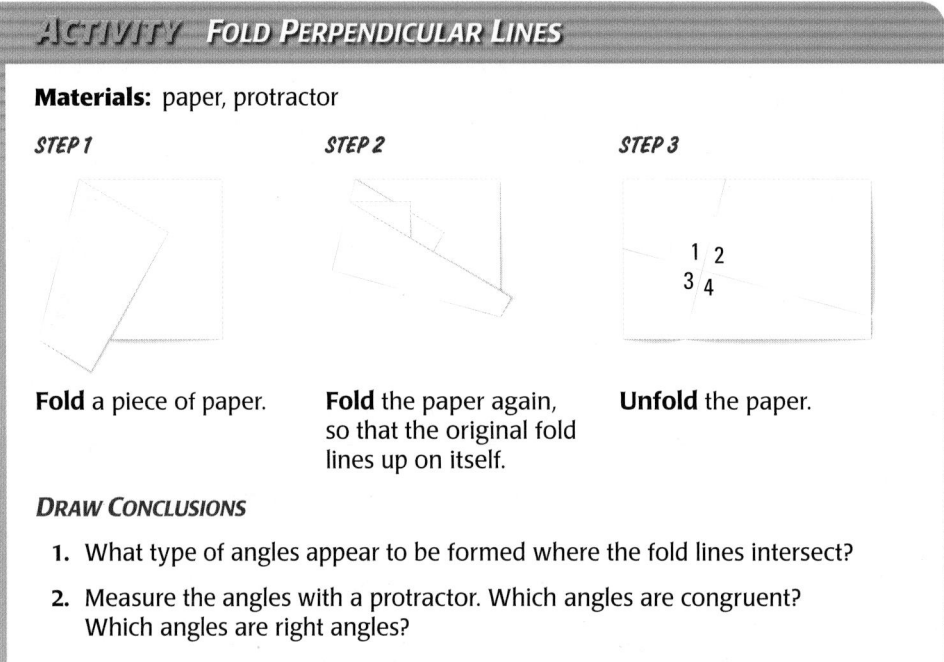

STEP 1

Fold a piece of paper.

STEP 2

Fold the paper again, so that the original fold lines up on itself.

STEP 3

1 2
3 4

Unfold the paper.

DRAW CONCLUSIONS

1. What type of angles appear to be formed where the fold lines intersect?

2. Measure the angles with a protractor. Which angles are congruent? Which angles are right angles?

The activity above suggests several properties of perpendicular lines.

THEOREMS *For Your Notebook*

THEOREM 3.8

If two lines intersect to form a linear pair of congruent angles, then the lines are perpendicular.

If $\angle 1 \cong \angle 2$, then $g \perp h$.

Proof: Ex. 31, p. 196

THEOREM 3.9

If two lines are perpendicular, then they intersect to form four right angles.

If $a \perp b$, then $\angle 1$, $\angle 2$, $\angle 3$, and $\angle 4$ are right angles.

Proof: Ex. 32, p. 196

EXAMPLE 1 **Draw conclusions**

In the diagram at the right, $\overleftrightarrow{AB} \perp \overleftrightarrow{BC}$. What can you conclude about $\angle 1$ and $\angle 2$?

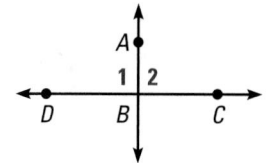

Solution

$\overleftrightarrow{AB}$ and $\overleftrightarrow{BC}$ are perpendicular, so by Theorem 3.9, they form four right angles. You can conclude that $\angle 1$ and $\angle 2$ are right angles, so $\angle 1 \cong \angle 2$.

THEOREM *For Your Notebook*

THEOREM 3.10

If two sides of two adjacent acute angles are perpendicular, then the angles are complementary.

If $\overrightarrow{BA} \perp \overrightarrow{BC}$, then $\angle 1$ and $\angle 2$ are complementary.

Proof: Example 2, below

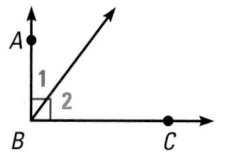

EXAMPLE 2 **Prove Theorem 3.10**

Prove that if two sides of two adjacent acute angles are perpendicular, then the angles are complementary.

GIVEN ▶ $\overrightarrow{ED} \perp \overrightarrow{EF}$

PROVE ▶ $\angle 7$ and $\angle 8$ are complementary.

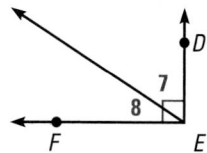

STATEMENTS	REASONS
1. $\overrightarrow{ED} \perp \overrightarrow{EF}$	1. Given
2. $\angle DEF$ is a right angle.	2. $\perp$ lines intersect to form 4 rt. $\angle$s. (Theorem 3.9)
3. $m\angle DEF = 90°$	3. Definition of a right angle
4. $m\angle 7 + m\angle 8 = m\angle DEF$	4. Angle Addition Postulate
5. $m\angle 7 + m\angle 8 = 90°$	5. Substitution Property of Equality
6. $\angle 7$ and $\angle 8$ are complementary.	6. Definition of complementary angles

---

✓ **GUIDED PRACTICE** for Examples 1 and 2

1. Given that $\angle ABC \cong \angle ABD$, what can you conclude about $\angle 3$ and $\angle 4$? *Explain* how you know.

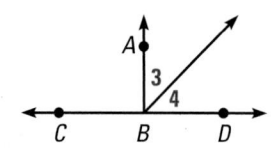

2. Write a plan for proof for Theorem 3.9, that if two lines are perpendicular, then they intersect to form four right angles.

THEOREM 3.11 Perpendicular Transversal Theorem

If a transversal is perpendicular to one of two parallel lines, then it is perpendicular to the other.

If $h \parallel k$ and $j \perp h$, then $j \perp k$.

Proof: Ex. 42, p. 160; Ex. 33, p. 196

THEOREM 3.12 Lines Perpendicular to a Transversal Theorem

In a plane, if two lines are perpendicular to the same line, then they are parallel to each other.

If $m \perp p$ and $n \perp p$, then $m \parallel n$.

Proof: Ex. 34, p. 196

EXAMPLE 3   **Draw conclusions**

Determine which lines, if any, must be parallel in the diagram. Explain your reasoning.

Solution

Lines p and q are both perpendicular to s, so by Theorem 3.12, $p \parallel q$. Also, lines s and t are both perpendicular to q, so by Theorem 3.12, $s \parallel t$.

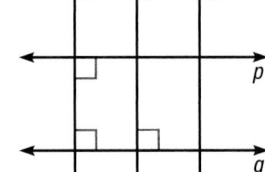

✔ **GUIDED PRACTICE**   for Example 3

Use the diagram at the right.

3. Is $b \parallel a$? *Explain* your reasoning.

4. Is $b \perp c$? *Explain* your reasoning.

DISTANCE FROM A LINE The **distance from a point to a line** is the length of the perpendicular segment from the point to the line. This perpendicular segment is the shortest distance between the point and the line. For example, the distance between point A and line k is AB. You will prove this in Chapter 5.

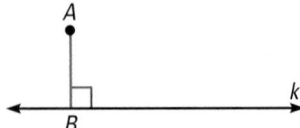

Distance from a point to a line

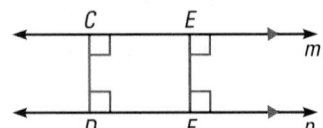

Distance between two parallel lines

The *distance between two parallel lines* is the length of any perpendicular segment joining the two lines. For example, the distance between line p and line m above is CD or EF.

EXAMPLE 4 **Find the distance between two parallel lines**

SCULPTURE The sculpture below is drawn on a graph where units are measured in inches. What is the approximate length of $\overline{SR}$, the depth of a seat?

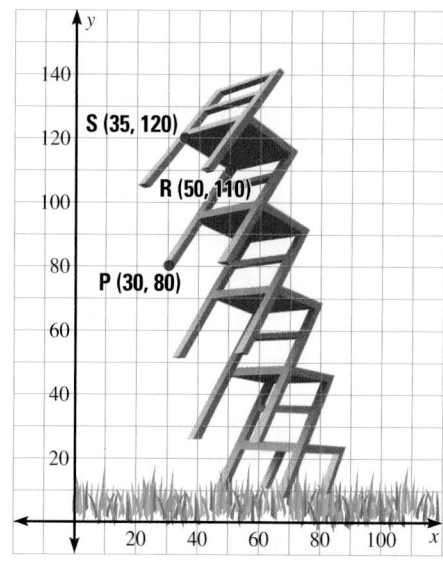

Solution

You need to find the length of a perpendicular segment from a back leg to a front leg on one side of the chair.

Using the points $P(30, 80)$ and $R(50, 110)$, the slope of each leg is

$$\frac{110 - 80}{50 - 30} = \frac{30}{20} = \frac{3}{2}.$$

The segment SR has a slope of

$$\frac{120 - 110}{35 - 50} = -\frac{10}{15} = -\frac{2}{3}.$$

The segment $\overline{SR}$ is perpendicular to the leg so the distance SR is

$$d = \sqrt{(35 - 50)^2 + (120 - 110)^2} \approx 18.0 \text{ inches}.$$

▶ The length of $\overline{SR}$ is about 18.0 inches.

✔ **GUIDED PRACTICE** **for Example 4**

Use the graph at the right for Exercises 5 and 6.

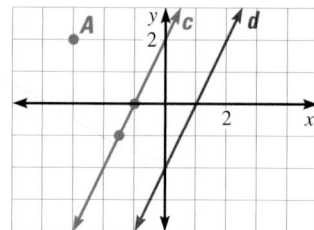

5. What is the distance from point A to line c?

6. What is the distance from line c to line d?

7. Graph the line $y = x + 1$. What point on the line is the shortest distance from the point $(4, 1)$? What is the distance? Round to the nearest tenth.

3.6 EXERCISES

HOMEWORK KEY

◯ = **WORKED-OUT SOLUTIONS**
on p. WS4 for Exs. 19, 23, and 29

★ = **STANDARDIZED TEST PRACTICE**
Exs. 11, 12, 21, 22, and 30

SKILL PRACTICE

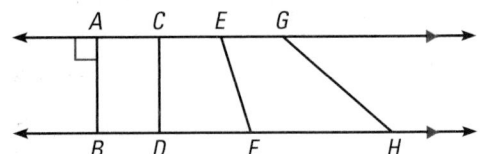

1. **VOCABULARY** The length of which segment shown is called the distance between the two parallel lines? *Explain.*

EXAMPLES 1 and 2
on p. 191
for Exs. 2–7

JUSTIFYING STATEMENTS Write the theorem that justifies the statement.

2. $j \perp k$

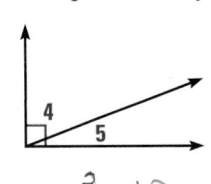

3. $\angle 4$ and $\angle 5$ are complementary.

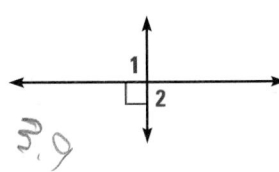

4. $\angle 1$ and $\angle 2$ are right angles.

APPLYING THEOREMS Find $m\angle 1$.

5.

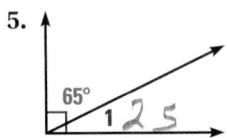

6.

7.

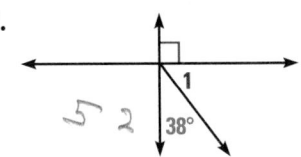

EXAMPLE 3
on p. 192
for Exs. 8–12

SHOWING LINES PARALLEL *Explain* how you would show that $m \parallel n$.

8.

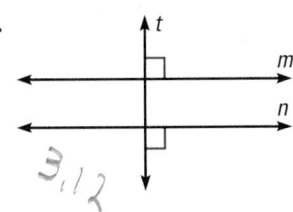

9.

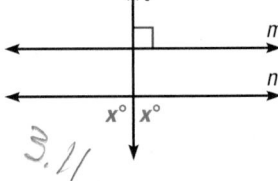

10.

11. ★ **SHORT RESPONSE** *Explain* how to draw two parallel lines using only a straightedge and a protractor.

12. ★ **SHORT RESPONSE** *Describe* how you can fold a sheet of paper to create two parallel lines that are perpendicular to the same line.

EXAMPLES 3 and 4
on pp. 192–193
for Exs. 13–14

ERROR ANALYSIS *Explain* why the statement about the figure is incorrect.

13.

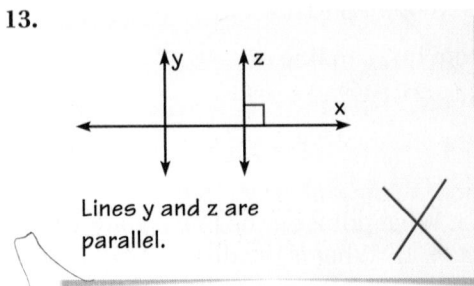

Lines y and z are parallel.

14.

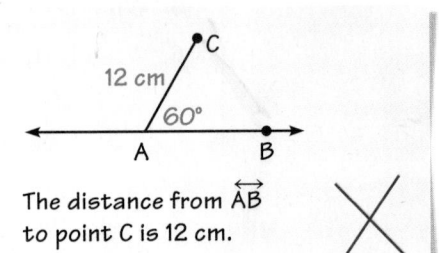

The distance from $\overleftrightarrow{AB}$ to point C is 12 cm.

FINDING ANGLE MEASURES In the diagram, $\overleftrightarrow{FG} \perp \overleftrightarrow{GH}$. Find the value of x.

15.

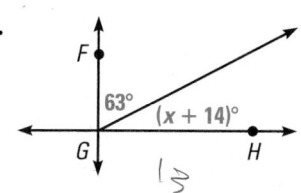

16.

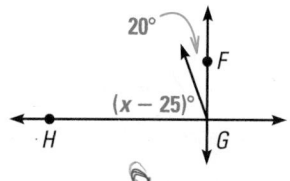

17.

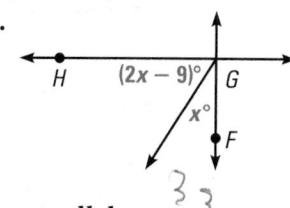

DRAWING CONCLUSIONS Determine which lines, if any, must be parallel. *Explain* your reasoning.

18.

(19.)

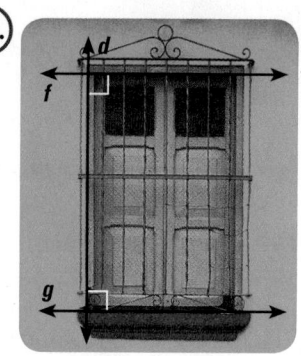

20.

21. ★ MULTIPLE CHOICE Which statement must be true if $c \perp d$?

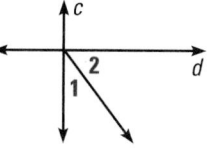

A $m\angle 1 + m\angle 2 = 90°$ **B** $m\angle 1 + m\angle 2 < 90°$

C $m\angle 1 + m\angle 2 > 90°$ **D** Cannot be determined

22. ★ WRITING *Explain* why the distance between two lines is only defined for parallel lines.

EXAMPLE 4 on p. 193 for Exs. 23–24

FINDING DISTANCES Use the Distance Formula to find the distance between the two parallel lines. Round to the nearest tenth, if necessary.

(23.)

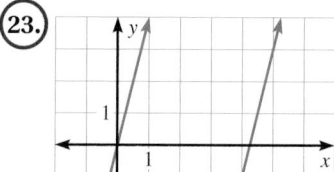

24.

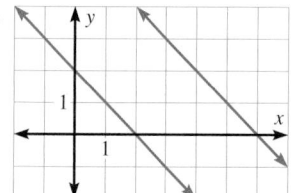

25. CONSTRUCTION You are given a line n and a point P not on n. Use a compass to find two points on n equidistant from P. Then use the steps for the construction of a segment bisector (page 33) to construct a line perpendicular to n through P.

26. FINDING ANGLES Find all the unknown angle measures in the diagram at the right. *Justify* your reasoning for each angle measure.

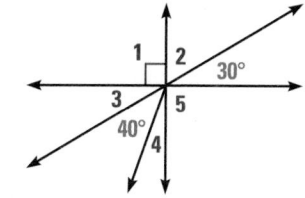

27. FINDING DISTANCES Find the distance between the lines with the equations $y = \frac{3}{2}x + 4$ and $-3x + 2y = -1$.

28. CHALLENGE *Describe* how you would find the distance from a point to a plane. Can you find the distance from a line to a plane? *Explain*.

29. **STREAMS** You are trying to cross a stream from point *A*. Which point should you jump to in order to jump the shortest distance? *Explain.*

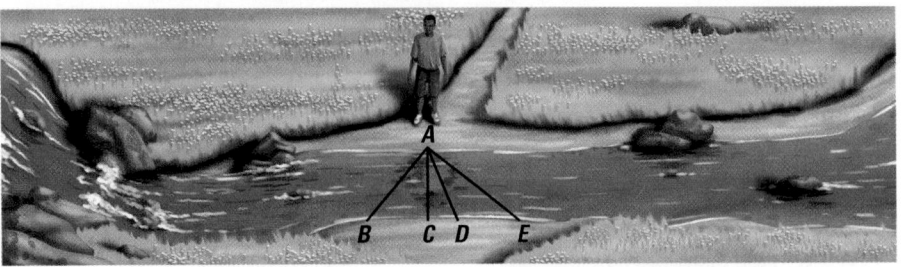

@HomeTutor for problem solving help at classzone.com

30. ★ **SHORT RESPONSE** The segments that form the path of a crosswalk are usually perpendicular to the crosswalk. Sketch what the segments would look like if they were perpendicular to the crosswalk. Which method requires less paint? *Explain.*

@HomeTutor for problem solving help at classzone.com

EXAMPLE 2
on p. 191
for Exs. 31–34

31. **PROVING THEOREM 3.8** Copy and complete the proof that if two lines intersect to form a linear pair of congruent angles, then the lines are perpendicular.

GIVEN ▶ ∠1 and ∠2 are a linear pair.
∠1 ≅ ∠2

PROVE ▶ $g \perp h$

STATEMENTS	REASONS
1. ∠1 and ∠2 are a linear pair.	1. Given
2. ∠1 and ∠2 are supplementary.	2. ?
3. ?	3. Definition of supplementary angles
4. ∠1 ≅ ∠2	4. Given
5. $m\angle 1 = m\angle 2$	5. ?
6. $m\angle 1 + m\angle 1 = 180°$	6. Substitution Property of Equality
7. $2(m\angle 1) = 180°$	7. Combine like terms.
8. $m\angle 1 = 90°$	8. ?
9. ?	9. Definition of a right angle
10. $g \perp h$	10. ?

PROVING THEOREMS Write a proof of the given theorem.

32. Theorem 3.9

33. Theorem 3.11, Perpendicular Transversal Theorem

34. Theorem 3.12, Lines Perpendicular to a Transversal Theorem

CHALLENGE Suppose the given statement is true. Determine whether $\overrightarrow{AB} \perp \overrightarrow{AC}$.

35. $\angle 1$ and $\angle 2$ are congruent.

36. $\angle 3$ and $\angle 4$ are complementary.

37. $m\angle 1 = m\angle 3$ and $m\angle 2 = m\angle 4$

38. $m\angle 1 = 40°$ and $m\angle 4 = 50°$

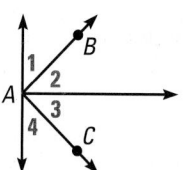

MIXED REVIEW

PREVIEW
Prepare for
Lesson 4.1
in Exs. 39–41.

Find the value of *x*. *(p. 24)*

39.

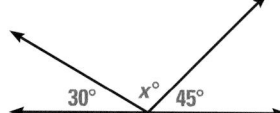

40.

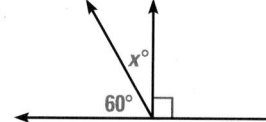

41.

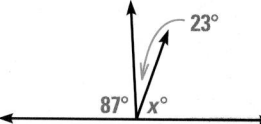

Find the circumference and area of the circle. Round to the nearest tenth.
(p. 49)

42.

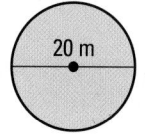

43.

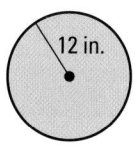

44.

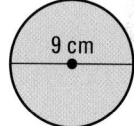

Find the value of *x* that makes $m \parallel n$. *(p. 161)*

45.

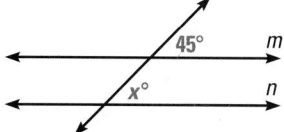

46.

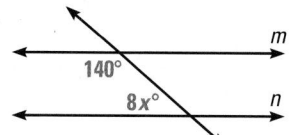

47.

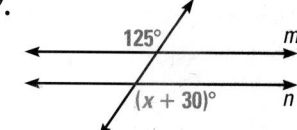

QUIZ *for Lessons 3.5–3.6*

Write an equation of the line that passes through point *P* and is parallel to the line with the given equation. *(p. 180)*

1. $P(0, 0)$, $y = -3x + 1$ **2.** $P(-5, -6)$, $y - 8 = 2x + 10$ **3.** $P(1, -2)$, $x = 15$

Write an equation of the line that passes through point *P* and is perpendicular to the line with the given equation. *(p. 180)*

4. $P(3, 4)$, $y = 2x - 1$ **5.** $P(2, 5)$, $y = -6$ **6.** $P(4, 0)$, $12x + 3y = 9$

Determine which lines, if any, must be parallel. *Explain.* *(p. 190)*

7.

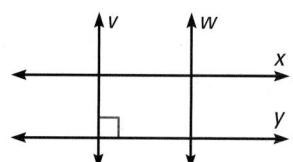

8.

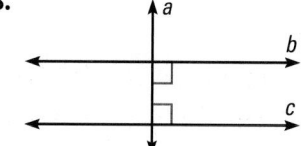

9.

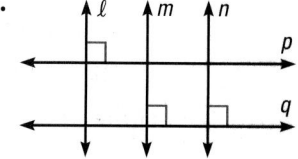

Taxicab Geometry

GOAL Find distances in a non-Euclidean geometry.

Key Vocabulary
• taxicab geometry

You have learned that the shortest distance between two points is the length of the straight line segment between them. This is true in the *Euclidean* geometry that you are studying. But think about what happens when you are in a city and want to get from point *A* to point *B*. You cannot walk through the buildings, so you have to go along the streets.

HISTORY NOTE
Euclidean geometry is named after a Greek mathematician. Euclid (circa third century B.C.) used postulates and deductive reasoning to prove the theorems you are studying in this book.
Non-Euclidean geometries start by assuming different postulates, so they result in different theorems.

Taxicab geometry is the non-Euclidean geometry that a taxicab or a pedestrian must obey.

In taxicab geometry, you can travel either horizontally or vertically parallel to the axes. In this geometry, the distance between two points is the shortest number of *blocks* between them.

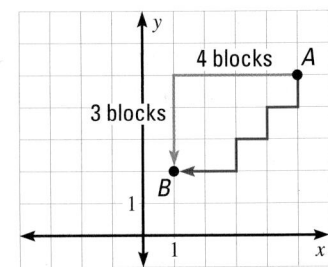

KEY CONCEPT
For Your Notebook

Taxicab Distance

The distance between two points is the sum of the differences in their coordinates.

$$AB = |x_2 - x_1| + |y_2 - y_1|$$

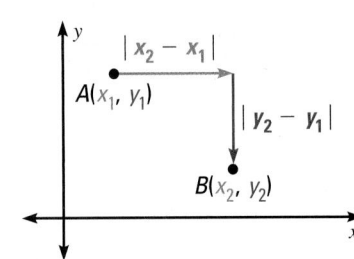

EXAMPLE 1 **Find a taxicab distance**

Find the taxicab distance from *A*(−1, 5) to *B*(4, 2). Draw two different shortest paths from *A* to *B*.

Solution

$$AB = |x_2 - x_1| + |y_2 - y_1|$$
$$= |4 - (-1)| + |2 - 5|$$
$$= |5| + |-3|$$
$$= 8$$

▶ The shortest path is 8 blocks. Two possible paths are shown.

REVIEW ABSOLUTE VALUE
For help with absolute value, see p. 870.

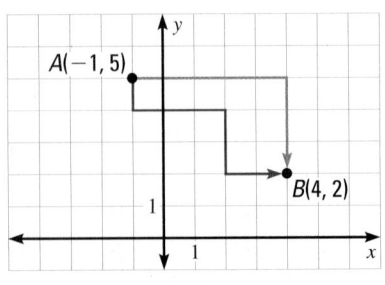

CIRCLES In Euclidean geometry, a *circle* is all points that are the same distance from a fixed point, called the *center*. That distance is the *radius*. Taxicab geometry uses the same definition for a circle, but taxicab circles are not round.

EXAMPLE 2 Draw a taxicab circle

Draw the taxicab circle with the given radius *r* and center *C*.

a. *r* = 2, *C*(1, 3)

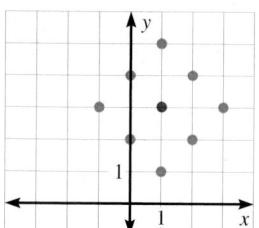

b. *r* = 1, *C*(−2, −4)

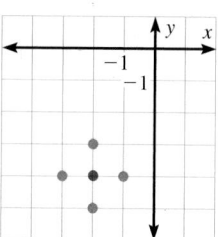

PRACTICE

EXAMPLE 1
on p. 198
for Exs. 1–6

FINDING DISTANCE Find the taxicab distance between the points.

1. (4, 2), (0, 0)

2. (3, 5), (6, 2)

3. (−6, 3), (8, 5)

4. (−1, −3), (5, −2)

5. (−3, 5), (−1, 5)

6. (−7, 3), (−7, −4)

EXAMPLE 2
on p. 199
for Exs. 7–9

DRAWING CIRCLES Draw the taxicab circle with radius *r* and center *C*.

7. *r* = 2, *C*(3, 4)

8. *r* = 4, *C*(0, 0)

9. *r* = 5, *C*(−1, 3)

FINDING MIDPOINTS A *midpoint* in taxicab geometry is a point where the distances to the endpoints are equal. Find all the midpoints of $\overline{AB}$.

10. *A*(2, 4), *B*(−2, −2)

11. *A*(1, −3), *B*(1, 3)

12. *A*(2, 2), *B*(−3, 0)

13. TRAVEL PLANNING A hotel's website claims that the hotel is an easy walk to a number of sites of interest. What are the coordinates of the hotel?

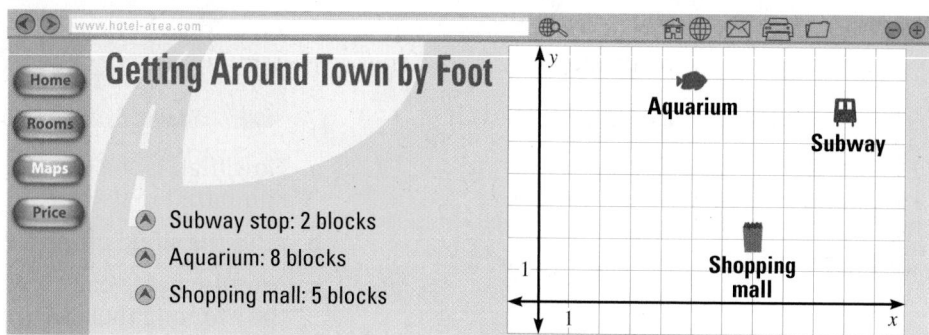

14. REASONING The taxicab distance between two points is always greater than or equal to the Euclidean distance between the two points. *Explain* what must be true about the points for both distances to be equal.

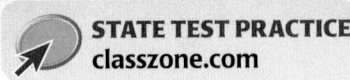
Lessons 3.4–3.6

1. MULTI-STEP PROBLEM You are planning a party. You would like to have the party at a roller skating rink or bowling alley. The table shows the total cost to rent the facilities by number of hours.

Hours	Roller skating rink cost ($)	Bowling alley cost ($)
1	35	20
2	70	40
3	105	60
4	140	80
5	175	100

  a. Use the data in the table. Write and graph two equations to represent the total cost y to rent the facilities, where x is the number of hours you rent the facility.

  b. Are the lines from part (a) parallel? *Explain* why or why not.

  c. What is the meaning of the slope in each equation from part (a)?

  d. Suppose the bowling alley charges an extra $25 set-up fee. Write and graph an equation to represent this situation. Is this line parallel to either of the lines from part (a)? *Explain* why or why not.

2. GRIDDED ANSWER The graph models the accumulated cost of buying a used guitar and taking lessons over the first several months. Find the slope of the line.

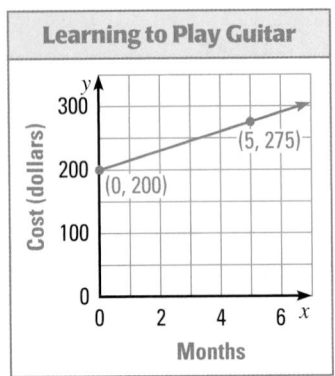

Learning to Play Guitar

(graph: Cost (dollars) vs. Months, with points (0, 200) and (5, 275))

3. OPEN-ENDED Write an equation of a line parallel to $2x + 3y = 6$. Then write an equation of a line perpendicular to your line.

4. SHORT RESPONSE You are walking across a field to get to a hiking path. Use the graph below to find the shortest distance you can walk to reach the path. *Explain* how you know you have the shortest distance.

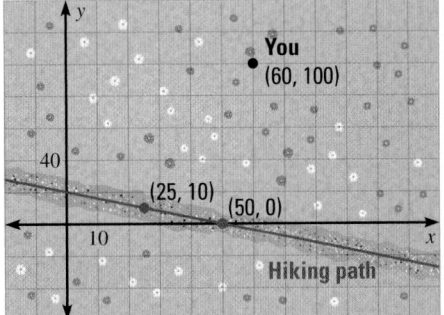

(graph: You (60, 100), (25, 10), (50, 0), Hiking path)

5. EXTENDED RESPONSE The Johnstown Inclined Plane in Johnstown, Pennsylvania, is a cable car that transports people up and down the side of a hill. During the cable car's climb, you move about 17 feet upward for every 25 feet you move forward. At the top of the incline, the horizontal distance from where you started is about 500 feet.

  a. How high is the car at the top of its climb compared to its starting height?

  b. Find the slope of the climb.

  c. Another cable car incline in Pennsylvania, the Monongahela Incline, climbs at a slope of about 0.7 for a horizontal distance of about 517 feet. *Compare* this climb to that of the Johnstown Inclined Plane. Which is steeper? *Justify* your answer.

BIG IDEAS
For Your Notebook

Big Idea ①

Using Properties of Parallel and Perpendicular Lines

When parallel lines are cut by a transversal, angle pairs are formed. Perpendicular lines form congruent right angles.

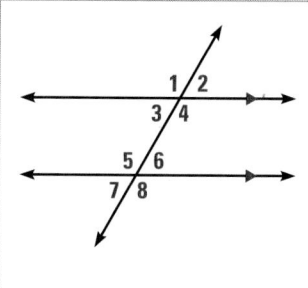

∠2 and ∠6 are corresponding angles, and they are congruent.

∠3 and ∠6 are alternate interior angles, and they are congruent.

∠1 and ∠8 are alternate exterior angles, and they are congruent.

∠3 and ∠5 are consecutive interior angles, and they are supplementary.

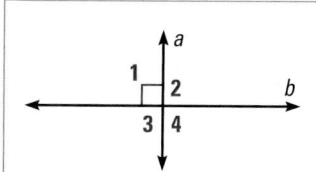

If $a \perp b$, then ∠1, ∠2, ∠3, and ∠4 are all right angles.

Big Idea ②

Proving Relationships Using Angle Measures

You can use the angle pairs formed by lines and a transversal to show that the lines are parallel. Also, if lines intersect to form a right angle, you know that the lines are perpendicular.

Through point A not on line q, there is only one line r parallel to q and one line s perpendicular to q.

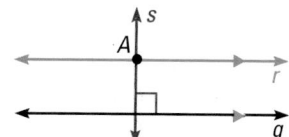

Big Idea ③

Making Connections to Lines in Algebra

In Algebra 1, you studied slope as a rate of change and linear equations as a way of modeling situations.

Slope and equations of lines are also a useful way to represent the lines and segments that you study in Geometry. For example, the slopes of parallel lines are the same ($a \parallel b$), and the product of the slopes of perpendicular lines is -1 ($a \perp c$, and $b \perp c$).

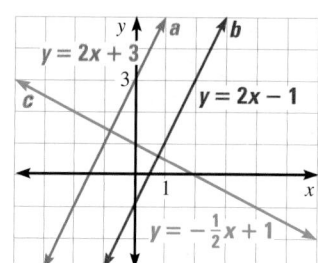

@HomeTutor

classzone.com
• Multi-Language Glossary
• Vocabulary practice

REVIEW KEY VOCABULARY

For a list of postulates and theorems, see pp. 926–931.

- parallel lines, *p. 147*
- skew lines, *p. 147*
- parallel planes, *p. 147*
- transversal, *p. 149*
- corresponding angles, *p. 149*
- alternate interior angles, *p. 149*
- alternate exterior angles, *p. 149*

- consecutive interior angles, *p. 149*
- paragraph proof, *p. 163*
- slope, *p. 171*
- slope-intercept form, *p. 180*
- standard form, *p. 182*
- distance from a point to a line, *p. 192*

VOCABULARY EXERCISES

1. Copy and complete: Two lines that do not intersect and are not coplanar are called __?__ .

2. **WRITING** *Compare* alternate interior angle pairs and consecutive interior angle pairs.

Copy and complete the statement using the figure at the right.

3. ∠1 and __?__ are corresponding angles.

4. ∠3 and __?__ are alternate interior angles.

5. ∠4 and __?__ are consecutive interior angles.

6. ∠7 and __?__ are alternate exterior angles.

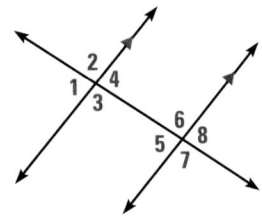

Identify the form of the equation as *slope-intercept form* or *standard form*.

7. $14x - 2y = 26$

8. $y = 7x - 13$

REVIEW EXAMPLES AND EXERCISES

Use the review examples and exercises below to check your understanding of the concepts you have learned in each lesson of Chapter 3.

3.1 Identify Pairs of Lines and Angles
pp. 147–152

EXAMPLE

Think of each segment in the rectangular box at the right as part of a line.

a. $\overleftrightarrow{BD}$, $\overleftrightarrow{AC}$, $\overleftrightarrow{BH}$, and $\overleftrightarrow{AG}$ appear perpendicular to $\overleftrightarrow{AB}$.

b. $\overleftrightarrow{CD}$, $\overleftrightarrow{GH}$, and $\overleftrightarrow{EF}$ appear parallel to $\overleftrightarrow{AB}$.

c. $\overleftrightarrow{CF}$ and $\overleftrightarrow{EG}$ appear skew to $\overleftrightarrow{AB}$.

d. Plane *EFG* appears parallel to plane *ABC*.

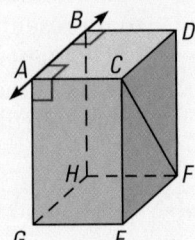

EXERCISES

EXAMPLE 1
on p. 147
for Exs. 9–12

Think of each segment in the diagram of a rectangular box as part of a line. Which line(s) or plane(s) contain point N and appear to fit the description?

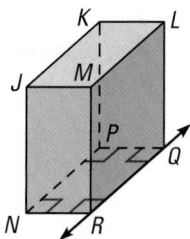

9. Line(s) perpendicular to $\overleftrightarrow{QR}$

10. Line(s) parallel to $\overleftrightarrow{QR}$

11. Line(s) skew to $\overleftrightarrow{QR}$

12. Plane(s) parallel to plane LMQ

3.2 Use Parallel Lines and Transversals
pp. 154–160

EXAMPLE

Use properties of parallel lines to find the value of x.

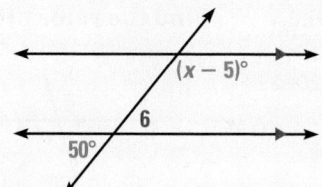

By the Vertical Angles Congruence Theorem, $m\angle 6 = 50°$.

$(x - 5)° + m\angle 6 = 180°$	**Consecutive Interior Angles Theorem**
$(x - 5)° + 50° = 180°$	**Substitute 50° for $m\angle 6$.**
$x = 135$	**Solve for x.**

EXERCISES

EXAMPLES
1 and 2
on pp. 154–155
for Exs. 13–19

Find $m\angle 1$ and $m\angle 2$. *Explain* your reasoning.

13.
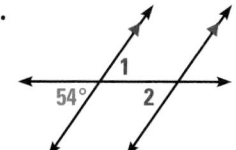

14.
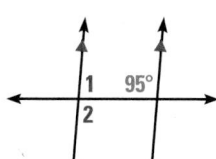

15.
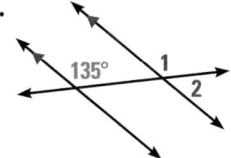

Find the values of x and y.

16.
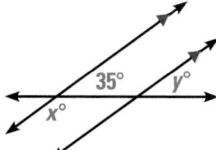

17.
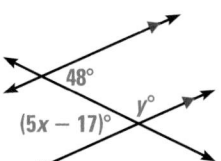

18.
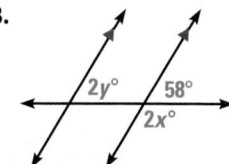

19. **FLAG OF PUERTO RICO** Sketch the rectangular flag of Puerto Rico as shown at the right. Find the measure of $\angle 1$ if $m\angle 3 = 55°$. *Justify* each step in your argument.

3.3 Prove Lines are Parallel

pp. 161–169

EXAMPLE

Find the value of *x* that makes *m* ∥ *n*.

Lines *m* and *n* are parallel when the marked corresponding angles are congruent.

$$(5x + 8)° = 53°$$
$$5x = 45$$
$$x = 9$$

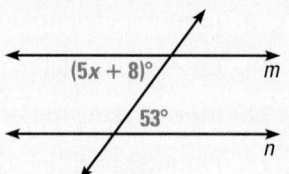

▶ The lines *m* and *n* are parallel when *x* = 9.

EXERCISES

EXAMPLE 1
on p. 161
for Exs. 20–22

Find the value of *x* that makes *m* ∥ *n*.

20.

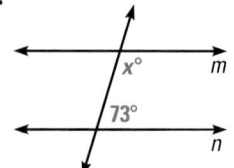

21.

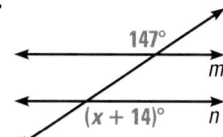

22.

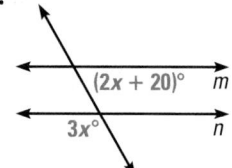

3.4 Find and Use Slopes of Lines

pp. 171–178

EXAMPLE

Find the slope of each line. Which lines are parallel?

$$\text{Slope of } \ell = \frac{-1 - 5}{-3 - (-5)} = \frac{-6}{2} = -3$$

$$\text{Slope of } m = \frac{1 - 5}{0 - (-1)} = \frac{-4}{1} = -4$$

$$\text{Slope of } n = \frac{0 - 4}{4 - 3} = \frac{-4}{1} = -4$$

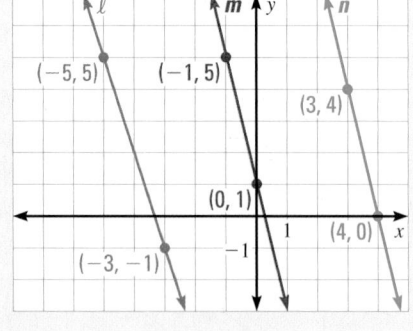

▶ Because *m* and *n* have the same slope, they are parallel. The slope of ℓ is different, so ℓ is not parallel to the other lines.

EXERCISES

EXAMPLES
2 and 3
on pp. 172–173
for Exs. 23–24

Tell whether the lines through the given points are *parallel*, *perpendicular*, or *neither*.

23. Line 1: (8, 12), (7, −5)
Line 2: (−9, 3), (8, 2)

24. Line 1: (3, −4), (−1, 4)
Line 2: (2, 7), (5, 1)

3.5 Write and Graph Equations of Lines
pp. 180–187

> **EXAMPLE**
>
> **Write an equation of the line k passing through the point $(-4, 1)$ that is perpendicular to the line n with the equation $y = 2x - 3$.**
>
> First, find the slope of line k. Line n has a slope of 2.
>
> $$2 \cdot m = -1$$
>
> $$m = -\frac{1}{2}$$
>
> Then, use the given point and the slope in the slope-intercept form to find the y-intercept.
>
> $$y = mx + b$$
>
> $$1 = -\frac{1}{2}(-4) + b$$
>
> $$-1 = b$$
>
> ▶ An equation of line k is $y = -\frac{1}{2}x - 1$.

EXERCISES

EXAMPLES
2 and 3
on pp. 180–181
for Exs. 25–26

Write equations of the lines that pass through point P and are (a) parallel and (b) perpendicular to the line with the given equation.

25. $P(3, -1)$, $y = 6x - 4$

26. $P(-6, 5)$, $7y + 4x = 2$

3.6 Prove Theorems About Perpendicular Lines
pp. 190–197

> **EXAMPLE**
>
> **Find the distance between $y = 2x + 3$ and $y = 2x + 8$.**
>
> Find the length of a perpendicular segment from one line to the other. Both lines have a slope of 2, so the slope of a perpendicular segment to each line is $-\frac{1}{2}$.
>
> The segment from $(0, 3)$ to $(-2, 4)$ has a slope of $\frac{4 - 3}{-2 - 0} = -\frac{1}{2}$. So, the distance between the lines is
>
> $$d = \sqrt{(-2 - 0)^2 + (4 - 3)^2} = \sqrt{5} \approx 2.2 \text{ units.}$$

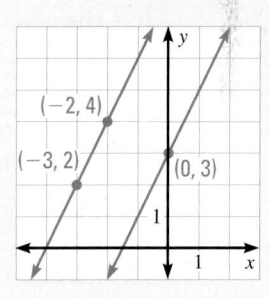

EXERCISES

EXAMPLE 4
on p. 193
for Exs. 27–28

Use the Distance Formula to find the distance between the two parallel lines. Round to the nearest tenth, if necessary.

27.

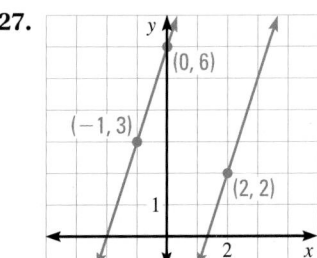

28.

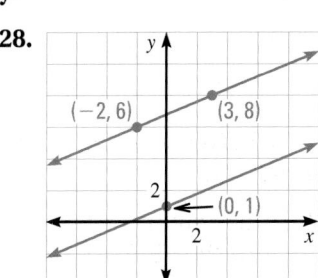

3 CHAPTER TEST

Classify the pairs of angles as *corresponding, alternate interior, alternate exterior,* or *consecutive interior.*

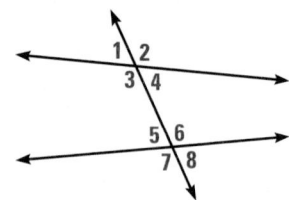

1. $\angle 1$ and $\angle 8$ **2.** $\angle 2$ and $\angle 6$ **3.** $\angle 3$ and $\angle 5$

4. $\angle 4$ and $\angle 5$ **5.** $\angle 3$ and $\angle 7$ **6.** $\angle 3$ and $\angle 6$

Find the value of *x*.

7.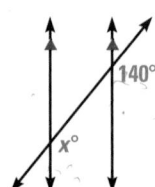

8.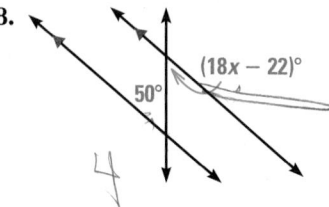

9.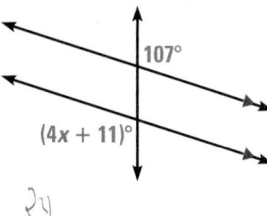

Find the value of *x* that makes $m \parallel n$.

10.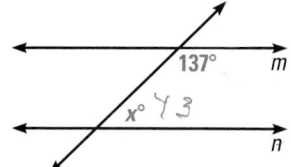

11.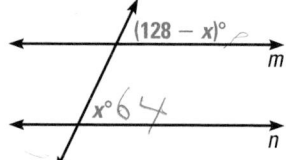

12.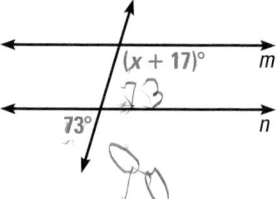

Find the slope of the line that passes through the points.

13. $(3, -1), (3, 4)$ **14.** $(2, 7), (-1, -3)$ **15.** $(0, 5), (-6, 12)$

Write an equation of the line that passes through the given point *P* and has the given slope *m*.

16. $P(-2, 4), m = 3$ **17.** $P(7, 12), m = -0.2$ **18.** $P(3, 5), m = -8$

Write an equation of the line that passes through point *P* and is perpendicular to the line with the given equation.

19. $P(1, 3), y = 2x - 1$ **20.** $P(0, 2), y = -x + 3$ **21.** $P(2, -3), x - y = 4$

In Exercises 22–24, $\overline{AB} \perp \overline{BC}$. Find the value of *x*.

22.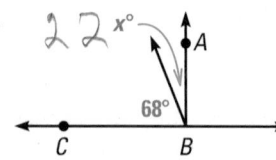

23.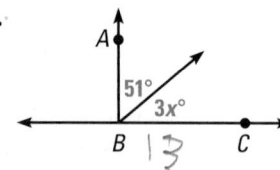

24.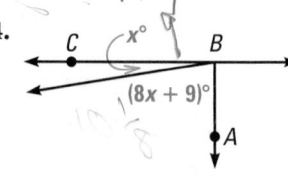

25. RENTAL COSTS The graph at the right models the cost of renting a moving van. Write an equation of the line. Then find the cost of renting the van for a 100 mile trip.

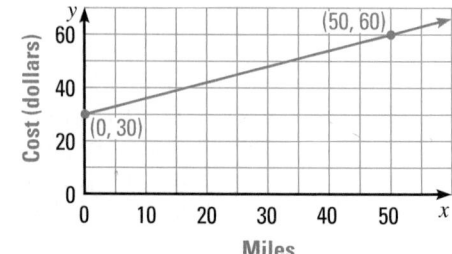

3 xy ALGEBRA REVIEW

GRAPH AND SOLVE LINEAR INEQUALITIES

xy **EXAMPLE 1** *Graph a linear inequality in two variables*

Graph the inequality $0 > 2x - 3 - y.$

Solution

Rewrite the inequality in slope-intercept form, $y > 2x - 3.$

The boundary line $y = 2x - 3$ is not part of the solution, so use a dashed line.

To decide where to shade, use a point not on the line, such as $(0, 0)$, as a test point. Because $0 > 2 \cdot 0 - 3$, $(0, 0)$ is a solution. Shade the half-plane that includes $(0, 0)$.

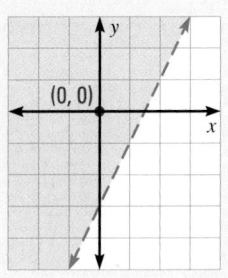

xy **EXAMPLE 2** *Use an inequality to solve a real-world problem*

SAVINGS Lily has saved $49. She plans to save $12 per week to buy a camera that costs $124. In how many weeks will she be able to buy the camera?

Solution

Let w represent the number of weeks needed.

$49 + 12w \geq 124$	**Write an algebraic model.**
$12w \geq 75$	**Subtract 49 from each side.**
$w \geq 6.25$	**Divide each side by 12.**

▶ She must save for 7 weeks to be able to buy the camera.

EXERCISES

EXAMPLE 1
for Exs. 1–8

Graph the linear inequality.

1. $y > -2x + 3$ **2.** $y \leq 0.5x - 4$ **3.** $-2.5x + y \geq 1.5$ **4.** $x < 3$

5. $y < -2$ **6.** $5x - y > -5$ **7.** $2x + 3y \geq -18$ **8.** $3x - 4y \leq 6$

EXAMPLE 2
for Exs. 9–11

Solve.

9. LOANS Eric borrowed $46 from his mother. He will pay her back at least $8 each month. At most, how many months will it take him?

10. GRADES Manuel's quiz scores in history are 76, 81, and 77. What score must he get on his fourth quiz to have an average of at least 80?

11. PHONE CALLS Company A charges a monthly fee of $5 and $.07 per minute for phone calls. Company B charges no monthly fee, but charges $.12 per minute. After how many minutes of calls is the cost of using Company A less than the cost of using Company B?

MULTIPLE CHOICE QUESTIONS

If you have difficulty solving a multiple choice problem directly, you may be able to use another approach to eliminate incorrect answer choices and obtain the correct answer.

PROBLEM 1

Which ordered pair is a solution of the equations $y = 2x - 5$ and $4x + 3y = 45$?

(A) (3, 11)   (B) (5, 5)   (C) (6, 7)   (D) (7, 6)

METHOD 1

SOLVE DIRECTLY Find the ordered pair that is the solution by using substitution.

Because the first equation is solved for y, substitute $y = 2x - 5$ into $4x + 3y = 45$.

$$4x + 3y = 45$$
$$4x + 3(2x - 5) = 45$$
$$4x + 6x - 15 = 45$$
$$10x - 15 = 45$$
$$10x = 60$$
$$x = 6$$

Solve for y by substituting 6 for x in the first equation.

$$y = 2x - 5$$
$$y = 2(6) - 5$$
$$y = 12 - 5$$
$$y = 7$$

So, the solution of the linear system is (6, 7), which is choice C. (A) (B) (C) (D)

METHOD 2

ELIMINATE CHOICES Another method is to eliminate incorrect answer choices.

Substitute choice A into the equations.

$$y = 2x - 5$$
$$11 \overset{?}{=} 2(3) - 5$$
$$11 \overset{?}{=} 6 - 5$$
$$11 \neq 1 \; ✗$$

The point is not a solution of $y = 2x - 5$, so there is no need to check the other equation. You can eliminate choice A.

Substitute choice B into the equations.

$$y = 2x - 5 \qquad\qquad 4x + 3y = 45$$
$$5 \overset{?}{=} 2(5) - 5 \qquad 4(5) + 3(5) \overset{?}{=} 45$$
$$5 \overset{?}{=} 10 - 5 \qquad\; 20 + 15 \overset{?}{=} 45$$
$$5 = 5 \; ✓ \qquad\qquad\quad 35 \neq 45 \; ✗$$

You can eliminate choice B.

Substitute choice C into the equations.

$$y = 2x - 5 \qquad\qquad 4x + 3y = 45$$
$$7 \overset{?}{=} 2(6) - 5 \qquad 4(6) + 3(7) \overset{?}{=} 45$$
$$7 \overset{?}{=} 12 - 5 \qquad\;\; 24 + 21 \overset{?}{=} 45$$
$$7 = 7 \; ✓ \qquad\qquad\quad 45 = 45 \; ✓$$

Choice C makes both equations true, so the answer is choice C. (A) (B) (C) (D)

PROBLEM 2

Which equation is an equation of the line through the point $(-1, 1)$ and perpendicular to the line through the points $(2, 4)$ and $(-4, 6)$?

A $y = -\frac{1}{3}x + \frac{2}{3}$ **B** $y = 3x + 4$

C $y = \frac{1}{3}x + \frac{4}{3}$ **D** $y = 3x - 2$

METHOD 1

SOLVE DIRECTLY Find the slope of the line through the points $(2, 4)$ and $(-4, 6)$.

$$m = \frac{6 - 4}{-4 - 2} = \frac{2}{-6} = -\frac{1}{3}$$

The slope of the line perpendicular to this line is 3, because $3 \cdot \left(-\frac{1}{3}\right) = -1$. Use $y = 3x + b$ and the point $(-1, 1)$ to find b.

$1 = 3(-1) + b$, so $b = 4$.

The equation of the line is $y = 3x + 4$. The correct answer is B. **A** **B** **C** **D**

METHOD 2

ELIMINATE CHOICES Another method to consider is to eliminate choices based on the slope, then substitute the point to find the correct equation.

$$m = \frac{6 - 4}{-4 - 2} = -\frac{1}{3}$$

The slope of the line perpendicular to this line is 3. Choices A and C do not have a slope of 3, so you can eliminate these choices. Next, try substituting the point $(-1, 1)$ into answer choice B.

$1 \stackrel{?}{=} 3(-1) + 4$ ✓

This is a true statement.

The correct answer is B. **A** **B** **C** **D**

PRACTICE

Explain why you can eliminate the highlighted answer choice.

1. Use the diagram below. Which pair of angles are alternate exterior angles?

    A 4 and 5   **B** 2 and 6

    C 1 and 8   **D** ✕ 1 and 10

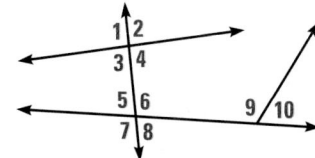

2. Which equation is an equation of the line parallel to the line through the points $(-1, 4)$ and $(1, 1)$?

    A $y = -\frac{3}{2}x - 3$ **B** $y = \frac{3}{2}x - 3$

    C ✕ $y = \frac{2}{3}x - 3$ **D** $y = 3x - 3$

MULTIPLE CHOICE

1. A line is to be drawn through point P in the graph so that it never crosses the y-axis. Through which point does it pass?

   Ⓐ $(-2, 3)$

   Ⓑ $(-3, -2)$

   Ⓒ $(3, 2)$

   Ⓓ $(-3, 2)$

   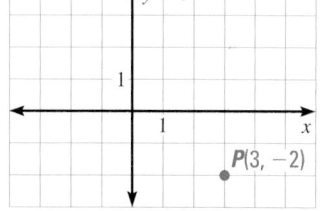

2. Which equation is an equation of a line parallel to $-2x + 3y = 15$?

   Ⓐ $y = -\frac{2}{3}x + 7$ Ⓑ $y = \frac{2}{3}x + 7$

   Ⓒ $y = -\frac{3}{2}x + 7$ Ⓓ $y = -6x + 7$

3. Two trains, E and F, travel along parallel tracks. Each track is 110 miles long. They begin their trips at the same time. Train E travels at a rate of 55 miles per hour and train F travels at a rate of 22 miles per hour. How many miles will train F have left to travel after train E completes its trip?

   Ⓐ 5 miles   Ⓑ 33 miles

   Ⓒ 60 miles   Ⓓ 66 miles

4. A line segment is parallel to the y-axis and is 9 units long. The two endpoints are $(3, 6)$ and (a, b). What is a value of b?

   Ⓐ -6 Ⓑ -3

   Ⓒ 3   Ⓓ 6

5. Which equation is an equation of a line perpendicular to $y = 5x + 7$?

   Ⓐ $y = -5x + 9$

   Ⓑ $y = 5x + 16$

   Ⓒ $y = \frac{1}{5}x + 7$

   Ⓓ $y = -\frac{1}{5}x + 7$

6. According to the graph, which is the closest approximation of the decrease in sales between week 4 and week 5?

   Ⓐ 24 DVD players

   Ⓑ 20 DVD players

   Ⓒ 18 DVD players

   Ⓓ 15 DVD players

7. In the diagram, $m \parallel n$. Which pair of angles have equal measures?

   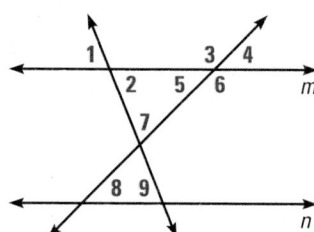

   Ⓐ $\angle 3$ and $\angle 5$ Ⓑ $\angle 4$ and $\angle 7$

   Ⓒ $\angle 1$ and $\angle 9$ Ⓓ $\angle 2$ and $\angle 6$

8. Five lines intersect as shown in the diagram. Lines a, b, and c are parallel. What is the value of $x + y$?

   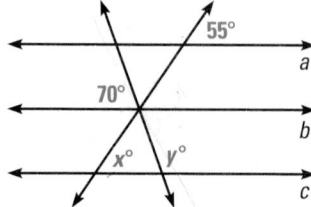

   Ⓐ 125   Ⓑ 165

   Ⓒ 195   Ⓓ 235

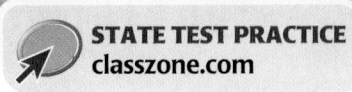
GRIDDED ANSWER

9. What is the slope of a line perpendicular to $5x - 3y = 9$?

10. What is the slope of the line passing through the points $(1, 1)$ and $(-2, -2)$?

11. What is the y-intercept of the line that is parallel to the line $2x - y = 3$ and passes through the point $(-3, 4)$?

12. What is the value of a if line j is parallel to line k?

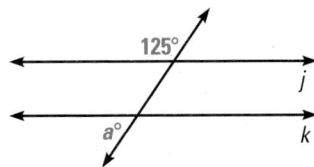

SHORT RESPONSE

13. *Explain* how you know that lines m and n are parallel to each other.

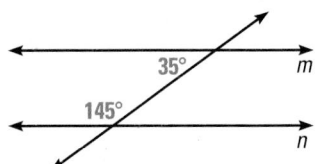

14. What is one possible value for the slope of a line passing through the point $(1, 1)$ and passing *between* the points $(-2, -2)$ and $(-2, -3)$ but not containing either one of them?

EXTENDED RESPONSE

15. Mrs. Smith needs a babysitter. Lauren who lives next door charges $5 per hour for her services. Zachary who lives across town charges $4 per hour plus $3 for bus fare.

    a. Using this information, write equations to represent Lauren and Zachary's babysitting fees. Let F represent their fees and h represent the number of hours.

    b. Graph the equations you wrote in part (a).

    c. Based on their fees, which babysitter would be a better choice for Mrs. Smith if she is going out for two hours? *Explain* your answer.

    d. Mrs. Smith needs to go out for four hours. Which babysitter would be the less expensive option for her? *Justify* your response.

16. In a game of pool, a cue ball is hit from point A and follows the path of arrows as shown on the pool table at the right. In the diagram, $\overline{AB} \parallel \overline{DC}$ and $\overline{BC} \parallel \overline{ED}$.

    a. *Compare* the slopes of $\overline{AB}$ and $\overline{BC}$. What can you conclude about $\angle ABC$?

    b. If $m\angle BCG = 45°$, what is $m\angle DCH$? *Explain* your reasoning.

    c. If the cue ball is hit harder, will it fall into Pocket F? *Justify* your answer.

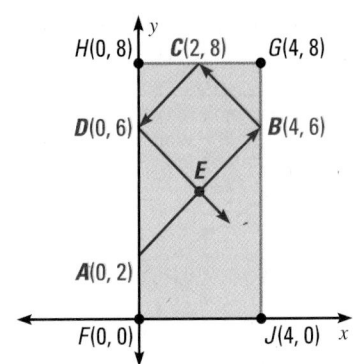

Line ℓ bisects the segment. Find the indicated lengths. *(p. 15)*

1. *GH* and *FH*

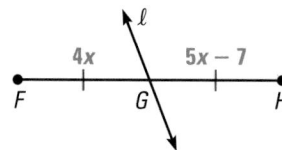

2. *XY* and *XZ*

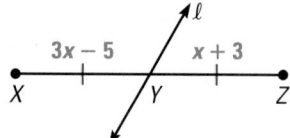

Classify the angle with the given measure as *acute, obtuse, right,* or *straight*. *(p. 24)*

3. $m\angle A = 28°$ **4.** $m\angle A = 113°$ **5.** $m\angle A = 79°$ **6.** $m\angle A = 90°$

Find the perimeter and area of the figure. *(p. 49)*

7.

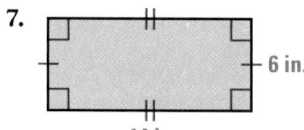

8.

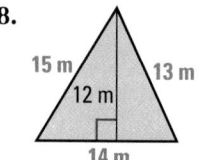

9.

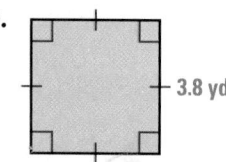

***Describe* the pattern in the numbers. Write the next number in the pattern.** *(p. 72)*

10. 1, 8, 27, 64, . . .   **11.** 128, 32, 8, 2, . . .   **12.** 2, −6, 18, −54, . . .

Use the Law of Detachment to make a valid conclusion. *(p. 87)*

13. If $6x < 42$, then $x < 7$. The value of $6x$ is 24.

14. If an angle measure is greater than 90°, then it is an obtuse angle. The measure of $\angle A$ is 103°.

15. If a musician plays a violin, then the musician plays a stringed instrument. The musician is playing a violin.

Solve the equation. Write a reason for each step. *(p. 105)*

16. $3x - 14 = 34$ **17.** $-4(x + 3) = -28$ **18.** $43 - 9(x - 7) = -x - 6$

Find the value of the variable(s). *(pp. 124, 154)*

19.

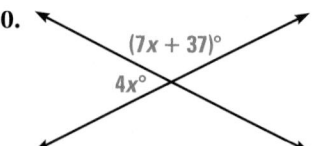

20.

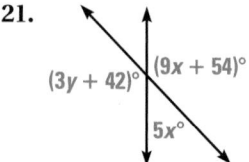

21.

22.

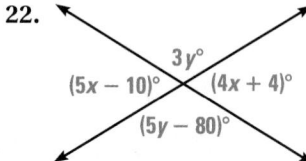

23.

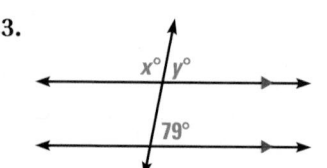

24.

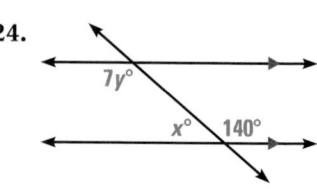

Find the slope of the line through the given points. *(p. 171)*

25. $(5, -2), (7, -2)$ **26.** $(8, 3), (3, 14)$ **27.** $(-1, 2), (0, 4)$

Write equations of the lines that pass through point *P* and are (a) parallel and (b) perpendicular to the line with the given equation. *(p. 180)*

28. $P(3, -2), y = 6x + 7$ **29.** $P(-2, 12), y = -x - 3$ **30.** $P(7, -1), 6y + 2x = 18$

31. Use the diagram at the right. If $\angle AEB \cong \angle AED$, is $\overleftrightarrow{AC} \perp \overleftrightarrow{DB}$? *Explain* how you know. *(p. 190)*

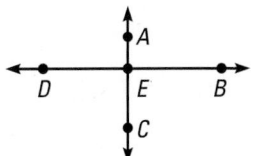

EVERYDAY INTERSECTIONS In Exercises 32–34, what kind of geometric intersection does the photograph suggest? *(p. 2)*

32.    **33.**    **34.**

35. MAPS The distance between Westville and Easton is 37 miles. The distance between Reading and Easton is 52 miles. How far is Westville from Reading? *(p. 9)*

36. GARDENING A rectangular garden is 40 feet long and 25 feet wide. What is the area of the garden? *(p. 49)*

ADVERTISING In Exercises 37 and 38, use the following advertising slogan: "Do you want the lowest prices on new televisions? Then come and see Matt's TV Warehouse." *(p. 79)*

37. Write the slogan in if-then form. What are the hypothesis and conclusion of the conditional statement?

38. Write the converse, inverse, and contrapositive of the conditional statement you wrote in Exercise 37.

39. CARPENTRY You need to cut eight wood planks that are the same size. You measure and cut the first plank. You cut the second piece using the first plank as a guide, as shown at the right. You use the second plank to cut the third plank. You continue this pattern. Is the last plank you cut the same length as the first? *Explain* your reasoning. *(p. 112)*

4 Congruent Triangles

- 4.1 **Apply Triangle Sum Properties**
- 4.2 **Apply Congruence and Triangles**
- 4.3 **Prove Triangles Congruent by SSS**
- 4.4 **Prove Triangles Congruent by SAS and HL**
- 4.5 **Prove Triangles Congruent by ASA and AAS**
- 4.6 **Use Congruent Triangles**
- 4.7 **Use Isosceles and Equilateral Triangles**
- 4.8 **Perform Congruence Transformations**

Before

In previous chapters, you learned the following skills, which you'll use in Chapter 4: classifying angles, solving linear equations, finding midpoints, and using angle relationships.

Prerequisite Skills

VOCABULARY CHECK

Classify the angle as *acute*, *obtuse*, *right*, or *straight*.

1. $m\angle A = 115°$ **2.** $m\angle B = 90°$ **3.** $m\angle C = 35°$ **4.** $m\angle D = 95°$

SKILLS AND ALGEBRA CHECK

Solve the equation. *(Review p. 65 for 4.1, 4.2.)*

5. $70 + 2y = 180$ **6.** $2x = 5x - 54$ **7.** $40 + x + 65 = 180$

Find the coordinates of the midpoint of $\overline{PQ}$. *(Review p. 15 for 4.3.)*

8. $P(2, -5), Q(-1, -2)$ **9.** $P(-4, 7), Q(1, -5)$ **10.** $P(h, k), Q(h, 0)$

Name the theorem or postulate that justifies the statement about the diagram. *(Review p. 154 for 4.3–4.5.)*

11. $\angle 2 \cong \angle 3$ **12.** $\angle 1 \cong \angle 4$

13. $\angle 2 \cong \angle 6$ **14.** $\angle 3 \cong \angle 5$

@HomeTutor Prerequisite skills practice at classzone.com

In Chapter 4, you will apply the big ideas listed below and reviewed in the Chapter Summary on page 281. You will also use the key vocabulary listed below.

Big Ideas

1. **Classifying triangles by sides and angles**
2. **Proving that triangles are congruent**
3. **Using coordinate geometry to investigate triangle relationships**

KEY VOCABULARY

- triangle, *p. 217*
  scalene, isosceles, equilateral, acute, right, obtuse, equiangular
- interior angles, *p. 218*
- exterior angles, *p. 218*

- corollary, *p. 220*
- congruent figures, *p. 225*
- corresponding parts, *p. 225*
- right triangle, *p. 241*
  legs, hypotenuse
- flow proof, *p. 250*

- isosceles triangle, *p. 264*
  legs, vertex angle, base, base angles
- transformation, *p. 272*
  translation, reflection, rotation

Why?

Triangles are used to add strength to structures in real-world situations. For example, the frame of a hang glider involves several triangles.

Animated Geometry

The animation illustrated below for Example 1 on page 256 helps you answer this question: What must be true about $\overline{QT}$ and $\overline{ST}$ for the hang glider to fly straight?

You will use congruent segments and angles in the hang glider to write a proof.

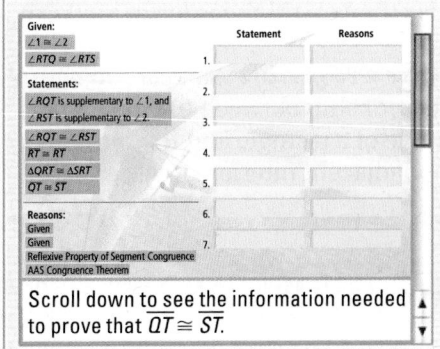

Scroll down to see the information needed to prove that $\overline{QT} \cong \overline{ST}$.

Animated Geometry at classzone.com

Other animations for Chapter 4: pages 234, 242, 250, 257, and 274

4.1 Angle Sums in Triangles

MATERIALS · paper · pencil · scissors · ruler

QUESTION What are some relationships among the *interior angles* of a triangle and *exterior angles* of a triangle?

EXPLORE 1 Find the sum of the measures of interior angles

STEP 1 *Draw triangles* Draw and cut out several different triangles.

STEP 2 *Tear off corners* For each triangle, tear off the three corners and place them next to each other, as shown in the diagram.

STEP 3 *Make a conjecture* Make a conjecture about the sum of the measures of the interior angles of a triangle.

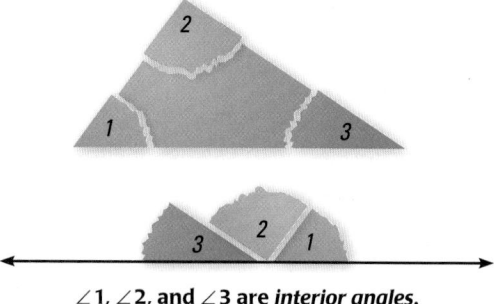

∠1, ∠2, and ∠3 are *interior angles*.

EXPLORE 2 Find the measure of an exterior angle of a triangle

STEP 1 *Draw exterior angle* Draw and cut out several different triangles. Place each triangle on a piece of paper and extend one side to form an *exterior angle*, as shown in the diagram.

STEP 2 *Tear off corners* For each triangle, tear off the corners that are not next to the exterior angle. Use them to fill the exterior angle, as shown.

STEP 3 *Make a conjecture* Make a conjecture about the relationship between the measure of an exterior angle of a triangle and the measures of the nonadjacent interior angles.

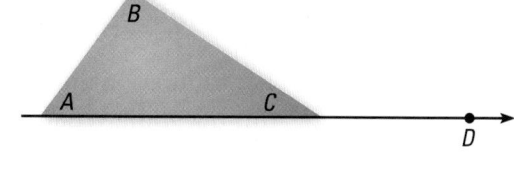

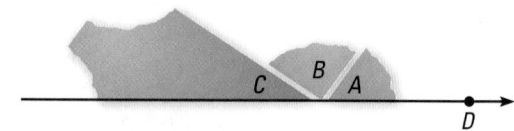

In the top figure, ∠*BCD* is an *exterior angle*.

DRAW CONCLUSIONS Use your observations to complete these exercises

1. Given the measures of two interior angles of a triangle, how can you find the measure of the third angle?

2. Draw several different triangles that each have one right angle. Show that the two acute angles of a right triangle are complementary.

4.1 Apply Triangle Sum Properties

Before You classified angles and found their measures.

Now You will classify triangles and find measures of their angles.

Why? So you can place actors on stage, as in Ex. 40.

Key Vocabulary
- **triangle**
  scalene, isosceles, equilateral, acute, right, obtuse, equiangular
- **interior angles**
- **exterior angles**
- **corollary to a theorem**

A **triangle** is a polygon with three sides. A triangle with vertices A, B, and C is called "triangle ABC" or "$\triangle ABC$."

KEY CONCEPT *For Your Notebook*

Classifying Triangles by Sides

Scalene Triangle	**Isosceles Triangle**	**Equilateral Triangle**
No congruent sides	At least 2 congruent sides	3 congruent sides

Classifying Triangles by Angles

Acute Triangle	**Right Triangle**	**Obtuse Triangle**	**Equiangular Triangle**
3 acute angles	1 right angle	1 obtuse angle	3 congruent angles

---

READ VOCABULARY

Notice that an equilateral triangle is also isosceles. An equiangular triangle is also acute.

EXAMPLE 1 Classify triangles by sides and by angles

SUPPORT BEAMS Classify the triangular shape of the support beams in the diagram by its sides and by measuring its angles.

Solution

The triangle has a pair of congruent sides, so it is isosceles. By measuring, the angles are 55°, 55°, and 70°. It is an acute isosceles triangle.

EXAMPLE 2 **Classify a triangle in a coordinate plane**

Classify △*PQO* by its sides. Then determine if the triangle is a right triangle.

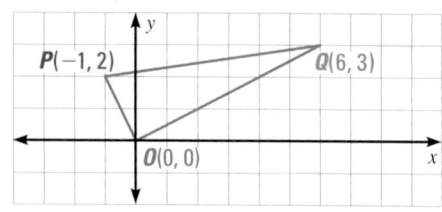

Solution

STEP 1 **Use** the distance formula to find the side lengths.

$$OP = \sqrt{(x_2 - x_1)^2 + (y_2 - y_1)^2} = \sqrt{((-1) - 0)^2 + (2 - 0)^2} = \sqrt{5} \approx 2.2$$

$$OQ = \sqrt{(x_2 - x_1)^2 + (y_2 - y_1)^2} = \sqrt{(6 - 0)^2 + (3 - 0)^2} = \sqrt{45} \approx 6.7$$

$$PQ = \sqrt{(x_2 - x_1)^2 + (y_2 - y_1)^2} = \sqrt{(6 - (-1))^2 + (3 - 2)^2} = \sqrt{50} \approx 7.1$$

STEP 2 **Check** for right angles. The slope of $\overline{OP}$ is $\dfrac{2 - 0}{-1 - 0} = -2$. The slope of $\overline{OQ}$ is $\dfrac{3 - 0}{6 - 0} = \dfrac{1}{2}$. The product of the slopes is $-2\left(\dfrac{1}{2}\right) = -1$, so $\overline{OP} \perp \overline{OQ}$ and $\angle POQ$ is a right angle.

▶ Therefore, △*PQO* is a right scalene triangle.

✓ **GUIDED PRACTICE**   **for Examples 1 and 2**

1. Draw an obtuse isosceles triangle and an acute scalene triangle.

2. Triangle *ABC* has the vertices *A*(0, 0), *B*(3, 3), and *C*(−3, 3). Classify it by its sides. Then determine if it is a right triangle.

ANGLES When the sides of a polygon are extended, other angles are formed. The original angles are the **interior angles**. The angles that form linear pairs with the interior angles are the **exterior angles**.

READ DIAGRAMS
Each vertex has a *pair* of congruent exterior angles. However, it is common to show only *one* exterior angle at each vertex.

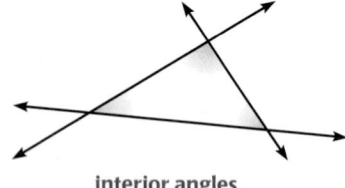

interior angles   exterior angles

THEOREM   *For Your Notebook*

THEOREM 4.1 Triangle Sum Theorem

The sum of the measures of the interior angles of a triangle is 180°.

Proof: p. 219; Ex. 53, p. 224

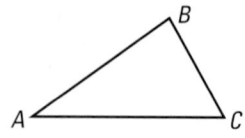

$m\angle A + m\angle B + m\angle C = 180°$

---

218   Chapter 4 Congruent Triangles

AUXILIARY LINES To prove certain theorems, you may need to add a line, a segment, or a ray to a given diagram. An *auxiliary* line is used in the proof of the Triangle Sum Theorem.

PROOF Triangle Sum Theorem

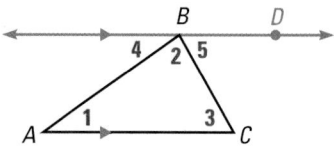

GIVEN ▶ $\triangle ABC$

PROVE ▶ $m\angle 1 + m\angle 2 + m\angle 3 = 180°$

Plan for Proof
a. Draw an auxiliary line through B and parallel to $\overline{AC}$.
b. Show that $m\angle 4 + m\angle 2 + m\angle 5 = 180°$, $\angle 1 \cong \angle 4$, and $\angle 3 \cong \angle 5$.
c. By substitution, $m\angle 1 + m\angle 2 + m\angle 3 = 180°$.

	STATEMENTS	REASONS
Plan in Action	a. **1.** Draw $\overleftrightarrow{BD}$ parallel to $\overline{AC}$.	**1.** Parallel Postulate
	b. **2.** $m\angle 4 + m\angle 2 + m\angle 5 = 180°$	**2.** Angle Addition Postulate and definition of straight angle
	3. $\angle 1 \cong \angle 4$, $\angle 3 \cong \angle 5$	**3.** Alternate Interior Angles Theorem
	4. $m\angle 1 = m\angle 4$, $m\angle 3 = m\angle 5$	**4.** Definition of congruent angles
	c. **5.** $m\angle 1 + m\angle 2 + m\angle 3 = 180°$	**5.** Substitution Property of Equality

---

THEOREM   *For Your Notebook*

THEOREM 4.2 Exterior Angle Theorem

The measure of an exterior angle of a triangle is equal to the sum of the measures of the two nonadjacent interior angles.

Proof: Ex. 50, p. 223

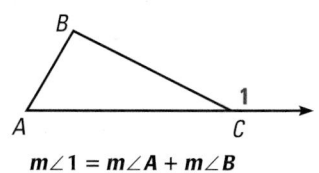

$m\angle 1 = m\angle A + m\angle B$

EXAMPLE 3 Find an angle measure

xy ALGEBRA Find $m\angle JKM$.

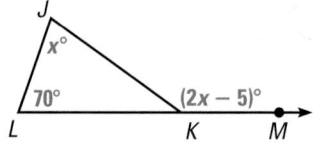

Solution

STEP 1 **Write** and solve an equation to find the value of x.

$(2x - 5)° = 70° + x°$ Apply the Exterior Angle Theorem.

$x = 75$ Solve for x.

STEP 2 **Substitute** 75 for x in $2x - 5$ to find $m\angle JKM$.

 $2x - 5 = 2 \cdot 75 - 5 = 145$

▶ The measure of $\angle JKM$ is 145°.

A **corollary to a theorem** is a statement that can be proved easily using the theorem. The corollary below follows from the Triangle Sum Theorem.

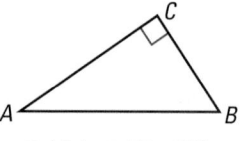
EXAMPLE 4 Find angle measures from a verbal description

ARCHITECTURE The tiled staircase shown forms a right triangle. The measure of one acute angle in the triangle is twice the measure of the other. Find the measure of each acute angle.

Solution

First, sketch a diagram of the situation. Let the measure of the smaller acute angle be $x°$. Then the measure of the larger acute angle is $2x°$. The Corollary to the Triangle Sum Theorem states that the acute angles of a right triangle are complementary.

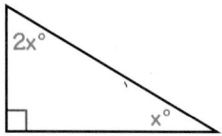

Use the corollary to set up and solve an equation.

$x° + 2x° = 90°$ **Corollary to the Triangle Sum Theorem**

$x = 30$ **Solve for x.**

▶ So, the measures of the acute angles are $30°$ and $2(30°) = 60°$.

✓ **GUIDED PRACTICE** for Examples 3 and 4

3. Find the measure of $\angle 1$ in the diagram shown.

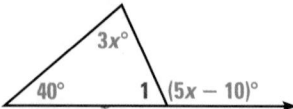

4. Find the measure of each interior angle of $\triangle ABC$, where $m\angle A = x°$, $m\angle B = 2x°$, and $m\angle C = 3x°$.

5. Find the measures of the acute angles of the right triangle in the diagram shown.

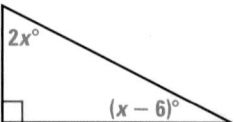

6. In Example 4, what is the measure of the obtuse angle formed between the staircase and a segment extending from the horizontal leg?

4.1 EXERCISES

HOMEWORK KEY

○ = **WORKED-OUT SOLUTIONS**
on p. WS4 for Exs. 9, 15, and 41

★ = **STANDARDIZED TEST PRACTICE**
Exs. 7, 20, 31, 43, and 51

SKILL PRACTICE

VOCABULARY Match the triangle description with the most specific name.

1. Angle measures: 30°, 60°, 90°   **A.** Isosceles
2. Side lengths: 2 cm, 2 cm, 2 cm   **B.** Scalene
3. Angle measures: 60°, 60°, 60°   **C.** Right
4. Side lengths: 6 m, 3 m, 6 m   **D.** Obtuse
5. Side lengths: 5 ft, 7 ft, 9 ft   **E.** Equilateral
6. Angle measures: 20°, 125°, 35°   **F.** Equiangular

7. ★ **WRITING** Can a right triangle also be obtuse? *Explain* why or why not.

EXAMPLE 1
on p. 217
for Exs. 8–10

CLASSIFYING TRIANGLES Copy the triangle and measure its angles. Classify the triangle by its sides and by its angles.

8.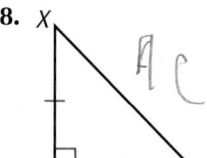

9.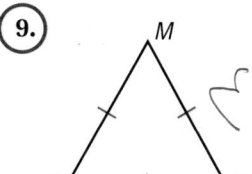

10.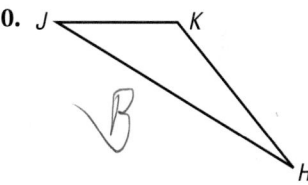

EXAMPLE 2
on p. 218
for Exs. 11–13

COORDINATE PLANE A triangle has the given vertices. Graph the triangle and classify it by its sides. Then determine if it is a right triangle.

11. $A(2, 3)$, $B(6, 3)$, $C(2, 7)$ 12. $A(3, 3)$, $B(6, 9)$, $C(6, -3)$ 13. $A(1, 9)$, $B(4, 8)$, $C(2, 5)$

EXAMPLE 3
on p. 219
for Exs. 14–19

FINDING ANGLE MEASURES Find the value of x. Then classify the triangle by its angles.

14.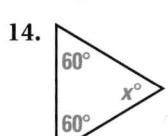

15.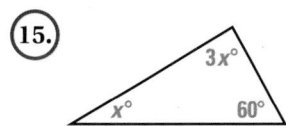

16.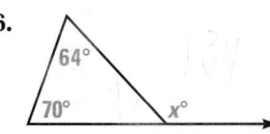

ⓧⓨ ALGEBRA Find the measure of the exterior angle shown.

17.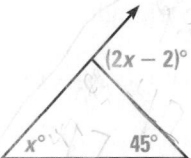

18.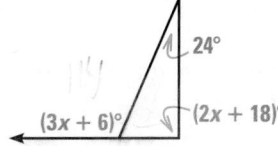

19.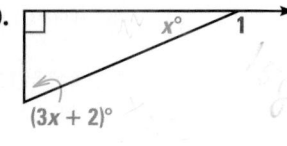

EXAMPLE 4
on p. 220
for Ex. 20

20. ★ **SHORT RESPONSE** *Explain* how to use the Corollary to the Triangle Sum Theorem to find the measure of each angle.

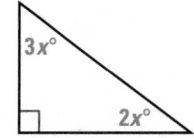

ANGLE RELATIONSHIPS Find the measure of the numbered angle.

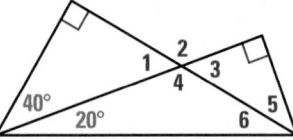

21. ∠1 5 0

22. ∠2 1 3 0

23. ∠3 5 0

24. ∠4 1 3 0

25. ∠5 4 0

26. ∠6 4 0

27. Ⓧ𝖞 **ALGEBRA** In △*PQR*, ∠*P* ≅ ∠*R* and the measure of ∠*Q* is twice the measure of ∠*R*. Find the measure of each angle.

28. Ⓧ𝖞 **ALGEBRA** In △*EFG*, $m\angle F = 3(m\angle G)$, and $m\angle E = m\angle F - 30°$. Find the measure of each angle.

ERROR ANALYSIS In Exercises 29 and 30, *describe* and correct the error.

29.

All equilateral triangles are also isosceles. So, if △ABC is isosceles, then it is equilateral as well.

30.
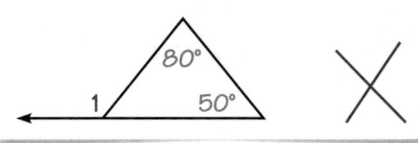
$m\angle 1 + 80° + 50° = 180°$

31. ★ **MULTIPLE CHOICE** Which of the following is not possible?

Ⓐ An acute scalene triangle

Ⓑ A triangle with two acute exterior angles

Ⓒ An obtuse isosceles triangle

Ⓓ An equiangular acute triangle

Ⓧ𝖞 **ALGEBRA** In Exercises 32–37, find the values of *x* and *y*.

32.
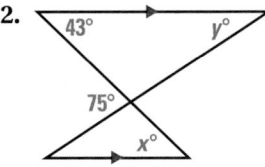

33.
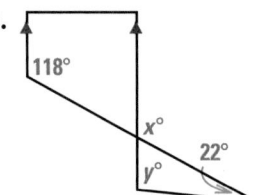

34.
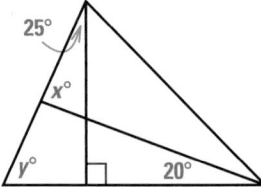

35.
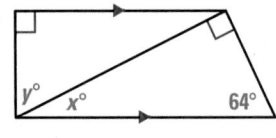

36.
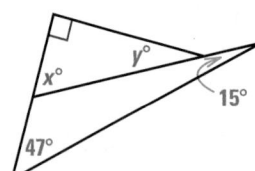

37.
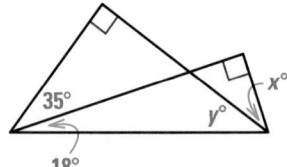

38. VISUALIZATION Is there an angle measure that is so small that any triangle with that angle measure will be an obtuse triangle? *Explain.*

39. CHALLENGE Suppose you have the equations $y = ax + b$, $y = cx + d$, and $y = ex + f$.

a. When will these three lines form a triangle?

b. Let $c = 1$, $d = 2$, $e = 4$, and $f = -7$. Find values of *a* and *b* so that no triangle is formed by the three equations.

c. Draw the triangle formed when $a = \frac{4}{3}$, $b = \frac{1}{3}$, $c = -\frac{4}{3}$, $d = \frac{41}{3}$, $e = 0$, and $f = -1$. Then classify the triangle by its sides.

○ = **WORKED-OUT SOLUTIONS** on p. WS1

★ = **STANDARDIZED TEST PRACTICE**

EXAMPLE 1
on p. 217
for Ex. 40

40. THEATER Three people are standing on a stage. The distances between the three people are shown in the diagram. Classify the triangle formed by its sides. Then copy the triangle, measure the angles, and classify the triangle by its angles.

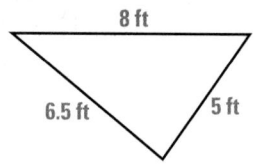

8 ft
6.5 ft
5 ft

@HomeTutor for problem solving help at classzone.com

(41.) KALEIDOSCOPES You are making a kaleidoscope. The directions state that you are to arrange three pieces of reflective mylar in an equilateral and equiangular triangle. You must cut three strips from a piece of mylar 6 inches wide. What are the side lengths of the triangle used to form the kaleidoscope? What are the measures of the angles? *Explain.*

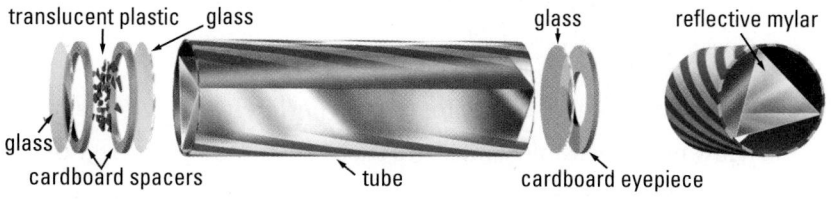

translucent plastic   glass   glass   reflective mylar

glass
cardboard spacers   tube   cardboard eyepiece

@HomeTutor for problem solving help at classzone.com

42. SCULPTURE You are bending a strip of metal into an isosceles triangle for a sculpture. The strip of metal is 20 inches long. The first bend is made 6 inches from one end. *Describe* two ways you could complete the triangle.

43. ★ MULTIPLE CHOICE Which inequality describes the possible measures of an angle of a triangle?

(A) $0° \leq x° \leq 180°$ **(B)** $0° \leq x° < 180°$ **(C)** $0° < x° < 180°$ **(D)** $0° < x° \leq 180°$

SLING CHAIRS The brace of a sling chair forms a triangle with the seat and legs of the chair. Suppose $m\angle 2 = 50°$ and $m\angle 3 = 65°$.

44. Find $m\angle 6$.   **45.** Find $m\angle 5$.

46. Find $m\angle 1$.   **47.** Find $m\angle 4$.

48. PROOF Prove the Corollary to the Triangle Sum Theorem on page 220.

49. MULTI-STEP PROBLEM The measures of the angles of a triangle are $(2\sqrt{2x})°$, $(5\sqrt{2x})°$, and $(2\sqrt{2x})°$.

a. Write an equation to show the relationship of the angles.

b. Find the measure of each angle.

c. Classify the triangle by its angles.

50. PROVING THEOREM 4.2 Prove the Exterior Angle Theorem. (*Hint:* Find two equations involving $m\angle ACB$.)

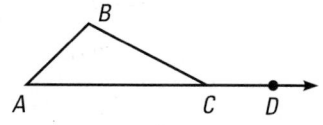

B

A   C   D

51. ★ **EXTENDED RESPONSE** The figure below shows an initial plan for a triangular flower bed that Mary and Tom plan to build along a fence. They are discussing what the measure of ∠1 should be.

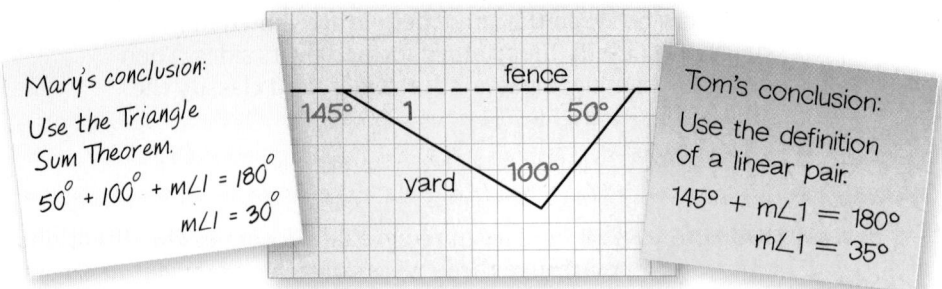

Mary's conclusion:
Use the Triangle
Sum Theorem.
$50° + 100° + m∠1 = 180°$
$m∠1 = 30°$

Tom's conclusion:
Use the definition
of a linear pair.
$145° + m∠1 = 180°$
$m∠1 = 35°$

Did Mary and Tom both reason correctly? If not, who made a mistake and what mistake was made? If they did both reason correctly, what can you conclude about their initial plan? *Explain.*

52. (xy) **ALGEBRA** △*ABC* is isosceles. $AB = x$ and $BC = 2x - 4$.

  a. Find two possible values for x if the perimeter of △*ABC* is 32.

  b. How many possible values are there for x if the perimeter of △*ABC* is 12?

53. **CHALLENGE** Use the diagram to write a proof of the Triangle Sum Theorem. Your proof should be different than the proof of the Triangle Sum Theorem on page 219.

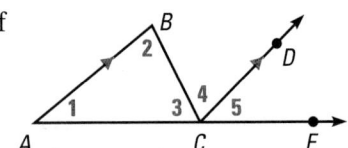

MIXED REVIEW

∠*A* and ∠*B* are complementary. Find *m*∠*A* and *m*∠*B*. (p. 35)

54. $m∠A = (3x + 16)°$
$m∠B = (4x - 3)°$

55. $m∠A = (4x - 2)°$
$m∠B = (7x + 4)°$

56. $m∠A = (3x + 4)°$
$m∠B = (2x + 6)°$

PREVIEW
Prepare for
Lesson 4.2
in Exs. 57–59.

Each figure is a regular polygon. Find the value of *x*. (p. 42)

57.

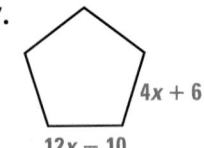

$4x + 6$
$12x - 10$

58.

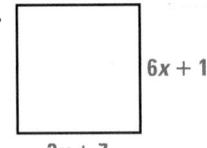

$6x + 1$
$3x + 7$

59.

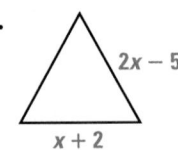

$2x - 5$
$x + 2$

60. Use the Symmetric Property of Congruence to complete the statement:
If ___?___ ≅ ___?___, then ∠*DEF* ≅ ∠*PQR*. (p. 112)

Use the diagram at the right. (p. 124)

61. If $m∠1 = 127°$, find $m∠2$, $m∠3$, and $m∠4$.

62. If $m∠4 = 170°$, find $m∠1$, $m∠2$, and $m∠3$.

63. If $m∠3 = 54°$, find $m∠1$, $m∠2$, and $m∠4$.

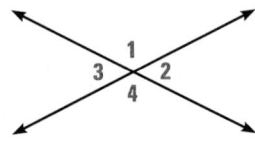

4.2 Apply Congruence and Triangles

Before	You identified congruent angles.
Now	You will identify congruent figures.
Why?	So you can determine if shapes are identical, as in Example 3.

Key Vocabulary
• congruent figures
• corresponding parts

Two geometric figures are *congruent* if they have exactly the same size and shape. Imagine cutting out one of the congruent figures. You could then position the cut-out figure so that it fits perfectly onto the other figure.

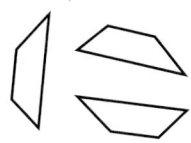

Congruent

Same size and shape

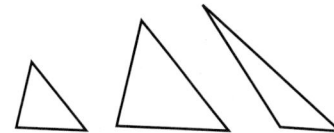

Not congruent

Different sizes or shapes

In two **congruent figures**, all the parts of one figure are congruent to the **corresponding parts** of the other figure. In congruent polygons, this means that the *corresponding sides* and the *corresponding angles* are congruent.

CONGRUENCE STATEMENTS When you write a congruence statement for two polygons, always list the corresponding vertices in the same order. You can write congruence statements in more than one way. Two possible congruence statements for the triangles at the right are $\triangle ABC \cong \triangle FED$ or $\triangle BCA \cong \triangle EDF$.

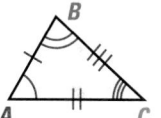

Corresponding angles $\angle A \cong \angle F$ $\angle B \cong \angle E$ $\angle C \cong \angle D$

Corresponding sides $\overline{AB} \cong \overline{FE}$ $\overline{BC} \cong \overline{ED}$ $\overline{AC} \cong \overline{FD}$

EXAMPLE 1   **Identify congruent parts**

VISUAL REASONING
To help you identify corresponding parts, turn $\triangle RST$.

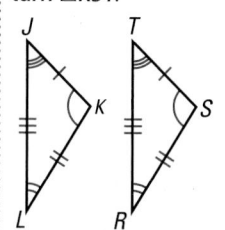

Write a congruence statement for the triangles. Identify all pairs of congruent corresponding parts.

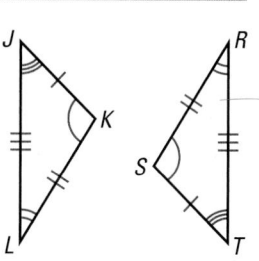

Solution

The diagram indicates that $\triangle JKL \cong \triangle TSR$.

Corresponding angles $\angle J \cong \angle T, \angle K \cong \angle S, \angle L \cong \angle R$

Corresponding sides $\overline{JK} \cong \overline{TS}, \overline{KL} \cong \overline{SR}, \overline{LJ} \cong \overline{RT}$

EXAMPLE 2   **Use properties of congruent figures**

In the diagram, $DEFG \cong SPQR$.

a. Find the value of x.

b. Find the value of y.

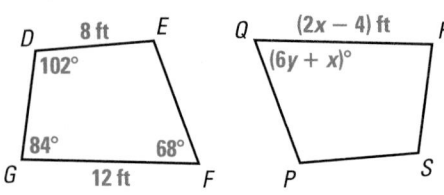

Solution

a. You know that $\overline{FG} \cong \overline{QR}$.

$$FG = QR$$
$$12 = 2x - 4$$
$$16 = 2x$$
$$8 = x$$

b. You know that $\angle F \cong \angle Q$.

$$m\angle F = m\angle Q$$
$$68° = (6y + x)°$$
$$68 = 6y + \mathbf{8}$$
$$10 = y$$

EXAMPLE 3   **Show that figures are congruent**

PAINTING If you divide the wall into orange and blue sections along $\overline{JK}$, will the sections of the wall be the same size and shape? *Explain.*

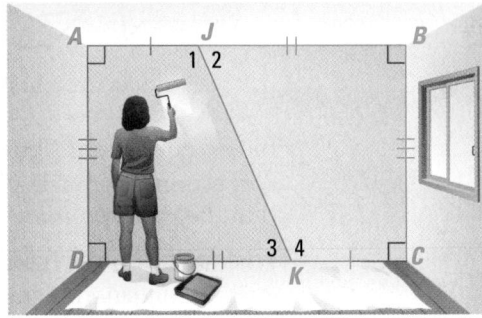

Solution

From the diagram, $\angle A \cong \angle C$ and $\angle D \cong \angle B$ because all right angles are congruent. Also, by the Lines Perpendicular to a Transversal Theorem, $\overline{AB} \parallel \overline{DC}$. Then, $\angle 1 \cong \angle 4$ and $\angle 2 \cong \angle 3$ by the Alternate Interior Angles Theorem. So, all pairs of corresponding angles are congruent.

The diagram shows $\overline{AJ} \cong \overline{CK}$, $\overline{KD} \cong \overline{JB}$, and $\overline{DA} \cong \overline{BC}$. By the Reflexive Property, $\overline{JK} \cong \overline{KJ}$. All corresponding parts are congruent, so $AJKD \cong CKJB$.

▶ Yes, the two sections will be the same size and shape.

✓ **GUIDED PRACTICE**   for Examples 1, 2, and 3

In the diagram at the right, $ABGH \cong CDEF$.

1. Identify all pairs of congruent corresponding parts.

2. Find the value of x and find $m\angle H$.

3. Show that $\triangle PTS \cong \triangle RTQ$.

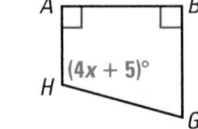

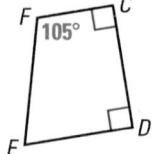

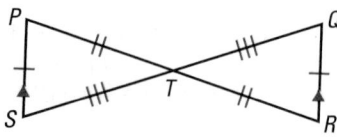

THEOREM 4.3 Third Angles Theorem

If two angles of one triangle are congruent to two angles of another triangle, then the third angles are also congruent.

Proof: Ex. 28, p. 230

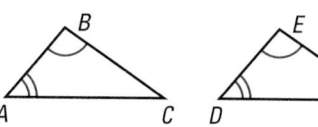

If ∠*A* ≅ ∠*D*, and ∠*B* ≅ ∠*E*, then ∠*C* ≅ ∠*F*.

EXAMPLE 4 **Use the Third Angles Theorem**

Find *m*∠*BDC*.

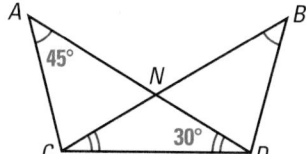

ANOTHER WAY

For an alternative method for solving the problem in Example 4, turn to page 232 for the **Problem Solving Workshop**.

Solution

∠*A* ≅ ∠*B* and ∠*ADC* ≅ ∠*BCD*, so by the Third Angles Theorem, ∠*ACD* ≅ ∠*BDC*. By the Triangle Sum Theorem, *m*∠*ACD* = 180° − 45° − 30° = 105°.

▶ So, *m*∠*ACD* = *m*∠*BDC* = 105° by the definition of congruent angles.

EXAMPLE 5 **Prove that triangles are congruent**

Write a proof.

GIVEN ▶ $\overline{AD} \cong \overline{CB}$, $\overline{DC} \cong \overline{BA}$, ∠*ACD* ≅ ∠*CAB*,
∠*CAD* ≅ ∠*ACB*

PROVE ▶ △*ACD* ≅ △*CAB*

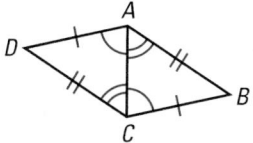

Plan for Proof
a. Use the Reflexive Property to show that $\overline{AC} \cong \overline{AC}$.
b. Use the Third Angles Theorem to show that ∠*B* ≅ ∠*D*.

	STATEMENTS	REASONS
Plan in Action	1. $\overline{AD} \cong \overline{CB}$, $\overline{DC} \cong \overline{BA}$	1. Given
a.	2. $\overline{AC} \cong \overline{AC}$	2. Reflexive Property of Congruence
	3. ∠*ACD* ≅ ∠*CAB*, ∠*CAD* ≅ ∠*ACB*	3. Given
b.	4. ∠*B* ≅ ∠*D*	4. Third Angles Theorem
	5. △*ACD* ≅ △*CAB*	5. Definition of ≅ figures

✓ **GUIDED PRACTICE** for Examples 4 and 5

4. In the diagram, what is *m*∠*DCN*?

5. By the definition of congruence, what additional information is needed to know that △*NDC* ≅ △*NSR*?

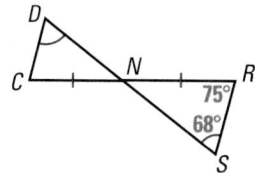

PROPERTIES OF CONGRUENT TRIANGLES The properties of congruence that are true for segments and angles are also true for triangles.

THEOREM *For Your Notebook*

THEOREM 4.4 Properties of Congruent Triangles

Reflexive Property of Congruent Triangles

For any triangle ABC, $\triangle ABC \cong \triangle ABC$.

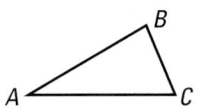

Symmetric Property of Congruent Triangles

If $\triangle ABC \cong \triangle DEF$, then $\triangle DEF \cong \triangle ABC$.

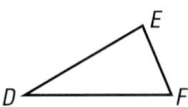

Transitive Property of Congruent Triangles

If $\triangle ABC \cong \triangle DEF$ and $\triangle DEF \cong \triangle JKL$, then $\triangle ABC \cong \triangle JKL$.

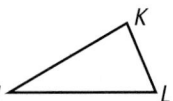

4.2 EXERCISES

HOMEWORK KEY
○ = WORKED-OUT SOLUTIONS
on p. WS4 for Exs. 9, 15, and 25

★ = STANDARDIZED TEST PRACTICE
Exs. 2, 18, 21, 24, 27, and 30

SKILL PRACTICE

1. **VOCABULARY** Copy the congruent triangles shown. Then label the vertices of the triangles so that $\triangle JKL \cong \triangle RST$. Identify all pairs of congruent *corresponding angles* and *corresponding sides*.

2. ★ **WRITING** Based on this lesson, what information do you need to prove that two triangles are congruent? *Explain*.

EXAMPLE 1
on p. 225
for Exs. 3–4

USING CONGRUENCE Identify all pairs of congruent corresponding parts. Then write another congruence statement for the figures.

3. $\triangle ABC \cong \triangle DEF$

4. $GHJK \cong QRST$

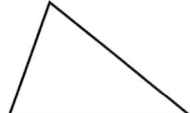

EXAMPLE 2
on p. 226
for Exs. 5–10

READING A DIAGRAM In the diagram, $\triangle XYZ \cong \triangle MNL$. Copy and complete the statement.

5. $m\angle Y = \underline{\ ?\ }$

6. $m\angle M = \underline{\ ?\ }$

7. $YX = \underline{\ ?\ }$

8. $\overline{YZ} \cong \underline{\ ?\ }$

9. $\triangle LNM \cong \underline{\ ?\ }$

10. $\triangle YXZ \cong \underline{\ ?\ }$

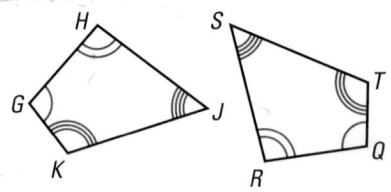

EXAMPLE 3
on p. 226
for Exs. 11–14

NAMING CONGRUENT FIGURES Write a congruence statement for any figures that can be proved congruent. *Explain* your reasoning.

11.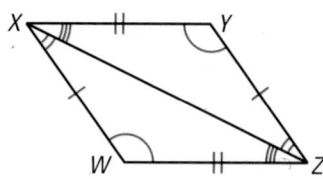

12.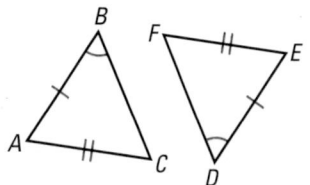

13.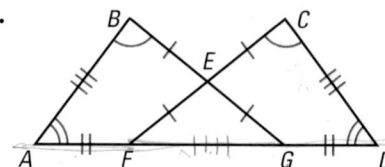

14.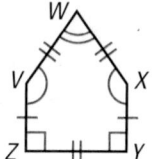

EXAMPLE 4
on p. 227
for Exs. 15–16

THIRD ANGLES THEOREM Find the value of *x*.

(15.)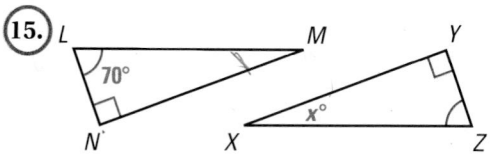

16.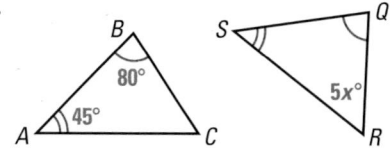

17. ERROR ANALYSIS A student says that △MNP ≅ △RSP because the corresponding angles of the triangles are congruent. *Describe* the error in this statement.

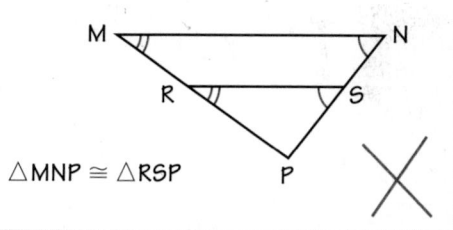

$$\triangle MNP \cong \triangle RSP$$

18. ★ OPEN-ENDED MATH Graph the triangle with vertices L(3, 1), M(8, 1), and N(8, 8). Then graph a triangle congruent to △LMN.

(xy) ALGEBRA Find the values of *x* and *y*.

19.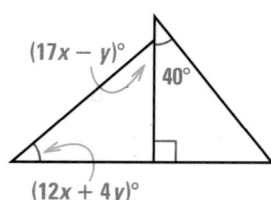

20.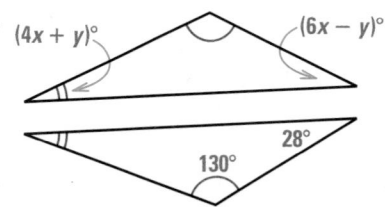

21. ★ MULTIPLE CHOICE Suppose △ABC ≅ △EFD, △EFD ≅ △GIH, m∠A = 90°, and m∠F = 20°. What is m∠H?

  (A) 20°   **(B)** 70°   **(C)** 90°   **(D)** Cannot be determined

22. CHALLENGE A hexagon is contained in a cube, as shown. Each vertex of the hexagon lies on the midpoint of an edge of the cube. This hexagon is equiangular. *Explain* why it is also regular.

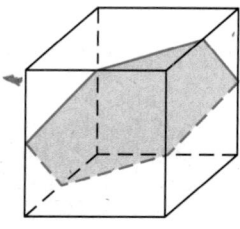

23. **RUG DESIGNS** The rug design is made of congruent triangles. One triangular shape is used to make all of the triangles in the design. Which property guarantees that all the triangles are congruent?

@HomeTutor for problem solving help at classzone.com

24. ★ **OPEN-ENDED MATH** Create a design for a rug made with congruent triangles that is different from the one in the photo above.

25. **CAR STEREO** A car stereo fits into a space in your dashboard. You want to buy a new car stereo, and it must fit in the existing space. What measurements need to be the same in order for the new stereo to be congruent to the old one?

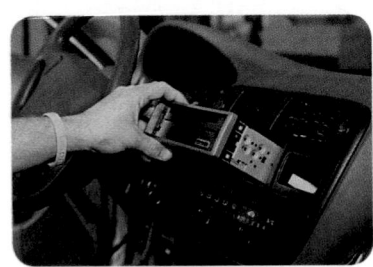

@HomeTutor for problem solving help at classzone.com

EXAMPLE 5
on p. 227
for Ex. 26

26. **PROOF** Copy and complete the proof.

GIVEN ▶ $\overline{AB} \cong \overline{ED}$, $\overline{BC} \cong \overline{DC}$, $\overline{CA} \cong \overline{CE}$, $\angle BAC \cong \angle DEC$

PROVE ▶ $\triangle ABC \cong \triangle EDC$

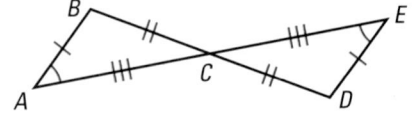

STATEMENTS	REASONS
1. $\overline{AB} \cong \overline{ED}$, $\overline{BC} \cong \overline{DC}$, $\overline{CA} \cong \overline{CE}$, $\angle BAC \cong \angle DEC$	1. Given
2. $\angle BCA \cong \angle DCE$	2. __?__
3. __?__	3. Third Angles Theorem
4. $\triangle ABC \cong \triangle EDC$	4. __?__

27. ★ **SHORT RESPONSE** Suppose $\triangle ABC \cong \triangle DCB$, and the triangles share vertices at points B and C. Draw a figure that illustrates this situation. Is $\overline{AC} \parallel \overline{BD}$? *Explain.*

28. **PROVING THEOREM 4.3** Use the plan to prove the Third Angles Theorem.

GIVEN ▶ $\angle A \cong \angle D$, $\angle B \cong \angle E$

PROVE ▶ $\angle C \cong \angle F$

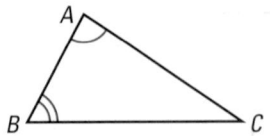 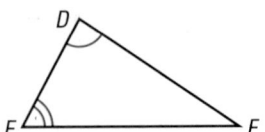

Plan for Proof Use the Triangle Sum Theorem to show that the sums of the angle measures are equal. Then use substitution to show $\angle C \cong \angle F$.

29. REASONING Given that $\triangle AFC \cong \triangle DFE$, must F be the midpoint of $\overline{AD}$ and $\overline{EC}$? Include a drawing with your answer.

30. ★ SHORT RESPONSE You have a set of tiles that come in two different shapes, as shown. You can put two of the triangular tiles together to make a quadrilateral that is the same size and shape as the quadrilateral tile.

Explain how you can find all of the angle measures of each tile by measuring only two angles.

31. MULTI-STEP PROBLEM In the diagram, quadrilateral $ABEF \cong$ quadrilateral $CDEF$.

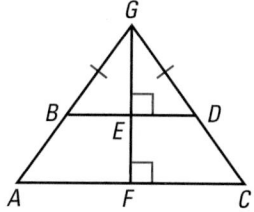

  a. *Explain* how you know that $\overline{BE} \cong \overline{DE}$ and $\angle ABE \cong \angle CDE$.

  b. *Explain* how you know that $\angle GBE \cong \angle GDE$.

  c. *Explain* how you know that $\angle GEB \cong \angle GED$.

  d. Do you have enough information to prove that $\triangle BEG \cong \triangle DEG$? *Explain*.

32. CHALLENGE Use the diagram to write a proof.

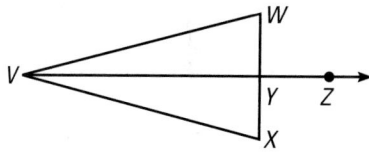

  GIVEN ▶ $\overline{WX} \perp \overrightarrow{VZ}$ at Y, Y is the midpoint of $\overline{WX}$, $\overline{VW} \cong \overline{VX}$, and $\overrightarrow{VZ}$ bisects $\angle WVX$.

  PROVE ▶ $\triangle VWY \cong \triangle VXY$

MIXED REVIEW

PREVIEW
Prepare for Lesson 4.3 in Exs. 33–35.

Use the Distance Formula to find the length of the segment. Round your answer to the nearest tenth of a unit. *(p. 15)*

33.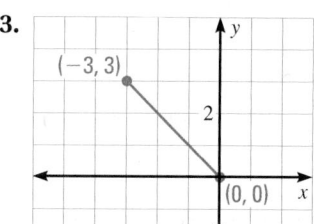

34.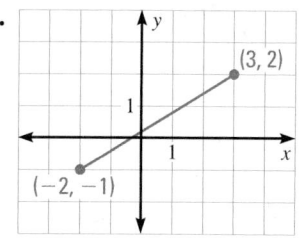

35.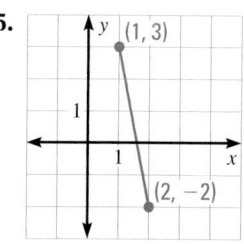

Line ℓ bisects the segment. Write a congruence statement. *(p. 15)*

36.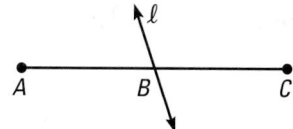

37.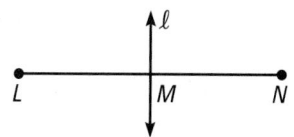

38.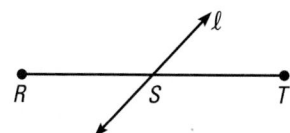

Write the converse of the statement. *(p. 79)*

39. If three points are coplanar, then they lie in the same plane.

40. If the sky is cloudy, then it is raining outside.

PROBLEM SOLVING WORKSHOP
LESSON 4.2

Using ALTERNATIVE METHODS

Another Way to Solve Example 4, page 227

MULTIPLE REPRESENTATIONS In Example 4 on page 227, you used congruencies in triangles that overlapped. When you solve problems like this, it may be helpful to redraw the art so that the triangles do not overlap.

PROBLEM

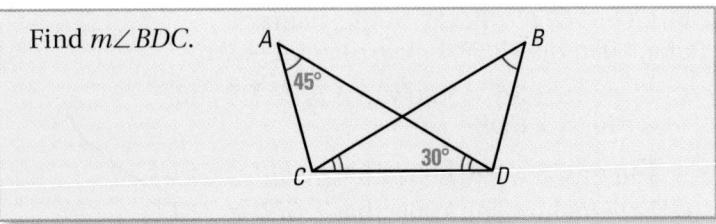

Find $m\angle BDC$.

METHOD **Drawing A Diagram**

STEP 1 **Identify** the triangles that overlap. Then redraw them so that they are separate. Copy all labels and markings.

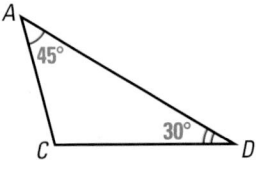
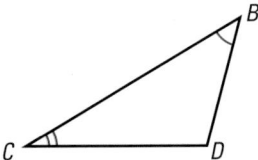

STEP 2 **Analyze** the situation. By the Triangle Sum Theorem, $m\angle ACD = 180° − 45° − 30° = 105°$.

Also, because $\angle A \cong \angle B$ and $\angle ADC \cong \angle BCD$, by the Third Angles Theorem, $\angle ACD \cong \angle BDC$, and $m\angle ACD = m\angle BDC = 105°$.

PRACTICE

1. **DRAWING FIGURES** Draw $\triangle HLM$ and $\triangle GJM$ so they do not overlap. Copy all labels and mark any known congruences.

   a. 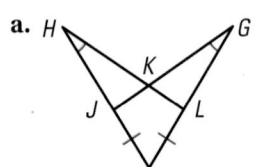 **b.**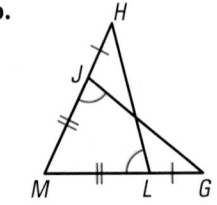

2. **ENVELOPE** Draw $\triangle PQS$ and $\triangle QPT$ so that they do not overlap. Find $m\angle PTS$.

   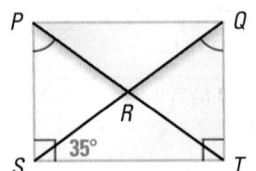

4.3 Investigate Congruent Figures

MATERIALS · straws · string · ruler · protractor

QUESTION How much information is needed to tell whether two figures are congruent?

EXPLORE 1 Compare triangles with congruent sides

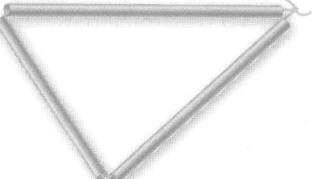

STEP 1

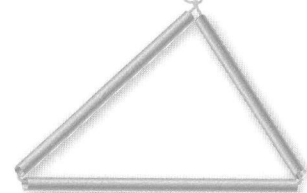

STEP 2

Make a triangle Cut straws to make side lengths of 8 cm, 10 cm, and 12 cm. Thread the string through the straws. Make a triangle by connecting the ends of the string.

Make another triangle Use the same length straws to make another triangle. If possible, make it different from the first. Compare the triangles. What do you notice?

EXPLORE 2 Compare quadrilaterals with congruent sides

STEP 1

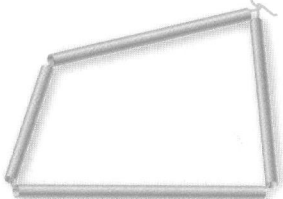

STEP 2

Make a quadrilateral Cut straws to make side lengths of 5 cm, 7 cm, 9 cm, and 11 cm. Thread the string through the straws. Make a quadrilateral by connecting the string.

Make another quadrilateral Make a second quadrilateral using the same length straws. If possible, make it different from the first. Compare the quadrilaterals. What do you notice?

DRAW CONCLUSIONS Use your observations to complete these exercises

1. Can you make two triangles with the same side lengths that are different shapes? *Justify* your answer.

2. If you know that three sides of a triangle are congruent to three sides of another triangle, can you say the triangles are congruent? *Explain.*

3. Can you make two quadrilaterals with the same side lengths that are different shapes? *Justify* your answer.

4. If four sides of a quadrilateral are congruent to four sides of another quadrilateral, can you say the quadrilaterals are congruent? *Explain.*

4.3 Prove Triangles Congruent by SSS

Before	You used the definition of congruent figures.
Now	You will use the side lengths to prove triangles are congruent.
Why	So you can determine if triangles in a tile floor are congruent, as in Ex. 22.

Key Vocabulary
• **congruent figures,** *p. 225*
• **corresponding parts,** *p. 225*

In the Activity on page 233, you saw that there is only one way to form a triangle given three side lengths. In general, any two triangles with the same three side lengths must be congruent.

POSTULATE   *For Your Notebook*

POSTULATE 19 **Side-Side-Side (SSS) Congruence Postulate**

If three sides of one triangle are congruent to three sides of a second triangle, then the two triangles are congruent.

If   Side $\overline{AB} \cong \overline{RS}$,
       Side $\overline{BC} \cong \overline{ST}$, and
       Side $\overline{CA} \cong \overline{TR}$,
then $\triangle ABC \cong \triangle RST$.

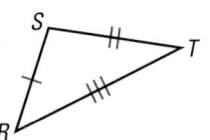

EXAMPLE 1   **Use the SSS Congruence Postulate**

Write a proof.

GIVEN ▶ $\overline{KL} \cong \overline{NL}$, $\overline{KM} \cong \overline{NM}$

PROVE ▶ $\triangle KLM \cong \triangle NLM$

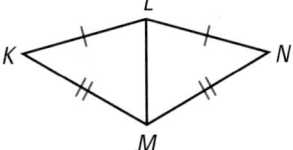

Proof It is given that $\overline{KL} \cong \overline{NL}$ and $\overline{KM} \cong \overline{NM}$. By the Reflexive Property, $\overline{LM} \cong \overline{LM}$. So, by the SSS Congruence Postulate, $\triangle KLM \cong \triangle NLM$.

Animated Geometry at classzone.com

✓ **GUIDED PRACTICE**   **for Example 1**

Decide whether the congruence statement is true. *Explain* **your reasoning.**

1. $\triangle DFG \cong \triangle HJK$

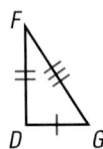 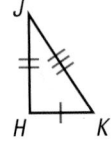

2. $\triangle ACB \cong \triangle CAD$

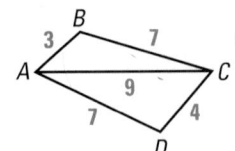

3. $\triangle QPT \cong \triangle RST$

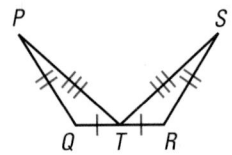

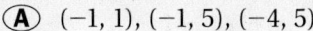 **EXAMPLE 2** **Standardized Test Practice**

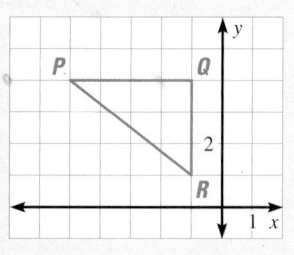

Which are the coordinates of the vertices of a triangle congruent to $\triangle PQR$?

Ⓐ $(-1, 1), (-1, 5), (-4, 5)$

Ⓑ $(-2, 4), (-7, 4), (-4, 6)$

Ⓒ $(-3, 2), (-1, 3), (-3, 1)$

Ⓓ $(-7, 7), (-7, 9), (-3, 7)$

Solution

ELIMINATE CHOICES
Once you know the side lengths of $\triangle PQR$, look for pairs of coordinates with the same x-coordinates or the same y-coordinates. In Choice C, $(-3, 2)$ and $(-3, 1)$ are only 1 unit apart. You can eliminate D in the same way.

By counting, $PQ = 4$ and $QR = 3$. Use the Distance Formula to find PR.

$$d = \sqrt{(x_2 - x_1)^2 + (y_2 - y_1)^2}$$

$$PR = \sqrt{(-1 - (-5))^2 + (1 - 4)^2} = \sqrt{4^2 + (-3)^2} = \sqrt{25} = 5$$

By the SSS Congruence Postulate, any triangle with side lengths 3, 4, and 5 will be congruent to $\triangle PQR$. The distance from $(-1, 1)$ to $(-1, 5)$ is 4. The distance from $(-1, 5)$ to $(-4, 5)$ is 3. The distance from $(-1, 1)$ to $(-4, 5)$ is $\sqrt{(5-1)^2 + ((-4) - (-1))^2} = \sqrt{4^2 + (-3)^2} = \sqrt{25} = 5$.

▶ The correct answer is A. Ⓐ Ⓑ Ⓒ Ⓓ

✓ **GUIDED PRACTICE** **for Example 2**

4. $\triangle JKL$ has vertices $J(-3, -2)$, $K(0, -2)$, and $L(-3, -8)$. $\triangle RST$ has vertices $R(10, 0)$, $S(10, -3)$, and $T(4, 0)$. Graph the triangles in the same coordinate plane and show that they are congruent.

ACTIVITY COPY A TRIANGLE

Follow the steps below to construct a triangle that is congruent to $\triangle ABC$.

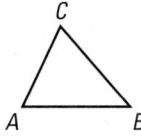

STEP 1

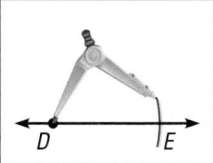

Construct $\overline{DE}$ so that it is congruent to $\overline{AB}$.

STEP 2

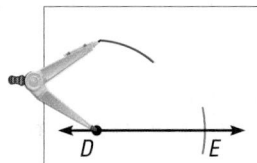

Open your compass to the length AC. Use this length to draw an arc with the compass point at D.

STEP 3

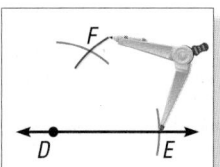

Draw an arc with radius BC and center E that intersects the arc from Step 2. Label the intersection point F.

STEP 4

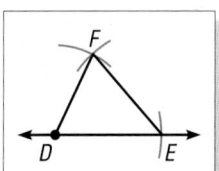

Draw $\triangle DEF$. By the SSS Congruence Postulate, $\triangle ABC \cong \triangle DEF$.

EXAMPLE 3 Solve a real-world problem

STRUCTURAL SUPPORT Explain why the bench with the diagonal support is stable, while the one without the support can collapse.

Solution

The bench with a diagonal support forms triangles with fixed side lengths. By the SSS Congruence Postulate, these triangles cannot change shape, so the bench is stable. The bench without a diagonal support is not stable because there are many possible quadrilaterals with the given side lengths.

✓ **GUIDED PRACTICE** for Example 3

Determine whether the figure is stable. *Explain* your reasoning.

5.

6.

7.

4.3 EXERCISES

○ = **WORKED-OUT SOLUTIONS**
on p. WS4 for Exs. 7, 9, and 25

★ = **STANDARDIZED TEST PRACTICE**
Exs. 16, 17, and 28

SKILL PRACTICE

VOCABULARY Tell whether the angles or sides are *corresponding angles*, *corresponding sides*, or *neither*.

1. $\angle C$ and $\angle L$

2. $\overline{AC}$ and $\overline{JK}$

3. $\overline{BC}$ and $\overline{KL}$

4. $\angle B$ and $\angle L$

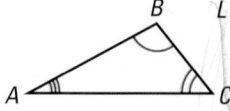

EXAMPLE 1
on p. 234
for Exs. 5–7

DETERMINING CONGRUENCE Decide whether the congruence statement is true. *Explain* your reasoning.

5. $\triangle RST \cong \triangle TQP$

6. $\triangle ABD \cong \triangle CDB$

7. $\triangle DEF \cong \triangle DGF$

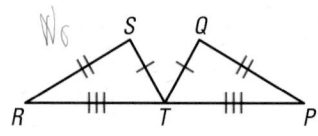

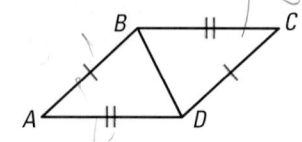

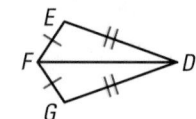

EXAMPLE 2
on p. 235
for Exs. 8–12

8. ERROR ANALYSIS *Describe* and correct the error in writing a congruence statement for the triangles in the coordinate plane.

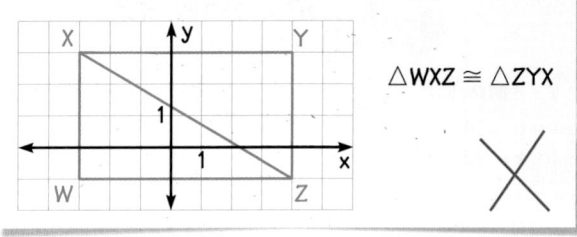

$\triangle WXZ \cong \triangle ZYX$

ALGEBRA Use the given coordinates to determine if $\triangle ABC \cong \triangle DEF$.

9. $A(-2, -2)$, $B(4, -2)$, $C(4, 6)$, $D(5, 7)$, $E(5, 1)$, $F(13, 1)$

10. $A(-2, 1)$, $B(3, -3)$, $C(7, 5)$, $D(3, 6)$, $E(8, 2)$, $F(10, 11)$

11. $A(0, 0)$, $B(6, 5)$, $C(9, 0)$, $D(0, -1)$, $E(6, -6)$, $F(9, -1)$

12. $A(-5, 7)$, $B(-5, 2)$, $C(0, 2)$, $D(0, 6)$, $E(0, 1)$, $F(4, 1)$

EXAMPLE 3
on p. 236
for Exs. 13–15

USING DIAGRAMS Decide whether the figure is stable. *Explain.*

13.

14.
15.

16. ★ MULTIPLE CHOICE Let $\triangle FGH$ be an equilateral triangle with point J as the midpoint of $\overline{FG}$. Which of the statements below is *not* true?

(A) $\overline{FH} \cong \overline{GH}$ (B) $\overline{FJ} \cong \overline{FH}$ (C) $\overline{FJ} \cong \overline{GJ}$ (D) $\triangle FHJ \cong \triangle GHJ$

17. ★ MULTIPLE CHOICE Let $ABCD$ be a rectangle separated into two triangles by $\overline{DB}$. Which of the statements below is *not* true?

(A) $\overline{AD} \cong \overline{CB}$ (B) $\overline{AB} \cong \overline{AD}$ (C) $\overline{AB} \cong \overline{CD}$ (D) $\triangle DAB \cong \triangle BCD$

APPLYING SEGMENT ADDITION Determine whether $\triangle ABC \cong \triangle DEF$. If they are congruent, write a congruence statement. *Explain* your reasoning.

18.
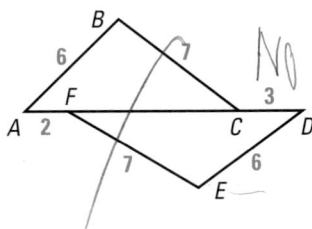

19.
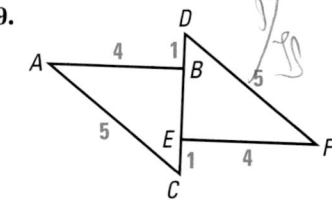

20. 3-D FIGURES In the diagram, $\overline{PK} \cong \overline{PL}$ and $\overline{JK} \cong \overline{JL}$. Show that $\triangle JPK \cong \triangle JPL$.

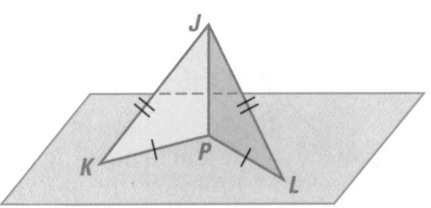

21. CHALLENGE Find all values of x that make the triangles congruent. *Explain.*

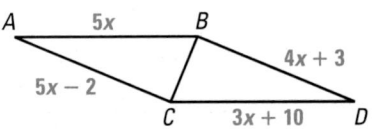

EXAMPLE 1
on p. 234
for Ex. 22

22. TILE FLOORS You notice two triangles in the tile floor of a hotel lobby. You want to determine if the triangles are congruent, but you only have a piece of string. Can you determine if the triangles are congruent? *Explain*.

@HomeTutor for problem solving help at classzone.com

EXAMPLE 3
on p. 236
for Ex. 23

23. GATES Which gate is stable? *Explain* your reasoning.

Gate 1   Gate 2

@HomeTutor for problem solving help at classzone.com

PROOF Write a proof.

24. GIVEN ▶ $\overline{GH} \cong \overline{JK}$, $\overline{HJ} \cong \overline{KG}$
   PROVE ▶ $\triangle GHJ \cong \triangle JKG$

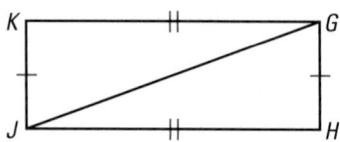

25. GIVEN ▶ $\overline{WX} \cong \overline{VZ}$, $\overline{WY} \cong \overline{VY}$, $\overline{YZ} \cong \overline{YX}$
   PROVE ▶ $\triangle VWX \cong \triangle WVZ$

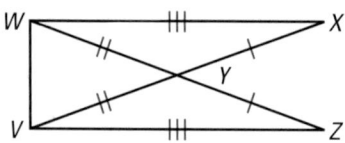

26. GIVEN ▶ $\overline{AE} \cong \overline{CE}$, $\overline{AB} \cong \overline{CD}$,
   E is the midpoint of $\overline{BD}$.
   PROVE ▶ $\triangle EAB \cong \triangle ECD$

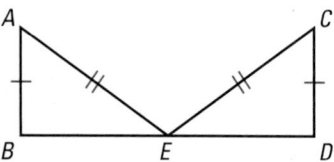

27. GIVEN ▶ $\overline{FM} \cong \overline{FN}$, $\overline{DM} \cong \overline{HN}$,
   $\overline{EF} \cong \overline{GF}$, $\overline{DE} \cong \overline{HG}$
   PROVE ▶ $\triangle DEN \cong \triangle HGM$

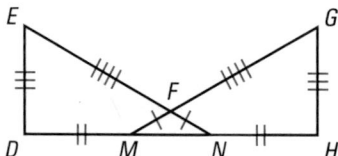

28. ★ EXTENDED RESPONSE When rescuers enter a partially collapsed building they often have to reinforce damaged doors for safety.

   a. Diagonal braces are added to Door 1 as shown below. *Explain* why the door is more stable with the braces.

   b. Would these braces be a good choice for rescuers needing to enter and exit the building through this doorway?

   c. In the diagram, Door 2 has only a corner brace. Does this solve the problem from part (b)?

   d. *Explain* why the corner brace makes the door more stable.

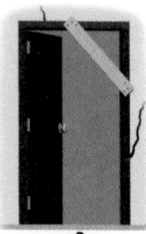

1   2

29. BASEBALL FIELD To create a baseball field, start by placing home plate. Then, place second base 127 feet $3\frac{3}{8}$ inches from home plate. Then, you can find first base using two tape measures. Stretch one from second base toward first base and the other from home plate toward first base. The point where the two tape measures cross at the 90 foot mark is first base. You can find third base in a similar manner. *Explain* how and why this process will always work.

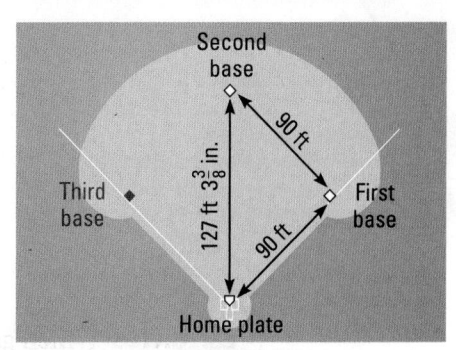

30. CHALLENGE Draw and label the figure described below. Then, identify what is given and write a two-column proof.

In an isosceles triangle, if a segment is added from the vertex between the congruent sides to the midpoint of the third side, then two congruent triangles are formed.

MIXED REVIEW

PREVIEW
Prepare for
Lesson 4.4 in
Exs. 31–33.

Find the slope of the line that passes through the points. *(p. 171)*

31. $A(3, 0)$, $B(7, 4)$ **32.** $F(1, 8)$, $G(-9, 2)$ **33.** $M(-4, -10)$, $N(6, 2)$

Use the *x*- and *y*-intercepts to write an equation of the line. *(p. 180)*

34. 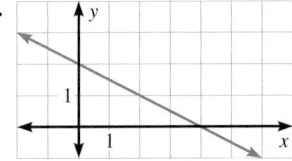   **35.** 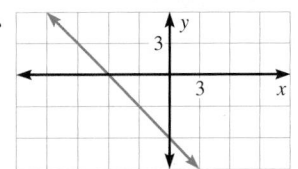   **36.**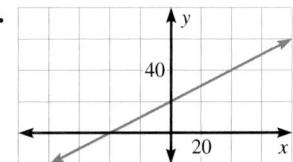

37. Write an equation of a line that passes through $(-3, -1)$ and is parallel to $y = 3x + 2$. *(p. 180)*

QUIZ *for Lessons 4.1–4.3*

A triangle has the given vertices. Graph the triangle and classify it by its sides. Then determine if it is a right triangle. *(p. 217)*

1. $A(-3, 0)$, $B(0, 4)$, $C(3, 0)$ **2.** $A(2, -4)$, $B(5, -1)$, $C(2, -1)$ **3.** $A(-7, 0)$, $B(1, 6)$, $C(-3, 4)$

In the diagram, $HJKL \cong NPQM$. *(p. 225)*

4. Find the value of x.

5. Find the value of y.

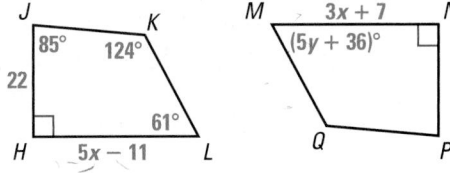

6. Write a proof. *(p. 234)*

   GIVEN ▶ $\overline{AB} \cong \overline{AC}$, $\overline{AD}$ bisects $\overline{BC}$.

   PROVE ▶ $\triangle ABD \cong \triangle ACD$

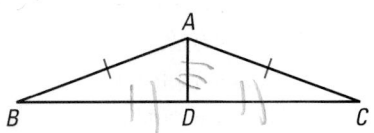

4.4 Prove Triangles Congruent by SAS and HL

Before	You used the SSS Congruence Postulate.
Now	You will use sides and angles to prove congruence.
Why?	So you can show triangles are congruent, as in Ex. 33.

Key Vocabulary
• leg of a right triangle
• hypotenuse

Consider a relationship involving two sides and the angle they form, their *included* angle. To picture the relationship, form an angle using two pencils.

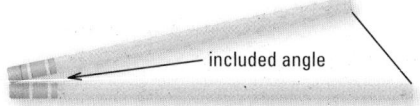

included angle

Any time you form an angle of the same measure with the pencils, the side formed by connecting the pencil points will have the same length. In fact, any two triangles formed in this way are congruent.

POSTULATE   *For Your Notebook*

POSTULATE 20 Side-Angle-Side (SAS) Congruence Postulate

If two sides and the included angle of one triangle are congruent to two sides and the included angle of a second triangle, then the two triangles are congruent.

If **Side** $\overline{RS} \cong \overline{UV}$,
   Angle $\angle R \cong \angle U$, and
   Side $\overline{RT} \cong \overline{UW}$,
then $\triangle RST \cong \triangle UVW$.

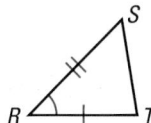 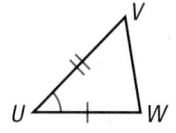

EXAMPLE 1   Use the SAS Congruence Postulate

Write a proof.

GIVEN ▶ $\overline{BC} \cong \overline{DA}$, $\overline{BC} \parallel \overline{AD}$
PROVE ▶ $\triangle ABC \cong \triangle CDA$

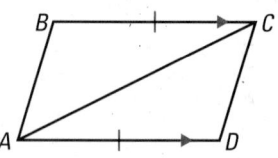

WRITE PROOFS
Make your proof easier to read by identifying the steps where you show congruent sides (S) and angles (A).

STATEMENTS	REASONS
S 1. $\overline{BC} \cong \overline{DA}$	1. Given
2. $\overline{BC} \parallel \overline{AD}$	2. Given
A 3. $\angle BCA \cong \angle DAC$	3. Alternate Interior Angles Theorem
S 4. $\overline{AC} \cong \overline{CA}$	4. Reflexive Property of Congruence
5. $\triangle ABC \cong \triangle CDA$	5. SAS Congruence Postulate

EXAMPLE 2 **Use SAS and properties of shapes**

In the diagram, $\overline{QS}$ and $\overline{RP}$ pass through the center *M* of the circle. What can you conclude about $\triangle MRS$ and $\triangle MPQ$?

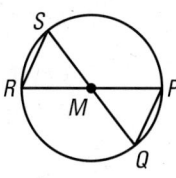

Solution

Because they are vertical angles, $\angle PMQ \cong \angle RMS$. All points on a circle are the same distance from the center, so *MP*, *MQ*, *MR*, and *MS* are all equal.

▶ $\triangle MRS$ and $\triangle MPQ$ are congruent by the SAS Congruence Postulate.

✓ **GUIDED PRACTICE** for Examples 1 and 2

In the diagram, *ABCD* is a square with four congruent sides and four right angles. *R*, *S*, *T*, and *U* are the midpoints of the sides of *ABCD*. Also, $\overline{RT} \perp \overline{SU}$ and $\overline{SV} \cong \overline{VU}$.

1. Prove that $\triangle SVR \cong \triangle UVR$.

2. Prove that $\triangle BSR \cong \triangle DUT$.

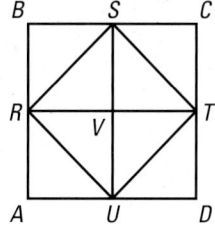

In general, if you know the lengths of two sides and the measure of an angle that is *not included* between them, you can create two different triangles.

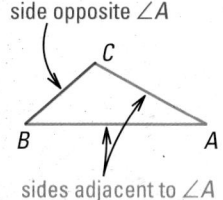
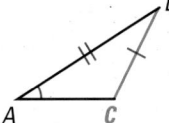 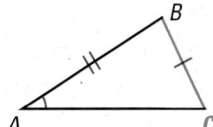

Therefore, SSA is *not* a valid method for proving that triangles are congruent, although there is a special case for right triangles.

RIGHT TRIANGLES In a right triangle, the sides adjacent to the right angle are called the **legs**. The side opposite the right angle is called the **hypotenuse** of the right triangle.

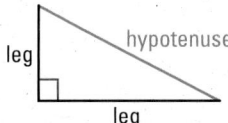

THEOREM *For Your Notebook*

THEOREM 4.5 Hypotenuse-Leg (HL) Congruence Theorem

If the hypotenuse and a leg of a right triangle are congruent to the hypotenuse and a leg of a second right triangle, then the two triangles are congruent.

Proofs: Ex. 37, p. 439; p. 932

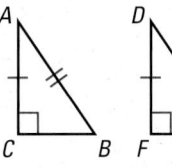

$\triangle ABC \cong \triangle DEF$

EXAMPLE 3 Use the Hypotenuse-Leg Congruence Theorem

USE DIAGRAMS
If you have trouble matching vertices to letters when you separate the overlapping triangles, leave the triangles in their original orientations.

Write a proof.

GIVEN ▶ $\overline{WY} \cong \overline{XZ}$, $\overline{WZ} \perp \overline{ZY}$, $\overline{XY} \perp \overline{ZY}$

PROVE ▶ $\triangle WYZ \cong \triangle XZY$

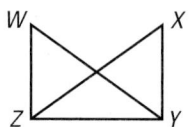

Solution

Redraw the triangles so they are side by side with corresponding parts in the same position. Mark the given information in the diagram.

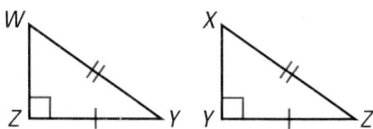

STATEMENTS	REASONS
H 1. $\overline{WY} \cong \overline{XZ}$	**1.** Given
2. $\overline{WZ} \perp \overline{ZY}$, $\overline{XY} \perp \overline{ZY}$	**2.** Given
3. $\angle Z$ and $\angle Y$ are right angles.	**3.** Definition of $\perp$ lines
4. $\triangle WYZ$ and $\triangle XZY$ are right triangles.	**4.** Definition of a right triangle
L 5. $\overline{ZY} \cong \overline{YZ}$	**5.** Reflexive Property of Congruence
6. $\triangle WYZ \cong \triangle XZY$	**6.** HL Congruence Theorem

Animated **Geometry** at classzone.com

EXAMPLE 4 Choose a postulate or theorem

SIGN MAKING You are making a canvas sign to hang on the triangular wall over the door to the barn shown in the picture. You think you can use two identical triangular sheets of canvas. You know that $\overline{RP} \perp \overline{QS}$ and $\overline{PQ} \cong \overline{PS}$. What postulate or theorem can you use to conclude that $\triangle PQR \cong \triangle PSR$?

Solution

You are given that $\overline{PQ} \cong \overline{PS}$. By the Reflexive Property, $\overline{RP} \cong \overline{RP}$. By the definition of perpendicular lines, both $\angle RPQ$ and $\angle RPS$ are right angles, so they are congruent. So, two sides and their included angle are congruent.

▶ You can use the SAS Congruence Postulate to conclude that $\triangle PQR \cong \triangle PSR$.

 GUIDED PRACTICE for Examples 3 and 4

Use the diagram at the right.

3. Redraw $\triangle ACB$ and $\triangle DBC$ side by side with corresponding parts in the same position.

4. Use the information in the diagram to prove that $\triangle ACB \cong \triangle DBC$.

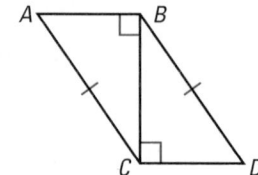

4.4 EXERCISES

SKILL PRACTICE

1. **VOCABULARY** Copy and complete: The angle between two sides of a triangle is called the __?__ angle.

2. ★ **WRITING** *Explain* the difference between proving triangles congruent using the SAS and SSS Congruence Postulates.

EXAMPLE 1
on p. 240
for Exs. 3–15

NAMING INCLUDED ANGLES Use the diagram to name the included angle between the given pair of sides.

3. $\overline{XY}$ and $\overline{YW}$ ∠ X Y W

4. $\overline{WZ}$ and $\overline{ZY}$ W Z Y

5. $\overline{ZW}$ and $\overline{YW}$ Z W Y

6. $\overline{WX}$ and $\overline{YX}$ W X Y

7. $\overline{XY}$ and $\overline{YZ}$ X Y Z

8. $\overline{WX}$ and $\overline{WZ}$ X W Z

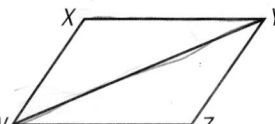

REASONING Decide whether enough information is given to prove that the triangles are congruent using the SAS Congruence Postulate.

9. $\triangle ABD$, $\triangle CDB$

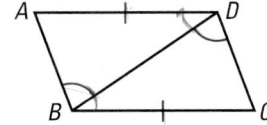

10. $\triangle LMN$, $\triangle NQP$

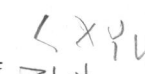 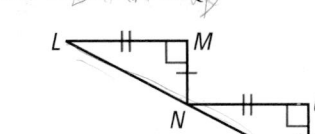

11. $\triangle YXZ$, $\triangle WXZ$

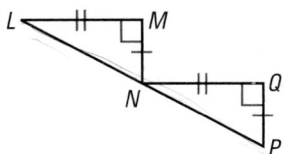

12. $\triangle QRV$, $\triangle TSU$

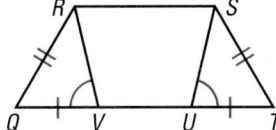

13.○ $\triangle EFH$, $\triangle GHF$

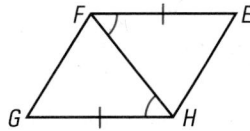

14. $\triangle KLM$, $\triangle MNK$

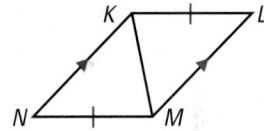

15. ★ **MULTIPLE CHOICE** Which of the following sets of information does not allow you to conclude that $\triangle ABC \cong \triangle DEF$?

  A $\overline{AB} \cong \overline{DE}$, $\overline{BC} \cong \overline{EF}$, $\angle B \cong \angle E$

  B $\overline{AB} \cong \overline{DF}$, $\overline{AC} \cong \overline{DE}$, $\angle C \cong \angle E$

  C $\overline{AC} \cong \overline{DF}$, $\overline{BC} \cong \overline{EF}$, $\overline{BA} \cong \overline{DE}$

  D $\overline{AB} \cong \overline{DE}$, $\overline{AC} \cong \overline{DF}$, $\angle A \cong \angle D$

EXAMPLE 2
on p. 241
for Exs. 16–18

APPLYING SAS In Exercises 16–18, use the given information to name two triangles that are congruent. *Explain* your reasoning.

16. *ABCD* is a square with four congruent sides and four congruent angles.

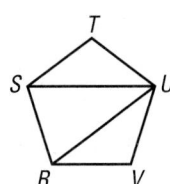

17. *RSTUV* is a regular pentagon.

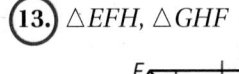

18. $\overline{MK} \perp \overline{MN}$ and $\overline{KL} \perp \overline{NL}$.

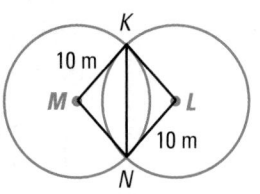

EXAMPLE 3
on p. 242
for Ex. 19

19. **OVERLAPPING TRIANGLES** Redraw △ACF and △EGB so they are side by side with corresponding parts in the same position. *Explain* how you know that △ACF ≅ △EGB.

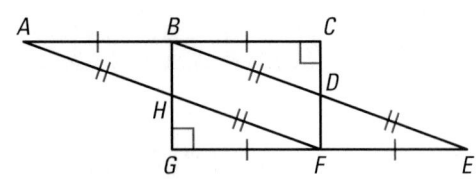

EXAMPLE 4
on p. 242
for Exs. 20–22

REASONING Decide whether enough information is given to prove that the triangles are congruent. If there is enough information, state the congruence postulate or theorem you would use.

20.

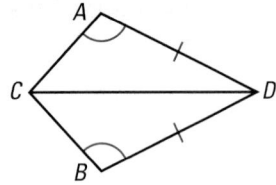

21. *Z* is the midpoint of $\overline{PY}$ and $\overline{XQ}$.

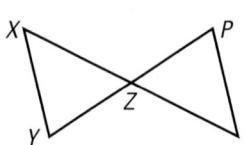

22.

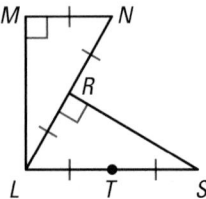

23. ★ **WRITING** Suppose both pairs of corresponding legs of two right triangles are congruent. Are the triangles congruent? *Explain*.

24. **ERROR ANALYSIS** *Describe* and correct the error in finding the value of *x*.

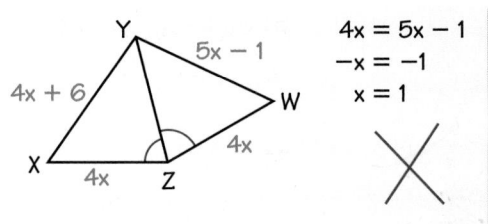

USING DIAGRAMS In Exercises 25–27, state the third congruence that must be given to prove that △ABC ≅ △DEF using the indicated postulate.

25. **GIVEN** ▶ $\overline{AB} \cong \overline{DE}$, $\overline{CB} \cong \overline{FE}$, _?_ ≅ _?_
Use the SSS Congruence Postulate.

26. **GIVEN** ▶ ∠A ≅ ∠D, $\overline{CA} \cong \overline{FD}$, _?_ ≅ _?_
Use the SAS Congruence Postulate.

27. **GIVEN** ▶ ∠B ≅ ∠E, $\overline{AB} \cong \overline{DE}$, _?_ ≅ _?_
Use the SAS Congruence Postulate.

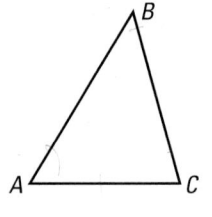
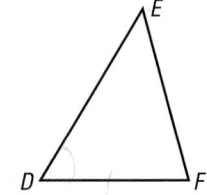

28. **USING ISOSCELES TRIANGLES** Suppose △KLN and △MLN are isosceles triangles with $\overline{KL} \cong \overline{LN}$ and $\overline{ML} \cong \overline{LN}$, and $\overline{NL}$ bisects ∠KLM. Is there enough information to prove that △KLN ≅ △MLN? *Explain*.

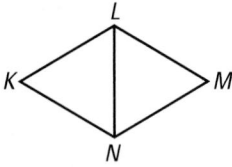

29. **REASONING** Suppose *M* is the midpoint of $\overline{PQ}$ in △PQR. If $\overline{RM} \perp \overline{PQ}$, *explain* why △RMP ≅ △RMQ.

30. **CHALLENGE** Suppose $\overline{AB} \cong \overline{AC}$, $\overline{AD} \cong \overline{AF}$, $\overline{AD} \perp \overline{AB}$, and $\overline{AF} \perp \overline{AC}$. *Explain* why you can conclude that △ACD ≅ △ABF.

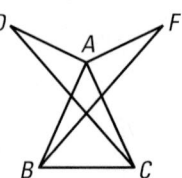

CONGRUENT TRIANGLES In Exercises 31 and 32, identify the theorem or postulate you would use to prove the triangles congruent.

31.

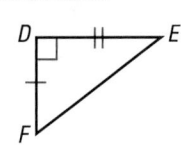

32.

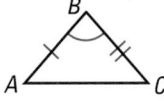 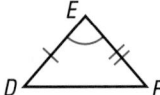

33. **SAILBOATS** Suppose you have two sailboats. What information do you need to know to prove that the triangular sails are congruent using SAS? using HL?

@HomeTutor for problem solving help at classzone.com

EXAMPLE 3
on p. 242
for Ex. 34

34. **DEVELOPING PROOF** Copy and complete the proof.

GIVEN ▶ Point M is the midpoint of $\overline{LN}$.
$\triangle PMQ$ is an isosceles triangle with $\overline{MP} \cong \overline{MQ}$.
$\angle L$ and $\angle N$ are right angles.

PROVE ▶ $\triangle LMP \cong \triangle NMQ$

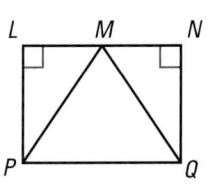

STATEMENTS	REASONS
1. $\angle L$ and $\angle N$ are right angles.	1. Given
2. $\triangle LMP$ and $\triangle NMQ$ are right triangles.	2. __?__
3. Point M is the midpoint of $\overline{LN}$.	3. __?__
4. __?__	4. Definition of midpoint
5. $\overline{MP} \cong \overline{MQ}$	5. Given
6. $\triangle LMP \cong \triangle NMQ$	6. __?__

@HomeTutor for problem solving help at classzone.com

PROOF In Exercises 35 and 36, write a proof.

35. **GIVEN** ▶ $\overline{PQ}$ bisects $\angle SPT$, $\overline{SP} \cong \overline{TP}$
    PROVE ▶ $\triangle SPQ \cong \triangle TPQ$

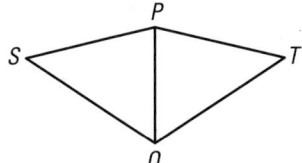

36. **GIVEN** ▶ $\overline{VX} \cong \overline{XY}$, $\overline{XW} \cong \overline{YZ}$, $\overline{XW} \parallel \overline{YZ}$
    PROVE ▶ $\triangle VXW \cong \triangle XYZ$

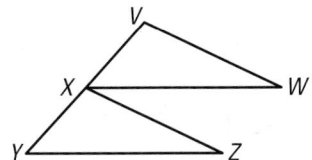

PROOF In Exercises 37 and 38, write a proof.

37. **GIVEN ▶** $\overline{JM} \cong \overline{LM}$
    PROVE ▶ $\triangle JKM \cong \triangle LKM$

38. **GIVEN ▶** D is the midpoint of $\overline{AC}$.
    PROVE ▶ $\triangle ABD \cong \triangle CBD$

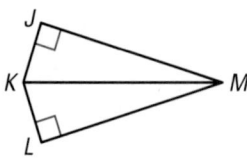

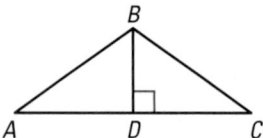

39. ★ **MULTIPLE CHOICE** Which triangle congruence can you prove, then use to prove that $\angle FED \cong \angle ABF$?

    (A) $\triangle ABE \cong \triangle ABF$

    (B) $\triangle AED \cong \triangle ABD$

    (C) $\triangle ACD \cong \triangle ADF$

    (D) $\triangle AEC \cong \triangle ABD$

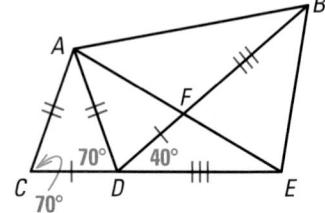

40. **PROOF** Write a two-column proof.

    GIVEN ▶ $\overline{CR} \cong \overline{CS}$, $\overline{QC} \perp \overline{CR}$, $\overline{QC} \perp \overline{CS}$
    PROVE ▶ $\triangle QCR \cong \triangle QCS$

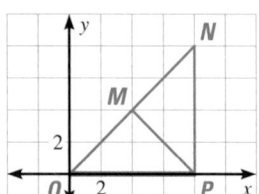

41. **CHALLENGE** *Describe* how to show that $\triangle PMO \cong \triangle PMN$ using the SSS Congruence Postulate. Then show that the triangles are congruent using the SAS Congruence Postulate without measuring any angles. *Compare* the two methods.

MIXED REVIEW

Draw a figure that fits the description. *(p. 42)*

42. A pentagon that is not regular.

43. A quadrilateral that is equilateral but not equiangular.

Write an equation of the line that passes through point *P* and is perpendicular to the line with the given equation. *(p. 180)*

44. $P(3, -1)$, $y = -x + 2$

45. $P(3, 3)$, $y = \frac{1}{3}x + 2$

46. $P(-4, -7)$, $y = -5$

PREVIEW
Prepare for
Lesson 4.5 in
Exs. 47–48.

Find the value of *x*. *(p. 225)*

47.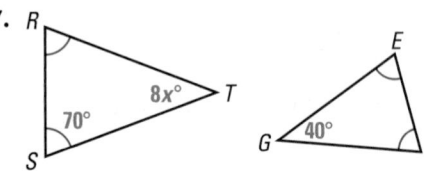

48.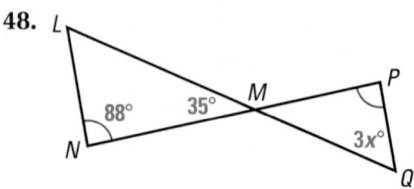

4.4 Investigate Triangles and Congruence

MATERIALS · graphing calculator or computer

QUESTION **Can you prove triangles are congruent by SSA?**

You can use geometry drawing software to show that if two sides and a nonincluded angle of one triangle are congruent to two sides and a nonincluded angle of another triangle, the triangles are not necessarily congruent.

EXAMPLE **Draw two triangles**

STEP 1

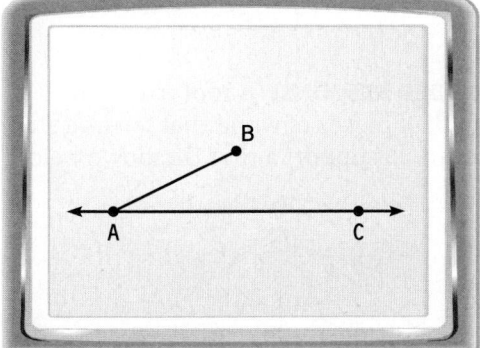

STEP 2

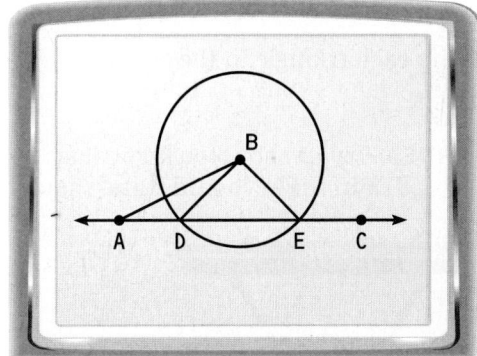

Draw a line Draw points *A* and *C*. Draw line $\overleftrightarrow{AC}$. Then choose point *B* so that $\angle BAC$ is acute. Draw $\overline{AB}$.

Draw a circle Draw a circle with center at *B* so that the circle intersects $\overleftrightarrow{AC}$ at two points. Label the points *D* and *E*. Draw $\overline{BD}$ and $\overline{BE}$. Save as "EXAMPLE".

STEP 3 ***Use your drawing***
Explain why $\overline{BD} \cong \overline{BE}$. In $\triangle ABD$ and $\triangle ABE$, what other sides are congruent? What angles are congruent?

PRACTICE

1. *Explain* how your drawing shows that $\triangle ABD \not\cong \triangle ABE$.

2. Change the diameter of your circle so that it intersects $\overleftrightarrow{AC}$ in only one point. Measure $\angle BDA$. *Explain* why there is exactly one triangle you can draw with the measures *AB*, *BD*, and a 90° angle at $\angle BDA$.

3. *Explain* why your results show that SSA cannot be used to show that two triangles are congruent but that HL can.

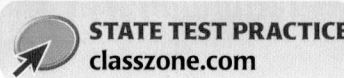
Lessons 4.1–4.4

1. **MULTI-STEP PROBLEM** In the diagram, $\overline{AC} \cong \overline{CD}$, $\overline{BC} \cong \overline{CG}$, $\overline{EC} \cong \overline{CF}$, and $\angle ACE \cong \angle DCF$.

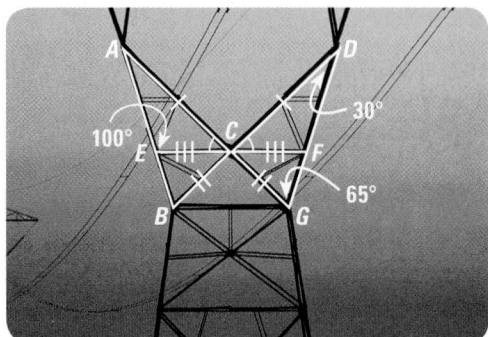

   a. Classify each triangle in the figure by angles.

   b. Classify each triangle in the figure by sides.

2. **OPEN-ENDED** *Explain* how you know that $\triangle PQR \cong \triangle STR$ in the keyboard stand shown.

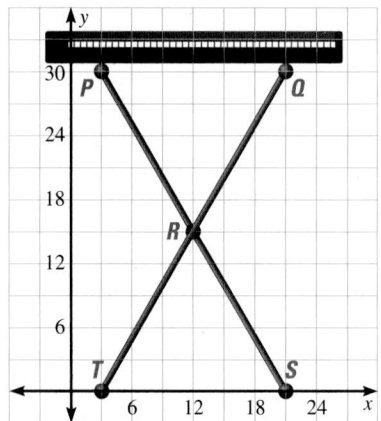

3. **GRIDDED ANSWER** In the diagram below, find the measure of $\angle 1$ in degrees.

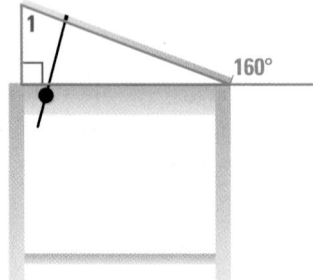

4. **SHORT RESPONSE** A rectangular "diver down" flag is used to indicate that scuba divers are in the water. On the flag, $\overline{AB} \cong \overline{FE}$, $\overline{AH} \cong \overline{DE}$, $\overline{CE} \cong \overline{AG}$, and $\overline{EG} \cong \overline{AC}$. Also, $\angle A$, $\angle C$, $\angle E$, and $\angle G$ are right angles. Is $\triangle BCD \cong \triangle FGH$? *Explain*.

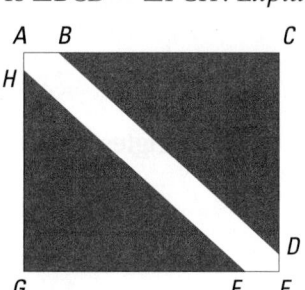

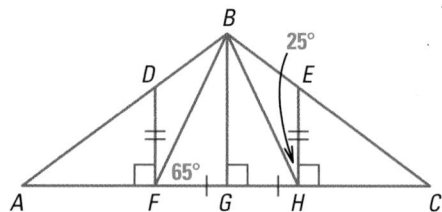

5. **EXTENDED RESPONSE** A roof truss is a network of pieces of wood that forms a stable structure to support a roof, as shown below.

   a. Prove that $\triangle FGB \cong \triangle HGB$.

   b. Is $\triangle BDF \cong \triangle BEH$? If so, prove it.

6. **GRIDDED ANSWER** In the diagram below, $BAFC \cong DEFC$. Find the value of x.

4.5 Prove Triangles Congruent by ASA and AAS

Before You used the SSS, SAS, and HL congruence methods.

Now You will use two more methods to prove congruences.

Why? So you can recognize congruent triangles in bikes, as in Exs. 23–24.

Key Vocabulary
• flow proof

Suppose you tear two angles out of a piece of paper and place them at a fixed distance on a ruler. Can you form more than one triangle with a given length and two given angle measures as shown below?

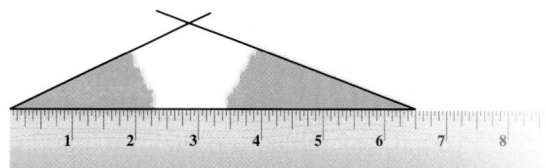

In a polygon, the side connecting the vertices of two angles is the *included* side. Given two angle measures and the length of the included side, you can make only one triangle. So, all triangles with those measurements are congruent.

THEOREMS   *For Your Notebook*

POSTULATE 21 Angle-Side-Angle (ASA) Congruence Postulate

If two angles and the included side of one triangle are congruent to two angles and the included side of a second triangle, then the two triangles are congruent.

If   Angle $\angle A \cong \angle D$,
       Side $\overline{AC} \cong \overline{DF}$, and
       Angle $\angle C \cong \angle F$,
then $\triangle ABC \cong \triangle DEF$.

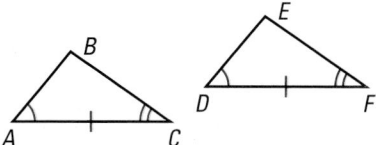

THEOREM 4.6 Angle-Angle-Side (AAS) Congruence Theorem

If two angles and a non-included side of one triangle are congruent to two angles and the corresponding non-included side of a second triangle, then the two triangles are congruent.

If   Angle $\angle A \cong \angle D$,
       Angle $\angle C \cong \angle F$, and
       Side $\overline{BC} \cong \overline{EF}$,
then $\triangle ABC \cong \triangle DEF$.

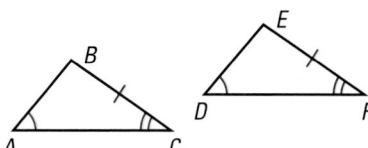

Proof: Example 2, p. 250

EXAMPLE 1   Identify congruent triangles

Can the triangles be proven congruent with the information given in the diagram? If so, state the postulate or theorem you would use.

a. 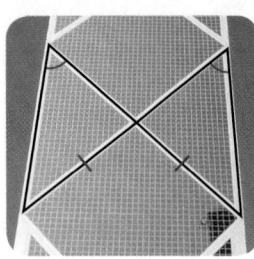 b.  c.

Solution

a. The vertical angles are congruent, so two pairs of angles and a pair of non-included sides are congruent. The triangles are congruent by the AAS Congruence Theorem.

AVOID ERRORS
You need at least one pair of congruent corresponding sides to prove two triangles congruent.

b. There is not enough information to prove the triangles are congruent, because no sides are known to be congruent.

c. Two pairs of angles and their included sides are congruent. The triangles are congruent by the ASA Congruence Postulate.

FLOW PROOFS You have written two-column proofs and paragraph proofs. A **flow proof** uses arrows to show the flow of a logical argument. Each reason is written below the statement it justifies.

EXAMPLE 2   Prove the AAS Congruence Theorem

Prove the Angle-Angle-Side Congruence Theorem.

GIVEN ▶ $\angle A \cong \angle D$, $\angle C \cong \angle F$, $\overline{BC} \cong \overline{EF}$

PROVE ▶ $\triangle ABC \cong \triangle DEF$

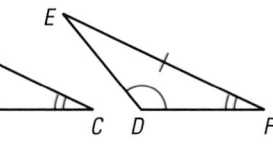

$\angle A \cong \angle D$	→	$\angle B \cong \angle E$
Given		Third ∠ Thm.

$\angle C \cong \angle F$
Given

$\triangle ABC \cong \triangle DEF$
ASA Congruence Post.

$\overline{BC} \cong \overline{EF}$
Given

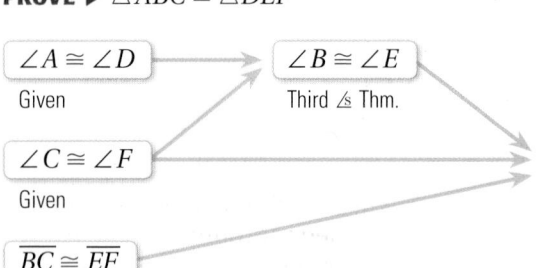

Animated Geometry at classzone.com

✓ **GUIDED PRACTICE**   for Examples 1 and 2

1. In the diagram at the right, what postulate or theorem can you use to prove that $\triangle RST \cong \triangle VUT$? *Explain.*

2. Rewrite the proof of the Triangle Sum Theorem on page 219 as a flow proof.

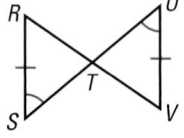

250   Chapter 4   Congruent Triangles

EXAMPLE 3 **Write a flow proof**

In the diagram, $\overline{CE} \perp \overline{BD}$ and $\angle CAB \cong \angle CAD$.
Write a flow proof to show $\triangle ABE \cong \triangle ADE$.

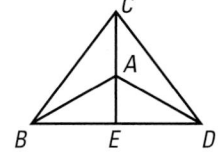

Solution

GIVEN ▶ $\overline{CE} \perp \overline{BD}$, $\angle CAB \cong \angle CAD$
PROVE ▶ $\triangle ABE \cong \triangle ADE$

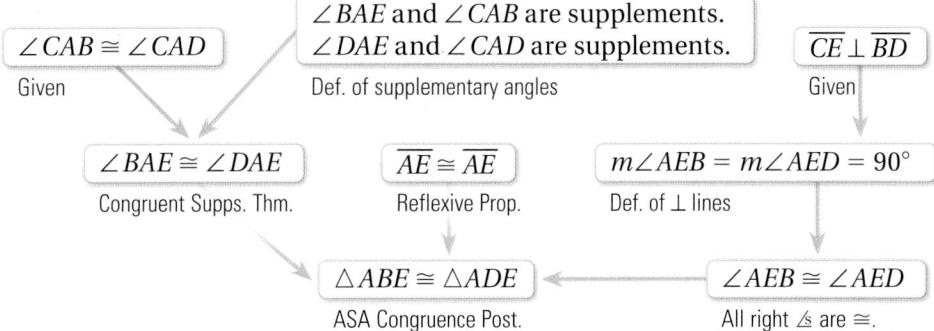

| $\angle CAB \cong \angle CAD$ | $\angle BAE$ and $\angle CAB$ are supplements. $\angle DAE$ and $\angle CAD$ are supplements. | $\overline{CE} \perp \overline{BD}$ |
| Given | Def. of supplementary angles | Given |

| $\angle BAE \cong \angle DAE$ | $\overline{AE} \cong \overline{AE}$ | $m\angle AEB = m\angle AED = 90°$ |
| Congruent Supps. Thm. | Reflexive Prop. | Def. of ⊥ lines |

| $\triangle ABE \cong \triangle ADE$ | $\angle AEB \cong \angle AED$ |
| ASA Congruence Post. | All right ∡ are ≅. |

EXAMPLE 4 **Standardized Test Practice**

FIRE TOWERS The forestry service uses fire tower lookouts to watch for forest fires. When the lookouts spot a fire, they measure the angle of their view and radio a dispatcher. The dispatcher then uses the angles to locate the fire. How many lookouts are needed to locate a fire?

Ⓐ 1   Ⓑ 2   Ⓒ 3   Ⓓ Not enough information

The locations of tower *A*, tower *B*, and the fire form a triangle. The dispatcher knows the distance from tower *A* to tower *B* and the measures of $\angle A$ and $\angle B$. So, the measures of two angles and an included side of the triangle are known.

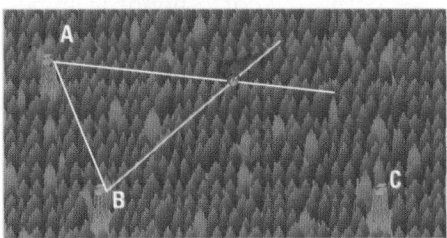

By the ASA Congruence Postulate, all triangles with these measures are congruent. So, the triangle formed is unique and the fire location is given by the third vertex. Two lookouts are needed to locate the fire.

▶ The correct answer is B. Ⓐ **Ⓑ** Ⓒ Ⓓ

✓ **GUIDED PRACTICE** for Examples 3 and 4

3. In Example 3, suppose $\angle ABE \cong \angle ADE$ is also given. What theorem or postulate besides ASA can you use to prove that $\triangle ABE \cong \triangle ADE$?

4. **WHAT IF?** In Example 4, suppose a fire occurs directly between tower *B* and tower *C*. Could towers *B* and *C* be used to locate the fire? *Explain.*

Triangle Congruence Postulates and Theorems

You have learned five methods for proving that triangles are congruent.

SSS	SAS	HL (right △ only)	ASA	AAS
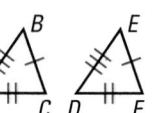	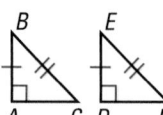	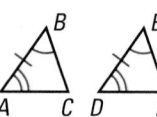	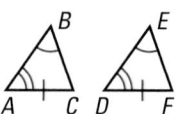	
All three sides are congruent.	Two sides and the included angle are congruent.	The hypotenuse and one of the legs are congruent.	Two angles and the included side are congruent.	Two angles and a (non-included) side are congruent.

In the Exercises, you will prove three additional theorems about the congruence of right triangles: **A**ngle-**L**eg, **L**eg-**L**eg, and **H**ypotenuse-**A**ngle.

4.5 EXERCISES

SKILL PRACTICE

1. **VOCABULARY** Name one advantage of using a flow proof rather than a two-column proof.

2. ★ **WRITING** You know that a pair of triangles has two pairs of congruent corresponding angles. What other information do you need to show that the triangles are congruent?

EXAMPLE 1
on p. 250
for Exs. 3–7

IDENTIFY CONGRUENT TRIANGLES **Is it possible to prove that the triangles are congruent? If so, state the postulate or theorem you would use.**

3. △ABC, △QRS

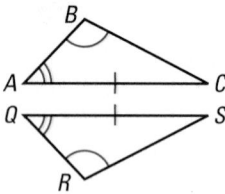

4. △XYZ, △JKL

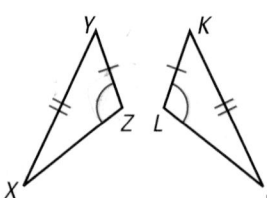

5. △PQR, △RSP

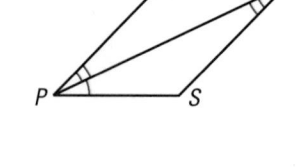

6. **ERROR ANALYSIS** *Describe* the error in concluding that △ABC ≅ △XYZ.

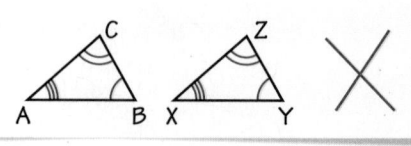

By AAA, △ABC ≅ △XYZ.

7. **★ MULTIPLE CHOICE** Which postulate or theorem can you use to prove that △ABC ≅ △HJK?

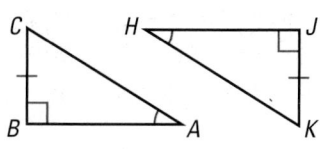

    (A) HL   (B) AAS

    (C) SAS   (D) Not enough information

EXAMPLE 2
on p. 250
for Exs. 8–13

DEVELOPING PROOF State the third congruence that is needed to prove that △*FGH* ≅ △*LMN* using the given postulate or theorem.

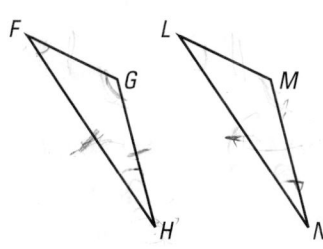

8. **GIVEN** ▶ $\overline{GH} \cong \overline{MN}$, $\angle G \cong \angle M$, __?__ ≅ __?__
    Use the AAS Congruence Theorem.

9. **GIVEN** ▶ $\overline{FG} \cong \overline{LM}$, $\angle G \cong \angle M$, __?__ ≅ __?__
    Use the ASA Congruence Postulate.

10. **GIVEN** ▶ $\overline{FH} \cong \overline{LN}$, $\angle H \cong \angle N$, __?__ ≅ __?__
    Use the SAS Congruence Postulate.

OVERLAPPING TRIANGLES *Explain* how you can prove that the indicated triangles are congruent using the given postulate or theorem.

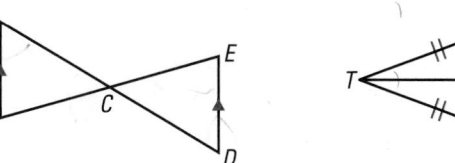

11. △*AFE* ≅ △*DFB* by SAS

12. △*AED* ≅ △*BDE* by AAS

13. △*AED* ≅ △*BDC* by ASA

DETERMINING CONGRUENCE Tell whether you can use the given information to determine whether △*ABC* ≅ △*DEF*. *Explain* your reasoning.

14. $\angle A \cong \angle D$, $\overline{AB} \cong \overline{DE}$, $\overline{AC} \cong \overline{DF}$
          15. $\angle A \cong \angle D$, $\angle B \cong \angle E$, $\angle C \cong \angle F$

16. $\angle B \cong \angle E$, $\angle C \cong \angle F$, $\overline{AC} \cong \overline{DE}$
        17. $\overline{AB} \cong \overline{EF}$, $\overline{BC} \cong \overline{FD}$, $\overline{AC} \cong \overline{DE}$

IDENTIFY CONGRUENT TRIANGLES Is it possible to prove that the triangles are congruent? If so, state the postulate(s) or theorem(s) you would use.

18. △*ABC*, △*DEC*   19. △*TUV*, △*TWV*   20. △*QML*, △*LPN*

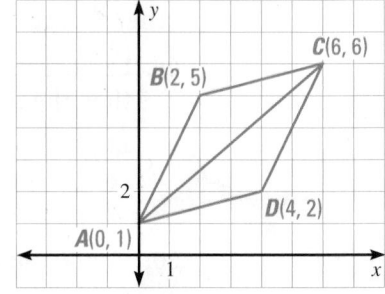

21. **★ EXTENDED RESPONSE** Use the graph at the right.

    a. Show that $\angle CAD \cong \angle ACB$. *Explain* your reasoning.

    b. Show that $\angle ACD \cong \angle CAB$. *Explain* your reasoning.

    c. Show that △*ABC* ≅ △*CDA*. *Explain* your reasoning.

22. **CHALLENGE** Use a coordinate plane.

    a. Graph the lines $y = 2x + 5$, $y = 2x - 3$, and $x = 0$ in the same coordinate plane.

    b. Consider the equation $y = mx + 1$. For what values of m will the graph of the equation form two triangles if added to your graph? For what values of m will those triangles be congruent? *Explain*.

CONGRUENCE IN BICYCLES *Explain* why the triangles are congruent.

23.

24.

@HomeTutor for problem solving help at classzone.com

EXAMPLE 3
on p. 251
for Ex. 25

25. FLOW PROOF Copy and complete the flow proof.

GIVEN ▶ $\overline{AD} \parallel \overline{CE}$, $\overline{BD} \cong \overline{BC}$

PROVE ▶ $\triangle ABD \cong \triangle EBC$

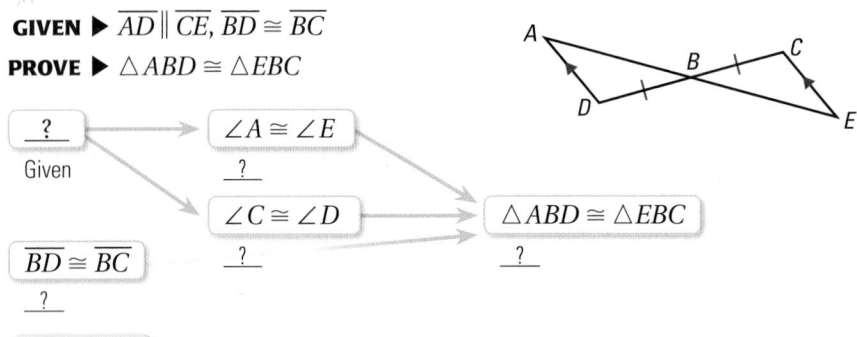

```
  ?          →      ∠A ≅ ∠E
─────                ──────
Given                  ?        →
                                     △ABD ≅ △EBC
                   ∠C ≅ ∠D     →    ─────────────
  BD ≅ BC            ──────              ?
─────────              ?
   ?
```

@HomeTutor for problem solving help at classzone.com

EXAMPLE 4
on p. 251
for Ex. 26

26. ★ SHORT RESPONSE You are making a map for an orienteering race. Participants start at a large oak tree, find a boulder 250 yards due east of the oak tree, and then find a maple tree that is 50° west of north of the boulder and 35° east of north of the oak tree. Sketch a map. Can you locate the maple tree? *Explain.*

27. AIRPLANE In the airplane at the right, $\angle C$ and $\angle F$ are right angles, $\overline{BC} \cong \overline{EF}$, and $\angle A \cong \angle D$. What postulate or theorem allows you to conclude that $\triangle ABC \cong \triangle DEF$?

RIGHT TRIANGLES In Lesson 4.4, you learned the Hypotenuse-Leg Theorem for right triangles. In Exercises 28–30, write a paragraph proof for these other theorems about right triangles.

28. Leg-Leg (LL) Theorem If the legs of two right triangles are congruent, then the triangles are congruent.

29. Angle-Leg (AL) Theorem If an angle and a leg of a right triangle are congruent to an angle and a leg of a second right triangle, then the triangles are congruent.

30. Hypotenuse-Angle (HA) Theorem If an angle and the hypotenuse of a right triangle are congruent to an angle and the hypotenuse of a second right triangle, then the triangles are congruent.

31. PROOF Write a two-column proof.

GIVEN ▶ $\overline{AK} \cong \overline{CJ}$, $\angle BJK \cong \angle BKJ$,
$\angle A \cong \angle C$

PROVE ▶ $\triangle ABK \cong \triangle CBJ$

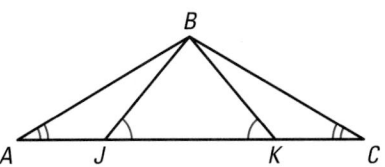

32. PROOF Write a flow proof.

GIVEN ▶ $\overline{VW} \cong \overline{UW}$, $\angle X \cong \angle Z$

PROVE ▶ $\triangle XWV \cong \triangle ZWU$

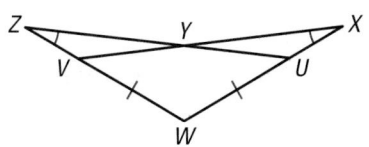

33. PROOF Write a proof.

GIVEN ▶ $\angle NKM \cong \angle LMK$, $\angle L \cong \angle N$

PROVE ▶ $\triangle NMK \cong \triangle LKM$

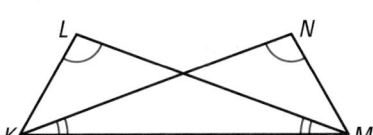

34. PROOF Write a proof.

GIVEN ▶ X is the midpoint of $\overline{VY}$ and $\overline{WZ}$.

PROVE ▶ $\triangle VWX \cong \triangle YZX$

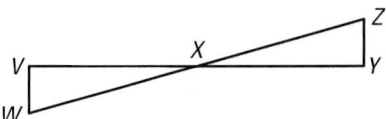

35. CHALLENGE Write a proof.

GIVEN ▶ $\triangle ABF \cong \triangle DFB$, F is the midpoint of $\overline{AE}$,
B is the midpoint of $\overline{AC}$.

PROVE ▶ $\triangle FDE \cong \triangle BCD \cong \triangle ABF$

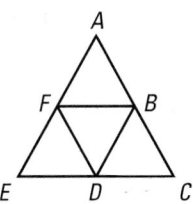

MIXED REVIEW

Find the value of x that makes $m \parallel n$. *(p. 161)*

36.

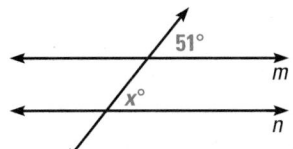

37.

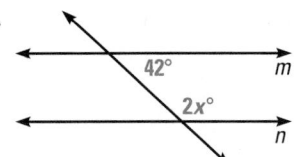

38.

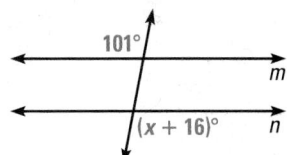

Write an equation of the line that passes through point P and is parallel to the line with the given equation. *(p. 180)*

39. $P(0, 3)$, $y = x - 8$

40. $P(-2, 4)$, $y = -2x + 3$

PREVIEW

Prepare for
Lesson 4.6 in
Exs. 41–43.

Decide which method, SSS, SAS, or HL, can be used to prove that the triangles are congruent. *(pp. 234, 240)*

41. $\triangle HJK \cong \triangle LKJ$

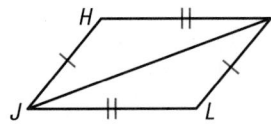

42. $\triangle UTV \cong \triangle WVT$

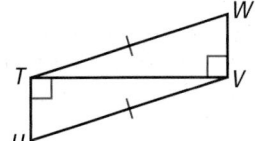

43. $\triangle XYZ \cong \triangle RQZ$

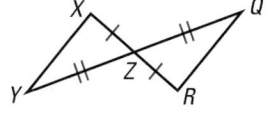

4.6 Use Congruent Triangles

Before You used corresponding parts to prove triangles congruent.

Now You will use congruent triangles to prove corresponding parts congruent.

Why? So you can find the distance across a half pipe, as in Ex. 30.

Key Vocabulary
• **corresponding parts,** *p. 225*

By definition, congruent triangles have congruent corresponding parts. So, if you can prove that two triangles are congruent, you know that their corresponding parts must be congruent as well.

EXAMPLE 1 Use congruent triangles

Explain how you can use the given information to prove that the hanglider parts are congruent.

GIVEN ▶ $\angle 1 \cong \angle 2$, $\angle RTQ \cong \angle RTS$

PROVE ▶ $\overline{QT} \cong \overline{ST}$

Solution

If you can show that $\triangle QRT \cong \triangle SRT$, you will know that $\overline{QT} \cong \overline{ST}$. First, copy the diagram and mark the given information. Then add the information that you can deduce. In this case, $\angle RQT$ and $\angle RST$ are supplementary to congruent angles, so $\angle RQT \cong \angle RST$. Also, $\overline{RT} \cong \overline{RT}$.

Mark given information.   Add deduced information.

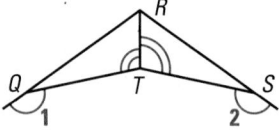   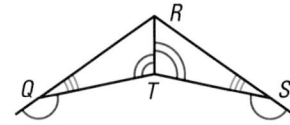

Two angle pairs and a non-included side are congruent, so by the AAS Congruence Theorem, $\triangle QRT \cong \triangle SRT$. Because corresponding parts of congruent triangles are congruent, $\overline{QT} \cong \overline{ST}$.

Animated **Geometry** at classzone.com

✓ **GUIDED PRACTICE** for Example 1

1. *Explain* how you can prove that $\angle A \cong \angle C$.

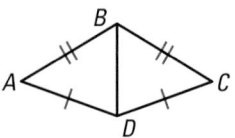

EXAMPLE 2 Use congruent triangles for measurement

INDIRECT MEASUREMENT
When you cannot easily measure a length directly, you can make conclusions about the length *indirectly*, usually by calculations based on known lengths.

SURVEYING Use the following method to find the distance across a river, from point *N* to point *P*.

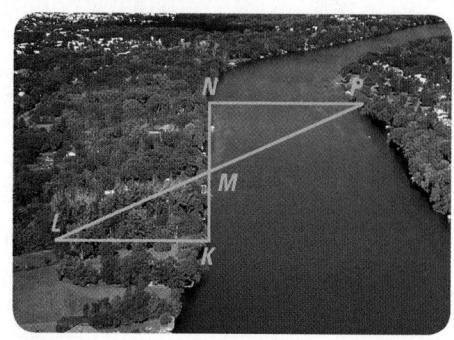

- Place a stake at *K* on the near side so that $\overline{NK} \perp \overline{NP}$.

- Find *M*, the midpoint of $\overline{NK}$.

- Locate the point *L* so that $\overline{NK} \perp \overline{KL}$ and *L*, *P*, and *M* are collinear.

- Explain how this plan allows you to find the distance.

Solution

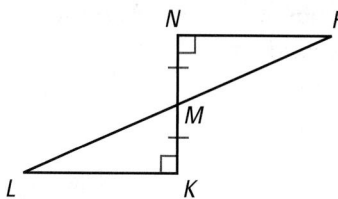

Because $\overline{NK} \perp \overline{NP}$ and $\overline{NK} \perp \overline{KL}$, $\angle N$ and $\angle K$ are congruent right angles. Because *M* is the midpoint of $\overline{NK}$, $\overline{NM} \cong \overline{KM}$. The vertical angles $\angle KML$ and $\angle NMP$ are congruent. So, $\triangle MLK \cong \triangle MPN$ by the ASA Congruence Postulate. Then, because corresponding parts of congruent triangles are congruent, $\overline{KL} \cong \overline{NP}$. So, you can find the distance *NP* across the river by measuring $\overline{KL}$.

EXAMPLE 3 Plan a proof involving pairs of triangles

Use the given information to write a plan for proof.

GIVEN ▶ $\angle 1 \cong \angle 2$, $\angle 3 \cong \angle 4$
PROVE ▶ $\triangle BCE \cong \triangle DCE$

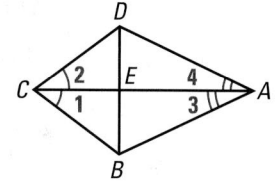

Solution

In $\triangle BCE$ and $\triangle DCE$, you know $\angle 1 \cong \angle 2$ and $\overline{CE} \cong \overline{CE}$. If you can show that $\overline{CB} \cong \overline{CD}$, you can use the SAS Congruence Postulate.

To prove that $\overline{CB} \cong \overline{CD}$, you can first prove that $\triangle CBA \cong \triangle CDA$. You are given $\angle 1 \cong \angle 2$ and $\angle 3 \cong \angle 4$. $\overline{CA} \cong \overline{CA}$ by the Reflexive Property. You can use the ASA Congruence Postulate to prove that $\triangle CBA \cong \triangle CDA$.

▶ **Plan for Proof** Use the ASA Congruence Postulate to prove that $\triangle CBA \cong \triangle CDA$. Then state that $\overline{CB} \cong \overline{CD}$. Use the SAS Congruence Postulate to prove that $\triangle BCE \cong \triangle DCE$.

Animated **Geometry** at classzone.com

✓ **GUIDED PRACTICE** | for Examples 2 and 3

2. In Example 2, does it matter how far from point *N* you place a stake at point *K*? *Explain.*

3. Using the information in the diagram at the right, write a plan to prove that $\triangle PTU \cong \triangle UQP$.

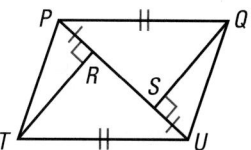

PROVING CONSTRUCTIONS On page 34, you learned how to use a compass and a straightedge to copy an angle. The construction is shown below. You can use congruent triangles to prove that this construction is valid.

STEP 1

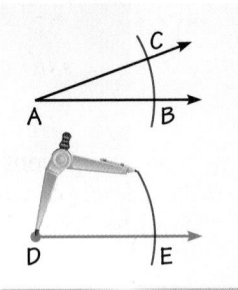

STEP 2

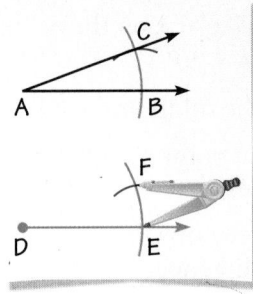

STEP 3

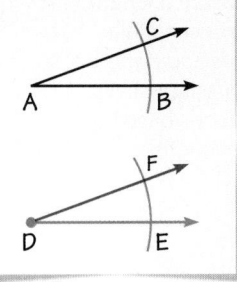

To copy ∠**A,** draw a segment with initial point *D*. Draw an arc with center *A*. Using the same radius, draw an arc with center *D*. Label points *B*, *C*, and *E*.

Draw an arc with radius *BC* and center *E*. Label the intersection *F*.

Draw $\overrightarrow{DF}$. In Example 4, you will prove that ∠*D* ≅ ∠*A*.

EXAMPLE 4   Prove a construction

Write a proof to verify that the construction for copying an angle is valid.

Solution

Add $\overline{BC}$ and $\overline{EF}$ to the diagram. In the construction, $\overline{AB}$, $\overline{DE}$, $\overline{AC}$, and $\overline{DF}$ are all determined by the same compass setting, as are $\overline{BC}$ and $\overline{EF}$. So, you can assume the following as given statements.

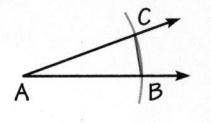

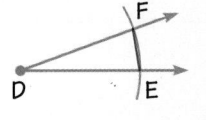

GIVEN ▶ $\overline{AB} \cong \overline{DE}$, $\overline{AC} \cong \overline{DF}$, $\overline{BC} \cong \overline{EF}$
PROVE ▶ ∠*D* ≅ ∠*A*

Plan for Proof   Show that △*CAB* ≅ △*FDE*, so you can conclude that the corresponding parts ∠*A* and ∠*D* are congruent.

	STATEMENTS	REASONS
Plan in Action	**1.** $\overline{AB} \cong \overline{DE}$, $\overline{AC} \cong \overline{DF}$, $\overline{BC} \cong \overline{EF}$	**1.** Given
	2. △*FDE* ≅ △*CAB*	**2.** SSS Congruence Postulate
	3. ∠*D* ≅ ∠*A*	**3.** Corresp. parts of ≅ △ are ≅.

✓ **GUIDED PRACTICE**   for Example 4

4. Look back at the construction of an angle bisector in Explore 4 on page 34. What segments can you assume are congruent?

4.6 EXERCISES

HOMEWORK KEY

○ = WORKED-OUT SOLUTIONS
on p. WS5 for Exs. 19, 23, and 31

★ = STANDARDIZED TEST PRACTICE
Exs. 2, 14, 31, and 36

SKILL PRACTICE

1. **VOCABULARY** Copy and complete: Corresponding parts of congruent triangles are __?__.

2. ★ **WRITING** *Explain* why you might choose to use congruent triangles to measure the distance across a river. Give another example where it may be easier to measure with congruent triangles rather than directly.

EXAMPLES 1 and 2
on p. 256–257 for Exs. 3–11

CONGRUENT TRIANGLES **Tell which triangles you can show are congruent in order to prove the statement. What postulate or theorem would you use?**

3. $\angle A \cong \angle D$

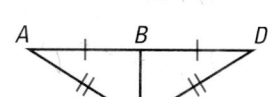

4. $\angle Q \cong \angle T$

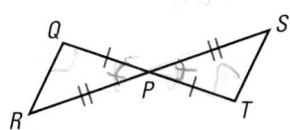

5. $\overline{JM} \cong \overline{LM}$

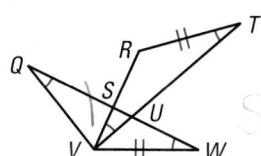

6. $\overline{AC} \cong \overline{BD}$

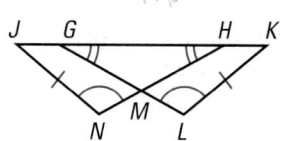

7. $\overline{GK} \cong \overline{HJ}$

8. $\overline{QW} \cong \overline{TV}$

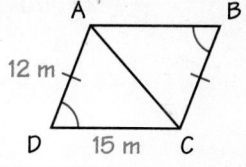

9. **ERROR ANALYSIS** *Describe* the error in the statement.

△ABC ≅ △CDA by SAS.
So, AB = 15 meters.

PLANNING FOR PROOF **Use the diagram to write a plan for proof.**

10. **PROVE** ▶ $\angle S \cong \angle U$

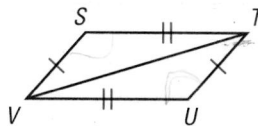

11. **PROVE** ▶ $\overline{LM} \cong \overline{LQ}$

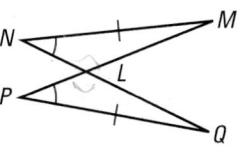

12. **PENTAGONS** *Explain* why segments connecting any pair of corresponding vertices of congruent pentagons are congruent. Make a sketch to support your answer.

13. **ALGEBRA** Given that $\triangle ABC \cong \triangle DEF$, $m\angle A = 70°$, $m\angle B = 60°$, $m\angle C = 50°$, $m\angle D = (3x + 10)°$, $m\angle E = \left(\dfrac{y}{3} + 20\right)°$, and $m\angle F = (z^2 + 14)°$, find the values of x, y, and z.

14. ★ MULTIPLE CHOICE Which set of given information does *not* allow you to conclude that $\overline{AD} \cong \overline{CD}$?

Ⓐ $\overline{AE} \cong \overline{CE}$, $m\angle BEA = 90°$

Ⓑ $\overline{BA} \cong \overline{BC}$, $\angle BDC \cong \angle BDA$

Ⓒ $\overline{AB} \cong \overline{CB}$, $\angle ABE \cong \angle CBE$

Ⓓ $\overline{AE} \cong \overline{CE}$, $\overline{AB} \cong \overline{CB}$

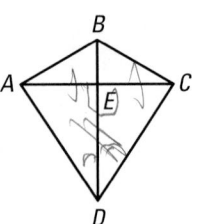

EXAMPLE 3
on p. 257
for Exs. 15–20

PLANNING FOR PROOF Use the information given in the diagram to write a plan for proving that $\angle 1 \cong \angle 2$.

15.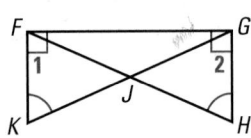

16.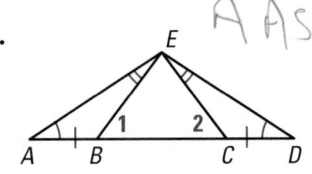

17.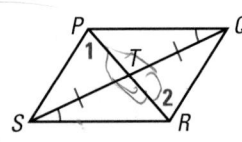

18.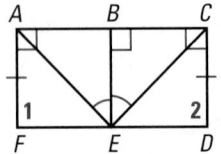

19.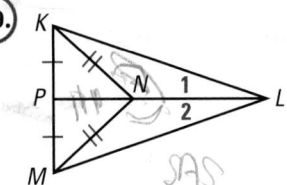

20.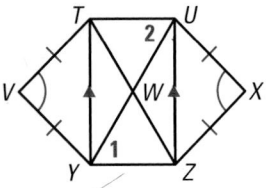

USING COORDINATES Use the vertices of $\triangle ABC$ and $\triangle DEF$ to show that $\angle A \cong \angle D$. *Explain* your reasoning.

21. $A(3, 7)$, $B(6, 11)$, $C(11, 13)$, $D(2, -4)$, $E(5, -8)$, $F(10, -10)$

22. $A(3, 8)$, $B(3, 2)$, $C(11, 2)$, $D(-1, 5)$, $E(5, 5)$, $F(5, 13)$

PROOF Use the information given in the diagram to write a proof.

23. **PROVE ▶** $\angle VYX \cong \angle WYZ$

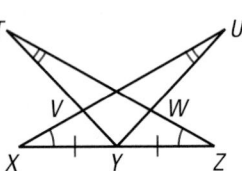

24. **PROVE ▶** $\overline{FL} \cong \overline{HN}$

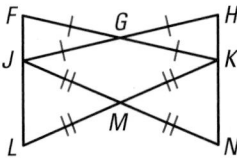

25. **PROVE ▶** $\triangle PUX \cong \triangle QSY$

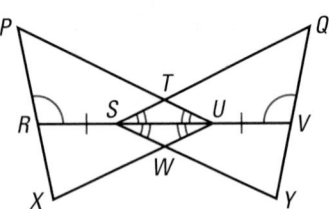

26. **PROVE ▶** $\overline{AC} \cong \overline{GE}$

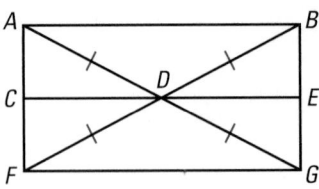

27. **CHALLENGE** Which of the triangles below are congruent?

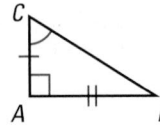
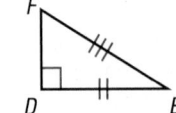
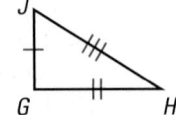
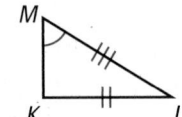
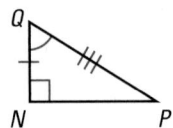

◯ = **WORKED-OUT SOLUTIONS**
on p. WS1

★ = **STANDARDIZED TEST PRACTICE**

EXAMPLE 2
on p. 257
for Ex. 28

28. CANYON *Explain* how you can find the distance across the canyon.

@HomeTutor for problem solving help at classzone.com

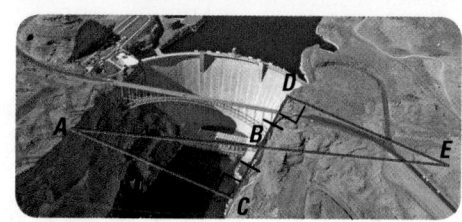

29. PROOF Use the given information and the diagram to write a two-column proof.

GIVEN ▸ $\overline{PQ} \parallel \overline{VS}$, $\overline{QU} \parallel \overline{ST}$, $\overline{PQ} \cong \overline{VS}$

PROVE ▸ $\angle Q \cong \angle S$

@HomeTutor for problem solving help at classzone.com

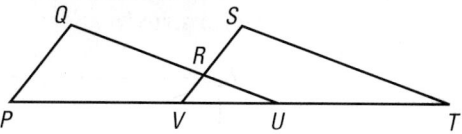

30. SNOWBOARDING In the diagram of the half pipe below, C is the midpoint of $\overline{BD}$. If $EC \approx 11.5$ m, and $CD \approx 2.5$ m, find the approximate distance across the half pipe. *Explain* your reasoning.

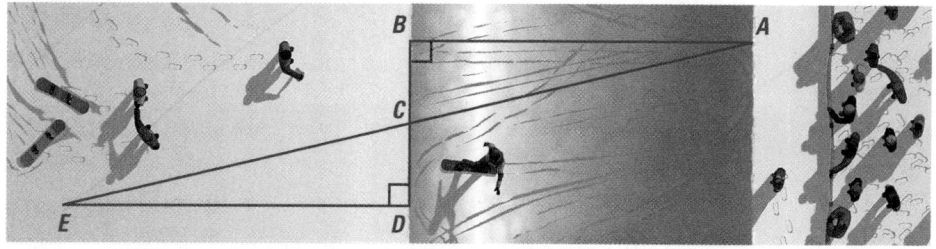

31. ★ **MULTIPLE CHOICE** Using the information in the diagram, you can prove that $\overline{WY} \cong \overline{ZX}$. Which reason would *not* appear in the proof?

A SAS Congruence Postulate

B AAS Congruence Theorem

C Alternate Interior Angles Theorem

D Right Angles Congruence Theorem

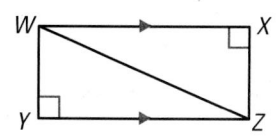

EXAMPLE 4
on p. 258
for Ex. 32

32. PROVING A CONSTRUCTION The diagrams below show the construction on page 34 used to bisect $\angle A$. By construction, you can assume that $\overline{AB} \cong \overline{AC}$ and $\overline{BG} \cong \overline{CG}$. Write a proof to verify that $\overrightarrow{AG}$ bisects $\angle A$.

STEP 1

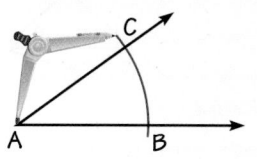

First draw an arc with center A. Label the points where the arc intersects the sides of the angle points B and C.

STEP 2

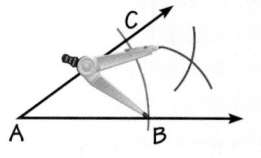

Draw an arc with center C. Using the same radius, draw an arc with center B. Label the intersection point G.

STEP 3

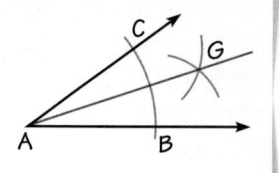

Draw $\overrightarrow{AG}$. It follows that $\angle BAG \cong \angle CAG$.

ARCHITECTURE Can you use the given information to determine that $\overline{AB} \cong \overline{BC}$? *Justify* your answer.

33. $\angle ABD \cong \angle CBD$, $AD = CD$

34. $\overline{AC} \perp \overline{BD}$, $\triangle ADE \cong \triangle CDE$

35. $\overline{BD}$ bisects $\overline{AC}$, $\overline{AD} \perp \overline{BD}$

36. ★ **EXTENDED RESPONSE** You can use the method described below to find the distance across a river. You will need a cap with a visor.

- Stand on one side of the river and look straight across to a point on the other side. Align the visor of your cap with that point.

- Without changing the inclination of your neck and head, turn sideways until the visor is in line with a point on your side of the stream.

- Measure the distance *BD* between your feet and that point.

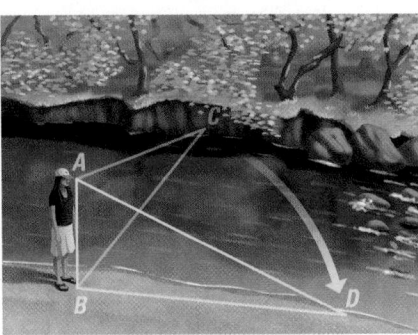

a. What corresponding parts of the two triangles can you assume are congruent? What postulate or theorem can you use to show that the two triangles are congruent?

b. *Explain* why *BD* is also the distance across the stream.

PROOF Use the given information and the diagram to prove that $\angle 1 \cong \angle 2$.

37. GIVEN ▶ $\overline{MN} \cong \overline{KN}$, $\angle PMN \cong \angle NKL$

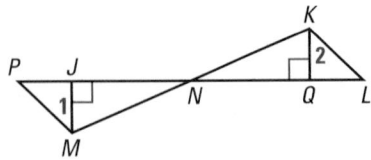

38. GIVEN ▶ $\overline{TS} \cong \overline{TV}$, $\overline{SR} \cong \overline{VW}$

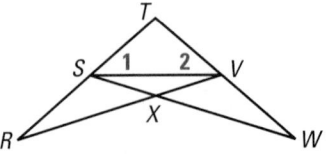

39. PROOF Write a proof.

GIVEN ▶ $\overline{BA} \cong \overline{BC}$, *D* and *E* are midpoints, $\angle A \cong \angle C$, $\overline{DF} \cong \overline{EF}$

PROVE ▶ $\overline{FG} \cong \overline{FH}$

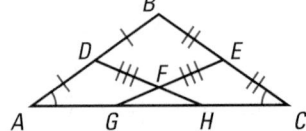

40. CHALLENGE In the diagram of pentagon $ABCDE$, $\overline{AB} \parallel \overline{EC}$, $\overline{AC} \parallel \overline{ED}$, $\overline{AB} \cong \overline{ED}$, and $\overline{AC} \cong \overline{EC}$. Write a proof that shows $\overline{AD} \cong \overline{EB}$.

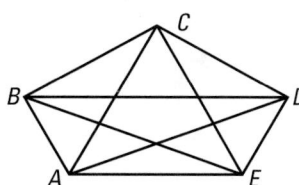

MIXED REVIEW

How many lines can be drawn that fit each description? Copy the diagram and sketch all the lines. *(p. 147)*

41. Line(s) through B and parallel to $\overleftrightarrow{AC}$

42. Line(s) through A and perpendicular to $\overleftrightarrow{BC}$

43. Line(s) through D and C

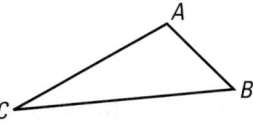

PREVIEW
Prepare for
Lesson 4.7 in
Exs. 44–46.

The variable expressions represent the angle measures of a triangle. Find the measure of each angle. Then classify the triangle by its angles. *(p. 217)*

44. $m\angle A = x°$
$m\angle B = (4x)°$
$m\angle C = (5x)°$

45. $m\angle A = x°$
$m\angle B = (5x)°$
$m\angle C = (x + 19)°$

46. $m\angle A = (x - 22)°$
$m\angle B = (x + 16)°$
$m\angle C = (2x - 14)°$

QUIZ *for Lessons 4.4–4.6*

Decide which method, SAS, ASA, AAS, or HL, can be used to prove that the triangles are congruent. *(pp. 240, 249)*

1.
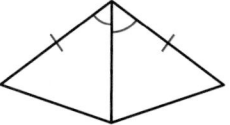

2.
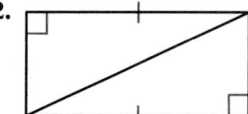

3.
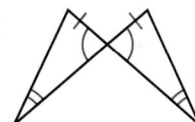

Use the given information to write a proof.

4. GIVEN ▶ $\angle BAC \cong \angle DCA$, $\overline{AB} \cong \overline{CD}$
PROVE ▶ $\triangle ABC \cong \triangle CDA$ *(p. 240)*

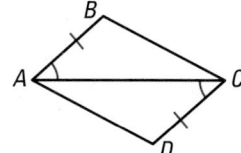

5. GIVEN ▶ $\angle W \cong \angle Z$, $\overline{VW} \cong \overline{YZ}$
PROVE ▶ $\triangle VWX \cong \triangle YZX$ *(p. 249)*

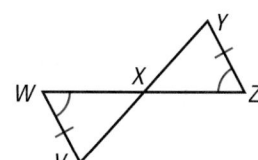

6. Write a plan for a proof. *(p. 256)*

GIVEN ▶ $\overline{PQ} \cong \overline{MN}$, $m\angle P = m\angle M = 90°$
PROVE ▶ $\overline{QL} \cong \overline{NL}$

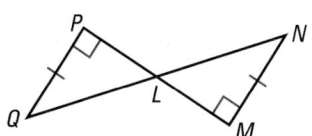

4.7 Use Isosceles and Equilateral Triangles

Before	You learned about isosceles and equilateral triangles.
Now	You will use theorems about isosceles and equilateral triangles.
Why?	So you can solve a problem about architecture, as in Ex. 40.

Key Vocabulary
• legs
• vertex angle
• base
• base angles

In Lesson 4.1, you learned that a triangle is isosceles if it has at least two congruent sides. When an isosceles triangle has exactly two congruent sides, these two sides are the **legs**. The angle formed by the legs is the **vertex angle**. The third side is the **base** of the isosceles triangle. The two angles adjacent to the base are called **base angles**.

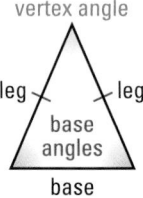

THEOREMS   *For Your Notebook*

THEOREM 4.7 Base Angles Theorem

If two sides of a triangle are congruent, then the angles opposite them are congruent.

If $\overline{AB} \cong \overline{AC}$, then $\angle B \cong \angle C$.

Proof: p. 265

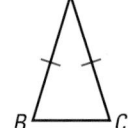

THEOREM 4.8 Converse of Base Angles Theorem

If two angles of a triangle are congruent, then the sides opposite them are congruent.

If $\angle B \cong \angle C$, then $\overline{AB} \cong \overline{AC}$.

Proof: Ex. 45, p. 269

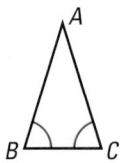

EXAMPLE 1   Apply the Base Angles Theorem

In △*DEF*, $\overline{DE} \cong \overline{DF}$. Name two congruent angles.

Solution

▶ $\overline{DE} \cong \overline{DF}$, so by the Base Angles Theorem, $\angle E \cong \angle F$.

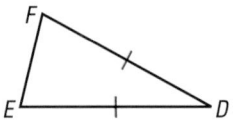

✓ **GUIDED PRACTICE**   for Example 1

Copy and complete the statement.

1. If $\overline{HG} \cong \overline{HK}$, then $\angle$ _?_ $\cong \angle$ _?_ .

2. If $\angle KHJ \cong \angle KJH$, then _?_ $\cong$ _?_ .

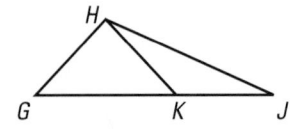

PROOF **Base Angles Theorem**

GIVEN ▶ $\overline{JK} \cong \overline{JL}$

PROVE ▶ $\angle K \cong \angle L$

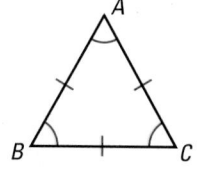

Plan for Proof
a. Draw $\overline{JM}$ so that it bisects $\overline{KL}$.
b. Use SSS to show that $\triangle JMK \cong \triangle JML$.
c. Use properties of congruent triangles to show that $\angle K \cong \angle L$.

	STATEMENTS	REASONS
Plan in Action	**1.** M is the midpoint of $\overline{KL}$.	**1.** Definition of midpoint
a.	**2.** Draw $\overline{JM}$.	**2.** Two points determine a line.
	3. $\overline{MK} \cong \overline{ML}$	**3.** Definition of midpoint
	4. $\overline{JK} \cong \overline{JL}$	**4.** Given
	5. $\overline{JM} \cong \overline{JM}$	**5.** Reflexive Property of Congruence
b.	**6.** $\triangle JMK \cong \triangle JML$	**6.** SSS Congruence Postulate
c.	**7.** $\angle K \cong \angle L$	**7.** Corresp. parts of $\cong$ ▵ are $\cong$.

Recall that an equilateral triangle has three congruent sides.

COROLLARIES *For Your Notebook*

WRITE A BICONDITIONAL
The corollaries state that a triangle is *equilateral* if and only if it is *equiangular*.

Corollary to the Base Angles Theorem

If a triangle is equilateral, then it is equiangular.

Corollary to the Converse of Base Angles Theorem

If a triangle is equiangular, then it is equilateral.

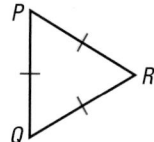

EXAMPLE 2 **Find measures in a triangle**

Find the measures of $\angle P$, $\angle Q$, and $\angle R$.

The diagram shows that $\triangle PQR$ is equilateral. Therefore, by the Corollary to the Base Angles Theorem, $\triangle PQR$ is equiangular. So, $m\angle P = m\angle Q = m\angle R$.

$3(m\angle P) = 180°$ **Triangle Sum Theorem**

$m\angle P = 60°$ **Divide each side by 3.**

▶ The measures of $\angle P$, $\angle Q$, and $\angle R$ are all 60°.

✓ **GUIDED PRACTICE** for Example 2

3. Find ST in the triangle at the right.

4. Is it possible for an equilateral triangle to have an angle measure other than 60°? *Explain.*

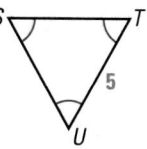

EXAMPLE 3 Use isosceles and equilateral triangles

xy ALGEBRA Find the values of *x* and *y* in the diagram.

Solution

STEP 1 **Find** the value of *y*. Because △*KLN* is equiangular, it is also equilateral and $\overline{KN} \cong \overline{KL}$. Therefore, *y* = 4.

STEP 2 **Find** the value of *x*. Because ∠*LNM* ≅ ∠*LMN*, $\overline{LN} \cong \overline{LM}$ and △*LMN* is isosceles. You also know that *LN* = 4 because △*KLN* is equilateral.

LN = *LM*	**Definition of congruent segments**
4 = *x* + 1	**Substitute 4 for *LN* and *x* + 1 for *LM*.**
3 = *x*	**Subtract 1 from each side.**

AVOID ERRORS
You cannot use ∠*N* to refer to ∠*LNM* because three angles have *N* as their vertex.

EXAMPLE 4 Solve a multi-step problem

LIFEGUARD TOWER In the lifeguard tower, $\overline{PS} \cong \overline{QR}$ and ∠*QPS* ≅ ∠*PQR*.

a. What congruence postulate can you use to prove that △*QPS* ≅ △*PQR*?

b. Explain why △*PQT* is isosceles.

c. Show that △*PTS* ≅ △*QTR*.

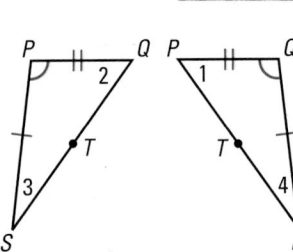

Solution

AVOID ERRORS
When you redraw the triangles so that they do not overlap, be careful to copy all given information and labels correctly.

a. Draw and label △*QPS* and △*PQR* so that they do not overlap. You can see that $\overline{PQ} \cong \overline{QP}$, $\overline{PS} \cong \overline{QR}$, and ∠*QPS* ≅ ∠*PQR*. So, by the SAS Congruence Postulate, △*QPS* ≅ △*PQR*.

b. From part (a), you know that ∠1 ≅ ∠2 because corresp. parts of ≅ ⧍ are ≅. By the Converse of the Base Angles Theorem, $\overline{PT} \cong \overline{QT}$, and △*PQT* is isosceles.

c. You know that $\overline{PS} \cong \overline{QR}$, and ∠3 ≅ ∠4 because corresp. parts of ≅ ⧍ are ≅. Also, ∠*PTS* ≅ ∠*QTR* by the Vertical Angles Congruence Theorem. So, △*PTS* ≅ △*QTR* by the AAS Congruence Theorem.

✓ **GUIDED PRACTICE** for Examples 3 and 4

5. Find the values of *x* and *y* in the diagram.

6. **REASONING** Use parts (b) and (c) in Example 4 and the SSS Congruence Postulate to give a different proof that △*QPS* ≅ △*PQR*.

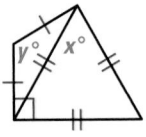

4.7 EXERCISES

SKILL PRACTICE

1. **VOCABULARY** Define the *vertex angle* of an isosceles triangle.

2. ★ **WRITING** What is the relationship between the base angles of an isosceles triangle? *Explain.*

EXAMPLE 1
on p. 264
for Exs. 3–6

USING DIAGRAMS In Exercises 3–6, use the diagram. Copy and complete the statement. Tell what theorem you used.

3. If $\overline{AE} \cong \overline{DE}$, then $\angle$ _?_ $\cong \angle$ _?_ .

4. If $\overline{AB} \cong \overline{EB}$, then $\angle$ _?_ $\cong \angle$ _?_ .

5. If $\angle D \cong \angle CED$, then _?_ $\cong$ _?_ .

6. If $\angle EBC \cong \angle ECB$, then _?_ $\cong$ _?_ .

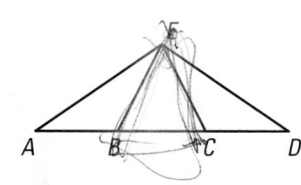

EXAMPLE 2
on p. 265
for Exs. 7–14

REASONING Find the unknown measure.

7.
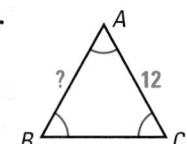

8.
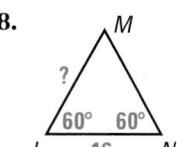

9.
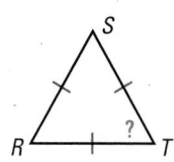

10. **DRAWING DIAGRAMS** A base angle in an isosceles triangle measures 37°. Draw and label the triangle. What is the measure of the vertex angle?

(xy) **ALGEBRA** Find the value of *x*.

11.
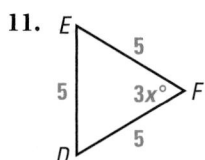

12.
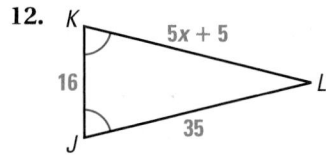

13.
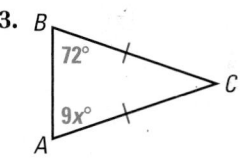

14. **ERROR ANALYSIS** *Describe* and correct the error made in finding *BC* in the diagram shown.

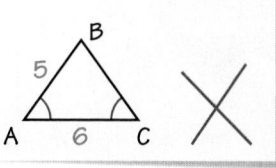

$\angle A \cong \angle C$, therefore
$\overline{AC} \cong \overline{BC}$. So,
$BC = 6$

EXAMPLE 3
on p. 266
for Exs. 15–17

(xy) **ALGEBRA** Find the values of *x* and *y*.

15.
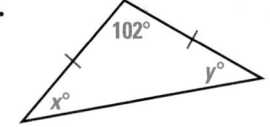

16.
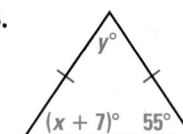

17.
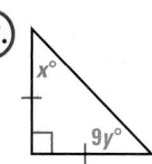

18. ★ **SHORT RESPONSE** Are isosceles triangles always acute triangles? *Explain* your reasoning.

19. ★ **MULTIPLE CHOICE** What is the value of x in the diagram?

(A) 5   (B) 6

(C) 7   (D) 9

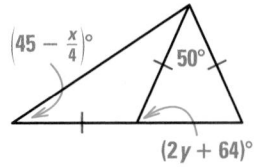

(xy) **ALGEBRA** Find the values of x and y, if possible. *Explain* your reasoning.

20.

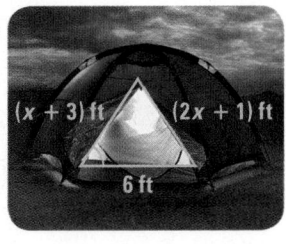

21.

22.

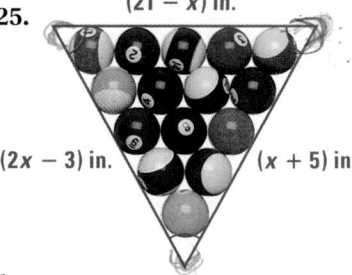

(xy) **ALGEBRA** Find the perimeter of the triangle.

23.

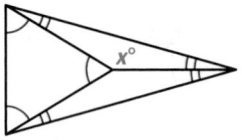

24.

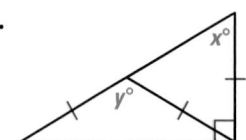

25.

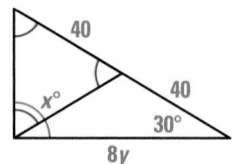

REASONING In Exercises 26–29, use the diagram. State whether the given values for x, y, and z are possible or not. If not, *explain*.

26. $x = 90$, $y = 68$, $z = 42$

27. $x = 40$, $y = 72$, $z = 36$

28. $x = 25$, $y = 25$, $z = 15$

29. $x = 42$, $y = 72$, $z = 33$

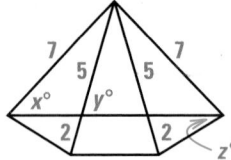

30. ★ **SHORT RESPONSE** In $\triangle DEF$, $m\angle D = (4x + 2)°$, $m\angle E = (6x - 30)°$, and $m\angle F = 3x°$. What type of triangle is $\triangle DEF$? *Explain* your reasoning.

31. ★ **SHORT RESPONSE** In $\triangle ABC$, D is the midpoint of $\overline{AC}$, and $\overline{BD}$ is perpendicular to $\overline{AC}$. *Explain* why $\triangle ABC$ is isosceles.

(xy) **ALGEBRA** Find the value(s) of the variable(s). *Explain* your reasoning.

32.

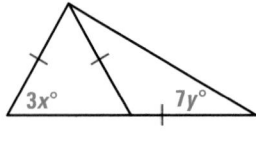

33.

34.

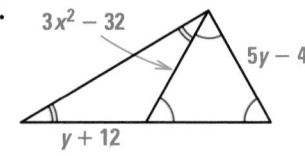

35. **REASONING** The measure of an exterior angle of an isosceles triangle is 130°. What are the possible angle measures of the triangle? *Explain.*

36. **PROOF** Let $\triangle ABC$ be isosceles with vertex angle $\angle A$. Suppose $\angle A$, $\angle B$, and $\angle C$ have integer measures. Prove that $m\angle A$ must be even.

37. **CHALLENGE** The measure of an exterior angle of an isosceles triangle is $x°$. What are the possible angle measures of the triangle in terms of x? *Describe* all the possible values of x.

○ = **WORKED-OUT SOLUTIONS**
on p. WS1

★ = **STANDARDIZED TEST PRACTICE**

38. SPORTS The dimensions of a sports pennant are given in the diagram. Find the values of *x* and *y*.

@HomeTutor for problem solving help at classzone.com

39. ADVERTISING A logo in an advertisement is an equilateral triangle with a side length of 5 centimeters. Sketch the logo and give the measure of each side and angle.

@HomeTutor for problem solving help at classzone.com

40. ARCHITECTURE The Transamerica Pyramid building shown in the photograph has four faces shaped like isosceles triangles. The measure of a base angle of one of these triangles is about 85°. What is the approximate measure of the vertex angle of the triangle?

EXAMPLE 4
on p. 266
for Exs. 41–42

41. MULTI-STEP PROBLEM To make a zig-zag pattern, a graphic designer sketches two parallel line segments. Then the designer draws blue and green triangles as shown below.

  a. Prove that △*ABC* ≅ △*BCD*.

  b. Name all the isosceles triangles in the diagram.

  c. Name four angles that are congruent to ∠*ABC*.

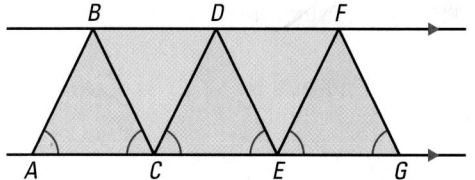

42. ★ VISUAL REASONING In the pattern below, each small triangle is an equilateral triangle with an area of 1 square unit.

Triangle				
Area	1 square unit	?	?	?

  a. Reasoning *Explain* how you know that any triangle made out of equilateral triangles will be an equilateral triangle.

  b. Area Find the areas of the first four triangles in the pattern.

  c. Make a Conjecture *Describe* any patterns in the areas. Predict the area of the seventh triangle in the pattern. *Explain* your reasoning.

43. REASONING Let △*PQR* be an isosceles right triangle with hypotenuse $\overline{QR}$. Find *m*∠*P*, *m*∠*Q*, and *m*∠*R*.

44. REASONING *Explain* how the Corollary to the Base Angles Theorem follows from the Base Angles Theorem.

45. PROVING THEOREM 4.8 Write a proof of the Converse of the Base Angles Theorem.

46. ★ **EXTENDED RESPONSE** Sue is designing fabric purses that she will sell at the school fair. Use the diagram of one of her purses.

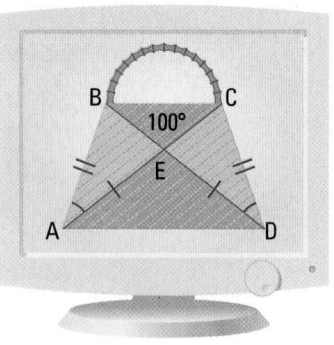

  a. Prove that $\triangle ABE \cong \triangle DCE$.

  b. Name the isosceles triangles in the purse.

  c. Name three angles that are congruent to $\angle EAD$.

  d. **What If?** If the measure of $\angle BEC$ changes, does your answer to part (c) change? *Explain.*

REASONING FROM DIAGRAMS Use the information in the diagram to answer the question. *Explain* your reasoning.

47. Is $p \parallel q$?

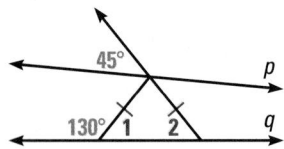

48. Is $\triangle ABC$ isosceles?

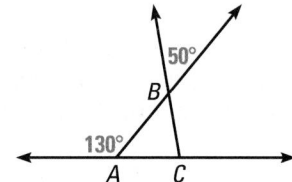

49. **PROOF** Write a proof.

  GIVEN ▶ $\triangle ABC$ is equilateral,
  $\angle CAD \cong \angle ABE \cong \angle BCF$.

  PROVE ▶ $\triangle DEF$ is equilateral.

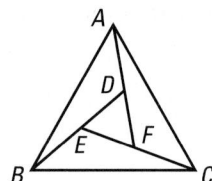

50. **COORDINATE GEOMETRY** The coordinates of two vertices of $\triangle TUV$ are $T(0, 4)$ and $U(4, 0)$. *Explain* why the triangle will always be an isosceles triangle if V is any point on the line $y = x$ except $(2, 2)$.

51. **CHALLENGE** The lengths of the sides of a triangle are $3t$, $5t - 12$, and $t + 20$. Find the values of t that make the triangle isosceles. *Explain.*

MIXED REVIEW

What quadrant contains the point? *(p. 878)*

52. $(-1, -3)$ **53.** $(-2, 4)$ **54.** $(5, -2)$

Copy and complete the given function table. *(p. 884)*

55.

x	-7	0	5
$y = x - 4$	?	?	?

56.

?	-2	0	1
?	-6	0	3

Use the Distance Formula to decide whether $\overline{AB} \cong \overline{AC}$. *(p. 15)*

57. $A(0, 0)$, $B(-5, -6)$, $C(6, 5)$ **58.** $A(3, -3)$, $B(0, 1)$, $C(-1, 0)$

59. $A(0, 1)$, $B(4, 7)$, $C(-6, 3)$ **60.** $A(-3, 0)$, $B(2, 2)$, $C(2, -2)$

PREVIEW
Prepare for
Lesson 4.8 in
Exs. 57–60.

4.8 Investigate Slides and Flips

MATERIALS · graph paper · pencil

QUESTION What happens when you slide or flip a triangle?

EXPLORE 1 Slide a triangle

STEP 1 *Draw a triangle* Draw a scalene right triangle with legs of length 3 units and 4 units on a piece of graph paper. Cut out the triangle.

STEP 2 *Draw coordinate plane* Draw axes on the graph paper. Place the cut-out triangle so that the coordinates of the vertices are integers. Trace around the triangle and label the vertices.

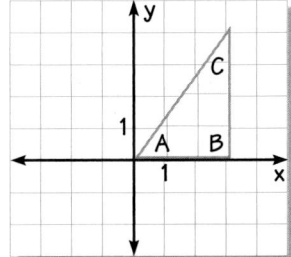

STEP 3 *Slide triangle* Slide the cut-out triangle so it moves left and down. Write a description of the *transformation* and record ordered pairs in a table like the one shown. Repeat this step three times, sliding the triangle left or right *and* up or down to various places in the coordinate plane.

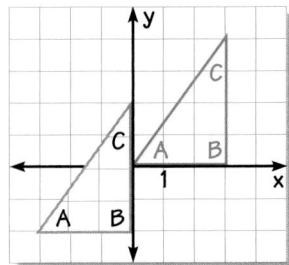

Slide 3 units left and 2 units down.		
Vertex	**Original position**	**New position**
A	(0, 0)	(−3, −2)
B	(3, 0)	(0, −2)
C	(3, 4)	(0, 2)

EXPLORE 2 Flip a triangle

STEP 1 *Draw a coordinate plane* Draw and label a second coordinate plane. Place the cut-out triangle so that one vertex is at the origin and one side is along the *y*-axis, as shown.

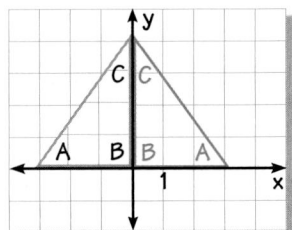

STEP 2 *Flip triangle* Flip the cut-out triangle over the *y*-axis. Record a description of the *transformation* and record the ordered pairs in a table. Repeat this step, flipping the triangle over the *x*-axis.

DRAW CONCLUSIONS Use your observations to complete these exercises

1. How are the coordinates of the original position of the triangle related to the new position in a slide? in a flip?

2. Is the original triangle congruent to the new triangle in a slide? in a flip? *Explain* your reasoning.

4.8 Perform Congruence Transformations

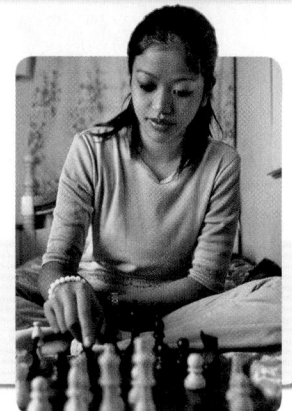

Before You determined whether two triangles are congruent.

Now You will create an image congruent to a given triangle.

Why So you can describe chess moves, as in Ex. 41.

Key Vocabulary
• transformation
• image
• translation
• reflection
• rotation
• congruence transformation

A **transformation** is an operation that moves or changes a geometric figure in some way to produce a new figure. The new figure is called the **image.** A transformation can be shown using an arrow.

The order of the vertices in the transformation statement tells you that *P* is the image of *A*, *Q* is the image of *B*, and *R* is the image of *C*.

$$\triangle ABC \ \rightarrow \ \triangle PQR$$

Original figure   Image

There are three main types of transformations. A **translation** moves every point of a figure the same distance in the same direction. A **reflection** uses a *line of reflection* to create a mirror image of the original figure. A **rotation** turns a figure about a fixed point, called the *center of rotation.*

EXAMPLE 1 Identify transformations

TRANSFORMATIONS
You will learn more about transformations in Lesson 6.7 and in Chapter 9.

Name the type of transformation demonstrated in each picture.

a.

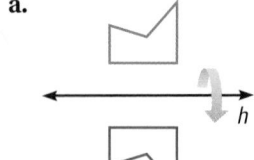

Reflection in a
horizontal line

b.

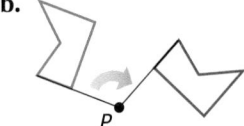

Rotation about a point

c.

Translation in a
straight path

✓ **GUIDED PRACTICE** for Example 1

1. Name the type of transformation shown.

CONGRUENCE Translations, reflections, and rotations are three types of *congruence transformations.* A **congruence transformation** changes the position of the figure without changing its size or shape.

TRANSLATIONS In a coordinate plane, a translation moves an object a given distance right or left and up or down. You can use coordinate notation to describe a translation.

KEY CONCEPT   *For Your Notebook*

Coordinate Notation for a Translation

You can describe a translation by the notation

$$(x, y) \rightarrow (x + a, y + b)$$

which shows that each point (x, y) of the blue figure is translated horizontally a units and vertically b units.

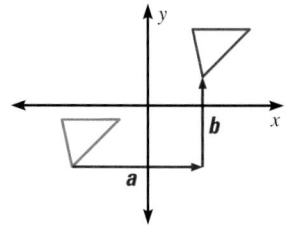

EXAMPLE 2   **Translate a figure in the coordinate plane**

Figure *ABCD* has the vertices $A(-4, 3)$, $B(-2, 4)$, $C(-1, 1)$, and $D(-3, 1)$. Sketch *ABCD* and its image after the translation $(x, y) \rightarrow (x + 5, y - 2)$.

Solution

First draw *ABCD*. Find the translation of each vertex by adding 5 to its *x*-coordinate and subtracting 2 from its *y*-coordinate. Then draw *ABCD* and its image.

$$(x, y) \rightarrow (x + 5, y - 2)$$

$A(-4, 3) \rightarrow (1, 1)$

$B(-2, 4) \rightarrow (3, 2)$

$C(-1, 1) \rightarrow (4, -1)$

$D(-3, 1) \rightarrow (2, -1)$

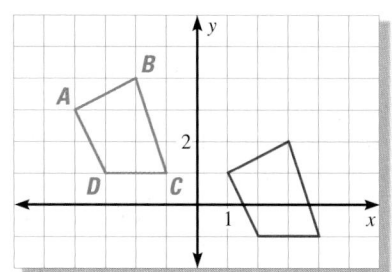

REFLECTIONS In this lesson, when a reflection is shown in a coordinate plane, the line of reflection is always the *x*-axis or the *y*-axis.

KEY CONCEPT   *For Your Notebook*

Coordinate Notation for a Reflection

Reflection in the x-axis   **Reflection in the y-axis**

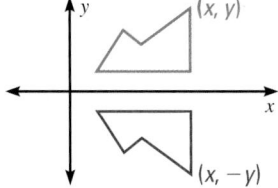   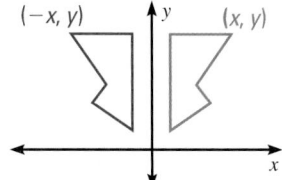

Multiply the *y*-coordinate by –1.   Multiply the *x*-coordinate by –1.
$(x, y) \rightarrow (x, -y)$ $(x, y) \rightarrow (-x, y)$

EXAMPLE 3 Reflect a figure in the *x*-axis

WOODWORK You are drawing a pattern for a wooden sign. Use a reflection in the *x*-axis to draw the other half of the pattern.

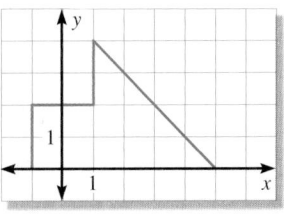

Solution

Multiply the *y*-coordinate of each vertex by −1 to find the corresponding vertex in the image.

$$(x, y) \rightarrow (x, -y)$$

$(-1, 0) \rightarrow (-1, 0)$ $(-1, 2) \rightarrow (-1, -2)$

$(1, 2) \rightarrow (1, -2)$ $(1, 4) \rightarrow (1, -4)$

$(5, 0) \rightarrow (5, 0)$

Use the vertices to draw the image. You can check your results by looking to see if each original point and its image are the same distance from the *x*-axis.

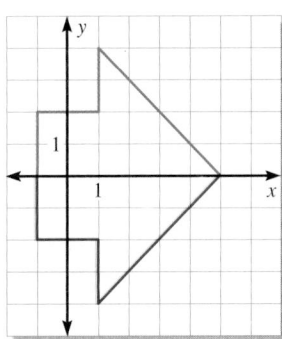

Animated Geometry at classzone.com

✓ **GUIDED PRACTICE**   for Examples 2 and 3

2. The vertices of △*ABC* are *A*(1, 2), *B*(0, 0), and *C*(4, 0). A translation of △*ABC* results in the image △*DEF* with vertices *D*(2, 1), *E*(1, −1), and *F*(5, −1). *Describe* the translation in words and in coordinate notation.

3. The endpoints of $\overline{RS}$ are *R*(4, 5) and *S*(1, −3). A reflection of $\overline{RS}$ results in the image $\overline{TU}$, with coordinates *T*(4, −5) and *U*(1, 3). Tell which axis $\overline{RS}$ was reflected in and write the coordinate rule for the reflection.

ROTATIONS In this lesson, if a rotation is shown in a coordinate plane, the center of rotation is the origin.

The direction of rotation can be either *clockwise* or *counterclockwise*. The *angle of rotation* is formed by rays drawn from the center of rotation through corresponding points on the original figure and its image.

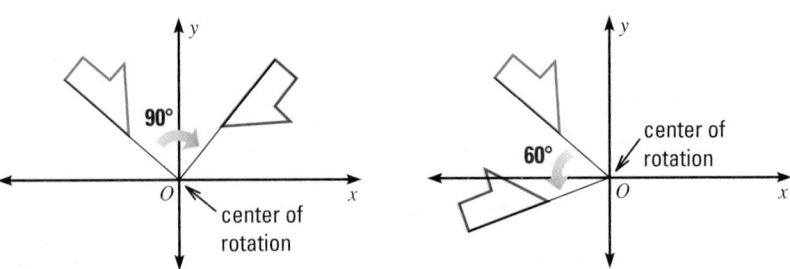

Notice that rotations preserve distances from the center of rotation. So, segments drawn from the center of rotation to corresponding points on the figures are congruent.

EXAMPLE 4 **Identify a rotation**

Graph $\overline{AB}$ and $\overline{CD}$. Tell whether $\overline{CD}$ is a rotation of $\overline{AB}$ about the origin. If so, give the angle and direction of rotation.

   a. $A(-3, 1)$, $B(-1, 3)$, $C(1, 3)$, $D(3, 1)$ **b.** $A(0, 1)$, $B(1, 3)$, $C(-1, 1)$, $D(-3, 2)$

Solution

a.
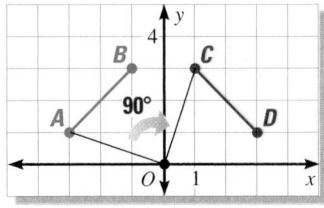

$m\angle AOC = m\angle BOD = 90°$
This is a 90° clockwise rotation.

b.
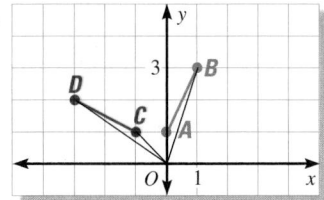

$m\angle AOC < m\angle BOD$
This is not a rotation.

EXAMPLE 5 **Verify congruence**

The vertices of $\triangle ABC$ are $A(4, 4)$, $B(6, 6)$, and $C(7, 4)$. The notation $(x, y) \rightarrow (x + 1, y - 3)$ describes the translation of $\triangle ABC$ to $\triangle DEF$. Show that $\triangle ABC \cong \triangle DEF$ to verify that the translation is a congruence transformation.

Solution

S You can see that $AC = DF = 3$, so $\overline{AC} \cong \overline{DF}$.

A Using the slopes, $\overline{AB} \parallel \overline{DE}$ and $\overline{AC} \parallel \overline{DF}$. If you extend $\overline{AB}$ and $\overline{DF}$ to form $\angle G$, the Corresponding Angles Postulate gives you $\angle BAC \cong \angle G$ and $\angle G \cong \angle EDF$. Then, $\angle BAC \cong \angle EDF$ by the Transitive Property of Congruence.

S Using the Distance Formula, $AB = DE = 2\sqrt{2}$ so $\overline{AB} \cong \overline{DE}$. So, $\triangle ABC \cong \triangle DEF$ by the SAS Congruence Postulate.

▶ Because $\triangle ABC \cong \triangle DEF$, the translation is a congruence transformation.

✓ **GUIDED PRACTICE**   for Examples 4 and 5

  4. Tell whether $\triangle PQR$ is a rotation of $\triangle STR$. If so, give the angle and direction of rotation.

  5. Show that $\triangle PQR \cong \triangle STR$ to verify that the transformation is a congruence transformation.

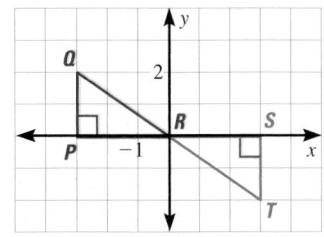

4.8 EXERCISES

HOMEWORK KEY

◯ = **WORKED-OUT SOLUTIONS**
on p. WS5 for Exs. 11, 23, and 39

★ = **STANDARDIZED TEST PRACTICE**
Exs. 2, 25, 40, 41, and 43

SKILL PRACTICE

1. **VOCABULARY** *Describe* the translation $(x, y) \rightarrow (x - 1, y + 4)$ in words.

2. ★ **WRITING** *Explain* why the term *congruence transformation* is used in describing translations, reflections, and rotations.

EXAMPLE 1
on p. 272
for Exs. 3–8

IDENTIFYING TRANSFORMATIONS **Name the type of transformation shown.**

3.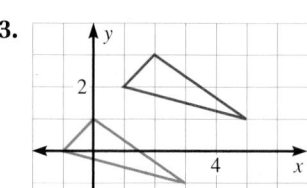

4.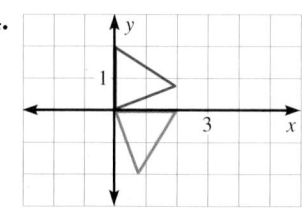

5.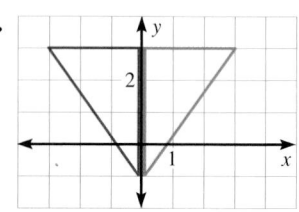

WINDOWS **Decide whether the moving part of the window is a translation.**

6. Double hung

7. Casement

8. Sliding

EXAMPLE 2
on p. 273
for Exs. 9–16

DRAWING A TRANSLATION **Copy figure** *ABCD* **and draw its image after the translation.**

9. $(x, y) \rightarrow (x + 2, y - 3)$

10. $(x, y) \rightarrow (x - 1, y - 5)$

⑪ $(x, y) \rightarrow (x + 4, y + 1)$

12. $(x, y) \rightarrow (x - 2, y + 3)$

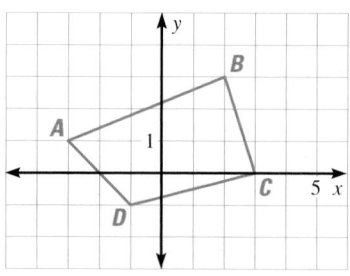

COORDINATE NOTATION **Use coordinate notation to** *describe* **the translation.**

13. 4 units to the left, 2 units down

14. 6 units to the right, 3 units up

15. 2 units to the right, 1 unit down

16. 7 units to the left, 9 units up

EXAMPLE 3
on p. 274
for Exs. 17–19

DRAWING **Use a reflection in the** *x*-**axis to draw the other half of the figure.**

17.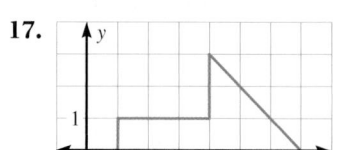

18.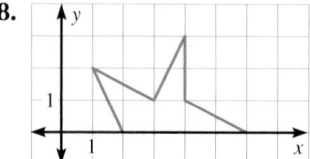

19.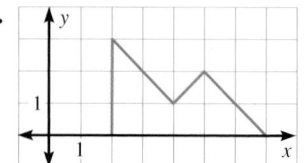

EXAMPLE 4
....
on p. 275
for Exs. 20–23

ROTATIONS Use the coordinates to graph $\overline{AB}$ and $\overline{CD}$. Tell whether $\overline{CD}$ is a rotation of $\overline{AB}$ about the origin. If so, give the angle and direction of rotation.

20. $A(1, 2), B(3, 4), C(2, -1), D(4, -3)$

21. $A(-2, -4), B(-1, -2), C(4, 3), D(2, 1)$

22. $A(-4, 0), B(-4, -4), C(4, 4), D(0, 4)$

23. $A(1, 2), B(3, 0), C(2, -1), D(2, -3)$

24. ERROR ANALYSIS A student says that the red triangle is a 120° clockwise rotation of the blue triangle about the origin. *Describe* and correct the error.

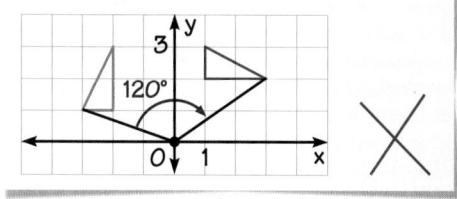

25. ★ WRITING Can a point or a line segment be its own image under a transformation? *Explain* and illustrate your answer.

APPLYING TRANSLATIONS Complete the statement using the description of the translation. In the description, points (0, 3) and (2, 5) are two vertices of a hexagon.

26. If (0, 3) translates to (0, 0), then (2, 5) translates to ___?___ .

27. If (0, 3) translates to (1, 2), then (2, 5) translates to ___?___ .

28. If (0, 3) translates to (−3, −2), then (2, 5) translates to ___?___ .

⟨xy⟩ ALGEBRA A point on an image and the translation are given. Find the corresponding point on the original figure.

29. Point on image: (4, 0); translation: $(x, y) \rightarrow (x + 2, y - 3)$

30. Point on image: (−3, 5); translation: $(x, y) \rightarrow (-x, y)$

31. Point on image: (6, −9); translation: $(x, y) \rightarrow (x - 7, y - 4)$

32. CONGRUENCE Show that the transformation in Exercise 3 is a congruence transformation.

DESCRIBING AN IMAGE State the segment or triangle that represents the image. You can use tracing paper to help you see the rotation.

33. 90° clockwise rotation of $\overline{ST}$ about E

34. 90° counterclockwise rotation of $\overline{BX}$ about E

35. 180° rotation of $\triangle BWX$ about E

36. 180° rotation of $\triangle TUA$ about E

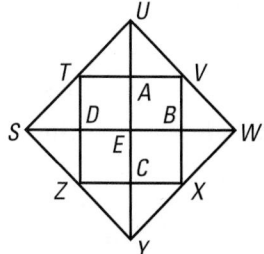

37. CHALLENGE Solve for the variables in the transformation of $\overline{AB}$ to $\overline{CD}$ and then to $\overline{EF}$.

$A(2, 3),$
$B(4, 2a)$ → Translation: $(x, y) \rightarrow (x - 2, y + 1)$ → $C(m - 3, 4),$
$D(n - 9, 5)$ → Reflection: in *x*-axis → $E(0, g - 6),$
$F(8h, -5)$

EXAMPLE 3
on p. 274
for Ex. 38

38. KITES The design for a kite shows the layout and dimensions for only half of the kite.

   a. What type of transformation can a designer use to create plans for the entire kite?

   b. What is the maximum width of the entire kite?

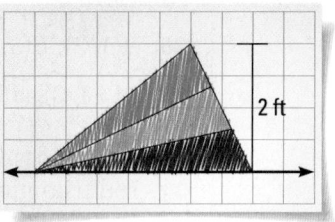

2 ft

@HomeTutor for problem solving help at classzone.com

39. STENCILING You are stenciling a room in your home. You want to use the stencil pattern below on the left to create the design shown. Give the angles and directions of rotation you will use to move the stencil from *A* to *B* and from *A* to *C*.

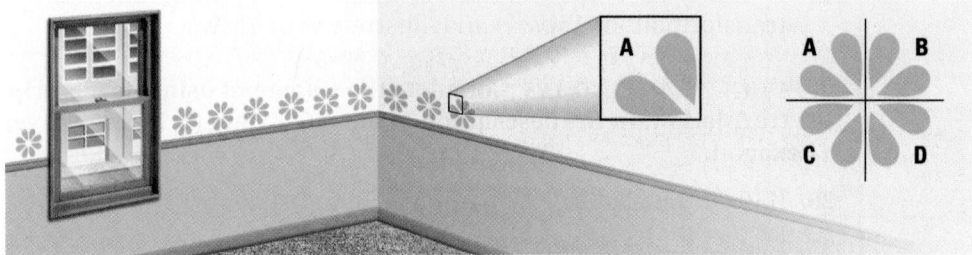

@HomeTutor for problem solving help at classzone.com

40. ★ OPEN-ENDED MATH Some words reflect onto themselves through a vertical line of reflection. An example is shown.

   a. Find two other words with vertical lines of reflection. Draw the line of reflection for each word.

   b. Find two words with horizontal lines of reflection. Draw the line of reflection for each word.

41. ★ SHORT RESPONSE In chess, six different kinds of pieces are moved according to individual rules. The Knight (shaped like a horse) moves in an "L" shape. It moves two squares horizontally or vertically and then one additional square perpendicular to its original direction. When a knight lands on a square with another piece, it *captures* that piece.

   a. *Describe* the translation used by the Black Knight to capture the White Pawn.

   b. *Describe* the translation used by the White Knight to capture the Black Pawn.

   c. After both pawns are captured, can the Black Knight capture the White Knight? *Explain.*

EXAMPLE 5
on p. 275
for Ex. 42

42. VERIFYING CONGRUENCE Show that $\triangle ABC$ and $\triangle DEF$ are right triangles and use the HL Congruence Theorem to verify that $\triangle DEF$ is a congruence transformation of $\triangle ABC$.

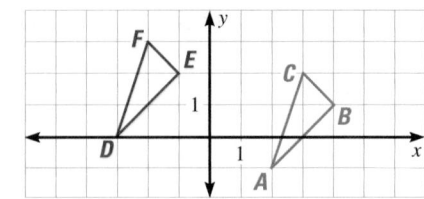

○ = **WORKED-OUT SOLUTIONS**
on p. WS1

★ = **STANDARDIZED TEST PRACTICE**

43. ★ **MULTIPLE CHOICE** A piece of paper is folded in half and some cuts are made, as shown. Which figure represents the unfolded piece of paper?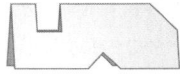

Ⓐ 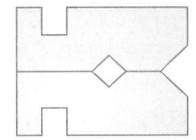 **Ⓑ** 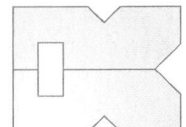 **Ⓒ** 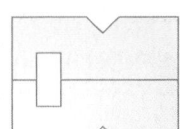 **Ⓓ**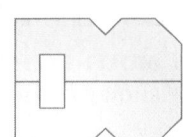

44. **CHALLENGE** A triangle is rotated 90° counterclockwise and then translated three units up. The vertices of the final image are $A(-4, 4)$, $B(-1, 6)$, and $C(-1, 4)$. Find the vertices of the original triangle. Would the final image be the same if the original triangle was translated 3 units up and then rotated 90° counterclockwise? *Explain* your reasoning.

MIXED REVIEW

PREVIEW
Prepare for Lesson 5.1 in Exs. 45–50.

Simplify the expression. Variables *a* and *b* are positive.

45. $\dfrac{-a - 0}{0 - (-b)}$ *(p. 870)*   **46.** $|(a + b) - a|$ *(p. 870)*   **47.** $\dfrac{2a + 2b}{2}$ *(p. 139)*

Simplify the expression. Variables *a* and *b* are positive. *(p. 139)*

48. $\sqrt{(-b)^2}$ **49.** $\sqrt{(2a)^2}$ **50.** $\sqrt{(2a - a)^2 + (0 - b)^2}$

51. Use the SSS Congruence Postulate to show $\triangle RST \cong \triangle UVW$. *(p. 234)*

$R(1, -4)$, $S(1, -1)$, $T(6, -1)$ $U(1, 4)$, $V(1, 1)$, $W(6, 1)$

QUIZ *for Lessons 4.7–4.8*

Find the value of *x*. *(p. 264)*

1.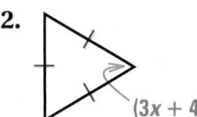

2.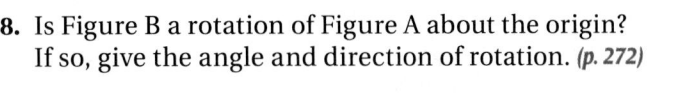

3.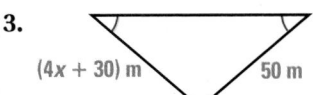

Copy $\triangle EFG$ and draw its image after the transformation. Identify the type of transformation. *(p. 272)*

4. $(x, y) \rightarrow (x + 4, y - 1)$ **5.** $(x, y) \rightarrow (-x, y)$

6. $(x, y) \rightarrow (x, -y)$ **7.** $(x, y) \rightarrow (x - 3, y + 2)$

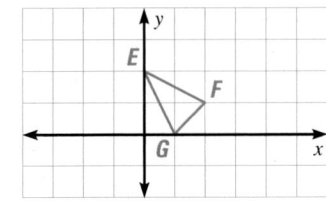

8. Is Figure B a rotation of Figure A about the origin? If so, give the angle and direction of rotation. *(p. 272)*

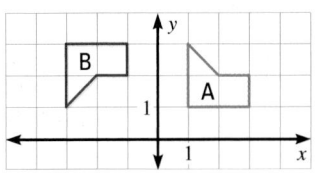

Lessons 4.5–4.8

1. MULTI-STEP PROBLEM Use the quilt pattern shown below.

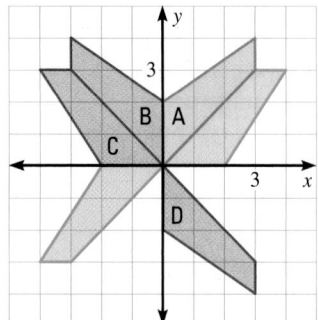

a. Figure B is the image of Figure A. Name and *describe* the transformation.

b. Figure C is the image of Figure A. Name and *describe* the transformation.

c. Figure D is the image of Figure A. Name and *describe* the transformation.

d. *Explain* how you could complete the quilt pattern using transformations of Figure A.

2. SHORT RESPONSE You are told that a triangle has sides that are 5 centimeters and 3 centimeters long. You are also told that the side that is 5 centimeters long forms an angle with the third side that measures 28°. Is there only one triangle that has these given dimensions? *Explain* why or why not.

3. OPEN-ENDED A friend has drawn a triangle on a piece of paper and she is describing the triangle so that you can draw one that is congruent to hers. So far, she has told you that the length of one side is 8 centimeters and one of the angles formed with this side is 34°. *Describe* three pieces of additional information you could use to construct the triangle.

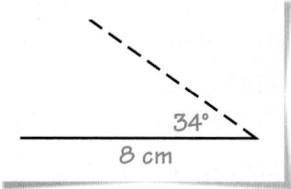

4. SHORT RESPONSE Can the triangles *ACD* and *BCE* be proven congruent using the information given in the diagram? Can you show that $\overline{AD} \cong \overline{BE}$? *Explain*.

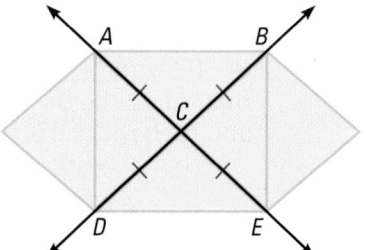

5. EXTENDED RESPONSE Use the information given in the diagram to prove the statements below.

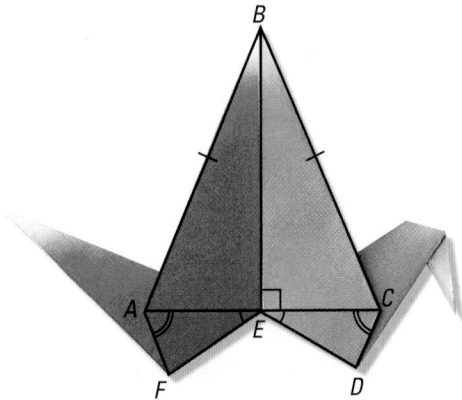

a. Prove that $\angle BCE \cong \angle BAE$.

b. Prove that $\overline{AF} \cong \overline{CD}$.

6. GRIDDED ANSWER Find the value of *x* in the diagram.

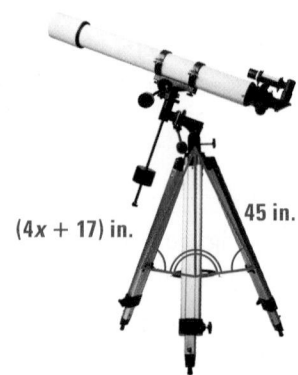

(4x + 17) in.

45 in.

BIG IDEAS

Big Idea ①

Classifying Triangles by Sides and Angles

	Equilateral	Isosceles	Scalene
Sides	 3 congruent sides	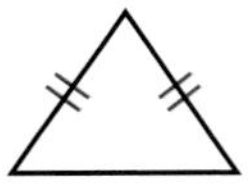 2 or 3 congruent sides	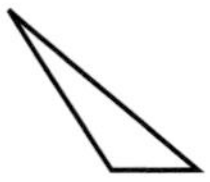 No congruent sides

	Acute	Equiangular	Right	Obtuse
Angles	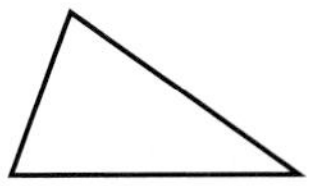 3 angles < 90°	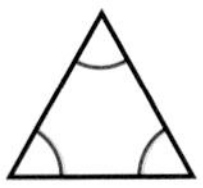 3 angles = 60°	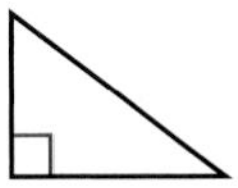 1 angle = 90°	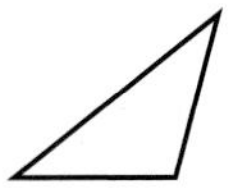 1 angle > 90°

Big Idea ②

Proving That Triangles Are Congruent

SSS	All three sides are congruent.	$\triangle ABC \cong \triangle DEF$ 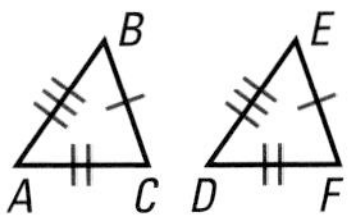
SAS	Two sides and the included angle are congruent.	$\triangle ABC \cong \triangle DEF$ 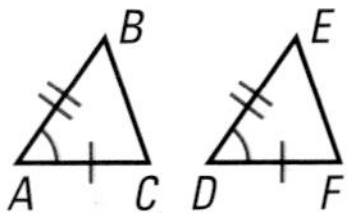
HL	The hypotenuse and one of the legs are congruent. (Right triangles only)	$\triangle ABC \cong \triangle DEF$ 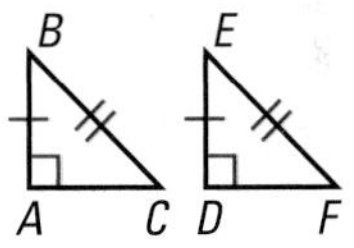
ASA	Two angles and the included side are congruent.	$\triangle ABC \cong \triangle DEF$ 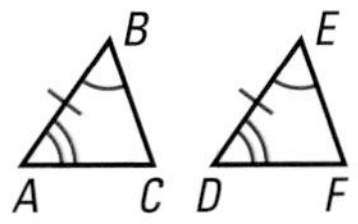
AAS	Two angles and a (non-included) side are congruent.	$\triangle ABC \cong \triangle DEF$ 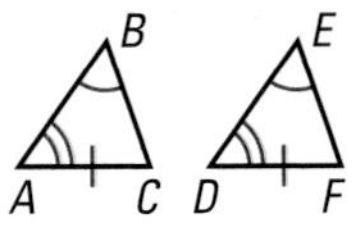

Big Idea ③

Using Coordinate Geometry to Investigate Triangle Relationships

You can use the Distance and Midpoint Formulas to apply postulates and theorems to triangles in the coordinate plane.

@HomeTutor
classzone.com
• Multi-Language Glossary
• Vocabulary practice

REVIEW KEY VOCABULARY

For a list of postulates and theorems, see pp. 926–931.

• triangle, *p. 217*
scalene, isosceles, equilateral, acute, right, obtuse, equiangular
• interior angles, *p. 218*
• exterior angles, *p. 218*
• corollary to a theorem, *p. 220*

• congruent figures, *p. 225*
• corresponding parts, *p. 225*
• right triangle, *p. 241*
legs, hypotenuse
• flow proof, *p. 250*

• isosceles triangle, *p. 264*
legs, vertex angle, base, base angles
• transformation, *p. 272*
• image, *p. 272*
• congruence transformation, *p. 272*
translation, reflection, rotation

VOCABULARY EXERCISES

1. Copy and complete: A triangle with three congruent angles is called __?__.

2. **WRITING** *Compare* vertex angles and base angles.

3. **WRITING** *Describe* the difference between isosceles and scalene triangles.

4. Sketch an acute scalene triangle. Label its interior angles 1, 2, and 3. Then draw and shade its exterior angles.

5. If $\triangle PQR \cong \triangle LMN$, which angles are corresponding angles? Which sides are corresponding sides?

REVIEW EXAMPLES AND EXERCISES

Use the review examples and exercises below to check your understanding of the concepts you have learned in each lesson of Chapter 4.

4.1 Apply Triangle Sum Properties
pp. 217–224

EXAMPLE

Find the measure of the exterior angle shown.

Use the Exterior Angle Theorem to write and solve an equation to find the value of x.

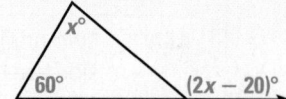

$(2x - 20)° = 60° + x°$ **Apply the Exterior Angle Theorem.**

$x = 80$ **Solve for x.**

The measure of the exterior angle is $(2 \cdot 80 - 20)°$, or $140°$.

EXERCISES

EXAMPLE 3
on p. 219
for Exs. 6–8

Find the measure of the exterior angle shown.

6.
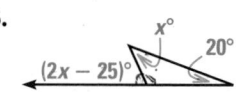

7.
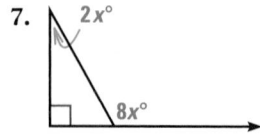

8.
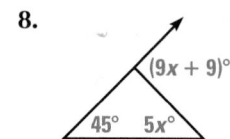

4.2 Apply Congruence and Triangles

pp. 225–231

EXAMPLE

Use the Third Angles Theorem to find $m\angle X$.

In the diagram, $\angle A \cong \angle Z$ and $\angle C \cong \angle Y$. By the Third Angles Theorem, $\angle B \cong \angle X$. Then by the Triangle Sum Theorem, $m\angle B = 180° − 65° − 51° = 64°$.

So, $m\angle X = m\angle B = 64°$ by the definition of congruent angles.

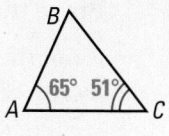
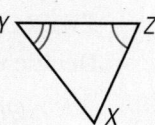

EXERCISES

EXAMPLES
2 and 4
on pp. 226–227
for Exs. 9–14

In the diagram, $\triangle ABC \cong \triangle VTU$.
Find the indicated measure.

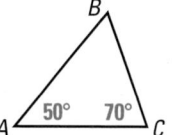
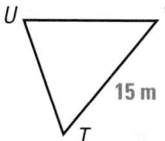

9. $m\angle B$

10. AB

11. $m\angle T$

12. $m\angle V$

Find the value of x.

13.

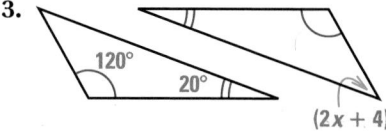

14.

4.3 Prove Triangles Congruent by SSS

pp. 234–239

EXAMPLE

Prove that $\triangle LMN \cong \triangle PMN$.

The marks on the diagram show that $\overline{LM} \cong \overline{PM}$ and $\overline{LN} \cong \overline{PN}$. By the Reflexive Property, $\overline{MN} \cong \overline{MN}$.

So, by the SSS Congruence Postulate, $\triangle LMN \cong \triangle PMN$.

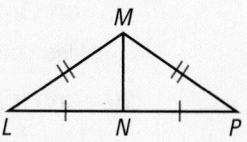

EXERCISES

EXAMPLE 1
on p. 234
for Exs. 15–16

Decide whether the congruence statement is true. *Explain* your reasoning.

15. $\triangle XYZ \cong \triangle RST$

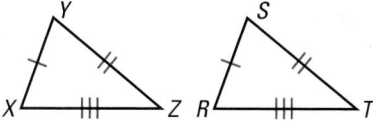

16. $\triangle ABC \cong \triangle DCB$

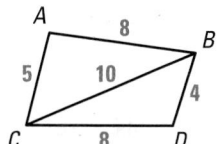

4.4 Prove Triangles Congruent by SAS and HL

pp. 240–246

EXAMPLE

Prove that △DEF ≅ △GHF.

From the diagram, $\overline{DE} \cong \overline{GH}$, $\angle E \cong \angle H$, and $\overline{EF} \cong \overline{HF}$. By the SAS Congruence Postulate, $\triangle DEF \cong \triangle GHF$.

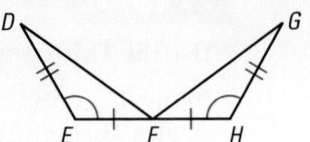

EXERCISES

Decide whether the congruence statement is true. *Explain* **your reasoning.**

EXAMPLES
1 and 3
on pp. 240, 242
for Exs. 17–18

17. △QRS ≅ △TUS

18. △DEF ≅ △GHF

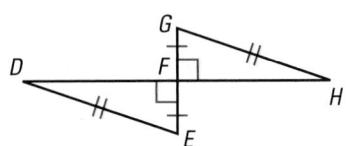

4.5 Prove Triangles Congruent by ASA and AAS

pp. 249–255

EXAMPLE

Prove that △DAC ≅ △BCA.

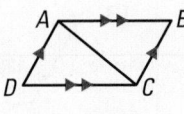

By the Reflexive Property, $\overline{AC} \cong \overline{AC}$. Because $\overline{AD} \parallel \overline{BC}$ and $\overline{AB} \parallel \overline{DC}$, $\angle DAC \cong \angle BCA$ and $\angle DCA \cong \angle BAC$ by the Alternate Interior Angles Theorem. So, by the ASA Congruence Postulate, $\triangle ADC \cong \triangle CBA$.

EXERCISES

State the third congruence that is needed to prove that △DEF ≅ △GHJ using the given postulate or theorem.

EXAMPLES
1 and 2
on p. 250
for Exs. 19–20

19. GIVEN ▶ $\overline{DE} \cong \overline{GH}$, $\angle D \cong \angle G$, ___?___ ≅ ___?___
    Use the AAS Congruence Theorem.

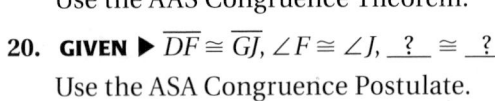

20. GIVEN ▶ $\overline{DF} \cong \overline{GJ}$, $\angle F \cong \angle J$, ___?___ ≅ ___?___
    Use the ASA Congruence Postulate.

4.6 Use Congruent Triangles

pp. 256–263

EXAMPLE

GIVEN ▶ $\overline{FG} \cong \overline{JG}$, $\overline{EG} \cong \overline{HG}$

PROVE ▶ $\overline{EF} \cong \overline{HJ}$

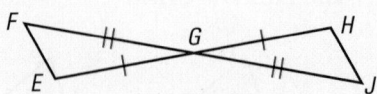

You are given that $\overline{FG} \cong \overline{JG}$ and $\overline{EG} \cong \overline{HG}$. By the Vertical Angles Congruence Theorem, $\angle FGE \cong \angle JGH$. So, $\triangle FGE \cong \triangle JGH$ by the SAS Congruence Postulate. Corresponding parts of ≅ △ are ≅, so $\overline{EF} \cong \overline{HJ}$.

EXERCISES

EXAMPLE 3
on p. 257
for Exs. 21–23

Write a plan for proving that $\angle 1 \cong \angle 2$.

21.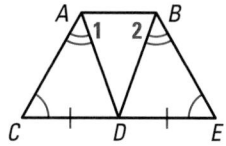

22.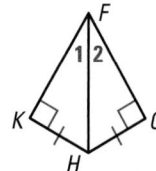

23.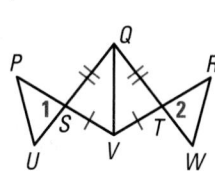

4.7 **Use Isosceles and Equilateral Triangles** *pp. 264–270*

EXAMPLE

$\triangle QRS$ is isosceles. Name two congruent angles.

$\overline{QR} \cong \overline{QS}$, so by the Base Angles Theorem, $\angle R \cong \angle S$.

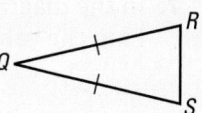

EXERCISES

EXAMPLE 3
on p. 266
for Exs. 24–26

Find the value of x.

24.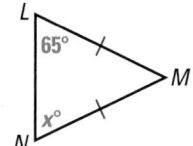

25.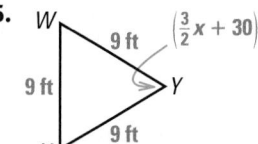

26.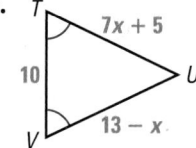

4.8 **Perform Congruence Transformations** *pp. 272–279*

EXAMPLE

Triangle ABC has vertices $A(-5, 1)$, $B(-4, 4)$, and $C(-2, 3)$. Sketch $\triangle ABC$ and its image after the translation $(x, y) \rightarrow (x + 5, y + 1)$.

$(x, y) \rightarrow (x + 5, y + 1)$

$A(-5, 1) \rightarrow (0, 2)$

$B(-4, 4) \rightarrow (1, 5)$

$C(-2, 3) \rightarrow (3, 4)$

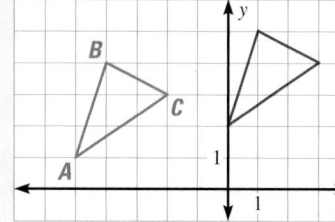

EXERCISES

EXAMPLES
2 and 3
on pp. 273–274
for Exs. 27–29

Triangle QRS has vertices $Q(2, -1)$, $R(5, -2)$, and $S(2, -3)$. Sketch $\triangle QRS$ and its image after the transformation.

27. $(x, y) \rightarrow (x - 1, y + 5)$ 28. $(x, y) \rightarrow (x, -y)$ 29. $(x, y) \rightarrow (-x, -y)$

Classify the triangle by its sides and by its angles.

1.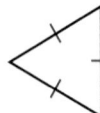

2.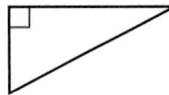

3.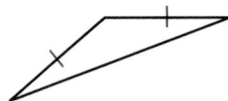

In Exercises 4–6, find the value of x.

4.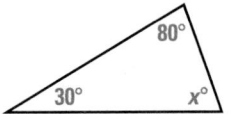

5.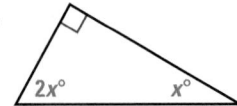

6.

7. In the diagram, $DEFG \cong WXFG$.
Find the values of x and y.

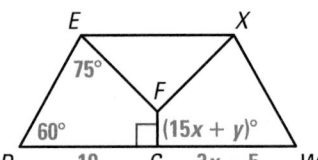

In Exercises 8–10, decide whether the triangles can be proven congruent by the given postulate.

8. $\triangle ABC \cong \triangle EDC$ by SAS

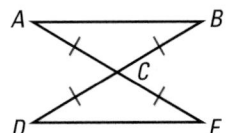

9. $\triangle FGH \cong \triangle JKL$ by ASA

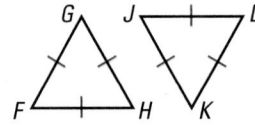

10. $\triangle MNP \cong \triangle PQM$ by SSS

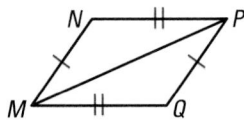

11. Write a proof.

GIVEN ▶ $\triangle ABC$ is isosceles with base $\overline{AC}$, $\overline{BD}$ bisects $\angle B$.

PROVE ▶ $\triangle ABD \cong \triangle CBD$

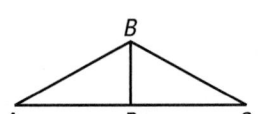

12. What is the third congruence needed to prove that $\triangle PQR \cong \triangle STU$ using the indicated theorem?

   a. HL

   b. AAS

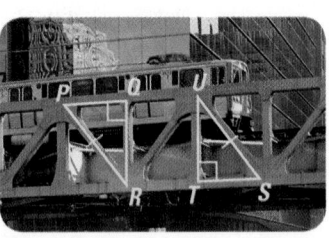

Decide whether the transformation is a *translation*, *reflection*, or *rotation*.

13.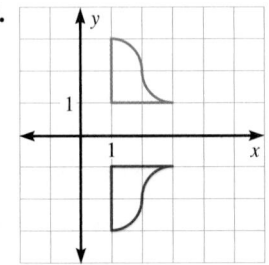

14.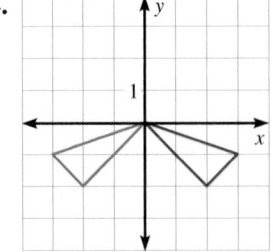

15.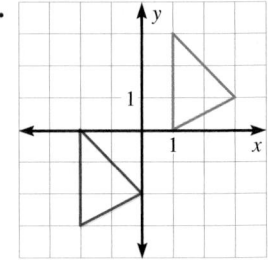

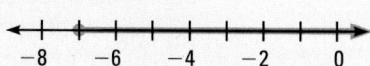
SOLVE INEQUALITIES AND ABSOLUTE VALUE EQUATIONS

×ʸ EXAMPLE 1 Solve inequalities

Solve $-3x + 7 \leq 28$. Then graph the solution.

When you multiply or divide each side of an inequality by a *negative* number, you must reverse the inequality symbol to obtain an equivalent inequality.

$-3x + 7 \leq 28$ **Write original inequality.**

$-3x \leq 21$ **Subtract 7 from both sides.**

$x \geq -7$ **Divide each side by -3. Reverse the inequality symbol.**

▶ The solutions are all real numbers greater than or equal to -7. The graph is shown at the right.

$$-8 \quad -6 \quad -4 \quad -2 \quad 0$$

×ʸ EXAMPLE 2 Solve absolute value equations

Solve $|2x + 1| = 5$.

The expression inside the absolute value bars can represent 5 or -5.

STEP 1 Assume $2x + 1$ represents 5.   **STEP 2** Assume $2x + 1$ represents -5.

$$2x + 1 = 5 \qquad\qquad 2x + 1 = -5$$

$$2x = 4 \qquad\qquad\qquad 2x = -6$$

$$x = 2 \qquad\qquad\qquad\quad x = -3$$

▶ The solutions are 2 and -3.

EXERCISES

EXAMPLE 1
for Exs. 1–12

Solve the inequality. Then graph the solution.

1. $x - 6 > -4$
2. $7 - c \leq -1$
3. $-54 \geq 6x$
4. $\dfrac{5}{2}t + 8 \leq 33$
5. $3(y + 2) < 3$
6. $\dfrac{1}{4}z < 2$
7. $5k + 1 \geq -11$
8. $13.6 > -0.8 - 7.2r$
9. $6x + 7 < 2x - 3$
10. $-v + 12 \leq 9 - 2v$
11. $4(n + 5) \geq 5 - n$
12. $5y + 3 \geq 2(y - 9)$

EXAMPLE 2
for Exs. 13–27

Solve the equation.

13. $|x - 5| = 3$
14. $|x + 6| = 2$
15. $|4 - x| = 4$
16. $|2 - x| = 0.5$
17. $|3x - 1| = 8$
18. $|4x + 5| = 7$
19. $|x - 1.3| = 2.1$
20. $|3x - 15| = 0$
21. $|6x - 2| = 4$
22. $|8x + 1| = 17$
23. $|9 - 2x| = 19$
24. $|0.5x - 4| = 2$
25. $|5x - 2| = 8$
26. $|7x + 4| = 11$
27. $|3x - 11| = 4$

CONTEXT-BASED MULTIPLE CHOICE QUESTIONS

Some of the information you need to solve a context-based multiple choice question may appear in a table, a diagram, or a graph.

PROBLEM 1

Five of six players on a lacrosse team are set up in a 2-3-1 formation. In this formation, the players form two congruent triangles. Three **attackmen** form one triangle. Three **midfielders** form the second triangle. In the diagram, where should player L stand so that $\triangle ABC \cong \triangle JKL$?

A (8, 8)   **B** (20, 60)

C (40, 40)   **D** (30, 15)

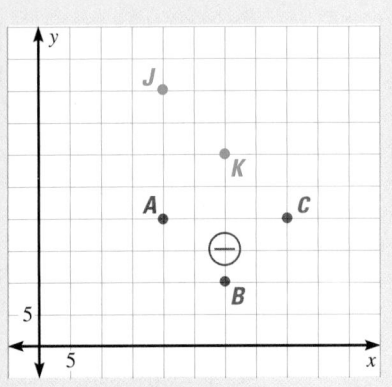

Plan

INTERPRET THE GRAPH Use the graph to determine the coordinates of each player. Use the Distance Formula to check the coordinates in the choices.

Solution

STEP 1
Find the coordinates of each vertex.

For $\triangle ABC$, the coordinates are $A(20, 20)$, $B(30, 10)$, and $C(40, 20)$. For $\triangle JKL$, the coordinates are $J(20, 40)$, $K(30, 30)$, and $L(\underline{\ ?\ }, \underline{\ ?\ })$.

STEP 2
Calculate BC and CA.

Because $\triangle ABC \cong \triangle JKL$, $BC = KL$ and $CA = LJ$. Find BC and CA.

By the Distance Formula, $BC = \sqrt{(40-30)^2 + (20-10)^2} = \sqrt{200} = 10\sqrt{2}$ yards.

Also, $CA = \sqrt{(20-40)^2 + (20-20)^2} = \sqrt{400} = 20$ yards.

STEP 3
Check the choices to find the coordinates that produce the congruent corresponding sides.

Check the coordinates given in the choices to see whether $LJ = CA = 20$ yards and $KL = BC = 10\sqrt{2}$ yards. As soon as one set of coordinates does not work for the first side length, you can move to the next set.

Choice A: $L(8, 8)$, so $LJ = \sqrt{(20-8)^2 + (40-8)^2} = 4\sqrt{73} \neq 20$ ✗

Choice B: $L(20, 60)$, so $LJ = \sqrt{(20-20)^2 + (40-60)^2} = \sqrt{400} = 20$ ✓

and $KL = \sqrt{(20-30)^2 + (60-30)^2} = \sqrt{1000} \neq 10\sqrt{2}$ ✗

Choice C: $L(40, 40)$, so $LJ = \sqrt{(20-40)^2 + (40-40)^2} = \sqrt{400} = 20$ ✓

and $KL = \sqrt{(40-30)^2 + (40-30)^2} = \sqrt{200} = 10\sqrt{2}$ ✓

Player L should stand at $(40, 40)$. The correct answer is C. **A** **B** **Ⓒ** **D**

Use the diagram to find the value of *y*.

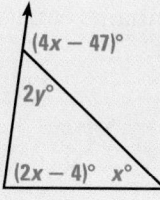

- **(A)** 15.5
- **(B)** 27.5
- **(C)** 43
- **(D)** 82

Plan

INTERPRET THE DIAGRAM All of the angle measures in the diagram are labeled with algebraic expressions. Use what you know about the angles in a triangle to find the value of *y*.

Solution

STEP 1
Find the value of *x*.

Use the Exterior Angle Theorem to find the value of *x*.

$(4x - 47)° = (2x - 4)° + x°$	Exterior Angle Theorem
$4x - 47 = 3x - 4$	Combine like terms.
$x = 43$	Solve for *x*.

STEP 2
Find the value of *y*.

Use the Linear Pair Postulate to find the value of *y*.

$(4x - 47)° + 2y° = 180°$	Linear Pair Postulate
$[4(43) - 47] + 2y = 180$	Substitute 43 for *x*.
$125 + 2y = 180$	Simplify.
$y = 27.5$	Solve for *y*.

The correct answer is B. **(A)** **(B)** **(C)** **(D)**

PRACTICE

1. In Problem 2, what are the measures of the interior angles of the triangle?
- **(A)** 27.5°, 43°, 109.5°
- **(B)** 27.5°, 51°, 86°
- **(C)** 40°, 60°, 80°
- **(D)** 43°, 55°, 82°

2. What are the coordinates of the vertices of the image of △*FGH* after the translation $(x, y) \rightarrow (x - 2, y + 3)$?

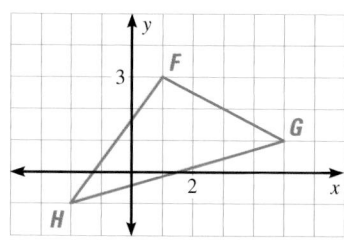

- **(A)** (3, 4), (−4, 4), (−1, 6)
- **(B)** (−2, −1), (1, 3), (5, 1)
- **(C)** (4, 1), (7, −1), (1, −3)
- **(D)** (−4, 2), (−1, 6), (3, 4)

MULTIPLE CHOICE

1. A teacher has the pennants shown below. Which pennants can you prove are congruent?

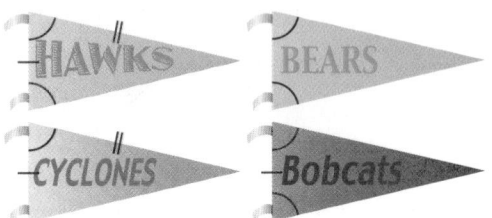

   (A) All of the pennants can be proven congruent.

   (B) The Hawks, Cyclones, and Bobcats pennants can be proven congruent.

   (C) The Bobcats and Bears pennants can be proven congruent.

   (D) None of the pennants can be proven congruent.

In Exercises 2 and 3, use the graph below.

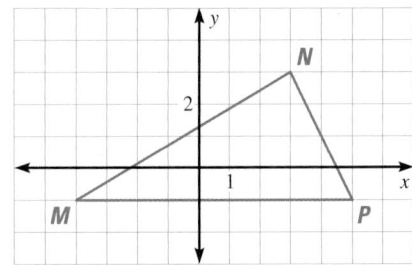

2. What type of triangle is △*MNP*?

   (A) Scalene

   (B) Isosceles

   (C) Right

   (D) Not enough information

3. Which are the coordinates of point *Q* such that △*MNP* ≅ △*QPN*?

   (A) (0, −3)

   (B) (−6, 3)

   (C) (12, 3)

   (D) (3, −5)

4. The diagram shows the final step in folding an origami butterfly. Use the congruent quadrilaterals, outlined in red, to find the value of $x + y$.

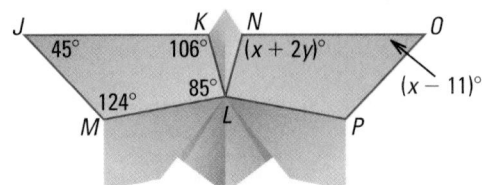

   (A) 25   **(B)** 56

   (C) 81   **(D)** 106

5. Which reason cannot be used to prove that ∠*A* ≅ ∠*D*?

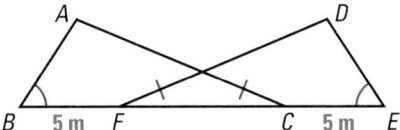

   (A) Base Angles Theorem

   (B) Segment Addition Postulate

   (C) SSS Congruence Postulate

   (D) Corresponding parts of congruent triangles are congruent.

6. Which coordinates are the vertices of a triangle congruent to △*JKL*?

   (A) (−5, 0), (−5, 6), (−1, 6)

   (B) (−1, −5), (−1, −1), (1, −5)

   (C) (2, 1), (2, 3), (5, 1)

   (D) (4, 6), (6, 6), (6, 4)

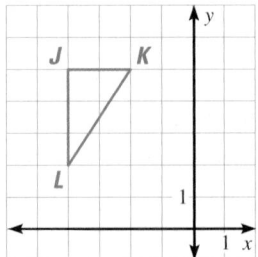

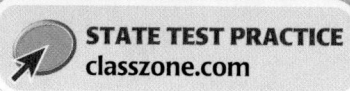
GRIDDED ANSWER

7. What is the perimeter of the triangle?

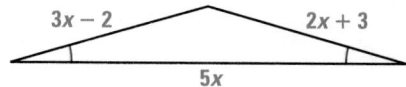

$3x - 2$ $2x + 3$
$5x$

8. Figure *ABCD* has vertices $A(0, 2)$, $B(-2, -4)$, $C(2, 7)$, and $D(5, 0)$. What is the *y*-coordinate of the image of vertex *B* after the translation $(x, y) \rightarrow (x + 8, y - 0.5)$?

9. What is the value of *x*?

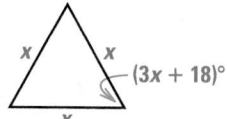

x x
$(3x + 18)°$
x

SHORT RESPONSE

10. If $\triangle ABE \cong \triangle EDC$, show that $\triangle EFA \cong \triangle CBE$.

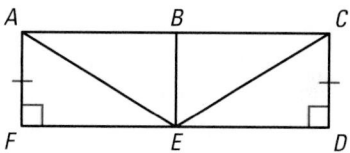

11. Two triangles have the same base and height. Are the triangles congruent? *Justify* your answer using an example.

12. If two people construct wooden frames for a triangular weaving loom using the instructions below, will the frames be congruent triangles? *Explain* your reasoning.

> Construct the frame so that the loom has a 90° angle at the bottom and 45° angles at the two upper corners. The piece of wood at the top should measure 72 inches.

EXTENDED RESPONSE

13. Use the diagram at the right.

   a. Copy the diagram onto a piece of graph paper. Reflect $\triangle ABC$ in the *x*-axis.

   b. Copy and complete the table. *Describe* what you notice about the coordinates of the image compared to the coordinates of $\triangle ABC$.

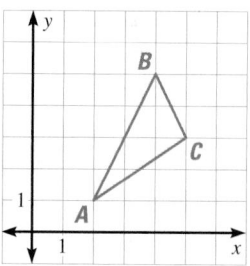

	A	B	C
Coordinates of △ABC	?	?	?
Coordinates of image	?	?	?

14. Kylie is designing a quilting pattern using two different fabrics. The diagram shows her progress so far.

   a. Use the markings on the diagram to prove that all of the white triangles are congruent.

   b. Prove that all of the blue triangles are congruent.

   c. Can you prove that the blue triangles are right triangles? *Explain.*

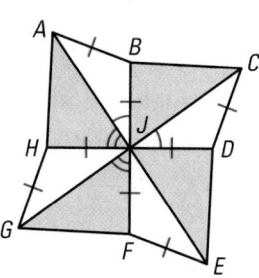

5 Relationships within Triangles

Before

In previous courses and in Chapters 1–4, you learned the following skills, which you'll use in Chapter 5: simplifying expressions, finding distances and slopes, using properties of triangles, and solving equations and inequalities.

Prerequisite Skills

VOCABULARY CHECK

1. Is the *distance from point P to line AB* equal to the length of $\overline{PQ}$? *Explain* why or why not.

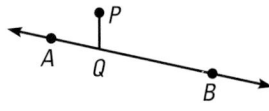

SKILLS AND ALGEBRA CHECK

Simplify the expression. All variables are positive. *(Review pp. 139, 870 for 5.1.)*

2. $\sqrt{(0-h)^2}$ 3. $\dfrac{2m + 2n}{2}$ 4. $|(x + a) - a|$ 5. $\sqrt{r^2 + r^2}$

$\triangle PQR$ **has the given vertices. Graph the triangle and classify it by its sides. Then determine if it is a right triangle.** *(Review p. 217 for 5.1, 5.4.)*

6. $P(2, 0)$, $Q(6, 6)$, and $R(12, 2)$ 7. $P(2, 3)$, $Q(4, 7)$, and $R(11, 3)$

Ray AD bisects $\angle BAC$ and point E bisects $\overline{CB}$. Find the measurement. *(Review pp. 15, 24, 217 for 5.2, 5.3, 5.5.)*

8. CE 9. $m\angle BAC$ 10. $m\angle ACB$

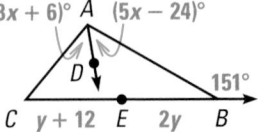

Solve. *(Review pp. 287, 882 for 5.3, 5.5.)*

11. $x^2 + 24^2 = 26^2$ 12. $48 + x^2 = 60$ 13. $43 > x + 35$

@HomeTutor Prerequisite skills practice at classzone.com

In Chapter 5, you will apply the big ideas listed below and reviewed in the Chapter Summary on page 343. You will also use the key vocabulary listed below.

Big Ideas

① Using properties of special segments in triangles

② Using triangle inequalities to determine what triangles are possible

③ Extending methods for justifying and proving relationships

KEY VOCABULARY

- midsegment of a triangle, *p. 295*
- coordinate proof, *p. 296*
- perpendicular bisector, *p. 303*
- equidistant, *p. 303*
- point of concurrency, *p. 305*
- circumcenter, *p. 306*

- incenter, *p. 312*
- median of a triangle, *p. 319*
- centroid, *p. 319*
- altitude of a triangle, *p. 320*
- orthocenter, *p. 321*
- indirect proof, *p. 337*

You can use triangle relationships to find and compare angle measures and distances. For example, if two sides of a triangle represent travel along two roads, then the third side represents the distance back to the starting point.

Animated Geometry

The animation illustrated below for Example 2 on page 336 helps you answer this question: After taking different routes, which group of bikers is farther from the camp?

Two groups of bikers head out from the same point and use different routes.

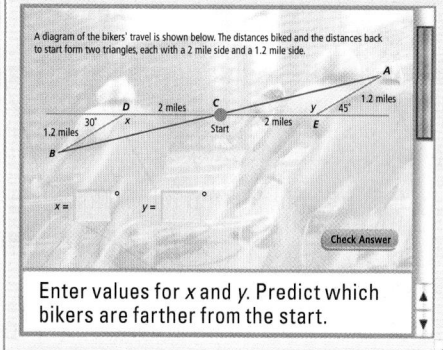

Enter values for *x* and *y*. Predict which bikers are farther from the start.

Animated Geometry at classzone.com

Other animations for Chapter 5: pages 296, 304, 312, 321, and 330

5.1 Investigate Segments in Triangles

MATERIALS · graph paper · ruler · pencil

QUESTION How are the midsegments of a triangle related to the sides of the triangle?

A *midsegment* of a triangle connects the midpoints of two sides of a triangle.

EXPLORE Draw and find a midsegment

| STEP 1 | *Draw a right triangle* | STEP 2 | *Draw the midsegment* | STEP 3 | *Make a table* |

STEP 1 *Draw a right triangle*

Draw a right triangle with legs on the *x*-axis and the *y*-axis. Use vertices *A*(0, 8), *B*(6, 0), and *O*(0, 0) as Case 1.

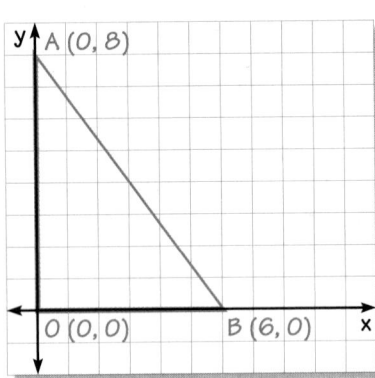

STEP 2 *Draw the midsegment*

Find the midpoints of $\overline{OA}$ and $\overline{OB}$. Plot the midpoints and label them *D* and *E*. Connect them to create the midsegment $\overline{DE}$.

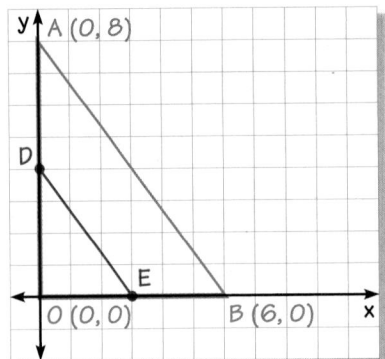

STEP 3 *Make a table*

Draw the Case 2 triangle below. Copy and complete the table.

	Case 1	Case 2
O	(0, 0)	(0, 0)
A	(0, 8)	(0, 11)
B	(6, 0)	(5, 0)
D	?	?
E	?	?
Slope of $\overline{AB}$	?	?
Slope of $\overline{DE}$	?	?
Length of $\overline{AB}$	?	?
Length of $\overline{DE}$	?	?

DRAW CONCLUSIONS Use your observations to complete these exercises

1. Choose two other right triangles with legs on the axes. Add these triangles as Cases 3 and 4 to your table.

2. Expand your table in Step 3 for Case 5 with *A*(0, *n*), *B*(*k*, 0), and *O*(0, 0).

3. Expand your table in Step 3 for Case 6 with *A*(0, 2*n*), *B*(2*k*, 0), and *O*(0, 0).

4. What do you notice about the slopes of $\overline{AB}$ and $\overline{DE}$? What do you notice about the lengths of $\overline{AB}$ and $\overline{DE}$?

5. In each case, is the midsegment $\overline{DE}$ parallel to $\overline{AB}$? *Explain*.

6. Are your observations true for the midsegment created by connecting the midpoints of $\overline{OA}$ and $\overline{AB}$? What about the midsegment connecting the midpoints of $\overline{AB}$ and $\overline{OB}$?

7. Make a conjecture about the relationship between a midsegment and a side of the triangle. Test your conjecture using an acute triangle.

5.1 Midsegment Theorem and Coordinate Proof

Before	You used coordinates to show properties of figures.
Now	You will use properties of midsegments and write coordinate proofs.
Why?	So you can use indirect measure to find a height, as in Ex. 35.

Key Vocabulary
• midsegment of a triangle
• coordinate proof

A **midsegment of a triangle** is a segment that connects the midpoints of two sides of the triangle. Every triangle has three midsegments.

The midsegments of $\triangle ABC$ at the right are $\overline{MP}$, $\overline{MN}$, and $\overline{NP}$.

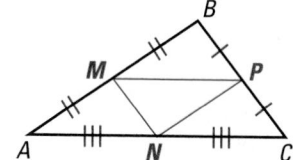

THEOREM *For Your Notebook*

THEOREM 5.1 Midsegment Theorem

The segment connecting the midpoints of two sides of a triangle is parallel to the third side and is half as long as that side.

Proof: Example 5, p. 297; Ex. 41, p. 300

$\overline{DE} \parallel \overline{AC}$ and $DE = \frac{1}{2}AC$

EXAMPLE 1 Use the Midsegment Theorem to find lengths

READ DIAGRAMS
In the diagram for Example 1, midsegment $\overline{UV}$ can be called "the midsegment opposite $\overline{RT}$."

CONSTRUCTION Triangles are used for strength in roof trusses. In the diagram, $\overline{UV}$ and $\overline{VW}$ are midsegments of $\triangle RST$. Find UV and RS.

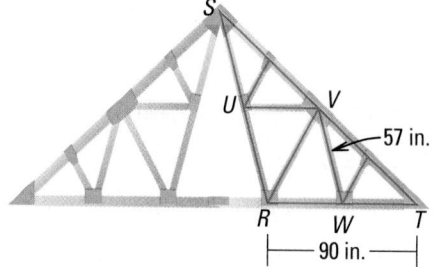

Solution

$UV = \frac{1}{2} \cdot RT = \frac{1}{2}(90 \text{ in.}) = 45 \text{ in.}$

$RS = 2 \cdot VW = 2(57 \text{ in.}) = 114 \text{ in.}$

✓ **GUIDED PRACTICE** for Example 1

1. Copy the diagram in Example 1. Draw and name the third midsegment.

2. In Example 1, suppose the distance UW is 81 inches. Find VS.

EXAMPLE 2 Use the Midsegment Theorem

In the kaleidoscope image, $\overline{AE} \cong \overline{BE}$ and $\overline{AD} \cong \overline{CD}$. Show that $\overline{CB} \parallel \overline{DE}$.

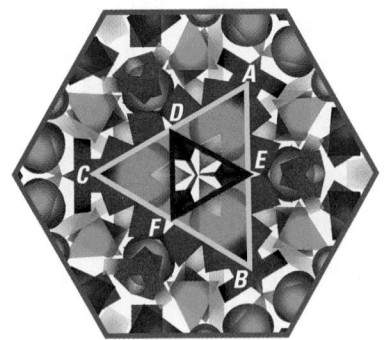

Solution

Because $\overline{AE} \cong \overline{BE}$ and $\overline{AD} \cong \overline{CD}$, E is the midpoint of $\overline{AB}$ and D is the midpoint of $\overline{AC}$ by definition. Then $\overline{DE}$ is a midsegment of $\triangle ABC$ by definition and $\overline{CB} \parallel \overline{DE}$ by the Midsegment Theorem.

COORDINATE PROOF A **coordinate proof** involves placing geometric figures in a coordinate plane. When you use variables to represent the coordinates of a figure in a coordinate proof, the results are true for all figures of that type.

EXAMPLE 3 Place a figure in a coordinate plane

Place each figure in a coordinate plane in a way that is convenient for finding side lengths. Assign coordinates to each vertex.

a. A rectangle

b. A scalene triangle

Solution

It is easy to find lengths of horizontal and vertical segments and distances from (0, 0), so place one vertex at the origin and one or more sides on an axis.

USE VARIABLES

The rectangle shown represents a general rectangle because the choice of coordinates is based only on the definition of a rectangle. If you use this rectangle to prove a result, the result will be true for all rectangles.

a. Let h represent the length and k represent the width.

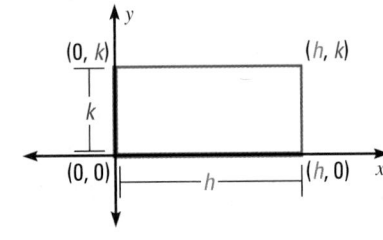

b. Notice that you need to use three different variables.

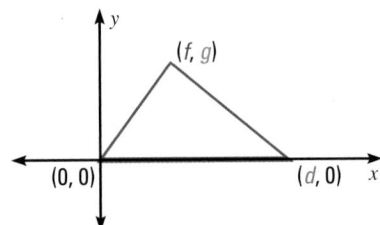

Animated Geometry at classzone.com

✓ **GUIDED PRACTICE** for Examples 2 and 3

3. In Example 2, if F is the midpoint of $\overline{CB}$, what do you know about $\overline{DF}$?

4. Show another way to place the rectangle in part (a) of Example 3 that is convenient for finding side lengths. Assign new coordinates.

5. Is it possible to find any of the side lengths in part (b) of Example 3 without using the Distance Formula? *Explain.*

6. A square has vertices (0, 0), (m, 0), and (0, m). Find the fourth vertex.

EXAMPLE 4 **Apply variable coordinates**

Place an isosceles right triangle in a coordinate plane. Then find the length of the hypotenuse and the coordinates of its midpoint *M*.

Solution

Place $\triangle PQO$ with the right angle at the origin. Let the length of the legs be k. Then the vertices are located at $P(0, k)$, $Q(k, 0)$, and $O(0, 0)$.

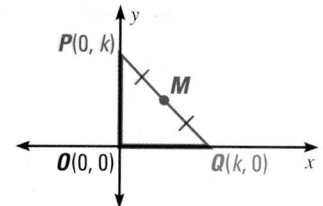

Use the Distance Formula to find PQ.

$$PQ = \sqrt{(k - 0)^2 + (0 - k)^2} = \sqrt{k^2 + (-k)^2} = \sqrt{k^2 + k^2} = \sqrt{2k^2} = k\sqrt{2}$$

Use the Midpoint Formula to find the midpoint M of the hypotenuse.

$$M\left(\frac{0 + k}{2}, \frac{k + 0}{2}\right) = M\left(\frac{k}{2}, \frac{k}{2}\right)$$

EXAMPLE 5 **Prove the Midsegment Theorem**

Write a coordinate proof of the Midsegment Theorem for one midsegment.

GIVEN ▶ $\overline{DE}$ is a midsegment of $\triangle OBC$.

PROVE ▶ $\overline{DE} \parallel \overline{OC}$ and $DE = \frac{1}{2}OC$

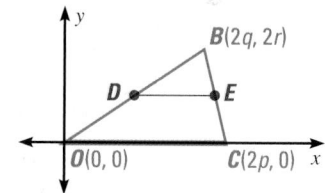

Solution

STEP 1 **Place** $\triangle OBC$ and assign coordinates. Because you are finding midpoints, use $2p$, $2q$, and $2r$. Then find the coordinates of D and E.

$$D\left(\frac{2q + 0}{2}, \frac{2r + 0}{2}\right) = D(q, r) \qquad E\left(\frac{2q + 2p}{2}, \frac{2r + 0}{2}\right) = E(q + p, r)$$

STEP 2 **Prove** $\overline{DE} \parallel \overline{OC}$. The y-coordinates of D and E are the same, so $\overline{DE}$ has a slope of 0. $\overline{OC}$ is on the x-axis, so its slope is 0.

▶ Because their slopes are the same, $\overline{DE} \parallel \overline{OC}$.

STEP 3 **Prove** $DE = \frac{1}{2}OC$. Use the Ruler Postulate to find $\overline{DE}$ and $\overline{OC}$.

$$DE = |(q + p) - q| = p \qquad OC = |2p - 0| = 2p$$

▶ So, the length of $\overline{DE}$ is half the length of $\overline{OC}$.

✓ **GUIDED PRACTICE** for Examples 4 and 5

7. In Example 5, find the coordinates of F, the midpoint of $\overline{OC}$. Then show that $\overline{EF} \parallel \overline{OB}$.

8. Graph the points $O(0, 0)$, $H(m, n)$, and $J(m, 0)$. Is $\triangle OHJ$ a right triangle? Find the side lengths and the coordinates of the midpoint of each side.

5.1 EXERCISES

○ = **WORKED-OUT SOLUTIONS**
on p. WS6 for Exs. 9, 21, and 37

★ = **STANDARDIZED TEST PRACTICE**
Exs. 2, 31, and 39

SKILL PRACTICE

1. **VOCABULARY** Copy and complete: In $\triangle ABC$, D is the midpoint of $\overline{AB}$ and E is the midpoint of $\overline{AC}$. $\overline{DE}$ is a __?__ of $\triangle ABC$.

2. ★ **WRITING** *Explain* why it is convenient to place a right triangle on the grid as shown when writing a coordinate proof. How might you want to relabel the coordinates of the vertices if the proof involves midpoints?

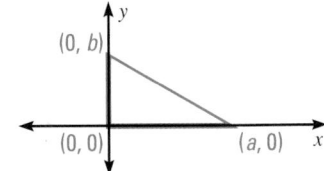

EXAMPLES 1 and 2
on pp. 295–296
for Exs. 3–11

FINDING LENGTHS $\overline{DE}$ is a midsegment of $\triangle ABC$. Find the value of x.

3.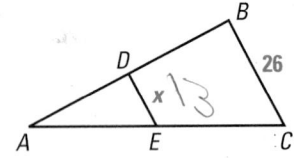

4.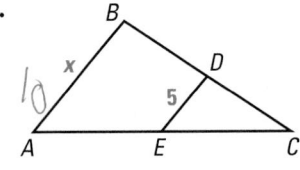

5.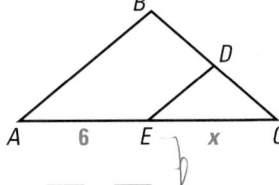

USING THE MIDSEGMENT THEOREM In $\triangle XYZ$, $\overline{XJ} \cong \overline{JY}$, $\overline{YL} \cong \overline{LZ}$, and $\overline{XK} \cong \overline{KZ}$. Copy and complete the statement.

6. $\overline{JK} \parallel$ __?__

7. $\overline{JL} \parallel$ __?__

8. $\overline{XY} \parallel$ __?__

9. $\overline{YJ} \cong$ __?__ $\cong$ __?__

10. $\overline{JL} \cong$ __?__ $\cong$ __?__

11. $\overline{JK} \cong$ __?__ $\cong$ __?__

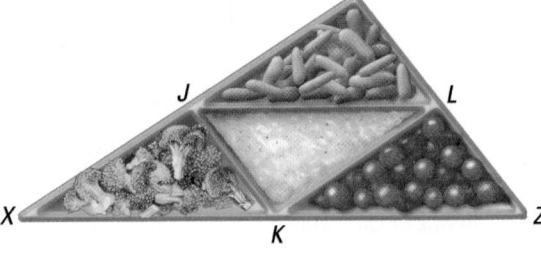

EXAMPLE 3
on p. 296
for Exs. 12–19

PLACING FIGURES Place the figure in a coordinate plane in a convenient way. Assign coordinates to each vertex.

12. Right triangle: leg lengths are 3 units and 2 units

13. Isosceles right triangle: leg length is 7 units

14. Square: side length is 3 units

15. Scalene triangle: one side length is $2m$

16. Rectangle: length is a and width is b

17. Square: side length is s

18. Isosceles right triangle: leg length is p

19. Right triangle: leg lengths are r and s

EXAMPLES 4 and 5
on p. 297
for Exs. 20–23

20. **COMPARING METHODS** Find the length of the hypotenuse in Exercise 19. Then place the triangle another way and use the new coordinates to find the length of the hypotenuse. Do you get the same result?

APPLYING VARIABLE COORDINATES Sketch $\triangle ABC$. Find the length and the slope of each side. Then find the coordinates of each midpoint. Is $\triangle ABC$ a right triangle? Is it isosceles? *Explain.* (Assume all variables are positive, $p \neq q$, and $m \neq n$.)

21. $A(0, 0)$, $B(p, q)$, $C(2p, 0)$

22. $A(0, 0)$, $B(h, h)$, $C(2h, 0)$

23. $A(0, n)$, $B(m, n)$, $C(m, 0)$

298 Chapter 5 Relationships within Triangles

xy ALGEBRA Use △*GHJ*, where *A*, *B*, and *C* are midpoints of the sides.

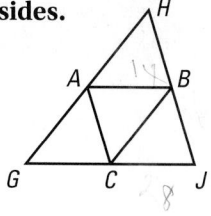

24. If $AB = 3x + 8$ and $GJ = 2x + 24$, what is AB? 14

25. If $AC = 3y - 5$ and $HJ = 4y + 2$, what is HB? 13

26. If $GH = 7z - 1$ and $BC = 4z - 3$, what is GH?
    34   17

27. **ERROR ANALYSIS** *Explain* why the conclusion is incorrect.

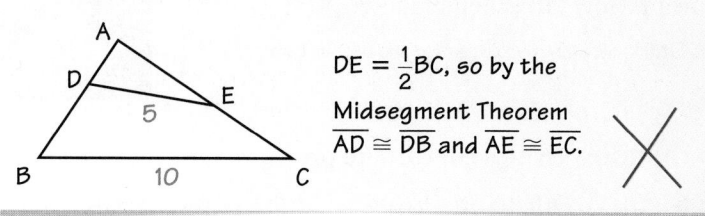

$DE = \frac{1}{2}BC$, so by the Midsegment Theorem $\overline{AD} \cong \overline{DB}$ and $\overline{AE} \cong \overline{EC}$.

28. **FINDING PERIMETER** The midpoints of the three sides of a triangle are $P(2, 0)$, $Q(7, 12)$, and $R(16, 0)$. Find the length of each midsegment and the perimeter of △*PQR*. Then find the perimeter of the original triangle.

APPLYING VARIABLE COORDINATES Find the coordinates of the red point(s) in the figure. Then show that the given statement is true.

29. △*OPQ* ≅ △*RSQ*

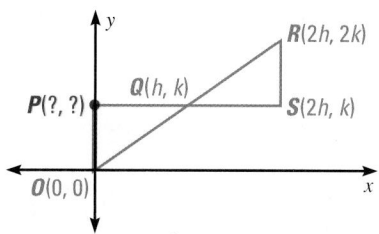

30. slope of $\overline{HE}$ = −(slope of $\overline{DG}$)

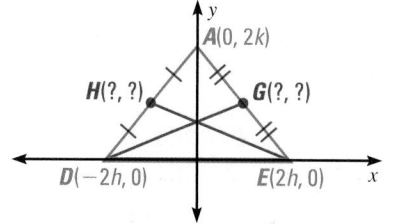

31. ★ **MULTIPLE CHOICE** A rectangle with side lengths $3h$ and k has a vertex at $(-h, k)$. Which point *cannot* be a vertex of the rectangle?

    (A) (h, k) (B) $(-h, 0)$ (C) $(2h, 0)$ (D) $(2h, k)$

32. **RECONSTRUCTING A TRIANGLE** The points $T(2, 1)$, $U(4, 5)$, and $V(7, 4)$ are the midpoints of the sides of a triangle. Graph the three midsegments. Then show how to use your graph and the properties of midsegments to draw the original triangle. Give the coordinates of each vertex.

33. **3-D FIGURES** Points *A*, *B*, *C*, and *D* are the vertices of a *tetrahedron* (a solid bounded by four triangles). $\overline{EF}$ is a midsegment of △*ABC*, $\overline{GE}$ is a midsegment of △*ABD*, and $\overline{FG}$ is a midsegment of △*ACD*.

    Show that Area of △*EFG* = $\frac{1}{4}$ · Area of △*BCD*.

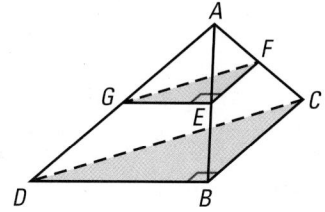

34. **CHALLENGE** In △*PQR*, the midpoint of $\overline{PQ}$ is $K(4, 12)$, the midpoint of $\overline{QR}$ is $L(5, 15)$, and the midpoint of $\overline{PR}$ is $M(6.4, 10.8)$. Show how to find the vertices of △*PQR*. *Compare* your work for this exercise with your work for Exercise 32. How were your methods different?

35. FLOODLIGHTS A floodlight on the edge of the stage shines upward onto the backdrop as shown. Constance is 5 feet tall. She stands halfway between the light and the backdrop, and the top of her head is at the midpoint of $\overline{AC}$. The edge of the light just reaches the top of her head. How tall is her shadow?

@*HomeTutor* for problem solving help at classzone.com

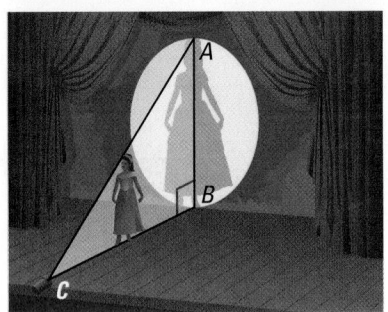

EXAMPLE 5
on p. 297
for Exs. 36–37

COORDINATE PROOF Write a coordinate proof.

36. GIVEN ▶ $P(0, k)$, $Q(h, 0)$, $R(-h, 0)$
PROVE ▶ $\triangle PQR$ is isosceles.

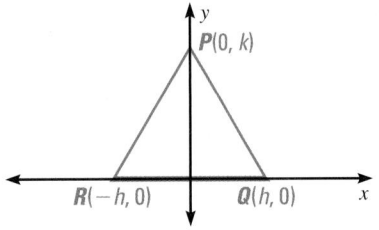

@*HomeTutor* for problem solving help at classzone.com

37. GIVEN ▶ $O(0, 0)$, $G(6, 6)$, $H(8, 0)$, $\overline{WV}$ is a midsegment.
PROVE ▶ $\overline{WV} \parallel \overline{OH}$ and $WV = \frac{1}{2}OH$

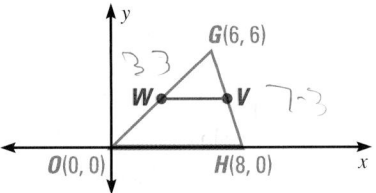

38. CARPENTRY In the set of shelves shown, the third shelf, labeled $\overline{CD}$, is closer to the bottom shelf, $\overline{EF}$, than midsegment $\overline{AB}$ is. If $\overline{EF}$ is 8 feet long, is it possible for $\overline{CD}$ to be 3 feet long? 4 feet long? 6 feet long? 8 feet long? *Explain.*

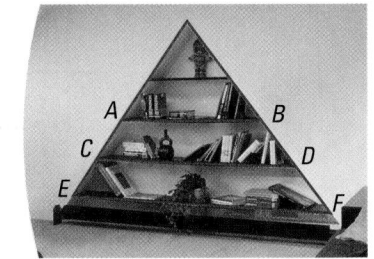

39. ★ **SHORT RESPONSE** Use the information in the diagram at the right. What is the length of side $\overline{AC}$ of $\triangle ABC$? *Explain* your reasoning.

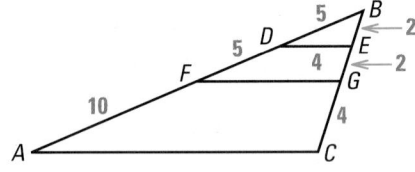

40. PLANNING FOR PROOF Copy and complete the plan for proof.

GIVEN ▶ $\overline{ST}$, $\overline{TU}$, and $\overline{SU}$ are midsegments of $\triangle PQR$.
PROVE ▶ $\triangle PST \cong \triangle SQU$

Use __?__ to show that $\overline{PS} \cong \overline{SQ}$. Use __?__ to show that $\angle QSU \cong \angle SPT$. Use __?__ to show that $\angle$ __?__ $\cong \angle$ __?__. Use __?__ to show that $\triangle PST \cong \triangle SQU$.

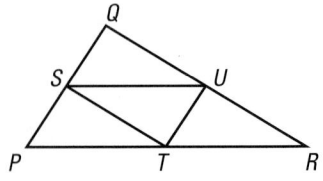

41. PROVING THEOREM 5.1 Use the figure in Example 5. Draw the midpoint F of $\overline{OC}$. Prove that $\overline{DF}$ is parallel to $\overline{BC}$ and $DF = \frac{1}{2}BC$.

42. COORDINATE PROOF Write a coordinate proof.

> **GIVEN** ▶ △*ABD* is a right triangle, with the right angle at vertex *A*.
> Point *C* is the midpoint of hypotenuse *BD*.
>
> **PROVE** ▶ Point *C* is the same distance from each vertex of △*ABD*.

43. MULTI-STEP PROBLEM To create the design below, shade the triangle formed by the three midsegments of a triangle. Then repeat the process for each unshaded triangle. Let the perimeter of the original triangle be 1.

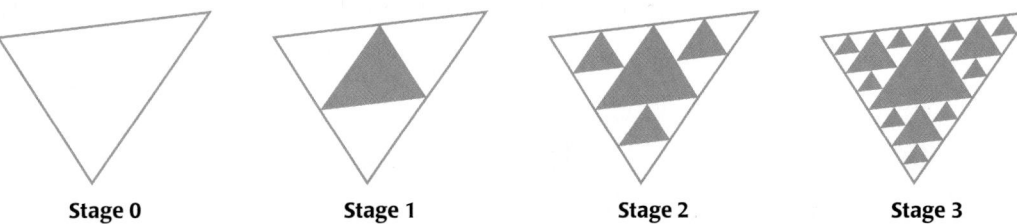

Stage 0   Stage 1   Stage 2   Stage 3

    a. What is the perimeter of the triangle that is shaded in Stage 1?

    b. What is the total perimeter of all the shaded triangles in Stage 2?

    c. What is the total perimeter of all the shaded triangles in Stage 3?

RIGHT ISOSCELES TRIANGLES In Exercises 44 and 45, write a coordinate proof.

44. Any right isosceles triangle can be subdivided into a pair of congruent right isosceles triangles. (*Hint:* Draw the segment from the right angle to the midpoint of the hypotenuse.)

45. Any two congruent right isosceles triangles can be combined to form a single right isosceles triangle.

46. CHALLENGE *XY* is a midsegment of △*LMN*. Suppose $\overline{DE}$ is called a "quarter-segment" of △*LMN*. What do you think an "eighth-segment" would be? Make a conjecture about the properties of a quarter-segment and of an eighth-segment. Use variable coordinates to verify your conjectures.

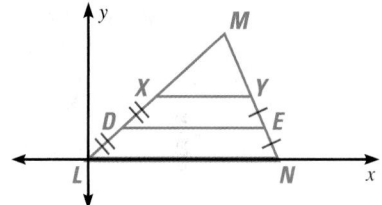

MIXED REVIEW

PREVIEW
Prepare for
Lesson 5.2
in Exs. 47–49.

Line ℓ bisects the segment. Find *LN*. *(p. 15)*

47.

$3x - 1$ $2x + 9$

L   *N*   *P*

48.

$6x - 10$ $4x$

L   *M*   *N*

49.

$4x + 22$ $7x + 1$

K   *L*   *N*

State which postulate or theorem you can use to prove that the triangles are congruent. Then write a congruence statement. *(pp. 225, 249)*

50.

X   *Y*

W   *Z*

51.

B

A   *C*

D

52.

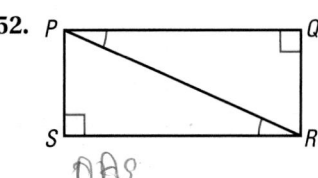

P   *Q*

S   *R*

Using ALTERNATIVE METHODS

Another Way to Solve Example 4, page 297

◆ **MULTIPLE REPRESENTATIONS** When you write a coordinate proof, you often have several options for how to place the figure in the coordinate plane and how to assign variables.

PROBLEM

> Place an isosceles right triangle in a coordinate plane. Then find the length of the hypotenuse and the coordinates of its midpoint M.

METHOD

Placing Hypotenuse on an Axis Place the triangle with point C at $(0, h)$ on the y-axis and the hypotenuse $\overline{AB}$ on the x-axis. To make $\angle ACB$ be a right angle, position A and B so that legs $\overline{CA}$ and $\overline{CB}$ have slopes of 1 and -1.

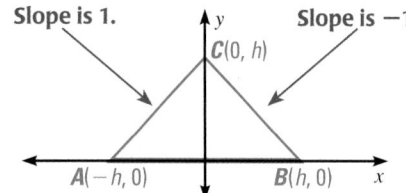

Length of hypotenuse $= 2h$

$$M = \left(\frac{-h + h}{2}, \frac{0 + 0}{2}\right) = (0, 0)$$

PRACTICE

1. **VERIFYING TRIANGLE PROPERTIES** Verify that $\angle C$ above is a right angle. Verify that $\triangle ABC$ is isosceles by showing $AC = BC$.

2. **MULTIPLES OF 2** Find the midpoint and length of each side using the placement below. What is the advantage of using $2h$ instead of h for the leg lengths?

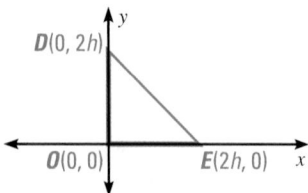

3. **OTHER ALTERNATIVES** Graph $\triangle JKL$ and verify that it is an isosceles right triangle. Then find the length and midpoint of $\overline{JK}$.

    a. $J(0, 0)$, $K(h, h)$, $L(h, 0)$

    b. $J(-2h, 0)$, $K(2h, 0)$, $L(0, 2h)$

4. **CHOOSE** Suppose you need to place a right isosceles triangle on a coordinate grid and assign variable coordinates. You know you will need to find all three side lengths and all three midpoints. How would you place the triangle? *Explain* your reasoning.

5. **RECTANGLES** Place rectangle $PQRS$ with length m and width n in the coordinate plane. Draw $\overline{PR}$ and $\overline{QS}$ connecting opposite corners of the rectangle. Then use coordinates to show that $\overline{PR} \cong \overline{QS}$.

6. **PARK** A square park has paths as shown. Use coordinates to determine whether a snack cart at point N is the same distance from each corner.

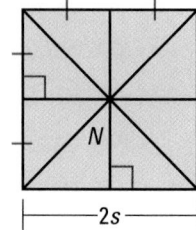

5.2 Use Perpendicular Bisectors

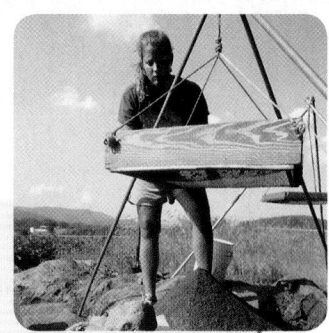

Before	You used segment bisectors and perpendicular lines.
Now	You will use perpendicular bisectors to solve problems.
Why?	So you can solve a problem in archaeology, as in Ex. 28.

Key Vocabulary
- **perpendicular bisector**
- **equidistant**
- **concurrent**
- **point of concurrency**
- **circumcenter**

In Lesson 1.3, you learned that a segment bisector intersects a segment at its midpoint. A segment, ray, line, or plane that is perpendicular to a segment at its midpoint is called a **perpendicular bisector**.

A point is **equidistant** from two figures if the point is the *same distance* from each figure. Points on the perpendicular bisector of a segment are equidistant from the segment's endpoints.

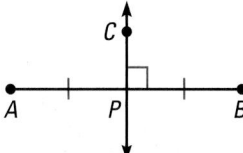

$\overleftrightarrow{CP}$ is a ⊥ bisector of $\overline{AB}$.

THEOREMS
For Your Notebook

THEOREM 5.2 Perpendicular Bisector Theorem

In a plane, if a point is on the perpendicular bisector of a segment, then it is equidistant from the endpoints of the segment.

If $\overleftrightarrow{CP}$ is the ⊥ bisector of $\overline{AB}$, then $CA = CB$.

Proof: Ex. 26, p. 308

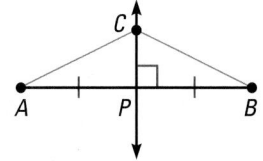

THEOREM 5.3 Converse of the Perpendicular Bisector Theorem

In a plane, if a point is equidistant from the endpoints of a segment, then it is on the perpendicular bisector of the segment.

If $DA = DB$, then D lies on the ⊥ bisector of $\overline{AB}$.

Proof: Ex. 27, p. 308

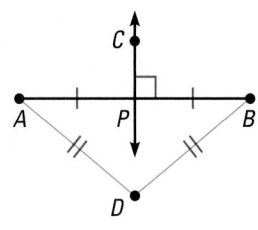

EXAMPLE 1 Use the Perpendicular Bisector Theorem

ALGEBRA $\overleftrightarrow{BD}$ is the perpendicular bisector of $\overline{AC}$. Find AD.

$AD = CD$	Perpendicular Bisector Theorem
$5x = 3x + 14$	Substitute.
$x = 7$	Solve for *x*.

▶ $AD = 5x = 5(7) = 35.$

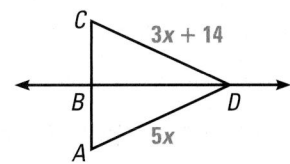

EXAMPLE 2   **Use perpendicular bisectors**

In the diagram, $\overleftrightarrow{WX}$ is the perpendicular bisector of $\overline{YZ}$.

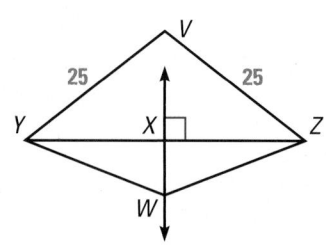

   a. What segment lengths in the diagram are equal?

   b. Is V on $\overleftrightarrow{WX}$?

Solution

   a. $\overleftrightarrow{WX}$ bisects $\overline{YZ}$, so $XY = XZ$. Because W is on the perpendicular bisector of $\overline{YZ}$, $WY = WZ$ by Theorem 5.2. The diagram shows that $VY = VZ = 25$.

   b. Because $VY = VZ$, V is equidistant from Y and Z. So, by the Converse of the Perpendicular Bisector Theorem, V is on the perpendicular bisector of $\overline{YZ}$, which is $\overleftrightarrow{WX}$.

Animated **Geometry** at classzone.com

  GUIDED PRACTICE   for Examples 1 and 2

In the diagram, $\overrightarrow{JK}$ is the perpendicular bisector of $\overline{NL}$.

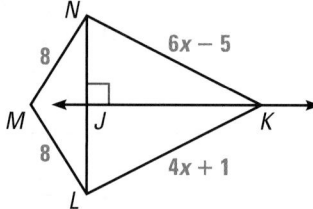

   1. What segment lengths are equal? *Explain* your reasoning.

   2. Find NK.

   3. *Explain* why M is on $\overleftrightarrow{JK}$.

ACTIVITY *FOLD THE PERPENDICULAR BISECTORS OF A TRIANGLE*

QUESTION Where do the perpendicular bisectors of a triangle meet?

Follow the steps below and answer the questions about perpendicular bisectors of triangles.

Materials:
• paper
• scissors
• ruler

STEP 1 Cut four large acute scalene triangles out of paper. Make each one different.

STEP 2 Choose one triangle. Fold it to form the perpendicular bisectors of the sides. Do the three bisectors intersect at the same point?

STEP 3 Repeat the process for the other three triangles. Make a conjecture about the perpendicular bisectors of a triangle.

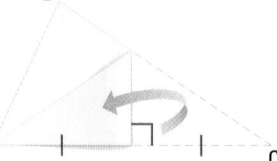

STEP 4 Choose one triangle. Label the vertices A, B, and C. Label the point of intersection of the perpendicular bisectors as P. Measure $\overline{AP}$, $\overline{BP}$, and $\overline{CP}$. What do you observe?

CONCURRENCY When three or more lines, rays, or segments intersect in the same point, they are called **concurrent** lines, rays, or segments. The point of intersection of the lines, rays, or segments is called the **point of concurrency**.

READ VOCABULARY
The perpendicular bisector of a side of a triangle can be referred to as a *perpendicular bisector of the triangle*.

As you saw in the Activity on page 304, the three perpendicular bisectors of a triangle are concurrent and the point of concurrency has a special property.

THEOREM   *For Your Notebook*

THEOREM 5.4 Concurrency of Perpendicular Bisectors of a Triangle

The perpendicular bisectors of a triangle intersect at a point that is equidistant from the vertices of the triangle.

If $\overline{PD}$, $\overline{PE}$, and $\overline{PF}$ are perpendicular bisectors, then $PA = PB = PC$.

Proof: p. 933

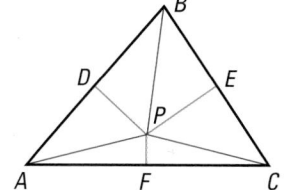

EXAMPLE 3   **Use the concurrency of perpendicular bisectors**

FROZEN YOGURT Three snack carts sell frozen yogurt from points A, B, and C outside a city. Each of the three carts is the same distance from the frozen yogurt distributor.

Find a location for the distributor that is equidistant from the three carts.

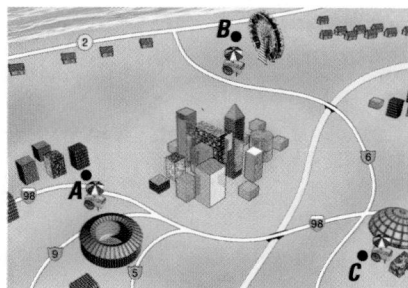

Solution

Theorem 5.4 shows you that you can find a point equidistant from three points by using the perpendicular bisectors of the triangle formed by those points.

Copy the positions of points A, B, and C and connect those points to draw $\triangle ABC$. Then use a ruler and protractor to draw the three perpendicular bisectors of $\triangle ABC$. The point of concurrency D is the location of the distributor.

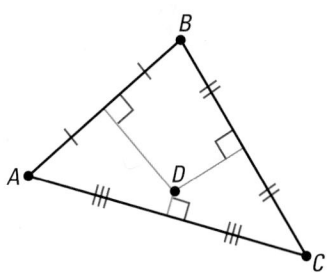

✓ **GUIDED PRACTICE**   for Example 3

4. **WHAT IF?** Hot pretzels are sold from points A and B and also from a cart at point E. Where could the pretzel distributor be located if it is equidistant from those three points? Sketch the triangle and show the location.

CIRCUMCENTER The point of concurrency of the three perpendicular bisectors of a triangle is called the **circumcenter** of the triangle. The circumcenter *P* is equidistant from the three vertices, so *P* is the center of a circle that passes through all three vertices.

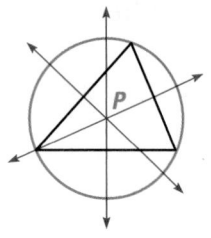
Acute triangle
P is inside triangle.

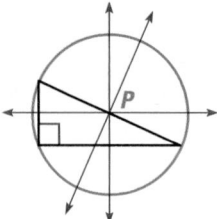
Right triangle
P is on triangle.

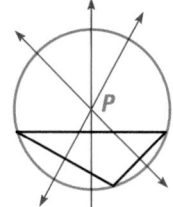
Obtuse triangle
P is outside triangle.

As shown above, the location of *P* depends on the type of triangle. The circle with the center *P* is said to be *circumscribed* about the triangle.

5.2 EXERCISES

SKILL PRACTICE

1. **VOCABULARY** Suppose you draw a circle with a compass. You choose three points on the circle to use as the vertices of a triangle. Copy and complete: The center of the circle is also the __?__ of the triangle.

2. ★ **WRITING** Consider $\overline{AB}$. How can you *describe* the set of all points in a plane that are equidistant from *A* and *B*?

⟨xy⟩ ALGEBRA Find the length of $\overline{AB}$.

3.

$5x$ B $4x + 3$

A D C

4.

$3x - 6$ C

A D

$x + 18$ B

5.

E

B D C

$9x + 1$ A $7x + 13$

REASONING Tell whether the information in the diagram allows you to conclude that *C* is on the perpendicular bisector of $\overline{AB}$.

6.
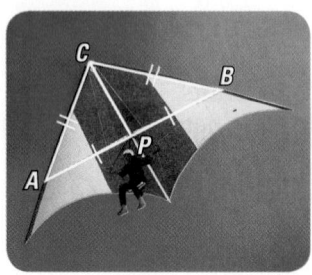

7.

8.

9. **★ MULTIPLE CHOICE** Point *P* is inside △*ABC* and is equidistant from points *A* and *B*. On which of the following segments must *P* be located?

- **A** $\overline{AB}$
- **B** The perpendicular bisector of $\overline{AB}$
- **C** The midsegment opposite $\overline{AB}$
- **D** The perpendicular bisector of $\overline{AC}$

10. **ERROR ANALYSIS** *Explain* why the conclusion is not correct given the information in the diagram.

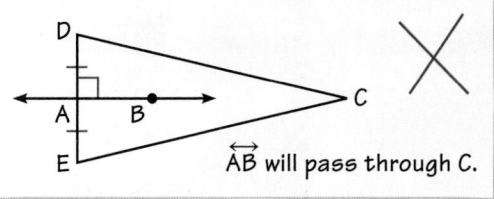

$\overleftrightarrow{AB}$ will pass through C.

PERPENDICULAR BISECTORS In Exercises 11–15, use the diagram. $\overrightarrow{JN}$ is the perpendicular bisector of $\overline{MK}$.

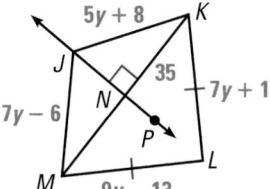

11. Find *NM*.
12. Find *JK*.
13. Find *KL*.
14. Find *ML*.
15. Is *L* on $\overleftrightarrow{JP}$? *Explain* your reasoning.

EXAMPLE 3
on p. 305
for Exs. 16–17

USING CONCURRENCY In the diagram, the perpendicular bisectors of △*ABC* meet at point *G* and are shown in blue. Find the indicated measure.

16. Find *BG*.

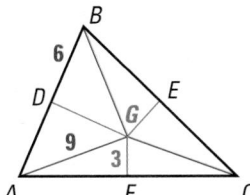

17. Find *GA*.

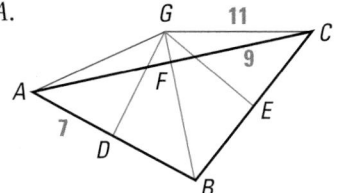

18. **CONSTRUCTING PERPENDICULAR BISECTORS** Use the construction shown on page 33 to construct the bisector of a segment. *Explain* why the bisector you constructed is actually the perpendicular bisector.

19. **CONSTRUCTION** Draw a right triangle. Use a compass and straightedge to find its circumcenter. Use a compass to draw the circumscribed circle.

ANALYZING STATEMENTS Copy and complete the statement with *always*, *sometimes*, or *never*. *Justify* your answer.

20. The circumcenter of a scalene triangle is __?__ inside the triangle.

21. If the perpendicular bisector of one side of a triangle goes through the opposite vertex, then the triangle is __?__ isosceles.

22. The perpendicular bisectors of a triangle intersect at a point that is __?__ equidistant from the midpoints of the sides of the triangle.

23. **CHALLENGE** Prove the statements in parts (a) – (c).

GIVEN ▶ Plane *P* is a perpendicular bisector of $\overline{XZ}$ at *Y*.

PROVE ▶ a. $\overline{XW} \cong \overline{ZW}$
  b. $\overline{XV} \cong \overline{ZV}$
  c. $\angle VXW \cong \angle VZW$

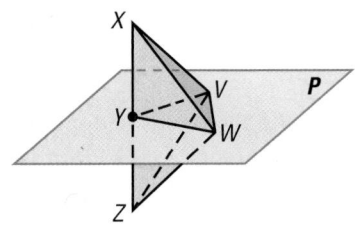

24. BRIDGE A cable-stayed bridge is shown below. Two cable lengths are given. Find the lengths of the blue cables. *Justify* your answer.

@HomeTutor for problem solving help at classzone.com

EXAMPLE 3
on p. 305
for Exs. 25, 28

(25.) ★ SHORT RESPONSE You and two friends plan to walk your dogs together. You want your meeting place to be the same distance from each person's house. *Explain* how you can use the diagram to locate the meeting place.

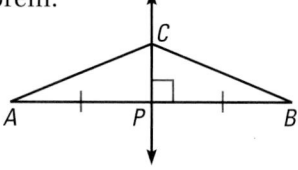

@HomeTutor for problem solving help at classzone.com

26. PROVING THEOREM 5.2 Prove the Perpendicular Bisector Theorem.

GIVEN ▶ $\overleftrightarrow{CP}$ is the perpendicular bisector of $\overline{AB}$.

PROVE ▶ $CA = CB$

Plan for Proof Show that right triangles $\triangle APC$ and $\triangle BPC$ are congruent. Then show that $\overline{CA} \cong \overline{CB}$.

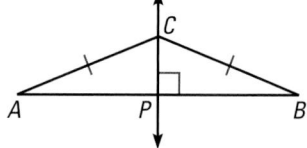

27. PROVING THEOREM 5.3 Prove the converse of Theorem 5.2. (*Hint:* Construct a line through C perpendicular to $\overline{AB}$.)

GIVEN ▶ $CA = CB$

PROVE ▶ C is on the perpendicular bisector of $\overline{AB}$.

28. ★ EXTENDED RESPONSE Archaeologists find three stones. They believe that the stones were once part of a circle of stones with a community firepit at its center. They mark the locations of Stones A, B, and C on a graph where distances are measured in feet.

a. *Explain* how the archaeologists can use a sketch to estimate the center of the circle of stones.

b. Copy the diagram and find the approximate coordinates of the point at which the archaeologists should look for the firepit.

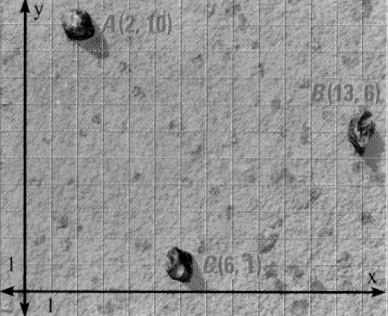

29. TECHNOLOGY Use geometry drawing software to construct $\overline{AB}$. Find the midpoint C. Draw the perpendicular bisector of $\overline{AB}$ through C. Construct a point D along the perpendicular bisector and measure $\overline{DA}$ and $\overline{DB}$. Move D along the perpendicular bisector. What theorem does this construction demonstrate?

○ = WORKED-OUT SOLUTIONS
on p. WS1

★ = STANDARDIZED
TEST PRACTICE

30. COORDINATE PROOF Where is the circumcenter located in any right triangle? Write a coordinate proof of this result.

PROOF Use the information in the diagram to prove the given statement.

31. $\overline{AB} \cong \overline{BC}$ if and only if D, E, and B are collinear.

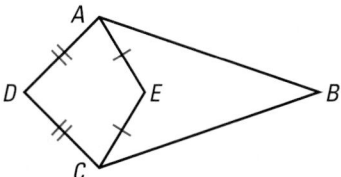

32. $\overline{PV}$ is the perpendicular bisector of $\overline{TQ}$ for regular polygon $PQRST$.

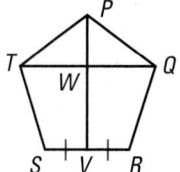

33. CHALLENGE The four towns on the map are building a common high school. They have agreed that the school should be an equal distance from each of the four towns. Is there a single point where they could agree to build the school? If so, find it. If not, *explain* why not. Use a diagram to *explain* your answer.

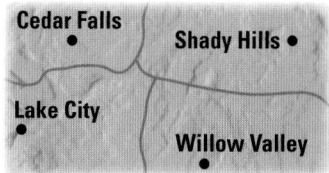

MIXED REVIEW

Solve the equation. Write your answer in simplest radical form. *(p. 882)*

34. $5^2 + x^2 = 13^2$

35. $x^2 + 15^2 = 17^2$

36. $x^2 + 10 = 38$

PREVIEW
Prepare for
Lesson 5.3 in
Exs. 37–38.

Ray $\overrightarrow{BD}$ bisects $\angle ABC$. Find the value of x. Then find $m\angle ABC$. *(p. 24)*

37.

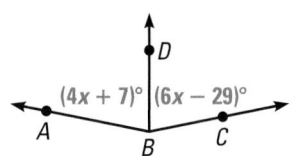

38.

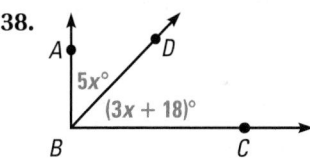

Describe the pattern in the numbers. Write the next number. *(p. 72)*

39. 21, 16, 11, 6, . . .

40. 2, 6, 18, 54, . . .

41. 3, 3, 4, 6, . . .

QUIZ *for Lessons 5.1–5.2*

Find the value of x. Identify the theorem used to find the answer. *(pp. 295, 303)*

1.

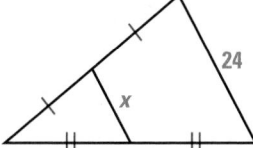

2.

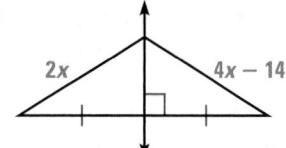

3.

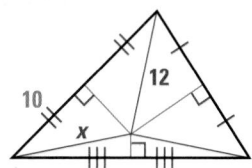

4. Graph the triangle with vertices $R(2a, 0)$, $S(0, 2b)$, and $T(2a, 2b)$, where a and b are positive. Find RT and ST. Then find the slope of $\overline{SR}$ and the coordinates of the midpoint of $\overline{SR}$. *(p. 295)*

EXTRA PRACTICE for Lesson 5.2, p. 904   🖈 **ONLINE QUIZ** at classzone.com   **309**

5.3 Use Angle Bisectors of Triangles

Before You used angle bisectors to find angle relationships.

Now You will use angle bisectors to find distance relationships.

Why? So you can apply geometry in sports, as in Example 2.

Key Vocabulary
- incenter
- angle bisector, *p. 28*
- distance from a point to a line, *p. 192*

Remember that an *angle bisector* is a ray that divides an angle into two congruent adjacent angles. Remember also that the *distance from a point to a line* is the length of the perpendicular segment from the point to the line.

So, in the diagram, $\overrightarrow{PS}$ is the bisector of $\angle QPR$ and the distance from *S* to $\overrightarrow{PQ}$ is *SQ*, where $\overline{SQ} \perp \overrightarrow{PQ}$.

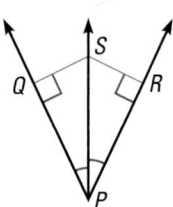

THEOREMS   *For Your Notebook*

THEOREM 5.5 Angle Bisector Theorem

If a point is on the bisector of an angle, then it is equidistant from the two sides of the angle.

If $\overrightarrow{AD}$ bisects $\angle BAC$ and $\overline{DB} \perp \overrightarrow{AB}$ and $\overline{DC} \perp \overrightarrow{AC}$, then **DB = DC**.

Proof: Ex. 34, p. 315

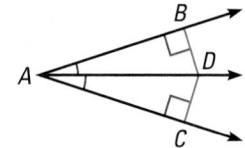

THEOREM 5.6 Converse of the Angle Bisector Theorem

If a point is in the interior of an angle and is equidistant from the sides of the angle, then it lies on the bisector of the angle.

If $\overline{DB} \perp \overrightarrow{AB}$ and $\overline{DC} \perp \overrightarrow{AC}$ and **DB = DC**, then $\overrightarrow{AD}$ bisects $\angle BAC$.

Proof: Ex. 35, p. 315

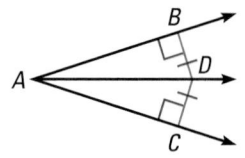

> **REVIEW DISTANCE**
> In Geometry, *distance* means the *shortest* length between two objects.

EXAMPLE 1   Use the Angle Bisector Theorems

Find the measure of $\angle GFJ$.

Solution

Because $\overline{JG} \perp \overrightarrow{FG}$ and $\overline{JH} \perp \overrightarrow{FH}$ and $JG = JH = 7$, $\overrightarrow{FJ}$ bisects $\angle GFH$ by the Converse of the Angle Bisector Theorem. So, $m\angle GFJ = m\angle HFJ = 42°$.

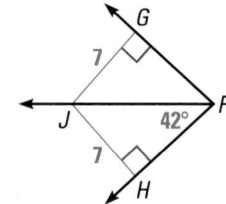

EXAMPLE 2 Solve a real-world problem

SOCCER A soccer goalie's position relative to the ball and goalposts forms congruent angles, as shown. Will the goalie have to move farther to block a shot toward the right goalpost R or the left goalpost L?

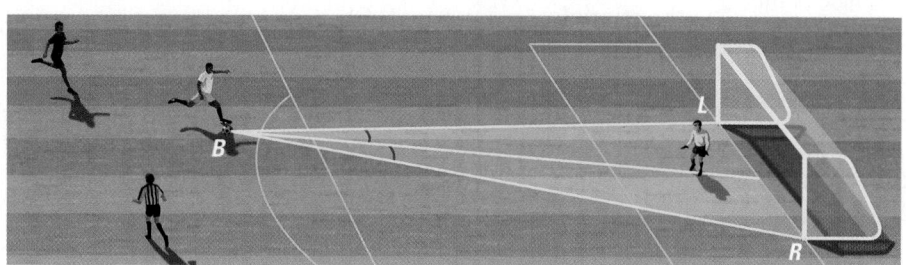

Solution

The congruent angles tell you that the goalie is on the bisector of $\angle LBR$. By the Angle Bisector Theorem, the goalie is equidistant from $\overrightarrow{BR}$ and $\overrightarrow{BL}$.

▶ So, the goalie must move the same distance to block either shot.

EXAMPLE 3 Use algebra to solve a problem

ALGEBRA For what value of x does P lie on the bisector of $\angle A$?

Solution

From the Converse of the Angle Bisector Theorem, you know that P lies on the bisector of $\angle A$ if P is equidistant from the sides of $\angle A$, so when $BP = CP$.

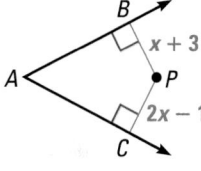

$BP = CP$ **Set segment lengths equal.**

$x + 3 = 2x - 1$ **Substitute expressions for segment lengths.**

$4 = x$ **Solve for x.**

▶ Point P lies on the bisector of $\angle A$ when $x = 4$.

✓ **GUIDED PRACTICE** for Examples 1, 2, and 3

In Exercises 1–3, find the value of x.

1.

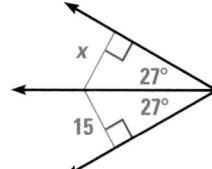

2.

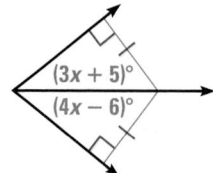

3.

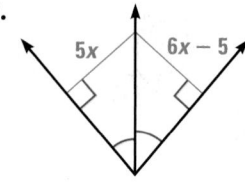

4. Do you have enough information to conclude that $\overrightarrow{QS}$ bisects $\angle PQR$? *Explain.*

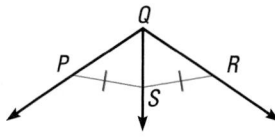

READ VOCABULARY

An *angle bisector of a triangle* is the bisector of an interior angle of the triangle.

THEOREM 5.7 Concurrency of Angle Bisectors of a Triangle

The angle bisectors of a triangle intersect at a point that is equidistant from the sides of the triangle.

If $\overline{AP}$, $\overline{BP}$, and $\overline{CP}$ are angle bisectors of $\triangle ABC$, then $PD = PE = PF$.

Proof: Ex. 36, p. 316

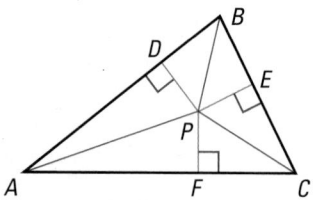

The point of concurrency of the three angle bisectors of a triangle is called the **incenter** of the triangle. The incenter always lies inside the triangle.

Because the incenter P is equidistant from the three sides of the triangle, a circle drawn using P as the center and the distance to one side as the radius will just touch the other two sides. The circle is said to be *inscribed* within the triangle.

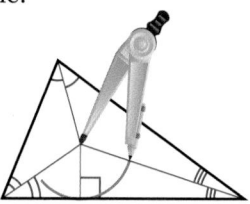 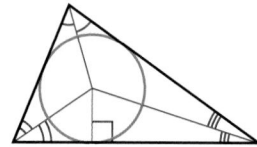

EXAMPLE 4 **Use the concurrency of angle bisectors**

In the diagram, N is the incenter of $\triangle ABC$. Find ND.

Solution

REVIEW QUADRATIC EQUATIONS

For help with solving a quadratic equation by taking square roots, see page 882. Use only the positive square root when finding a distance, as in Example 4.

By the Concurrency of Angle Bisectors of a Triangle Theorem, the incenter N is equidistant from the sides of $\triangle ABC$. So, to find ND, you can find NF in $\triangle NAF$. Use the Pythagorean Theorem stated on page 18.

$c^2 = a^2 + b^2$ **Pythagorean Theorem**

$20^2 = NF^2 + 16^2$ **Substitute known values.**

$400 = NF^2 + 256$ **Multiply.**

$144 = NF^2$ **Subtract 256 from each side.**

$12 = NF$ **Take the positive square root of each side.**

▶ Because $NF = ND$, $ND = 12$.

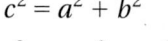 *Animated* Geometry at classzone.com

---

✓ **GUIDED PRACTICE** for Example 4

5. WHAT IF? In Example 4, suppose you are not given AF or AN, but you are given that $BF = 12$ and $BN = 13$. Find ND.

5.3 EXERCISES

HOMEWORK KEY

○ = WORKED-OUT SOLUTIONS
on p. WS6 for Exs. 7, 15, and 29

★ = STANDARDIZED TEST PRACTICE
Exs. 2, 18, 23, 30, and 31

SKILL PRACTICE

1. **VOCABULARY** Copy and complete: Point *C* is in the interior of ∠*ABD*. If ∠*ABC* and ∠*DBC* are congruent, then $\overrightarrow{BC}$ is the __?__ of ∠*ABD*.

2. ★ **WRITING** How are perpendicular bisectors and angle bisectors of a triangle different? How are they alike?

EXAMPLE 1
on p. 310
for Exs. 3–5

FINDING MEASURES Use the information in the diagram to find the measure.

3. Find *m*∠*ABD*.

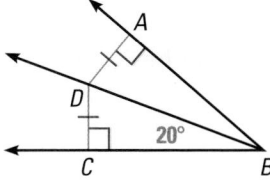

4. Find *PS*.

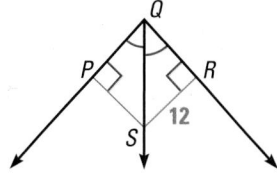

5. *m*∠*YXW* = 60°. Find *WZ*.

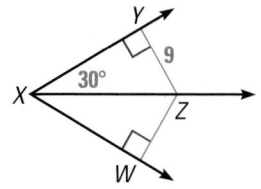

EXAMPLE 2
on p. 311
for Exs. 6–11

ANGLE BISECTOR THEOREM Is *DB* = *DC*? *Explain*.

6.

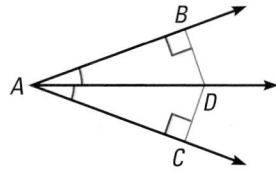

7.

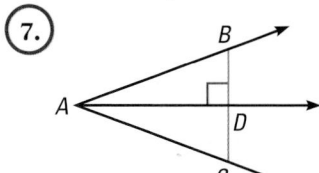

8.

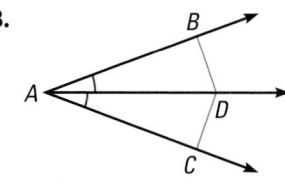

REASONING Can you conclude that $\overrightarrow{EH}$ bisects ∠*FEG*? *Explain*.

9.

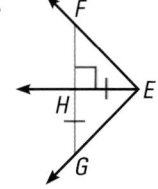

10.

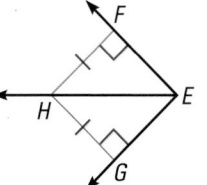

11.

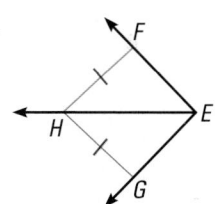

EXAMPLE 3
on p. 311
for Exs. 12–18

ALGEBRA Find the value of *x*.

12.

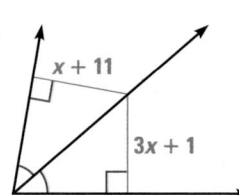

13.

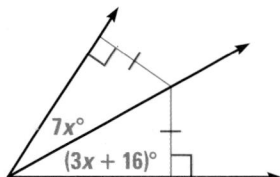

14.

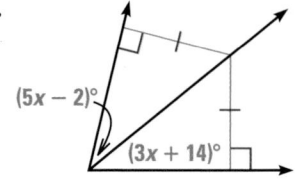

RECOGNIZING MISSING INFORMATION Can you find the value of *x*? *Explain*.

15.

16.

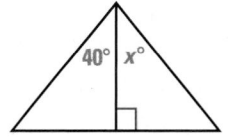

17.

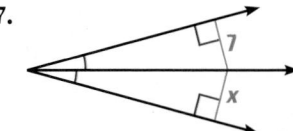

18. ★ **MULTIPLE CHOICE** What is the value of x in the diagram?

Ⓐ 13   Ⓑ 18

Ⓒ 33   Ⓓ Not enough information

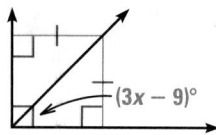

EXAMPLE 4
on p. 312
for Exs. 19–22

USING INCENTERS Find the indicated measure.

19. Point D is the incenter of $\triangle XYZ$. Find DB.

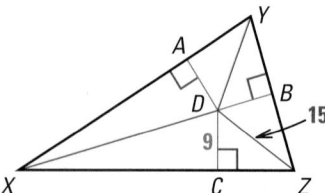

20. Point L is the incenter of $\triangle EGJ$. Find HL.

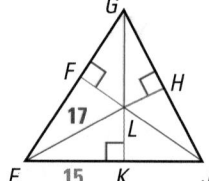

ERROR ANALYSIS *Describe* the error in reasoning. Then state a correct conclusion about distances that can be deduced from the diagram.

21.

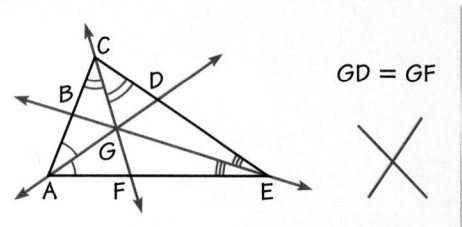

GD = GF

22.

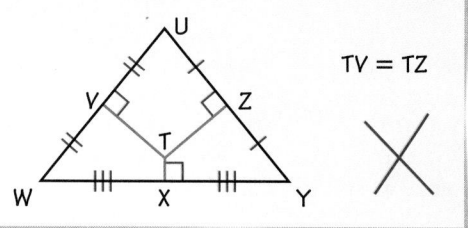

TV = TZ

23. ★ **MULTIPLE CHOICE** In the diagram, N is the incenter of $\triangle GHJ$. Which statement cannot be deduced from the given information?

Ⓐ $\overline{NM} \cong \overline{NK}$ Ⓑ $\overline{NL} \cong \overline{NM}$

Ⓒ $\overline{NG} \cong \overline{NJ}$ Ⓓ $\overline{HK} \cong \overline{HM}$

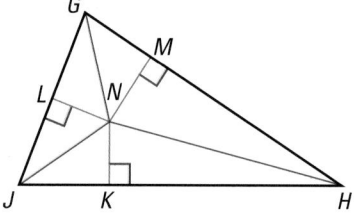

ALGEBRA Find the value of x that makes N the incenter of the triangle.

24.

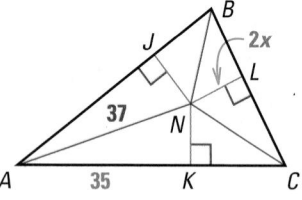

25.

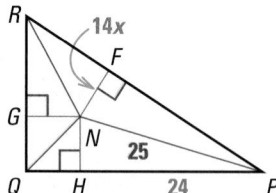

26. **CONSTRUCTION** Use a compass and a straightedge to draw $\triangle ABC$ with incenter D. Label the angle bisectors and the perpendicular segments from D to each of the sides of $\triangle ABC$. Measure each segment. What do you notice? What theorem have you verified for your $\triangle ABC$?

27. **CHALLENGE** Point D is the incenter of $\triangle ABC$. Write an expression for the length x in terms of the three side lengths AB, AC, and BC.

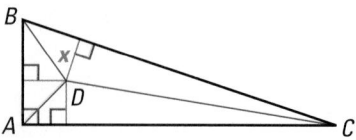

○ = **WORKED-OUT SOLUTIONS**
on p. WS1

★ = **STANDARDIZED TEST PRACTICE**

EXAMPLE 2
on p. 311
for Ex. 28

28. FIELD HOCKEY In a field hockey game, the goalkeeper is at point *G* and a player from the opposing team hits the ball from point *B*. The goal extends from left goalpost *L* to right goalpost *R*. Will the goalkeeper have to move farther to keep the ball from hitting *L* or *R*? *Explain.*

@HomeTutor for problem solving help at classzone.com

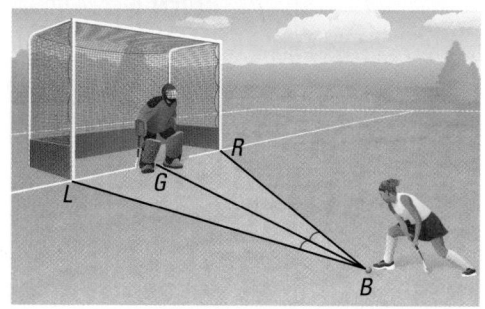

29. KOI POND You are constructing a fountain in a triangular koi pond. You want the fountain to be the same distance from each edge of the pond. Where should you build the fountain? *Explain* your reasoning. Use a sketch to support your answer.

@HomeTutor for problem solving help at classzone.com

30. ★ SHORT RESPONSE What congruence postulate or theorem would you use to prove the Angle Bisector Theorem? to prove the Converse of the Angle Bisector Theorem? Use diagrams to show your reasoning.

31. ★ EXTENDED RESPONSE Suppose you are given a triangle and are asked to draw all of its perpendicular bisectors and angle bisectors.

  a. For what type of triangle would you need the fewest segments? What is the minimum number of segments you would need? *Explain.*

  b. For what type of triangle would you need the most segments? What is the maximum number of segments you would need? *Explain.*

CHOOSING A METHOD In Exercises 32 and 33, tell whether you would use *perpendicular bisectors* or *angle bisectors*. Then solve the problem.

32. BANNER To make a banner, you will cut a triangle from an $8\frac{1}{2}$ inch by 11 inch sheet of white paper and paste a red circle onto it as shown. The circle should just touch each side of the triangle. Use a model to decide whether the circle's radius should be *more* or *less* than $2\frac{1}{2}$ inches. Can you cut the circle from a 5 inch by 5 inch red square? *Explain.*

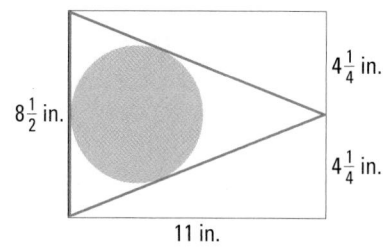

$8\frac{1}{2}$ in. $4\frac{1}{4}$ in. $4\frac{1}{4}$ in.   11 in.

33. CAMP A map of a camp shows a pool at (10, 20), a nature center at (16, 2), and a tennis court at (2, 4). A new circular walking path will connect the three locations. Graph the points and find the approximate center of the circle. Estimate the radius of the circle if each unit on the grid represents 10 yards. Then use the formula $C = 2\pi r$ to estimate the length of the path.

PROVING THEOREMS 5.5 AND 5.6 Use Exercise 30 to prove the theorem.

34. Angle Bisector Theorem

35. Converse of the Angle Bisector Theorem

36. PROVING THEOREM 5.7 Write a proof of the Concurrency of Angle Bisectors of a Triangle Theorem.

GIVEN ▶ $\triangle ABC$, $\overline{AD}$ bisects $\angle CAB$, $\overline{BD}$ bisects $\angle CBA$, $\overline{DE} \perp \overline{AB}$, $\overline{DF} \perp \overline{BC}$, $\overline{DG} \perp \overline{CA}$

PROVE ▶ The angle bisectors intersect at D, which is equidistant from $\overline{AB}$, $\overline{BC}$, and $\overline{CA}$.

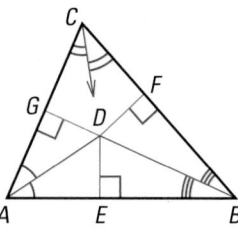

37. CELEBRATION You are planning a graduation party in the triangular courtyard shown. You want to fit as large a circular tent as possible on the site without extending into the walkway.

a. Copy the triangle and show how to place the tent so that it just touches each edge. Then *explain* how you can be sure that there is no place you could fit a larger tent on the site. Use sketches to support your answer.

b. Suppose you want to fit as large a tent as possible while leaving at least one foot of space around the tent. Would you put the center of the tent in the same place as you did in part (a)? *Justify* your answer.

38. CHALLENGE You have seen that there is a point inside any triangle that is equidistant from the three sides of the triangle. Prove that if you extend the sides of the triangle to form lines, you can find three points outside the triangle, each of which is equidistant from those three lines.

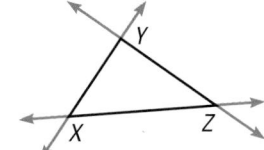

MIXED REVIEW

PREVIEW
Prepare for
Lesson 5.4 in
Exs. 39–41.

Find the length of $\overline{AB}$ and the coordinates of the midpoint of $\overline{AB}$. *(p. 15)*

39. $A(-2, 2)$, $B(-10, 2)$ **40.** $A(0, 6)$, $B(5, 8)$ **41.** $A(-1, -3)$, $B(7, -5)$

Explain **how to prove the given statement.** *(p. 256)*

42. $\angle QNP \cong \angle LNM$ **43.** $\overline{JG}$ bisects $\angle FGH$.   **44.** $\triangle ZWX \cong \triangle ZYX$

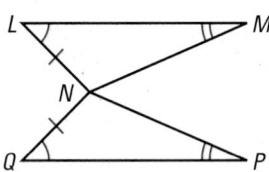 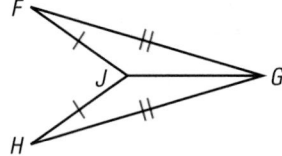 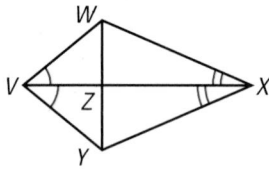

Find the coordinates of the red points in the figure if necessary. Then find OR **and the coordinates of the midpoint M of $\overline{RT}$.** *(p. 295)*

45.   **46.**   **47.**

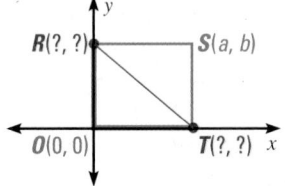 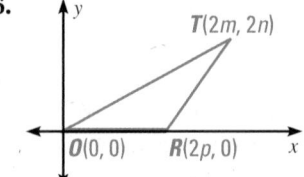 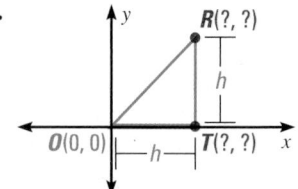

MIXED REVIEW of Problem Solving

Lessons 5.1–5.3

1. **SHORT RESPONSE** A committee has decided to build a park in Deer County. The committee agreed that the park should be equidistant from the three largest cities in the county, which are labeled *X*, *Y*, and *Z* in the diagram. *Explain* why this may not be the best place to build the park. Use a sketch to support your answer.

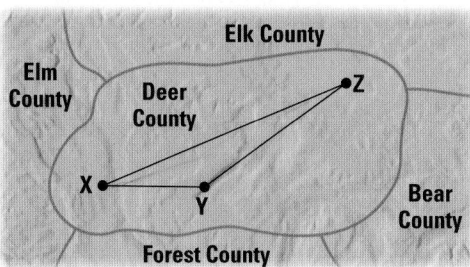

2. **EXTENDED RESPONSE** A woodworker is trying to cut as large a wheel as possible from a triangular scrap of wood. The wheel just touches each side of the triangle as shown below.

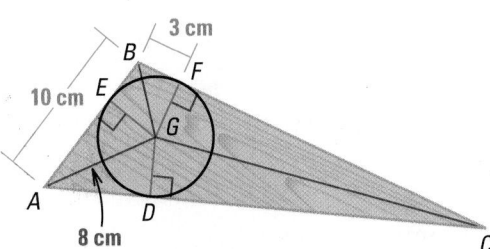

   a. Which point of concurrency is the woodworker using for the center of the circle? What type of special segment are $\overline{BG}$, $\overline{CG}$, and $\overline{AG}$?

   b. Which postulate or theorem can you use to prove that $\triangle BGF \cong \triangle BGE$?

   c. Find the radius of the wheel to the nearest tenth of a centimeter. *Explain* your reasoning.

3. **SHORT RESPONSE** Graph $\triangle GHJ$ with vertices $G(2, 2)$, $H(6, 8)$, and $J(10, 4)$ and draw its midsegments. Each midsegment is contained in a line. Which of those lines has the greatest *y*-intercept? Write the equation of that line. *Justify* your answer.

4. **GRIDDED ANSWER** Three friends are practicing disc golf, in which a flying disk is thrown into a set of targets. Each player is 15 feet from the target. Two players are 24 feet from each other along one edge of the nearby football field. How far is the target from that edge of the football field?

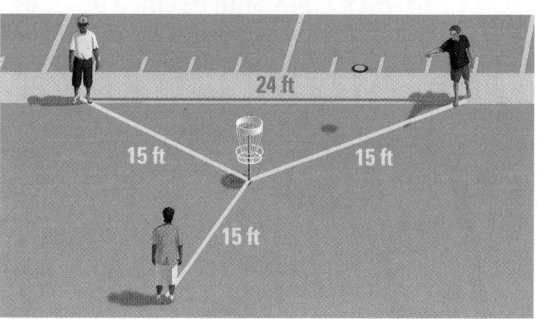

5. **MULTI-STEP PROBLEM** An artist created a large floor mosaic consisting of eight triangular sections. The grey segments are the midsegments of the two black triangles.

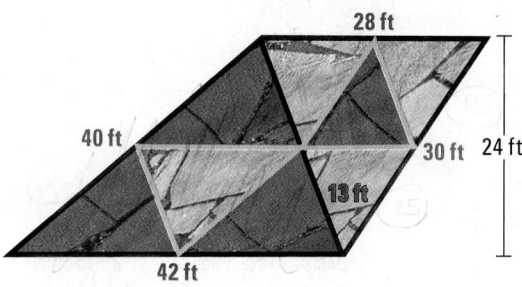

   a. The gray and black edging was created using special narrow tiles. What is the total length of all the edging used?

   b. What is the total area of the mosaic?

6. **OPEN-ENDED** If possible, draw a triangle whose incenter and circumcenter are the same point. *Describe* this triangle as specifically as possible.

7. **SHORT RESPONSE** Points *S*, *T*, and *U* are the midpoints of the sides of $\triangle PQR$. Which angles are congruent to $\angle QST$? *Justify* your answer.

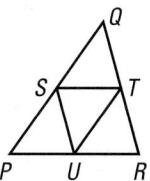

5.4 Intersecting Medians

MATERIALS • cardboard • straightedge • scissors • metric ruler

> **QUESTION** What is the relationship between segments formed by the medians of a triangle?

> **EXPLORE 1** Find the balance point of a triangle

STEP 1

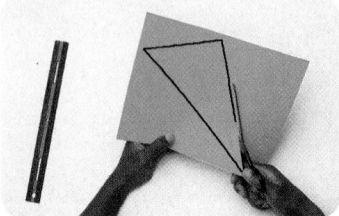

Cut out triangle Draw a triangle on a piece of cardboard. Then cut it out.

STEP 2

Balance the triangle Balance the triangle on the eraser end of a pencil.

STEP 3

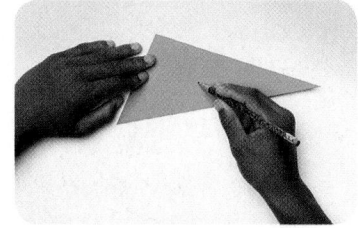

Mark the balance point Mark the point on the triangle where it balanced on the pencil.

> **EXPLORE 2** Construct the medians of a triangle

STEP 1

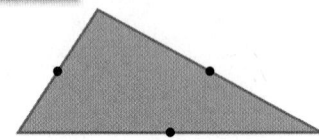

Find the midpoint Use a ruler to find the midpoint of each side of the triangle.

STEP 2

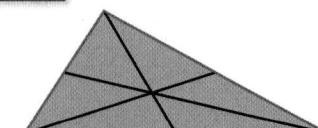

Draw medians Draw a segment, or *median*, from each midpoint to the vertex of the opposite angle.

STEP 3

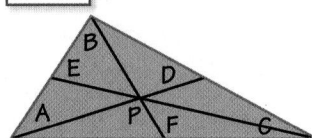

Label points Label your triangle as shown. What do you notice about point *P* and the balance point in Explore 1?

> **DRAW CONCLUSIONS** Use your observations to complete these exercises

1. Copy and complete the table. Measure in millimeters.

Length of segment from vertex to midpoint of opposite side	*AD* = ?	*BF* = ?	*CE* = ?
Length of segment from vertex to *P*	*AP* = ?	*BP* = ?	*CP* = ?
Length of segment from *P* to midpoint	*PD* = ?	*PF* = ?	*PE* = ?

2. How does the length of the segment from a vertex to *P* compare with the length of the segment from *P* to the midpoint of the opposite side?

3. How does the length of the segment from a vertex to *P* compare with the length of the segment from the vertex to the midpoint of the opposite side?

5.4 Use Medians and Altitudes

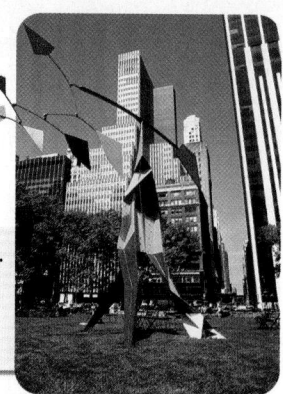

Before	You used perpendicular bisectors and angle bisectors of triangles.
Now	You will use medians and altitudes of triangles.
Why?	So you can find the balancing point of a triangle, as in Ex. 37.

Key Vocabulary
- **median of a triangle**
- **centroid**
- **altitude of a triangle**
- **orthocenter**

As shown by the Activity on page 318, a triangle will balance at a particular point. This point is the intersection of the *medians* of the triangle.

A **median of a triangle** is a segment from a vertex to the midpoint of the opposite side. The three medians of a triangle are concurrent. The point of concurrency, called the **centroid**, is inside the triangle.

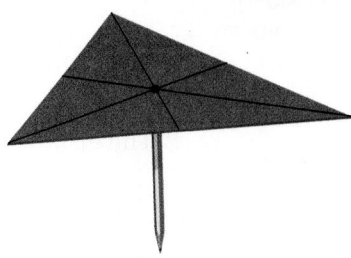

Three medians meet at the centroid.

THEOREM *For Your Notebook*

THEOREM 5.8 Concurrency of Medians of a Triangle

The medians of a triangle intersect at a point that is two thirds of the distance from each vertex to the midpoint of the opposite side.

The medians of $\triangle ABC$ meet at P and

$AP = \frac{2}{3}AE$, $BP = \frac{2}{3}BF$, and $CP = \frac{2}{3}CD$.

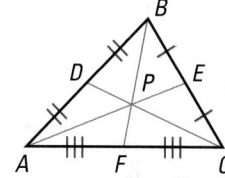

Proof: Ex. 32, p. 323; p. 934

EXAMPLE 1 Use the centroid of a triangle

In $\triangle RST$, Q is the centroid and $SQ = 8$. Find QW and SW.

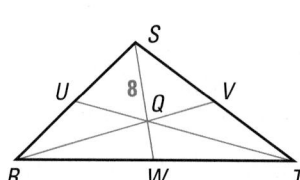

Solution

$SQ = \frac{2}{3}SW$ **Concurrency of Medians of a Triangle Theorem**

$8 = \frac{2}{3}SW$ **Substitute 8 for *SQ*.**

$12 = SW$ **Multiply each side by the reciprocal, $\frac{3}{2}$.**

Then $QW = SW - SQ = 12 - 8 = 4$.

▸ So, $QW = 4$ and $SW = 12$.

The vertices of △*FGH* are *F*(2, 5), *G*(4, 9), and *H*(6, 1). Which ordered pair gives the coordinates of the centroid *P* of △*FGH*?

Ⓐ (3, 5)   Ⓑ (4, 5)   Ⓒ (4, 7)   Ⓓ (5, 3)

Solution

Sketch △*FGH*. Then use the Midpoint Formula to find the midpoint *K* of $\overline{FH}$ and sketch median $\overline{GK}$.

$$K\left(\frac{2+6}{2}, \frac{5+1}{2}\right) = K(4, 3).$$

The centroid is two thirds of the distance from each vertex to the midpoint of the opposite side.

The distance from vertex *G*(4, 9) to *K*(4, 3) is

$9 - 3 = 6$ units. So, the centroid is $\frac{2}{3}(6) = 4$ units down from *G* on $\overline{GK}$.

The coordinates of the centroid *P* are (4, 9 − 4), or (4, 5).

▶ The correct answer is B. Ⓐ Ⓑ Ⓒ Ⓓ

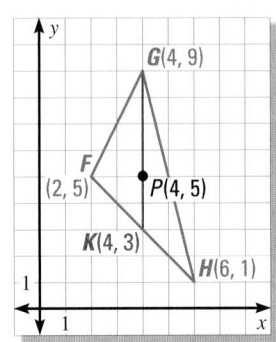

✓ **GUIDED PRACTICE**   for Examples 1 and 2

There are three paths through a triangular park. Each path goes from the midpoint of one edge to the opposite corner. The paths meet at point *P*.

1. If *SC* = 2100 feet, find *PS* and *PC*.

2. If *BT* = 1000 feet, find *TC* and *BC*.

3. If *PT* = 800 feet, find *PA* and *TA*.

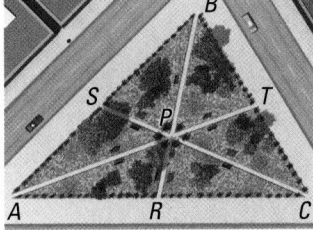

MEASURES OF TRIANGLES

In the area formula for a triangle, $A = \frac{1}{2}bh$, you can use the length of any side for the base *b*. The height *h* is the length of the altitude to that side from the opposite vertex.

ALTITUDES An **altitude of a triangle** is the perpendicular segment from a vertex to the opposite side or to the line that contains the opposite side.

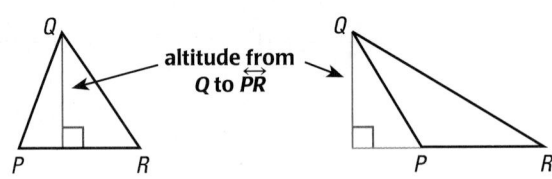

altitude from *Q* to $\overleftrightarrow{PR}$

THEOREM   *For Your Notebook*

THEOREM 5.9 Concurrency of Altitudes of a Triangle

The lines containing the altitudes of a triangle are concurrent.

The lines containing $\overline{AF}$, $\overline{BE}$, and $\overline{CD}$ meet at *G*.

Proof: Exs. 29–31, p. 323; p. 936

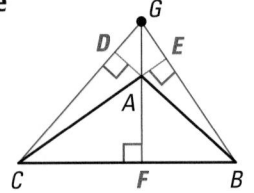

CONCURRENCY OF ALTITUDES The point at which the lines containing the three altitudes of a triangle intersect is called the **orthocenter** of the triangle.

EXAMPLE 3 **Find the orthocenter**

Find the orthocenter *P* in an acute, a right, and an obtuse triangle.

Solution

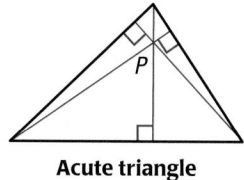 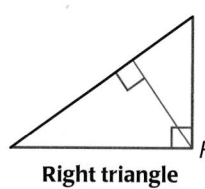 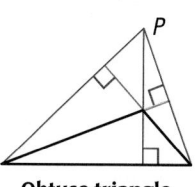

Acute triangle
P is inside triangle.

Right triangle
P is on triangle.

Obtuse triangle
P is outside triangle.

Animated Geometry at classzone.com

ISOSCELES TRIANGLES In an isosceles triangle, the perpendicular bisector, angle bisector, median, and altitude from the vertex angle to the base are all the same segment. In an equilateral triangle, this is true for the special segment from any vertex.

EXAMPLE 4 **Prove a property of isosceles triangles**

Prove that the median to the base of an isosceles triangle is an altitude.

Solution

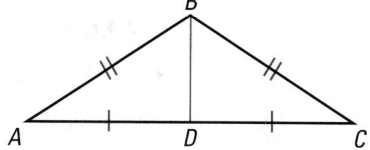

GIVEN ▶ $\triangle ABC$ is isosceles, with base $\overline{AC}$.
     $\overline{BD}$ is the median to base $\overline{AC}$.

PROVE ▶ $\overline{BD}$ is an altitude of $\triangle ABC$.

Proof Legs $\overline{AB}$ and $\overline{BC}$ of isosceles $\triangle ABC$ are congruent. $\overline{CD} \cong \overline{AD}$ because $\overline{BD}$ is the median to $\overline{AC}$. Also, $\overline{BD} \cong \overline{BD}$. Therefore, $\triangle ABD \cong \triangle CBD$ by the SSS Congruence Postulate.

$\angle ADB \cong \angle CDB$ because corresponding parts of $\cong \triangle$ are $\cong$. Also, $\angle ADB$ and $\angle CDB$ are a linear pair. $\overline{BD}$ and $\overline{AC}$ intersect to form a linear pair of congruent angles, so $\overline{BD} \perp \overline{AC}$ and $\overline{BD}$ is an altitude of $\triangle ABC$.

✓ **GUIDED PRACTICE** for Examples 3 and 4

4. Copy the triangle in Example 4 and find its orthocenter.

5. **WHAT IF?** In Example 4, suppose you wanted to show that median $\overline{BD}$ is also an angle bisector. How would your proof be different?

6. Triangle *PQR* is an isoscleles triangle and segment $\overline{OQ}$ is an altitude. What else do you know about $\overline{OQ}$? What are the coordinates of *P*?

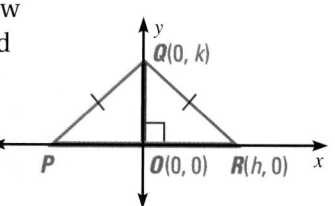

5.4 EXERCISES

HOMEWORK KEY
○ = WORKED-OUT SOLUTIONS
on p. WS6 for Exs. 5, 21, and 39

★ = STANDARDIZED TEST PRACTICE
Exs. 2, 7, 11, 12, 28, 40, and 44

SKILL PRACTICE

1. **VOCABULARY** Name the four types of points of concurrency introduced in Lessons 5.2–5.4. When is each type inside the triangle? on the triangle? outside the triangle?

2. ★ **WRITING** *Compare* a perpendicular bisector and an altitude of a triangle. *Compare* a perpendicular bisector and a median of a triangle.

EXAMPLE 1
on p. 319
for Exs. 3–7

FINDING LENGTHS *G* is the centroid of △*ABC*, *BG* = 6, *AF* = 12, and *AE* = 15. Find the length of the segment.

3. $\overline{FC}$

4. $\overline{BF}$

5. $\overline{AG}$

6. $\overline{GE}$

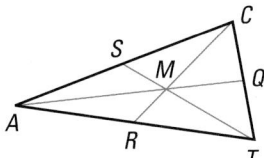

7. ★ **MULTIPLE CHOICE** In the diagram, *M* is the centroid of △*ACT*, *CM* = 36, *MQ* = 30, and *TS* = 56. What is *AM*?

Ⓐ 15   Ⓑ 30

Ⓒ 36   Ⓓ 60

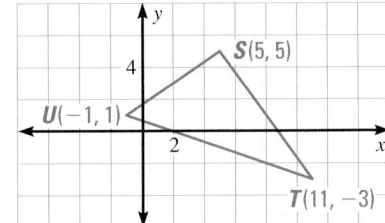

EXAMPLE 2
on p. 320
for Exs. 8–11

8. **FINDING A CENTROID** Use the graph shown.

   a. Find the coordinates of *P*, the midpoint of $\overline{ST}$. Use the median $\overline{UP}$ to find the coordinates of the centroid *Q*.

   b. Find the coordinates of *R*, the midpoint of $\overline{TU}$. Verify that $SQ = \frac{2}{3}SR$.

GRAPHING CENTROIDS Find the coordinates of the centroid *P* of △*ABC*.

9. *A*(−1, 2), *B*(5, 6), *C*(5, −2)   10. *A*(0, 4), *B*(3, 10), *C*(6, −2)

11. ★ **OPEN-ENDED MATH** Draw a large right triangle and find its centroid.

EXAMPLE 3
on p. 321
for Exs. 12–16

12. ★ **OPEN-ENDED MATH** Draw a large obtuse, scalene triangle and find its orthocenter.

IDENTIFYING SEGMENTS Is $\overline{BD}$ a *perpendicular bisector* of △*ABC*? Is $\overline{BD}$ a *median*? an *altitude*?

13.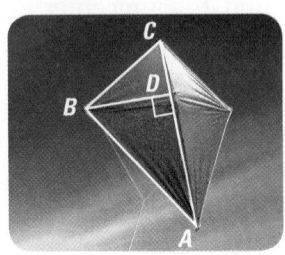

14.

15.

16. ERROR ANALYSIS A student uses the fact that T is a point of concurrency to conclude that $NT = \frac{2}{3}NQ$. *Explain* what is wrong with this reasoning.

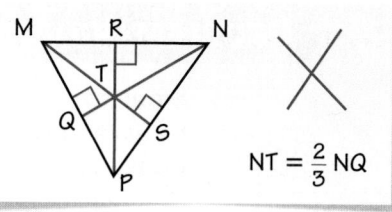

$$NT = \frac{2}{3}NQ$$

EXAMPLE 4
on p. 321
for Exs. 17–22

REASONING Use the diagram shown and the given information to decide whether $\overline{YW}$ is a *perpendicular bisector*, an *angle bisector*, a *median*, or an *altitude* of $\triangle XYZ$. There may be more than one right answer.

17. $\overline{YW} \perp \overline{XZ}$

18. $\angle XYW \cong \angle ZYW$

19. $\overline{XW} \cong \overline{ZW}$

20. $\overline{YW} \perp \overline{XZ}$ and $\overline{XW} \cong \overline{ZW}$

21. $\triangle XYW \cong \triangle ZYW$

22. $\overline{YW} \perp \overline{XZ}$ and $\overline{XY} \cong \overline{ZY}$

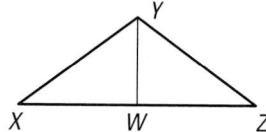

ISOSCELES TRIANGLES Find the measurements. *Explain* your reasoning.

23. Given that $\overline{DB} \perp \overline{AC}$, find DC and $m\angle ABD$.

24. Given that $AD = DC$, find $m\angle ADB$ and $m\angle ABD$.

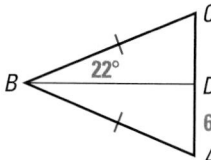

RELATING LENGTHS Copy and complete the statement for $\triangle DEF$ with medians $\overline{DH}$, $\overline{EJ}$, and $\overline{FG}$, and centroid K.

25. $EJ = \underline{\ ?\ } KJ$

26. $DK = \underline{\ ?\ } KH$

27. $FG = \underline{\ ?\ } KF$

28. ★ **SHORT RESPONSE** Any isosceles triangle can be placed in the coordinate plane with its base on the x-axis and the opposite vertex on the y-axis as in Guided Practice Exercise 6 on page 321. *Explain* why.

CONSTRUCTION Verify the Concurrency of Altitudes of a Triangle by drawing a triangle of the given type and constructing its altitudes. (*Hint:* To construct an altitude, use the construction in Exercise 25 on page 195.)

29. Equilateral triangle

30. Right scalene triangle

31. Obtuse isosceles triangle

32. **VERIFYING THEOREM 5.8** Use Example 2 on page 320. Verify that Theorem 5.8, the Concurrency of Medians of a Triangle, holds for the median from vertex F and for the median from vertex H.

(xy) ALGEBRA Point D is the centroid of $\triangle ABC$. Use the given information to find the value of x.

33. $BD = 4x + 5$ and $BF = 9x$

34. $GD = 2x - 8$ and $GC = 3x + 3$

35. $AD = 5x$ and $DE = 3x - 2$

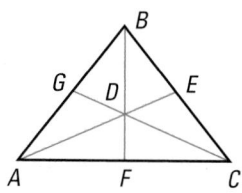

36. **CHALLENGE** $\overline{KM}$ is a median of $\triangle JKL$. Find the areas of $\triangle JKM$ and $\triangle LKM$. Compare the areas. Do you think that the two areas will always compare in this way, regardless of the shape of the triangle? *Explain*.

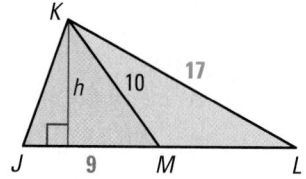

37. MOBILES To complete the mobile, you need to balance the red triangle on the tip of a metal rod. Copy the triangle and decide if you should place the rod at *A* or *B*. *Explain.*

@HomeTutor for problem solving help at classzone.com

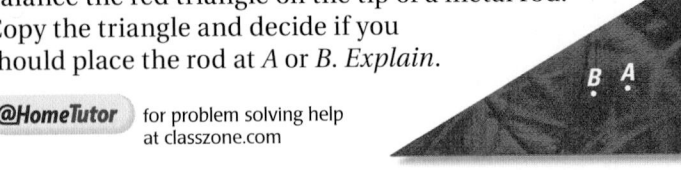

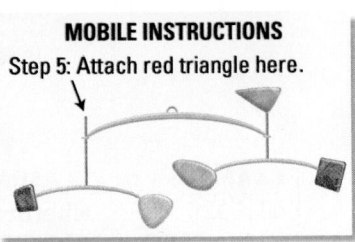

MOBILE INSTRUCTIONS
Step 5: Attach red triangle here.

38. DEVELOPING PROOF Show two different ways that you can place an isosceles triangle with base *2n* and height *h* on the coordinate plane. Label the coordinates for each vertex.

@HomeTutor for problem solving help at classzone.com

39. PAPER AIRPLANE Find the area of the triangular part of the paper airplane wing that is outlined in red. Which special segment of the triangle did you use?

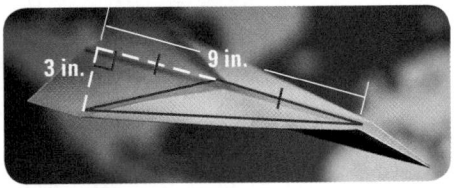

3 in.   9 in.

40. ★ SHORT RESPONSE In what type(s) of triangle can a vertex of the triangle be one of the points of concurrency of the triangle? *Explain.*

41. COORDINATE GEOMETRY Graph the lines on the same coordinate plane and find the centroid of the triangle formed by their intersections.

$$y_1 = 3x - 4 \qquad\qquad y_2 = \frac{3}{4}x + 5 \qquad\qquad y_3 = -\frac{3}{2}x - 4$$

EXAMPLE 4
on p. 321
for Ex. 42

42. PROOF Write proofs using different methods.

GIVEN ▸ $\triangle ABC$ is equilateral.
$\overline{BD}$ is an altitude of $\triangle ABC$.

PROVE ▸ $\overline{BD}$ is also a perpendicular bisector of $\overline{AC}$.

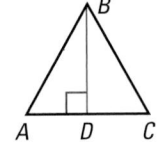

a. Write a proof using congruent triangles.

b. Write a proof using the Perpendicular Postulate on page 148.

43. TECHNOLOGY Use geometry drawing software.

a. Construct a triangle and its medians. Measure the areas of the blue, green, and red triangles.

b. What do you notice about the triangles?

c. If a triangle is of uniform thickness, what can you conclude about the weight of the three interior triangles? How does this support the idea that a triangle will balance on its centroid?

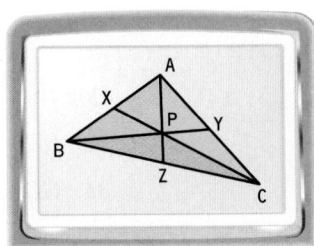

44. ★ EXTENDED RESPONSE Use *P*(0, 0), *Q*(8, 12), and *R*(14, 0).

a. What is the slope of the altitude from *R* to $\overline{PQ}$?

b. Write an equation for each altitude of $\triangle PQR$. Find the orthocenter by finding the ordered pair that is a solution of the three equations.

c. How would your steps change if you were finding the circumcenter?

○ = **WORKED-OUT SOLUTIONS**
on p. WS1

★ = **STANDARDIZED TEST PRACTICE**

45. CHALLENGE Prove the results in parts (a) – (c).

GIVEN ▶ $\overrightarrow{LP}$ and $\overline{MQ}$ are medians of scalene $\triangle LMN$. Point R is on $\overrightarrow{LP}$ such that $\overline{LP} \cong \overline{PR}$. Point S is on $\overrightarrow{MQ}$ such that $\overline{MQ} \cong \overline{QS}$.

PROVE ▶ **a.** $\overline{NS} \cong \overline{NR}$

        b. $\overline{NS}$ and $\overline{NR}$ are both parallel to $\overline{LM}$.

        c. R, N, and S are collinear.

MIXED REVIEW

In Exercises 46–48, write an equation of the line that passes through points *A* and *B*. *(p. 180)*

46. $A(0, 7)$, $B(1, 10)$
47. $A(4, -8)$, $B(-2, -5)$
48. $A(5, -21)$, $B(0, 4)$

49. In the diagram, $\triangle JKL \cong \triangle RST$. Find the value of x. *(p. 225)*

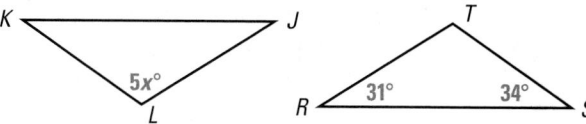

PREVIEW

Prepare for Lesson 5.5 in Exs. 50–52.

Solve the inequality. *(p. 287)*

50. $2x + 13 < 35$
51. $12 > -3x - 6$
52. $6x < x + 20$

In the diagram, $\overline{LM}$ is the perpendicular bisector of $\overline{PN}$. *(p. 303)*

53. What segment lengths are equal?

54. What is the value of x?

55. Find MN.

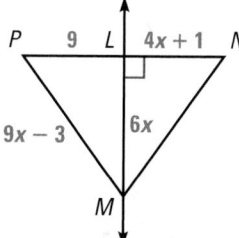

QUIZ *for Lessons 5.3–5.4*

Find the value of *x*. Identify the theorem used to find the answer. *(p. 310)*

1.

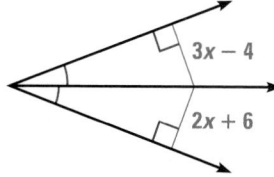

2.

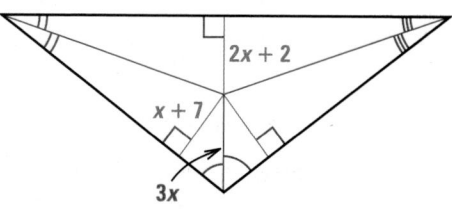

In the figure, *P* is the centroid of $\triangle XYZ$, $YP = 12$, $LX = 15$, and $LZ = 18$. *(p. 319)*

3. Find the length of $\overline{LY}$.

4. Find the length of $\overline{YN}$.

5. Find the length of $\overline{LP}$.

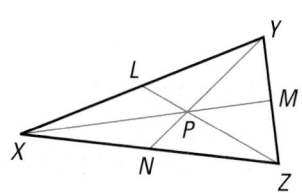

5.4 Investigate Points of Concurrency

MATERIALS · graphing calculator or computer

QUESTION How are the points of concurrency in a triangle related?

You can use geometry drawing software to investigate concurrency.

EXAMPLE 1 Draw the perpendicular bisectors of a triangle

STEP 1

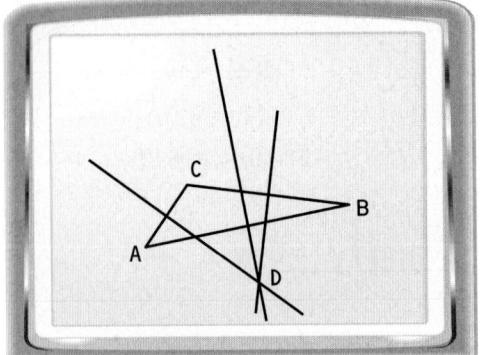

Draw perpendicular bisectors Draw a line perpendicular to each side of a △ABC at the midpoint. Label the point of concurrency D.

STEP 2

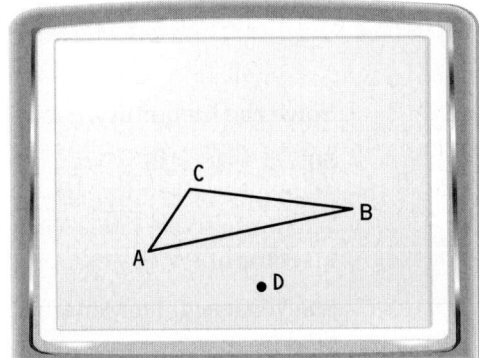

Hide the lines Use the HIDE feature to hide the perpendicular bisectors. Save as "EXAMPLE1."

EXAMPLE 2 Draw the medians of the triangle

STEP 1

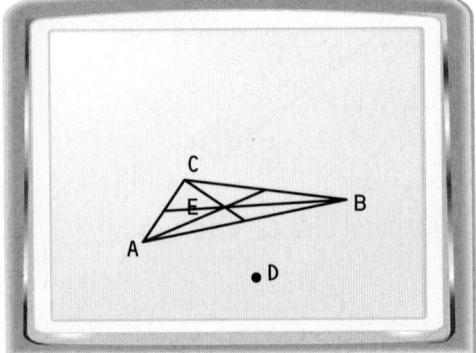

Draw medians Start with the figure you saved as "EXAMPLE1." Draw the medians of △ABC. Label the point of concurrency E.

STEP 2

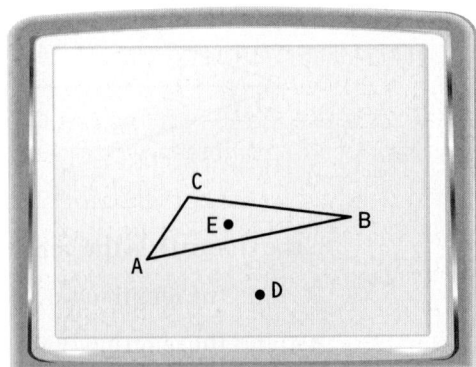

Hide the lines Use the HIDE feature to hide the medians. Save as "EXAMPLE2."

EXAMPLE 3 Draw the altitudes of the triangle

STEP 1

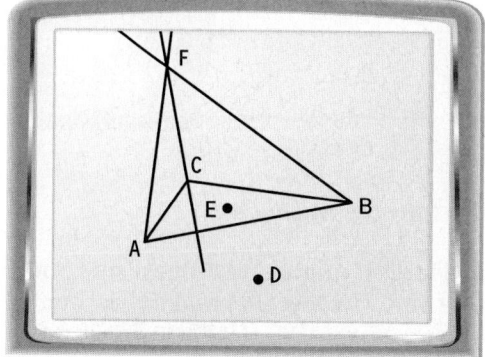

STEP 2

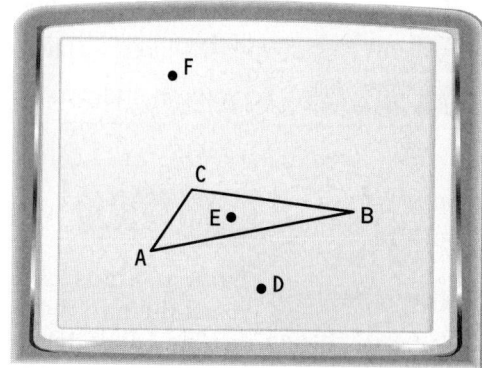

Draw altitudes Start with the figure you saved as "EXAMPLE2." Draw the altitudes of △*ABC*. Label the point of concurrency *F*.

Hide the lines Use the *HIDE* feature to hide the altitudes. Save as "EXAMPLE3."

PRACTICE

1. Try to draw a line through points *D*, *E*, and *F*. Are the points collinear?

2. Try dragging point *A*. Do points *D*, *E*, and *F* remain collinear?

In Exercises 3–5, use the triangle you saved as "EXAMPLE3."

3. Draw the angle bisectors. Label the point of concurrency as point *G*.

4. How does point *G* relate to points *D*, *E*, and *F*?

5. Try dragging point *A*. What do you notice about points *D*, *E*, *F*, and *G*?

DRAW CONCLUSIONS

In 1765, Leonhard Euler (pronounced "oi´-ler") proved that the circumcenter, the centroid, and the orthocenter are all collinear. The line containing these three points is called *Euler's line*. Save the triangle from Exercise 5 as "EULER" and use that for Exercises 6–8.

6. Try moving the triangle's vertices. Can you verify that the same three points lie on Euler's line whatever the shape of the triangle? *Explain.*

7. Notice that some of the four points can be outside of the triangle. Which points lie outside the triangle? Why? What happens when you change the shape of the triangle? Are there any points that never lie outside the triangle? Why?

8. Draw the three midsegments of the triangle. Which, if any, of the points seem contained in the triangle formed by the midsegments? Do those points stay there when the shape of the large triangle is changed?

5.5 Use Inequalities in a Triangle

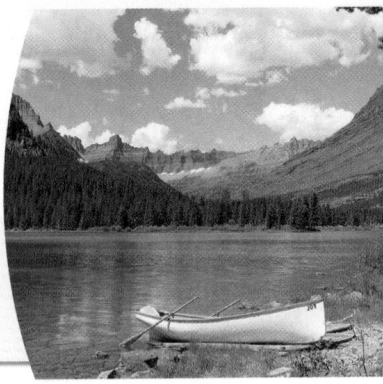

Before You found what combinations of angles are possible in a triangle.

Now You will find possible side lengths of a triangle.

Why? So you can find possible distances, as in Ex. 39.

Key Vocabulary
- **side opposite,** *p. 241*
- **inequality,** *p. 876*

EXAMPLE 1 Relate side length and angle measure

Draw an obtuse scalene triangle. Find the largest angle and longest side and mark them in red. Find the smallest angle and shortest side and mark them in blue. What do you notice?

Solution

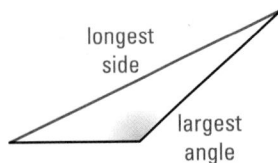

The longest side and largest angle are opposite each other.

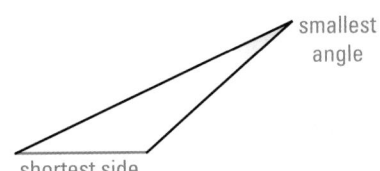

The shortest side and smallest angle are opposite each other.

The relationships in Example 1 are true for all triangles as stated in the two theorems below. These relationships can help you to decide whether a particular arrangement of side lengths and angle measures in a triangle may be possible.

THEOREMS   *For Your Notebook*

AVOID ERRORS

Be careful not to confuse the symbol ∠ meaning *angle* with the symbol < meaning *is less than*. Notice that the bottom edge of the angle symbol is horizontal.

THEOREM 5.10

If one side of a triangle is longer than another side, then the angle opposite the longer side is larger than the angle opposite the shorter side.

Proof: p. 329

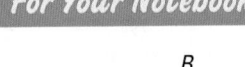

AB > BC, so *m∠C > m∠A.*

THEOREM 5.11

If one angle of a triangle is larger than another angle, then the side opposite the larger angle is longer than the side opposite the smaller angle.

Proof: Ex. 24, p. 340

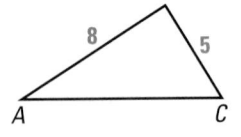

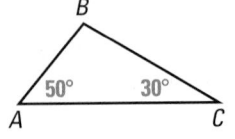

m∠A > m∠C, so *BC > AB.*

STAGE PROP You are constructing a stage prop that shows a large triangular mountain. The bottom edge of the mountain is about 27 feet long, the left slope is about 24 feet long, and the right slope is about 20 feet long. You are told that one of the angles is about 46° and one is about 59°. What is the angle measure of the peak of the mountain?

   A 46°   **B** 59°   **C** 75°   **D** 85°

ELIMINATE CHOICES
You can eliminate choice D because a triangle with a 46° angle and a 59° angle cannot have an 85° angle. The sum of the three angles in a triangle must be 180°, but the sum of 46, 59, and 85 is 190, not 180.

Solution

Draw a diagram and label the side lengths. The peak angle is opposite the longest side so, by Theorem 5.10, the peak angle is the largest angle.

The angle measures sum is 180°, so the third angle measure is $180° - (46° + 59°) = 75°$. You can now label the angle measures in your diagram.

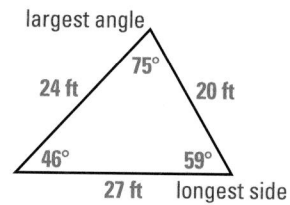

▶ The greatest angle measure is 75°, so the correct answer is C. **A** **B** **C** **D**

 GUIDED PRACTICE   for Examples 1 and 2

1. List the sides of $\triangle RST$ in order from shortest to longest.

2. Another stage prop is a right triangle with sides that are 6, 8, and 10 feet long and angles of 90°, about 37°, and about 53°. Sketch and label a diagram with the shortest side on the bottom and the right angle at the left.

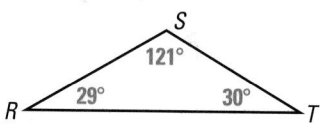

PROOF   **Theorem 5.10**

GIVEN ▶ $BC > AB$
PROVE ▶ $m\angle BAC > m\angle C$

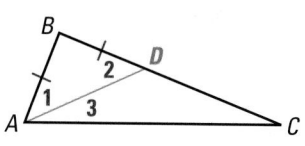

Locate a point **D** on $\overline{BC}$ such that $DB = BA$. Then draw $\overline{AD}$. In the isosceles triangle $\triangle ABD$, $\angle 1 \cong \angle 2$.

Because $m\angle BAC = m\angle 1 + m\angle 3$, it follows that $m\angle BAC > m\angle 1$. Substituting $m\angle 2$ for $m\angle 1$ produces $m\angle BAC > m\angle 2$.

By the Exterior Angle Theorem, $m\angle 2 = m\angle 3 + m\angle C$, so it follows that $m\angle 2 > m\angle C$ (see Exercise 27, page 332). Finally, because $m\angle BAC > m\angle 2$ and $m\angle 2 > m\angle C$, you can conclude that $m\angle BAC > m\angle C$.

THE TRIANGLE INEQUALITY Not every group of three segments can be used to form a triangle. The lengths of the segments must fit a certain relationship.

For example, three attempted triangle constructions for sides with given lengths are shown below. Only the first set of side lengths forms a triangle.

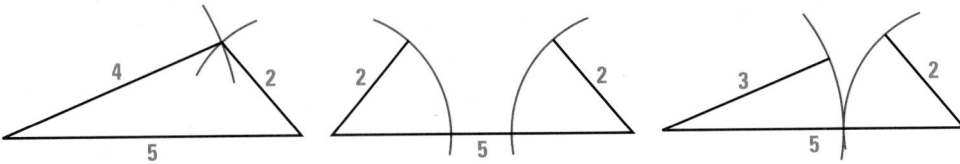

If you start with the longest side and attach the other two sides at its endpoints, you can see that the other two sides are not long enough to form a triangle in the second and third figures. This leads to the *Triangle Inequality Theorem*.

Animated Geometry at classzone.com

THEOREM   *For Your Notebook*

THEOREM 5.12 Triangle Inequality Theorem

The sum of the lengths of any two sides of a triangle is greater than the length of the third side.

$$AB + BC > AC \qquad AC + BC > AB \qquad AB + AC > BC$$

Proof: Ex. 47, p. 334

EXAMPLE 3 **Find possible side lengths**

ALGEBRA A triangle has one side of length 12 and another of length 8. Describe the possible lengths of the third side.

Solution

Let x represent the length of the third side. Draw diagrams to help visualize the small and large values of x. Then use the Triangle Inequality Theorem to write and solve inequalities.

USE SYMBOLS

You can combine the two inequalities, $x > 4$ and $x < 20$, to write the compound inequality $4 < x < 20$. This can be read as *x is between 4 and 20.*

Small values of x	Large values of x

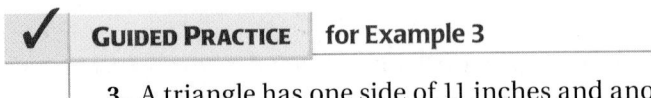

$$x + 8 > 12 \qquad\qquad 8 + 12 > x$$
$$x > 4 \qquad\qquad\qquad 20 > x, \text{ or } x < 20$$

▶ The length of the third side must be greater than 4 and less than 20.

✓ **GUIDED PRACTICE**   for Example 3

3. A triangle has one side of 11 inches and another of 15 inches. *Describe* the possible lengths of the third side.

5.5 EXERCISES

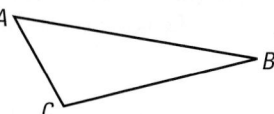
SKILL PRACTICE

1. **VOCABULARY** Use the diagram at the right. For each angle, name the side that is *opposite* that angle.

2. ★ **WRITING** How can you tell from the angle measures of a triangle which side of the triangle is the longest? the shortest?

EXAMPLE 1
on p. 328
for Exs. 3–5

MEASURING Use a ruler and protractor to draw the given type of triangle. Mark the largest angle and longest side in red and the smallest angle and shortest side in blue. What do you notice?

3. Acute scalene

4. Right scalene

5. Obtuse isosceles

EXAMPLE 2
on p. 329
for Exs. 6–15

WRITING MEASUREMENTS IN ORDER List the sides and the angles in order from smallest to largest.

6.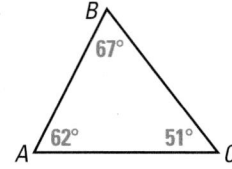

7.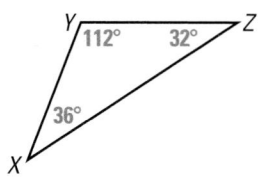

8.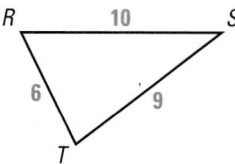

9.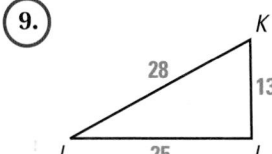

10.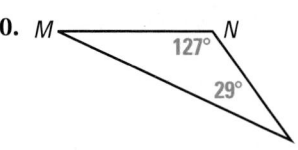

11.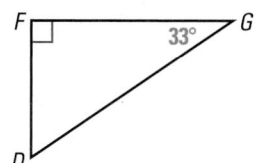

12. ★ **MULTIPLE CHOICE** In △RST, which is a possible side length for ST?

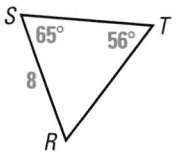

Ⓐ 7

Ⓑ 8

Ⓒ 9

Ⓓ Cannot be determined

DRAWING TRIANGLES Sketch and label the triangle described.

13. Side lengths: about 3 m, 7 m, and 9 m, with longest side on the bottom
Angle measures: 16°, 41°, and 123°, with smallest angle at the left

14. Side lengths: 37 ft, 35 ft, and 12 ft, with shortest side at the right
Angle measures: about 71°, about 19°, and 90°, with right angle at the top

15. Side lengths: 11 in., 13 in., and 14 in., with middle-length side at the left
Two angle measures: about 48° and 71°, with largest angle at the top

EXAMPLE 3
on p. 330
for Exs. 16–26

IDENTIFYING POSSIBLE TRIANGLES Is it possible to construct a triangle with the given side lengths? If not, *explain* why not.

16. 6, 7, 11

17. 3, 6, 9

18. 28, 34, 39

19. 35, 120, 125

20. ★ MULTIPLE CHOICE Which group of side lengths can be used to construct a triangle?

    (A) 3 yd, 4 ft, 5 yd   **(B)** 3 yd, 5 ft, 8 ft

    (C) 11 in., 16 in., 27 in.   **(D)** 2 ft, 11 in., 12 in.

POSSIBLE SIDE LENGTHS *Describe* the possible lengths of the third side of the triangle given the lengths of the other two sides.

21. 5 inches, 12 inches   **22.** 3 meters, 4 meters   **23.** 12 feet, 18 feet

24. 10 yards, 23 yards   **25.** 2 feet, 40 inches   **26.** 25 meters, 25 meters

27. EXTERIOR ANGLE INEQUALITY Another triangle inequality relationship is given by the Exterior Angle Inequality Theorem. It states:

The measure of an exterior angle of a triangle is greater than the measure of either of the nonadjacent interior angles.

Use a relationship from Chapter 4 to *explain* how you know that $m\angle 1 > m\angle A$ and $m\angle 1 > m\angle B$ in $\triangle ABC$ with exterior angle $\angle 1$.

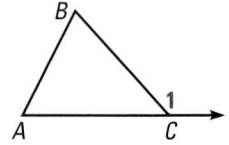

ERROR ANALYSIS **Use Theorems 5.10–5.12 and the theorem in Exercise 27 to** *explain* **why the diagram must be incorrect.**

28.

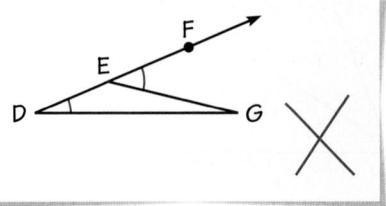

29.

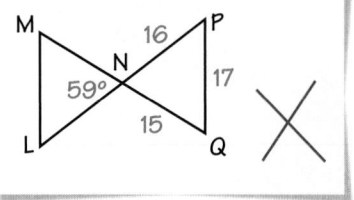

30. ★ SHORT RESPONSE *Explain* why the hypotenuse of a right triangle must always be longer than either leg.

ORDERING MEASURES **Is it possible to build a triangle using the given side lengths? If so, list the angles of the triangle in order from least to greatest measure.**

31. $PQ = \sqrt{58}$, $QR = 2\sqrt{13}$, $PR = 5\sqrt{2}$ **32.** $ST = \sqrt{29}$, $TU = 2\sqrt{17}$, $SU = 13.9$

(XY) ALGEBRA *Describe* the possible values of *x*.

33.

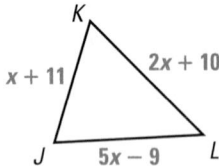

34.

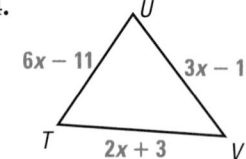

35. USING SIDE LENGTHS Use the diagram at the right. Suppose $\overline{XY}$ bisects $\angle WYZ$. List all six angles of $\triangle XYZ$ and $\triangle WXY$ in order from smallest to largest. *Explain* your reasoning.

36. CHALLENGE The perimeter of $\triangle HGF$ must be between what two integers? *Explain* your reasoning.

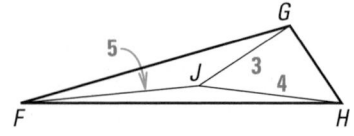

◯ = **WORKED-OUT SOLUTIONS** on p. WS1   ★ = **STANDARDIZED TEST PRACTICE**

37. TRAY TABLE In the tray table shown, $\overline{PQ} \cong \overline{PR}$ and $QR < PQ$. Write two inequalities about the angles in $\triangle PQR$. What other angle relationship do you know?

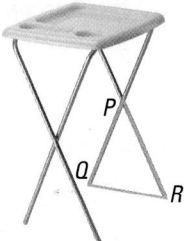

@HomeTutor for problem solving help at classzone.com

38. INDIRECT MEASUREMENT You can estimate the width of the river at point A by taking several sightings to the tree across the river at point B. The diagram shows the results for locations C and D along the riverbank. Using $\triangle BCA$ and $\triangle BDA$, what can you conclude about AB, the width of the river at point A? What could you do if you wanted a closer estimate?

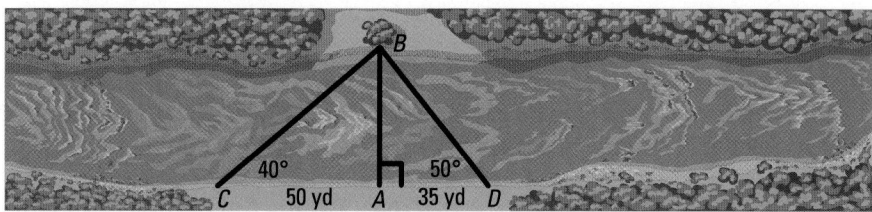

@HomeTutor for problem solving help at classzone.com

EXAMPLE 3
on p. 330
for Ex. 39

39. ★ **EXTENDED RESPONSE** You are planning a vacation to Montana. You want to visit the destinations shown in the map.

a. A brochure states that the distance between Granite Peak and Fort Peck Lake is 1080 kilometers. *Explain* how you know that this distance is a misprint.

b. Could the distance from Granite Peak to Fort Peck Lake be 40 kilometers? *Explain.*

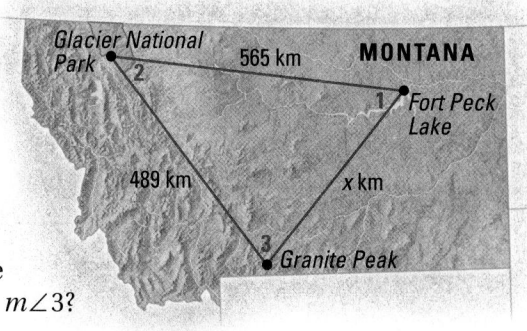

c. Write two inequalities to represent the range of possible distances from Granite Peak to Fort Peck Lake.

d. What can you say about the distance between Granite Peak and Fort Peck Lake if you know that $m\angle 2 < m\angle 1$ and $m\angle 2 < m\angle 3$?

FORMING TRIANGLES In Exercises 40–43, you are given a 24 centimeter piece of string. You want to form a triangle out of the string so that the length of each side is a whole number. Draw figures accurately.

40. Can you decide if three side lengths form a triangle without checking all three inequalities shown for Theorem 5.12? If so, *describe* your shortcut.

41. Draw four possible isosceles triangles and label each side length. Tell whether each of the triangles you formed is *acute*, *right*, or *obtuse*.

42. Draw three possible scalene triangles and label each side length. Try to form at least one scalene acute triangle and one scalene obtuse triangle.

43. List three combinations of side lengths that will not produce triangles.

44. SIGHTSEEING You get off the Washington, D.C., subway system at the Smithsonian Metro station. First you visit the Museum of Natural History. Then you go to the Air and Space Museum. You record the distances you walk on your map as shown. *Describe* the range of possible distances you might have to walk to get back to the Smithsonian Metro station.

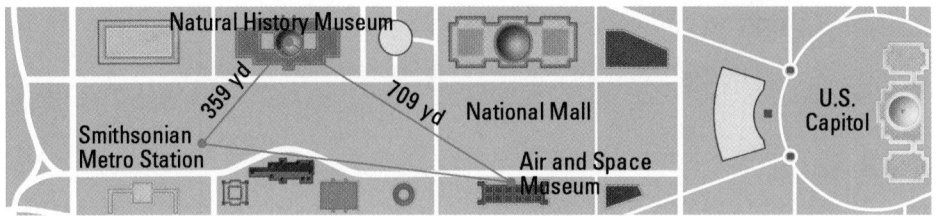

45. ★ **SHORT RESPONSE** Your house is 2 miles from the library. The library is $\frac{3}{4}$ mile from the grocery store. What do you know about the distance from your house to the grocery store? *Explain.* Include the special case when the three locations are all in a straight line.

46. ISOSCELES TRIANGLES For what combinations of angle measures in an isosceles triangle are the congruent sides shorter than the base of the triangle? longer than the base of the triangle?

47. PROVING THEOREM 5.12 Prove the Triangle Inequality Theorem.

    GIVEN ▶ $\triangle ABC$

    PROVE ▶ (1) $AB + BC > AC$
              (2) $AC + BC > AB$
              (3) $AB + AC > BC$

Plan for Proof One side, say $\overline{BC}$, is longer than or at least as long as each of the other sides. Then (1) and (2) are true. To prove (3), extend $\overline{AC}$ to D so that $\overline{AB} \cong \overline{AD}$ and use Theorem 5.11 to show that $DC > BC$.

48. CHALLENGE Prove the following statements.

    a. The length of any one median of a triangle is less than half the perimeter of the triangle.

    b. The sum of the lengths of the three medians of a triangle is greater than half the perimeter of the triangle.

MIXED REVIEW

PREVIEW
Prepare for
Lesson 5.6 in
Exs. 49–50.

In Exercises 49 and 50, write the if-then form, the converse, the inverse, and the contrapositive of the given statement. *(p. 79)*

49. A redwood is a large tree.   **50.** $5x - 2 = 18$, because $x = 4$.

51. A triangle has vertices $A(22, 21)$, $B(0, 0)$, and $C(22, 2)$. Graph $\triangle ABC$ and classify it by its sides. Then determine if it is a right triangle. *(p. 217)*

Graph figure *LMNP* **with vertices** $L(-4, 6)$, $M(4, 8)$, $N(2, 2)$, **and** $P(-4, 0)$. **Then draw its image after the transformation.** *(p. 272)*

52. $(x, y) \rightarrow (x + 3, y - 4)$ **53.** $(x, y) \rightarrow (x, -y)$ **54.** $(x, y) \rightarrow (-x, y)$

5.6 Inequalities in Two Triangles and Indirect Proof

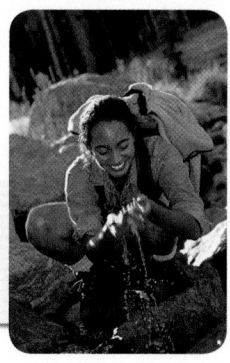

Before	You used inequalities to make comparisons in one triangle.
Now	You will use inequalities to make comparisons in two triangles.
Why?	So you can compare the distances hikers traveled, as in Ex. 22.

Key Vocabulary
• **indirect proof**
• **included angle**, *p. 240*

Imagine a gate between fence posts *A* and *B* that has hinges at *A* and swings open at *B*.

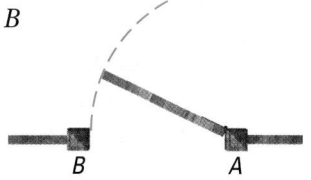

As the gate swings open, you can think of △*ABC*, with side $\overline{AC}$ formed by the gate itself, side $\overline{AB}$ representing the distance between the fence posts, and side $\overline{BC}$ representing the opening between post *B* and the outer edge of the gate.

 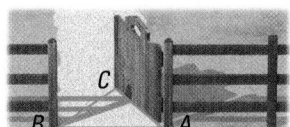 

Notice that as the gate opens wider, both the measure of ∠*A* and the distance *CB* increase. This suggests the *Hinge Theorem*.

THEOREMS
For Your Notebook

THEOREM 5.13 Hinge Theorem

If two sides of one triangle are congruent to two sides of another triangle, and the included angle of the first is larger than the included angle of the second, then the third side of the first is longer than the third side of the second.

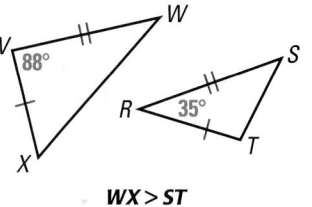

WX > ST

Proof: Ex. 28, p. 341

THEOREM 5.14 Converse of the Hinge Theorem

If two sides of one triangle are congruent to two sides of another triangle, and the third side of the first is longer than the third side of the second, then the included angle of the first is larger than the included angle of the second.

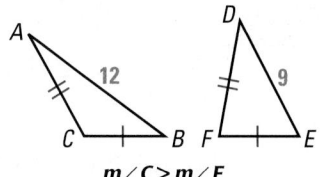

m∠C > m∠F

Proof: Example 4, p. 338

EXAMPLE 1 Use the Converse of the Hinge Theorem

Given that $\overline{ST} \cong \overline{PR}$**, how does** $\angle PST$ **compare to** $\angle SPR$**?**

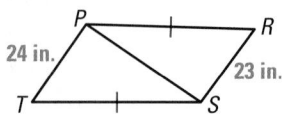

Solution

You are given that $\overline{ST} \cong \overline{PR}$ and you know that $\overline{PS} \cong \overline{PS}$ by the Reflexive Property. Because 24 inches > 23 inches, $PT > RS$. So, two sides of $\triangle STP$ are congruent to two sides of $\triangle PRS$ and the third side in $\triangle STP$ is longer.

▶ By the Converse of the Hinge Theorem, $m\angle PST > m\angle SPR$.

EXAMPLE 2 Solve a multi-step problem

BIKING Two groups of bikers leave the same camp heading in opposite directions. Each group goes 2 miles, then changes direction and goes 1.2 miles. Group A starts due east and then turns 45° toward north as shown. Group B starts due west and then turns 30° toward south.

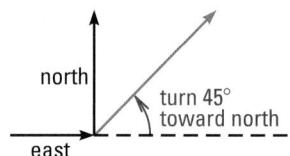

Which group is farther from camp? Explain your reasoning.

Solution

Draw a diagram and mark the given measures. The distances biked and the distances back to camp form two triangles, with congruent 2 mile sides and congruent 1.2 mile sides. Add the third sides of the triangles to your diagram.

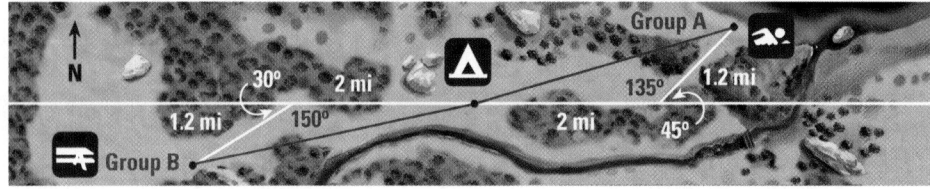

Next use linear pairs to find and mark the included angles of 150° and 135°.

▶ Because 150° > 135°, Group B is farther from camp by the Hinge Theorem.

Animated **Geometry** at classzone.com

✓ **GUIDED PRACTICE** for Examples 1 and 2

Use the diagram at the right.

1. If $PR = PS$ and $m\angle QPR > m\angle QPS$, which is longer, $\overline{SQ}$ or $\overline{RQ}$?

2. If $PR = PS$ and $RQ < SQ$, which is larger, $\angle RPQ$ or $\angle SPQ$?

3. **WHAT IF?** In Example 2, suppose Group C leaves camp and goes 2 miles due north. Then they turn 40° toward east and continue 1.2 miles. *Compare* the distances from camp for all three groups.

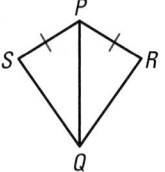

INDIRECT REASONING Suppose a student looks around the cafeteria, concludes that hamburgers are not being served, and explains as follows.

> *At first I assumed that we are having hamburgers because today is Tuesday and Tuesday is usually hamburger day.*
>
> *There is always ketchup on the table when we have hamburgers, so I looked for the ketchup, but I didn't see any.*
>
> *So, my assumption that we are having hamburgers must be false.*

The student used *indirect* reasoning. So far in this book, you have reasoned *directly* from given information to prove desired conclusions.

In an **indirect proof**, you start by making the temporary assumption that the desired conclusion is false. By then showing that this assumption leads to a logical impossibility, you prove the original statement true *by contradiction*.

KEY CONCEPT
For Your Notebook

How to Write an Indirect Proof

STEP 1 **Identify** the statement you want to prove. **Assume** temporarily that this statement is false by assuming that its opposite is true.

STEP 2 **Reason** logically until you reach a contradiction.

STEP 3 **Point out** that the desired conclusion must be true because the contradiction proves the temporary assumption false.

EXAMPLE 3 Write an indirect proof

Write an indirect proof that an odd number is not divisible by 4.

GIVEN ▶ x is an odd number.

PROVE ▶ x is not divisible by 4.

Solution

STEP 1 Assume temporarily that x is divisible by 4. This means that $\frac{x}{4} = n$ for some whole number n. So, multiplying both sides by 4 gives $x = 4n$.

STEP 2 If x is odd, then, by definition, x cannot be divided evenly by 2. However, $x = 4n$ so $\frac{x}{2} = \frac{4n}{2} = 2n$. We know that $2n$ is a whole number because n is a whole number, so x *can* be divided evenly by 2. This contradicts the given statement that x is odd.

STEP 3 Therefore, the assumption that x is divisible by 4 must be false, which proves that x is not divisible by 4.

READ VOCABULARY
You have reached a *contradiction* when you have two statements that cannot both be true at the same time.

✓ **GUIDED PRACTICE** for Example 3

4. Suppose you wanted to prove the statement "If $x + y \neq 14$ and $y = 5$, then $x \neq 9$." What temporary assumption could you make to prove the conclusion indirectly? How does that assumption lead to a contradiction?

EXAMPLE 4 Prove the Converse of the Hinge Theorem

Write an indirect proof of Theorem 5.14.

GIVEN ▶ $\overline{AB} \cong \overline{DE}$
$\overline{BC} \cong \overline{EF}$
$AC > DF$

PROVE ▶ $m\angle B > m\angle E$

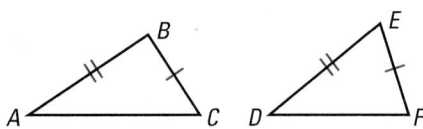

Proof Assume temporarily that $m\angle B \not> m\angle E$. Then, it follows that either $m\angle B = m\angle E$ or $m\angle B < m\angle E$.

Case 1 If $m\angle B = m\angle E$, then $\angle B \cong \angle E$. So, $\triangle ABC \cong \triangle DEF$ by the SAS Congruence Postulate and $AC = DF$.

Case 2 If $m\angle B < m\angle E$, then $AC < DF$ by the Hinge Theorem.

Both conclusions contradict the given statement that $AC > DF$. So, the temporary assumption that $m\angle B \not> m\angle E$ cannot be true. This proves that $m\angle B > m\angle E$.

✓ **GUIDED PRACTICE** for Example 4

5. Write a temporary assumption you could make to prove the Hinge Theorem indirectly. What two cases does that assumption lead to?

5.6 EXERCISES

HOMEWORK KEY

○ = WORKED-OUT SOLUTIONS
 on p. WS7 for Exs. 5, 7, and 23

★ = STANDARDIZED TEST PRACTICE
 Exs. 2, 9, 19, and 25

SKILL PRACTICE

1. **VOCABULARY** Why is indirect proof also called *proof by contradiction*?

2. ★ **WRITING** *Explain* why the name "Hinge Theorem" is used for Theorem 5.13.

EXAMPLE 1
on p. 336
for Exs. 3–10

APPLYING THEOREMS Copy and complete with <, >, or =. *Explain.*

3. *AD* __?__ *CD*

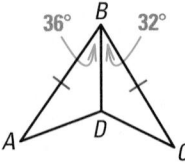

4. *MN* __?__ *LK*

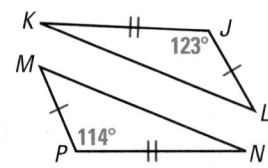

5. *TR* __?__ *UR*

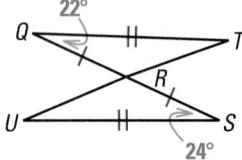

6. $m\angle 1$ __?__ $m\angle 2$

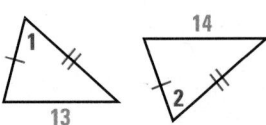

7. $m\angle 1$ __?__ $m\angle 2$

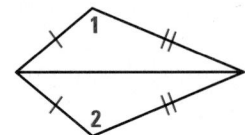

8. $m\angle 1$ __?__ $m\angle 2$

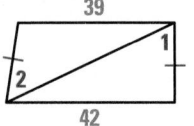

9. ★ **MULTIPLE CHOICE** Which is a possible measure for ∠JKM?

   Ⓐ 20°   Ⓑ 25°

   Ⓒ 30°   Ⓓ Cannot be determined

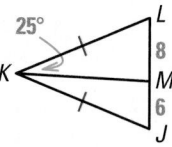

10. **USING A DIAGRAM** The path from *E* to *F* is longer than the path from *E* to *D*. The path from *G* to *D* is the same length as the path from *G* to *F*. What can you conclude about the angles of the paths? *Explain* your reasoning.

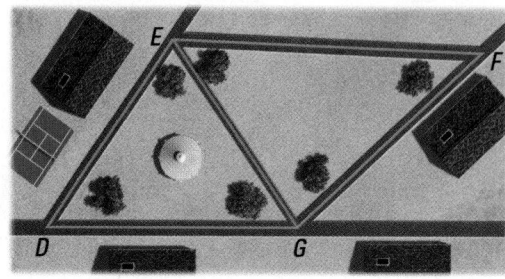

EXAMPLES
3 and 4
on pp. 337–338
for Exs. 11–13

STARTING AN INDIRECT PROOF In Exercises 11 and 12, write a temporary assumption you could make to prove the conclusion indirectly.

11. If *x* and *y* are odd integers, then *xy* is odd.

12. In △*ABC*, if *m*∠*A* = 100°, then ∠*B* is not a right angle.

13. **REASONING** Your study partner is planning to write an indirect proof to show that ∠*A* is an obtuse angle. She states "Assume temporarily that ∠*A* is an acute angle." What has your study partner overlooked?

ERROR ANALYSIS *Explain* why the student's reasoning is not correct.

14.

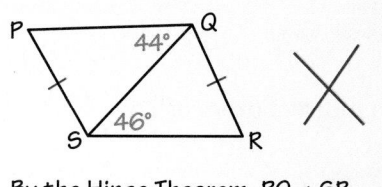

By the Hinge Theorem, PQ < SR.

15.

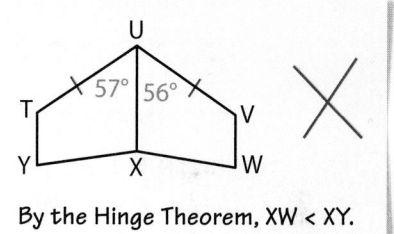

By the Hinge Theorem, XW < XY.

🆇🆈 **ALGEBRA** Use the Hinge Theorem or its converse and properties of triangles to write and solve an inequality to describe a restriction on the value of *x*.

16.

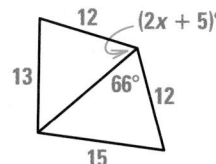

17.

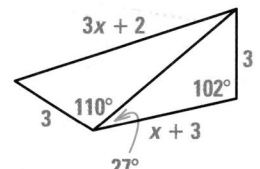

18.

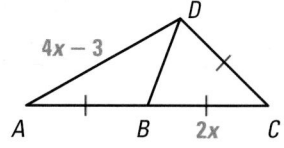

19. ★ **SHORT RESPONSE** If $\overline{NR}$ is a median of △*NPQ* and *NQ* > *NP*, *explain* why ∠*NRQ* is obtuse.

20. **ANGLE BISECTORS** In △*EFG*, the bisector of ∠*F* intersects the bisector of ∠*G* at point *H*. *Explain* why $\overline{FG}$ must be longer than $\overline{FH}$ or $\overline{HG}$.

21. **CHALLENGE** In △*ABC*, the altitudes from *B* and *C* meet at *D*. What is true about △*ABC* if *m*∠*BAC* > *m*∠*BDC*? *Justify* your answer.

EXAMPLE 2
on p. 336
for Ex. 22

22. HIKING Two hikers start at the visitor center. The first hikes 4 miles due west, then turns 40° toward south and hikes 1.8 miles. The second hikes 4 miles due east, then turns 52° toward north and and hikes 1.8 miles. Which hiker is farther from the visitor center? *Explain* how you know.

@*HomeTutor* for problem solving help at classzone.com

EXAMPLES
3 and 4
on pp. 337–338
for Exs. 23–24

23. INDIRECT PROOF Arrange statements A–E in order to write an indirect proof of the corollary: If △*PQR* is *equilateral*, then it is *equiangular*.

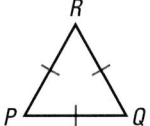

GIVEN ▶ △*PQR* is equilateral.

A. That means that for some pair of vertices, say *P* and *Q*, $m\angle P > m\angle Q$.

B. But this contradicts the given statement that △*PQR* is equilateral.

C. The contradiction shows that the temporary assumption that △*PQR* is not equiangular is false. This proves that △*PQR* is equiangular.

D. Then, by Theorem 5.11, you can conclude that $QR > PR$.

E. Temporarily assume that △*PQR* is not equiangular.

@*HomeTutor* for problem solving help at classzone.com

24. PROVING THEOREM 5.11 Write an indirect proof of Theorem 5.11, page 328.

GIVEN ▶ $m\angle D > m\angle E$

PROVE ▶ $EF > DF$

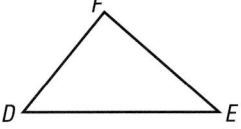

Plan for Proof In Case 1, assume that $EF < DF$. In Case 2, assume that $EF = DF$.

25. ★ EXTENDED RESPONSE A scissors lift can be used to adjust the height of a platform.

a. Interpret As the mechanism expands, $\overline{KL}$ gets longer. As *KL* increases, what happens to $m\angle LNK$? to $m\angle KNM$?

b. Apply Name a distance that decreases as $\overline{KL}$ gets longer.

c. Writing *Explain* how the adjustable mechanism illustrates the Hinge Theorem.

26. PROOF Write a proof that the shortest distance from a point to a line is the length of the perpendicular segment from the point to the line.

GIVEN ▶ Line *k*; point *A* not on *k*; point *B* on *k* such that $\overline{AB} \perp k$

PROVE ▶ $\overline{AB}$ is the shortest segment from *A* to *k*.

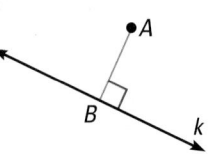

Plan for Proof Assume that there is a shorter segment from *A* to *k* and use Theorem 5.10 to show that this leads to a contradiction.

27. USING A CONTRAPOSITIVE Because the contrapositive of a conditional is equivalent to the original statement, you can prove the statement by proving its contrapositive. Look back at the conditional in Example 3 on page 337. Write a proof of the contrapositive that uses direct reasoning. How is your proof similar to the indirect proof of the original statement?

28. CHALLENGE Write a proof of Theorem 5.13, the Hinge Theorem.

> **GIVEN** ▶ $\overline{AB} \cong \overline{DE}$, $\overline{BC} \cong \overline{EF}$,
> $m\angle ABC > m\angle DEF$
>
> **PROVE** ▶ $AC > DF$

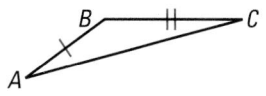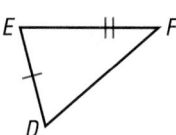

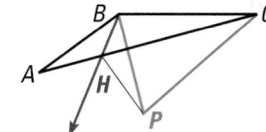

Plan for Proof

1. Because $m\angle ABC > m\angle DEF$, you can locate a point P in the interior of $\angle ABC$ so that $\angle CBP \cong \angle FED$ and $\overline{BP} \cong \overline{ED}$. Draw $\overline{BP}$ and show that $\triangle PBC \cong \triangle DEF$.

2. Locate a point H on $\overline{AC}$ so that $\overrightarrow{BH}$ bisects $\angle PBA$ and show that $\triangle ABH \cong \triangle PBH$.

3. Give reasons for each statement below to show that $AC > DF$.
   $AC = AH + HC = PH + HC > PC = DF$

MIXED REVIEW

PREVIEW
Prepare for Lesson 6.1 in Exs. 29–31.

Write the conversion factor you would multiply by to change units as specified. *(p. 886)*

29. inches to feet   **30.** liters to kiloliters   **31.** pounds to ounces

Solve the equation. Write a reason for each step. *(p. 105)*

32. $1.5(x + 4) = 5(2.4)$ **33.** $-3(-2x + 5) = 12$ **34.** $2(5x) = 3(4x + 6)$

35. Simplify the expression $\dfrac{-6xy^2}{21x^2y}$ if possible. *(p. 139)*

QUIZ for Lessons 5.5–5.6

1. Is it possible to construct a triangle with side lengths 5, 6, and 12? If not, *explain* why not. *(p. 328)*

2. The lengths of two sides of a triangle are 15 yards and 27 yards. *Describe* the possible lengths of the third side of the triangle. *(p. 328)*

3. In $\triangle PQR$, $m\angle P = 48°$ and $m\angle Q = 79°$. List the sides of $\triangle PQR$ in order from shortest to longest. *(p. 328)*

Copy and complete with <, >, or =. *(p. 335)*

4. BA _?_ DA

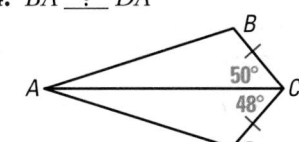

5. $m\angle 1$ _?_ $m\angle 2$

MIXED REVIEW *of Problem Solving*

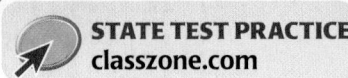

Lessons 5.4–5.6

1. **MULTI-STEP PROBLEM** In the diagram below, the entrance to the path is halfway between your house and your friend's house.

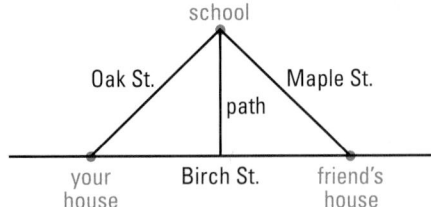

a. Can you conclude that you and your friend live the same distance from the school if the path bisects the angle formed by Oak and Maple Streets?

b. Can you conclude that you and your friend live the same distance from the school if the path is perpendicular to Birch Street?

c. Your answers to parts (a) and (b) show that a triangle must be isosceles if which two special segments are equal in length?

2. **SHORT RESPONSE** The map shows your driving route from Allentown to Bakersville and from Allentown to Dawson. Which city, Bakersville or Dawson, is located closer to Allentown? *Explain* your reasoning.

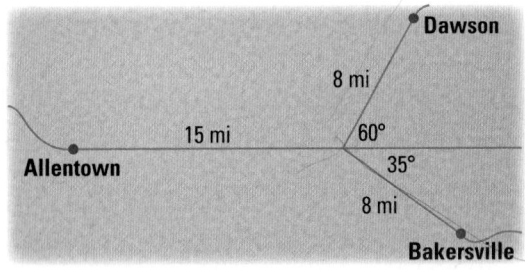

3. **GRIDDED RESPONSE** Find the length of $\overline{AF}$.

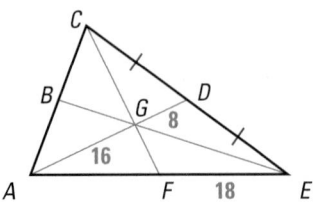

4. **SHORT RESPONSE** In the instructions for creating the terrarium shown, you are given a pattern for the pieces that form the roof. Does the diagram for the red triangle appear to be correct? *Explain* why or why not.

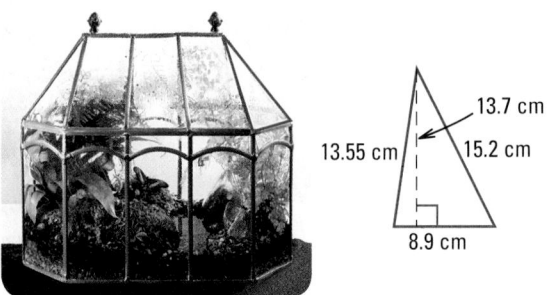

5. **EXTENDED RESPONSE** You want to create a triangular fenced pen for your dog. You have the two pieces of fencing shown, so you plan to move those to create two sides of the pen.

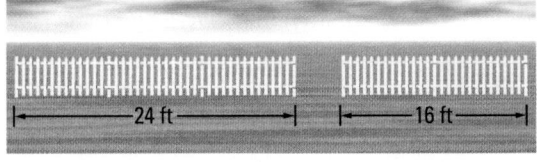

a. *Describe* the possible lengths for the third side of the pen.

b. The fencing is sold in 8 foot sections. If you use whole sections, what lengths of fencing are possible for the third side?

c. You want your dog to have a run within the pen that is at least 25 feet long. Which pen(s) could you use? *Explain.*

6. **OPEN-ENDED** In the gem shown, give a possible side length of $\overline{DE}$ if $m\angle EFD > 90°$, $DF = 0.4$ mm, and $EF = 0.63$ mm.

BIG IDEAS
For Your Notebook

Big Idea 1

Using Properties of Special Segments in Triangles

Special segment	*Properties to remember*
Midsegment	Parallel to side opposite it and half the length of side opposite it
Perpendicular bisector	Concurrent at the circumcenter, which is: • equidistant from 3 vertices of △ • center of *circumscribed* circle that passes through 3 vertices of △
Angle bisector	Concurrent at the incenter, which is: • equidistant from 3 sides of △ • center of *inscribed* circle that just touches each side of △
Median (connects vertex to midpoint of opposite side)	Concurrent at the centroid, which is: • located two thirds of the way from vertex to midpoint of opposite side • balancing point of △
Altitude (perpendicular to side of △ through opposite vertex)	Concurrent at the orthocenter Used in finding area: If b is length of any side and h is length of altitude to that side, then $A = \frac{1}{2}bh$.

Big Idea 2

Using Triangle Inequalities to Determine What Triangles are Possible

Sum of lengths of any two sides of a △ is greater than length of third side.		$AB + BC > AC$ $AB + AC > BC$ $BC + AC > AB$
In a △, longest side is opposite largest angle and shortest side is opposite smallest angle.		If $AC > AB > BC$, then $m\angle B > m\angle C > m\angle A$. If $m\angle B > m\angle C > m\angle A$, then $AC > AB > BC$.
If two sides of a △ are ≅ to two sides of another △, then the △ with longer third side also has larger included angle.	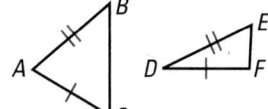	If $BC > EF$, then $m\angle A > m\angle D$. If $m\angle A > m\angle D$, then $BC > EF$.

Big Idea 3

Extending Methods for Justifying and Proving Relationships

Coordinate proof uses the coordinate plane and variable coordinates. *Indirect proof* involves assuming the conclusion is false and then showing that the assumption leads to a contradiction.

REVIEW KEY VOCABULARY

For a list of postulates and theorems, see pp. 926–931.

• midsegment of a triangle, *p. 295*
• coordinate proof, *p. 296*
• perpendicular bisector, *p. 303*
• equidistant, *p. 303*
• concurrent, *p. 305*
• point of concurrency, *p. 305*
• circumcenter, *p. 306*

• incenter, *p. 312*
• median of a triangle, *p. 319*
• centroid, *p. 319*
• altitude of a triangle, *p. 320*
• orthocenter, *p. 321*
• indirect proof, *p. 337*

VOCABULARY EXERCISES

1. Copy and complete: A __?__ is a segment, ray, line, or plane that is perpendicular to a segment at its midpoint.

2. **WRITING** *Explain* how to draw a circle that is circumscribed about a triangle. What is the center of the circle called? *Describe* its radius.

In Exercises 3–5, match the term with the correct definition.

3. Incenter

4. Centroid

5. Orthocenter

A. The point of concurrency of the medians of a triangle

B. The point of concurrency of the angle bisectors of a triangle

C. The point of concurrency of the altitudes of a triangle

REVIEW EXAMPLES AND EXERCISES

Use the review examples and exercises below to check your understanding of the concepts you have learned in each lesson of Chapter 5.

5.1 Midsegment Theorem and Coordinate Proof   *pp. 295–301*

EXAMPLE

In the diagram, $\overline{DE}$ is a midsegment of $\triangle ABC$. Find AC.

By the Midsegment Theorem, $DE = \frac{1}{2}AC$.

So, $AC = 2DE = 2(51) = 102$.

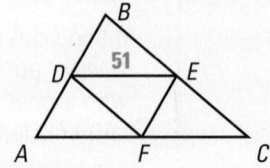

EXERCISES

**EXAMPLES
1, 4, and 5**
on pp. 295, 297
for Exs. 6–8

Use the diagram above where $\overline{DF}$ and $\overline{EF}$ are midsegments of $\triangle ABC$.

6. If $AB = 72$, find EF.

7. If $DF = 45$, find EC.

8. Graph $\triangle PQO$, with vertices $P(2a, 2b)$, $Q(2a, 0)$, and $O(0, 0)$. Find the coordinates of midpoint S of $\overline{PQ}$ and midpoint T of $\overline{QO}$. Show $\overline{ST} \parallel \overline{PO}$.

5.2 Use Perpendicular Bisectors

pp. 303–309

EXAMPLE

Use the diagram at the right to find XZ.

$\overleftrightarrow{WZ}$ is the perpendicular bisector of $\overline{XY}$.

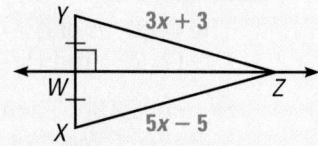

$5x - 5 = 3x + 3$ **By the Perpendicular Bisector Theorem, $ZX = ZY$.**

$x = 4$ **Solve for x.**

▶ So, $XZ = 5x - 5 = 5(4) - 5 = 15$.

EXERCISES

EXAMPLES
1 and 2
on pp. 303–304
for Exs. 9–11

In the diagram, $\overleftrightarrow{BD}$ is the perpendicular bisector of $\overline{AC}$.

9. What segment lengths are equal?

10. What is the value of x?

11. Find AB.

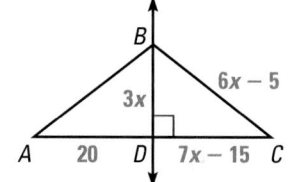

5.3 Use Angle Bisectors of Triangles

pp. 310–316

EXAMPLE

In the diagram, N is the incenter of $\triangle XYZ$. Find NL.

Use the Pythagorean Theorem to find NM in $\triangle NMY$.

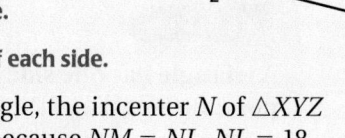

$c^2 = a^2 + b^2$ **Pythagorean Theorem**

$30^2 = NM^2 + 24^2$ **Substitute known values.**

$900 = NM^2 + 576$ **Multiply.**

$324 = NM^2$ **Subtract 576 from each side.**

$18 = NM$ **Take positive square root of each side.**

▶ By the Concurrency of Angle Bisectors of a Triangle, the incenter N of $\triangle XYZ$ is equidistant from all three sides of $\triangle XYZ$. So, because $NM = NL$, $NL = 18$.

EXERCISES

EXAMPLE 4
on p. 312
for Exs. 12–13

Point D is the incenter of the triangle. Find the value of x.

12.

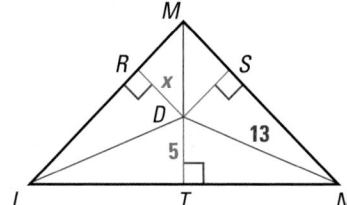

13.

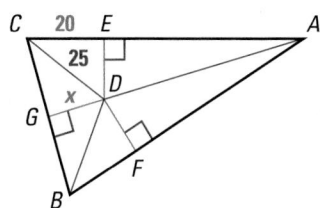

5.4 Use Medians and Altitudes

pp. 319–325

EXAMPLE

The vertices of △ABC are A(−6, 8), B(0, −4), and C(−12, 2). Find the coordinates of its centroid P.

Sketch △ABC. Then find the midpoint M of $\overline{BC}$ and sketch median $\overline{AM}$.

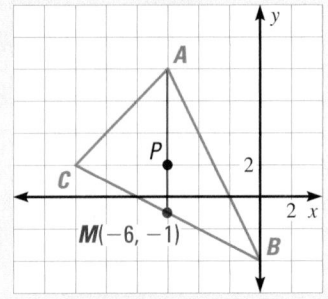

$$M\left(\frac{-12 + 0}{2}, \frac{2 + (-4)}{2}\right) = M(-6, -1)$$

The centroid is two thirds of the distance from a vertex to the midpoint of the opposite side.

The distance from vertex A(−6, 8) to midpoint M(−6, −1) is 8 − (−1) = 9 units.

So, the centroid P is $\frac{2}{3}(9) = 6$ units down from A on $\overline{AM}$.

▶ The coordinates of the centroid P are (−6, 8 − 6), or (−6, 2).

EXERCISES

**EXAMPLES
1, 2, and 3**
on pp. 319–321
for Exs. 14–18

Find the coordinates of the centroid D of △RST.

14. R(−4, 0), S(2, 2), T(2, −2)   **15.** R(−6, 2), S(−2, 6), T(2, 4)

Point Q is the centroid of △XYZ.

16. Find XQ.   **17.** Find XM.

18. Draw an obtuse △ABC. Draw its three altitudes. Then label its orthocenter D.

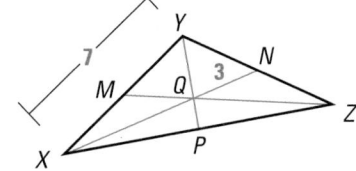

5.5 Use Inequalities in a Triangle

pp. 328–334

EXAMPLE

A triangle has one side of length 9 and another of length 14. Describe the possible lengths of the third side.

Let x represent the length of the third side. Draw diagrams and use the Triangle Inequality Theorem to write inequalities involving x.

$x + 9 > 14$ $9 + 14 > x$

$x > 5$ $23 > x$, or $x < 23$

▶ The length of the third side must be greater than 5 and less than 23.

EXERCISES

EXAMPLES
1, 2, and 3
on pp. 328–330
for Exs. 19–24

Describe the possible lengths of the third side of the triangle given the lengths of the other two sides.

19. 4 inches, 8 inches   **20.** 6 meters, 9 meters   **21.** 12 feet, 20 feet

List the sides and the angles in order from smallest to largest.

22.

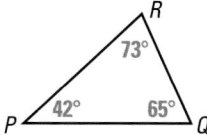

23.

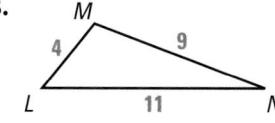

24.

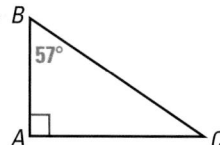

5.6 Inequalities in Two Triangles and Indirect Proof   *pp. 335–341*

EXAMPLE

How does the length of $\overline{DG}$ compare to the length of $\overline{FG}$?

▶ Because 27° > 23°, $m\angle GEF > m\angle GED$. You are given that $\overline{DE} \cong \overline{FE}$ and you know that $\overline{EG} \cong \overline{EG}$. Two sides of $\triangle GEF$ are congruent to two sides of $\triangle GED$ and the included angle is larger so, by the Hinge Theorem, $FG > DG$.

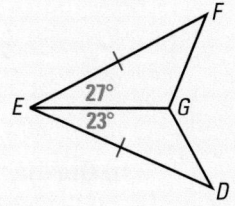

EXERCISES

EXAMPLES
1, 3, and 4
on pp. 336–338
for Exs. 25–27

Copy and complete with <, >, or =.

25. $m\angle BAC$ _?_ $m\angle DAC$

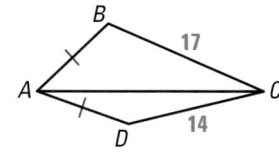

26. LM _?_ KN

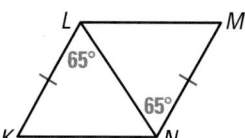

27. Arrange statements A–D in correct order to write an indirect proof of the statement: *If two lines intersect, then their intersection is exactly one point.*

GIVEN ▶ Intersecting lines m and n

PROVE ▶ The intersection of lines m and n is exactly one point.

A. But this contradicts Postulate 5, which states that through any two points there is exactly one line.

B. Then there are two lines (m and n) through points P and Q.

C. Assume that there are two points, P and Q, where m and n intersect.

D. It is false that m and n can intersect in two points, so they must intersect in exactly one point.

Two midsegments of △ABC are $\overline{DE}$ and $\overline{DF}$.

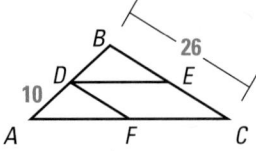

1. Find DB.

2. Find DF.

3. What can you conclude about $\overline{EF}$?

Find the value of *x*. Explain your reasoning.

4.

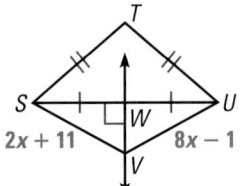

5.

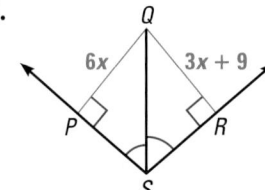

6.

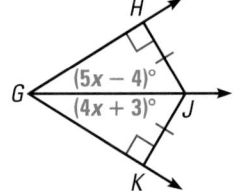

7. In Exercise 4, is point *T* on the perpendicular bisector of $\overline{SU}$? *Explain.*

8. In the diagram at the right, the angle bisectors of △XYZ meet at point *D*. Find *DB*.

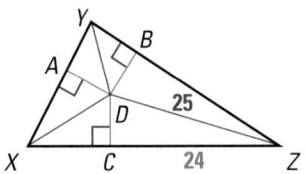

In the diagram at the right, *P* is the centroid of △RST.

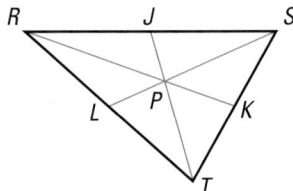

9. If *LS* = 36, find *PL* and *PS*.

10. If *TP* = 20, find *TJ* and *PJ*.

11. If *JR* = 25, find *JS* and *RS*.

12. Is it possible to construct a triangle with side lengths 9, 12, and 22? If not, *explain* why not.

13. In △ABC, AB = 36, BC = 18, and AC = 22. Sketch and label the triangle. List the angles in order from smallest to largest.

In the diagram for Exercises 14 and 15, *JL = MK*.

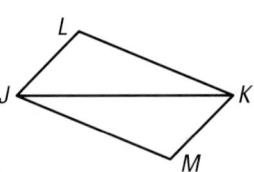

14. If *m∠JKM > m∠LJK*, which is longer, $\overline{LK}$ or $\overline{MJ}$? *Explain.*

15. If *MJ < LK*, which is larger, *∠LJK* or *∠JKM*? *Explain.*

16. Write a temporary assumption you could make to prove the conclusion indirectly: *If RS + ST ≠ 12 and ST = 5, then RS ≠ 7.*

Use the diagram in Exercises 17 and 18.

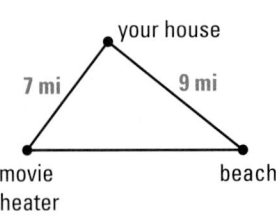

17. *Describe* the range of possible distances from the beach to the movie theater.

18. A market is the same distance from your house, the movie theater, and the beach. Copy the diagram and locate the market.

USE RATIOS AND PERCENT OF CHANGE

 EXAMPLE 1 *Write a ratio in simplest form*

A team won 18 of its 30 games and lost the rest. Find its win-loss ratio.

The ratio of a to b, $b \neq 0$, can be written as a to b, $a:b$, and $\dfrac{a}{b}$.

$$\dfrac{\text{wins}}{\text{losses}} = \dfrac{18}{30 - 18} \qquad \text{To find losses, subtract wins from total.}$$

$$= \dfrac{18}{12} = \dfrac{3}{2} \qquad \text{Simplify.}$$

▶ The team's win-loss ratio is $3:2$.

xy **EXAMPLE 2** *Find and interpret a percent of change*

A \$50 sweater went on sale for \$28. What is the percent of change in price? The new price is what percent of the old price?

$$\text{Percent of change} = \dfrac{\text{Amount of increase or decrease}}{\text{Original amount}} = \dfrac{50 - 28}{50} = \dfrac{22}{50} = 0.44$$

▶ The price went down, so the change is a decrease. The percent of decrease is 44%. So, the new price is $100\% - 44\% = 56\%$ of the original price.

EXERCISES

EXAMPLE 1
for Exs. 1–3

1. A team won 12 games and lost 4 games. Write each ratio in simplest form.

    a. wins to losses   **b.** losses out of total games

2. A scale drawing that is 2.5 feet long by 1 foot high was used to plan a mural that is 15 feet long by 6 feet high. Write each ratio in simplest form.

    a. length to height of mural   **b.** length of scale drawing to length of mural

3. There are 8 males out of 18 members in the school choir. Write the ratio of females to males in simplest form.

EXAMPLE 2
for Exs. 4–13

Find the percent of change.

4. From 75 campsites to 120 campsites   **5.** From 150 pounds to 136.5 pounds

6. From \$480 to \$408   **7.** From 16 employees to 18 employees

8. From 24 houses to 60 houses   **9.** From 4000 ft^2 to 3990 ft^2

Write the percent comparing the new amount to the original amount. Then find the new amount.

10. 75 feet increased by 4%   **11.** 45 hours decreased by 16%

12. \$16,500 decreased by 85%   **13.** 80 people increased by 7.5%

SHORT RESPONSE QUESTIONS

> **PROBLEM**
>
> The coordinates of the vertices of a triangle are $O(0, 0)$, $M(k, k\sqrt{3})$, and $N(2k, 0)$. Classify $\triangle OMN$ by its side lengths. *Justify* your answer.

Below are sample solutions to the problem. Read each solution and the comments in blue to see why the sample represents full credit, partial credit, or no credit.

SAMPLE 1: Full credit solution

A sample triangle is graphed and an explanation is given.

Begin by graphing $\triangle OMN$ for a given value of k. I chose a value of k that makes $\triangle OMN$ easy to graph. In the diagram, $k = 4$, so the coordinates are $O(0, 0)$, $M(4, 4\sqrt{3})$, and $N(8, 0)$.

From the graph, it appears that $\triangle OMN$ is equilateral.

The Distance Formula is applied correctly.

To verify that $\triangle OMN$ is equilateral, use the Distance Formula. Show that $OM = MN = ON$ for all values of k.

$$OM = \sqrt{(k - 0)^2 + (k\sqrt{3} - 0)^2} = \sqrt{k^2 + 3k^2} = \sqrt{4k^2} = 2|k|$$

$$MN = \sqrt{(2k - k)^2 + (0 - k\sqrt{3})^2} = \sqrt{k^2 + 3k^2} = \sqrt{4k^2} = 2|k|$$

$$ON = \sqrt{(2k - 0)^2 + (0 - 0)^2} = \sqrt{4k^2} = 2|k|$$

The answer is correct.

Because all of its side lengths are equal, $\triangle OMN$ is an equilateral triangle.

SAMPLE 2: Partial credit solution

Use the Distance Formula to find the side lengths.

A calculation error is made in finding OM and MN. The value of $(k\sqrt{3})^2$ is $k^2 \cdot (\sqrt{3})^2$, or $3k^2$, not $9k^2$.

$$OM = \sqrt{(k - 0)^2 + (k\sqrt{3} - 0)^2} = \sqrt{k^2 + 9k^2} = \sqrt{10k^2} = k\sqrt{10}$$

$$MN = \sqrt{(2k - k)^2 + (0 - k\sqrt{3})^2} = \sqrt{k^2 + 9k^2} = \sqrt{10k^2} = k\sqrt{10}$$

$$ON = \sqrt{(2k - 0)^2 + (0 - 0)^2} = \sqrt{4k^2} = 2k$$

The answer is incorrect.

Two of the side lengths are equal, so $\triangle OMN$ is an isosceles triangle.

SAMPLE 3: Partial credit solution

The answer is correct, but the explanation does not justify the answer.

Graph △*OMN* and compare the side lengths.

From *O*(0, 0), move right *k* units and up $k\sqrt{3}$ units to *M*($k, k\sqrt{3}$). Draw $\overline{OM}$. To draw $\overline{MN}$, move *k* units right and $k\sqrt{3}$ units down from *M* to *N*(2*k*, 0). Then draw $\overline{ON}$, which is 2*k* units long. All side lengths appear to be equal, so △*OMN* is equilateral.

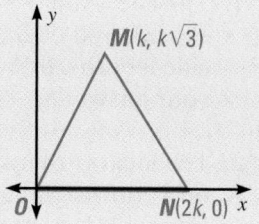

SAMPLE 4: No credit solution

The reasoning and the answer are incorrect.

You are not given enough information to classify △*OMN* because you need to know the value of *k*.

PRACTICE   Apply the Scoring Rubric

Use the rubric on page 350 to score the solution to the problem below as *full credit*, *partial credit*, or *no credit*. *Explain* your reasoning.

PROBLEM You are a goalie guarding the goal $\overline{NQ}$. To make a goal, Player *P* must send the ball across $\overline{NQ}$. Is the distance you may need to move to block the shot greater if you stand at Position *A* or at Position *B*? *Explain*.

1. At either position, you are on the angle bisector of ∠NPQ. So, in both cases you are equidistant from the angle's sides. Therefore, the distance you need to move to block the shot from the two positions is the same.

2. Both positions lie on the angle bisector of ∠NPQ. So, each is equidistant from $\overline{PN}$ and $\overline{PQ}$.

   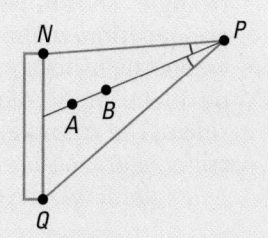

   The sides of an angle are farther from the angle bisector as you move away from the vertex. So, *A* is farther from $\overline{PN}$ and from $\overline{PQ}$ than *B* is.

   The distance may be greater if you stand at Position *A* than if you stand at Position *B*.

3. Because Position *B* is farther from the goal, you may need to move a greater distance to block the shot if you stand at Position *B*.

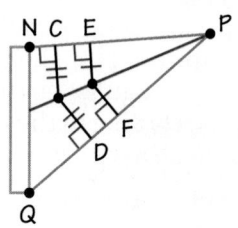

SHORT RESPONSE

1. The coordinates of $\triangle OPQ$ are $O(0, 0)$, $P(a, a)$, and $Q(2a, 0)$. Classify $\triangle OPQ$ by its side lengths. Is $\triangle OPQ$ a right triangle? *Justify* your answer.

2. The local gardening club is planting flowers on a traffic triangle. They divide the triangle into four sections, as shown. The perimeter of the middle triangle is 10 feet. What is the perimeter of the traffic triangle? *Explain* your reasoning.

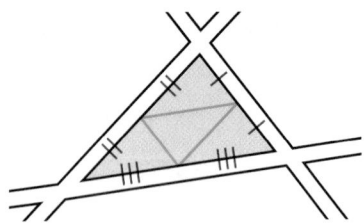

3. A wooden stepladder with a metal support is shown. The legs of the stepladder form a triangle. The support is parallel to the floor, and positioned about five inches above where the midsegment of the triangle would be. Is the length of the support from one side of the triangle to the other side of the triangle *greater than*, *less than*, or *equal to* 8 inches? *Explain* your reasoning.

16 in.

4. You are given instructions for making a triangular earring from silver wire. According to the instructions, you must first bend a wire into a triangle with side lengths of $\frac{3}{4}$ inch, $\frac{5}{8}$ inch, and $1\frac{1}{2}$ inches. *Explain* what is wrong with the first part of the instructions.

5. The centroid of $\triangle ABC$ is located at $P(-1, 2)$. The coordinates of A and B are $A(0, 6)$ and $B(-2, 4)$. What are the coordinates of vertex C? *Explain* your reasoning.

6. A college club wants to set up a booth to attract more members. They want to put the booth at a spot that is equidistant from three important buildings on campus. Without measuring, decide which spot, A or B, is the correct location for the booth. *Explain* your reasoning.

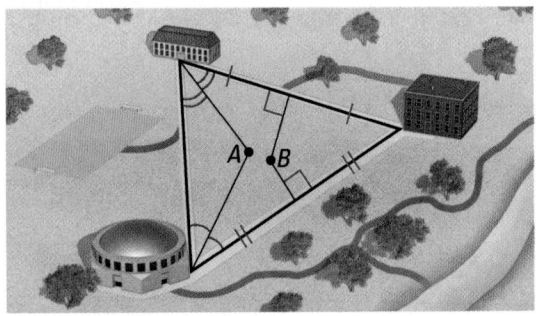

7. Contestants on a television game show must run to a well (point W), fill a bucket with water, empty it at either point A or B, and then run back to the starting point (point P). To run the shortest distance possible, which point should contestants choose, A or B? *Explain* your reasoning.

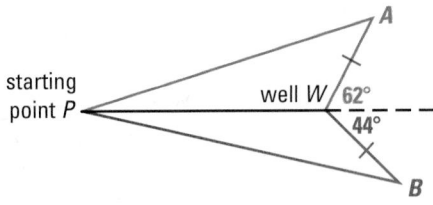

starting point P · well W · 62° · 44° · A · B

8. How is the area of the triangle formed by the midsegments of a triangle related to the area of the original triangle? Use an example to *justify* your answer.

9. You are bending an 18 inch wire to form an isosceles triangle. *Describe* the possible lengths of the base if the vertex angle is larger than 60°. *Explain* your reasoning.

MULTIPLE CHOICE

10. If △*ABC* is obtuse, which statement is always true about its circumcenter *P*?

 A *P* is equidistant from $\overline{AB}$, $\overline{BC}$, and $\overline{AC}$.

 B *P* is inside △*ABC*.

 C *P* is on △*ABC*.

 D *P* is outside △*ABC*.

11. Which conclusion about the value of *x* can be made from the diagram?

 A *x* < 8

 B *x* = 8

 C *x* > 8

 D No conclusion can be made.

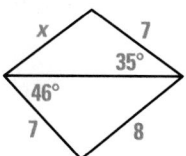

GRIDDED ANSWER

12. Find the perimeter of △*RST*.

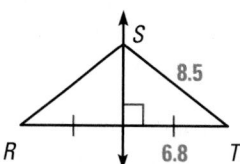

13. In the diagram, *N* is the incenter of △*ABC*. Find *NF*.

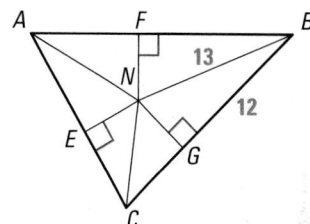

EXTENDED RESPONSE

14. A new sport is to be played on the triangular playing field shown with a basket located at a point that is equidistant from each side line.

 a. Copy the diagram and show how to find the location of the basket. *Describe* your method.

 b. What theorem can you use to verify that the location you chose in part (a) is correct? *Explain*.

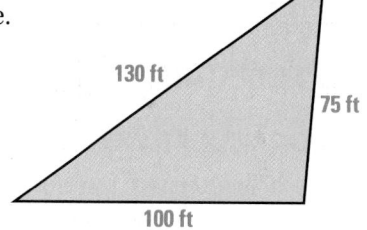

15. A segment has endpoints *A*(8, −1) and *B*(6, 3).

 a. Graph $\overline{AB}$. Then find the midpoint *C* of $\overline{AB}$ and the slope of $\overline{AB}$.

 b. Use what you know about slopes of perpendicular lines to find the slope of the perpendicular bisector of $\overline{AB}$. Then sketch the perpendicular bisector of $\overline{AB}$ and write an equation of the line. *Explain* your steps.

 c. Find a point *D* that is a solution to the equation you wrote in part (b). Find *AD* and *BD*. What do you notice? What theorem does this illustrate?

16. The coordinates of △*JKL* are *J*(−2, 2), *K*(4, 8), and *L*(10, −4).

 a. Find the coordinates of the centroid *M*. Show your steps.

 b. Find the mean of the *x*-coordinates of the three vertices and the mean of the *y*-coordinates of the three vertices. *Compare* these results with the coordinates of the centroid. What do you notice?

 c. Is the relationship in part (b) true for △*JKP* with *P*(1, −1)? *Explain*.

6 Similarity

Before

In previous courses and in Chapters 1–5, you learned the following skills, which you'll use in Chapter 6: using properties of parallel lines, using properties of triangles, simplifying expressions, and finding perimeter.

Prerequisite Skills

VOCABULARY CHECK

1. The alternate interior angles formed when a transversal intersects two __?__ lines are congruent.

2. Two triangles are congruent if and only if their corresponding parts are __?__.

SKILLS AND ALGEBRA CHECK

Simplify the expression. *(Review pp. 870, 874 for 6.1.)*

3. $\dfrac{9 \cdot 20}{15}$ 4. $\dfrac{15}{25}$ 5. $\dfrac{3 + 4 + 5}{6 + 8 + 10}$ 6. $\sqrt{5(5 \cdot 7)}$

Find the perimeter of the rectangle with the given dimensions.
(Review p. 49 for 6.1, 6.2.)

7. $\ell = 5$ in., $w = 12$ in.   8. $\ell = 30$ ft, $w = 10$ ft   9. $A = 56$ m^2, $\ell = 8$ m

10. Find the slope of a line parallel to the line whose equation is $y - 4 = 7(x + 2)$. *(Review p. 171 for 6.5.)*

@HomeTutor Prerequisite skills practice at classzone.com

In Chapter 6, you will apply the big ideas listed below and reviewed in the Chapter Summary on page 417. You will also use the key vocabulary listed below.

Big Ideas

1 Using ratios and proportions to solve geometry problems
2 Showing that triangles are similar
3 Using indirect measurement and similarity

KEY VOCABULARY

- ratio, *p. 356*
- proportion, *p. 358*
  means, extremes
- geometric mean, *p. 359*
- scale drawing, *p. 365*

- scale, *p. 365*
- similar polygons, *p. 372*
- scale factor of two similar polygons, *p. 373*
- dilation, *p. 409*

- center of dilation, *p. 409*
- scale factor of a dilation, *p. 409*
- reduction, *p. 409*
- enlargement, *p. 409*

You can use similarity to measure lengths indirectly. For example, you can use similar triangles to find the height of a tree.

Animated Geometry

The animation illustrated below for Exercise 33 on page 394 helps you answer this question: What is the height of the tree?

You can use proportional reasoning to estimate the height of a tall tree.

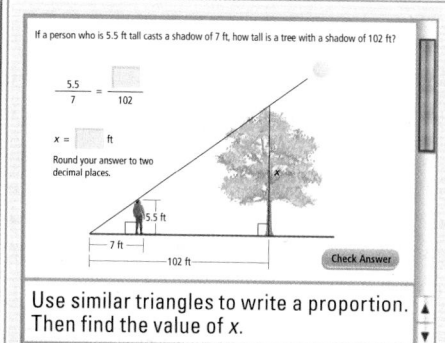

If a person who is 5.5 ft tall casts a shadow of 7 ft, how tall is a tree with a shadow of 102 ft?

$$\frac{5.5}{7} = \frac{}{102}$$

$x =$ ___ ft

Round your answer to two decimal places.

5.5 ft
7 ft
102 ft

Check Answer

Use similar triangles to write a proportion. Then find the value of *x*.

Animated Geometry at classzone.com

Other animations for Chapter 6: pages 365, 375, 391, 407, and 414

6.1 Ratios, Proportions, and the Geometric Mean

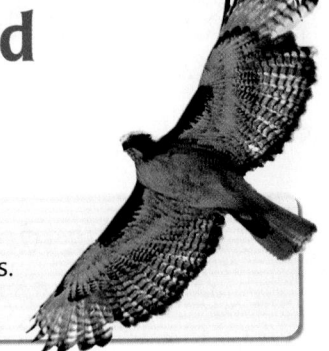

Before	You solved problems by writing and solving equations.
Now	You will solve problems by writing and solving proportions.
Why?	So you can estimate bird populations, as in Ex. 62.

Key Vocabulary
• ratio
• proportion
  means, extremes
• geometric mean

If a and b are two numbers or quantities and $b \neq 0$, then the **ratio of a to b** is $\frac{a}{b}$. The ratio of a to b can also be written as $a:b$.

For example, the ratio of a side length in $\triangle ABC$ to a side length in $\triangle DEF$ can be written as $\frac{2}{1}$ or $2:1$.

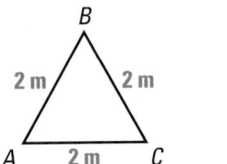
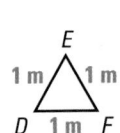

Ratios are usually expressed in simplest form. Two ratios that have the same simplified form are called *equivalent ratios*. The ratios $7:14$ and $1:2$ in the example below are *equivalent*.

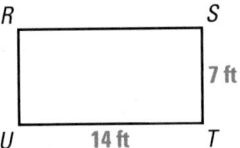

$$\frac{\text{width of } RSTU}{\text{length of } RSTU} = \frac{7 \text{ ft}}{14 \text{ ft}} = \frac{1}{2}$$

EXAMPLE 1 Simplify ratios

Simplify the ratio.

a. $64 \text{ m} : 6 \text{ m}$

b. $\dfrac{5 \text{ ft}}{20 \text{ in.}}$

Solution

REVIEW UNIT ANALYSIS
For help with measures and conversion factors, see p. 886 and the Table of Measures on p. 921.

a. Write $64 \text{ m} : 6 \text{ m}$ as $\dfrac{64 \text{ m}}{6 \text{ m}}$. Then divide out the units and simplify.

$$\frac{64 \text{ m}}{6 \text{ m}} = \frac{32}{3} = 32:3$$

b. To simplify a ratio with unlike units, multiply by a conversion factor.

$$\frac{5 \text{ ft}}{20 \text{ in.}} = \frac{5 \text{ ft}}{20 \text{ in.}} \cdot \frac{12 \text{ in.}}{1 \text{ ft}} = \frac{60}{20} = \frac{3}{1}$$

 GUIDED PRACTICE for Example 1

Simplify the ratio.

1. 24 yards to 3 yards

2. $150 \text{ cm} : 6 \text{ m}$

EXAMPLE 2 **Use a ratio to find a dimension**

PAINTING You are planning to paint a mural on a rectangular wall. You know that the perimeter of the wall is 484 feet and that the ratio of its length to its width is 9 : 2. Find the area of the wall.

Solution

WRITE EXPRESSIONS

Because the ratio in Example 2 is 9 : 2, you can write an equivalent ratio to find expressions for the length and width.

$$\frac{\text{length}}{\text{width}} = \frac{9}{2}$$
$$= \frac{9}{2} \cdot \frac{x}{x}$$
$$= \frac{9x}{2x}.$$

STEP 1 **Write** expressions for the length and width. Because the ratio of length to width is 9 : 2, you can represent the length by $9x$ and the width by $2x$.

STEP 2 **Solve** an equation to find x.

$2\ell + 2w = P$	**Formula for perimeter of rectangle**
$2(9x) + 2(2x) = 484$	**Substitute for ℓ, w, and P.**
$22x = 484$	**Multiply and combine like terms.**
$x = 22$	**Divide each side by 22.**

STEP 3 **Evaluate** the expressions for the length and width. Substitute the value of x into each expression.

$$\text{Length} = 9x = 9(22) = 198 \qquad \text{Width} = 2x = 2(22) = 44$$

▸ The wall is 198 feet long and 44 feet wide, so its area is 198 ft • 44 ft = 8712 ft^2.

EXAMPLE 3 **Use extended ratios**

ALGEBRA The measures of the angles in $\triangle CDE$ are in the *extended ratio* of 1 : 2 : 3. Find the measures of the angles.

Solution

Begin by sketching the triangle. Then use the extended ratio of 1 : 2 : 3 to label the measures as $x°$, $2x°$, and $3x°$.

$x° + 2x° + 3x° = 180°$	**Triangle Sum Theorem**
$6x = 180$	**Combine like terms.**
$x = 30$	**Divide each side by 6.**

▸ The angle measures are $30°$, $2(30°) = 60°$, and $3(30°) = 90°$.

 GUIDED PRACTICE for Examples 2 and 3

3. The perimeter of a room is 48 feet and the ratio of its length to its width is 7 : 5. Find the length and width of the room.

4. A triangle's angle measures are in the extended ratio of 1 : 3 : 5. Find the measures of the angles.

PROPORTIONS An equation that states that two ratios are equal is called a **proportion**.

$$\text{extreme} \longrightarrow \frac{a}{b} = \frac{c}{d} \longleftarrow \text{mean}$$
$$\text{mean} \longrightarrow \qquad \qquad \longleftarrow \text{extreme}$$

The numbers b and c are the **means** of the proportion. The numbers a and d are the **extremes** of the proportion.

The property below can be used to solve proportions. To *solve a proportion*, you find the value of any variable in the proportion.

KEY CONCEPT *For Your Notebook*

A Property of Proportions

1. **Cross Products Property** In a proportion, the product of the extremes equals the product of the means.

If $\dfrac{a}{b} = \dfrac{c}{d}$ where $b \neq 0$ and $d \neq 0$, then $ad = bc$.

$$\frac{2}{3} = \frac{4}{6} \qquad \begin{array}{l} 3 \cdot 4 = 12 \\ 2 \cdot 6 = 12 \end{array}$$

PROPORTIONS
You will learn more properties of proportions on p. 364.

EXAMPLE 4 Solve proportions

xy ALGEBRA Solve the proportion.

a. $\dfrac{5}{10} = \dfrac{x}{16}$

b. $\dfrac{1}{y + 1} = \dfrac{2}{3y}$

Solution

ANOTHER WAY
In part (a), you could multiply each side by the denominator, 16. Then $16 \cdot \dfrac{5}{10} = 16 \cdot \dfrac{x}{16}$, so $8 = x$.

a. $\dfrac{5}{10} = \dfrac{x}{16}$ Write original proportion.

$5 \cdot 16 = 10 \cdot x$ Cross Products Property

$80 = 10x$ Multiply.

$8 = x$ Divide each side by 10.

b. $\dfrac{1}{y + 1} = \dfrac{2}{3y}$ Write original proportion.

$1 \cdot 3y = 2(y + 1)$ Cross Products Property

$3y = 2y + 2$ Distributive Property

$y = 2$ Subtract 2y from each side.

✓ **GUIDED PRACTICE** for Example 4

Solve the proportion.

5. $\dfrac{2}{x} = \dfrac{5}{8}$

6. $\dfrac{1}{x - 3} = \dfrac{4}{3x}$

7. $\dfrac{y - 3}{7} = \dfrac{y}{14}$

EXAMPLE 5 Solve a real-world problem

SCIENCE As part of an environmental study, you need to estimate the number of trees in a 150 acre area. You count 270 trees in a 2 acre area and you notice that the trees seem to be evenly distributed. Estimate the total number of trees.

Solution

Write and solve a proportion involving two ratios that compare the number of trees with the area of the land.

$$\frac{270}{2} = \frac{n}{150} \quad \longleftarrow \text{ number of trees} \atop \longleftarrow \text{ area in acres}$$ Write proportion.

$$270 \cdot 150 = 2 \cdot n$$ Cross Products Property

$$20{,}250 = n$$ Simplify.

▶ There are about 20,250 trees in the 150 acre area.

KEY CONCEPT *For Your Notebook*

Geometric Mean

The **geometric mean** of two positive numbers a and b is the positive number x that satisfies $\frac{a}{x} = \frac{x}{b}$. So, $x^2 = ab$ and $x = \sqrt{ab}$.

EXAMPLE 6 Find a geometric mean

Find the geometric mean of 24 and 48.

Solution

$$x = \sqrt{ab}$$ Definition of geometric mean

$$= \sqrt{24 \cdot 48}$$ Substitute 24 for a and 48 for b.

$$= \sqrt{24 \cdot 24 \cdot 2}$$ Factor.

$$= 24\sqrt{2}$$ Simplify.

▶ The geometric mean of 24 and 48 is $24\sqrt{2} \approx 33.9$.

 GUIDED PRACTICE for Examples 5 and 6

8. WHAT IF? In Example 5, suppose you count 390 trees in a 3 acre area of the 150 acre area. Make a new estimate of the total number of trees.

Find the geometric mean of the two numbers.

9. 12 and 27　　　　**10.** 18 and 54　　　　**11.** 16 and 18

6.1 EXERCISES

HOMEWORK KEY

○ = **WORKED-OUT SOLUTIONS**
on p. WS7 for Exs. 5, 27, and 59

★ = **STANDARDIZED TEST PRACTICE**
Exs. 2, 47, 48, 52, and 63

◆ = **MULTIPLE REPRESENTATIONS**
Ex. 66

SKILL PRACTICE

1. **VOCABULARY** Copy the proportion $\frac{m}{n} = \frac{p}{q}$. Identify the means of the proportion and the extremes of the proportion.

2. ★ **WRITING** Write three ratios that are equivalent to the ratio $3:4$. *Explain* how you found the ratios.

EXAMPLE 1
on p. 356
for Exs. 3–17

SIMPLIFYING RATIOS Simplify the ratio.

3. $\$20:\$5$

4. $\dfrac{15 \text{ cm}^2}{12 \text{ cm}^2}$

5. $6 \text{ L}:10 \text{ mL}$

6. $\dfrac{1 \text{ mi}}{20 \text{ ft}}$

7. $\dfrac{7 \text{ ft}}{12 \text{ in.}}$

8. $\dfrac{80 \text{ cm}}{2 \text{ m}}$

9. $\dfrac{3 \text{ lb}}{10 \text{ oz}}$

10. $\dfrac{2 \text{ gallons}}{18 \text{ quarts}}$

WRITING RATIOS Find the ratio of the width to the length of the rectangle. Then simplify the ratio.

11.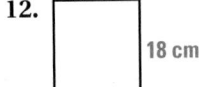
5 in.
15 in.

12.
18 cm
16 cm

13.
320 cm
10 m

FINDING RATIOS Use the number line to find the ratio of the distances.

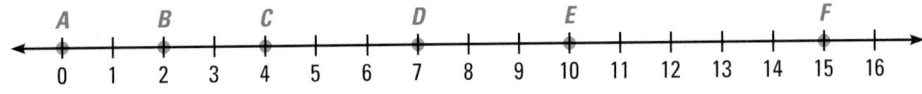

14. $\dfrac{AD}{CF}$

15. $\dfrac{BD}{AB}$

16. $\dfrac{CE}{EF}$

17. $\dfrac{BE}{CE}$

EXAMPLE 2
on p. 357
for Exs. 18–19

18. **PERIMETER** The perimeter of a rectangle is 154 feet. The ratio of the length to the width is $10:1$. Find the length and the width.

19. **SEGMENT LENGTHS** In the diagram, $AB:BC$ is $2:7$ and $AC = 36$. Find AB and BC.

36
A   B   C

EXAMPLE 3
on p. 357
for Exs. 20–22

USING EXTENDED RATIOS The measures of the angles of a triangle are in the extended ratio given. Find the measures of the angles of the triangle.

20. $3:5:10$

21. $2:7:9$

22. $11:12:13$

EXAMPLE 4
on p. 358
for Exs. 23–30

ALGEBRA Solve the proportion.

23. $\dfrac{6}{x} = \dfrac{3}{2}$

24. $\dfrac{y}{20} = \dfrac{3}{10}$

25. $\dfrac{2}{7} = \dfrac{12}{z}$

26. $\dfrac{j+1}{5} = \dfrac{4}{10}$

27. $\dfrac{1}{c+5} = \dfrac{3}{24}$

28. $\dfrac{4}{a-3} = \dfrac{2}{5}$

29. $\dfrac{1+3b}{4} = \dfrac{5}{2}$

30. $\dfrac{3}{2p+5} = \dfrac{1}{9p}$

EXAMPLE 6
on p. 359
for Exs. 31–36

GEOMETRIC MEAN **Find the geometric mean of the two numbers.**

31. 2 and 18　　　　　**32.** 4 and 25　　　　　**33.** 32 and 8

34. 4 and 16　　　　　**35.** 2 and 25　　　　　**36.** 6 and 20

37. ERROR ANALYSIS A student incorrectly simplified the ratio. *Describe* and correct the student's error.

$$\frac{8 \text{ in.}}{3 \text{ ft}} = \frac{8 \text{ in.}}{3 \text{ ft}} \cdot \frac{12 \text{ in.}}{1 \text{ ft}} = \frac{96 \text{ in.}}{3 \text{ ft}} = \frac{32 \text{ in.}}{1 \text{ ft}}$$

WRITING RATIOS Let $x = 10$, $y = 3$, and $z = 8$. **Write the ratio in simplest form.**

38. $x : z$　　**39.** $\dfrac{8y}{x}$　　**40.** $\dfrac{4}{2x + 2z}$　　**41.** $\dfrac{2x - z}{3y}$

ALGEBRA **Solve the proportion.**

42. $\dfrac{2x + 5}{3} = \dfrac{x - 5}{4}$　　**43.** $\dfrac{2 - s}{3} = \dfrac{2s + 1}{5}$　　**44.** $\dfrac{15}{m} = \dfrac{m}{5}$　　**45.** $\dfrac{7}{q + 1} = \dfrac{q - 1}{5}$

46. ANGLE MEASURES The ratio of the measures of two supplementary angles is 5 : 3. Find the measures of the angles.

47. ★ SHORT RESPONSE The ratio of the measure of an exterior angle of a triangle to the measure of the adjacent interior angle is 1 : 4. Is the triangle *acute* or *obtuse*? *Explain* how you found your answer.

48. ★ SHORT RESPONSE Without knowing its side lengths, can you determine the ratio of the perimeter of a square to the length of one of its sides? *Explain.*

ALGEBRA **In Exercises 49–51, the ratio of two side lengths for the triangle is given. Solve for the variable.**

49. $AB : BC$ is 3 : 8.　　**50.** $AB : BC$ is 3 : 4.　　**51.** $AB : BC$ is 5 : 9.

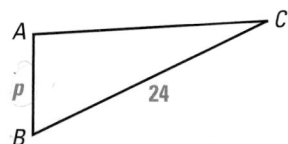　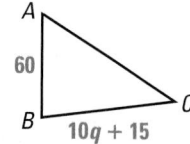　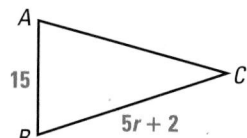

52. ★ MULTIPLE CHOICE What is a value of x that makes $\dfrac{x}{3} = \dfrac{4x}{x + 3}$ true?

  (A) 3　　　　**(B)** 4　　　　**(C)** 9　　　　**(D)** 12

53. AREA The area of a rectangle is 4320 square inches. The ratio of the width to the length is 5 : 6. Find the length and the width.

54. COORDINATE GEOMETRY The points $(-3, 2)$, $(1, 1)$, and $(x, 0)$ are collinear. Use slopes to write a proportion to find the value of x.

55. ALGEBRA Use the proportions $\dfrac{a + b}{2a - b} = \dfrac{5}{4}$ and $\dfrac{b}{a + 9} = \dfrac{5}{9}$ to find a and b.

56. CHALLENGE Find the ratio of x to y given that $\dfrac{5}{y} + \dfrac{7}{x} = 24$ and $\dfrac{12}{y} + \dfrac{2}{x} = 24$.

EXAMPLE 2
on p. 357
for Ex. 57

57. TILING The perimeter of a room is 66 feet. The ratio of its length to its width is 6 : 5. You want to tile the floor with 12 inch square tiles. Find the length and width of the room, and the area of the floor. How many tiles will you need? The tiles cost $1.98 each. What is the total cost to tile the floor?

@HomeTutor for problem solving help at classzone.com

58. GEARS The *gear ratio* of two gears is the ratio of the number of teeth of the larger gear to the number of teeth of the smaller gear. In a set of three gears, the ratio of Gear A to Gear B is equal to the ratio of Gear B to Gear C. Gear A has 36 teeth and Gear C has 16 teeth. How many teeth does Gear B have?

@HomeTutor for problem solving help at classzone.com

59. TRAIL MIX You need to make 36 one-half cup bags of trail mix for a class trip. The recipe calls for peanuts, chocolate chips, and raisins in the extended ratio 5 : 1 : 4. How many cups of each item do you need?

60. PAPER SIZES International standard paper sizes are commonly used all over the world. The various sizes all have the same width-to-length ratios. Two sizes of paper are shown, called A3 and A2. The distance labeled x is the geometric mean of 297 mm and 594 mm. Find the value of x.

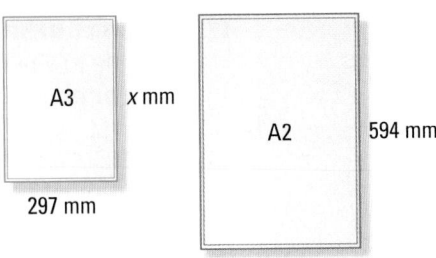

61. BATTING AVERAGE The batting average of a baseball player is the ratio of the number of hits to the number of official at-bats. In 2004, Johnny Damon of the Boston Red Sox had 621 official at-bats and a batting average of .304. Use the proportion to find the number of hits made by Johnny Damon.

$$\frac{\text{Number of hits}}{\text{Number of at-bats}} = \frac{\text{Batting average}}{1.000}$$

EXAMPLE 5
on p. 359
for Ex. 62

62. MULTI-STEP PROBLEM The population of Red-tailed hawks is increasing in many areas of the United States. One long-term survey of bird populations suggests that the Red-tailed hawk population is increasing nationally by 2.7% each year.

a. Write the ratio of hawks in year n to hawks in year $(n - 1)$.

b. In 2004, observers in Corpus Christi, TX, spotted 180 migrating Red-tailed hawks. Assuming this population follows the national trend, about how many Red-tailed hawks can they expect to see in 2005?

c. Observers in Lipan Point, AZ, spotted 951 migrating Red-tailed hawks in 2004. Assuming this population follows the national trend, about how many Red-tailed hawks can they expect to see in 2006?

63. ★ **SHORT RESPONSE** Some common computer screen resolutions are 1024 : 768, 800 : 600, and 640 : 480. *Explain* why these ratios are equivalent.

64. **BIOLOGY** The larvae of the Mother-of-Pearl moth is the fastest moving caterpillar. It can run at a speed of 15 inches per second. When threatened, it can curl itself up and roll away 40 times faster than it can run. How fast can it run in miles per hour? How fast can it roll?

65. **CURRENCY EXCHANGE** Emily took 500 U.S. dollars to the bank to exchange for Canadian dollars. The exchange rate on that day was 1.2 Canadian dollars per U.S. dollar. How many Canadian dollars did she get in exchange for the 500 U.S. dollars?

66. ◆ **MULTIPLE REPRESENTATIONS** Let x and y be two positive numbers whose geometric mean is 6.

    a. Making a Table Make a table of ordered pairs (x, y) such that $\sqrt{xy} = 6$.

    b. Drawing a Graph Use the ordered pairs to make a scatter plot. Connect the points with a smooth curve.

    c. Analyzing Data Is the data linear? Why or why not?

67. **xy ALGEBRA** Use algebra to verify Property 1, the Cross Products Property.

68. **xy ALGEBRA** Show that the geometric mean of two numbers is equal to the arithmetic mean (or average) of the two numbers only when the numbers are equal. (*Hint*: Solve $\sqrt{xy} = \dfrac{x + y}{2}$ with $x, y \geq 0$.)

CHALLENGE In Exercises 69–71, use the given information to find the value(s) of x. Assume that the given quantities are nonnegative.

69. The geometric mean of the quantities $\left(\sqrt{x}\right)$ and $\left(3\sqrt{x}\right)$ is $(x - 6)$.

70. The geometric mean of the quantities $(x + 1)$ and $(2x + 3)$ is $(x + 3)$.

71. The geometric mean of the quantities $(2x + 1)$ and $(6x + 1)$ is $(4x - 1)$.

MIXED REVIEW

PREVIEW
Prepare for
Lesson 6.2
in Exs. 72–75.

Find the reciprocal. *(p. 869)*

72. -6 **73.** $\dfrac{1}{13}$ **74.** $\dfrac{-36}{3}$ **75.** -0.2

Solve the quadratic equation. *(p. 882)*

76. $5x^2 = 35$ **77.** $x^2 - 20 = 29$ **78.** $(x - 3)(x + 3) = 27$

Write the equation of the line with the given description. *(p. 180)*

79. Parallel to $y = 3x - 7$, passing through $(1, 2)$

80. Perpendicular to $y = \dfrac{1}{4}x + 5$, passing through $(0, 24)$

6.2 Use Proportions to Solve Geometry Problems

Before	You wrote and solved proportions.
Now	You will use proportions to solve geometry problems.
Why?	So you can calculate building dimensions, as in Ex. 22.

Key Vocabulary
• scale drawing
• scale

In Lesson 6.1, you learned to use the Cross Products Property to write equations that are equivalent to a given proportion. Three more ways to do this are given by the properties below.

REVIEW RECIPROCALS
For help with reciprocals, see p. 869.

KEY CONCEPT *For Your Notebook*

Additional Properties of Proportions

2. **Reciprocal Property** If two ratios are equal, then their reciprocals are also equal.

   If $\frac{a}{b} = \frac{c}{d}$, then $\frac{b}{a} = \frac{d}{c}$.

3. If you interchange the means of a proportion, then you form another true proportion.

   If $\frac{a}{b} = \frac{c}{d}$, then $\frac{a}{c} = \frac{b}{d}$.

4. In a proportion, if you add the value of each ratio's denominator to its numerator, then you form another true proportion.

   If $\frac{a}{b} = \frac{c}{d}$, then $\frac{a+b}{b} = \frac{c+d}{d}$.

EXAMPLE 1 Use properties of proportions

In the diagram, $\frac{MN}{RS} = \frac{NP}{ST}$.
Write four true proportions.

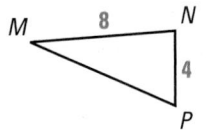
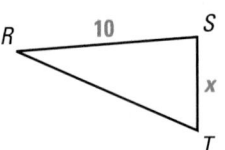

Solution

Because $\frac{MN}{RS} = \frac{NP}{ST}$, then $\frac{8}{10} = \frac{4}{x}$.

By the Reciprocal Property, the reciprocals are equal, so $\frac{10}{8} = \frac{x}{4}$.

By Property 3, you can interchange the means, so $\frac{8}{4} = \frac{10}{x}$.

By Property 4, you can add the denominators to the numerators, so $\frac{8+10}{10} = \frac{4+x}{x}$, or $\frac{18}{10} = \frac{4+x}{x}$.

EXAMPLE 2 Use proportions with geometric figures

ALGEBRA In the diagram, $\dfrac{BD}{DA} = \dfrac{BE}{EC}$.
Find *BA* and *BD*.

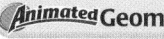

Solution

$\dfrac{BD}{DA} = \dfrac{BE}{EC}$	**Given**
$\dfrac{BD + DA}{DA} = \dfrac{BE + EC}{EC}$	**Property of Proportions (Property 4)**
$\dfrac{x}{3} = \dfrac{18 + 6}{6}$	**Substitution Property of Equality**
$6x = 3(18 + 6)$	**Cross Products Property**
$x = 12$	**Solve for *x*.**

▶ So, $BA = 12$ and $BD = 12 - 3 = 9$.

Animated Geometry at classzone.com

SCALE DRAWING A **scale drawing** is a drawing that is the same shape as the object it represents. The **scale** is a ratio that describes how the dimensions in the drawing are related to the actual dimensions of the object.

EXAMPLE 3 Find the scale of a drawing

BLUEPRINTS The blueprint shows a scale drawing of a cell phone. The length of the antenna on the blueprint is 5 centimeters. The actual length of the antenna is 2 centimeters. What is the scale of the blueprint?

Solution

To find the scale, write the ratio of a length in the drawing to an actual length, then rewrite the ratio so that the denominator is 1.

$$\frac{\text{length on blueprint}}{\text{length of antenna}} = \frac{5 \text{ cm}}{2 \text{ cm}} = \frac{5 \div 2}{2 \div 2} = \frac{2.5}{1}$$

▶ The scale of the blueprint is 2.5 cm : 1 cm.

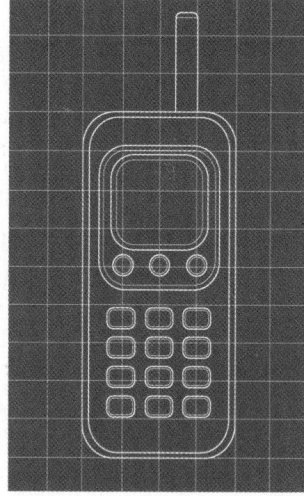

✓ **GUIDED PRACTICE** for Examples 1, 2, and 3

1. In Example 1, find the value of *x*.

2. In Example 2, $\dfrac{DE}{AC} = \dfrac{BE}{BC}$. Find *AC*.

3. **WHAT IF?** In Example 3, suppose the length of the antenna on the blueprint is 10 centimeters. Find the new scale of the blueprint.

EXAMPLE 4 Use a scale drawing

MAPS The scale of the map at the right is 1 inch : 26 miles. Find the actual distance from Pocahontas to Algona.

Solution

Use a ruler. The distance from Pocahontas to Algona on the map is about 1.25 inches. Let x be the actual distance in miles.

$$\frac{1.25 \text{ in.}}{x \text{ mi}} = \frac{1 \text{ in.}}{26 \text{ mi}} \quad \begin{array}{l} \leftarrow \text{ distance on map} \\ \leftarrow \text{ actual distance} \end{array}$$

$x = 1.25(26)$ **Cross Products Property**

$x = 32.5$ **Simplify.**

▶ The actual distance from Pocahontas to Algona is about 32.5 miles.

EXAMPLE 5 Solve a multi-step problem

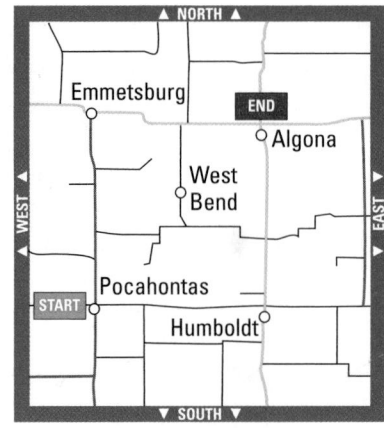

SCALE MODEL You buy a 3-D scale model of the Reunion Tower in Dallas, TX. The actual building is 560 feet tall. Your model is 10 inches tall, and the diameter of the dome on your scale model is about 2.1 inches.

a. What is the diameter of the actual dome?

b. About how many times as tall as your model is the actual building?

Solution

a. $\dfrac{10 \text{ in.}}{560 \text{ ft}} = \dfrac{2.1 \text{ in.}}{x \text{ ft}} \quad \begin{array}{l} \leftarrow \text{ measurement on model} \\ \leftarrow \text{ measurement on actual building} \end{array}$

$10x = 1176$ **Cross Products Property**

$x = 117.6$ **Solve for x.**

▶ The diameter of the actual dome is about 118 feet.

b. To simplify a ratio with unlike units, multiply by a conversion factor.

$$\frac{560 \text{ ft}}{10 \text{ in.}} = \frac{560 \cancel{\text{ft}}}{10 \cancel{\text{in.}}} \cdot \frac{12 \cancel{\text{in.}}}{1 \cancel{\text{ft}}} = 672$$

▶ The actual building is 672 times as tall as the model.

✓ **GUIDED PRACTICE** for Examples 4 and 5

4. Two cities are 96 miles from each other. The cities are 4 inches apart on a map. Find the scale of the map.

5. **WHAT IF?** Your friend has a model of the Reunion Tower that is 14 inches tall. What is the diameter of the dome on your friend's model?

6.2 EXERCISES

SKILL PRACTICE

1. **VOCABULARY** Copy and complete: A __?__ is a drawing that has the same shape as the object it represents.

2. ★ **WRITING** Suppose the scale of a model of the Eiffel Tower is 1 inch : 20 feet. *Explain* how to determine how many times taller the actual tower is than the model.

EXAMPLE 1
on p. 364
for Exs. 3–10

REASONING Copy and complete the statement.

3. If $\frac{8}{x} = \frac{3}{y}$, then $\frac{8}{3} = \frac{?}{?}$.

4. If $\frac{x}{9} = \frac{y}{20}$, then $\frac{x}{y} = \frac{?}{?}$.

5. If $\frac{x}{6} = \frac{y}{15}$, then $\frac{x+6}{6} = \frac{?}{?}$.

6. If $\frac{14}{3} = \frac{x}{y}$, then $\frac{17}{3} = \frac{?}{?}$.

REASONING Decide whether the statement is *true* or *false*.

7. If $\frac{8}{m} = \frac{n}{9}$, then $\frac{8+m}{m} = \frac{n+9}{9}$.

8. If $\frac{5}{7} = \frac{a}{b}$, then $\frac{7}{5} = \frac{a}{b}$.

9. If $\frac{d}{2} = \frac{g+10}{11}$, then $\frac{d}{g+10} = \frac{2}{11}$.

10. If $\frac{4+x}{4} = \frac{3+y}{y}$, then $\frac{x}{4} = \frac{3}{y}$.

EXAMPLE 2
on p. 365
for Exs. 11–12

PROPERTIES OF PROPORTIONS Use the diagram and the given information to find the unknown length.

(11.) Given $\frac{CB}{BA} = \frac{DE}{EF}$, find *BA*.

12. Given $\frac{XW}{XV} = \frac{YW}{ZV}$, find *ZV*.

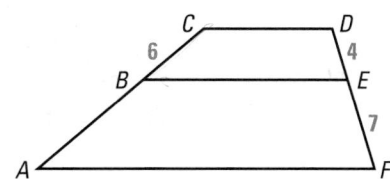

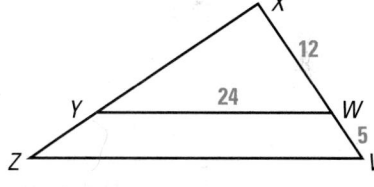

EXAMPLES 3 and 4
on pp. 365–366
for Exs. 13–14

SCALE DIAGRAMS In Exercises 13 and 14, use the diagram of the field hockey field in which 1 inch = 50 yards. Use a ruler to approximate the dimension.

(13.) Find the actual length of the field.

14. Find the actual width of the field.

15. **ERROR ANALYSIS** *Describe* and correct the error made in the reasoning.

If $\frac{a}{3} = \frac{c}{4}$, then $\frac{a+3}{3} = \frac{c+3}{4}$. ✗

PROPERTIES OF PROPORTIONS Use the diagram and the given information to find the unknown length.

16. Given $\dfrac{CA}{CB} = \dfrac{AE}{BD}$, find BD.

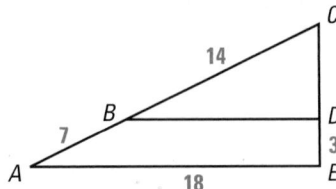

17. Given $\dfrac{SQ}{SR} = \dfrac{TV}{TU}$, find RQ.

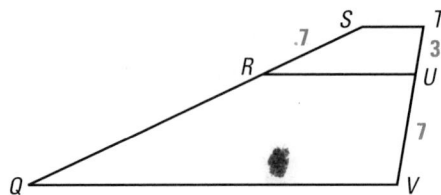

18. ★ **MULTIPLE CHOICE** If x, y, z, and q are four different numbers, and the proportion $\dfrac{x}{y} = \dfrac{z}{q}$ is true, which of the following is false?

(A) $\dfrac{y}{x} = \dfrac{q}{z}$ (B) $\dfrac{x}{z} = \dfrac{y}{q}$ (C) $\dfrac{y}{x} = \dfrac{z}{q}$ (D) $\dfrac{x+y}{y} = \dfrac{z+q}{q}$

CHALLENGE Two number patterns are *proportional* if there is a nonzero number k such that $(a_1, b_1, c_1, \ldots) = k(a_2, b_2, c_2, \ldots) = ka_2, kb_2, kc_2, \ldots$.

19. Given the relationship $(8, 16, 20) = k(2, 4, 5)$, find k.

20. Given that $a_1 = ka_2$, $b_1 = kb_2$, and $c_1 = kc_2$, show that $\dfrac{a_1}{a_2} = \dfrac{b_1}{b_2} = \dfrac{c_1}{c_2}$.

21. Given that $a_1 = ka_2$, $b_1 = kb_2$, and $c_1 = kc_2$, show that $\dfrac{a_1 + b_1 + c_1}{a_2 + b_2 + c_2} = k$.

PROBLEM SOLVING

EXAMPLE 5
on p. 366
for Ex. 22

22. **ARCHITECTURE** A basket manufacturer has headquarters in an office building that has the same shape as a basket they sell.

   a. The bottom of the basket is a rectangle with length 15 inches and width 10 inches. The base of the building is a rectangle with length 192 feet. What is the width of the base of the building?

   b. About how many times as long as the bottom of the basket is the base of the building?

   @HomeTutor for problem solving help at classzone.com

Longaberger Company Home Office
Newark, Ohio

23. **MAP SCALE** A street on a map is 3 inches long. The actual street is 1 mile long. Find the scale of the map.

   @HomeTutor for problem solving help at classzone.com

24. ★ **MULTIPLE CHOICE** A model train engine is 12 centimeters long. The actual engine is 18 meters long. What is the scale of the model?

(A) 3 cm : 2 m   (B) 1 cm : 1.5 m   (C) 1 cm : 3 m   (D) 200 cm : 3 m

○ = **WORKED-OUT SOLUTIONS**
    on p. WS1

★ = **STANDARDIZED TEST PRACTICE**

MAP READING The map of a hiking trail has a scale of 1 inch : 3.2 miles. Use a ruler to approximate the actual distance between the two shelters.

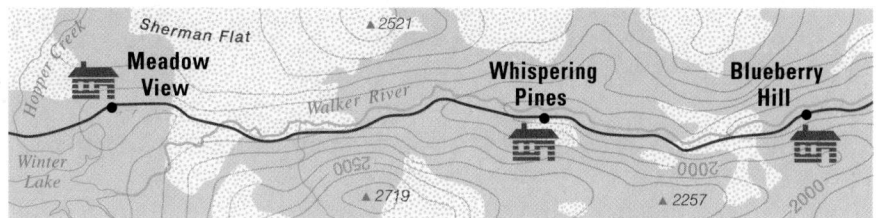

25. Meadow View and Whispering Pines

26. Whispering Pines and Blueberry Hill

27. POLLEN The photograph shows a particle of goldenrod pollen that has been magnified under a microscope. The scale of the photograph is 900 : 1. Use a ruler to estimate the width in millimeters of the particle.

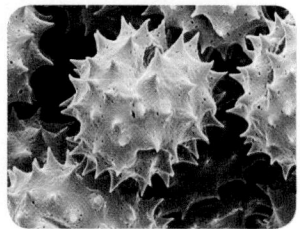

RAMP DESIGN Assume that the wheelchair ramps described each have a slope of $\frac{1}{12}$, which is the maximum slope recommended for a wheelchair ramp.

28. A wheelchair ramp has a 21 foot run. What is its rise?

29. A wheelchair ramp rises 4 feet. What is its run?

30. STATISTICS Researchers asked 4887 people to pick a number between 1 and 10. The results are shown in the table below.

Answer	1	2	3	4	5
Percent	4.2%	5.1%	11.4%	10.5%	10.7%
Answer	6	7	8	9	10
Percent	10.0%	27.2%	8.8%	6.0%	6.1%

a. Estimate the number of people who picked the number 3.

b. You ask a participant what number she picked. Is the participant more likely to answer 6 or 7? *Explain.*

c. Conduct this experiment with your classmates. Make a table in which you compare the new percentages with the ones given in the original survey. Why might they be different?

XY ALGEBRA Use algebra to verify the property of proportions.

31. Property 2   **32.** Property 3   **33.** Property 4

REASONING Use algebra to *explain* why the property of proportions is true.

34. If $\dfrac{a-b}{a+b} = \dfrac{c-d}{c+d}$, then $\dfrac{a}{b} = \dfrac{c}{d}$.

35. If $\dfrac{a+c}{b+d} = \dfrac{a-c}{b-d}$, then $\dfrac{a}{b} = \dfrac{c}{d}$.

36. If $\dfrac{a}{b} = \dfrac{c}{d} = \dfrac{e}{f}$, then $\dfrac{a+c+e}{b+d+f} = \dfrac{a}{b}$. (*Hint:* Let $\dfrac{a}{b} = r$.)

37. **CHALLENGE** When fruit is dehydrated, water is removed from the fruit. The water content in fresh apricots is about 86%. In dehydrated apricots, the water content is about 75%. Suppose 5 kilograms of raw apricots are dehydrated. How many kilograms of water are removed from the fruit? What is the approximate weight of the dehydrated apricots?

MIXED REVIEW

38. Over the weekend, Claudia drove a total of 405 miles, driving twice as far on Saturday as on Sunday. How far did Claudia travel each day? *(p. 65)*

Prepare for Lesson 6.3 in Exs. 39–40.

Identify all pairs of congruent corresponding parts. Then write another congruence statement for the figures. *(p. 225)*

39. $\triangle XYZ \cong \triangle LMN$

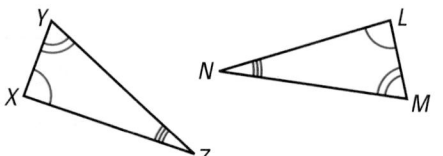

40. $DEFG \cong QRST$

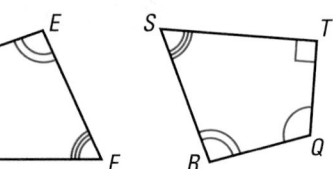

QUIZ *for Lessons 6.1–6.2*

Solve the proportion. *(p. 356)*

1. $\dfrac{10}{y} = \dfrac{5}{2}$ **2.** $\dfrac{x}{6} = \dfrac{9}{3}$ **3.** $\dfrac{1}{a+3} = \dfrac{4}{16}$ **4.** $\dfrac{6}{d-6} = \dfrac{4}{8}$

Copy and complete the statement. *(p. 364)*

5. If $\dfrac{9}{x} = \dfrac{5}{2}$, then $\dfrac{9}{5} = \dfrac{?}{?}$.

6. If $\dfrac{x}{15} = \dfrac{y}{21}$, then $\dfrac{x}{y} = \dfrac{?}{?}$.

7. If $\dfrac{x}{8} = \dfrac{y}{12}$, then $\dfrac{x+8}{8} = \dfrac{?}{?}$.

8. If $\dfrac{32}{5} = \dfrac{x}{y}$, then $\dfrac{37}{5} = \dfrac{?}{?}$.

9. In the diagram, $AD = 10$, B is the midpoint of $\overline{AD}$, and AC is the geometric mean of AB and AD. Find AC. *(p. 364)*

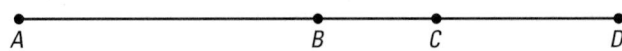

370 **EXTRA PRACTICE** for Lesson 6.2, p. 906   **ONLINE QUIZ** at classzone.com

6.3 Similar Polygons

MATERIALS · metric ruler · protractor

QUESTION **When a figure is reduced, how are the corresponding angles related? How are the corresponding lengths related?**

EXPLORE **Compare measures of lengths and angles in two photos**

STEP 1 *Measure segments* Photo 2 is a reduction of Photo 1. In each photo, find *AB* to the nearest millimeter. Write the ratio of the length of $\overline{AB}$ in Photo 1 to the length of $\overline{AB}$ in Photo 2.

STEP 2 *Measure angles* Use a protractor to find the measure of ∠1 in each photo. Write the ratio of *m*∠1 in Photo 1 to *m*∠1 in Photo 2.

STEP 3 *Find measurements* Copy and complete the table. Use the same units for each measurement. Record your results in a table.

Photo 1

Measurement	Photo 1	Photo 2	Photo 1 / Photo 2
AB	?	?	?
AC	?	?	?
DE	?	?	?
m∠1	?	?	?
m∠2	?	?	?

Photo 2

DRAW CONCLUSIONS **Use your observations to complete these exercises**

1. Make a conjecture about the relationship between corresponding lengths when a figure is reduced.

2. Make a conjecture about the relationship between corresponding angles when a figure is reduced.

3. Suppose the measure of an angle in Photo 2 is 35°. What is the measure of the corresponding angle in Photo 1?

4. Suppose a segment in Photo 2 is 1 centimeter long. What is the measure of the corresponding segment in Photo 1?

5. Suppose a segment in Photo 1 is 5 centimeters long. What is the measure of the corresponding segment in Photo 2?

6.3 Use Similar Polygons

Before	You used proportions to solve geometry problems.
Now	You will use proportions to identify similar polygons.
Why?	So you can solve science problems, as in Ex. 34.

Key Vocabulary
• **similar polygons**
• **scale factor**

Two polygons are **similar polygons** if corresponding angles are congruent and corresponding side lengths are proportional.

In the diagram below, *ABCD* is similar to *EFGH*. You can write "*ABCD* is similar to *EFGH*" as *ABCD* ~ *EFGH*. Notice in the similarity statement that the corresponding vertices are listed in the same order.

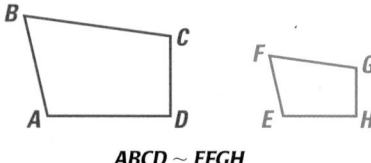

ABCD ~ *EFGH*

Corresponding angles

$\angle A \cong \angle E, \angle B \cong \angle F, \angle C \cong \angle G,$ and $\angle D \cong \angle H$

Ratios of corresponding sides

$$\frac{AB}{EF} = \frac{BC}{FG} = \frac{CD}{GH} = \frac{DA}{HE}$$

EXAMPLE 1 Use similarity statements

In the diagram, $\triangle RST \sim \triangle XYZ$.

a. List all pairs of congruent angles.

b. Check that the ratios of corresponding side lengths are equal.

READ VOCABULARY

In a *statement of proportionality,* any pair of ratios forms a true proportion.

c. Write the ratios of the corresponding side lengths in a *statement of proportionality.*

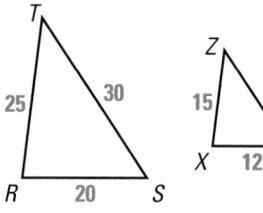

Solution

a. $\angle R \cong \angle X, \angle S \cong \angle Y,$ and $\angle T \cong \angle Z.$

b. $\dfrac{RS}{XY} = \dfrac{20}{12} = \dfrac{5}{3}$ $\dfrac{ST}{YZ} = \dfrac{30}{18} = \dfrac{5}{3}$ $\dfrac{TR}{ZX} = \dfrac{25}{15} = \dfrac{5}{3}$

c. Because the ratios in part (b) are equal, $\dfrac{RS}{XY} = \dfrac{ST}{YZ} = \dfrac{TR}{ZX}.$

 GUIDED PRACTICE for Example 1

1. Given $\triangle JKL \sim \triangle PQR$, list all pairs of congruent angles. Write the ratios of the corresponding side lengths in a statement of proportionality.

SCALE FACTOR If two polygons are similar, then the ratio of the lengths of two corresponding sides is called the **scale factor**. In Example 1, the common ratio of $\frac{5}{3}$ is the scale factor of $\triangle RST$ to $\triangle XYZ$.

EXAMPLE 2 **Find the scale factor**

Determine whether the polygons are similar. If they are, write a similarity statement and find the scale factor of *ZYXW* to *FGHJ*.

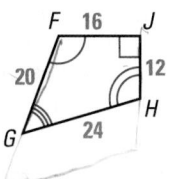 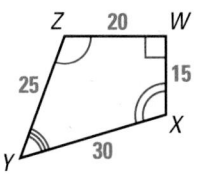

Solution

STEP 1 **Identify** pairs of congruent angles. From the diagram, you can see that $\angle Z \cong \angle F$, $\angle Y \cong \angle G$, and $\angle X \cong \angle H$. Angles W and J are right angles, so $\angle W \cong \angle J$. So, the corresponding angles are congruent.

STEP 2 **Show** that corresponding side lengths are proportional.

$$\frac{ZY}{FG} = \frac{25}{20} = \frac{5}{4} \qquad \frac{YX}{GH} = \frac{30}{24} = \frac{5}{4} \qquad \frac{XW}{HJ} = \frac{15}{12} = \frac{5}{4} \qquad \frac{WZ}{JF} = \frac{20}{16} = \frac{5}{4}$$

The ratios are equal, so the corresponding side lengths are proportional.

▶ So $ZYXW \sim FGHJ$. The scale factor of $ZYXW$ to $FGHJ$ is $\frac{5}{4}$.

EXAMPLE 3 **Use similar polygons**

XY ALGEBRA In the diagram, $\triangle DEF \sim \triangle MNP$. Find the value of x.

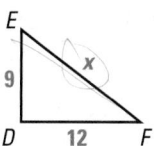 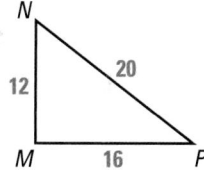

Solution

The triangles are similar, so the corresponding side lengths are proportional.

ANOTHER WAY

There are several ways to write the proportion. For example, you could write $\frac{DF}{MP} = \frac{EF}{NP}$.

$$\frac{MN}{DE} = \frac{NP}{EF} \qquad \text{Write proportion.}$$

$$\frac{12}{9} = \frac{20}{x} \qquad \text{Substitute.}$$

$$12x = 180 \qquad \text{Cross Products Property}$$

$$x = 15 \qquad \text{Solve for } x.$$

✓ **GUIDED PRACTICE** for Examples 2 and 3

In the diagram, $ABCD \sim QRST$.

2. What is the scale factor of *QRST* to *ABCD*?

3. Find the value of x.

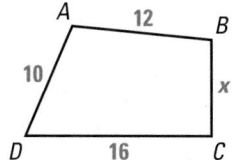 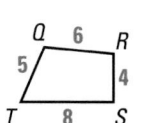

PERIMETERS The ratio of lengths in similar polygons is the same as the scale factor. Theorem 6.1 shows this is true for the perimeters of the polygons.

THEOREM *For Your Notebook*

THEOREM 6.1 Perimeters of Similar Polygons

If two polygons are similar, then the ratio of their perimeters is equal to the ratios of their corresponding side lengths.

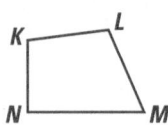 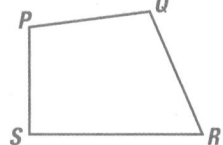

If $KLMN \sim PQRS$, then $\dfrac{KL + LM + MN + NK}{PQ + QR + RS + SP} = \dfrac{KL}{PQ} = \dfrac{LM}{QR} = \dfrac{MN}{RS} = \dfrac{NK}{SP}$.

Proof: Ex. 38, p. 379

EXAMPLE 4 **Find perimeters of similar figures**

SWIMMING A town is building a new swimming pool. An Olympic pool is rectangular with length 50 meters and width 25 meters. The new pool will be similar in shape, but only 40 meters long.

a. Find the scale factor of the new pool to an Olympic pool.

b. Find the perimeter of an Olympic pool and the new pool.

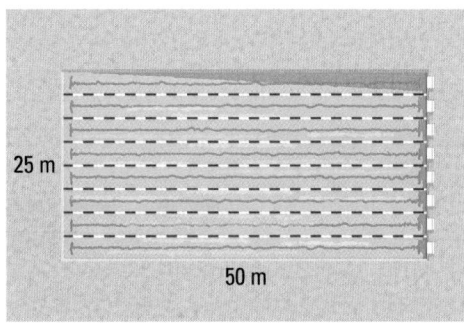

25 m

50 m

Solution

ANOTHER WAY
Another way to solve Example 4 is to write the scale factor as the decimal 0.8. Then, multiply the perimeter of the Olympic pool by the scale factor to get the perimeter of the new pool:
0.8(150) = 120.

a. Because the new pool will be similar to an Olympic pool, the scale factor is the ratio of the lengths, $\dfrac{40}{50} = \dfrac{4}{5}$.

b. The perimeter of an Olympic pool is 2(50) + 2(25) = 150 meters. You can use Theorem 6.1 to find the perimeter x of the new pool.

$\dfrac{x}{150} = \dfrac{4}{5}$ Use Theorem 6.1 to write a proportion.

$x = 120$ Multiply each side by 150 and simplify.

▶ The perimeter of the new pool is 120 meters.

✓ **GUIDED PRACTICE** for Example 4

In the diagram, $ABCDE \sim FGHJK$.

4. Find the scale factor of $FGHJK$ to $ABCDE$.

5. Find the value of x.

6. Find the perimeter of $ABCDE$.

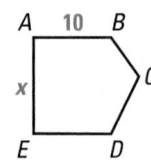 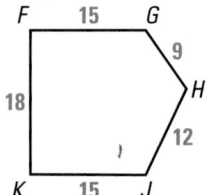

SIMILARITY AND CONGRUENCE Notice that any two congruent figures are also similar. Their scale factor is $1:1$. In $\triangle ABC$ and $\triangle DEF$, the scale factor is $\frac{5}{5} = 1$. You can write $\triangle ABC \sim \triangle DEF$ and $\triangle ABC \cong \triangle DEF$.

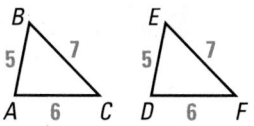

READ VOCABULARY

Corresponding lengths in similar triangles include side lengths, altitudes, medians, midsegments, and so on.

CORRESPONDING LENGTHS You know that perimeters of similar polygons are in the same ratio as corresponding side lengths. You can extend this concept to other segments in polygons.

KEY CONCEPT *For Your Notebook*

Corresponding Lengths in Similar Polygons

If two polygons are similar, then the ratio of any two corresponding lengths in the polygons is equal to the scale factor of the similar polygons.

EXAMPLE 5 Use a scale factor

In the diagram, $\triangle TPR \sim \triangle XPZ$.
Find the length of the altitude $\overline{PS}$.

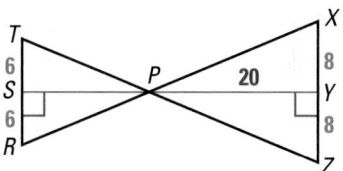

Solution

First, find the scale factor of $\triangle TPR$ to $\triangle XPZ$.

$$\frac{TR}{XZ} = \frac{6+6}{8+8} = \frac{12}{16} = \frac{3}{4}$$

Because the ratio of the lengths of the altitudes in similar triangles is equal to the scale factor, you can write the following proportion.

$\dfrac{PS}{PY} = \dfrac{3}{4}$ **Write proportion.**

$\dfrac{PS}{20} = \dfrac{3}{4}$ **Substitute 20 for PY.**

$PS = 15$ **Multiply each side by 20 and simplify.**

▶ The length of the altitude $\overline{PS}$ is 15.

Animated Geometry at classzone.com

✓ **GUIDED PRACTICE** for Example 5

7. In the diagram, $\triangle JKL \sim \triangle EFG$. Find the length of the median $\overline{KM}$.

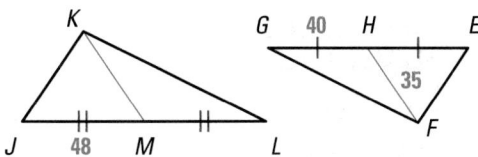

6.3 EXERCISES

HOMEWORK KEY

○ = WORKED-OUT SOLUTIONS
on p. WS7 for Exs. 3, 7, and 31

★ = STANDARDIZED TEST PRACTICE
Exs. 2, 6, 18, 27, 28, 35, 36, and 37

◆ = MULTIPLE REPRESENTATIONS
Ex. 33

SKILL PRACTICE

1. **VOCABULARY** Copy and complete: Two polygons are similar if corresponding angles are __?__ and corresponding side lengths are __?__ .

2. ★ **WRITING** If two polygons are congruent, must they be similar? If two polygons are similar, must they be congruent? *Explain*.

EXAMPLE 1
on p. 372
for Exs. 3–6

USING SIMILARITY List all pairs of congruent angles for the figures. Then write the ratios of the corresponding sides in a statement of proportionality.

3. $\triangle ABC \sim \triangle LMN$

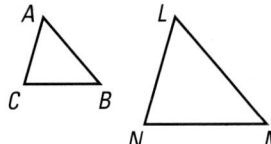

4. $DEFG \sim PQRS$

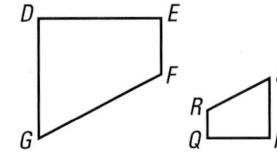

5. $HJKL \sim WXYZ$

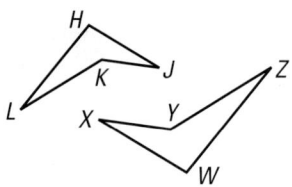

6. ★ **MULTIPLE CHOICE** Triangles *ABC* and *DEF* are similar. Which statement is *not* correct?

Ⓐ $\dfrac{BC}{EF} = \dfrac{AC}{DF}$ Ⓑ $\dfrac{AB}{DE} = \dfrac{CA}{FD}$ Ⓒ $\dfrac{CA}{FD} = \dfrac{BC}{EF}$ Ⓓ $\dfrac{AB}{EF} = \dfrac{BC}{DE}$

EXAMPLES 2 and 3
on p. 373
for Exs. 7–10

DETERMINING SIMILARITY Determine whether the polygons are similar. If they are, write a similarity statement and find the scale factor.

7.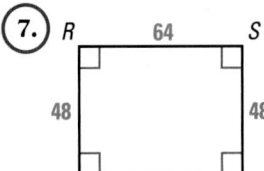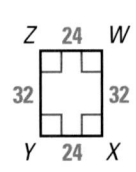

8.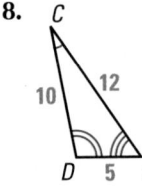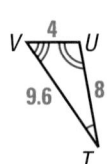

USING SIMILAR POLYGONS In the diagram, $JKLM \sim EFGH$.

9. Find the scale factor of *JKLM* to *EFGH*.

10. Find the values of *x*, *y*, and *z*.

11. Find the perimeter of each polygon.

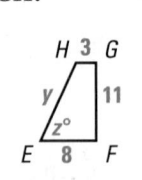 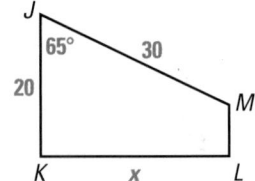

EXAMPLE 4
on p. 374
for Exs. 11–13

12. **PERIMETER** Two similar FOR SALE signs have a scale factor of 5 : 3. The large sign's perimeter is 60 inches. Find the small sign's perimeter.

13. **ERROR ANALYSIS** The triangles are similar. *Describe* and correct the error in finding the perimeter of Triangle B.

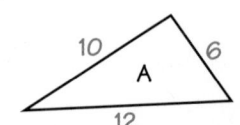 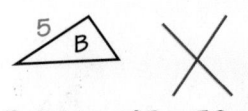

Perimeter of B = 56

REASONING Are the polygons *always*, *sometimes*, or *never* similar?

14. Two isosceles triangles

15. Two equilateral triangles

16. A right triangle and an isosceles triangle

17. A scalene triangle and an isosceles triangle

18. ★ **SHORT RESPONSE** The scale factor of Figure A to Figure B is $1 : x$. What is the scale factor of Figure B to Figure A? *Explain* your reasoning.

SIMILAR TRIANGLES The black triangles are similar. Identify the type of special segment shown in blue, and find the value of the variable.

19.

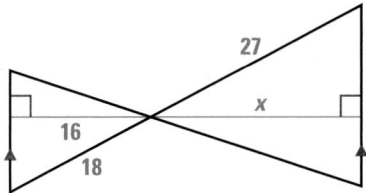

20.

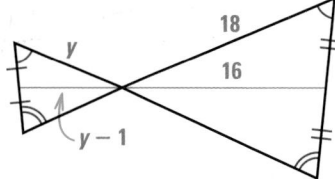

EXAMPLE 5 on p. 375 for Exs. 21–22

USING SCALE FACTOR **Triangles *NPQ* and *RST* are similar. The side lengths of △*NPQ* are 6 inches, 8 inches, and 10 inches, and the length of an altitude is 4.8 inches. The shortest side of △*RST* is 8 inches long.**

21. Find the lengths of the other two sides of △*RST*.

22. Find the length of the corresponding altitude in △*RST*.

USING SIMILAR TRIANGLES **In the diagram, △*ABC* ~ △*DEF*.**

23. Find the scale factor of △*ABC* to △*DEF*.

24. Find the unknown side lengths in both triangles.

25. Find the length of the altitude shown in △*ABC*.

26. Find and compare the areas of both triangles.

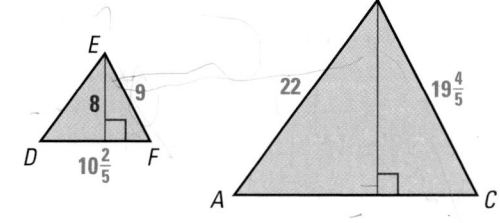

27. ★ **SHORT RESPONSE** Suppose you are told that △*PQR* ~ △*XYZ* and that the extended ratio of the angle measures in △*PQR* is $x : x + 30 : 3x$. Do you need to know anything about △*XYZ* to be able to write its extended ratio of angle measures? *Explain* your reasoning.

28. ★ **MULTIPLE CHOICE** The lengths of the legs of right triangle *ABC* are 3 feet and 4 feet. The shortest side of △*UVW* is 4.5 feet and △*UVW* ~ △*ABC*. How long is the hypotenuse of △*UVW*?

    A 1.5 ft   **B** 5 ft   **C** 6 ft   **D** 7.5 ft

29. **CHALLENGE** Copy the figure at the right and divide it into two similar figures.

30. **REASONING** Is similarity reflexive? symmetric? transitive? Give examples to support your answers.

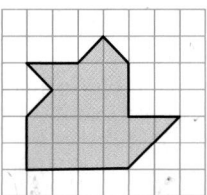

EXAMPLE 2
on p. 373 for
Exs. 31–32

31. **TENNIS** In table tennis, the table is a rectangle 9 feet long and 5 feet wide. A tennis court is a rectangle 78 feet long and 36 feet wide. Are the two surfaces similar? *Explain.* If so, find the scale factor of the tennis court to the table.

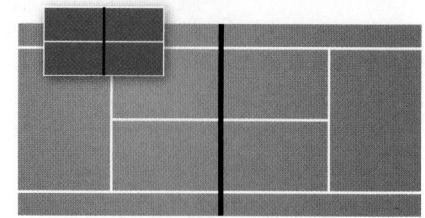

@HomeTutor for problem solving help at classzone.com

32. **DIGITAL PROJECTOR** You are preparing a computer presentation to be digitally projected onto the wall of your classroom. Your computer screen is 13.25 inches wide and 10.6 inches high. The projected image on the wall is 53 inches wide and 42.4 inches high. Are the two shapes similar? If so, find the scale factor of the computer screen to the projected image.

@HomeTutor for problem solving help at classzone.com

33. ◆ **MULTIPLE REPRESENTATIONS** Use the similar figures shown. The scale factor of Figure 1 to Figure 2 is 7 : 10.

a. **Making a Table** Copy and complete the table.

	AB	BC	CD	DE	EA
Figure 1	3.5	?	?	?	?
Figure 2	5.0	4.0	6.0	8.0	3.0

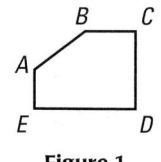
Figure 1

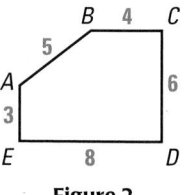
Figure 2

b. **Drawing a Graph** Graph the data in the table. Let x represent the length of a side in Figure 1 and let y represent the length of the corresponding side in Figure 2. Is the relationship linear?

c. **Writing an Equation** Write an equation that relates x and y. What is its slope? How is the slope related to the scale factor?

34. **MULTI-STEP PROBLEM** During a total eclipse of the sun, the moon is directly in line with the sun and blocks the sun's rays. The distance ED between Earth and the moon is 240,000 miles, the distance DA between Earth and the sun is 93,000,000 miles, and the radius AB of the sun is 432,500 miles.

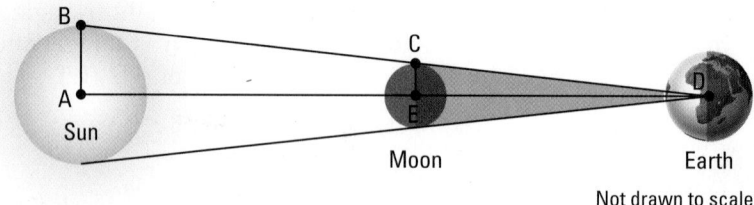

Not drawn to scale

a. Copy the diagram and label the known distances.

b. In the diagram, $\triangle BDA \sim \triangle CDE$. Use this fact to explain a total eclipse of the sun.

c. Estimate the radius CE of the moon.

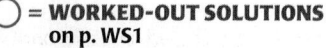
= WORKED-OUT SOLUTIONS
on p. WS1

= STANDARDIZED
TEST PRACTICE

= MULTIPLE
REPRESENTATIONS

17. ERROR ANALYSIS A student uses the proportion $\frac{4}{6} = \frac{5}{x}$ to find the value of *x* in the figure. *Explain* why this proportion is incorrect and write a correct proportion.

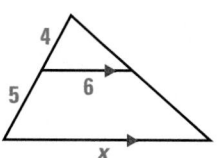

★ **OPEN-ENDED MATH** In Exercises 18 and 19, make a sketch that can be used to show that the statement is false.

18. If two pairs of sides of two triangles are congruent, then the triangles are similar.

19. If the ratios of two pairs of sides of two triangles are proportional, then the triangles are similar.

20. ★ **MULTIPLE CHOICE** In the figure at the right, find the length of $\overline{BD}$.

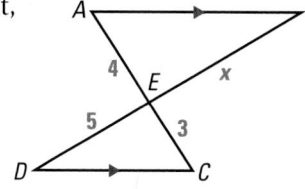

Ⓐ $\frac{35}{3}$ Ⓑ $\frac{37}{5}$

Ⓒ $\frac{20}{3}$ Ⓓ $\frac{12}{5}$

 ALGEBRA Find coordinates for point *E* so that $\triangle ABC \sim \triangle ADE$.

21. $A(0, 0)$, $B(0, 4)$, $C(8, 0)$, $D(0, 5)$, $E(x, y)$

22. $A(0, 0)$, $B(0, 3)$, $C(4, 0)$, $D(0, 7)$, $E(x, y)$

23. $A(0, 0)$, $B(0, 1)$, $C(6, 0)$, $D(0, 4)$, $E(x, y)$

24. $A(0, 0)$, $B(0, 6)$, $C(3, 0)$, $D(0, 9)$, $E(x, y)$

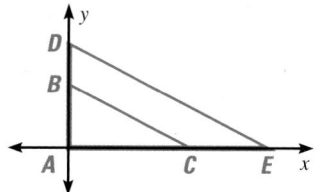

25. MULTI-STEP PROBLEM In the diagram, $\overleftrightarrow{AB} \parallel \overleftrightarrow{DC}$, $AE = 6$, $AB = 8$, $CE = 15$, and $DE = 10$.

   a. Copy the diagram and mark all given information.

   b. List two pairs of congruent angles in the diagram.

   c. Name a pair of similar triangles and write a similarity statement.

   d. Find *BE* and *DC*.

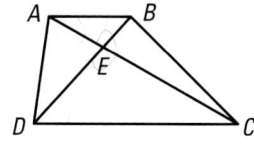

REASONING In Exercises 26–29, is it possible for $\triangle JKL$ and $\triangle XYZ$ to be similar? *Explain* why or why not.

26. $m\angle J = 71°$, $m\angle K = 52°$, $m\angle X = 71°$, and $m\angle Z = 57°$

27. $\triangle JKL$ is a right triangle and $m\angle X + m\angle Y = 150°$.

28. $m\angle J = 87°$ and $m\angle Y = 94°$

29. $m\angle J + m\angle K = 85°$ and $m\angle Y + m\angle Z = 80°$

30. CHALLENGE If $PT = x$, $PQ = 3x$, and $SR = \frac{8}{3}x$, find *PS* in terms of *x*. *Explain* your reasoning.

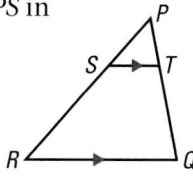

EXAMPLE 3
on p. 383
for Exs. 31–32

31. AIR HOCKEY An air hockey player returns the puck to his opponent by bouncing the puck off the wall of the table as shown. From physics, the angles that the path of the puck makes with the wall are congruent. What is the distance *d* between the puck and the wall when the opponent returns it?

@HomeTutor for problem solving help at classzone.com

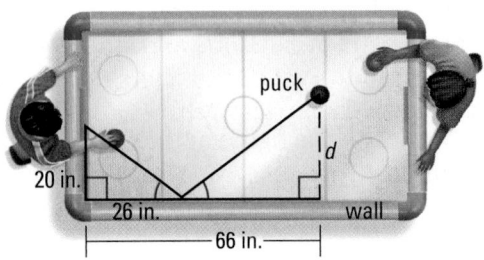

32. LAKES You can measure the width of the lake using a surveying technique, as shown in the diagram.

a. What postulate or theorem can you use to show that the triangles are similar?

b. Find the width of the lake, *WX*.

c. If *XY* = 10 meters, find *VX*.

@HomeTutor for problem solving help at classzone.com

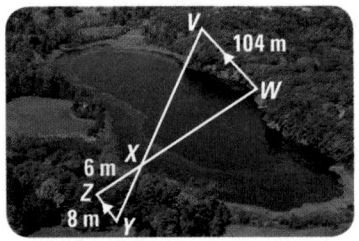

33. ★ SHORT RESPONSE *Explain* why all equilateral triangles are similar. Include sketches in your answer.

34. AERIAL PHOTOGRAPHY Low-level aerial photos can be taken using a remote-controlled camera suspended from a blimp. You want to take an aerial photo that covers a ground distance *g* of 50 meters. Use the proportion $\frac{f}{h} = \frac{n}{g}$ to estimate the altitude *h* that the blimp should fly at to take the photo. In the proportion, use *f* = 8 centimeters and *n* = 3 centimeters. These two variables are determined by the type of camera used.

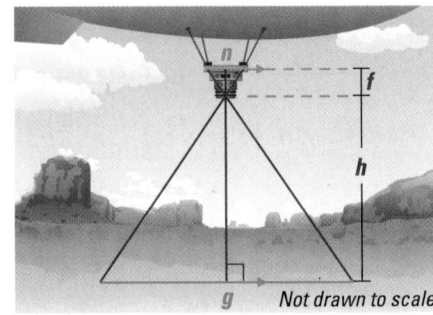

35. PROOF Use the given information to draw a sketch. Then write a proof.

GIVEN ▶ △*STU* ~ △*PQR*
Point *V* lies on $\overline{TU}$ so that $\overline{SV}$ bisects ∠*TSU*.
Point *N* lies on $\overline{QR}$ so that $\overline{PN}$ bisects ∠*QPR*.

PROVE ▶ $\dfrac{SV}{PN} = \dfrac{ST}{PQ}$

36. PROOF Prove that if an acute angle in one right triangle is congruent to an acute angle in another right triangle, then the triangles are similar.

37. **TECHNOLOGY** Use a graphing calculator or computer.

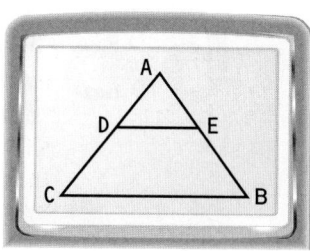

a. Draw $\triangle ABC$. Draw $\overline{DE}$ through two sides of the triangle, parallel to the third side.

b. Measure $\angle ADE$ and $\angle ACB$. Measure $\angle AED$ and $\angle ABC$. What do you notice?

c. What does a postulate in this lesson tell you about $\triangle ADE$ and $\triangle ACB$?

d. Measure all the sides. Show that corresponding side lengths are proportional.

e. Move vertex A to form new triangles. How do your measurements in parts (b) and (d) change? Are the new triangles still similar? *Explain.*

38. ★ **EXTENDED RESPONSE** *Explain* how you could use similar triangles to show that any two points on a line can be used to calculate its slope.

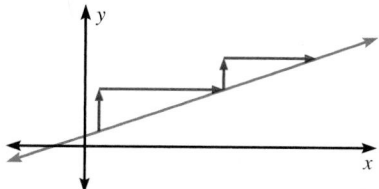

39. **CORRESPONDING LENGTHS** Without using the Corresponding Lengths Property on page 375, prove that the ratio of two corresponding angle bisectors in similar triangles is equal to the scale factor.

40. **CHALLENGE** Prove that if the lengths of two sides of a triangle are a and b respectively, then the lengths of the corresponding altitudes to those sides are in the ratio $\dfrac{b}{a}$.

MIXED REVIEW

PREVIEW

Prepare for Lesson 6.5 in Exs. 41–44.

In Exercises 41–44, use the diagram.

41. Name three pairs of corresponding angles. *(p. 147)*

42. Name two pairs of alternate interior angles. *(p. 147)*

43. Name two pairs of alternate exterior angles. *(p. 147)*

44. Find $m\angle 1 + m\angle 7$. *(p. 154)*

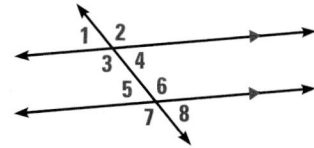

45. **CONGRUENCE** Explain why $\triangle ABE \cong \triangle CDE$. *(p. 240)*

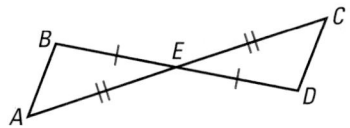

Simplify the ratio. *(p. 356)*

46. $\dfrac{4}{20}$

47. $\dfrac{36}{18}$

48. $21:63$

49. $42:28$

6.5 Prove Triangles Similar by SSS and SAS

Before	You used the AA Similarity Postulate to prove triangles similar.
Now	You will use the SSS and SAS Similarity Theorems.
Why?	So you can show that triangles are similar, as in Ex. 28.

Key Vocabulary
• **ratio,** *p. 356*
• **proportion,** *p. 358*
• **similar polygons,** *p. 372*

In addition to using congruent corresponding angles to show that two triangles are similar, you can use proportional corresponding side lengths.

THEOREM   *For Your Notebook*

THEOREM 6.2 Side-Side-Side (SSS) Similarity Theorem

If the corresponding side lengths of two triangles are proportional, then the triangles are similar.

If $\dfrac{AB}{RS} = \dfrac{BC}{ST} = \dfrac{CA}{TR}$, then $\triangle ABC \sim \triangle RST$.

Proof: p. 389

EXAMPLE 1   Use the SSS Similarity Theorem

Is either $\triangle DEF$ or $\triangle GHJ$ similar to $\triangle ABC$?

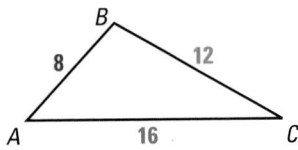
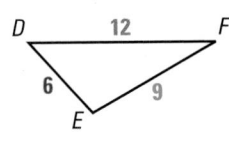
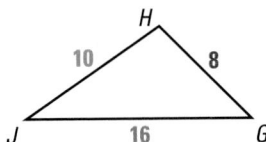

Solution

APPLY THEOREMS

When using the SSS Similarity Theorem, compare the shortest sides, the longest sides, and then the remaining sides.

Compare $\triangle ABC$ and $\triangle DEF$ by finding ratios of corresponding side lengths.

Shortest sides	Longest sides	Remaining sides
$\dfrac{AB}{DE} = \dfrac{8}{6} = \dfrac{4}{3}$	$\dfrac{CA}{FD} = \dfrac{16}{12} = \dfrac{4}{3}$	$\dfrac{BC}{EF} = \dfrac{12}{9} = \dfrac{4}{3}$

▶ All of the ratios are equal, so $\triangle ABC \sim \triangle DEF$.

Compare $\triangle ABC$ and $\triangle GHJ$ by finding ratios of corresponding side lengths.

Shortest sides	Longest sides	Remaining sides
$\dfrac{AB}{GH} = \dfrac{8}{8} = 1$	$\dfrac{CA}{JG} = \dfrac{16}{16} = 1$	$\dfrac{BC}{HJ} = \dfrac{12}{10} = \dfrac{6}{5}$

▶ The ratios are not all equal, so $\triangle ABC$ and $\triangle GHJ$ are not similar.

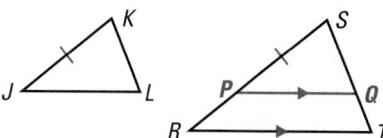

PROOF SSS Similarity Theorem

GIVEN ▶ $\dfrac{RS}{JK} = \dfrac{ST}{KL} = \dfrac{TR}{LJ}$

PROVE ▶ $\triangle RST \sim \triangle JKL$

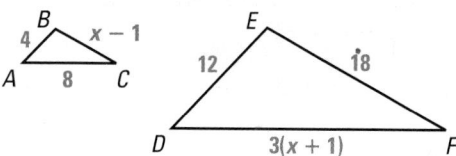

USE AN AUXILIARY LINE
The Parallel Postulate allows you to draw an auxiliary line $\overleftrightarrow{PQ}$ in $\triangle RST$. There is only one line through point P parallel to $\overleftrightarrow{RT}$, so you are able to draw it.

Locate P on $\overline{RS}$ so that $PS = JK$. Draw $\overline{PQ}$ so that $\overline{PQ} \parallel \overline{RT}$. Then $\triangle RST \sim \triangle PSQ$ by the AA Similarity Postulate, and $\dfrac{RS}{PS} = \dfrac{ST}{SQ} = \dfrac{TR}{QP}$.

You can use the given proportion and the fact that $PS = JK$ to deduce that $SQ = KL$ and $QP = LJ$. By the SSS Congruence Postulate, it follows that $\triangle PSQ \cong \triangle JKL$. Finally, use the definition of congruent triangles and the AA Similarity Postulate to conclude that $\triangle RST \sim \triangle JKL$.

EXAMPLE 2 Use the SSS Similarity Theorem

ALGEBRA Find the value of x that makes $\triangle ABC \sim \triangle DEF$.

Solution

STEP 1 **Find** the value of x that makes corresponding side lengths proportional.

CHOOSE A METHOD
You can use either $\dfrac{AB}{DE} = \dfrac{BC}{EF}$ or $\dfrac{AB}{DE} = \dfrac{AC}{DF}$ in Step 1.

$\dfrac{4}{12} = \dfrac{x-1}{18}$ **Write proportion.**

$4 \cdot 18 = 12(x-1)$ **Cross Products Property**

$72 = 12x - 12$ **Simplify.**

$7 = x$ **Solve for x.**

STEP 2 **Check** that the side lengths are proportional when $x = 7$.

$BC = x - 1 = 6$ $DF = 3(x + 1) = 24$

$\dfrac{AB}{DE} \overset{?}{=} \dfrac{BC}{EF} \implies \dfrac{4}{12} = \dfrac{6}{18}$ ✓ $\dfrac{AB}{DE} \overset{?}{=} \dfrac{AC}{DF} \implies \dfrac{4}{12} = \dfrac{8}{24}$ ✓

▶ When $x = 7$, the triangles are similar by the SSS Similarity Theorem.

✓ **GUIDED PRACTICE** for Examples 1 and 2

1. Which of the three triangles are similar? Write a similarity statement.

2. The shortest side of a triangle similar to $\triangle RST$ is 12 units long. Find the other side lengths of the triangle.

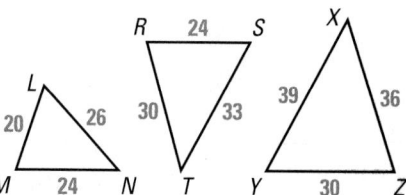

THEOREM 6.3 Side-Angle-Side (SAS) Similarity Theorem

If an angle of one triangle is congruent to an angle of a second triangle and the lengths of the sides including these angles are proportional, then the triangles are similar.

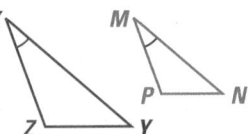

If $\angle X \cong \angle M$ and $\dfrac{ZX}{PM} = \dfrac{XY}{MN}$, then $\triangle XYZ \sim \triangle MNP$.

Proof: Ex. 37, p. 395

EXAMPLE 3 Use the SAS Similarity Theorem

LEAN-TO SHELTER You are building a lean-to shelter starting from a tree branch, as shown. Can you construct the right end so it is similar to the left end using the angle measure and lengths shown?

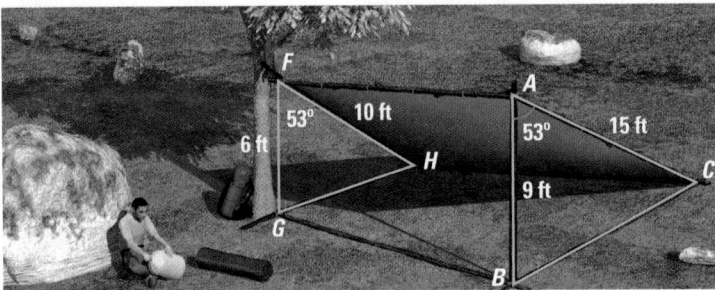

Solution

Both $m\angle A$ and $m\angle F$ equal 53°, so $\angle A \cong \angle F$. Next, compare the ratios of the lengths of the sides that include $\angle A$ and $\angle F$.

Shorter sides $\dfrac{AB}{FG} = \dfrac{9}{6} = \dfrac{3}{2}$ Longer sides $\dfrac{AC}{FH} = \dfrac{15}{10} = \dfrac{3}{2}$

The lengths of the sides that include $\angle A$ and $\angle F$ are proportional.

▶ So, by the SAS Similarity Theorem, $\triangle ABC \sim \triangle FGH$. Yes, you can make the right end similar to the left end of the shelter.

CONCEPT SUMMARY *For Your Notebook*

Triangle Similarity Postulate and Theorems

AA Similarity Postulate

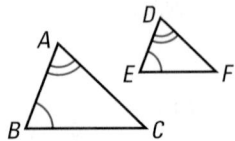

If $\angle A \cong \angle D$ and $\angle B \cong \angle E$, then $\triangle ABC \sim \triangle DEF$.

SSS Similarity Theorem

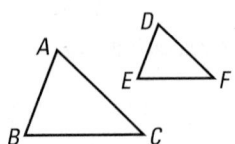

If $\dfrac{AB}{DE} = \dfrac{BC}{EF} = \dfrac{AC}{DF}$, then $\triangle ABC \sim \triangle DEF$.

SAS Similarity Theorem

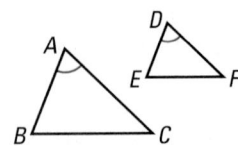

If $\angle A \cong \angle D$ and $\dfrac{AB}{DE} = \dfrac{AC}{DF}$, then $\triangle ABC \sim \triangle DEF$.

EXAMPLE 4 **Choose a method**

To identify corresponding parts, redraw the triangles so that the corresponding parts have the same orientation.

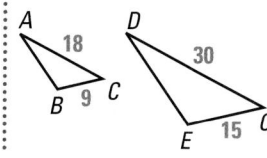

Tell what method you would use to show that the triangles are similar.

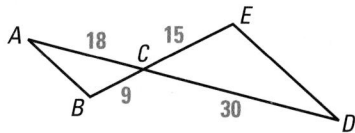

Solution

Find the ratios of the lengths of the corresponding sides.

Shorter sides $\dfrac{BC}{EC} = \dfrac{9}{15} = \dfrac{3}{5}$ Longer sides $\dfrac{CA}{CD} = \dfrac{18}{30} = \dfrac{3}{5}$

The corresponding side lengths are proportional. The included angles $\angle ACB$ and $\angle DCE$ are congruent because they are vertical angles. So, $\triangle ACB \sim \triangle DCE$ by the SAS Similarity Theorem.

Animated Geometry at classzone.com

✓ **GUIDED PRACTICE** for Examples 3 and 4

Explain how to show that the indicated triangles are similar.

3. $\triangle SRT \sim \triangle PNQ$

4. $\triangle XZW \sim \triangle YZX$

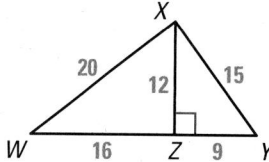

6.5 EXERCISES

○ = **WORKED-OUT SOLUTIONS**
on p. WS7 for Exs. 3, 7, and 31

★ = **STANDARDIZED TEST PRACTICE**
Exs. 2, 14, 32, 34, and 36

SKILL PRACTICE

1. **VOCABULARY** You plan to prove that $\triangle ACB$ is similar to $\triangle PXQ$ by the SSS Similarity Theorem. Copy and complete the proportion that is needed to use this theorem: $\dfrac{AC}{?} = \dfrac{?}{XQ} = \dfrac{AB}{?}$.

2. ★ **WRITING** If you know two triangles are similar by the SAS Similarity Theorem, what additional piece(s) of information would you need to know to show that the triangles are congruent?

**EXAMPLES
1 and 2**
on pp. 388–389
for Exs. 3–6

SSS SIMILARITY THEOREM Verify that $\triangle ABC \sim \triangle DEF$. Find the scale factor of $\triangle ABC$ to $\triangle DEF$.

3. $\triangle ABC$: $BC = 18$, $AB = 15$, $AC = 12$
$\triangle DEF$: $EF = 12$, $DE = 10$, $DF = 8$

4. $\triangle ABC$: $AB = 10$, $BC = 16$, $CA = 20$
$\triangle DEF$: $DE = 25$, $EF = 40$, $FD = 50$

5. SSS SIMILARITY THEOREM Is either △*JKL* or △*RST* similar to △*ABC*?

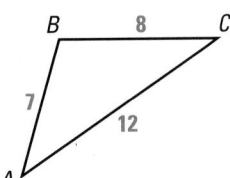 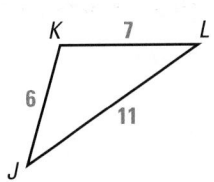 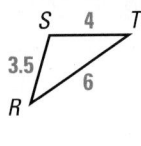

6. SSS SIMILARITY THEOREM Is either △*JKL* or △*RST* similar to △*ABC*?

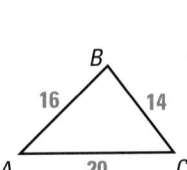 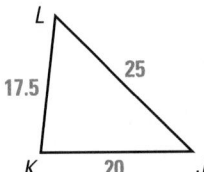 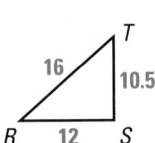

EXAMPLE 3
on p. 390
for Exs. 7–9

SAS SIMILARITY THEOREM **Determine whether the two triangles are similar. If they are similar, write a similarity statement and find the scale factor of Triangle B to Triangle A.**

⑦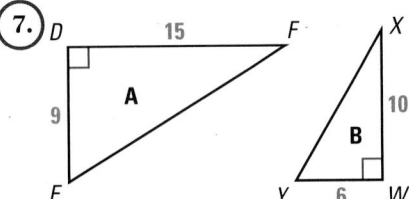

8.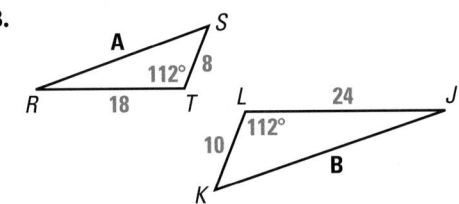

9. 🆇🆈 **ALGEBRA** Find the value of *n* that makes △*PQR* ~ △*XYZ* when *PQ* = 4, *QR* = 5, *XY* = 4(*n* + 1), *YZ* = 7*n* − 1, and ∠*Q* ≅ ∠*Y*. Include a sketch.

EXAMPLE 4
on p. 391
for Exs. 10–12

SHOWING SIMILARITY **Show that the triangles are similar and write a similarity statement.** *Explain* your reasoning.

10.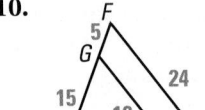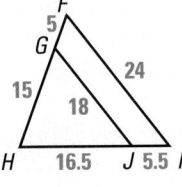

11.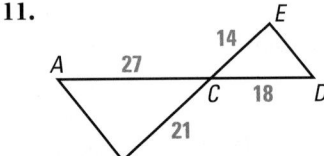

12.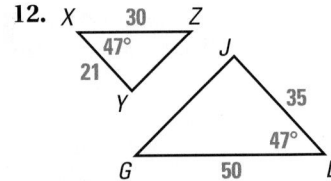

13. ERROR ANALYSIS *Describe* and correct the student's error in writing the similarity statement.

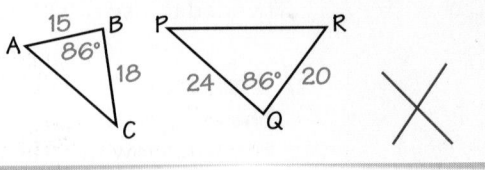

△*ABC* ~ △*PQR* by SAS Similarity Theorem

14. ★ **MULTIPLE CHOICE** In the diagram, $\dfrac{MN}{MR} = \dfrac{MP}{MQ}$.
Which of the statements must be true?

(A) ∠1 ≅ ∠2

(B) $\overline{QR} \parallel \overline{NP}$

(C) ∠1 ≅ ∠4

(D) △*MNP* ~ △*MRQ*

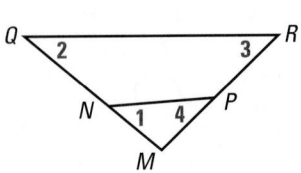

○ = **WORKED-OUT SOLUTIONS**
on p. WS1

★ = **STANDARDIZED TEST PRACTICE**

DRAWING TRIANGLES Sketch the triangles using the given description. *Explain* whether the two triangles can be similar.

15. In $\triangle XYZ$, $m\angle X = 66°$ and $m\angle Y = 34°$. In $\triangle LMN$, $m\angle M = 34°$ and $m\angle N = 80°$.

16. In $\triangle RST$, $RS = 20$, $ST = 32$, and $m\angle S = 16°$. In $\triangle FGH$, $GH = 30$, $HF = 48$, and $m\angle H = 24°$.

17. The side lengths of $\triangle ABC$ are 24, $8x$, and 54, and the side lengths of $\triangle DEF$ are 15, 25, and $7x$.

FINDING MEASURES In Exercises 18–23, use the diagram to copy and complete the statements.

18. $m\angle NQP = \underline{\ ?\ }$ 19. $m\angle QPN = \underline{\ ?\ }$

20. $m\angle PNQ = \underline{\ ?\ }$ 21. $RN = \underline{\ ?\ }$

22. $PQ = \underline{\ ?\ }$ 23. $NM = \underline{\ ?\ }$

24. **SIMILAR TRIANGLES** In the diagram at the right, name the three pairs of triangles that are similar.

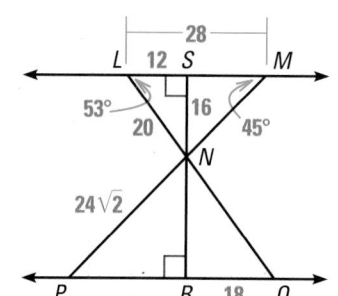

CHALLENGE In the figure at the right, $\triangle ABC \sim \triangle VWX$.

25. Find the scale factor of $\triangle VWX$ to $\triangle ABC$.

26. Find the ratio of the area of $\triangle VWX$ to the area of $\triangle ABC$.

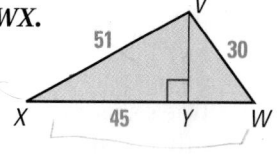

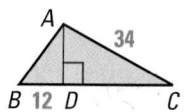

27. Make a conjecture about the relationship between the scale factor in Exercise 25 and the ratio in Exercise 26. *Justify* your conjecture.

PROBLEM SOLVING

28. **RACECAR NET** Which postulate or theorem could you use to show that the three triangles that make up the racecar window net are similar? *Explain.*

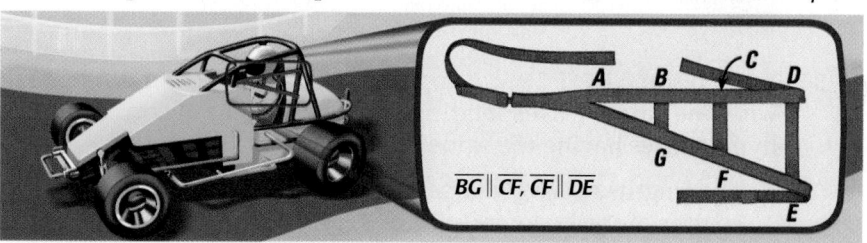

$\overline{BG} \parallel \overline{CF}$, $\overline{CF} \parallel \overline{DE}$

@HomeTutor for problem solving help at classzone.com

EXAMPLE 1
on p. 388
for Ex. 29

29. **STAINED GLASS** Certain sections of stained glass are sold in triangular *beveled* pieces. Which of the three beveled pieces, if any, are similar?

3 in.   3 in.   5 in.

7 in.   4 in.   4 in.

5.25 in.   3 in.   3 in.

@HomeTutor for problem solving help at classzone.com

SHUFFLEBOARD In the portion of the shuffleboard court shown, $\frac{BC}{AC} = \frac{BD}{AE}$.

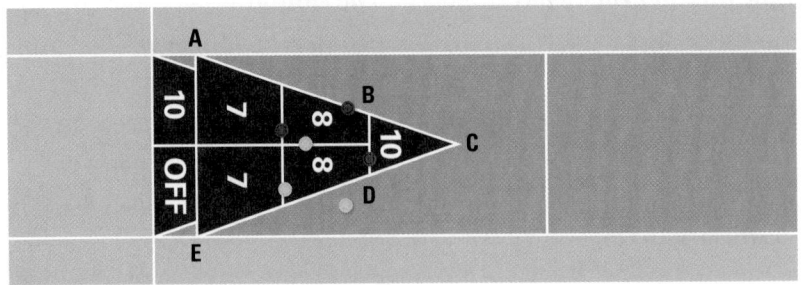

30. What additional piece of information do you need in order to show that △BCD ~ △ACE using the SSS Similarity Theorem?

31. What additional piece of information do you need in order to show that △BCD ~ △ACE using the SAS Similarity Theorem?

32. ★ **OPEN-ENDED MATH** Use a diagram to show why there is no Side-Side-Angle Similarity Postulate.

EXAMPLE 4
on p. 391
for Ex. 33

33. **MULTI-STEP PROBLEM** Ruby is standing in her back yard and she decides to estimate the height of a tree. She stands so that the tip of her shadow coincides with the tip of the tree's shadow, as shown. Ruby is 66 inches tall. The distance from the tree to Ruby is 95 feet and the distance between the tip of the shadows and Ruby is 7 feet.

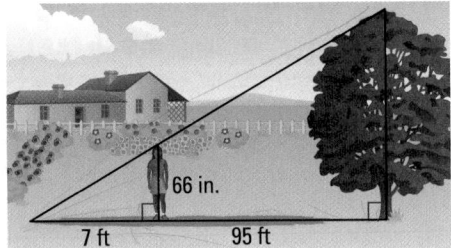

   a. What postulate or theorem can you use to show that the triangles in the diagram are similar?

   b. About how tall is the tree, to the nearest foot?

   c. **What If?** Curtis is 75 inches tall. At a different time of day, he stands so that the tip of his shadow and the tip of the tree's shadow coincide, as described above. His shadow is 6 feet long. How far is Curtis from the tree?

   Animated Geometry at classzone.com

34. ★ **EXTENDED RESPONSE** Suppose you are given two right triangles with one pair of corresponding legs and the pair of corresponding hypotenuses having the same length ratios.

   a. The lengths of the given pair of corresponding legs are 6 and 18, and the lengths of the hypotenuses are 10 and 30. Use the Pythagorean Theorem to solve for the lengths of the other pair of corresponding legs. Draw a diagram.

   b. Write the ratio of the lengths of the second pair of corresponding legs.

   c. Are these triangles similar? Does this suggest a Hypotenuse-Leg Similarity Theorem for right triangles?

35. **PROOF** Given that △ABC is a right triangle and D, E, and F are midpoints, prove that $m\angle DEF = 90°$.

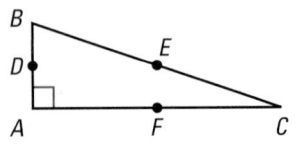

36. ★ **WRITING** Can two triangles have all pairs of corresponding angles in proportion? *Explain.*

37. PROVING THEOREM 6.3 Write a paragraph proof of the SAS Similarity Theorem.

GIVEN ▶ $\angle A \cong \angle D$, $\dfrac{AB}{DE} = \dfrac{AC}{DF}$

PROVE ▶ $\triangle ABC \sim \triangle DEF$

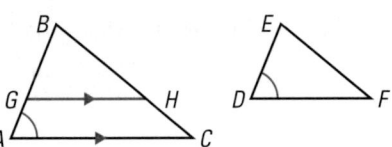

38. CHALLENGE A portion of a water slide in an amusement park is shown. Find the length of $\overline{EF}$. (*Note:* The posts form right angles with the ground.)

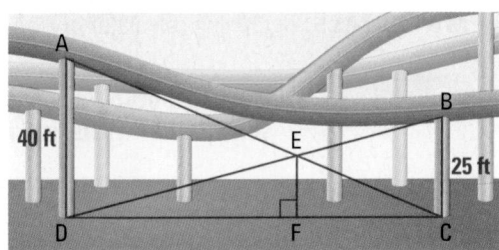

MIXED REVIEW

Find the slope of the line that passes through the given points. *(p. 171)*

39. $(0, -8)$, $(4, 16)$ **40.** $(-2, -9)$, $(1, -3)$ **41.** $(-3, 9)$, $(7, 2)$

42. State the postulate or theorem you would use to prove the triangles congruent. Then write a congruence statement. *(p. 249)*

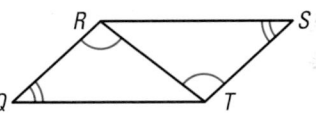

PREVIEW
Prepare for Lesson 6.6 in Exs. 43–44.

Find the value of x.

43. $\overline{DE}$ is a midsegment of $\triangle ABC$. *(p. 295)*   **44.** $\dfrac{GK}{GH} = \dfrac{JK}{FH}$ *(p. 364)*

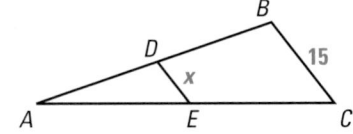
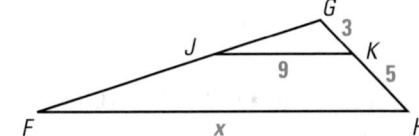

QUIZ *for Lessons 6.3–6.5*

In the diagram, *ABCD* ~ *KLMN*. *(p. 372)*

1. Find the scale factor of *ABCD* to *KLMN*.

2. Find the values of x, y, and z.

3. Find the perimeter of each polygon.

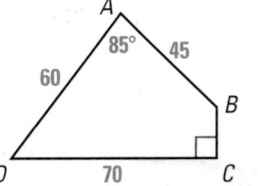
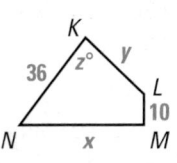

Determine whether the triangles are similar. If they are similar, write a similarity statement. *(pp. 381, 388)*

4.   **5.**   **6.**

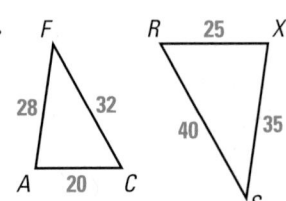
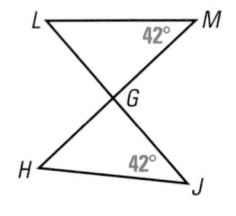

EXTRA PRACTICE for Lesson 6.5, p. 907   ⊘ **ONLINE QUIZ** at classzone.com   **395**

6.6 Investigate Proportionality

MATERIALS · graphing calculator or computer

QUESTION How can you use geometry drawing software to compare segment lengths in triangles?

EXPLORE 1 Construct a line parallel to a triangle's third side

STEP 1 *Draw a triangle* Draw a triangle. Label the vertices *A*, *B*, and *C*. Draw a point on $\overline{AB}$. Label the point *D*.

STEP 2 *Draw a parallel line* Draw a line through *D* that is parallel to $\overline{AC}$. Label the intersection of the line and $\overline{BC}$ as point *E*.

STEP 3 *Measure segments* Measure $\overline{BD}$, $\overline{DA}$, $\overline{BE}$, and $\overline{EC}$. Calculate the ratios $\frac{BD}{DA}$ and $\frac{BE}{EC}$.

STEP 4 *Compare ratios* Move one or more of the triangle's vertices to change its shape. *Compare* the ratios from Step 3 as the shape changes. Save as "EXPLORE1."

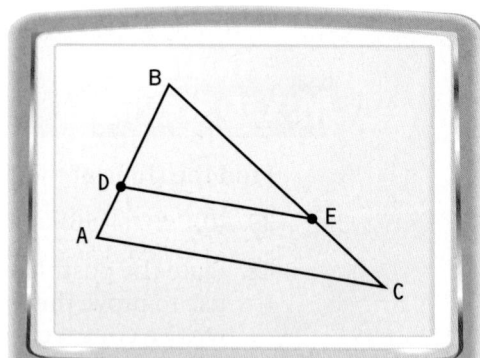

EXPLORE 2 Construct an angle bisector of a triangle

STEP 1 *Draw a triangle* Draw a triangle. Label the vertices *P*, *Q*, and *R*. Draw the angle bisector of ∠*QPR*. Label the intersection of the angle bisector and $\overline{QR}$ as point *B*.

STEP 2 *Measure segments* Measure $\overline{BR}$, $\overline{RP}$, $\overline{BQ}$, and $\overline{QP}$. Calculate the ratios $\frac{BR}{BQ}$ and $\frac{RP}{QP}$.

STEP 3 *Compare ratios* Move one or more of the triangle's vertices to change its shape. *Compare* the ratios from Step 3. Save as "EXPLORE2."

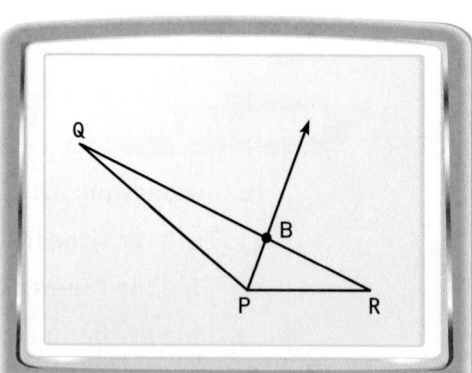

DRAW CONCLUSIONS Use your observations to complete these exercises

1. Make a conjecture about the ratios of the lengths of the segments formed when two sides of a triangle are cut by a line parallel to the triangle's third side.

2. Make a conjecture about how the ratio of the lengths of two sides of a triangle is related to the ratio of the lengths of the segments formed when an angle bisector is drawn to the third side.

6.6 Use Proportionality Theorems

Before You used proportions with similar triangles.

Now You will use proportions with a triangle or parallel lines.

Why? So you can use perspective drawings, as in Ex. 28.

Key Vocabulary
- **corresponding angles,** *p. 147*
- **ratio,** *p. 356*
- **proportion,** *p. 358*

The Midsegment Theorem, which you learned on page 295, is a special case of the Triangle Proportionality Theorem and its converse.

THEOREMS
For Your Notebook

THEOREM 6.4 Triangle Proportionality Theorem

If a line parallel to one side of a triangle intersects the other two sides, then it divides the two sides proportionally.

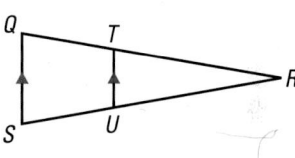

Proof: Ex. 22, p. 402

If $\overline{TU} \parallel \overline{QS}$, then $\dfrac{RT}{TQ} = \dfrac{RU}{US}$.

THEOREM 6.5 Converse of the Triangle Proportionality Theorem

If a line divides two sides of a triangle proportionally, then it is parallel to the third side.

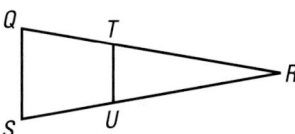

Proof: Ex. 26, p. 402

If $\dfrac{RT}{TQ} = \dfrac{RU}{US}$, then $\overline{TU} \parallel \overline{QS}$.

EXAMPLE 1   Find the length of a segment

In the diagram, $\overline{QS} \parallel \overline{UT}$, $RS = 4$, $ST = 6$, and $QU = 9$. What is the length of $\overline{RQ}$?

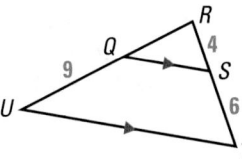

Solution

$\dfrac{RQ}{QU} = \dfrac{RS}{ST}$ **Triangle Proportionality Theorem**

$\dfrac{RQ}{9} = \dfrac{4}{6}$ **Substitute.**

$RQ = 6$ **Multiply each side by 9 and simplify.**

REASONING Theorems 6.4 and 6.5 also tell you that if the lines are *not* parallel, then the proportion is *not* true, and vice-versa.

So if $\overline{TU} \nparallel \overline{QS}$, then $\frac{RT}{TQ} \neq \frac{RU}{US}$. Also, if $\frac{RT}{TQ} \neq \frac{RU}{US}$, then $\overline{TU} \nparallel \overline{QS}$.

EXAMPLE 2 Solve a real-world problem

SHOERACK On the shoerack shown, $AB = 33$ cm, $BC = 27$ cm, $CD = 44$ cm, and $DE = 25$ cm. *Explain* why the gray shelf is not parallel to the floor.

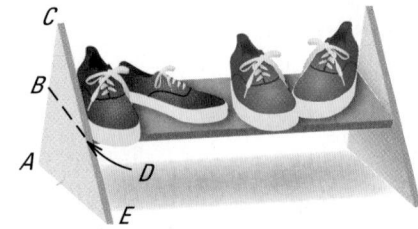

Solution

Find and simplify the ratios of lengths determined by the shoerack.

$$\frac{CD}{DE} = \frac{44}{25} \qquad \frac{CB}{BA} = \frac{27}{33} = \frac{9}{11}$$

▶ Because $\frac{44}{25} \neq \frac{9}{11}$, $\overline{BD}$ is not parallel to $\overline{AE}$. So, the shelf is not parallel to the floor.

 GUIDED PRACTICE   for Examples 1 and 2

1. Find the length of $\overline{YZ}$.

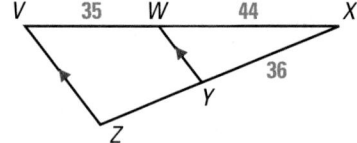

2. Determine whether $\overline{PS} \parallel \overline{QR}$.

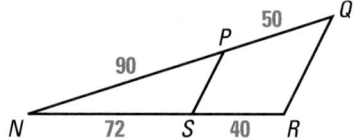

THEOREMS   *For Your Notebook*

THEOREM 6.6

If three parallel lines intersect two transversals, then they divide the transversals proportionally.

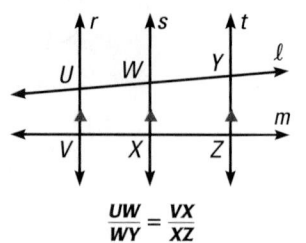

$$\frac{UW}{WY} = \frac{VX}{XZ}$$

Proof: Ex. 23, p. 402

THEOREM 6.7

If a ray bisects an angle of a triangle, then it divides the opposite side into segments whose lengths are proportional to the lengths of the other two sides.

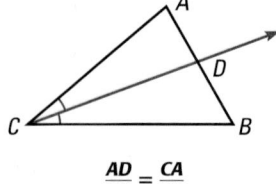

$$\frac{AD}{DB} = \frac{CA}{CB}$$

Proof: Ex. 27, p. 403

EXAMPLE 3   Use Theorem 6.6

CITY TRAVEL In the diagram, $\angle 1$, $\angle 2$, and $\angle 3$ are all congruent and $GF = 120$ yards, $DE = 150$ yards, and $CD = 300$ yards. Find the distance HF between Main Street and South Main Street.

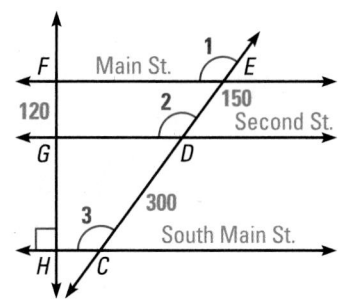

Solution

Corresponding angles are congruent, so $\overleftrightarrow{FE}$, $\overleftrightarrow{GD}$, and $\overleftrightarrow{HC}$ are parallel. Use Theorem 6.6.

$$\frac{HG}{GF} = \frac{CD}{DE}$$ **Parallel lines divide transversals proportionally.**

$$\frac{HG + GF}{GF} = \frac{CD + DE}{DE}$$ **Property of proportions (Property 4)**

$$\frac{HF}{120} = \frac{300 + 150}{150}$$ **Substitute.**

$$\frac{HF}{120} = \frac{450}{150}$$ **Simplify.**

$$HF = 360$$ **Multiply each side by 120 and simplify.**

▶ The distance between Main Street and South Main Street is 360 yards.

ANOTHER WAY

For alternative methods for solving the problem in Example 3, turn to page 404 for the **Problem Solving Workshop**.

EXAMPLE 4   Use Theorem 6.7

In the diagram, $\angle QPR \cong \angle RPS$. Use the given side lengths to find the length of $\overline{RS}$.

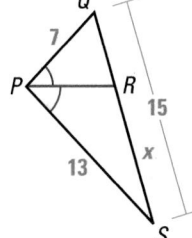

Solution

Because $\overrightarrow{PR}$ is an angle bisector of $\angle QPS$, you can apply Theorem 6.7. Let $RS = x$. Then $RQ = 15 - x$.

$$\frac{RQ}{RS} = \frac{PQ}{PS}$$ **Angle bisector divides opposite side proportionally.**

$$\frac{15 - x}{x} = \frac{7}{13}$$ **Substitute.**

$$7x = 195 - 13x$$ **Cross Products Property**

$$x = 9.75$$ **Solve for x.**

✓ **GUIDED PRACTICE**   for Examples 3 and 4

Find the length of $\overline{AB}$.

3.

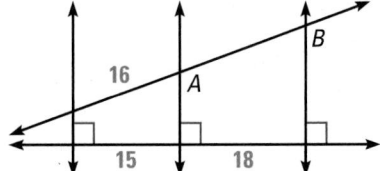

4.

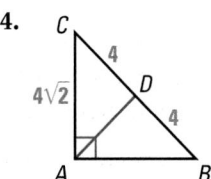

6.6 EXERCISES

SKILL PRACTICE

1. **VOCABULARY** State the Triangle Proportionality Theorem. Draw a diagram.

2. ★ **WRITING** *Compare* the Midsegment Theorem (see page 295) and the Triangle Proportionality Theorem. How are they related?

EXAMPLE 1
on p. 397
for Exs. 3–4

FINDING THE LENGTH OF A SEGMENT Find the length of $\overline{AB}$.

3.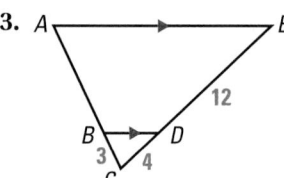

4.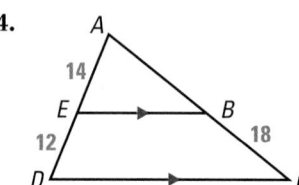

EXAMPLE 2
on p. 398
for Exs. 5–7

REASONING Use the given information to determine whether $\overline{KM} \parallel \overline{JN}$. *Explain* your reasoning.

5.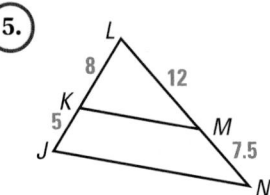

6.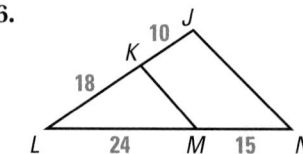

7.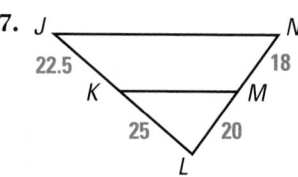

EXAMPLE 3
on p. 399
for Ex. 8

8. ★ **MULTIPLE CHOICE** For the figure at the right, which statement is *not* necessarily true?

Ⓐ $\dfrac{PQ}{QR} = \dfrac{UT}{TS}$ Ⓑ $\dfrac{TS}{UT} = \dfrac{QR}{PQ}$

Ⓒ $\dfrac{QR}{RS} = \dfrac{TS}{RS}$ Ⓓ $\dfrac{PQ}{PR} = \dfrac{UT}{US}$

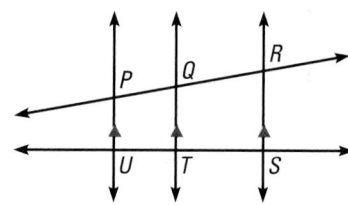

EXAMPLE 4
on p. 399
for Exs. 9–12

⚹ **ALGEBRA** Find the value of the variable.

9.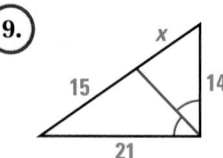

10.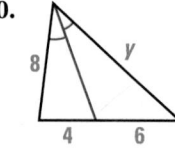

11.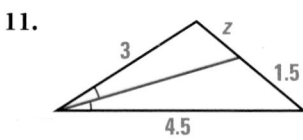

12. **ERROR ANALYSIS** A student begins to solve for the length of $\overline{AD}$ as shown. *Describe* and correct the student's error.

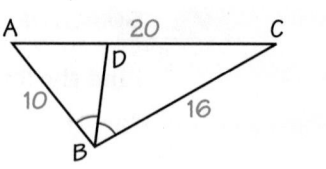

$$\frac{AB}{BC} = \frac{AD}{CD} \implies \frac{10}{16} = \frac{20 - x}{20}$$

13. ★ MULTIPLE CHOICE Find the value of x.

Ⓐ $\frac{1}{2}$　　Ⓑ 1

Ⓒ 2　　Ⓓ 3

ⓧⓨ ALGEBRA Find the value of the variable.

14.

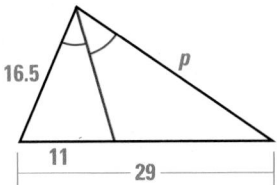

15.

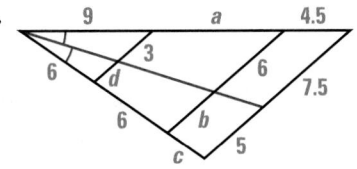

FINDING SEGMENT LENGTHS Use the diagram to find the value of each variable.

16.

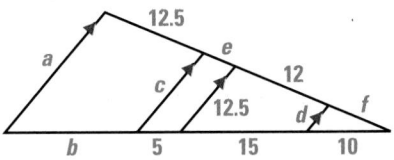

17.

18. ERROR ANALYSIS A student claims that $AB = AC$ using the method shown. *Describe* and correct the student's error.

By Theorem 6.7, $\frac{BD}{CD} = \frac{AB}{AC}$. Because $BD = CD$, it follows that $AB = AC$.

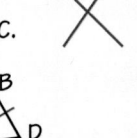

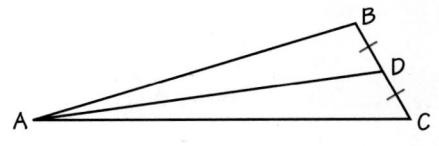

19. CONSTRUCTION Follow the instructions for constructing a line segment that is divided into four equal parts.

a. Draw a line segment that is about 3 inches long, and label its endpoints A and B. Choose any point C not on $\overline{AB}$. Draw $\overrightarrow{AC}$.

b. Using any length, place the compass point at A and make an arc intersecting $\overrightarrow{AC}$ at D. Using the same compass setting, make additional arcs on $\overrightarrow{AC}$. Label the points E, F, and G so that $AD = DE = EF = FG$.

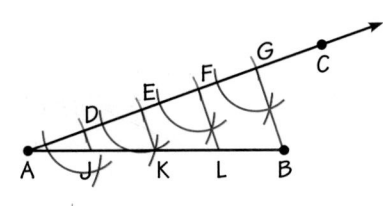

c. Draw $\overline{GB}$. Construct a line parallel to $\overline{GB}$ through D. Continue constructing parallel lines and label the points as shown. *Explain* why $AJ = JK = KL = LB$.

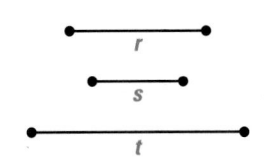

20. CHALLENGE Given segments with lengths r, s, and t, construct a segment of length x, such that $\frac{r}{s} = \frac{t}{x}$.

21. CITY MAP On the map below, Idaho Avenue bisects the angle between University Avenue and Walter Street. To the nearest yard, what is the distance along University Avenue from 12th Street to Washington Street?

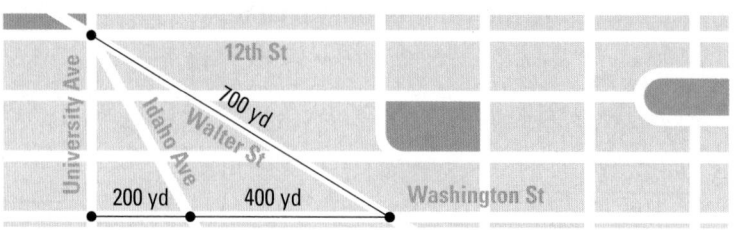

@HomeTutor for problem solving help at classzone.com

22. PROVING THEOREM 6.4 Prove the Triangle Proportionality Theorem.

GIVEN ▶ $\overline{QS} \parallel \overline{TU}$

PROVE ▶ $\dfrac{QT}{TR} = \dfrac{SU}{UR}$

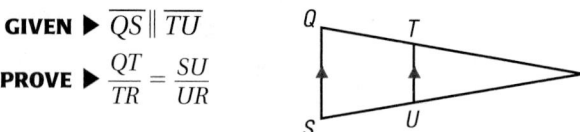

@HomeTutor for problem solving help at classzone.com

23. PROVING THEOREM 6.6 Use the diagram with the auxiliary line drawn to write a paragraph proof of Theorem 6.6.

GIVEN ▶ $k_1 \parallel k_2$, $k_2 \parallel k_3$

PROVE ▶ $\dfrac{CB}{BA} = \dfrac{DE}{EF}$

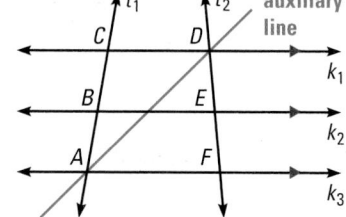

24. MULTI-STEP PROBLEM The real estate term *lake frontage* refers to the distance along the edge of a piece of property that touches a lake.

a. Find the lake frontage (to the nearest tenth of a yard) for each lot shown.

b. In general, the more lake frontage a lot has, the higher its selling price. Which of the lots should be listed for the highest price?

c. Suppose that lot prices are in the same ratio as lake frontages. If the least expensive lot is $100,000, what are the prices of the other lots? *Explain* your reasoning.

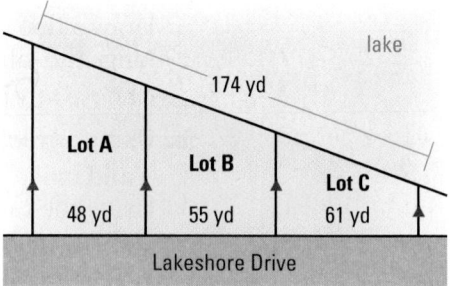

25. ★ SHORT RESPONSE Sketch an isosceles triangle. Draw a ray that bisects the angle opposite the base. This ray divides the base into two segments. By Theorem 6.7, the ratio of the legs is proportional to the ratio of these two segments. *Explain* why this ratio is 1 : 1 for an isosceles triangle.

26. PLAN FOR PROOF Use the diagram given for the proof of Theorem 6.4 in Exercise 22 to write a plan for proving Theorem 6.5, the Triangle Proportionality Converse.

◯ = **WORKED-OUT SOLUTIONS** on p. WS1   ★ = **STANDARDIZED TEST PRACTICE**

27. PROVING THEOREM 6.7 Use the diagram with the auxiliary lines drawn to write a paragraph proof of Theorem 6.7.

GIVEN ▶ $\angle YXW \cong \angle WXZ$

PROVE ▶ $\dfrac{YW}{WZ} = \dfrac{XY}{XZ}$

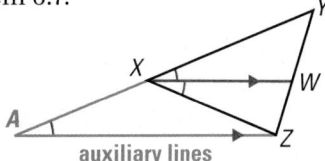

auxiliary lines

28. ★ EXTENDED RESPONSE In *perspective drawing*, lines that are parallel in real life must meet at a vanishing point on the horizon. To make the train cars in the drawing appear equal in length, they are drawn so that the lines connecting the opposite corners of each car are parallel.

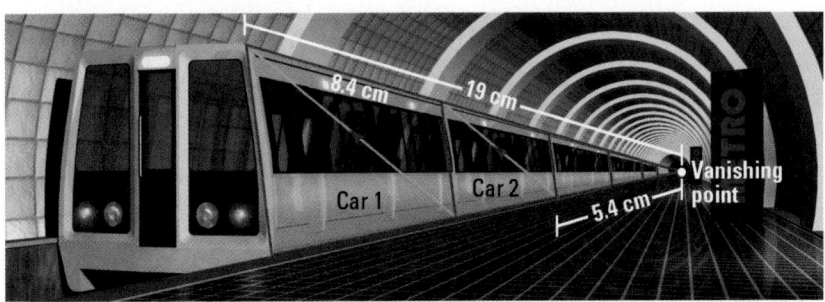

a. Use the dimensions given and the red parallel lines to find the length of the bottom edge of the drawing of Car 2.

b. What other set of parallel lines exist in the figure? *Explain* how these can be used to form a set of similar triangles.

c. Find the length of the top edge of the drawing of Car 2.

29. CHALLENGE Prove *Ceva's Theorem:* If P is any point inside $\triangle ABC$, then $\dfrac{AY}{YC} \cdot \dfrac{CX}{XB} \cdot \dfrac{BZ}{ZA} = 1$. (*Hint:* Draw lines parallel to $\overline{BY}$ through A and C. Apply Theorem 6.4 to $\triangle ACM$. Show that $\triangle APN \sim \triangle MPC$, $\triangle CXM \sim \triangle BXP$, and $\triangle BZP \sim \triangle AZN$.)

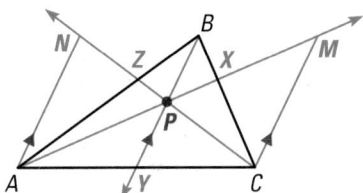

MIXED REVIEW

PREVIEW

Prepare for Lesson 6.7 in Exs. 30–36.

Perform the following operations. Then simplify.

30. $(-3) \cdot \dfrac{7}{2}$ *(p. 869)*

31. $\dfrac{4}{3} \cdot \dfrac{1}{2}$ *(p. 869)*

32. $5\left(\dfrac{1}{2}\right)^2$ *(p. 871)*

33. $\left(\dfrac{5}{4}\right)^3$ *(p. 871)*

Describe the translation in words and write the coordinate rule for the translation. *(p. 272)*

34.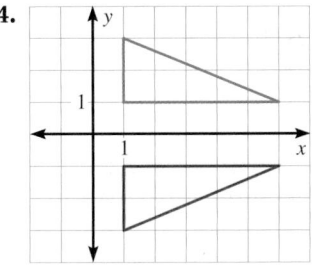

35.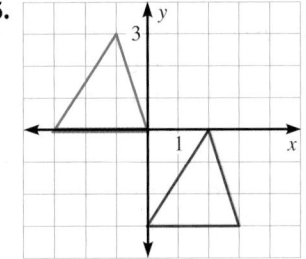

36.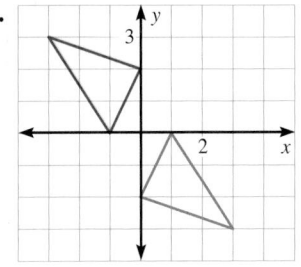

Using ALTERNATIVE METHODS

Another Way to Solve Example 3, page 399

MULTIPLE REPRESENTATIONS In Lesson 6.6, you used proportionality theorems to find lengths of segments formed when transversals intersect two or more parallel lines. Now, you will learn two different ways to solve Example 3 on page 399.

PROBLEM

CITY TRAVEL In the diagram, $\angle 1$, $\angle 2$, and $\angle 3$ are all congruent and $GF = 120$ yards, $DE = 150$ yards, and $CD = 300$ yards. Find the distance HF between Main Street and South Main Street.

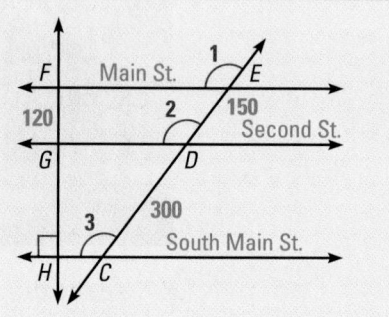

METHOD 1 **Applying a Ratio** One alternative approach is to look for ratios in the diagram.

STEP 1 **Read** the problem. Because Main Street, Second Street, and South Main Street are all parallel, the lengths of the segments of the cross streets will be in proportion, so they have the same ratio.

STEP 2 **Apply** a ratio. Notice that on $\overleftrightarrow{CE}$, the distance CD between South Main Street and Second Street is twice the distance DE between Second Street and Main Street. So the same will be true for the distances HG and GF.

$$HG = 2 \cdot GF \qquad \text{Write equation.}$$
$$= 2 \cdot 120 \qquad \text{Substitute.}$$
$$= 240 \qquad \text{Simplify.}$$

STEP 3 **Calculate** the distance. Line HF is perpendicular to both Main Street and South Main Street, so the distance between Main Street and South Main Street is this perpendicular distance, HF.

$$HF = HG + GF \qquad \text{Segment Addition Postulate}$$
$$= 120 + 240 \qquad \text{Substitute.}$$
$$= 360 \qquad \text{Simplify.}$$

STEP 4 **Check** page 399 to verify your answer, and confirm that it is the same.

METHOD 2 **Writing a Proportion** Another alternative approach is to use a graphic organizer to set up a proportion.

STEP 1 **Make** a table to compare the distances.

	$\overleftrightarrow{CE}$	$\overleftrightarrow{HF}$
Total distance	300 + 150, or 450	x
Partial distance	150	120

STEP 2 **Write** and solve a proportion.

$$\frac{450}{150} = \frac{x}{120}$$ **Write proportion.**

$$360 = x$$ **Multiply each side by 120 and simplify.**

▶ The distance is 360 yards.

PRACTICE

1. MAPS Use the information on the map.

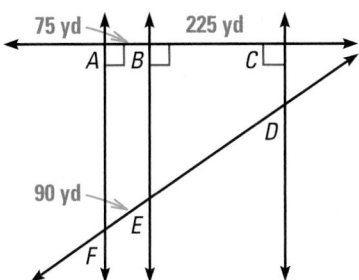

    a. Find *DE*.

    b. **What If?** Suppose there is an alley one fourth of the way from $\overline{BE}$ to $\overline{CD}$ and parallel to $\overline{BE}$. What is the distance from *E* to the alley along $\overleftrightarrow{FD}$?

2. REASONING Given the diagram below, *explain* why the three given proportions are true.

$$\frac{a}{a+b} = \frac{d}{e}$$

$$\frac{a}{a+b+c} = \frac{d}{f}$$

$$\frac{a+b}{a+b+c} = \frac{e}{f}$$

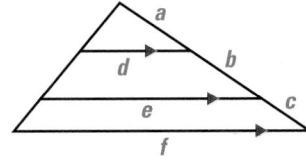

3. WALKING Two people leave points *A* and *B* at the same time. They intend to meet at point *C* at the same time. The person who leaves point *A* walks at a speed of 3 miles per hour. How fast must the person who leaves point *B* walk?

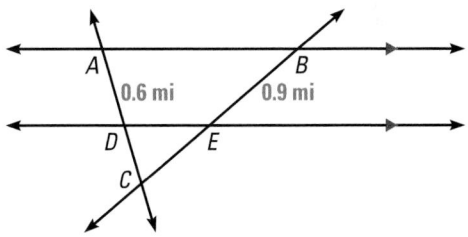

4. ERROR ANALYSIS A student who attempted to solve the problem in Exercise 3 claims that you need to know the length of $\overline{AC}$ to solve the problem. *Describe* and correct the error that the student made.

5. **XY** **ALGEBRA** Use the diagram to find the values of *x* and *y*.

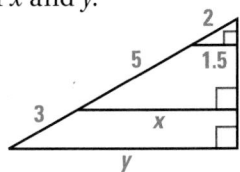

Extension
Use after Lesson 6.6

Fractals

GOAL Explore the properties of fractals.

Key Vocabulary
- fractal
- self-similarity
- iteration

A **fractal** is an object that is *self-similar*. An object is **self-similar** if one part of the object can be enlarged to look like the whole object. In nature, fractals can be found in ferns and branches of a river. Scientists use fractals to map out clouds in order to predict rain.

Many fractals are formed by a repetition of a sequence of the steps called **iteration**. The first stage of drawing a fractal is considered Stage 0. Helge van Koch (1870–1924) described a fractal known as the *Koch snowflake*, shown in Example 1.

A Mandelbrot fractal

HISTORY NOTE

Computers made it easier to study mathematical iteration by reducing the time needed to perform calculations. Using fractals, mathematicians have been able to create better models of coastlines, clouds, and other natural objects.

EXAMPLE 1 Draw a fractal

Use the directions below to draw a Koch snowflake.

Starting with an equilateral triangle, at each stage each side is divided into thirds and a new equilateral triangle is formed using the middle third as the triangle side length.

Solution

STAGE 0 **Draw** an equilateral triangle with a side length of one unit.

STAGE 1 **Replace** the middle third of each side with an equilateral triangle.

STAGE 2 **Repeat** Stage 1 with the six smaller equilateral triangles.

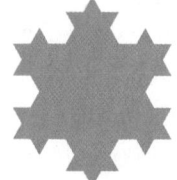

STAGE 3 **Repeat** Stage 1 with the eighteen smaller equilateral triangles.

MEASUREMENT Benoit Mandelbrot (b. 1924) was the first mathematician to formalize the idea of fractals when he observed methods used to measure the lengths of coastlines. Coastlines cannot be measured as straight lines because of the inlets and rocks. Mandelbrot used fractals to model coastlines.

EXAMPLE 2 Find lengths in a fractal

Make a table to study the lengths of the sides of a Koch snowflake at different stages.

Stage number	Edge length	Number of edges	Perimeter
0	1	3	3
1	$\frac{1}{3}$	$3 \cdot 4 = 12$	4
2	$\frac{1}{9}$	$12 \cdot 4 = 48$	$\frac{48}{9} = 5\frac{1}{3}$
3	$\frac{1}{27}$	$48 \cdot 4 = 192$	$\frac{192}{27} = 7\frac{1}{9}$
n	$\frac{1}{3^n}$	$3 \cdot 4^n$	$\frac{4^n}{3^{n-1}}$

Animated **Geometry** at classzone.com

PRACTICE

EXAMPLES
1 and 2
for Exs. 1–3

1. **PERIMETER** Find the ratio of the edge length of the triangle in Stage 0 of a Koch snowflake to the edge length of the triangle in Stage 1. How is the perimeter of the triangle in Stage 0 related to the perimeter of the triangle in Stage 1? *Explain.*

2. **MULTI-STEP PROBLEM** Use the *Cantor set*, which is a fractal whose iteration consists of dividing a segment into thirds and erasing the middle third.

   a. Draw Stage 0 through Stage 5 of the Cantor set. Stage 0 has a length of one unit.

   b. Make a table showing the stage number, number of segments, segment length, and total length of the Cantor set.

   c. What is the total length of the Cantor set at Stage 10? Stage 20? Stage n?

3. **EXTENDED RESPONSE** A *Sierpinski carpet* starts with a square with side length one unit. At each stage, divide the square into nine equal squares with the middle square shaded a different color.

   a. Draw Stage 0 through Stage 3 of a Sierpinski carpet.

   b. *Explain* why the carpet is said to be *self-similar* by comparing the upper left hand square to the whole square.

   c. Make a table to find the total area of the colored squares at Stage 3.

6.7 Dilations

MATERIALS • graph paper • straightedge • compass • ruler

QUESTION How can you construct a similar figure?

EXPLORE Construct a similar triangle

STEP 1

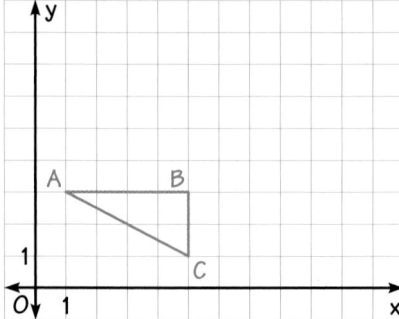

Draw a triangle Plot the points $A(1, 3)$, $B(5, 3)$, and $C(5, 1)$ in a coordinate plane. Draw $\triangle ABC$.

STEP 2

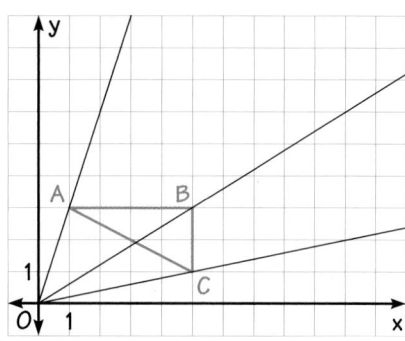

Draw rays Using the origin as an endpoint O, draw $\overrightarrow{OA}$, $\overrightarrow{OB}$, and $\overrightarrow{OC}$.

STEP 3

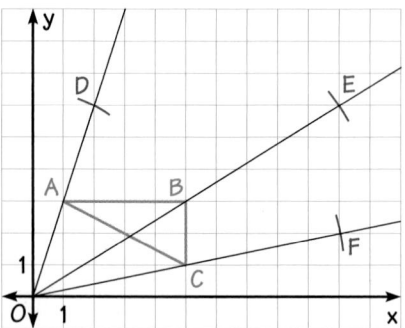

Draw equal segments Use a compass to mark a point D on $\overrightarrow{OA}$ so $OA = AD$. Mark a point E on $\overrightarrow{OB}$ so $OB = BE$. Mark a point F on $\overrightarrow{OC}$ so $OC = CF$.

STEP 4

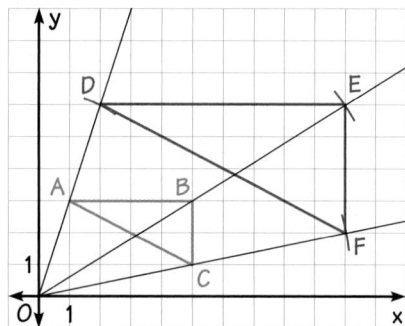

Draw the image Connect points D, E, and F to form a right triangle.

DRAW CONCLUSIONS Use your observations to complete these exercises

1. Measure $\overline{AB}$, $\overline{BC}$, $\overline{DE}$, and $\overline{EF}$. Calculate the ratios $\dfrac{DE}{AB}$ and $\dfrac{EF}{BC}$. Using this information, show that the two triangles are similar.

2. Repeat the steps in the Explore to construct $\triangle GHJ$ so that $3 \cdot OA = AG$, $3 \cdot OB = BH$, and $3 \cdot OC = CJ$.

6.7 Perform Similarity Transformations

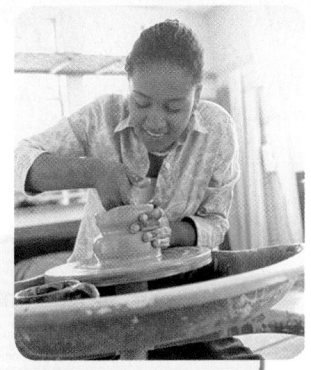

Before You performed congruence transformations.

Now You will perform dilations.

Why? So you can solve problems in art, as in Ex. 26.

Key Vocabulary
- dilation
- center of dilation
- scale factor of a dilation
- reduction
- enlargement
- transformation, *p. 272*

A **dilation** is a transformation that stretches or shrinks a figure to create a similar figure. A dilation is a type of *similarity transformation*.

In a dilation, a figure is enlarged or reduced with respect to a fixed point called the **center of dilation**.

The **scale factor of a dilation** is the ratio of a side length of the image to the corresponding side length of the original figure. In the figure shown, $\triangle XYZ$ is the image of $\triangle ABC$. The center of dilation is $(0, 0)$ and the scale factor is $\dfrac{XY}{AB}$.

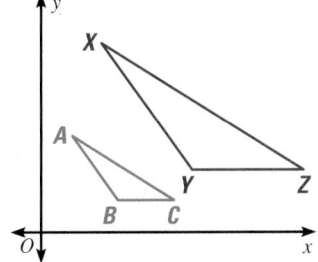

KEY CONCEPT
For Your Notebook

Coordinate Notation for a Dilation

You can describe a dilation with respect to the origin with the notation $(x, y) \rightarrow (kx, ky)$, where k is the scale factor.

If $0 < k < 1$, the dilation is a **reduction**. If $k > 1$, the dilation is an **enlargement**.

EXAMPLE 1   Draw a dilation with a scale factor greater than 1

> **READ DIAGRAMS**
> All of the dilations in this lesson are in the coordinate plane and each center of dilation is the origin.

Draw a dilation of quadrilateral *ABCD* with vertices *A*(2, 1), *B*(4, 1), *C*(4, −1), and *D*(1, −1). Use a scale factor of 2.

Solution

First draw *ABCD*. Find the dilation of each vertex by multiplying its coordinates by 2. Then draw the dilation.

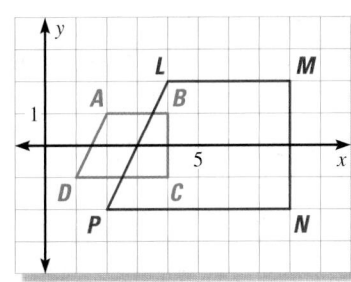

$$(x, y) \rightarrow (2x, 2y)$$

$$A(2, 1) \rightarrow L(4, 2)$$

$$B(4, 1) \rightarrow M(8, 2)$$

$$C(4, -1) \rightarrow N(8, -2)$$

$$D(1, -1) \rightarrow P(2, -2)$$

EXAMPLE 2 **Verify that a figure is similar to its dilation**

A triangle has the vertices $A(4, -4)$, $B(8, 2)$, and $C(8, -4)$. The image of $\triangle ABC$ after a dilation with a scale factor of $\frac{1}{2}$ is $\triangle DEF$.

a. Sketch $\triangle ABC$ and $\triangle DEF$.

b. Verify that $\triangle ABC$ and $\triangle DEF$ are similar.

Solution

a. The scale factor is less than one, so the dilation is a reduction.

$$(x, y) \rightarrow \left(\frac{1}{2}x, \frac{1}{2}y\right)$$

$$A(4, -4) \rightarrow D(2, -2)$$

$$B(8, 2) \rightarrow E(4, 1)$$

$$C(8, -4) \rightarrow F(4, -2)$$

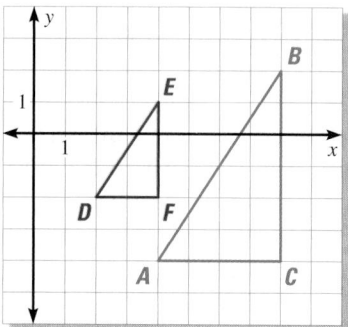

b. Because $\angle C$ and $\angle F$ are both right angles, $\angle C \cong \angle F$. Show that the lengths of the sides that include $\angle C$ and $\angle F$ are proportional. Find the horizontal and vertical lengths from the coordinate plane.

$$\frac{AC}{DF} \stackrel{?}{=} \frac{BC}{EF} \implies \frac{4}{2} = \frac{6}{3} \checkmark$$

So, the lengths of the sides that include $\angle C$ and $\angle F$ are proportional.

▶ Therefore, $\triangle ABC \sim \triangle DEF$ by the SAS Similarity Theorem.

 GUIDED PRACTICE for Examples 1 and 2

Find the coordinates of L, M, and N so that $\triangle LMN$ is a dilation of $\triangle PQR$ with a scale factor of k. Sketch $\triangle PQR$ and $\triangle LMN$.

1. $P(-2, -1)$, $Q(-1, 0)$, $R(0, -1)$; $k = 4$ **2.** $P(5, -5)$, $Q(10, -5)$, $R(10, 5)$; $k = 0.4$

EXAMPLE 3 **Find a scale factor**

PHOTO STICKERS You are making your own photo stickers. Your photo is 4 inches by 4 inches. The image on the stickers is 1.1 inches by 1.1 inches. What is the scale factor of the reduction?

Solution

The scale factor is the ratio of a side length of the sticker image to a side length of the original photo, or $\frac{1.1 \text{ in.}}{4 \text{ in.}}$. In simplest form, the scale factor is $\frac{11}{40}$.

READING DIAGRAMS Generally, for a center of dilation at the origin, a point of the figure and its image lie on the same ray from the origin. However, if a point of the figure *is* the origin, its image is also the origin.

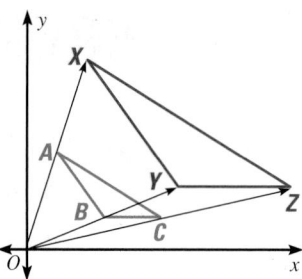

★ **EXAMPLE 4** **Standardized Test Practice**

You want to create a quadrilateral *EFGH* that is similar to quadrilateral *PQRS*. What are the coordinates of *H*?

ELIMINATE CHOICES
You can eliminate choice A, because you can tell by looking at the graph that *H* is in Quadrant I. The point (12, −15) is in Quadrant IV.

Ⓐ (12, −15)

Ⓑ (7, 8)

Ⓒ (12, 15)

Ⓓ (15, 18)

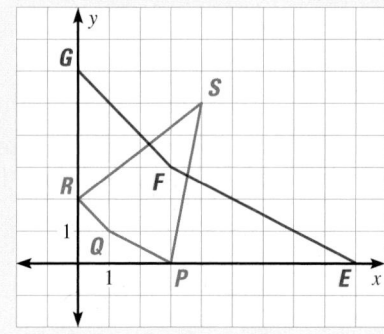

Solution

Determine if *EFGH* is a dilation of *PQRS* by checking whether the same scale factor can be used to obtain *E*, *F*, and *G* from *P*, *Q*, and *R*.

$(x, y) \rightarrow (kx, ky)$

$P(3, 0) \rightarrow E(9, 0)$ $k = 3$

$Q(1, 1) \rightarrow F(3, 3)$ $k = 3$

$R(0, 2) \rightarrow G(0, 6)$ $k = 3$

Because *k* is the same in each case, the image is a dilation with a scale factor of 3. So, you can use the scale factor to find the image *H* of point *S*.

$S(4, 5) \rightarrow H(3 \cdot 4, 3 \cdot 5) = H(12, 15)$

▶ The correct answer is C. Ⓐ Ⓑ Ⓒ Ⓓ

CHECK Draw rays from the origin through each point and its image.

✓ **GUIDED PRACTICE** for Examples 3 and 4

3. **WHAT IF?** In Example 3, what is the scale factor of the reduction if your photo is 5.5 inches by 5.5 inches?

4. Suppose a figure containing the origin is dilated. *Explain* why the corresponding point in the image of the figure is also the origin.

6.7 EXERCISES

HOMEWORK KEY

○ = **WORKED-OUT SOLUTIONS**
on p. WS8 for Exs. 5, 11, and 27

★ = **STANDARDIZED TEST PRACTICE**
Exs. 2, 13, 21, 22, 28, 30, and 31

SKILL PRACTICE

1. **VOCABULARY** Copy and complete: In a dilation, the image is __?__ to the original figure.

2. ★ **WRITING** *Explain* how to find the scale factor of a dilation. How do you know whether a dilation is an enlargement or a reduction?

EXAMPLES
1 and 2
on pp. 409–410
for Exs. 3–8

DRAWING DILATIONS **Draw a dilation of the polygon with the given vertices using the given scale factor *k*.**

3. $A(-2, 1)$, $B(-4, 1)$, $C(-2, 4)$; $k = 2$

4. $A(-5, 5)$, $B(-5, -10)$, $C(10, 0)$; $k = \dfrac{3}{5}$

5. $A(1, 1)$, $B(6, 1)$, $C(6, 3)$; $k = 1.5$

6. $A(2, 8)$, $B(8, 8)$, $C(16, 4)$; $k = 0.25$

7. $A(-8, 0)$, $B(0, 8)$, $C(4, 0)$, $D(0, -4)$; $k = \dfrac{3}{8}$

8. $A(0, 0)$, $B(0, 3)$, $C(2, 4)$, $D(2, -1)$; $k = \dfrac{13}{2}$

EXAMPLE 3
on p. 410
for Exs. 9–12

IDENTIFYING DILATIONS **Determine whether the dilation from Figure A to Figure B is a *reduction* or an *enlargement*. Then find its scale factor.**

9.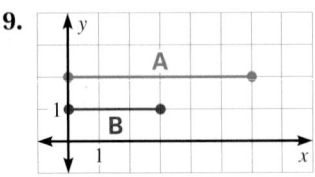

10.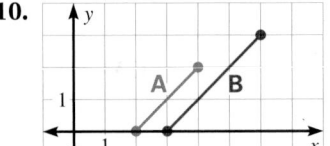

11.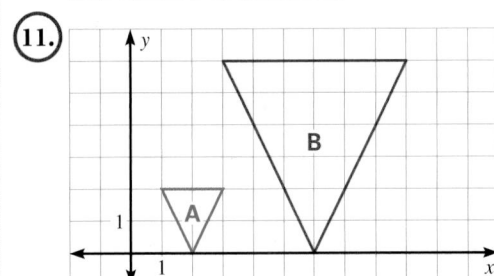

12.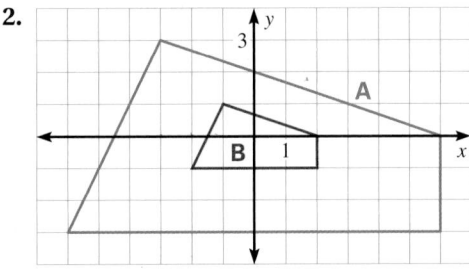

EXAMPLE 4
on p. 411
for Ex. 13

13. ★ **MULTIPLE CHOICE** You want to create a quadrilateral *PQRS* that is similar to quadrilateral *JKLM*. What are the coordinates of *S*?

Ⓐ (2, 4)

Ⓑ (4, −2)

Ⓒ (−2, −4)

Ⓓ (−4, −2)

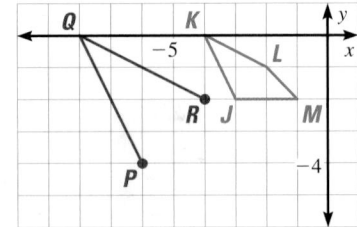

14. **ERROR ANALYSIS** A student found the scale factor of the dilation from $\overline{AB}$ to $\overline{CD}$ to be $\dfrac{2}{5}$. *Describe* and correct the student's error.

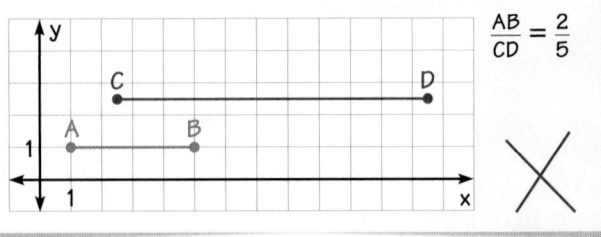

$$\dfrac{AB}{CD} = \dfrac{2}{5}$$

15. ERROR ANALYSIS A student says that the figure shown represents a dilation. What is wrong with this statement?

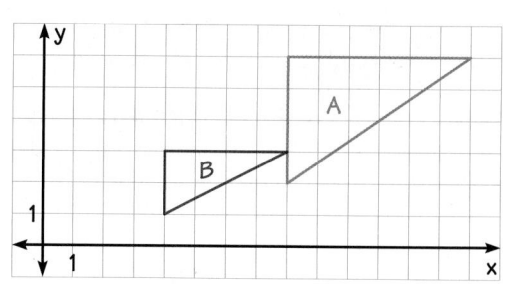

IDENTIFYING TRANSFORMATIONS Determine whether the transformation shown is a *translation, reflection, rotation,* or *dilation.*

16.
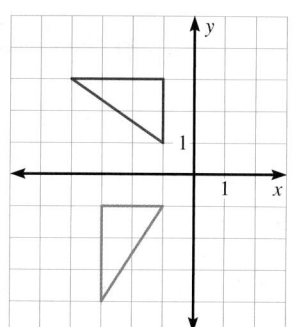

17.
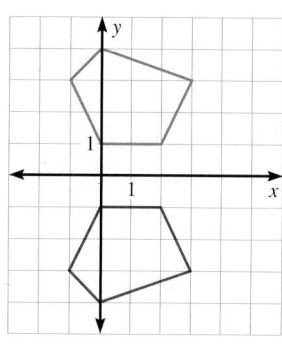

18.
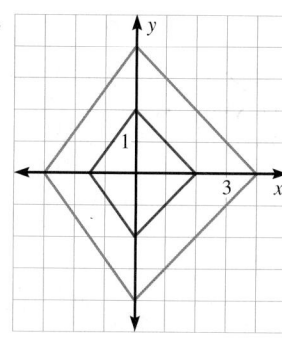

FINDING SCALE FACTORS Find the scale factor of the dilation of Figure A to Figure B. Then give the unknown lengths of Figure A.

19.
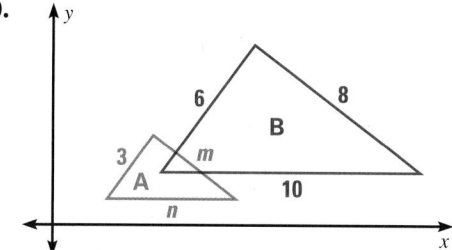

20.
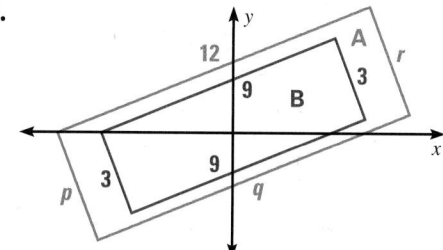

21. ★ MULTIPLE CHOICE In the diagram shown, $\triangle ABO$ is a dilation of $\triangle DEO$. The length of a median of $\triangle ABO$ is what percent of the length of the corresponding median of $\triangle DEO$?

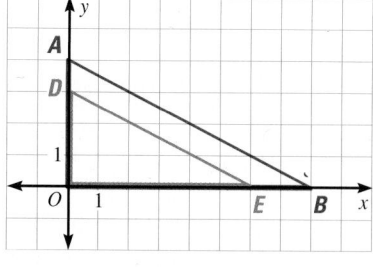

(A) 50%

(B) 75%

(C) $133\frac{1}{3}\%$

(D) 200%

22. ★ SHORT RESPONSE Suppose you dilate a figure using a scale factor of 2. Then, you dilate the image using a scale factor of $\frac{1}{2}$. *Describe* the size and shape of this new image.

CHALLENGE *Describe* the two transformations, the first followed by the second, that combined will transform $\triangle ABC$ into $\triangle DEF$.

23. $A(-3, 3), B(-3, 1), C(0, 1)$
$D(6, 6), E(6, 2), F(0, 2)$

24. $A(6, 0), B(9, 6), C(12, 6)$
$D(0, 3), E(1, 5), F(2, 5)$

EXAMPLE 3
on p. 410 for
Exs. 25–27

25. BILLBOARD ADVERTISEMENT A billboard advertising agency requires each advertisement to be drawn so that it fits in a 12-inch by 6-inch rectangle. The agency uses a scale factor of 24 to enlarge the advertisement to create the billboard. What are the dimensions of a billboard, in feet?

@HomeTutor for problem solving help at classzone.com

26. POTTERY Your pottery is used on a poster for a student art show. You want to make postcards using the same image. On the poster, the image is 8 inches in width and 6 inches in height. If the image on the postcard can be 5 inches wide, what scale should you use for the image on the postcard?

Student Art Show
Main Gallery
May 14 – June 12

@HomeTutor for problem solving help at classzone.com

27. SHADOWS You and your friend are walking at night. You point a flashlight at your friend, and your friend's shadow is cast on the building behind him. The shadow is an enlargement, and is 15 feet tall. Your friend is 6 feet tall. What is the scale factor of the enlargement?

28. ★ OPEN-ENDED MATH *Describe* how you can use dilations to create the figure shown below.

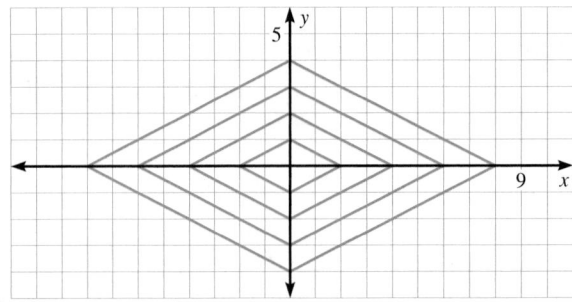

Animated Geometry at classzone.com

29. MULTI-STEP PROBLEM $\triangle ABC$ has vertices $A(3, -3)$, $B(3, 6)$, and $C(15, 6)$.

  a. Draw a dilation of $\triangle ABC$ using a scale factor of $\frac{2}{3}$.

  b. Find the ratio of the perimeter of the image to the perimeter of the original figure. How does this ratio compare to the scale factor?

  c. Find the ratio of the area of the image to the area of the original figure. How does this ratio compare to the scale factor?

30. ★ EXTENDED RESPONSE Look at the coordinate notation for a dilation on page 409. Suppose the definition of dilation allowed $k < 0$.

  a. *Describe* the dilation if $-1 < k < 0$.

  b. *Describe* the dilation if $k < -1$.

  c. Use a rotation to describe a dilation with $k = -1$.

31. ★ **SHORT RESPONSE** *Explain* how you can use dilations to make a perspective drawing with the center of dilation as a vanishing point. Draw a diagram.

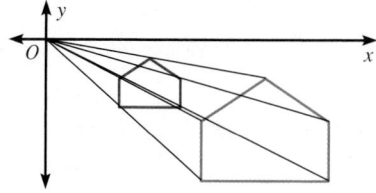

32. **MIDPOINTS** Let $\overline{XY}$ be a dilation of $\overline{PQ}$ with scale factor k. Show that the image of the midpoint of $\overline{PQ}$ is the midpoint of $\overline{XY}$.

33. **REASONING** In Exercise 32, show that $\overline{XY} \parallel \overline{PQ}$.

34. **CHALLENGE** A rectangle has vertices $A(0, 0)$, $B(0, 6)$, $C(9, 6)$, and $D(9, 0)$. *Explain* how to dilate the rectangle to produce an image whose area is twice the area of the original rectangle. Make a conjecture about how to dilate any polygon to produce an image whose area is n times the area of the original polygon.

MIXED REVIEW

Simplify the expression. *(p. 873)*

35. $(3x + 2)^2 + (x - 5)^2$ **36.** $4\left(\frac{1}{2}ab\right) + (b - a)^2$ **37.** $(a + b)^2 - (a - b)^2$

Find the distance between each pair of points. *(p. 15)*

38. $(0, 5)$ and $(4, 3)$ **39.** $(-3, 0)$ and $(2, 4)$ **40.** $(-2, -4)$ and $(3, -2)$

PREVIEW
Prepare for
Lesson 7.1
in Exs. 41–43.

Find the value(s) of the variable(s).

41. Area = 6 in.^{2} *(p. 49)*   **42.** $\triangle ABC \cong \triangle DCB$ *(p. 256)*   **43.** $\triangle PQR$ is isosceles. *(p. 303)*

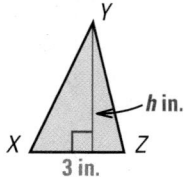   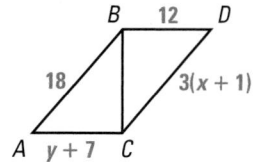   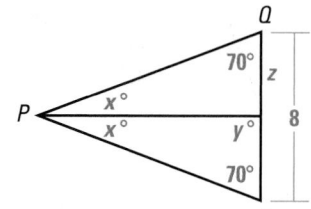

QUIZ *for Lessons 6.6–6.7*

Find the value of x. *(p. 397)*

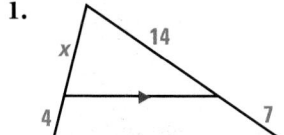

1.   **2.**   **3.**

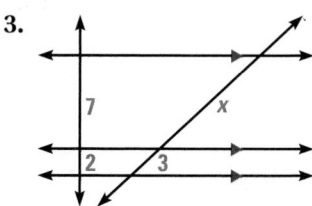

Draw a dilation of $\triangle ABC$ with the given vertices and scale factor k. *(p. 409)*

4. $A(-5, 5)$, $B(-5, -10)$, $C(10, 0)$; $k = 0.4$ **5.** $A(-2, 1)$, $B(-4, 1)$, $C(-2, 4)$; $k = 2.5$

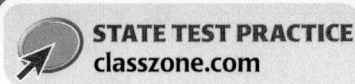
Lessons 6.4–6.7

1. **OPEN-ENDED** The diagram shows the front of a house. What information would you need in order to show that $\triangle WXY \sim \triangle VXZ$ using the SAS Similarity Theorem?

2. **EXTENDED RESPONSE** You leave your house to go to the mall. You drive due north 8 miles, due east 7.5 miles, and due north again 2 miles.

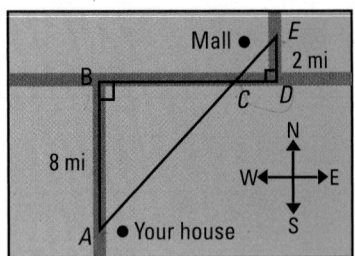

   a. *Explain* how to prove that $\triangle ABC \sim \triangle EDC$.

   b. Find CD.

   c. Find AE, the distance between your house and the mall.

3. **SHORT RESPONSE** The Cardon cactus found in the Sonoran Desert in Mexico is the tallest type of cactus in the world. Marco stands 76 feet from the cactus so that his shadow coincides with the cactus' shadow. Marco is 6 feet tall and his shadow is 8 feet long. How tall is the Cardon cactus? *Explain.*

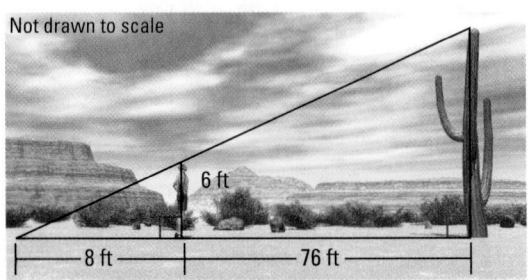

Not drawn to scale

6 ft

8 ft   76 ft

4. **SHORT RESPONSE** In the diagram, is it *always*, *sometimes*, or *never* true that $l_1 \parallel l_2 \parallel l_3$? *Explain.*

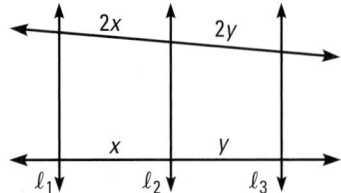

5. **GRIDDED ANSWER** In the diagram of the roof truss, $HK = 7$ meters, $KM = 8$ meters, $JL = 4.7$ meters, and $\angle 1 \cong \angle 2$. Find LM to the nearest tenth of a meter.

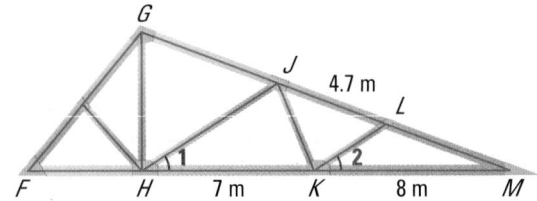

6. **GRIDDED ANSWER** You are designing a catalog for a greeting card company.

   The catalog features a $2\frac{4}{5}$ inch by 2 inch photograph of each card. The actual dimensions of a greeting card are 7 inches by 5 inches. What is the scale factor of the reduction?

7. **MULTI-STEP PROBLEM** Rectangle $ABCD$ has vertices $A(2, 2)$, $B(4, 2)$, $C(4, -4)$, and $D(2, -4)$.

   a. Draw rectangle $ABCD$. Then draw a dilation of rectangle $ABCD$ using a scale factor of $\frac{5}{4}$. Label the image $PQRS$.

   b. Find the ratio of the perimeter of the image to the perimeter of the original figure. How does this ratio compare to the scale factor?

   c. Find the ratio of the area of the image to the area of the original figure. How does this ratio compare to the scale factor?

BIG IDEAS

For Your Notebook

Big Idea 1

Using Ratios and Proportions to Solve Geometry Problems

You can use properties of proportions to solve a variety of algebraic and geometric problems.

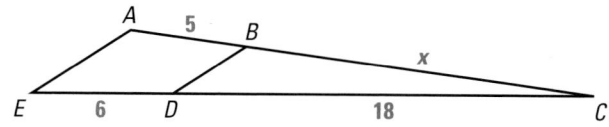

For example, in the diagram above, suppose you know that $\dfrac{AB}{BC} = \dfrac{ED}{DC}$. Then you can write any of the following relationships.

$$\frac{5}{x} = \frac{6}{18} \qquad 5 \cdot 18 = 6x \qquad \frac{x}{5} = \frac{18}{6} \qquad \frac{5}{6} = \frac{x}{18} \qquad \frac{5 + x}{x} = \frac{6 + 18}{18}$$

Big Idea 2

Showing that Triangles are Similar

You learned three ways to prove two triangles are similar.

AA Similarity Postulate	**SSS Similarity Theorem**	**SAS Similarity Theorem**
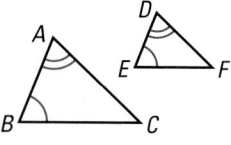	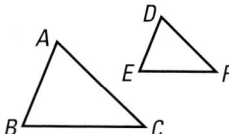	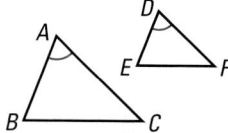
If $\angle A \cong \angle D$ and $\angle B \cong \angle E$, then $\triangle ABC \sim \triangle DEF$.	If $\dfrac{AB}{DE} = \dfrac{BC}{EF} = \dfrac{AC}{DF}$, then $\triangle ABC \sim \triangle DEF$.	If $\angle A \cong \angle D$ and $\dfrac{AB}{DE} = \dfrac{AC}{DF}$, then $\triangle ABC \sim \triangle DEF$.

Big Idea 3

Using Indirect Measurement and Similarity

You can use triangle similarity theorems to apply indirect measurement in order to find lengths that would be inconvenient or impossible to measure directly.

Consider the diagram shown. Because the two triangles formed by the person and the tree are similar by the AA Similarity Postulate, you can write the following proportion to find the height of the tree.

$$\frac{\text{height of person}}{\text{length of person's shadow}} = \frac{\text{height of tree}}{\text{length of tree's shadow}}$$

You also learned about dilations, a type of similarity transformation. In a dilation, a figure is either enlarged or reduced in size.

@HomeTutor
classzone.com
• Multi-Language Glossary
• Vocabulary practice

REVIEW KEY VOCABULARY

For a list of postulates and theorems, see pp. 926–931.

- ratio, *p. 356*
- proportion, *p. 358* means, extremes
- geometric mean, *p. 359*
- scale drawing, *p. 365*

- scale, *p. 365*
- similar polygons, *p. 372*
- scale factor of two similar polygons, *p. 373*
- dilation, *p. 409*

- center of dilation, *p. 409*
- scale factor of a dilation, *p. 409*
- reduction, *p. 409*
- enlargement, *p. 409*

VOCABULARY EXERCISES

Copy and complete the statement.

1. A __?__ is a transformation in which the original figure and its image are similar.

2. If $\triangle PQR \sim \triangle XYZ$, then $\dfrac{PQ}{XY} = \dfrac{?}{YZ} = \dfrac{?}{?}$.

3. **WRITING** *Describe* the relationship between a ratio and a proportion. Give an example of each.

REVIEW EXAMPLES AND EXERCISES

Use the review examples and exercises below to check your understanding of the concepts you have learned in each lesson of Chapter 6.

6.1 Ratios, Proportions, and the Geometric Mean   *pp. 356–363*

EXAMPLE

The measures of the angles in $\triangle ABC$ are in the extended ratio of $3:4:5$. Find the measures of the angles.

Use the extended ratio of $3:4:5$ to label the angle measures as $3x°$, $4x°$, and $5x°$.

$3x° + 4x° + 5x° = 180°$	**Triangle Sum Theorem**
$12x = 180$	**Combine like terms.**
$x = 15$	**Divide each side by 12.**

So, the angle measures are $3(15°) = 45°$, $4(15°) = 60°$, and $5(15°) = 75°$.

EXERCISES

EXAMPLES
1, 3, and 6
on pp. 356–359
for Exs. 4–6

4. The length of a rectangle is 20 meters and the width is 15 meters. Find the ratio of the width to the length of the rectangle. Then simplify the ratio.

5. The measures of the angles in $\triangle UVW$ are in the extended ratio of $1:1:2$. Find the measures of the angles.

6. Find the geometric mean of 8 and 12.

6.2 Use Proportions to Solve Geometry Problems
pp. 364–370

EXAMPLE

In the diagram, $\frac{BA}{DA} = \frac{BC}{EC}$. Find *BD*.

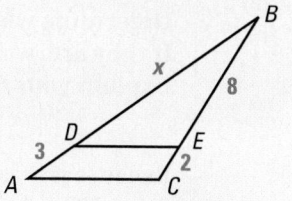

$\frac{x+3}{3} = \frac{8+2}{2}$ **Substitution Property of Equality**

$2x + 6 = 30$ **Cross Products Property**

$x = 12$ **Solve for *x*.**

EXERCISES

EXAMPLE 2
on p. 365
for Exs. 7–8

Use the diagram and the given information to find the unknown length.

7. Given $\frac{RN}{RP} = \frac{QM}{QL}$, find *RP*.

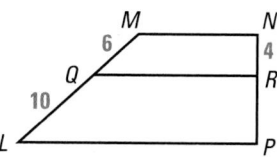

8. Given $\frac{CD}{DB} = \frac{CE}{EA}$, find *CD*.

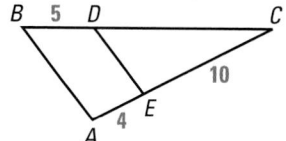

6.3 Use Similar Polygons
pp. 372–379

EXAMPLE

In the diagram, *EHGF* ~ *KLMN*. Find the scale factor.

From the diagram, you can see that $\overline{EH}$ and $\overline{KL}$ correspond. So, the scale factor of *EHGF* to *KLMN* is $\frac{EH}{KL} = \frac{12}{18} = \frac{2}{3}$.

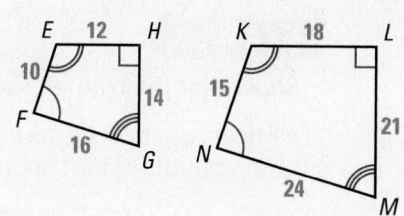

EXERCISES

**EXAMPLES
2 and 4**
on pp. 373–374
for Exs. 9–11

In Exercises 9 and 10, determine whether the polygons are similar. If they are, write a similarity statement and find the scale factor.

9.

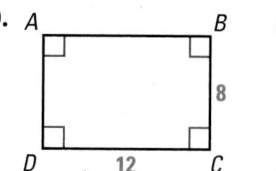 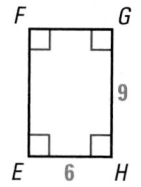

10.

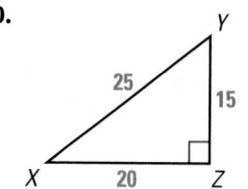 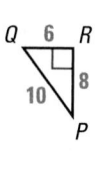

11. POSTERS Two similar posters have a scale factor of 4 : 5. The large poster's perimeter is 85 inches. Find the small poster's perimeter.

6.4 Prove Triangles Similar by AA

pp. 381–387

EXAMPLE

Determine whether the triangles are similar. If they are, write a similarity statement. Explain your reasoning.

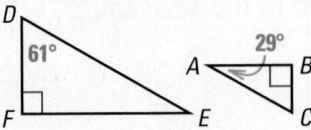

Because they are right angles, $\angle F \cong \angle B$. By the Triangle Sum Theorem, $61° + 90° + m\angle E = 180°$, so $m\angle E = 29°$ and $\angle E \cong \angle A$. Then, two angles of $\triangle DFE$ are congruent to two angles of $\triangle CBA$. So, $\triangle DFE \sim \triangle CBA$.

EXERCISES

EXAMPLES 2 and 3
on pp. 382–383
for Exs. 12–14

Use the AA Similarity Postulate to show that the triangles are similar.

12.
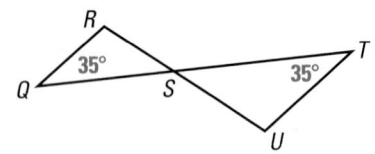

13.
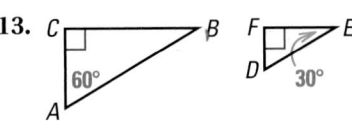

14. **CELL TOWER** A cellular telephone tower casts a shadow that is 72 feet long, while a tree nearby that is 27 feet tall casts a shadow that is 6 feet long. How tall is the tower?

6.5 Prove Triangles Similar by SSS and SAS

pp. 388–395

EXAMPLE

Show that the triangles are similar.

Notice that the lengths of two pairs of corresponding sides are proportional.

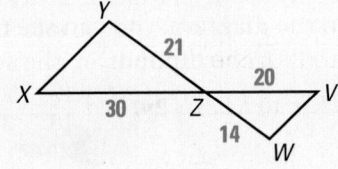

$$\frac{WZ}{YZ} = \frac{14}{21} = \frac{2}{3} \qquad \frac{VZ}{XZ} = \frac{20}{30} = \frac{2}{3}$$

The included angles for these sides, $\angle XZY$ and $\angle VZW$, are vertical angles, so $\angle XZY \cong \angle VZW$. Then $\triangle XYZ \sim \triangle VWZ$ by the SAS Similarity Theorem.

EXERCISES

EXAMPLE 4
on p. 391
for Exs. 15–16

Use the SSS Similarity Theorem or SAS Similarity Theorem to show that the triangles are similar.

15.
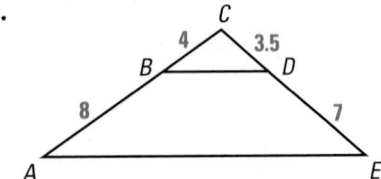

16.
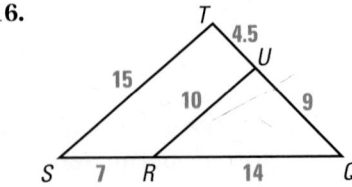

6.6 Use Proportionality Theorems

pp. 397–403

EXAMPLE

Determine whether $\overline{MP} \parallel \overline{LQ}$.

Begin by finding and simplifying ratios of lengths determined by $\overline{MP}$.

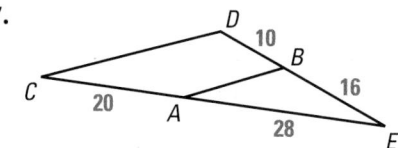

$$\frac{NM}{ML} = \frac{8}{4} = \frac{2}{1} \qquad \frac{NP}{PQ} = \frac{24}{12} = \frac{2}{1}$$

Because $\frac{NM}{ML} = \frac{NP}{PQ}$, $\overline{MP}$ is parallel to $\overline{LQ}$ by Theorem 6.5, the Triangle Proportionality Converse.

EXERCISES

EXAMPLE 2
on p. 398
for Exs. 17–18

Use the given information to determine whether $\overline{AB} \parallel \overline{CD}$.

17.

18.

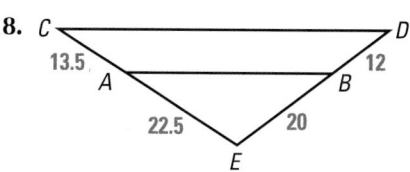

6.7 Perform Similarity Transformations

pp. 409–415

EXAMPLE

Draw a dilation of quadrilateral *FGHJ* with vertices *F*(1, 1), *G*(2, 2), *H*(4, 1), and *J*(2, −1). Use a scale factor of 2.

First draw *FGHJ*. Find the dilation of each vertex by multiplying its coordinates by 2. Then draw the dilation.

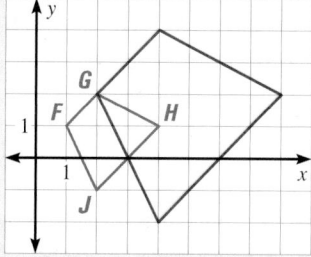

$$(x, y) \rightarrow (2x, 2y)$$

$$F(1, 1) \rightarrow (2, 2)$$

$$G(2, 2) \rightarrow (4, 4)$$

$$H(4, 1) \rightarrow (8, 2)$$

$$J(2, -1) \rightarrow (4, -2)$$

EXERCISES

EXAMPLE 1
on p. 409
for Exs. 19–21

Draw a dilation of the polygon with the given vertices using the given scale factor *k*.

19. *T*(0, 8), *U*(6, 0), *V*(0, 0); $k = \frac{3}{2}$

20. *A*(6, 0), *B*(3, 9), *C*(0, 0), *D*(3, 1); $k = 4$

21. *P*(8, 2), *Q*(4, 0), *R*(3, 1), *S*(6, 4); $k = 0.5$

Solve the proportion.

1. $\dfrac{6}{x} = \dfrac{9}{24}$

2. $\dfrac{5}{4} = \dfrac{y-5}{12}$

3. $\dfrac{3-2b}{4} = \dfrac{3}{2}$

4. $\dfrac{7}{2a+8} = \dfrac{1}{a-1}$

In Exercises 5–7, use the diagram where $\triangle PQR \sim \triangle ABC$.

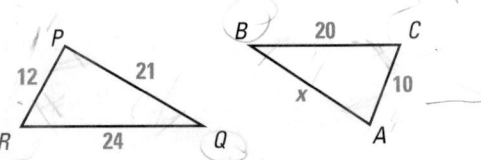

5. List all pairs of congruent angles.

6. Write the ratios of the corresponding sides in a statement of proportionality.

7. Find the value of x.

Determine whether the triangles are similar. If so, write a similarity statement and the postulate or theorem that justifies your answer.

8.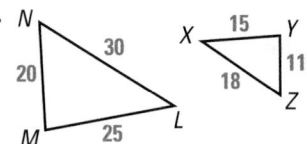

9.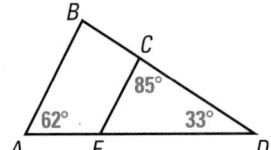

10.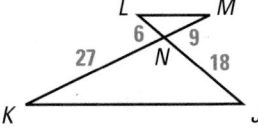

In Exercises 11–13, find the length of $\overline{AB}$.

11.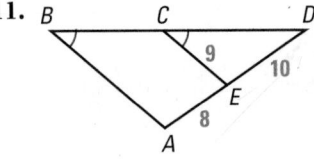

12.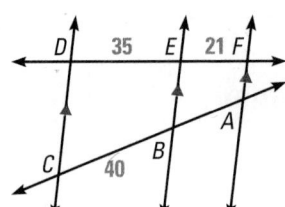

13.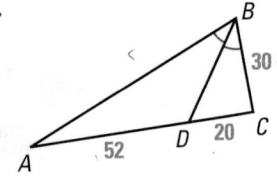

Determine whether the dilation from Figure A to Figure B is a *reduction* or an *enlargement*. Then find its scale factor.

14.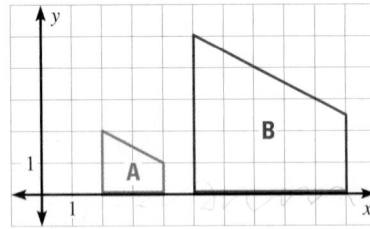

15.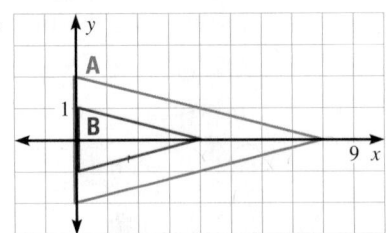

16. SCALE MODEL You are making a scale model of your school's baseball diamond as part of an art project. The distance between two consecutive bases is 90 feet. If you use a scale factor of $\dfrac{1}{180}$ to build your model, what will be the distance around the bases on your model?

SOLVE QUADRATIC EQUATIONS AND SIMPLIFY RADICALS

A radical expression is *simplified* when the radicand has no perfect square factor except 1, there is no fraction in the radicand, and there is no radical in a denominator.

xy **EXAMPLE 1** *Solve quadratic equations by finding square roots*

Solve the equation $4x^2 - 3 = 109$.

$4x^2 - 3 = 109$	Write original equation.
$4x^2 = 112$	Add 3 to each side.
$x^2 = 28$	Divide each side by 4.
$x = \pm\sqrt{28}$	$\sqrt{ab} = \sqrt{a} \cdot \sqrt{b}$, so $\sqrt{28} = \pm\sqrt{4} \cdot \sqrt{7}$.
$x = \pm 2\sqrt{7}$	Simplify.

xy **EXAMPLE 2** *Simplify quotients with radicals*

Simplify the expression.

a. $\sqrt{\dfrac{10}{8}}$

b. $\sqrt{\dfrac{1}{5}}$

Solution

a. $\sqrt{\dfrac{10}{8}} = \sqrt{\dfrac{5}{4}}$ Simplify fraction.

$= \dfrac{\sqrt{5}}{\sqrt{4}}$ $\sqrt{\dfrac{a}{b}} = \dfrac{\sqrt{a}}{\sqrt{b}}$.

$= \dfrac{\sqrt{5}}{2}$ Simplify.

b. $\sqrt{\dfrac{1}{5}} = \dfrac{1}{\sqrt{5}}$ $\sqrt{\dfrac{a}{b}} = \dfrac{\sqrt{a}}{\sqrt{b}}$ and $\sqrt{1} = 1$.

$= \dfrac{1}{\sqrt{5}} \cdot \dfrac{\sqrt{5}}{\sqrt{5}}$ Multiply numerator and denominator by $\sqrt{5}$.

$= \dfrac{\sqrt{5}}{5}$ Multiply fractions. $\sqrt{a} \cdot \sqrt{a} = a$.

EXERCISES

EXAMPLE 1
for Exs. 1–9

Solve the equation or write *no solution*.

1. $x^2 + 8 = 108$ **2.** $2x^2 - 1 = 49$ **3.** $x^2 - 9 = 8$

4. $5x^2 + 11 = 1$ **5.** $2(x^2 - 7) = 6$ **6.** $9 = 21 + 3x^2$

7. $3x^2 - 17 = 43$ **8.** $56 - x^2 = 20$ **9.** $-3(-x^2 + 5) = 39$

EXAMPLE 2
for Exs. 10–17

Simplify the expression.

10. $\sqrt{\dfrac{7}{81}}$ **11.** $\sqrt{\dfrac{3}{5}}$ **12.** $\sqrt{\dfrac{24}{27}}$ **13.** $\dfrac{3\sqrt{7}}{\sqrt{12}}$

14. $\sqrt{\dfrac{75}{64}}$ **15.** $\dfrac{\sqrt{2}}{\sqrt{200}}$ **16.** $\dfrac{9}{\sqrt{27}}$ **17.** $\sqrt{\dfrac{21}{42}}$

EXTENDED RESPONSE QUESTIONS

> **PROBLEM**

To find the height of a tree, a student 63 inches in height measures the length of the tree's shadow and the length of his own shadow, as shown. The student casts a shadow 81 inches in length and the tree casts a shadow 477 inches in length.

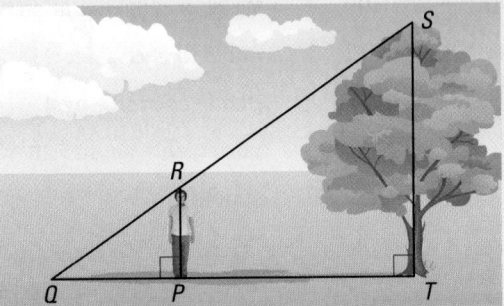

a. Explain why $\triangle PQR \sim \triangle TQS$.

b. Find the height of the tree.

c. Suppose the sun is a little lower in the sky. Can you still use this method to measure the height of the tree? *Explain.*

Below are sample solutions to the problem. Read each solution and the comments in blue to see why the sample represents full credit, partial credit, or no credit.

SAMPLE 1: Full credit solution

The reasoning is complete.

a. Because they are both right angles, $\angle QPR \cong \angle QTS$. Also, $\angle Q \cong \angle Q$ by the Reflexive Property. So, $\triangle PQR \sim \triangle TQS$ by the AA Similarity Postulate.

The proportion and calculations are correct.

b.
$$\frac{PR}{PQ} = \frac{TS}{TQ}$$

$$\frac{63}{81} = \frac{TS}{477}$$

$$63(477) = 81 \cdot TS$$

$$371 = TS$$

The height of the tree is 371 inches.

In part (b), the question is answered correctly.

c. As long as the sun creates two shadows, I can use this method. Angles *RPQ* and *T* will always be right angles. The measure of $\angle Q$ will change as the sun's position changes, but the angle will still be congruent to itself. So, $\triangle PQR$ and $\triangle TQS$ will still be similar, and I can write a proportion.

In part (c), the reasoning is complete and correct.

Scoring Rubric

Full Credit
• solution is complete and correct

Partial Credit
• solution is complete but has errors,
  or
• solution is without error but is incomplete

No Credit
• no solution is given,
  or
• solution makes no sense

SAMPLE 2: Partial credit solution

> In part (a), there is no explanation of why the postulate can be applied.

a. $\triangle PQR \sim \triangle TQS$ by the Angle-Angle Similarity Postulate.

b.
$$\frac{PR}{PQ} = \frac{TS}{TP}$$

> In part (b), the proportion is incorrect, which leads to an incorrect solution.

$$\frac{63}{81} = \frac{TS}{396}$$

$$308 = TS$$

The height of the tree is 308 inches.

> In part (c), a partial explanation is given.

c. As long as the sun creates two shadows, I can use this method because the triangles will always be similar.

SAMPLE 3: No credit solution

> The reasoning in part (a) is incomplete.

a. The triangles are similar because the lines are parallel and the angles are congruent.

> In part (b), no work is shown.

b. $TS = 371$ inches

> The answer in part (c) is incorrect.

c. No. The angles in the triangle will change, so you can't write a proportion.

PRACTICE Apply the Scoring Rubric

1. A student's solution to the problem on the previous page is given below. Score the solution as *full credit, partial credit,* or *no credit. Explain* your reasoning. If you choose *partial credit* or *no credit, explain* how you would change the solution so that it earns a score of full credit.

a. $\angle QPR \cong \angle PTS$, and $\angle Q$ is in both triangles. So, $\triangle PQR \sim \triangle TQS$.

b.
$$\frac{PR}{PQ} = \frac{QT}{ST}$$

$$\frac{63}{81} = \frac{477}{x}$$

$$63x = 81(477)$$

$$x \approx 613.3$$

The tree is about 613.3 inches tall.

c. The method will still work because the triangles will still be similar if the sun changes position. The right angles will stay right angles, and $\angle Q$ is in both triangles, so it does not matter if its measure changes.

EXTENDED RESPONSE

1. Use the diagram.

   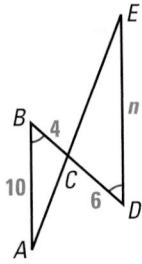

   a. *Explain* how you know that △*ABC* ~ △*EDC*.

   b. Find the value of *n*.

   c. The perimeter of △*ABC* is 22. What is the perimeter of △*EDC*? *Justify* your answer.

2. On the easel shown at the right, $\overline{AB} \parallel \overline{HC} \parallel \overline{GD}$, and $\overline{AG} \cong \overline{BD}$.

   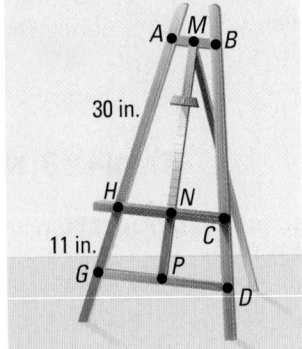

   a. Find *BD*, *BC*, and *CD*. *Justify* your answer.

   b. On the easel, $\overline{MP}$ is a support bar attached to $\overline{AB}$, $\overline{HC}$, and $\overline{GD}$. On this support bar, *NP* = 10 inches. Find the length of $\overline{MP}$ to the nearest inch. *Justify* your answer.

   c. The support bar $\overline{MP}$ bisects $\overline{AB}$, $\overline{HC}$, and $\overline{GD}$. Does this mean that polygons *AMNH* and *AMPG* are similar? *Explain*.

3. A handmade rectangular rug is available in two sizes at a rug store. A small rug is 24 inches long and 16 inches wide. A large rug is 36 inches long and 24 inches wide.

   a. Are the rugs similar? If so, what is the ratio of their corresponding sides? *Explain*.

   b. Find the perimeter and area of each rug. Then find the ratio of the perimeters (large rug to small rug) and the ratio of the areas (large rug to small rug).

   c. It takes 250 feet of wool yarn to make 1 square foot of either rug. How many inches of yarn are used for each rug? *Explain*.

   d. The price of a large rug is 1.5 times the price of a small rug. The store owner wants to change the prices for the rugs, so that the price for each rug is based on the amount of yarn used to make the rug. If the owner changes the prices, about how many times as much will the price of a large rug be than the price of a small rug? *Explain*.

4. In the diagram shown at the right, $\overleftrightarrow{OQ}$ passes through the origin.

   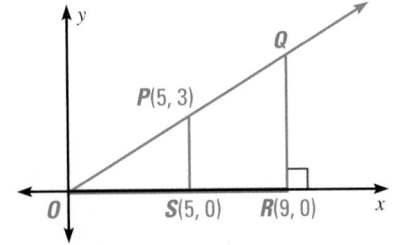

   a. Explain how you know that △*OPS* ~ △*OQR*.

   b. Find the coordinates of point *Q*. *Justify* your answer.

   c. The *x*-coordinate of a point on $\overleftrightarrow{OQ}$ is *a*. Write the *y*-coordinate of this point in terms of *a*. *Justify* your answer.

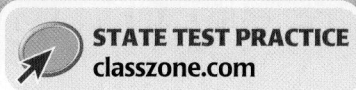
MULTIPLE CHOICE

5. If △*PQR* ~ △*STU*, which proportion is not necessarily true?

   Ⓐ $\dfrac{PQ}{QR} = \dfrac{ST}{TU}$ Ⓑ $\dfrac{PQ}{SU} = \dfrac{PR}{TU}$

   Ⓒ $\dfrac{PR}{SU} = \dfrac{QR}{TU}$ Ⓓ $\dfrac{PQ}{PR} = \dfrac{ST}{SU}$

6. On a map, the distance between two cities is $2\frac{3}{4}$ inches. The scale on the map is 1 in.:80 mi. What is the actual distance between the two cities?

   Ⓐ 160 mi   Ⓑ 180 mi

   Ⓒ 200 mi   Ⓓ 220 mi

7. In the diagram, what is the scale factor of the dilation from △*PQR* to △*TUV*?

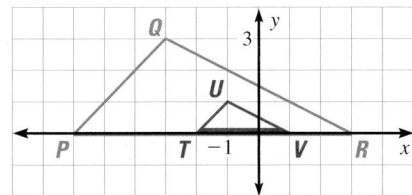

   Ⓐ $\dfrac{1}{2}$ Ⓑ $\dfrac{1}{3}$

   Ⓒ 2   Ⓓ 3

GRIDDED ANSWER

8. Find the value of *x*.

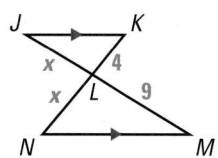

9. In the diagram below, △*PQM* ~ △*NMR*, and $\overline{MR} \cong \overline{QR}$. If *NR* = 12, find *PM*.

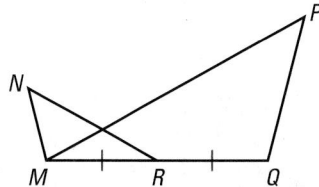

10. Given *GE* = 10, find *HE*.

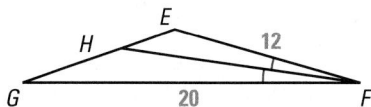

11. In an acute isosceles triangle, the measures of two of the angles are in the ratio 4 : 1. Find the measure of a base angle in the triangle.

SHORT RESPONSE

12. On a school campus, the gym is 400 feet from the art studio.

   a. Suppose you draw a map of the school campus using a scale of $\frac{1}{4}$ inch: 100 feet. How far will the gym be from the art studio on your map?

   b. Suppose you draw a map of the school campus using a scale of $\frac{1}{2}$ inch : 100 feet. Will the distance from the gym to the art studio on this map be *greater than* or *less than* the distance on the map in part (a)? *Explain.*

13. Rectangles *ABCD* and *EFGH* are similar, and the ratio of *AB* to *EF* is 1 : 3. In each rectangle, the length is twice the width. The area of *ABCD* is 32 square inches. Find the length, width, and area of *EFGH*. *Explain.*

Find $m\angle 2$ **if** $\angle 1$ **and** $\angle 2$ **are (a) complementary angles and (b) supplementary angles.** *(p. 35)*

  1. $m\angle 1 = 57°$ **2.** $m\angle 1 = 23°$ **3.** $m\angle 1 = 88°$ **4.** $m\angle 1 = 46°$

Solve the equation and write a reason for each step. *(p. 105)*

  5. $3x - 19 = 47$ **6.** $30 - 4(x - 3) = -x + 18$ **7.** $-5(x + 2) = 25$

State the postulate or theorem that justifies the statement. *(pp. 147, 154)*

  8. $\angle 1 \cong \angle 8$ **9.** $\angle 3 \cong \angle 6$

  10. $m\angle 3 + m\angle 5 = 180°$ **11.** $\angle 3 \cong \angle 7$

  12. $\angle 2 \cong \angle 3$ **13.** $m\angle 7 + m\angle 8 = 180°$

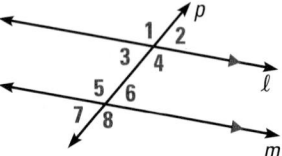

The variable expressions represent the angle measures of a triangle. Find the measure of each angle. Then classify the triangle by its angles. *(p. 217)*

  14. $m\angle A = x°$ **15.** $m\angle A = 2x°$ **16.** $m\angle A = (3x - 15)°$
  $\quad m\angle B = 3x°$ $\quad m\angle B = 2x°$ $\quad m\angle B = (x + 5)°$
  $\quad m\angle C = 4x°$ $\quad m\angle C = (x - 15)°$ $\quad m\angle C = (x - 20)°$

Determine whether the triangles are congruent. If so, write a congruence statement and state the postulate or theorem you used. *(pp. 234, 240, 249)*

17. 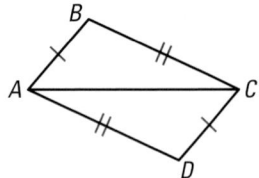   **18.** 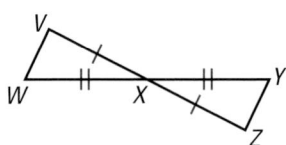   **19.**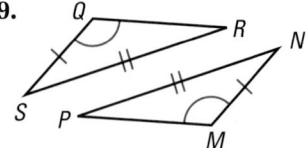

Find the value of x. *(pp. 295, 303, 310)*

20. 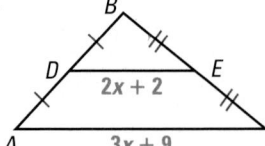   **21.** 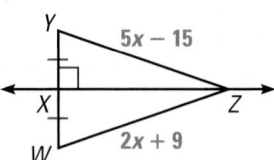   **22.**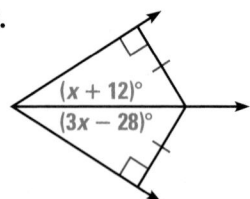

Determine whether the triangles are similar. If they are, write a similarity statement and state the postulate or theorem you used. *(pp. 381, 388)*

23. 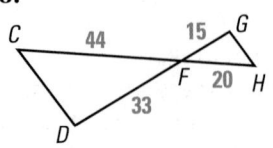   **24.** 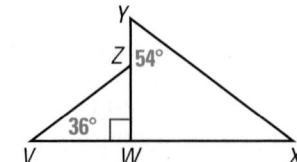   **25.**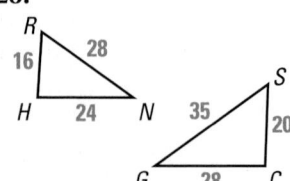

26. **PROFITS** A company's profits for two years are shown in the table. Plot and connect the points (x, y). Use the Midpoint Formula to estimate the company's profits in 2003. (Assume that profits followed a linear pattern.) *(p. 15)*

Years since 2000, x	1	5
Profit, y (in dollars)	21,000	36,250

27. **TENNIS MEMBERSHIP** The graph at the right models the accumulated cost for an individual adult tennis club membership for several months. *(p. 180)*

    a. Write an equation of the line.

    b. Tell what the slope and y-intercept mean in this situation.

    c. Find the accumulated cost for one year.

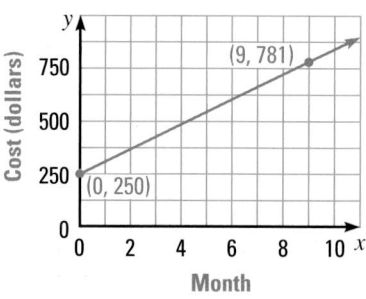

PROOF Write a two-column proof or a paragraph proof. *(pp. 234, 240, 249)*

28. **GIVEN** ▶ $\overline{FG} \cong \overline{HJ}$, $\overline{MH} \cong \overline{KG}$, $\overline{MF} \perp \overline{FJ}$, $\overline{KJ} \perp \overline{FJ}$

    PROVE ▶ $\triangle FHM \cong \triangle JGK$

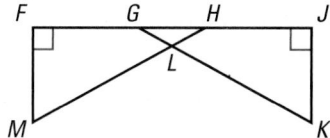

29. **GIVEN** ▶ $\overline{BC} \parallel \overline{AD}$, $\overline{BC} \cong \overline{AD}$

    PROVE ▶ $\triangle BCD \cong \triangle DAB$

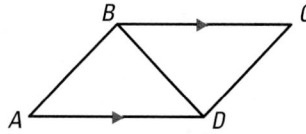

30. **COMMUNITY CENTER** A building committee needs to choose a site for a new community center. The committee decides that the new center should be located so that it is the same distance from each of the three local schools. Use the diagram to make a sketch of the triangle formed by the three schools. *Explain* how you can use this triangle to locate the site for the new community center. *(p. 303)*

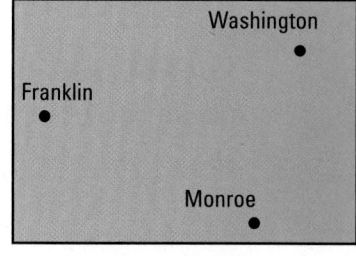

31. **GEOGRAPHY** The map shows the distances between three cities in North Dakota. *Describe* the range of possible distances from Bowman to Ellendale. *(p. 328)*

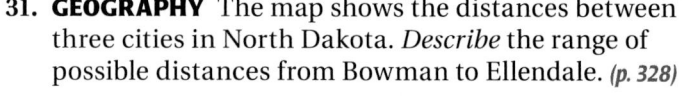

32. **CALENDAR** You send 12 photos to a company that makes personalized wall calendars. The company enlarges the photos and inserts one for each month on the calendar. Each photo is 4 inches by 6 inches. The image for each photo on the calendar is 10 inches by 15 inches. What is the scale factor of the enlargement? *(p. 409)*

7 Right Triangles and Trigonometry

- 7.1 Apply the Pythagorean Theorem
- 7.2 Use the Converse of the Pythagorean Theorem
- 7.3 Use Similar Right Triangles
- 7.4 Special Right Triangles
- 7.5 Apply the Tangent Ratio
- 7.6 Apply the Sine and Cosine Ratios
- 7.7 Solve Right Triangles

Before

In previous courses and in Chapters 1–6, you learned the following skills, which you'll use in Chapter 7: classifying triangles, simplifying radicals, and solving proportions.

Prerequisite Skills

VOCABULARY CHECK

Classify the triangle shown.

1.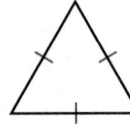
2.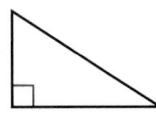
3.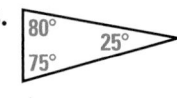
4.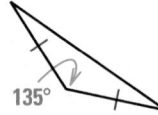

SKILLS AND ALGEBRA CHECK

Simplify the radical. *(Review p. 874 for 7.1, 7.2, 7.4.)*

5. $\sqrt{45}$ 6. $\left(3\sqrt{7}\right)^2$ 7. $\sqrt{3} \cdot \sqrt{5}$ 8. $\dfrac{7}{\sqrt{2}}$

Solve the proportion. *(Review p. 356 for 7.3, 7.5–7.7.)*

9. $\dfrac{3}{x} = \dfrac{12}{16}$ 10. $\dfrac{2}{3} = \dfrac{x}{18}$ 11. $\dfrac{x+5}{4} = \dfrac{1}{2}$ 12. $\dfrac{x+4}{x-4} = \dfrac{6}{5}$

@**Home**Tutor Prerequisite skills practice at classzone.com

Now

In Chapter 7, you will apply the big ideas listed below and reviewed in the Chapter Summary on page 493. You will also use the key vocabulary listed below.

Big Ideas

① Using the Pythagorean Theorem and its converse
② Using special relationships in right triangles
③ Using trigonometric ratios to solve right triangles

KEY VOCABULARY
- Pythagorean triple, *p. 435*
- trigonometric ratio, *p. 466*
- tangent, *p. 466*
- sine, *p. 473*

- cosine, *p. 473*
- angle of elevation, *p. 475*
- angle of depression, *p. 475*
- solve a right triangle, *p. 483*

- inverse tangent, *p. 483*
- inverse sine, *p. 483*
- inverse cosine, *p. 483*

Why?

You can use trigonometric ratios to find unknown side lengths and angle measures in right triangles. For example, you can find the length of a ski slope.

Animated Geometry

The animation illustrated below for Example 4 on page 475 helps you answer this question: How far will you ski down the mountain?

You can use right triangles to find the distance you ski down a mountain.

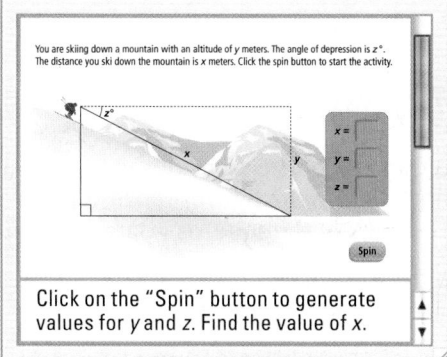

You are skiing down a mountain with an altitude of *y* meters. The angle of depression is *z*°. The distance you ski down the mountain is *x* meters. Click the spin button to start the activity.

Click on the "Spin" button to generate values for *y* and *z*. Find the value of *x*.

Animated Geometry at classzone.com

Other animations for Chapter 7: pages 434, 442, 450, 460, and 462

7.1 Pythagorean Theorem

MATERIALS · graph paper · ruler · pencil · scissors

QUESTION **What relationship exists among the sides of a right triangle?**

Recall that a square is a four sided figure with four right angles and four congruent sides.

EXPLORE **Make and use a tangram set**

STEP 1 *Make a tangram set* On your graph paper, copy the tangram set as shown. Label each piece with the given letters. Cut along the solid black lines to make seven pieces.

STEP 2 *Trace a triangle* On another piece of paper, trace one of the large triangles P of the tangram set.

STEP 3 *Assemble pieces along the legs* Use all of the tangram pieces to form two squares along the legs of your triangle so that the length of each leg is equal to the side length of the square. Trace all of the pieces.

STEP 4 *Assemble pieces along the hypotenuse* Use all of the tangram pieces to form a square along the hypotenuse so that the side length of the square is equal to the length of the hypotenuse. Trace all of the pieces.

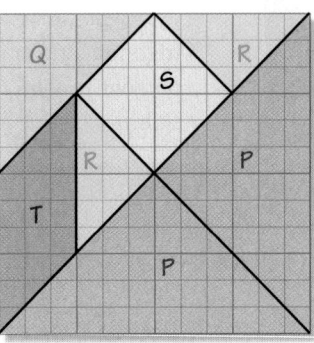

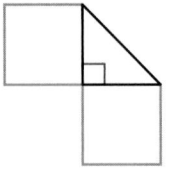

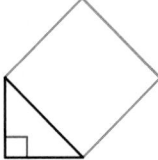

DRAW CONCLUSIONS **Use your observations to complete these exercises**

1. Find the sum of the areas of the two squares formed in Step 3. Let the letters labeling the figures represent the area of the figure. How are the side lengths of the squares related to Triangle P?

2. Find the area of the square formed in Step 4. How is the side length of the square related to Triangle P?

3. Compare your answers from Exercises 1 and 2. Make a conjecture about the relationship between the legs and hypotenuse of a right triangle.

4. The triangle you traced in Step 2 is an isosceles right triangle. Why? Do you think that your conjecture is true for all isosceles triangles? Do you think that your conjecture is true for all right triangles? *Justify* your answers.

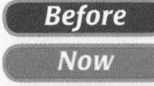 **7.1 Apply the Pythagorean Theorem**

Before You learned about the relationships within triangles.

Now You will find side lengths in right triangles.

Why? So you can find the shortest distance to a campfire, as in Ex. 35.

Key Vocabulary
• **Pythagorean triple**
• **right triangle,** *p. 217*
• **leg of a right triangle,** *p. 241*
• **hypotenuse,** *p. 241*

One of the most famous theorems in mathematics is the Pythagorean Theorem, named for the ancient Greek mathematician Pythagoras (around 500 B.C.). This theorem can be used to find information about the lengths of the sides of a right triangle.

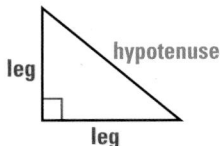

THEOREM   *For Your Notebook*

THEOREM 7.1 Pythagorean Theorem

In a right triangle, the square of the length of the hypotenuse is equal to the sum of the squares of the lengths of the legs.

Proof: p. 434; Ex. 32, p. 455

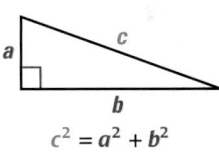

$$c^2 = a^2 + b^2$$

EXAMPLE 1   **Find the length of a hypotenuse**

Find the length of the hypotenuse of the right triangle.

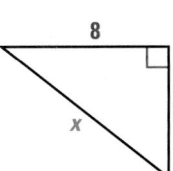

Solution

$$(\text{hypotenuse})^2 = (\text{leg})^2 + (\text{leg})^2 \qquad \text{Pythagorean Theorem}$$
$$x^2 = 6^2 + 8^2 \qquad \text{Substitute.}$$
$$x^2 = 36 + 64 \qquad \text{Multiply.}$$
$$x^2 = 100 \qquad \text{Add.}$$
$$x = 10 \qquad \text{Find the positive square root.}$$

ABBREVIATE
In the equation for the Pythagorean Theorem, "length of hypotenuse" and "length of leg" was shortened to "hypotenuse" and "leg".

✓ **GUIDED PRACTICE**   for Example 1

Identify the unknown side as a *leg* or *hypotenuse*. Then, find the unknown side length of the right triangle. Write your answer in simplest radical form.

1.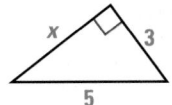

2.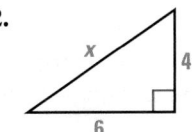

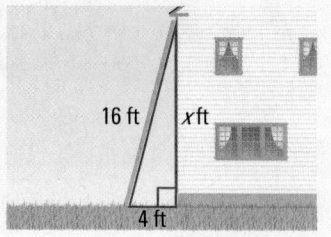

A 16 foot ladder rests against the side of the house, and the base of the ladder is 4 feet away. Approximately how high above the ground is the top of the ladder?

(A) 240 feet **(B)** 20 feet

(C) 16.5 feet **(D)** 15.5 feet

16 ft x ft

4 ft

Solution

$$\left(\begin{array}{c}\text{Length}\\\text{of ladder}\end{array}\right)^2 = \left(\begin{array}{c}\text{Distance}\\\text{from house}\end{array}\right)^2 + \left(\begin{array}{c}\text{Height}\\\text{of ladder}\end{array}\right)^2$$

$16^2 = 4^2 + x^2$	**Substitute.**
$256 = 16 + x^2$	**Multiply.**
$240 = x^2$	**Subtract 16 from each side.**
$\sqrt{240} = x$	**Find positive square root.**
$15.491 \approx x$	**Approximate with a calculator.**

> **APPROXIMATE**
> ....
> In real-world applications, it is usually appropriate to use a calculator to approximate the square root of a number. Round your answer to the nearest tenth.

The ladder is resting against the house at about 15.5 feet above the ground.

▶ The correct answer is D. (A) (B) (C) (●)

✔ **GUIDED PRACTICE** for Example 2

3. The top of a ladder rests against a wall, 23 feet above the ground. The base of the ladder is 6 feet away from the wall. What is the length of the ladder?

4. The Pythagorean Theorem is only true for what type of triangle?

PROVING THE PYTHAGOREAN THEOREM There are many proofs of the Pythagorean Theorem. An informal proof is shown below. You will write another proof in Exercise 32 on page 455.

In the figure at the right, the four right triangles are congruent, and they form a small square in the middle. The area of the large square is equal to the area of the four triangles plus the area of the smaller square.

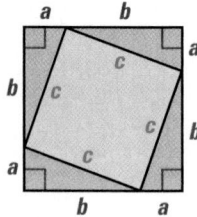

$$\begin{array}{c}\text{Area of}\\\text{large square}\end{array} = \begin{array}{c}\text{Area of}\\\text{four triangles}\end{array} + \begin{array}{c}\text{Area of}\\\text{smaller square}\end{array}$$

> **REVIEW AREA**
> ....
> Recall that the area of a square with side length s is $A = s^2$. The area of a triangle with base b and height h is $A = \frac{1}{2}bh$.

$(a + b)^2 = 4\left(\frac{1}{2}ab\right) + c^2$	**Use area formulas.**
$a^2 + 2ab + b^2 = 2ab + c^2$	**Multiply.**
$a^2 + b^2 = c^2$	**Subtract $2ab$ from each side.**

Animated Geometry at classzone.com

>

EXAMPLE 3 **Find the area of an isosceles triangle**

Find the area of the isosceles triangle with side lengths 10 meters,
13 meters, and 13 meters.

Solution

STEP 1 **Draw** a sketch. By definition, the length of an altitude
is the height of a triangle. In an isosceles triangle, the
altitude to the base is also a perpendicular bisector.
So, the altitude divides the triangle into two right
triangles with the dimensions shown.

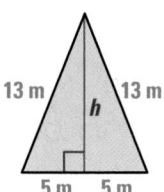

STEP 2 **Use** the Pythagorean Theorem to find the height
of the triangle.

$c^2 = a^2 + b^2$	**Pythagorean Theorem**
$13^2 = 5^2 + h^2$	**Substitute.**
$169 = 25 + h^2$	**Multiply.**
$144 = h^2$	**Subtract 25 from each side.**
$12 = h$	**Find the positive square root.**

STEP 3 **Find** the area.

$$\text{Area} = \frac{1}{2}(\text{base})(\text{height}) = \frac{1}{2}(10)(12) = 60 \text{ m}^2$$

▶ The area of the triangle is 60 square meters.

READ TABLES
You may find it helpful
to use the Table of
Squares and Square
Roots on p. 924.

✓ **GUIDED PRACTICE** for Example 3

Find the area of the triangle.

5.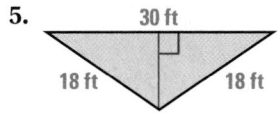

6.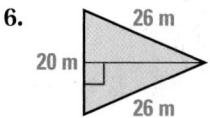

PYTHAGOREAN TRIPLES A **Pythagorean triple** is a set of three positive
integers a, b, and c that satisfy the equation $c^2 = a^2 + b^2$.

STANDARDIZED TESTS
You may find it helpful
to memorize the basic
Pythagorean triples,
shown in **bold**, for
standardized tests.

KEY CONCEPT *For Your Notebook*

Common Pythagorean Triples and Some of Their Multiples

3, 4, 5	**5, 12, 13**	**8, 15, 17**	**7, 24, 25**
6, 8, 10	10, 24, 26	16, 30, 34	14, 48, 50
9, 12, 15	15, 36, 39	24, 45, 51	21, 72, 75
30, 40, 50	50, 120, 130	80, 150, 170	70, 240, 250
$3x, 4x, 5x$	$5x, 12x, 13x$	$8x, 15x, 17x$	$7x, 24x, 25x$

The most common Pythagorean triples are in bold. The other triples are the
result of multiplying each integer in a bold face triple by the same factor.

EXAMPLE 4 **Find the length of a hypotenuse using two methods**

Find the length of the hypotenuse of the right triangle.

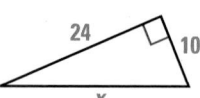

Solution

Method 1: Use a Pythagorean triple.

A common Pythagorean triple is **5**, **12**, **13**. Notice that if you multiply the lengths of the legs of the Pythagorean triple by 2, you get the lengths of the legs of this triangle: **5** • 2 = 10 and **12** • 2 = 24. So, the length of the hypotenuse is **13** • 2 = 26.

Method 2: Use the Pythagorean Theorem.

$x^2 = 10^2 + 24^2$ **Pythagorean Theorem**

$x^2 = 100 + 576$ **Multiply.**

$x^2 = 676$ **Add.**

$x = 26$ **Find the positive square root.**

✓ **GUIDED PRACTICE**   for Example 4

Find the unknown side length of the right triangle using the Pythagorean Theorem. Then use a Pythagorean triple.

7.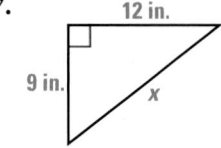

8.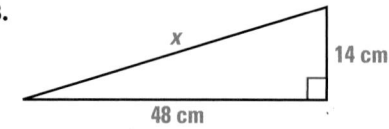

7.1 EXERCISES

HOMEWORK KEY

○ = **WORKED-OUT SOLUTIONS**
on p. WS8 for Exs. 9, 11, and 33

★ = **STANDARDIZED TEST PRACTICE**
Exs. 2, 17, 27, 33, and 36

◆ = **MULTIPLE REPRESENTATIONS**
Ex. 35

SKILL PRACTICE

1. **VOCABULARY** Copy and complete: A set of three positive integers a, b, and c that satisfy the equation $c^2 = a^2 + b^2$ is called a __?__ .

2. ★ **WRITING** *Describe* the information you need to have in order to use the Pythagorean Theorem to find the length of a side of a triangle.

EXAMPLE 1
on p. 433
for Exs. 3–7

xy **ALGEBRA** Find the length of the hypotenuse of the right triangle.

3.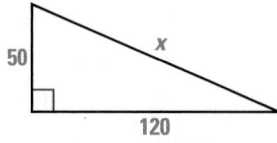

4.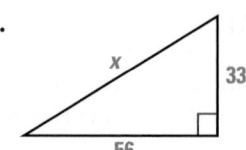

5.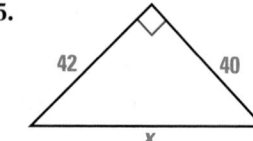

ERROR ANALYSIS *Describe* and correct the error in using the Pythagorean Theorem.

6.

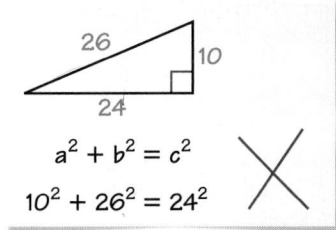

$$a^2 + b^2 = c^2$$
$$10^2 + 26^2 = 24^2$$

✗

7.

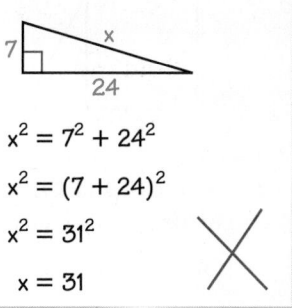

$$x^2 = 7^2 + 24^2$$
$$x^2 = (7 + 24)^2$$
$$x^2 = 31^2$$
$$x = 31$$

✗

EXAMPLE 2
on p. 434
for Exs. 8–10

FINDING A LENGTH Find the unknown leg length *x*.

8.

9.

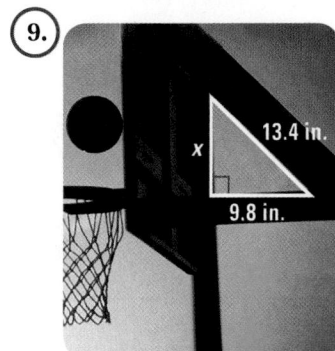

10.

EXAMPLE 3
on p. 435
for Exs. 11–13

FINDING THE AREA Find the area of the isosceles triangle.

11.

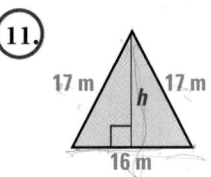

12.

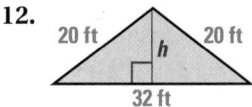

13.

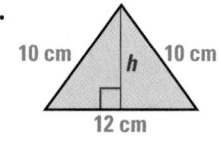

EXAMPLE 4
on p. 436
for Exs. 14–17

FINDING SIDE LENGTHS Find the unknown side length of the right triangle using the Pythagorean Theorem or a Pythagorean triple.

14.

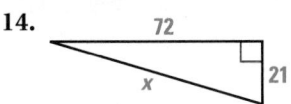

15.

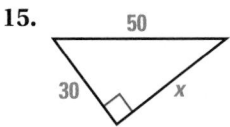

16.

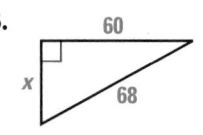

17. ★ **MULTIPLE CHOICE** What is the length of the hypotenuse of a right triangle with leg lengths of 8 inches and 15 inches?

Ⓐ 13 inches   Ⓑ 17 inches   Ⓒ 21 inches   Ⓓ 25 inches

PYTHAGOREAN TRIPLES The given lengths are two sides of a right triangle. All three side lengths of the triangle are integers and together form a Pythagorean triple. Find the length of the third side and tell whether it is a leg or the hypotenuse.

18. 24 and 51   **19.** 20 and 25   **20.** 28 and 96

21. 20 and 48   **22.** 75 and 85   **23.** 72 and 75

FINDING SIDE LENGTHS Find the unknown side length *x*. Write your answer in simplest radical form.

24.
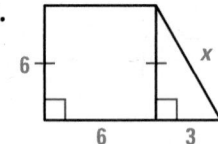

25.
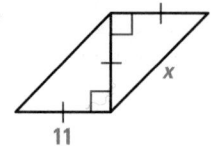

26.
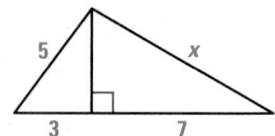

27. ★ **MULTIPLE CHOICE** What is the area of a right triangle with a leg length of 15 feet and a hypotenuse length of 39 feet?

    A 270 ft²   **B** 292.5 ft²   **C** 540 ft²   **D** 585 ft²

28. ⓧⓨ **ALGEBRA** Solve for *x* if the lengths of the two legs of a right triangle are $2x$ and $2x + 4$, and the length of the hypotenuse is $4x - 4$.

CHALLENGE In Exercises 29 and 30, solve for *x*.

29.
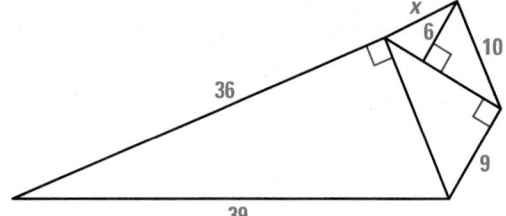

30.
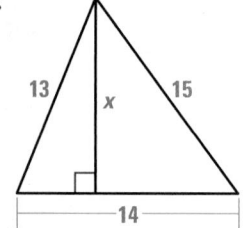

PROBLEM SOLVING

EXAMPLE 2
on p. 434
for Exs. 31–32

31. BASEBALL DIAMOND In baseball, the distance of the paths between each pair of consecutive bases is 90 feet and the paths form right angles. How far does the ball need to travel if it is thrown from home plate directly to second base?

    @HomeTutor for problem solving help at classzone.com

32. APPLE BALLOON You tie an apple balloon to a stake in the ground. The rope is 10 feet long. As the wind picks up, you observe that the balloon is now 6 feet away from the stake. How far above the ground is the balloon now?

    @HomeTutor for problem solving help at classzone.com

33. ★ **SHORT RESPONSE** Three side lengths of a right triangle are 25, 65, and 60. *Explain* how you know which side is the hypotenuse.

34. MULTI-STEP PROBLEM In your town, there is a field that is in the shape of a right triangle with the dimensions shown.

    a. Find the perimeter of the field.

    b. You are going to plant dogwood seedlings about every ten feet around the field's edge. How many trees do you need?

    c. If each dogwood seedling sells for $12, how much will the trees cost?

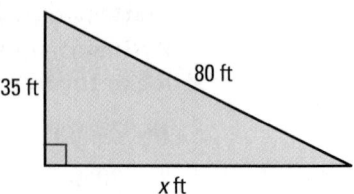

○ = **WORKED-OUT SOLUTIONS** on p. WS1   ★ = **STANDARDIZED TEST PRACTICE**   ◆ = **MULTIPLE REPRESENTATIONS**

35. ◆ **MULTIPLE REPRESENTATIONS** As you are gathering leaves for a science project, you look back at your campsite and see that the campfire is not completely out. You want to get water from a nearby river to put out the flames with the bucket you are using to collect leaves. Use the diagram and the steps below to determine the shortest distance you must travel.

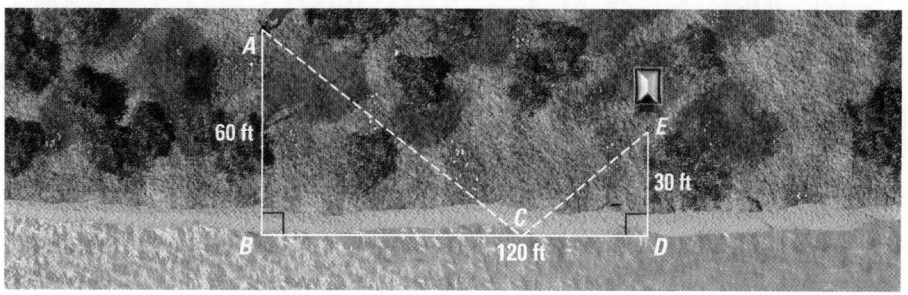

a. **Making a Table** Make a table with columns labeled *BC*, *AC*, *CE*, and *AC* + *CE*. Enter values of *BC* from 10 to 120 in increments of 10.

b. **Calculating Values** Calculate *AC*, *CE*, and *AC* + *CE* for each value of *BC*, and record the results in the table. Then, use your table of values to determine the shortest distance you must travel.

c. **Drawing a Picture** Draw an accurate picture to scale of the shortest distance.

36. ★ **SHORT RESPONSE** *Justify* the Distance Formula using the Pythagorean Theorem.

37. **PROVING THEOREM 4.5** Find the Hypotenuse-Leg (HL) Congruence Theorem on page 241. Assign variables for the side lengths in the diagram. Use your variables to write GIVEN and PROVE statements. Use the Pythagorean Theorem and congruent triangles to prove Theorem 4.5.

38. **CHALLENGE** Trees grown for sale at nurseries should stand at least five feet from one another while growing. If the trees are grown in parallel rows, what is the smallest allowable distance between rows?

MIXED REVIEW

PREVIEW
Prepare for
Lesson 7.2
in Exs. 39–42.

Evaluate the expression. *(p. 874)*

39. $(\sqrt{7})^2$ **40.** $(4\sqrt{3})^2$ **41.** $(-6\sqrt{81})^2$ **42.** $(-8\sqrt{2})^2$

Describe the possible lengths of the third side of the triangle given the lengths of the other two sides. *(p. 328)*

43. 3 feet, 6 feet   **44.** 5 inches, 11 inches   **45.** 14 meters, 21 meters

46. 12 inches, 27 inches   **47.** 18 yards, 18 yards   **48.** 27 meters, 39 meters

Determine whether the two triangles are similar. If they are similar, write a similarity statement and find the scale factor of Triangle B to Triangle A. *(p. 388)*

49.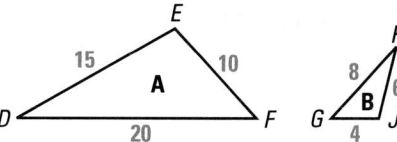

50.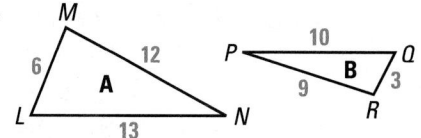

7.2 Converse of the Pythagorean Theorem

MATERIALS · graphing calculator or computer

QUESTION How can you use the side lengths in a triangle to classify the triangle by its angle measures?

You can use geometry drawing software to construct and measure triangles.

EXPLORE Construct a triangle

STEP 1 *Draw a triangle* Draw any $\triangle ABC$ with the largest angle at C. Measure $\angle C$, $\overline{AB}$, $\overline{AC}$, and $\overline{CB}$.

STEP 2 *Calculate* Use your measurements to calculate AB^2, AC^2, CB^2, and $(AC^2 + CB^2)$.

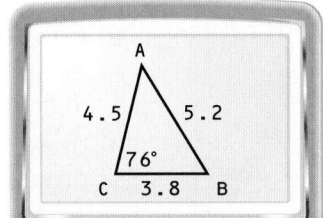

STEP 3 *Complete a table* Copy the table below and record your results in the first row. Then move point A to different locations and record the values for each triangle in your table. Make sure $\overline{AB}$ is always the longest side of the triangle. Include triangles that are acute, right, and obtuse.

$m\angle C$	AB	AB^2	AC	CB	$AC^2 + CB^2$
76°	5.2	27.04	4.5	3.8	34.69
?	?	?	?	?	?
?	?	?	?	?	?

DRAW CONCLUSIONS Use your observations to complete these exercises

1. The Pythagorean Theorem states that "In a right triangle, the square of the length of the hypotenuse is equal to the sum of the squares of the lengths of the legs." Write the Pythagorean Theorem in if-then form. Then write its converse.

2. Is the converse of the Pythagorean Theorem true? *Explain.*

3. Make a conjecture about the relationship between the measure of the largest angle in a triangle and the squares of the side lengths.

Copy and complete the statement.

4. If $AB^2 > AC^2 + CB^2$, then the triangle is a(n) __?__ triangle.

5. If $AB^2 < AC^2 + CB^2$, then the triangle is a(n) __?__ triangle.

6. If $AB^2 = AC^2 + CB^2$, then the triangle is a(n) __?__ triangle.

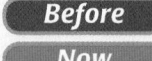 **Use the Converse of the Pythagorean Theorem**

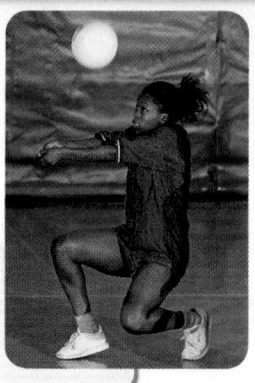

Before	You used the Pythagorean Theorem to find missing side lengths.
Now	You will use its converse to determine if a triangle is a right triangle.
Why?	So you can determine if a volleyball net is set up correctly, as in Ex. 38.

Key Vocabulary
• **acute triangle,** p. 217
• **obtuse triangle,** p. 217

The converse of the Pythagorean Theorem is also true. You can use it to verify that a triangle with given side lengths is a right triangle.

THEOREM *For Your Notebook*

THEOREM 7.2 Converse of the Pythagorean Theorem

If the square of the length of the longest side of a triangle is equal to the sum of the squares of the lengths of the other two sides, then the triangle is a right triangle.

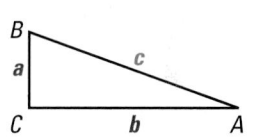

If $c^2 = a^2 + b^2$, then $\triangle ABC$ is a right triangle.

Proof: Ex. 42, p. 446

EXAMPLE 1 **Verify right triangles**

Tell whether the given triangle is a right triangle.

a.
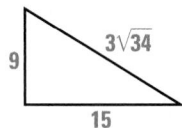

b.
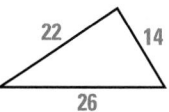

Let c represent the length of the longest side of the triangle. Check to see whether the side lengths satisfy the equation $c^2 = a^2 + b^2$.

REVIEW ALGEBRA

Use a square root table or a calculator to find the decimal representation. So, $3\sqrt{34} \approx 17.493$ is the length of the longest side in part (a).

a. $\left(3\sqrt{34}\right)^2 \overset{?}{=} 9^2 + 15^2$

$9 \cdot 34 \overset{?}{=} 81 + 225$

$306 = 306$ ✓

The triangle is a right triangle.

b. $26^2 \overset{?}{=} 22^2 + 14^2$

$676 \overset{?}{=} 484 + 196$

$676 \neq 680$

The triangle is not a right triangle.

 GUIDED PRACTICE for Example 1

Tell whether a triangle with the given side lengths is a right triangle.

1. $4, 4\sqrt{3}, 8$ **2.** $10, 11,$ and 14 **3.** $5, 6,$ and $\sqrt{61}$

CLASSIFYING TRIANGLES The Converse of the Pythagorean Theorem is used to verify that a given triangle is a right triangle. The theorems below are used to verify that a given triangle is acute or obtuse.

THEOREMS
For Your Notebook

THEOREM 7.3

If the square of the length of the longest side of a triangle is less than the sum of the squares of the lengths of the other two sides, then the triangle is an acute triangle.

If $c^2 < a^2 + b^2$, then the triangle is acute.

Proof: Ex. 40, p. 446

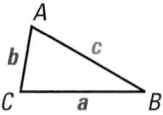

THEOREM 7.4

If the square of the length of the longest side of a triangle is greater than the sum of the squares of the lengths of the other two sides, then the triangle is an obtuse triangle.

If $c^2 > a^2 + b^2$, then triangle *ABC* is obtuse.

Proof: Ex. 41, p. 446

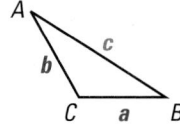

EXAMPLE 2   Classify triangles

Can segments with lengths of 4.3 feet, 5.2 feet, and 6.1 feet form a triangle? If so, would the triangle be *acute, right,* or *obtuse*?

Solution

APPLY THEOREMS

The Triangle Inequality Theorem on page 330 states that the sum of the lengths of any two sides of a triangle is greater than the length of the third side.

STEP 1 **Use** the Triangle Inequality Theorem to check that the segments can make a triangle.

$4.3 + 5.2 = 9.5$	$4.3 + 6.1 = 10.4$	$5.2 + 6.1 = 11.3$
$9.5 > 6.1$	$10.4 > 5.2$	$11.3 > 4.3$

▸ The side lengths 4.3 feet, 5.2 feet, and 6.1 feet can form a triangle.

STEP 2 **Classify** the triangle by comparing the square of the length of the longest side with the sum of squares of the lengths of the shorter sides.

$c^2 \ \underline{\ ?\ } \ a^2 + b^2$	Compare c^2 with $a^2 + b^2$.
$6.1^2 \ \underline{\ ?\ } \ 4.3^2 + 5.2^2$	Substitute.
$37.21 \ \underline{\ ?\ } \ 18.49 + 27.04$	Simplify.
$37.21 \ < \ 45.53$	c^2 is less than $a^2 + b^2$.

▸ The side lengths 4.3 feet, 5.2 feet, and 6.1 feet form an acute triangle.

Animated **Geometry** at classzone.com

EXAMPLE 3   **Use the Converse of the Pythagorean Theorem**

CATAMARAN You are part of a crew that is installing the mast on a catamaran. When the mast is fastened properly, it is perpendicular to the trampoline deck. How can you check that the mast is perpendicular using a tape measure?

Solution

To show a line is perpendicular to a plane you must show that the line is perpendicular to two lines in the plane.

Think of the mast as a line and the deck as a plane. Use a 3-4-5 right triangle and the Converse of the Pythagorean Theorem to show that the mast is perpendicular to different lines on the deck.

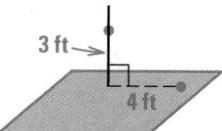 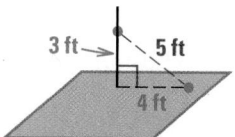 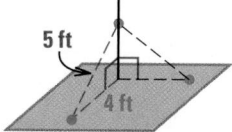

First place a mark 3 feet up the mast and a mark on the deck 4 feet from the mast.

Use the tape measure to check that the distance between the two marks is 5 feet. The mast makes a right angle with the line on the deck.

Finally, repeat the procedure to show that the mast is perpendicular to another line on the deck.

✓ **GUIDED PRACTICE**   for Examples 2 and 3

4. Show that segments with lengths 3, 4, and 6 can form a triangle and classify the triangle as *acute, right,* or *obtuse.*

5. **WHAT IF?** In Example 3, could you use triangles with side lengths 2, 3, and 4 to verify that you have perpendicular lines? *Explain.*

CLASSIFYING TRIANGLES You can use the theorems from this lesson to classify a triangle as acute, right, or obtuse based on its side lengths.

CONCEPT SUMMARY   *For Your Notebook*

Methods for Classifying a Triangle by Angles Using its Side Lengths

Theorem 7.2	Theorem 7.3	Theorem 7.4
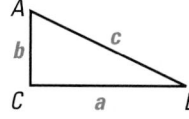	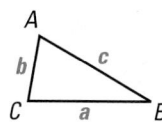	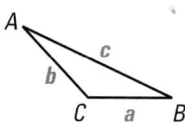
If $c^2 = a^2 + b^2$, then $m\angle C = 90°$ and $\triangle ABC$ is a right triangle.	If $c^2 < a^2 + b^2$, then $m\angle C < 90°$ and $\triangle ABC$ is an acute triangle.	If $c^2 > a^2 + b^2$, then $m\angle C > 90°$ and $\triangle ABC$ is an obtuse triangle.

7.2 EXERCISES

HOMEWORK KEY

○ = WORKED-OUT SOLUTIONS
on p. WS8 for Exs. 7, 17, and 37

★ = STANDARDIZED TEST PRACTICE
Exs. 2, 24, 25, 32, 38, 39, and 43

SKILL PRACTICE

1. **VOCABULARY** What is the longest side of a right triangle called?

2. ★ **WRITING** *Explain* how the side lengths of a triangle can be used to classify it as acute, right, or obtuse.

EXAMPLE 1
on p. 441
for Exs. 3–14

VERIFYING RIGHT TRIANGLES Tell whether the triangle is a right triangle.

3.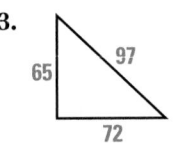

4.

5.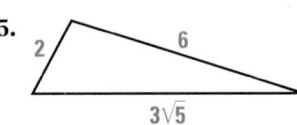

6.

7.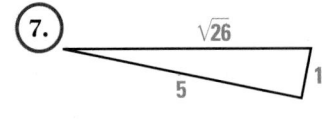

8.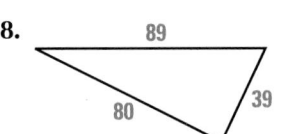

VERIFYING RIGHT TRIANGLES Tell whether the given side lengths of a triangle can represent a right triangle.

9. 9, 12, and 15

10. 9, 10, and 15

11. 36, 48, and 60

12. 6, 10, and $2\sqrt{34}$

13. 7, 14, and $7\sqrt{5}$

14. 10, 12, and 20

EXAMPLE 2
on p. 442
for Exs. 15–23

CLASSIFYING TRIANGLES In Exercises 15–23, decide if the segment lengths form a triangle. If so, would the triangle be *acute, right,* or *obtuse?*

15. 10, 11, and 14

16. 10, 15, and $5\sqrt{13}$

17. 24, 30, and $6\sqrt{43}$

18. 5, 6, and 7

19. 12, 16, and 20

20. 8, 10, and 12

21. 15, 20, and 36

22. 6, 8, and 10

23. 8.2, 4.1, and 12.2

24. ★ **MULTIPLE CHOICE** Which side lengths do not form a right triangle?

Ⓐ 5, 12, 13   Ⓑ 10, 24, 28   Ⓒ 15, 36, 39   Ⓓ 50, 120, 130

25. ★ **MULTIPLE CHOICE** What type of triangle has side lengths of 4, 7, and 9?

Ⓐ Acute scalene   Ⓑ Right scalene

Ⓒ Obtuse scalene   Ⓓ None of the above

26. **ERROR ANALYSIS** A student tells you that if you double all the sides of a right triangle, the new triangle is obtuse. *Explain* why this statement is incorrect.

GRAPHING TRIANGLES Graph points *A*, *B*, and *C*. Connect the points to form △*ABC*. Decide whether △*ABC* is *acute, right,* or *obtuse.*

27. *A*(−2, 4), *B*(6, 0), *C*(−5, −2)

28. *A*(0, 2), *B*(5, 1), *C*(1, −1)

29.  **ALGEBRA** Tell whether a triangle with side lengths $5x$, $12x$, and $13x$ (where $x > 0$) is *acute*, *right*, or *obtuse*.

USING DIAGRAMS In Exercises 30 and 31, copy and complete the statement with <, >, or =, if possible. If it is not possible, *explain* why.

30. $m\angle A \underline{\ ?\ } m\angle D$

31. $m\angle B + m\angle C \underline{\ ?\ } m\angle E + m\angle F$

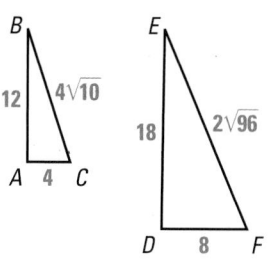

32. ★ **OPEN-ENDED MATH** The side lengths of a triangle are 6, 8, and x (where $x > 0$). What are the values of x that make the triangle a right triangle? an acute triangle? an obtuse triangle?

33.  **ALGEBRA** The sides of a triangle have lengths x, $x + 4$, and 20. If the length of the longest side is 20, what values of x make the triangle acute?

34. **CHALLENGE** The sides of a triangle have lengths $4x + 6$, $2x + 1$, and $6x - 1$. If the length of the longest side is $6x - 1$, what values of x make the triangle obtuse?

PROBLEM SOLVING

EXAMPLE 3
on p. 443
for Ex. 35

35. **PAINTING** You are making a canvas frame for a painting using stretcher bars. The rectangular painting will be 10 inches long and 8 inches wide. Using a ruler, how can you be certain that the corners of the frame are 90°?

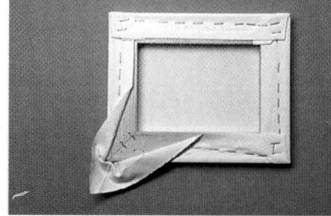

@HomeTutor for problem solving help at classzone.com

36. **WALKING** You walk 749 feet due east to the gym from your home. From the gym you walk 800 feet southwest to the library. Finally, you walk 305 feet from the library back home. Do you live directly north of the library? *Explain.*

@HomeTutor for problem solving help at classzone.com

37. **MULTI-STEP PROBLEM** Use the diagram shown.

   a. Find BC.

   b. Use the Converse of the Pythagorean Theorem to show that $\triangle ABC$ is a right triangle.

   c. Draw and label a similar diagram where $\triangle DBC$ remains a right triangle, but $\triangle ABC$ is not.

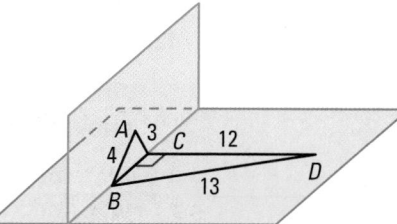

38. ★ SHORT RESPONSE You are setting up a volleyball net. To stabilize the pole, you tie one end of a rope to the pole 7 feet from the ground. You tie the other end of the rope to a stake that is 4 feet from the pole. The rope between the pole and stake is about 8 feet 4 inches long. Is the pole perpendicular to the ground? *Explain.* If it is not, how can you fix it?

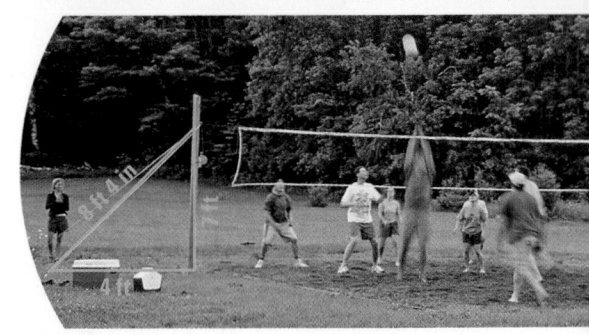

39. ★ EXTENDED RESPONSE You are considering buying a used car. You would like to know whether the frame is sound. A sound frame of the car should be rectangular, so it has four right angles. You plan to measure the shadow of the car on the ground as the sun shines directly on the car.

  a. You make a triangle with three tape measures on one corner. It has side lengths 12 inches, 16 inches, and 20 inches. Is this a right triangle? *Explain.*

  b. You make a triangle on a second corner with side lengths 9 inches, 12 inches, and 18 inches. Is this a right triangle? *Explain.*

  c. The car owner says the car was never in an accident. Do you believe this claim? *Explain.*

40. PROVING THEOREM 7.3 Copy and complete the proof of Theorem 7.3.

  GIVEN ▶ In $\triangle ABC$, $c^2 < a^2 + b^2$ where c is the length of the longest side.

  PROVE ▶ $\triangle ABC$ is an acute triangle.

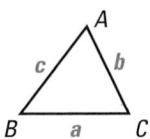 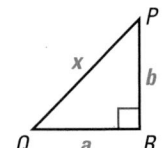

Plan for Proof Draw right $\triangle PQR$ with side lengths a, b, and x, where $\angle R$ is a right angle and x is the length of the longest side. Compare lengths c and x.

STATEMENTS	REASONS
1. In $\triangle ABC$, $c^2 < a^2 + b^2$ where c is the length of the longest side. In $\triangle PQR$, $\angle R$ is a right angle.	**1.** __?__
2. $a^2 + b^2 = x^2$	**2.** __?__
3. $c^2 < x^2$	**3.** __?__
4. $c < x$	**4.** A property of square roots
5. $m\angle R = 90°$	**5.** __?__
6. $m\angle C < m\angle$ __?__	**6.** Converse of the Hinge Theorem
7. $m\angle C < 90°$	**7.** __?__
8. $\angle C$ is an acute angle.	**8.** __?__
9. $\triangle ABC$ is an acute triangle.	**9.** __?__

41. PROVING THEOREM 7.4 Prove Theorem 7.4. Include a diagram and GIVEN and PROVE statements. (*Hint*: Look back at Exercise 40.)

42. PROVING THEOREM 7.2 Prove the Converse of the Pythagorean Theorem.

  GIVEN ▶ In $\triangle LMN$, $\overline{LM}$ is the longest side, and $c^2 = a^2 + b^2$.

  PROVE ▶ $\triangle LMN$ is a right triangle.

  Plan for Proof Draw right $\triangle PQR$ with side lengths a, b, and x. Compare lengths c and x.

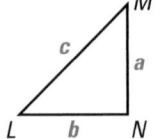 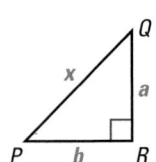

43. ★ **SHORT RESPONSE** *Explain* why ∠D must be a right angle.

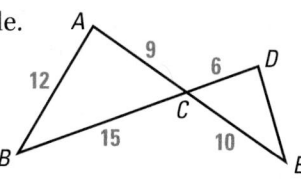

44. **COORDINATE PLANE** Use graph paper.

  a. Graph △ABC with A(−7, 2), B(0, 1) and C(−4, 4).

  b. Use the slopes of the sides of △ABC to determine whether it is a right triangle. *Explain.*

  c. Use the lengths of the sides of △ABC to determine whether it is a right triangle. *Explain.*

  d. Did you get the same answer in parts (b) and (c)? If not, *explain* why.

45. **CHALLENGE** Find the values of *x* and *y*.

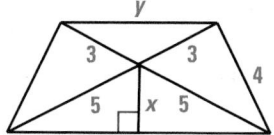

MIXED REVIEW

PREVIEW

Prepare for Lesson 7.3 in Exs. 46–48.

In Exercises 46–48, copy the triangle and draw one of its altitudes. *(p. 319)*

46. 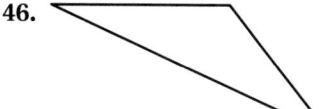   **47.**    **48.**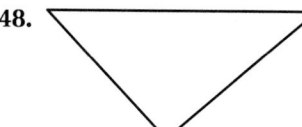

Copy and complete the statement. *(p. 364)*

49. If $\dfrac{10}{x} = \dfrac{7}{y}$, then $\dfrac{10}{7} = \dfrac{?}{?}$.   **50.** If $\dfrac{x}{15} = \dfrac{y}{2}$, then $\dfrac{x}{y} = \dfrac{?}{?}$.   **51.** If $\dfrac{x}{8} = \dfrac{y}{9}$, then $\dfrac{x+8}{8} = \dfrac{?}{?}$.

52. The perimeter of a rectangle is 135 feet. The ratio of the length to the width is 8 : 1. Find the length and the width. *(p. 372)*

QUIZ *for Lessons 7.1–7.2*

Find the unknown side length. Write your answer in simplest radical form.
(p. 433)

1. 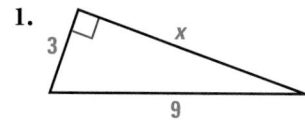   **2.** 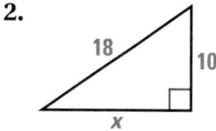   **3.**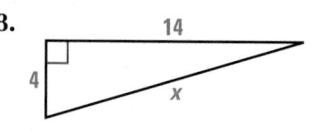

Classify the triangle formed by the side lengths as *acute, right,* **or** *obtuse.* *(p. 441)*

4. 6, 7, and 9   **5.** 10, 12, and 16   **6.** 8, 16, and $8\sqrt{6}$

7. 20, 21, and 29   **8.** 8, 3, $\sqrt{73}$ **9.** 8, 10, and 12

7.3 Similar Right Triangles

MATERIALS · rectangular piece of paper · ruler · scissors · colored pencils

QUESTION How are geometric means related to the altitude of a right triangle?

EXPLORE Compare right triangles

STEP 1

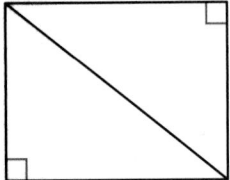

Draw a diagonal Draw a diagonal on your rectangular piece of paper to form two congruent right triangles.

STEP 2

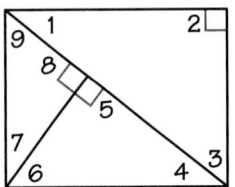

Draw an altitude Fold the paper to make an altitude to the hypotenuse of one of the triangles.

STEP 3

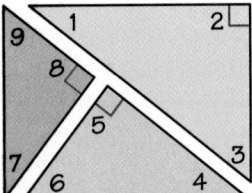

Cut and label triangles Cut the rectangle into the three right triangles that you drew. Label the angles and color the triangles as shown.

STEP 4

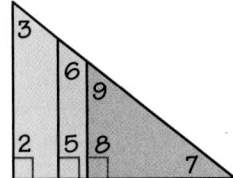

Arrange the triangles Arrange the triangles so ∠1, ∠4, and ∠7 are on top of each other as shown.

DRAW CONCLUSIONS Use your observations to complete these exercises

1. How are the two smaller right triangles related to the large triangle?

2. *Explain* how you would show that the green triangle is similar to the red triangle.

3. *Explain* how you would show that the red triangle is similar to the blue triangle.

4. The *geometric mean* of a and b is x if $\frac{a}{x} = \frac{x}{b}$. Write a proportion involving the side lengths of two of your triangles so that one side length is the geometric mean of the other two lengths in the proportion.

7.3 Use Similar Right Triangles

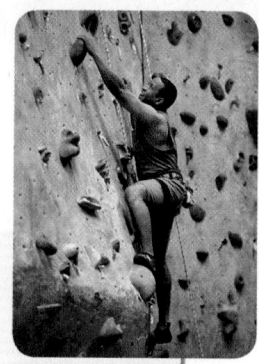

Before	You identified the altitudes of a triangle.
Now	You will use properties of the altitude of a right triangle.
Why?	So you can determine the height of a wall, as in Example 4.

Key Vocabulary
- **altitude of a triangle,** *p. 320*
- **geometric mean,** *p. 359*
- **similar polygons,** *p. 372*

When the altitude is drawn to the hypotenuse of a right triangle, the two smaller triangles are similar to the original triangle and to each other.

THEOREM *For Your Notebook*

THEOREM 7.5

If the altitude is drawn to the hypotenuse of a right triangle, then the two triangles formed are similar to the original triangle and to each other.

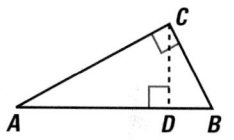

$\triangle CBD \sim \triangle ABC$, $\triangle ACD \sim \triangle ABC$, and $\triangle CBD \sim \triangle ACD$.

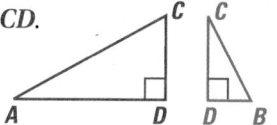

Proof: below; Ex. 35, p. 456

Plan for Proof of Theorem 7.5 First prove that $\triangle CBD \sim \triangle ABC$. Each triangle has a right angle and each triangle includes $\angle B$. The triangles are similar by the AA Similarity Postulate. Use similar reasoning to show that $\triangle ACD \sim \triangle ABC$.

To show $\angle CBD \sim \triangle ACD$, begin by showing $\angle ACD \cong \angle B$ because they are both complementary to $\angle DCB$. Each triangle also has a right angle, so you can use the AA Similarity Postulate.

EXAMPLE 1 Identify similar triangles

Identify the similar triangles in the diagram.

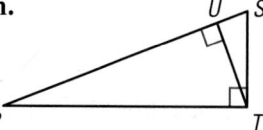

Solution

Sketch the three similar right triangles so that the corresponding angles and sides have the same orientation.

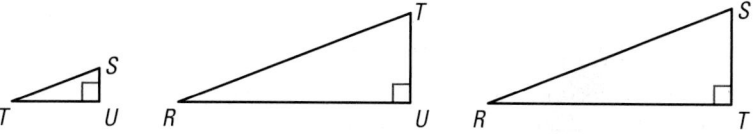

▶ $\triangle TSU \sim \triangle RTU \sim \triangle RST$

EXAMPLE 2 **Find the length of the altitude to the hypotenuse**

SWIMMING POOL The diagram below shows a cross-section of a swimming pool. What is the maximum depth of the pool?

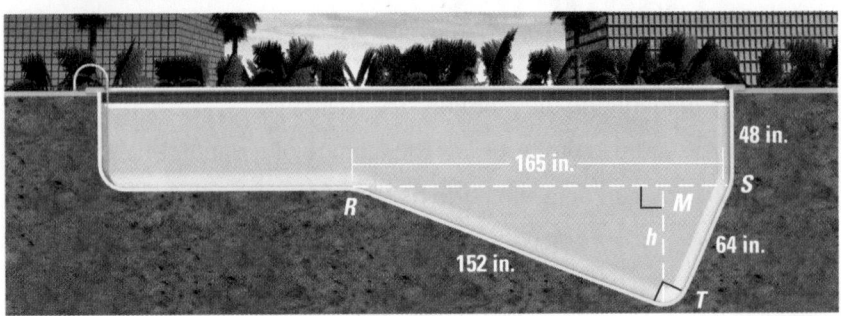

Solution

STEP 1 **Identify** the similar triangles and sketch them.

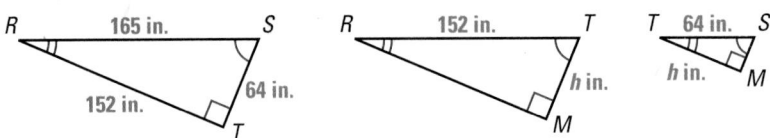

$$\triangle RST \sim \triangle RTM \sim \triangle TSM$$

AVOID ERRORS
Notice that if you tried to write a proportion using $\triangle RTM$ and $\triangle TSM$, there would be two unknowns, so you would not be able to solve for h.

STEP 2 **Find** the value of h. Use the fact that $\triangle RST \sim \triangle RTM$ to write a proportion.

$\dfrac{TM}{ST} = \dfrac{TR}{SR}$ **Corresponding side lengths of similar triangles are in proportion.**

$\dfrac{h}{64} = \dfrac{152}{165}$ **Substitute.**

$165h = 64(152)$ **Cross Products Property**

$h \approx 59$ **Solve for h.**

STEP 3 **Read** the diagram above. You can see that the maximum depth of the pool is $h + 48$, which is about $59 + 48 = 107$ inches.

▸ The maximum depth of the pool is about 107 inches.

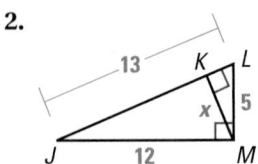 at classzone.com

---

✓ **GUIDED PRACTICE** for Examples 1 and 2

Identify the similar triangles. Then find the value of x.

1.

E, H, 5, 3, x, G, 4, F

2.

13, K, L, 5, x, J, 12, M

GEOMETRIC MEANS In Lesson 6.1, you learned that the *geometric mean* of two numbers a and b is the positive number x such that $\frac{a}{x} = \frac{x}{b}$. Consider right $\triangle ABC$. From Theorem 7.5, you know that altitude $\overline{CD}$ forms two smaller triangles so that $\triangle CBD \sim \triangle ACD \sim \triangle ABC$.

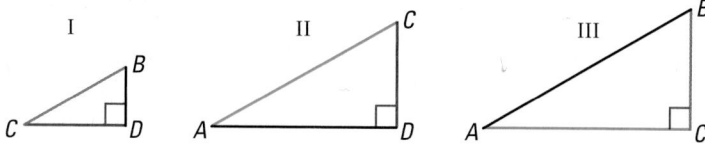

READ SYMBOLS
Remember that an altitude is defined as a segment. So, $\overline{CD}$ refers to an altitude in $\triangle ABC$ and CD refers to its length.

Notice that $\overline{CD}$ is the longer leg of $\triangle CBD$ and the shorter leg of $\triangle ACD$. When you write a proportion comparing the leg lengths of $\triangle CBD$ and $\triangle ACD$, you can see that CD is the geometric mean of BD and AD. As you see below, CB and AC are also geometric means of segment lengths in the diagram.

Proportions Involving Geometric Means in Right $\triangle ABC$

length of shorter leg of I $\longrightarrow$ $\dfrac{BD}{CD} = \dfrac{CD}{AD}$ $\longleftarrow$ length of longer leg of I
length of shorter leg of II   length of longer leg of II

length of hypotenuse of III $\longrightarrow$ $\dfrac{AB}{CB} = \dfrac{CB}{DB}$ $\longleftarrow$ length of shorter leg of III
length of hypotenuse of I   length of shorter leg of I

length of hypotenuse of III $\longrightarrow$ $\dfrac{AB}{AC} = \dfrac{AC}{AD}$ $\longleftarrow$ length of longer leg of III
length of hypotenuse of II   length of longer leg of II

EXAMPLE 3   **Use a geometric mean**

xy **Find the value of y. Write your answer in simplest radical form.**

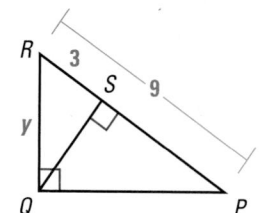

Solution

REVIEW SIMILARITY
Notice that $\triangle RQS$ and $\triangle RPQ$ both contain the side with length y, so these are the similar triangles to use to solve for y.

STEP 1   **Draw** the three similar triangles.

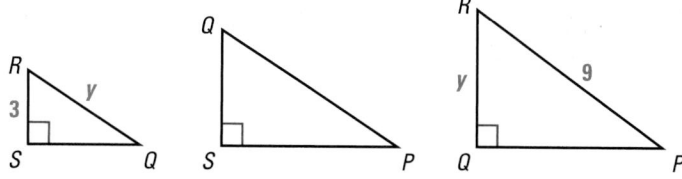

STEP 2   **Write** a proportion.

$$\frac{\text{length of hyp. of } \triangle RPQ}{\text{length of hyp. of } \triangle RQS} = \frac{\text{length of shorter leg of } \triangle RPQ}{\text{length of shorter leg of } \triangle RQS}$$

$\dfrac{9}{y} = \dfrac{y}{3}$ **Substitute.**

$27 = y^2$ **Cross Products Property**

$\sqrt{27} = y$ **Take the positive square root of each side.**

$3\sqrt{3} = y$ **Simplify.**

WRITE PROOFS

In Exercise 32 on page 455, you will use the geometric mean theorems to prove the Pythagorean Theorem.

THEOREM 7.6 **Geometric Mean (Altitude) Theorem**

In a right triangle, the altitude from the right angle to the hypotenuse divides the hypotenuse into two segments.

The length of the altitude is the geometric mean of the lengths of the two segments.

Proof: Ex. 36, p. 456

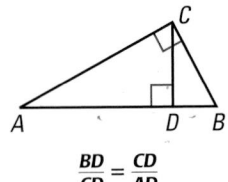

$$\frac{BD}{CD} = \frac{CD}{AD}$$

THEOREM 7.7 **Geometric Mean (Leg) Theorem**

In a right triangle, the altitude from the right angle to the hypotenuse divides the hypotenuse into two segments.

The length of each leg of the right triangle is the geometric mean of the lengths of the hypotenuse and the segment of the hypotenuse that is adjacent to the leg.

Proof: Ex. 37, p. 456

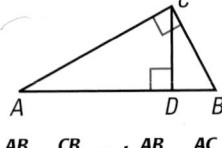
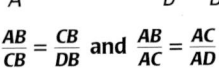

$$\frac{AB}{CB} = \frac{CB}{DB} \text{ and } \frac{AB}{AC} = \frac{AC}{AD}$$

EXAMPLE 4 **Find a height using indirect measurement**

ROCK CLIMBING WALL To find the cost of installing a rock wall in your school gymnasium, you need to find the height of the gym wall.

You use a cardboard square to line up the top and bottom of the gym wall. Your friend measures the vertical distance from the ground to your eye and the distance from you to the gym wall. Approximate the height of the gym wall.

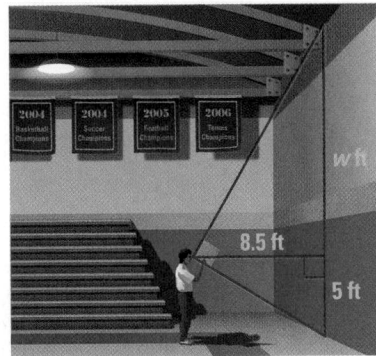

Solution

By Theorem 7.6, you know that 8.5 is the geometric mean of w and 5.

$$\frac{w}{8.5} = \frac{8.5}{5} \qquad \text{Write a proportion.}$$

$$w \approx 14.5 \qquad \text{Solve for } w.$$

▸ So, the height of the wall is $5 + w \approx 5 + 14.5 = 19.5$ feet.

✓ **GUIDED PRACTICE** | for Examples 3 and 4

   3. In Example 3, which theorem did you use to solve for y? *Explain.*

   4. Mary is 5.5 feet tall. How far from the wall in Example 4 would she have to stand in order to measure its height?

7.3 EXERCISES

HOMEWORK KEY

○ = WORKED-OUT SOLUTIONS
on p. WS8 for Exs. 5, 15, and 29

★ = STANDARDIZED TEST PRACTICE
Exs. 2, 19, 20, 31, and 34

SKILL PRACTICE

1. VOCABULARY Copy and complete: Two triangles are ? if their corresponding angles are congruent and their corresponding side lengths are proportional.

2. ★ WRITING In your own words, explain *geometric mean*.

EXAMPLE 1
on p. 449
for Exs. 3–4

IDENTIFYING SIMILAR TRIANGLES Identify the three similar right triangles in the given diagram.

3.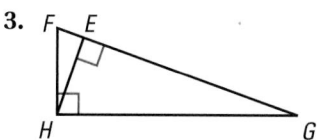

4.

EXAMPLE 2
on p. 450
for Exs. 5–7

FINDING ALTITUDES Find the length of the altitude to the hypotenuse. Round decimal answers to the nearest tenth.

5.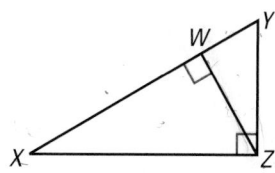

6.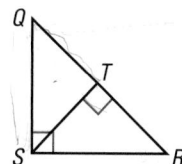

7.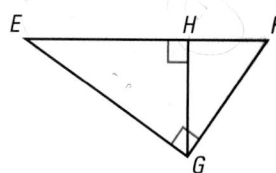

EXAMPLES 3 and 4
on pp. 451–452
for Exs. 8–18

COMPLETING PROPORTIONS Write a similarity statement for the three similar triangles in the diagram. Then complete the proportion.

8. $\dfrac{XW}{?} = \dfrac{ZW}{YW}$

9. $\dfrac{?}{SQ} = \dfrac{SQ}{TQ}$

10. $\dfrac{EF}{EG} = \dfrac{EG}{?}$

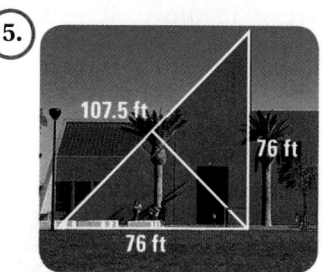

ERROR ANALYSIS *Describe* and correct the error in writing a proportion for the given diagram.

11.

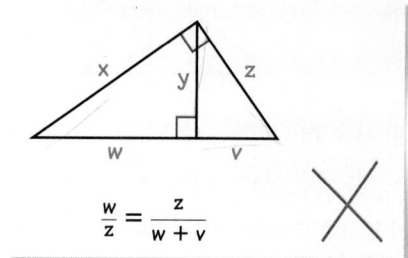

$$\frac{w}{z} = \frac{z}{w+v}$$

12.

$$\frac{e}{d} = \frac{d}{f}$$

FINDING LENGTHS Find the value of the variable. Round decimal answers to the nearest tenth.

13.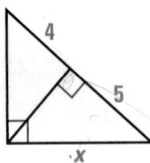

14.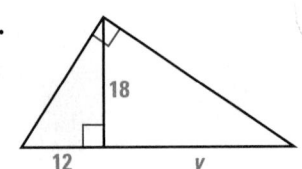

15.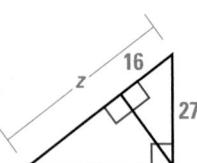

16.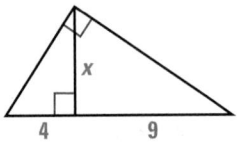

17.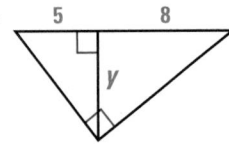

18.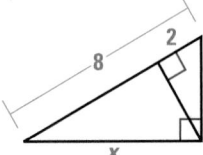

19. ★ **MULTIPLE CHOICE** Use the diagram at the right. Decide which proportion is false.

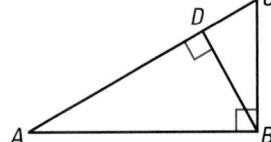

    A $\dfrac{DB}{DC} = \dfrac{DA}{DB}$ **B** $\dfrac{CA}{AB} = \dfrac{AB}{AD}$

    C $\dfrac{CA}{BA} = \dfrac{BA}{CA}$ **D** $\dfrac{DC}{BC} = \dfrac{BC}{CA}$

20. ★ **MULTIPLE CHOICE** In the diagram in Exercise 19 above, $AC = 36$ and $BC = 18$. Find AD. If necessary, round to the nearest tenth.

    A 9   **B** 15.6   **C** 27   **D** 31.2

ALGEBRA Find the value(s) of the variable(s).

21.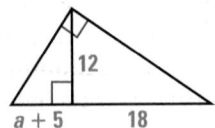

22.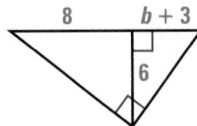

23.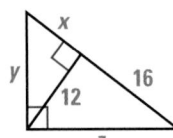

USING THEOREMS Tell whether the triangle is a right triangle. If so, find the length of the altitude to the hypotenuse. Round decimal answers to the nearest tenth.

24.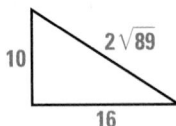

25.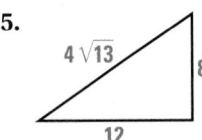

26.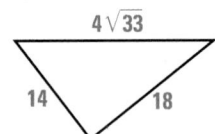

27. **FINDING LENGTHS** Use the Geometric Mean Theorems to find AC and BD.

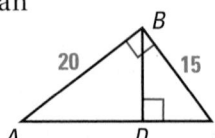

28. **CHALLENGE** Draw a right isosceles triangle and label the two leg lengths x. Then draw the altitude to the hypotenuse and label its length y. Now draw the three similar triangles and label any side length that is equal to either x or y. What can you conclude about the relationship between the two smaller triangles? *Explain.*

○ = **WORKED-OUT SOLUTIONS** on p. WS1   ★ = **STANDARDIZED TEST PRACTICE**

29. **DOGHOUSE** The peak of the doghouse shown forms a right angle. Use the given dimensions to find the height of the roof.

1.5 ft   1.5 ft

@HomeTutor for problem solving help at classzone.com

EXAMPLE 4
on p. 452
for Exs. 30–31

30. **MONUMENT** You want to determine the height of a monument at a local park. You use a cardboard square to line up the top and bottom of the monument. Mary measures the vertical distance from the ground to your eye and the distance from you to the monument. Approximate the height of the monument (as shown at the left below).

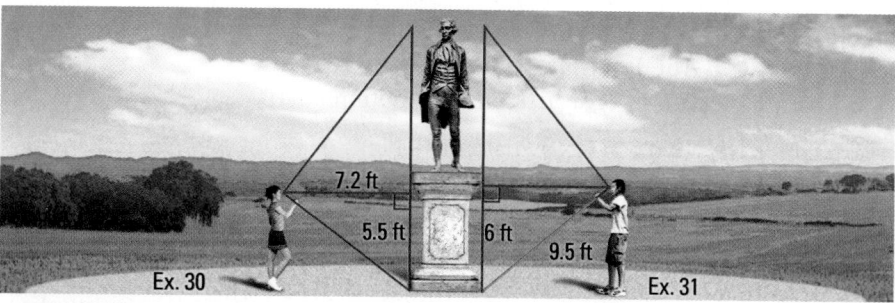

7.2 ft

5.5 ft   6 ft

9.5 ft

Ex. 30   Ex. 31

@HomeTutor for problem solving help at classzone.com

31. ★ **SHORT RESPONSE** Paul is standing on the other side of the monument in Exercise 30 (as shown at the right above). He has a piece of rope staked at the base of the monument. He extends the rope to the cardboard square he is holding lined up to the top and bottom of the monument. Use the information in the diagram above to approximate the height of the monument. Do you get the same answer as in Exercise 30? *Explain.*

32. **PROVING THEOREM 7.1** Use the diagram of $\triangle ABC$. Copy and complete the proof of the Pythagorean Theorem.

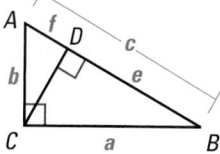

GIVEN ▶ In $\triangle ABC$, $\angle BCA$ is a right angle.
PROVE ▶ $c^2 = a^2 + b^2$

STATEMENTS	REASONS
1. Draw $\triangle ABC$. $\angle BCA$ is a right angle.	1. ?
2. Draw a perpendicular from C to $\overline{AB}$.	2. Perpendicular Postulate
3. $\dfrac{c}{a} = \dfrac{a}{e}$ and $\dfrac{c}{b} = \dfrac{b}{f}$	3. ?
4. $ce = a^2$ and $cf = b^2$	4. ?
5. $ce + b^2 = \underline{\ ?\ } + b^2$	5. Addition Property of Equality
6. $ce + cf = a^2 + b^2$	6. ?
7. $c(e + f) = a^2 + b^2$	7. ?
8. $e + f = \underline{\ ?\ }$	8. Segment Addition Postulate
9. $c \cdot c = a^2 + b^2$	9. ?
10. $c^2 = a^2 + b^2$	10. Simplify.

33. MULTI-STEP PROBLEM Use the diagram.

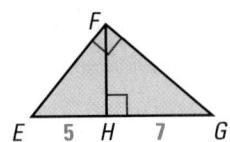

a. Name all the altitudes in $\triangle EGF$. *Explain.*

b. Find *FH*.

c. Find the area of the triangle.

34. ★ **EXTENDED RESPONSE** Use the diagram.

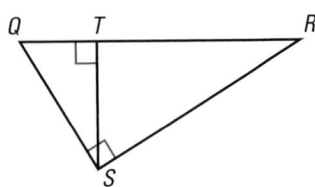

a. Sketch the three similar triangles in the diagram. Label the vertices. *Explain* how you know which vertices correspond.

b. Write similarity statements for the three triangles.

c. Which segment's length is the geometric mean of *RT* and *RQ*? *Explain* your reasoning.

PROVING THEOREMS In Exercises 35–37, use the diagram and GIVEN statements below.

GIVEN ▶ $\triangle ABC$ is a right triangle.
Altitude $\overline{CD}$ is drawn to hypotenuse $\overline{AB}$.

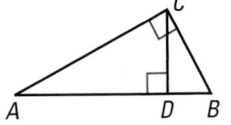

35. Prove Theorem 7.5 by using the Plan for Proof on page 449.

36. Prove Theorem 7.6 by showing $\dfrac{BD}{CD} = \dfrac{CD}{AD}$.

37. Prove Theorem 7.7 by showing $\dfrac{AB}{CB} = \dfrac{CB}{DB}$ and $\dfrac{AB}{AC} = \dfrac{AC}{AD}$.

38. CHALLENGE The *harmonic mean* of *a* and *b* is $\dfrac{2ab}{a+b}$. The Greek mathematician Pythagoras found that three equally taut strings on stringed instruments will sound harmonious if the length of the middle string is equal to the harmonic mean of the lengths of the shortest and longest string.

a. Find the harmonic mean of 10 and 15.

b. Find the harmonic mean of 6 and 14.

c. Will equally taut strings whose lengths have the ratio 4 : 6 : 12 sound harmonious? *Explain* your reasoning.

MIXED REVIEW

PREVIEW
Prepare for
Lesson 7.4 in
Exs. 39–46.

Simplify the expression. *(p. 874)*

39. $\sqrt{27} \cdot \sqrt{2}$

40. $\sqrt{8} \cdot \sqrt{10}$

41. $\sqrt{12} \cdot \sqrt{7}$

42. $\sqrt{18} \cdot \sqrt{12}$

43. $\dfrac{5}{\sqrt{7}}$

44. $\dfrac{8}{\sqrt{11}}$

45. $\dfrac{15}{\sqrt{27}}$

46. $\dfrac{12}{\sqrt{24}}$

Tell whether the lines through the given points are *parallel, perpendicular*, or *neither. Justify* your answer. *(p. 171)*

47. Line 1: (2, 4), (4, 2)
Line 2: (3, 5), (−1, 1)

48. Line 1: (0, 2), (−1, −1)
Line 2: (3, 1), (1, −5)

49: Line 1: (1, 7), (4, 7)
Line 2: (5, 2), (7, 4)

7.4 Special Right Triangles

Before   You found side lengths using the Pythagorean Theorem.

Now   You will use the relationships among the sides in special right triangles.

Why?   So you can find the height of a drawbridge, as in Ex. 28.

Key Vocabulary
- **isosceles triangle**, p. 217

A 45°-45°-90° triangle is an *isosceles right triangle* that can be formed by cutting a square in half as shown.

THEOREM   *For Your Notebook*

THEOREM 7.8   **45°-45°-90° Triangle Theorem**

USE RATIOS
The extended ratio of the side lengths of a 45°-45°-90° triangle is 1:1:$\sqrt{2}$.

In a 45°-45°-90° triangle, the hypotenuse is $\sqrt{2}$ times as long as each leg.

hypotenuse = leg · $\sqrt{2}$

Proof: Ex. 30, p. 463

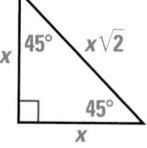

EXAMPLE 1   **Find hypotenuse length in a 45°-45°-90° triangle**

Find the length of the hypotenuse.

a.

b.

Solution

a. By the Triangle Sum Theorem, the measure of the third angle must be 45°. Then the triangle is a 45°-45°-90° triangle, so by Theorem 7.8, the hypotenuse is $\sqrt{2}$ times as long as each leg.

     hypotenuse = leg · $\sqrt{2}$ **45°-45°-90° Triangle Theorem**

           = $8\sqrt{2}$ **Substitute.**

REVIEW ALGEBRA
Remember the following properties of radicals:

$\sqrt{a} \cdot \sqrt{b} = \sqrt{a \cdot b}$

$\sqrt{a} \cdot a = a$

For a review of radical expressions, see p. 874.

b. By the Base Angles Theorem and the Corollary to the Triangle Sum Theorem, the triangle is a 45°-45°-90° triangle.

     hypotenuse = leg · $\sqrt{2}$ **45°-45°-90° Triangle Theorem**

           = $3\sqrt{2} \cdot \sqrt{2}$ **Substitute.**

           = $3 \cdot 2$ **Product of square roots**

           = 6   **Simplify.**

EXAMPLE 2 Find leg lengths in a 45°-45°-90° triangle

Find the lengths of the legs in the triangle.

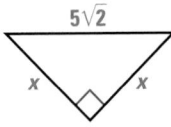

Solution

By the Base Angles Theorem and the Corollary to the Triangle Sum Theorem, the triangle is a 45°-45°-90° triangle.

$$\text{hypotenuse} = \text{leg} \cdot \sqrt{2} \qquad \text{45°-45°-90° Triangle Theorem}$$

$$5\sqrt{2} = x \cdot \sqrt{2} \qquad \text{Substitute.}$$

$$\frac{5\sqrt{2}}{\sqrt{2}} = \frac{x\sqrt{2}}{\sqrt{2}} \qquad \text{Divide each side by } \sqrt{2}.$$

$$5 = x \qquad \text{Simplify.}$$

★ **EXAMPLE 3** Standardized Test Practice

Triangle *WXY* is a right triangle.
Find the length of $\overline{WX}$.

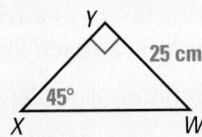

A 50 cm

B $25\sqrt{2}$ cm

C 25 cm

D $\frac{25\sqrt{2}}{2}$ cm

ELIMINATE CHOICES
You can eliminate choices C and D because the hypotenuse has to be longer than the leg.

Solution

By the Corollary to the Triangle Sum Theorem, the triangle is a 45°-45°-90° triangle.

$$\text{hypotenuse} = \text{leg} \cdot \sqrt{2} \qquad \text{45°-45°-90° Triangle Theorem}$$

$$WX = 25\sqrt{2} \qquad \text{Substitute.}$$

▶ The correct answer is B. **A** **B** **C** **D**

✓ **GUIDED PRACTICE** for Examples 1, 2, and 3

Find the value of the variable.

1.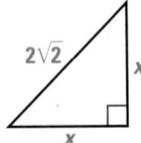

2.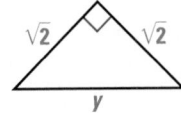

3.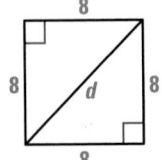

4. Find the leg length of a 45°-45°-90° triangle with a hypotenuse length of 6.

A 30°-60°-90° triangle can be formed by dividing an equilateral triangle in half.

THEOREM 7.9 30°-60°-90° Triangle Theorem

In a 30°-60°-90° triangle, the hypotenuse is twice as long as the shorter leg, and the longer leg is $\sqrt{3}$ times as long as the shorter leg.

hypotenuse = 2 • shorter leg

longer leg = shorter leg • $\sqrt{3}$

Proof: Ex. 32, p. 463

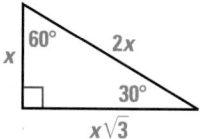

USE RATIOS

The extended ratio of the side lengths of a 30°-60°-90° triangle is $1 : \sqrt{3} : 2$.

EXAMPLE 4   **Find the height of an equilateral triangle**

LOGO The logo on the recycling bin at the right resembles an equilateral triangle with side lengths of 6 centimeters. What is the approximate height of the logo?

Solution

Draw the equilateral triangle described. Its altitude forms the longer leg of two 30°-60°-90° triangles. The length h of the altitude is approximately the height of the logo.

longer leg = shorter leg • $\sqrt{3}$

$h = 3 \cdot \sqrt{3} \approx 5.2$ cm

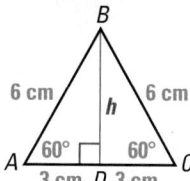

REVIEW MEDIAN

Remember that in an equilateral triangle, the altitude to a side is also the median to that side. So, altitude $\overline{BD}$ bisects $\overline{AC}$.

EXAMPLE 5   **Find lengths in a 30°-60°-90° triangle**

xy Find the values of x and y. Write your answer in simplest radical form.

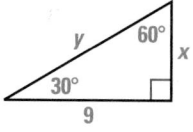

STEP 1   **Find** the value of x.

longer leg = shorter leg • $\sqrt{3}$ 30°-60°-90° Triangle Theorem

$9 = x\sqrt{3}$ Substitute.

$\dfrac{9}{\sqrt{3}} = x$ Divide each side by $\sqrt{3}$.

$\dfrac{9}{\sqrt{3}} \cdot \dfrac{\sqrt{3}}{\sqrt{3}} = x$ Multiply numerator and denominator by $\sqrt{3}$.

$\dfrac{9\sqrt{3}}{3} = x$ Multiply fractions.

$3\sqrt{3} = x$ Simplify.

STEP 2   **Find** the value of y.

hypotenuse = 2 • shorter leg   30°-60°-90° Triangle Theorem

$y = 2 \cdot 3\sqrt{3} = 6\sqrt{3}$ Substitute and simplify.

EXAMPLE 6 **Find a height**

DUMP TRUCK The body of a dump truck is raised to empty a load of sand. How high is the 14 foot body from the frame when it is tipped upward at the given angle?

a. 45° angle   **b.** 60° angle

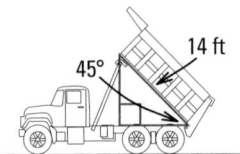

Solution

a. When the body is raised 45° above the frame, the height h is the length of a leg of a 45°-45°-90° triangle. The length of the hypotenuse is 14 feet.

$14 = h \cdot \sqrt{2}$ **45°-45°-90° Triangle Theorem**

$\dfrac{14}{\sqrt{2}} = h$ **Divide each side by $\sqrt{2}$.**

$9.9 \approx h$ **Use a calculator to approximate.**

REWRITE MEASURES

To write 9.9 ft in feet and inches, multiply the decimal part by 12.

$12 \cdot 0.9 = 10.8$

So, 9.9 ft is about 9 feet 11 inches.

▸ When the angle of elevation is 45°, the body is about 9 feet 11 inches above the frame.

b. When the body is raised 60°, the height h is the length of the longer leg of a 30°-60°-90° triangle. The length of the hypotenuse is 14 feet.

hypotenuse = 2 · shorter leg   **30°-60°-90° Triangle Theorem**

$14 = 2 \cdot s$ **Substitute.**

$7 = s$ **Divide each side by 2.**

longer leg = shorter leg · $\sqrt{3}$ **30°-60°-90° Triangle Theorem**

$h = 7\sqrt{3}$ **Substitute.**

$h \approx 12.1$ **Use a calculator to approximate.**

▸ When the angle of elevation is 60°, the body is about 12 feet 1 inch above the frame.

Animated Geometry at classzone.com

✓ **GUIDED PRACTICE**   for Examples 4, 5, and 6

Find the value of the variable.

5.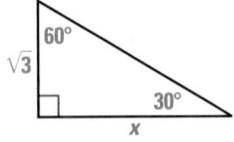

6.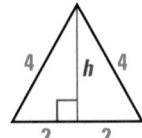

7. WHAT IF? In Example 6, what is the height of the body of the dump truck if it is raised 30° above the frame?

8. In a 30°-60°-90° triangle, *describe* the location of the shorter side. *Describe* the location of the longer side?

7.4 EXERCISES

HOMEWORK KEY

◯ = **WORKED-OUT SOLUTIONS**
on p. WS8 for Exs. 5, 9, and 27

★ = **STANDARDIZED TEST PRACTICE**
Exs. 2, 6, 19, 22, 29, and 34

SKILL PRACTICE

1. **VOCABULARY** Copy and complete: A triangle with two congruent sides and a right angle is called __?__ .

2. ★ **WRITING** *Explain* why the acute angles in an isosceles right triangle always measure 45°.

EXAMPLES 1 and 2
on pp. 457–458
for Exs. 3–5

45°-45°-90° TRIANGLES **Find the value of *x*. Write your answer in simplest radical form.**

3.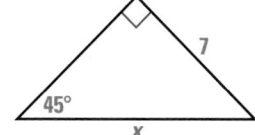

4.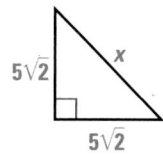

5.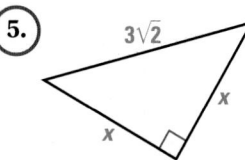

EXAMPLE 3
on p. 458
for Exs. 6–7

6. ★ **MULTIPLE CHOICE** Find the length of $\overline{AC}$.

Ⓐ $7\sqrt{2}$ in.   Ⓑ $2\sqrt{7}$ in.

Ⓒ $\dfrac{7\sqrt{2}}{2}$ in.   Ⓓ $\sqrt{14}$ in.

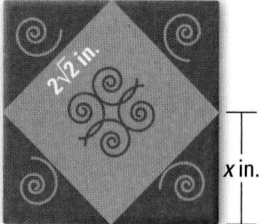

7. **ISOSCELES RIGHT TRIANGLE** The square tile shown has painted corners in the shape of congruent 45°-45°-90° triangles. What is the value of *x*? What is the side length of the tile?

EXAMPLES 4 and 5
on p. 459
for Exs. 8–10

30°-60°-90° TRIANGLES **Find the value of each variable. Write your answers in simplest radical form.**

8.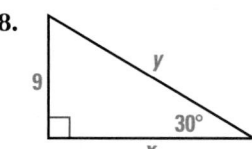

9.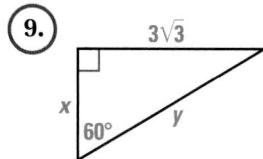

10.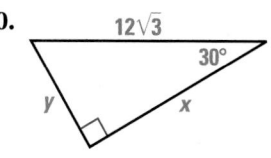

SPECIAL RIGHT TRIANGLES **Copy and complete the table.**

11.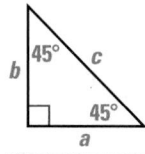

a	7	?	?	?	$\sqrt{5}$
b	?	11	?	?	?
c	?	?	10	$6\sqrt{2}$	?

12.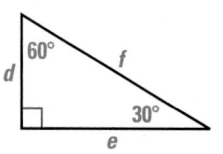

d	5	?	?	?	?
e	?	?	$8\sqrt{3}$	?	12
f	?	14	?	$18\sqrt{3}$	?

ALGEBRA Find the value of each variable. Write your answers in simplest radical form.

13.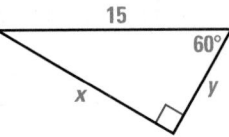

14.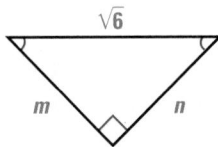

15.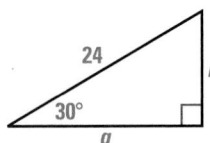

16.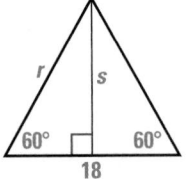

17.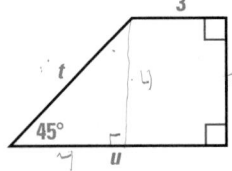

18.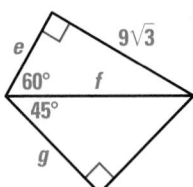

Animated Geometry at classzone.com

19. ★ **MULTIPLE CHOICE** Which side lengths do *not* represent a 30°-60°-90° triangle?

Ⓐ $\frac{1}{2}, \frac{\sqrt{3}}{2}, 1$

Ⓑ $\sqrt{2}, \sqrt{6}, 2\sqrt{2}$

Ⓒ $\frac{5}{2}, \frac{5\sqrt{3}}{2}, 10$

Ⓓ $3, 3\sqrt{3}, 6$

ERROR ANALYSIS *Describe* and correct the error in finding the length of the hypotenuse.

20.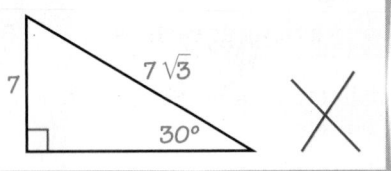

21.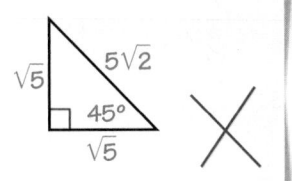

22. ★ **WRITING** Abigail solved Example 5 on page 459 in a different way. Instead of dividing each side by $\sqrt{3}$, she multiplied each side by $\sqrt{3}$. Does her method work? *Explain* why or why not.

ALGEBRA Find the value of each variable. Write your answers in simplest radical form.

23.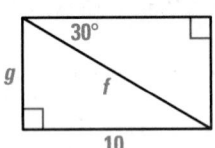

24.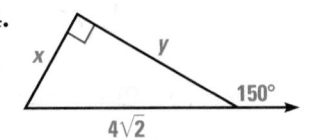

25.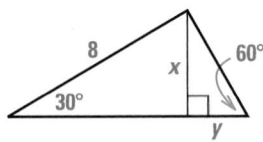

26. **CHALLENGE** △*ABC* is a 30°-60°-90° triangle. Find the coordinates of *A*.

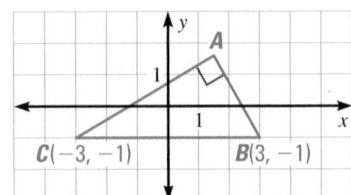

○ = **WORKED-OUT SOLUTIONS** on p. WS1

★ = **STANDARDIZED TEST PRACTICE**

EXAMPLE 6
on p. 460
for Ex. 27

27. **KAYAK RAMP** A ramp is used to launch a kayak. What is the height of an 11 foot ramp when its angle is 30° as shown?

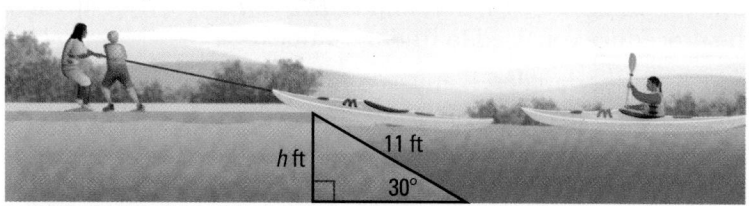

h ft   11 ft   30°

@HomeTutor for problem solving help at classzone.com

28. **DRAWBRIDGE** Each half of the drawbridge is about 284 feet long, as shown. How high does a seagull who is on the end of the drawbridge rise when the angle with measure *x*° is 30°? 45°? 60°?

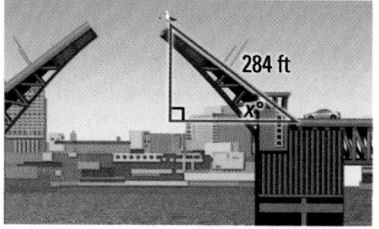

284 ft

x°

@HomeTutor for problem solving help at classzone.com

29. ★ **SHORT RESPONSE** *Describe* two ways to show that all isosceles right triangles are similar to each other.

30. **PROVING THEOREM 7.8** Write a paragraph proof of the 45°-45°-90° Triangle Theorem.

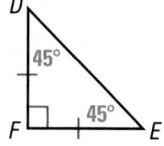

GIVEN ▶ △*DEF* is a 45°-45°-90° triangle.

PROVE ▶ The hypotenuse is $\sqrt{2}$ times as long as each leg.

31. **EQUILATERAL TRIANGLE** If an equilateral triangle has a side length of 20 inches, find the height of the triangle.

32. **PROVING THEOREM 7.9** Write a paragraph proof of the 30°-60°-90° Triangle Theorem.

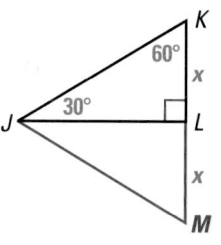

GIVEN ▶ △*JKL* is a 30°-60°-90° triangle.

PROVE ▶ The hypotenuse is twice as long as the shorter leg and the longer leg is $\sqrt{3}$ times as long as the shorter leg.

Plan for Proof Construct △*JML* congruent to △*JKL*. Then prove that △*JKM* is equilateral. Express the lengths of $\overline{JK}$ and $\overline{JL}$ in terms of *x*.

33. **MULTI-STEP PROBLEM** You are creating a quilt that will have a traditional "flying geese" border, as shown below.

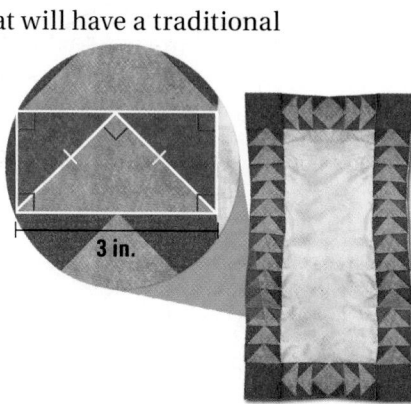

3 in.

a. Find all the angle measures of the small blue triangles and the large orange triangles.

b. The width of the border is to be 3 inches. To create the large triangle, you cut a square of fabric in half. Not counting any extra fabric needed for seams, what size square do you need?

c. What size square do you need to create each small triangle?

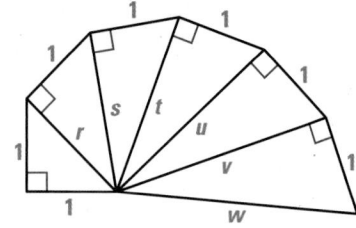

34. ★ **EXTENDED RESPONSE** Use the figure at the right. You can use the fact that the converses of the 45°-45°-90° Triangle Theorem and the 30°-60°-90° Triangle Theorem are true.

   a. Find the values of *r*, *s*, *t*, *u*, *v*, and *w*. *Explain* the procedure you used to find the values.

   b. Which of the triangles, if any, is a 45°-45°-90° triangle? *Explain.*

   c. Which of the triangles, if any, is a 30°-60°-90° triangle? *Explain.*

35. **CHALLENGE** In quadrilateral *QRST*, m∠*R* = 60°, m∠*T* = 90°, *QR* = *RS*, *ST* = 8, *TQ* = 8, and $\overline{RT}$ and $\overline{QS}$ intersect at point *Z*.

   a. Draw a diagram.

   b. *Explain* why △*RQT* ≅ △*RST*.

   c. Which is longer, *QS* or *RT*? *Explain.*

MIXED REVIEW

In the diagram, $\overleftrightarrow{BD}$ is the perpendicular bisector of $\overline{AC}$. *(p. 303)*

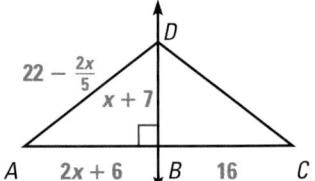

36. Which pairs of segment lengths are equal?

37. What is the value of *x*?

38. Find *CD*.

Is it possible to build a triangle using the given side lengths? *(p. 328)*

39. 4, 4, and 7   40. 3, 3, and $9\sqrt{2}$ 41. 7, 15, and 21

PREVIEW
....
Prepare for
Lesson 7.5 in
Exs. 42–44.

Tell whether the given side lengths form a right triangle. *(p. 441)*

42. 21, 22, and $5\sqrt{37}$ 43. $\frac{3}{2}$, 2, and $\frac{5}{2}$ 44. 8, 10, and 14

QUIZ *for Lessons 7.3–7.4*

In Exercises 1 and 2, use the diagram. *(p. 449)*

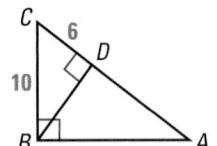

   1. Which segment's length is the geometric mean of *AC* and *CD*?

   2. Find *BD*, *AD*, and *AB*.

Find the values of the variable(s). Write your answer(s) in simplest radical form. *(p. 457)*

3.   4.   5.

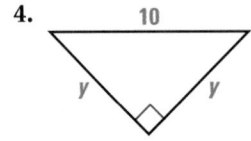   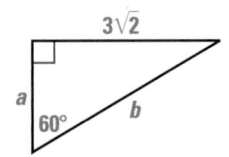

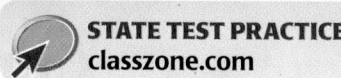
Lessons 7.1–7.4

1. GRIDDED ANSWER Find the direct distance, in paces, from the treasure to the stump.

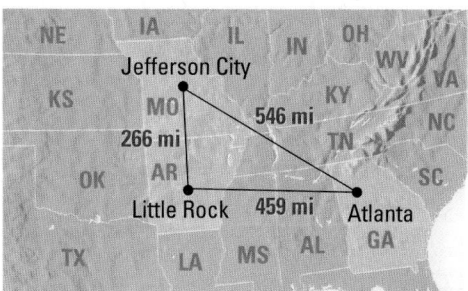

From the old stump, take 30 paces east, then 20 paces north, 6 paces west, and then another 25 paces north to find the hidden treasure.

2. MULTI-STEP PROBLEM On a map of the United States, you put a pushpin on three state capitols you want to visit: Jefferson City, Missouri; Little Rock, Arkansas; and Atlanta, Georgia.

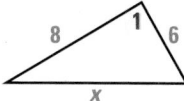

a. Draw a diagram to model the triangle.

b. Do the pushpins form a right triangle? If not, what type of triangle do they form?

3. SHORT RESPONSE Bob and John started running at 10 A.M. Bob ran east at 4 miles per hour while John ran south at 5 miles per hour. How far apart were they at 11:30 A.M.? *Describe* how you calculated the answer.

4. EXTENDED RESPONSE Give all values of x that make the statement true for the given diagram.

a. ∠1 is a right angle. *Explain.*

b. ∠1 is an obtuse angle. *Explain.*

c. ∠1 is an acute angle. *Explain.*

d. The triangle is isosceles. *Explain.*

e. No triangle is possible. *Explain.*

5. EXTENDED RESPONSE A Chinese checker board is made of triangles. Use the picture below to answer the questions.

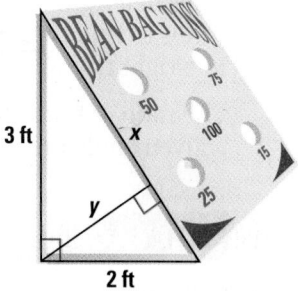

a. Count the marble holes in the purple triangle. What kind of triangle is it?

b. If a side of the purple triangle measures 8 centimeters, find the area of the purple triangle.

c. How many marble holes are in the center hexagon? Assuming each marble hole takes up the same amount of space, what is the relationship between the purple triangle and center hexagon?

d. Find the area of the center hexagon. *Explain* your reasoning.

6. MULTI-STEP PROBLEM You build a beanbag toss game. The game is constructed from a sheet of plywood supported by two boards. The two boards form a right angle and their lengths are 3 feet and 2 feet.

a. Find the length x of the plywood.

b. You put in a support that is the altitude y to the hypotenuse of the right triangle. What is the length of the support?

c. Where does the support attach to the plywood? *Explain.*

7.5 Apply the Tangent Ratio

Before You used congruent or similar triangles for indirect measurement.

Now You will use the tangent ratio for indirect measurement.

Why? So you can find the height of a roller coaster, as in Ex. 32.

Key Vocabulary
• trigonometric ratio
• tangent

Materials: metric ruler, protractor, calculator

STEP 1 Draw a 30° angle and mark a point every 5 centimeters on a side as shown. Draw perpendicular segments through the 3 points.

STEP 2 Measure the legs of each right triangle. Copy and complete the table.

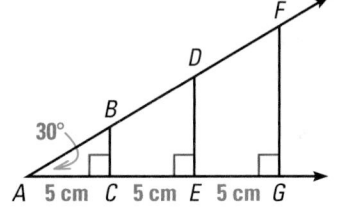

Triangle	Adjacent leg	Opposite leg	Opposite leg / Adjacent leg
△ABC	5 cm	?	?
△ADE	10 cm	?	?
△AFG	15 cm	?	?

STEP 3 Explain why the proportions $\frac{BC}{DE} = \frac{AC}{AE}$ and $\frac{BC}{AC} = \frac{DE}{AE}$ are true.

STEP 4 Make a conjecture about the ratio of the lengths of the legs in a right triangle. Test your conjecture by using different acute angle measures.

A **trigonometric ratio** is a ratio of the lengths of two sides in a right triangle. You will use trigonometric ratios to find the measure of a side or an acute angle in a right triangle.

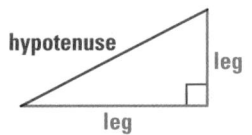

The ratio of the lengths of the legs in a right triangle is constant for a given angle measure. This ratio is called the **tangent** of the angle.

KEY CONCEPT *For Your Notebook*

ABBREVIATE
Remember these abbreviations:
tangent → tan
opposite → opp.
adjacent → adj.

Tangent Ratio

Let △ABC be a right triangle with acute ∠A. The tangent of ∠A (written as tan A) is defined as follows:

$$\tan A = \frac{\text{length of leg opposite } \angle A}{\text{length of leg adjacent to } \angle A} = \frac{BC}{AC}$$

COMPLEMENTARY ANGLES In the right triangle, $\angle A$ and $\angle B$ are complementary so you can use the same diagram to find the tangent of $\angle A$ and the tangent of $\angle B$. Notice that the leg adjacent to $\angle A$ is the leg *opposite* $\angle B$ and the leg opposite $\angle A$ is the leg *adjacent* to $\angle B$.

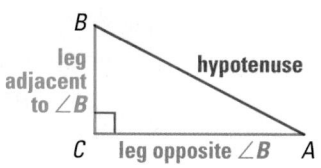

EXAMPLE 1 Find tangent ratios

Find tan S and tan R. Write each answer as a fraction and as a decimal rounded to four places.

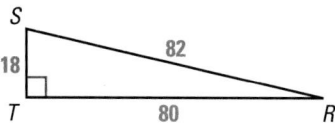

APPROXIMATE

Unless told otherwise, you should round the values of trigonometric ratios to the ten-thousandths' place and round lengths to the tenths' place.

Solution

$$\tan S = \frac{\text{opp. } \angle S}{\text{adj. to } \angle S} = \frac{RT}{ST} = \frac{80}{18} = \frac{40}{9} \approx 4.4444$$

$$\tan R = \frac{\text{opp. } \angle R}{\text{adj. to } \angle R} = \frac{ST}{RT} = \frac{18}{80} = \frac{9}{40} = 0.2250$$

✓ **GUIDED PRACTICE** for Example 1

Find tan J and tan K. Round to four decimal places.

1.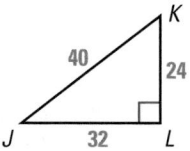

2.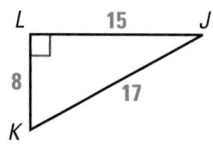

EXAMPLE 2 Find a leg length

XY ALGEBRA Find the value of x.

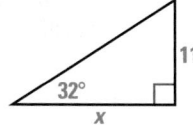

Solution

Use the tangent of an acute angle to find a leg length.

$\tan 32° = \dfrac{\text{opp.}}{\text{adj.}}$	**Write ratio for tangent of 32°.**
$\tan 32° = \dfrac{11}{x}$	**Substitute.**
$x \cdot \tan 32° = 11$	**Multiply each side by x.**
$x = \dfrac{11}{\tan 32°}$	**Divide each side by tan 32°.**
$x \approx \dfrac{11}{0.6249}$	**Use a calculator to find tan 32°.**
$x \approx 17.6$	**Simplify.**

ANOTHER WAY

You can also use the Table of Trigonometric Ratios on p. 925 to find the decimal values of trigonometric ratios.

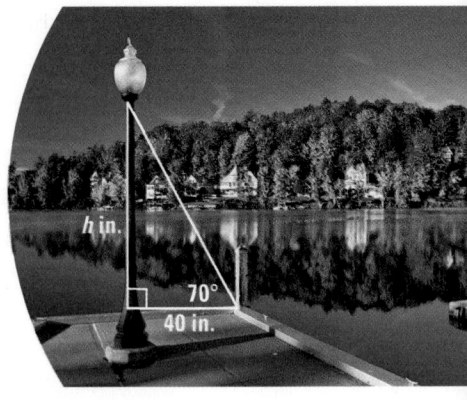

EXAMPLE 3 Estimate height using tangent

LAMPPOST Find the height h of the lamppost to the nearest inch.

$\tan 70° = \dfrac{\text{opp.}}{\text{adj.}}$ **Write ratio for tangent of 70°.**

$\tan 70° = \dfrac{h}{40}$ **Substitute.**

$40 \cdot \tan 70° = h$ **Multiply each side by 40.**

$109.9 \approx h$ **Use a calculator to simplify.**

▶ The lamppost is about 110 inches tall.

SPECIAL RIGHT TRIANGLES You can find the tangent of an acute angle measuring 30°, 45°, or 60° by applying what you know about special right triangles.

EXAMPLE 4 Use a special right triangle to find a tangent

Use a special right triangle to find the tangent of a 60° angle.

SIMILAR TRIANGLES
The tangents of all 60° angles are the same constant ratio. Any right triangle with a 60° angle can be used to determine this value.

STEP 1 Because all 30°-60°-90° triangles are similar, you can simplify your calculations by choosing 1 as the length of the shorter leg. Use the 30°-60°-90° Triangle Theorem to find the length of the longer leg.

longer leg = shorter leg $\cdot \sqrt{3}$ **30°-60°-90° Triangle Theorem**

$x = 1 \cdot \sqrt{3}$ **Substitute.**

$x = \sqrt{3}$ **Simplify.**

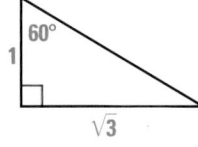

STEP 2 Find $\tan 60°$.

$\tan 60° = \dfrac{\text{opp.}}{\text{adj.}}$ **Write ratio for tangent of 60°.**

$\tan 60° = \dfrac{\sqrt{3}}{1}$ **Substitute.**

$\tan 60° = \sqrt{3}$ **Simplify.**

▶ The tangent of any 60° angle is $\sqrt{3} \approx 1.7321$.

✓ GUIDED PRACTICE for Examples 2, 3, and 4

Find the value of x. Round to the nearest tenth.

3.

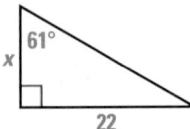

4.

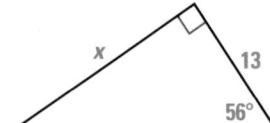

5. **WHAT IF?** In Example 4, suppose the side length of the shorter leg is 5 instead of 1. Show that the tangent of 60° is still equal to $\sqrt{3}$.

7.5 EXERCISES

HOMEWORK KEY

◯ = WORKED-OUT SOLUTIONS
on p. WS9 for Exs. 5, 7, and 31

★ = STANDARDIZED TEST PRACTICE
Exs. 2, 15, 16, 17, 35, and 37

SKILL PRACTICE

1. **VOCABULARY** Copy and complete: The tangent ratio compares the length of __?__ to the length of __?__.

2. ★ **WRITING** *Explain* how you know that all right triangles with an acute angle measuring $n°$ are similar to each other.

EXAMPLE 1
on p. 467
for Exs. 3–5

FINDING TANGENT RATIOS Find tan *A* and tan *B*. Write each answer as a fraction and as a decimal rounded to four places.

3.

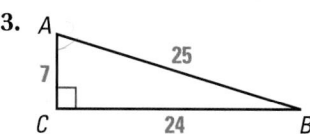

4.

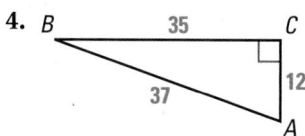

5.

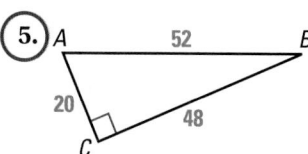

EXAMPLE 2
on p. 467
for Exs. 6–8

FINDING LEG LENGTHS Find the value of *x* to the nearest tenth.

6.

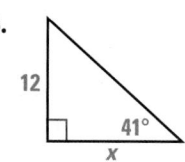

7.

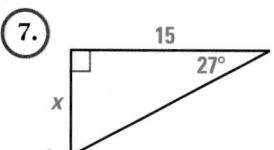

8.

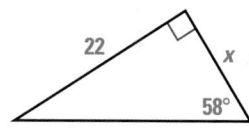

EXAMPLE 4
on p. 468
for Exs. 9–12

FINDING LEG LENGTHS Find the value of *x* using the definition of tangent. Then find the value of *x* using the 45°-45°-90° Theorem or the 30°-60°-90° Theorem. *Compare* the results.

9.

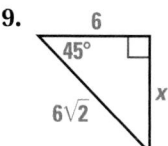

10.

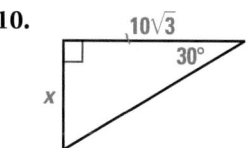

11.

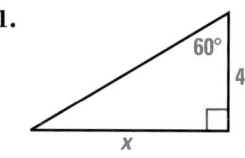

12. **SPECIAL RIGHT TRIANGLES** Find tan 30° and tan 45° using the 45°-45°-90° Triangle Theorem and the 30°-60°-90° Triangle Theorem.

ERROR ANALYSIS *Describe* the error in the statement of the tangent ratio. Correct the statement, if possible. Otherwise, write *not possible*.

13.

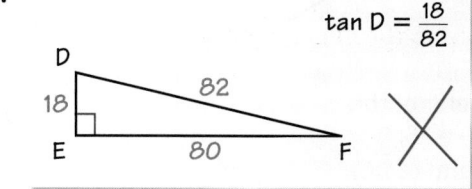

14.

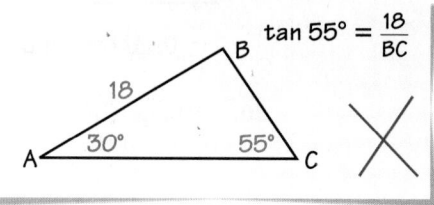

15. ★ **WRITING** *Describe* what you must know about a triangle in order to use the tangent ratio.

16. ★ MULTIPLE CHOICE Which expression can be used to find the value of x in the triangle shown?

    A $x = 20 \cdot \tan 40°$

    B $x = \dfrac{\tan 40°}{20}$

    C $x = \dfrac{20}{\tan 40°}$

    D $x = \dfrac{20}{\tan 50°}$

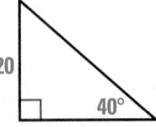

17. ★ MULTIPLE CHOICE What is the approximate value of x in the triangle shown?

    A   0.4   **B**   2.7

    C   7.5   **D**   19.2

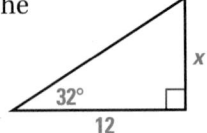

FINDING LEG LENGTHS Use a tangent ratio to find the value of x. Round to the nearest tenth. Check your solution using the tangent of the other acute angle.

18.
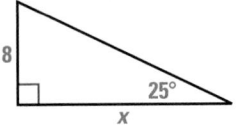

19.
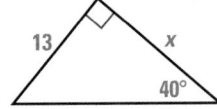

20.
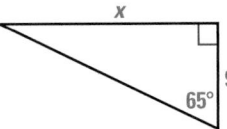

FINDING AREA Find the area of the triangle. Round to the nearest tenth.

21.
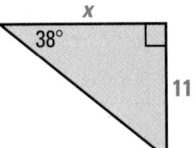

22.
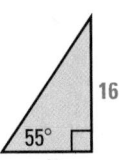

23.
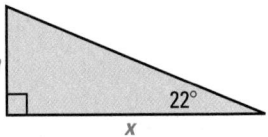

FINDING PERIMETER Find the perimeter of the triangle. Round to the nearest tenth.

24.
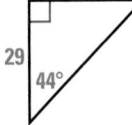

25.

26.
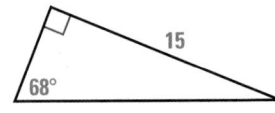

FINDING LENGTHS Find y. Then find z. Round to the nearest tenth.

27.
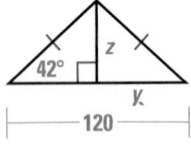

28.
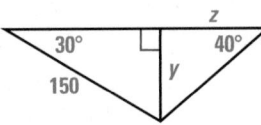

29.
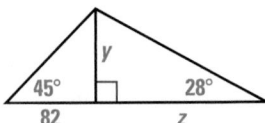

30. CHALLENGE Find the perimeter of the figure at the right, where $AC = 26$, $AD = BF$, and D is the midpoint of $\overline{AC}$.

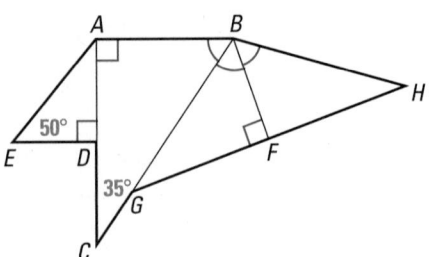

○ = **WORKED-OUT SOLUTIONS**
    on p. WS1

★ = **STANDARDIZED TEST PRACTICE**

EXAMPLE 3
on p. 468
for Exs. 31–32

31. **WASHINGTON MONUMENT** A surveyor is standing 118 feet from the base of the Washington Monument. The surveyor measures the angle between the ground and the top of the monument to be 78°. Find the height *h* of the Washington Monument to the nearest foot.

@HomeTutor for problem solving help at classzone.com

32. **ROLLER COASTERS** A roller coaster makes an angle of 52° with the ground. The horizontal distance from the crest of the hill to the bottom of the hill is about 121 feet, as shown. Find the height *h* of the roller coaster to the nearest foot.

@HomeTutor for problem solving help at classzone.com

CLASS PICTURE Use this information and diagram for Exercises 33 and 34.

Your class is having a class picture taken on the lawn. The photographer is positioned 14 feet away from the center of the class. If she looks toward either end of the class, she turns 50°.

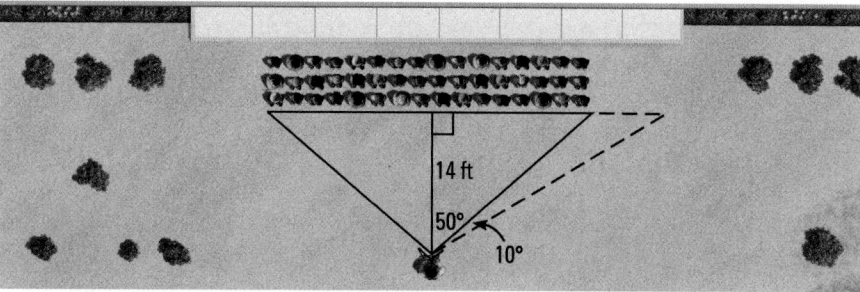

33. **ISOSCELES TRIANGLE** What is the distance between the ends of the class?

34. **MULTI-STEP PROBLEM** The photographer wants to estimate how many more students can fit at the end of the first row. The photographer turns 50° to see the last student and another 10° to see the end of the camera range.

   a. Find the distance from the center to the last student in the row.

   b. Find the distance from the center to the end of the camera range.

   c. Use the results of parts (a) and (b) to estimate the length of the empty space.

   d. If each student needs 2 feet of space, about how many more students can fit at the end of the first row? *Explain* your reasoning.

35. ★ **SHORT RESPONSE** Write expressions for the tangent of each acute angle in the triangle. *Explain* how the tangent of one acute angle is related to the tangent of the other acute angle. What kind of angle pair are ∠A and ∠B?

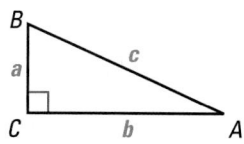

36. EYE CHART You are looking at an eye chart that is 20 feet away. Your eyes are level with the bottom of the "E" on the chart. To see the top of the "E," you look up 1°. How tall is the "E"?

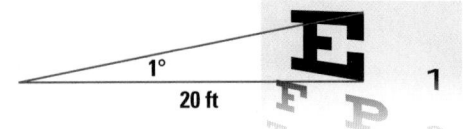

Not drawn to scale

37. ★ EXTENDED RESPONSE According to the Americans with Disabilities Act, a ramp cannot have an incline that is greater than 5°. The regulations also state that the maximum rise of a ramp is 30 inches. When a ramp needs to reach a height greater than 30 inches, a series of ramps connected by 60 inch landings can be used, as shown below.

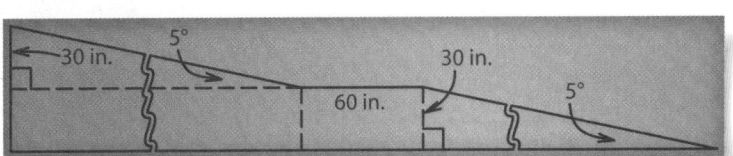

a. What is the maximum horizontal length of the base of one ramp, in feet? Round to the nearest foot.

b. If a doorway is 7.5 feet above the ground, what is the least number of ramps and landings you will need to lead to the doorway? Draw and label a diagram to *justify* your answer.

c. To the nearest foot, what is the total length of the base of the system of ramps and landings in part (b)?

38. CHALLENGE The road salt shown is stored in a cone-shaped pile. The base of the cone has a circumference of 80 feet. The cone rises at an angle of 32°. Find the height *h* of the cone. Then find the length *s* of the cone-shaped pile.

MIXED REVIEW

The expressions given represent the angle measures of a triangle. Find the measure of each angle. Then classify the triangle by its angles. *(p. 217)*

39. $m\angle A = x°$
$m\angle B = 4x°$
$m\angle C = 4x°$

40. $m\angle A = x°$
$m\angle B = x°$
$m\angle C = (5x - 60)°$

41. $m\angle A = (x + 20)°$
$m\angle B = (3x + 15)°$
$m\angle C = (x - 30)°$

Copy and complete the statement with <, >, or =. *Explain.* *(p. 335)*

42. $m\angle 1 \underline{\ ?\ } m\angle 2$

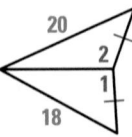

43. $m\angle 1 \underline{\ ?\ } m\angle 2$

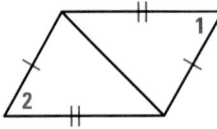

44. $m\angle 1 \underline{\ ?\ } m\angle 2$

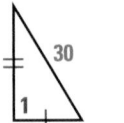 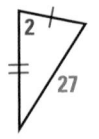

PREVIEW
·············
Prepare for
Lesson 7.6 in
Exs. 45–47.

Find the unknown side length of the right triangle. *(p. 433)*

45.

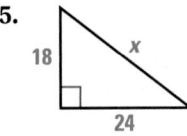

46.

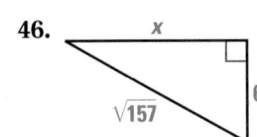

47.

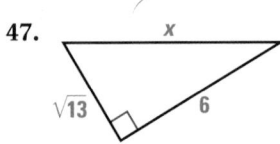

EXTRA PRACTICE for Lesson 7.5, p. 909   **ONLINE QUIZ** at classzone.com

7.6 Apply the Sine and Cosine Ratios

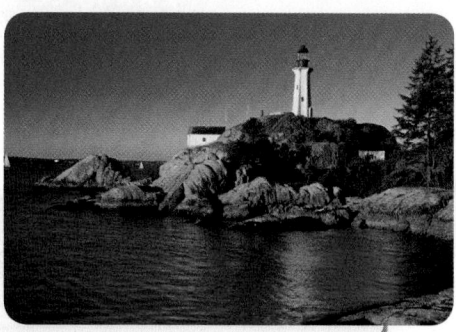

Before	You used the tangent ratio.
Now	You will use the sine and cosine ratios.
Why	So you can find distances, as in Ex. 39.

Key Vocabulary
- sine
- cosine
- angle of elevation
- angle of depression

The **sine** and **cosine** ratios are trigonometric ratios for acute angles that involve the lengths of a leg and the hypotenuse of a right triangle.

KEY CONCEPT   *For Your Notebook*

Sine and Cosine Ratios

Let $\triangle ABC$ be a right triangle with acute $\angle A$. The sine of $\angle A$ and cosine of $\angle A$ (written sin A and cos A) are defined as follows:

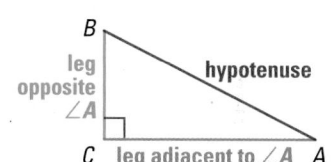

$$\sin A = \frac{\text{length of leg opposite } \angle A}{\text{length of hypotenuse}} = \frac{BC}{AB}$$

$$\cos A = \frac{\text{length of leg adjacent to } \angle A}{\text{length of hypotenuse}} = \frac{AC}{AB}$$

ABBREVIATE
Remember these abbreviations:
sine → sin
cosine → cos
hypotenuse → hyp

EXAMPLE 1 Find sine ratios

Find sin S and sin R. Write each answer as a fraction and as a decimal rounded to four places.

Solution

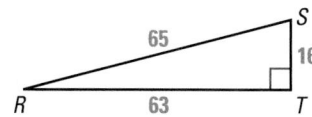

$$\sin S = \frac{\text{opp. } \angle S}{\text{hyp.}} = \frac{RT}{SR} = \frac{63}{65} \approx 0.9692$$

$$\sin R = \frac{\text{opp. } \angle R}{\text{hyp.}} = \frac{ST}{SR} = \frac{16}{65} \approx 0.2462$$

✓ **GUIDED PRACTICE** for Example 1

Find sin X and sin Y. Write each answer as a fraction and as a decimal. Round to four decimal places, if necessary.

1.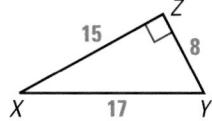

2.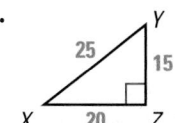

EXAMPLE 2 Find cosine ratios

Find cos *U* and cos *W*. Write each answer as a
fraction and as a decimal.

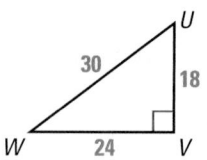

Solution

$$\cos U = \frac{\text{adj. to } \angle U}{\text{hyp.}} = \frac{UV}{UW} = \frac{18}{30} = \frac{3}{5} = 0.6000$$

$$\cos W = \frac{\text{adj. to } \angle W}{\text{hyp.}} = \frac{WV}{UW} = \frac{24}{30} = \frac{4}{5} = 0.8000$$

EXAMPLE 3 Use a trigonometric ratio to find a hypotenuse

DOG RUN You want to string cable to
make a dog run from two corners of
a building, as shown in the diagram.
Write and solve a proportion using a
trigonometric ratio to approximate the
length of cable you will need.

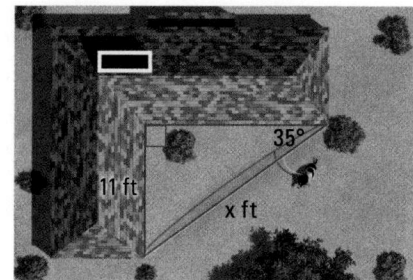

Solution

$$\sin 35° = \frac{\text{opp.}}{\text{hyp.}} \qquad \textbf{Write ratio for sine of 35°.}$$

$$\sin 35° = \frac{11}{x} \qquad \textbf{Substitute.}$$

$$x \cdot \sin 35° = 11 \qquad \textbf{Multiply each side by } x.$$

$$x = \frac{11}{\sin 35°} \qquad \textbf{Divide each side by sin 35°.}$$

$$x \approx \frac{11}{0.5736} \qquad \textbf{Use a calculator to find sin 35°.}$$

$$x \approx 19.2 \qquad \textbf{Simplify.}$$

▶ You will need a little more than 19 feet of cable.

✓ **GUIDED PRACTICE** for Examples 2 and 3

In Exercises 3 and 4, find cos *R* and cos *S*. Write each answer as a decimal.
Round to four decimal places, if necessary.

3.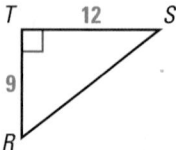

4.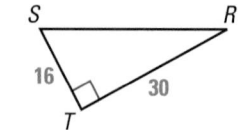

5. In Example 3, use the cosine ratio to find the length of the other leg of the
   triangle formed.

ANGLES If you look up at an object, the angle your line of sight makes with a horizontal line is called the **angle of elevation**. If you look down at an object, the angle your line of sight makes with a horizontal line is called the **angle of depression**.

APPLY THEOREMS

Notice that the angle of elevation and the angle of depression are congruent by the Alternate Interior Angles Theorem on page 155.

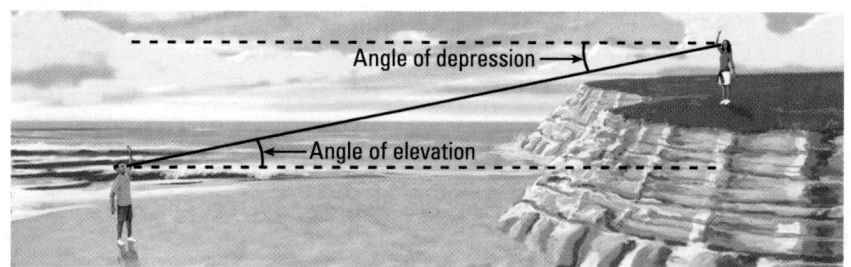

Angle of depression

Angle of elevation

EXAMPLE 4 Find a hypotenuse using an angle of depression

SKIING You are skiing on a mountain with an altitude of 1200 meters. The angle of depression is 21°. About how far do you ski down the mountain?

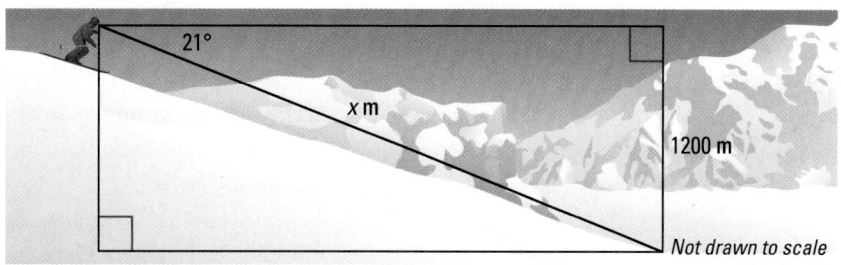

21°

x m

1200 m

Not drawn to scale

Solution

$$\sin 21° = \frac{\text{opp.}}{\text{hyp.}}$$ **Write ratio for sine of 21°.**

$$\sin 21° = \frac{1200}{x}$$ **Substitute.**

$$x \cdot \sin 21° = 1200$$ **Multiply each side by x.**

$$x = \frac{1200}{\sin 21°}$$ **Divide each side by sin 21°.**

$$x \approx \frac{1200}{0.3584}$$ **Use a calculator to find sin 21°.**

$$x \approx 3348.2$$ **Simplify.**

▶ You ski about 3348 meters down the mountain.

Animated **Geometry** at classzone.com

✔ **GUIDED PRACTICE** for Example 4

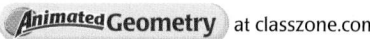

6. **WHAT IF?** Suppose the angle of depression in Example 4 is 28°. About how far would you ski?

EXAMPLE 5 Find leg lengths using an angle of elevation

SKATEBOARD RAMP You want to build a skateboard ramp with a length of 14 feet and an angle of elevation of 26°. You need to find the height and length of the base of the ramp.

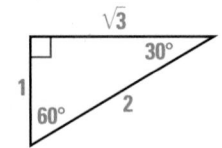
14 ft
x ft
26°
y ft

Solution

ANOTHER WAY

For alternative methods for solving the problem in Example 5, turn to page 481 for the **Problem Solving Workshop**.

STEP 1 Find the height.

$$\sin 26° = \frac{\text{opp.}}{\text{hyp.}}$$ **Write ratio for sine of 26°.**

$$\sin 26° = \frac{x}{14}$$ **Substitute.**

$$14 \cdot \sin 26° = x$$ **Multiply each side by 14.**

$$6.1 \approx x$$ **Use a calculator to simplify.**

▶ The height is about 6.1 feet.

STEP 2 Find the length of the base.

$$\cos 26° = \frac{\text{adj.}}{\text{hyp.}}$$ **Write ratio for cosine of 26°.**

$$\cos 26° = \frac{y}{14}$$ **Substitute.**

$$14 \cdot \cos 26° = y$$ **Multiply each side by 14.**

$$12.6 \approx y$$ **Use a calculator to simplify.**

▶ The length of the base is about 12.6 feet.

EXAMPLE 6 Use a special right triangle to find a sine and cosine

Use a special right triangle to find the sine and cosine of a 60° angle.

Solution

DRAW DIAGRAMS

As in Example 4 on page 468, to simplify calculations you can choose 1 as the length of the shorter leg.

Use the 30°-60°-90° Triangle Theorem to draw a right triangle with side lengths of 1, $\sqrt{3}$, and 2. Then set up sine and cosine ratios for the 60° angle.

$$\sin 60° = \frac{\text{opp.}}{\text{hyp.}} = \frac{\sqrt{3}}{2} \approx 0.8660$$

$$\cos 60° = \frac{\text{adj.}}{\text{hyp.}} = \frac{1}{2} = 0.5000$$

√3
30°
1
60°   2

✓ **GUIDED PRACTICE** for Examples 5 and 6

7. **WHAT IF?** In Example 5, suppose the angle of elevation is 35°. What is the new height and base length of the ramp?

8. Use a special right triangle to find the sine and cosine of a 30° angle.

7.6 EXERCISES

HOMEWORK KEY
○ = WORKED-OUT SOLUTIONS
on p. WS9 for Exs. 5, 9, and 33

★ = STANDARDIZED TEST PRACTICE
Exs. 2, 17, 18, 29, 35, and 37

◆ = MULTIPLE REPRESENTATIONS
Ex. 39

SKILL PRACTICE

1. **VOCABULARY** Copy and complete: The sine ratio compares the length of __?__ to the length of __?__.

2. ★ **WRITING** *Explain* how to tell which side of a right triangle is adjacent to an angle and which side is the hypotenuse.

EXAMPLE 1
on p. 473
for Exs. 3–6

FINDING SINE RATIOS Find sin *D* and sin *E*. Write each answer as a fraction and as a decimal. Round to four decimal places, if necessary.

3.
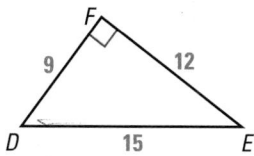

4.
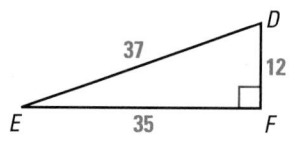

5. ○
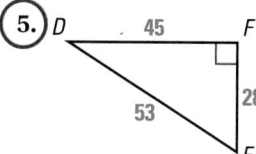

6. **ERROR ANALYSIS** *Explain* why the student's statement is incorrect. Write a correct statement for the sine of the angle.

$\sin A = \dfrac{5}{13}$

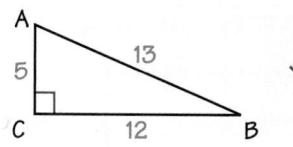

EXAMPLE 2
on p. 474
for Exs. 7–9

FINDING COSINE RATIOS Find cos *X* and cos *Y*. Write each answer as a fraction and as a decimal. Round to four decimal places, if necessary.

7.
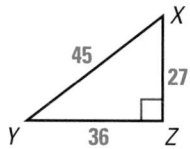

8.
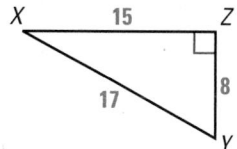

9. ○
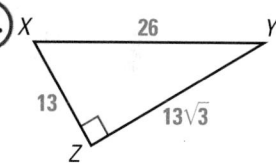

EXAMPLE 3
on p. 474
for Exs. 10–15

USING SINE AND COSINE RATIOS Use a sine or cosine ratio to find the value of each variable. Round decimals to the nearest tenth.

10.
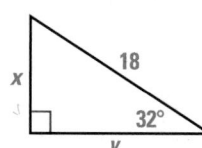

11.
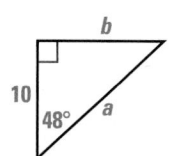

12.
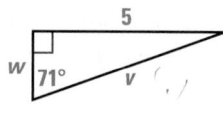

13.
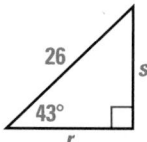

14.
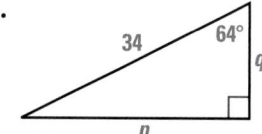

15.
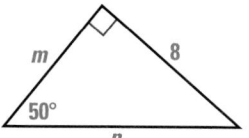

EXAMPLE 6
on p. 476
for Ex. 16

16. **SPECIAL RIGHT TRIANGLES** Use the 45°-45°-90° Triangle Theorem to find the sine and cosine of a 45° angle.

17. ★ **WRITING** *Describe* what you must know about a triangle in order to use the sine ratio and the cosine ratio.

18. ★ **MULTIPLE CHOICE** In △*PQR*, which expression can be used to find *PQ*?

A 10 · cos 29°   **B** 10 · sin 29°

C $\dfrac{10}{\sin 29°}$ **D** $\dfrac{10}{\cos 29°}$

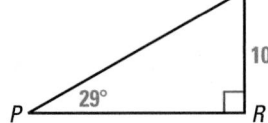

(XY) ALGEBRA Find the value of *x*. Round decimals to the nearest tenth.

19.

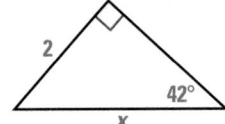

20.

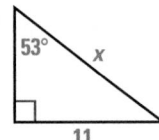

21.

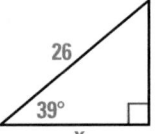

FINDING SINE AND COSINE RATIOS Find the unknown side length. Then find sin *X* and cos *X*. Write each answer as a fraction in simplest form and as a decimal. Round to four decimal places, if necessary.

22.

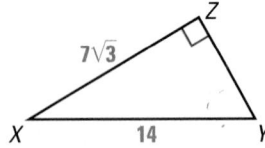

23.

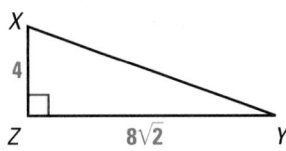

24.

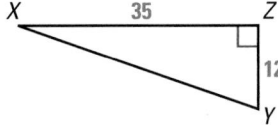

25.

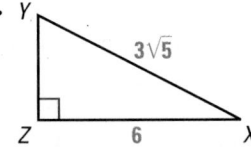

26.

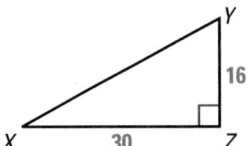

27.

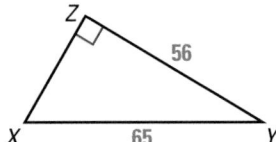

28. **ANGLE MEASURE** Make a prediction about how you could use trigonometric ratios to find angle measures in a triangle.

29. ★ **MULTIPLE CHOICE** In △*JKL*, *m∠L* = 90°. Which statement about △*JKL* *cannot* be true?

A sin *J* = 0.5   **B** sin *J* = 0.1071

C sin *J* = 0.8660   **D** sin *J* = 1.1

PERIMETER Find the approximate perimeter of the figure.

30.

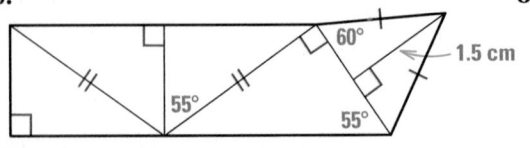

31.

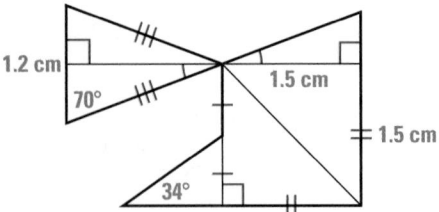

32. **CHALLENGE** Let *A* be any acute angle of a right triangle. Show that

(a) $\tan A = \dfrac{\sin A}{\cos A}$ and (b) $(\sin A)^2 + (\cos A)^2 = 1$.

○ = **WORKED-OUT SOLUTIONS**
on p. WS1

★ = **STANDARDIZED TEST PRACTICE**

**EXAMPLES
4 and 5**
on pp. 475–476
for Exs. 33–36

33. **AIRPLANE RAMP** The airplane door is 19 feet off the ground and the ramp has a 31° angle of elevation. What is the length y of the ramp?

@*HomeTutor* for problem solving help at classzone.com

34. **BLEACHERS** Find the horizontal distance h the bleachers cover. Round to the nearest foot.

@*HomeTutor* for problem solving help at classzone.com

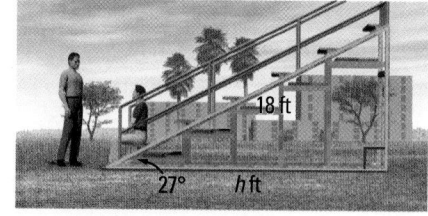

35. **SHORT RESPONSE** You are flying a kite with 20 feet of string extended. The angle of elevation from the spool of string to the kite is 41°.

  a. Draw and label a diagram to represent the situation.

  b. How far off the ground is the kite if you hold the spool 5 feet off the ground? *Describe* how the height where you hold the spool affects the height of the kite.

36. **MULTI-STEP PROBLEM** You want to hang a banner that is 29 feet tall from the third floor of your school. You need to know how tall the wall is, but there is a large bush in your way.

  a. You throw a 38 foot rope out of the window to your friend. She extends it to the end and measures the angle of elevation to be 70°. How high is the window?

  b. The bush is 6 feet tall. Will your banner fit above the bush?

  c. **What If?** Suppose you need to find how far from the school your friend needs to stand. Which trigonometric ratio should you use?

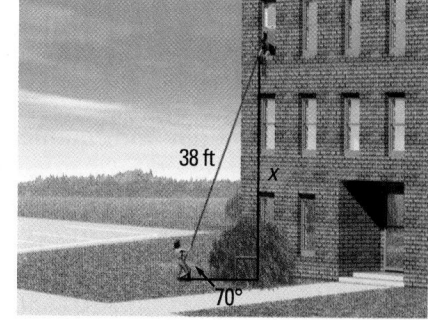

37. ★ **SHORT RESPONSE** Nick uses the equation $\sin 49° = \frac{x}{16}$ to find BC in $\triangle ABC$. Tim uses the equation $\cos 41° = \frac{x}{16}$. Which equation produces the correct answer? *Explain*.

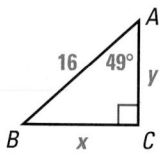

38. **TECHNOLOGY** Use geometry drawing software to construct an angle. Mark three points on one side of the angle and construct segments perpendicular to that side at the points. Measure the legs of each triangle and calculate the sine of the angle. Is the sine the same for each triangle?

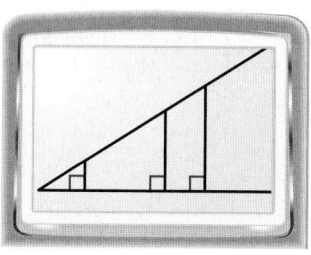

39. ◆ **MULTIPLE REPRESENTATIONS** You are standing on a cliff 30 feet above an ocean. You see a sailboat on the ocean.

   a. **Drawing a Diagram** Draw and label a diagram of the situation.

   b. **Making a Table** Make a table showing the angle of depression and the length of your line of sight. Use the angles 40°, 50°, 60°, 70°, and 80°.

   c. **Drawing a Graph** Graph the values you found in part (b), with the angle measures on the *x*-axis.

   d. **Making a Prediction** Predict the length of the line of sight when the angle of depression is 30°.

40. ⓧⓨ **ALGEBRA** If △*EQU* is equilateral and △*RGT* is a right triangle with $RG = 2$, $RT = 1$, and $m\angle T = 90°$, show that $\sin E = \cos G$.

41. **CHALLENGE** Make a conjecture about the relationship between sine and cosine values.

   a. Make a table that gives the sine and cosine values for the acute angles of a 45°-45°-90° triangle, a 30°-60°-90° triangle, a 34°-56°-90° triangle, and a 17°-73°-90° triangle.

   b. Compare the sine and cosine values. What pattern(s) do you notice?

   c. Make a conjecture about the sine and cosine values in part (b).

   d. Is the conjecture in part (c) true for right triangles that are not special right triangles? *Explain*.

MIXED REVIEW

Rewrite the equation so that *x* is a function of *y*. *(p. 877)*

42. $y = \sqrt{x}$

43. $y = 3x - 10$

44. $y = \dfrac{x}{9}$

PREVIEW
Prepare for
Lesson 7.7 in
Exs. 45–47.

Copy and complete the table. *(p. 884)*

45.

x	$\sqrt{x}$
?	0
?	1
?	$\sqrt{2}$
?	2
?	4

46.

x	$\dfrac{1}{x}$
?	1
?	$\dfrac{1}{2}$
?	3
?	$\dfrac{2}{7}$
?	7

47.

x	$\dfrac{2}{7}x + 4$
?	0
?	2
?	6
?	8
?	10

48. Find the values of *x* and *y* in the triangle at the right. *(p. 449)*

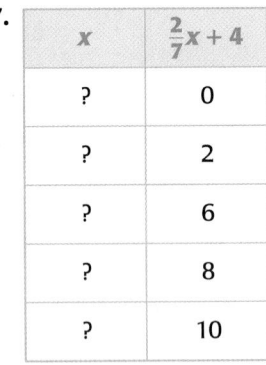

 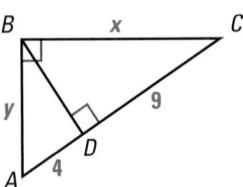

Using ALTERNATIVE METHODS

Another Way to Solve Example 5, page 476

MULTIPLE REPRESENTATIONS You can use the Pythagorean Theorem, tangent ratio, sine ratio, or cosine ratio to find the length of an unknown side of a right triangle. The decision of which method to use depends upon what information you have. In some cases, you can use more than one method to find the unknown length.

PROBLEM

SKATEBOARD RAMP You want to build a skateboard ramp with a length of 14 feet and an angle of elevation of 26°. You need to find the height and base of the ramp.

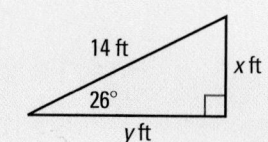

14 ft
x ft
26°
y ft

METHOD 1

Using a Cosine Ratio and the Pythagorean Theorem

STEP 1 **Find** the measure of the third angle.

$$26° + 90° + m\angle 3 = 180°$$ **Triangle Sum Theorem**

$$116° + m\angle 3 = 180°$$ **Combine like terms.**

$$m\angle 3 = 64°$$ **Subtact 116° from each side.**

STEP 2 **Use** the cosine ratio to find the height of the ramp.

$$\cos 64° = \frac{adj.}{hyp.}$$ **Write ratio for cosine of 64°.**

$$\cos 64° = \frac{x}{14}$$ **Substitute.**

$$14 \cdot \cos 64° = x$$ **Multiply each side by 14.**

$$6.1 \approx x$$ **Use a calculator to simplify.**

▶ The height is about 6.1 feet.

STEP 3 **Use** the Pythagorean Theorem to find the length of the base of the ramp.

$$(\text{hypotenuse})^2 = (\text{leg})^2 + (\text{leg})^2$$ **Pythagorean Theorem**

$$14^2 = 6.1^2 + y^2$$ **Substitute.**

$$196 = 37.21 + y^2$$ **Multiply.**

$$158.79 = y^2$$ **Subtract 37.21 from each side.**

$$12.6 \approx y$$ **Find the positive square root.**

▶ The length of the base is about 12.6 feet.

Using a Tangent Ratio

Use the tangent ratio and $h = 6.1$ feet to find the length of the base of the ramp.

$$\tan 26° = \frac{\text{opp.}}{\text{adj.}}$$ **Write ratio for tangent of 26°.**

$$\tan 26° = \frac{6.1}{y}$$ **Substitute.**

$$y \cdot \tan 26° = 6.1$$ **Multiply each side by y.**

$$y = \frac{6.1}{\tan 26°}$$ **Divide each side by tan 26°.**

$$y \approx 12.5$$ **Use a calculator to simplify.**

▸ The length of the base is about 12.5 feet.

Notice that when using the Pythagorean Theorem, the length of the base is 12.6 feet, but when using the tangent ratio, the length of the base is 12.5 feet. The tenth of a foot difference is due to the rounding error introduced when finding the height of the ramp and using that rounded value to calculate the length of the base.

PRACTICE

1. **WHAT IF?** Suppose the length of the skateboard ramp is 20 feet. Find the height and base of the ramp.

2. **SWIMMER** The angle of elevation from the swimmer to the lifeguard is 35°. Find the distance x from the swimmer to the base of the lifeguard chair. Find the distance y from the swimmer to the lifeguard.

3. **xy ALGEBRA** Use the triangle below to write three different equations you can use to find the unknown leg length.

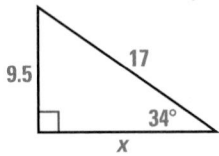

4. **SHORT RESPONSE** *Describe* how you would decide whether to use the Pythagorean Theorem or trigonometric ratios to find the lengths of unknown sides of a right triangle.

5. **ERROR ANALYSIS** *Explain* why the student's statement is incorrect. Write a correct statement for the cosine of the angle.

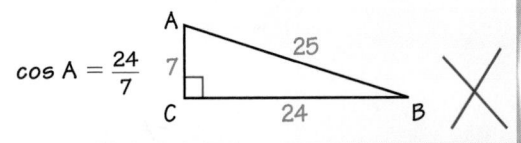
$$\cos A = \frac{24}{7}$$

6. **EXTENDED RESPONSE** You want to find the height of a tree in your yard. The tree's shadow is 15 feet long and you measure the angle of elevation from the end of the shadow to the top of tree to be 75°.

   a. Find the height of the tree. *Explain* the method you chose to solve the problem.

   b. What else would you need to know to solve this problem using similar triangles.

   c. *Explain* why you cannot use the sine ratio to find the height of the tree.

7.7 Solve Right Triangles

Before	You used tangent, sine, and cosine ratios.
Now	You will use inverse tangent, sine, and cosine ratios.
Why?	So you can build a saddlerack, as in Ex. 39.

Key Vocabulary
• solve a right triangle
• inverse tangent
• inverse sine
• inverse cosine

To **solve a right triangle** means to find the measures of all of its sides and angles. You can solve a right triangle if you know either of the following:

• Two side lengths

• One side length and the measure of one acute angle

In Lessons 7.5 and 7.6, you learned how to use the side lengths of a right triangle to find trigonometric ratios for the acute angles of the triangle. Once you know the tangent, the sine, or the cosine of an acute angle, you can use a calculator to find the measure of the angle.

KEY CONCEPT   *For Your Notebook*

Inverse Trigonometric Ratios

Let $\angle A$ be an acute angle.

READ VOCABULARY

The expression "$\tan^{-1}x$" is read as "the inverse tangent of x."

Inverse Tangent If $\tan A = x$, then $\tan^{-1} x = m\angle A$. $\tan^{-1}\dfrac{BC}{AC} = m\angle A$

Inverse Sine If $\sin A = y$, then $\sin^{-1} y = m\angle A$. $\sin^{-1}\dfrac{BC}{AB} = m\angle A$

Inverse Cosine If $\cos A = z$, then $\cos^{-1} z = m\angle A$. $\cos^{-1}\dfrac{AC}{AB} = m\angle A$

EXAMPLE 1   Use an inverse tangent to find an angle measure

Use a calculator to approximate the measure of $\angle A$ to the nearest tenth of a degree.

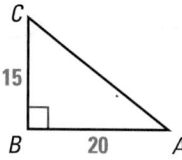

Solution

Because $\tan A = \dfrac{15}{20} = \dfrac{3}{4} = 0.75$, $\tan^{-1} 0.75 = m\angle A$. Use a calculator.

$\tan^{-1} 0.75 \approx 36.86989765 \cdots$

▶ So, the measure of $\angle A$ is approximately $36.9°$.

EXAMPLE 2 **Use an inverse sine and an inverse cosine**

Let $\angle A$ and $\angle B$ be acute angles in two right triangles. Use a calculator to approximate the measures of $\angle A$ and $\angle B$ to the nearest tenth of a degree.

a. $\sin A = 0.87$

b. $\cos B = 0.15$

Solution

a. $m\angle A = \sin^{-1} 0.87 \approx 60.5°$

b. $m\angle B = \cos^{-1} 0.15 \approx 81.4°$

✔ **GUIDED PRACTICE** for Examples 1 and 2

1. Look back at Example 1. Use a calculator and an inverse tangent to approximate $m\angle C$ to the nearest tenth of a degree.

2. Find $m\angle D$ to the nearest tenth of a degree if $\sin D = 0.54$.

EXAMPLE 3 **Solve a right triangle**

Solve the right triangle. Round decimal answers to the nearest tenth.

Solution

STEP 1 Find $m\angle B$ by using the Triangle Sum Theorem.

$180° = 90° + 42° + m\angle B$

$48° = m\angle B$

STEP 2 Approximate BC by using a tangent ratio.

$\tan 42° = \dfrac{BC}{70}$ Write ratio for tangent of 42°.

$70 \cdot \tan 42° = BC$ Multiply each side by 70.

$70 \cdot 0.9004 \approx BC$ Approximate tan 42°.

$63 \approx BC$ Simplify and round answer.

STEP 3 Approximate AB using a cosine ratio.

$\cos 42° = \dfrac{70}{AB}$ Write ratio for cosine of 42°.

$AB \cdot \cos 42° = 70$ Multiply each side by AB.

$AB = \dfrac{70}{\cos 42°}$ Divide each side by cos 42°.

$AB \approx \dfrac{70}{0.7431}$ Use a calculator to find cos 42°.

$AB \approx 94.2$ Simplify .

▶ The angle measures are 42°, 48°, and 90°. The side lengths are 70 feet, about 63 feet, and about 94 feet.

EXAMPLE 4 **Solve a real-world problem**

THEATER DESIGN Suppose your school is building a *raked stage*. The stage will be 30 feet long from front to back, with a total rise of 2 feet. A rake (angle of elevation) of 5° or less is generally preferred for the safety and comfort of the actors. Is the raked stage you are building within the range suggested?

Solution

Use the sine and inverse sine ratios to find the degree measure *x* of the rake.

$$\sin x° = \frac{\text{opp.}}{\text{hyp.}} = \frac{2}{30} \approx 0.0667$$

$$x \approx \sin^{-1} 0.0667 \approx 3.824$$

▶ The rake is about 3.8°, so it is within the suggested range of 5° or less.

✓ **GUIDED PRACTICE** for Examples 3 and 4

3. Solve a right triangle that has a 40° angle and a 20 inch hypotenuse.

4. **WHAT IF?** In Example 4, suppose another raked stage is 20 feet long from front to back with a total rise of 2 feet. Is this raked stage safe? *Explain.*

7.7 EXERCISES

SKILL PRACTICE

1. **VOCABULARY** Copy and complete: To solve a right triangle means to find the measures of all of its __?__ and __?__ .

2. ★ **WRITING** *Explain* when to use a trigonometric ratio to find a side length of a right triangle and when to use the Pythagorean Theorem.

EXAMPLE 1
on p. 483
for Exs. 3–5

USING INVERSE TANGENTS Use a calculator to approximate the measure of ∠*A* to the nearest tenth of a degree.

3.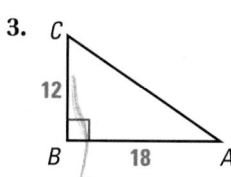

4.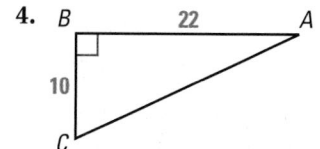

5.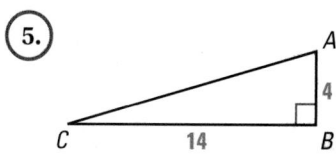

EXAMPLE 2
on p. 484
for Exs. 6–9

USING INVERSE SINES AND COSINES Use a calculator to approximate the measure of ∠A to the nearest tenth of a degree.

6.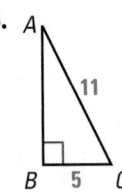

7.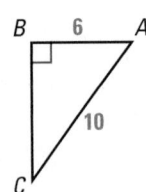

8.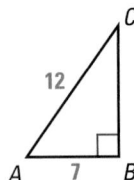

9. ★ **MULTIPLE CHOICE** Which expression is correct?

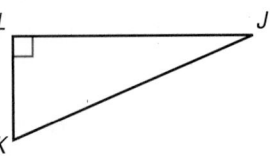

Ⓐ $\sin^{-1}\dfrac{JL}{JK} = m\angle J$ Ⓑ $\tan^{-1}\dfrac{KL}{JL} = m\angle J$

Ⓒ $\cos^{-1}\dfrac{JL}{JK} = m\angle K$ Ⓓ $\sin^{-1}\dfrac{JL}{KL} = m\angle K$

EXAMPLE 3
on p. 484
for Exs. 10–18

SOLVING RIGHT TRIANGLES Solve the right triangle. Round decimal answers to the nearest tenth.

10.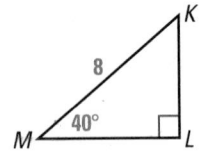

11.

12.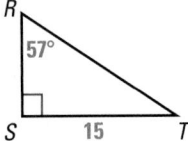

13.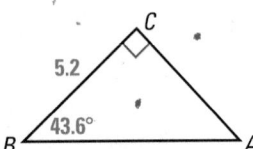

14.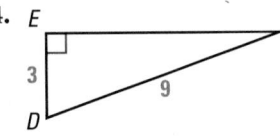

15.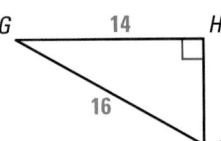

16.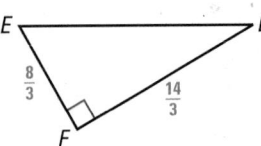

17.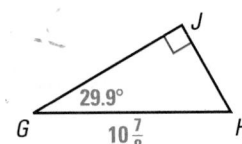

18.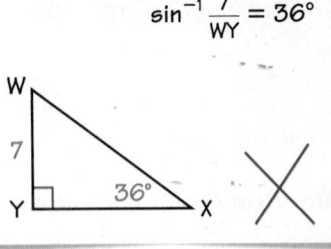

ERROR ANALYSIS *Describe* and correct the student's error in using an inverse trigonometric ratio.

19.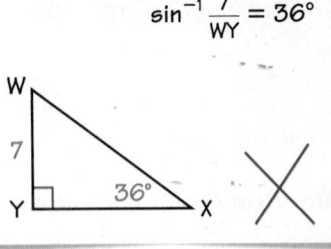

$$\sin^{-1}\dfrac{7}{WY} = 36°$$

20.

$$\cos^{-1}\dfrac{8}{15} = m\angle T$$

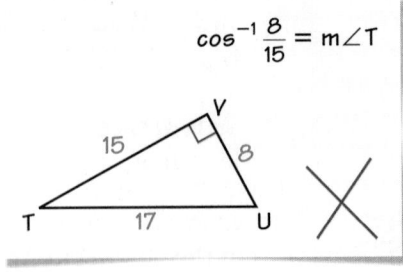

CALCULATOR Let ∠A be an acute angle in a right triangle. Approximate the measure of ∠A to the nearest tenth of a degree.

21. $\sin A = 0.5$ **22.** $\sin A = 0.75$ **23.** $\cos A = 0.33$ **24.** $\cos A = 0.64$

25. $\tan A = 1.0$ **26.** $\tan A = 0.28$ **27.** $\sin A = 0.19$ **28.** $\cos A = 0.81$

○ = **WORKED-OUT SOLUTIONS**
on p. WS1

★ = **STANDARDIZED
TEST PRACTICE**

29. ★ **MULTIPLE CHOICE** Which additional information would *not* be enough to solve △*PRQ*?

(**A**) $m\angle P$ and PR (**B**) $m\angle P$ and $m\angle R$

(**C**) PQ and PR (**D**) $m\angle P$ and PQ

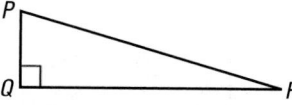

30. ★ **WRITING** *Explain* why it is incorrect to say that $\tan^{-1} x = \dfrac{1}{\tan x}$.

31. **SPECIAL RIGHT TRIANGLES** If $\sin A = \frac{1}{2}\sqrt{2}$, what is $m\angle A$? If $\sin B = \frac{1}{2}\sqrt{3}$, what is $m\angle B$?

32. **TRIGONOMETRIC VALUES** Use the *Table of Trigonometric Ratios* on page 925 to answer the questions.

    a. What angles have nearly the same sine and tangent values?

    b. What angle has the greatest difference in its sine and tangent value?

    c. What angle has a tangent value that is double its sine value?

    d. Is $\sin 2x$ equal to $2 \cdot \sin x$?

33. **CHALLENGE** The perimeter of rectangle *ABCD* is 16 centimeters, and the ratio of its width to its length is $1:3$. Segment *BD* divides the rectangle into two congruent triangles. Find the side lengths and angle measures of one of these triangles.

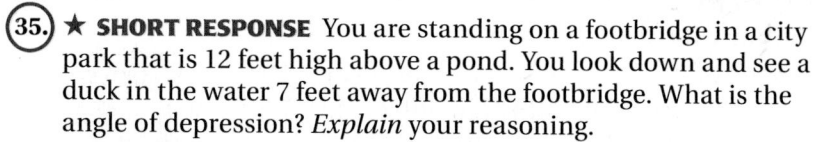

EXAMPLE 4
on p. 485
for Exs. 34–36

34. **SOCCER** A soccer ball is placed 10 feet away from the goal, which is 8 feet high. You kick the ball and it hits the crossbar along the top of the goal. What is the angle of elevation of your kick?

(*@HomeTutor*) for problem solving help at classzone.com

35. ★ **SHORT RESPONSE** You are standing on a footbridge in a city park that is 12 feet high above a pond. You look down and see a duck in the water 7 feet away from the footbridge. What is the angle of depression? *Explain* your reasoning.

(*@HomeTutor*) for problem solving help at classzone.com

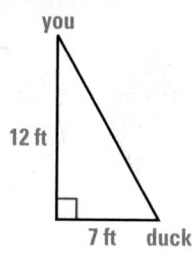

36. **CLAY** In order to unload clay easily, the body of a dump truck must be elevated to at least 55°. If the body of the dump truck is 14 feet long and has been raised 10 feet, will the clay pour out easily?

37. **REASONING** For △*ABC* shown, each of the expressions $\sin^{-1}\dfrac{BC}{AB}$, $\cos^{-1}\dfrac{AC}{AB}$, and $\tan^{-1}\dfrac{BC}{AC}$ can be used to approximate the measure of $\angle A$. Which expression would you choose? *Explain* your choice.

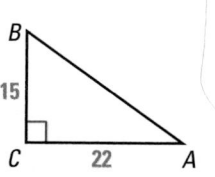

38. MULTI-STEP PROBLEM You are standing on a plateau that is 800 feet above a basin where you can see two hikers.

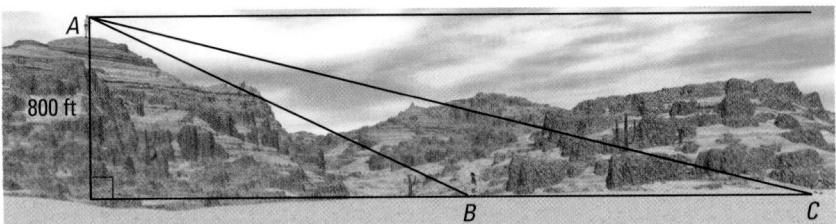

800 ft

A

B

C

a. If the angle of depression from your line of sight to the hiker at *B* is 25°, how far is the hiker from the base of the plateau?

b. If the angle of depression from your line of sight to the hiker at *C* is 15°, how far is the hiker from the base of the plateau?

c. How far apart are the two hikers? *Explain.*

39. ◆ **MULTIPLE REPRESENTATIONS** A local ranch offers trail rides to the public. It has a variety of different sized saddles to meet the needs of horse and rider. You are going to build saddle racks that are 11 inches high. To save wood, you decide to make each rack fit each saddle.

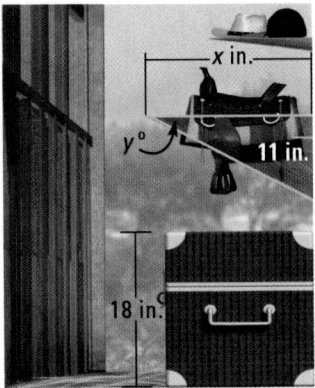

x in.

y°

11 in.

18 in.

a. Making a Table The lengths of the saddles range from 20 inches to 27 inches. Make a table showing the saddle rack length *x* and the measure of the adjacent angle *y*°.

b. Drawing a Graph Use your table to draw a scatterplot.

c. Making a Conjecture Make a conjecture about the relationship between the length of the rack and the angle needed.

40. ★ **OPEN-ENDED MATH** *Describe* a real-world problem you could solve using a trigonometric ratio.

41. ★ **EXTENDED RESPONSE** Your town is building a wind generator to create electricity for your school. The builder wants your geometry class to make sure that the guy wires are placed so that the tower is secure. By safety guidelines, the distance along the ground from the tower to the guy wire's connection with the ground should be between 50% to 75% of the height of the guy wire's connection with the tower.

a. The tower is 64 feet tall. The builders plan to have the distance along the ground from the tower to the guy wire's connection with the ground be 60% of the height of the tower. How far apart are the tower and the ground connection of the wire?

b. How long will a guy wire need to be that is attached 60 feet above the ground?

c. How long will a guy wire need to be that is attached 30 feet above the ground?

d. Find the angle of elevation of each wire. Are the right triangles formed by the ground, tower, and wires *congruent*, *similar*, or *neither*? *Explain.*

e. *Explain* which trigonometric ratios you used to solve the problem.

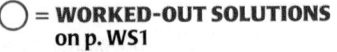

○ = **WORKED-OUT SOLUTIONS**
on p. WS1

★ = **STANDARDIZED TEST PRACTICE**

◆ = **MULTIPLE REPRESENTATIONS**

42. CHALLENGE Use the diagram of △ABC.

   GIVEN ▸ △ABC with altitude $\overline{CD}$.

   PROVE ▸ $\dfrac{\sin A}{a} = \dfrac{\sin B}{b}$

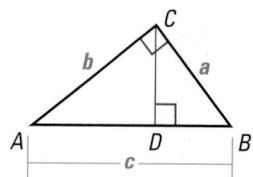

MIXED REVIEW

PREVIEW

Prepare for
Lesson 8.1
in Ex. 43.

43. Copy and complete the table. *(p. 42)*

Number of sides	Type of polygon
5	?
12	?
?	Octagon
?	Triangle
7	?

Number of sides	Type of polygon
?	*n*-gon
?	Quadrilateral
10	?
9	?
?	Hexagon

A point on an image and the transformation are given. Find the corresponding point on the original figure. *(p. 272)*

44. Point on image: (5, 1); translation: $(x, y) \rightarrow (x + 3, y - 2)$

45. Point on image: (4, −6); reflection: $(x, y) \rightarrow (x, -y)$

46. Point on image: (−2, 3); translation: $(x, y) \rightarrow (x - 5, y + 7)$

Draw a dilation of the polygon with the given vertices using the given scale factor *k*. *(p. 409)*

47. $A(2, 2)$, $B(-1, -3)$, $C(5, -3)$; $k = 2$ **48.** $A(-4, -2)$, $B(-2, 4)$, $C(3, 6)$, $D(6, 3)$; $k = \dfrac{1}{2}$

QUIZ *for Lessons 7.5–7.7*

Find the value of *x* to the nearest tenth.

1. *(p. 466)*   **2.** *(p. 473)*   **3.** *(p. 473)*

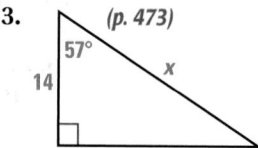

Solve the right triangle. Round decimal answers to the nearest tenth. *(p. 483)*

4.   **5.**   **6.**

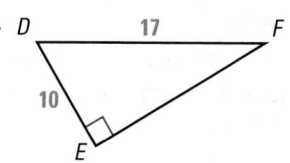
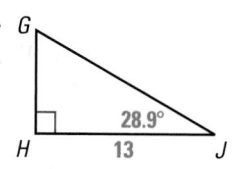

Law of Sines and Law of Cosines

GOAL Use trigonometry with acute and obtuse triangles.

The trigonometric ratios you have seen so far in this chapter can be used to find angle and side measures in right triangles. You can use the Law of Sines to find angle and side measures in *any* triangle.

KEY CONCEPT *For Your Notebook*

Law of Sines

If $\triangle ABC$ has sides of length a, b, and c as shown, then $\dfrac{\sin A}{a} = \dfrac{\sin B}{b} = \dfrac{\sin C}{c}$.

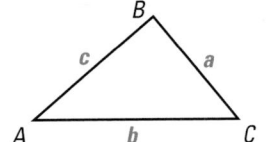

EXAMPLE 1 **Find a distance using Law of Sines**

DISTANCE Use the information in the diagram to determine how much closer you live to the music store than your friend does.

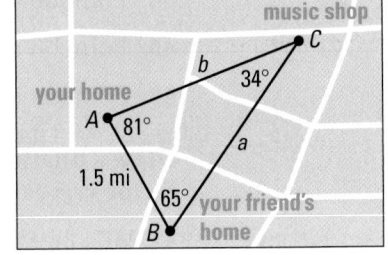

Solution

STEP 1 **Use** the Law of Sines to find the distance a from your friend's home to the music store.

$$\frac{\sin A}{a} = \frac{\sin C}{c} \qquad \text{Write Law of Sines.}$$

$$\frac{\sin 81°}{a} = \frac{\sin 34°}{1.5} \qquad \text{Substitute.}$$

$$a \approx 2.6 \qquad \text{Solve for } a.$$

STEP 2 **Use** the Law of Sines to find the distance b from your home to the music store.

$$\frac{\sin B}{b} = \frac{\sin C}{c} \qquad \text{Write Law of Sines.}$$

$$\frac{\sin 65°}{b} = \frac{\sin 34°}{1.5} \qquad \text{Substitute.}$$

$$b \approx 2.4 \qquad \text{Solve for } b.$$

STEP 3 **Subtract** the distances.

$$a - b \approx 2.6 - 2.4 = 0.2$$

▶ You live about 0.2 miles closer to the music store.

LAW OF COSINES You can also use the Law of Cosines to solve any triangle.

KEY CONCEPT   *For Your Notebook*

Law of Cosines

If $\triangle ABC$ has sides of length a, b, and c, then:

$$a^2 = b^2 + c^2 - 2bc \cos A$$

$$b^2 = a^2 + c^2 - 2ac \cos B$$

$$c^2 = a^2 + b^2 - 2ab \cos C$$

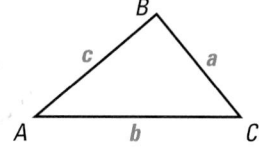

EXAMPLE 2 **Find an angle measure using Law of Cosines**

In $\triangle ABC$ at the right, $a = 11$ cm, $b = 17$ cm, and $c = 19$ cm. Find $m\angle C$.

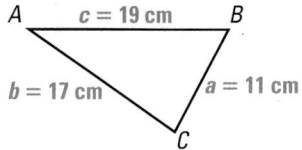

Solution

$c^2 = a^2 + b^2 - 2ab \cos C$	**Write Law of Cosines.**
$19^2 = 11^2 + 17^2 - 2(11)(17) \cos C$	**Substitute.**
$0.1310 = \cos C$	**Solve for cos C.**
$m\angle C \approx 82°$	**Find $\cos^{-1}$ (0.1310).**

PRACTICE

EXAMPLE 1
for Exs. 1–3

LAW OF SINES Use the Law of Sines to solve the triangle. Round decimal answers to the nearest tenth.

1.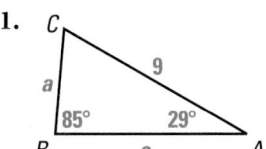

2.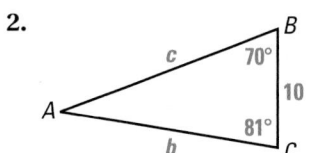

3.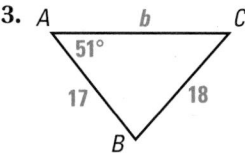

EXAMPLE 2
for Exs. 4–7

LAW OF COSINES Use the Law of Cosines to solve the triangle. Round decimal answers to the nearest tenth.

4.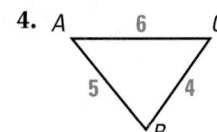

5.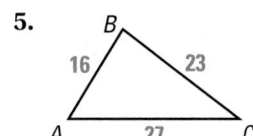

6.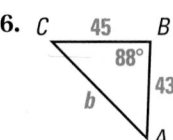

7. **DISTANCE** Use the diagram at the right. Find the straight distance between the zoo and movie theater.

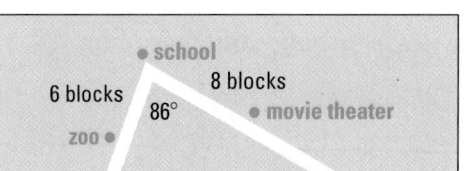

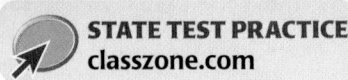
Lessons 7.5–7.7

1. **MULTI-STEP PROBLEM** A *reach stacker* is a vehicle used to lift objects and move them between ships and land.

a. The vehicle's arm is 10.9 meters long. The maximum measure of ∠A is 60°. What is the greatest height *h* the arm can reach if the vehicle is 3.6 meters tall?

b. The vehicle's arm can extend to be 16.4 meters long. What is the greatest height its extended arm can reach?

c. What is the difference between the two heights the arm can reach above the ground?

2. **EXTENDED RESPONSE** You and a friend are standing the same distance from the edge of a canyon. Your friend looks directly across the canyon at a rock. You stand 10 meters from your friend and estimate the angle between your friend and the rock to be 85°.

a. Sketch the situation.

b. *Explain* how to find the distance across the canyon.

c. Suppose the actual angle measure is 87°. How far off is your estimate of the distance?

3. **SHORT RESPONSE** The international rules of basketball state the rim of the net should be 3.05 meters above the ground. If your line of sight to the rim is 34° and you are 1.7 meters tall, what is the distance from you to the rim? *Explain* your reasoning.

4. **GRIDDED ANSWER** The specifications for a *yield ahead* pavement marking are shown. Find the height *h* in feet of this isosceles triangle to the nearest tenth.

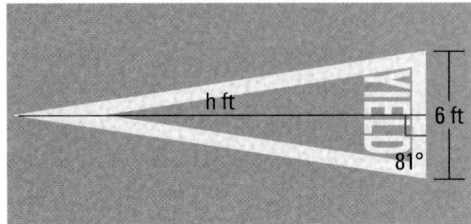

5. **EXTENDED RESPONSE** Use the diagram to answer the questions.

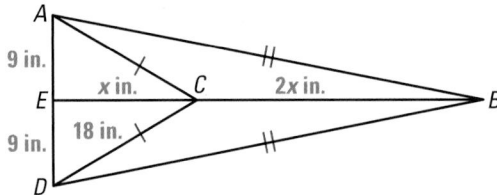

a. Solve for *x*. *Explain* the method you chose.

b. Find *m∠ABC*. *Explain* the method you chose.

c. *Explain* a different method for finding each of your answers in parts (a) and (b).

6. **SHORT RESPONSE** The triangle on the staircase below has a 52° angle and the distance along the stairs is 14 feet. What is the height *h* of the staircase? What is the length *b* of the base of the staircase?

7. **GRIDDED ANSWER** The base of an isosceles triangle is 70 centimeters long. The altitude to the base is 75 centimeters long. Find the measure of a base angle to the nearest degree.

BIG IDEAS
For Your Notebook

Big Idea ①

Using the Pythagorean Theorem and Its Converse

The Pythagorean Theorem states that in a right triangle the square of the length of the hypotenuse c is equal to the sum of the squares of the lengths of the legs a and b, so that $c^2 = a^2 + b^2$.

The Converse of the Pythagorean Theorem can be used to determine if a triangle is a right triangle.

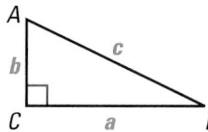 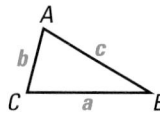 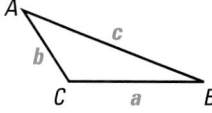

If $c^2 = a^2 + b^2$, then $m\angle C = 90°$ and $\triangle ABC$ is a right triangle.

If $c^2 < a^2 + b^2$, then $m\angle C < 90°$ and $\triangle ABC$ is an acute triangle.

If $c^2 > a^2 + b^2$, then $m\angle C > 90°$ and $\triangle ABC$ is an obtuse triangle.

Big Idea ②

Using Special Relationships in Right Triangles

GEOMETRIC MEAN In right $\triangle ABC$, altitude $\overline{CD}$ forms two smaller triangles so that $\triangle CBD \sim \triangle ACD \sim \triangle ABC$.

Also, $\dfrac{BD}{CD} = \dfrac{CD}{AD}$, $\dfrac{AB}{CB} = \dfrac{CB}{DB}$, and $\dfrac{AB}{AC} = \dfrac{AC}{AD}$.

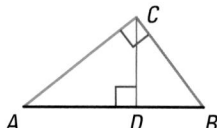

SPECIAL RIGHT TRIANGLES

45°-45°-90° Triangle

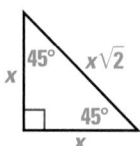

hypotenuse = leg · $\sqrt{2}$

30°-60°-90° Triangle

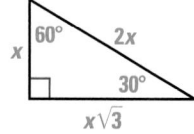

hypotenuse = 2 · shorter leg
longer leg = shorter leg · $\sqrt{3}$

Big Idea ③

Using Trigonometric Ratios to Solve Right Triangles

The tangent, sine, and cosine ratios can be used to find unknown side lengths and angle measures of right triangles. The values of tan $x°$, sin $x°$, and cos $x°$ depend only on the angle measure and not on the side length.

$\tan A = \dfrac{\text{opp.}}{\text{adj.}} = \dfrac{BC}{AC}$ $\tan^{-1} \dfrac{BC}{AC} = m\angle A$

$\sin A = \dfrac{\text{opp.}}{\text{hyp.}} = \dfrac{BC}{AB}$ $\sin^{-1} \dfrac{BC}{AB} = m\angle A$

$\cos A = \dfrac{\text{adj.}}{\text{hyp.}} = \dfrac{AC}{AB}$ $\cos^{-1} \dfrac{AC}{AB} = m\angle A$

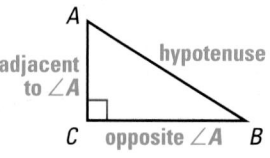

@Home Tutor

classzone.com
• Multi-Language Glossary
• Vocabulary practice

REVIEW KEY VOCABULARY

For a list of postulates and theorems, see pp. 926–931.

• Pythagorean triple, *p. 435*
• trigonometric ratio, *p. 466*
• tangent, *p. 466*
• sine, *p. 473*

• cosine, *p. 473*
• angle of elevation, *p. 475*
• angle of depression, *p. 475*
• solve a right triangle, *p. 483*

• inverse tangent, *p. 483*
• inverse sine, *p. 483*
• inverse cosine, *p. 483*

VOCABULARY EXERCISES

1. Copy and complete: A Pythagorean triple is a set of three positive integers *a*, *b*, and *c* that satisfy the equation __?__ .

2. **WRITING** What does it mean to solve a right triangle? What do you need to know to solve a right triangle?

3. **WRITING** *Describe* the difference between an angle of depression and an angle of elevation.

REVIEW EXAMPLES AND EXERCISES

Use the review examples and exercises below to check your understanding of the concepts you have learned in each lesson of Chapter 7.

7.1 Apply the Pythagorean Theorem   *pp. 433–439*

EXAMPLE

Find the value of *x*.

Because *x* is the length of the hypotenuse of a right triangle, you can use the Pythagorean Theorem to find its value.

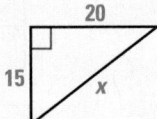

$$(\text{hypotenuse})^2 = (\text{leg})^2 + (\text{leg})^2 \qquad \textbf{Pythagorean Theorem}$$
$$x^2 = 15^2 + 20^2 \qquad \textbf{Substitute.}$$
$$x^2 = 625 \qquad \textbf{Simplify.}$$
$$x = 25 \qquad \textbf{Find the positive square root.}$$

EXERCISES

EXAMPLES 1 and 2 on pp. 433–434 for Exs. 4–6

Find the unknown side length *x*.

4.
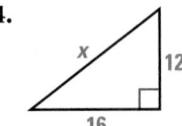

5.
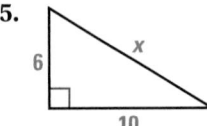

6.
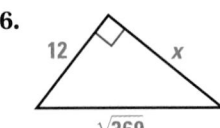

7.2 Use the Converse of the Pythagorean Theorem

pp. 441–447

EXAMPLE

Tell whether the given triangle is a right triangle.

Check to see whether the side lengths satisfy the equation $c^2 = a^2 + b^2$.

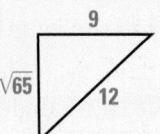

$12^2 \stackrel{?}{=} (\sqrt{65})^2 + 9^2$

$144 \stackrel{?}{=} 65 + 81$

$144 < 146$

The triangle is not a right triangle. It is an acute triangle.

EXERCISES

EXAMPLE 2
on p. 442
for Exs. 7–12

Classify the triangle formed by the side lengths as *acute*, *right*, or *obtuse*.

7. 6, 8, 9

8. 4, 2, 5

9. $10, 2\sqrt{2}, 6\sqrt{3}$

10. 15, 20, 15

11. $3, 3, 3\sqrt{2}$

12. $13, 18, 3\sqrt{55}$

7.3 Use Similar Right Triangles

pp. 449–456

EXAMPLE

Find the value of x.

By Theorem 7.6, you know that 4 is the geometric mean of x and 2.

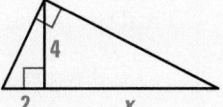

$\dfrac{x}{4} = \dfrac{4}{2}$ **Write a proportion.**

$2x = 16$ **Cross Products Property**

$x = 8$ **Divide.**

EXERCISES

EXAMPLES
2 and 3
on pp. 450–451
for Exs. 13–18

Find the value of x.

13.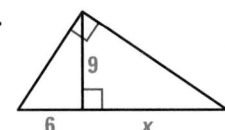

14.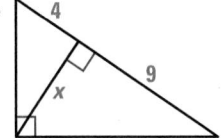

15.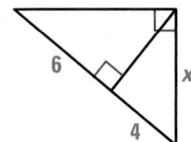

16.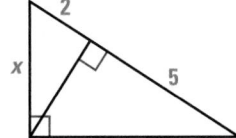

17.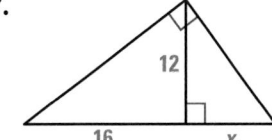

18.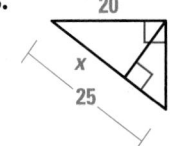

Chapter Review   **495**

7.4 Special Right Triangles

pp. 457–464

EXAMPLE

Find the length of the hypotenuse.

By the Triangle Sum Theorem, the measure of
the third angle must be 45°. Then the triangle is
a 45°-45°-90° triangle.

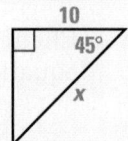

hypotenuse = leg • $\sqrt{2}$ **45°-45°-90° Triangle Theorem**

$x = 10\sqrt{2}$ **Substitute.**

EXERCISES

**EXAMPLES
1, 2, and 5**
on pp. 457–459
for Exs. 19–21

Find the value of *x*. Write your answer in simplest radical form.

19.

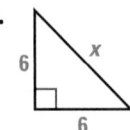

20.

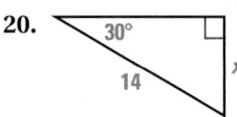

21.

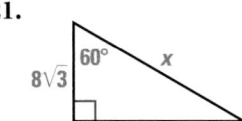

7.5 Apply the Tangent Ratio

pp. 466–472

EXAMPLE

Find the value of *x*.

$\tan 37° = \dfrac{\text{opp.}}{\text{adj.}}$ **Write ratio for tangent of 37°.**

$\tan 37° = \dfrac{x}{8}$ **Substitute.**

$8 \cdot \tan 37° = x$ **Multiply each side by 8.**

$6 \approx x$ **Use a calculator to simplify.**

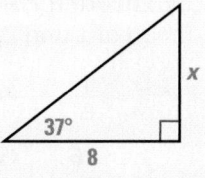

EXERCISES

EXAMPLE 2
on p. 467
for Exs. 22–26

In Exercises 22 and 23, use the diagram.

22. The angle between the bottom of a fence and the top of a
tree is 75°. The tree is 4 feet from the fence. How tall is the
tree? Round your answer to the nearest foot.

23. In Exercise 22, how tall is the tree if the angle is 55°?

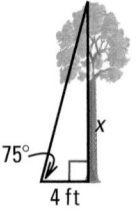

Find the value of *x* to the nearest tenth.

24.

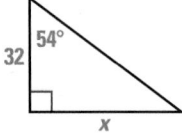

25.

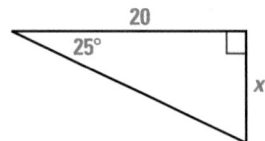

26.

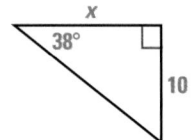

7.6 Apply the Sine and Cosine Ratios

pp. 473–480

EXAMPLE

Find sin A and sin B.

$$\sin A = \frac{\text{opp.}}{\text{hyp.}} = \frac{BC}{BA} = \frac{15}{17} \approx 0.8824$$

$$\sin B = \frac{\text{opp.}}{\text{hyp.}} = \frac{AC}{AB} = \frac{8}{17} \approx 0.4706$$

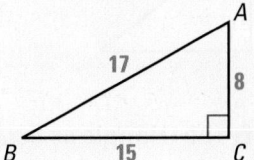

EXERCISES

EXAMPLES
1 and 2
on pp. 473–474
for Exs. 27–29

Find sin X and cos X. Write each answer as a fraction, and as a decimal. Round to four decimals places, if necessary.

27.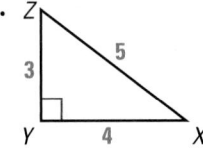

28.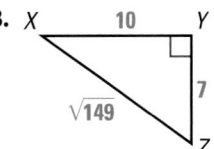

29.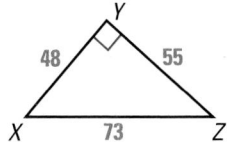

7.7 Solve Right Triangles

pp. 483–489

EXAMPLE

Use a calculator to approximate the measure of ∠A to the nearest tenth of a degree.

Because $\tan A = \frac{18}{12} = \frac{3}{2} = 1.5$, $\tan^{-1} 1.5 = m\angle A$.

Use a calculator to evaluate this expression.

$$\tan^{-1} 1.5 \approx 56.3099324\ldots$$

So, the measure of ∠A is approximately 56.3°.

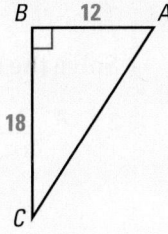

EXERCISES

EXAMPLE 3
on p. 484
for Exs. 30–33

Solve the right triangle. Round decimal answers to the nearest tenth.

30.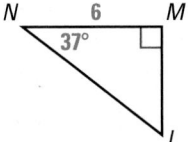

31.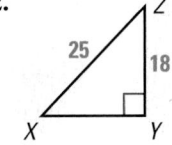

32.

33. Find the measures of ∠GED, ∠GEF, and ∠EFG. Find the lengths of $\overline{EG}$, $\overline{DF}$, $\overline{EF}$.

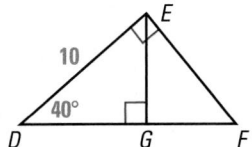

Find the value of *x*. Write your answer in simplest radical form.

1.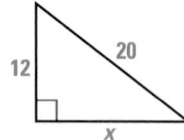
12, 20, *x*

2.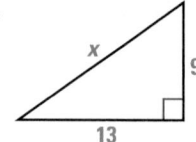
x, 9, 13

3.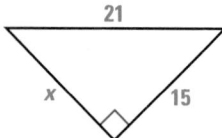
21, *x*, 15

Classify the triangle as *acute*, *right*, or *obtuse*.

4. $5, 15, 5\sqrt{10}$

5. $4.3, 6.7, 8.2$

6. $5, 7, 8$

Find the value of *x*. Round decimal answers to the nearest tenth.

7.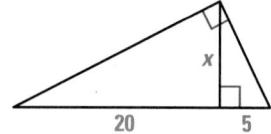
x, 20, 5

8.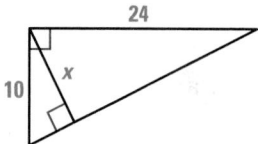
24, *x*, 10

9.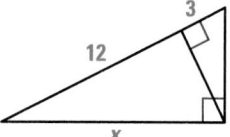
3, 12, *x*

Find the value of each variable. Write your answer in simplest radical form.

10.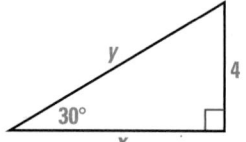
y, 4, 30°, *x*

11.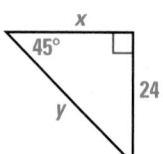
x, 45°, 24, *y*

12.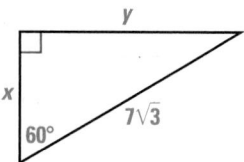
y, *x*, 60°, $7\sqrt{3}$

Solve the right triangle. Round decimal answers to the nearest tenth.

13.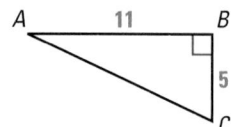
A, 11, B, 5, C

14.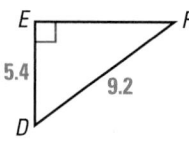
E, F, 5.4, 9.2, D

15.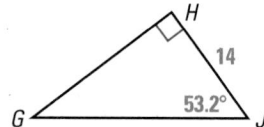
H, 14, 53.2°, G, J

16. FLAGPOLE Julie is 6 feet tall. If she stands 15 feet from the flagpole and holds a cardboard square, the edges of the square line up with the top and bottom of the flagpole. Approximate the height of the flagpole.

17. HILLS The length of a hill in your neighborhood is 2000 feet. The height of the hill is 750 feet. What is the angle of elevation of the hill?

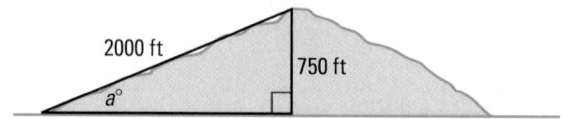
2000 ft, 750 ft, a°

Animated Algebra
classzone.com

GRAPH AND SOLVE QUADRATIC EQUATIONS

The graph of $y = ax^2 + bx + c$ is a parabola that opens upward if $a > 0$ and opens downward if $a < 0$. The x-coordinate of the vertex is $-\frac{b}{2a}$. The axis of symmetry is the vertical line $x = -\frac{b}{2a}$.

---

xy **EXAMPLE 1** *Graph a quadratic function*

Graph the equation $y = -x^2 + 4x - 3$.

Because $a = -1$ and $-1 < 0$, the graph opens downward.

The vertex has x-coordinate $-\frac{b}{2a} = -\frac{4}{2(-1)} = 2$.

The y-coordinate of the vertex is $-(2)^2 + 4(2) - 3 = 1$.

So, the vertex is $(2, 1)$ and the axis of symmetry is $x = 2$.

Use a table of values to draw a parabola through the plotted points.

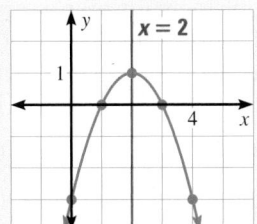

---

xy **EXAMPLE 2** *Solve a quadratic equation by graphing*

Solve the equation $x^2 - 2x = 3$.

Write the equation in the standard form $ax^2 + bx + c = 0$:

$x^2 - 2x - 3 = 0$.

Graph the related quadratic function $y = x^2 - 2x - 3$, as shown.

The x-intercepts of the graph are -1 and 3.

So, the solutions of $x^2 - 2x = 3$ are -1 and 3.

Check the solution algebraically.

$(-1)^2 - 2(-1) \stackrel{?}{=} 3 \rightarrow 1 + 2 = 3$ $(3)^2 - 2(3) \stackrel{?}{=} 3 \rightarrow 9 - 6 = 3$ ✓

EXERCISES

EXAMPLE 1
for Exs. 1–6

Graph the quadratic function. Label the vertex and axis of symmetry.

1. $y = x^2 - 6x + 8$ **2.** $y = -x^2 - 4x + 2$ **3.** $y = 2x^2 - x - 1$

4. $y = 3x^2 - 9x + 2$ **5.** $y = \frac{1}{2}x^2 - x + 3$ **6.** $y = -4x^2 + 6x - 5$

EXAMPLE 2
for Exs. 7–18

Solve the quadratic equation by graphing. Check solutions algebraically.

7. $x^2 = x + 6$ **8.** $4x + 4 = -x^2$ **9.** $2x^2 = -8$ **10.** $3x^2 + 2 = 14$

11. $-x^2 + 4x - 5 = 0$ **12.** $2x - x^2 = -15$ **13.** $\frac{1}{4}x^2 = 2x$ **14.** $x^2 + 3x = 4$

15. $x^2 + 8 = 6x$ **16.** $x^2 = 9x - 1$ **17.** $-25 = x^2 + 10x$ **18.** $x^2 + 6x = 0$

MULTIPLE CHOICE QUESTIONS

If you have difficulty solving a multiple choice question directly, you may be able to use another approach to eliminate incorrect answer choices and obtain the correct answer.

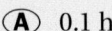

PROBLEM 1

You ride your bike at an average speed of 10 miles per hour. How long does it take you to ride one time around the triangular park shown in the diagram?

A 0.1 h   **B** 0.2 h

C 0.3 h   **D** 0.4 h

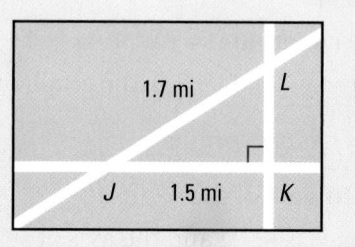

1.7 mi   *L*

J   1.5 mi   *K*

METHOD 1

SOLVE DIRECTLY The park is a right triangle. Use the Pythagorean Theorem to find *KL*. Find the perimeter of △*JKL*. Then find how long it takes to ride around the park.

STEP 1 Find *KL*. Use the Pythagorean Theorem.

$$JK^2 + KL^2 = JL^2$$
$$1.5^2 + KL^2 = 1.7^2$$
$$2.25 + KL^2 = 2.89$$
$$KL^2 = 0.64$$
$$KL = 0.8$$

STEP 2 Find the perimeter of △*JKL*.

$$P = JK + JL + KL$$
$$= 1.5 + 1.7 + 0.8$$
$$= 4 \text{ mi}$$

STEP 3 Find the time *t* (in hours) it takes you to go around the park.

Rate × Time = Distance

$$(10 \text{ mi/h}) \cdot t = 4 \text{ mi}$$
$$t = 0.4 \text{ h}$$

The correct answer is D. **A** **B** **C** **D**

METHOD 2

ELIMINATE CHOICES Another method is to find how far you can travel in the given times to eliminate choices that are not reasonable.

STEP 1 Find how far you will travel in each of the given times. Use the formula $rt = d$.

Choice A: 0.1(10) = 1 mi

Choice B: 0.2(10) = 2 mi

Choice C: 0.3(10) = 3 mi

Choice D: 0.4(10) = 4 mi

The distance around two sides of the park is 1.5 + 1.7 = 3.2 mi. But you need to travel around all three sides, which is longer.

Since 1 < 3.2, 2 < 3.2, and 3 < 3.2. You can eliminate choices A, B, and C.

STEP 2 Check that D is the correct answer. If the distance around the park is 4 miles, then

$$KL = 4 - JK - JL$$
$$= 4 - 1.5 - 1.7 = 0.8 \text{ mi.}$$

Apply the Converse of the Pythagorean Theorem.

$$0.8^2 + 1.5^2 \stackrel{?}{=} 1.7^2$$
$$0.64 + 2.25 \stackrel{?}{=} 2.89$$
$$2.89 = 2.89 \checkmark$$

The correct answer is D. **A** **B** **C** **D**

PROBLEM 2

What is the height of △*WXY*?

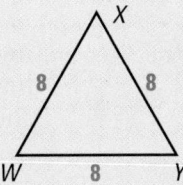

A 4

B 4√3

C 8

D 8√3

METHOD 1

SOLVE DIRECTLY Draw altitude $\overline{XZ}$ to form two congruent 30°-60°-90° triangles.

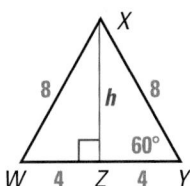

Let *h* be the length of the longer leg of △*XZY*.
The length of the shorter leg is 4.

longer leg = √3 · shorter leg

$$h = 4\sqrt{3}$$

The correct answer is B. Ⓐ **Ⓑ** Ⓒ Ⓓ

METHOD 2

ELIMINATE CHOICES Another method is to use theorems about triangles to eliminate incorrect choices. Draw altitude $\overline{XZ}$ to form two congruent right triangles.

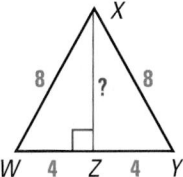

Consider △*XZW*. By the Triangle Inequality Theorem, *XW* < *WZ* + *XZ*. So, 8 < 4 + *XZ* and *XZ* > 4. You can eliminate choice A. Also, *XZ* must be less than the hypotenuse of △*XWZ*. You can eliminate choices C and D.

The correct answer is B. Ⓐ **Ⓑ** Ⓒ Ⓓ

PRACTICE

Explain why you can eliminate the highlighted answer choice.

1. In the figure shown, what is the length of $\overline{EF}$?

   A 9

   B ✗ 9√2

   C 18

   D 9√5

   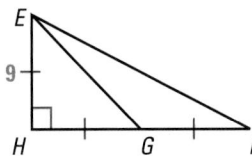

2. Which of the following lengths are side lengths of a right triangle?

   A ✗ 2, 21, 23   **B** 3, 4, 5   **C** 9, 16, 18   **D** 11, 16, 61

3. In △*PQR*, *PQ* = *QR* = 13 and *PR* = 10. What is the length of the altitude drawn from vertex *Q*?

   A 10   **B** 11   **C** 12   **D** ✗ 13

MULTIPLE CHOICE

1. Which expression gives the correct length for *XW* in the diagram below?

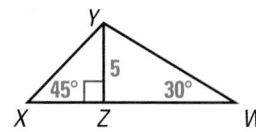

A $5 + 5\sqrt{2}$ **B** $5 + 5\sqrt{3}$

C $5\sqrt{3} + 5\sqrt{2}$ **D** $5 + 10$

2. The area of △*EFG* is 400 square meters. To the nearest tenth of a meter, what is the length of side $\overline{EG}$?

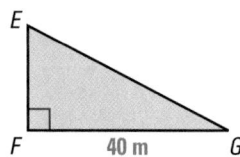

A 10.0 meters **B** 20.0 meters

C 44.7 meters **D** 56.7 meters

3. Which expression can be used to find the value of *x* in the diagram below?

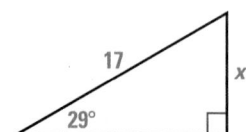

A $\tan 29° = \dfrac{x}{17}$ **B** $\cos 29° = \dfrac{x}{17}$

C $\tan 61° = \dfrac{x}{17}$ **D** $\cos 61° = \dfrac{x}{17}$

4. A fire station, a police station, and a hospital are not positioned in a straight line. The distance from the police station to the fire station is 4 miles. The distance from the fire station to the hospital is 3 miles. Which of the following could *not* be the distance from the police station to the hospital?

A 1 mile **B** 2 miles

C 5 miles **D** 6 miles

5. It takes 14 minutes to walk from your house to your friend's house on the path shown in red. If you walk at the same speed, about how many minutes will it take on the path shown in blue?

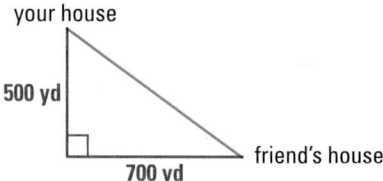

A 6 minutes **B** 8 minutes

C 10 minutes **D** 13 minutes

6. Which equation can be used to find *QR* in the diagram below?

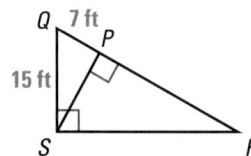

A $\dfrac{QR}{15} = \dfrac{15}{7}$

B $\dfrac{15}{QR} = \dfrac{QR}{8}$

C $QR = \sqrt{15^2 + 27^2}$

D $\dfrac{QR}{7} = \dfrac{7}{15}$

7. Stitches are sewn along the black line segments in the potholder shown below. There are 10 stitches per inch. Which is the closest estimate of the number of stitches used?

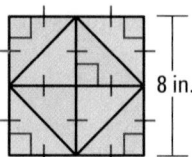

A 480 **B** 550

C 656 **D** 700

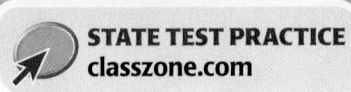
GRIDDED ANSWER

8. A design on a T-shirt is made of a square and four equilateral triangles. The side length of the square is 4 inches. Find the distance (in inches) from point A to point B. Round to the nearest tenth.

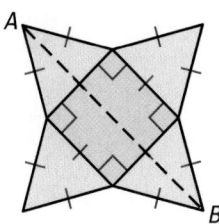

9. Use the diagram below. Find KM to the nearest tenth of a unit.

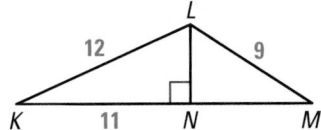

SHORT RESPONSE

10. The diagram shows the side of a set of stairs. In the diagram, the smaller right triangles are congruent. *Explain* how to find the lengths x, y, and z.

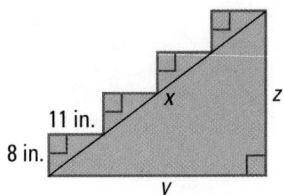

11. You drive due north from Dalton to Bristol. Next, you drive from Bristol to Hilldale. Finally, you drive from Hilldale to Dalton. Is Hilldale due west of Bristol? *Explain*.

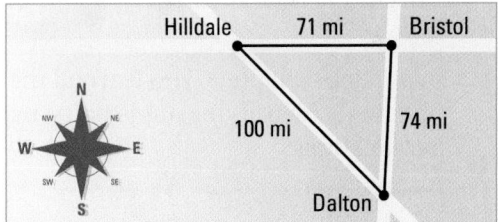

EXTENDED RESPONSE

12. The design for part of a water ride at an amusement park is shown. The ride carries people up a track along ramp $\overline{AB}$. Then riders travel down a water chute along ramp $\overline{BC}$.

  a. How high is the ride above point D? *Explain*.

  b. What is the total distance from point A to point B to point C? *Explain*.

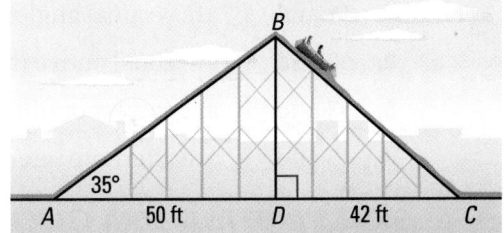

13. A formula for the area A of a triangle is *Heron's Formula*. For a triangle with side lengths EF, FG, and EG, the formula is

$A = \sqrt{s(s - EF)(s - FG)(s - EG)}$, where $s = \frac{1}{2}(EF + FG + EG)$.

  a. In $\triangle EFG$ shown, $EF = FG = 15$, and $EG = 18$. Use Heron's formula to find the area of $\triangle EFG$.

  b. Use the formula $A = \frac{1}{2}bh$ to find the area of $\triangle EFG$.

  c. Use Heron's formula to *justify* that the area of an equilateral triangle

   with side length x is $A = \frac{x^2}{4}\sqrt{3}$.

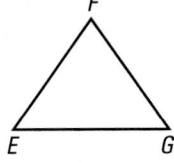

8 Quadrilaterals

- **8.1** Find Angle Measures in Polygons
- **8.2** Use Properties of Parallelograms
- **8.3** Show that a Quadrilateral is a Parallelogram
- **8.4** Properties of Rhombuses, Rectangles, and Squares
- **8.5** Use Properties of Trapezoids and Kites
- **8.6** Identify Special Quadrilaterals

Before

In previous chapters, you learned the following skills, which you'll use in Chapter 8: identifying angle pairs, using the Triangle Sum Theorem, and using parallel lines.

Prerequisite Skills

VOCABULARY CHECK

Copy and complete the statement.

1. $\angle 1$ and __?__ are vertical angles.

2. $\angle 3$ and __?__ are consecutive interior angles.

3. $\angle 7$ and __?__ are corresponding angles.

4. $\angle 5$ and __?__ are alternate interior angles.

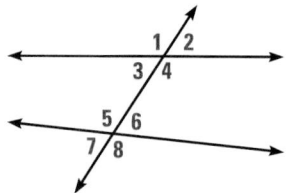

SKILLS AND ALGEBRA CHECK

5. In $\triangle ABC$, $m\angle A = x°$, $m\angle B = 3x°$, and $m\angle C = (4x - 12)°$. Find the measures of the three angles. *(Review p. 217 for 8.1.)*

Find the measure of the indicated angle. *(Review p. 154 for 8.2–8.5.)*

6. If $m\angle 3 = 105°$, then $m\angle 2 =$ __?__ .

7. If $m\angle 1 = 98°$, then $m\angle 3 =$ __?__ .

8. If $m\angle 4 = 82°$, then $m\angle 1 =$ __?__ .

9. If $m\angle 2 = 102°$, then $m\angle 4 =$ __?__ .

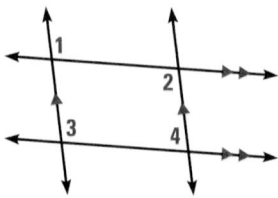

@HomeTutor Prerequisite skills practice at classzone.com

In Chapter 8, you will apply the big ideas listed below and reviewed in the Chapter Summary on page 559. You will also use the key vocabulary listed below.

Big Ideas

① **Using angle relationships in polygons**
② **Using properties of parallelograms**
③ **Classifying quadrilaterals by their properties**

KEY VOCABULARY

- diagonal, *p. 507*
- parallelogram, *p. 515*
- rhombus, *p. 533*
- rectangle, *p. 533*

- square, *p. 533*
- trapezoid, *p. 542*
  bases, base angles, legs
- isosceles trapezoid, *p. 543*

- midsegment of a trapezoid, *p. 544*
- kite, *p. 545*

You can use properties of quadrilaterals and other polygons to find side lengths and angle measures.

Animated Geometry

The animation illustrated below for Example 4 on page 545 helps you answer this question: How can classifying a quadrilateral help you draw conclusions about its sides and angles?

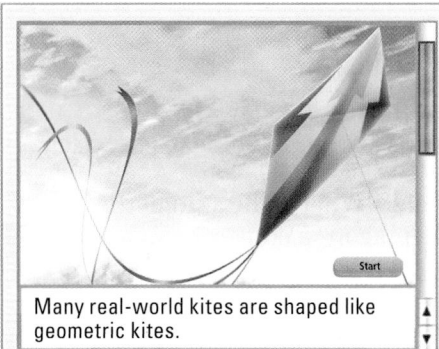

Many real-world kites are shaped like geometric kites.

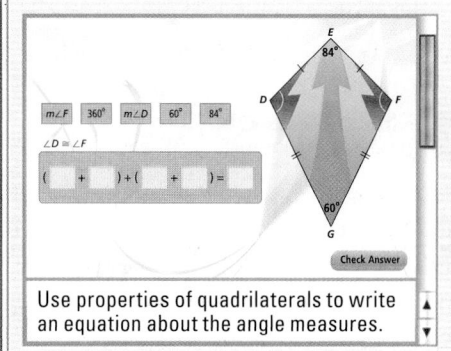

Use properties of quadrilaterals to write an equation about the angle measures.

Animated **Geometry** at classzone.com

Other animations for Chapter 8: pages 509, 519, 527, 535, 551, and 553

8.1 Investigate Angle Sums in Polygons

MATERIALS • straightedge • ruler

QUESTION What is the sum of the measures of the interior angles of a convex *n*-gon?

Recall from page 43 that an *n*-gon is a polygon with *n* sides and *n* vertices.

EXPLORE Find sums of interior angle measures

STEP 1 *Draw polygons* Use a straightedge to draw convex polygons with three sides, four sides, five sides, and six sides. An example is shown.

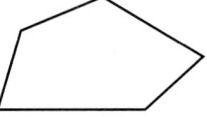

STEP 2 *Draw diagonals* In each polygon, draw all the diagonals from one vertex. A *diagonal* is a segment that joins two nonconsecutive vertices. Notice that the diagonals divide the polygon into triangles.

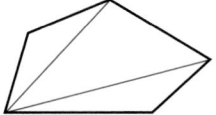

STEP 3 *Make a table* Copy the table below. By the Triangle Sum Theorem, the sum of the measures of the interior angles of a triangle is 180°. Use this theorem to complete the table.

Polygon	Number of sides	Number of triangles	Sum of measures of interior angles
Triangle	3	1	$1 \cdot 180° = 180°$
Quadrilateral	?	?	$2 \cdot 180° = 360°$
Pentagon	?	?	?
Hexagon	?	?	?

DRAW CONCLUSIONS Use your observations to complete these exercises

1. Look for a pattern in the last column of the table. What is the sum of the measures of the interior angles of a convex heptagon? a convex octagon? *Explain* your reasoning.

2. Write an expression for the sum of the measures of the interior angles of a convex *n*-gon.

3. Measure the side lengths in the hexagon you drew. Compare the lengths with those in hexagons drawn by other students. Do the side lengths affect the sum of the interior angle measures of a hexagon? *Explain*.

8.1 Find Angle Measures in Polygons

Before	You classified polygons.
Now	You will find angle measures in polygons.
Why?	So you can describe a baseball park, as in Exs. 28–29.

Key Vocabulary
• **diagonal**
• **interior angle,** p. 218
• **exterior angle,** p. 218

In a polygon, two vertices that are endpoints of the same side are called *consecutive vertices*. A **diagonal** of a polygon is a segment that joins two *nonconsecutive vertices*. Polygon *ABCDE* has two diagonals from vertex *B*, $\overline{BD}$ and $\overline{BE}$.

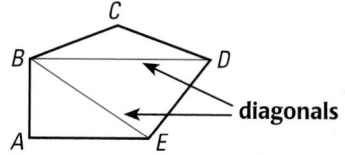

diagonals

As you can see, the diagonals from one vertex form triangles. In the Activity on page 506, you used these triangles to find the sum of the interior angle measures of a polygon. Your results support the following theorem and corollary.

THEOREMS   *For Your Notebook*

THEOREM 8.1 Polygon Interior Angles Theorem

The sum of the measures of the interior angles of a convex *n*-gon is $(n - 2) \cdot 180°$.

$m\angle 1 + m\angle 2 + \cdots + m\angle n = (n - 2) \cdot 180°$

Proof: Ex. 33, p. 512 (for pentagons)

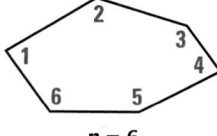

n = 6

COROLLARY TO THEOREM 8.1 Interior Angles of a Quadrilateral

The sum of the measures of the interior angles of a quadrilateral is 360°.

Proof: Ex. 34, p. 512

EXAMPLE 1   **Find the sum of angle measures in a polygon**

Find the sum of the measures of the interior angles of a convex octagon.

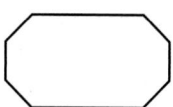

Solution

An octagon has 8 sides. Use the Polygon Interior Angles Theorem.

$(n - 2) \cdot 180° = (8 - 2) \cdot 180°$ **Substitute 8 for *n*.**

$= 6 \cdot 180°$ **Subtract.**

$= 1080°$ **Multiply.**

▶ The sum of the measures of the interior angles of an octagon is 1080°.

EXAMPLE 2   **Find the number of sides of a polygon**

The sum of the measures of the interior angles of a convex polygon is 900°. Classify the polygon by the number of sides.

Solution

Use the Polygon Interior Angles Theorem to write an equation involving the number of sides n. Then solve the equation to find the number of sides.

$(n - 2) \cdot 180° = 900°$ **Polygon Interior Angles Theorem**

$n - 2 = 5$ **Divide each side by 180°.**

$n = 7$ **Add 2 to each side.**

▶ The polygon has 7 sides. It is a heptagon.

✔ **GUIDED PRACTICE**   for Examples 1 and 2

1. The coin shown is in the shape of a regular 11-gon. Find the sum of the measures of the interior angles.

2. The sum of the measures of the interior angles of a convex polygon is 1440°. Classify the polygon by the number of sides.

EXAMPLE 3   **Find an unknown interior angle measure**

 ALGEBRA Find the value of x in the diagram shown.

Solution

The polygon is a quadrilateral. Use the Corollary to the Polygon Interior Angles Theorem to write an equation involving x. Then solve the equation.

$x° + 108° + 121° + 59° = 360°$ **Corollary to Theorem 8.1**

$x + 288 = 360$ **Combine like terms.**

$x = 72$ **Subtract 288 from each side.**

▶ The value of x is 72.

✔ **GUIDED PRACTICE**   for Example 3

3. Use the diagram at the right. Find $m\angle S$ and $m\angle T$.

4. The measures of three of the interior angles of a quadrilateral are 89°, 110°, and 46°. Find the measure of the fourth interior angle.

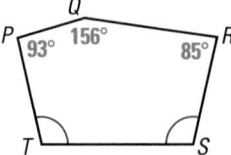

EXTERIOR ANGLES Unlike the sum of the interior angle measures of a convex polygon, the sum of the exterior angle measures does *not* depend on the number of sides of the polygon. The diagrams below suggest that the sum of the measures of the exterior angles, one at each vertex, of a pentagon is 360°. In general, this sum is 360° for any convex polygon.

VISUALIZE IT

A circle contains two straight angles. So, there are 180° + 180°, or 360°, in a circle.

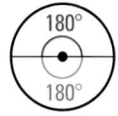

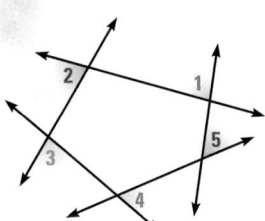

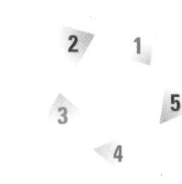

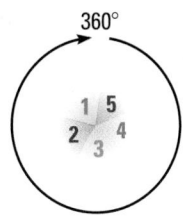

360°

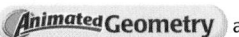

STEP 1 **Shade** one exterior angle at each vertex.

STEP 2 **Cut** out the exterior angles.

STEP 3 **Arrange** the exterior angles to form 360°.

Animated **Geometry** at classzone.com

THEOREM *For Your Notebook*

THEOREM 8.2 **Polygon Exterior Angles Theorem**

The sum of the measures of the exterior angles of a convex polygon, one angle at each vertex, is 360°.

$m\angle 1 + m\angle 2 + \cdots + m\angle n = 360°$

Proof: Ex. 35, p. 512

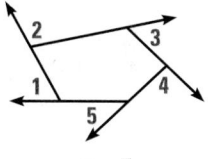

$n = 5$

⭐ **EXAMPLE 4** **Standardized Test Practice**

What is the value of *x* in the diagram shown?

Ⓐ 67　　　Ⓑ 68

Ⓒ 91　　　Ⓓ 136

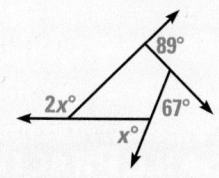

ELIMINATE CHOICES

You can quickly eliminate choice *D*. If *x* were equal to 136, then the sum of only two of the angle measures (*x*° and 2*x*°) would be greater than 360°.

Solution

Use the Polygon Exterior Angles Theorem to write and solve an equation.

$x° + 2x° + 89° + 67° = 360°$　　　**Polygon Exterior Angles Theorem**

$3x + 156 = 360$　　　**Combine like terms.**

$x = 68$　　　**Solve for x.**

▸ The correct answer is B. Ⓐ **Ⓑ** Ⓒ Ⓓ

✓ **GUIDED PRACTICE** for Example 4

5. A convex hexagon has exterior angles with measures 34°, 49°, 58°, 67°, and 75°. What is the measure of an exterior angle at the sixth vertex?

EXAMPLE 5 Find angle measures in regular polygons

READ VOCABULARY
Recall that a *dodecagon* is a polygon with 12 sides and 12 vertices.

TRAMPOLINE The trampoline shown is shaped like a regular dodecagon. Find (a) the measure of each interior angle and (b) the measure of each exterior angle.

Solution

a. Use the Polygon Interior Angles Theorem to find the sum of the measures of the interior angles.

$$(n - 2) \cdot 180° = (12 - 2) \cdot 180° = 1800°$$

Then find the measure of one interior angle. A regular dodecagon has 12 congruent interior angles. Divide 1800° by 12: $1800° \div 12 = 150°$.

▶ The measure of each interior angle in the dodecagon is 150°.

b. By the Polygon Exterior Angles Theorem, the sum of the measures of the exterior angles, one angle at each vertex, is 360°. Divide 360° by 12 to find the measure of one of the 12 congruent exterior angles: $360° \div 12 = 30°$.

▶ The measure of each exterior angle in the dodecagon is 30°.

✓ **GUIDED PRACTICE** for Example 5

6. An interior angle and an adjacent exterior angle of a polygon form a linear pair. How can you use this fact as another method to find the exterior angle measure in Example 5?

8.1 EXERCISES

HOMEWORK KEY
◯ = **WORKED-OUT SOLUTIONS**
on p. WS9 for Exs. 9, 11, and 29
★ = **STANDARDIZED TEST PRACTICE**
Exs. 2, 18, 23, and 37
◆ = **MULTIPLE REPRESENTATIONS**
Ex. 36

SKILL PRACTICE

1. **VOCABULARY** Sketch a convex hexagon. Draw all of its diagonals.

2. ★ **WRITING** How many exterior angles are there in an *n*-gon? Are all the exterior angles considered when you use the Polygon Exterior Angles Theorem? *Explain.*

EXAMPLES
1 and 2
on pp. 507–508
for Exs. 3–10

INTERIOR ANGLE SUMS Find the sum of the measures of the interior angles of the indicated convex polygon.

3. Nonagon
4. 14-gon
5. 16-gon
6. 20-gon

FINDING NUMBER OF SIDES The sum of the measures of the interior angles of a convex polygon is given. Classify the polygon by the number of sides.

7. 360°
8. 720°
9. 1980°
10. 2340°

ALGEBRA Find the value of *x*.

(11.)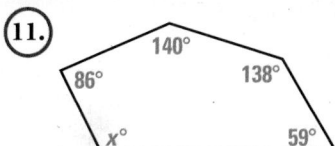

12.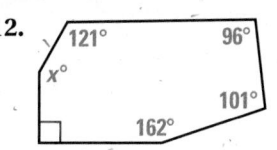

13.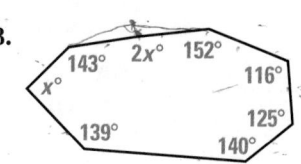

14.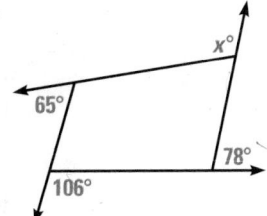

15.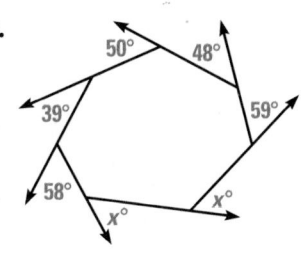

16.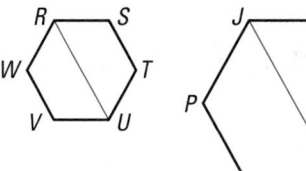

17. **ERROR ANALYSIS** A student claims that the sum of the measures of the exterior angles of an octagon is greater than the sum of the measures of the exterior angles of a hexagon. The student justifies this claim by saying that an octagon has two more sides than a hexagon. *Describe* and correct the error the student is making.

18. ★ **MULTIPLE CHOICE** The measures of the interior angles of a quadrilateral are $x°$, $2x°$, $3x°$, and $4x°$. What is the measure of the largest interior angle?

   (A) 120°   (B) 144°   (C) 160°   (D) 360°

EXAMPLE 5
on p. 510
for Exs. 19–21

REGULAR POLYGONS Find the measures of an interior angle and an exterior angle of the indicated regular polygon.

19. Regular pentagon   20. Regular 18-gon   21. Regular 90-gon

22. **DIAGONALS OF SIMILAR FIGURES**
Hexagons *RSTUVW* and *JKLMNP* are similar. $\overline{RU}$ and $\overline{JM}$ are diagonals. Given $ST = 6$, $KL = 10$, and $RU = 12$, find *JM*.

23. ★ **SHORT RESPONSE** *Explain* why any two regular pentagons are similar.

REGULAR POLYGONS Find the value of *n* for each regular *n*-gon described.

24. Each interior angle of the regular *n*-gon has a measure of 156°.

25. Each exterior angle of the regular *n*-gon has a measure of 9°.

26. **POSSIBLE POLYGONS** Determine if it is possible for a regular polygon to have an interior angle with the given angle measure. *Explain* your reasoning.

   a. 165°   **b.** 171°   **c.** 75°   **d.** 40°

27. **CHALLENGE** Sides are added to a convex polygon so that the sum of its interior angle measures is increased by 540°. How many sides are added to the polygon? *Explain* your reasoning.

EXAMPLE 1
on p. 507
for Exs. 28–29

BASEBALL The outline of the playing field at a baseball park is a polygon, as shown. Find the sum of the measures of the interior angles of the polygon.

28.

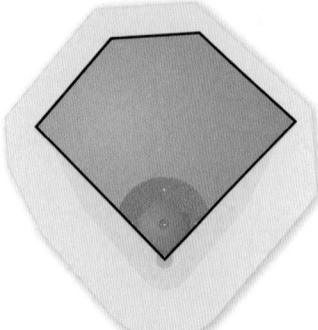

(29.)

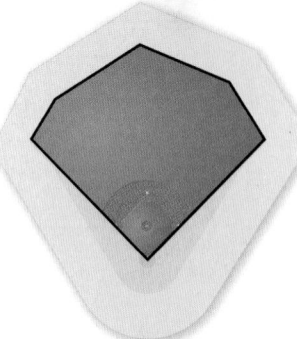

@HomeTutor for problem solving help at classzone.com

EXAMPLE 5
on p. 510
for Exs. 30–31

30. JEWELRY BOX The base of a jewelry box is shaped like a regular hexagon. What is the measure of each interior angle of the hexagon?

@HomeTutor for problem solving help at classzone.com

31. GREENHOUSE The floor of the greenhouse shown is a shaped like a regular decagon. Find the measure of an interior angle of the regular decagon. Then find the measure of an exterior angle.

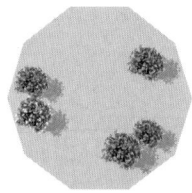

32. MULTI-STEP PROBLEM In pentagon $PQRST$, $\angle P$, $\angle Q$, and $\angle S$ are right angles, and $\angle R \cong \angle T$.

   a. Draw a Diagram Sketch pentagon $PQRST$. Mark the right angles and the congruent angles.

   b. Calculate Find the sum of the interior angle measures of $PQRST$.

   c. Calculate Find $m\angle R$ and $m\angle T$.

33. PROVING THEOREM 8.1 FOR PENTAGONS The Polygon Interior Angles Theorem states that the sum of the measures of the interior angles of an n-gon is $(n - 2) \cdot 180°$. Write a paragraph proof of this theorem for the case when $n = 5$.

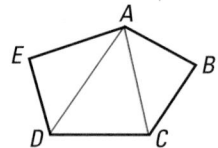

34. PROVING A COROLLARY Write a paragraph proof of the Corollary to the Polygon Interior Angles Theorem.

35. PROVING THEOREM 8.2 Use the plan below to write a paragraph proof of the Polygon Exterior Angles Theorem.

   Plan for Proof In a convex n-gon, the sum of the measures of an interior angle and an adjacent exterior angle at any vertex is 180°. Multiply by n to get the sum of all such sums at each vertex. Then subtract the sum of the interior angles derived by using the Polygon Interior Angles Theorem.

36. ◆ **MULTIPLE REPRESENTATIONS** The formula for the measure of each interior angle in a regular polygon can be written in function notation.

    a. Writing a Function Write a function $h(n)$, where n is the number of sides in a regular polygon and $h(n)$ is the measure of any interior angle in the regular polygon.

    b. Using a Function Use the function from part (a) to find $h(9)$. Then use the function to find n if $h(n) = 150°$.

    c. Graphing a Function Graph the function from part (a) for $n = 3, 4, 5, 6, 7,$ and 8. Based on your graph, *describe* what happens to the value of $h(n)$ as n increases. *Explain* your reasoning.

37. ★ **EXTENDED RESPONSE** In a concave polygon, at least one interior angle measure is greater than 180°. For example, the measure of the shaded angle in the concave quadrilateral below is 210°.

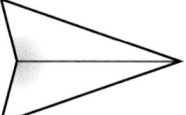  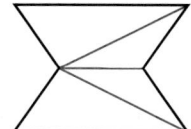 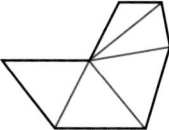

    a. In the diagrams above, the interiors of a concave quadrilateral, pentagon, hexagon, and heptagon are divided into triangles. Make a table like the one in the Activity on page 506. For each of the polygons shown above, record the number of sides, the number of triangles, and the sum of the measures of the interior angles.

    b. Write a function that you can use to find the sum of the measures of the interior angles of a concave polygon. *Explain.*

38. **CHALLENGE** Polygon $ABCDEFGH$ is a regular octagon. Suppose sides $\overline{AB}$ and $\overline{CD}$ are extended to meet at a point P. Find $m\angle BPC$. *Explain* your reasoning. Include a diagram with your answer.

MIXED REVIEW

PREVIEW
Prepare for
Lesson 8.2
in Exs. 39–41.

Find $m\angle 1$ and $m\angle 2$. Explain your reasoning. *(p. 154)*

39.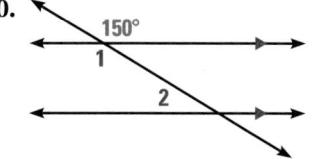

40.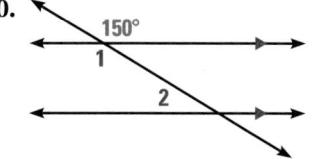

41.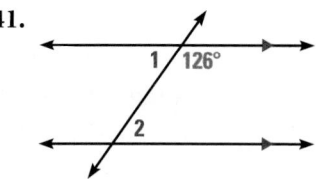

42. Quadrilaterals $JKLM$ and $PQRS$ are similar. If $JK = 3.6$ centimeters and $PQ = 1.2$ centimeters, find the scale factor of $JKLM$ to $PQRS$. *(p. 372)*

43. Quadrilaterals $ABCD$ and $EFGH$ are similar. The scale factor of $ABCD$ to $EFGH$ is $8:5$, and the perimeter of $ABCD$ is 90 feet. Find the perimeter of $EFGH$. *(p. 372)*

Let $\angle A$ be an acute angle in a right triangle. Approximate the measure of $\angle A$ to the nearest tenth of a degree. *(p. 483)*

44. $\sin A = 0.77$ 45. $\sin A = 0.35$ 46. $\cos A = 0.81$ 47. $\cos A = 0.23$

8.2 Investigate Parallelograms

MATERIALS · graphing calculator or computer

QUESTION **What are some of the properties of a parallelogram?**

You can use geometry drawing software to investigate relationships in special quadrilaterals.

EXPLORE **Draw a quadrilateral**

STEP 1 *Draw parallel lines* Construct $\overleftrightarrow{AB}$ and a line parallel to $\overleftrightarrow{AB}$ through point C. Then construct $\overleftrightarrow{BC}$ and a line parallel to $\overleftrightarrow{BC}$ through point A. Finally, construct a point D at the intersection of the line drawn parallel to $\overleftrightarrow{AB}$ and the line drawn parallel to $\overleftrightarrow{BC}$.

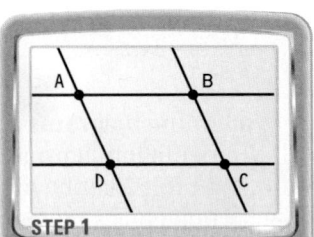

STEP 2 *Draw quadrilateral* Construct segments to form the sides of quadrilateral $ABCD$. After you construct $\overline{AB}$, $\overline{BC}$, $\overline{CD}$, and $\overline{DA}$, hide the parallel lines that you drew in Step 1.

STEP 3 *Measure side lengths* Measure the side lengths AB, BC, CD, and DA. Drag point A or point B to change the side lengths of $ABCD$. What do you notice about the side lengths?

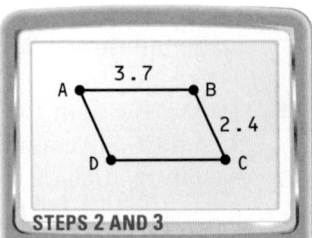

STEP 4 *Measure angles* Find the measures of $\angle A$, $\angle B$, $\angle C$, and $\angle D$. Drag point A or point B to change the angle measures of $ABCD$. What do you notice about the angle measures?

DRAW CONCLUSIONS **Use your observations to complete these exercises**

1. The quadrilateral you drew in the Explore is called a *parallelogram*. Why do you think this type of quadrilateral has this name?

2. Based on your observations, make a conjecture about the side lengths of a parallelogram and a conjecture about the angle measures of a parallelogram.

3. **REASONING** Draw a parallelogram and its diagonals. Measure the distance from the intersection of the diagonals to each vertex of the parallelogram. Make and test a conjecture about the diagonals of a parallelogram.

8.2 Use Properties of Parallelograms

Before	You used a property of polygons to find angle measures.
Now	You will find angle and side measures in parallelograms.
Why?	So you can solve a problem about airplanes, as in Ex. 38.

Key Vocabulary
• **parallelogram**

A **parallelogram** is a quadrilateral with both pairs of opposite sides parallel. The term "parallelogram *PQRS*" can be written as □*PQRS*. In □*PQRS*, $\overline{PQ} \parallel \overline{RS}$ and $\overline{QR} \parallel \overline{PS}$ by definition. The theorems below describe other properties of parallelograms.

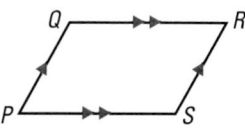

THEOREMS   *For Your Notebook*

THEOREM 8.3

If a quadrilateral is a parallelogram, then its opposite sides are congruent.

If *PQRS* is a parallelogram, then $\overline{PQ} \cong \overline{RS}$ and $\overline{QR} \cong \overline{PS}$.

Proof: p. 516

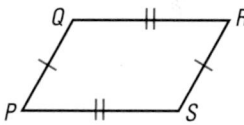

THEOREM 8.4

If a quadrilateral is a parallelogram, then its opposite angles are congruent.

If *PQRS* is a parallelogram, then $\angle P \cong \angle R$ and $\angle Q \cong \angle S$.

Proof: Ex. 42, p. 520

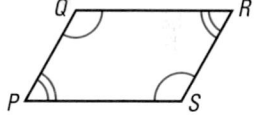

EXAMPLE 1   **Use properties of parallelograms**

ALGEBRA **Find the values of *x* and *y*.**

ABCD is a parallelogram by the definition of a parallelogram. Use Theorem 8.3 to find the value of *x*.

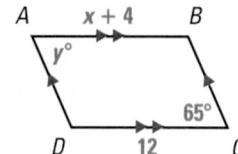

$AB = CD$ Opposite sides of a □ are ≅.

$x + 4 = 12$ Substitute *x* + 4 for **AB** and 12 for **CD**.

$x = 8$ Subtract 4 from each side.

By Theorem 8.4, $\angle A \cong \angle C$, or $m\angle A = m\angle C$. So, $y° = 65°$.

▶ In □*ABCD*, $x = 8$ and $y = 65$.

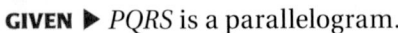
If a quadrilateral is a parallelogram, then its opposite sides are congruent.

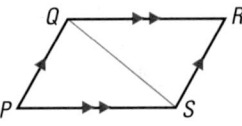

GIVEN ▶ *PQRS* is a parallelogram.

PROVE ▶ $\overline{PQ} \cong \overline{RS}$, $\overline{QR} \cong \overline{PS}$

Plan for Proof
a. Draw diagonal $\overline{QS}$ to form $\triangle PQS$ and $\triangle RSQ$.
b. Use the ASA Congruence Postulate to show that $\triangle PQS \cong \triangle RSQ$.
c. Use congruent triangles to show that $\overline{PQ} \cong \overline{RS}$ and $\overline{QR} \cong \overline{PS}$.

	STATEMENTS	REASONS
Plan in Action	a. 1. *PQRS* is a ▱.	1. Given
	2. Draw $\overline{QS}$.	2. Through any 2 points there exists exactly 1 line.
	3. $\overline{PQ} \parallel \overline{RS}$, $\overline{QR} \parallel \overline{PS}$	3. Definition of parallelogram
	b. 4. $\angle PQS \cong \angle RSQ$, $\angle PSQ \cong \angle RQS$	4. Alternate Interior Angles Theorem
	5. $\overline{QS} \cong \overline{QS}$	5. Reflexive Property of Congruence
	6. $\triangle PQS \cong \triangle RSQ$	6. ASA Congruence Postulate
	c. 7. $\overline{PQ} \cong \overline{RS}$, $\overline{QR} \cong \overline{PS}$	7. Corresp. parts of $\cong \triangle$ are $\cong$.

✓ **GUIDED PRACTICE** for Example 1

1. Find *FG* and $m\angle G$.

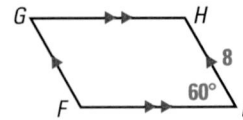

2. Find the values of *x* and *y*.

INTERIOR ANGLES The Consecutive Interior Angles Theorem (page 155) states that if two parallel lines are cut by a transversal, then the pairs of consecutive interior angles formed are supplementary.

A pair of consecutive angles in a parallelogram are like a pair of consecutive interior angles between parallel lines. This similarity suggests Theorem 8.5.

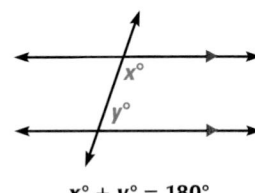

$x° + y° = 180°$

THEOREM *For Your Notebook*

THEOREM 8.5

If a quadrilateral is a parallelogram, then its consecutive angles are supplementary.

If *PQRS* is a parallelogram, then $x° + y° = 180°$.

Proof: Ex. 43, p. 520

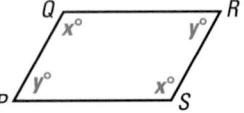

EXAMPLE 2 **Use properties of a parallelogram**

DESK LAMP As shown, part of the extending arm of a desk lamp is a parallelogram. The angles of the parallelogram change as the lamp is raised and lowered. Find $m\angle BCD$ when $m\angle ADC = 110°$.

Solution

By Theorem 8.5, the consecutive angle pairs in $\square ABCD$ are supplementary. So, $m\angle ADC + m\angle BCD = 180°$. Because $m\angle ADC = 110°$, $m\angle BCD = 180° - 110° = 70°$.

THEOREM *For Your Notebook*

THEOREM 8.6

If a quadrilateral is a parallelogram, then its diagonals bisect each other.

Proof: Ex. 44, p. 521

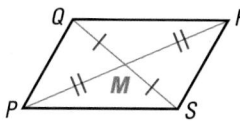

$\overline{QM} \cong \overline{SM}$ and $\overline{PM} \cong \overline{RM}$

 EXAMPLE 3 **Standardized Test Practice**

The diagonals of $\square LMNO$ intersect at point P. What are the coordinates of P?

(A) $\left(\dfrac{7}{2}, 2\right)$ (B) $\left(2, \dfrac{7}{2}\right)$

(C) $\left(\dfrac{5}{2}, 2\right)$ (D) $\left(2, \dfrac{5}{2}\right)$

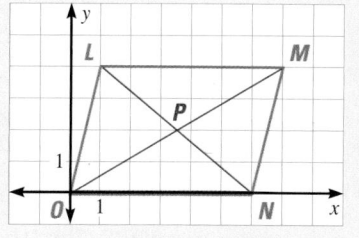

SIMPLIFY CALCULATIONS

In Example 3, you can use either diagonal to find the coordinates of P. Using $\overline{OM}$ simplifies calculations because one endpoint is $(0, 0)$.

Solution

By Theorem 8.6, the diagonals of a parallelogram bisect each other. So, P is the midpoint of diagonals $\overline{LN}$ and $\overline{OM}$. Use the Midpoint Formula.

Coordinates of midpoint P of $\overline{OM} = \left(\dfrac{7 + 0}{2}, \dfrac{4 + 0}{2}\right) = \left(\dfrac{7}{2}, 2\right)$

▶ The correct answer is A. (A) (B) (C) (D)

✓ **GUIDED PRACTICE** for Examples 2 and 3

Find the indicated measure in $\square JKLM$.

3. NM **4.** KM

5. $m\angle JML$ **6.** $m\angle KML$

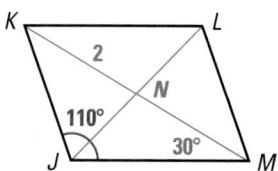

8.2 EXERCISES

HOMEWORK KEY

◯ = **WORKED-OUT SOLUTIONS**
on p. WS1 for Exs. 9, 13, and 39

★ = **STANDARDIZED TEST PRACTICE**
Exs. 2, 16, 29, 35, and 41

SKILL PRACTICE

1. **VOCABULARY** What property of a parallelogram is included in the definition of a parallelogram? What properties are described by the theorems in this lesson?

2. ★ **WRITING** In parallelogram *ABCD*, *m*∠*A* = 65°. *Explain* how you would find the other angle measures of ▱ *ABCD*.

EXAMPLE 1
on p. 515
for Exs. 3–8

ALGEBRA Find the value of each variable in the parallelogram.

3.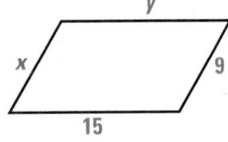

4.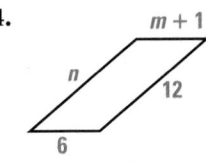

5.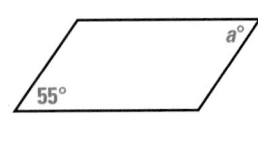

6.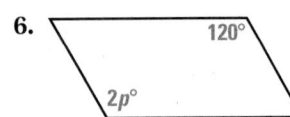

7.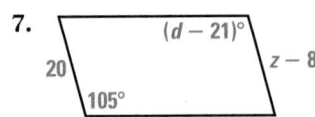

8.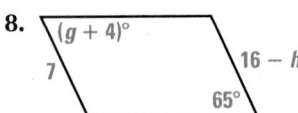

EXAMPLE 2
on p. 517
for Exs. 9–12

FINDING ANGLE MEASURES Find the measure of the indicated angle in the parallelogram.

9. Find *m*∠*B*.

10. Find *m*∠*L*.

11. Find *m*∠*Y*.

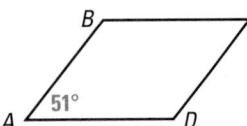
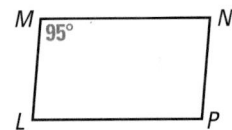
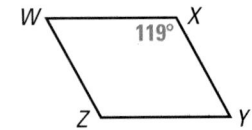

12. **SKETCHING** In ▱ *PQRS*, *m*∠*R* is 24 degrees more than *m*∠*S*. Sketch ▱ *PQRS*. Find the measure of each interior angle. Then label each angle with its measure.

EXAMPLE 3
on p. 517
for Exs. 13–16

ALGEBRA Find the value of each variable in the parallelogram.

13.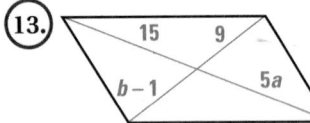

14.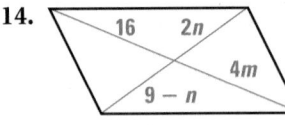

15.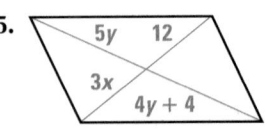

16. ★ **MULTIPLE CHOICE** The diagonals of parallelogram *OPQR* intersect at point *M*. What are the coordinates of point *M*?

Ⓐ $\left(1, \frac{5}{2}\right)$

Ⓑ $\left(2, \frac{5}{2}\right)$

Ⓒ $\left(1, \frac{3}{2}\right)$

Ⓓ $\left(2, \frac{3}{2}\right)$

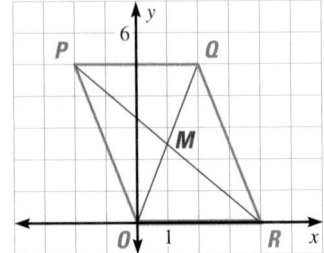

17. $\overline{AD} \cong$?

18. $\angle DAB \cong$?

19. $\angle BCA \cong$?

20. $m\angle ABC =$?

21. $m\angle CAB =$?

22. $m\angle CAD =$?

USING A DIAGRAM Find the indicated measure in $\square EFGH$. *Explain.*

23. $m\angle EJF$

24. $m\angle EGF$

25. $m\angle HFG$

26. $m\angle GEF$

27. $m\angle HGF$

28. $m\angle EHG$

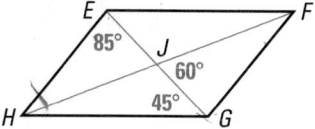

 **Geometry** at classzone.com

29. ★ **MULTIPLE CHOICE** In parallelogram $ABCD$, $AB = 14$ inches and $BC = 20$ inches. What is the perimeter (in inches) of $\square ABCD$?

(A) 28   (B) 40   (C) 68   (D) 280

30. **xy ALGEBRA** The measure of one interior angle of a parallelogram is 0.25 times the measure of another angle. Find the measure of each angle.

31. **xy ALGEBRA** The measure of one interior angle of a parallelogram is 50 degrees more than 4 times the measure of another angle. Find the measure of each angle.

32. **ERROR ANALYSIS** In $\square ABCD$, $m\angle B = 50°$. A student says that $m\angle A = 50°$. *Explain* why this statement is incorrect.

33. **USING A DIAGRAM** In the diagram, $QRST$ and $STUV$ are parallelograms. Find the values of x and y. *Explain* your reasoning.

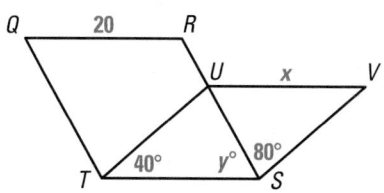

34. **FINDING A PERIMETER** The sides of $\square MNPQ$ are represented by the expressions below. Sketch $\square MNPQ$ and find its perimeter.

$MQ = -2x + 37$ $QP = y + 14$ $NP = x - 5$ $MN = 4y + 5$

35. ★ **SHORT RESPONSE** In $ABCD$, $m\angle B = 124°$, $m\angle A = 66°$, and $m\angle C = 124°$. *Explain* why $ABCD$ cannot be a parallelogram.

36. **FINDING ANGLE MEASURES** In $\square LMNP$ shown at the right, $m\angle MLN = 32°$, $m\angle NLP = (x^2)°$, $m\angle MNP = 12x°$, and $\angle MNP$ is an acute angle. Find $m\angle NLP$.

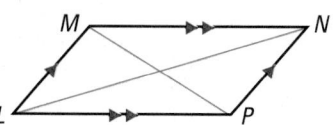

37. **CHALLENGE** Points $A(1, 2)$, $B(3, 6)$, and $C(6, 4)$ are three vertices of a parallelogram. Find the coordinates of each point that could be vertex D. Sketch each possible parallelogram in a separate coordinate plane. *Justify* your answers.

EXAMPLE 2
on p. 517
for Ex. 38

38. AIRPLANE The diagram shows the mechanism for opening the canopy on a small airplane. Two pivot arms attach at four pivot points *A*, *B*, *C*, and *D*. These points form the vertices of a parallelogram. Find $m\angle D$ when $m\angle C = 40°$. *Explain* your reasoning.

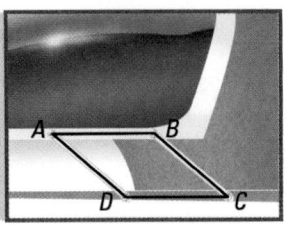

@HomeTutor for problem solving help at classzone.com

39. MIRROR The mirror shown is attached to the wall by an arm that can extend away from the wall. In the figure, points *P*, *Q*, *R*, and *S* are the vertices of a parallelogram. This parallelogram is one of several that change shape as the mirror is extended.

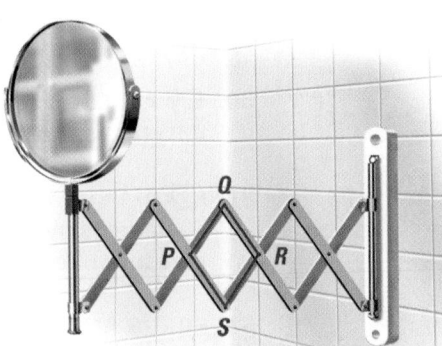

a. If *PQ* = 3 inches, find *RS*.

b. If $m\angle Q = 70°$, what is $m\angle S$?

c. What happens to $m\angle P$ as $m\angle Q$ increases? What happens to *QS* as $m\angle Q$ decreases? *Explain*.

@HomeTutor for problem solving help at classzone.com

40. USING RATIOS In □*LMNO*, the ratio of *LM* to *MN* is 4 : 3. Find *LM* if the perimeter of *LMNO* is 28.

41. ★ **OPEN-ENDED MATH** Draw a triangle. Copy the triangle and combine the two triangles to form a quadrilateral. Show that the quadrilateral is a parallelogram. Then show how you can make additional copies of the triangle to form a larger parallelogram that is similar to the first parallelogram. *Justify* your method.

42. PROVING THEOREM 8.4 Use the diagram of quadrilateral *ABCD* with the auxiliary line segment drawn to write a two-column proof of Theorem 8.4.

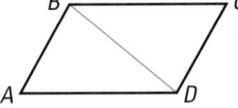

GIVEN ▶ *ABCD* is a parallelogram.

PROVE ▶ $\angle A \cong \angle C$, $\angle B \cong \angle D$

43. PROVING THEOREM 8.5 Use properties of parallel lines to prove Theorem 8.5.

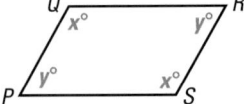

GIVEN ▶ *PQRS* is a parallelogram.

PROVE ▶ $x° + y° = 180°$

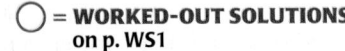
= **WORKED-OUT SOLUTIONS**
on p. WS1

★ = **STANDARDIZED TEST PRACTICE**

44. PROVING THEOREM 8.6 Theorem 8.6 states that if a quadrilateral is a parallelogram, then its diagonals bisect each other. Write a two-column proof of Theorem 8.6.

45. CHALLENGE Suppose you choose a point on the base of an isosceles triangle. You draw segments from that point perpendicular to the legs of the triangle. Prove that the sum of the lengths of those segments is equal to the length of the altitude drawn to one leg.

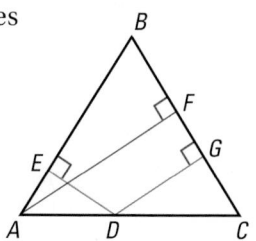

GIVEN ▶ $\triangle ABC$ is isosceles with base $\overline{AC}$,
$\overline{AF}$ is the altitude drawn to $\overline{BC}$,
$\overline{DE} \perp \overline{AB}, \overline{DG} \perp \overline{BC}$

PROVE ▶ For D anywhere on $\overline{AC}$, $DE + DG = AF$.

MIXED REVIEW

PREVIEW
Prepare for
Lesson 8.3
in Exs. 46–48.

Tell whether the lines through the given points are *parallel*, *perpendicular*, or *neither*. Justify your answer. *(p. 171)*

46. Line 1: (2, 4), (4, 1)
Line 2: (5, 7), (9, 0)

47. Line 1: (−6, 7), (−2, 3)
Line 2: (9, −1), (2, 6)

48. Line 1: (−3, 0), (−6, 5)
Line 2: (3, −5), (5, −10)

Decide if the side lengths form a triangle. If so, would the triangle be *acute*, *right*, or *obtuse*? *(p. 441)*

49. 9, 13, and 6

50. 10, 12, and 7

51. 5, 9, and $\sqrt{106}$

52. 8, 12, and 4

53. 24, 10, and 26

54. 9, 10, and 11

Find the value of *x*. Write your answer in simplest radical form. *(p. 457)*

55.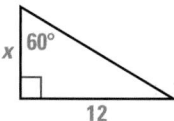

56.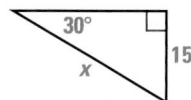

57.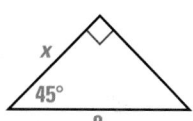

QUIZ *for Lessons 8.1–8.2*

Find the value of *x*. *(p. 507)*

1.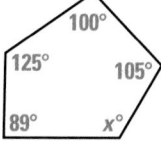

2.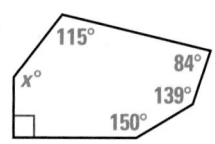

3.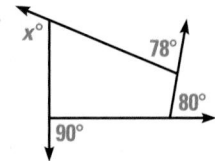

Find the value of each variable in the parallelogram. *(p. 515)*

4.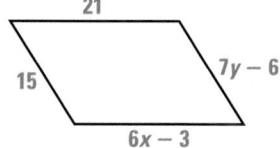

5.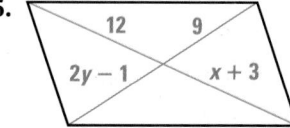

6.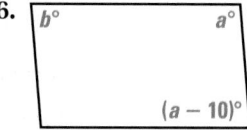

8.3 Show that a Quadrilateral is a Parallelogram

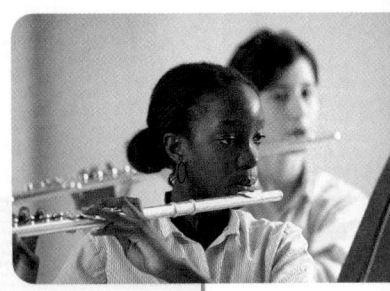

Before	You identified properties of parallelograms.
Now	You will use properties to identify parallelograms.
Why?	So you can describe how a music stand works, as in Ex. 32.

Key Vocabulary
• **parallelogram,**
  p. 515

Given a parallelogram, you can use Theorem 8.3 and Theorem 8.4 to prove statements about the angles and sides of the parallelogram. The converses of Theorem 8.3 and Theorem 8.4 are stated below. You can use these and other theorems in this lesson to prove that a quadrilateral with certain properties is a parallelogram.

THEOREMS *For Your Notebook*

THEOREM 8.7

If both pairs of opposite sides of a quadrilateral are congruent, then the quadrilateral is a parallelogram.

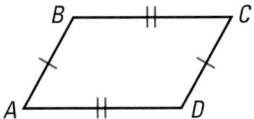

If $\overline{AB} \cong \overline{CD}$ and $\overline{BC} \cong \overline{AD}$, then *ABCD* is a parallelogram.

Proof: below

THEOREM 8.8

If both pairs of opposite angles of a quadrilateral are congruent, then the quadrilateral is a parallelogram.

If $\angle A \cong \angle C$ and $\angle B \cong \angle D$, then *ABCD* is a parallelogram.

Proof: Ex. 38, p. 529

PROOF Theorem 8.7

GIVEN ▶ $\overline{AB} \cong \overline{CD}$, $\overline{BC} \cong \overline{AD}$

PROVE ▶ *ABCD* is a parallelogram.

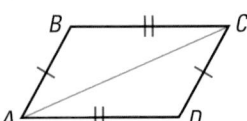

Proof Draw $\overline{AC}$, forming $\triangle ABC$ and $\triangle CDA$. You are given that $\overline{AB} \cong \overline{CD}$ and $\overline{BC} \cong \overline{AD}$. Also, $\overline{AC} \cong \overline{AC}$ by the Reflexive Property of Congruence. So, $\triangle ABC \cong \triangle CDA$ by the SSS Congruence Postulate. Because corresponding parts of congruent triangles are congruent, $\angle BAC \cong \angle DCA$ and $\angle BCA \cong DAC$. Then, by the Alternate Interior Angles Converse, $\overline{AB} \parallel \overline{CD}$ and $\overline{BC} \parallel \overline{AD}$. By definition, *ABCD* is a parallelogram.

EXAMPLE 1 **Solve a real-world problem**

RIDE An amusement park ride has a moving platform attached to four swinging arms. The platform swings back and forth, higher and higher, until it goes over the top and around in a circular motion. In the diagram below, $\overline{AD}$ and $\overline{BC}$ represent two of the swinging arms, and $\overline{DC}$ is parallel to the ground (line ℓ). *Explain* why the moving platform $\overline{AB}$ is always parallel to the ground.

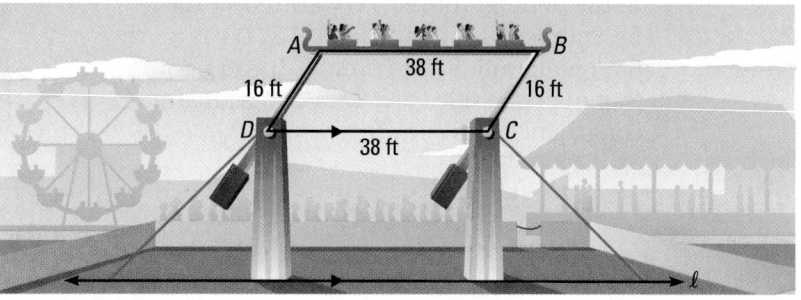

Solution

The shape of quadrilateral *ABCD* changes as the moving platform swings around, but its side lengths do not change. Both pairs of opposite sides are congruent, so *ABCD* is a parallelogram by Theorem 8.7.

By the definition of a parallelogram, $\overline{AB} \parallel \overline{DC}$. Because $\overline{DC}$ is parallel to line ℓ, $\overline{AB}$ is also parallel to line ℓ by the Transitive Property of Parallel Lines. So, the moving platform is parallel to the ground.

✓ **GUIDED PRACTICE** | **for Example 1**

1. In quadrilateral *WXYZ*, $m\angle W = 42°$, $m\angle X = 138°$, $m\angle Y = 42°$. Find $m\angle Z$. Is *WXYZ* a parallelogram? *Explain* your reasoning.

THEOREMS *For Your Notebook*

THEOREM 8.9

If one pair of opposite sides of a quadrilateral are congruent and parallel, then the quadrilateral is a parallelogram.

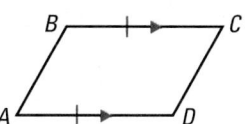

If $\overline{BC} \parallel \overline{AD}$ and $\overline{BC} \cong \overline{AD}$, then *ABCD* is a parallelogram.

Proof: Ex. 33, p. 528

THEOREM 8.10

If the diagonals of a quadrilateral bisect each other, then the quadrilateral is a parallelogram.

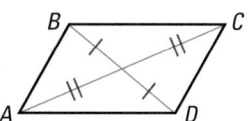

If $\overline{BD}$ and $\overline{AC}$ bisect each other, then *ABCD* is a parallelogram.

Proof: Ex. 39, p. 529

EXAMPLE 2 **Identify a parallelogram**

ARCHITECTURE The doorway shown is part of a building in England. Over time, the building has leaned sideways. *Explain* how you know that $SV = TU$.

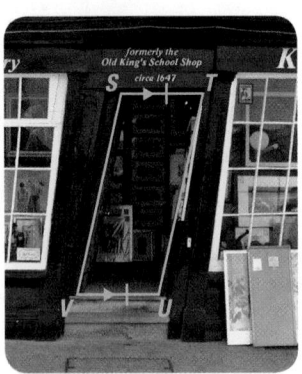

Solution

In the photograph, $\overline{ST} \parallel \overline{UV}$ and $\overline{ST} \cong \overline{UV}$. By Theorem 8.9, quadrilateral $STUV$ is a parallelogram. By Theorem 8.3, you know that opposite sides of a parallelogram are congruent. So, $SV = TU$.

EXAMPLE 3 **Use algebra with parallelograms**

xy ALGEBRA For what value of x is quadrilateral $CDEF$ a parallelogram?

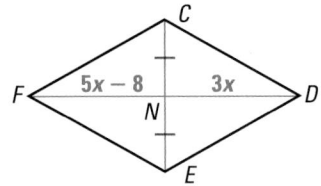

Solution

By Theorem 8.10, if the diagonals of $CDEF$ bisect each other, then it is a parallelogram. You are given that $\overline{CN} \cong \overline{EN}$. Find x so that $\overline{FN} \cong \overline{DN}$.

$FN = DN$	Set the segment lengths equal.
$5x - 8 = 3x$	Substitute $5x - 8$ for FN and $3x$ for DN.
$2x - 8 = 0$	Subtract $3x$ from each side.
$2x = 8$	Add 8 to each side.
$x = 4$	Divide each side by 2.

When $x = 4$, $FN = 5(4) - 8 = 12$ and $DN = 3(4) = 12$.

▶ Quadrilateral $CDEF$ is a parallelogram when $x = 4$.

✓ **GUIDED PRACTICE** **for Examples 2 and 3**

What theorem can you use to show that the quadrilateral is a parallelogram?

2.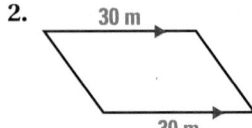

3.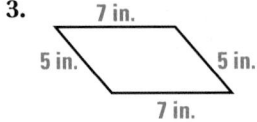

4.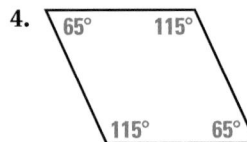

5. For what value of x is quadrilateral $MNPQ$ a parallelogram? *Explain* your reasoning.

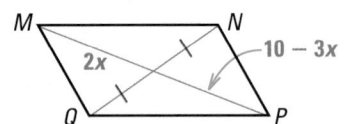

CONCEPT SUMMARY

For Your Notebook

Ways to Prove a Quadrilateral is a Parallelogram

1. Show both pairs of opposite sides are parallel.
   (DEFINITION)

   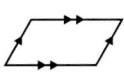

2. Show both pairs of opposite sides are congruent.
   (THEOREM 8.7)

   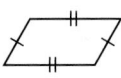

3. Show both pairs of opposite angles are congruent.
   (THEOREM 8.8)

   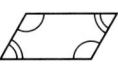

4. Show one pair of opposite sides are congruent and parallel.
   (THEOREM 8.9)

   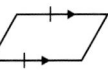

5. Show the diagonals bisect each other.
   (THEOREM 8.10)

EXAMPLE 4   Use coordinate geometry

Show that quadrilateral *ABCD* is a parallelogram.

ANOTHER WAY

For alternative methods for solving the problem in Example 4, turn to page 530 for the **Problem Solving Workshop**.

Solution

One way is to show that a pair of sides are congruent and parallel. Then apply Theorem 8.9.

First use the Distance Formula to show that $\overline{AB}$ and $\overline{CD}$ are congruent.

$$AB = \sqrt{[2 - (-3)]^2 + (5 - 3)^2} = \sqrt{29} \qquad CD = \sqrt{(5 - 0)^2 + (2 - 0)^2} = \sqrt{29}$$

Because $AB = CD = \sqrt{29}$, $\overline{AB} \cong \overline{CD}$.

Then use the slope formula to show that $\overline{AB} \parallel \overline{CD}$.

$$\text{Slope of } \overline{AB} = \frac{5 - (3)}{2 - (-3)} = \frac{2}{5} \qquad \text{Slope of } \overline{CD} = \frac{2 - 0}{5 - 0} = \frac{2}{5}$$

Because $\overline{AB}$ and $\overline{CD}$ have the same slope, they are parallel.

▶ $\overline{AB}$ and $\overline{CD}$ are congruent and parallel. So, *ABCD* is a parallelogram by Theorem 8.9.

 GUIDED PRACTICE   for Example 4

6. Refer to the Concept Summary above. *Explain* how other methods can be used to show that quadrilateral *ABCD* in Example 4 is a parallelogram.

8.3 EXERCISES

HOMEWORK KEY

○ = WORKED-OUT SOLUTIONS
on p. WS9 for Exs. 5, 11, and 31

★ = STANDARDIZED TEST PRACTICE
Exs. 2, 7, 18, and 37

SKILL PRACTICE

1. **VOCABULARY** *Explain* how knowing that $\overline{AB} \parallel \overline{CD}$ and $\overline{AD} \parallel \overline{BC}$ allows you to show that quadrilateral *ABCD* is a parallelogram.

2. ★ **WRITING** A quadrilateral has four congruent sides. Is the quadrilateral a parallelogram? *Justify* your answer.

3. **ERROR ANALYSIS** A student claims that because two pairs of sides are congruent, quadrilateral *DEFG* shown at the right is a parallelogram. *Describe* the error that the student is making.

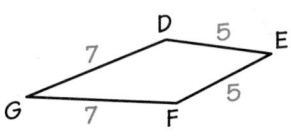

DEFG is a parallelogram.

EXAMPLES 1 and 2
on pp. 523–524
for Exs. 4–7

REASONING What theorem can you use to show that the quadrilateral is a parallelogram?

4.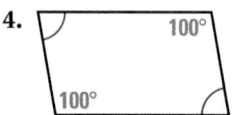

5.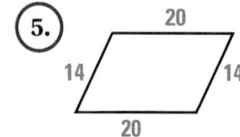

6.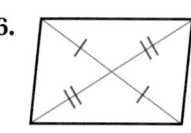

7. ★ **SHORT RESPONSE** When you shift gears on a bicycle, a mechanism called a *derailleur* moves the chain to a new gear. For the derailleur shown below, $JK = 5.5$ cm, $KL = 2$ cm, $ML = 5.5$ cm, and $MJ = 2$ cm. *Explain* why $\overline{JK}$ and $\overline{ML}$ are always parallel as the derailleur moves.

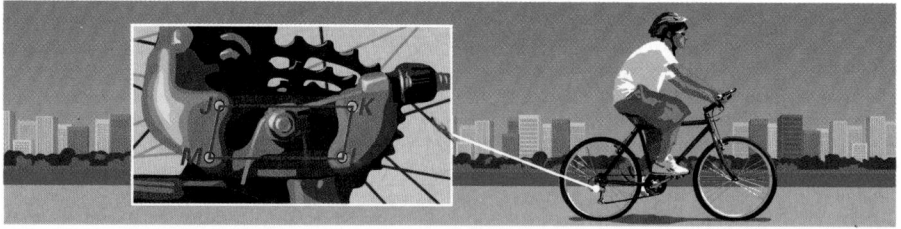

EXAMPLE 3
on p. 524
for Exs. 8–10

ALGEBRA For what value of *x* is the quadrilateral a parallelogram?

8.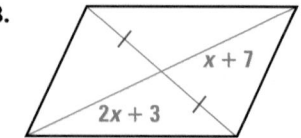

9.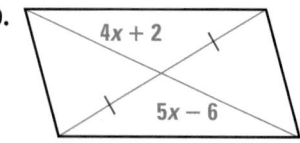

10.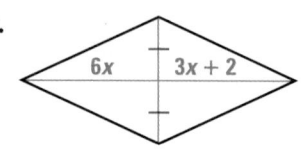

EXAMPLE 4
on p. 525
for Exs. 11–14

COORDINATE GEOMETRY The vertices of quadrilateral *ABCD* are given. Draw *ABCD* in a coordinate plane and show that it is a parallelogram.

11. $A(0, 1)$, $B(4, 4)$, $C(12, 4)$, $D(8, 1)$

12. $A(-3, 0)$, $B(-3, 4)$, $C(3, -1)$, $D(3, -5)$

13. $A(-2, 3)$, $B(-5, 7)$, $C(3, 6)$, $D(6, 2)$

14. $A(-5, 0)$, $B(0, 4)$, $C(3, 0)$, $D(-2, -4)$

REASONING *Describe* how to prove that *ABCD* is a parallelogram.

15.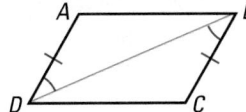

16.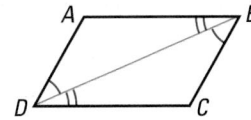

17.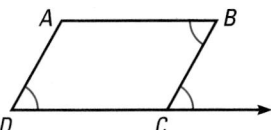

Animated Geometry at classzone.com

18. ★ **MULTIPLE CHOICE** In quadrilateral *WXYZ*, $\overline{WZ}$ and $\overline{XY}$ are congruent and parallel. Which statement below is not necessarily true?

Ⓐ $m\angle Y + m\angle W = 180°$

Ⓑ $\angle X \cong \angle Z$

Ⓒ $\overline{WX} \cong \overline{ZY}$

Ⓓ $\overline{WX} \parallel \overline{ZY}$

XV **ALGEBRA** For what value of *x* is the quadrilateral a parallelogram?

19.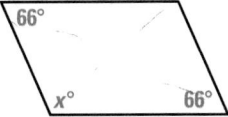

20.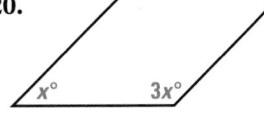

21.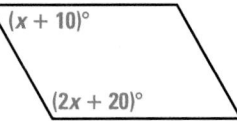

BICONDITIONALS Write the indicated theorems as a biconditional statement.

22. Theorem 8.3, page 515 and Theorem 8.7, page 522

23. Theorem 8.4, page 515 and Theorem 8.8, page 522

24. **REASONING** Follow the steps below to draw a parallelogram. *Explain* why this method works. State a theorem to support your answer.

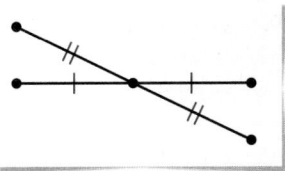

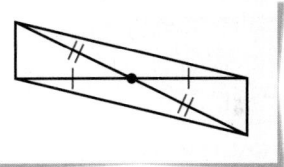

STEP 1 Use a ruler to draw two segments that intersect at their midpoints.

STEP 2 Connect the endpoints of the segments to form a quadrilateral.

COORDINATE GEOMETRY Three of the vertices of ▱*ABCD* are given. Find the coordinates of point *D*. Show your method.

25. $A(-2, -3)$, $B(4, -3)$, $C(3, 2)$, $D(x, y)$

26. $A(-4, 1)$, $B(-1, 5)$, $C(6, 5)$, $D(x, y)$

27. $A(-4, 4)$, $B(4, 6)$, $C(3, -1)$, $D(x, y)$

28. $A(-1, 0)$, $B(0, -4)$, $C(8, -6)$, $D(x, y)$

29. **CONSTRUCTION** There is more than one way to use a compass and a straightedge to construct a parallelogram. *Describe* a method that uses Theorem 8.7 or Theorem 8.9. Then use your method to construct a parallelogram.

30. **CHALLENGE** In the diagram, *ABCD* is a parallelogram, *BF* = *DE* = 12, and *CF* = 8. Find *AE*. *Explain* your reasoning.

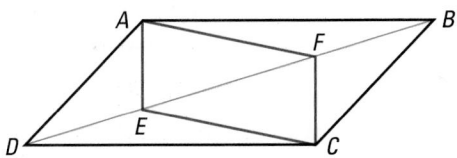

EXAMPLES
1 and 2
on pp. 523–524
for Exs. 31–32

31. **AUTOMOBILE REPAIR** The diagram shows an automobile lift. A bus drives on to the ramp ($\overline{EG}$). Levers ($\overline{EK}$, $\overline{FJ}$, and $\overline{GH}$) raise the bus. In the diagram, $\overline{EG} \cong \overline{KH}$ and $EK = FJ = GH$. Also, F is the midpoint of $\overline{EG}$, and J is the midpoint of $\overline{KH}$.

a. Identify all the quadrilaterals in the automobile lift. *Explain* how you know that each one is a parallelogram.

b. *Explain* why $\overline{EG}$ is always parallel to $\overline{KH}$.

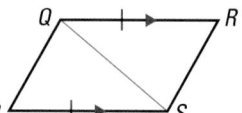

@HomeTutor for problem solving help at classzone.com

32. **MUSIC STAND** A music stand can be folded up, as shown below. In the diagrams, $\angle A \cong \angle EFD$, $\angle D \cong \angle AEF$, $\angle C \cong \angle BEF$, and $\angle B \cong \angle CFE$. *Explain* why $\overline{AD}$ and $\overline{BC}$ remain parallel as the stand is folded up. Which other labeled segments remain parallel?

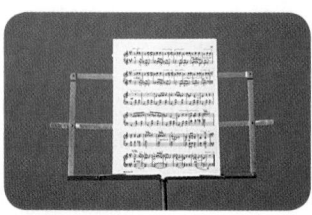 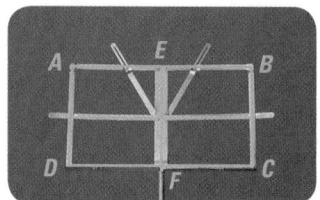 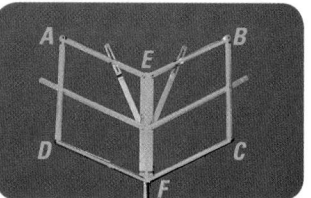

@HomeTutor for problem solving help at classzone.com

33. **PROVING THEOREM 8.9** Use the diagram of *PQRS* with the auxiliary line segment drawn. Copy and complete the flow proof of Theorem 8.9.

GIVEN ▶ $\overline{QR} \parallel \overline{PS}$, $\overline{QR} \cong \overline{PS}$

PROVE ▶ *PQRS* is a parallelogram.

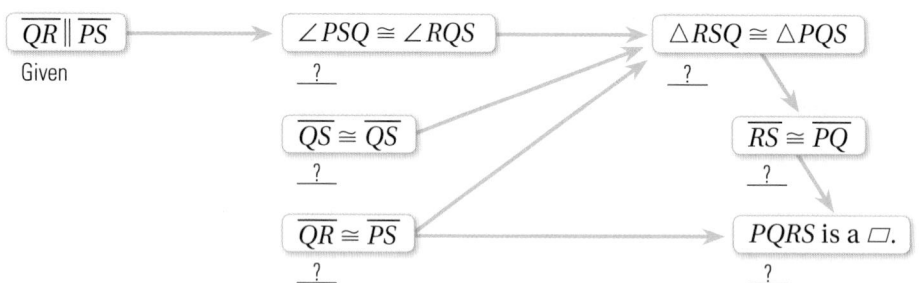

$\overline{QR} \parallel \overline{PS}$	$\angle PSQ \cong \angle RQS$	$\triangle RSQ \cong \triangle PQS$
Given	___?___	___?___
	$\overline{QS} \cong \overline{QS}$	$\overline{RS} \cong \overline{PQ}$
	___?___	___?___
	$\overline{QR} \cong \overline{PS}$	*PQRS* is a ▱.
	___?___	___?___

REASONING A student claims incorrectly that the marked information can be used to show that the figure is a parallelogram. Draw a quadrilateral with the marked properties that is clearly *not* a parallelogram. *Explain*.

34.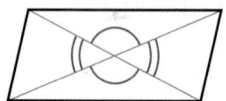

35.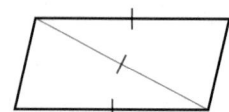

36.

○ = **WORKED-OUT SOLUTIONS**
on p. WS1

★ = **STANDARDIZED**
TEST PRACTICE

37. ★ **EXTENDED RESPONSE** Theorem 8.5 states that if a quadrilateral is a parallelogram, then its consecutive angles are supplementary. Write the converse of Theorem 8.5. Then write a plan for proving the converse of Theorem 8.5. Include a diagram.

38. **PROVING THEOREM 8.8** Prove Theorem 8.8.

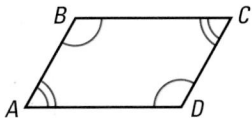

> **GIVEN** ▶ $\angle A \cong \angle C$, $\angle B \cong \angle D$
> **PROVE** ▶ $ABCD$ is a parallelogram.

Hint: Let $x°$ represent $m\angle A$ and $m\angle C$, and let $y°$ represent $m\angle B$ and $m\angle D$. Write and simplify an equation involving x and y.

39. **PROVING THEOREM 8.10** Prove Theorem 8.10.

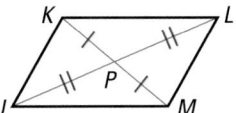

> **GIVEN** ▶ Diagonals $\overline{JL}$ and $\overline{KM}$ bisect each other.
> **PROVE** ▶ $JKLM$ is a parallelogram.

40. **PROOF** Use the diagram at the right.

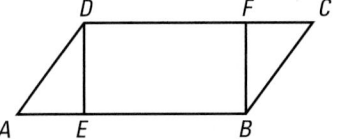

> **GIVEN** ▶ $DEBF$ is a parallelogram, $AE = CF$
> **PROVE** ▶ $ABCD$ is a parallelogram.

41. **REASONING** In the diagram, the midpoints of the sides of a quadrilateral have been joined to form what appears to be a parallelogram. Show that a quadrilateral formed by connecting the midpoints of the sides of any quadrilateral is *always* a parallelogram. (*Hint:* Draw a diagram. Include a diagonal of the larger quadrilateral. Show how two sides of the smaller quadrilateral are related to the diagonal.)

42. **CHALLENGE** Show that if $ABCD$ is a parallelogram with its diagonals intersecting at E, then you can connect the midpoints F, G, H, and J of $\overline{AE}$, $\overline{BE}$, $\overline{CE}$, and $\overline{DE}$, respectively, to form another parallelogram, $FGHJ$.

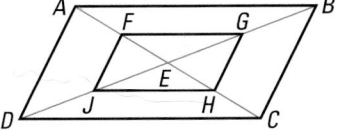

MIXED REVIEW

PREVIEW
Prepare for
Lesson 8.4
in Exs. 43–45.

In Exercises 43–45, draw a figure that fits the description. *(p. 42)*

43. A quadrilateral that is equilateral but not equiangular

44. A quadrilateral that is equiangular but not equilateral

45. A quadrilateral that is concave

46. The width of a rectangle is 4 centimeters less than its length. The perimeter of the rectangle is 42 centimeters. Find its area. *(p. 49)*

47. Find the values of x and y in the triangle shown at the right. Write your answers in simplest radical form. *(p. 457)*

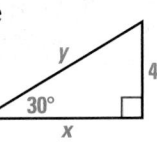

PROBLEM SOLVING WORKSHOP

LESSON 8.3

Using ALTERNATIVE METHODS

Another Way to Solve Example 4, page 525

MULTIPLE REPRESENTATIONS In Example 4 on page 525, the problem is solved by showing that one pair of opposite sides are congruent and parallel using the Distance Formula and the slope formula. There are other ways to show that a quadrilateral is a parallelogram.

PROBLEM

Show that quadrilateral *ABCD* is a parallelogram.

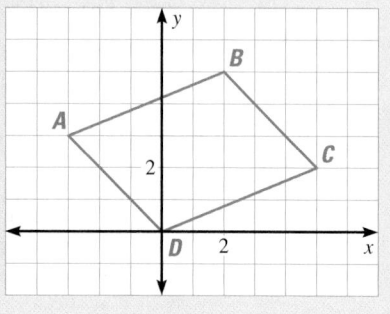

METHOD 1

Use Opposite Sides You can show that both pairs of opposite sides are congruent.

STEP 1 Draw two right triangles. Use $\overline{AB}$ as the hypotenuse of $\triangle AEB$ and $\overline{CD}$ as the hypotenuse of $\triangle CFD$.

STEP 2 Show that $\triangle AEB \cong \triangle CFD$. From the graph, $AE = 2$, $BE = 5$, and $\angle E$ is a right angle. Similarly, $CF = 2$, $DF = 5$, and $\angle F$ is a right angle. So, $\triangle AEB \cong \triangle CFD$ by the SAS Congruence Postulate.

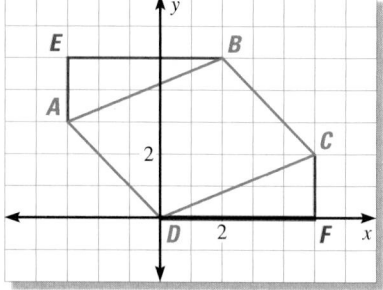

STEP 3 Use the fact that corresponding parts of congruent triangles are congruent to show that $\overline{AB} \cong \overline{CD}$.

STEP 4 Repeat Steps 1–3 for sides $\overline{AD}$ and $\overline{BC}$. You can prove that $\triangle AHD \cong \triangle CGB$. So, $\overline{AD} \cong \overline{CB}$.

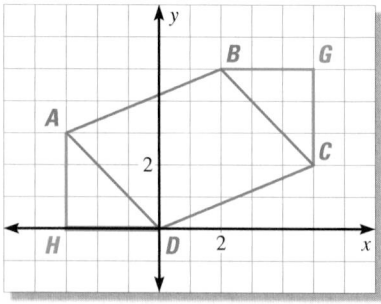

▶ The pairs of opposite sides, $\overline{AB}$ and $\overline{CD}$ and $\overline{AD}$ and $\overline{CB}$, are congruent. So, *ABCD* is a parallelogram by Theorem 8.7.

METHOD 2 **Use Diagonals** You can show that the diagonals bisect each other.

STEP 1 **Use** the Midpoint Formula to find the midpoint of diagonal $\overline{AC}$.

The coordinates of the endpoints of $\overline{AC}$ are $A(-3, 3)$ and $C(5, 2)$.

$$\left(\frac{x_1 + x_2}{2}, \frac{y_1 + y_2}{2}\right) = \left(\frac{-3 + 5}{2}, \frac{3 + 2}{2}\right) = \left(\frac{2}{2}, \frac{5}{2}\right) = \left(1, \frac{5}{2}\right)$$

STEP 2 **Use** the Midpoint Formula to find the midpoint of diagonal $\overline{BD}$.

The coordinates of the endpoints of $\overline{BD}$ are $B(2, 5)$ and $D(0, 0)$.

$$\left(\frac{x_1 + x_2}{2}, \frac{y_1 + y_2}{2}\right) = \left(\frac{2 + 0}{2}, \frac{5 + 0}{2}\right) = \left(\frac{2}{2}, \frac{5}{2}\right) = M\left(1, \frac{5}{2}\right)$$

▶ Because the midpoints of both diagonals are the same point, the diagonals bisect each other. So, *ABCD* is a parallelogram by Theorem 8.10.

PRACTICE

1. **SLOPE** Show that quadrilateral *ABCD* in the problem on page 530 is a parallelogram by showing that both pairs of opposite sides are parallel.

2. **PARALLELOGRAMS** Use two methods to show that *EFGH* is a parallelogram.

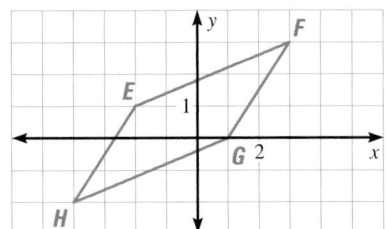

3. **MAP** Do the four towns on the map form the vertices of a parallelogram? *Explain.*

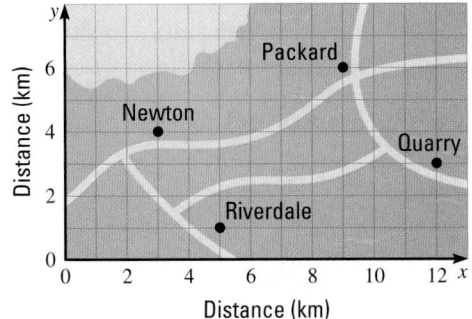

4. **QUADRILATERALS** Is the quadrilateral a parallelogram? *Justify* your answer.

   a. $A(1, 0)$, $B(5, 0)$, $C(7, 2)$, $D(3, 2)$

   b. $E(3, 4)$ $F(6, 8)$, $G(9, 5)$, $H(6, 0)$

   c. $J(-1, 0)$, $K(2, -2)$, $L(2, 2)$, $M(-1, 4)$

5. **ERROR ANALYSIS** Quadrilateral *PQRS* has vertices $P(2, 2)$, $Q(3, 4)$, $R(6, 5)$, and $S(5, 3)$. A student makes the conclusion below. *Describe* and correct the error(s) made by the student.

   $\overline{PQ}$ and $\overline{QR}$ are opposite sides, so they should be congruent.

   $PQ = \sqrt{(3 - 2)^2 + (4 - 2)^2} = \sqrt{5}$

   $QR = \sqrt{(6 - 3)^2 + (5 - 4)^2} = \sqrt{10}$

   But $\overline{PQ} \not\cong \overline{QR}$. So, *PQRS* is not a parallelogram.

   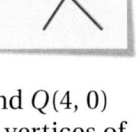

6. **WRITING** Points $O(0, 0)$, $P(3, 5)$, and $Q(4, 0)$ are vertices of $\triangle OPQ$, and are also vertices of a parallelogram. Find all points *R* that could be the other vertex of the parallelogram. *Explain* your reasoning.

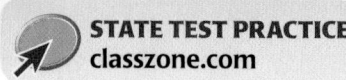
Lessons 8.1–8.3

1. **MULTI-STEP PROBLEM** The shape of Iowa can be approximated by a polygon, as shown.

IOWA

Des Moines
★

   a. How many sides does the polygon have? Classify the polygon.

   b. What is the sum of the measures of the interior angles of the polygon?

   c. What is the sum of the measures of the exterior angles of the polygon?

2. **SHORT RESPONSE** A graphic designer is creating an electronic image of a house. In the drawing, $\angle B$, $\angle D$, and $\angle E$ are right angles, and $\angle A \cong \angle C$. *Explain* how to find $m\angle A$ and $m\angle C$.

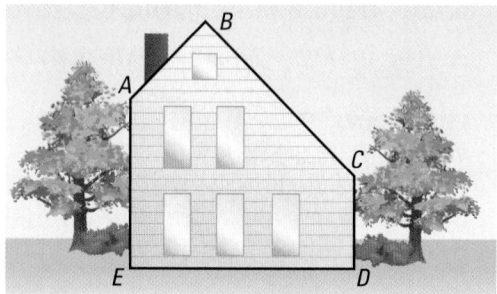

3. **SHORT RESPONSE** Quadrilateral *STUV* shown below is a parallelogram. Find the values of *x* and *y*. *Explain* your reasoning.

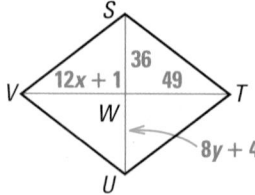

4. **GRIDDED ANSWER** A convex decagon has interior angles with measures 157°, 128°, 115°, 162°, 169°, 131°, 155°, 168°, *x*°, and 2*x*°. Find the value of *x*.

5. **SHORT RESPONSE** The measure of an angle of a parallelogram is 12 degrees less than 3 times the measure of an adjacent angle. *Explain* how to find the measures of all the interior angles of the parallelogram.

6. **EXTENDED RESPONSE** A stand to hold binoculars in place uses a quadrilateral in its design. Quadrilateral *EFGH* shown below changes shape as the binoculars are moved. In the photograph, $\overline{EF}$ and $\overline{GH}$ are congruent and parallel.

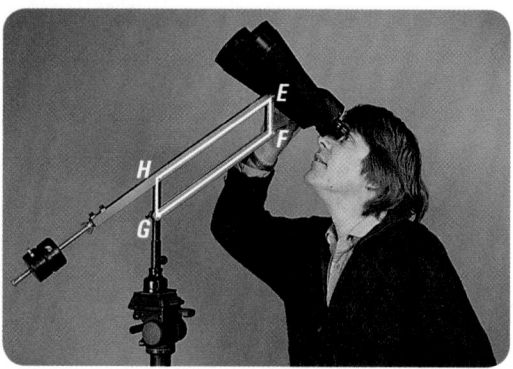

   a. *Explain* why $\overline{EF}$ and $\overline{GH}$ remain parallel as the shape of *EFGH* changes. *Explain* why $\overline{EH}$ and $\overline{FG}$ remain parallel.

   b. As *EFGH* changes shape, $m\angle E$ changes from 55° to 50°. *Describe* how $m\angle F$, $m\angle G$, and $m\angle H$ will change. *Explain*.

7. **EXTENDED RESPONSE** The vertices of quadrilateral *MNPQ* are $M(-8, 1)$, $N(3, 4)$, $P(7, -1)$, and $Q(-4, -4)$.

   a. Use what you know about slopes of lines to prove that *MNPQ* is a parallelogram. *Explain* your reasoning.

   b. Use the Distance Formula to show that *MNPQ* is a parallelogram. *Explain*.

8. **EXTENDED RESPONSE** In $\square ABCD$, $\overline{BX} \perp \overline{AC}$, $\overline{DY} \perp \overline{AC}$. Show that *XBYD* is a parallelogram.

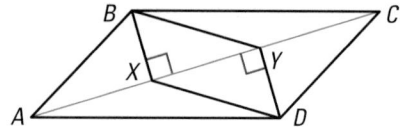

8.4 Properties of Rhombuses, Rectangles, and Squares

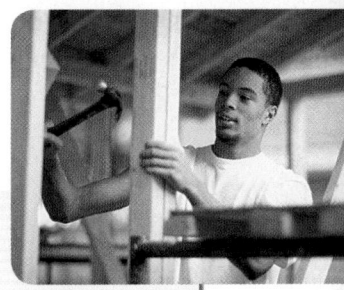

Before	You used properties of parallelograms.
Now	You will use properties of rhombuses, rectangles, and squares.
Why?	So you can solve a carpentry problem, as in Example 4.

Key Vocabulary
• rhombus
• rectangle
• square

In this lesson, you will learn about three special types of parallelograms: *rhombuses*, *rectangles*, and *squares*.

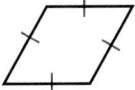

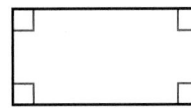

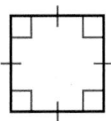

A rhombus is a parallelogram with four congruent sides.

A rectangle is a parallelogram with four right angles.

A square is a parallelogram with four congruent sides and four right angles.

You can use the corollaries below to prove that a quadrilateral is a rhombus, rectangle, or square, without first proving that the quadrilateral is a parallelogram.

COROLLARIES
For Your Notebook

RHOMBUS COROLLARY

A quadrilateral is a rhombus if and only if it has four congruent sides.

ABCD is a rhombus if and only if $\overline{AB} \cong \overline{BC} \cong \overline{CD} \cong \overline{AD}$.

Proof: Ex. 57, p. 539

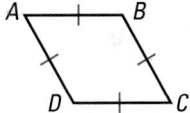

RECTANGLE COROLLARY

A quadrilateral is a rectangle if and only if it has four right angles.

ABCD is a rectangle if and only if $\angle A$, $\angle B$, $\angle C$, and $\angle D$ are right angles.

Proof: Ex. 58, p. 539

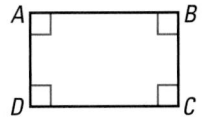

SQUARE COROLLARY

A quadrilateral is a square if and only if it is a rhombus and a rectangle.

ABCD is a square if and only if $\overline{AB} \cong \overline{BC} \cong \overline{CD} \cong \overline{AD}$ and $\angle A$, $\angle B$, $\angle C$, and $\angle D$ are right angles.

Proof: Ex. 59, p. 539

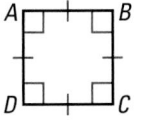

The *Venn diagram* below illustrates some important relationships among parallelograms, rhombuses, rectangles, and squares. For example, you can see that a square is a rhombus because it is a parallelogram with four congruent sides. Because it has four right angles, a square is also a rectangle.

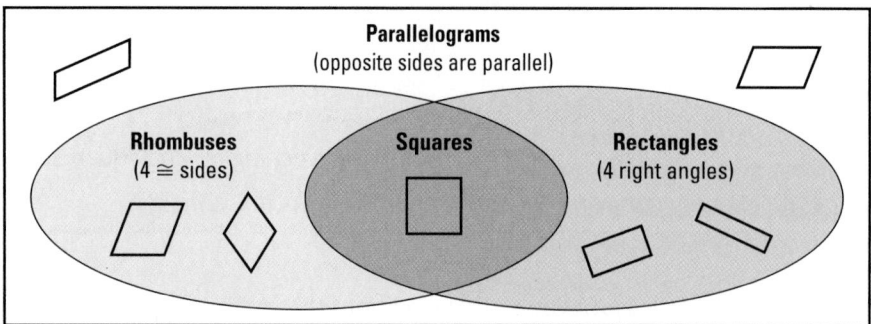

Parallelograms
(opposite sides are parallel)

Rhombuses
(4 ≅ sides)

Squares

Rectangles
(4 right angles)

EXAMPLE 1 **Use properties of special quadrilaterals**

For any rhombus *QRST*, decide whether the statement is *always* or *sometimes* true. Draw a sketch and explain your reasoning.

a. ∠*Q* ≅ ∠*S*   **b.** ∠*Q* ≅ ∠*R*

Solution

a. By definition, a rhombus is a parallelogram with four congruent sides. By Theorem 8.4, opposite angles of a parallelogram are congruent. So, ∠*Q* ≅ ∠*S*. The statement is *always* true.

b. If rhombus *QRST* is a square, then all four angles are congruent right angles. So, ∠*Q* ≅ ∠*R* if *QRST* is a square. Because not all rhombuses are also squares, the statement is *sometimes* true.

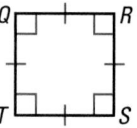

EXAMPLE 2 **Classify special quadrilaterals**

Classify the special quadrilateral. Explain your reasoning.

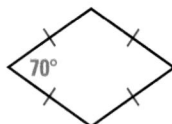

70°

Solution

The quadrilateral has four congruent sides. One of the angles is not a right angle, so the rhombus is not also a square. By the Rhombus Corollary, the quadrilateral is a rhombus.

✓ **GUIDED PRACTICE** | for Examples 1 and 2

1. For any rectangle *EFGH*, is it *always* or *sometimes* true that $\overline{FG} \cong \overline{GH}$? *Explain* your reasoning.

2. A quadrilateral has four congruent sides and four congruent angles. Sketch the quadrilateral and classify it.

DIAGONALS The theorems below describe some properties of the diagonals of rhombuses and rectangles.

THEOREM 8.11

A parallelogram is a rhombus if and only if its diagonals are perpendicular.

▱*ABCD* is a rhombus if and only if $\overline{AC} \perp \overline{BD}$.

Proof: p. 536; Ex. 56, p. 539

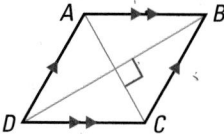

THEOREM 8.12

A parallelogram is a rhombus if and only if each diagonal bisects a pair of opposite angles.

▱*ABCD* is a rhombus if and only if $\overline{AC}$ bisects ∠*BCD* and ∠*BAD* and $\overline{BD}$ bisects ∠*ABC* and ∠*ADC*.

Proof: Exs. 60–61, p. 539

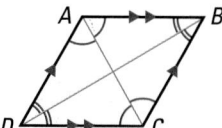

THEOREM 8.13

A parallelogram is a rectangle if and only if its diagonals are congruent.

▱*ABCD* is a rectangle if and only if $\overline{AC} \cong \overline{BD}$.

Proof: Exs. 63–64, p. 540

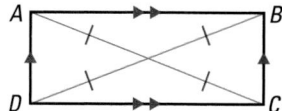

EXAMPLE 3   **List properties of special parallelograms**

Sketch rectangle *ABCD*. List everything that you know about it.

Solution

By definition, you need to draw a figure with the following properties:

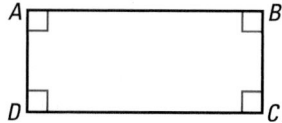

- The figure is a parallelogram.
- The figure has four right angles.

Because *ABCD* is a parallelogram, it also has these properties:

- Opposite sides are parallel and congruent.
- Opposite angles are congruent. Consecutive angles are supplementary.
- Diagonals bisect each other.

By Theorem 8.13, the diagonals of *ABCD* are congruent.

Animated Geometry at classzone.com

✓ **GUIDED PRACTICE**   for Example 3

3. Sketch square *PQRS*. List everything you know about the square.

BICONDITIONALS Recall that biconditionals such as Theorem 8.11 can be rewritten as two parts. To prove a biconditional, you must prove both parts.

Conditional statement If the diagonals of a parallelogram are perpendicular, then the parallelogram is a rhombus.

Converse If a parallelogram is a rhombus, then its diagonals are perpendicular.

PROOF Part of Theorem 8.11

PROVE THEOREMS
You will prove the other part of Theorem 8.11 in Exercise 56 on page 539.

If the diagonals of a parallelogram are perpendicular, then the parallelogram is a rhombus.

GIVEN ▶ *ABCD* is a parallelogram; $\overline{AC} \perp \overline{BD}$
PROVE ▶ *ABCD* is a rhombus.

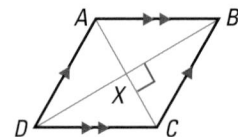

Proof *ABCD* is a parallelogram, so $\overline{AC}$ and $\overline{BD}$ bisect each other, and $\overline{BX} \cong \overline{DX}$. Also, $\angle BXC$ and $\angle CXD$ are congruent right angles, and $\overline{CX} \cong \overline{CX}$. So, $\triangle BXC \cong \triangle DXC$ by the SAS Congruence Postulate. Corresponding parts of congruent triangles are congruent, so $\overline{BC} \cong \overline{DC}$. Opposite sides of a $\square ABCD$ are congruent, so $\overline{AD} \cong \overline{BC} \cong \overline{DC} \cong \overline{AB}$. By definition, *ABCD* is a rhombus.

EXAMPLE 4 Solve a real-world problem

CARPENTRY You are building a frame for a window. The window will be installed in the opening shown in the diagram.

a. The opening must be a rectangle. Given the measurements in the diagram, can you assume that it is? *Explain.*

b. You measure the diagonals of the opening. The diagonals are 54.8 inches and 55.3 inches. What can you conclude about the shape of the opening?

Solution

a. No, you cannot. The boards on opposite sides are the same length, so they form a parallelogram. But you do not know whether the angles are right angles.

b. By Theorem 8.13, the diagonals of a rectangle are congruent. The diagonals of the quadrilateral formed by the boards are not congruent, so the boards do not form a rectangle.

✓ **GUIDED PRACTICE** for Example 4

4. Suppose you measure only the diagonals of a window opening. If the diagonals have the same measure, can you conclude that the opening is a rectangle? *Explain.*

8.4 EXERCISES

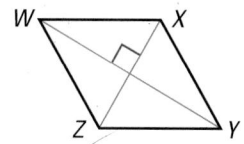
SKILL PRACTICE

1. **VOCABULARY** What is another name for an equilateral rectangle?

2. ★ **WRITING** Do you have enough information to identify the figure at the right as a rhombus? *Explain.*

EXAMPLES
1, 2, and 3
on pp. 534–535
for Exs. 3–25

RHOMBUSES For any rhombus *JKLM*, decide whether the statement is *always* or *sometimes* true. Draw a diagram and *explain* your reasoning.

3. $\angle L \cong \angle M$

4. $\angle K \cong \angle M$

5. $\overline{JK} \cong \overline{KL}$

6. $\overline{JM} \cong \overline{KL}$

7. $\overline{JL} \cong \overline{KM}$

8. $\angle JKM \cong \angle LKM$

RECTANGLES For any rectangle *WXYZ*, decide whether the statement is *always* or *sometimes* true. Draw a diagram and *explain* your reasoning.

9. $\angle W \cong \angle X$

10. $\overline{WX} \cong \overline{YZ}$

11. $\overline{WX} \cong \overline{XY}$

12. $\overline{WY} \cong \overline{XZ}$

13. $\overline{WY} \perp \overline{XZ}$

14. $\angle WXZ \cong \angle YXZ$

CLASSIFYING Classify the quadrilateral. *Explain* your reasoning.

15.

16.

17.

18. **USING PROPERTIES** Sketch rhombus *STUV. Describe* everything you know about the rhombus.

USING PROPERTIES Name each quadrilateral—*parallelogram, rectangle, rhombus,* and *square*—for which the statement is true.

19. It is equiangular.

20. It is equiangular and equilateral.

21. Its diagonals are perpendicular.

22. Opposite sides are congruent.

23. The diagonals bisect each other.

24. The diagonals bisect opposite angles.

25. **ERROR ANALYSIS** Quadrilateral *PQRS* is a rectangle. *Describe* and correct the error made in finding the value of *x*.

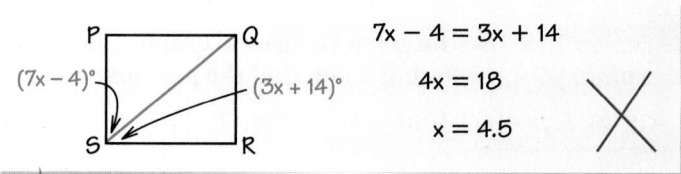

ALGEBRA Classify the special quadrilateral. *Explain* your reasoning. Then find the values of *x* and *y*.

26.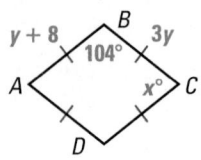

27.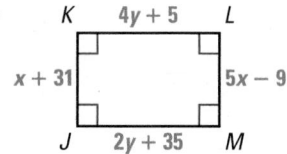

28.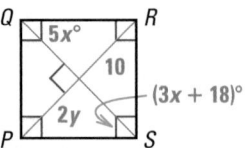

29.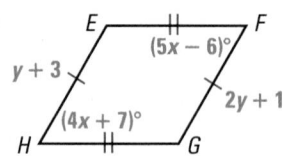

30. ★ **SHORT RESPONSE** The diagonals of a rhombus are 6 inches and 8 inches. What is the perimeter of the rhombus? *Explain.*

31. ★ **MULTIPLE CHOICE** Rectangle *ABCD* is similar to rectangle *FGHJ*. If *AC* = 5, *CD* = 4, and *FM* = 5, what is *HJ*?

    (A) 4   **(B)** 5

    (C) 8   **(D)** 10

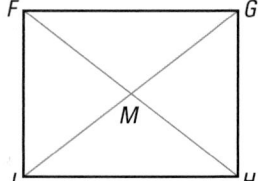

RHOMBUS The diagonals of rhombus *ABCD* intersect at *E*. Given that $m\angle BAC = 53°$ and *DE* = 8, find the indicated measure.

32. $m\angle DAC$ 33. $m\angle AED$

34. $m\angle ADC$ 35. *DB*

36. *AE*   37. *AC*

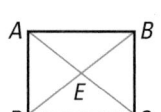

RECTANGLE The diagonals of rectangle *QRST* intersect at *P*. Given that $m\angle PTS = 34°$ and *QS* = 10, find the indicated measure.

38. $m\angle SRT$ 39. $m\angle QPR$

40. *QP*   41. *RP*

42. *QR*   43. *RS*

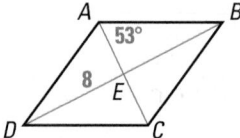

SQUARE The diagonals of square *LMNP* intersect at *K*. Given that *LK* = 1, find the indicated measure.

44. $m\angle MKN$ 45. $m\angle LMK$

46. $m\angle LPK$ 47. *KN*

48. *MP*   49. *LP*

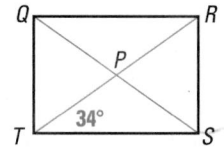

COORDINATE GEOMETRY Use the given vertices to graph ▱*JKLM*. Classify ▱*JKLM* and *explain* your reasoning. Then find the perimeter of ▱*JKLM*.

50. *J*(−4, 2), *K*(0, 3), *L*(1, −1), *M*(−3, −2)   51. *J*(−2, 7), *K*(7, 2), *L*(−2, −3), *M*(−11, 2)

○ = **WORKED-OUT SOLUTIONS** on p. WS1   ★ = **STANDARDIZED TEST PRACTICE**

52. REASONING Are all rhombuses similar? Are all squares similar? *Explain* your reasoning.

53. CHALLENGE Quadrilateral *ABCD* shown at the right is a rhombus. Given that *AC* = 10 and *BD* = 16, find all side lengths and angle measures. *Explain* your reasoning.

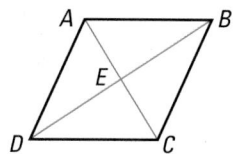

PROBLEM SOLVING

EXAMPLE 2
on p. 534
for Ex. 54

54. MULTI-STEP PROBLEM In the window shown at the right, $\overline{BD} \cong \overline{DF} \cong \overline{BH} \cong \overline{HF}$. Also, $\angle HAB$, $\angle BCD$, $\angle DEF$, and $\angle FGH$ are right angles.

a. Classify *HBDF* and *ACEG*. *Explain* your reasoning.

b. What can you conclude about the lengths of the diagonals $\overline{AE}$ and $\overline{GC}$? Given that these diagonals intersect at *J*, what can you conclude about the lengths of $\overline{AJ}$, $\overline{JE}$, $\overline{CJ}$, and $\overline{JG}$? *Explain*.

@HomeTutor for problem solving help at classzone.com

EXAMPLE 4
on p. 536
for Ex. 55

55. PATIO You want to mark off a square region in your yard for a patio. You use a tape measure to mark off a quadrilateral on the ground. Each side of the quadrilateral is 2.5 meters long. *Explain* how you can use the tape measure to make sure that the quadrilateral you drew is a square.

@HomeTutor for problem solving help at classzone.com

56. PROVING THEOREM 8.11 Use the plan for proof below to write a paragraph proof for the converse statement of Theorem 8.11.

GIVEN ▶ *ABCD* is a rhombus.
PROVE ▶ $\overline{AC} \perp \overline{BD}$

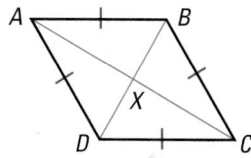

Plan for Proof Because *ABCD* is a parallelogram, its diagonals bisect each other at *X*. Show that $\triangle AXB \cong \triangle CXB$. Then show that $\overline{AC}$ and $\overline{BD}$ intersect to form congruent adjacent angles, $\angle AXB$ and $\angle CXB$.

PROVING COROLLARIES Write the corollary as a conditional statement and its converse. Then *explain* why each statement is true.

57. Rhombus Corollary   **58.** Rectangle Corollary   **59.** Square Corollary

PROVING THEOREM 8.12 In Exercises 60 and 61, prove both parts of Theorem 8.12.

60. GIVEN ▶ *PQRS* is a parallelogram.
$\overline{PR}$ bisects $\angle SPQ$ and $\angle QRS$.
$\overline{SQ}$ bisects $\angle PSR$ and $\angle RQP$.
PROVE ▶ *PQRS* is a rhombus.

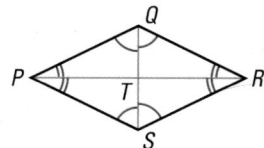

61. GIVEN ▶ *WXYZ* is a rhombus.
PROVE ▶ $\overline{WY}$ bisects $\angle ZWX$ and $\angle XYZ$.
$\overline{ZX}$ bisects $\angle WZY$ and $\angle YXW$.

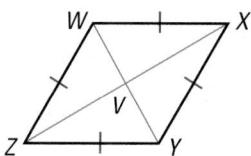

62. ★ **EXTENDED RESPONSE** In $ABCD$, $\overline{AB} \parallel \overline{CD}$, and $\overline{DB}$ bisects $\angle ADC$.

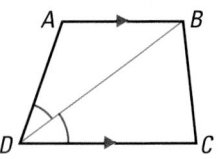

  a. Show that $\angle ABD \cong \angle CDB$. What can you conclude about $\angle ADB$ and $\angle ABD$? What can you conclude about $\overline{AB}$ and $\overline{AD}$? *Explain.*

  b. Suppose you also know that $\overline{AD} \parallel \overline{BC}$. Classify $ABCD$. *Explain.*

63. **PROVING THEOREM 8.13** Write a coordinate proof of the following statement, which is part of Theorem 8.13.

  If a quadrilateral is a rectangle, then its diagonals are congruent.

64. **CHALLENGE** Write a coordinate proof of part of Theorem 8.13.

  GIVEN ▶ $DFGH$ is a parallelogram, $\overline{DG} \cong \overline{HF}$

  PROVE ▶ $DFGH$ is a rectangle.

  Plan for Proof Write the coordinates of the vertices in terms of a and b. Find and compare the slopes of the sides.

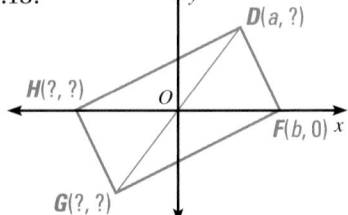

MIXED REVIEW

PREVIEW

Prepare for Lesson 8.5 in Ex. 65.

65. In $\triangle JKL$, $KL = 54.2$ centimeters. Point M is the midpoint of $\overline{JK}$ and N is the midpoint of $\overline{JL}$. Find MN. *(p. 295)*

Find the sine and cosine of the indicated angle. Write each answer as a fraction and a decimal. *(p. 473)*

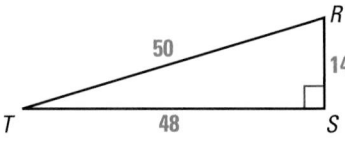

66. $\angle R$ **67.** $\angle T$

Find the value of x. *(p. 507)*

68.   **69.**   **70.**

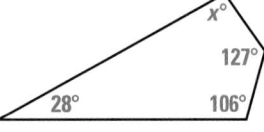      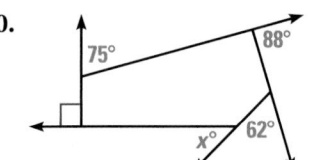

QUIZ *for Lessons 8.3–8.4*

For what value of x is the quadrilateral a parallelogram? *(p. 522)*

1.   **2.**   **3.**

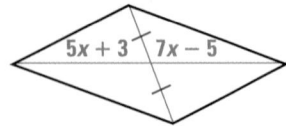   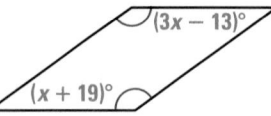   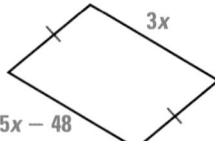

Classify the quadrilateral. *Explain* **your reasoning.** *(p. 533)*

4.   **5.**   **6.**

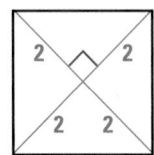   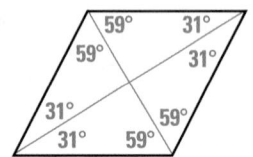   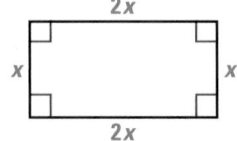

8.5 Midsegment of a Trapezoid

MATERIALS · graphing calculator or computer

QUESTION What are the properties of the midsegment of a trapezoid?

You can use geometry drawing software to investigate properties
of trapezoids.

EXPLORE Draw a trapezoid and its midsegment

STEP 1 *Draw parallel lines* Draw $\overleftrightarrow{AB}$. Draw a point C
not on $\overleftrightarrow{AB}$ and construct a line parallel to $\overleftrightarrow{AB}$
through point C.

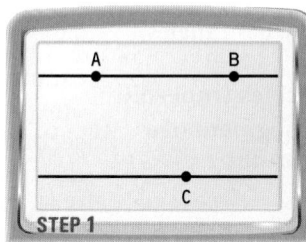

STEP 2 *Draw trapezoid* Construct a point D on the same
line as point C. Then draw $\overline{AD}$ and $\overline{BC}$ so that the
segments are not parallel. Draw $\overline{AB}$ and $\overline{DC}$.
Quadrilateral $ABCD$ is called a *trapezoid*. A trapezoid
is a quadrilateral with exactly one pair of parallel sides.

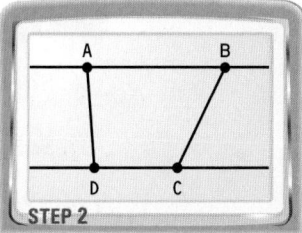

STEP 3 *Draw midsegment* Construct the midpoints of $\overline{AD}$ and
$\overline{BC}$. Label the points E and F. Draw $\overline{EF}$. $\overline{EF}$ is called a
midsegment of trapezoid $ABCD$. The midsegment of a
trapezoid connects the midpoints of its nonparallel sides.

STEP 4 *Measure lengths* Measure $\overline{AB}$, $\overline{DC}$, and $\overline{EF}$.

STEP 5 *Compare lengths* The average of AB and DC is $\frac{AB + DC}{2}$.
Calculate and compare this average to EF. What do you
notice? Drag point A or point B to change the shape of
trapezoid $ABCD$. Do not allow $\overline{AD}$ to intersect $\overline{BC}$. What
do you notice about EF and $\frac{AB + DC}{2}$?

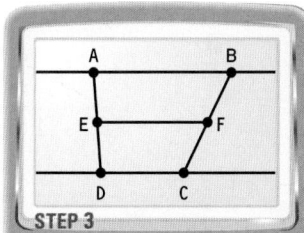

DRAW CONCLUSIONS Use your observations to complete these exercises

1. Make a conjecture about the length of the midsegment of a trapezoid.

2. The midsegment of a trapezoid is parallel to the two parallel sides of
   the trapezoid. What measurements could you make to show that the
   midsegment in the *Explore* is parallel to $\overline{AB}$ and $\overline{CD}$? *Explain.*

3. In Lesson 5.1 (page 295), you learned a theorem about the midsegment
   of a triangle. How is the midsegment of a trapezoid similar to the
   midsegment of a triangle? How is it different?

8.5 Use Properties of Trapezoids and Kites

Before You used properties of special parallelograms.

Now You will use properties of trapezoids and kites.

Why? So you can measure part of a building, as in Example 2.

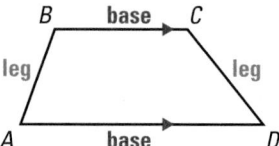

Key Vocabulary
- **trapezoid**
  bases, base angles, legs
- **isosceles trapezoid**
- **midsegment of a trapezoid**
- **kite**

A **trapezoid** is a quadrilateral with exactly one pair of parallel sides. The parallel sides are the **bases**.

A trapezoid has two pairs of **base angles**. For example, in trapezoid $ABCD$, $\angle A$ and $\angle D$ are one pair of base angles, and $\angle B$ and $\angle C$ are the second pair. The nonparallel sides are the **legs** of the trapezoid.

EXAMPLE 1 Use a coordinate plane

Show that *ORST* is a trapezoid.

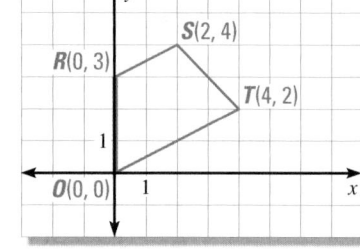

Solution

Compare the slopes of opposite sides.

Slope of $\overline{RS} = \dfrac{4-3}{2-0} = \dfrac{1}{2}$

Slope of $\overline{OT} = \dfrac{2-0}{4-0} = \dfrac{2}{4} = \dfrac{1}{2}$

The slopes of $\overline{RS}$ and $\overline{OT}$ are the same, so $\overline{RS} \parallel \overline{OT}$.

Slope of $\overline{ST} = \dfrac{2-4}{4-2} = \dfrac{-2}{2} = -1$

Slope of $\overline{OR} = \dfrac{3-0}{0-0} = \dfrac{3}{0}$, which is undefined.

The slopes of $\overline{ST}$ and $\overline{OR}$ are not the same, so $\overline{ST}$ is not parallel to $\overline{OR}$.

▶ Because quadrilateral $ORST$ has exactly one pair of parallel sides, it is a trapezoid.

✓ **GUIDED PRACTICE** for Example 1

1. **WHAT IF?** In Example 1, suppose the coordinates of point S are $(4, 5)$. What type of quadrilateral is $ORST$? *Explain.*

2. In Example 1, which of the interior angles of quadrilateral $ORST$ are supplementary angles? *Explain* your reasoning.

ISOSCELES TRAPEZOIDS If the legs of a trapezoid are congruent, then the trapezoid is an **isosceles trapezoid**.

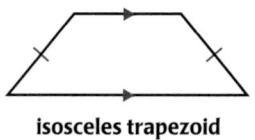

isosceles trapezoid

THEOREMS *For Your Notebook*

THEOREM 8.14

If a trapezoid is isosceles, then each pair of base angles is congruent.

If trapezoid *ABCD* is isosceles, then ∠*A* ≅ ∠*D* and ∠*B* ≅ ∠*C*.

Proof: Ex. 37, p. 548

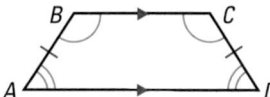

THEOREM 8.15

If a trapezoid has a pair of congruent base angles, then it is an isosceles trapezoid.

If ∠*A* ≅ ∠*D* (or if ∠*B* ≅ ∠*C*), then trapezoid *ABCD* is isosceles.

Proof: Ex. 38, p. 548

THEOREM 8.16

A trapezoid is isosceles if and only if its diagonals are congruent.

Trapezoid *ABCD* is isosceles if and only if $\overline{AC} \cong \overline{BD}$.

Proof: Exs. 39 and 43, p. 549

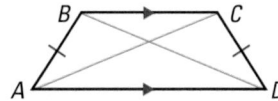

EXAMPLE 2 **Use properties of isosceles trapezoids**

ARCH The stone above the arch in the diagram is an isosceles trapezoid. Find *m*∠*K*, *m*∠*M*, and *m*∠*J*.

Solution

STEP 1 Find *m*∠*K*. *JKLM* is an isosceles trapezoid, so ∠*K* and ∠*L* are congruent base angles, and *m*∠*K* = *m*∠*L* = 85°.

STEP 2 Find *m*∠*M*. Because ∠*L* and ∠*M* are consecutive interior angles formed by $\overleftrightarrow{LM}$ intersecting two parallel lines, they are supplementary. So, *m*∠*M* = 180° − 85° = 95°.

STEP 3 Find *m*∠*J*. Because ∠*J* and ∠*M* are a pair of base angles, they are congruent, and *m*∠*J* = *m*∠*M* = 95°.

▶ So, *m*∠*J* = 95°, *m*∠*K* = 85°, and *m*∠*M* = 95°.

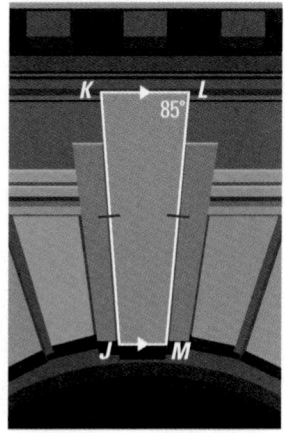

MIDSEGMENTS Recall that a midsegment of a triangle is a segment that connects the midpoints of two sides of the triangle. The **midsegment of a trapezoid** is the segment that connects the midpoints of its legs.

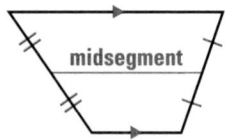

The theorem below is similar to the Midsegment Theorem for Triangles.

THEOREM *For Your Notebook*

THEOREM 8.17 Midsegment Theorem for Trapezoids

The midsegment of a trapezoid is parallel to each base and its length is one half the sum of the lengths of the bases.

If $\overline{MN}$ is the midsegment of trapezoid $ABCD$, then $\overline{MN} \parallel \overline{AB}$, $\overline{MN} \parallel \overline{DC}$, and $MN = \frac{1}{2}(AB + CD)$.

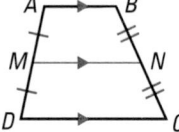

Justification: Ex. 40, p. 549
Proof: p. 937

EXAMPLE 3 **Use the midsegment of a trapezoid**

In the diagram, $\overline{MN}$ is the midsegment of trapezoid $PQRS$. Find MN.

Solution

Use Theorem 8.17 to find MN.

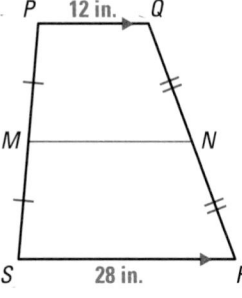

$MN = \frac{1}{2}(PQ + SR)$ **Apply Theorem 8.17.**

$\quad = \frac{1}{2}(12 + 28)$ **Substitute 12 for PQ and 28 for XU.**

$\quad = 20$ **Simplify.**

▶ The length MN is 20 inches.

✓ **GUIDED PRACTICE**   for Examples 2 and 3

In Exercises 3 and 4, use the diagram of trapezoid $EFGH$.

3. If $EG = FH$, is trapezoid $EFGH$ isosceles? *Explain.*

4. If $m\angle HEF = 70°$ and $m\angle FGH = 110°$, is trapezoid $EFGH$ isosceles? *Explain.*

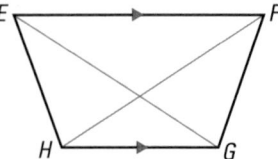

5. In trapezoid $JKLM$, $\angle J$ and $\angle M$ are right angles, and $JK = 9$ cm. The length of the midsegment $\overline{NP}$ of trapezoid $JKLM$ is 12 cm. Sketch trapezoid $JKLM$ and its midsegment. Find ML. *Explain* your reasoning.

KITES A **kite** is a quadrilateral that has two pairs of consecutive congruent sides, but opposite sides are not congruent.

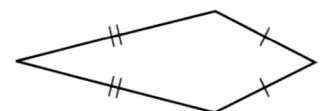

THEOREM 8.18

If a quadrilateral is a kite, then its diagonals are perpendicular.

If quadrilateral *ABCD* is a kite, then $\overline{AC} \perp \overline{BD}$.

Proof: Ex. 41, p. 549

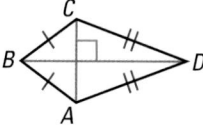

THEOREM 8.19

If a quadrilateral is a kite, then exactly one pair of opposite angles are congruent.

If quadrilateral *ABCD* is a kite and $\overline{BC} \cong \overline{BA}$, then $\angle A \cong \angle C$ and $\angle B \not\cong \angle D$.

Proof: Ex. 42, p. 549

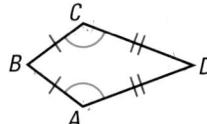

EXAMPLE 4   **Apply Theorem 8.19**

Find $m\angle D$ in the kite shown at the right.

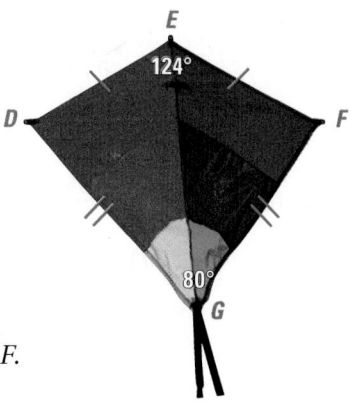

Solution

By Theorem 8.19, *DEFG* has exactly one pair of congruent opposite angles. Because $\angle E \not\cong \angle G$, $\angle D$ and $\angle F$ must be congruent. So, $m\angle D = m\angle F$. Write and solve an equation to find $m\angle D$.

$m\angle D + m\angle F + 124° + 80° = 360°$	**Corollary to Theorem 8.1**
$m\angle D + m\angle D + 124° + 80° = 360°$	**Substitute $m\angle D$ for $m\angle F$.**
$2(m\angle D) + 204° = 360°$	**Combine like terms.**
$m\angle D = 78°$	**Solve for $m\angle D$.**

Animated **Geometry** at classzone.com

✓ **GUIDED PRACTICE**   **for Example 4**

6. In a kite, the measures of the angles are $3x°$, 75°, 90°, and 120°. Find the value of *x*. What are the measures of the angles that are congruent?

8.5 EXERCISES

HOMEWORK KEY

○ = **WORKED-OUT SOLUTIONS**
on p. WS10 for Exs. 11, 19, and 35

★ = **STANDARDIZED TEST PRACTICE**
Exs. 2, 16, 28, 31, and 36

SKILL PRACTICE

1. **VOCABULARY** In trapezoid $PQRS$, $\overline{PQ} \parallel \overline{RS}$. Sketch $PQRS$ and identify its bases and its legs.

2. ★ **WRITING** *Describe* the differences between a kite and a trapezoid.

EXAMPLES 1 and 2
on pp. 542–543
for Exs. 3–12

COORDINATE PLANE Points A, B, C, and D are the vertices of a quadrilateral. **Determine whether $ABCD$ is a trapezoid.**

3. $A(0, 4)$, $B(4, 4)$, $C(8, -2)$, $D(2, 1)$

4. $A(-5, 0)$, $B(2, 3)$, $C(3, 1)$, $D(-2, -2)$

5. $A(2, 1)$, $B(6, 1)$, $C(3, -3)$, $D(-1, -4)$

6. $A(-3, 3)$, $B(-1, 1)$, $C(1, -4)$, $D(-3, 0)$

FINDING ANGLE MEASURES Find $m\angle J$, $m\angle L$, and $m\angle M$.

7.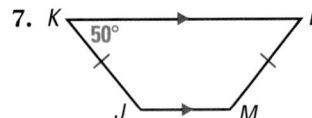

8.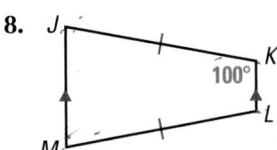

9.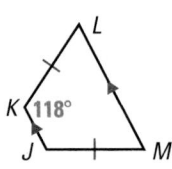

REASONING Determine whether the quadrilateral is a trapezoid. *Explain.*

10. A◁...▷B
D◁...▷C

(11.)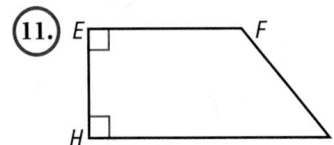

12.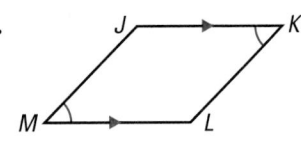

EXAMPLE 3
on p. 544
for Exs. 13–16

FINDING MIDSEGMENTS Find the length of the midsegment of the trapezoid.

13.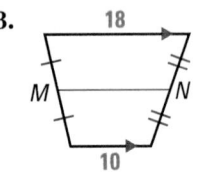

14.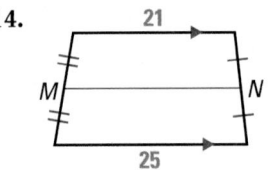

15.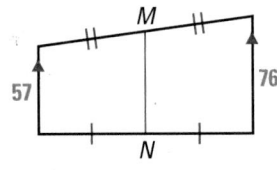

16. ★ **MULTIPLE CHOICE** Which statement is not always true?

Ⓐ The base angles of an isosceles trapezoid are congruent.

Ⓑ The midsegment of a trapezoid is parallel to the bases.

Ⓒ The bases of a trapezoid are parallel.

Ⓓ The legs of a trapezoid are congruent.

EXAMPLE 4
on p. 545
for Exs. 17–20

17. **ERROR ANALYSIS** *Describe* and correct the error made in finding $m\angle A$.

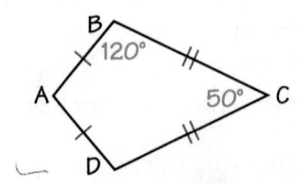

Opposite angles of a kite are congruent, so $m\angle A = 50°$.

ANGLES OF KITES *EFGH* is a kite. Find $m\angle G$.

18.
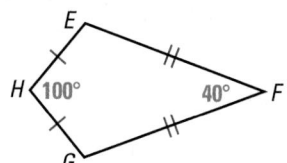

19.
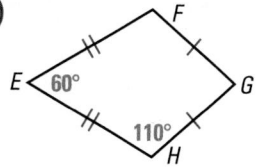

20.
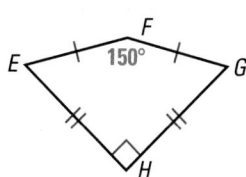

DIAGONALS OF KITES Use Theorem 8.18 and the Pythagorean Theorem to find the side lengths of the kite. Write the lengths in simplest radical form.

21.
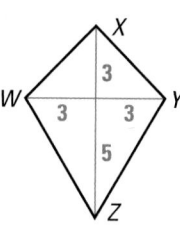

22.
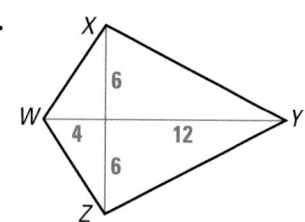

23.
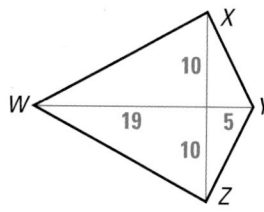

24. **ERROR ANALYSIS** In trapezoid *ABCD*, $\overline{MN}$ is the midsegment. *Describe* and correct the error made in finding *DC*.

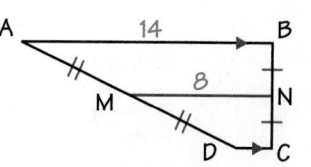

$DC = AB - MN$
$DC = 14 - 8$
$DC = 6$

XY ALGEBRA Find the value of *x*.

25.
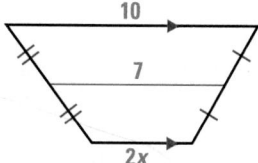

26.
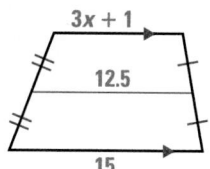

27.
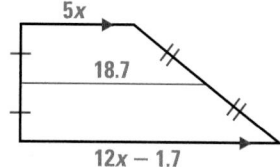

28. ★ **SHORT RESPONSE** The points $M(-3, 5)$, $N(-1, 5)$, $P(3, -1)$, and $Q(-5, -1)$ form the vertices of a trapezoid. Draw *MNPQ* and find *MP* and *NQ*. What do your results tell you about the trapezoid? *Explain.*

29. **DRAWING** In trapezoid *JKLM*, $\overline{JK} \parallel \overline{LM}$ and $JK = 17$. The midsegment of *JKLM* is $\overline{XY}$, and $XY = 37$. Sketch *JKLM* and its midsegment. Then find *LM*.

30. **RATIOS** The ratio of the lengths of the bases of a trapezoid is $1:3$. The length of the midsegment is 24. Find the lengths of the bases.

31. ★ **MULTIPLE CHOICE** In trapezoid *PQRS*, $\overline{PQ} \parallel \overline{RS}$ and $\overline{MN}$ is the midsegment of *PQRS*. If $RS = 5 \cdot PQ$, what is the ratio of *MN* to *RS*?

　　Ⓐ $3:5$　　　Ⓑ $5:3$　　　Ⓒ $2:1$　　　Ⓓ $3:1$

32. **CHALLENGE** The figure shown at the right is a trapezoid with its midsegment. Find all the possible values of *x*. What is the length of the midsegment? *Explain.* (The figure may not be drawn to scale.)

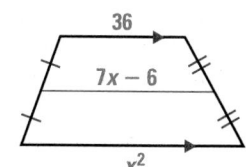

33. **REASONING** *Explain* why a kite and a general quadrilateral are the only quadrilaterals that can be concave.

**EXAMPLES
3 and 4**
on pp. 544–545
for Exs. 34–35

34. FURNITURE In the photograph of a chest of drawers, $\overline{HC}$ is the midsegment of trapezoid *ABDG*, $\overline{GD}$ is the midsegment of trapezoid *HCEF*, *AB* = 13.9 centimeters, and *GD* = 50.5 centimeters. Find *HC*. Then find *FE*.

@HomeTutor for problem solving help at classzone.com

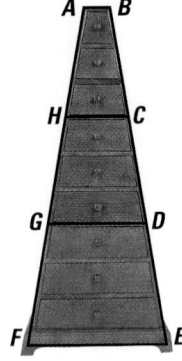

35. GRAPHIC DESIGN You design a logo in the shape of a convex kite. The measure of one angle of the kite is 90°. The measure of another angle is 30°. Sketch a kite that matches this description. Give the measures of all the angles and mark any congruent sides.

@HomeTutor for problem solving help at classzone.com

36. ★ EXTENDED RESPONSE The bridge below is designed to fold up into an octagon shape. The diagram shows a section of the bridge.

a. Classify the quadrilaterals shown in the diagram.

b. As the bridge folds up, what happens to the length of $\overline{BF}$? What happens to $m\angle BAF$, $m\angle ABC$, $m\angle BCF$, and $m\angle CFA$?

c. Given $m\angle CFE = 65°$, find $m\angle DEF$, $m\angle FCD$, and $m\angle CDE$. *Explain.*

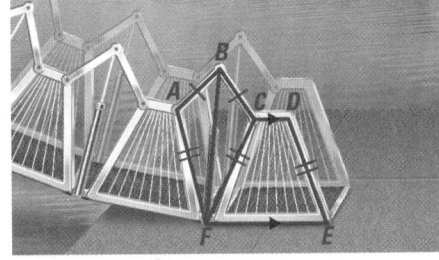

37. PROVING THEOREM 8.14 Use the diagram and the auxiliary segment to prove Theorem 8.14. In the diagram, $\overline{EC}$ is drawn parallel to $\overline{AB}$.

GIVEN ▶ *ABCD* is an isosceles trapezoid, $\overline{BC} \parallel \overline{AD}$

PROVE ▶ $\angle A \cong \angle D$, $\angle B \cong \angle BCD$

Hint: Find a way to show that $\triangle ECD$ is an isosceles triangle.

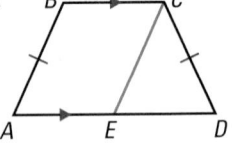

38. PROVING THEOREM 8.15 Use the diagram and the auxiliary segment to prove Theorem 8.15. In the diagram, $\overline{JG}$ is drawn parallel to $\overline{EF}$.

GIVEN ▶ *EFGH* is a trapezoid, $\overline{FG} \parallel \overline{EH}$, $\angle E \cong \angle H$

PROVE ▶ *EFGH* is an isosceles trapezoid.

Hint: Find a way to show that $\triangle JGH$ is an isosceles triangle.

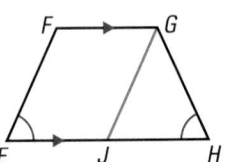

39. PROVING THEOREM 8.16 Prove part of Theorem 8.16.

   GIVEN ▶ *JKLM* is an isosceles trapezoid.
   $\overline{KL} \parallel \overline{JM}$, $\overline{JK} \cong \overline{LM}$
   PROVE ▶ $\overline{JL} \cong \overline{KM}$

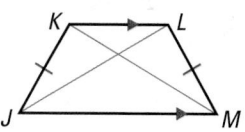

40. REASONING In the diagram below, $\overline{BG}$ is the midsegment of $\triangle ACD$ and $\overline{GE}$ is the midsegment of $\triangle ADF$. *Explain* why the midsegment of trapezoid *ACDF* is parallel to each base and why its length is one half the sum of the lengths of the bases.

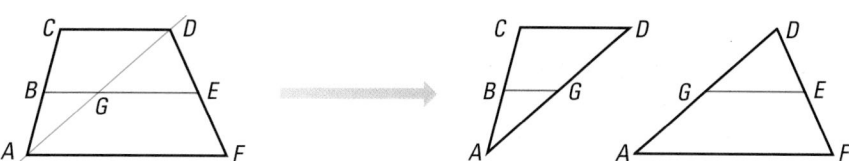

41. PROVING THEOREM 8.18 Prove Theorem 8.18.

   GIVEN ▶ *ABCD* is a kite.
   $\overline{AB} \cong \overline{CB}$, $\overline{AD} \cong \overline{CD}$
   PROVE ▶ $\overline{AC} \perp \overline{BD}$

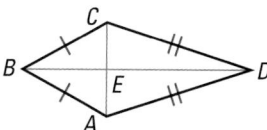

42. PROVING THEOREM 8.19 Write a paragraph proof of Theorem 8.19.

   GIVEN ▶ *EFGH* is a kite.
   $\overline{EF} \cong \overline{GF}$, $\overline{EH} \cong \overline{GH}$
   PROVE ▶ $\angle E \cong \angle G$, $\angle F \not\cong \angle H$

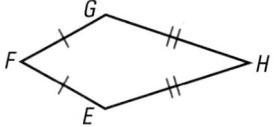

Plan for Proof First show that $\angle E \cong \angle G$. Then use an indirect argument to show that $\angle F \not\cong \angle H$: If $\angle F \cong \angle H$, then *EFGH* is a parallelogram. But opposite sides of a parallelogram are congruent. This result contradicts the definition of a kite.

43. CHALLENGE In Exercise 39, you proved that part of Theorem 8.16 is true. Write the other part of Theorem 8.16 as a conditional statement. Then prove that the statement is true.

MIXED REVIEW

44. Place a right triangle in a coordinate plane in a way that is convenient for finding side lengths. Assign coordinates to each vertex. *(p. 295)*

Use the diagram to complete the proportion. *(p. 449)*

45. $\dfrac{AB}{AC} = \dfrac{?}{AB}$

46. $\dfrac{AB}{BC} = \dfrac{BD}{?}$

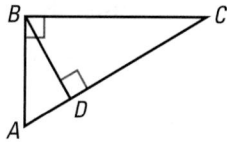

Three of the vertices of $\square ABCD$ are given. Find the coordinates of point *D*. Show your method. *(p. 522)*

47. $A(-1, -2)$, $B(4, -2)$, $C(6, 2)$, $D(x, y)$

48. $A(1, 4)$, $B(0, 1)$, $C(4, 1)$, $D(x, y)$

PREVIEW
Prepare for
Lesson 8.6 in
Exs. 47–48.

Draw Three-Dimensional Figures

GOAL Create isometric drawings and orthographic projections of three-dimensional figures.

Key Vocabulary
• isometric drawing
• orthographic projection

Technical drawings are drawings that show different viewpoints of an object. Engineers and architects create technical drawings of products and buildings before actually constructing the actual objects.

EXAMPLE 1 **Draw a rectangular box**

Draw a rectangular box.

Solution

STEP 1 **Draw** the bases. They are rectangular, but you need to draw them tilted.

STEP 2 **Connect** the bases using vertical lines.

STEP 3 **Erase** parts of the hidden edges so that they are dashed lines.

ISOMETRIC DRAWINGS Technical drawings may include **isometric drawings**. These drawings look three-dimensional and can be created on a grid of dots using three axes that intersect to form 120° angles.

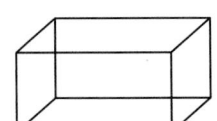
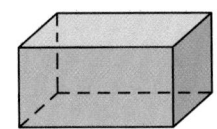

EXAMPLE 2 **Create an isometric drawing**

Create an isometric drawing of the rectangular box in Example 1.

Solution

STEP 1 **Draw** three axes on isometric dot paper.

STEP 2 **Draw** the box so that the edges of the box are parallel to the three axes.

STEP 3 **Add** depth to the drawing by using different shading for the front, top, and sides.

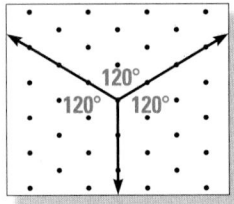

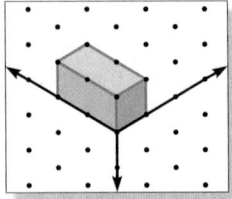

ANOTHER VIEW Technical drawings may also include an *orthographic projection*. An **orthographic projection** is a two-dimensional drawing of the front, top, and side views of an object. The interior lines in these two-dimensional drawings represent edges of the object.

EXAMPLE 3 Create an orthographic projection

Create an orthographic projection of the solid.

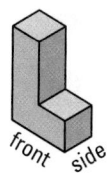

VISUAL REASONING
In this Extension, you can think of the solids as being constructed from cubes. You can assume there are no cubes hidden from view except those needed to support the visible ones.

Solution

On graph paper, draw the front, top, and side views of the solid.

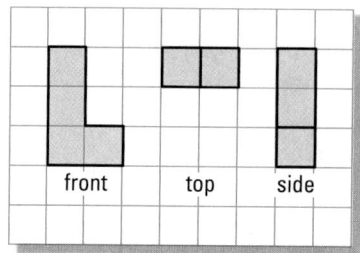

Animated **Geometry** at classzone.com

PRACTICE

EXAMPLE 1
on p. 550
for Exs. 1–3

EXAMPLES 2 and 3
on pp. 550–551
for Exs. 4–12

DRAWING BOXES Draw a box with the indicated base.

1. Equilateral triangle   **2.** Regular hexagon   **3.** Square

DRAWING SOLIDS Create an isometric drawing of the solid. Then create an orthographic projection of the solid.

4. 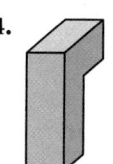   **5.** 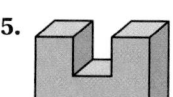   **6.**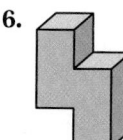

7. 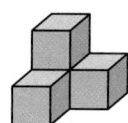   **8.**    **9.**

CREATING ISOMETRIC DRAWINGS Create an isometric drawing of the orthographic projection.

10. 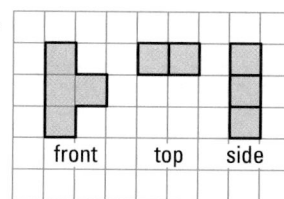   **11.** 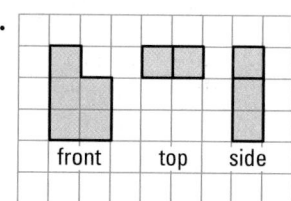   **12.**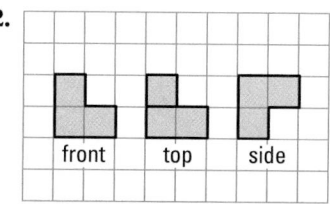

8.6 Identify Special Quadrilaterals

Before	You identified polygons.
Now	You will identify special quadrilaterals.
Why?	So you can describe part of a pyramid, as in Ex. 36.

Key Vocabulary
- **parallelogram,** *p. 515*
- **rhombus,** *p. 533*
- **rectangle,** *p. 533*
- **square,** *p. 533*
- **trapezoid,** *p. 542*
- **kite,** *p. 545*

The diagram below shows relationships among the special quadrilaterals you have studied in Chapter 8. Each shape in the diagram has the properties of the shapes linked above it. For example, a rhombus has the properties of a parallelogram and a quadrilateral.

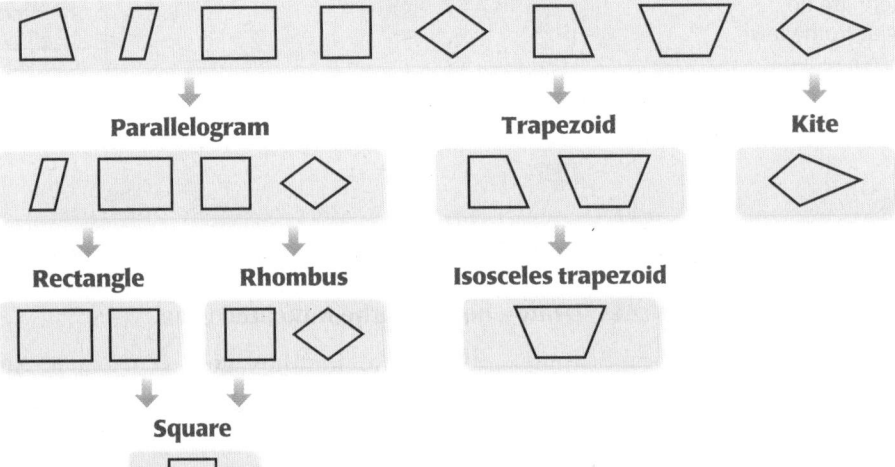

EXAMPLE 1 Identify quadrilaterals

Quadrilateral *ABCD* has at least one pair of opposite angles congruent. What types of quadrilaterals meet this condition?

Solution

There are many possibilities.

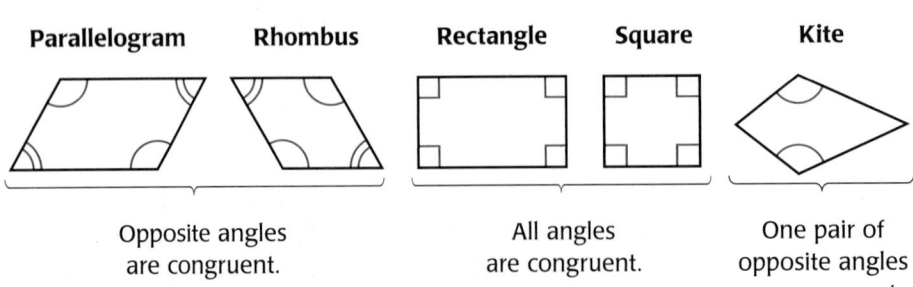

| Parallelogram | Rhombus | Rectangle | Square | Kite |

Opposite angles are congruent. · All angles are congruent. · One pair of opposite angles are congruent.

EXAMPLE 2 Standardized Test Practice

What is the most specific name for quadrilateral *ABCD*?

Ⓐ Parallelogram   Ⓑ Rhombus

Ⓒ Square   Ⓓ Rectangle

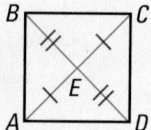

Solution

The diagram shows $\overline{AE} \cong \overline{CE}$ and $\overline{BE} \cong \overline{DE}$. So, the diagonals bisect each other. By Theorem 8.10, *ABCD* is a parallelogram.

Rectangles, rhombuses and squares are also parallelograms. However, there is no information given about the side lengths or angle measures of *ABCD*. So, you cannot determine whether it is a rectangle, a rhombus, or a square.

▶ The correct answer is A. Ⓐ Ⓑ Ⓒ Ⓓ

EXAMPLE 3 Identify a quadrilateral

Is enough information given in the diagram to show that quadrilateral *PQRS* is an isosceles trapezoid? Explain.

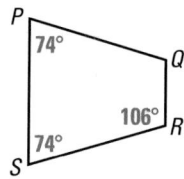

Solution

STEP 1 **Show** that *PQRS* is a trapezoid. ∠*R* and ∠*S* are supplementary, but ∠*P* and ∠*S* are not. So, $\overline{PS} \parallel \overline{QR}$, but $\overline{PQ}$ is not parallel to $\overline{SR}$. By definition, *PQRS* is a trapezoid.

STEP 2 **Show** that trapezoid *PQRS* is isosceles. ∠*P* and ∠*S* are a pair of congruent base angles. So, *PQRS* is an isosceles trapezoid by Theorem 8.15.

▶ Yes, the diagram is sufficient to show that *PQRS* is an isosceles trapezoid.

Animated Geometry at classzone.com

✓ **GUIDED PRACTICE** for Examples 1, 2, and 3

1. Quadrilateral *DEFG* has at least one pair of opposite sides congruent. What types of quadrilaterals meet this condition?

Give the most specific name for the quadrilateral. *Explain* your reasoning.

2.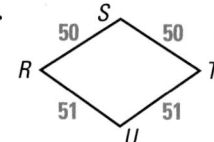

3.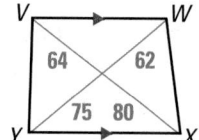

4.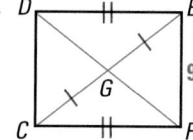

5. **ERROR ANALYSIS** A student knows the following information about quadrilateral *MNPQ*: $\overline{MN} \parallel \overline{PQ}$, $\overline{MP} \cong \overline{NQ}$, and ∠*P* ≅ ∠*Q*. The student concludes that *MNPQ* is an isosceles trapezoid. *Explain* why the student cannot make this conclusion.

8.6 EXERCISES

HOMEWORK KEY

◯ = **WORKED-OUT SOLUTIONS**
on p. WS10 for Exs. 3, 15, and 33

★ = **STANDARDIZED TEST PRACTICE**
Exs. 2, 13, 37, and 38

SKILL PRACTICE

1. **VOCABULARY** Copy and complete: A quadrilateral that has exactly one pair of parallel sides and diagonals that are congruent is a(n) __?__.

2. ★ **WRITING** *Describe* three methods you could use to prove that a parallelogram is a rhombus.

EXAMPLE 1
on p. 552
for Exs. 3–12

PROPERTIES OF QUADRILATERALS Copy the chart. Put an X in the box if the shape *always* has the given property.

Property	▱	Rectangle	Rhombus	Square	Kite	Trapezoid
3. All sides are ≅.	?	?	?	?	?	?
4. Both pairs of opp. sides are ≅.	?	?	?	?	?	?
5. Both pairs of opp. sides are ∥.	?	?	?	?	?	?
6. Exactly 1 pair of opp. sides are ∥.	?	?	?	?	?	?
7. All ∠ are ≅.	?	?	?	?	?	?
8. Exactly 1 pair of opp. ∠ are ≅.	?	?	?	?	?	?
9. Diagonals are ⊥.	?	?	?	?	?	?
10. Diagonals are ≅.	?	?	?	?	?	?
11. Diagonals bisect each other.	?	?	?	?	?	?

12. **ERROR ANALYSIS** *Describe* and correct the error in classifying the quadrilateral.

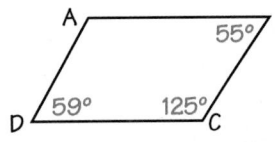

∠B and ∠C are supplements, so $\overline{AB} \parallel \overline{CD}$. So, ABCD is a parallelogram.

EXAMPLE 2
on p. 553
for Exs. 13–17

13. ★ **MULTIPLE CHOICE** What is the most specific name for the quadrilateral shown at the right?

Ⓐ Rectangle Ⓑ Parallelogram

Ⓒ Trapezoid Ⓓ Isosceles trapezoid

CLASSIFYING QUADRILATERALS Give the most specific name for the quadrilateral. *Explain.*

14.
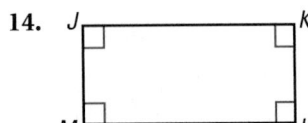

15.
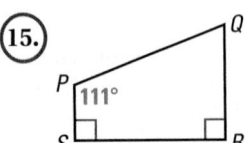

16.
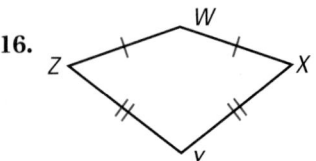

17. DRAWING Draw a quadrilateral with congruent diagonals and exactly one pair of congruent sides. What is the most specific name for this quadrilateral?

EXAMPLE 3
on p. 553
for Exs. 18–20

IDENTIFYING QUADRILATERALS Tell whether enough information is given in the diagram to classify the quadrilateral by the indicated name. *Explain.*

18. Rhombus

19. Isosceles trapezoid

20. Square

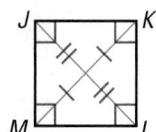

COORDINATE PLANE Points *P, Q, R,* and *S* are the vertices of a quadrilateral. Give the most specific name for *PQRS*. *Justify* your answer.

21. *P*(1, 0), *Q*(1, 2), *R*(6, 5), *S*(3, 0)

22. *P*(2, 1), *Q*(6, 1), *R*(5, 8), *S*(3, 8)

23. *P*(2, 7), *Q*(6, 9), *R*(9, 3), *S*(5, 1)

24. *P*(1, 7), *Q*(5, 8), *R*(6, 2), *S*(2, 1)

25. TECHNOLOGY Use geometry drawing software to draw points *A, B, C,* and segments *AC* and *BC*. Draw a circle with center *A* and radius *AC*. Draw a circle with center *B* and radius *BC*. Label the other intersection of the circles *D*. Draw $\overline{BD}$ and $\overline{AD}$.

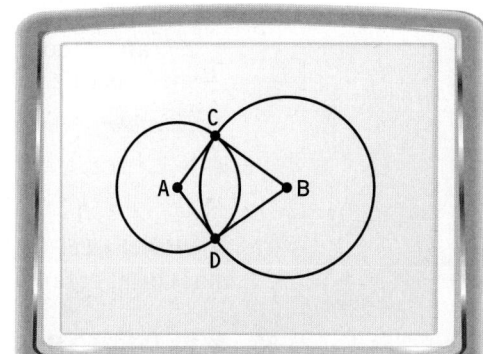

  a. Drag point *A, B, C,* or *D* to change the shape of *ABCD*. What types of quadrilaterals can be formed?

  b. Are there types of quadrilaterals that cannot be formed? *Explain.*

DEVELOPING PROOF Which pairs of segments or angles must be congruent so that you can prove that *ABCD* is the indicated quadrilateral? *Explain.* There may be more than one right answer.

26. Square

27. Isosceles trapezoid

28. Parallelogram

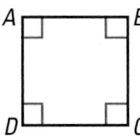

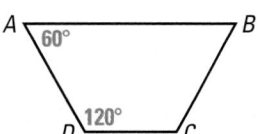

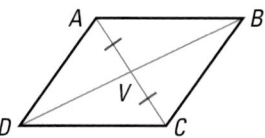

TRAPEZOIDS In Exercises 29–31, determine whether there is enough information to prove that *JKLM* is an isosceles trapezoid. *Explain.*

29. GIVEN ▶ $\overline{JK} \parallel \overline{LM}$, ∠*JKL* ≅ ∠*KJM*

30. GIVEN ▶ $\overline{JK} \parallel \overline{LM}$, ∠*JML* ≅ ∠*KLM*, *m*∠*KLM* ≠ 90°

31. GIVEN ▶ $\overline{JL} \cong \overline{KM}$, $\overline{JK} \parallel \overline{LM}$, *JK* > *LM*

32. CHALLENGE Draw a rectangle and bisect its angles. What type of quadrilateral is formed by the intersecting bisectors? *Justify* your answer.

REAL-WORLD OBJECTS What type of special quadrilateral is outlined?

33.

34.

35.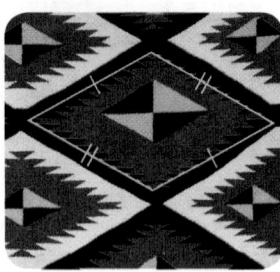

@*HomeTutor* for problem solving help at classzone.com

36. PYRAMID Use the photo of the Pyramid of Kukulcan in Mexico.

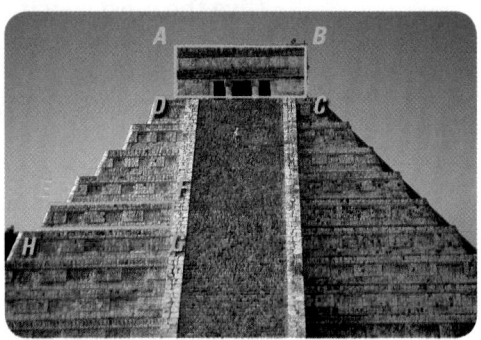

  a. $\overline{EF} \parallel \overline{HG}$, and $\overline{EH}$ and $\overline{FG}$ are not parallel. What shape is this part of the pyramid?

  b. $\overline{AB} \parallel \overline{DC}$, $\overline{AD} \parallel \overline{BC}$, and $\angle A$, $\angle B$, $\angle C$, and $\angle D$ are all congruent to each other. What shape is this part of the pyramid?

@*HomeTutor* for problem solving help at classzone.com

37. ★ **SHORT RESPONSE** *Explain* why a parallelogram with one right angle must be a rectangle.

38. ★ **EXTENDED RESPONSE** Segments *AC* and *BD* bisect each other.

  a. Suppose that $\overline{AC}$ and $\overline{BD}$ are congruent, but not perpendicular. Draw quadrilateral *ABCD* and classify it. *Justify* your answer.

  b. Suppose that $\overline{AC}$ and $\overline{BD}$ are perpendicular, but not congruent. Draw quadrilateral *ABCD* and classify it. *Justify* your answer.

39. MULTI-STEP PROBLEM Polygon *QRSTUV* shown at the right is a regular hexagon, and $\overline{QU}$ and $\overline{RT}$ are diagonals. Follow the steps below to classify quadrilateral *QRTU*. *Explain* your reasoning in each step.

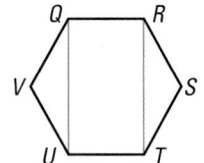

  a. Show that $\triangle QVU$ and $\triangle RST$ are congruent isosceles triangles.

  b. Show that $\overline{QR} \cong \overline{UT}$ and that $\overline{QU} \cong \overline{RT}$.

  c. Show that $\angle UQR \cong \angle QRT \cong \angle RTU \cong \angle TUQ$. Find the measure of each of these angles.

  d. Classify quadrilateral *QRTU*.

40. REASONING In quadrilateral *WXYZ*, $\overline{WY}$ and $\overline{XZ}$ intersect each other at point *V*. $\overline{WV} \cong \overline{XV}$ and $\overline{YV} \cong \overline{ZV}$, but $\overline{WY}$ and $\overline{XZ}$ do not bisect each other. Draw $\overline{WY}$, $\overline{XY}$, and *WXYZ*. What special type of quadrilateral is *WXYZ*? Write a plan for a proof of your answer.

CHALLENGE What special type of quadrilateral is *EFGH*? Write a paragraph proof to show that your answer is correct.

41. **GIVEN** ▶ *PQRS* is a square.
    E, *F*, *G*, and *H* are midpoints
    of the sides of the square.

    PROVE ▶ *EFGH* is a __?__ .

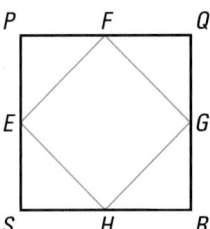

42. **GIVEN** ▶ In the three-dimensional figure,
    $\overline{JK} \cong \overline{LM}$; *E*, *F*, *G*, and *H* are the
    midpoints of $\overline{JL}$, $\overline{KL}$, $\overline{KM}$, and $\overline{JM}$.

    PROVE ▶ *EFGH* is a __?__ .

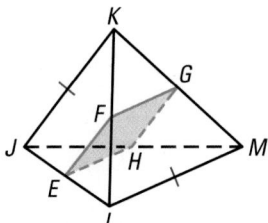

MIXED REVIEW

In Exercises 43 and 44, use the diagram. *(p. 264)*

43. Find the values of *x* and *y*. *Explain* your reasoning.

44. Find *m∠ADC*, *m∠DAC*, and *m∠DCA*. *Explain* your reasoning.

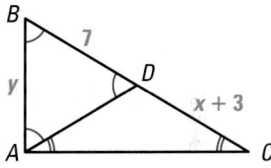

PREVIEW
Prepare for
Lesson 9.1
in Exs. 45–46.

The vertices of quadrilateral *ABCD* are *A*(−2, 1), *B*(2, 5), *C*(3, 2), and *D*(1, −1). Draw *ABCD* in a coordinate plane. Then draw its image after the indicated translation. *(p. 272)*

45. $(x, y) \rightarrow (x + 1, y - 3)$

46. $(x, y) \rightarrow (x - 2, y - 2)$

Use the diagram of ▱*WXYZ* to find the indicated length. *(p. 515)*

47. *YZ*   48. *WZ*

49. *XV*   50. *XZ*

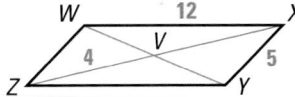

QUIZ *for Lessons 8.5–8.6*

Find the unknown angle measures. *(p. 542)*

1.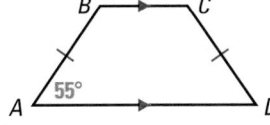

2.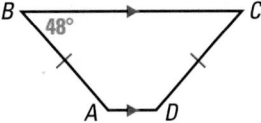

3.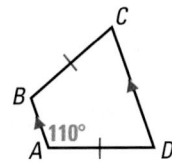

4. The diagonals of quadrilateral *ABCD* are congruent and bisect each other. What types of quadrilaterals match this description? *(p. 552)*

5. In quadrilateral *EFGH*, ∠*E* ≅ ∠*G*, ∠*F* ≅ ∠*H*, and $\overline{EF} \cong \overline{EH}$. What is the most specific name for quadrilateral *EFGH*? *(p. 552)*

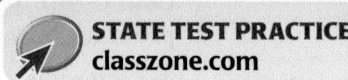
Lessons 8.4–8.6

1. **MULTI-STEP PROBLEM** In the photograph shown below, quadrilateral *ABCD* represents the front view of the roof.

   a. *Explain* how you know that the shape of the roof is a trapezoid.

   b. Do you have enough information to determine that the roof is an isosceles trapezoid? *Explain* your reasoning.

2. **SHORT RESPONSE** Is enough information given in the diagram to show that quadrilateral *JKLM* is a square? *Explain* your reasoning.

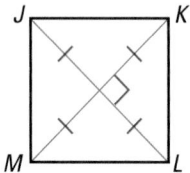

3. **EXTENDED RESPONSE** In the photograph, quadrilateral *QRST* is a kite.

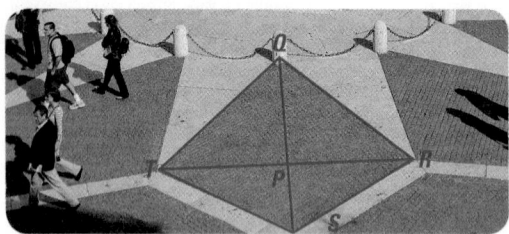

   a. If $m\angle TQR = 102°$ and $m\angle RST = 125°$, find $m\angle QTS$. *Explain* your reasoning.

   b. If $QS = 11$ ft, $TR = 14$ ft, and $\overline{TP} \cong \overline{QP} \cong \overline{RP}$, find QR, RS, ST, and TQ. Round your answers to the nearest foot. Show your work.

4. **GRIDDED ANSWER** The top of the table shown is shaped like an isosceles trapezoid. In *ABCD*, $AB = 48$ inches, $BC = 19$ inches, $CD = 24$ inches, and $DA = 19$ inches. Find the length (in inches) of the midsegment of *ABCD*.

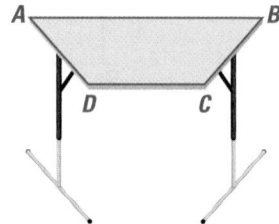

5. **SHORT RESPONSE** Rhombus *PQRS* is similar to rhombus *VWXY*. In the diagram below, $QS = 32$, $QR = 20$, and $WZ = 20$. Find *WX*. *Explain* your reasoning.

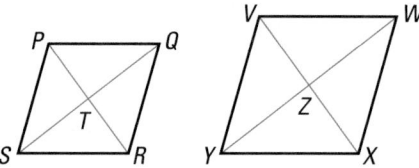

6. **OPEN-ENDED** In quadrilateral *MNPQ*, $\overline{MP} \cong \overline{NQ}$.

   a. What types of quadrilaterals could *MNPQ* be? Use the most specific names. *Explain*.

   b. For each of your answers in part (a), tell what additional information would allow you to conclude that *MNPQ* is that type of quadrilateral. *Explain* your reasoning. (There may be more than one correct answer.)

7. **EXTENDED RESPONSE** Three of the vertices of quadrilateral *EFGH* are *E*(0, 4), *F*(2, 2), and *G*(4, 4).

   a. Suppose that *EFGH* is a rhombus. Find the coordinates of vertex *H*. *Explain* why there is only one possible location for *H*.

   b. Suppose that *EFGH* is a convex kite. Show that there is more than one possible set of coordinates for vertex *H*. *Describe* what all the possible sets of coordinates have in common.

BIG IDEAS

For Your Notebook

Using Angle Relationships in Polygons

You can use theorems about the interior and exterior angles of convex polygons to solve problems.

Polygon Interior Angles Theorem	Polygon Exterior Angles Theorem
The sum of the interior angle measures of a convex n-gon is $(n - 2) \cdot 180°$.	The sum of the exterior angle measures of a convex n-gon is $360°$.

Using Properties of Parallelograms

By definition, a parallelogram is a quadrilateral with both pairs of opposite sides parallel. Other properties of parallelograms:

- Opposite sides are congruent.
- Opposite angles are congruent.
- Diagonals bisect each other.
- Consecutive angles are supplementary.

Ways to show that a quadrilateral is a parallelogram:

- Show both pairs of opposite sides are parallel.
- Show both pairs of opposite sides or opposite angles are congruent.
- Show one pair of opposite sides are congruent and parallel.
- Show the diagonals bisect each other.

Classifying Quadrilaterals by Their Properties

Special quadrilaterals can be classified by their properties. In a parallelogram, both pairs of opposite sides are parallel. In a trapezoid, only one pair of sides are parallel. A kite has two pairs of consecutive congruent sides, but opposite sides are not congruent.

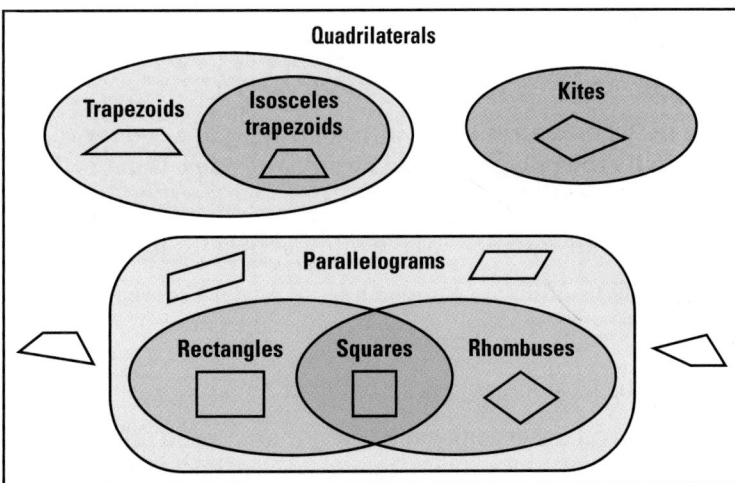

REVIEW KEY VOCABULARY

For a list of postulates and theorems, see pp. 926–931.

• diagonal, *p. 507*
• parallelogram, *p. 515*
• rhombus, *p. 533*
• rectangle, *p. 533*

• square, *p. 533*
• trapezoid, *p. 542*
• bases of a trapezoid, *p. 542*
• base angles of a trapezoid, *p. 542*

• legs of a trapezoid, *p. 542*
• isosceles trapezoid, *p. 543*
• midsegment of a trapezoid, *p. 544*
• kite, *p. 545*

VOCABULARY EXERCISES

In Exercises 1 and 2, copy and complete the statement.

1. The __?__ of a trapezoid is parallel to the bases.

2. A(n) __?__ of a polygon is a segment whose endpoints are nonconsecutive vertices.

3. **WRITING** *Describe* the different ways you can show that a trapezoid is an isosceles trapezoid.

In Exercises 4–6, match the figure with the most specific name.

4.

5.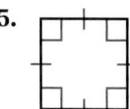

6.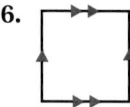

A. Square

B. Parallelogram

C. Rhombus

REVIEW EXAMPLES AND EXERCISES

Use the review examples and exercises below to check your understanding of the concepts you have learned in each lesson of Chapter 8.

8.1 Find Angle Measures in Polygons
pp. 507–513

EXAMPLE

The sum of the measures of the interior angles of a convex regular polygon is 1080°. Classify the polygon by the number of sides. What is the measure of each interior angle?

Write and solve an equation for the number of sides *n*.

$(n - 2) \cdot 180° = 1080°$ **Polygon Interior Angles Theorem**

$n = 8$ **Solve for *n*.**

The polygon has 8 sides, so it is an octagon.

A regular octagon has 8 congruent interior angles, so divide to find the measure of each angle: $1080° \div 8 = 135°$. The measure of each interior angle is 135°.

EXERCISES

EXAMPLES
2, 3, 4, and 5
on pp. 508–510
for Exs. 7–11

7. The sum of the measures of the interior angles of a convex regular polygon is 3960°. Classify the polygon by the number of sides. What is the measure of each interior angle?

In Exercises 8–10, find the value of *x*.

8.
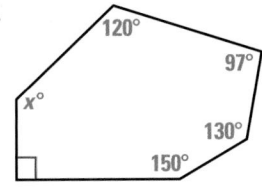

9.
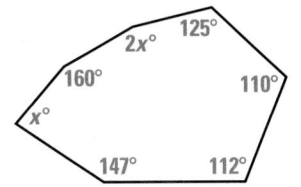

10.
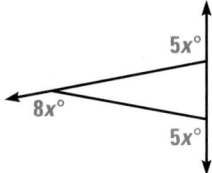

11. In a regular nonagon, the exterior angles are all congruent. What is the measure of one of the exterior angles? *Explain.*

8.2 Use Properties of Parallelograms
pp. 515–521

EXAMPLE

Quadrilateral *WXYZ* is a parallelogram. Find the values of *x* and *y*.

To find the value of *x*, apply Theorem 8.3.

$XY = WZ$ **Opposite sides of a ▱ are ≅.**

$x - 9 = 15$ **Substitute.**

$x = 24$ **Add 9 to each side.**

By Theorem 8.4, $\angle W \cong \angle Y$, or $m\angle W = m\angle Y$. So, $y = 60$.

EXERCISES

EXAMPLES
1, 2, and 3
on pp. 515, 517
for Exs. 12–17

Find the value of each variable in the parallelogram.

12.
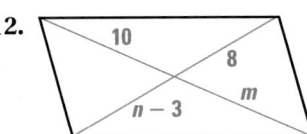

13.
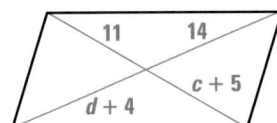

14.
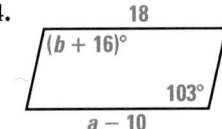

15. In ▱*PQRS*, $PQ = 5$ centimeters, $QR = 10$ centimeters, and $m\angle PQR = 36°$. Sketch *PQRS*. Find and label all of its side lengths and interior angle measures.

16. The perimeter of ▱*EFGH* is 16 inches. If *EF* is 5 inches, find the lengths of all the other sides of *EFGH*. *Explain* your reasoning.

17. In ▱*JKLM*, the ratio of the measure of $\angle J$ to the measure of $\angle M$ is 5 : 4. Find $m\angle J$ and $m\angle M$. *Explain* your reasoning.

8.3 Show that a Quadrilateral is a Parallelogram
pp. 522–529

EXAMPLE

For what value of *x* is quadrilateral *ABCD* a parallelogram?

If the diagonals bisect each other, then *ABCD* is a parallelogram. The diagram shows that $\overline{BE} \cong \overline{DE}$. You need to find the value of *x* that makes $\overline{AE} \cong \overline{CE}$.

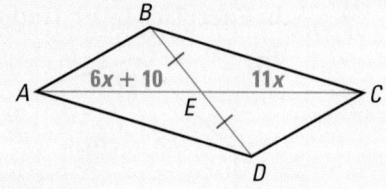

$AE = CE$	**Set the segment lengths equal.**
$6x + 10 = 11x$	**Substitute expressions for the lengths.**
$x = 2$	**Solve for *x*.**

When $x = 2$, $AE = 6(2) + 10 = 22$ and $CE = 11(2) = 22$. So, $\overline{AE} \cong \overline{CE}$.

Quadrilateral *ABCD* is a parallelogram when $x = 2$.

EXERCISES

EXAMPLE 3
on p. 524
for Exs. 18–19

For what value of *x* is the quadrilateral a parallelogram?

18.

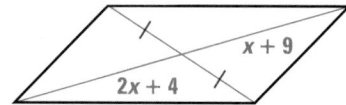

19.

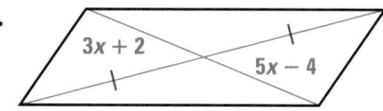

8.4 Properties of Rhombuses, Rectangles, and Squares
pp. 533–540

EXAMPLE

Classify the special quadrilateral.

In quadrilateral *UVWX*, the diagonals bisect each other. So, *UVWX* is a parallelogram. Also, $\overline{UY} \cong \overline{VY} \cong \overline{WY} \cong \overline{XY}$. So, $UY + YW = VY + XY$. Because $UY + YW = UW$, and $VY + XY = VX$, you can conclude that $\overline{UW} \cong \overline{VX}$. By Theorem 8.13, *UVWX* is a rectangle.

EXERCISES

EXAMPLES 2 and 3
on pp. 534–535
for Exs. 20–22

Classify the special quadrilateral. Then find the values of *x* and *y*.

20.

21.

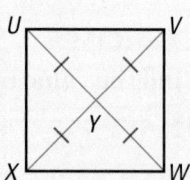

22. The diagonals of a rhombus are 10 centimeters and 24 centimeters. Find the length of a side. *Explain.*

8.5 Use Properties of Trapezoids and Kites

pp. 542–549

EXAMPLE

Quadrilateral *ABCD* is a kite. Find *m∠B* and *m∠D*.

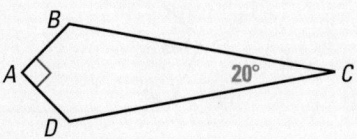

A kite has exactly one pair of congruent opposite angles. Because $\angle A \not\cong \angle C$, $\angle B$ and $\angle D$ must be congruent. Write and solve an equation.

$90° + 20° + m\angle B + m\angle D = 360°$ **Corollary to Theorem 8.1**

$110° + m\angle B° + m\angle D = 360°$ **Combine like terms.**

$m\angle B + m\angle D = 250°$ **Subtract 110° from each side.**

Because $\angle B \cong \angle D$, you can substitute $m\angle B$ for $m\angle D$ in the last equation. Then $m\angle B + m\angle B = 250°$, and $m\angle B = m\angle D = 125°$.

EXERCISES

**EXAMPLES
2 and 3**
on pp. 543–544
for Exs. 20–22

In Exercises 23 and 24, use the diagram of a recycling container. One end of the container is an isosceles trapezoid with $\overline{FG} \parallel \overline{JH}$ and $m\angle F = 79°$.

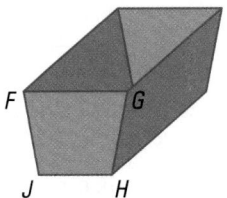

23. Find $m\angle G$, $m\angle H$, and $m\angle J$.

24. Copy trapezoid *FGHJ* and sketch its midsegment. If the midsegment is 16.5 inches long and $\overline{FG}$ is 19 inches long, find *JH*.

8.6 Identify Special Quadrilaterals

pp. 552–557

EXAMPLE

Give the most specific name for quadrilateral *LMNP*.

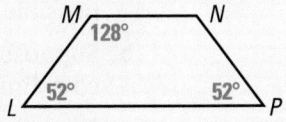

In *LMNP*, $\angle L$ and $\angle M$ are supplementary, but $\angle L$ and $\angle P$ are not. So, $\overline{MN} \parallel \overline{LP}$, but $\overline{LM}$ is not parallel to $\overline{NP}$. By definition, *LMNP* is a trapezoid.

Also, $\angle L$ and $\angle P$ are a pair of base angles and $\angle L \cong \angle P$. So, *LMNP* is an isosceles trapezoid by Theorem 8.15.

EXERCISES

EXAMPLE 2
on p. 553
for Exs. 25–28

Give the most specific name for the quadrilateral. *Explain* your reasoning.

25.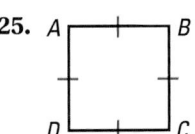

26.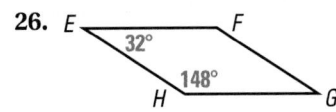

27.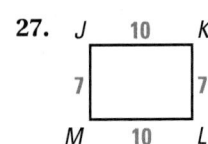

28. In quadrilateral *RSTU*, $\angle R$, $\angle T$, and $\angle U$ are right angles, and $RS = ST$. What is the most specific name for quadrilateral *RSTU*? *Explain.*

Find the value of x.

1.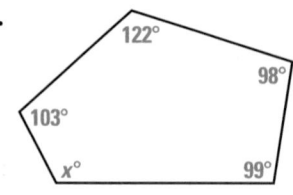

2.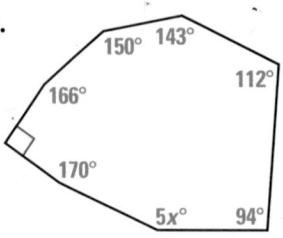

3.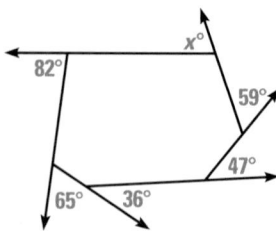

4. In ▱*EFGH*, *m∠F* is 40° greater than *m∠G*. Sketch ▱*EFGH* and label each angle with its correct angle measure. *Explain* your reasoning.

Are you given enough information to determine whether the quadrilateral is a parallelogram? *Explain* **your reasoning.**

5.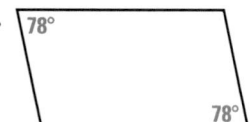

6.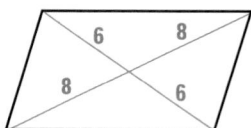

7.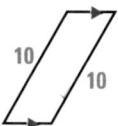

In Exercises 8–11, list each type of quadrilateral—*parallelogram, rectangle, rhombus,* and *square*—for which the statement is always true.

8. It is equilateral.

9. Its interior angles are all right angles.

10. The diagonals are congruent.

11. Opposite sides are parallel.

12. The vertices of quadrilateral *PQRS* are *P*(−2, 0), *Q*(0, 3), *R*(6, −1), and *S*(1, −2). Draw *PQRS* in a coordinate plane. Show that it is a trapezoid.

13. One side of a quadrilateral *JKLM* is longer than another side.

   a. Suppose *JKLM* is an isosceles trapezoid. In a coordinate plane, find possible coordinates for the vertices of *JKLM*. *Justify* your answer.

   b. Suppose *JKLM* is a kite. In a coordinate plane, find possible coordinates for the vertices of *JKLM*. *Justify* your answer.

   c. Name other special quadrilaterals that *JKLM* could be.

Give the most specific name for the quadrilateral. *Explain* **your reasoning.**

14.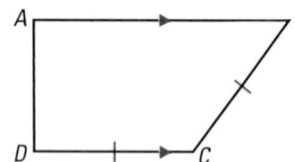

15.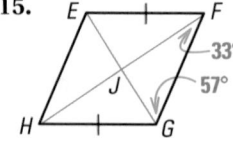

16.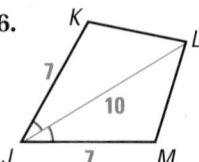

17. In trapezoid *WXYZ*, $\overline{WX} \parallel \overline{YZ}$, and *YZ* = 4.25 centimeters. The midsegment of trapezoid *WXYZ* is 2.75 centimeters long. Find *WX*.

18. In ▱*RSTU*, $\overline{RS}$ is 3 centimeters shorter than $\overline{ST}$. The perimeter of ▱*RSTU* is 42 centimeters. Find *RS* and *ST*.

GRAPH NONLINEAR FUNCTIONS

⟨xy⟩ **EXAMPLE 1** *Graph a quadratic function in vertex form*

Graph $y = 2(x - 3)^2 - 1$.

The *vertex form* of a quadratic function is $y = a(x - h)^2 + k$. Its graph is a parabola with vertex at (h, k) and axis of symmetry $x = h$.

The given function is in vertex form. So, $a = 2$, $h = 3$, and $k = -1$. Because $a > 0$, the parabola opens up.

Graph the vertex at $(3, -1)$. Sketch the axis of symmetry, $x = 3$. Use a table of values to find points on each side of the axis of symmetry. Draw a parabola through the points.

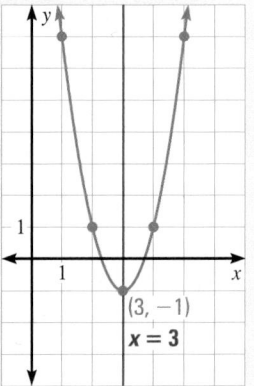

x	3	1	2	4	5
y	−1	7	1	1	7

⟨xy⟩ **EXAMPLE 2** *Graph an exponential function*

Graph $y = 2^x$.

Make a table by choosing a few values for x and finding the values for y. Plot the points and connect them with a smooth curve.

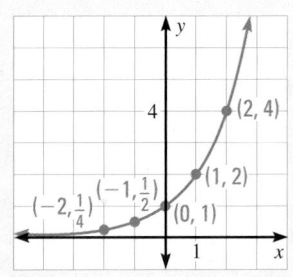

x	−2	−1	0	1	2
y	$\frac{1}{4}$	$\frac{1}{2}$	1	2	4

EXERCISES

EXAMPLE 1
for Exs. 1–6

Graph the quadratic function. Label the vertex and sketch the axis of symmetry.

1. $y = 3x^2 + 5$
2. $y = -2x^2 + 4$
3. $y = 0.5x^2 - 3$

4. $y = 3(x + 3)^2 - 3$
5. $y = -2(x - 4)^2 - 1$
6. $y = \frac{1}{2}(x - 4)^2 + 3$

EXAMPLE 2
for Exs. 7–10

Graph the exponential function.

7. $y = 3^x$
8. $y = 8^x$
9. $y = 2.2^x$
10. $y = \left(\frac{1}{3}\right)^x$

Use a table of values to graph the cubic or absolute value function.

11. $y = x^3$
12. $y = x^3 - 2$
13. $y = 3x^3 - 1$

14. $y = 2|x|$
15. $y = 2|x| - 4$
16. $y = -|x| - 1$

CONTEXT-BASED MULTIPLE CHOICE QUESTIONS

Some of the information you need to solve a context-based multiple choice question may appear in a table, a diagram, or a graph.

> ### PROBLEM 1
>
> Which of the statements about the rhombus-shaped ring is not always true?
>
> **(A)** $m\angle SPT = m\angle TPQ$ **(B)** $PT = TR$
>
> **(C)** $m\angle STR = 90°$ **(D)** $PR = SQ$
>
>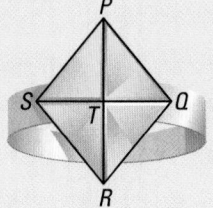

Plan

INTERPRET THE DIAGRAM The diagram shows rhombus *PQRS* with its diagonals intersecting at point *T*. Use properties of rhombuses to figure out which statement is not always true.

Solution

STEP 1
....
Evaluate choice A.

➤ Consider choice A: $m\angle SPT = m\angle TPQ$.

Each diagonal of a rhombus bisects each of a pair of opposite angles. The diagonal $\overline{PR}$ bisects $\angle SPQ$, so $m\angle SPT = m\angle TPQ$. Choice A is true.

STEP 2
....
Evaluate choice B.

➤ Consider choice B: $PT = TR$.

The diagonals of a parallelogram bisect each other. A rhombus is also a parallelogram, so the diagonals of *PQRS* bisect each other. So, $PT = TR$. Choice B is true.

STEP 3
....
Evaluate choice C.

➤ Consider choice C: $m\angle STR = 90°$.

The diagonals of a rhombus are perpendicular. *PQRS* is a rhombus, so its diagonals are perpendicular. Therefore, $m\angle STR = 90°$. Choice C is true.

STEP 3
....
Evaluate choice D.

➤ Consider choice D: $PR = SQ$.

If the diagonals of a parallelogram are congruent, then it is a rectangle. But *PQRS* is a rhombus. Only in the special case where it is also a square (a type of rhombus that is also a rectangle), would choice D be true. So, choice D is not always true.

The correct answer is D. **(A)** **(B)** **(C)** **(D)**

PROBLEM 2

The official dimensions of home plate in professional baseball are shown on the diagram. What is the value of *x*?

(A) 90 **(B)** 108

(C) 135 **(D)** 150

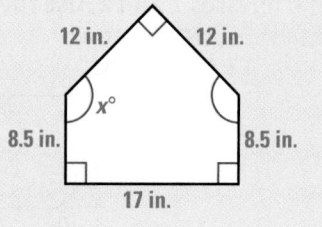

Plan

INTERPRET THE DIAGRAM From the diagram, you can see that home plate is a pentagon. Use what you know about the interior angles of a polygon and the markings given on the diagram to find the value of *x*.

Solution

STEP 1
Find the sum of the measures of the interior angles.

Home plate has 5 sides. Use the Polygon Interior Angles Theorem to find the sum of the measures of the interior angles.

$$(n - 2) \cdot 180° = (5 - 2) \cdot 180°$$ **Substitute 5 for *n*.**

$$= 3 \cdot 180°$$ **Subtract.**

$$= 540°$$ **Multiply.**

STEP 2
Write and solve an equation.

From the diagram, you know that three interior angles are right angles. The two other angles are congruent, including the one whose measure is *x*°. Use this information to write an equation. Then solve the equation.

$$3 \cdot 90° + 2 \cdot x° = 540°$$ **Write equation.**

$$270 + 2x = 540$$ **Multiply.**

$$2x = 270$$ **Subtract 270 from each side.**

$$x = 135$$ **Divide each side by 2.**

The correct answer is C. **(A)** **(B)** **(C)** **(D)**

PRACTICE

In Exercises 1 and 2, use the part of the quilt shown.

1. What is the value of *x*?

   (A) 3 **(B)** 3.4

   (C) 3.8 **(D)** 5.5

2. What is the value of *z*?

   (A) 35 **(B)** 55

   (C) 125 **(D)** 145

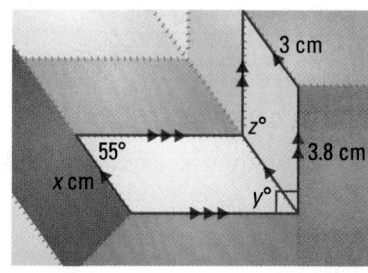

MULTIPLE CHOICE

In Exercises 1 and 2, use the diagram of rhombus *ABCD* below.

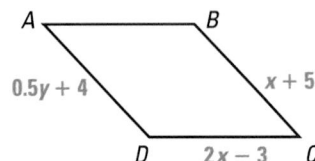

1. What is the value of *x*?

   (A) 2   **(B)** 4.6

   (C) 8   **(D)** 13

2. What is the value of *y*?

   (A) 1.8   **(B)** 2

   (C) 8   **(D)** 18

3. In the design shown below, a green regular hexagon is surrounded by yellow equilateral triangles and blue isosceles triangles. What is the measure of ∠1?

   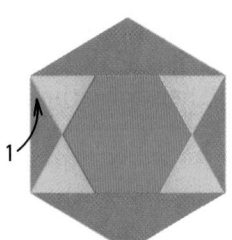

   (A) 30°   **(B)** 40°

   (C) 50°   **(D)** 60°

4. Which statement about *EFGH* can be concluded from the given information?

   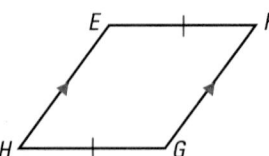

   (A) It is not a kite.

   (B) It is not an isosceles trapezoid.

   (C) It is not a square.

   (D) It is not a rhombus.

5. What is the most specific name for quadrilateral *FGHJ*?

   (A) Parallelogram

   (B) Rhombus

   (C) Rectangle

   (D) Square

   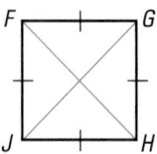

6. What is the measure of the smallest interior angle of the hexagon shown?

   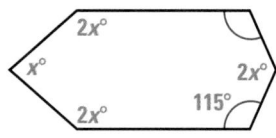

   (A) 50°   **(B)** 60°

   (C) 70°   **(D)** 80°

In Exercises 7 and 8, use the diagram of a cardboard container. In the diagram, ∠*S* ≅ ∠*R*, $\overline{PQ} \parallel \overline{SR}$, and $\overline{PS}$ and $\overline{QR}$ are not parallel.

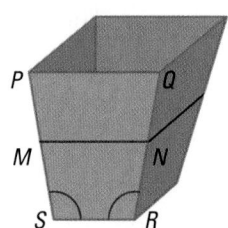

7. Which statement is true?

   (A) $PR = SQ$

   (B) $m\angle S + m\angle R = 180°$

   (C) $PQ = 2 \cdot SR$

   (D) $PQ = QR$

8. The bases of trapezoid *PQRS* are $\overline{PQ}$ and $\overline{SR}$, and the midsegment is $\overline{MN}$. Given $PQ = 9$ centimeters, and $MN = 7.2$ centimeters, what is *SR*?

   (A) 5.4 cm   **(B)** 8.1 cm

   (C) 10.8 cm   **(D)** 12.6 cm

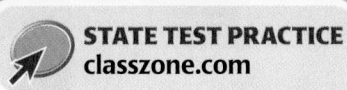

GRIDDED ANSWER

9. How many degrees greater is the measure of an interior angle of a regular octagon than the measure of an interior angle of a regular pentagon?

10. Parallelogram *ABCD* has vertices *A*(−3, −1), *B*(−1, 3), *C*(4, 3), and *D*(2, −1). What is the sum of the *x*- and *y*-coordinates of the point of intersection of the diagonals of *ABCD*?

11. For what value of *x* is the quadrilateral shown below a parallelogram?

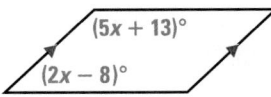

12. In kite *JKLM*, the ratio of *JK* to *KL* is 3 : 2. The perimeter of *JKLM* is 30 inches. Find the length (in inches) of $\overline{JK}$.

SHORT RESPONSE

13. The vertices of quadrilateral *EFGH* are *E*(−1, −2), *F*(−1, 3), *G*(2, 4), and *H*(3, 1). What type of quadrilateral is *EFGH*? *Explain.*

14. In the diagram below, *PQRS* is an isosceles trapezoid with $\overline{PQ} \parallel \overline{RS}$. *Explain* how to show that $\triangle PTS \cong \triangle QTR$.

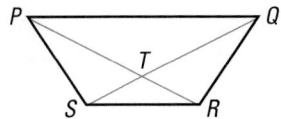

15. In trapezoid *ABCD*, $\overline{AB} \parallel \overline{CD}$, $\overline{XY}$ is the midsegment of *ABCD*, and $\overline{CD}$ is twice as long as $\overline{AB}$. Find the ratio of *XY* to *AB*. *Justify* your answer.

EXTENDED RESPONSE

16. The diagram shows a regular pentagon and diagonals drawn from vertex *F*.

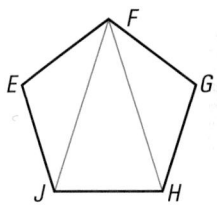

   a. The diagonals divide the pentagon into three triangles. Classify the triangles by their angles and side measures. *Explain* your reasoning.

   b. Which triangles are congruent? *Explain* how you know.

   c. For each triangle, find the interior angle measures. *Explain* your reasoning.

17. In parts (a)–(c), you are given information about a quadrilateral with vertices *A*, *B*, *C*, *D*. In each case, *ABCD* is a different quadrilateral.

   a. Suppose that $\overline{AB} \parallel \overline{CD}$, *AB* = *DC*, and ∠*C* is a right angle. Draw quadrilateral *ABCD* and give the most specific name for *ABCD*. *Justify* your answer.

   b. Suppose that $\overline{AB} \parallel \overline{CD}$ and *ABCD* has *exactly* two right angles, one of which is ∠*C*. Draw quadrilateral *ABCD* and give the most specific name for *ABCD*. *Justify* your answer.

   c. Suppose you are given only that $\overline{AB} \parallel \overline{CD}$. What additional information would you need to know about $\overline{AC}$ and $\overline{BD}$ to conclude that *ABCD* is a rhombus? *Explain.*

9 Properties of Transformations

Before

In previous chapters, you learned the following skills, which you'll use in Chapter 9: translating, reflecting, and rotating polygons, and using similar triangles.

Prerequisite Skills

VOCABULARY CHECK

Match the transformation of Triangle A with its graph.

1. Translation of Triangle A

2. Reflection of Triangle A

3. Rotation of Triangle A

SKILLS AND ALGEBRA CHECK

The vertices of *JKLM* are *J*(−1, 6), *K*(2, 5), *L*(2, 2), and *M*(−1, 1). Graph its image after the transformation described. *(Review p. 272 for 9.1, 9.3.)*

4. Translate 3 units left and 1 unit down.

5. Reflect in the *y*-axis.

In the diagram, *ABCD* ~ *EFGH*.
(Review p. 372 for 9.7.)

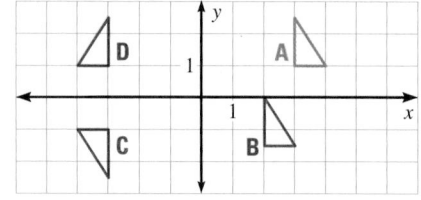

6. Find the scale factor of *ABCD* to *EFGH*.

7. Find the values of *x*, *y*, and *z*.

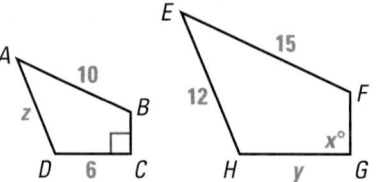

@HomeTutor Prerequisite skills practice at classzone.com

In Chapter 9, you will apply the big ideas listed below and reviewed in the Chapter Summary on page 635. You will also use the key vocabulary listed below.

Big Ideas

① Performing congruence and similarity transformations

② Making real-world connections to symmetry and tessellations

③ Applying matrices and vectors in Geometry

KEY VOCABULARY

- image, *p. 572*
- preimage, *p. 572*
- isometry, *p. 573*
- vector, *p. 574*
- component form, *p. 574*
- matrix, *p. 580*

- element, *p. 580*
- dimensions, *p. 580*
- line of reflection, *p. 589*
- center of rotation, *p. 598*
- angle of rotation, *p. 598*
- glide reflection, *p. 608*

- composition of transformations, *p. 609*
- line symmetry, *p. 619*
- rotational symmetry, *p. 620*
- scalar multiplication, *p. 627*

Why?

You can use properties of shapes to determine whether shapes tessellate. For example, you can use angle measurements to determine which shapes can be used to make a tessellation.

Animated Geometry

The animation illustrated below for Example 3 on page 617 helps you answer this question: How can you use tiles to tessellate a floor?

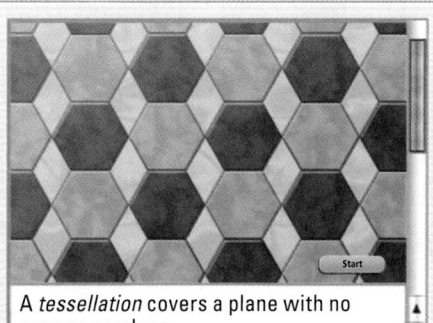

A *tessellation* covers a plane with no gaps or overlaps.

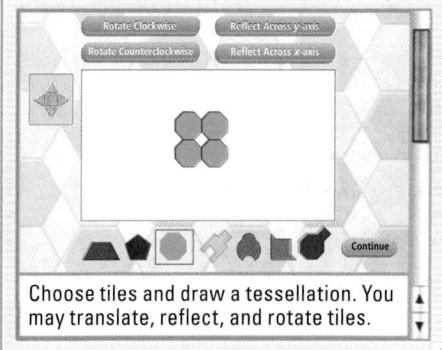

Choose tiles and draw a tessellation. You may translate, reflect, and rotate tiles.

Animated Geometry at classzone.com

Other animations for Chapter 9: pages 582, 590, 599, 602, 611, 619, and 626

9.1 Translate Figures and Use Vectors

Before	You used a coordinate rule to translate a figure.
Now	You will use a vector to translate a figure.
Why?	So you can find a distance covered on snowshoes, as in Exs. 35–37.

Key Vocabulary
• **image**
• **preimage**
• **isometry**
• **vector**
  initial point, terminal point, horizontal component, vertical component
• **component form**
• **translation,** *p. 272*

In Lesson 4.8, you learned that a *transformation* moves or changes a figure in some way to produce a new figure called an **image**. Another name for the original figure is the **preimage**.

Recall that a *translation* moves every point of a figure the same distance in the same direction. More specifically, a translation maps, or moves, the points P and Q of a plane figure to the points P' (read "P prime") and Q', so that one of the following statements is true:

• $PP' = QQ'$ and $\overline{PP'} \parallel \overline{QQ'}$, or
• $PP' = QQ'$ and $\overline{PP'}$ and $\overline{QQ'}$ are collinear.

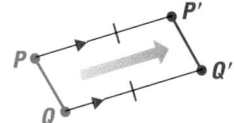

EXAMPLE 1   Translate a figure in the coordinate plane

Graph quadrilateral $ABCD$ with vertices $A(-1, 2)$, $B(-1, 5)$, $C(4, 6)$, and $D(4, 2)$. Find the image of each vertex after the translation $(x, y) \rightarrow (x + 3, y - 1)$. Then graph the image using prime notation.

Solution

USE NOTATION
You can use *prime notation* to name an image. For example, if the preimage is $\triangle ABC$, then its image is $\triangle A'B'C'$, read as *"triangle A prime, B prime, C prime."*

First, draw $ABCD$. Find the translation of each vertex by adding 3 to its x-coordinate and subtracting 1 from its y-coordinate. Then graph the image.

$$(x, y) \rightarrow (x + 3, y - 1)$$

$$A(-1, 2) \rightarrow A'(2, 1)$$
$$B(-1, 5) \rightarrow B'(2, 4)$$
$$C(4, 6) \rightarrow C'(7, 5)$$
$$D(4, 2) \rightarrow D'(7, 1)$$

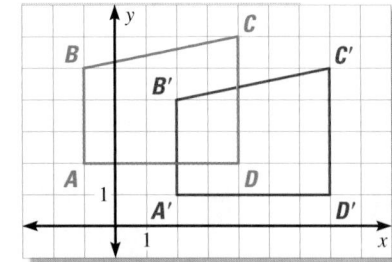

✓ **GUIDED PRACTICE** for Example 1

1. Draw $\triangle RST$ with vertices $R(2, 2)$, $S(5, 2)$, and $T(3, 5)$. Find the image of each vertex after the translation $(x, y) \rightarrow (x + 1, y + 2)$. Graph the image using prime notation.

2. The image of $(x, y) \rightarrow (x + 4, y - 7)$ is $\overline{P'Q'}$ with endpoints $P'(-3, 4)$ and $Q'(2, 1)$. Find the coordinates of the endpoints of the preimage.

ISOMETRY An **isometry** is a transformation that preserves length and angle measure. Isometry is another word for congruence transformation (page 272).

EXAMPLE 2 Write a translation rule and verify congruence

Write a rule for the translation of $\triangle ABC$ to $\triangle A'B'C'$. Then verify that the transformation is an isometry.

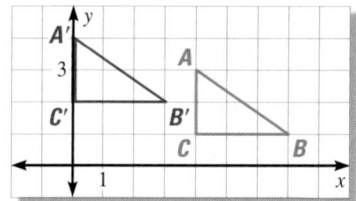

Solution

To go from A to A', move 4 units left and 1 unit up. So, a rule for the translation is $(x, y) \rightarrow (x - 4, y + 1)$.

Use the SAS Congruence Postulate. Notice that $CB = C'B' = 3$, and $AC = A'C' = 2$. The slopes of $\overline{CB}$ and $\overline{C'B'}$ are 0, and the slopes of $\overline{CA}$ and $\overline{C'A'}$ are undefined, so the sides are perpendicular. Therefore, $\angle C$ and $\angle C'$ are congruent right angles. So, $\triangle ABC \cong \triangle A'B'C'$. The translation is an isometry.

✓ **GUIDED PRACTICE** for Example 2

3. In Example 2, write a rule to translate $\triangle A'B'C'$ back to $\triangle ABC$.

THEOREM *For Your Notebook*

THEOREM 9.1 Translation Theorem

A translation is an isometry.

Proof: below; Ex. 46, p. 579

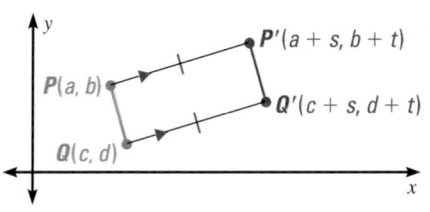

$\triangle ABC \cong \triangle A'B'C'$

PROOF Translation Theorem

A translation is an isometry.

GIVEN ▶ $P(a, b)$ and $Q(c, d)$ are two points on a figure translated by $(x, y) \rightarrow (x + s, y + t)$.

PROVE ▶ $PQ = P'Q'$

The translation maps $P(a, b)$ to $P'(a + s, b + t)$ and $Q(c, d)$ to $Q'(c + s, d + t)$.

Use the Distance Formula to find PQ and $P'Q'$. $PQ = \sqrt{(c - a)^2 + (d - b)^2}$.

$$P'Q' = \sqrt{[(c + s) - (a + s)]^2 + [(d + t) - (b + t)]^2}$$
$$= \sqrt{(c + s - a - s)^2 + (d + t - b - t)^2}$$
$$= \sqrt{(c - a)^2 + (d - b)^2}$$

Therefore, $PQ = P'Q'$ by the Transitive Property of Equality.

VECTORS Another way to describe a translation is by using a vector. A **vector** is a quantity that has both direction and *magnitude,* or size. A vector is represented in the coordinate plane by an arrow drawn from one point to another.

Vectors

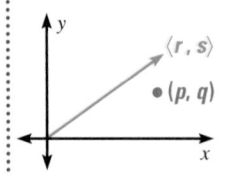
The diagram shows a vector named $\overrightarrow{FG}$, read as "vector *FG.*"

The **initial point**, or starting point, of the vector is *F*.

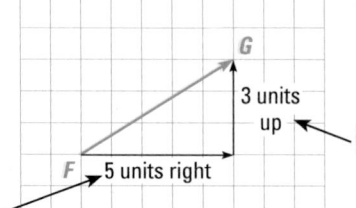

The **terminal point**, or ending point, of the vector is *G*.

horizontal component

The **component form** of a vector combines the horizontal and vertical components. So, the component form of $\overrightarrow{FG}$ is $\langle 5, 3 \rangle$.

EXAMPLE 3   **Identify vector components**

Name the vector and write its component form.

a.
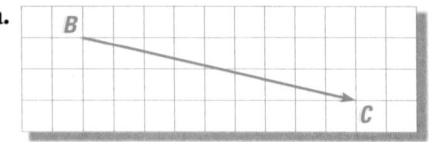

b.

Solution

a. The vector is $\overrightarrow{BC}$. From initial point *B* to terminal point *C*, you move 9 units right and 2 units down. So, the component form is $\langle 9, -2 \rangle$.

b. The vector is $\overrightarrow{ST}$. From initial point *S* to terminal point *T*, you move 8 units left and 0 units vertically. The component form is $\langle -8, 0 \rangle$.

EXAMPLE 4   **Use a vector to translate a figure**

The vertices of $\triangle ABC$ are *A*(0, 3), *B*(2, 4), and *C*(1, 0). Translate $\triangle ABC$ using the vector $\langle 5, -1 \rangle$.

Solution

First, graph $\triangle ABC$. Use $\langle 5, -1 \rangle$ to move each vertex 5 units to the right and 1 unit down. Label the image vertices. Draw $\triangle A'B'C'$. Notice that the vectors drawn from preimage to image vertices are parallel.

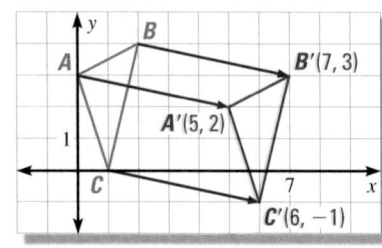

Name the vector and write its component form.

4.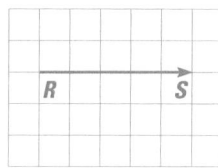

5.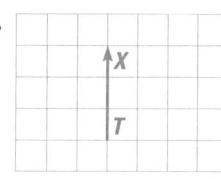

6.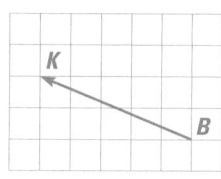

7. The vertices of △LMN are L(2, 2), M(5, 3), and N(9, 1). Translate △LMN using the vector ⟨−2, 6⟩.

EXAMPLE 5 **Solve a multi-step problem**

NAVIGATION A boat heads out from point D on one island toward point D on another. The boat encounters a storm at B, 12 miles east and 4 miles north of its starting point. The storm pushes the boat off course to point C, as shown.

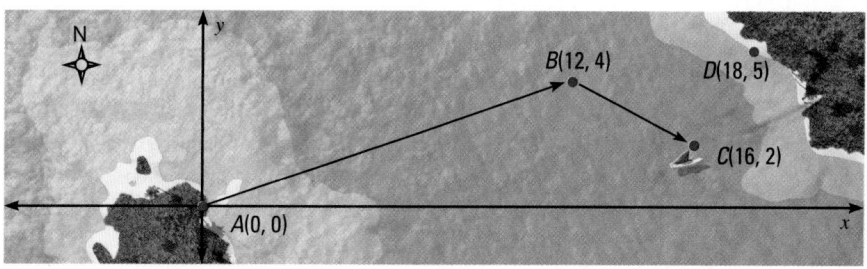

a. Write the component form of $\overrightarrow{AB}$.

b. Write the component form of $\overrightarrow{BC}$.

c. Write the component form of the vector that describes the straight line path from the boat's current position C to its intended destination D.

Solution

a. The component form of the vector from A(0, 0) to B(12, 4) is
$$\overrightarrow{AB} = \langle 12 - 0, 4 - 0 \rangle = \langle 12, 4 \rangle.$$

b. The component form of the vector from B(12, 4) to C(16, 2) is
$$\overrightarrow{BC} = \langle 16 - 12, 2 - 4 \rangle = \langle 4, -2 \rangle.$$

c. The boat is currently at point C and needs to travel to D.
The component form of the vector from C(16, 2) to D(18, 5) is
$$\overrightarrow{CD} = \langle 18 - 16, 5 - 2 \rangle = \langle 2, 3 \rangle.$$

✓ **GUIDED PRACTICE** for Example 5

8. **WHAT IF?** In Example 5, suppose there is no storm. Write the component form of the vector that describes the straight path from the boat's starting point A to its final destination D.

9.1 EXERCISES

HOMEWORK KEY

○ = WORKED-OUT SOLUTIONS
on p. WS10 for Exs. 7, 11, and 35

★ = STANDARDIZED TEST PRACTICE
Exs. 2, 14, and 42

SKILL PRACTICE

1. **VOCABULARY** Copy and complete: A __?__ is a quantity that has both __?__ and magnitude.

2. ★ **WRITING** *Describe* the difference between a vector and a ray.

EXAMPLE 1
on p. 572
for Exs. 3–10

IMAGE AND PREIMAGE Use the translation $(x, y) \rightarrow (x - 8, y + 4)$.

3. What is the image of $A(2, 6)$?

4. What is the image of $B(-1, 5)$?

5. What is the preimage of $C'(-3, -10)$?

6. What is the preimage of $D'(4, -3)$?

GRAPHING AN IMAGE The vertices of $\triangle PQR$ are $P(-2, 3)$, $Q(1, 2)$, and $R(3, -1)$. Graph the image of the triangle using prime notation.

7. $(x, y) \rightarrow (x + 4, y + 6)$

8. $(x, y) \rightarrow (x + 9, y - 2)$

9. $(x, y) \rightarrow (x - 2, y - 5)$

10. $(x, y) \rightarrow (x - 1, y + 3)$

EXAMPLE 2
on p. 573
for Exs. 11–14

WRITING A RULE $\triangle A'B'C'$ is the image of $\triangle ABC$ after a translation. Write a rule for the translation. Then *verify* that the translation is an isometry.

11.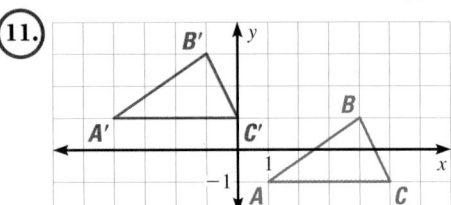

12.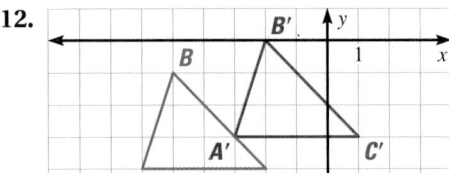

13. **ERROR ANALYSIS** *Describe* and correct the error in graphing the translation of quadrilateral *EFGH*.

$(x, y) \rightarrow (x - 1, y - 2)$

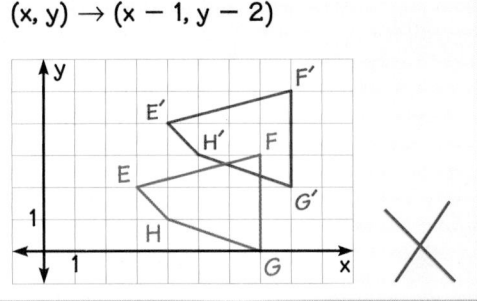

14. ★ **MULTIPLE CHOICE** Translate $Q(0, -8)$ using $(x, y) \rightarrow (x - 3, y + 2)$.

Ⓐ $Q'(-2, 5)$　　Ⓑ $Q'(3, -10)$　　Ⓒ $Q'(-3, -6)$　　Ⓓ $Q'(2, -11)$

EXAMPLE 3
on p. 574
for Exs. 15–23

IDENTIFYING VECTORS Name the vector and write its component form.

15.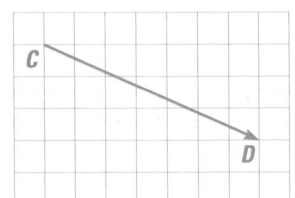

16.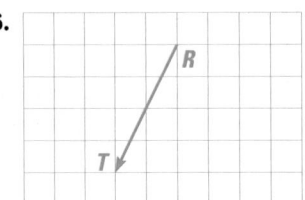

17.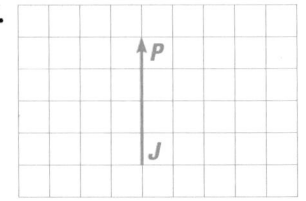

VECTORS Use the point $P(-3, 6)$. Find the component form of the vector that describes the translation to P'.

18. $P'(0, 1)$ **19.** $P'(-4, 8)$ **20.** $P'(-2, 0)$ **21.** $P'(-3, -5)$

TRANSLATIONS Think of each translation as a vector. *Describe* the vertical component of the vector. *Explain.*

22.    **23.**

EXAMPLE 4
on p. 574
for Exs. 24–27

TRANSLATING A TRIANGLE The vertices of $\triangle DEF$ are $D(2, 5)$, $E(6, 3)$, and $F(4, 0)$. Translate $\triangle DEF$ using the given vector. Graph $\triangle DEF$ and its image.

24. $\langle 6, 0 \rangle$ **25.** $\langle 5, -1 \rangle$ **26.** $\langle -3, -7 \rangle$ **27.** $\langle -2, -4 \rangle$

ALGEBRA Find the value of each variable in the translation.

28. 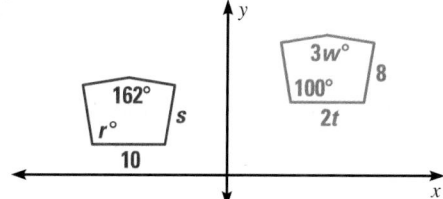   **29.**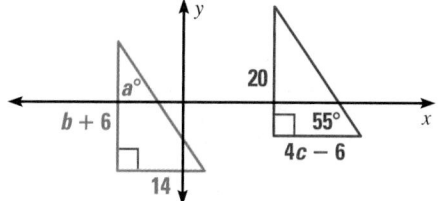

30. **ALGEBRA** Translation A maps (x, y) to $(x + n, y + m)$. Translation B maps (x, y) to $(x + s, y + t)$.

     a. Translate a point using Translation A, then Translation B. Write a rule for the final image of the point.

     b. Translate a point using Translation B, then Translation A. Write a rule for the final image of the point.

     c. *Compare* the rules you wrote in parts (a) and (b). Does it matter which translation you do first? *Explain.*

31. **MULTI-STEP PROBLEM** The vertices of a rectangle are $Q(2, -3)$, $R(2, 4)$, $S(5, 4)$, and $T(5, -3)$.

     a. Translate $QRST$ 3 units left and 2 units down. Find the areas of $QRST$ and $Q'R'S'T'$.

     b. *Compare* the areas. Make a conjecture about the areas of a preimage and its image after a translation.

32. **CHALLENGE** The vertices of $\triangle ABC$ are $A(2, 2)$, $B(4, 2)$, and $C(3, 4)$.

     a. Graph the image of $\triangle ABC$ after the transformation $(x, y) \rightarrow (x + y, y)$. Is the transformation an isometry? *Explain.* Are the areas of $\triangle ABC$ and $\triangle A'B'C'$ the same?

     b. Graph a new triangle, $\triangle DEF$, and its image after the transformation given in part (a). Are the areas of $\triangle DEF$ and $\triangle D'E'F'$ the same?

EXAMPLE 2
on p. 573
for Exs. 33–34

HOME DESIGN Designers can use computers to make patterns in fabrics or floors. On the computer, a copy of the design in Rectangle A is used to cover an entire floor. The translation $(x, y) \rightarrow (x + 3, y)$ maps Rectangle A to Rectangle B.

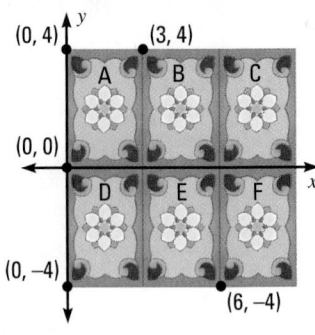

33. Use coordinate notation to describe the translations that map Rectangle A to Rectangles C, D, E, and F.

@HomeTutor for problem solving help at classzone.com

34. Write a rule to translate Rectangle F back to Rectangle A.

@HomeTutor for problem solving help at classzone.com

EXAMPLE 5
on p. 575
for Exs. 35–37

SNOWSHOEING You are snowshoeing in the mountains. The distances in the diagram are in miles. Write the component form of the vector.

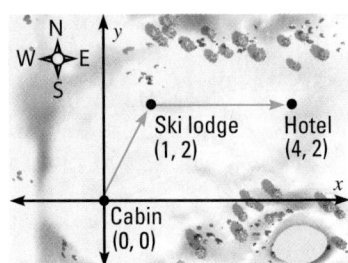

35. From the cabin to the ski lodge

36. From the ski lodge to the hotel

37. From the hotel back to your cabin

HANG GLIDING A hang glider travels from point *A* to point *D*. At point *B*, the hang glider changes direction, as shown in the diagram. The distances in the diagram are in kilometers.

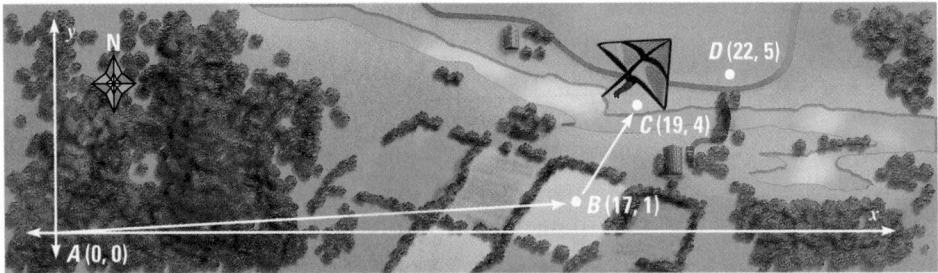

38. Write the component form for $\overrightarrow{AB}$ and $\overrightarrow{BC}$.

39. Write the component form of the vector that describes the path from the hang glider's current position *C* to its intended destination *D*.

40. What is the total distance the hang glider travels?

41. Suppose the hang glider went straight from *A* to *D*. Write the component form of the vector that describes this path. What is this distance?

42. ★ **EXTENDED RESPONSE** Use the equation $2x + y = 4$.

   a. Graph the line and its image after the translation $\langle -5, 4 \rangle$. What is an equation of the image of the line?

   b. *Compare* the line and its image. What are the slopes? the *y*-intercepts? the *x*-intercepts?

   c. Write an equation of the image of $2x + y = 4$ after the translation $\langle 2, -6 \rangle$ *without* using a graph. *Explain* your reasoning.

43. SCIENCE You are studying an amoeba through a microscope. Suppose the amoeba moves on a grid-indexed microscope slide in a straight line from square B3 to square G7.

a. *Describe* the translation.

b. Each grid square is 2 millimeters on a side. How far does the amoeba travel?

c. Suppose the amoeba moves from B3 to G7 in 24.5 seconds. What is its speed in millimeters per second?

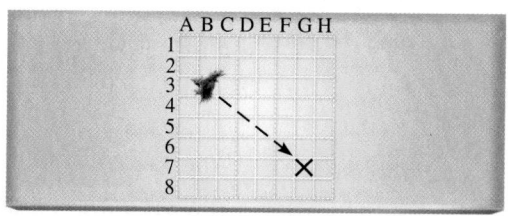

44. MULTI-STEP PROBLEM You can write the equation of a parabola in the form $y = (x - h)^2 + k$, where (h, k) is the *vertex* of the parabola. In the graph, an equation of Parabola 1 is $y = (x - 1)^2 + 3$, with vertex $(1, 3)$. Parabola 2 is the image of Parabola 1 after a translation.

a. Write a rule for the translation.

b. Write an equation of Parabola 2.

c. Suppose you translate Parabola 1 using the vector $\langle -4, 8 \rangle$. Write an equation of the image.

d. An equation of Parabola 3 is $y = (x + 5)^2 - 3$. Write a rule for the translation of Parabola 1 to Parabola 3. *Explain* your reasoning.

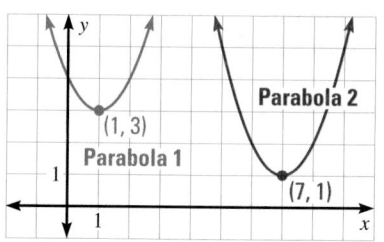

45. TECHNOLOGY The standard form of an exponential equation is $y = a^x$, where $a > 0$ and $a \neq 1$. Use the equation $y = 2^x$.

a. Use a graphing calculator to graph $y = 2^x$ and $y = 2^x - 4$. *Describe* the translation from $y = 2^x$ to $y = 2^x - 4$.

b. Use a graphing calculator to graph $y = 2^x$ and $y = 2^{x-4}$. *Describe* the translation from $y = 2^x$ to $y = 2^{x-4}$.

46. CHALLENGE Use properties of congruent triangles to prove part of Theorem 9.1, that a translation preserves angle measure.

MIXED REVIEW

PREVIEW
Prepare for Lesson 9.2 in Exs. 47–50.

Find the sum, difference, product, or quotient. *(p. 869)*

47. $-16 - 7$

48. $6 + (-12)$

49. $(13)(-2)$

50. $16 \div (-4)$

Determine whether the two triangles are similar. If they are, write a similarity statement. *(pp. 381, 388)*

51.

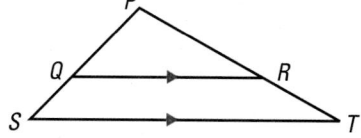

52.

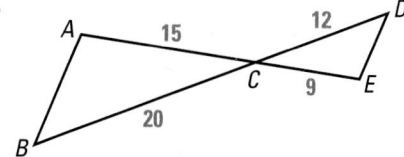

Points *A*, *B*, *C*, and *D* are the vertices of a quadrilateral. Give the most specific name for *ABCD*. *Justify* your answer. *(p. 552)*

53. $A(2, 0), B(7, 0), C(4, 4), D(2, 4)$

54. $A(3, 0), B(7, 2), C(3, 4), D(1, 2)$

EXTRA PRACTICE for Lesson 9.1, p. 912   **ONLINE QUIZ** at classzone.com

9.2 Use Properties of Matrices

Before	You performed translations using vectors.
Now	You will perform translations using matrix operations.
Why?	So you can calculate the total cost of art supplies, as in Ex. 36.

Key Vocabulary
• matrix
• element
• dimensions

A **matrix** is a rectangular arrangement of numbers in rows and columns. (The plural of matrix is *matrices*.) Each number in a matrix is called an **element**.

$$\text{row} \begin{bmatrix} 5 & 4 & 4 & 9 \\ -3 & 5 & 2 & 6 \\ 3 & -7 & 8 & 7 \end{bmatrix} \xleftarrow{\hspace{0.5cm}}$$

column

The element in the second row and third column is 2.

READ VOCABULARY

An element of a matrix may also be called an *entry*.

The **dimensions** of a matrix are the numbers of rows and columns. The matrix above has three rows and four columns, so the dimensions of the matrix are 3×4 (read "3 by 4").

You can represent a figure in the coordinate plane using a matrix with two rows. The first row has the x-coordinate(s) of the vertices. The second row has the corresponding y-coordinate(s). Each column represents a vertex, so the number of columns depends on the number of vertices of the figure.

EXAMPLE 1 Represent figures using matrices

Write a matrix to represent the point or polygon.

a. Point A

b. Quadrilateral $ABCD$

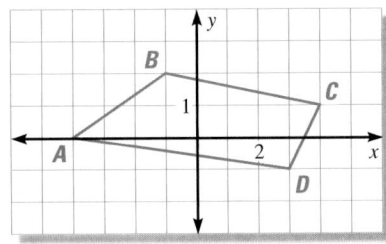

Solution

AVOID ERRORS

The columns in a polygon matrix follow the consecutive order of the vertices of the polygon.

a. Point matrix for A

$$\begin{bmatrix} -4 \\ 0 \end{bmatrix} \begin{matrix} \leftarrow x\text{-coordinate} \\ \leftarrow y\text{-coordinate} \end{matrix}$$

b. Polygon matrix for $ABCD$

$$\begin{matrix} A & B & C & D \end{matrix}$$
$$\begin{bmatrix} -4 & -1 & 4 & 3 \\ 0 & 2 & 1 & -1 \end{bmatrix} \begin{matrix} \leftarrow x\text{-coordinates} \\ \leftarrow y\text{-coordinates} \end{matrix}$$

✓ **GUIDED PRACTICE** for Example 1

1. Write a matrix to represent $\triangle ABC$ with vertices $A(3, 5)$, $B(6, 7)$ and $C(7, 3)$.

2. How many rows and columns are in a matrix for a hexagon?

ADDING AND SUBTRACTING To add or subtract matrices, you add or subtract corresponding elements. The matrices must have the same dimensions.

EXAMPLE 2 Add and subtract matrices

a. $\begin{bmatrix} 5 & -3 \\ 6 & -6 \end{bmatrix} + \begin{bmatrix} 1 & 2 \\ 3 & -4 \end{bmatrix} = \begin{bmatrix} 5+1 & -3+2 \\ 6+3 & -6+(-4) \end{bmatrix} = \begin{bmatrix} 6 & -1 \\ 9 & -10 \end{bmatrix}$

b. $\begin{bmatrix} 6 & 8 & 5 \\ 4 & 9 & -1 \end{bmatrix} - \begin{bmatrix} 1 & -7 & 0 \\ 4 & -2 & 3 \end{bmatrix} = \begin{bmatrix} 6-1 & 8-(-7) & 5-0 \\ 4-4 & 9-(-2) & -1-3 \end{bmatrix} = \begin{bmatrix} 5 & 15 & 5 \\ 0 & 11 & -4 \end{bmatrix}$

TRANSLATIONS You can use matrix addition to represent a translation in the coordinate plane. The image matrix for a translation is the sum of the translation matrix and the matrix that represents the preimage.

EXAMPLE 3 Represent a translation using matrices

The matrix $\begin{bmatrix} 1 & 5 & 3 \\ 1 & 0 & -1 \end{bmatrix}$ represents $\triangle ABC$. Find the image matrix that represents the translation of $\triangle ABC$ 1 unit left and 3 units up. Then graph $\triangle ABC$ and its image.

Solution

The translation matrix is $\begin{bmatrix} -1 & -1 & -1 \\ 3 & 3 & 3 \end{bmatrix}$.

Add this to the polygon matrix for the preimage to find the image matrix.

$$\begin{bmatrix} -1 & -1 & -1 \\ 3 & 3 & 3 \end{bmatrix} + \overset{A \quad B \quad C}{\begin{bmatrix} 1 & 5 & 3 \\ 1 & 0 & -1 \end{bmatrix}} = \overset{A' \quad B' \quad C'}{\begin{bmatrix} 0 & 4 & 2 \\ 4 & 3 & 2 \end{bmatrix}}$$

Translation   Polygon   Image
matrix   matrix   matrix

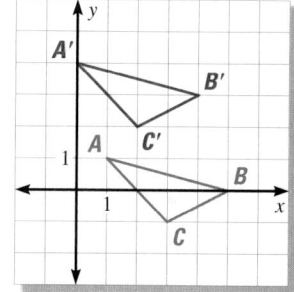

AVOID ERRORS

In order to add two matrices, they must have the same dimensions, so the translation matrix here must have three columns like the polygon matrix.

✓ **GUIDED PRACTICE** for Examples 2 and 3

In Exercises 3 and 4, add or subtract.

3. $\begin{bmatrix} -3 & 7 \end{bmatrix} + \begin{bmatrix} 2 & -5 \end{bmatrix}$

4. $\begin{bmatrix} 1 & -4 \\ 3 & -5 \end{bmatrix} - \begin{bmatrix} 2 & 3 \\ 7 & 8 \end{bmatrix}$

5. The matrix $\begin{bmatrix} 1 & 2 & 6 & 7 \\ 2 & -1 & 1 & 3 \end{bmatrix}$ represents quadrilateral *JKLM*. Write the translation matrix and the image matrix that represents the translation of *JKLM* 4 units right and 2 units down. Then graph *JKLM* and its image.

MULTIPLYING MATRICES The product of two matrices A and B is defined only when the number of columns in A is equal to the number of rows in B. If A is an $m \times n$ matrix and B is an $n \times p$ matrix, then the product AB is an $m \times p$ matrix.

$$
\begin{array}{ccccc}
A & \cdot & B & = & AB \\
(m \text{ by } n) & \cdot & (n \text{ by } p) & = & (m \text{ by } p)
\end{array}
$$

equal   dimensions of AB

You will use matrix multiplication in later lessons to represent transformations.

EXAMPLE 4 · Multiply matrices

Multiply $\begin{bmatrix} 1 & 0 \\ 4 & 5 \end{bmatrix} \begin{bmatrix} 2 & -3 \\ -1 & 8 \end{bmatrix}$.

Solution

The matrices are both 2×2, so their product is defined. Use the following steps to find the elements of the product matrix.

STEP 1 **Multiply** the numbers in the first row of the first matrix by the numbers in the first column of the second matrix. Put the result in the first row, first column of the product matrix.

$$\begin{bmatrix} 1 & 0 \\ 4 & 5 \end{bmatrix} \begin{bmatrix} 2 & -3 \\ -1 & 8 \end{bmatrix} = \begin{bmatrix} 1(2) + 0(-1) & ? \\ ? & ? \end{bmatrix}$$

STEP 2 **Multiply** the numbers in the first row of the first matrix by the numbers in the second column of the second matrix. Put the result in the first row, second column of the product matrix.

$$\begin{bmatrix} 1 & 0 \\ 4 & 5 \end{bmatrix} \begin{bmatrix} 2 & -3 \\ -1 & 8 \end{bmatrix} = \begin{bmatrix} 1(2) + 0(-1) & 1(-3) + 0(8) \\ ? & ? \end{bmatrix}$$

STEP 3 **Multiply** the numbers in the second row of the first matrix by the numbers in the first column of the second matrix. Put the result in the second row, first column of the product matrix.

$$\begin{bmatrix} 1 & 0 \\ 4 & 5 \end{bmatrix} \begin{bmatrix} 2 & -3 \\ -1 & 8 \end{bmatrix} = \begin{bmatrix} 1(2) + 0(-1) & 1(-3) + 0(8) \\ 4(2) + 5(-1) & ? \end{bmatrix}$$

STEP 4 **Multiply** the numbers in the second row of the first matrix by the numbers in the second column of the second matrix. Put the result in the second row, second column of the product matrix.

$$\begin{bmatrix} 1 & 0 \\ 4 & 5 \end{bmatrix} \begin{bmatrix} 2 & -3 \\ -1 & 8 \end{bmatrix} = \begin{bmatrix} 1(2) + 0(-1) & 1(-3) + 0(8) \\ 4(2) + 5(-1) & 4(-3) + 5(8) \end{bmatrix}$$

STEP 5 **Simplify** the product matrix.

$$\begin{bmatrix} 1(2) + 0(-1) & 1(-3) + 0(8) \\ 4(2) + 5(-1) & 4(-3) + 5(8) \end{bmatrix} = \begin{bmatrix} 2 & -3 \\ 3 & 28 \end{bmatrix}$$

Animated Geometry at classzone.com

EXAMPLE 5 **Solve a real-world problem**

SOFTBALL Two softball teams submit equipment lists for the season. A bat costs $20, a ball costs $5, and a uniform costs $40. Use matrix multiplication to find the total cost of equipment for each team.

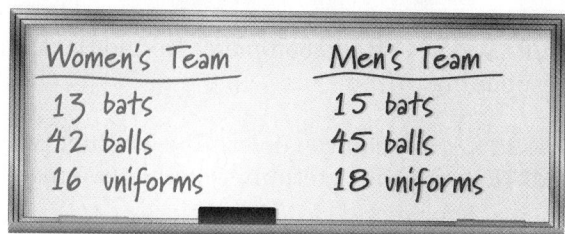

Women's Team
13 bats
42 balls
16 uniforms

Men's Team
15 bats
45 balls
18 uniforms

Solution

ANOTHER WAY
You could solve this problem arithmetically, multiplying the number of bats by the price of bats, and so on, then adding the costs for each team.

First, write the equipment lists and the costs per item in matrix form. You will use matrix multiplication, so you need to set up the matrices so that the number of columns of the equipment matrix matches the number of rows of the cost per item matrix.

$$
\begin{array}{c}
\textbf{EQUIPMENT} \\
\begin{array}{c}
 \\
\begin{array}{ccc} \textbf{Bats} & \textbf{Balls} & \textbf{Uniforms} \end{array} \\
\begin{array}{c} \textbf{Women} \\ \textbf{Men} \end{array}
\begin{bmatrix} 13 & 42 & 16 \\ 15 & 45 & 18 \end{bmatrix}
\end{array}
\end{array}
\cdot
\begin{array}{c}
\textbf{COST} \\
\textbf{Dollars} \\
\begin{array}{c} \textbf{Bats} \\ \textbf{Balls} \\ \textbf{Uniforms} \end{array}
\begin{bmatrix} 20 \\ 5 \\ 40 \end{bmatrix}
\end{array}
=
\begin{array}{c}
\textbf{TOTAL COST} \\
\textbf{Dollars} \\
\begin{array}{c} \textbf{Women} \\ \textbf{Men} \end{array}
\begin{bmatrix} ? \\ ? \end{bmatrix}
\end{array}
$$

You can find the total cost of equipment for each team by multiplying the equipment matrix by the cost per item matrix. The equipment matrix is 2×3 and the cost per item matrix is 3×1, so their product is a 2×1 matrix.

$$
\begin{bmatrix} 13 & 42 & 16 \\ 15 & 45 & 18 \end{bmatrix}
\begin{bmatrix} 20 \\ 5 \\ 40 \end{bmatrix}
=
\begin{bmatrix} 13(20) + 42(5) + 16(40) \\ 15(20) + 45(5) + 18(40) \end{bmatrix}
=
\begin{bmatrix} 1110 \\ 1245 \end{bmatrix}
$$

▶ The total cost of equipment for the women's team is $1110, and the total cost for the men's team is $1245.

✓ **GUIDED PRACTICE** for Examples 4 and 5

Use the matrices below. Is the product defined? *Explain.*

$$
A = \begin{bmatrix} -3 \\ 4 \end{bmatrix} \qquad B = \begin{bmatrix} 2 & 1 \end{bmatrix} \qquad C = \begin{bmatrix} 6.7 & 0 \\ -9.3 & 5.2 \end{bmatrix}
$$

6. AB **7.** BA **8.** AC

Multiply.

9. $\begin{bmatrix} 1 & 0 \\ 0 & -1 \end{bmatrix} \begin{bmatrix} 3 & 8 \\ -4 & 7 \end{bmatrix}$ **10.** $\begin{bmatrix} 5 & 1 \end{bmatrix} \begin{bmatrix} -3 \\ -2 \end{bmatrix}$ **11.** $\begin{bmatrix} 5 & 1 \\ 1 & -1 \end{bmatrix} \begin{bmatrix} 2 & -4 \\ 5 & 1 \end{bmatrix}$

12. WHAT IF? In Example 5, find the total cost for each team if a bat costs $25, a ball costs $4, and a uniform costs $35.

9.2 EXERCISES

HOMEWORK KEY

○ = **WORKED-OUT SOLUTIONS**
on p. WS11 for Exs. 13, 19, and 31

★ = **STANDARDIZED TEST PRACTICE**
Exs. 2, 17, 24, 25, and 35

SKILL PRACTICE

1. **VOCABULARY** Copy and complete: To find the sum of two matrices, add corresponding __?__.

2. ★ **WRITING** How can you determine whether two matrices can be added? How can you determine whether two matrices can be multiplied?

EXAMPLE 1
on p. 580
for Exs. 3–6

USING A DIAGRAM Use the diagram to write a matrix to represent the given polygon.

3. △*EBC*

4. △*ECD*

5. Quadrilateral *BCDE*

6. Pentagon *ABCDE*

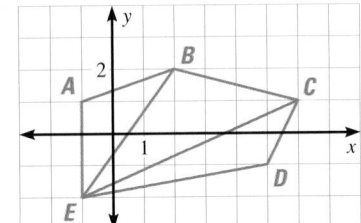

EXAMPLE 2
on p. 581
for Exs. 7–12

MATRIX OPERATIONS Add or subtract.

7. $\begin{bmatrix} 3 & 5 \end{bmatrix} + \begin{bmatrix} 9 & 2 \end{bmatrix}$

8. $\begin{bmatrix} -12 & 5 \\ 1 & -4 \end{bmatrix} + \begin{bmatrix} 2 & -3 \\ 0 & 8 \end{bmatrix}$

9. $\begin{bmatrix} 9 & 8 \\ -2 & 3 \\ 0 & -4 \end{bmatrix} + \begin{bmatrix} 7 & 1 \\ 2 & -3 \\ -5 & 1 \end{bmatrix}$

10. $\begin{bmatrix} 4.6 & 8.1 \end{bmatrix} - \begin{bmatrix} 3.8 & -2.1 \end{bmatrix}$

11. $\begin{bmatrix} -5 & 6 \\ -8 & 9 \end{bmatrix} - \begin{bmatrix} 8 & 10 \\ 4 & -7 \end{bmatrix}$

12. $\begin{bmatrix} 1.2 & 6 \\ 5.3 & 1.1 \end{bmatrix} - \begin{bmatrix} 2.5 & -3.3 \\ 7 & 4 \end{bmatrix}$

EXAMPLE 3
on p. 581
for Exs. 13–17

TRANSLATIONS Find the image matrix that represents the translation of the polygon. Then graph the polygon and its image.

13. $\begin{matrix} A & B & C \\ \begin{bmatrix} -2 & 2 & 1 \\ 4 & 1 & -3 \end{bmatrix} \end{matrix}$; 4 units up

14. $\begin{matrix} F & G & H & J \\ \begin{bmatrix} 2 & 5 & 8 & 5 \\ 2 & 3 & 1 & -1 \end{bmatrix} \end{matrix}$; 2 units left and 3 units down

15. $\begin{matrix} L & M & N & P \\ \begin{bmatrix} 2 & 0 & 2 & 3 \\ -1 & 3 & 3 & -1 \end{bmatrix} \end{matrix}$; 4 units right and 2 units up

16. $\begin{matrix} Q & R & S \\ \begin{bmatrix} -5 & 0 & 1 \\ 1 & 4 & 2 \end{bmatrix} \end{matrix}$; 3 units right and 1 unit down

17. ★ **MULTIPLE CHOICE** The matrix that represents quadrilateral *ABCD* is $\begin{bmatrix} 3 & 8 & 9 & 7 \\ 3 & 7 & 3 & 1 \end{bmatrix}$. Which matrix represents the image of the quadrilateral after translating it 3 units right and 5 units up?

Ⓐ $\begin{bmatrix} 6 & 11 & 12 & 10 \\ 8 & 12 & 8 & 6 \end{bmatrix}$

Ⓑ $\begin{bmatrix} 0 & 5 & 6 & 4 \\ 8 & 12 & 8 & 6 \end{bmatrix}$

Ⓒ $\begin{bmatrix} 6 & 11 & 12 & 10 \\ -2 & 2 & -2 & -4 \end{bmatrix}$

Ⓓ $\begin{bmatrix} 0 & 6 & 6 & 4 \\ -2 & 3 & -2 & -4 \end{bmatrix}$

EXAMPLE 4
....
on p. 582
for Exs. 18–26

MATRIX OPERATIONS **Multiply.**

18. $\begin{bmatrix} 5 & 2 \end{bmatrix} \begin{bmatrix} 4 \\ 3 \end{bmatrix}$

(19.) $\begin{bmatrix} 1.2 & 3 \end{bmatrix} \begin{bmatrix} -2 \\ -1.5 \end{bmatrix}$

20. $\begin{bmatrix} 6 & 7 \\ -5 & 8 \end{bmatrix} \begin{bmatrix} 2 & 1 \\ 9 & -3 \end{bmatrix}$

21. $\begin{bmatrix} 0.4 & 6 \\ -6 & 2.3 \end{bmatrix} \begin{bmatrix} 5 & 8 \\ -1 & 2 \end{bmatrix}$

22. $\begin{bmatrix} 4 & 8 & -1 \end{bmatrix} \begin{bmatrix} 3 \\ 2 \\ 5 \end{bmatrix}$

23. $\begin{bmatrix} 9 & 1 & 2 \\ 8 & -1 & 4 \end{bmatrix} \begin{bmatrix} 4 \\ 0 \\ 1 \end{bmatrix}$

24. ★ **MULTIPLE CHOICE** Which product is not defined?

Ⓐ $\begin{bmatrix} 1 & 7 \\ 3 & 12 \end{bmatrix} \begin{bmatrix} 6 \\ 15 \end{bmatrix}$ Ⓑ $\begin{bmatrix} 3 & 20 \end{bmatrix} \begin{bmatrix} 9 \\ 30 \end{bmatrix}$ Ⓒ $\begin{bmatrix} 15 \\ -3 \end{bmatrix} \begin{bmatrix} 1 & 6 \\ 4 & 0 \end{bmatrix}$ Ⓓ $\begin{bmatrix} 30 \\ -7 \end{bmatrix} \begin{bmatrix} 5 & 5 \end{bmatrix}$

25. ★ **OPEN-ENDED MATH** Write two matrices that have a defined product.
Then find the product.

26. **ERROR ANALYSIS** *Describe* and correct the error in the computation.

$$\begin{bmatrix} 9 & -2 \\ 4 & 10 \end{bmatrix} \begin{bmatrix} -6 & 12 \\ 3 & -6 \end{bmatrix} = \begin{bmatrix} 9(-6) & -2(12) \\ 4(3) & 10(-6) \end{bmatrix} \quad ✗$$

TRANSLATIONS **Use the described translation and the graph of the image to
find the matrix that represents the preimage.**

27. 4 units right and 2 units down

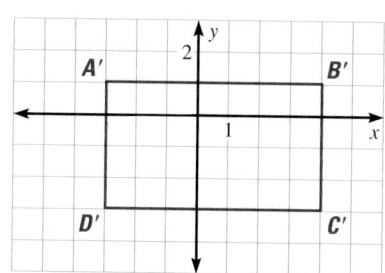

28. 6 units left and 5 units up

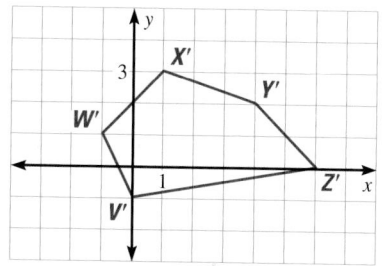

29. **MATRIX EQUATION** Use the description of a translation of a triangle to
find the value of each variable. *Explain* your reasoning. What are the
coordinates of the vertices of the image triangle?

$$\begin{bmatrix} 12 & 12 & w \\ -7 & v & -7 \end{bmatrix} + \begin{bmatrix} 9 & a & b \\ 6 & -2 & c \end{bmatrix} = \begin{bmatrix} m & 20 & -8 \\ n & -9 & 13 \end{bmatrix}$$

30. **CHALLENGE** A point in space has three coordinates
(x, y, z), as shown at the right. From the origin, a point
can be forward or back on the x-axis, left or right on the
y-axis, and up or down on the z-axis.

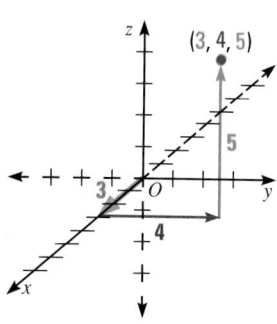

a. You translate a point three units forward, four units
right, and five units up. Write a translation matrix for
the point.

b. You translate a figure that has five vertices. Write a
translation matrix to move the figure five units back,
ten units left, and six units down.

EXAMPLE 5
on p. 583
for Ex. 31

31. **COMPUTERS** Two computer labs submit equipment lists. A mouse costs $10, a package of CDs costs $32, and a keyboard costs $15. Use matrix multiplication to find the total cost of equipment for each lab.

Lab 1	Lab 2
25 Mice	15 Mice
10 CDs	20 CDs
18 Keyboards	12 Keyboards

@HomeTutor for problem solving help at classzone.com

32. **SWIMMING** Two swim teams submit equipment lists. The women's team needs 30 caps and 26 goggles. The men's team needs 15 caps and 25 goggles. A cap costs $10 and goggles cost $15.

a. Use matrix addition to find the total number of caps and the total number of goggles for each team.

b. Use matrix multiplication to find the total equipment cost for each team.

c. Find the total cost for both teams.

@HomeTutor for problem solving help at classzone.com

MATRIX PROPERTIES In Exercises 33–35, use matrices *A*, *B*, and *C*.

$$A = \begin{bmatrix} 5 & 1 \\ 10 & -2 \end{bmatrix} \qquad B = \begin{bmatrix} -1 & 3 \\ 2 & 0 \end{bmatrix} \qquad C = \begin{bmatrix} 2 & 4 \\ -5 & 1 \end{bmatrix}$$

33. **MULTI-STEP PROBLEM** Use the 2 × 2 matrices above to explore the Commutative Property of Multiplication.

a. What does it mean that multiplication is *commutative*?

b. Find and *compare AB* and *BA*.

c. Based on part (b), make a conjecture about whether matrix multiplication is commutative.

34. **MULTI-STEP PROBLEM** Use the 2 × 2 matrices above to explore the Associative Property of Multiplication.

a. What does it mean that multiplication is *associative*?

b. Find and *compare A(BC)* and *(AB)C*.

c. Based on part (b), make a conjecture about whether matrix multiplication is associative.

35. ★ **SHORT RESPONSE** Find and *compare A(B + C)* and *AB + AC*. Make a conjecture about matrices and the Distributive Property.

36. **ART** Two art classes are buying supplies. A brush is $4 and a paint set is $10. Each class has only $225 to spend. Use matrix multiplication to find the maximum number of brushes Class A can buy and the maximum number of paint sets Class B can buy. *Explain.*

Class A	Class B
x brushes	18 brushes
12 paint sets	*y* paint sets

37. CHALLENGE The total United States production of corn was 8,967 million bushels in 2002, and 10,114 million bushels in 2003. The table shows the percents of the total grown by four states.

   a. Use matrix multiplication to find the number of bushels (in millions) harvested in each state each year.

   b. How many bushels (in millions) were harvested in these two years in Iowa?

   c. The price for a bushel of corn in Nebraska was $2.32 in 2002, and $2.45 in 2003. Use matrix multiplication to find the total value of corn harvested in Nebraska in these two years.

	2002	2003
Iowa	21.5%	18.6%
Illinois	16.4%	17.9%
Nebraska	10.5%	11.1%
Minnesota	11.7%	9.6%

MIXED REVIEW

PREVIEW

Prepare for Lesson 9.3 in Exs. 38–39.

Copy the figure and draw its image after the reflection. *(p. 272)*

38. Reflect the figure in the *x*-axis.

39. Reflect the figure in the *y*-axis.

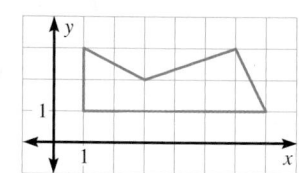

Find the value of *x* to the nearest tenth. *(p. 466)*

40.

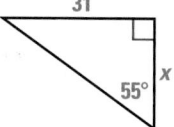

41.

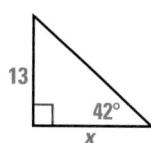

42.

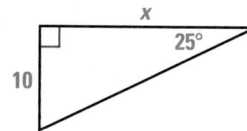

The diagonals of rhombus *WXYZ* intersect at *V*. Given that $m\angle XYW = 62°$, find the indicated measure. *(p. 533)*

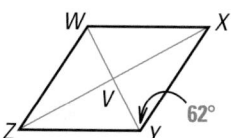

43. $m\angle ZYW = \underline{}$ **44.** $m\angle WXY = \underline{}$ **45.** $m\angle XVY = \underline{}$

QUIZ *for Lessons 9.1–9.2*

1. In the diagram shown, name the vector and write its component form. *(p. 572)*

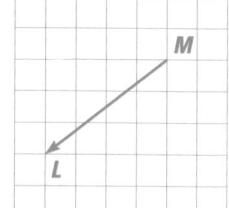

Use the translation $(x, y) \rightarrow (x + 3, y - 2)$. *(p. 572)*

2. What is the image of $(-1, 5)$?

3. What is the image of $(6, 3)$?

4. What is the preimage of $(-4, -1)$?

Add, subtract, or multiply. *(p. 580)*

5. $\begin{bmatrix} 5 & -3 \\ 8 & -2 \end{bmatrix} + \begin{bmatrix} -9 & 6 \\ 4 & -7 \end{bmatrix}$ **6.** $\begin{bmatrix} -6 & 1 \\ 3 & 12 \end{bmatrix} - \begin{bmatrix} 4 & 15 \\ -7 & 8 \end{bmatrix}$ **7.** $\begin{bmatrix} 7 & -6 & 2 \\ 8 & 3 & 5 \end{bmatrix} \begin{bmatrix} 5 & 2 \\ -9 & 0 \\ 3 & -7 \end{bmatrix}$

9.3 Reflections in the Plane

MATERIALS · graph paper · straightedge

QUESTION What is the relationship between the line of reflection and the segment connecting a point and its image?

EXPLORE Graph a reflection of a triangle

STEP 1

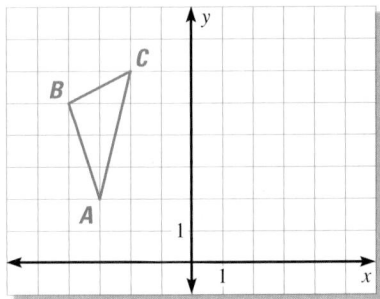

Draw a triangle Graph $A(-3, 2)$, $B(-4, 5)$, and $C(-2, 6)$. Connect the points to form $\triangle ABC$.

STEP 2

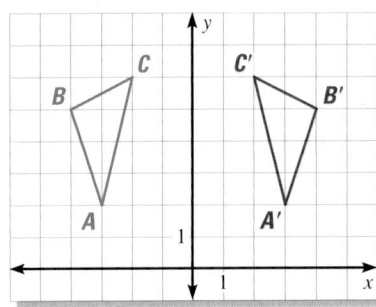

Graph a reflection Reflect $\triangle ABC$ in the y-axis. Label points A', B', and C' appropriately.

STEP 3

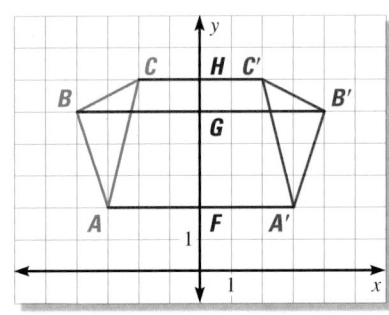

Draw segments Draw $\overline{AA'}$, $\overline{BB'}$, and $\overline{CC'}$. Label the points where these segments intersect the y-axis as F, G, and H, respectively.

DRAW CONCLUSIONS Use your observations to complete these exercises

1. Find the lengths of $\overline{CH}$ and $\overline{HC'}$, $\overline{BG}$ and $\overline{GB'}$, and $\overline{AF}$ and $\overline{FA'}$. *Compare* the lengths of each pair of segments.

2. Find the measures of $\angle CHG$, $\angle BGF$, and $\angle AFG$. *Compare* the angle measures.

3. How is the y-axis related to $\overline{AA'}$, $\overline{BB'}$, and $\overline{CC'}$?

4. Use the graph at the right.

   a. $\overline{K'L'}$ is the reflection of $\overline{KL}$ in the x-axis. Copy the diagram and draw $\overline{K'L'}$.

   b. Draw $\overline{KK'}$ and $\overline{LL'}$. Label the points where the segments intersect the x-axis as J and M.

   c. How is the x-axis related to $\overline{KK'}$ and $\overline{LL'}$?

5. How is the line of reflection related to the segment connecting a point and its image?

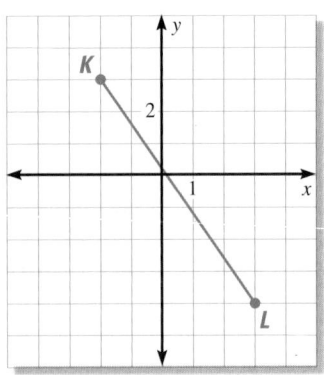

9.3 Perform Reflections

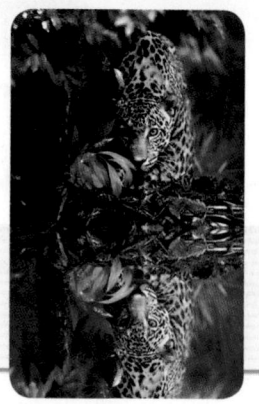

Before	You reflected a figure in the *x*- or *y*-axis.
Now	You will reflect a figure in any given line.
Why?	So you can identify reflections, as in Exs. 31–33.

Key Vocabulary
• **line of reflection**
• reflection, *p. 272*

In Lesson 4.8, you learned that a *reflection* is a transformation that uses a line like a mirror to reflect an image. The mirror line is called the **line of reflection**.

A reflection in a line *m* maps every point *P* in the plane to a point *P'*, so that for each point one of the following properties is true:

• If *P* is not on *m*, then *m* is the perpendicular bisector of $\overline{PP'}$, or

• If *P* is on *m*, then *P = P'*.

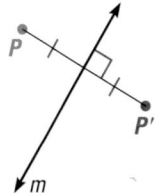

Point P not on m

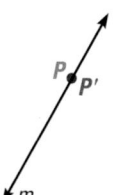

Point P on m

EXAMPLE 1 Graph reflections in horizontal and vertical lines

The vertices of △*ABC* are *A*(1, 3), *B*(5, 2), and *C*(2, 1). Graph the reflection of △*ABC* described.

a. In the line *n*: *x* = 3 **b.** In the line *m*: *y* = 1

Solution

a. Point *A* is 2 units left of *n*, so its reflection *A'* is 2 units right of *n* at (5, 3). Also, *B'* is 2 units left of *n* at (1, 2), and *C'* is 1 unit right of *n* at (4, 1).

b. Point *A* is 2 units above *m*, so *A'* is 2 units below *m* at (1, −1). Also, *B'* is 1 unit below *m* at (5, 0). Because point *C* is on line *m*, you know that *C = C'*.

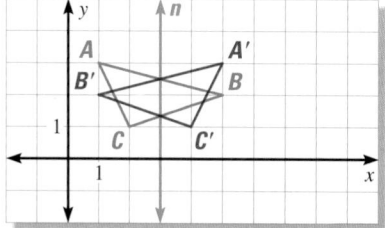

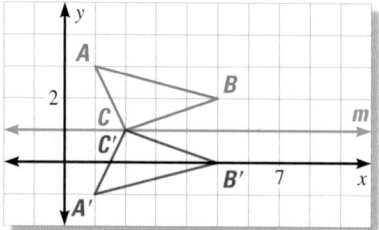

✓ **GUIDED PRACTICE** for Example 1

Graph a reflection of △*ABC* from Example 1 in the given line.

1. *y* = 4   **2.** *x* = −3   **3.** *y* = 2

EXAMPLE 2 **Graph a reflection in** *y* = *x*

The endpoints of $\overline{FG}$ are *F*(−1, 2) and *G*(1, 2). Reflect the segment in the line *y* = *x*. Graph the segment and its image.

Solution

REVIEW SLOPE

The product of the slopes of perpendicular lines is −1.

The slope of *y* = *x* is 1. The segment from *F* to its image, $\overline{FF'}$, is perpendicular to the line of reflection *y* = *x*, so the slope of $\overline{FF'}$ will be −1 (because 1(−1) = −1). From *F*, move 1.5 units right and 1.5 units down to *y* = *x*. From that point, move 1.5 units right and 1.5 units down to locate *F'*(2, −1).

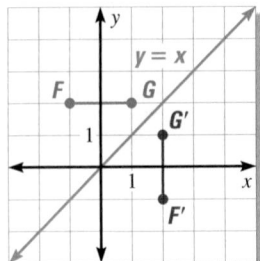

The slope of $\overline{GG'}$ will also be −1. From *G*, move 0.5 units right and 0.5 units down to *y* = *x*. Then move 0.5 units right and 0.5 units down to locate *G'*(2, 1).

COORDINATE RULES You can use coordinate rules to find the images of points reflected in four special lines.

KEY CONCEPT   *For Your Notebook*

Coordinate Rules for Reflections

- If (*a*, *b*) is reflected in the *x*-axis, its image is the point (*a*, −*b*).
- If (*a*, *b*) is reflected in the *y*-axis, its image is the point (−*a*, *b*).
- If (*a*, *b*) is reflected in the line *y* = *x*, its image is the point (*b*, *a*).
- If (*a*, *b*) is reflected in the line *y* = −*x*, its image is the point (−*b*, −*a*).

EXAMPLE 3 **Graph a reflection in** *y* = −*x*

Reflect $\overline{FG}$ from Example 2 in the line *y* = −*x*. Graph $\overline{FG}$ and its image.

Solution

Use the coordinate rule for reflecting in *y* = −*x*.

$$(a, b) \rightarrow (-b, -a)$$

$$F(-1, 2) \rightarrow F'(-2, 1)$$

$$G(1, 2) \rightarrow G'(-2, -1)$$

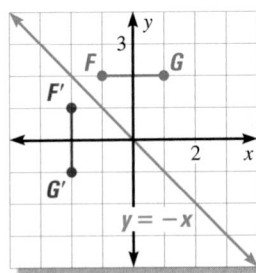

Animated Geometry at classzone.com

✓ **GUIDED PRACTICE** for Examples 2 and 3

4. Graph △*ABC* with vertices *A*(1, 3), *B*(4, 4), and *C*(3, 1). Reflect △*ABC* in the lines *y* = −*x* and *y* = *x*. Graph each image.

5. In Example 3, *verify* that $\overline{FF'}$ is perpendicular to *y* = −*x*.

REFLECTION THEOREM You saw in Lesson 9.1 that the image of a translation is congruent to the original figure. The same is true for a reflection.

THEOREM   *For Your Notebook*

THEOREM 9.2 Reflection Theorem

A reflection is an isometry.

Proof: Exs. 35–38, p. 595

$\triangle ABC \cong \triangle A'B'C'$

WRITE PROOFS
Some theorems, such as the Reflection Theorem, have more than one case. To prove this type of theorem, each case must be proven.

PROVING THE THEOREM To prove the Reflection Theorem, you need to show that a reflection preserves the length of a segment. Consider a segment $\overline{PQ}$ that is reflected in a line m to produce $\overline{P'Q'}$. There are four cases to prove:

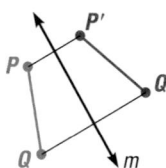   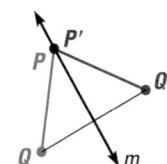   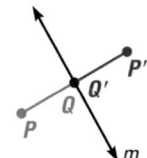

Case 1 P and Q are on the same side of m.

Case 2 P and Q are on opposite sides of m.

Case 3 P lies on m, and $\overline{PQ}$ is not $\perp$ to m.

Case 4 Q lies on m, and $\overline{PQ} \perp m$.

EXAMPLE 4 **Find a minimum distance**

PARKING You are going to buy books. Your friend is going to buy CDs. Where should you park to minimize the distance you both will walk?

Solution

Reflect B in line m to obtain B'. Then draw $\overline{AB'}$. Label the intersection of $\overline{AB'}$ and m as C. Because AB' is the shortest distance between A and B' and $BC = B'C$, park at point C to minimize the combined distance, $AC + BC$, you both have to walk.

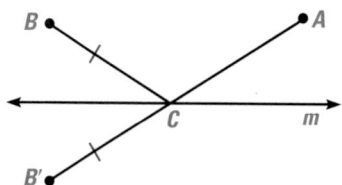

✔ **GUIDED PRACTICE** for Example 4

6. Look back at Example 4. Answer the question by using a reflection of point A instead of point B.

REFLECTION MATRIX You can find the image of a polygon reflected in the *x*-axis or *y*-axis using matrix multiplication. Write the reflection matrix to the *left* of the polygon matrix, then multiply.

Notice that because matrix multiplication is not commutative, the order of the matrices in your product is important. The reflection matrix must be first followed by the polygon matrix.

KEY CONCEPT   *For Your Notebook*

Reflection Matrices

Reflection in the *x*-axis

$$\begin{bmatrix} 1 & 0 \\ 0 & -1 \end{bmatrix}$$

Reflection in the *y*-axis

$$\begin{bmatrix} -1 & 0 \\ 0 & 1 \end{bmatrix}$$

EXAMPLE 5 **Use matrix multiplication to reflect a polygon**

The vertices of $\triangle DEF$ are $D(1, 2)$, $E(3, 3)$, and $F(4, 0)$. Find the reflection of $\triangle DEF$ in the *y*-axis using matrix multiplication. Graph $\triangle DEF$ and its image.

Solution

STEP 1 **Multiply** the polygon matrix by the matrix for a reflection in the *y*-axis.

$$\begin{matrix} & D & E & F \end{matrix}$$
$$\begin{bmatrix} -1 & 0 \\ 0 & 1 \end{bmatrix}\begin{bmatrix} 1 & 3 & 4 \\ 2 & 3 & 0 \end{bmatrix} = \begin{bmatrix} -1(1) + 0(2) & -1(3) + 0(3) & -1(4) + 0(0) \\ 0(1) + 1(2) & 0(3) + 1(3) & 0(4) + 1(0) \end{bmatrix}$$

Reflection Polygon
  matrix   matrix

$$\begin{matrix} & D' & E' & F' \end{matrix}$$
$$= \begin{bmatrix} -1 & -3 & -4 \\ 2 & 3 & 0 \end{bmatrix} \quad \text{Image matrix}$$

STEP 2 **Graph** $\triangle DEF$ and $\triangle D'E'F'$.

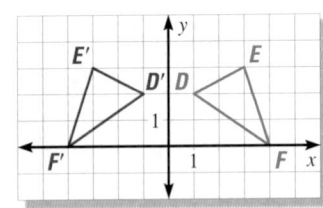

✓ **GUIDED PRACTICE** for Example 5

The vertices of $\triangle LMN$ are $L(-3, 3)$, $M(1, 2)$, and $N(-2, 1)$. Find the described reflection using matrix multiplication.

7. Reflect $\triangle LMN$ in the *x*-axis.   **8.** Reflect $\triangle LMN$ in the *y*-axis.

9.3 EXERCISES

HOMEWORK KEY
○ = WORKED-OUT SOLUTIONS
on p. WS11 for Exs. 5, 13, and 33

★ = STANDARDIZED TEST PRACTICE
Exs. 2, 12, 25, and 40

SKILL PRACTICE

1. **VOCABULARY** What is a *line of reflection*?

2. ★ **WRITING** *Explain* how to find the distance from a point to its image if you know the distance from the point to the line of reflection.

REFLECTIONS Graph the reflection of the polygon in the given line.

EXAMPLE 1
on p. 589
for Exs. 3–8

3. *x*-axis

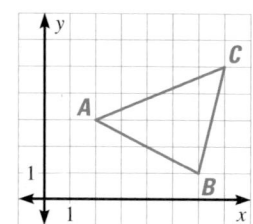

4. *y*-axis

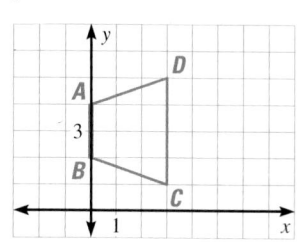

5. *y* = 2

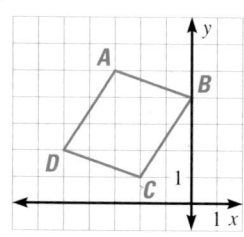

6. *x* = −1

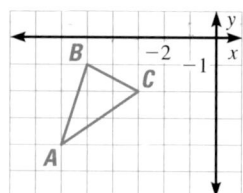

7. *y*-axis

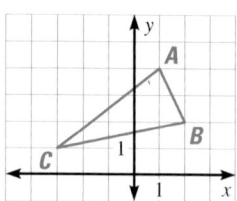

8. *y* = −3

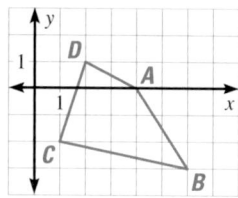

EXAMPLES 2 and 3
on p. 590
for Exs. 9–12

9. *y* = *x*

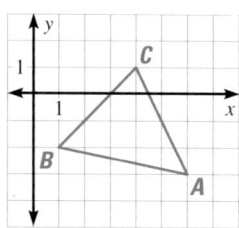

10. *y* = −*x*

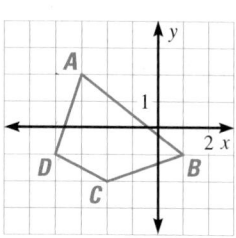

11. *y* = *x*

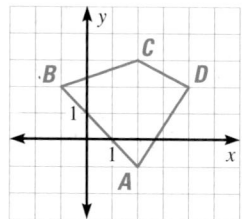

12. ★ **MULTIPLE CHOICE** What is the line of reflection for △*ABC* and its image?

(A) *y* = 0 (the *x*-axis)   (B) *y* = −*x*

(C) *x* = 1   (D) *y* = *x*

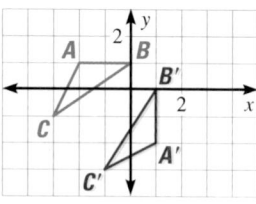

EXAMPLE 5
on p. 592
for Exs. 13–17

USING MATRIX MULTIPLICATION Use matrix multiplication to find the image. Graph the polygon and its image.

13. Reflect $\begin{bmatrix} A & B & C \\ -2 & 3 & 4 \\ 5 & -3 & 6 \end{bmatrix}$ in the *x*-axis.

14. Reflect $\begin{bmatrix} P & Q & R & S \\ 2 & 6 & 5 & 2 \\ -2 & -3 & -8 & -5 \end{bmatrix}$ in the *y*-axis.

FINDING IMAGE MATRICES Write a matrix for the polygon. Then find the image matrix that represents the polygon after a reflection in the given line.

15. *y*-axis

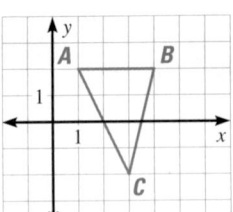

16. *x*-axis

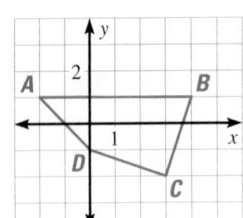

17. *y*-axis

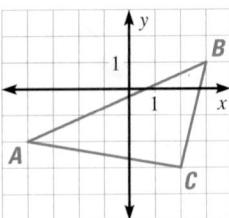

18. ERROR ANALYSIS *Describe* and correct the error in finding the image matrix of △*PQR* reflected in the *y*-axis.

$$\begin{bmatrix} 1 & 0 \\ 0 & -1 \end{bmatrix}\begin{bmatrix} -5 & 4 & -2 \\ 4 & 8 & -1 \end{bmatrix} = \begin{bmatrix} -5 & 4 & -2 \\ -4 & -8 & -1 \end{bmatrix}$$

MINIMUM DISTANCE Find point *C* on the *x*-axis so *AC* + *BC* is a minimum.

19. *A*(1, 4), *B*(6, 1)

20. *A*(4, −3), *B*(12, −5)

21. *A*(−8, 4), *B*(−1, 3)

TWO REFLECTIONS The vertices of △*FGH* are *F*(3, 2), *G*(1, 5), and *H*(−1, 2). Reflect △*FGH* in the first line. Then reflect △*F′G′H′* in the second line. Graph △*F′G′H′* and △*F″G″H″*.

22. In *y* = 2, then in *y* = −1

23. In *y* = −1, then in *x* = 2

24. In *y* = *x*, then in *x* = −3

25. ★ **SHORT RESPONSE** Use your graphs from Exercises 22–24. What do you notice about the order of vertices in the preimages and images?

26. CONSTRUCTION Use these steps to construct a reflection of △*ABC* in line *m* using a straightedge and a compass.

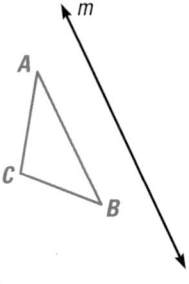

STEP 1 Draw △*ABC* and line *m*.

STEP 2 Use one compass setting to find two points that are equidistant from *A* on line *m*. Use the same compass setting to find a point on the other side of *m* that is the same distance from line *m*. Label that point *A′*.

STEP 3 Repeat Step 2 to find points *B′* and *C′*. Draw △*A′B′C′*.

27. ⓧⓨ **ALGEBRA** The line *y* = 3*x* + 2 is reflected in the line *y* = −1. What is the equation of the image?

28. ⓧⓨ **ALGEBRA** Reflect the graph of the quadratic equation *y* = 2*x*² − 5 in the *x*-axis. What is the equation of the image?

29. REFLECTING A TRIANGLE Reflect △*MNQ* in the line *y* = −2*x*.

30. CHALLENGE Point *B′*(1, 4) is the image of *B*(3, 2) after a reflection in line *c*. Write an equation of line *c*.

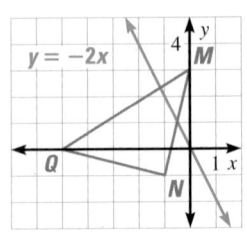

○ = **WORKED-OUT SOLUTIONS**
on p. WS1

★ = **STANDARDIZED TEST PRACTICE**

REFLECTIONS Identify the case of the Reflection Theorem represented.

31.

32.

(33.)

EXAMPLE 4
....
on p. 591
for Ex. 34

34. DELIVERING PIZZA You park at some point K on line n. You deliver a pizza to house H, go back to your car, and deliver a pizza to house J. Assuming that you can cut across both lawns, how can you determine the parking location K that minimizes the total walking distance?

@HomeTutor for problem solving help at classzone.com

35. PROVING THEOREM 9.2 Prove Case 1 of the Reflection Theorem.

Case 1 The segment does not intersect the line of reflection.

GIVEN ▶ A reflection in m maps P to P' and Q to Q'.

PROVE ▶ $PQ = P'Q'$

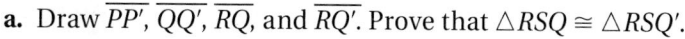

Plan for Proof

a. Draw $\overline{PP'}$, $\overline{QQ'}$, $\overline{RQ}$, and $\overline{RQ'}$. Prove that $\triangle RSQ \cong \triangle RSQ'$.

b. Use the properties of congruent triangles and perpendicular bisectors to prove that $PQ = P'Q'$.

@HomeTutor for problem solving help at classzone.com

PROVING THEOREM 9.2 In Exercises 36–38, write a proof for the given case of the Reflection Theorem. (Refer to the diagrams on page 591.)

36. Case 2 The segment intersects the line of reflection.

GIVEN ▶ A reflection in m maps P to P' and Q to Q'.
Also, $\overline{PQ}$ intersects m at point R.

PROVE ▶ $PQ = P'Q'$

37. Case 3 One endpoint is on the line of reflection, and the segment is not perpendicular to the line of reflection.

GIVEN ▶ A reflection in m maps P to P' and Q to Q'.
Also, P lies on line m, and $\overline{PQ}$ is not perpendicular to m.

PROVE ▶ $PQ = P'Q'$

38. Case 4 One endpoint is on the line of reflection, and the segment is perpendicular to the line of reflection.

GIVEN ▶ A reflection in m maps P to P' and Q to Q'.
Also, Q lies on line m, and $\overline{PQ}$ is perpendicular to line m.

PROVE ▶ $PQ = P'Q'$

39. REFLECTING POINTS Use $C(1, 3)$.

    a. Point A has coordinates $(-1, 1)$. Find point B on $\overrightarrow{AC}$ so $AC = CB$.

    b. The endpoints of $\overline{FG}$ are $F(2, 0)$ and $G(3, 2)$. Find point H on $\overrightarrow{FC}$ so $FC = CH$. Find point J on $\overrightarrow{GC}$ so $GC = CJ$.

    c. Explain why parts (a) and (b) can be called *reflection in a point*.

PHYSICS **The Law of Reflection states that the angle of incidence is congruent to the angle of reflection. Use this information in Exercises 40 and 41.**

angle of incidence   angle of reflection

40. ★ **SHORT RESPONSE** Suppose a billiard table has a coordinate grid on it. If a ball starts at the point $(0, 1)$ and rolls at a 45° angle, it will eventually return to its starting point. Would this happen if the ball started from other points on the *y*-axis between $(0, 0)$ and $(0, 4)$? *Explain.*

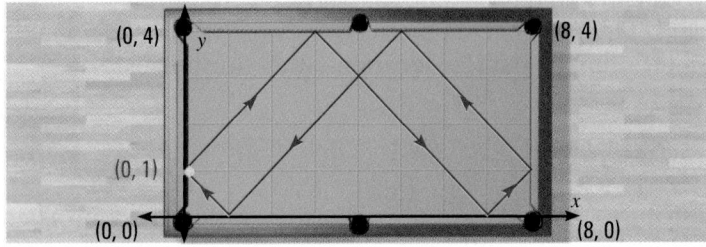

41. CHALLENGE Use the diagram to prove that you can see your full self in a mirror that is only half of your height. Assume that you and the mirror are both perpendicular to the floor.

    a. Think of a light ray starting at your foot and reflected in a mirror. Where does it have to hit the mirror in order to reflect to your eye?

    b. Think of a light ray starting at the top of your head and reflected in a mirror. Where does it have to hit the mirror in order to reflect to your eye?

    c. Show that the distance between the points you found in parts (a) and (b) is half your height.

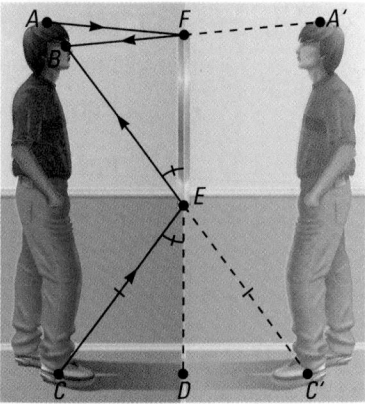

MIXED REVIEW

PREVIEW
Prepare for
Lesson 9.4 in
Exs. 42–43.

Tell whether the lines through the given points are *parallel*, *perpendicular*, or *neither*. *Justify* your answer. *(p. 171)*

42. Line 1: $(3, 7)$ and $(9, 7)$
    Line 2: $(-2, 8)$ and $(-2, 1)$

43. Line 1: $(-4, -1)$ and $(-8, -4)$
    Line 2: $(1, -3)$ and $(5, 0)$

Quadrilateral *EFGH* is a kite. Find $m\angle G$. *(p. 542)*

44. 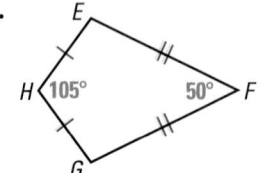   **45.** 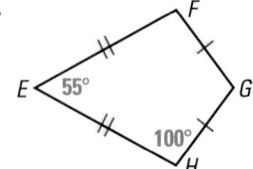   **46.**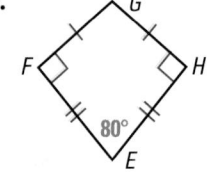

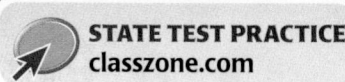
Lessons 9.1–9.3

1. **MULTI-STEP PROBLEM** $\triangle R'S'T'$ is the image of $\triangle RST$ after a translation.

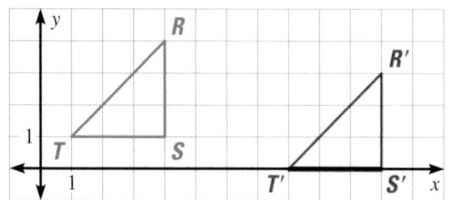

   a. Write a rule for the translation.

   b. *Verify* that the transformation is an isometry.

   c. Suppose $\triangle R'S'T'$ is translated using the rule $(x, y) \rightarrow (x + 4, y - 2)$. What are the coordinates of the vertices of $\triangle R''S''T''$?

2. **SHORT RESPONSE** During a marching band routine, a band member moves directly from point A to point B. Write the component form of the vector $\overrightarrow{AB}$. *Explain* your answer.

3. **SHORT RESPONSE** Trace the picture below. Reflect the image in line m. How is the distance from X to line m related to the distance from X' to line m? Write the property that makes this true.

4. **SHORT RESPONSE** The endpoints of $\overline{AB}$ are $A(2, 4)$ and $B(4, 0)$. The endpoints of $\overline{CD}$ are $C(3, 3)$ and $D(7, -1)$. Is the transformation from $\overline{AB}$ to $\overline{CD}$ an isometry? *Explain.*

5. **GRIDDED ANSWER** The vertices of $\triangle FGH$ are $F(-4, 3)$, $G(3, -1)$, and $H(1, -2)$. The coordinates of F' are $(-1, 4)$ after a translation. What is the x-coordinate of G'?

6. **OPEN-ENDED** Draw a triangle in a coordinate plane. Reflect the triangle in an axis. Write the reflection matrix that would yield the same result.

7. **EXTENDED RESPONSE** Two cross-country teams submit equipment lists for a season. A pair of running shoes costs $60, a pair of shorts costs $18, and a shirt costs $15.

Women's Team	Men's Team
14 pairs of shoes	10 pairs of shoes
16 pairs of shorts	13 pairs of shorts
16 shirts	13 shirts

   a. Use matrix multiplication to find the total cost of equipment for each team.

   b. How much money will the teams need to raise if the school gives each team $200?

   c. Repeat parts (a) and (b) if a pair of shoes costs $65 and a shirt costs $10. Does the change in prices change which team needs to raise more money? *Explain.*

8. **MULTI-STEP PROBLEM** Use the polygon as the preimage.

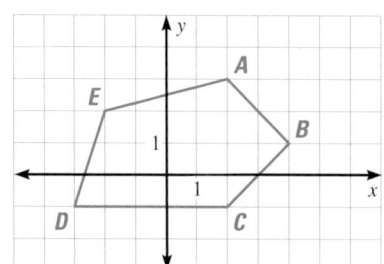

   a. Reflect the preimage in the y-axis.

   b. Reflect the preimage in the x-axis.

   c. *Compare* the order of vertices in the preimage with the order in each image.

9.4 Perform Rotations

Before You rotated figures about the origin.

Now You will rotate figures about a point.

Why? So you can classify transformations, as in Exs. 3–5.

Key Vocabulary
• center of rotation
• angle of rotation
• rotation, *p. 272*

Recall from Lesson 4.8 that a *rotation* is a transformation in which a figure is turned about a fixed point called the **center of rotation**. Rays drawn from the center of rotation to a point and its image form the **angle of rotation**.

A rotation about a point *P* through an angle of *x*° maps every point *Q* in the plane to a point *Q'* so that one of the following properties is true:

• If *Q* is not the center of rotation *P*, then $QP = Q'P$ and $m\angle QPQ' = x°$, or

• If *Q* is the center of rotation *P*, then the image of *Q* is *Q*.

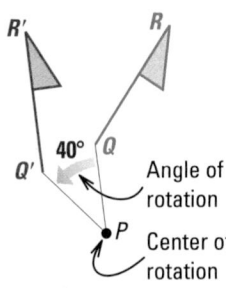

DIRECTION OF ROTATION

A 40° counterclockwise rotation is shown at the right. Rotations can be *clockwise* or *counterclockwise*. In this chapter, all rotations are counterclockwise.

clockwise

counterclockwise

EXAMPLE 1 Draw a rotation

Draw a 120° rotation of △*ABC* about *P*.

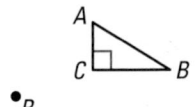

Solution

STEP 1 **Draw** a segment from *A* to *P*.

STEP 2 **Draw** a ray to form a 120° angle with $\overline{PA}$.

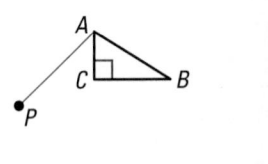

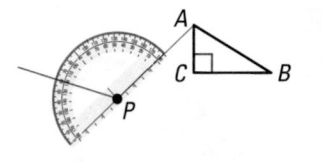

STEP 3 **Draw** *A'* so that $PA' = PA$.

STEP 4 **Repeat** Steps 1–3 for each vertex. Draw △*A'B'C'*.

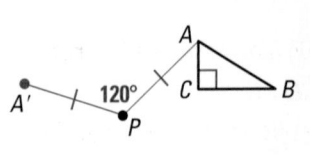

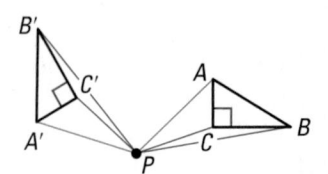

ROTATIONS ABOUT THE ORIGIN You can rotate a figure more than 180°. The diagram shows rotations of point *A* 130°, 220°, and 310° about the origin. A rotation of 360° returns a figure to its original coordinates.

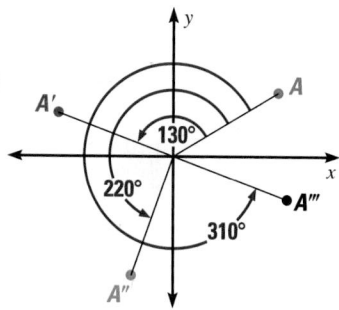

USE ROTATIONS
You can rotate a figure more than 360°. However, the effect is the same as rotating the figure by the angle minus 360°.

There are coordinate rules that can be used to find the coordinates of a point after rotations of 90°, 180°, or 270° about the origin.

KEY CONCEPT *For Your Notebook*

Coordinate Rules for Rotations about the Origin

When a point (a, b) is rotated counterclockwise about the origin, the following are true:

1. For a rotation of 90°, $(a, b) \rightarrow (-b, a)$.
2. For a rotation of 180°, $(a, b) \rightarrow (-a, -b)$.
3. For a rotation of 270°, $(a, b) \rightarrow (b, -a)$.

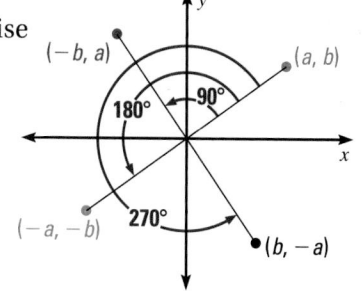

EXAMPLE 2 **Rotate a figure using the coordinate rules**

Graph quadrilateral *RSTU* with vertices *R*(3, 1), *S*(5, 1), *T*(5, −3), and *U*(2, −1). Then rotate the quadrilateral 270° about the origin.

Solution

Graph *RSTU*. Use the coordinate rule for a 270° rotation to find the images of the vertices.

$(a, b) \rightarrow (b, -a)$

$R(3, 1) \rightarrow R'(1, -3)$

$S(5, 1) \rightarrow S'(1, -5)$

$T(5, -3) \rightarrow T'(-3, -5)$

$U(2, -1) \rightarrow U'(-1, -2)$

Graph the image *R'S'T'U'*.

ANOTHER WAY
For an alternative method for solving the problem in Example 2, turn to page 606 for the **Problem Solving Workshop**.

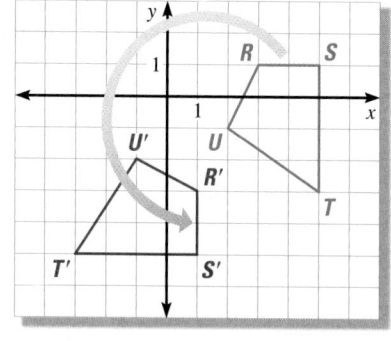

Animated **Geometry** at classzone.com

✔ **GUIDED PRACTICE** for Examples 1 and 2

1. Trace △*DEF* and *P*. Then draw a 50° rotation of △*DEF* about *P*.

2. Graph △*JKL* with vertices *J*(3, 0), *K*(4, 3), and *L*(6, 0). Rotate the triangle 90° about the origin.

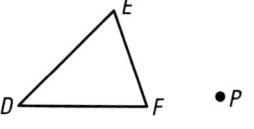

USING MATRICES You can find certain images of a polygon rotated about the origin using matrix multiplication. Write the rotation matrix to the left of the polygon matrix, then multiply.

KEY CONCEPT   *For Your Notebook*

Rotation Matrices (Counterclockwise)

90° rotation

$$\begin{bmatrix} 0 & -1 \\ 1 & 0 \end{bmatrix}$$

180° rotation

$$\begin{bmatrix} -1 & 0 \\ 0 & -1 \end{bmatrix}$$

270° rotation

$$\begin{bmatrix} 0 & 1 \\ -1 & 0 \end{bmatrix}$$

360° rotation

$$\begin{bmatrix} 1 & 0 \\ 0 & 1 \end{bmatrix}$$

READ VOCABULARY

Notice that a 360° rotation returns the figure to its original position. Multiplying by the matrix that represents this rotation gives you the polygon matrix you started with, which is why it is also called the *identity matrix*.

EXAMPLE 3   **Use matrices to rotate a figure**

Trapezoid *EFGH* has vertices $E(-3, 2)$, $F(-3, 4)$, $G(1, 4)$, and $H(2, 2)$. Find the image matrix for a 180° rotation of *EFGH* about the origin. Graph *EFGH* and its image.

Solution

STEP 1 **Write** the polygon matrix:
$$\begin{matrix} E & F & G & H \end{matrix}$$
$$\begin{bmatrix} -3 & -3 & 1 & 2 \\ 2 & 4 & 4 & 2 \end{bmatrix}$$

AVOID ERRORS

Because matrix multiplication is not commutative, you should always write the rotation matrix first, then the polygon matrix.

STEP 2 **Multiply** by the matrix for a 180° rotation.

$$\begin{bmatrix} -1 & 0 \\ 0 & -1 \end{bmatrix} \overset{\begin{matrix} E & F & G & H \end{matrix}}{\begin{bmatrix} -3 & -3 & 1 & 2 \\ 2 & 4 & 4 & 2 \end{bmatrix}} = \overset{\begin{matrix} E' & F' & G' & H' \end{matrix}}{\begin{bmatrix} 3 & 3 & -1 & -2 \\ -2 & -4 & -4 & -2 \end{bmatrix}}$$

Rotation matrix   Polygon matrix   Image matrix

STEP 3 **Graph** the preimage *EFGH*. Graph the image *E'F'G'H'*.

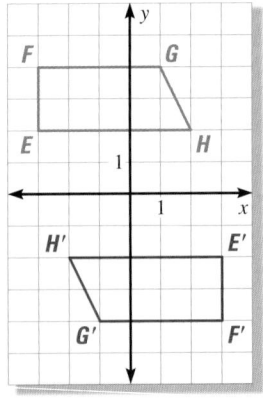

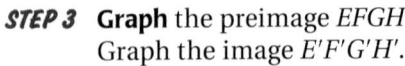

GUIDED PRACTICE for Example 3

Use the quadrilateral *EFGH* in Example 3. Find the image matrix after the rotation about the origin. Graph the image.

3. 90°   **4.** 270°   **5.** 360°

THEOREM 9.3 **Rotation Theorem**

A rotation is an isometry.

Proof: Exs. 33–35, p. 604

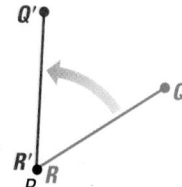

$\triangle ABC \cong \triangle A'B'C'$

CASES OF THEOREM 9.3 To prove the Rotation Theorem, you need to show that a rotation preserves the length of a segment. Consider a segment $\overline{QR}$ rotated about point P to produce $\overline{Q'R'}$. There are three cases to prove:

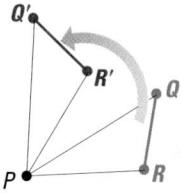

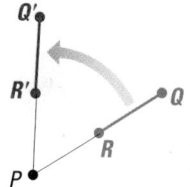

Case 1 R, Q, and P are noncollinear.

Case 2 R, Q, and P are collinear.

Case 3 P and R are the same point.

 EXAMPLE 4 **Standardized Test Practice**

> The quadrilateral is rotated about P. **What is the value of y?**
>
> **(A)** $\dfrac{8}{5}$ **(B)** 2
>
> **(C)** 3   **(D)** 10

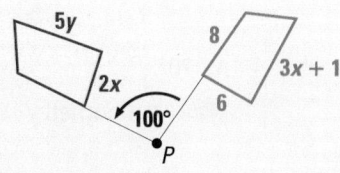

Solution

By Theorem 9.3, the rotation is an isometry, so corresponding side lengths are equal. Then $2x = 6$, so $x = 3$. Now set up an equation to solve for y.

$5y = 3x + 1$	**Corresponding lengths in an isometry are equal.**
$5y = 3(3) + 1$	**Substitute 3 for x.**
$y = 2$	**Solve for y.**

▶ The correct answer is B. **(A)** **(B)** **(C)** **(D)**

✔ **GUIDED PRACTICE** **for Example 4**

6. Find the value of r in the rotation of the triangle.

(A) 3   **(B)** 5

(C) 6   **(D)** 15

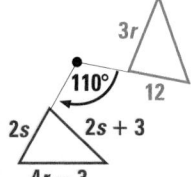

9.4 EXERCISES

HOMEWORK KEY

○ = WORKED-OUT SOLUTIONS
on p. WS11 for Exs. 13, 15, and 29

★ = STANDARDIZED TEST PRACTICE
Exs. 2, 20, 21, 23, 24, and 37

SKILL PRACTICE

1. **VOCABULARY** What is a *center of rotation*?

2. ★ **WRITING** *Compare* the coordinate rules and the rotation matrices for a rotation of 90°.

EXAMPLE 1
on p. 598
for Exs. 3–11

IDENTIFYING TRANSFORMATIONS **Identify the type of transformation,** *translation,* *reflection,* **or** *rotation,* **in the photo.** *Explain* **your reasoning.**

3.

4.

5.

ANGLE OF ROTATION **Match the diagram with the angle of rotation.**

6.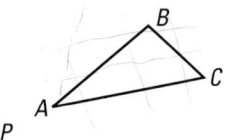

7.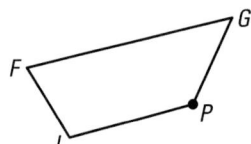

8.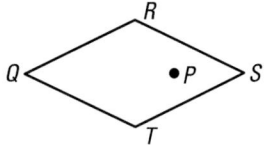

A. 70°   **B.** 100°   **C.** 150°

Animated **Geometry** at classzone.com

ROTATING A FIGURE **Trace the polygon and point *P* on paper. Then draw a rotation of the polygon the given number of degrees about *P*.**

9. 30°

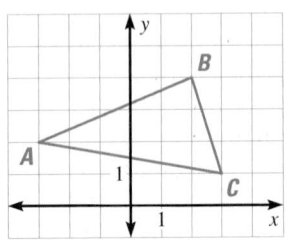

10. 150°

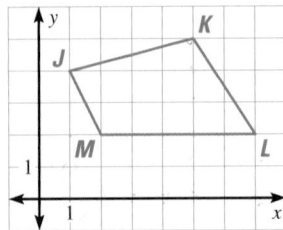

11. 130°

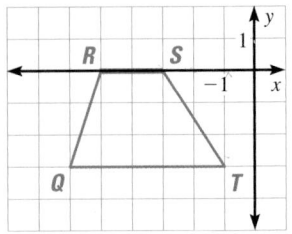

EXAMPLE 2
on p. 599
for Exs. 12–14

USING COORDINATE RULES **Rotate the figure the given number of degrees about the origin. List the coordinates of the vertices of the image.**

12. 90°

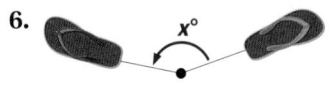

(13.) 180°

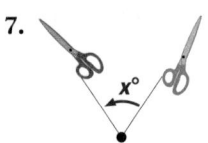

14. 270°

EXAMPLE 3
....
on p. 600
for Exs. 15–19

USING MATRICES Find the image matrix that represents the rotation of the polygon about the origin. Then graph the polygon and its image.

15. $\begin{array}{c} A \quad B \quad C \\ \begin{bmatrix} 1 & 5 & 4 \\ 4 & 6 & 3 \end{bmatrix} \end{array}$; 90°

16. $\begin{array}{c} J \quad K \quad L \\ \begin{bmatrix} 1 & 2 & 0 \\ 1 & -1 & -3 \end{bmatrix} \end{array}$; 180°

17. $\begin{array}{c} P \quad Q \quad R \quad S \\ \begin{bmatrix} -4 & 2 & 2 & -4 \\ -4 & -2 & -5 & -7 \end{bmatrix} \end{array}$; 270°

ERROR ANALYSIS The endpoints of $\overline{AB}$ are $A(-1, 1)$ and $B(2, 3)$. *Describe and correct the error in setting up the matrix multiplication for a 270° rotation about the origin.*

18.

270° rotation of $\overline{AB}$

$$\begin{bmatrix} 0 & -1 \\ 1 & 0 \end{bmatrix} \begin{bmatrix} -1 & 2 \\ 1 & 3 \end{bmatrix}$$ ✗

19.

270° rotation of $\overline{AB}$

$$\begin{bmatrix} -1 & 2 \\ 1 & 3 \end{bmatrix} \begin{bmatrix} 0 & 1 \\ -1 & 0 \end{bmatrix}$$ ✗

EXAMPLE 4
....
on p. 601
for Exs. 20–21

20. ★ **MULTIPLE CHOICE** What is the value of y in the rotation of the triangle about P?

Ⓐ 4 Ⓑ 5 Ⓒ $\dfrac{17}{3}$ Ⓓ 10

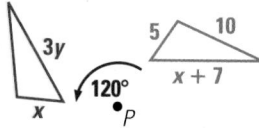

21. ★ **MULTIPLE CHOICE** Suppose quadrilateral $QRST$ is rotated 180° about the origin. In which quadrant is Q'?

Ⓐ I Ⓑ II Ⓒ III Ⓓ IV

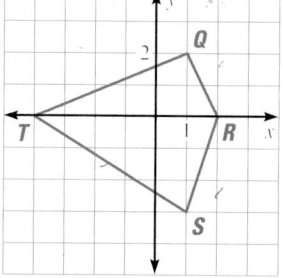

22. **FINDING A PATTERN** The vertices of $\triangle ABC$ are $A(2, 0)$, $B(3, 4)$, and $C(5, 2)$. Make a table to show the vertices of each image after a 90°, 180°, 270°, 360°, 450°, 540°, 630°, and 720° rotation. What would be the coordinates of A' after a rotation of 1890°? *Explain.*

23. ★ **MULTIPLE CHOICE** A rectangle has vertices at $(4, 0)$, $(4, 2)$, $(7, 0)$, and $(7, 2)$. Which image has a vertex at the origin?

Ⓐ Translation right 4 units and down 2 units

Ⓑ Rotation of 180° about the origin

Ⓒ Reflection in the line $x = 4$

Ⓓ Rotation of 180° about the point $(2, 0)$

24. ★ **SHORT RESPONSE** Rotate the triangle in Exercise 12 90° about the origin. Show that corresponding sides of the preimage and image are perpendicular. *Explain.*

25. **VISUAL REASONING** A point in space has three coordinates (x, y, z). What is the image of point $(3, 2, 0)$ rotated 180° about the origin in the xz-plane? (*See* Exercise 30, page 585.)

CHALLENGE Rotate the line the given number of degrees (a) about the x-intercept and (b) about the y-intercept. Write the equation of each image.

26. $y = 2x - 3$; 90°

27. $y = -x + 8$; 180°

28. $y = \dfrac{1}{2}x + 5$; 270°

ANGLE OF ROTATION Use the photo to find the angle of rotation that maps *A* onto *A'*. *Explain* your reasoning.

(29.)

30.

31.

@HomeTutor for problem solving help at classzone.com

32. **REVOLVING DOOR** You enter a revolving door and rotate the door 180°. What does this mean in the context of the situation? Now, suppose you enter a revolving door and rotate the door 360°. What does this mean in the context of the situation? *Explain.*

@HomeTutor for problem solving help at classzone.com

33. **PROVING THEOREM 9.3** Copy and complete the proof of Case 1.

Case 1 The segment is noncollinear with the center of rotation.

GIVEN ▶ A rotation about *P* maps *Q* to *Q'* and *R* to *R'*.
PROVE ▶ *QR* = *Q'R'*

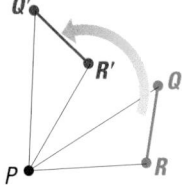

STATEMENTS	REASONS
1. $PQ = PQ'$, $PR = PR'$, $m\angle QPQ' = m\angle RPR'$	1. Definition of __?__
2. $m\angle QPQ' = m\angle QPR' + m\angle R'PQ'$ $m\angle RPR' = m\angle RPQ + m\angle QPR'$	2. __?__
3. $m\angle QPR' + m\angle R'PQ' = m\angle RPQ + m\angle QPR'$	3. __?__ Property of Equality
4. $m\angle QPR = m\angle Q'PR'$	4. __?__ Property of Equality
5. __?__ ≅ __?__	5. SAS Congruence Postulate
6. $\overline{QR} \cong \overline{Q'R'}$	6. __?__
7. $QR = Q'R'$	7. __?__

PROVING THEOREM 9.3 Write a proof for Case 2 and Case 3. (Refer to the diagrams on page 601.)

34. **Case 2** The segment is collinear with the center of rotation.

   GIVEN ▶ A rotation about *P* maps *Q* to *Q'* and *R* to *R'*.
   P, *Q*, and *R* are collinear.
   PROVE ▶ *QR* = *Q'R'*

35. **Case 3** The center of rotation is one endpoint of the segment.

   GIVEN ▶ A rotation about *P* maps *Q* to *Q'* and *R* to *R'*.
   P and *R* are the same point.
   PROVE ▶ *QR* = *Q'R'*

○ = WORKED-OUT SOLUTIONS on p. WS1   ★ = STANDARDIZED TEST PRACTICE

36. MULTI-STEP PROBLEM Use the graph of $y = 2x - 3$.

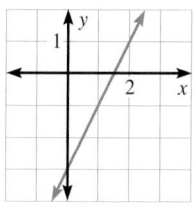

   a. Rotate the line 90°, 180°, 270°, and 360° about the origin. *Describe* the relationship between the equation of the preimage and each image.

   b. Do you think that the relationships you described in part (a) are true for *any* line? *Explain* your reasoning.

37. ★ EXTENDED RESPONSE Use the graph of the quadratic equation $y = x^2 + 1$ at the right.

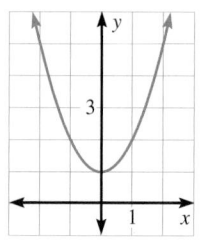

   a. Rotate the *parabola* by replacing y with x and x with y in the original equation, then graph this new equation.

   b. What is the angle of rotation?

   c. Are the image and the preimage both functions? *Explain.*

TWO ROTATIONS The endpoints of $\overline{FG}$ are $F(1, 2)$ and $G(3, 4)$. Graph $\overline{F'G'}$ and $\overline{F''G''}$ after the given rotations.

38. Rotation: 90° about the origin
Rotation: 180° about (0, 4)

39. Rotation: 270° about the origin
Rotation: 90° about (−2, 0)

40. CHALLENGE A polar coordinate system locates a point in a plane by its distance from the origin O and by the measure of an angle with its vertex at the origin. For example, the point $A(2, 30°)$ at the right is 2 units from the origin and $m\angle XOA = 30°$. What are the polar coordinates of the image of point A after a 90° rotation? 180° rotation? 270° rotation? *Explain.*

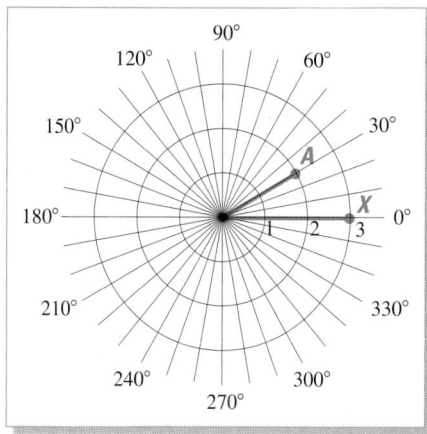

MIXED REVIEW

PREVIEW
Prepare for
Lesson 9.5
in Exs. 41–43.

In the diagram, $\overrightarrow{DC}$ is the perpendicular bisector of $\overline{AB}$. *(p. 303)*

41. What segment lengths are equal?

42. What is the value of x?

43. Find BD. *(p. 433)*

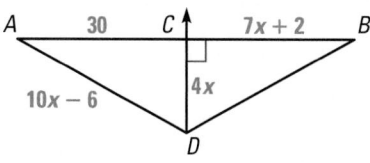

Use a sine or cosine ratio to find the value of each variable. Round decimals to the nearest tenth. *(p. 473)*

44.

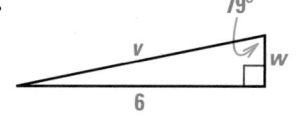

45.

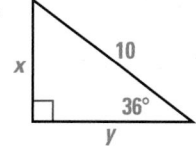

46.

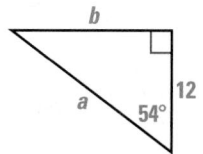

Using ALTERNATIVE METHODS

Another Way to Solve Example 2, page 599

MULTIPLE REPRESENTATIONS In Example 2 on page 599, you saw how to use a coordinate rule to rotate a figure. You can also *use tracing paper* and move a copy of the figure around the coordinate plane.

PROBLEM

Graph quadrilateral *RSTU* with vertices *R*(3, 1), *S*(5, 1), *T*(5, −3), and *U*(2, −1). Then rotate the quadrilateral 270° about the origin.

METHOD

Using Tracing Paper You can use tracing paper to rotate a figure.

STEP 1 **Graph** the original figure in the coordinate plane.

STEP 2 **Trace** the quadrilateral and the axes on tracing paper.

STEP 3 **Rotate** the tracing paper 270°. Then transfer the resulting image onto the graph paper.

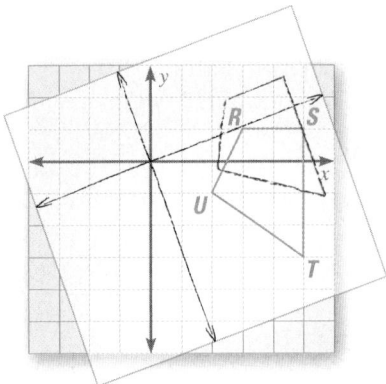

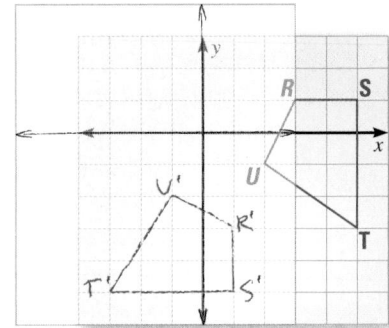

PRACTICE

1. **GRAPH** Graph quadrilateral *ABCD* with vertices *A*(2, −2), *B*(5, −3), *C*(4, −5), and *D*(2, −4). Then rotate the quadrilateral 180° about the origin using tracing paper.

2. **GRAPH** Graph △*RST* with vertices *R*(0, 6), *S*(1, 4), and *T*(−2, 3). Then rotate the triangle 270° about the origin using tracing paper.

3. **SHORT RESPONSE** *Explain* why rotating a figure 90° clockwise is the same as rotating the figure 270° counterclockwise.

4. **SHORT RESPONSE** *Explain* how you could use tracing paper to do a reflection.

5. **REASONING** If you rotate the point (3, 4) 90° about the origin, what happens to the *x*-coordinate? What happens to the *y*-coordinate?

6. **GRAPH** Graph △*JKL* with vertices *J*(4, 8), *K*(4, 6), and *L*(2, 6). Then rotate the triangle 90° about the point (−1, 4) using tracing paper.

9.5 Double Reflections

MATERIALS · graphing calculator or computer

QUESTION What happens when you reflect a figure in two lines in a plane?

EXPLORE 1 Double reflection in parallel lines

STEP 1 *Draw a scalene triangle* Construct a scalene triangle like the one at the right. Label the vertices *D*, *E*, and *F*.

STEP 2 *Draw parallel lines* Construct two parallel lines *p* and *q* on one side of the triangle. Make sure that the lines do not intersect the triangle. Save as "EXPLORE1".

STEP 3 *Reflect triangle* Reflect △*DEF* in line *p*. Reflect △*D'E'F'* in line *q*. How is △*D"E"F"* related to △*DEF*?

STEP 4 *Make conclusion* Drag line *q*. Does the relationship appear to be true if *p* and *q* are not on the same side of the figure?

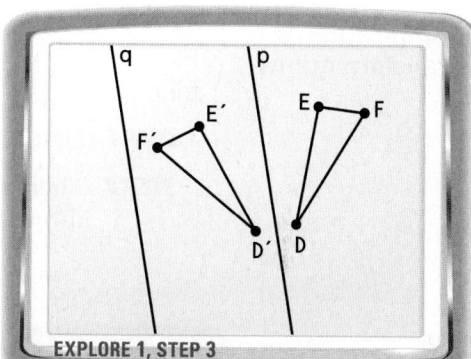

EXPLORE 1, STEP 3

EXPLORE 2 Double reflection in intersecting lines

STEP 1 *Draw intersecting lines* Follow Step 1 in Explore 1 for △*ABC*. Change Step 2 from parallel lines to intersecting lines *k* and *m*. Make sure that the lines do not intersect the triangle. Label the point of intersection of lines *k* and *m* as *P*. Save as "EXPLORE2".

STEP 2 *Reflect triangle* Reflect △*ABC* in line *k*. Reflect △*A'B'C'* in line *m*. How is △*A"B"C"* related to △*ABC*?

STEP 3 *Measure angles* Measure ∠*APA"* and the acute angle formed by lines *k* and *m*. What is the relationship between these two angles? Does this relationship remain true when you move lines *k* and *m*?

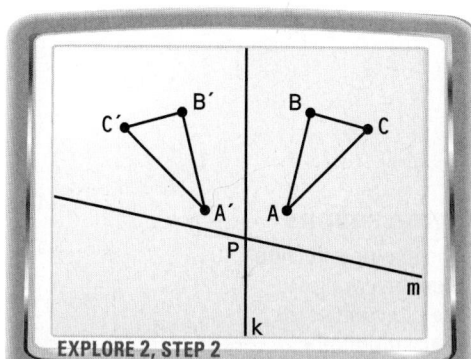

EXPLORE 2, STEP 2

DRAW CONCLUSIONS Use your observations to complete these exercises

1. What other transformation maps a figure onto the same image as a reflection in two parallel lines?

2. What other transformation maps a figure onto the same image as a reflection in two intersecting lines?

9.5 Apply Compositions of Transformations

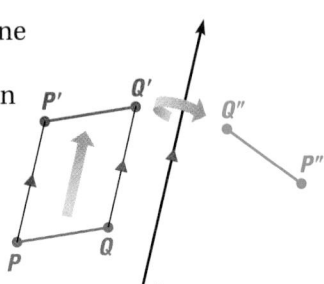

Before	You performed rotations, reflections, or translations.
Now	You will perform combinations of two or more transformations.
Why?	So you can describe the transformations that represent a rowing crew, as in Ex. 30.

Key Vocabulary
• glide reflection
• composition of transformations

A translation followed by a reflection can be performed one after the other to produce a *glide reflection*. A translation can be called a glide. A **glide reflection** is a transformation in which every point *P* is mapped to a point *P″* by the following steps.

> **STEP 1** First, a translation maps *P* to *P′*.
>
> **STEP 2** Then, a reflection in a line *k* parallel to the direction of the translation maps *P′* to *P″*.

EXAMPLE 1 Find the image of a glide reflection

The vertices of △ABC are A(3, 2), B(6, 3), and C(7, 1). Find the image of △ABC after the glide reflection.

> **Translation:** $(x, y) \rightarrow (x - 12, y)$
> **Reflection:** in the *x*-axis

Solution

Begin by graphing △ABC. Then graph △A′B′C′ after a translation 12 units left. Finally, graph △A″B″C″ after a reflection in the *x*-axis.

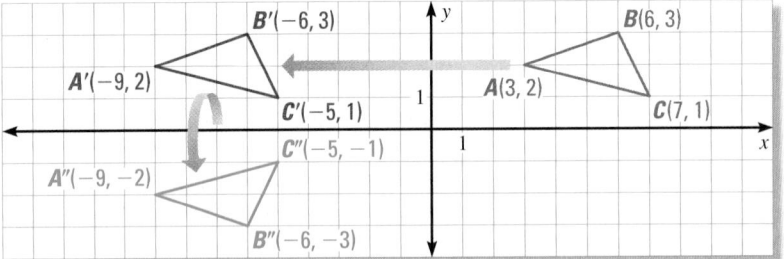

✓ GUIDED PRACTICE for Example 1

1. Suppose △ABC in Example 1 is translated 4 units down, then reflected in the *y*-axis. What are the coordinates of the vertices of the image?

2. In Example 1, *describe* a glide reflection from △A″B″C″ to △ABC.

COMPOSITIONS When two or more transformations are combined to form a single transformation, the result is a **composition of transformations**. A glide reflection is an example of a composition of transformations.

In this lesson, a composition of transformations uses isometries, so the final image is congruent to the preimage. This suggests the Composition Theorem.

THEOREM   *For Your Notebook*

THEOREM 9.4 Composition Theorem

The composition of two (or more) isometries is an isometry.

Proof: Exs. 35–36, p. 614

EXAMPLE 2 **Find the image of a composition**

The endpoints of $\overline{RS}$ are $R(1, -3)$ and $S(2, -6)$. Graph the image of $\overline{RS}$ after the composition.

> **Reflection:** in the y-axis
> **Rotation:** 90° about the origin

Solution

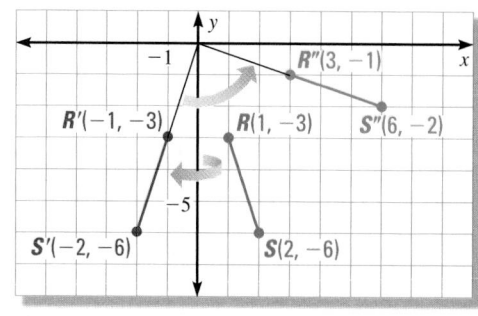

STEP 1 Graph $\overline{RS}$.

AVOID ERRORS
Unless you are told otherwise, do the transformations in the order given.

STEP 2 Reflect $\overline{RS}$ in the y-axis. $\overline{R'S'}$ has endpoints $R'(-1, -3)$ and $S'(-2, -6)$.

STEP 3 Rotate $\overline{R'S'}$ 90° about the origin. $\overline{R''S''}$ has endpoints $R''(3, -1)$ and $S''(6, -2)$.

TWO REFLECTIONS Compositions of two reflections result in either a translation or a rotation, as described in Theorems 9.5 and 9.6.

THEOREM   *For Your Notebook*

THEOREM 9.5 Reflections in Parallel Lines Theorem

If lines k and m are parallel, then a reflection in line k followed by a reflection in line m is the same as a translation.

If P'' is the image of P, then:

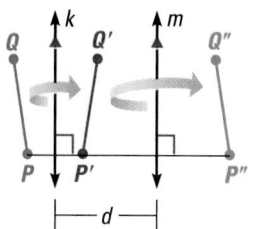

1. $\overline{PP''}$ is perpendicular to k and m, and

2. $PP'' = 2d$, where d is the distance between k and m.

Proof: Ex. 37, p. 614

EXAMPLE 3   **Use Theorem 9.5**

In the diagram, a reflection in line *k* maps $\overline{GH}$ to $\overline{G'H'}$. A reflection in line *m* maps $\overline{G'H'}$ to $\overline{G''H''}$. Also, *HB* = 9 and *DH''* = 4.

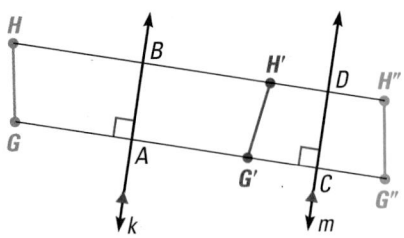

a. Name any segments congruent to each segment: $\overline{HG}$, $\overline{HB}$, and $\overline{GA}$.

b. Does *AC* = *BD*? Explain.

c. What is the length of $\overline{GG''}$?

Solution

a. $\overline{HG} \cong \overline{H'G'}$, and $\overline{HG} \cong \overline{H''G''}$. $\overline{HB} \cong \overline{H'B}$. $\overline{GA} \cong \overline{G'A}$.

b. Yes, *AC* = *BD* because $\overline{GG''}$ and $\overline{HH''}$ are perpendicular to both *k* and *m*, so $\overline{BD}$ and $\overline{AC}$ are opposite sides of a rectangle.

c. By the properties of reflections, *H'B* = 9 and *H'D* = 4. Theorem 9.5 implies that *GG''* = *HH''* = 2 · *BD*, so the length of $\overline{GG''}$ is 2(9 + 4), or 26 units.

✓   **GUIDED PRACTICE**   **for Examples 2 and 3**

3. Graph $\overline{RS}$ from Example 2. Do the rotation first, followed by the reflection. Does the order of the transformations matter? *Explain.*

4. In Example 3, part (c), *explain* how you know that *GG''* = *HH''*.

Use the figure below for Exercises 5 and 6. The distance between line *k* and line *m* is 1.6 centimeters.

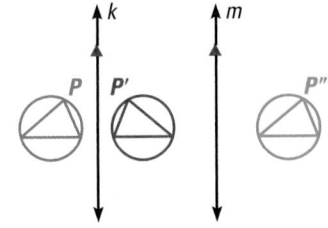

5. The preimage is reflected in line *k*, then in line *m*. *Describe* a single transformation that maps the blue figure to the green figure.

6. What is the distance between *P* and *P''*? If you draw $\overline{PP'}$, what is its relationship with line *k*? *Explain.*

THEOREM   *For Your Notebook*

THEOREM 9.6 Reflections in Intersecting Lines Theorem

If lines *k* and *m* intersect at point *P*, then a reflection in *k* followed by a reflection in *m* is the same as a rotation about point *P*.

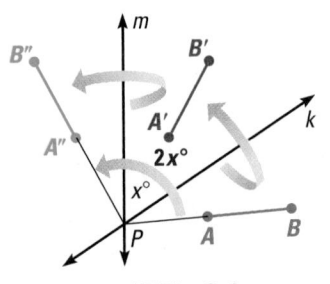

The angle of rotation is 2*x*°, where *x*° is the measure of the acute or right angle formed by *k* and *m*.

Proof: Ex. 38, p. 614

$m\angle BPB'' = 2x°$

EXAMPLE 4 Use Theorem 9.6

In the diagram, the figure is reflected in line _k_. The image is then reflected in line _m_. Describe a single transformation that maps _F_ to _F″_.

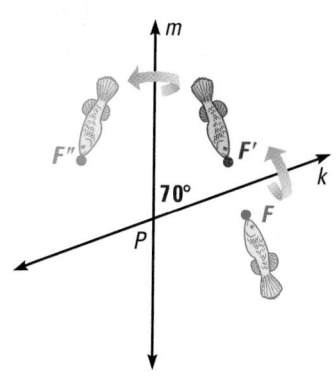

Solution

The measure of the acute angle formed between lines _k_ and _m_ is 70°. So, by Theorem 9.6, a single transformation that maps _F_ to _F″_ is a 140° rotation about point _P_.

You can check that this is correct by tracing lines _k_ and _m_ and point _F_, then rotating the point 140°.

Animated Geometry at classzone.com

✓ **GUIDED PRACTICE**   for Example 4

7. In the diagram at the right, the preimage is reflected in line _k_, then in line _m_. *Describe* a single transformation that maps the blue figure onto the green figure.

8. A rotation of 76° maps _C_ to _C′_. To map _C_ to _C′_ using two reflections, what is the angle formed by the intersecting lines of reflection?

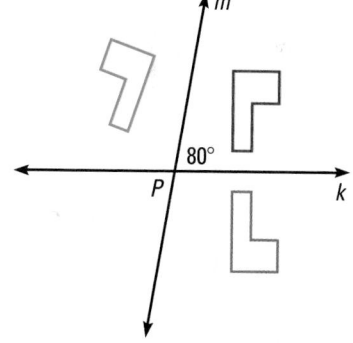

9.5 **EXERCISES**

HOMEWORK KEY
○ = **WORKED-OUT SOLUTIONS**
on p. WS12 for Exs. 7, 17, and 27

★ = **STANDARDIZED TEST PRACTICE**
Exs. 2, 25, 29, and 34

SKILL PRACTICE

1. VOCABULARY Copy and complete: In a glide reflection, the direction of the translation must be __?__ to the line of reflection.

2. ★ **WRITING** *Explain* why a glide reflection is an isometry.

EXAMPLE 1
on p. 608
for Exs. 3–6

GLIDE REFLECTION The endpoints of $\overline{CD}$ are _C_(2, −5) and _D_(4, 0). **Graph the image of $\overline{CD}$ after the glide reflection.**

3. Translation: $(x, y) \rightarrow (x, y - 1)$
Reflection: in the _y_-axis

4. Translation: $(x, y) \rightarrow (x - 3, y)$
Reflection: in $y = -1$

5. Translation: $(x, y) \rightarrow (x, y + 4)$
Reflection: in $x = 3$

6. Translation: $(x, y) \rightarrow (x + 2, y + 2)$
Reflection: in $y = x$

EXAMPLE 2
on p. 609
for Exs. 7–14

GRAPHING COMPOSITIONS The vertices of $\triangle PQR$ are $P(2, 4)$, $Q(6, 0)$, and $R(7, 2)$. Graph the image of $\triangle PQR$ after a composition of the transformations in the order they are listed.

7. Translation: $(x, y) \rightarrow (x, y - 5)$
Reflection: in the y-axis

8. Translation: $(x, y) \rightarrow (x - 3, y + 2)$
Rotation: 90° about the origin

9. Translation: $(x, y) \rightarrow (x + 12, y + 4)$
Translation: $(x, y) \rightarrow (x - 5, y - 9)$

10. Reflection: in the x-axis
Rotation: 90° about the origin

REVERSING ORDERS Graph $\overline{F''G''}$ after a composition of the transformations in the order they are listed. Then perform the transformations in reverse order. Does the order affect the final image $\overline{F''G''}$?

11. $F(-5, 2)$, $G(-2, 4)$
Translation: $(x, y) \rightarrow (x + 3, y - 8)$
Reflection: in the x-axis

12. $F(-1, -8)$, $G(-6, -3)$
Reflection: in the line $y = 2$
Rotation: 90° about the origin

DESCRIBING COMPOSITIONS *Describe* the composition of transformations.

13.
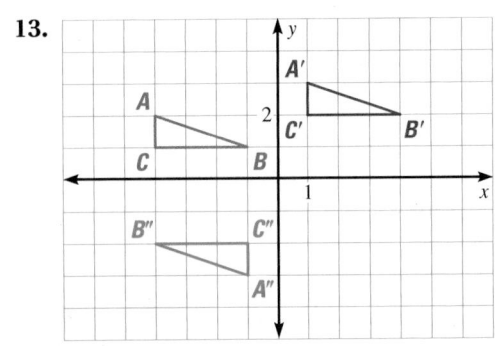

14.
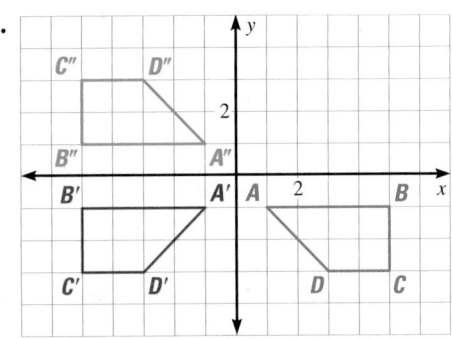

EXAMPLE 3
on p. 610
for Exs. 15–19

USING THEOREM 9.5 In the diagram, $k \parallel m$, $\triangle ABC$ is reflected in line k, and $\triangle A'B'C'$ is reflected in line m.

15. A translation maps $\triangle ABC$ onto which triangle?

16. Which lines are perpendicular to $\overleftrightarrow{AA''}$?

17. Name two segments parallel to $\overleftrightarrow{BB''}$.

18. If the distance between k and m is 2.6 inches, what is the length of $\overline{CC''}$?

19. Is the distance from B' to m the same as the distance from B'' to m? *Explain.*

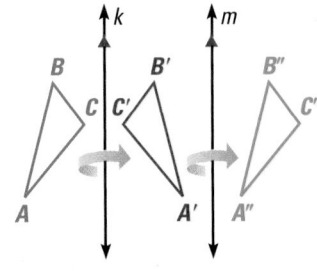

EXAMPLE 4
on p. 611
for Exs. 20–21

USING THEOREM 9.6 Find the angle of rotation that maps A onto A''.

20.
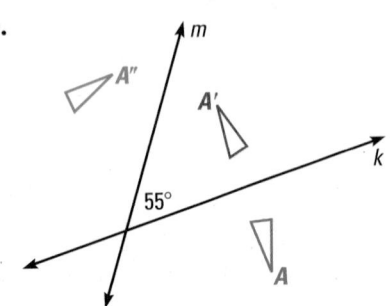

21.
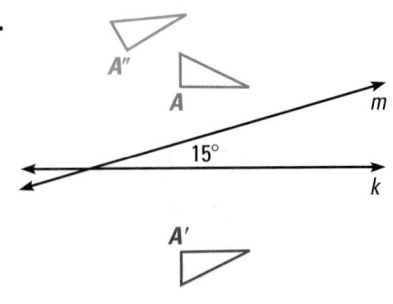

$\bigcirc$ = **WORKED-OUT SOLUTIONS**
on p. WS1

★ = **STANDARDIZED
TEST PRACTICE**

22. ERROR ANALYSIS A student described the translation of $\overline{AB}$ to $\overline{A'B'}$ followed by the reflection of $\overline{A'B'}$ to $\overline{A''B''}$ in the y-axis as a glide reflection. *Describe* and correct the student's error.

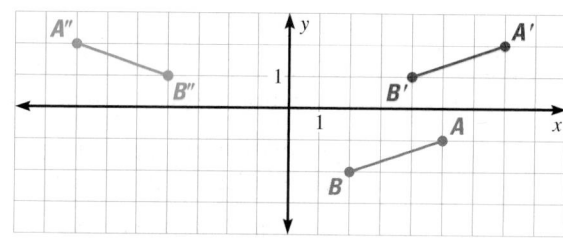

USING MATRICES The vertices of $\triangle PQR$ are $P(1, 4)$, $Q(3, -2)$, and $R(7, 1)$. Use matrix operations to find the image matrix that represents the composition of the given transformations. Then graph $\triangle PQR$ and its image.

23. Translation: $(x, y) \rightarrow (x, y + 5)$
Reflection: in the y-axis

24. Reflection: in the x-axis
Translation: $(x, y) \rightarrow (x - 9, y - 4)$

25. ★ **OPEN-ENDED MATH** Sketch a polygon. Apply three transformations of your choice on the polygon. What can you say about the congruence of the preimage and final image after multiple transformations? *Explain.*

26. CHALLENGE The vertices of $\triangle JKL$ are $J(1, -3)$, $K(2, 2)$, and $L(3, 0)$. Find the image of the triangle after a 180° rotation about the point $(-2, 2)$, followed by a reflection in the line $y = -x$.

PROBLEM SOLVING

EXAMPLE 1
on p. 608
for Exs. 27–30

ANIMAL TRACKS The left and right prints in the set of animal tracks can be related by a glide reflection. Copy the tracks and *describe* a translation and reflection that combine to create the glide reflection.

27. bald eagle (2 legs)

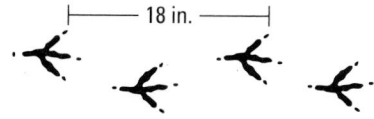

28. armadillo (4 legs)

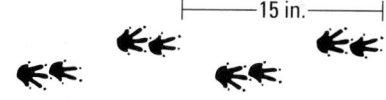

@HomeTutor for problem solving help at classzone.com

29. ★ **MULTIPLE CHOICE** Which is *not* a glide reflection?

Ⓐ The teeth of a closed zipper

Ⓑ The tracks of a walking duck

Ⓒ The keys on a computer keyboard

Ⓓ The red squares on two adjacent rows of a checkerboard

@HomeTutor for problem solving help at classzone.com

30. ROWING *Describe* the transformations that are combined to represent an eight-person rowing shell.

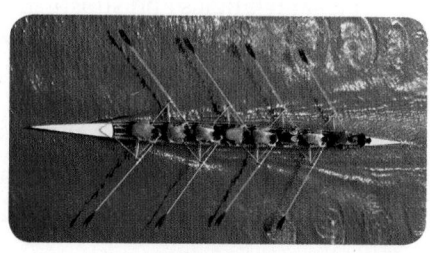

SWEATER PATTERNS In Exercises 31–33, *describe* the transformations that are combined to make each sweater pattern.

31.

32.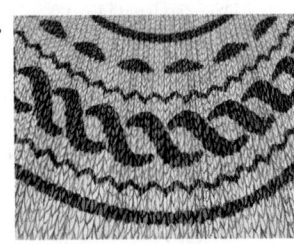

33.

34. ★ **SHORT RESPONSE** Use Theorem 9.5 to *explain* how you can make a glide reflection using three reflections. How are the lines of reflection related?

35. **PROVING THEOREM 9.4** Write a plan for proof for one case of the Composition Theorem.

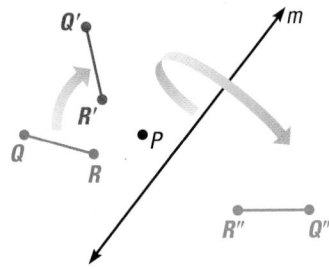

    GIVEN ▶ A rotation about P maps Q to Q' and R to R'. A reflection in m maps Q' to Q'' and R' to R''.

    PROVE ▶ $QR = Q''R''$

36. **PROVING THEOREM 9.4** A composition of a rotation and a reflection, as in Exercise 35, is one case of the Composition Theorem. List all possible cases, and prove the theorem for another pair of compositions.

37. **PROVING THEOREM 9.5** Prove the Reflection in Parallel Lines Theorem.

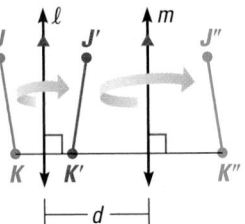

    GIVEN ▶ A reflection in line ℓ maps $\overline{JK}$ to $\overline{J'K'}$, a reflection in line m maps $\overline{J'K'}$ to $\overline{J''K''}$, and $\ell \parallel m$.

    PROVE ▶ **a.** $\overleftrightarrow{KK''}$ is perpendicular to ℓ and m.

              b. $KK'' = 2d$, where d is the distance between ℓ and m.

38. **PROVING THEOREM 9.6** Prove the Reflection in Intersecting Lines Theorem.

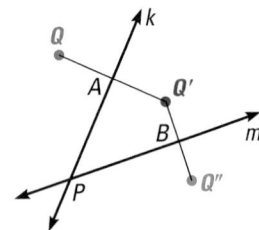

    GIVEN ▶ Lines k and m intersect at point P. Q is any point not on k or m.

    PROVE ▶ **a.** If you reflect point Q in k, and then reflect its image Q' in m, Q'' is the image of Q after a rotation about point P.

              b. $m\angle QPQ'' = 2(m\angle APB)$

Plan for Proof First show $k \perp \overline{QQ'}$ and $\overline{QA} \cong \overline{Q'A}$. Then show $\triangle QAP \cong \triangle Q'AP$. In the same way, show $\triangle Q'BP \cong \triangle Q''BP$. Use congruent triangles and substitution to show that $\overline{QP} \cong \overline{Q''P}$. That proves part (a) by the definition of a rotation. Then use congruent triangles to prove part (b).

39. **VISUAL REASONING** You are riding a bicycle along a flat street.

    a. What two transformations does the wheel's motion use?

    b. *Explain* why this is not a composition of transformations.

★ = **STANDARDIZED TEST PRACTICE**

40. MULTI-STEP PROBLEM A point in space has three coordinates (x, y, z). From the origin, a point can be forward or back on the x-axis, left or right on the y-axis, and up or down on the z-axis. The endpoints of segment $\overline{AB}$ in space are $A(2, 0, 0)$ and $B(2, 3, 0)$, as shown at the right.

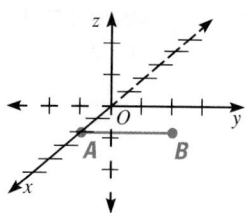

    a. Rotate $\overline{AB}$ 90° about the x-axis with center of rotation A. What are the coordinates of $\overline{A'B'}$?

    b. Translate $\overline{A'B'}$ using the vector $\langle 4, 0, -1 \rangle$. What are the coordinates of $\overline{A''B''}$?

41. CHALLENGE *Justify* the following conjecture or provide a counterexample.

    Conjecture When performing a composition of two transformations of the *same type*, order does not matter.

MIXED REVIEW

Find the unknown side length. Write your answer in simplest radical form. *(p. 433)*

42.

43.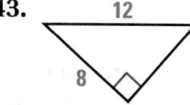

44.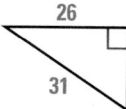

PREVIEW
Prepare for
Lesson 9.6 in
Exs. 45–48.

The coordinates of $\triangle PQR$ are $P(3, 1)$, $Q(3, 3)$, and $R(6, 1)$. Graph the image of the triangle after the translation. *(p. 572)*

45. $(x, y) \rightarrow (x + 3, y)$ **46.** $(x, y) \rightarrow (x - 3, y)$

47. $(x, y) \rightarrow (x, y + 2)$ **48.** $(x, y) \rightarrow (x + 3, y + 2)$

QUIZ *for Lessons 9.3–9.5*

The vertices of $\triangle ABC$ are $A(7, 1)$, $B(3, 5)$, and $C(10, 7)$. Graph the reflection in the line. *(p. 589)*

    1. y-axis   **2.** $x = -4$ **3.** $y = -x$

Find the coordinates of the image of $P(2, -3)$ after the rotation about the origin. *(p. 598)*

    4. 180° rotation   **5.** 90° rotation   **6.** 270° rotation

The vertices of $\triangle PQR$ are $P(-8, 8)$, $Q(-5, 0)$, and $R(-1, 3)$. Graph the image of $\triangle PQR$ after a composition of the transformations in the order they are listed. *(p. 608)*

    7. Translation: $(x, y) \rightarrow (x + 6, y)$ **8. Reflection:** in the line $y = -2$
        Reflection: in the y-axis   **Rotation:** 90° about the origin

    9. Translation: $(x, y) \rightarrow (x - 5, y)$ **10. Rotation:** 180° about the origin
        Translation: $(x, y) \rightarrow (x + 2, y + 7)$ **Translation:** $(x, y) \rightarrow (x + 4, y - 3)$

Tessellations

GOAL   Make tessellations and discover their properties.

Key Vocabulary
• tessellation

A **tessellation** is a collection of figures that cover a plane with no gaps or overlaps. You can use transformations to make tessellations.

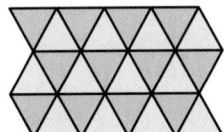 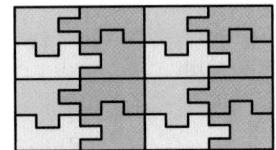

A *regular tessellation* is a tessellation of congruent regular polygons. In the figures above, the tessellation of equilateral triangles is a regular tessellation.

EXAMPLE 1   **Determine whether shapes tessellate**

Does the shape tessellate? If so, tell whether the tessellation is regular.

a. Regular octagon   **b.** Trapezoid   **c.** Regular hexagon

        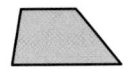   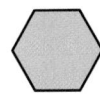

Solution

AVOID ERRORS
The sum of the angles surrounding every vertex of a tessellation is 360°. This means that no regular polygon with more than six sides can be used in a *regular* tesssellation.

a. A regular octagon does not tessellate.

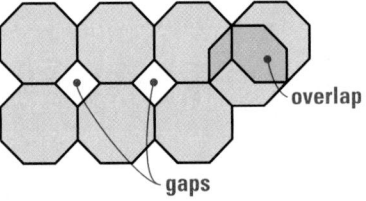

overlap

gaps

b. The trapezoid tessellates. The tessellation is not regular because the trapezoid is not a regular polygon.

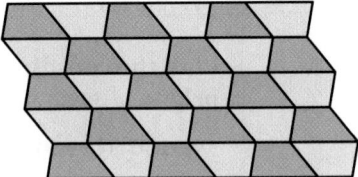

c. A regular hexagon tessellates using translations. The tessellation is regular because it is made of congruent regular hexagons.

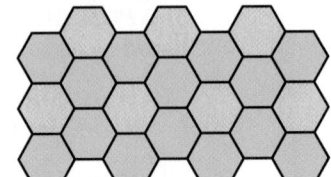

EXAMPLE 2 Draw a tessellation using one shape

Change a triangle to make a tessellation.

Solution

STEP 1

Cut a piece from the triangle.

STEP 2

Slide the piece to another side.

STEP 3

Translate and reflect the figure to make a tessellation.

EXAMPLE 3 Draw a tessellation using two shapes

Draw a tessellation using the given floor tiles.

Solution

READ VOCABULARY
Notice that in the tessellation in Example 3, the same combination of regular polygons meet at each vertex. This type of tessellation is called *semi-regular*.

STEP 1

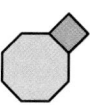

Combine one octagon and one square by connecting sides of the same length.

STEP 2

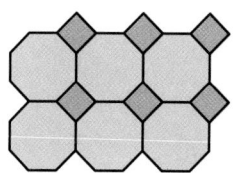

Translate the pair of polygons to make a tessellation

Animated Geometry at classzone.com

PRACTICE

EXAMPLE 1
on p. 616
for Exs. 1–4

REGULAR TESSELLATIONS **Does the shape tessellate? If so, tell whether the tessellation is regular.**

1. Equilateral triangle

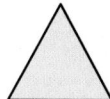

2. Circle

3. Kite

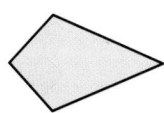

4. ★ **OPEN-ENDED MATH** Draw a rectangle. Use the rectangle to make two different tessellations.

5. MULTI-STEP PROBLEM Choose a tessellation and measure the angles at three vertices.

    a. What is the sum of the measures of the angles? What can you conclude?

    b. *Explain* how you know that any *quadrilateral* will tessellate.

EXAMPLE 2
on p. 617
for Exs. 6–9

DRAWING TESSELLATIONS **In Exercises 6–8, use the steps in Example 2 to make a figure that will tessellate.**

  6. Make a tessellation using a triangle as the base figure.

  7. Make a tessellation using a square as the base figure. Change both pairs of opposite sides.

  8. Make a tessellation using a hexagon as the base figure. Change all three pairs of opposite sides.

  9. ROTATION TESSELLATION Use these steps to make another tessellation based on a regular hexagon *ABCDEF*.

    a. Connect points *A* and *B* with a curve. Rotate the curve 120° about *A* so that *B* coincides with *F*.

    b. Connect points *E* and *F* with a curve. Rotate the curve 120° about *E* so that *F* coincides with *D*.

    c. Connect points *C* and *D* with a curve. Rotate the curve 120° about *C* so that *D* coincides with *B*.

    d. Use this figure to draw a tessellation.

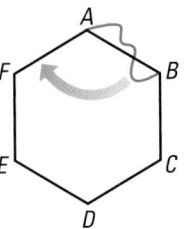

EXAMPLE 3
on p. 617
for Exs. 10–12

USING TWO POLYGONS **Draw a tessellation using the given polygons.**

  10.    **11.**    **12.**

  13. ★ **OPEN-ENDED MATH** Draw a tessellation using three different polygons.

TRANSFORMATIONS *Describe* the transformation(s) used to make the tessellation.

  14. 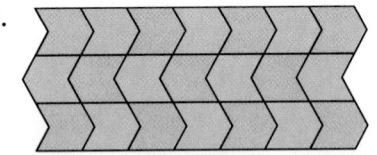   **15.**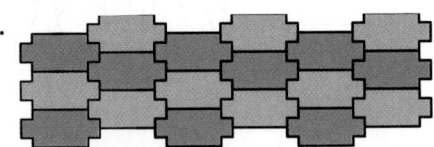

  16. 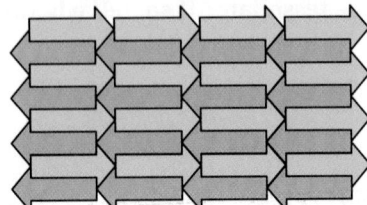   **17.**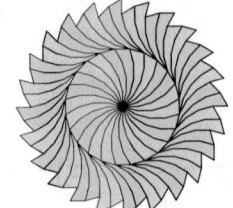

  18. USING SHAPES On graph paper, outline a capital H. Use this shape to make a tessellation. What transformations did you use?

9.6 Identify Symmetry

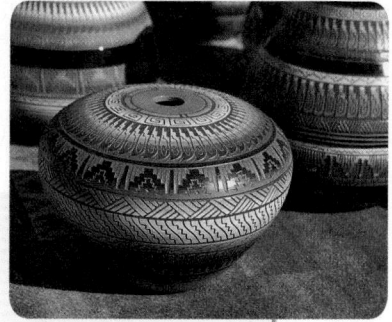

Before	You reflected or rotated figures.
Now	You will identify line and rotational symmetries of a figure.
Why?	So you can identify the symmetry in a bowl, as in Ex. 11.

Key Vocabulary
• **line symmetry**
• **line of symmetry**
• **rotational symmetry**
• **center of symmetry**

A figure in the plane has **line symmetry** if the figure can be mapped onto itself by a reflection in a line. This line of reflection is a **line of symmetry**, such as line *m* at the right. A figure can have more than one line of symmetry.

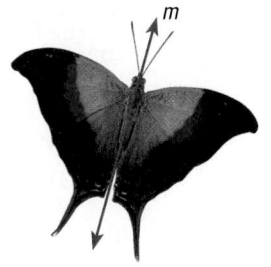

EXAMPLE 1 **Identify lines of symmetry**

How many lines of symmetry does the hexagon have?

a. 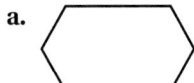   b.    c.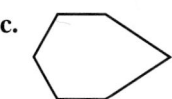

Solution

a. Two lines of symmetry

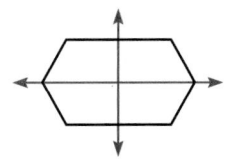

b. Six lines of symmetry

c. One line of symmetry

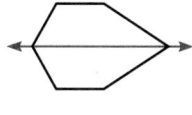

Animated Geometry at classzone.com

✓ **GUIDED PRACTICE** for Example 1

How many lines of symmetry does the object appear to have?

1.    2.    3.

4. Draw a hexagon with no lines of symmetry.

ROTATIONAL SYMMETRY A figure in a plane has **rotational symmetry** if the figure can be mapped onto itself by a rotation of 180° or less about the center of the figure. This point is the **center of symmetry**. Note that the rotation can be either clockwise or counterclockwise.

REVIEW ROTATION
For a figure with rotational symmetry, the *angle of rotation* is the smallest angle that maps the figure onto itself.

For example, the figure below has rotational symmetry, because a rotation of either 90° or 180° maps the figure onto itself (although a rotation of 45° does not).

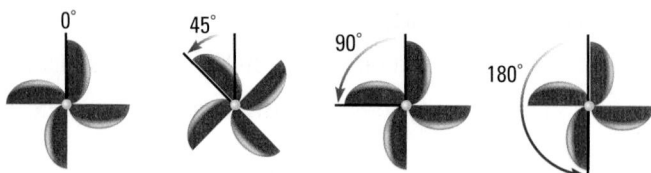

The figure above also has *point symmetry*, which is 180° rotational symmetry.

EXAMPLE 2 **Identify rotational symmetry**

Does the figure have rotational symmetry? If so, describe any rotations that map the figure onto itself.

a. Parallelogram

b. Regular octagon

c. Trapezoid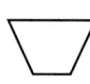

Solution

a. The parallelogram has rotational symmetry. The center is the intersection of the diagonals. A 180° rotation about the center maps the parallelogram onto itself.

b. The regular octagon has rotational symmetry. The center is the intersection of the diagonals. Rotations of 45°, 90°, 135°, or 180° about the center all map the octagon onto itself.

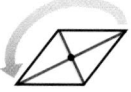

c. The trapezoid does not have rotational symmetry because no rotation of 180° or less maps the trapezoid onto itself.

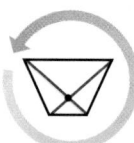

✓ **GUIDED PRACTICE** for Example 2

Does the figure have rotational symmetry? If so, *describe* any rotations that map the figure onto itself.

5. Rhombus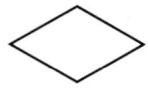

6. Octagon

7. Right triangle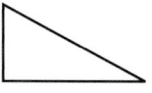

EXAMPLE 3 **Standardized Test Practice**

Identify the line symmetry and rotational symmetry of the equilateral triangle at the right.

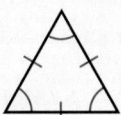

- Ⓐ 3 lines of symmetry, 60° rotational symmetry
- Ⓑ 3 lines of symmetry, 120° rotational symmetry
- Ⓒ 1 line of symmetry, 180° rotational symmetry
- Ⓓ 1 line of symmetry, no rotational symmetry

Solution

ELIMINATE CHOICES
An equilateral triangle can be mapped onto itself by reflecting over any of three different lines. So, you can eliminate choices C and D.

The triangle has line symmetry. Three lines of symmetry can be drawn for the figure.

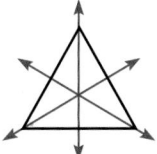

For a figure with *s* lines of symmetry, the smallest rotation that maps the figure onto itself has the measure $\frac{360°}{s}$. So, the equilateral triangle has $\frac{360°}{3}$, or 120° rotational symmetry.

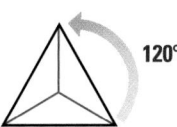
120°

▶ The correct answer is B. Ⓐ Ⓑ Ⓒ Ⓓ

✓ **GUIDED PRACTICE** for Example 3

8. *Describe* the lines of symmetry and rotational symmetry of a non-equilateral isosceles triangle.

9.6 **EXERCISES**

HOMEWORK KEY
○ = **WORKED-OUT SOLUTIONS**
on p. WS12 for Exs. 7, 13, and 31

★ = **STANDARDIZED TEST PRACTICE**
Exs. 2, 13, 14, 21, and 23

SKILL PRACTICE

1. **VOCABULARY** What is a *center of symmetry*?

2. ★ **WRITING** Draw a figure that has one line of symmetry and does not have rotational symmetry. Can a figure have two lines of symmetry and no rotational symmetry?

EXAMPLE 1
on p. 619
for Exs. 3–5

LINE SYMMETRY How many lines of symmetry does the triangle have?

3.
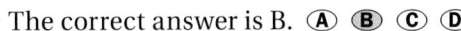

4.

5.
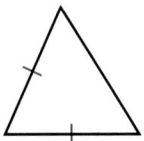

ROTATIONAL SYMMETRY Does the figure have rotational symmetry? If so, *describe* any rotations that map the figure onto itself.

6.    7.    8. 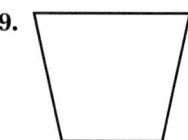   9.

SYMMETRY Determine whether the figure has *line symmetry* and whether it has *rotational symmetry*. Identify all lines of symmetry and angles of rotation that map the figure onto itself.

10. 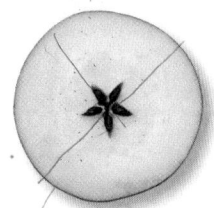   11.   12.

13. ★ **MULTIPLE CHOICE** Identify the line symmetry and rotational symmetry of the figure at the right.

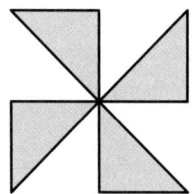

   (A) 1 line of symmetry, no rotational symmetry

   (B) 1 line of symmetry, 180° rotational symmetry

   (C) No lines of symmetry, 90° rotational symmetry

   (D) No lines of symmetry, no rotational symmetry

14. ★ **MULTIPLE CHOICE** Which statement best describes the rotational symmetry of a square?

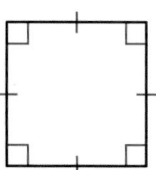

   (A) The square has no rotational symmetry.

   (B) The square has 90° rotational symmetry.

   (C) The square has point symmetry.

   (D) Both B and C are correct.

ERROR ANALYSIS *Describe* and correct the error made in describing the symmetry of the figure.

15.

The figure has 1 line of symmetry and 180° rotational symmetry.

16.

The figure has 1 line of symmetry and 180° rotational symmetry.

DRAWING FIGURES In Exercises 17–20, use the description to draw a figure. If not possible, write *not possible*.

17. A quadrilateral with no line of symmetry

18. An octagon with exactly two lines of symmetry

19. A hexagon with no point symmetry

20. A trapezoid with rotational symmetry

21. ★ **OPEN-ENDED MATH** Draw a polygon with 180° rotational symmetry and with exactly two lines of symmetry.

22. **POINT SYMMETRY** In the graph, $\overline{AB}$ is reflected in the point C to produce the image $\overline{A'B'}$. To make a reflection in a point C for each point N on the preimage, locate N' so that $N'C = NC$ and N' is on $\overleftrightarrow{NC}$. *Explain* what kind of rotation would produce the same image. What kind of symmetry does quadrilateral $AB'A'B$ have?

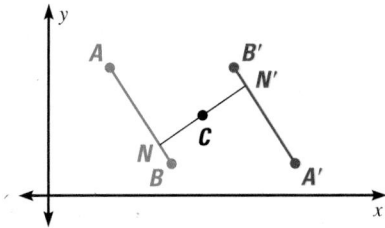

23. ★ **SHORT RESPONSE** A figure has more than one line of symmetry. Can two of the lines of symmetry be parallel? *Explain.*

24. **REASONING** How many lines of symmetry does a circle have? How many angles of rotational symmetry does a circle have? *Explain.*

25. **VISUAL REASONING** How many planes of symmetry does a cube have?

26. **CHALLENGE** What can you say about the rotational symmetry of a regular polygon with n sides? *Explain.*

PROBLEM SOLVING

EXAMPLES 1 and 2 on pp. 619–620 for Exs. 27–30

WORDS Identify the line symmetry and rotational symmetry (if any) of each word.

27. MOW **28.** RADAR **29.** OHIO **30.** pod

@HomeTutor for problem solving help at classzone.com

KALEIDOSCOPES In Exercises 31–33, use the following information about kaleidoscopes.

Inside a kaleidoscope, two mirrors are placed next to each other to form a V, as shown at the right. The angle between the mirrors determines the number of lines of symmetry in the image. Use the formula $n(m\angle 1) = 180°$ to find the measure of $\angle 1$ between the mirrors or the number n of lines of symmetry in the image.

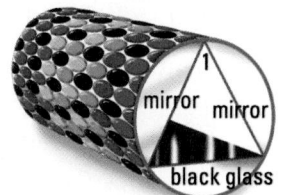

Calculate the angle at which the mirrors must be placed for the image of a kaleidoscope to make the design shown.

31.

32.

33.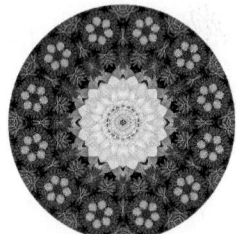

@HomeTutor for problem solving help at classzone.com

34. CHEMISTRY The diagram at the right shows two forms of the amino acid *alanine*. One form is laevo-alanine and the other is dextro-alanine. How are the structures of these two molecules related? *Explain.*

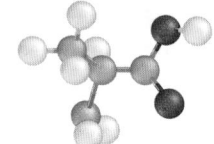 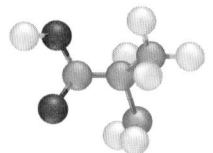

35. MULTI-STEP PROBLEM The *Castillo de San Marcos* in St. Augustine, Florida, has the shape shown.

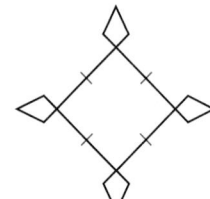 

   a. What kind(s) of symmetry does the shape of the building show?

   b. Imagine the building on a three-dimensional coordinate system. Copy and complete the following statement: The lines of symmetry in part (a) are now described as __?__ of symmetry and the rotational symmetry about the center is now described as rotational symmetry about the __?__.

36. CHALLENGE Spirals have a type of symmetry called spiral, or helical, symmetry. *Describe* the two transformations involved in a spiral staircase. Then *explain* the difference in transformations between the two staircases at the right.

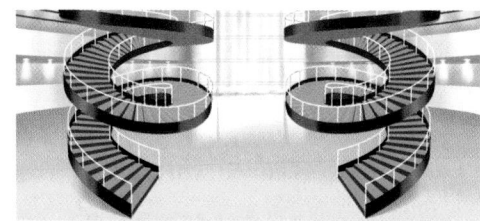

MIXED REVIEW

PREVIEW
Prepare for Lesson 9.7 in Exs. 37–39.

Solve the proportion. *(p. 356)*

37. $\dfrac{5}{x} = \dfrac{15}{27}$ **38.** $\dfrac{a + 4}{7} = \dfrac{49}{56}$ **39.** $\dfrac{5}{2b - 3} = \dfrac{1}{3b + 1}$

Determine whether the dilation from Figure A to Figure B is a *reduction* or an *enlargement*. Then find its scale factor. *(p. 409)*

40. 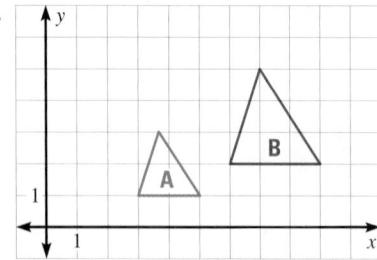   **41.**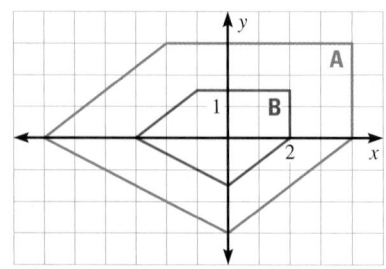

Write a matrix to represent the given polygon. *(p. 580)*

42. Triangle A in Exercise 40   **43.** Triangle B in Exercise 40

44. Pentagon A in Exercise 41   **45.** Pentagon B in Exercise 41

9.7 Investigate Dilations

MATERIALS • straightedge • compass • ruler

QUESTION How do you construct a dilation of a figure?

Recall from Lesson 6.7 that a dilation enlarges or reduces a figure to make a similar figure. You can use construction tools to make enlargement dilations.

EXPLORE Construct an enlargement dilation

Use a compass and straightedge to construct a dilation of $\triangle PQR$ with a scale factor of 2, using a point C outside the triangle as the center of dilation.

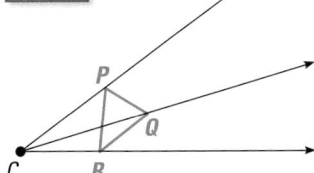

Draw a triangle Draw $\triangle PQR$ and choose the center of the dilation C outside the triangle. Draw lines from C through the vertices of the triangle.

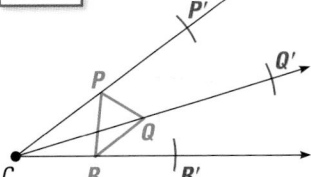

Use a compass Use a compass to locate P' on $\overrightarrow{CP}$ so that $CP' = 2(CP)$. Locate Q' and R' in the same way.

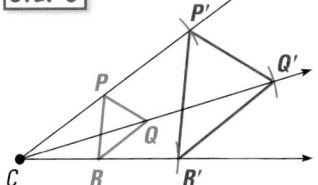

Connect points Connect points P', Q', and R' to form $\triangle P'Q'R'$.

DRAW CONCLUSIONS Use your observations to complete these exercises

1. Find the ratios of corresponding side lengths of $\triangle PQR$ and $\triangle P'Q'R'$. Are the triangles similar? *Explain.*

2. Draw $\triangle DEF$. Use a compass and straightedge to construct a dilation with a scale factor of 3, using point D on the triangle as the center of dilation.

3. Find the ratios of corresponding side lengths of $\triangle DEF$ and $\triangle D'E'F'$. Are the triangles similar? *Explain.*

4. Draw $\triangle JKL$. Use a compass and straightedge to construct a dilation with a scale factor of 2, using a point A inside the triangle as the center of dilation.

5. Find the ratios of corresponding side lengths of $\triangle JKL$ and $\triangle J'K'L'$. Are the triangles similar? *Explain.*

6. What can you conclude about the corresponding angle measures of a triangle and an enlargement dilation of the triangle?

9.7 Identify and Perform Dilations

Before	You used a coordinate rule to draw a dilation.
Now	You will use drawing tools and matrices to draw dilations.
Why?	So you can determine the scale factor of a photo, as in Ex. 37.

Key Vocabulary
- scalar multiplication
- dilation, *p. 409*
- reduction, *p. 409*
- enlargement, *p. 409*

Recall from Lesson 6.7 that a dilation is a transformation in which the original figure and its image are similar.

A dilation with center C and scale factor k maps every point P in a figure to a point P' so that one of the following statements is true:

- If P is not the center point C, then the image point P' lies on $\overrightarrow{CP}$. The scale factor k is a positive number such that $k = \dfrac{CP'}{CP}$ and $k \neq 1$, or

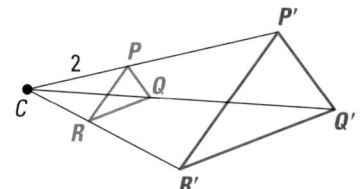

- If P is the center point C, then $P = P'$.

As you learned in Lesson 6.7, the dilation is a *reduction* if $0 < k < 1$ and it is an *enlargement* if $k > 1$.

EXAMPLE 1 Identify dilations

Find the scale factor of the dilation. Then tell whether the dilation is a *reduction* or an *enlargement*.

a.

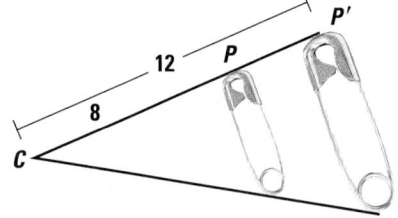

b.

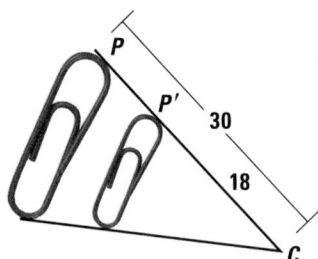

Solution

a. Because $\dfrac{CP'}{CP} = \dfrac{12}{8}$, the scale factor is $k = \dfrac{3}{2}$. The image P' is an enlargement.

b. Because $\dfrac{CP'}{CP} = \dfrac{18}{30}$, the scale factor is $k = \dfrac{3}{5}$. The image P' is a reduction.

Animated Geometry at classzone.com

EXAMPLE 2 Draw a dilation

Draw and label □DEFG. Then construct a dilation of □DEFG with point D as the center of dilation and a scale factor of 2.

Solution

STEP 1

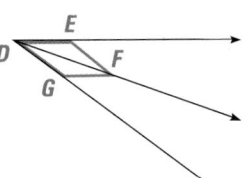

STEP 2

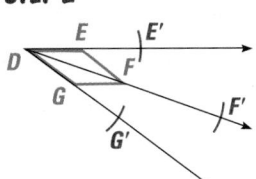

STEP 3

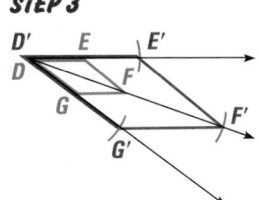

Draw *DEFG*. Draw rays from *D* through vertices *E*, *F*, and *G*.

Open the compass to the length of $\overline{DE}$. Locate *E'* on $\overrightarrow{DE}$ so $DE' = 2(DE)$. Locate *F'* and *G'* the same way.

Add a second label *D'* to point *D*. Draw the sides of *D'E'F'G'*.

 GUIDED PRACTICE for Examples 1 and 2

1. In a dilation, $CP' = 3$ and $CP = 12$. Tell whether the dilation is a *reduction* or an *enlargement* and find its scale factor.

2. Draw and label $\triangle RST$. Then construct a dilation of $\triangle RST$ with *R* as the center of dilation and a scale factor of 3.

MATRICES **Scalar multiplication** is the process of multiplying each element of a matrix by a real number or *scalar*.

EXAMPLE 3 Scalar multiplication

Simplify the product: $4 \begin{bmatrix} 3 & 0 & 1 \\ 2 & -1 & -3 \end{bmatrix}$.

Solution

$$4 \begin{bmatrix} 3 & 0 & 1 \\ 2 & -1 & -3 \end{bmatrix} = \begin{bmatrix} 4(3) & 4(0) & 4(1) \\ 4(2) & 4(-1) & 4(-3) \end{bmatrix}$$ Multiply each element in the matrix by 4.

$$= \begin{bmatrix} 12 & 0 & 4 \\ 8 & -4 & -12 \end{bmatrix}$$ Simplify.

✓ **GUIDED PRACTICE** for Example 3

Simplify the product.

3. $5 \begin{bmatrix} 2 & 1 & -10 \\ 3 & -4 & 7 \end{bmatrix}$

4. $-2 \begin{bmatrix} -4 & 1 & 0 \\ 9 & -5 & -7 \end{bmatrix}$

DILATIONS USING MATRICES You can use scalar multiplication to represent a dilation centered at the origin in the coordinate plane. To find the image matrix for a dilation centered at the origin, use the scale factor as the scalar.

EXAMPLE 4 Use scalar multiplication in a dilation

The vertices of quadrilateral *KLMN* are *K*(−6, 6), *L*(−3, 6), *M*(0, 3), and *N*(−6, 0). Use scalar multiplication to find the image of *KLMN* after a dilation with its center at the origin and a scale factor of $\frac{1}{3}$. Graph *KLMN* and its image.

Solution

$$\frac{1}{3}\begin{matrix} K & L & M & N \\ \begin{bmatrix} -6 & -3 & 0 & -6 \\ 6 & 6 & 3 & 0 \end{bmatrix} \end{matrix} = \begin{matrix} K' & L' & M' & N' \\ \begin{bmatrix} -2 & -1 & 0 & -2 \\ 2 & 2 & 1 & 0 \end{bmatrix} \end{matrix}$$

Scale factor　**Polygon matrix**　**Image matrix**

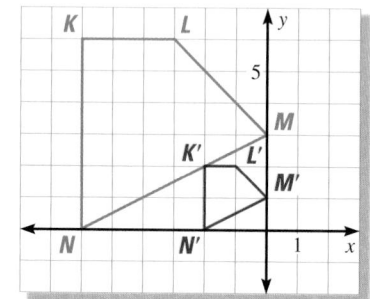

EXAMPLE 5 Find the image of a composition

The vertices of △*ABC* are *A*(−4, 1), *B*(−2, 2), and *C*(−2, 1). Find the image of △*ABC* after the given composition.

Translation: $(x, y) \rightarrow (x + 5, y + 1)$
Dilation: centered at the origin with a scale factor of 2

Solution

STEP 1 **Graph** the preimage △*ABC* on the coordinate plane.

STEP 2 **Translate** △*ABC* 5 units to the right and 1 unit up. Label it △*A'B'C'*.

STEP 3 **Dilate** △*A'B'C'* using the origin as the center and a scale factor of 2 to find △*A"B"C"*.

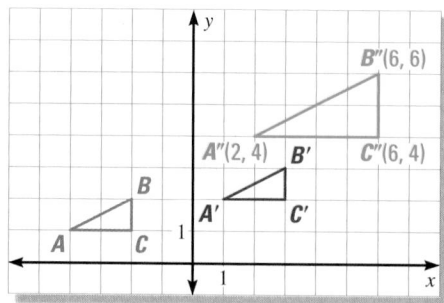

✓ **GUIDED PRACTICE** for Examples 4 and 5

5. The vertices of △*RST* are *R*(1, 2), *S*(2, 1), and *T*(2, 2). Use scalar multiplication to find the vertices of △*R'S'T'* after a dilation with its center at the origin and a scale factor of 2.

6. A segment has the endpoints *C*(−1, 1) and *D*(1, 1). Find the image of $\overline{CD}$ after a 90° rotation about the origin followed by a dilation with its center at the origin and a scale factor of 2.

9.7 EXERCISES

SKILL PRACTICE

1. **VOCABULARY** What is a *scalar*?

2. ★ **WRITING** If you know the scale factor, *explain* how to determine if an image is larger or smaller than the preimage.

EXAMPLE 1
on p. 626 for Exs. 3–6

IDENTIFYING DILATIONS **Find the scale factor. Tell whether the dilation is a** *reduction* **or an** *enlargement.* **Find the value of x.**

3.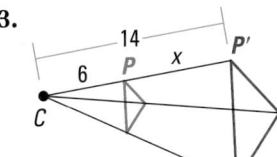

4.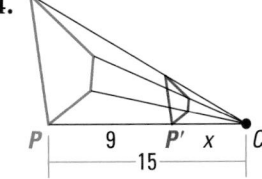

5.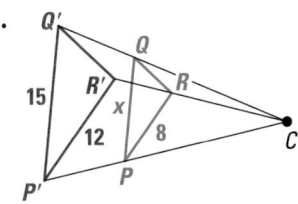

6. **ERROR ANALYSIS** *Describe* and correct the error in finding the scale factor k of the dilation.

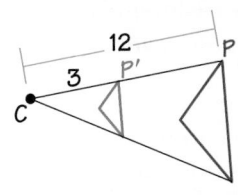

$$k = \frac{CP}{CP'}$$
$$k = \frac{12}{3} = 4$$ ✗

EXAMPLE 2
on p. 627 for Exs. 7–14

CONSTRUCTION **Copy the diagram. Then draw the given dilation.**

7. Center H; $k = 2$ 8. Center H; $k = 3$

9. Center J; $k = 2$ 10. Center F; $k = 2$

11. Center J; $k = \frac{1}{2}$ 12. Center F; $k = \frac{3}{2}$

13. Center D; $k = \frac{3}{2}$ 14. Center G; $k = \frac{1}{2}$

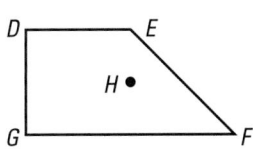

EXAMPLE 3
on p. 627 for Exs. 15–17

SCALAR MULTIPLICATION **Simplify the product.**

15. $4 \begin{bmatrix} 3 & 7 & 4 \\ 0 & 9 & -1 \end{bmatrix}$ 16. $-5 \begin{bmatrix} -2 & -5 & 7 & 3 \\ 1 & 4 & 0 & -1 \end{bmatrix}$ 17. $9 \begin{bmatrix} 0 & 3 & 2 \\ -1 & 7 & 0 \end{bmatrix}$

EXAMPLE 4
on p. 628 for Exs. 18–20

DILATIONS WITH MATRICES **Find the image matrix that represents a dilation of the polygon centered at the origin with the given scale factor. Then graph the polygon and its image.**

18. $\begin{array}{ccc} D & E & F \end{array}$
$\begin{bmatrix} 2 & 3 & 5 \\ 1 & 6 & 4 \end{bmatrix}$; $k = 2$
19. $\begin{array}{ccc} G & H & J \end{array}$
$\begin{bmatrix} -2 & 0 & 6 \\ -4 & 2 & -2 \end{bmatrix}$; $k = \frac{1}{2}$
20. $\begin{array}{cccc} J & L & M & N \end{array}$
$\begin{bmatrix} -6 & -3 & 3 & 3 \\ 0 & 3 & 0 & -3 \end{bmatrix}$; $k = \frac{2}{3}$

EXAMPLE 5
....
on p. 628
for Exs. 21–23

COMPOSING TRANSFORMATIONS The vertices of △ *FGH* are *F*(−2, −2), *G*(−2, −4), and *H*(−4, −4). Graph the image of the triangle after a composition of the transformations in the order they are listed.

21. **Translation:** $(x, y) \rightarrow (x + 3, y + 1)$
    Dilation: centered at the origin with a scale factor of 2

22. **Dilation:** centered at the origin with a scale factor of $\frac{1}{2}$
    Reflection: in the *y*-axis

23. **Rotation:** 90° about the origin
    Dilation: centered at the origin with a scale factor of 3

24. ★ **WRITING** Is a composition of transformations that includes a dilation ever an isometry? *Explain*.

25. ★ **MULTIPLE CHOICE** In the diagram, the center of the dilation of ▱*PQRS* is point *C*. The length of a side of ▱*P'Q'R'S'* is what percent of the length of the corresponding side of ▱*PQRS*?

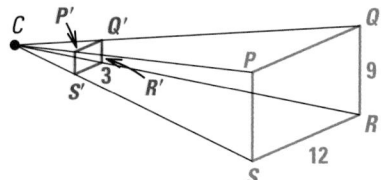

   (A) 25%   **(B)** 33%   **(C)** 300%   **(D)** 400%

26. **REASONING** The distance from the center of dilation to the image of a point is shorter than the distance from the center of dilation to the preimage. Is the dilation a *reduction* or an *enlargement*? *Explain*.

27. ★ **SHORT RESPONSE** Graph a triangle in the coordinate plane. Rotate the triangle, then dilate it. Then do the same dilation first, followed by the rotation. In this composition of transformations, does it matter in which order the triangle is dilated and rotated? *Explain* your answer.

28. **REASONING** A dilation maps *A*(5, 1) to *A'*(2, 1) and *B*(7, 4) to *B'*(6, 7).
    a. Find the scale factor of the dilation.
    b. Find the center of the dilation.

29. ★ **MULTIPLE CHOICE** Which transformation of (x, y) is a dilation?
    (A) $(3x, y)$ **(B)** $(-x, 3y)$ **(C)** $(3x, 3y)$ **(D)** $(x + 3, y + 3)$

30. **ⓧⓨ ALGEBRA** Graph parabolas of the form $y = ax^2$ using three different values of *a*. Describe the effect of changing the value of *a*. Is this a dilation? *Explain*.

31. **REASONING** In the graph at the right, determine whether △ *D'E'F'* is a dilation of △ *DEF*. *Explain*.

32. **CHALLENGE** △*ABC* has vertices *A*(4, 2), *B*(4, 6), and *C*(7, 2). Find the vertices that represent a dilation of △*ABC* centered at (4, 0) with a scale factor of 2.

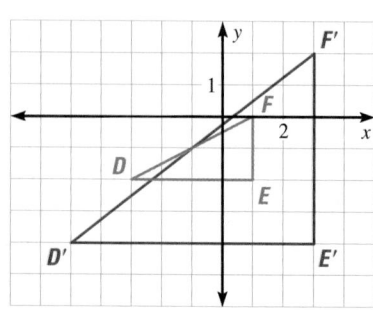

○ = **WORKED-OUT SOLUTIONS**
on p. WS1

★ = **STANDARDIZED**
TEST PRACTICE

EXAMPLE 1
on p. 626
for Exs. 33–35

SCIENCE You are using magnifying glasses. Use the length of the insect and the magnification level to determine the length of the image seen through the magnifying glass.

33. Emperor moth
magnification 5x

←———— 60 mm ————→

34. Ladybug
magnification 10x

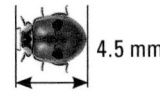

4.5 mm

35. Dragonfly
magnification 20x

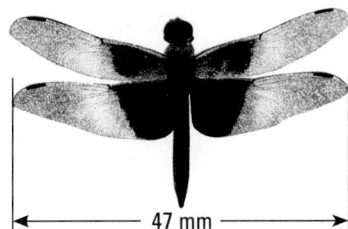

←———— 47 mm ————→

@HomeTutor for problem solving help at classzone.com

36. MURALS A painter sketches plans for a mural. The plans are 2 feet by 4 feet. The actual mural will be 25 feet by 50 feet. What is the scale factor? Is this a dilation? *Explain.*

@HomeTutor for problem solving help at classzone.com

37. PHOTOGRAPHY By adjusting the distance between the negative and the enlarged print in a photographic enlarger, you can make prints of different sizes. In the diagram shown, you want the enlarged print to be 9 inches wide (*A′B′*). The negative is 1.5 inches wide (*AB*), and the distance between the light source and the negative is 1.75 inches (*CD*).

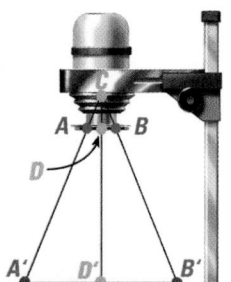

a. What is the scale factor of the enlargement?

b. What is the distance between the negative and the enlarged print?

38. ★ **OPEN-ENDED MATH** Graph a polygon in a coordinate plane. Draw a figure that is similar but not congruent to the polygon. What is the scale factor of the dilation you drew? What is the center of the dilation?

39. MULTI-STEP PROBLEM Use the figure at the right.

a. Write a polygon matrix for the figure. Multiply the matrix by the scalar −2.

b. Graph the polygon represented by the new matrix.

c. Repeat parts (a) and (b) using the scalar $-\frac{1}{2}$.

d. Make a conjecture about the effect of multiplying a polygon matrix by a negative scale factor.

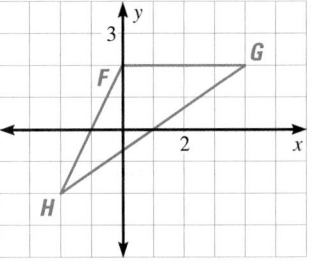

40. AREA You have an 8 inch by 10 inch photo.

a. What is the area of the photo?

b. You photocopy the photo at 50%. What are the dimensions of the image? What is the area of the image?

c. How many images of this size would you need to cover the original photo?

41. REASONING You put a reduction of a page on the original page. *Explain* why there is a point that is in the same place on both pages.

42. CHALLENGE Draw two concentric circles with center *A*. Draw $\overline{AB}$ and $\overline{AC}$ to the larger circle to form a 45° angle. Label points *D* and *F*, where $\overline{AB}$ and $\overline{AC}$ intersect the smaller circle. Locate point *E* at the intersection of $\overline{BF}$ and $\overline{CD}$. Choose a point *G* and draw quadrilateral *DEFG*. Use *A* as the center of the dilation and a scale factor of $\frac{1}{2}$. Dilate *DEFG*, $\triangle DBE$, and $\triangle CEF$ two times. Sketch each image on the circles. *Describe* the result.

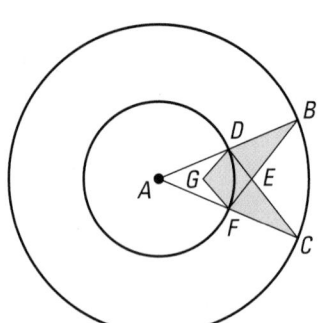

MIXED REVIEW

PREVIEW
Prepare for
Lesson 10.1 in
Exs. 43–45.

Find the unknown leg length *x*. *(p. 433)*

43.
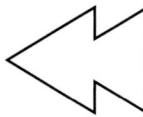

44.
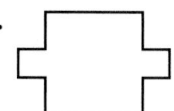

45.
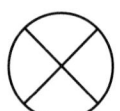

Find the sum of the measures of the interior angles of the indicated convex polygon. *(p. 507)*

46. Hexagon   **47.** 13-gon   **48.** 15-gon   **49.** 18-gon

---

QUIZ *for Lessons 9.6–9.7*

Determine whether the figure has *line symmetry* and/or *rotational symmetry*. Identify the number of lines of symmetry and/or the rotations that map the figure onto itself. *(p. 619)*

1.   **2.**   **3.**   **4.**

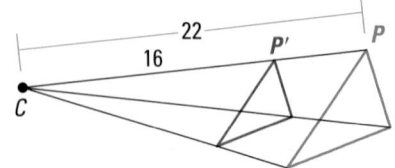

Tell whether the dilation is a *reduction* or an *enlargement* and find its scale factor. *(p. 626)*

5.   **6.**

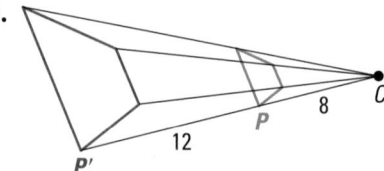

7. The vertices of $\triangle RST$ are *R*(3, 1), *S*(0, 4), and *T*(−2, 2). Use scalar multiplication to find the image of the triangle after a dilation centered at the origin with scale factor $4\frac{1}{2}$. *(p. 626)*

9.7 Compositions With Dilations

MATERIALS • graphing calculator or computer

QUESTION **How can you graph compositions with dilations?**

You can use geometry drawing software to perform compositions with dilations.

EXAMPLE **Perform a reflection and dilation**

STEP 1 **Draw triangle** Construct a scalene triangle like △*ABC* at the right. Label the vertices *A*, *B*, and *C*. Construct a line that does not intersect the triangle. Label the line *p*.

STEP 2 **Reflect triangle** Select Reflection from the F4 menu. To reflect △*ABC* in line *p*, choose the triangle, then the line.

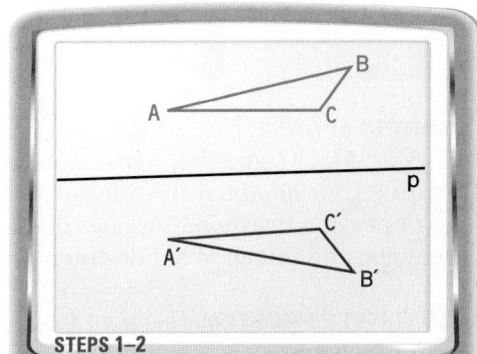

STEP 3 **Dilate triangle** Select Hide/Show from the F5 menu and show the axes. To set the scale factor, select Alpha-Num from the F5 menu, press ENTER when the cursor is where you want the number, and then enter 0.5 for the scale factor.

Next, select Dilation from the F4 menu. Choose the image of △*ABC*, then choose the origin as the center of dilation, and finally choose 0.5 as the scale factor to dilate the triangle. Save this as "DILATE".

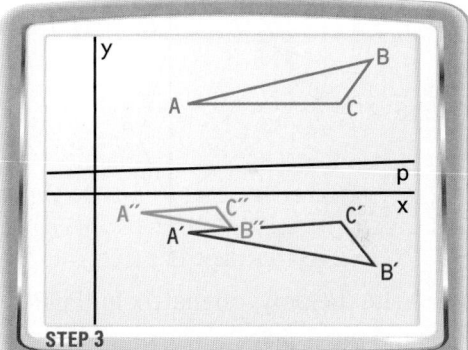

PRACTICE

1. Move the line of reflection. How does the final image change?

2. To change the scale factor, select the Alpha-Num tool. Place the cursor over the scale factor. Press ENTER, then DELETE. Enter a new scale. How does the final image change?

3. Dilate with a center not at the origin. How does the final image change?

4. Use △*ABC* and line *p*, and the dilation and reflection from the Example. Dilate the triangle first, then reflect it. How does the final image change?

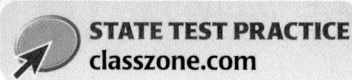
Lessons 9.4–9.7

1. GRIDDED ANSWER What is the angle of rotation, in degrees, that maps *A* to *A'* in the photo of the ceiling fan below?

2. SHORT RESPONSE The vertices of △*DEF* are *D*(−3, 2), *E*(2, 3), and *F*(3, −1). Graph △*DEF*. Rotate △*DEF* 90° about the origin. Compare the slopes of corresponding sides of the preimage and image. What do you notice?

3. MULTI–STEP PROBLEM Use pentagon *PQRST* shown below.

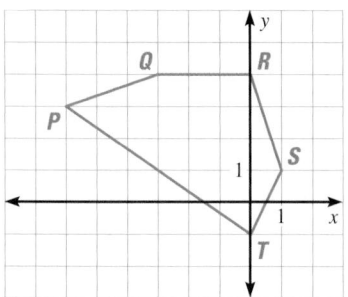

  a. Write the polygon matrix for *PQRST*.

  b. Find the image matrix for a 270° rotation about the origin.

  c. Graph the image.

4. SHORT RESPONSE *Describe* the transformations that can be found in the quilt pattern below.

5. MULTI-STEP PROBLEM The diagram shows the pieces of a puzzle.

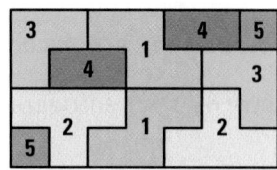

  a. Which pieces are translated?

  b. Which pieces are reflected?

  c. Which pieces are glide reflected?

6. OPEN-ENDED Draw a figure that has the given type(s) of symmetry.

  a. Line symmetry only

  b. Rotational symmetry only

  c. Both line symmetry and rotational symmetry

7. EXTENDED RESPONSE In the graph below, △*A'B'C'* is a dilation of △*ABC*.

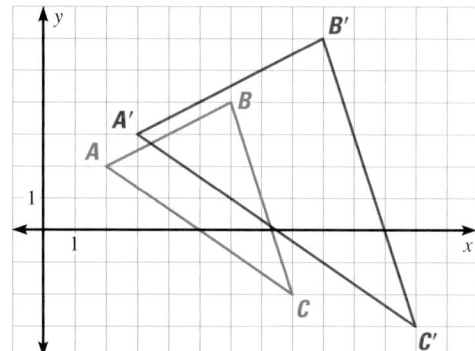

  a. Is the dilation a *reduction* or an *enlargement*?

  b. What is the scale factor? *Explain* your steps.

  c. What is the polygon matrix? What is the image matrix?

  d. When you perform a composition of a dilation and a translation on a figure, does order matter? *Justify* your answer using the translation (*x*, *y*) → (*x* + 3, *y* − 1) and the dilation of △*ABC*.

BIG IDEAS

Big Idea 1

Performing Congruence and Similarity Transformations

Translation

Translate a figure right or left, up or down.

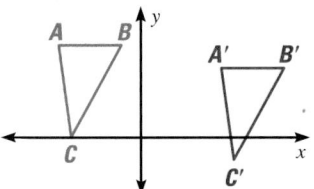

Reflection

Reflect a figure in a line.

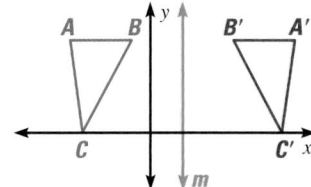

Rotation

Rotate a figure about a point.

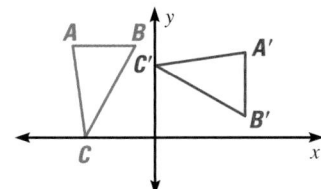

Dilation

Dilate a figure to change the size but not the shape.

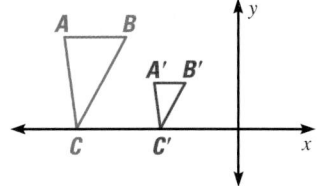

You can combine congruence and similarity transformations to make a composition of transformations, such as a glide reflection.

Big Idea 2

Making Real-World Connections to Symmetry and Tessellations

Line symmetry

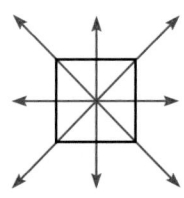

4 lines of symmetry

Rotational symmetry

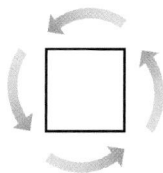

90° rotational symmetry

Big Idea 3

Applying Matrices and Vectors in Geometry

You can use matrices to represent points and polygons in the coordinate plane. Then you can use matrix addition to represent translations, matrix multiplication to represent reflections and rotations, and scalar multiplication to represent dilations. You can also use vectors to represent translations.

REVIEW KEY VOCABULARY

For a list of postulates and theorems, see pp. 926–931.

• image, *p. 572*
• preimage, *p. 572*
• isometry, *p. 573*
• vector, *p. 574*
  initial point, terminal point, horizontal component, vertical component
• component form, *p. 574*

• matrix, *p. 580*
• element, *p. 580*
• dimensions, *p. 580*
• line of reflection, *p. 589*
• center of rotation, *p. 598*
• angle of rotation, *p. 598*
• glide reflection, *p. 608*

• composition of transformations, *p. 609*
• line symmetry, *p. 619*
• line of symmetry, *p. 619*
• rotational symmetry, *p. 620*
• center of symmetry, *p. 620*
• scalar multiplication, *p. 627*

VOCABULARY EXERCISES

1. Copy and complete: A(n) __?__ is a transformation that preserves lengths.

2. Draw a figure with exactly one line of symmetry.

3. **WRITING** *Explain* how to identify the dimensions of a matrix. Include an example with your explanation.

Match the point with the appropriate name on the vector.

4. *T*   **A.** Initial point

5. *H*   **B.** Terminal point

REVIEW EXAMPLES AND EXERCISES

Use the review examples and exercises below to check your understanding of the concepts you have learned in each lesson of Chapter 9.

9.1 Translate Figures and Use Vectors   *pp. 572–579*

EXAMPLE

Name the vector and write its component form.

The vector is $\overrightarrow{EF}$. From initial point *E* to terminal point *F*, you move 4 units right and 1 unit down. So, the component form is ⟨4, 1⟩.

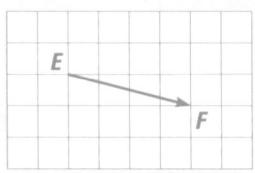

EXERCISES

EXAMPLES
1 and 4
on pp. 572, 574
for Exs. 6–7

6. The vertices of △*ABC* are *A*(2, 3), *B*(1, 0), and *C*(−2, 4). Graph the image of △*ABC* after the translation $(x, y) \rightarrow (x + 3, y − 2)$.

7. The vertices of △*DEF* are *D*(−6, 7), *E*(−5, 5), and *F*(−8, 4). Graph the image of △*DEF* after the translation using the vector ⟨−1, 6⟩.

9.2 Use Properties of Matrices
pp. 580–587

EXAMPLE

Add $\begin{bmatrix} -9 & 12 \\ 5 & -4 \end{bmatrix} + \begin{bmatrix} 20 & 18 \\ 11 & 25 \end{bmatrix}$.

These two matrices have the same dimensions, so you can perform the addition. To add matrices, you add corresponding elements.

$$\begin{bmatrix} -9 & 12 \\ 5 & -4 \end{bmatrix} + \begin{bmatrix} 20 & 18 \\ 11 & 25 \end{bmatrix} = \begin{bmatrix} -9+20 & 12+18 \\ 5+11 & -4+25 \end{bmatrix} = \begin{bmatrix} 11 & 30 \\ 16 & 21 \end{bmatrix}$$

EXERCISES

EXAMPLE 3
on p. 581
for Exs. 8–9

Find the image matrix that represents the translation of the polygon. Then graph the polygon and its image.

8. $\begin{array}{ccc} A & B & C \\ \begin{bmatrix} 2 & 8 & 1 \\ 4 & 3 & 2 \end{bmatrix} \end{array}$;

   5 units up and 3 units left

9. $\begin{array}{cccc} D & E & F & G \\ \begin{bmatrix} -2 & 3 & 4 & -1 \\ 3 & 6 & 4 & -1 \end{bmatrix} \end{array}$;

   2 units down

9.3 Perform Reflections
pp. 589–596

EXAMPLE

The vertices of △*MLN* are *M*(4, 3), *L*(6, 3), and *N*(5, 1). Graph the reflection of △*MLN* in the line *p* with equation *x* = 2.

Point *M* is 2 units to the right of *p*, so its reflection *M*′ is 2 units to the left of *p* at (0, 3). Similarly, *L*′ is 4 units to the left of *p* at (−2, 3) and *N*′ is 3 units to the left of *p* at (−1, 1).

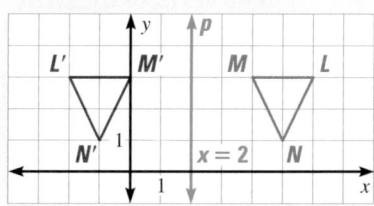

EXERCISES

**EXAMPLES
1 and 2**
on pp. 589–590
for Exs. 10–12

Graph the reflection of the polygon in the given line.

10. $x = 4$

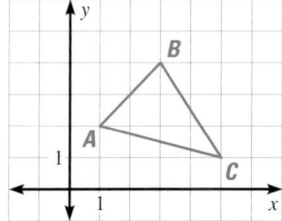

11. $y = 3$

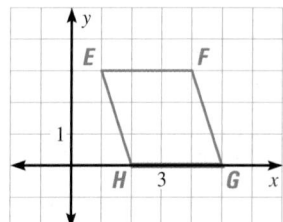

12. $y = x$

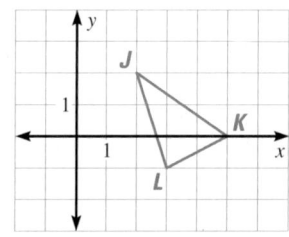

9.4 Perform Rotations

pp. 598–605

EXAMPLE

**Find the image matrix that represents the 90°
rotation of *ABCD* about the origin.**

The polygon matrix for *ABCD* is $\begin{bmatrix} -2 & 1 & 2 & -3 \\ 4 & 4 & 2 & 2 \end{bmatrix}$.

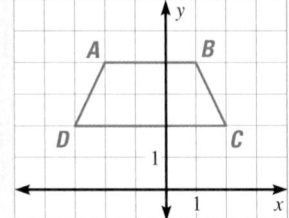

Multiply by the matrix for a 90° rotation.

$$\begin{bmatrix} 0 & -1 \\ 1 & 0 \end{bmatrix} \overset{\begin{matrix} A & B & C & D \end{matrix}}{\begin{bmatrix} -2 & 1 & 2 & -3 \\ 4 & 4 & 2 & 2 \end{bmatrix}} = \overset{\begin{matrix} A' & B' & C' & D' \end{matrix}}{\begin{bmatrix} -4 & -4 & -2 & -2 \\ -2 & 1 & 2 & -3 \end{bmatrix}}$$

EXERCISES

EXAMPLE 3
on p. 600
for Exs. 13–14

**Find the image matrix that represents the given rotation of the polygon
about the origin. Then graph the polygon and its image.**

13. $\overset{\begin{matrix} Q & R & S \end{matrix}}{\begin{bmatrix} 3 & 4 & 1 \\ 0 & 5 & -2 \end{bmatrix}}$; 180°

14. $\overset{\begin{matrix} L & M & N & P \end{matrix}}{\begin{bmatrix} -1 & 3 & 5 & -2 \\ 6 & 5 & 0 & -3 \end{bmatrix}}$; 270°

9.5 Apply Compositions of Transformations

pp. 608–615

EXAMPLE

**The vertices of $\triangle ABC$ are $A(4, -4)$, $B(3, -2)$, and $C(8, -3)$. Graph the image
of $\triangle ABC$ after the glide reflection.**

Translation: $(x, y) \rightarrow (x, y + 5)$
Reflection: in the y-axis

Begin by graphing $\triangle ABC$.
Then graph the image
$\triangle A'B'C'$ after a translation
of 5 units up. Finally, graph
the image $\triangle A''B''C''$ after a
reflection in the y-axis.

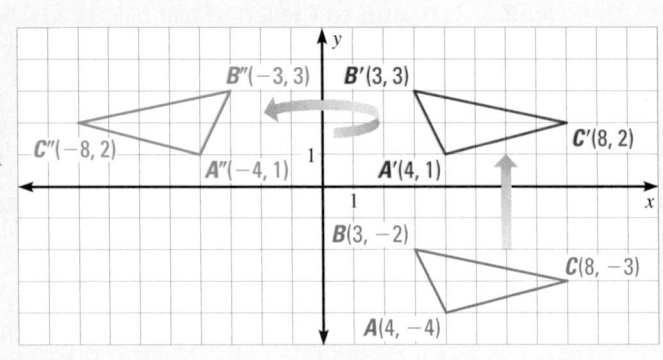

EXERCISES

EXAMPLE 1
on p. 608
for Exs. 15–16

Graph the image of $H(-4, 5)$ after the glide reflection.

15. **Translation:** $(x, y) \rightarrow (x + 6, y - 2)$
    Reflection: in $x = 3$

16. **Translation:** $(x, y) \rightarrow (x - 4, y - 5)$
    Reflection: in $y = x$

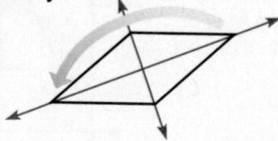

9.6 Identify Symmetry

pp. 619–624

EXAMPLE

Determine whether the rhombus has *line symmetry* and/or *rotational symmetry.* Identify the number of lines of symmetry and/or the rotations that map the figure onto itself.

The rhombus has two lines of symmetry. It also has rotational symmetry, because a 180° rotation maps the rhombus onto itself.

EXERCISES

**EXAMPLES
1 and 2**
on pp. 619–620
for Exs. 17–19

Determine whether the figure has *line symmetry* and/or *rotational symmetry.* Identify the number of lines of symmetry and/or the rotations that map the figure onto itself.

17.

18.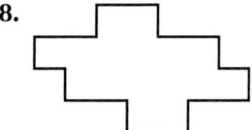

19.

9.7 Identify and Perform Dilations

pp. 626–632

EXAMPLE

Quadrilateral *ABCD* has vertices *A*(1, 1), *B*(1, 3), *C*(3, 2), and *D*(3, 1). Use scalar multiplication to find the image of *ABCD* after a dilation with its center at the origin and a scale factor of 2. Graph *ABCD* and its image.

To find the image matrix, multiply each element of the polygon matrix by the scale factor.

$$2\begin{bmatrix} \overset{A}{1} & \overset{B}{1} & \overset{C}{3} & \overset{D}{3} \\ 1 & 3 & 2 & 1 \end{bmatrix} = \begin{bmatrix} \overset{A'}{2} & \overset{B'}{2} & \overset{C'}{6} & \overset{D'}{6} \\ 2 & 6 & 4 & 2 \end{bmatrix}$$

Scale factor   Polygon matrix   Image matrix

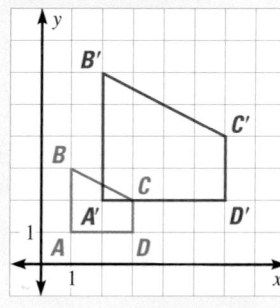

EXERCISES

EXAMPLE 4
on p. 628
for Exs. 20–21

Find the image matrix that represents a dilation of the polygon centered at the origin with the given scale factor. Then graph the polygon and its image.

20. $\begin{bmatrix} \overset{Q}{2} & \overset{R}{4} & \overset{S}{8} \\ 2 & 4 & 2 \end{bmatrix}; k = \frac{1}{4}$

21. $\begin{bmatrix} \overset{L}{-1} & \overset{M}{1} & \overset{N}{2} \\ -2 & 3 & 4 \end{bmatrix}; k = 3$

Write a rule for the translation of △*ABC* to △*A'B'C'*. Then verify that the translation is an isometry.

1.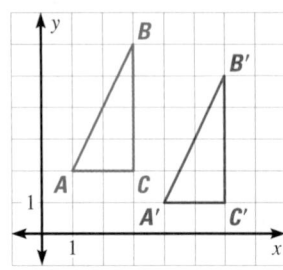

2.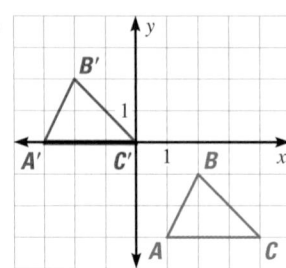

3.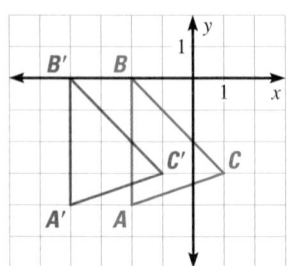

Add, subtract, or multiply.

4. $\begin{bmatrix} 3 & -8 \\ 9 & 4.3 \end{bmatrix} + \begin{bmatrix} -10 & 2 \\ 5.1 & -5 \end{bmatrix}$

5. $\begin{bmatrix} -2 & 2.6 \\ 0.8 & 4 \end{bmatrix} - \begin{bmatrix} 6 & 9 \\ -1 & 3 \end{bmatrix}$

6. $\begin{bmatrix} 7 & -3 & 2 \\ 5 & 1 & -4 \end{bmatrix} \begin{bmatrix} 1 \\ 0 \\ 3 \end{bmatrix}$

Graph the image of the polygon after the reflection in the given line.

7. *x*-axis

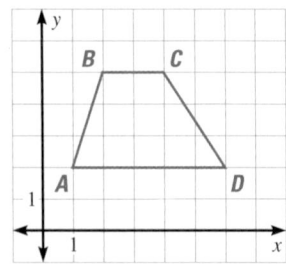

8. $y = 3$

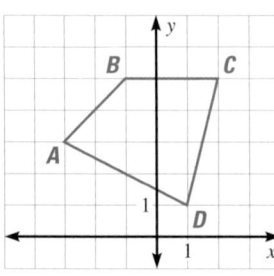

9. $y = -x$

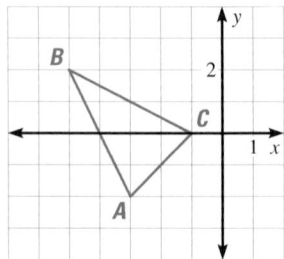

Find the image matrix that represents the rotation of the polygon. Then graph the polygon and its image.

10. △*ABC*: $\begin{bmatrix} 2 & 4 & 6 \\ 2 & 5 & 1 \end{bmatrix}$; 90° rotation

11. *KLMN*: $\begin{bmatrix} -5 & -2 & -3 & -5 \\ 0 & 3 & -1 & -3 \end{bmatrix}$; 180° rotation

The vertices of △*PQR* are *P*(−5, 1), *Q*(−4, 6), and *R*(−2, 3). Graph △*P″Q″R″* after a composition of the transformations in the order they are listed.

12. **Translation:** $(x, y) \rightarrow (x - 8, y)$
Dilation: centered at the origin, $k = 2$

13. **Reflection:** in the *y*-axis
Rotation: 90° about the origin

Determine whether the flag has *line symmetry* and/or *rotational symmetry*. Identify all lines of symmetry and/or angles of rotation that map the figure onto itself.

14.

15.

16.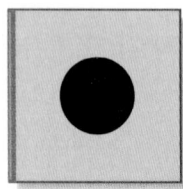

MULTIPLY BINOMIALS AND USE QUADRATIC FORMULA

_xy_ **EXAMPLE 1** **_Multiply binomials_**

Find the product $(2x + 3)(x - 7)$.

Solution

Use the **FOIL** pattern: Multiply the First, Outer, Inner, and Last terms.

$$\begin{array}{cccc} \textbf{First} & \textbf{Outer} & \textbf{Inner} & \textbf{Last} \\ \downarrow & \downarrow & \downarrow & \downarrow \end{array}$$

$(2x + 3)(x - 7) = 2x(x) + 2x(-7) + 3(x) + 3(-7)$	Write the products of terms.
$= 2x^2 - 14x + 3x - 21$	Multiply.
$= 2x^2 - 11x - 21$	Combine like terms.

_xy_ **EXAMPLE 2** **_Solve a quadratic equation using the quadratic formula_**

Solve $2x^2 + 1 = 5x$.

Solution

Write the equation in standard form to be able to use the quadratic formula.

$2x^2 + 1 = 5x$	Write the original equation.
$2x^2 - 5x + 1 = 0$	Write in standard form.
$x = \dfrac{-b \pm \sqrt{b^2 - 4ac}}{2a}$	Write the quadratic formula.
$x = \dfrac{-(-5) \pm \sqrt{(-5)^2 - 4(2)(1)}}{2(2)}$	Substitute values in the quadratic formula: $a = 2$, $b = -5$, and $c = 1$.
$x = \dfrac{5 \pm \sqrt{25 - 8}}{4} = \dfrac{5 \pm \sqrt{17}}{4}$	Simplify.

▶ The solutions are $\dfrac{5 + \sqrt{17}}{4} \approx 2.28$ and $\dfrac{5 - \sqrt{17}}{4} \approx 0.22$.

EXERCISES

EXAMPLE 1
for Exs. 1–9

Find the product.

1. $(x + 3)(x - 2)$ **2.** $(x - 8)^2$ **3.** $(x + 4)(x - 4)$

4. $(x - 5)(x - 1)$ **5.** $(7x + 6)^2$ **6.** $(3x - 1)(x + 9)$

7. $(2x + 1)(2x - 1)$ **8.** $(-3x + 1)^2$ **9.** $(x + y)(2x + y)$

EXAMPLE 2
for Exs. 10–18

Use the quadratic formula to solve the equation.

10. $3x^2 - 2x - 5 = 0$ **11.** $x^2 - 7x + 12 = 0$ **12.** $x^2 + 5x - 2 = 0$

13. $4x^2 + 9x + 2 = 0$ **14.** $3x^2 + 4x - 10 = 0$ **15.** $x^2 + x = 7$

16. $3x^2 = 5x - 1$ **17.** $x^2 = -11x - 4$ **18.** $5x^2 + 6 = 17x$

SHORT RESPONSE QUESTIONS

PROBLEM

The vertices of $\triangle PQR$ are $P(1, -1)$, $Q(4, -1)$, and $R(0, -3)$. What are the coordinates of the image of $\triangle PQR$ after the given composition? *Describe* your steps. Include a graph with your answer.

Translation: $(x, y) \rightarrow (x - 6, y)$
Reflection: in the x-axis

Below are sample solutions to the problem. Read each solution and the comments in blue to see why the sample represents full credit, partial credit, or no credit.

SAMPLE 1: Full credit solution

The reasoning is correct, and the graphs are correct.

First, graph $\triangle PQR$. Next, to translate $\triangle PQR$ 6 units left, subtract 6 from the x-coordinate of each vertex.

$P(1, -1) \rightarrow P'(-5, -1)$

$Q(4, -1) \rightarrow Q'(-2, -1)$

$R(0, -3) \rightarrow R'(-6, -3)$

Finally, reflect $\triangle P'Q'R'$ in the x-axis by multiplying the y-coordinates by -1.

$P'(-5, -1) \rightarrow P''(-5, 1)$

$Q'(-2, -1) \rightarrow Q''(-2, 1)$

$R'(-6, -3) \rightarrow R''(-6, 3)$

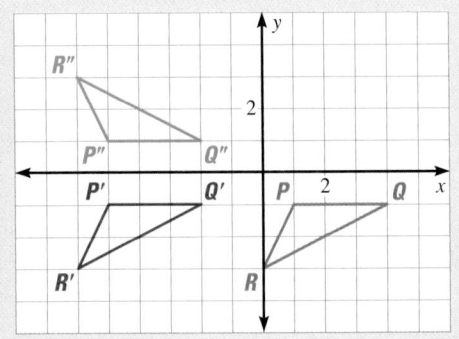

SAMPLE 2: Partial credit solution

Each transformation is performed correctly. However, the transformations are not performed in the order given in the problem.

First, graph $\triangle PQR$. Next, reflect $\triangle PQR$ over the x-axis by multiplying each y-coordinate by -1. Finally, to translate $\triangle P'Q'R'$ 6 units left, subtract 6 from each x-coordinate.

The coordinates of the image of $\triangle PQR$ after the composition are $P''(-5, 1)$, $Q''(-2, 1)$, and $R''(-6, 3)$.

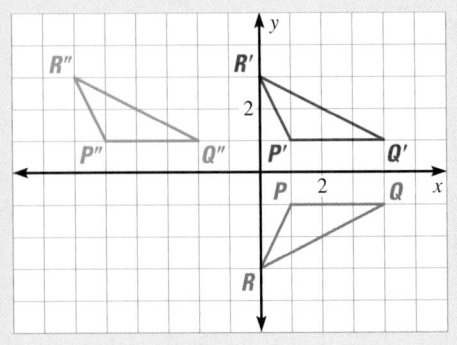

In Chapter 10, you will apply the big ideas listed below and reviewed in the Chapter Summary on page 707. You will also use the key vocabulary listed below.

Big Ideas

1. **Using properties of segments that intersect circles**
2. **Applying angle relationships in circles**
3. **Using circles in the coordinate plane**

KEY VOCABULARY

- circle, *p. 651*
  center, radius, diameter
- chord, *p. 651*
- secant, *p. 651*
- tangent, *p. 651*

- central angle, *p. 659*
- minor arc, *p. 659*
- major arc, *p. 659*
- semicircle, *p. 659*
- congruent circles, *p. 660*

- congruent arcs, *p. 660*
- inscribed angle, *p. 672*
- intercepted arc, *p. 672*
- standard equation of a circle, *p. 699*

Circles can be used to model a wide variety of natural phenomena. You can use properties of circles to investigate the Northern Lights.

Animated Geometry

The animation illustrated below for Example 4 on page 682 helps you answer this question: From what part of Earth are the Northern Lights visible?

Your goal is to determine from what part of Earth you can see the Northern Lights.

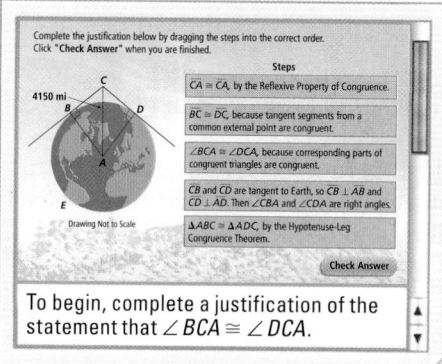

To begin, complete a justification of the statement that ∠ *BCA* ≅ ∠ *DCA*.

Animated Geometry at classzone.com

Other animations for Chapter 10: pages 655, 661, 671, 691, and 701

10.1 Explore Tangent Segments

MATERIALS · compass · ruler

QUESTION How are the lengths of tangent segments related?

A line can intersect a circle at 0, 1, or 2 points. If a line is in the plane of a circle and intersects the circle at 1 point, the line is a *tangent*.

EXPLORE Draw tangents to a circle

STEP 1	STEP 2	STEP 3
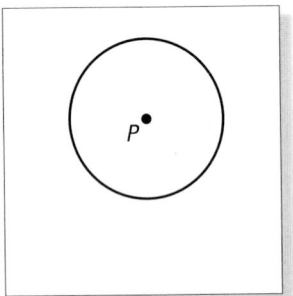	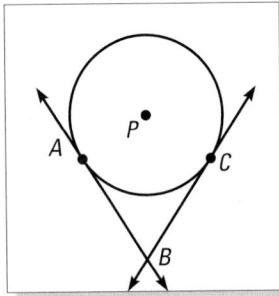	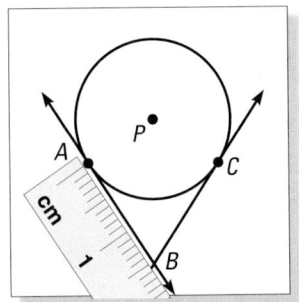

Draw a circle Use a compass to draw a circle. Label the center *P*.

Draw tangents Draw lines $\overleftrightarrow{AB}$ and $\overleftrightarrow{CB}$ so that they intersect $\odot P$ only at *A* and *C*, respectively. These lines are called *tangents*.

Measure segments $\overline{AB}$ and $\overline{CB}$ are called *tangent segments*. Measure and compare the lengths of the tangent segments.

DRAW CONCLUSIONS Use your observations to complete these exercises

1. Repeat Steps 1–3 with three different circles.

2. Use your results from Exercise 1 to make a conjecture about the lengths of tangent segments that have a common endpoint.

3. In the diagram, *L*, *Q*, *N*, and *P* are points of tangency. Use your conjecture from Exercise 2 to find *LQ* and *NP* if *LM* = 7 and *MP* = 5.5.

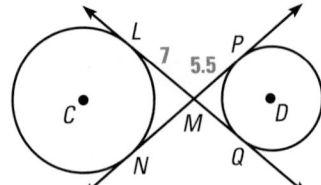

4. In the diagram below, *A*, *B*, *D*, and *E* are points of tangency. Use your conjecture from Exercise 2 to explain why $\overline{AB} \cong \overline{ED}$.

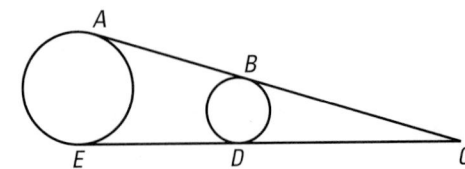

10.1 Use Properties of Tangents

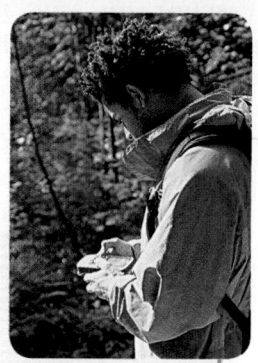

Before You found the circumference and area of circles.

Now You will use properties of a tangent to a circle.

Why? So you can find the range of a GPS satellite, as in Ex. 37.

Key Vocabulary
• **circle**
  center, radius, diameter
• **chord**
• **secant**
• **tangent**

A **circle** is the set of all points in a plane that are equidistant from a given point called the **center** of the circle. A circle with center *P* is called "circle *P*" and can be written ⊙*P*. A segment whose endpoints are the center and any point on the circle is a **radius**.

A **chord** is a segment whose endpoints are on a circle. A **diameter** is a chord that contains the center of the circle.

A **secant** is a line that intersects a circle in two points. A **tangent** is a line in the plane of a circle that intersects the circle in exactly one point, the *point of tangency*. The *tangent ray* $\overrightarrow{AB}$ and the *tangent segment* $\overline{AB}$ are also called tangents.

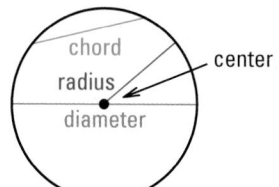

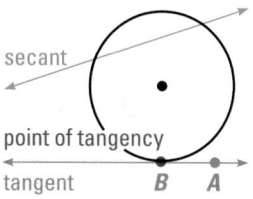

EXAMPLE 1 Identify special segments and lines

Tell whether the line, ray, or segment is best described as a *radius, chord, diameter, secant,* or *tangent* of ⊙*C.*

a. $\overline{AC}$ b. $\overline{AB}$

c. $\overrightarrow{DE}$ d. $\overleftrightarrow{AE}$

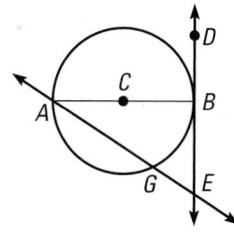

Solution

a. $\overline{AC}$ is a radius because *C* is the center and *A* is a point on the circle.

b. $\overline{AB}$ is a diameter because it is a chord that contains the center *C*.

c. $\overrightarrow{DE}$ is a tangent ray because it is contained in a line that intersects the circle at only one point.

d. $\overleftrightarrow{AE}$ is a secant because it is a line that intersects the circle in two points.

 GUIDED PRACTICE for Example 1

1. In Example 1, what word best describes $\overline{AG}$? $\overline{CB}$?

2. In Example 1, name a tangent and a tangent segment.

RADIUS AND DIAMETER The words *radius* and *diameter* are used for lengths as well as segments. For a given circle, think of *a radius* and *a diameter* as segments and *the radius* and *the diameter* as lengths.

EXAMPLE 2 Find lengths in circles in a coordinate plane

Use the diagram to find the given lengths.

a. Radius of $\odot A$

b. Diameter of $\odot A$

c. Radius of $\odot B$

d. Diameter of $\odot B$

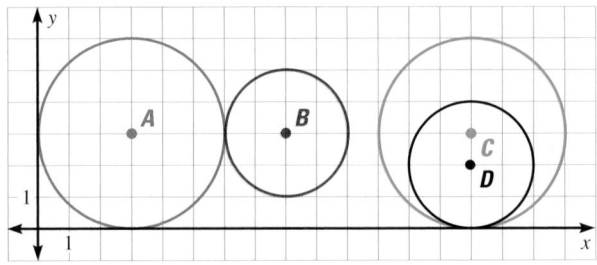

Solution

a. The radius of $\odot A$ is 3 units.

b. The diameter of $\odot A$ is 6 units.

c. The radius of $\odot B$ is 2 units.

d. The diameter of $\odot B$ is 4 units.

 GUIDED PRACTICE for Example 2

3. Use the diagram in Example 2 to find the radius and diameter of $\odot C$ and $\odot D$.

COPLANAR CIRCLES Two circles can intersect in two points, one point, or no points. Coplanar circles that intersect in one point are called *tangent circles*. Coplanar circles that have a common center are called *concentric*.

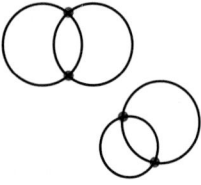

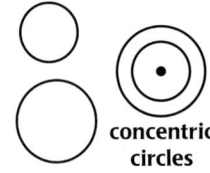

2 points of intersection

1 point of intersection (tangent circles)

no points of intersection

COMMON TANGENTS A line, ray, or segment that is tangent to two coplanar circles is called a *common tangent*.

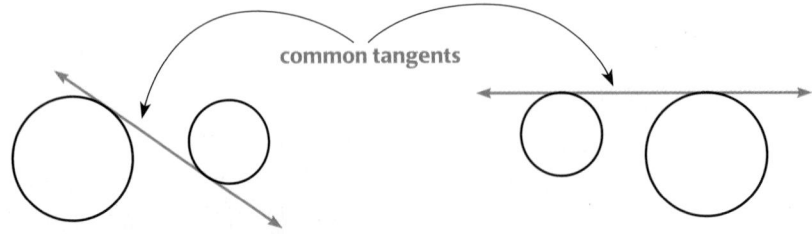

common tangents

EXAMPLE 3 Draw common tangents

Tell how many common tangents the circles have and draw them.

a.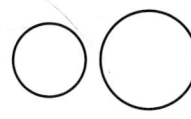

b.

c.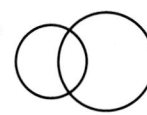

Solution

a. 4 common tangents

b. 3 common tangents

c. 2 common tangents

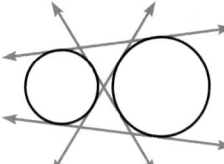

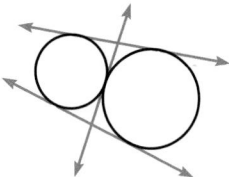

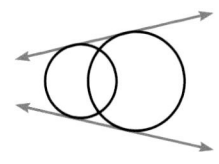

✓ **GUIDED PRACTICE** for Example 3

Tell how many common tangents the circles have and draw them.

4.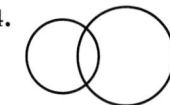

5.

6.

THEOREM   *For Your Notebook*

THEOREM 10.1

In a plane, a line is tangent to a circle if and only if the line is perpendicular to a radius of the circle at its endpoint on the circle.

Proof: Exs. 39–40, p. 658

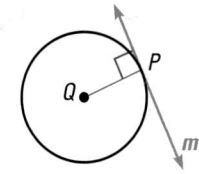

Line *m* is tangent to ⊙*Q* if and only if *m* ⊥ $\overline{QP}$.

EXAMPLE 4 Verify a tangent to a circle

In the diagram, $\overline{PT}$ is a radius of ⊙*P*. Is $\overline{ST}$ tangent to ⊙*P*?

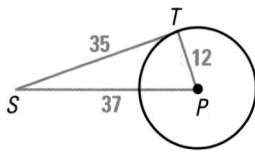

Solution

Use the Converse of the Pythagorean Theorem. Because $12^2 + 35^2 = 37^2$, △*PST* is a right triangle and $\overline{ST} \perp \overline{PT}$. So, $\overline{ST}$ is perpendicular to a radius of ⊙*P* at its endpoint on ⊙*P*. By Theorem 10.1, $\overline{ST}$ is tangent to ⊙*P*.

EXAMPLE 5 **Find the radius of a circle**

In the diagram, *B* is a point of tangency.
Find the radius *r* of ⊙*C*.

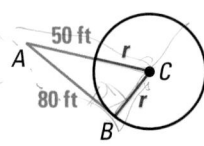

Solution

You know from Theorem 10.1 that $\overline{AB} \perp \overline{BC}$, so △*ABC* is a right triangle.
You can use the Pythagorean Theorem.

$$AC^2 = BC^2 + AB^2 \qquad \text{Pythagorean Theorem}$$

$$(r + 50)^2 = r^2 + 80^2 \qquad \text{Substitute.}$$

$$r^2 + 100r + 2500 = r^2 + 6400 \qquad \text{Multiply.}$$

$$100r = 3900 \qquad \text{Subtract from each side.}$$

$$r = 39 \text{ ft} \qquad \text{Divide each side by 100.}$$

THEOREM *For Your Notebook*

THEOREM 10.2

Tangent segments from a common external
point are congruent.

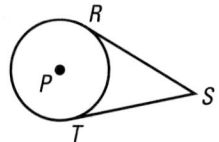

If $\overline{SR}$ and $\overline{ST}$ are tangent
segments, then $\overline{SR} \cong \overline{ST}$.

Proof: Ex. 41, p. 658

EXAMPLE 6 **Use properties of tangents**

$\overline{RS}$ is tangent to ⊙*C* at *S* and $\overline{RT}$ is tangent
to ⊙*C* at *T*. Find the value of *x*.

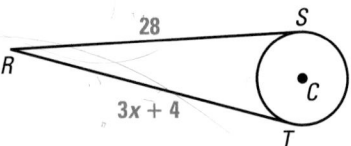

Solution

$RS = RT$ Tangent segments from the same point are ≅.

$28 = 3x + 4$ Substitute.

$8 = x$ Solve for *x*.

✓ **GUIDED PRACTICE**   for Examples 4, 5, and 6

7. Is $\overline{DE}$ tangent to ⊙*C*?

8. $\overline{ST}$ is tangent to ⊙*Q*.
Find the value of *r*.

9. Find the value(s)
of *x*.

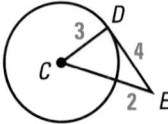

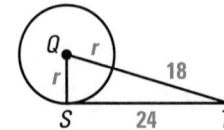

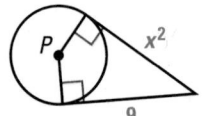

10.1 EXERCISES

HOMEWORK KEY

○ = **WORKED-OUT SOLUTIONS**
on p. WS12 for Exs. 7, 19, and 37

★ = **STANDARDIZED TEST PRACTICE**
Exs. 2, 29, 33, and 38

SKILL PRACTICE

1. **VOCABULARY** Copy and complete: The points *A* and *B* are on ⊙*C*. If *C* is a point on $\overline{AB}$, then $\overline{AB}$ is a __?__ .

2. ★ **WRITING** Explain how you can determine from the context whether the words *radius* and *diameter* are referring to a segment or a length.

EXAMPLE 1
on p. 651
for Exs. 3–11

MATCHING TERMS Match the notation with the term that best describes it.

3. *B*   **A.** Center
4. $\overleftrightarrow{BH}$ **B.** Radius
5. $\overline{AB}$ **C.** Chord
6. $\overleftrightarrow{AB}$ **D.** Diameter
7. $\overleftrightarrow{AE}$ **E.** Secant
8. *G*   **F.** Tangent
9. $\overline{CD}$ **G.** Point of tangency
10. $\overline{BD}$ **H.** Common tangent

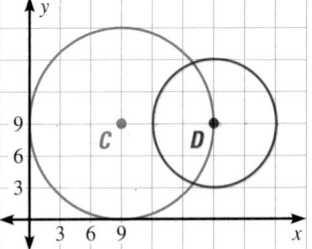

Animated Geometry at classzone.com

11. **ERROR ANALYSIS** *Describe* and correct the error in the statement about the diagram.

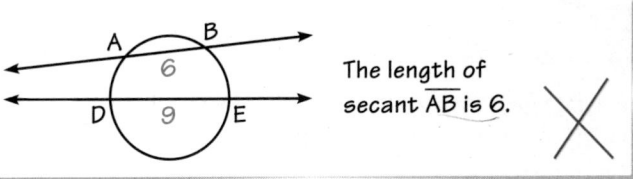

The length of secant $\overline{AB}$ is 6.

EXAMPLES 2 and 3
on pp. 652–653
for Exs. 12–17

COORDINATE GEOMETRY Use the diagram at the right.

12. What are the radius and diameter of ⊙*C*?

13. What are the radius and diameter of ⊙*D*?

14. Copy the circles. Then draw all the common tangents of the two circles.

DRAWING TANGENTS Copy the diagram. Tell how many common tangents the circles have and draw them.

15. 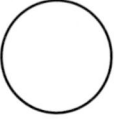   16.   17.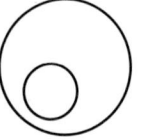

EXAMPLE 4
on p. 653
for Exs. 18–20

DETERMINING TANGENCY Determine whether $\overline{AB}$ is tangent to $\odot C$. *Explain.*

18.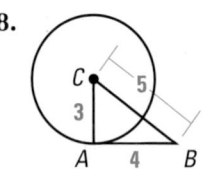

19.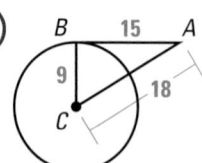

20.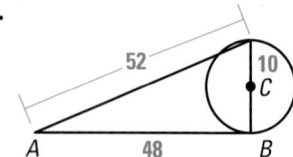

EXAMPLES
5 and 6
on p. 654
for Exs. 21–26

ⓧⓨ ALGEBRA Find the value(s) of the variable. In Exercises 24–26, B and D are points of tangency.

21.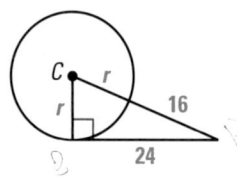

22.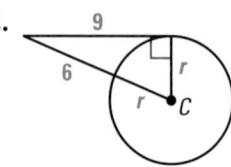

23.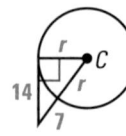

24.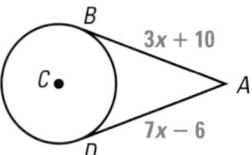

25.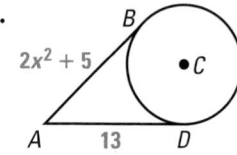

26.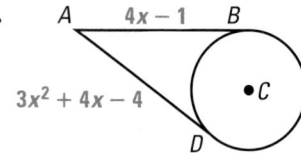

COMMON TANGENTS A *common internal tangent* intersects the segment that joins the centers of two circles. A *common external* tangent does not intersect the segment that joins the centers of the two circles. Determine whether the common tangents shown are *internal* or *external*.

27.

28.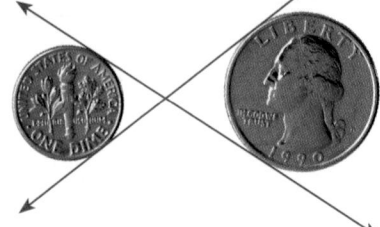

29. ★ **MULTIPLE CHOICE** In the diagram, $\odot P$ and $\odot Q$ are tangent circles. $\overline{RS}$ is a common tangent. Find RS.

Ⓐ $-2\sqrt{15}$

Ⓑ 4

Ⓒ $2\sqrt{15}$

Ⓓ 8

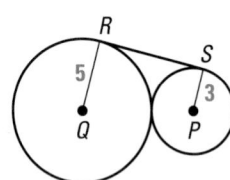

30. **REASONING** In the diagram, $\overrightarrow{PB}$ is tangent to $\odot Q$ and $\odot R$. *Explain* why $\overline{PA} \cong \overline{PB} \cong \overline{PC}$ even though the radius of $\odot Q$ is not equal to the radius of $\odot R$.

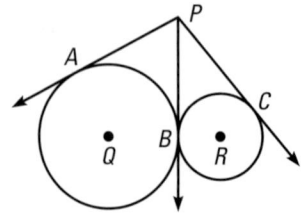

31. **TANGENT LINES** When will two lines tangent to the same circle not intersect? Use Theorem 10.1 to *explain* your answer.

32. ANGLE BISECTOR In the diagram at right, A and D are points of tangency on $\odot C$. *Explain* how you know that $\overrightarrow{BC}$ bisects $\angle ABD$. (*Hint:* Use Theorem 5.6, page 310.)

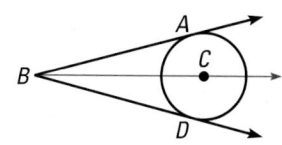

33. ★ **SHORT RESPONSE** For any point outside of a circle, is there ever only one tangent to the circle that passes through the point? Are there ever more than two such tangents? *Explain* your reasoning.

34. CHALLENGE In the diagram at the right, $AB = AC = 12$, $BC = 8$, and all three segments are tangent to $\odot P$. What is the radius of $\odot P$?

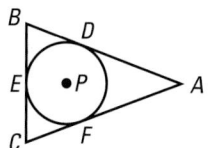

PROBLEM SOLVING

BICYCLES On modern bicycles, rear wheels usually have *tangential spokes*. Occasionally, front wheels have *radial spokes*. Use the definitions of *tangent* and *radius* to determine if the wheel shown has *tangential spokes* or *radial spokes*.

35.

36.

@HomeTutor for problem solving help at classzone.com

EXAMPLE 4
on p. 653
for Ex. 37

37. GLOBAL POSITIONING SYSTEM (GPS) GPS satellites orbit about 11,000 miles above Earth. The mean radius of Earth is about 3959 miles. Because GPS signals cannot travel through Earth, a satellite can transmit signals only as far as points A and C from point B, as shown. Find BA and BC to the nearest mile.

@HomeTutor for problem solving help at classzone.com

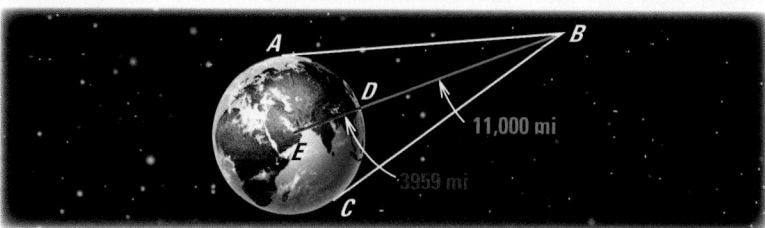

38. ★ **SHORT RESPONSE** In the diagram, $\overline{RS}$ is a common internal tangent (see Exercises 27–28) to $\odot A$ and $\odot B$. Use similar triangles to *explain* why $\dfrac{AC}{BC} = \dfrac{RC}{SC}$.

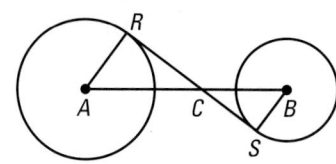

39. PROVING THEOREM 10.1 Use parts (a)–(c) to prove indirectly that if a line is tangent to a circle, then it is perpendicular to a radius.

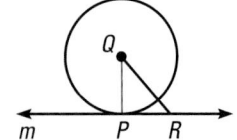

GIVEN ▶ Line *m* is tangent to ⊙*Q* at *P*.

PROVE ▶ $m \perp \overline{QP}$

a. Assume *m* is not perpendicular to $\overline{QP}$. Then the perpendicular segment from *Q* to *m* intersects *m* at some other point *R*. Because *m* is a tangent, *R* cannot be inside ⊙*Q*. *Compare* the length *QR* to *QP*.

b. Because $\overline{QR}$ is the perpendicular segment from *Q* to *m*, $\overline{QR}$ is the shortest segment from *Q* to *m*. Now *compare* *QR* to *QP*.

c. Use your results from parts (a) and (b) to complete the indirect proof.

40. PROVING THEOREM 10.1 Write an indirect proof that if a line is perpendicular to a radius at its endpoint, the line is a tangent.

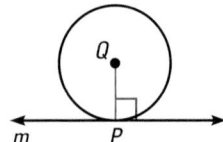

GIVEN ▶ $m \perp \overline{QP}$

PROVE ▶ Line *m* is tangent to ⊙*Q*.

41. PROVING THEOREM 10.2 Write a proof that tangent segments from a common external point are congruent.

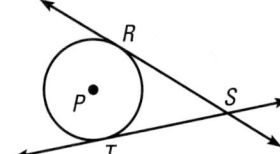

GIVEN ▶ $\overline{SR}$ and $\overline{ST}$ are tangent to ⊙*P*.

PROVE ▶ $\overline{SR} \cong \overline{ST}$

Plan for Proof Use the Hypotenuse–Leg Congruence Theorem to show that △*SRP* ≅ △*STP*.

42. CHALLENGE Point *C* is located at the origin. Line ℓ is tangent to ⊙*C* at (−4, 3). Use the diagram at the right to complete the problem.

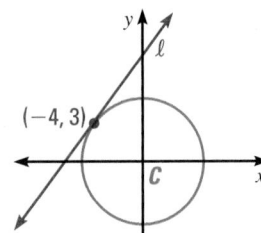

a. Find the slope of line ℓ.

b. Write the equation for ℓ.

c. Find the radius of ⊙*C*.

d. Find the distance from ℓ to ⊙*C* along the *y*-axis.

MIXED REVIEW

PREVIEW

Prepare for Lesson 10.2 in Ex. 43.

43. *D* is in the interior of ∠*ABC*. If *m*∠*ABD* = 25° and *m*∠*ABC* = 70°, find *m*∠*DBC*. *(p. 24)*

Find the values of *x* and *y*. *(p. 154)*

44.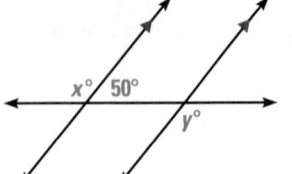

45.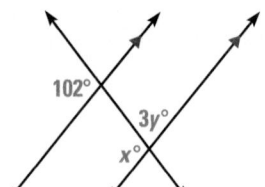

46.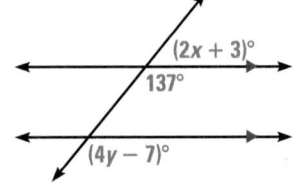

47. A triangle has sides of lengths 8 and 13. Use an inequality to describe the possible length of the third side. What if two sides have lengths 4 and 11? *(p. 328)*

10.2 Find Arc Measures

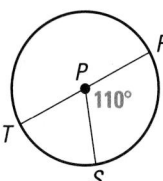

Before	You found angle measures.
Now	You will use angle measures to find arc measures.
Why?	So you can describe the arc made by a bridge, as in Ex. 22.

Key Vocabulary
- central angle
- minor arc
- major arc
- semicircle
- measure
  minor arc, major arc
- congruent circles
- congruent arcs

A **central angle** of a circle is an angle whose vertex is the center of the circle. In the diagram, $\angle ACB$ is a central angle of $\odot C$.

If $m\angle ACB$ is less than $180°$, then the points on $\odot C$ that lie in the interior of $\angle ACB$ form a **minor arc** with endpoints A and B. The points on $\odot C$ that do not lie on minor arc $\widehat{AB}$ form a **major arc** with endpoints A and B. A **semicircle** is an arc with endpoints that are the endpoints of a diameter.

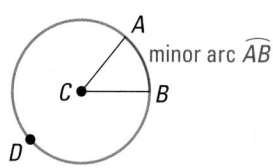

NAMING ARCS Minor arcs are named by their endpoints. The minor arc associated with $\angle ACB$ is named $\widehat{AB}$. Major arcs and semicircles are named by their endpoints and a point on the arc. The major arc associated with $\angle ACB$ can be named $\widehat{ADB}$.

KEY CONCEPT *For Your Notebook*

Measuring Arcs

The **measure of a minor arc** is the measure of its central angle. The expression $m\widehat{AB}$ is read as "the measure of arc AB."

The measure of the entire circle is $360°$. The **measure of a major arc** is the difference between $360°$ and the measure of the related minor arc. The measure of a semicircle is $180°$.

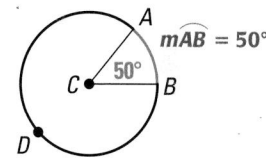

EXAMPLE 1 **Find measures of arcs**

Find the measure of each arc of $\odot P$, where $\overline{RT}$ is a diameter.

  a. $\widehat{RS}$ **b.** $\widehat{RTS}$ **c.** $\widehat{RST}$

Solution

  a. $\widehat{RS}$ is a minor arc, so $m\widehat{RS} = m\angle RPS = 110°$.

  b. $\widehat{RTS}$ is a major arc, so $m\widehat{RTS} = 360° - 110° = 250°$.

  c. $\overline{RT}$ is a diameter, so $\widehat{RST}$ is a semicircle, and $m\widehat{RST} = 180°$.

ADJACENT ARCS Two arcs of the same circle are *adjacent* if they have a common endpoint. You can add the measures of two adjacent arcs.

POSTULATE   *For Your Notebook*

POSTULATE 23 Arc Addition Postulate

The measure of an arc formed by two adjacent arcs is the sum of the measures of the two arcs.

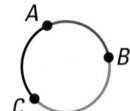

$$m\overset{\frown}{ABC} = m\overset{\frown}{AB} + m\overset{\frown}{BC}$$

EXAMPLE 2   **Find measures of arcs**

SURVEY A recent survey asked teenagers if they would rather meet a famous musician, athlete, actor, inventor, or other person. The results are shown in the circle graph. Find the indicated arc measures.

a. $m\overset{\frown}{AC}$ **b.** $m\overset{\frown}{ACD}$

c. $m\overset{\frown}{ADC}$ **d.** $m\overset{\frown}{EBD}$

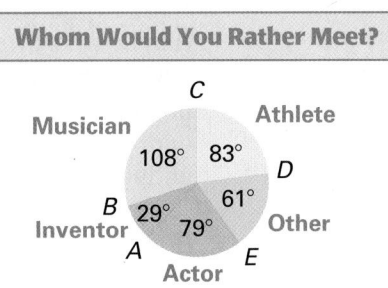

Whom Would You Rather Meet?

Solution

ARC MEASURES

The measure of a minor arc is less than 180°. The measure of a major arc is greater than 180°.

a. $m\overset{\frown}{AC} = m\overset{\frown}{AB} + m\overset{\frown}{BC}$
$= 29° + 108°$
$= 137°$

b. $m\overset{\frown}{ACD} = m\overset{\frown}{AC} + m\overset{\frown}{CD}$
$= 137° + 83°$
$= 220°$

c. $m\overset{\frown}{ADC} = 360° - m\overset{\frown}{AC}$
$= 360° - 137°$
$= 223°$

d. $m\overset{\frown}{EBD} = 360° - m\overset{\frown}{ED}$
$= 360° - 61°$
$= 299°$

✓ **GUIDED PRACTICE**   for Examples 1 and 2

Identify the given arc as a *major arc, minor arc,* or *semicircle*, and find the measure of the arc.

1. $\overset{\frown}{TQ}$ **2.** $\overset{\frown}{QRT}$ **3.** $\overset{\frown}{TQR}$

4. $\overset{\frown}{QS}$ **5.** $\overset{\frown}{TS}$ **6.** $\overset{\frown}{RST}$

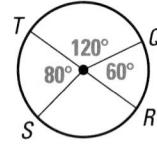

CONGRUENT CIRCLES AND ARCS Two circles are **congruent circles** if they have the same radius. Two arcs are **congruent arcs** if they have the same measure and they are arcs of the same circle or of congruent circles. If $\odot C$ is congruent to $\odot D$, then you can write $\odot C \cong \odot D$.

EXAMPLE 3 **Identify congruent arcs**

Tell whether the red arcs are congruent. Explain why or why not.

a.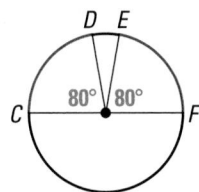

b.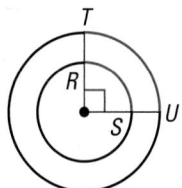

c.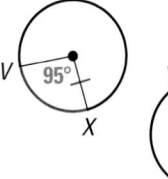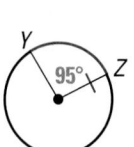

Solution

a. $\overarc{CD} \cong \overarc{EF}$ because they are in the same circle and $m\overarc{CD} = m\overarc{EF}$.

b. $\overarc{RS}$ and $\overarc{TU}$ have the same measure, but are not congruent because they are arcs of circles that are not congruent.

c. $\overarc{VX} \cong \overarc{YZ}$ because they are in congruent circles and $m\overarc{VX} = m\overarc{YZ}$.

Animated Geometry at classzone.com

✓ **GUIDED PRACTICE** | for Example 3

Tell whether the red arcs are congruent. *Explain* why or why not.

7.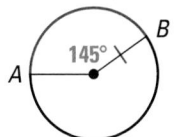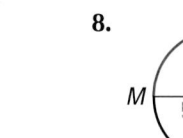

8.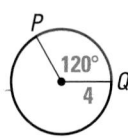

10.2 EXERCISES

HOMEWORK KEY

○ = **WORKED-OUT SOLUTIONS**
on p. WS12 for Exs. 5, 13, and 23

★ = **STANDARDIZED TEST PRACTICE**
Exs. 2, 11, 17, 18, and 24

SKILL PRACTICE

1. **VOCABULARY** Copy and complete: If $\angle ACB$ and $\angle DCE$ are congruent central angles of $\odot C$, then $\overarc{AB}$ and $\overarc{DE}$ are ___?___.

2. ★ **WRITING** What do you need to know about two circles to show that they are congruent? *Explain.*

EXAMPLES
1 and 2
on pp. 659–660
for Exs. 3–11

MEASURING ARCS $\overline{AC}$ and $\overline{BE}$ are diameters of $\odot F$. Determine whether the arc is a *minor arc*, a *major arc*, or a *semicircle* of $\odot F$. Then find the measure of the arc.

3. $\overarc{BC}$

4. $\overarc{DC}$

5. $\overarc{DB}$

6. $\overarc{AE}$

7. $\overarc{AD}$

8. $\overarc{ABC}$

9. $\overarc{ACD}$

10. $\overarc{EAC}$

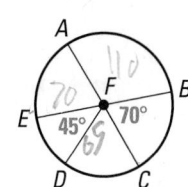

11. ★ **MULTIPLE CHOICE** In the diagram, $\overline{QS}$ is a diameter of $\odot P$. Which arc represents a semicircle?

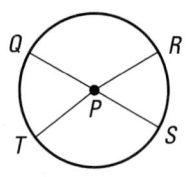

Ⓐ $\overset{\frown}{QR}$ Ⓑ $\overset{\frown}{RQT}$

Ⓒ $\overset{\frown}{QRS}$ Ⓓ $\overset{\frown}{QRT}$

EXAMPLE 3
on p. 661
for Exs. 12–14

CONGRUENT ARCS Tell whether the red arcs are congruent. *Explain* why or why not.

12.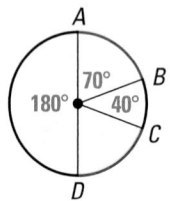

13.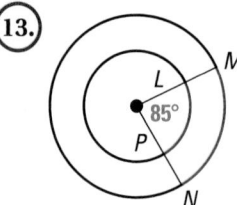

14.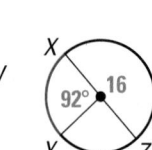

15. ERROR ANALYSIS *Explain* what is wrong with the statement.

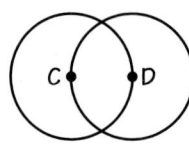

> You cannot tell if $\odot C \cong \odot D$ because the radii are not given.

16. ARCS Two diameters of $\odot P$ are $\overline{AB}$ and $\overline{CD}$. If $m\overset{\frown}{AD} = 20°$, find $m\overset{\frown}{ACD}$ and $m\overset{\frown}{AC}$.

17. ★ **MULTIPLE CHOICE** $\odot P$ has a radius of 3 and $\overset{\frown}{AB}$ has a measure of 90°. What is the length of $\overline{AB}$?

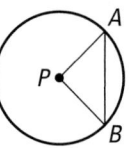

Ⓐ $3\sqrt{2}$ Ⓑ $3\sqrt{3}$

Ⓒ 6   Ⓓ 9

18. ★ **SHORT RESPONSE** On $\odot C$, $m\overset{\frown}{EF} = 100°$, $m\overset{\frown}{FG} = 120°$, and $m\overset{\frown}{EFG} = 220°$. If H is on $\odot C$ so that $m\overset{\frown}{GH} = 150°$, *explain* why H must be on $\overset{\frown}{EF}$.

19. REASONING In $\odot R$, $m\overset{\frown}{AB} = 60°$, $m\overset{\frown}{BC} = 25°$, $m\overset{\frown}{CD} = 70°$, and $m\overset{\frown}{DE} = 20°$. Find two possible values for $m\overset{\frown}{AE}$.

20. CHALLENGE In the diagram shown, $\overline{PQ} \perp \overline{AB}$, $\overline{QA}$ is tangent to $\odot P$, and $m\overset{\frown}{AVB} = 60°$. What is $m\overset{\frown}{AUB}$?

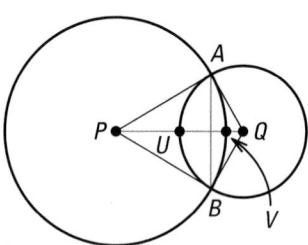

21. CHALLENGE In the coordinate plane shown, C is at the origin. Find the following arc measures on $\odot C$.

  a. $m\overset{\frown}{BD}$

  b. $m\overset{\frown}{AD}$

  c. $m\overset{\frown}{AB}$

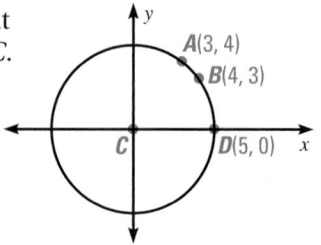

EXAMPLE 1
on p. 659
for Ex. 22

22. BRIDGES The deck of a bascule bridge creates an arc when it is moved from the closed position to the open position. Find the measure of the arc.

@HomeTutor for problem solving help at classzone.com

23. DARTS On a regulation dartboard, the outermost circle is divided into twenty congruent sections. What is the measure of each arc in this circle?

@HomeTutor for problem solving help at classzone.com

24. ★ EXTENDED RESPONSE A surveillance camera is mounted on a corner of a building. It rotates clockwise and counterclockwise continuously between Wall A and Wall B at a rate of 10° per minute.

  a. What is the measure of the arc surveyed by the camera?

  b. How long does it take the camera to survey the entire area once?

  c. If the camera is at an angle of 85° from Wall B while rotating counterclockwise, how long will it take for the camera to return to that same position?

  d. The camera is rotating counterclockwise and is 50° from Wall A. Find the location of the camera after 15 minutes.

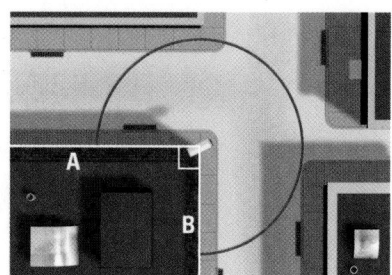

25. CHALLENGE A clock with hour and minute hands is set to 1:00 P.M.

  a. After 20 minutes, what will be the measure of the minor arc formed by the hour and minute hands?

  b. At what time before 2:00 P.M., to the nearest minute, will the hour and minute hands form a diameter?

PREVIEW
Prepare for
Lesson 10.3
in Exs. 26–27.

Determine if the lines with the given equations are parallel. *(p. 180)*

26. $y = 5x + 2$, $y = 5(1 - x)$ **27.** $2y + 2x = 5$, $y = 4 - x$

28. Trace $\triangle XYZ$ and point P. Draw a counterclockwise rotation of $\triangle XYZ$ 145° about P. *(p. 598)*

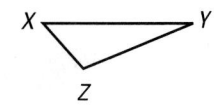

Find the product. *(p. 641)*

29. $(x + 2)(x + 3)$ **30.** $(2y - 5)(y + 7)$ **31.** $(x + 6)(x - 6)$

32. $(z - 3)^2$ **33.** $(3x + 7)(5x + 4)$ **34.** $(z - 1)(z - 4)$

10.3 Apply Properties of Chords

Before	You used relationships of central angles and arcs in a circle.
Now	You will use relationships of arcs and chords in a circle.
Why?	So you can design a logo for a company, as in Ex. 25.

Key Vocabulary
• chord, *p. 651*
• arc, *p. 659*
• semicircle, *p. 659*

Recall that a *chord* is a segment with endpoints on a circle. Because its endpoints lie on the circle, any chord divides the circle into two arcs. A diameter divides a circle into two semicircles. Any other chord divides a circle into a minor arc and a major arc.

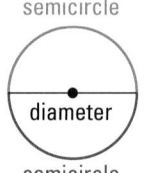

THEOREM *For Your Notebook*

THEOREM 10.3

In the same circle, or in congruent circles, two minor arcs are congruent if and only if their corresponding chords are congruent.

Proof: Exs. 27–28, p. 669

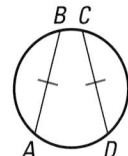

$\overset{\frown}{AB} \cong \overset{\frown}{CD}$ if and only if $\overline{AB} \cong \overline{CD}$.

EXAMPLE 1 Use congruent chords to find an arc measure

In the diagram, $\odot P \cong \odot Q$, $\overline{FG} \cong \overline{JK}$, and $m\overset{\frown}{JK} = 80°$. Find $m\overset{\frown}{FG}$.

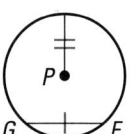
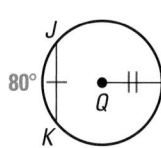

Solution

Because $\overline{FG}$ and $\overline{JK}$ are congruent chords in congruent circles, the corresponding minor arcs $\overset{\frown}{FG}$ and $\overset{\frown}{JK}$ are congruent.

▶ So, $m\overset{\frown}{FG} = m\overset{\frown}{JK} = 80°$.

✓ **GUIDED PRACTICE** for Example 1

Use the diagram of $\odot D$.

1. If $m\overset{\frown}{AB} = 110°$, find $m\overset{\frown}{BC}$.

2. If $m\overset{\frown}{AC} = 150°$, find $m\overset{\frown}{AB}$.

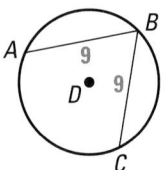

BISECTING ARCS If $\overset{\frown}{XY} \cong \overset{\frown}{YZ}$, then the point Y, and any line, segment, or ray that contains Y, bisects $\overset{\frown}{XYZ}$.

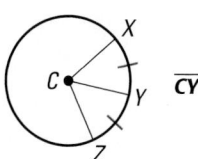

$\overline{CY}$ bisects $\overset{\frown}{XYZ}$.

THEOREMS
For Your Notebook

THEOREM 10.4

If one chord is a perpendicular bisector of another chord, then the first chord is a diameter.

If $\overline{QS}$ is a perpendicular bisector of $\overline{TR}$, then $\overline{QS}$ is a diameter of the circle.

Proof: Ex. 31, p. 670

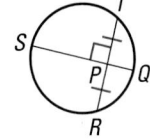

THEOREM 10.5

If a diameter of a circle is perpendicular to a chord, then the diameter bisects the chord and its arc.

If $\overline{EG}$ is a diameter and $\overline{EG} \perp \overline{DF}$, then $\overline{HD} \cong \overline{HF}$ and $\overset{\frown}{GD} \cong \overset{\frown}{GF}$.

Proof: Ex. 32, p. 670

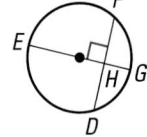

EXAMPLE 2 **Use perpendicular bisectors**

GARDENING Three bushes are arranged in a garden as shown. Where should you place a sprinkler so that it is the same distance from each bush?

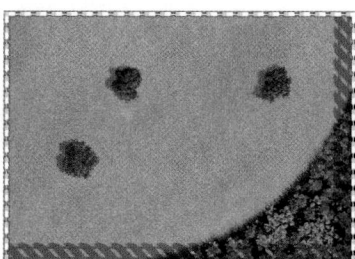

Solution

STEP 1

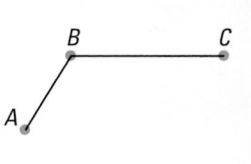

Label the bushes A, B, and C, as shown. Draw segments $\overline{AB}$ and $\overline{BC}$.

STEP 2

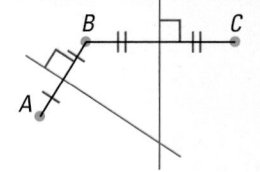

Draw the perpendicular bisectors of $\overline{AB}$ and $\overline{BC}$. By Theorem 10.4, these are diameters of the circle containing A, B, and C.

STEP 3

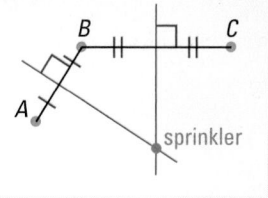

Find the point where these bisectors intersect. This is the center of the circle through A, B, and C, and so it is equidistant from each point.

EXAMPLE 3 Use a diameter

Use the diagram of ⊙E to find the length of $\overline{AC}$. Tell what theorem you use.

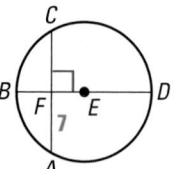

Solution

Diameter $\overline{BD}$ is perpendicular to $\overline{AC}$. So, by Theorem 10.5, $\overline{BD}$ bisects $\overline{AC}$, and $CF = AF$. Therefore, $AC = 2(AF) = 2(7) = 14$.

✓ **GUIDED PRACTICE** | for Examples 2 and 3

Find the measure of the indicated arc in the diagram.

3. $\overset{\frown}{CD}$ 4. $\overset{\frown}{DE}$ 5. $\overset{\frown}{CE}$

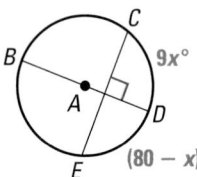

THEOREM   *For Your Notebook*

THEOREM 10.6

In the same circle, or in congruent circles, two chords are congruent if and only if they are equidistant from the center.

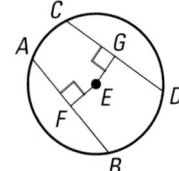

Proof: Ex. 33, p. 670

$\overline{AB} \cong \overline{CD}$ if and only if $EF = EG$.

EXAMPLE 4 Use Theorem 10.6

In the diagram of ⊙C, QR = ST = 16. Find CU.

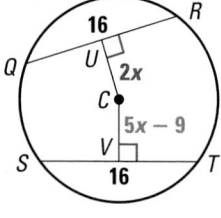

Solution

Chords $\overline{QR}$ and $\overline{ST}$ are congruent, so by Theorem 10.6 they are equidisant from C. Therefore, $CU = CV$.

$CU = CV$	Use Theorem 10.6.
$2x = 5x - 9$	Substitute.
$x = 3$	Solve for *x*.

▶ So, $CU = 2x = 2(3) = 6$.

✓ **GUIDED PRACTICE** | for Example 4

In the diagram in Example 4, suppose ST = 32, and CU = CV = 12. Find the given length.

6. *QR*   7. *QU*   8. The radius of ⊙C

10.3 EXERCISES

HOMEWORK KEY

○ = WORKED-OUT SOLUTIONS
on p. WS13 for Exs. 7, 9, and 25

★ = STANDARDIZED TEST PRACTICE
Exs. 2, 15, 22, and 26

SKILL PRACTICE

1. **VOCABULARY** *Describe* what it means to *bisect* an arc.

2. ★ **WRITING** Two chords of a circle are perpendicular and congruent. Does one of them have to be a diameter? *Explain* your reasoning.

EXAMPLES 1 and 3
on pp. 664, 666
for Exs. 3–5

FINDING ARC MEASURES Find the measure of the red arc or chord in ⊙C.

3.
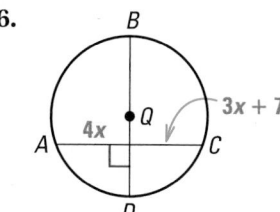

4.
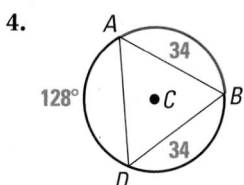

5.
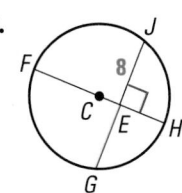

EXAMPLES 3 and 4
on p. 666
for Exs. 6–11

ALGEBRA Find the value of *x* in ⊙Q. *Explain* your reasoning.

6.
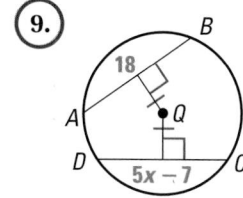

7.
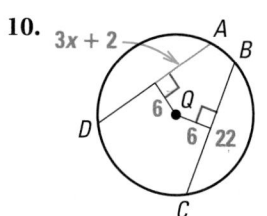

8.
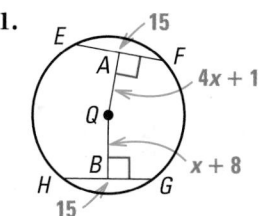

9.
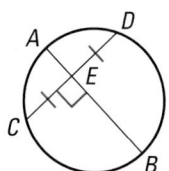

10.
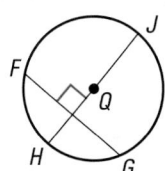

11.
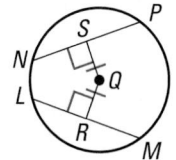

REASONING In Exercises 12–14, what can you conclude about the diagram shown? State a theorem that justifies your answer.

12.
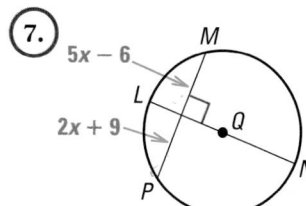

13.
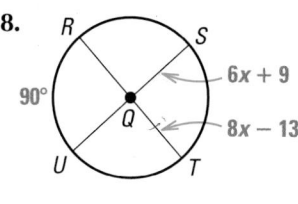

14.

15. ★ **MULTIPLE CHOICE** In the diagram of ⊙R, which congruence relation is not necessarily true?

Ⓐ $\overline{PQ} \cong \overline{QN}$

Ⓑ $\overline{NL} \cong \overline{LP}$

Ⓒ $\overarc{MN} \cong \overarc{MP}$

Ⓓ $\overline{PN} \cong \overline{PL}$

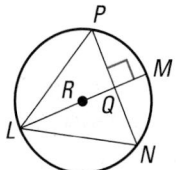

10.3 Apply Properties of Chords **667**

16. ERROR ANALYSIS *Explain* what is wrong with the diagram of ⊙P.

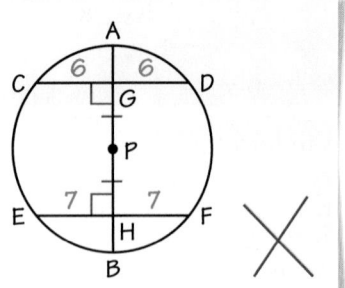

17. ERROR ANALYSIS *Explain* why the congruence statement is wrong.

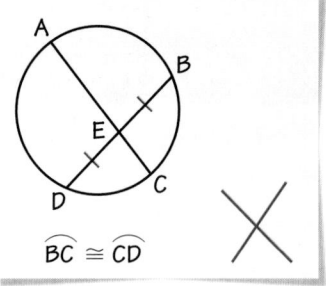

$\overarc{BC} \cong \overarc{CD}$

IDENTIFYING DIAMETERS Determine whether $\overline{AB}$ is a diameter of the circle. *Explain* your reasoning.

18.

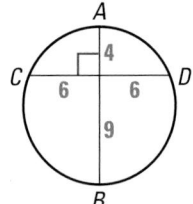

19.

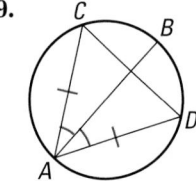

20.

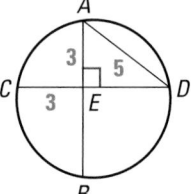

21. REASONING In the diagram of semicircle $\overarc{QCR}$, $\overline{PC} \cong \overline{AB}$ and $m\overarc{AC} = 30°$. *Explain* how you can conclude that $\triangle ADC \cong \triangle BDC$.

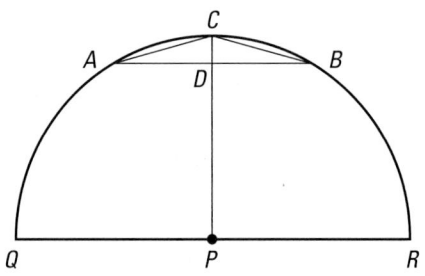

22. ★ WRITING Theorem 10.4 is nearly the converse of Theorem 10.5.

a. Write the converse of Theorem 10.5. *Explain* how it is different from Theorem 10.4.

b. Copy the diagram of ⊙C and draw auxiliary segments $\overline{PC}$ and $\overline{RC}$. Use congruent triangles to prove the converse of Theorem 10.5.

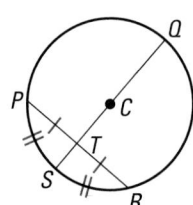

c. Use the converse of Theorem 10.5 to show that $QP = QR$ in the diagram of ⊙C.

23. XY ALGEBRA In ⊙P below, $\overline{AC}$, $\overline{BC}$, and all arcs have integer measures. Show that x must be even.

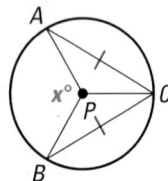

24. CHALLENGE In ⊙P below, the lengths of the parallel chords are 20, 16, and 12. Find $m\overarc{AB}$.

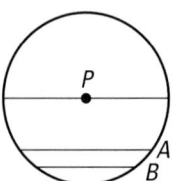

○ = **WORKED-OUT SOLUTIONS** on p. WS1   ★ = **STANDARDIZED TEST PRACTICE**

25. **LOGO DESIGN** The owner of a new company would like the company logo to be a picture of an arrow inscribed in a circle, as shown. For symmetry, she wants $\overset{\frown}{AB}$ to be congruent to $\overset{\frown}{BC}$. How should $\overline{AB}$ and $\overline{BC}$ be related in order for the logo to be exactly as desired?

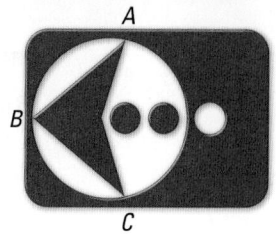

@HomeTutor for problem solving help at classzone.com

EXAMPLE 2
on p. 665
for Ex. 26

26. ★ **OPEN-ENDED MATH** In the cross section of the submarine shown, the control panels are parallel and the same length. *Explain* two ways you can find the center of the cross section.

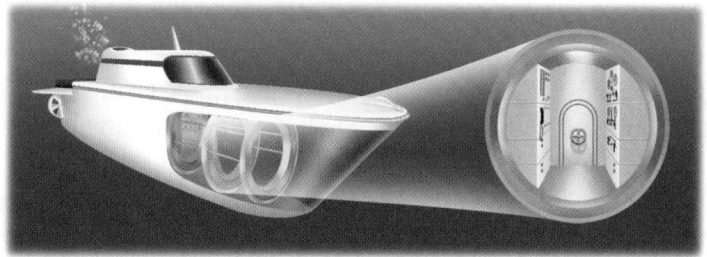

@HomeTutor for problem solving help at classzone.com

PROVING THEOREM 10.3 In Exercises 27 and 28, prove Theorem 10.3.

27. **GIVEN** ▶ $\overline{AB}$ and $\overline{CD}$ are congruent chords.
PROVE ▶ $\overset{\frown}{AB} \cong \overset{\frown}{CD}$

28. **GIVEN** ▶ $\overline{AB}$ and $\overline{CD}$ are chords and $\overset{\frown}{AB} \cong \overset{\frown}{CD}$.
PROVE ▶ $\overline{AB} \cong \overline{CD}$

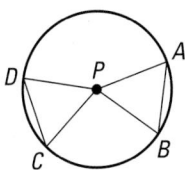

29. **CHORD LENGTHS** Make and prove a conjecture about chord lengths.

  a. Sketch a circle with two noncongruent chords. Is the *longer* chord or the *shorter* chord closer to the center of the circle? Repeat this experiment several times.

  b. Form a conjecture related to your experiment in part (a).

  c. Use the Pythagorean Theorem to prove your conjecture.

30. **MULTI-STEP PROBLEM** If a car goes around a turn too quickly, it can leave tracks that form an arc of a circle. By finding the radius of the circle, accident investigators can estimate the speed of the car.

  a. To find the radius, choose points A and B on the tire marks. Then find the midpoint C of $\overline{AB}$. Measure $\overline{CD}$, as shown. Find the radius r of the circle.

  b. The formula $S = 3.86\sqrt{fr}$ can be used to estimate a car's speed in miles per hours, where f is the *coefficient of friction* and r is the radius of the circle in feet. The coefficient of friction measures how slippery a road is. If $f = 0.7$, estimate the car's speed in part (a).

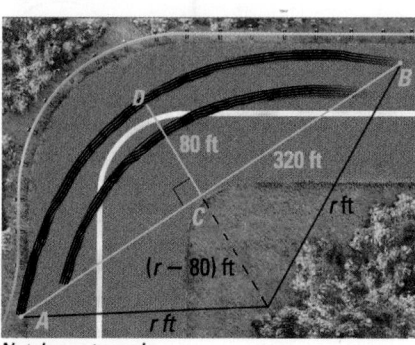

Not drawn to scale

31. **GIVEN** ▶ $\overline{QS}$ is the perpendicular bisector of $\overline{RT}$.

PROVE ▶ $\overline{QS}$ is a diameter of $\odot L$.

Plan for Proof Use indirect reasoning. Assume center L is not on $\overline{QS}$. Prove that $\triangle RLP \cong \triangle TLP$, so $\overline{PL} \perp \overline{RT}$. Then use the Perpendicular Postulate.

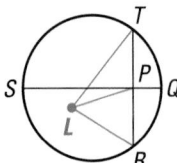

32. **GIVEN** ▶ $\overline{EG}$ is a diameter of $\odot L$.
$\overline{EG} \perp \overline{DF}$

PROVE ▶ $\overline{CD} \cong \overline{CF}$, $\overparen{DG} \cong \overparen{FG}$

Plan for Proof Draw $\overline{LD}$ and $\overline{LF}$. Use congruent triangles to show $\overline{CD} \cong \overline{CF}$ and $\angle DLG \cong \angle FLG$. Then show $\overparen{DG} \cong \overparen{FG}$.

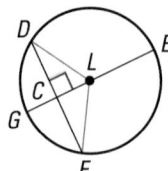

33. **PROVING THEOREM 10.6** For Theorem 10.6, prove both cases of the biconditional. Use the diagram shown for the theorem on page 666.

34. **CHALLENGE** A car is designed so that the rear wheel is only partially visible below the body of the car, as shown. The bottom panel is parallel to the ground. Prove that the point where the tire touches the ground bisects $\overparen{AB}$.

MIXED REVIEW

PREVIEW
Prepare for
Lesson 10.4 in
Exs. 35–37.

35. The measures of the interior angles of a quadrilateral are $100°$, $140°$, $(x + 20)°$, and $(2x + 10)°$. Find the value of x. **(p. 507)**

Quadrilateral *JKLM* is a parallelogram. Graph ▱ *JKLM*. Decide whether it is best described as a *rectangle*, a *rhombus*, or a *square*. (p. 552)

36. $J(-3, 5)$, $K(2, 5)$, $L(2, -1)$, $M(-3, -1)$ **37.** $J(-5, 2)$, $K(1, 1)$, $L(2, -5)$, $M(-4, -4)$

QUIZ *for Lessons 10.1–10.3*

Determine whether $\overline{AB}$ is tangent to $\odot C$. *Explain* your reasoning. (p. 651)

1.

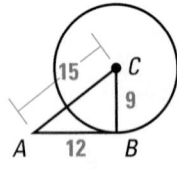

2.

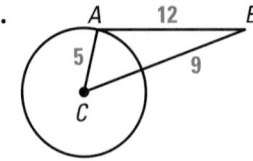

3. If $m\overparen{EFG} = 195°$, and $m\overparen{EF} = 80°$, find $m\overparen{FG}$ and $m\overparen{EG}$. **(p. 659)**

4. The points A, B, and D are on $\odot C$, $\overline{AB} \cong \overline{BD}$, and $m\overparen{ABD} = 194°$. What is the measure of $\overparen{AB}$? **(p. 664)**

10.4 Explore Inscribed Angles

MATERIALS · compass · straightedge · protractor

QUESTION How are inscribed angles related to central angles?

The vertex of a central angle is at the center of the circle. The vertex of an *inscribed angle* is on the circle, and its sides form chords of the circle.

EXPLORE Construct inscribed angles of a circle

STEP 1	STEP 2	STEP 3
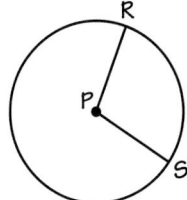	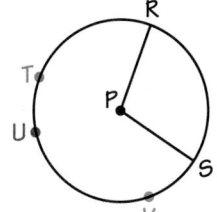	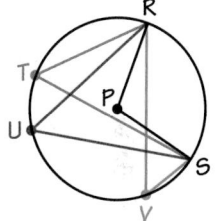

Draw a central angle Use a compass to draw a circle. Label the center *P*. Use a straightedge to draw a central angle. Label it ∠*RPS*.

Draw points Locate three points on ⊙*P* in the exterior of ∠*RPS* and label them *T, U,* and *V.*

Measure angles Draw ∠*RTS*, ∠*RUS*, and ∠*RVS*. These are called *inscribed angles*. Measure each angle.

Animated Geometry at classzone.com

DRAW CONCLUSIONS Use your observations to complete these exercises

1. Copy and complete the table.

	Central angle	Inscribed angle 1	Inscribed angle 2	Inscribed angle 3
Name	∠*RPS*	∠*RTS*	∠*RUS*	∠*RVS*
Measure	?	?	?	?

2. Draw two more circles. Repeat Steps 1–3 using different central angles. Record the measures in a table similar to the one above.

3. Use your results to make a conjecture about how the measure of an inscribed angle is related to the measure of the corresponding central angle.

10.4 Use Inscribed Angles and Polygons

Before	You used central angles of circles.
Now	You will use inscribed angles of circles.
Why?	So you can take a picture from multiple angles, as in Example 4.

Key Vocabulary
• inscribed angle
• intercepted arc
• inscribed polygon
• circumscribed circle

An **inscribed angle** is an angle whose vertex is on a circle and whose sides contain chords of the circle. The arc that lies in the interior of an inscribed angle and has endpoints on the angle is called the **intercepted arc** of the angle.

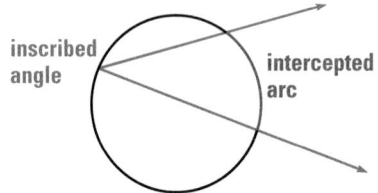

THEOREM · *For Your Notebook*

THEOREM 10.7 Measure of an Inscribed Angle Theorem

The measure of an inscribed angle is one half the measure of its intercepted arc.

Proof: Exs. 31–33, p. 678

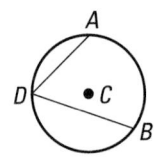

$$m\angle ADB = \tfrac{1}{2}m\widehat{AB}$$

The proof of Theorem 10.7 in Exercises 31–33 involves three cases.

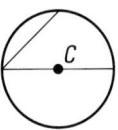
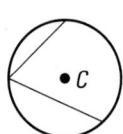
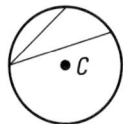

Case 1 Center *C* is on a side of the inscribed angle.

Case 2 Center *C* is inside the inscribed angle.

Case 3 Center *C* is outside the inscribed angle.

EXAMPLE 1 · Use inscribed angles

Find the indicated measure in ⊙*P*.

a. $m\angle T$ **b.** $m\widehat{QR}$

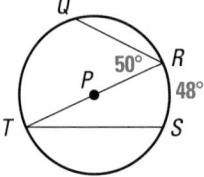

Solution

a. $m\angle T = \tfrac{1}{2}m\widehat{RS} = \tfrac{1}{2}(48°) = 24°$

b. $m\widehat{TQ} = 2m\angle R = 2 \cdot 50° = 100°$. Because $\widehat{TQR}$ is a semicircle,
$m\widehat{QR} = 180° - m\widehat{TQ} = 180° - 100° = 80°$. So, $m\widehat{QR} = 80°$.

EXAMPLE 2 **Find the measure of an intercepted arc**

Find $m\widehat{RS}$ and $m\angle STR$. What do you notice about $\angle STR$ and $\angle RUS$?

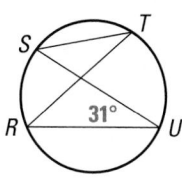

Solution

From Theorem 10.7, you know that $m\widehat{RS} = 2m\angle RUS = 2(31°) = 62°$.

Also, $m\angle STR = \frac{1}{2}m\widehat{RS} = \frac{1}{2}(62°) = 31°$. So, $\angle STR \cong \angle RUS$.

INTERCEPTING THE SAME ARC Example 2 suggests Theorem 10.8.

THEOREM *For Your Notebook*

THEOREM 10.8

If two inscribed angles of a circle intercept the same arc, then the angles are congruent.

Proof: Ex. 34, p. 678

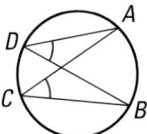

$\angle ADB \cong \angle ACB$

★ **EXAMPLE 3** **Standardized Test Practice**

Name two pairs of congruent angles in the figure.

(A) $\angle JKM \cong \angle KJL$, $\angle JLM \cong \angle KML$

(B) $\angle JLM \cong \angle KJL$, $\angle JKM \cong \angle KML$

(C) $\angle JKM \cong \angle JLM$, $\angle KJL \cong \angle KML$

(D) $\angle JLM \cong \angle KJL$, $\angle JLM \cong \angle JKM$

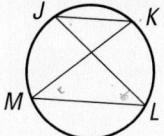

Solution

ELIMINATE CHOICES
You can eliminate choices A and B, because they do not include the pair $\angle JKM \cong \angle JLM$.

Notice that $\angle JKM$ and $\angle JLM$ intercept the same arc, and so $\angle JKM \cong \angle JLM$ by Theorem 10.8. Also, $\angle KJL$ and $\angle KML$ intercept the same arc, so they must also be congruent. Only choice C contains both pairs of angles.

▸ So, by Theorem 10.8, the correct answer is C. Ⓐ Ⓑ Ⓒ Ⓓ

✓ **GUIDED PRACTICE** for Examples 1, 2, and 3

Find the measure of the red arc or angle.

1.

2.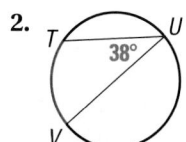

3.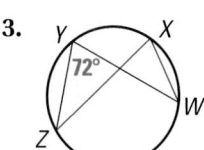

POLYGONS A polygon is an **inscribed polygon** if all of its vertices lie on a circle. The circle that contains the vertices is a **circumscribed circle**.

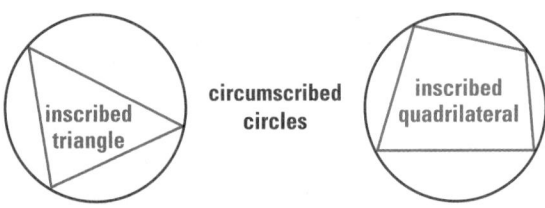

inscribed triangle

circumscribed circles

inscribed quadrilateral

THEOREM   *For Your Notebook*

THEOREM 10.9

If a right triangle is inscribed in a circle, then the hypotenuse is a diameter of the circle. Conversely, if one side of an inscribed triangle is a diameter of the circle, then the triangle is a right triangle and the angle opposite the diameter is the right angle.

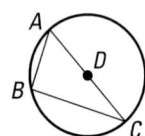

m∠ABC = 90° if and only if $\overline{AC}$ is a diameter of the circle.

Proof: Ex. 35, p. 678

EXAMPLE 4   **Use a circumscribed circle**

PHOTOGRAPHY Your camera has a 90° field of vision and you want to photograph the front of a statue. You move to a spot where the statue is the only thing captured in your picture, as shown. You want to change your position. Where else can you stand so that the statue is perfectly framed in this way?

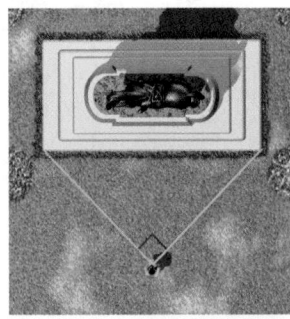

Solution

From Theorem 10.9, you know that if a right triangle is inscribed in a circle, then the hypotenuse of the triangle is a diameter of the circle. So, draw the circle that has the front of the statue as a diameter. The statue fits perfectly within your camera's 90° field of vision from any point on the semicircle in front of the statue.

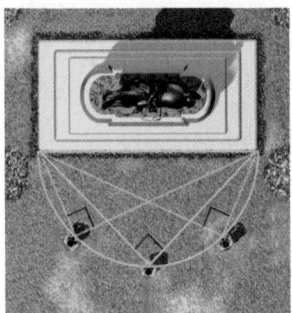

✓ **GUIDED PRACTICE**   for Example 4

  4. **WHAT IF?** In Example 4, *explain* how to find locations if you want to frame the front and left side of the statue in your picture.

INSCRIBED QUADRILATERAL Only certain quadrilaterals can be inscribed in a circle. Theorem 10.10 describes these quadrilaterals.

THEOREM   *For Your Notebook*

THEOREM 10.10

A quadrilateral can be inscribed in a circle if and only if its opposite angles are supplementary.

D, E, F, and G lie on $\odot C$ if and only if $m\angle D + m\angle F = m\angle E + m\angle G = 180°$.

Proof: Ex. 30, p. 678; p. 938

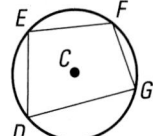

EXAMPLE 5   **Use Theorem 10.10**

Find the value of each variable.

a.

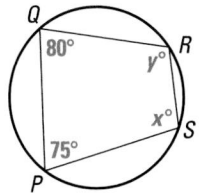

b.

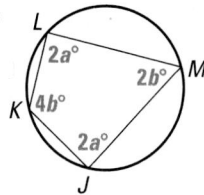

Solution

a. *PQRS* is inscribed in a circle, so opposite angles are supplementary.

$m\angle P + m\angle R = 180°$ $\qquad$ $m\angle Q + m\angle S = 180°$

$75° + y° = 180°$ $\qquad\qquad$ $80° + x° = 180°$

$y = 105$ $\qquad\qquad\qquad$ $x = 100$

b. *JKLM* is inscribed in a circle, so opposite angles are supplementary.

$m\angle J + m\angle L = 180°$ $\qquad$ $m\angle K + m\angle M = 180°$

$2a° + 2a° = 180°$ $\qquad\qquad$ $4b° + 2b° = 180°$

$4a = 180$ $\qquad\qquad\qquad$ $6b = 180$

$a = 45$ $\qquad\qquad\qquad$ $b = 30$

✓ **GUIDED PRACTICE**   for Example 5

Find the value of each variable.

5.

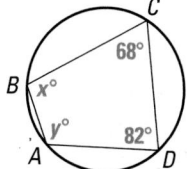

6.

10.4 EXERCISES

HOMEWORK KEY

○ = WORKED-OUT SOLUTIONS
on p. WS13 for Exs. 11, 13, and 29

★ = STANDARDIZED TEST PRACTICE
Exs. 2, 16, 18, 29, and 36

SKILL PRACTICE

1. **VOCABULARY** Copy and complete: If a circle is circumscribed about a polygon, then the polygon is __?__ in the circle.

2. ★ **WRITING** *Explain* why the diagonals of a rectangle inscribed in a circle are diameters of the circle.

EXAMPLES 1 and 2
on pp. 672–673
for Exs. 3–9

INSCRIBED ANGLES Find the indicated measure.

3. $m\angle A$

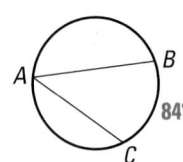

4. $m\angle G$

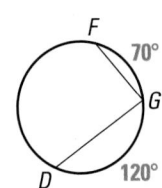

5. $m\angle N$

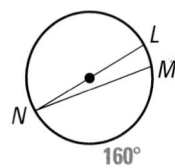

6. $m\overarc{RS}$

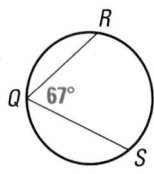

7. $m\overarc{VU}$

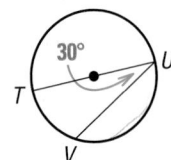

8. $m\overarc{WX}$

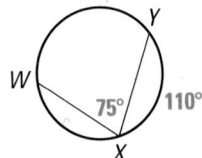

9. **ERROR ANALYSIS** *Describe* the error in the diagram of ⊙C. Find two ways to correct the error.

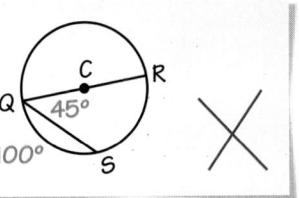

EXAMPLE 3
on p. 673
for Exs. 10–12

CONGRUENT ANGLES Name two pairs of congruent angles.

10.

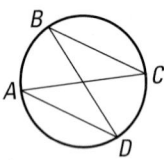

11.

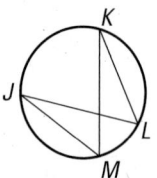

12.

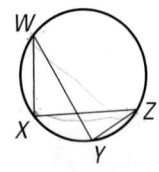

EXAMPLE 5
on p. 675
for Exs. 13–15

ALGEBRA Find the values of the variables.

13.

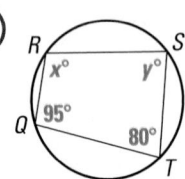

14.

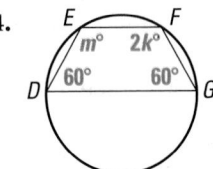

15.

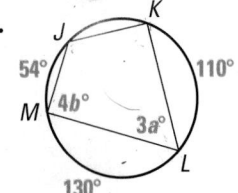

EXAMPLE 4 | **Graph a circle**

USE EQUATIONS

If you know the equation of a circle, you can graph the circle by identifying its center and radius.

The equation of a circle is $(x - 4)^2 + (y + 2)^2 = 36$. Graph the circle.

Solution

Rewrite the equation to find the center and radius.

$$(x - 4)^2 + (y + 2)^2 = 36$$

$$(x - 4)^2 + [y - (-2)]^2 = 6^2$$

The center is $(4, -2)$ and the radius is 6. Use a compass to graph the circle.

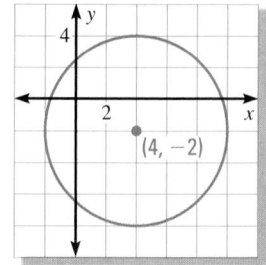

EXAMPLE 5 | **Use graphs of circles**

EARTHQUAKES The epicenter of an earthquake is the point on Earth's surface directly above the earthquake's origin. A seismograph can be used to determine the distance to the epicenter of an earthquake. Seismographs are needed in three different places to locate an earthquake's epicenter.

Use the seismograph readings from locations A, B, and C to find the epicenter of an earthquake.

- The epicenter is 7 miles away from $A(-2, 2.5)$.

- The epicenter is 4 miles away from $B(4, 6)$.

- The epicenter is 5 miles away from $C(3, -2.5)$.

Solution

The set of all points equidistant from a given point is a circle, so the epicenter is located on each of the following circles.

⊙A with center $(-2, 2.5)$ and radius 7

⊙B with center $(4, 6)$ and radius 4

⊙C with center $(3, -2.5)$ and radius 5

To find the epicenter, graph the circles on a graph where units are measured in miles. Find the point of intersection of all three circles.

▶ The epicenter is at about $(5, 2)$.

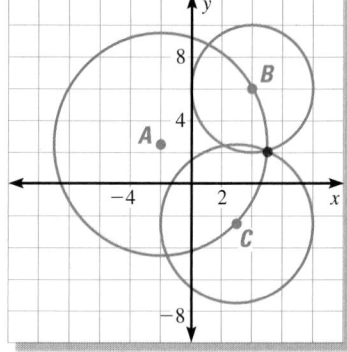

Animated **Geometry** at classzone.com

 GUIDED PRACTICE | for Examples 4 and 5

5. The equation of a circle is $(x - 4)^2 + (y + 3)^2 = 16$. Graph the circle.

6. The equation of a circle is $(x + 8)^2 + (y + 5)^2 = 121$. Graph the circle.

7. Why are three seismographs needed to locate an earthquake's epicenter?

10.7 EXERCISES

HOMEWORK
KEY

◯ = WORKED-OUT SOLUTIONS
on p. WS13 for Exs. 7, 17, and 37

★ = STANDARDIZED TEST PRACTICE
Exs. 2, 16, 26, and 42

SKILL PRACTICE

1. **VOCABULARY** Copy and complete: The standard equation of a circle can be written for any circle with known __?__ and __?__ .

2. ★ **WRITING** *Explain* why the location of the center and one point on a circle is enough information to draw the rest of the circle.

EXAMPLES 1 and 2
on pp. 699–700
for Exs. 3–16

WRITING EQUATIONS Write the standard equation of the circle.

3.
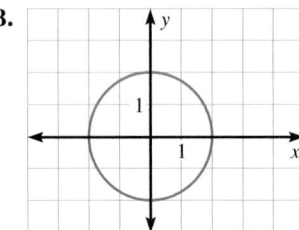

4.
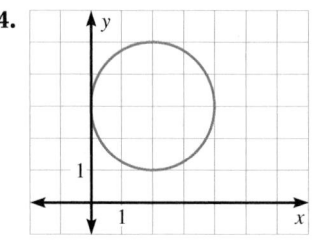

5.
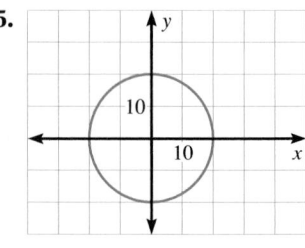

6.
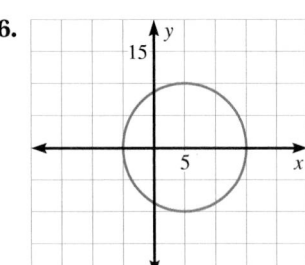

7.
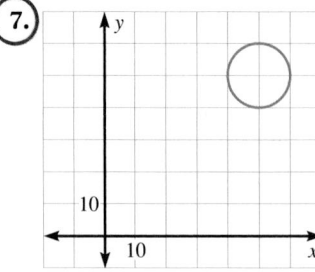

8.
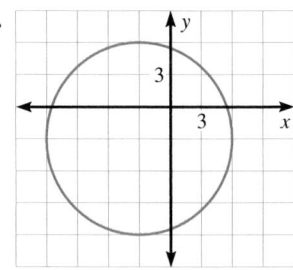

WRITING EQUATIONS Write the standard equation of the circle with the given center and radius.

9. Center (0, 0), radius 7
10. Center (−4, 1), radius 1
11. Center (7, −6), radius 8

12. Center (4, 1), radius 5
13. Center (3, −5), radius 7
14. Center (−3, 4), radius 5

15. **ERROR ANALYSIS** *Describe* and correct the error in writing the equation of a circle.

> An equation of a circle with center (−3, −5) and radius 3 is $(x − 3)^2 + (y − 5)^2 = 9$.

16. ★ **MULTIPLE CHOICE** The standard equation of a circle is $(x − 2)^2 + (y + 1)^2 = 16$. What is the diameter of the circle?

Ⓐ 2   Ⓑ 4   Ⓒ 8   Ⓓ 16

EXAMPLE 3
on p. 700
for Exs. 17–19

WRITING EQUATIONS Use the given information to write the standard equation of the circle.

17. The center is (0, 0), and a point on the circle is (0, 6).

18. The center is (1, 2), and a point on the circle is (4, 2).

19. The center is (−3, 5), and a point on the circle is (1, 8).

EXAMPLE 4
·····················
on p. 701
for Exs. 20–25

GRAPHING CIRCLES **Graph the equation.**

20. $x^2 + y^2 = 49$

21. $(x - 3)^2 + y^2 = 16$

22. $x^2 + (y + 2)^2 = 36$

23. $(x - 4)^2 + (y - 1)^2 = 1$

24. $(x + 5)^2 + (y - 3)^2 = 9$

25. $(x + 2)^2 + (y + 6)^2 = 25$

26. ★ **MULTIPLE CHOICE** Which of the points does not lie on the circle described by the equation $(x + 2)^2 + (y - 4)^2 = 25$?

(A) $(-2, -1)$ **(B)** $(1, 8)$ **(C)** $(3, 4)$ **(D)** $(0, 5)$

(xy) ALGEBRA **Determine whether the given equation defines a circle. If the equation defines a circle, rewrite the equation in standard form.**

27. $x^2 + y^2 - 6y + 9 = 4$

28. $x^2 - 8x + 16 + y^2 + 2y + 4 = 25$

29. $x^2 + y^2 + 4y + 3 = 16$

30. $x^2 - 2x + 5 + y^2 = 81$

IDENTIFYING TYPES OF LINES **Use the given equations of a circle and a line to determine whether the line is a *tangent, secant, secant that contains a diameter,* or none of these.**

31. Circle: $(x - 4)^2 + (y - 3)^2 = 9$
Line: $y = -3x + 6$

32. Circle: $(x + 2)^2 + (y - 2)^2 = 16$
Line: $y = 2x - 4$

33. Circle: $(x - 5)^2 + (y + 1)^2 = 4$
Line: $y = \frac{1}{5}x - 3$

34. Circle: $(x + 3)^2 + (y - 6)^2 = 25$
Line: $y = -\frac{4}{3}x + 2$

35. **CHALLENGE** Four tangent circles are centered on the x-axis. The radius of $\odot A$ is twice the radius of $\odot O$. The radius of $\odot B$ is three times the radius of $\odot O$. The radius of $\odot C$ is four times the radius of $\odot O$. All circles have integer radii and the point $(63, 16)$ is on $\odot C$. What is the equation of $\odot A$?

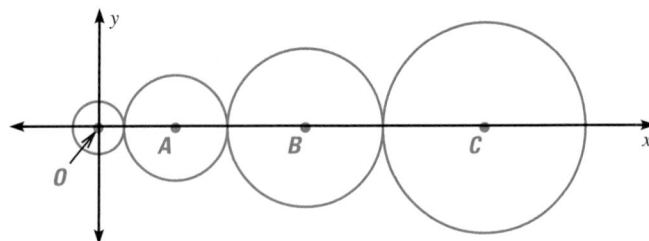

PROBLEM SOLVING

EXAMPLE 5
·····················
on p. 701
for Ex. 36

36. **COMMUTER TRAINS** A city's commuter system has three zones covering the regions described. Zone 1 covers people living within three miles of the city center. Zone 2 covers those between three and seven miles from the center, and Zone 3 covers those over seven miles from the center.

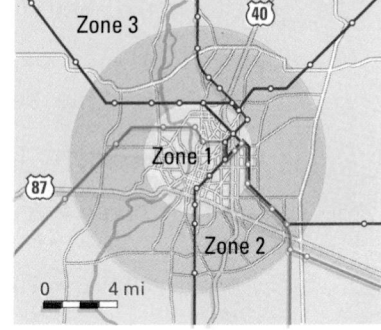

a. Graph this situation with the city center at the origin, where units are measured in miles.

b. Find which zone covers people living at $(3, 4)$, $(6, 5)$, $(1, 2)$, $(0, 3)$, and $(1, 6)$.

@HomeTutor for problem solving help at classzone.com

37. **COMPACT DISCS** The diameter of a CD is about 4.8 inches. The diameter of the hole in the center is about 0.6 inches. You place a CD on the coordinate plane with center at (0, 0). Write the equations for the outside edge of the disc and the edge of the hole in the center.

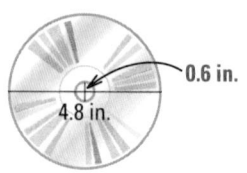
0.6 in.
4.8 in.

@HomeTutor for problem solving help at classzone.com

REULEAUX POLYGONS In Exercises 38–41, use the following information.

The figure at the right is called a *Reuleaux polygon*. It is not a true polygon because its sides are not straight. $\triangle ABC$ is equilateral.

38. $\overset{\frown}{JD}$ lies on a circle with center A and radius AD. Write an equation of this circle.

39. $\overset{\frown}{DE}$ lies on a circle with center B and radius BD. Write an equation of this circle.

40. **CONSTRUCTION** The remaining arcs of the polygon are constructed in the same way as $\overset{\frown}{JD}$ and $\overset{\frown}{DE}$ in Exercises 38 and 39. Construct a Reuleaux polygon on a piece of cardboard.

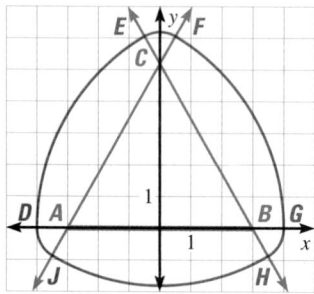

41. Cut out the Reuleaux polygon from Exercise 40. Roll it on its edge like a wheel and measure its height when it is in different orientations. *Explain* why a Reuleaux polygon is said to have constant width.

42. ★ **EXTENDED RESPONSE** Telecommunication towers can be used to transmit cellular phone calls. Towers have a range of about 3 km. A graph with units measured in kilometers shows towers at points (0, 0), (0, 5), and (6, 3).

a. Draw the graph and locate the towers. Are there any areas that may receive calls from more than one tower?

b. Suppose your home is located at (2, 6) and your school is at (2.5, 3). Can you use your cell phone at either or both of these locations?

c. City A is located at $(-2, 2.5)$ and City B is at (5, 4). Each city has a radius of 1.5 km. Which city seems to have better cell phone coverage? *Explain.*

43. **REASONING** The lines $y = \frac{3}{4}x + 2$ and $y = -\frac{3}{4}x + 16$ are tangent to $\odot C$ at the points (4, 5) and (4, 13), respectively.

a. Find the coordinates of C and the radius of $\odot C$. *Explain* your steps.

b. Write the standard equation of $\odot C$ and draw its graph.

44. **PROOF** Write a proof.

GIVEN ▶ A circle passing through the points $(-1, 0)$ and $(1, 0)$

PROVE ▶ The equation of the circle is $x^2 - 2yk + y^2 = 1$ with center at $(0, k)$.

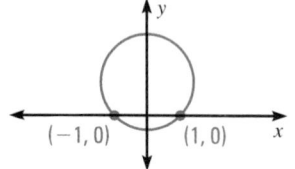

45. CHALLENGE The intersecting lines *m* and *n* are tangent to ⊙*C* at the points (8, 6) and (10, 8), respectively.

    a. What is the intersection point of *m* and *n* if the radius *r* of ⊙*C* is 2? What is their intersection point if *r* is 10? What do you notice about the two intersection points and the center *C*?

    b. Write the equation that describes the locus of intersection points of *m* and *n* for all possible values of *r*.

MIXED REVIEW

PREVIEW

Prepare for Lesson 11.1 in Exs. 46–48.

Find the perimeter of the figure.

46. *(p. 49)*

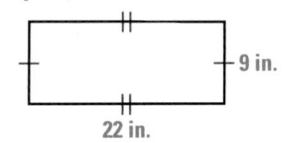

9 in.

22 in.

47. *(p. 49)*

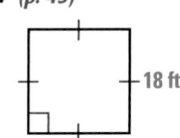

18 ft

48. *(p. 433)*

40 m

57 m

Find the circumference of the circle with given radius *r* or diameter *d*. Use π = 3.14. *(p. 49)*

49. *r* = 7 cm

50. *d* = 160 in.

51. *d* = 48 yd

Find the radius *r* of ⊙*C*. *(p. 651)*

52.

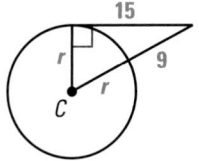

15

9

r

r

C

53.

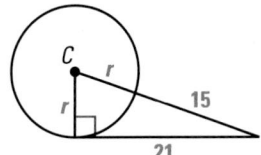

C

r

r

15

21

54.

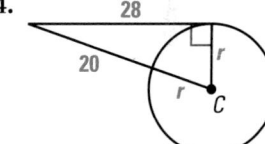

28

20

r

r

C

QUIZ *for Lessons 10.6–10.7*

Find the value of *x*. *(p. 689)*

1.

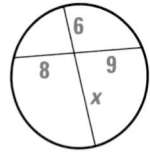

6

8

9

x

2.

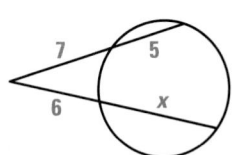

7

6

5

x

3.

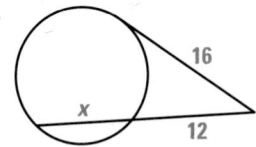

16

x

12

In Exercises 4 and 5, use the given information to write the standard equation of the circle. *(p. 699)*

  4. The center is (1, 4), and the radius is 6.

  5. The center is (5, −7), and a point on the circle is (5, −3).

  6. TIRES The diameter of a certain tire is 24.2 inches. The diameter of the rim in the center is 14 inches. Draw the tire in a coordinate plane with center at (−4, 3). Write the equations for the outer edge of the tire and for the rim where units are measured in inches. *(p. 699)*

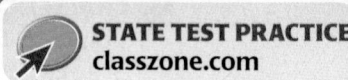
Lessons 10.6–10.7

1. SHORT RESPONSE A local radio station can broadcast its signal 20 miles. The station is located at the point (20, 30) where units are measured in miles.

 a. Write an inequality that represents the area covered by the radio station.

 b. Determine whether you can receive the radio station's signal when you are located at each of the following points: $E(25, 25)$, $F(10, 10)$, $G(20, 16)$, and $H(35, 30)$.

2. EXTENDED RESPONSE Cell phone towers are used to transmit calls. An area has cell phone towers at points (2, 3), (4, 5), and (5, 3) where units are measured in miles. Each tower has a transmission radius of 2 miles.

 a. Draw the area on a graph and locate the three cell phone towers. Are there any areas that can transmit calls using more than one tower?

 b. Suppose you live at (3, 5) and your friend lives at (1, 7). Can you use your cell phone at either or both of your homes?

 c. City A is located at $(-1, 1)$ and City B is located at (4, 7). Each city has a radius of 5 miles. Which city has better coverage from the cell phone towers?

3. SHORT RESPONSE You are standing at point *P* inside a go-kart track. To determine if the track is a circle, you measure the distance to four points on the track, as shown in the diagram. What can you conclude about the shape of the track? *Explain.*

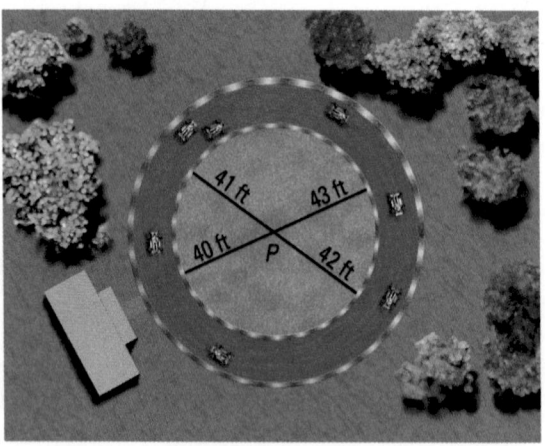

4. SHORT RESPONSE You are at point *A*, about 6 feet from a circular aquarium tank. The distance from you to a point of tangency on the tank is 17 feet.

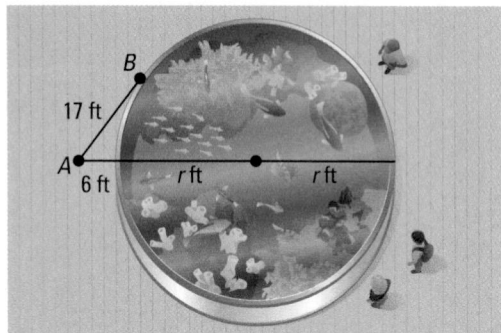

 a. What is the radius of the tank?

 b. Suppose you are standing 4 feet from another aquarium tank that has a diameter of 12 feet. How far, in feet, are you from a point of tangency?

5. EXTENDED RESPONSE You are given seismograph readings from three locations.

 • At $A(-2, 3)$, the epicenter is 4 miles away.

 • At $B(5, -1)$, the epicenter is 5 miles away.

 • At $C(2, 5)$, the epicenter is 2 miles away.

 a. Graph circles centered at *A*, *B*, and *C* with radii of 4, 5, and 2 miles, respectively.

 b. Locate the epicenter.

 c. The earthquake could be felt up to 12 miles away. If you live at (14, 16), could you feel the earthquake? *Explain.*

6. MULTI-STEP PROBLEM Use the diagram.

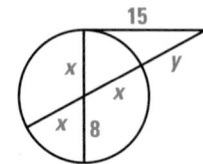

 a. Use Theorem 10.16 and the quadratic formula to write an equation for *y* in terms of *x*.

 b. Find the value of *x*.

 c. Find the value of *y*.

BIG IDEAS
For Your Notebook

Big Idea 1

Using Properties of Segments that Intersect Circles

You learned several relationships between tangents, secants, and chords.

Some of these relationships can help you determine that two chords or tangents are congruent. For example, tangent segments from the same exterior point are congruent.

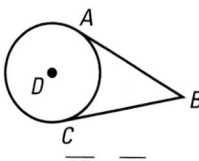

$$\overline{AB} \cong \overline{CB}$$

Other relationships allow you to find the length of a secant or chord if you know the length of related segments. For example, with the Segments of a Chord Theorem you can find the length of an unknown chord segment.

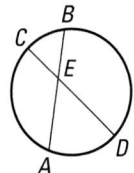

$$EA \cdot EB = EC \cdot ED$$

Big Idea 2

Applying Angle Relationships in Circles

You learned to find the measures of angles formed inside, outside, and on circles.

Angles formed on circles

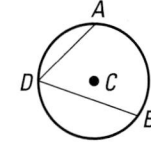

$$m\angle ADB = \tfrac{1}{2}m\widehat{AB}$$

Angles formed inside circles

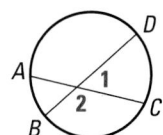

$$m\angle 1 = \tfrac{1}{2}\left(m\widehat{AB} + m\widehat{CD}\right),$$
$$m\angle 2 = \tfrac{1}{2}\left(m\widehat{AD} + m\widehat{BC}\right)$$

Angles formed outside circles

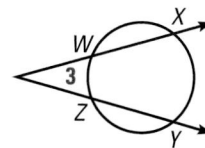

$$m\angle 3 = \tfrac{1}{2}\left(m\widehat{XY} - m\widehat{WZ}\right)$$

Big Idea 3

Using Circles in the Coordinate Plane

The standard equation of $\odot C$ is:

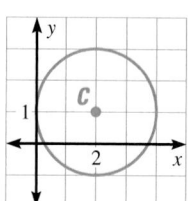

$$(x - h)^2 + (y - k)^2 = r^2$$
$$(x - 2)^2 + (y - 1)^2 = 2^2$$
$$(x - 2)^2 + (y - 1)^2 = 4$$

@HomeTutor
classzone.com
• Multi-Language Glossary
• Vocabulary practice

REVIEW KEY VOCABULARY

For a list of postulates and theorems, see pp. 926–931.

• circle, *p. 651*
  center, radius, diameter
• chord, *p. 651*
• secant, *p. 651*
• tangent, *p. 651*
• central angle, *p. 659*
• minor arc, *p. 659*

• major arc, *p. 659*
• semicircle, *p. 659*
• measure of a minor arc, *p. 659*
• measure of a major arc, *p. 659*
• congruent circles, *p. 660*
• congruent arcs, *p. 660*
• inscribed angle, *p. 672*

• intercepted arc, *p. 672*
• inscribed polygon, *p. 674*
• circumscribed circle, *p. 674*
• segments of a chord, *p. 689*
• secant segment, *p. 690*
• external segment, *p. 690*
• standard equation of a circle, *p. 699*

VOCABULARY EXERCISES

1. Copy and complete: If a chord passes through the center of a circle, then it is called a(n) __?__.

2. Draw and *describe* an inscribed angle and an intercepted arc.

3. **WRITING** *Describe* how the measure of a central angle of a circle relates to the measure of the minor arc and the measure of the major arc created by the angle.

In Exercises 4–6, match the term with the appropriate segment.

4. Tangent segment   **A.** $\overline{LM}$

5. Secant segment   **B.** $\overline{KL}$

6. External segment   **C.** $\overline{LN}$

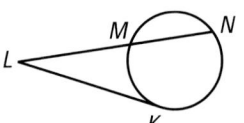

REVIEW EXAMPLES AND EXERCISES

Use the review examples and exercises below to check your understanding of the concepts you have learned in each lesson of Chapter 10.

10.1 Use Properties of Tangents
pp. 651–658

EXAMPLE

In the diagram, *B* and *D* are points of tangency on ⊙*C*. Find the value of *x*.

Use Theorem 10.2 to find *x*.

$AB = AD$	Tangent segments from the same point are ≅.
$2x + 5 = 33$	Substitute.
$x = 14$	Solve for *x*.

EXERCISES

EXAMPLES
5 and 6
on p. 654
for Exs. 7–9

Find the value of the variable. Y and Z are points of tangency on $\odot W$.

7.

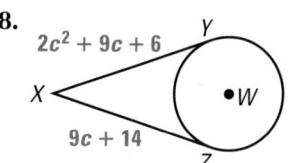

$9a^2 - 30$
$3a$

8.

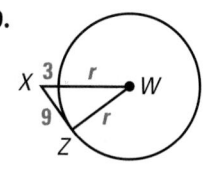

$2c^2 + 9c + 6$
$9c + 14$

9.

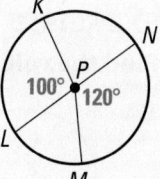

10.2 Find Arc Measures

pp. 659–663

EXAMPLE

Find the measure of the arc of $\odot P$. In the diagram, $\overline{LN}$ is a diameter.

a. $\overset{\frown}{MN}$ b. $\overset{\frown}{NLM}$ c. $\overset{\frown}{NML}$

a. $\overset{\frown}{MN}$ is a minor arc, so $m\overset{\frown}{MN} = m\angle MPN = 120°$.

b. $\overset{\frown}{NLM}$ is a major arc, so $m\overset{\frown}{NLM} = 360° - 120° = 240°$.

c. $\overset{\frown}{NML}$ is a semicircle, so $m\overset{\frown}{NML} = 180°$.

EXAMPLES
1 and 2
on pp. 659–660
for Exs. 10–13

EXERCISES

Use the diagram above to find the measure of the indicated arc.

10. $\overset{\frown}{KL}$ 11. $\overset{\frown}{LM}$ 12. $\overset{\frown}{KM}$ 13. $\overset{\frown}{KN}$

10.3 Apply Properties of Chords

pp. 664–670

EXAMPLE

In the diagram, $\odot A \cong \odot B$, $\overline{CD} \cong \overline{FE}$, and $m\overset{\frown}{FE} = 75°$. Find $m\overset{\frown}{CD}$.

By Theorem 10.3, $\overline{CD}$ and $\overline{FE}$ are congruent chords in congruent circles, so the corresponding minor arcs $\overset{\frown}{FE}$ and $\overset{\frown}{CD}$ are congruent. So, $m\overset{\frown}{CD} = m\overset{\frown}{FE} = 75°$.

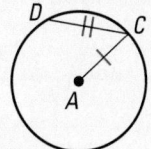

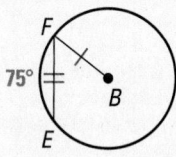

EXAMPLES
1, 3, and 4
on pp. 664, 666
for Exs. 14–16

EXERCISES

Find the measure of $\overset{\frown}{AB}$.

14.

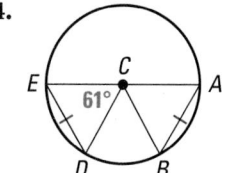

15.

16.

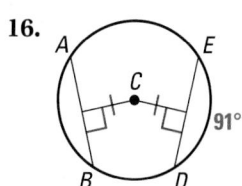

10.4 Use Inscribed Angles and Polygons
pp. 672–679

EXAMPLE

Find the value of each variable.

LMNP is inscribed in a circle, so by Theorem 10.10, opposite angles are supplementary.

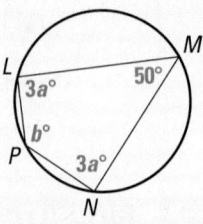

$$m\angle L + m\angle N = 180° \qquad m\angle P + m\angle M = 180°$$

$$3a° + 3a° = 180° \qquad\qquad b° + 50° = 180°$$

$$6a = 180 \qquad\qquad\qquad b = 130$$

$$a = 30$$

EXERCISES

EXAMPLES
1, 2, and 5
on pp. 672–675
for Exs. 17–19

Find the value(s) of the variable(s).

17.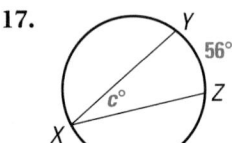

18.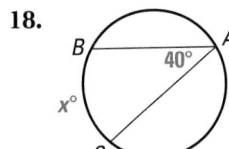

19.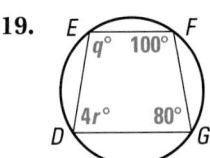

10.5 Apply Other Angle Relationships in Circles
pp. 680–686

EXAMPLE

Find the value of y.

The tangent $\overrightarrow{RQ}$ and secant $\overrightarrow{RT}$ intersect outside the circle, so you can use Theorem 10.13 to find the value of *y*.

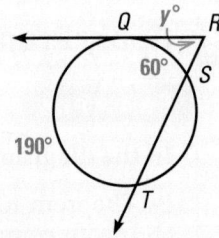

$$y° = \frac{1}{2}\left(m\widehat{QT} - m\widehat{SQ}\right) \qquad \text{Use Theorem 10.13.}$$

$$y° = \frac{1}{2}(190° - 60°) \qquad \text{Substitute.}$$

$$y = 65 \qquad\qquad\qquad \text{Simplify.}$$

EXERCISES

EXAMPLES
2 and 3
on pp. 681–682
for Exs. 20–22

Find the value of x.

20.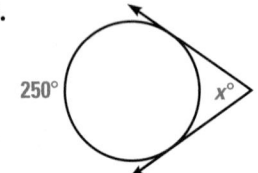

21.

22.

10.6 Find Segment Lengths in Circles

pp. 689–695

EXAMPLE

Find the value of x.

The chords $\overline{EG}$ and $\overline{FH}$ intersect inside the circle, so you can use Theorem 10.14 to find the value of x.

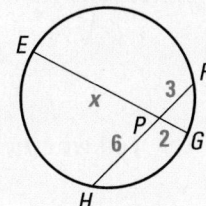

$EP \cdot PG = FP \cdot PH$ **Use Theorem 10.14.**

$x \cdot 2 = 3 \cdot 6$ **Substitute.**

$x = 9$ **Solve for x.**

EXERCISE

EXAMPLE 4
on p. 692
for Ex. 23

23. SKATING RINK A local park has a circular ice skating rink. You are standing at point A, about 12 feet from the edge of the rink. The distance from you to a point of tangency on the rink is about 20 feet. Estimate the radius of the rink.

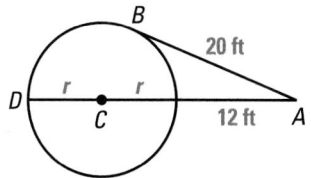

10.7 Write and Graph Equations of Circles

pp. 699–705

EXAMPLE

Write an equation of the circle shown.

The radius is 4 and the center is at $(-2, 4)$.

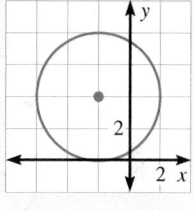

$(x - h)^2 + (y - k)^2 = r^2$ **Standard equation of a circle**

$(x - (-2))^2 + (y - 4)^2 = 4^2$ **Substitute.**

$(x + 2)^2 + (y - 4)^2 = 16$ **Simplify.**

EXERCISES

EXAMPLES
1, 2, and 3
on pp. 699–700
for Exs. 24–32

Write an equation of the circle shown.

24.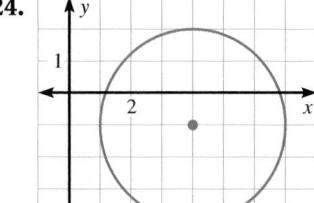

25.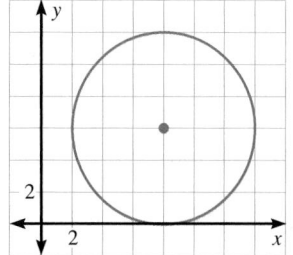

26.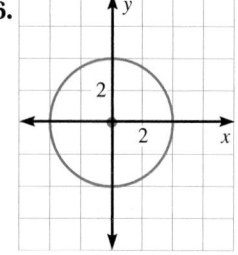

Write the standard equation of the circle with the given center and radius.

27. Center $(0, 0)$, radius 9   **28.** Center $(-5, 2)$, radius 1.3   **29.** Center $(6, 21)$, radius 4

30. Center $(-3, 2)$, radius 16   **31.** Center $(10, 7)$, radius 3.5   **32.** Center $(0, 0)$, radius 5.2

In ⊙C, B and D are points of tangency. Find the value of the variable.

1.

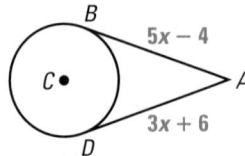

2.

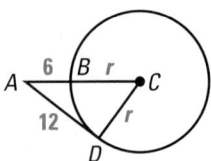

3.

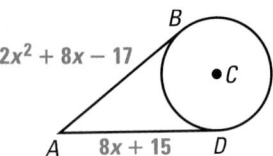

Tell whether the red arcs are congruent. *Explain* why or why not.

4.

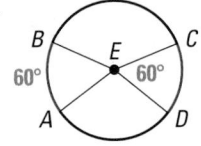

5.

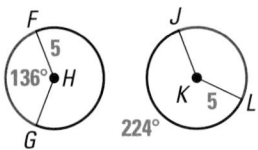

6.

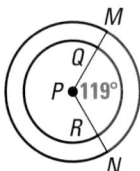

Determine whether $\overline{AB}$ is a diameter of the circle. *Explain* your reasoning.

7.

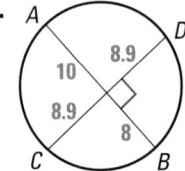

8.

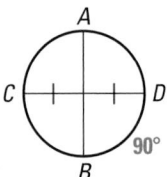

9.

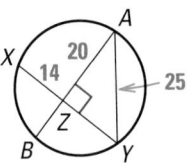

Find the indicated measure.

10. $m\angle ABC$

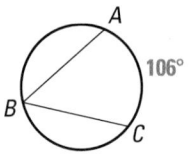

11. $m\widehat{DF}$

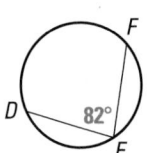

12. $m\widehat{GHJ}$

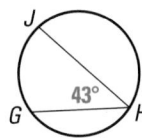

13. $m\angle 1$

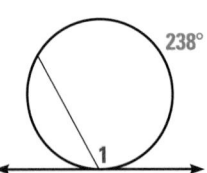

14. $m\angle 2$

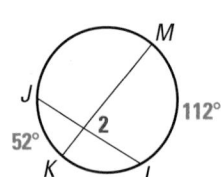

15. $m\widehat{AC}$

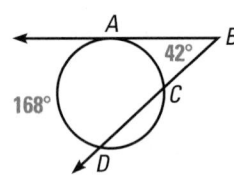

Find the value of x. Round decimal answers to the nearest tenth.

16.

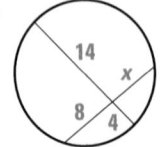

17.

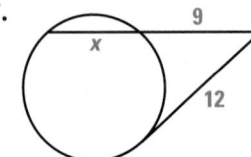

18.

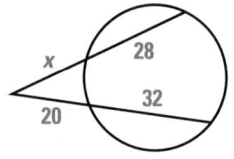

19. Find the center and radius of a circle that has the standard equation
$(x + 2)^2 + (y - 5)^2 = 169$.

10 ^{xy} ALGEBRA REVIEW

FACTOR BINOMIALS AND TRINOMIALS

EXAMPLE 1 *Factor using greatest common factor*

Factor $2x^3 + 6x^2$.

Identify the *greatest common factor* of the terms. The greatest common factor (GCF) is the product of all the common factors.

First, factor each term. $2x^3 = 2 \cdot x \cdot x \cdot x$ and $6x^2 = 2 \cdot 3 \cdot x \cdot x$

Then, write the product of the common terms. $GCF = 2 \cdot x \cdot x = 2x^2$

Finally, use the distributive property with the GCF. $2x^3 + 6x^2 = 2x^2(x + 3)$

EXAMPLE 2 *Factor binomials and trinomials*

Factor.

a. $2x^2 - 5x + 3$

b. $x^2 - 9$

Solution

a. Make a table of possible factorizations. Because the middle term, $-5x$, is negative, both factors of the third term, 3, must be negative.

Factors of 2	Factors of 3	Possible factorization	Middle term when multiplied	
1, 2	−3, −1	$(x - 3)(2x - 1)$	$-x - 6x = -7x$	✗
1, 2	−1, −3	$(x - 1)(2x - 3)$	$-3x - 2x = -5x$	← Correct

b. Use the special factoring pattern $a^2 - b^2 = (a + b)(a - b)$.

$x^2 - 9 = x^2 - 3^2$ Write in the form $a^2 - b^2$.

$= (x + 3)(x - 3)$ Factor using the pattern.

EXERCISES

Factor.

EXAMPLE 1
for Exs. 1–9

1. $6x^2 + 18x^4$
2. $16a^2 - 24b$
3. $9r^2 - 15rs$
4. $14x^5 + 27x^3$
5. $8t^4 + 6t^2 - 10t$
6. $9z^3 + 3z + 21z^2$
7. $5y^6 - 4y^5 + 2y^3$
8. $30v^7 - 25v^5 - 10v^4$
9. $6x^3y + 15x^2y^3$

EXAMPLE 2
for Exs. 10–24

10. $x^2 + 6x + 8$
11. $y^2 - y - 6$
12. $a^2 - 64$
13. $z^2 - 8z + 16$
14. $3s^2 + 2s - 1$
15. $5b^2 - 16b + 3$
16. $4x^4 - 49$
17. $25r^2 - 81$
18. $4x^2 + 12x + 9$
19. $x^2 + 10x + 21$
20. $z^2 - 121$
21. $y^2 + y - 6$
22. $z^2 + 12z + 36$
23. $x^2 - 49$
24. $2x^2 - 12x - 14$

MULTIPLE CHOICE QUESTIONS

If you have difficulty solving a multiple choice question directly, you may be able to use another approach to eliminate incorrect answer choices and obtain the correct answer.

PROBLEM 1

In the diagram, $\triangle PQR$ is inscribed in a circle. The ratio of the angle measures of $\triangle PQR$ is $4:7:7$. What is $m\overset{\frown}{QR}$?

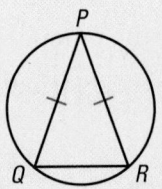

(**A**) $20°$ (**B**) $40°$

(**C**) $80°$ (**D**) $140°$

METHOD 1

SOLVE DIRECTLY Use the Interior Angles Theorem to find $m\angle QPR$. Then use the fact that $\angle QPR$ intercepts $\overset{\frown}{QR}$ to find $m\overset{\frown}{QR}$.

STEP 1 **Use** the ratio of the angle measures to write an equation. Because $\triangle PQR$ is isosceles, its base angles are congruent. Let $4x° = m\angle QPR$. Then $m\angle Q = m\angle R = 7x°$. You can write:

$$m\angle QPR + m\angle Q + m\angle R = 180°$$
$$4x° + 7x° + 7x° = 180°$$

STEP 2 **Solve** the equation to find the value of x.

$$4x° + 7x° + 7x° = 180°$$
$$18x° = 180°$$
$$x = 10$$

STEP 3 **Find** $m\angle QPR$. From Step 1, $m\angle QPR = 4x°$, so $m\angle QPR = 4 \cdot 10° = 40°$.

STEP 4 **Find** $m\overset{\frown}{QR}$. Because $\angle QPR$ intercepts $\overset{\frown}{QR}$, $m\overset{\frown}{QR} = 2 \cdot m\angle QPR$. So, $m\overset{\frown}{QR} = 2 \cdot 40° = 80°$.

The correct answer is C. (**A**) (**B**) (**C**) (**D**)

METHOD 2

ELIMINATE CHOICES Because $\angle QPR$ intercepts $\overset{\frown}{QR}$, $m\angle QPR = \frac{1}{2} \cdot m\overset{\frown}{QR}$. Also, because $\triangle PQR$ is isosceles, its base angles, $\angle Q$ and $\angle R$, are congruent. For each choice, find $m\angle QPR$, $m\angle Q$, and $m\angle R$. Determine whether the ratio of the angle measures is $4:7:7$.

Choice A: If $m\overset{\frown}{QR} = 20°$, $m\angle QPR = 10°$. So, $m\angle Q + m\angle R = 180° - 10° = 170°$, and $m\angle Q = m\angle R = \frac{170}{2} = 85°$. The angle measures $10°$, $85°$, and $85°$ are not in the ratio $4:7:7$, so Choice A is not correct.

Choice B: If $m\overset{\frown}{QR} = 40°$, $m\angle QPR = 20°$. So, $m\angle Q + m\angle R = 180° - 20° = 160°$, and $m\angle Q = m\angle R = 80°$. The angle measures $20°$, $80°$, and $80°$ are not in the ratio $4:7:7$, so Choice B is not correct.

Choice C: If $m\overset{\frown}{QR} = 80°$, $m\angle QPR = 40°$. So, $m\angle Q + m\angle R = 180° - 40° = 140°$, and $m\angle Q = m\angle R = 70°$. The angle measures $40°$, $70°$, and $70°$ are in the ratio $4:7:7$. So, $m\overset{\frown}{QR} = 80°$.

The correct answer is C. (**A**) (**B**) (**C**) (**D**)

PROBLEM 2

In the circle shown, $\overline{JK}$ intersects $\overline{LM}$ at point N.
What is the value of x?

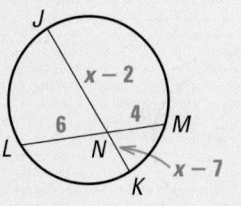

- **A** −1
- **B** 2
- **C** 7
- **D** 10

METHOD 1

SOLVE DIRECTLY Write and solve an equation.

STEP 1 Write an equation. By the Segments of a Chord Theorem, $NJ \cdot NK = NL \cdot NM$. You can write $(x - 2)(x - 7) = 6 \cdot 4 = 24$.

STEP 2 Solve the equation.

$$(x - 2)(x - 7) = 24$$
$$x^2 - 9x + 14 = 24$$
$$x^2 - 9x - 10 = 0$$
$$(x - 10)(x + 1) = 0$$

So, $x = 10$ or $x = -1$.

STEP 3 Decide which value makes sense. If $x = -1$, then $NJ = -1 - 2 = -3$. But a distance cannot be negative. If $x = 10$, then $NJ = 10 - 2 = 8$, and $NK = 10 - 7 = 3$. So, $x = 10$.

The correct answer is D. (A) (B) (C) (**D**)

METHOD 2

ELIMINATE CHOICES Check to see if any choices do not make sense.

STEP 1 Check to see if any choices give impossible values for NJ and NK. Use the fact that $NJ = x - 2$ and $NK = x - 7$.

Choice A: If $x = -1$, then $NJ = -3$ and $NK = -8$. A distance cannot be negative, so you can eliminate Choice A.

Choice B: If $x = 2$, then $NJ = 0$ and $NK = -5$. A distance cannot be negative or 0, so you can eliminate Choice B.

Choice C: If $x = 7$, then $NJ = 5$ and $NK = 0$. A distance cannot be 0, so you can eliminate Choice C.

STEP 2 Verify that Choice D is correct. By the Segments of a Chord Theorem, $(x - 7)(x - 2) = 6(4)$. This equation is true when $x = 10$.

The correct answer is D. (A) (B) (C) (**D**)

EXERCISES

Explain why you can eliminate the highlighted answer choice.

1. In the diagram, what is $m\overset{\frown}{NQ}$?

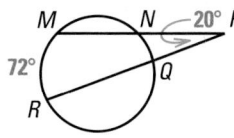

- **A** 20°
- **B** 26°
- **C** 40°
- **D** 52°

2. Isosceles trapezoid *EFGH* is inscribed in a circle, $m\angle E = (x + 8)°$, and $m\angle G = (3x + 12)°$. What is the value of x?

- **A** −17
- **B** 10
- **C** 40
- **D** 72

MULTIPLE CHOICE

1. In $\odot L$, $\overline{MN} \cong \overline{PQ}$. Which statement is not necessarily true?

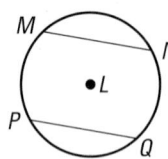

(A) $\overarc{MN} \cong \overarc{PQ}$ **(B)** $\overarc{NQP} \cong \overarc{QNM}$

(C) $\overarc{MP} \cong \overarc{NQ}$ **(D)** $\overarc{MPQ} \cong \overarc{NMP}$

2. In $\odot T$, $PV = 5x - 2$ and $PR = 4x + 14$. What is the value of x?

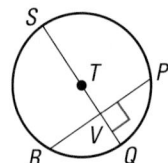

(A) -10 **(B)** 3

(C) 12 **(D)** 16

3. What are the coordinates of the center of a circle with equation $(x + 2)^2 + (y - 4)^2 = 9$?

(A) $(-2, -4)$ **(B)** $(-2, 4)$

(C) $(2, -4)$ **(D)** $(2, 4)$

4. In the circle shown below, what is $m\overarc{QR}$?

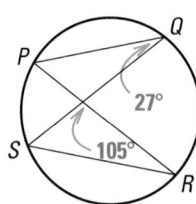

(A) $24°$ **(B)** $27°$

(C) $48°$ **(D)** $96°$

5. Regular hexagon *FGHJKL* is inscribed in a circle. What is $m\overarc{KL}$?

(A) $6°$ **(B)** $60°$

(C) $120°$ **(D)** $240°$

6. In the design for a jewelry store sign, *STUV* is inscribed inside a circle, $ST = TU = 12$ inches, and $SV = UV = 18$ inches. What is the approximate diameter of the circle?

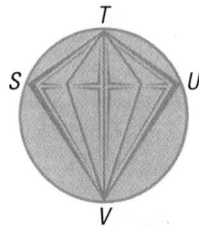

(A) 17 in.   **(B)** 22 in.

(C) 25 in.   **(D)** 30 in.

7. In the diagram shown, $\overleftrightarrow{QS}$ is tangent to $\odot N$ at R. What is $m\overarc{RPT}$?

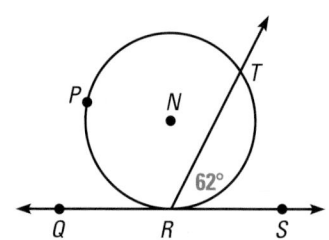

(A) $62°$ **(B)** $118°$

(C) $124°$ **(D)** $236°$

8. Two distinct circles intersect. What is the maximum number of common tangents?

(A) 1   **(B)** 2

(C) 3   **(D)** 4

9. In the circle shown, $m\overarc{EFG} = 146°$ and $m\overarc{FGH} = 172°$. What is the value of x?

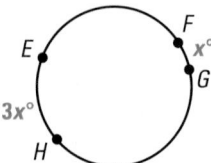

(A) 10.5   **(B)** 21

(C) 42   **(D)** 336

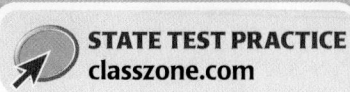
GRIDDED ANSWER

10. $\overline{LK}$ is tangent to $\odot T$ at K. $\overline{LM}$ is tangent to $\odot T$ at M. Find the value of x.

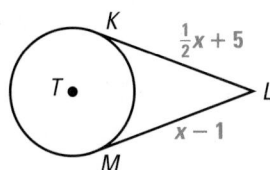

11. In $\odot H$, find $m\angle AHB$ in degrees.

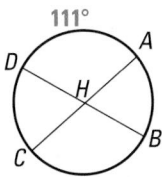

12. Find the value of x.

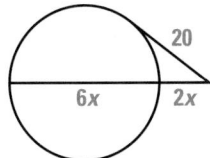

SHORT RESPONSE

13. *Explain* why $\triangle PSR$ is similar to $\triangle TQR$.

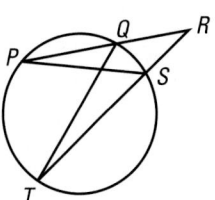

14. Let $x°$ be the measure of an inscribed angle, and let $y°$ be the measure of its intercepted arc. Graph y as a function of x for all possible values of x. Give the slope of the graph.

15. In $\odot J$, $\overline{JD} \cong \overline{JH}$. Write two true statements about congruent arcs and two true statements about congruent segments in $\odot J$. *Justify* each statement.

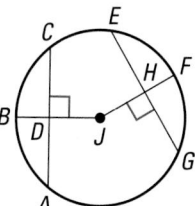

EXTENDED RESPONSE

16. The diagram shows a piece of broken pottery found by an archaeologist. The archaeologist thinks that the pottery is part of a circular plate and wants to estimate the diameter of the plate.

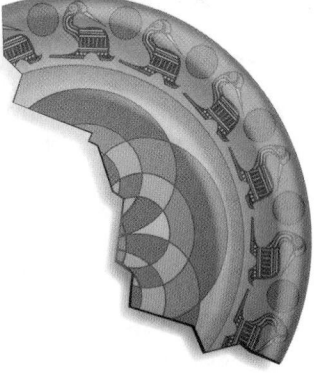

 a. Trace the outermost arc of the diagram on a piece of paper. Draw any two chords whose endpoints lie on the arc.

 b. Construct the perpendicular bisector of each chord. Mark the point of intersection of the perpendiculars bisectors. How is this point related to the circular plate?

 c. Based on your results, *describe* a method the archaeologist could use to estimate the diameter of the actual plate. *Explain* your reasoning.

17. The point $P(3, -8)$ lies on a circle with center $C(-2, 4)$.

 a. Write an equation for $\odot C$.

 b. Write an equation for the line that contains radius $\overline{CP}$. *Explain*.

 c. Write an equation for the line that is tangent to $\odot C$ at point P. *Explain*.

11 Measuring Length and Area

Before

In previous chapters, you learned the following skills, which you'll use in Chapter 11: applying properties of circles and polygons, using formulas, solving for lengths in right triangles, and using ratios and proportions.

Prerequisite Skills

VOCABULARY CHECK

Give the indicated measure for $\odot P$.

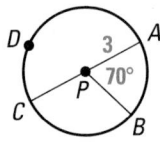

1. The radius   2. The diameter   3. $m\overarc{ADB}$

SKILLS AND ALGEBRA CHECK

4. Use a formula to find the width w of the rectangle that has a perimeter of 24 centimeters and a length of 9 centimeters. *(Review p. 49 for 11.1.)*

In $\triangle ABC$, angle C is a right angle. Use the given information to find AC.
(Review pp. 433, 457, 473 for 11.1, 11.6.)

5. $AB = 14, BC = 6$ 6. $m\angle A = 35°, AB = 25$ 7. $m\angle B = 60°, BC = 5$

8. Which special quadrilaterals have diagonals that bisect each other?
   (Review pp. 533, 542 for 11.2.)

9. Use a proportion to find XY if $\triangle UVW \sim \triangle XYZ$.
   (Review p. 372 for 11.3.)

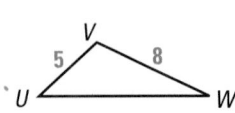
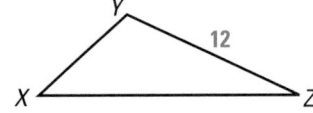

@HomeTutor Prerequisite skills practice at classzone.com

In Chapter 11, you will apply the big ideas listed below and reviewed in the Chapter Summary on page 779. You will also use the key vocabulary listed below.

Big Ideas

1. **Using area formulas for polygons**
2. **Relating length, perimeter, and area ratios in similar polygons**
3. **Comparing measures for parts of circles and the whole circle**

KEY VOCABULARY

- bases of a parallelogram, *p. 720*
- height of a parallelogram, *p. 720*
- height of a trapezoid, *p. 730*
- circumference, *p. 746*
- arc length, *p. 747*
- sector of a circle, *p. 756*

- center of a polygon, *p. 762*
- radius of a polygon, *p. 762*
- apothem of a polygon, *p. 762*
- central angle of a regular polygon, *p. 762*
- probability, *p. 771*
- geometric probability, *p. 771*

You can apply formulas for perimeter, circumference, and area to find and compare measures. To find lengths along a running track, you can break the track into straight sides and semicircles.

𝐴𝑛𝑖𝑚𝑎𝑡𝑒𝑑 Geometry

The animation illustrated below for Example 5 on page 749 helps you answer this question: How far does a runner travel to go around a track?

Your goal is to find the distances traveled by two runners in different track lanes.

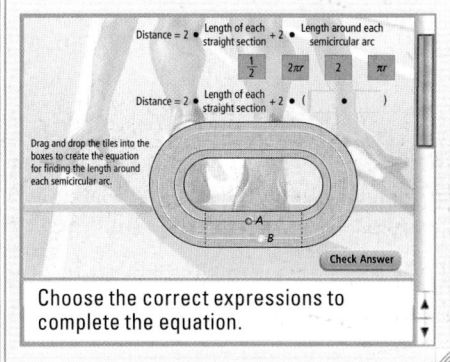

Choose the correct expressions to complete the equation.

𝐴𝑛𝑖𝑚𝑎𝑡𝑒𝑑 Geometry at classzone.com

Other animations for Chapter 11: pages 720, 739, 759, 765, and 771

11.1 Areas of Triangles and Parallelograms

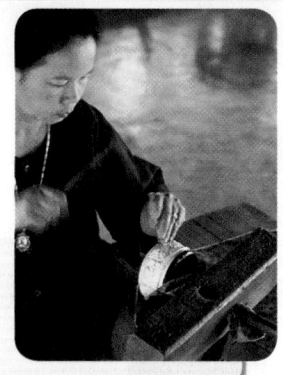

Before	You learned properties of triangles and parallelograms.
Now	You will find areas of triangles and parallelograms.
Why?	So you can plan a jewelry making project, as in Ex. 44.

Key Vocabulary
- **bases of a parallelogram**
- **height of a parallelogram**
- **area,** *p. 49*
- **perimeter,** *p. 49*

POSTULATES
For Your Notebook

POSTULATE 24 Area of a Square Postulate

The area of a square is the square of the length of its side.

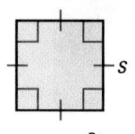

$A = s^2$

POSTULATE 25 Area Congruence Postulate

If two polygons are congruent, then they have the same area.

POSTULATE 26 Area Addition Postulate

The area of a region is the sum of the areas of its nonoverlapping parts.

RECTANGLES A rectangle that is b units by h units can be split into $b \cdot h$ unit squares, so the area formula for a rectangle follows from Postulates 24 and 26.

THEOREM
For Your Notebook

THEOREM 11.1 Area of a Rectangle

The area of a rectangle is the product of its base and height.

Justification: Ex. 46, p. 726

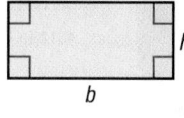

$A = bh$

READ DIAGRAMS
The word *base* can refer to a segment or to its length. The segment used for the height must be perpendicular to the bases used.

PARALLELOGRAMS Either pair of parallel sides can be used as the **bases** of a parallelogram. The **height** is the perpendicular distance between these bases.

If you transform a rectangle to form other parallelograms with the same base and height, the area stays the same.

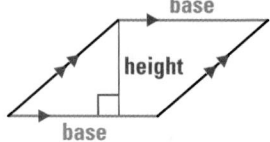

Animated Geometry at classzone.com

THEOREM 11.2 Area of a Parallelogram

The area of a parallelogram is the product of a base and its corresponding height.

Justification: Ex. 42, p. 725

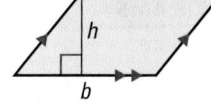

$A = bh$

THEOREM 11.3 Area of a Triangle

The area of a triangle is one half the product of a base and its corresponding height.

Justification: Ex. 43, p. 726

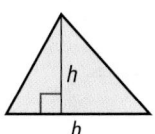

$A = \frac{1}{2}bh$

RELATING AREA FORMULAS As illustrated below, the area formula for a parallelogram is related to the formula for a rectangle, and the area formula for a triangle is related to the formula for a parallelogram. You will write a justification of these relationships in Exercises 42 and 43 on pages 725–726.

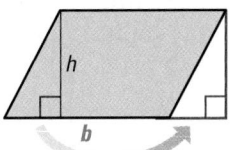

Area of □ = Area of Rectangle

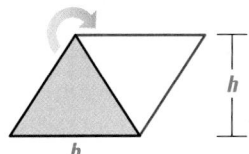

Area of △ = $\frac{1}{2}$ • Area of □

EXAMPLE 1 Use a formula to find area

Find the area of □ *PQRS*.

Solution

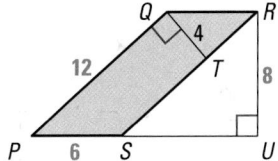

Method 1 Use $\overline{PS}$ as the base.
The base is extended to measure the height *RU*. So, $b = 6$ and $h = 8$.

Area $= bh = 6(8) = 48$ square units

Method 2 Use $\overline{PQ}$ as the base.
Then the height is *QT*. So, $b = 12$ and $h = 4$.

Area $= bh = 12(4) = 48$ square units

✓ **GUIDED PRACTICE**   for Example 1

Find the perimeter and area of the polygon.

1.
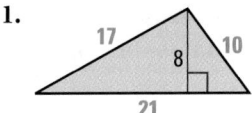

2.
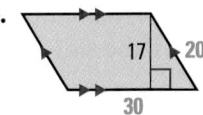

3.

EXAMPLE 2 Solve for unknown measures

DRAW DIAGRAMS

Note that there are other ways you can draw the triangle described in Example 2.

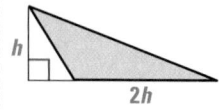

ALGEBRA The base of a triangle is twice its height. The area of the triangle is 36 square inches. Find the base and height.

Let h represent the height of the triangle. Then the base is $2h$.

$A = \frac{1}{2}bh$ **Write formula.**

$36 = \frac{1}{2}(2h)(h)$ **Substitute 36 for *A* and 2*h* for *b*.**

$36 = h^2$ **Simplify.**

$6 = h$ **Find positive square root of each side.**

▶ The height of the triangle is 6 inches, and the base is 6 · 2 = 12 inches.

EXAMPLE 3 Solve a multi-step problem

PAINTING You need to buy paint so that you can paint the side of a barn. A gallon of paint covers 350 square feet. How many gallons should you buy?

Solution

You can use a right triangle and a rectangle to approximate the area of the side of the barn.

ANOTHER WAY

In Example 3, you have a 45°-45°-90° triangle, so you can also find x by using trigonometry or special right angles.

STEP 1 **Find** the length x of each leg of the triangle.

$26^2 = x^2 + x^2$ **Use Pythagorean Theorem.**

$676 = 2x^2$ **Simplify.**

$\sqrt{338} = x$ **Solve for the positive value of *x*.**

STEP 2 **Find** the approximate area of the side of the barn.

Area = **Area of rectangle** + Area of triangle

$= \mathbf{26(18)} + \frac{1}{2} \cdot \left[(\sqrt{338})(\sqrt{338}) \right] = 637 \text{ ft}^2$

STEP 3 **Determine** how many gallons of paint you need.

$637 \text{ ft}^2 \cdot \frac{1 \text{ gal}}{350 \text{ ft}^2} \approx 1.82 \text{ gal}$ **Use unit analysis.**

▶ Round up so you will have enough paint. You need to buy 2 gallons of paint.

✓ **GUIDED PRACTICE** for Examples 2 and 3

4. A parallelogram has an area of 153 square inches and a height of 17 inches. What is the length of the base?

5. **WHAT IF?** In Example 3, suppose there is a 5 foot by 10 foot rectangular window on the side of the barn. What is the approximate area you need to paint?

11.1 EXERCISES

SKILL PRACTICE

1. **VOCABULARY** Copy and complete: Either pair of parallel sides of a parallelogram can be called its __?__, and the perpendicular distance between these sides is called the __?__.

2. ★ **WRITING** What are the two formulas you have learned for the area of a rectangle? *Explain* why these formulas give the same results.

EXAMPLE 1
on p. 721
for Exs. 3–15

FINDING AREA Find the area of the polygon.

3.
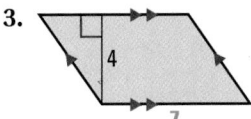

4.
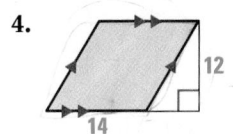

5.
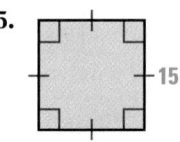

6.
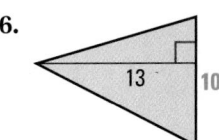

⑦.
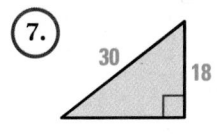

8.
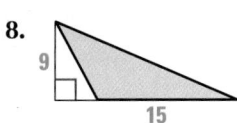

9. **COMPARING METHODS** Show two different ways to calculate the area of parallelogram *ABCD*. *Compare* your results.

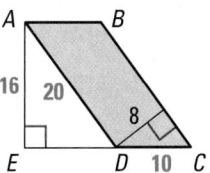

ERROR ANALYSIS *Describe* and correct the error in finding the area of the parallelogram.

10.

$A = bh$
$= (6)(5)$
$= 30$

11.

$A = bh$
$= (7)(4)$
$= 28$

PYTHAGOREAN THEOREM The lengths of the hypotenuse and one leg of a right triangle are given. Find the perimeter and area of the triangle.

12. Hypotenuse: 15 in.; leg: 12 in.

13. Hypotenuse: 34 ft; leg: 16 ft

14. Hypotenuse: 85 m; leg: 84 m

15. Hypotenuse: 29 cm; leg: 20 cm

EXAMPLE 2
on p. 722
for Exs. 16–21

ALGEBRA Find the value of *x*.

16. $A = 36$ in.^{2}
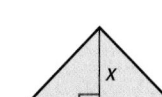
12 in.

17. $A = 276$ ft^2
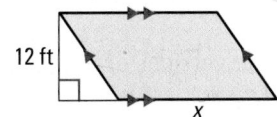
12 ft

18. $A = 476$ cm^2
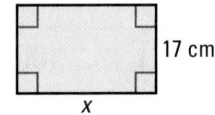
17 cm

19. **XY ALGEBRA** The area of a triangle is 4 square feet. The height of the triangle is half its base. Find the base and the height.

20. **XY ALGEBRA** The area of a parallelogram is 507 square centimeters, and its height is three times its base. Find the base and the height.

21. ★ **OPEN-ENDED MATH** A polygon has an area of 80 square meters and a height of 10 meters. Make scale drawings of three different triangles and three different parallelograms that match this description. Label the base and the height.

EXAMPLE 3
on p. 722
for Exs. 22–27

FINDING AREA Find the area of the shaded polygon.

22.

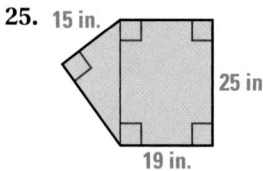

5 ft
8 ft
17 ft

23.

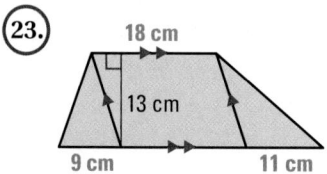

18 cm
13 cm
9 cm   11 cm

24.

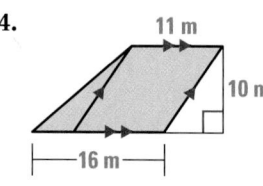

11 m
10 m
16 m

25.

15 in.
25 in.
19 in.

26.

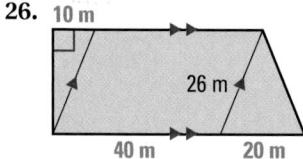

10 m
26 m
40 m   20 m

27.

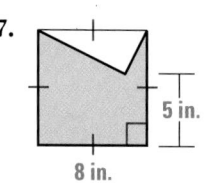

5 in.
8 in.

COORDINATE GRAPHING Graph the points and connect them to form a polygon. Find the area of the polygon.

28. $A(3, 3)$, $B(10, 3)$, $C(8, -3)$, $D(1, -3)$

29. $E(-2, -2)$, $F(5, 1)$, $G(3, -2)$

30. ★ **MULTIPLE CHOICE** What is the area of the parallelogram shown at the right?

A 8 ft^2 6 in.^{2}

B 1350 in.

C 675 in.^{2}

D 9.375 ft^2

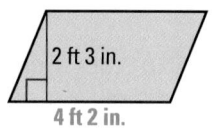

2 ft 3 in.
4 ft 2 in.

31. **TECHNOLOGY** Use geometry drawing software to draw a line ℓ and a line m parallel to ℓ. Then draw $\triangle ABC$ so that C is on line ℓ and $\overline{AB}$ is on line m. Find the base AB, the height CD, and the area of $\triangle ABC$. Move point C to change the shape of $\triangle ABC$. What do you notice about the base, height, and area of $\triangle ABC$?

32. **USING TRIGONOMETRY** In $\square ABCD$, base AD is 15 and AB is 8. What are the height and area of $\square ABCD$ if $m\angle DAB$ is 20°? if $m\angle DAB$ is 50°?

33. **XY ALGEBRA** Find the area of a right triangle with side lengths 12 centimeters, 35 centimeters, and 37 centimeters. Then find the length of the altitude drawn to the hypotenuse.

34. **XY ALGEBRA** Find the area of a triangle with side lengths 5 feet, 5 feet, and 8 feet. Then find the lengths of all three altitudes of the triangle.

35. **CHALLENGE** The vertices of quadrilateral $ABCD$ are $A(2, -2)$, $B(6, 4)$, $C(-1, 5)$, and $D(-5, 2)$. Without using the Distance Formula, find the area of $ABCD$. Show your steps.

○ = **WORKED-OUT SOLUTIONS**
on p. WS1

★ = **STANDARDIZED TEST PRACTICE**

36. SAILING Sails A and B are right triangles. The lengths of the legs of Sail A are 65 feet and 35 feet. The lengths of the legs of Sail B are 29.5 feet and 10.5 feet. Find the area of each sail to the nearest square foot. About how many times as great is the area of Sail A as the area of Sail B?

@HomeTutor for problem solving help at classzone.com

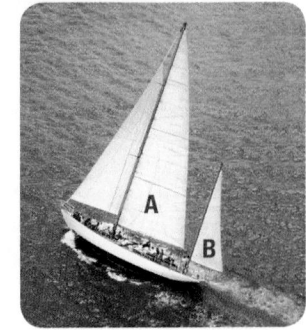

EXAMPLE 3
on p. 722
for Ex. 37

37. MOWING You can mow 10 square yards of grass in one minute. How long does it take you to mow a triangular plot with height 25 yards and base 24 yards? How long does it take you to mow a rectangular plot with base 24 yards and height 36 yards?

@HomeTutor for problem solving help at classzone.com

38. CARPENTRY You are making a tabletop in the shape of a parallelogram to replace an old 24 inch by 15 inch rectangular one. You want the areas of the tabletops to be equal. The base of the parallelogram is 20 inches. What should the height be?

39. ★ SHORT RESPONSE A *4 inch square* is a square that has a side length of 4 inches. Does a 4 inch square have an area of 4 square inches? If not, what size square does have an area of 4 square inches? *Explain.*

40. PAINTING You are earning money by painting a shed. You plan to paint two sides of the shed today. Each of the two sides has the dimensions shown at the right. You can paint 200 square feet per hour, and you charge $20 per hour. About how much will you get paid for painting those two sides of the shed?

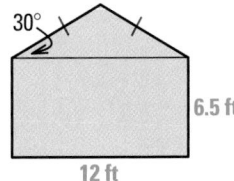

41. ENVELOPES The pattern below shows how to make an envelope to fit a card that is 17 centimeters by 14 centimeters. What are the dimensions of the rectangle you need to start with? What is the area of the paper that is actually used in the envelope? of the paper that is cut off?

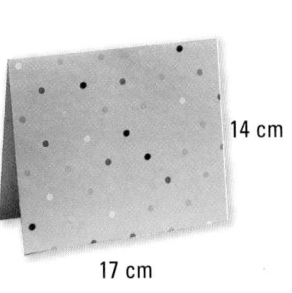

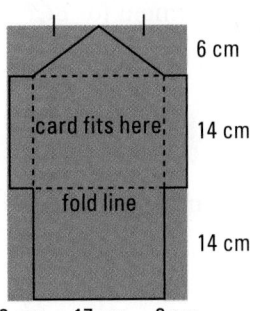

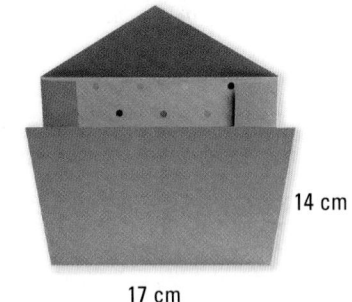

42. JUSTIFYING THEOREM 11.2 You can use the area formula for a rectangle to justify the area formula for a parallelogram. First draw ▱*PQRS* with base *b* and height *h*, as shown. Then draw a segment perpendicular to $\overleftrightarrow{PS}$ through point *R*. Label point *V*.

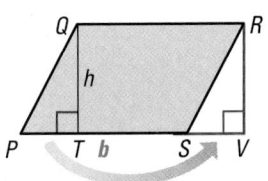

a. In the diagram, *explain* how you know that △*PQT* ≅ △*SRV*.

b. *Explain* how you know that the area of *PQRS* is equal to the area of *QRVT*. How do you know that Area of *PQRS* = *bh*?

43. JUSTIFYING THEOREM 11.3 You can use the area formula for a parallelogram to justify the area formula for a triangle. Start with two congruent triangles with base b and height h. Place and label them as shown. *Explain* how you know that $XYZW$ is a parallelogram and that Area of $\triangle XYW = \frac{1}{2}bh$.

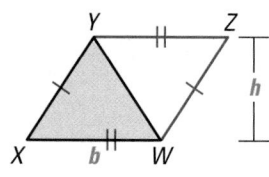

44. MULTI-STEP PROBLEM You have enough silver to make a pendant with an area of 4 square centimeters. The pendant will be an equilateral triangle. Let s be the side length of the triangle.

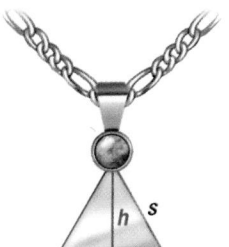

  a. Find the height h of the triangle in terms of s. Then write a formula for the area of the triangle in terms of s.

  b. Find the side length of the triangle. Round to the nearest centimeter.

45. ★ **EXTENDED RESPONSE** The base of a parallelogram is 7 feet and the height is 3 feet. *Explain* why the perimeter cannot be determined from the given information. Is there a least possible perimeter for the parallelogram? Is there a greatest possible perimeter? *Explain*.

46. JUSTIFYING THEOREM 11.1 You can use the diagram to show that the area of a rectangle is the product of its base b and height h.

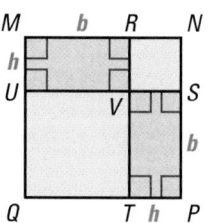

  a. Figures $MRVU$ and $VSPT$ are congruent rectangles with base b and height h. *Explain* why $RNSV$, $UVTQ$, and $MNPQ$ are squares. Write expressions in terms of b and h for the areas of the squares.

  b. Let A be the area of $MRVU$. Substitute A and the expressions from part (a) into the equation below. Solve to find an expression for A.

    Area of $MNPQ$ = Area of $MRVU$ + Area of $UVTQ$ + Area of $RNSV$ + Area of $VSPT$

47. CHALLENGE An equation of $\overleftrightarrow{AB}$ is $y = x$. An equation of $\overleftrightarrow{AC}$ is $y = 2$. Suppose $\overleftrightarrow{BC}$ is placed so that $\triangle ABC$ is isosceles with an area of 4 square units. Find two different lines that fit these conditions. Give an equation for each line. Is there another line that could fit this requirement for $\overleftrightarrow{BC}$? *Explain*.

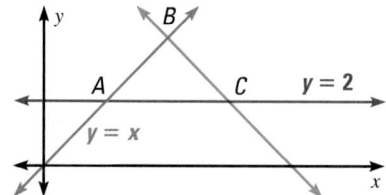

MIXED REVIEW

PREVIEW
Prepare for Lesson 11.2 in Exs. 48–50.

Find the length of the midsegment $\overline{MN}$ of the trapezoid. *(p. 542)*

48.

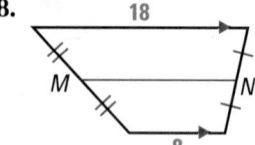

49.

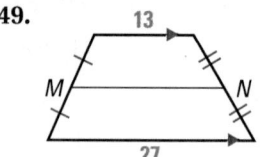

50.

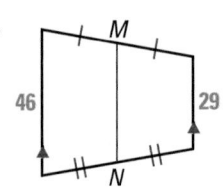

The coordinates of $\triangle PQR$ are $P(-4, 1)$, $Q(2, 5)$, and $R(1, -4)$. Graph the image of the triangle after the translation. Use prime notation. *(p. 572)*

51. $(x, y) \rightarrow (x + 1, y + 4)$ **52.** $(x, y) \rightarrow (x + 3, y - 5)$

53. $(x, y) \rightarrow (x - 3, y - 2)$ **54.** $(x, y) \rightarrow (x - 2, y + 3)$

Determine Precision and Accuracy

GOAL Determine the precision and accuracy of measurements.

Key Vocabulary
- unit of measure
- greatest possible error
- relative error

All measurements are approximations. The length of each segment below, *to the nearest inch*, is 2 inches. The measurement is to the nearest inch, so the **unit of measure** is 1 inch.

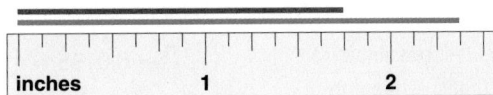

If you are told that an object is 2 inches long, you know that its exact length is between $1\frac{1}{2}$ inches and $2\frac{1}{2}$ inches, or within $\frac{1}{2}$ inch of 2 inches. The **greatest possible error** of a measurement is equal to one half of the unit of measure.

When the unit of measure is smaller, the greatest possible error is smaller and the measurement is *more precise*. Using one-eighth inch as the unit of measure for the segments above gives lengths of $1\frac{6}{8}$ inches and $2\frac{3}{8}$ inches and a greatest possible error of $\frac{1}{16}$ inch.

EXAMPLE 1 **Find greatest possible error**

AMUSEMENT PARK The final drop of a log flume ride is listed in the park guide as 52.3 feet. Find the unit of measure and the greatest possible error.

Solution

The measurement 52.3 feet is given to the nearest tenth of a foot. So, the unit of measure is $\frac{1}{10}$ foot. The greatest possible error is half the unit of measure. Because $\frac{1}{2}\left(\frac{1}{10}\right) = \frac{1}{20} = 0.05$, the greatest possible error is 0.05 foot.

READ VOCABULARY

The *precision* of a measurement depends only on the unit of measure. The *accuracy* of a measurement depends on both the unit of measure and on the size of the object being measured.

RELATIVE ERROR The diameter of a bicycle tire is 26 inches. The diameter of a key ring is 1 inch. In each case, the greatest possible error is $\frac{1}{2}$ inch, but a half-inch error has a much greater effect on the diameter of a smaller object. The **relative error** of a measurement is the ratio $\frac{\text{greatest possible error}}{\text{measured length}}$.

Bicycle tire diameter	Key ring diameter
Rel. error $= \frac{0.5 \text{ in.}}{26 \text{ in.}} \approx 0.01923 \approx 1.9\%$	Rel. error $= \frac{0.5 \text{ in.}}{1 \text{ in.}} = 0.5 = 50\%$

The measurement with the smaller relative error is said to be *more accurate*.

EXAMPLE 2 Find relative error

PLAYING AREAS An air hockey table is 3.7 feet wide. An ice rink is 85 feet wide. Find the relative error of each measurement. Which measurement is more accurate?

	Air hockey table (3.7 feet)	Ice rink (85 feet)
Unit of measure	0.1 ft	1 ft
Greatest possible error $\frac{1}{2}$ · (unit of measure)	$\frac{1}{2}$(0.1 ft) = 0.05 ft	$\frac{1}{2}$(1 ft) = 0.5 ft
Relative error $\dfrac{\text{greatest possible error}}{\text{measured length}}$	$\dfrac{0.05 \text{ ft}}{3.7 \text{ ft}} \approx 0.0135 \approx 1.4\%$	$\dfrac{0.5 \text{ ft}}{85 \text{ ft}} \approx 0.00588 \approx 0.6\%$

▶ The ice rink width has the smaller relative error, so it is more accurate.

PRACTICE

1. **VOCABULARY** *Describe* the difference between the *precision* of a measurement and the *accuracy* of a measurement. Give an example that illustrates the difference.

EXAMPLE 1
on p. 727
for Exs. 2–5

GREATEST POSSIBLE ERROR **Find the unit of measure. Then find the greatest possible error.**

2. 14.6 in. 3. 6 m 4. 8.217 km 5. $4\frac{5}{16}$ yd

EXAMPLE 2
on p. 728
for Exs. 6–9

RELATIVE ERROR **Find the relative error of the measurement.**

6. 4.0 cm 7. 28 in. 8. 4.6 m 9. 12.16 mm

10. **CHOOSING A UNIT** You are estimating the amount of paper needed to make book covers for your textbooks. Which unit of measure, 1 foot, 1 inch, or $\frac{1}{16}$ inch, should you use to measure your textbooks? *Explain.*

11. **REASONING** The greatest possible error of a measurement is $\frac{1}{16}$ inch. *Explain* how such a measurement could be more accurate in one situation than in another situation.

PRECISION AND ACCURACY **Tell which measurement is more precise. Then tell which of the two measurements is more accurate.**

12. 17 cm; 12 cm 13. 18.65 ft; 25.6 ft 14. 6.8 in.; 13.4 ft 15. 3.5 ft; 35 in.

16. **PERIMETER** A side of the eraser shown is a parallelogram. What is the greatest possible error for the length of each side of the parallelogram? for the perimeter of the parallelogram? Find the greatest and least possible perimeter of the parallelogram.

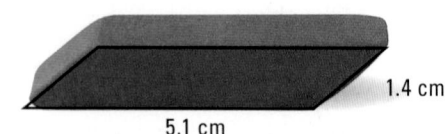

1.4 cm

5.1 cm

11.2 Areas of Trapezoids and Kites

MATERIALS • graph paper • straightedge • scissors • tape

QUESTION **How can you use a parallelogram to find other areas?**

A trapezoid or a kite can be cut out and rearranged to form a parallelogram.

EXPLORE 1 **Use two congruent trapezoids to form a parallelogram**

STEP 1

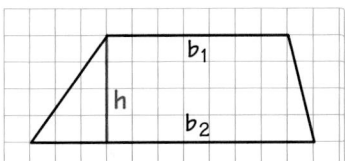

STEP 2

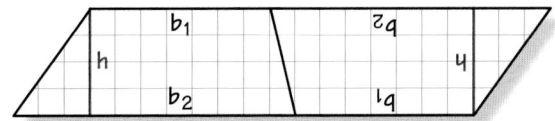

Draw a trapezoid Fold graph paper in half and draw a trapezoid. Cut out two congruent trapezoids. Label as shown.

Create a parallelogram Arrange the two trapezoids from Step 1 to form a parallelogram. Then tape them together.

EXPLORE 2 **Use one kite to form a rectangle**

STEP 1

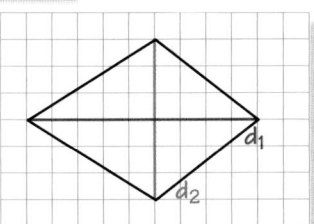

STEP 2

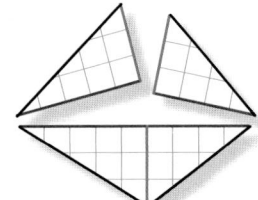

STEP 3

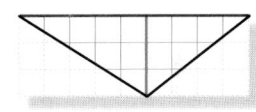

Draw a kite Draw a kite and its perpendicular diagonals. Label the diagonal that is a line of symmetry d_1. Label the other diagonal d_2.

Cut triangles Cut out the kite. Cut along d_1 to form two congruent triangles. Then cut one triangle along part of d_2 to form two right triangles.

Create a rectangle Turn over the right triangles. Place each with its hypotenuse along a side of the larger triangle to form a rectangle. Then tape the pieces together.

DRAW CONCLUSIONS **Use your observations to complete these exercises**

1. In Explore 1, how does the area of one trapezoid compare to the area of the parallelogram formed from two trapezoids? Write expressions in terms of b_1, b_2, and h for the base, height, and area of the parallelogram. Then write a formula for the area of a trapezoid.

2. In Explore 2, how do the base and height of the rectangle compare to d_1 and d_2? Write an expression for the area of the rectangle in terms of d_1 and d_2. Then use that expression to write a formula for the area of a kite.

11.2 Areas of Trapezoids, Rhombuses, and Kites

Before	You found areas of triangles and parallelograms.
Now	You will find areas of other types of quadrilaterals.
Why?	So you can solve a problem in sports, as in Example 1.

Key Vocabulary
• **height of a trapezoid**
• **diagonal,** *p. 507*
• **bases of a trapezoid,** *p. 542*

As you saw in the Activity on page 729, you can use the area formula for a parallelogram to develop area formulas for other special quadrilaterals. The areas of the figures below are related to the lengths of the marked segments.

The **height of a trapezoid** is the perpendicular distance between its bases.

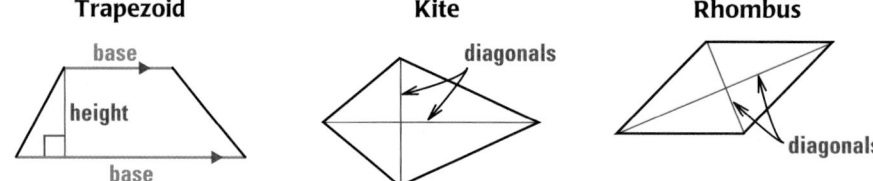

Trapezoid　　　　　Kite　　　　　Rhombus

THEOREM　　　　　*For Your Notebook*

THEOREM 11.4　Area of a Trapezoid

The area of a trapezoid is one half the product of the height and the sum of the lengths of the bases.

Proof: Ex. 40, p. 736

$$A = \frac{1}{2}h(b_1 + b_2)$$

EXAMPLE 1　Find the area of a trapezoid

BASKETBALL The free-throw lane on an international basketball court is shaped like a trapezoid. Find the area of the free-throw lane.

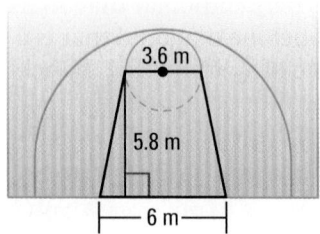

3.6 m
5.8 m
6 m

ANOTHER WAY

In a trapezoid, the average of the lengths of the bases is also the length of the midsegment. So, you can also find the area by multiplying the midsegment by the height.

Solution

The height of the trapezoid is 5.8 meters. The lengths of the bases are 3.6 meters and 6 meters.

$A = \frac{1}{2}h(b_1 + b_2)$　　　**Formula for area of a trapezoid**

$= \frac{1}{2}(5.8)(3.6 + 6)$　　　**Substitute 5.8 for h, 3.6 for b_1, and 6 for b_2.**

$= 27.84$　　　　**Simplify.**

▶ The area of the free-throw lane is about 27.8 square meters.

THEOREMS

For Your Notebook

THEOREM 11.5 Area of a Rhombus

The area of a rhombus is one half the product of the lengths of its diagonals.

Justification: Ex. 39, p. 735

$$A = \frac{1}{2}d_1 d_2$$

THEOREM 11.6 Area of a Kite

The area of a kite is one half the product of the lengths of its diagonals.

Proof: Ex. 41, p. 736

$$A = \frac{1}{2}d_1 d_2$$

EXAMPLE 2 **Find the area of a rhombus**

MUSIC Rhombus *PQRS* represents one of the inlays on the guitar in the photo. Find the area of the inlay.

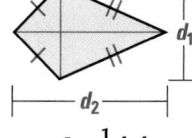

Solution

STEP 1 **Find** the length of each diagonal. The diagonals of a rhombus bisect each other, so $QN = NS$ and $PN = NR$.

$QS = QN + NS = 9 + 9 = 18$ mm

$PR = PN + NR = 12 + 12 = 24$ mm

STEP 2 **Find** the area of the rhombus. Let d_1 represent QS and d_2 represent PR.

$A = \frac{1}{2}d_1 d_2$ **Formula for area of a rhombus**

$= \frac{1}{2}(18)(24)$ **Substitute.**

$= 216$ **Simplify.**

▸ The area of the inlay is 216 square millimeters.

✓ **GUIDED PRACTICE**   for Examples 1 and 2

Find the area of the figure.

1.
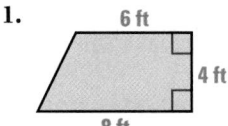

2.
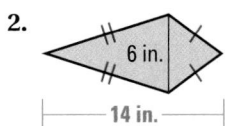

3.
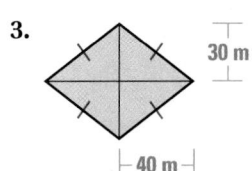

EXAMPLE 3 **Standardized Test Practice**

> One diagonal of a kite is twice as long as the other diagonal. The area of the kite is 72.25 square inches. What are the lengths of the diagonals?
>
> (A) 6 in., 6 in. (B) 8.5 in., 8.5 in. (C) 8.5 in., 17 in. (D) 6 in., 12 in.

ELIMINATE CHOICES

In Example 3, you can eliminate choices A and B because in each case, one diagonal is not twice as long as the other diagonal.

Solution

Draw and label a diagram. Let x be the length of one diagonal. The other diagonal is twice as long, so label it $2x$. Use the formula for the area of a kite to find the value of x.

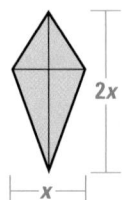

$$A = \frac{1}{2}d_1 d_2 \qquad \text{Formula for area of a kite}$$

$$72.25 = \frac{1}{2}(x)(2x) \qquad \text{Substitute 72.25 for } A, x \text{ for } d_1, \text{ and } 2x \text{ for } d_2.$$

$$72.25 = x^2 \qquad \text{Simplify.}$$

$$8.5 = x \qquad \text{Find the positive square root of each side.}$$

The lengths of the diagonals are 8.5 inches and $2(8.5) = 17$ inches.

▶ The correct answer is C. (A) (B) (C) (D)

EXAMPLE 4 Find an area in the coordinate plane

CITY PLANNING You have a map of a city park. Each grid square represents a 10 meter by 10 meter square. Find the area of the park.

Solution

STEP 1 **Find** the lengths of the bases and the height of trapezoid $ABCD$.

$$b_1 = BC = |70 - 30| = 40 \text{ m}$$
$$b_2 = AD = |80 - 10| = 70 \text{ m}$$
$$h = BE = |60 - 10| = 50 \text{ m}$$

STEP 2 **Find** the area of $ABCD$.

$$A = \frac{1}{2}h(b_1 + b_2) = \frac{1}{2}(50)(40 + 70) = 2750$$

▶ The area of the park is 2750 square meters.

✓ **GUIDED PRACTICE** for Examples 3 and 4

4. The area of a kite is 80 square feet. One diagonal is 4 times as long as the other. Find the diagonal lengths.

5. Find the area of a rhombus with vertices $M(1, 3)$, $N(5, 5)$, $P(9, 3)$, and $Q(5, 1)$.

11.2 EXERCISES

SKILL PRACTICE

1. **VOCABULARY** Copy and complete: The perpendicular distance between the bases of a trapezoid is called the __?__ of the trapezoid.

2. ★ **WRITING** Sketch a kite and its diagonals. *Describe* what you know about the segments and angles formed by the intersecting diagonals.

EXAMPLE 1
on p. 730
for Exs. 3–6

FINDING AREA Find the area of the trapezoid.

3.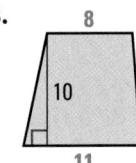
8
10
11

4.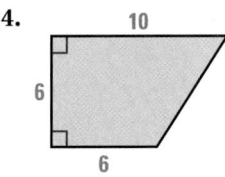
10
6
6

5.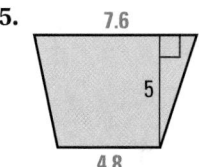
7.6
5
4.8

6. **DRAWING DIAGRAMS** The lengths of the bases of a trapezoid are 5.4 centimeters and 10.2 centimeters. The height is 8 centimeters. Draw and label a trapezoid that matches this description. Then find its area.

EXAMPLE 2
on p. 731
for Exs. 7–14

FINDING AREA Find the area of the rhombus or kite.

7.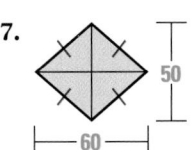
50
60

8.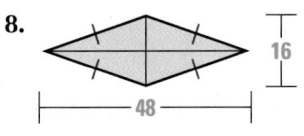
16
48

9.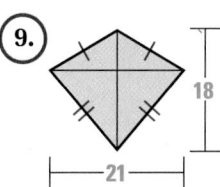
18
21

10.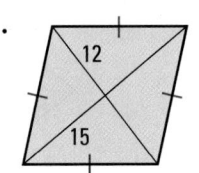
10
19

11.
12
15

12.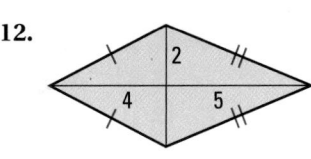
2
4
5

ERROR ANALYSIS *Describe* and correct the error in finding the area.

13.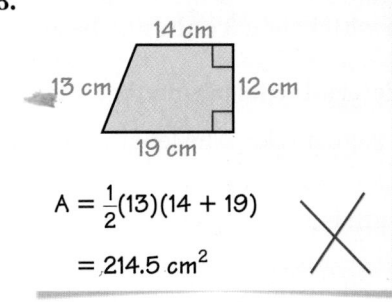
14 cm
13 cm
12 cm
19 cm

$A = \frac{1}{2}(13)(14 + 19)$

$= 214.5 \text{ cm}^2$

14.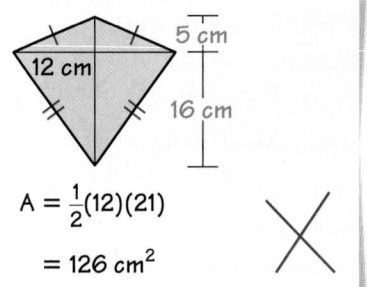
5 cm
12 cm
16 cm

$A = \frac{1}{2}(12)(21)$

$= 126 \text{ cm}^2$

EXAMPLE 3
on p. 732
for Exs. 15–18

15. ★ **MULTIPLE CHOICE** One diagonal of a rhombus is three times as long as the other diagonal. The area of the rhombus is 24 square feet. What are the lengths of the diagonals?

(A) 8 ft, 11 ft   (B) 4 ft, 12 ft   (C) 2 ft, 6 ft   (D) 6 ft, 24 ft

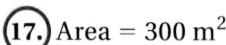 **ALGEBRA** Use the given information to find the value of *x*.

16. Area = 108 ft²

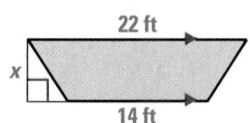

22 ft
x
14 ft

17. Area = 300 m²

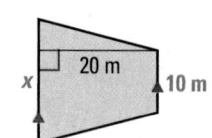

20 m
x
10 m

18. Area = 100 yd²

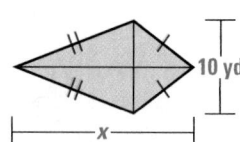

10 yd
x

EXAMPLE 4
on p. 732
for Exs. 19–21

COORDINATE GEOMETRY Find the area of the figure.

19.

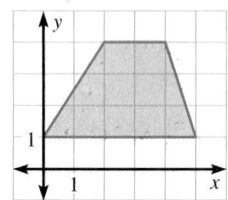

20.

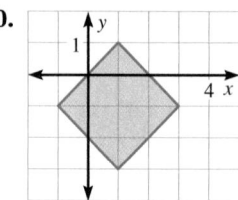

21.

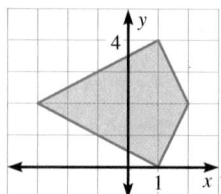

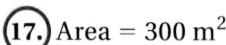 **ALGEBRA** Find the lengths of the bases of the trapezoid described.

22. The height is 3 feet. One base is twice as long as the other base. The area is 13.5 square feet.

23. One base is 8 centimeters longer than the other base. The height is 6 centimeters and the area is 54 square centimeters.

FINDING AREA Find the area of the shaded region.

24.

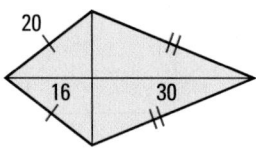

20
16
30

25.

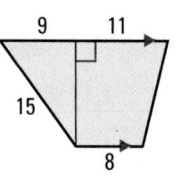

9   11
15
8

26.

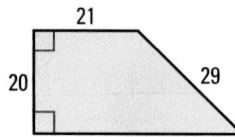

21
20
29

27.

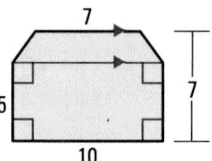

7
5
7
10

28.

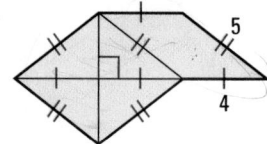

5
4

29.

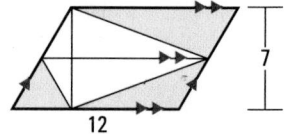

7
12

30. ★ **OPEN-ENDED MATH** Draw three examples of trapezoids that match this description: The height of the trapezoid is 3 units and its area is the same as the area of a parallelogram with height 3 units and base 8 units.

VISUALIZING Sketch the figure. Then determine its perimeter and area.

31. The figure is a trapezoid. It has two right angles. The lengths of its bases are 7 and 15. Its height is 6.

32. The figure is a rhombus. Its side length is 13. The length of one of its diagonals is 24.

33. **CHALLENGE** In the diagram shown at the right, *ABCD* is a parallelogram and *BF* = 16. Find the area of ▱*ABCD*. *Explain* your reasoning. (*Hint:* Draw auxiliary lines through point *A* and through point *D* that are parallel to $\overline{EH}$.)

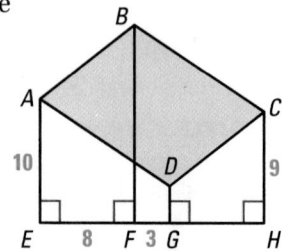

B
A   C
10   9
D
E   8   F 3 G   H

○ = **WORKED-OUT SOLUTIONS**
on p. WS1

★ = **STANDARDIZED
TEST PRACTICE**

EXAMPLE 1
on p. 730
for Ex. 34

34. TRUCKS The windshield in a truck is in the shape of a trapezoid. The lengths of the bases of the trapezoid are 70 inches and 79 inches. The height is 35 inches. Find the area of the glass in the windshield.

@*HomeTutor* for problem solving help at classzone.com

EXAMPLE 2
on p. 731
for Ex. 35

35. INTERNET You are creating a kite-shaped logo for your school's website. The diagonals of the logo are 8 millimeters and 5 millimeters long. Find the area of the logo. Draw two different possible shapes for the logo.

@*HomeTutor* for problem solving help at classzone.com

36. DESIGN You are designing a wall hanging that is in the shape of a rhombus. The area of the wall hanging is 432 square inches and the length of one diagonal is 36 inches. Find the length of the other diagonal.

37. MULTI-STEP PROBLEM As shown, a baseball stadium's playing field is shaped like a pentagon. To find the area of the playing field shown at the right, you can divide the field into two smaller polygons.

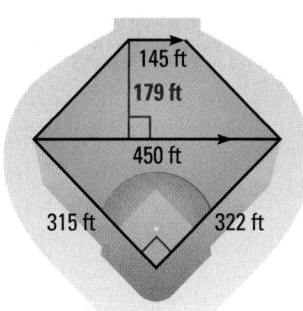

145 ft
179 ft
450 ft
315 ft   322 ft

a. Classify the two polygons.

b. Find the area of the playing field in square feet. Round to the nearest square foot. Then express your answer in square yards.

38. VISUAL REASONING Follow the steps in parts (a)–(c).

a. Analyze Copy the table and extend it to include a column for $n = 5$. Complete the table for $n = 4$ and $n = 5$.

Rhombus number, n	1	2	3	4
Diagram				?
Area, A	2	4	6	?

b. Use Algebra *Describe* the relationship between the rhombus number n and the area of the rhombus. Then write an algebraic rule for finding the area of the nth rhombus.

c. Compare In each rhombus, the length of one diagonal (d_1) is 2. What is the length of the other diagonal (d_2) for the nth rhombus? Use the formula for the area of a rhombus to write a rule for finding the area of the nth rhombus. *Compare* this rule with the one you wrote in part (b).

39. ★ SHORT RESPONSE Look back at the Activity on page 729. *Explain* how the results for kites in Explore 2 can be used to justify Theorem 11.5, the formula for the area of a rhombus.

PROVING THEOREMS 11.4 AND 11.6 Use the triangle area formula and the triangles in the diagram to write a plan for the proof.

40. Show that the area A of the trapezoid shown is $\frac{1}{2}h(b_1 + b_2)$.

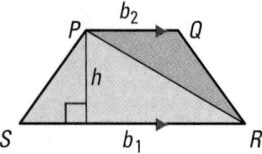

41. Show that the area A of the kite shown is $\frac{1}{2}d_1 d_2$.

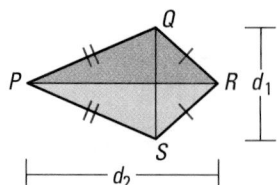

42. ★ **EXTENDED RESPONSE** You will explore the effect of moving a diagonal.

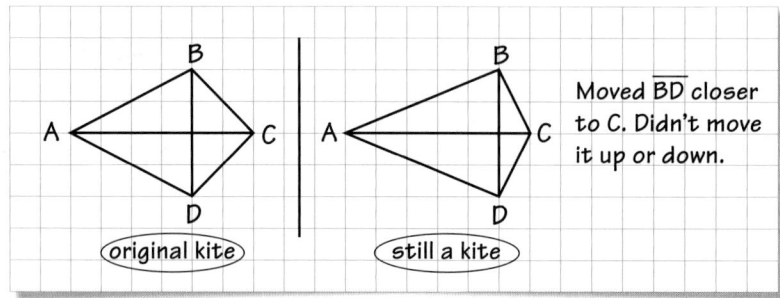

Moved $\overline{BD}$ closer to C. Didn't move it up or down.

original kite   still a kite

a. Investigate Draw a kite in which the longer diagonal is horizontal. Suppose this diagonal is fixed and you can slide the vertical diagonal left or right and up or down. You can keep sliding as long as the diagonals continue to intersect. Draw and identify each type of figure you can form.

b. Justify Is it possible to form any shapes that are not quadrilaterals? *Explain.*

c. Compare Compare the areas of the different shapes you found in part (b). What do you notice about the areas? *Explain.*

43. CHALLENGE James A. Garfield, the twentieth president of the United States, discovered a proof of the Pythagorean Theorem in 1876. His proof involved the fact that a trapezoid can be formed from two congruent right triangles and an isosceles right triangle. Use the diagram to show that $a^2 + b^2 = c^2$.

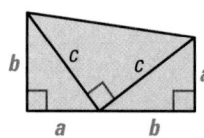

MIXED REVIEW

Solve for the indicated variable. Write a reason for each step. *(p. 105)*

44. $d = rt$; solve for t **45.** $A = \frac{1}{2}bh$; solve for h **46.** $P = 2\ell + 2w$; solve for w

47. Find the angle measures of an isosceles triangle if the measure of a base angle is 4 times the measure of the vertex angle. *(p. 264)*

PREVIEW

Prepare for Lesson 11.3 in Ex. 48.

48. In the diagram at the right, $\triangle PQR \sim \triangle STU$. The perimeter of $\triangle STU$ is 81 inches. Find the height h and the perimeter of $\triangle PQR$. *(p. 372)*

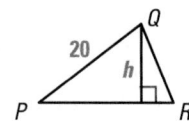

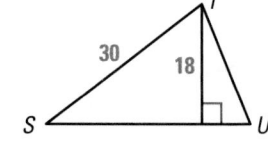

11.3 Perimeter and Area of Similar Figures

Before	You used ratios to find perimeters of similar figures.
Now	You will use ratios to find areas of similar figures.
Why	So you can apply similarity in cooking, as in Example 3.

Key Vocabulary
- **regular polygon,** *p. 43*
- **corresponding sides,** *p. 225*
- **similar polygons,** *p. 372*

In Chapter 6 you learned that if two polygons are similar, then the ratio of their perimeters, or of any two corresponding lengths, is equal to the ratio of their corresponding side lengths. As shown below, the areas have a different ratio.

Ratio of perimeters

$$\frac{\text{Blue}}{\text{Red}} = \frac{10t}{10} = t$$

Ratio of areas

$$\frac{\text{Blue}}{\text{Red}} = \frac{6t^2}{6} = t^2$$

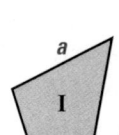

THEOREM   *For Your Notebook*

THEOREM 11.7 Areas of Similar Polygons

If two polygons are similar with the lengths of corresponding sides in the ratio of $a:b$, then the ratio of their areas is $a^2:b^2$.

$$\frac{\text{Side length of Polygon I}}{\text{Side length of Polygon II}} = \frac{a}{b}$$

$$\frac{\text{Area of Polygon I}}{\text{Area of Polygon II}} = \frac{a^2}{b^2}$$

Justification: Ex. 30, p. 742

Polygon I ~ Polygon II

EXAMPLE 1   **Find ratios of similar polygons**

In the diagram, $\triangle ABC \sim \triangle DEF$. Find the indicated ratio.

a. Ratio (red to blue) of the perimeters

b. Ratio (red to blue) of the areas

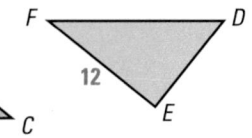

INTERPRET RATIOS

You can also compare the measures with fractions. The perimeter of $\triangle ABC$ is two thirds of the perimeter of $\triangle DEF$. The area of $\triangle ABC$ is four ninths of the area of $\triangle DEF$.

Solution

The ratio of the lengths of corresponding sides is $\frac{8}{12} = \frac{2}{3}$, or $2:3$.

a. By Theorem 6.1 on page 374, the ratio of the perimeters is $2:3$.

b. By Theorem 11.7 above, the ratio of the areas is $2^2:3^2$, or $4:9$.

EXAMPLE 2 **Standardized Test Practice**

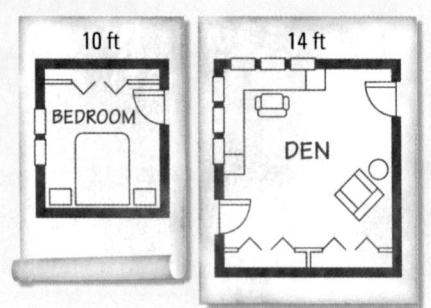

You are installing the same carpet in a bedroom and den. The floors of the rooms are similar. The carpet for the bedroom costs $225. Carpet is sold by the square foot. How much does it cost to carpet the den?

(A) $115   (B) $161

(C) $315   (D) $441

USE ESTIMATION

The cost for the den is $\frac{49}{25}$ times the cost for the bedroom. Because $\frac{49}{25}$ is a little less than 2, the cost for the den is a little less than twice $225. The only possible choice is D.

Solution

The ratio of a side length of the den to the corresponding side length of the bedroom is $14:10$, or $7:5$. So, the ratio of the areas is $7^2:5^2$, or $49:25$. This ratio is also the ratio of the carpeting costs. Let x be the cost for the den.

$\frac{49}{25} = \frac{x}{225}$ ← cost of carpet for den
← cost of carpet for bedroom

$x = 441$ **Solve for x.**

▶ It costs $441 to carpet the den. The correct answer is D. (A) (B) (C) **(D)**

 GUIDED PRACTICE | for Examples 1 and 2

1. The perimeter of $\triangle ABC$ is 16 feet, and its area is 64 square feet. The perimeter of $\triangle DEF$ is 12 feet. Given $\triangle ABC \sim \triangle DEF$, find the ratio of the area of $\triangle ABC$ to the area of $\triangle DEF$. Then find the area of $\triangle DEF$.

EXAMPLE 3 **Use a ratio of areas**

COOKING A large rectangular baking pan is 15 inches long and 10 inches wide. A smaller pan is similar to the large pan. The area of the smaller pan is 96 square inches. Find the width of the smaller pan.

ANOTHER WAY

For an alternative method for solving the problem in Example 3, turn to page 744 for the **Problem Solving Workshop**.

Solution

First draw a diagram to represent the problem. Label dimensions and areas.

Then use Theorem 11.7. If the area ratio is $a^2:b^2$, then the length ratio is $a:b$.

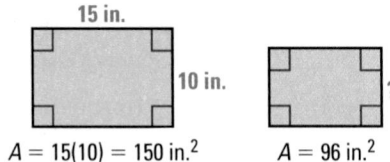

$\frac{\text{Area of smaller pan}}{\text{Area of large pan}} = \frac{96}{150} = \frac{16}{25}$ **Write ratio of known areas. Then simplify.**

$\frac{\text{Length in smaller pan}}{\text{Length in large pan}} = \frac{4}{5}$ **Find square root of area ratio.**

▶ Any length in the smaller pan is $\frac{4}{5}$, or 0.8, of the corresponding length in the large pan. So, the width of the smaller pan is 0.8(10 inches) = 8 inches.

REGULAR POLYGONS Consider two regular polygons with the same number of sides. All of the angles are congruent. The lengths of all pairs of corresponding sides are in the same ratio. So, any two such polygons are similar. Also, any two circles are similar.

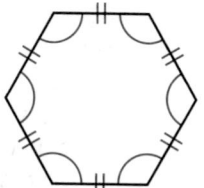

EXAMPLE 4 Solve a multi-step problem

GAZEBO The floor of the gazebo shown is a regular octagon. Each side of the floor is 8 feet, and the area is about 309 square feet. You build a small model gazebo in the shape of a regular octagon. The perimeter of the floor of the model gazebo is 24 inches. Find the area of the floor of the model gazebo to the nearest tenth of a square inch.

Solution

All regular octagons are similar, so the floor of the model is similar to the floor of the full-sized gazebo.

ANOTHER WAY

In Step 1, instead of finding the perimeter of the full-sized and comparing perimeters, you can find the side length of the model and compare side lengths. $24 \div 8 = 3$, so the ratio of side lengths is $\dfrac{8 \text{ ft.}}{3 \text{ in.}} = \dfrac{96 \text{ in.}}{3 \text{ in.}} = \dfrac{32}{1}$.

STEP 1 **Find** the ratio of the lengths of the two floors by finding the ratio of the perimeters. Use the same units for both lengths in the ratio.

$$\frac{\text{Perimeter of full-sized}}{\text{Perimeter of model}} = \frac{8(8 \text{ ft})}{24 \text{ in.}} = \frac{64 \text{ ft}}{24 \text{ in.}} = \frac{64 \text{ ft}}{2 \text{ ft}} = \frac{32}{1}$$

So, the ratio of corresponding lengths (full-sized to model) is $32 : 1$.

STEP 2 **Calculate** the area of the model gazebo's floor. Let x be this area.

$$\frac{(\text{Length in full-sized})^2}{(\text{Length in model})^2} = \frac{\text{Area of full-sized}}{\text{Area of model}} \qquad \textbf{Theorem 11.7}$$

$$\frac{32^2}{1^2} = \frac{309 \text{ ft}^2}{x \text{ ft}^2} \qquad \textbf{Substitute.}$$

$$1024x = 309 \qquad \textbf{Cross Products Property}$$

$$x \approx 0.302 \text{ ft}^2 \qquad \textbf{Solve for } \textit{x.}$$

STEP 3 **Convert** the area to square inches.

$$0.302 \text{ ft}^2 \cdot \frac{144 \text{ in.}^2}{1 \text{ ft}^2} \approx 43.5 \text{ in.}^2$$

▶ The area of the floor of the model gazebo is about 43.5 square inches.

Animated **Geometry** at classzone.com

✓ **GUIDED PRACTICE** for Examples 3 and 4

2. The ratio of the areas of two regular decagons is $20 : 36$. What is the ratio of their corresponding side lengths in simplest radical form?

3. Rectangles I and II are similar. The perimeter of Rectangle I is 66 inches. Rectangle II is 35 feet long and 20 feet wide. Show the steps you would use to find the ratio of the areas and then find the area of Rectangle I.

11.3 EXERCISES

HOMEWORK
KEY

○ = WORKED-OUT SOLUTIONS
on p. WS14 for Exs. 7, 17, and 27

★ = STANDARDIZED TEST PRACTICE
Exs. 2, 12, 18, 28, 32, and 33

SKILL PRACTICE

1. **VOCABULARY** Sketch two similar triangles. Use your sketch to explain what is meant by *corresponding side lengths*.

2. ★ **WRITING** Two regular *n*-gons are similar. The ratio of their side lengths is 3:4. Do you need to know the value of *n* to find the ratio of the perimeters or the ratio of the areas of the polygons? *Explain*.

EXAMPLES
1 and 2
on pp. 737–738
for Exs. 3–8

FINDING RATIOS Copy and complete the table of ratios for similar polygons.

Ratio of corresponding side lengths	Ratio of perimeters	Ratio of areas
3. 6:11	?	?
4. ?	20:36 = ?	?

RATIOS AND AREAS Corresponding lengths in similar figures are given. Find the ratios (red to blue) of the perimeters and areas. Find the unknown area.

5.
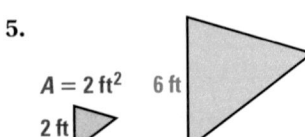
$A = 2$ ft² 6 ft
2 ft

6.
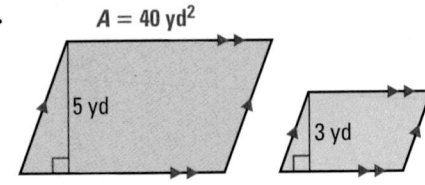
15 cm
20 cm
$A = 240$ cm²

(7.)
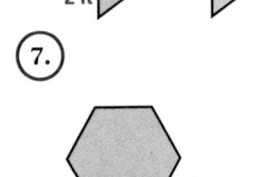
$A = 210$ in.²
7 in.
9 in.

8.
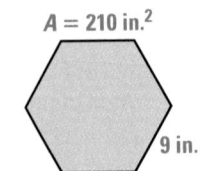
$A = 40$ yd²
5 yd
3 yd

EXAMPLE 3
on p. 738
for Exs. 9–15

FINDING LENGTH RATIOS The ratio of the areas of two similar figures is given. Write the ratio of the lengths of corresponding sides.

9. Ratio of areas = 49:16   10. Ratio of areas = 16:121   11. Ratio of areas = 121:144

12. ★ **MULTIPLE CHOICE** The area of △LMN is 18 ft² and the area of △FGH is 24 ft². If △LMN ~ △FGH, what is the ratio of LM to FG?

(A) 3:4   (B) 9:16   (C) √3:2   (D) 4:3

FINDING SIDE LENGTHS Use the given area to find XY.

13. △DEF ~ △XYZ
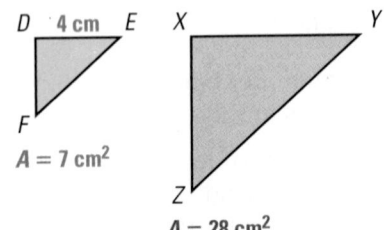
D 4 cm E   X   Y
F
$A = 7$ cm²
Z
$A = 28$ cm²

14. UVWXY ~ LMNPQ
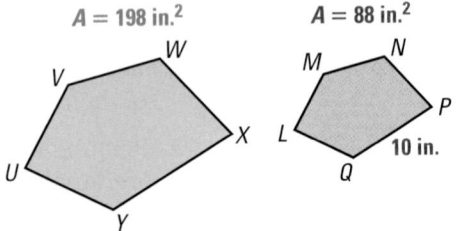
$A = 198$ in.² $A = 88$ in.²
V   W   M   N
U   X   L   P
Y   Q   10 in.

15. ERROR ANALYSIS In the diagram, Rectangles *DEFG* and *WXYZ* are similar. The ratio of the area of *DEFG* to the area of *WXYZ* is 1 : 4. *Describe* and correct the error in finding *ZY*.

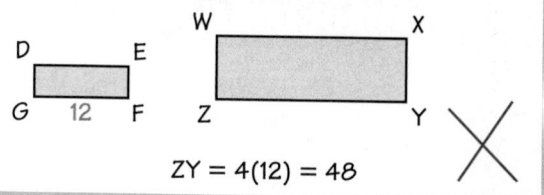

ZY = 4(12) = 48

EXAMPLE 4
on p. 739
for Exs. 16–17

16. REGULAR PENTAGONS Regular pentagon *QRSTU* has a side length of 12 centimeters and an area of about 248 square centimeters. Regular pentagon *VWXYZ* has a perimeter of 140 centimeters. Find its area.

(17.) RHOMBUSES Rhombuses *MNPQ* and *RSTU* are similar. The area of *RSTU* is 28 square feet. The diagonals of *MNPQ* are 25 feet long and 14 feet long. Find the area of *MNPQ*. Then use the ratio of the areas to find the lengths of the diagonals of *RSTU*.

18. ★ SHORT RESPONSE You enlarge the same figure three different ways. In each case, the enlarged figure is similar to the original. List the enlargements in order from smallest to largest. *Explain.*

Case 1 The side lengths of the original figure are multiplied by 3.
Case 2 The perimeter of the original figure is multiplied by 4.
Case 3 The area of the original figure is multiplied by 5.

REASONING In Exercises 19 and 20, copy and complete the statement using *always*, *sometimes*, or *never*. *Explain* your reasoning.

19. Doubling the side length of a square ___?___ doubles the area.

20. Two similar octagons ___?___ have the same perimeter.

21. FINDING AREA The sides of △*ABC* are 4.5 feet, 7.5 feet, and 9 feet long. The area is about 17 square feet. *Explain* how to use the area of △*ABC* to find the area of a △*DEF* with side lengths 6 feet, 10 feet, and 12 feet.

22. RECTANGLES Rectangles *ABCD* and *DEFG* are similar. The length of *ABCD* is 24 feet and the perimeter is 84 feet. The width of *DEFG* is 3 yards. Find the ratio of the area of *ABCD* to the area of *DEFG*.

SIMILAR TRIANGLES *Explain* why the red and blue triangles are similar. Find the ratio (red to blue) of the areas of the triangles. Show your steps.

23.

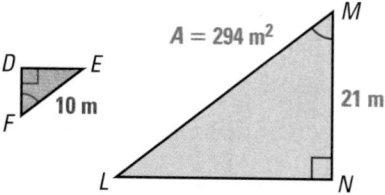

24.

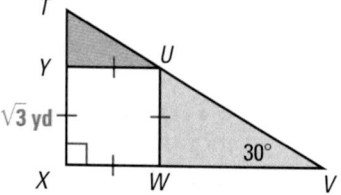

25. CHALLENGE In the diagram shown, *ABCD* is a parallelogram. The ratio of the area of △*AGB* to the area of △*CGE* is 9 : 25, *CG* = 10, and *GE* = 15.

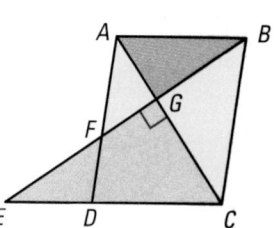

    a. Find *AG*, *GB*, *GF*, and *FE*. Show your methods.

    b. Give two area ratios other than 9 : 25 or 25 : 9 for pairs of similar triangles in the figure. *Explain.*

26. BANNER Two rectangular banners from this year's music festival are shown. Organizers of next year's festival want to design a new banner that will be similar to the banner whose dimensions are given in the photograph. The length of the longest side of the new banner will be 5 feet. Find the area of the new banner.

@HomeTutor for problem solving help at classzone.com

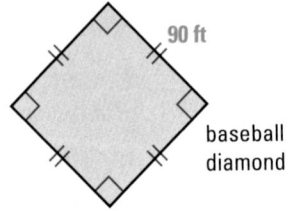

3 ft

1 ft

EXAMPLE 3
on p. 738
for Ex. 27

27. PATIO A new patio will be an irregular hexagon. The patio will have two long parallel sides and an area of 360 square feet. The area of a similar shaped patio is 250 square feet, and its long parallel sides are 12.5 feet apart. What will be the corresponding distance on the new patio?

@HomeTutor for problem solving help at classzone.com

28. ★ MULTIPLE CHOICE You need 20 pounds of grass seed to plant grass inside the baseball diamond shown. About how many pounds do you need to plant grass inside the softball diamond?

(A) 6 (B) 9

(C) 13 (D) 20

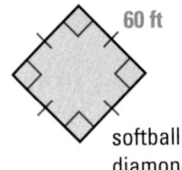

60 ft

softball
diamond

90 ft

baseball
diamond

29. MULTI-STEP PROBLEM Use graph paper for parts (a) and (b).

a. Draw a triangle and label its vertices. Find the area of the triangle.

b. Mark and label the midpoint of each side of the triangle. Connect the midpoints to form a smaller triangle. Show that the larger and smaller triangles are similar. Then use the fact that the triangles are similar to find the area of the smaller triangle.

30. JUSTIFYING THEOREM 11.7 Choose a type of polygon for which you know the area formula. Use algebra and the area formula to prove Theorem 11.7 for that polygon. (*Hint:* Use the ratio for the corresponding side lengths in two similar polygons to express each dimension in one polygon as $\frac{a}{b}$ times the corresponding dimension in the other polygon.)

31. MISLEADING GRAPHS A student wants to show that the students in a science class prefer mysteries to science fiction books. Over a two month period, the students in the class read 50 mysteries, but only 25 science fiction books. The student makes a bar graph of these data. *Explain* why the graph is visually misleading. Show how the student could redraw the bar graph.

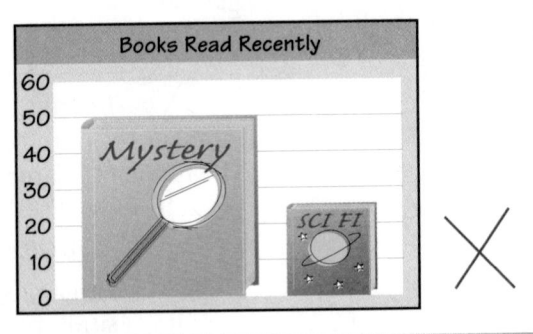

Books Read Recently

60
50
40
30
20
10
0

Mystery

SCI FI

32. ★ **OPEN-ENDED MATH** The ratio of the areas of two similar polygons is 9 : 6. Draw two polygons that fit this description. Find the ratio of their perimeters. Then write the ratio in simplest radical form.

33. ★ **EXTENDED RESPONSE** Use the diagram shown at the right.

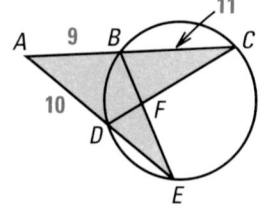

 a. Name as many pairs of similar triangles as you can. *Explain* your reasoning.

 b. Find the ratio of the areas for one pair of similar triangles.

 c. Show two ways to find the length of $\overline{DE}$.

34. **CHALLENGE** In the diagram, the solid figure is a cube. Quadrilateral *JKNM* is on a plane that cuts through the cube, with *JL* = *KL*.

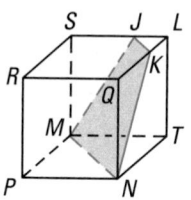

 a. *Explain* how you know that $\triangle JKL \sim \triangle MNP$.

 b. Suppose $\dfrac{JK}{MN} = \dfrac{1}{3}$. Find the ratio of the area of $\triangle JKL$ to the area of one face of the cube.

 c. Find the ratio of the area of $\triangle JKL$ to the area of pentagon *JKQRS*.

MIXED REVIEW

PREVIEW
Prepare for
Lesson 11.4 in
Exs. 35–38.

Find the circumference of the circle with the given radius *r* or diameter *d*. Use $\pi \approx 3.14$. Round your answers to the nearest hundredth. *(p. 49)*

35. $d = 4$ cm   **36.** $d = 10$ ft   **37.** $r = 2.5$ yd   **38.** $r = 3.1$ m

Find the value of *x*.

39. *(p. 295)*
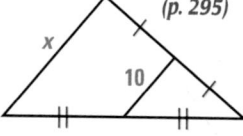

40. *(p. 672)*
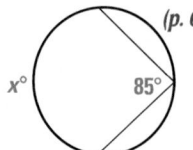

41. *(p. 680)*
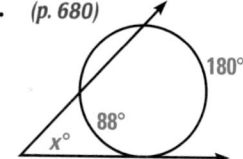

QUIZ *for Lessons 11.1–11.3*

1. The height of □*ABCD* is 3 times its base. Its area is 108 square feet. Find the base and the height. *(p. 720)*

Find the area of the figure.

2. *(p. 720)*
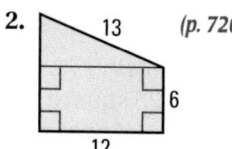

3. *(p. 730)*
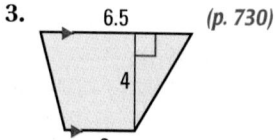

4. *(p. 730)*
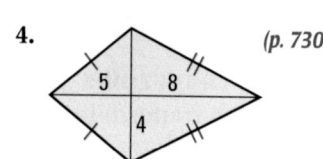

5. The ratio of the lengths of corresponding sides of two similar heptagons is 7 : 20. Find the ratio of their perimeters and their areas. *(p. 737)*

6. Triangles *PQR* and *XYZ* are similar. The area of $\triangle PQR$ is 1200 ft² and the area of $\triangle XYZ$ is 48 ft². Given *PQ* = 50 ft, find *XY*. *(p. 737)*

Using ALTERNATIVE METHODS

Another Way to Solve Example 3, page 738

MULTIPLE REPRESENTATIONS In Example 3 on page 738, you used proportional reasoning to solve a problem about cooking. You can also solve the problem by using an area formula.

PROBLEM

> **COOKING** A large rectangular baking pan is 15 inches long and 10 inches wide. A smaller pan is similar to the large pan. The area of the smaller pan is 96 square inches. Find the width of the smaller pan.

METHOD

Using a Formula You can use what you know about side lengths of similar figures to find the width of the pan.

STEP 1 **Use** the given dimensions of the large pan to write expressions for the dimensions of the smaller pan. Let x represent the width of the smaller pan.

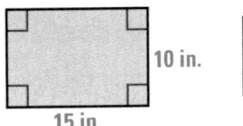
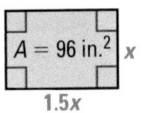

The length of the larger pan is 1.5 times its width. So, the length of the smaller pan is also 1.5 times its width, or $1.5x$.

STEP 2 **Use** the formula for the area of a rectangle to write an equation.

$A = \ell w$	Formula for area of a rectangle
$96 = 1.5x \cdot x$	Substitute $1.5x$ for ℓ and x for w.
$8 = x$	Solve for a positive value of x.

▶ The width of the smaller pan is 8 inches.

PRACTICE

1. **COOKING** A third pan is similar to the large pan shown above and has 1.44 times its area. Find the length of the third pan.

2. **TRAPEZOIDS** Trapezoid *PQRS* is similar to trapezoid *WXYZ*. The area of *WXYZ* is 28 square units. Find *WZ*.

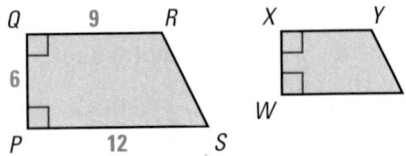

3. **SQUARES** One square has sides of length s. If another square has twice the area of the first square, what is its side length?

4. **REASONING** $\triangle ABC \sim \triangle DEF$ and the area of $\triangle DEF$ is 11.25 square centimeters. Find *DE* and *DF*. *Explain* your reasoning.

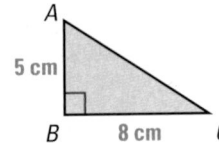
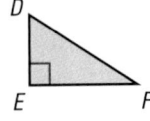

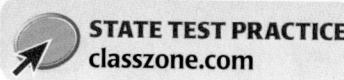
Lessons 11.1–11.3

1. MULTI-STEP PROBLEM The diagram below represents a rectangular flower bed. In the diagram, $AG = 9.5$ feet and $GE = 15$ feet.

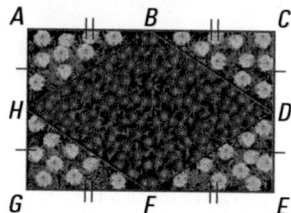

a. *Explain* how you know that *BDFH* is a rhombus.

b. Find the area of rectangle *ACEG* and the area of rhombus *BDFH*.

c. You want to plant asters inside rhombus *BDFH* and marigolds in the other parts of the flower bed. It costs about $.30 per square foot to plant marigolds and about $.40 per square foot to plant asters. How much will you spend on flowers?

2. OPEN-ENDED A polygon has an area of 48 square meters and a height of 8 meters. Draw three different triangles that fit this description and three different parallelograms. *Explain* your thinking.

3. EXTENDED RESPONSE You are tiling a 12 foot by 21 foot rectangular floor. Prices are shown below for two sizes of square tiles.

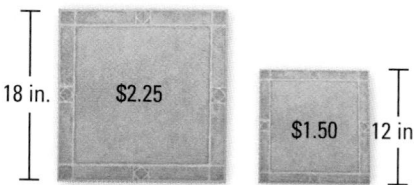

a. How many small tiles would you need for the floor? How many large tiles?

b. Find the cost of buying large tiles for the floor and the cost of buying small tiles for the floor. Which tile should you use if you want to spend as little as possible?

c. *Compare* the side lengths, the areas, and the costs of the two tiles. Is the cost per tile based on side length or on area? *Explain.*

4. SHORT RESPONSE What happens to the area of a rhombus if you double the length of each diagonal? if you triple the length of each diagonal? *Explain* what happens to the area of a rhombus if each diagonal is multiplied by the same number *n*.

5. MULTI-STEP PROBLEM The pool shown is a right triangle with legs of length 40 feet and 41 feet. The path around the pool is 40 inches wide.

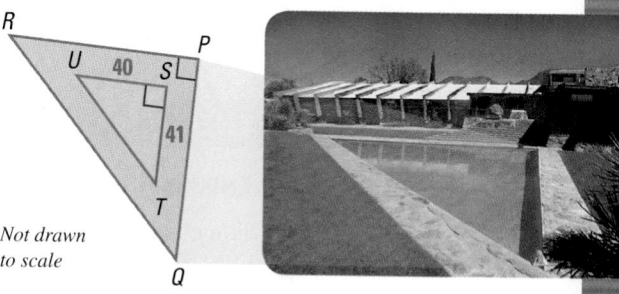

Not drawn to scale

a. Find the area of △*STU*.

b. In the diagram, △*PQR* ~ △*STU*, and the scale factor of the two triangles is 1.3 : 1. Find the perimeter of △*PQR*.

c. Find the area of △*PQR*. Then find the area of the path around the pool.

6. GRIDDED ANSWER In trapezoid *ABCD*, $\overline{AB} \parallel \overline{CD}$, $m\angle D = 90°$, $AD = 5$ inches, and $CD = 3 \cdot AB$. The area of trapezoid *ABCD* is 1250 square inches. Find the length (in inches) of $\overline{CD}$.

7. EXTENDED RESPONSE In the diagram below, △*EFH* is an isosceles right triangle, and △*FGH* is an equilateral triangle.

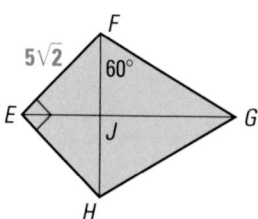

a. Find *FH*. *Explain* your reasoning.

b. Find *EG*. *Explain* your reasoning.

c. Find the area of *EFGH*.

11.4 Circumference and Arc Length

Before	You found the circumference of a circle.
Now	You will find arc lengths and other measures.
Why?	So you can find a running distance, as in Example 5.

Key Vocabulary
• circumference
• arc length
• radius, *p. 651*
• diameter, *p. 651*
• measure of an arc, *p. 659*

The **circumference** of a circle is the distance around the circle. For all circles, the ratio of the circumference to the diameter is the same. This ratio is known as π, or *pi*. In Chapter 1, you used 3.14 to approximate the value of π. Throughout this chapter, you should use the π key on a calculator, then round to the hundredths place unless instructed otherwise.

THEOREM
For Your Notebook

THEOREM 11.8 Circumference of a Circle

The circumference C of a circle is $C = \pi d$ or $C = 2\pi r$, where d is the diameter of the circle and r is the radius of the circle.

Justification: Ex. 2, p. 769

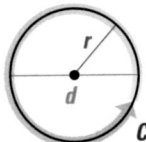

$C = \pi d = 2\pi r$

EXAMPLE 1 Use the formula for circumference

Find the indicated measure.

a. Circumference of a circle with radius 9 centimeters

b. Radius of a circle with circumference 26 meters

Solution

a. $C = 2\pi r$ Write circumference formula.

      $= 2 \cdot \pi \cdot 9$ Substitute 9 for *r*.

      $= 18\pi$ Simplify.

      ≈ 56.55 Use a calculator.

   ▶ The circumference is about 56.55 centimeters.

> **ANOTHER WAY**
> You can give an exact measure in terms of π. In Example 1, part (a), the exact circumference is 18π. The exact radius in Example 1, part (b) is $\frac{26}{2\pi}$, or $\frac{13}{\pi}$.

b. $C = 2\pi r$ Write circumference formula.

    $26 = 2\pi r$ Substitute 26 for *C*.

    $\dfrac{26}{2\pi} = r$ Divide each side by 2π.

    $4.14 \approx r$ Use a calculator.

   ▶ The radius is about 4.14 meters.

EXAMPLE 2 **Use circumference to find distance traveled**

TIRE REVOLUTIONS The dimensions of a car tire are shown at the right. To the nearest foot, how far does the tire travel when it makes 15 revolutions?

5.5 in.

15 in.

5.5 in.

Solution

STEP 1 **Find** the diameter of the tire.

$d = 15 + 2(5.5) = 26$ in.

STEP 2 **Find** the circumference of the tire.

$C = \pi d = \pi(26) \approx 81.68$ in.

STEP 3 **Find** the distance the tire travels in 15 revolutions. In one revolution, the tire travels a distance equal to its circumference. In 15 revolutions, the tire travels a distance equal to 15 times its circumference.

Distance traveled	=	Number of revolutions	·	Circumference

$\approx 15 \cdot 81.68$ in.

$= 1225.2$ in.

AVOID ERRORS
Always pay attention to units. In Example 2, you need to convert units to get a correct answer.

STEP 4 **Use** unit analysis. Change 1225.2 inches to feet.

$1225.2 \text{ in.} \cdot \dfrac{1 \text{ ft}}{12 \text{ in.}} = 102.1 \text{ ft}$

▶ The tire travels approximately 102 feet.

✔ **GUIDED PRACTICE** for Examples 1 and 2

1. Find the circumference of a circle with diameter 5 inches. Find the diameter of a circle with circumference 17 feet.

2. A car tire has a diameter of 28 inches. How many revolutions does the tire make while traveling 500 feet?

ARC LENGTH An **arc length** is a portion of the circumference of a circle. You can use the measure of the arc (in degrees) to find its length (in linear units).

COROLLARY *For Your Notebook*

ARC LENGTH COROLLARY

In a circle, the ratio of the length of a given arc to the circumference is equal to the ratio of the measure of the arc to 360°.

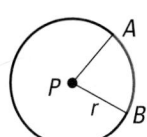

$\dfrac{\text{Arc length of } \overset{\frown}{AB}}{2\pi r} = \dfrac{m\overset{\frown}{AB}}{360°}$, or Arc length of $\overset{\frown}{AB} = \dfrac{m\overset{\frown}{AB}}{360°} \cdot 2\pi r$

EXAMPLE 3 Find arc lengths

Find the length of each red arc.

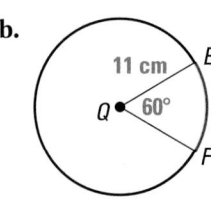

a.

b.

c.

INTERPRET DIAGRAMS

In Example 3, $\overset{\frown}{AB}$ and $\overset{\frown}{EF}$ have the same measure. However, they have different lengths because they are in circles with different circumferences.

Solution

a. Arc length of $\overset{\frown}{AB} = \dfrac{60°}{360°} \cdot 2\pi(8) \approx 8.38$ centimeters

b. Arc length of $\overset{\frown}{EF} = \dfrac{60°}{360°} \cdot 2\pi(11) \approx 11.52$ centimeters

c. Arc length of $\overset{\frown}{GH} = \dfrac{120°}{360°} \cdot 2\pi(11) \approx 23.04$ centimeters

EXAMPLE 4 Use arc lengths to find measures

Find the indicated measure.

a. Circumference C of $\odot Z$

b. $m\overset{\frown}{RS}$

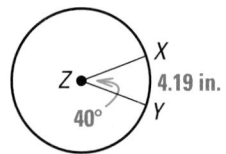

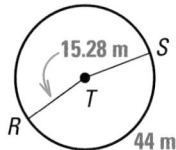

Solution

a.
$$\frac{\text{Arc length of } \overset{\frown}{XY}}{C} = \frac{m\overset{\frown}{XY}}{360°}$$

$$\frac{4.19}{C} = \frac{40°}{360°}$$

$$\frac{4.19}{C} = \frac{1}{9}$$

▶ 37.71 in. $= C$

b.
$$\frac{\text{Arc length of } \overset{\frown}{RS}}{2\pi r} = \frac{m\overset{\frown}{RS}}{360°}$$

$$\frac{44}{2\pi(15.28)} = \frac{m\overset{\frown}{RS}}{360°}$$

$$360° \cdot \frac{44}{2\pi(15.28)} = m\overset{\frown}{RS}$$

▶ $165° \approx m\overset{\frown}{RS}$

✓ **GUIDED PRACTICE** for Examples 3 and 4

Find the indicated measure.

3. Length of $\overset{\frown}{PQ}$

4. Circumference of $\odot N$

5. Radius of $\odot G$

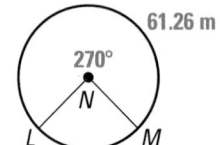

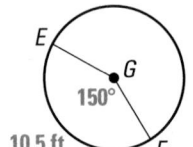

EXAMPLE 5 **Use arc length to find distances**

TRACK The curves at the ends of the track shown are 180° arcs of circles. The radius of the arc for a runner on the red path shown is 36.8 meters. About how far does this runner travel to go once around the track? Round to the nearest tenth of a meter.

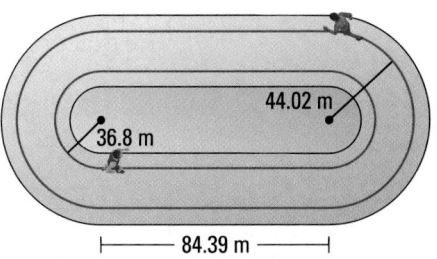

Solution

The arc length of a semicircle is half the circumference of the circle with the same radius. So, the arc length of a semicircle is $\frac{1}{2} \cdot 2\pi r$, or πr.

The path of a runner is made of two straight sections and two semicircles. To find the total distance, find the sum of the lengths of each part.

$$\text{Distance} = \begin{array}{c} 2 \cdot \text{Length of each} \\ \text{straight section} \end{array} + \begin{array}{c} 2 \cdot \text{Length of} \\ \text{each semicircle} \end{array}$$

$$= 2(84.39) + 2 \cdot \left(\frac{1}{2} \cdot 2\pi \cdot 36.8 \right)$$

$$\approx 400.0 \text{ meters}$$

▶ The runner on the red path travels about 400 meters.

Animated **Geometry** at classzone.com

✓ **GUIDED PRACTICE** for Example 5

6. In Example 5, the radius of the arc for a runner on the blue path is 44.02 meters, as shown in the diagram. About how far does this runner travel to go once around the track? Round to the nearest tenth of a meter.

11.4 EXERCISES

○ = **WORKED-OUT SOLUTIONS**
on p. WS15 for Exs. 23, 25, and 35

★ = **STANDARDIZED TEST PRACTICE**
Exs. 2, 31, 32, and 38

SKILL PRACTICE

In Exercises 1 and 2, refer to the diagram of ⊙P shown.

1. **VOCABULARY** Copy and complete the equation: $\dfrac{?}{2\pi r} = \dfrac{m\widehat{AB}}{?}$.

2. ★ **WRITING** *Describe* the difference between the *arc measure* and the *arc length* of $\widehat{AB}$.

EXAMPLE 1
on p. 746
for Exs. 3–7

USING CIRCUMFERENCE Use the diagram to find the indicated measure.

3. Find the circumference.   4. Find the circumference.   5. Find the radius.

 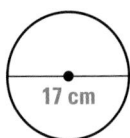 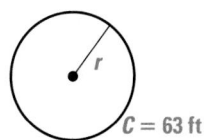

FINDING EXACT MEASURES Find the indicated measure.

6. The exact circumference of a circle with diameter 5 inches

7. The exact radius of a circle with circumference 28π meters

EXAMPLE 2
on p. 747
for Exs. 8–10

FINDING CIRCUMFERENCE Find the circumference of the red circle.

8.
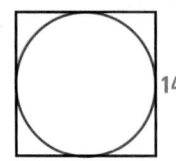

9.
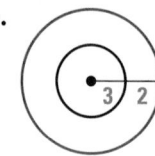

10.
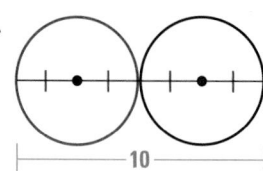

EXAMPLE 3
on p. 748
for Exs. 11–20

FINDING ARC LENGTHS Find the length of $\overarc{AB}$.

11.
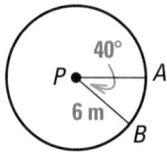

12.
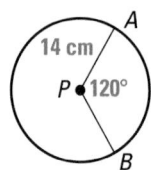

13.
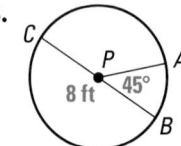

14. **ERROR ANALYSIS** A student says that two arcs from different circles have the same arc length if their central angles have the same measure. *Explain* the error in the student's reasoning.

FINDING MEASURES In $\odot P$ shown at the right, $\angle QPR \cong \angle RPS$. Find the indicated measure.

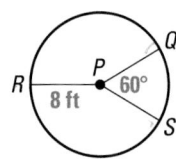

15. $m\overarc{QRS}$ 16. Length of $\overarc{QRS}$ 17. $m\overarc{QR}$

18. $m\overarc{RSQ}$ 19. Length of $\overarc{QR}$ 20. Length of $\overarc{RSQ}$

EXAMPLE 4
on p. 748
for Exs. 21–23

USING ARC LENGTH Find the indicated measure.

21. $m\overarc{AB}$ 22. Circumference of $\odot Q$ **23.** Radius of $\odot Q$

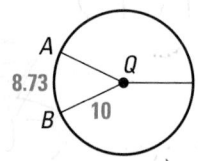

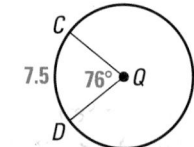

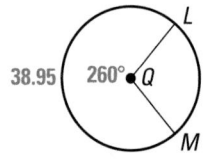

EXAMPLE 5
on p. 749
for Exs. 24–25

FINDING PERIMETERS Find the perimeter of the shaded region.

24.
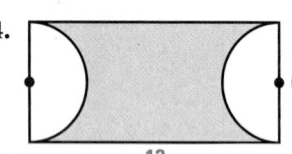

25.
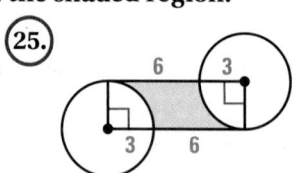

COORDINATE GEOMETRY The equation of a circle is given. Find the circumference of the circle. Write the circumference in terms of π.

26. $x^2 + y^2 = 16$ 27. $(x + 2)^2 + (y - 3)^2 = 9$ 28. $x^2 + y^2 = 18$

29. **xy ALGEBRA** Solve the formula $C = 2\pi r$ for r. Solve the formula $C = \pi d$ for d. Use the rewritten formulas to find r and d when $C = 26\pi$.

◯ = **WORKED-OUT SOLUTIONS**
on p. WS1

★ = **STANDARDIZED**
TEST PRACTICE

30. FINDING VALUES In the table below, $\overset{\frown}{AB}$ refers to the arc of a circle. Copy and complete the table.

Radius	?	2	0.8	4.2	?	$4\sqrt{2}$
$m\overset{\frown}{AB}$	45°	60°	?	183°	90°	?
Length of $\overset{\frown}{AB}$	4	?	0.3	?	3.22	2.86

31. ★ SHORT RESPONSE Suppose $\overset{\frown}{EF}$ is an arc on a circle with radius r. Let $x°$ be the measure of $\overset{\frown}{EF}$. *Describe* the effect on the length of $\overset{\frown}{EF}$ if you (a) double the radius of the circle, and (b) double the measure of $\overset{\frown}{EF}$.

32. ★ MULTIPLE CHOICE In the diagram, $\overline{WY}$ and $\overline{XZ}$ are diameters of $\odot T$, and $WY = XZ = 6$. If $m\overset{\frown}{XY} = 140°$, what is the length of $\overset{\frown}{YZ}$?

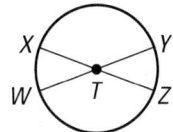

(A) $\frac{2}{3}\pi$ **(B)** $\frac{4}{3}\pi$ **(C)** 6π **(D)** 4π

33. CHALLENGE Find the circumference of a circle inscribed in a rhombus with diagonals that are 12 centimeters and 16 centimeters long. *Explain*.

34. FINDING CIRCUMFERENCE In the diagram, the measure of the shaded red angle is 30°. The arc length a is 2. *Explain* how to find the circumference of the blue circle without finding the radius of either the red or the blue circles.

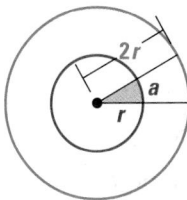

PROBLEM SOLVING

35. TREES A group of students wants to find the diameter of the trunk of a young sequoia tree. The students wrap a rope around the tree trunk, then measure the length of rope needed to wrap one time around the trunk. This length is 21 feet 8 inches. *Explain* how they can use this length to estimate the diameter of the tree trunk to the nearest half foot.

@HomeTutor for problem solving help at classzone.com

36. INSCRIBED SQUARE A square with side length 6 units is inscribed in a circle so that all four vertices are on the circle. Draw a sketch to represent this problem. Find the circumference of the circle.

@HomeTutor for problem solving help at classzone.com

EXAMPLE 2
on p. 747
for Ex. 37

37. MEASURING WHEEL As shown, a measuring wheel is used to calculate the length of a path. The diameter of the wheel is 8 inches. The wheel rotates 87 times along the length of the path. About how long is the path?

38. ★ EXTENDED RESPONSE A motorized scooter has a chain drive. The chain goes around the front and rear sprockets.

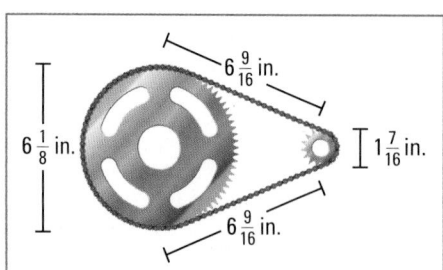

a. About how long is the chain? *Explain.*

b. Each sprocket has teeth that grip the chain. There are 76 teeth on the larger sprocket, and 15 teeth on the smaller sprocket. About how many teeth are gripping the chain at any given time? *Explain.*

39. SCIENCE Over 2000 years ago, the Greek scholar Eratosthenes estimated Earth's circumference by assuming that the Sun's rays are parallel. He chose a day when the Sun shone straight down into a well in the city of Syene. At noon, he measured the angle the Sun's rays made with a vertical stick in the city of Alexandria. Eratosthenes assumed that the distance from Syene to Alexandria was equal to about 575 miles.

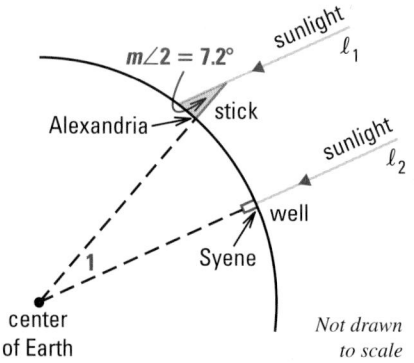

Find $m\angle 1$. Then estimate Earth's circumference.

CHALLENGE Suppose $\overline{AB}$ is divided into four congruent segments, and semicircles with radius r are drawn.

40. What is the sum of the four arc lengths if the radius of each arc is r?

41. Suppose that $\overline{AB}$ is divided into n congruent segments and that semicircles are drawn, as shown. What will the sum of the arc lengths be for 8 segments? for 16 segments? for n segments? *Explain* your thinking.

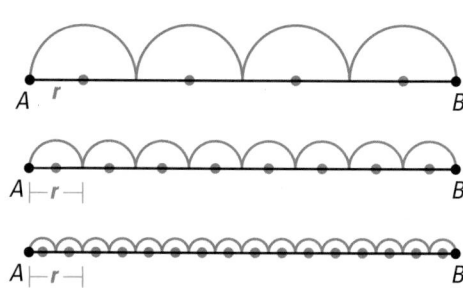

MIXED REVIEW

PREVIEW
Prepare for
Lesson 11.5 in
Exs. 42–45.

Find the area of a circle with radius r. Round to the nearest hundredth. *(p. 49)*

42. $r = 6$ cm

43. $r = 4.2$ in.

44. $r = 8\frac{3}{4}$ mi

45. $r = 1\frac{3}{8}$ in.

Find the value of x. *(p. 689)*

46.

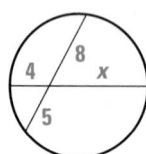

47.

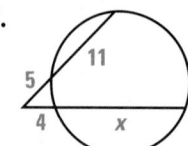

48.

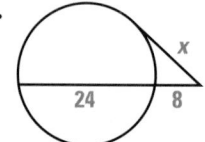

Geometry on a Sphere

GOAL Compare Euclidean and spherical geometries.

Key Vocabulary
• **great circle**

In Euclidean geometry, a plane is a flat surface that extends without end in all directions. A line in the plane is a set of points that extends without end in two opposite directions. Geometry on a sphere is different.

In *spherical geometry*, a plane is the surface of a sphere. A line is defined as a **great circle**, which is a circle on the sphere whose center is the center of the sphere.

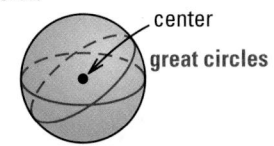

KEY CONCEPT *For Your Notebook*

Euclidean Geometry

Plane *P* contains line ℓ and point *A* not on the line ℓ.

Spherical Geometry

Sphere *S* contains great circle *m* and point *A* not on *m*. Great circle *m* is a line.

HISTORY NOTE

Spherical geometry is sometimes called *Riemann geometry* after Bernhard Riemann, who wrote the first description of it in 1854.

Some properties and postulates in Euclidean geometry are true in spherical geometry. Others are not, or are true only under certain circumstances. For example, in Euclidean geometry, Postulate 5 states that through any two points there exists exactly one line. On a sphere, this postulate is true only for points that are not the endpoints of a diameter of the sphere.

EXAMPLE 1 **Compare Euclidean and spherical geometry**

Tell whether the following postulate in Euclidean geometry is also true in spherical geometry. Draw a diagram to support your answer.

Parallel Postulate: If there is a line ℓ and a point *A* not on the line, then there is exactly one line through the point *A* parallel to the given line ℓ.

Solution

Parallel lines do not intersect. The sphere shows a line ℓ (a great circle) and a point *A* not on ℓ. Several lines are drawn through *A*. Each great circle containing *A* intersects ℓ. So, there can be no line parallel to ℓ. The parallel postulate is not true in spherical geometry.

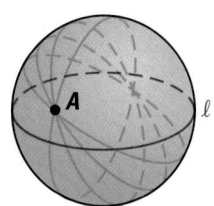

DISTANCES In Euclidean geometry, there is exactly one distance that can be measured between any two points. On a sphere, there are two distances that can be measured between two points. These distances are the lengths of the major and minor arcs of the great circle drawn through the points.

EXAMPLE 2 Find distances on a sphere

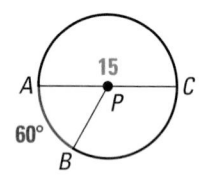
The diameter of the sphere shown is 15, and $m\overarc{AB} = 60°$. Find the distances between A and B.

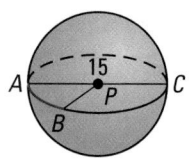

Solution

Find the lengths of the minor arc $\overarc{AB}$ and the major arc $\overarc{ACB}$ of the great circle shown. In each case, let x be the arc length.

$$\frac{\text{Arc length of } \overarc{AB}}{2\pi r} = \frac{m\overarc{AB}}{360°} \qquad\qquad \frac{\text{Arc length of } \overarc{ACB}}{2\pi r} = \frac{m\overarc{ACB}}{360°}$$

$$\frac{x}{15\pi} = \frac{60°}{360°} \qquad\qquad\qquad \frac{x}{15\pi} = \frac{360° - 60°}{360°}$$

$$x = 2.5\pi \qquad\qquad\qquad\qquad x = 12.5\pi$$

▶ The distances are 2.5π and 12.5π.

PRACTICE

1. **WRITING** Lines of latitude and longitude are used to identify positions on Earth. Which of the lines shown in the figure are great circles? Which are not? *Explain* your reasoning.

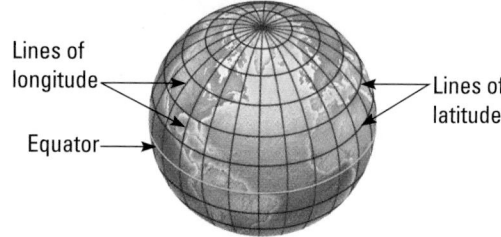

Lines of longitude

Lines of latitude

Equator

2. **COMPARING GEOMETRIES** Draw sketches to show that there is more than one line through the endpoints of a diameter of a sphere, but only one line through two points that are *not* endpoints of a diameter.

3. **COMPARING GEOMETRIES** The following statement is true in Euclidean geometry: If two lines intersect, then their intersection is exactly one point. Rewrite this statement to be true for lines on a sphere.

FINDING DISTANCES Use the diagram and the given arc measure to find the distances between points A and B. Leave your answers in terms of π.

4. $m\overarc{AB} = 120°$

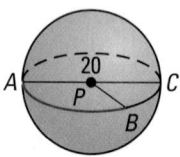

5. $m\overarc{AB} = 90°$

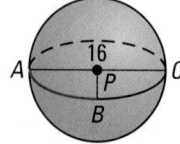

6. $m\overarc{AB} = 140°$

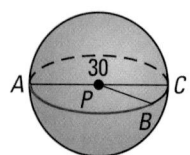

11.5 Areas of Circles and Sectors

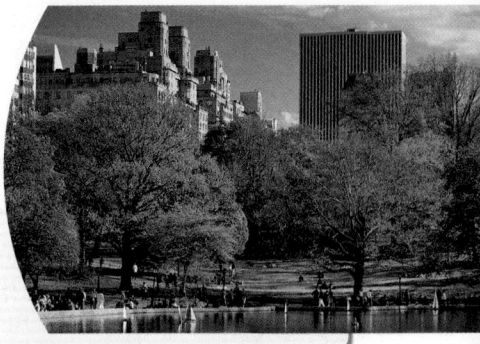

Before	You found circumferences of circles.
Now	You will find the areas of circles and sectors.
Why	So you can estimate walking distances, as in Ex. 38.

Key Vocabulary
• sector of a circle

In Chapter 1, you used the formula for the area of a circle. This formula is presented below as Theorem 11.9.

THEOREM *For Your Notebook*

THEOREM 11.9 Area of a Circle

The area of a circle is π times the square of the radius.

Justification: Ex. 43, p. 761; Ex. 3, p. 769

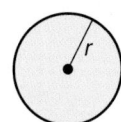

$A = \pi r^2$

EXAMPLE 1 Use the formula for area of a circle

Find the indicated measure.

a. Area

$r = 2.5$ cm

b. Diameter

$A = 113.1$ cm^2

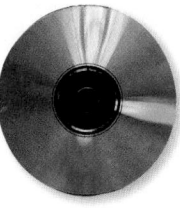

Solution

a. $A = \pi r^2$ — **Write formula for the area of a circle.**

$= \pi \cdot (2.5)^2$ — **Substitute 2.5 for *r*.**

$= 6.25\pi$ — **Simplify.**

≈ 19.63 — **Use a calculator.**

▶ The area of $\odot A$ is about 19.63 square centimeters.

b. $A = \pi r^2$ — **Write formula for the area of a circle.**

$113.1 = \pi r^2$ — **Substitute 113.1 for *A*.**

$\dfrac{113.1}{\pi} = r^2$ — **Divide each side by π.**

$6 \approx r$ — **Find the positive square root of each side.**

▶ The radius is about 6 cm, so the diameter is about 12 centimeters.

SECTORS A **sector of a circle** is the region bounded by two radii of the circle and their intercepted arc. In the diagram below, sector APB is bounded by $\overline{AP}$, $\overline{BP}$, and $\widehat{AB}$. Theorem 11.10 gives a method for finding the area of a sector.

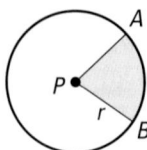

THEOREM *For Your Notebook*

THEOREM 11.10 Area of a Sector

The ratio of the area of a sector of a circle to the area of the whole circle (πr^2) is equal to the ratio of the measure of the intercepted arc to 360°.

$$\frac{\text{Area of sector } APB}{\pi r^2} = \frac{m\widehat{AB}}{360°}, \text{ or Area of sector } APB = \frac{m\widehat{AB}}{360°} \cdot \pi r^2$$

EXAMPLE 2   **Find areas of sectors**

Find the areas of the sectors formed by $\angle UTV$.

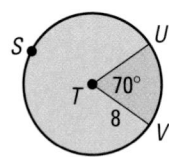

Solution

STEP 1 **Find** the measures of the minor and major arcs.

Because $m\angle UTV = 70°$, $m\widehat{UV} = 70°$ and $m\widehat{USV} = 360° - 70° = 290°$.

STEP 2 **Find** the areas of the small and large sectors.

$$\text{Area of small sector} = \frac{m\widehat{UV}}{360°} \cdot \pi r^2 \qquad \text{Write formula for area of a sector.}$$

$$= \frac{70°}{360°} \cdot \pi \cdot 8^2 \qquad \text{Substitute.}$$

$$\approx 39.10 \qquad \text{Use a calculator.}$$

$$\text{Area of large sector} = \frac{m\widehat{USV}}{360°} \cdot \pi r^2 \qquad \text{Write formula for area of a sector.}$$

$$= \frac{290°}{360°} \cdot \pi \cdot 8^2 \qquad \text{Substitute.}$$

$$\approx 161.97 \qquad \text{Use a calculator.}$$

▶ The areas of the small and large sectors are about 39.10 square units and 161.97 square units, respectively.

✓ **GUIDED PRACTICE**   for Examples 1 and 2

Use the diagram to find the indicated measure.

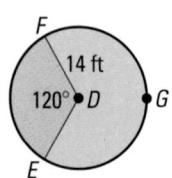

1. Area of $\odot D$

2. Area of red sector

3. Area of blue sector

EXAMPLE 3   **Use the Area of a Sector Theorem**

Use the diagram to find the area of ⊙V.

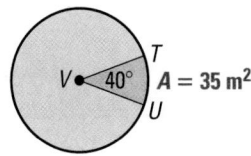

Solution

$$\text{Area of sector } TVU = \frac{m\overset{\frown}{TU}}{360°} \cdot \text{Area of } \odot V \qquad \text{Write formula for area of a sector.}$$

$$35 = \frac{40°}{360°} \cdot \text{Area of } \odot V \qquad \text{Substitute.}$$

$$315 = \text{Area of } \odot V \qquad \text{Solve for Area of } \odot V.$$

▶ The area of ⊙V is 315 square meters.

EXAMPLE 4   **Standardized Test Practice**

A rectangular wall has an entrance cut into it. You want to paint the wall. To the nearest square foot, what is the area of the region you need to paint?

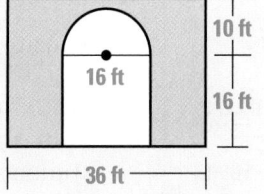

A 357 ft^2 **B** 479 ft^2

C 579 ft^2 **D** 936 ft^2

Solution

AVOID ERRORS
Use the radius (8 ft), not the diameter (16 ft) when you calculate the area of the semicircle.

The area you need to paint is the area of the rectangle minus the area of the entrance. The entrance can be divided into a **semicircle** and a **square**.

Area of wall	=	Area of rectangle	−	(Area of semicircle + Area of square)

$$= \qquad 36(26) \qquad - \qquad \left[\frac{180°}{360°} \cdot (\pi \cdot 8^2) + \quad 16^2\right]$$

$$= 936 - [32\pi + 256]$$

$$\approx 579.47$$

The area is about 579 square feet.

▶ The correct answer is C.   **A** **B** **C** **D**

✓ **GUIDED PRACTICE**   for Examples 3 and 4

4. Find the area of ⊙H.

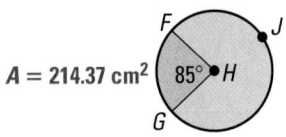

$A = 214.37$ cm^2

5. Find the area of the figure.

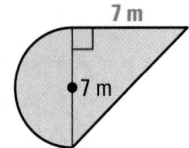

6. If you know the area and radius of a sector of a circle, can you find the measure of the intercepted arc? *Explain.*

11.5 EXERCISES

HOMEWORK KEY

○ = WORKED-OUT SOLUTIONS
on p. WS15 for Exs. 7, 17, and 39

★ = STANDARDIZED TEST PRACTICE
Exs. 2, 19, 40, and 42

SKILL PRACTICE

1. **VOCABULARY** Copy and complete: A _?_ of a circle is the region bounded by two radii of the circle and their intercepted arc.

2. ★ **WRITING** Suppose you double the arc measure of a sector in a given circle. Will the area of the sector also be doubled? *Explain.*

EXAMPLE 1
on p. 755
for Exs. 3–9

FINDING AREA Find the exact area of a circle with the given radius *r* or diameter *d*. Then find the area to the nearest hundredth.

3. *r* = 5 in.   4. *d* = 16 ft   5. *d* = 23 cm   6. *r* = 1.5 km

USING AREA In Exercises 7–9, find the indicated measure.

7. The area of a circle is 154 square meters. Find the radius.

8. The area of a circle is 380 square inches. Find the radius.

9. The area of a circle is 676π square centimeters. Find the diameter.

EXAMPLE 2
on p. 756
for Exs. 10–13

10. **ERROR ANALYSIS** In the diagram at the right, the area of ⊙Z is 48 square feet. A student writes a proportion to find the area of sector *XZY*. *Describe* and correct the error in writing the proportion. Then find the area of sector *XZY*.

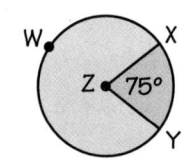

Let n be the area of sector XZY.

$$\frac{n}{360°} = \frac{48}{285°}$$

FINDING AREA OF SECTORS Find the areas of the sectors formed by ∠*DFE*.

11.
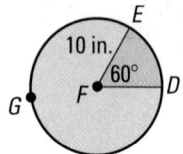

12.
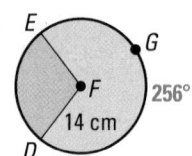

13.
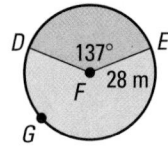

EXAMPLE 3
on p. 757
for Exs. 14–16

USING AREA OF A SECTOR Use the diagram to find the indicated measure.

14. Find the area of ⊙*M*.
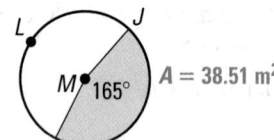

15. Find the area of ⊙*M*.
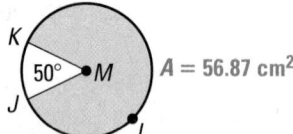

16. Find the radius of ⊙*M*.
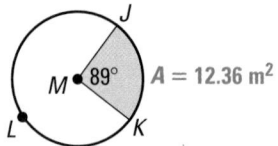

EXAMPLE 4
on p. 757
for Exs. 17–19

FINDING AREA Find the area of the shaded region.

17.
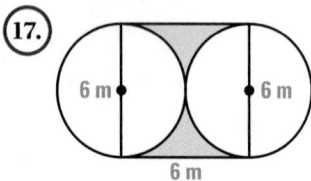

18.
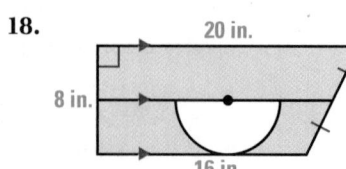

19. ★ **MULTIPLE CHOICE** The diagram shows the shape of a putting green at a miniature golf course. One part of the green is a sector of a circle. To the nearest square foot, what is the area of the putting green?

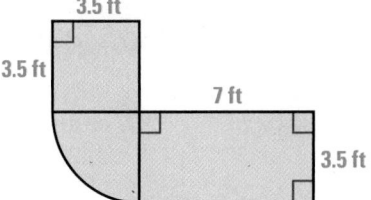

(A) 46 ft²   (B) 49 ft²

(C) 56 ft²   (D) 75 ft²

FINDING MEASURES The area of ⊙*M* is 260.67 square inches. The area of sector *KML* is 42 square inches. Find the indicated measure.

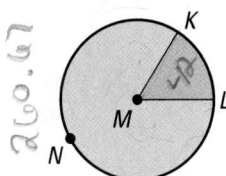

20. Radius of ⊙*M*

21. Circumference of ⊙*M*

22. $m\widehat{KL}$

23. Perimeter of blue region

24. Length of $\widehat{KL}$

25. Perimeter of red region

FINDING AREA Find the area of the shaded region.

26.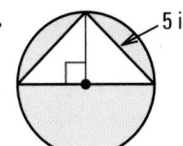

27.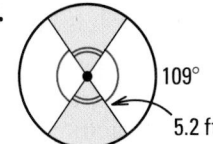

28.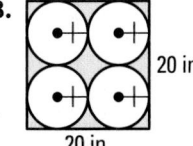

29.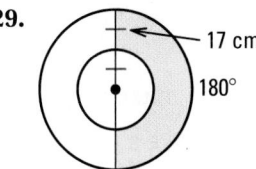

30.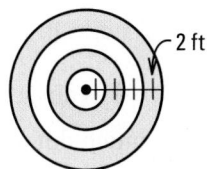

31.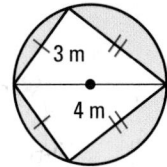

Animated Geometry at classzone.com

32. **TANGENT CIRCLES** In the diagram at the right, ⊙*Q* and ⊙*P* are tangent, and *P* lies on ⊙*Q*. The measure of $\widehat{RS}$ is 108°. Find the area of the red region, the area of the blue region, and the area of the yellow region. Leave your answers in terms of π.

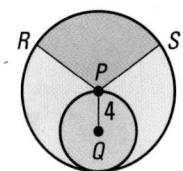

33. **SIMILARITY** Look back at the Perimeters of Similar Polygons Theorem on page 374 and the Areas of Similar Polygons Theorem on page 737. How would you rewrite these theorems to apply to circles? *Explain.*

34. **ERROR ANALYSIS** The ratio of the lengths of two arcs in a circle is 2:1. A student claims that the ratio of the areas of the sectors bounded by these arcs is 4:1, because $\left(\frac{2}{1}\right)^2 = \frac{4}{1}$. *Describe* and correct the error.

35. **DRAWING A DIAGRAM** A square is inscribed in a circle. The same square is also circumscribed about a smaller circle. Draw a diagram. Find the ratio of the area of the large circle to the area of the small circle.

36. **CHALLENGE** In the diagram at the right, $\widehat{FG}$ and $\widehat{EH}$ are arcs of concentric circles, and $\overline{EF}$ and $\overline{GH}$ lie on radii of the larger circle. Find the area of the shaded region.

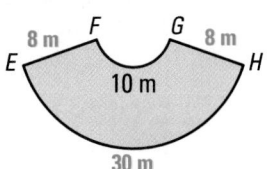

EXAMPLE 1
on p. 755
for Ex. 37

37. METEOROLOGY The *eye of a hurricane* is a relatively calm circular region in the center of the storm. The diameter of the eye is typically about 20 miles. If the eye of a hurricane is 20 miles in diameter, what is the area of the land that is underneath the eye?

@HomeTutor for problem solving help at classzone.com

38. WALKING The area of a circular pond is about 138,656 square feet. You are going to walk around the entire edge of the pond. About how far will you walk? Give your answer to the nearest foot.

@HomeTutor for problem solving help at classzone.com

(39.) CIRCLE GRAPH The table shows how students get to school.

  a. *Explain* why a circle graph is appropriate for the data.

  b. You will represent each method by a sector of a circle graph. Find the central angle to use for each sector. Then use a protractor and a compass to construct the graph. Use a radius of 2 inches.

  c. Find the area of each sector in your graph.

Method	% of Students
Bus	65%
Walk	25%
Other	10%

40. ★ SHORT RESPONSE It takes about $\frac{1}{4}$ cup of dough to make a tortilla with a 6 inch diameter. How much dough does it take to make a tortilla with a 12 inch diameter? *Explain* your reasoning.

41. HIGHWAY SIGNS A new typeface has been designed to make highway signs more readable. One change was to redesign the form of the letters to increase the space inside letters.

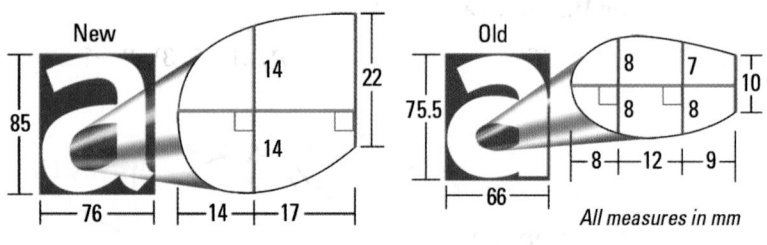

All measures in mm

  a. Estimate the interior area for the old and the new "a." Then find the percent increase in interior area.

  b. Do you think the change in interior area is just a result of a change in height and width of the letter *a*? *Explain*.

42. ★ EXTENDED RESPONSE A circular pizza with a 12 inch diameter is enough for you and 2 friends. You want to buy pizza for yourself and 7 friends. A 10 inch diameter pizza with one topping costs $6.99 and a 14 inch diameter pizza with one topping costs $12.99. How many 10 inch and 14 inch pizzas should you buy in each situation below? *Explain*.

  a. You want to spend as little money as possible.

  b. You want to have three pizzas, each with a different topping.

  c. You want to have as much of the thick outer crust as possible.

43. JUSTIFYING THEOREM 11.9 You can follow the steps below to justify the formula for the area of a circle with radius *r*.

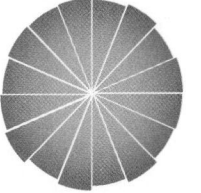

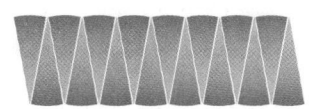

Divide a circle into 16 congruent sectors. Cut out the sectors.

Rearrange the 16 sectors to form a shape resembling a parallelogram.

a. Write expressions in terms of *r* for the approximate height and base of the parallelogram. Then write an expression for its area.

b. *Explain* how your answers to part (a) justify Theorem 11.9.

44. CHALLENGE Semicircles with diameters equal to the three sides of a right triangle are drawn, as shown. Prove that the sum of the areas of the two shaded crescents equals the area of the triangle.

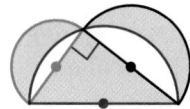

MIXED REVIEW

PREVIEW

Prepare for Lesson 11.6 In Exs. 45–47.

Triangle *DEG* is isosceles with altitude $\overline{DF}$. Find the given measurement. *Explain* your reasoning. *(p. 319)*

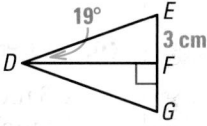

45. $m\angle DFG$ **46.** $m\angle FDG$ **47.** FG

Sketch the indicated figure. Draw all of its lines of symmetry. *(p. 619)*

48. Isosceles trapezoid **49.** Regular hexagon

Graph $\triangle ABC$. Then find its area. *(p. 720)*

50. $A(2, 2)$, $B(9, 2)$, $C(4, 16)$ **51.** $A(-8, 3)$, $B(-3, 3)$, $C(-1, -10)$

QUIZ *for Lessons 11.4–11.5*

Find the indicated measure. *(p. 746)*

1. Length of $\overarc{AB}$

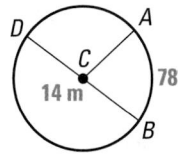

2. Circumference of $\odot F$

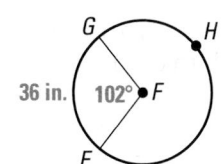

3. Radius of $\odot L$

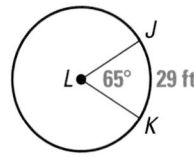

Find the area of the shaded region. *(p. 755)*

4.

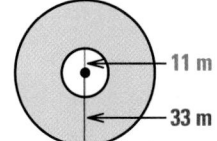

5.

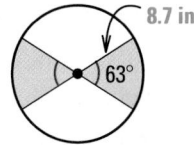

6.

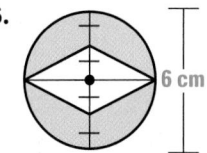

EXTRA PRACTICE for Lesson 11.5, p. 917   **ONLINE QUIZ** at classzone.com   **761**

11.6 Areas of Regular Polygons

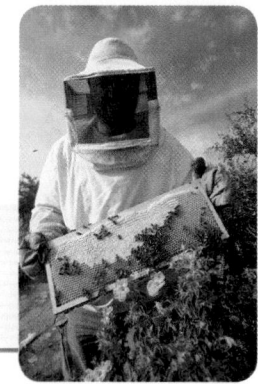

Before	You found areas of circles.
Now	You will find areas of regular polygons inscribed in circles.
Why?	So you can understand the structure of a honeycomb, as in Ex. 44.

Key Vocabulary
• center of a polygon
• radius of a polygon
• apothem of a polygon
• central angle of a regular polygon

The diagram shows a regular polygon inscribed in a circle. The **center of the polygon** and the **radius of the polygon** are the center and the radius of its circumscribed circle.

The distance from the center to any side of the polygon is called the **apothem of the polygon**. The apothem is the height to the base of an isosceles triangle that has two radii as legs.

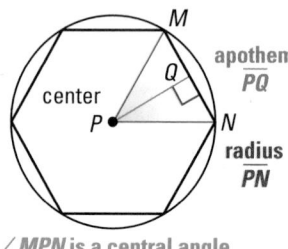

∠*MPN* is a central angle.

A **central angle of a regular polygon** is an angle formed by two radii drawn to consecutive vertices of the polygon. To find the measure of each central angle, divide 360° by the number of sides.

EXAMPLE 1 **Find angle measures in a regular polygon**

In the diagram, *ABCDE* is a regular pentagon inscribed in ⊙*F*. Find each angle measure.

   a. *m*∠*AFB*   **b.** *m*∠*AFG*   **c.** *m*∠*GAF*

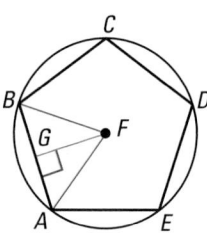

READ DIAGRAMS
A segment whose length is *the apothem* is sometimes called *an apothem*. The segment is an altitude of an isosceles triangle, so it is also a median and angle bisector of the isosceles triangle.

Solution

  a. ∠*AFB* is a central angle, so *m*∠*AFB* = $\frac{360°}{5}$, or 72°.

  b. $\overline{FG}$ is an apothem, which makes it an altitude of isosceles △*AFB*. So, $\overline{FG}$ bisects ∠*AFB* and *m*∠*AFG* = $\frac{1}{2}$ *m*∠*AFB* = 36°.

  c. The sum of the measures of right △*GAF* is 180°. So, 90° + 36° + *m*∠*GAF* = 180°, and *m*∠*GAF* = 54°.

✓ **GUIDED PRACTICE**   for Example 1

In the diagram, *WXYZ* is a square inscribed in ⊙*P*.

  1. Identify the center, a radius, an apothem, and a central angle of the polygon.

  2. Find *m*∠*XPY*, *m*∠*XPQ*, and *m*∠*PXQ*.

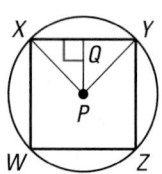

AREA OF AN *n*-GON You can find the area of any regular *n*-gon by dividing it into congruent triangles.

A = Area of one triangle • Number of triangles

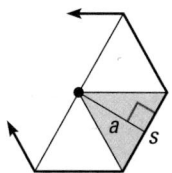

READ DIAGRAMS
In this book, a point shown inside a regular polygon marks the center of the circle that can be circumscribed about the polygon.

$$= \left(\frac{1}{2} \cdot s \cdot a\right) \cdot n$$ 　 **Base of triangle is *s* and height of triangle is *a*. Number of triangles is *n*.**

$$= \frac{1}{2} \cdot a \cdot (n \cdot s)$$ 　 **Commutative and Associative Properties of Equality**

$$= \frac{1}{2} a \cdot P$$ 　 **There are *n* congruent sides of length *s*, so perimeter *P* is *n* · *s*.**

THEOREM 　　　　　　　　　　　　　　　*For Your Notebook*

THEOREM 11.11　Area of a Regular Polygon

The area of a regular *n*-gon with side length *s* is one half the product of the apothem *a* and the perimeter *P*, so $A = \frac{1}{2}aP$, or $A = \frac{1}{2}a \cdot ns$.

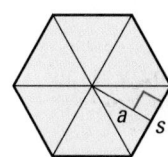

EXAMPLE 2 　 **Find the area of a regular polygon**

DECORATING You are decorating the top of a table by covering it with small ceramic tiles. The table top is a regular octagon with 15 inch sides and a radius of about 19.6 inches. What is the area you are covering?

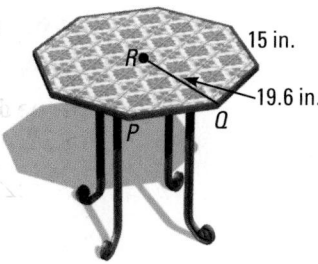

15 in.
19.6 in.

Solution

STEP 1 　 **Find** the perimeter *P* of the table top. An octagon has 8 sides, so *P* = 8(15) = 120 inches.

STEP 2 　 **Find** the apothem *a*. The apothem is height *RS* of △*PQR*. Because △*PQR* is isosceles, altitude $\overline{RS}$ bisects $\overline{QP}$.

So, $QS = \frac{1}{2}(QP) = \frac{1}{2}(15) = 7.5$ inches.

To find *RS*, use the Pythagorean Theorem for △*RQS*.

$a = RS \approx \sqrt{19.6^2 - 7.5^2} = \sqrt{327.91} \approx 18.108$

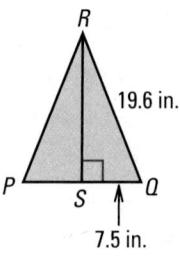

R
19.6 in.
P 　 *S* 　 *Q*
7.5 in.

ROUNDING
In general, your answer will be more accurate if you avoid rounding until the last step. Round your final answers to the nearest tenth unless you are told otherwise.

STEP 3 　 **Find** the area *A* of the table top.

$A = \frac{1}{2}aP$ 　 **Formula for area of regular polygon**

$\approx \frac{1}{2}(18.108)(120)$ 　 **Substitute.**

≈ 1086.5 　 **Simplify.**

▶ So, the area you are covering with tiles is about 1086.5 square inches.

EXAMPLE 3   Find the perimeter and area of a regular polygon

A regular nonagon is inscribed in a circle with radius 4 units. Find the perimeter and area of the nonagon.

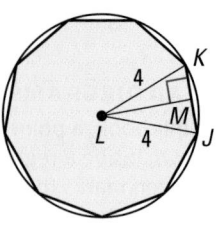

Solution

The measure of central $\angle JLK$ is $\dfrac{360°}{9}$, or 40°. Apothem $\overline{LM}$

bisects the central angle, so $m\angle KLM$ is 20°. To find the lengths of the legs, use trigonometric ratios for right $\triangle KLM$.

$$\sin 20° = \frac{MK}{LK} \qquad\qquad \cos 20° = \frac{LM}{LK}$$

$$\sin 20° = \frac{MK}{4} \qquad\qquad \cos 20° = \frac{LM}{4}$$

$$4 \cdot \sin 20° = MK \qquad\qquad 4 \cdot \cos 20° = LM$$

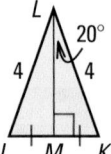

The regular nonagon has side length $s = 2MK = 2(4 \cdot \sin 20°) = 8 \cdot \sin 20°$ and apothem $a = LM = 4 \cdot \cos 20°$.

▶ So, the perimeter is $P = 9s = 9(8 \cdot \sin 20°) = 72 \cdot \sin 20° \approx 24.6$ units,

and the area is $A = \frac{1}{2}aP = \frac{1}{2}(4 \cdot \cos 20°)(72 \cdot \sin 20°) \approx 46.3$ square units.

✔ **GUIDED PRACTICE** | for Examples 2 and 3

Find the perimeter and the area of the regular polygon.

3.
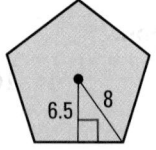

4.
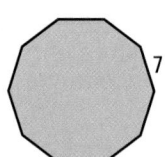

5.
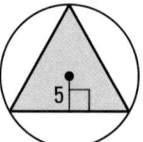

6. Which of Exercises 3–5 above can be solved using special right triangles?

CONCEPT SUMMARY   *For Your Notebook*

Finding Lengths in a Regular *n*-gon

To find the area of a regular *n*-gon with radius *r*, you may need to first find the apothem ***a*** or the side length ***s***.

You can use . . .	. . . when you know *n* and . . .	. . . as in . . .
Pythagorean Theorem: $\left(\dfrac{1}{2}s\right)^2 + a^2 = r^2$	Two measures: *r* and *a*, or *r* and *s*	Example 2 and Guided Practice Ex. 3.
Special Right Triangles	Any one measure: *r* or *a* or *s* **And** the value of *n* is 3, 4, or 6	Guided Practice Ex. 5.
Trigonometry	Any one measure: *r* or *a* or *s*	Example 3 and Guided Practice Exs. 4 and 5.

11.6 EXERCISES

HOMEWORK KEY

○ = **WORKED-OUT SOLUTIONS**
on p. WS15 for Exs. 7, 21, and 37

★ = **STANDARDIZED TEST PRACTICE**
Exs. 5, 18, 22, and 44

SKILL PRACTICE

VOCABULARY In Exercises 1–4, use the diagram shown.

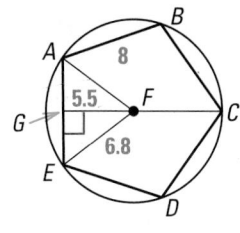

1. Identify the *center* of regular polygon *ABCDE*.

2. Identify a *central angle* of the polygon.

3. What is the *radius* of the polygon?

4. What is the *apothem*?

5. ★ **WRITING** *Explain* how to find the measure of a *central angle* of a regular polygon with *n* sides.

EXAMPLE 1
on p. 762
for Exs. 6–13

MEASURES OF CENTRAL ANGLES Find the measure of a central angle of a regular polygon with the given number of sides. Round answers to the nearest tenth of a degree, if necessary.

6. 10 sides ⑦ 18 sides 8. 24 sides 9. 7 sides

FINDING ANGLE MEASURES Find the given angle measure for the regular octagon shown.

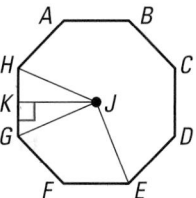

10. $m\angle GJH$

11. $m\angle GJK$

12. $m\angle KGJ$

13. $m\angle EJH$

EXAMPLE 2
on p. 763
for Exs. 14–17

FINDING AREA Find the area of the regular polygon.

14.
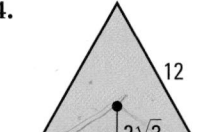

15.
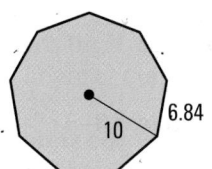

16.
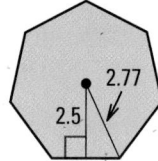

Animated Geometry at classzone.com

17. **ERROR ANALYSIS** *Describe* and correct the error in finding the area of the regular hexagon.

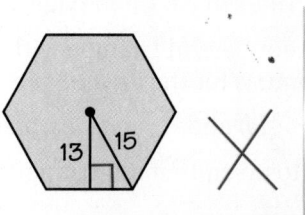

$$\sqrt{15^2 - 13^2} \approx 7.5$$

$$A = \frac{1}{2}a \cdot ns$$

$$A = \frac{1}{2}(13)(6)(7.5) = 292.5$$

EXAMPLE 3
on p. 764
for Exs. 18–25

18. ★ **MULTIPLE CHOICE** Which expression gives the apothem for a regular dodecagon with side length 8?

Ⓐ $a = \dfrac{4}{\tan 30°}$ Ⓑ $a = \dfrac{4}{\tan 15°}$ Ⓒ $a = \dfrac{8}{\tan 15°}$ Ⓓ $a = 8 \cdot \cos 15°$

PERIMETER AND AREA Find the perimeter and area of the regular polygon.

19.
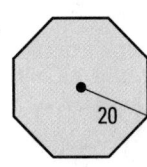
20

20.
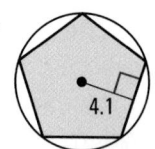
4.1

21.
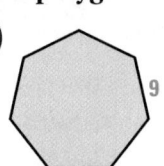
9

22. ★ **SHORT RESPONSE** The perimeter of a regular nonagon is 18 inches. Is that enough information to find the area? If so, find the area and *explain* your steps. If not, *explain* why not.

CHOOSE A METHOD Identify any unknown length(s) you need to know to find the area of the regular polygon. Which methods in the table on page 764 can you use to find those lengths? Choose a method and find the area.

23.
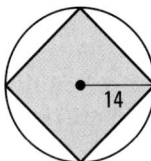
14

24.
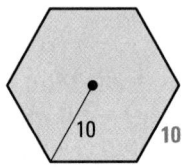
10   10

25.
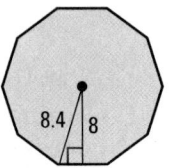
8.4   8

26. **INSCRIBED SQUARE** Find the area of the *unshaded* region in Exercise 23.

POLYGONS IN CIRCLES Find the area of the shaded region.

27.

12

28.
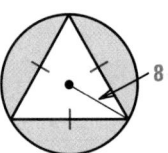
8

29.
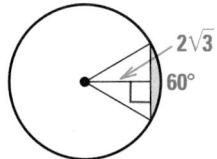
$2\sqrt{3}$
60°

30. **COORDINATE GEOMETRY** Find the area of a regular pentagon inscribed in a circle whose equation is given by $(x - 4)^2 + (y + 2)^2 = 25$.

REASONING Decide whether the statement is *true* or *false*. *Explain*.

31. The area of a regular *n*-gon of fixed radius *r* increases as *n* increases.

32. The apothem of a regular polygon is always less than the radius.

33. The radius of a regular polygon is always less than the side length.

34. **FORMULAS** In Exercise 44 on page 726, the formula $A = \dfrac{\sqrt{3}s^2}{4}$ for the area *A* of an equilateral triangle with side length *s* was developed. Show that the formulas for the area of a triangle and for the area of a regular polygon, $A = \frac{1}{2}bh$ and $A = \frac{1}{2}a \cdot ns$, also result in this formula when they are applied to an equilateral triangle with side length *s*.

35. **CHALLENGE** An equilateral triangle is shown inside a square inside a regular pentagon inside a regular hexagon. Write an expression for the exact area of the shaded regions in the figure. Then find the approximate area of the entire shaded region, rounded to the nearest whole unit.

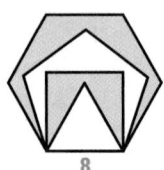
8

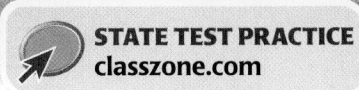
MULTIPLE CHOICE

5. In the diagram, J is the center of two circles, and K lies on $\overline{JL}$. Given $JL = 6$ and $KL = 2$, what is the ratio of the area of the smaller circle to the area of the larger circle?

Ⓐ $\sqrt{2} : \sqrt{3}$

Ⓑ $1 : 3$

Ⓒ $2 : 3$

Ⓓ $4 : 9$

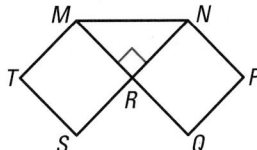

6. In the diagram, $TMRS$ and $RNPQ$ are congruent squares, and $\triangle MNR$ is a right triangle. What is the probability that a randomly chosen point on the diagram lies inside $\triangle MNR$?

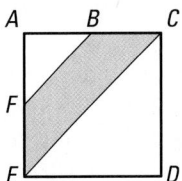

Ⓐ 0.2 Ⓑ 0.25

Ⓒ 0.5 Ⓓ 0.75

GRIDDED ANSWER

7. You are buying fertilizer for a lawn that is shaped like a parallelogram. Two sides of the parallelogram are each 300 feet long, and the perpendicular distance between these sides is 150 feet. One bag of fertilizer covers 5000 square feet and costs $14. How much (in dollars) will you spend?

8. In square $ACDE$, $ED = 2$, $AB = BC$, and $AF = FE$. What is the area (in square units) of the shaded region?

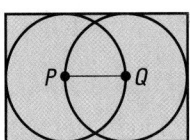

9. In the diagram, a rectangle's sides are tangent to two circles with centers at points P and Q. The circumference of each circle is 8π square units. What is the area (in square units) of the rectangle?

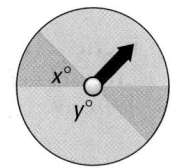

SHORT RESPONSE

10. You are designing a spinner for a board game. An arrow is attached to the center of a circle with diameter 7 inches. The arrow is spun until it stops. The arrow has an equally likely chance of stopping anywhere.

a. If $x° = 45°$, what is the probability that the arrow points to a red sector? *Explain.*

b. You want to change the spinner so the probability that the arrow points to a blue sector is half the probability that it points to a red sector. What values should you use for x and y? *Explain.*

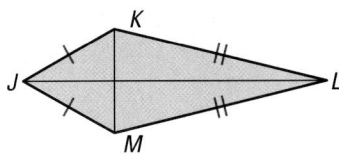

11. In quadrilateral $JKLM$, $JL = 3 \cdot KM$. The area of $JKLM$ is 54 square centimeters.

a. Find JL and KM.

b. Quadrilateral $NPQR$ is similar to $JKLM$, and its area is 486 square centimeters. Sketch $NPQR$ and its diagonals. Then find the length of $\overline{NQ}$. *Explain* your reasoning.

12 Surface Area and Volume of Solids

Before

In previous chapters, you learned the following skills, which you'll use in Chapter 12: properties of similar polygons, areas and perimeters of two-dimensional figures, and right triangle trigonometry.

Prerequisite Skills

VOCABULARY CHECK

1. Copy and complete: The area of a regular polygon is given by the formula $A = \underline{\ ?\ }$.

2. *Explain* what it means for two polygons to be similar.

SKILLS AND ALGEBRA CHECK

Use trigonometry to find the value of x. *(Review pp. 466, 473 for 12.2–12.5.)*

3.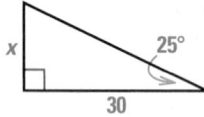

4.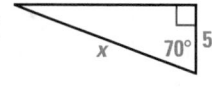

5.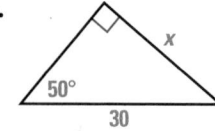

Find the circumference and area of the circle with the given dimension.
(Review pp. 746, 755 for 12.2–12.5.)

6. $r = 2$ m

7. $d = 3$ in.

8. $r = 2\sqrt{5}$ cm

@HomeTutor Prerequisite skills practice at classzone.com

In Chapter 12, you will apply the big ideas listed below and reviewed in the Chapter Summary on page 856. You will also use the key vocabulary listed below.

Big Ideas

① **Exploring solids and their properties**
② **Solving problems using surface area and volume**
③ **Connecting similarity to solids**

KEY VOCABULARY

- polyhedron, *p. 794* face, edge, vertex
- Platonic solids, *p. 796*
- cross section, *p. 797*
- prism, *p. 803*
- surface area, *p. 803*
- lateral area, *p. 803*

- net, *p. 803*
- right prism, *p. 804*
- oblique prism, *p. 804*
- cylinder, *p. 805*
- right cylinder, *p. 805*
- pyramid, *p. 810*
- regular pyramid, *p. 810*

- cone, *p. 812*
- right cone, *p. 812*
- volume, *p. 819*
- sphere, *p. 838*
- great circle, *p. 839*
- hemisphere, *p. 839*
- similar solids, *p. 847*

Knowing how to use surface area and volume formulas can help you solve problems in three dimensions. For example, you can use a formula to find the volume of a column in a building.

Animated Geometry

The animation illustrated below for Exercise 31 on page 825 helps you answer this question: What is the volume of the column?

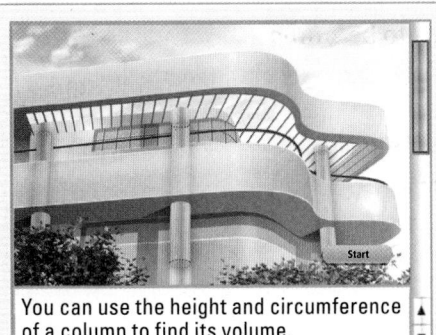

You can use the height and circumference of a column to find its volume.

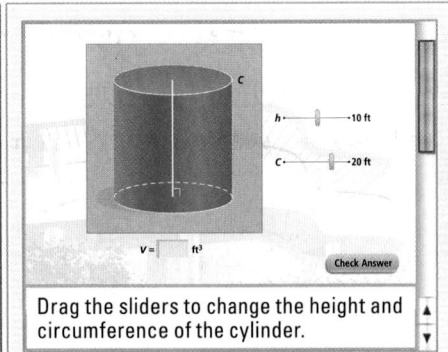

Drag the sliders to change the height and circumference of the cylinder.

Animated Geometry at classzone.com

Other animations for Chapter 12: pages 795, 805, 821, 833, 841, and 852

12.1 Investigate Solids

MATERIALS · poster board · scissors · tape · straightedge

QUESTION **What solids can be made using congruent regular polygons?**

Platonic solids, named after the Greek philosopher Plato (427 B.C.–347 B.C.), are solids that have the same congruent regular polygon as each *face,* or side of the solid.

EXPLORE 1 **Make a solid using four equilateral triangles**

STEP 1

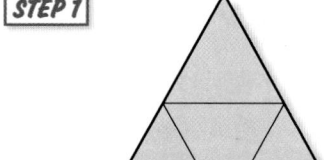

STEP 2

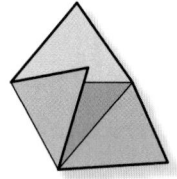

Make a net Copy the full-sized triangle from page 793 on poster board to make a template. Trace the triangle four times to make a *net* like the one shown.

Make a solid Cut out your net. Fold along the lines. Tape the edges together to form a solid. How many faces meet at each *vertex*?

EXPLORE 2 **Make a solid using eight equilateral triangles**

STEP 1

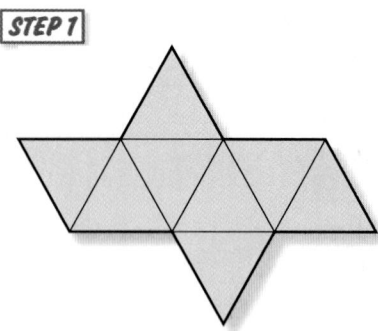

STEP 2

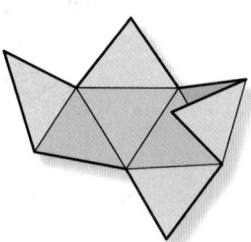

Make a net Trace your triangle template from Explore 1 eight times to make a net like the one shown.

Make a solid Cut out your net. Fold along the lines. Tape the edges together to form a solid. How many faces meet at each vertex?

EXPLORE 3 Make a solid using six squares

STEP 1

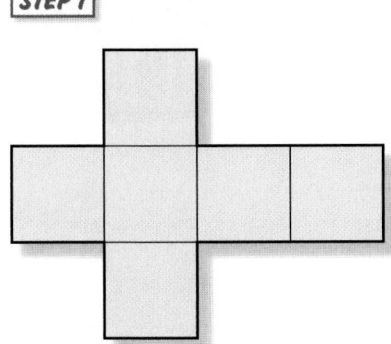

STEP 2

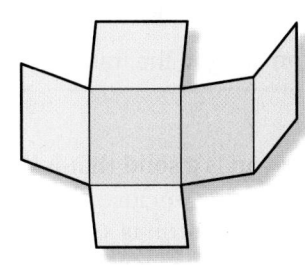

Make a net Copy the full-sized square from the bottom of the page on poster board to make a template. Trace the square six times to make a net like the one shown.

Make a solid Cut out your net. Fold along the lines. Tape the edges together to form a solid. How many faces meet at each vertex?

DRAW CONCLUSIONS Use your observations to complete these exercises

1. The two other convex solids that you can make using congruent, regular faces are shown below. For each of these solids, how many faces meet at each vertex?

a.
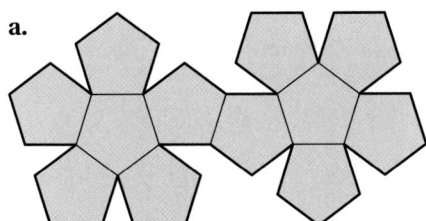

b.
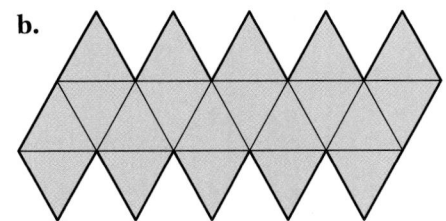

2. *Explain* why it is not possible to make a solid that has six congruent equilateral triangles meeting at each vertex.

3. *Explain* why it is not possible to make a solid that has three congruent regular hexagons meeting at each vertex.

4. Count the number of vertices *V*, edges *E*, and faces *F* for each solid you made. Make a conjecture about the relationship between the sum $F + V$ and the value of *E*.

Templates:

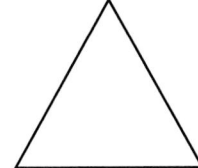
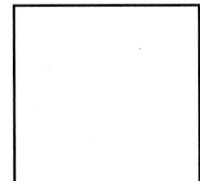

12.1 Explore Solids

Before   You identified polygons.

Now   You will identify solids.

Why   So you can analyze the frame of a house, as in Example 2.

Key Vocabulary
- polyhedron
  face, edge, vertex
- base
- regular polyhedron
- convex polyhedron
- Platonic solids
- cross section

A **polyhedron** is a solid that is bounded by polygons, called **faces**, that enclose a single region of space. An **edge** of a polyhedron is a line segment formed by the intersection of two faces. A **vertex** of a polyhedron is a point where three or more edges meet. The plural of polyhedron is *polyhedra* or *polyhedrons*.

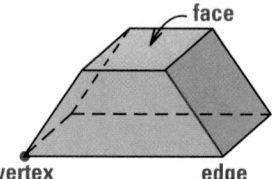

KEY CONCEPT   *For Your Notebook*

Types of Solids

Polyhedra   **Not Polyhedra**

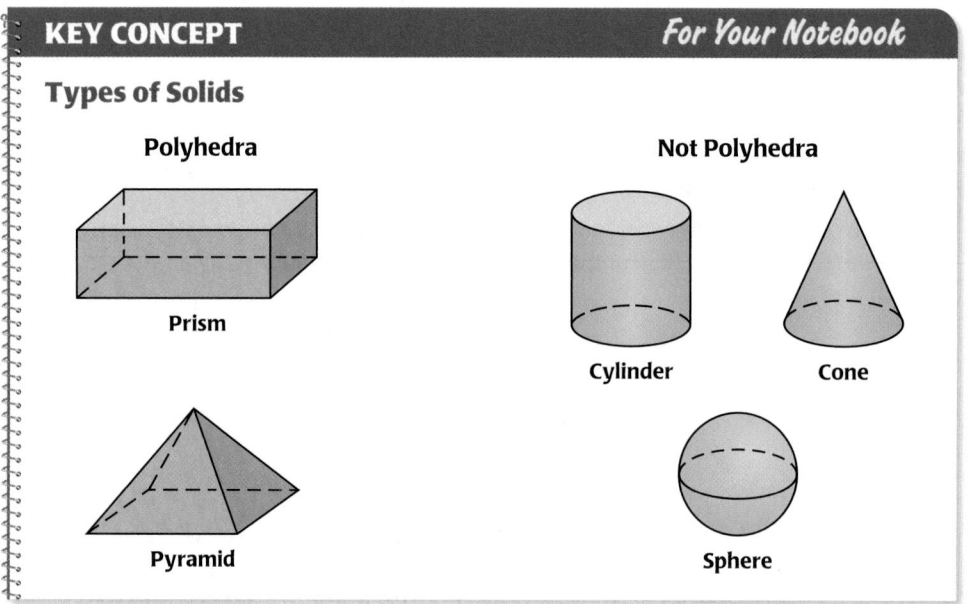

Prism   Cylinder   Cone

Pyramid   Sphere

CLASSIFYING SOLIDS Of the five solids above, the prism and the pyramid are polyhedra. To name a prism or a pyramid, use the shape of the *base*.

Pentagonal prism   **Triangular pyramid**

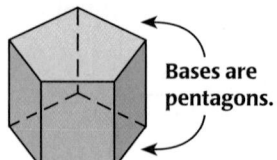
Bases are pentagons.

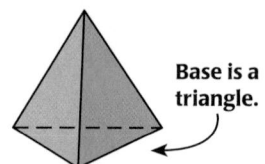
Base is a triangle.

The two **bases** of a prism are congruent polygons in parallel planes.

The **base** of a pyramid is a polygon.

EXAMPLE 1 **Identify and name polyhedra**

Tell whether the solid is a polyhedron. If it is, name the polyhedron and find the number of faces, vertices, and edges.

a. 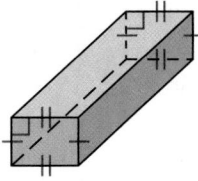 b. 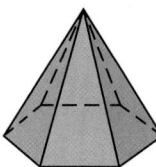 c.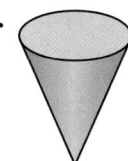

Solution

a. The solid is formed by polygons, so it is a polyhedron. The two bases are congruent rectangles, so it is a rectangular prism. It has 6 faces, 8 vertices, and 12 edges.

b. The solid is formed by polygons, so it is a polyhedron. The base is a hexagon, so it is a hexagonal pyramid. It has 7 faces, consisting of 1 base, 3 visible triangular faces, and 3 non-visible triangular faces. The polyhedron has 7 faces, 7 vertices, and 12 edges.

c. The cone has a curved surface, so it is not a polyhedron.

Animated Geometry at classzone.com

 GUIDED PRACTICE for Example 1

Tell whether the solid is a polyhedron. If it is, name the polyhedron and find the number of faces, vertices, and edges.

1. 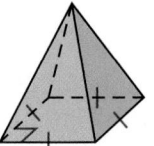 2. 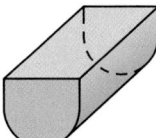 3.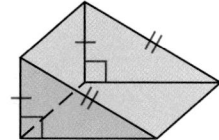

EULER'S THEOREM Notice in Example 1 that the sum of the number of faces and vertices of the polyhedra is two more than the number of edges. This suggests the following theorem, proved by the Swiss mathematician Leonhard Euler (pronounced "oi'-ler"), who lived from 1707 to 1783.

THEOREM *For Your Notebook*

THEOREM 12.1 Euler's Theorem

The number of faces (*F*), vertices (*V*), and edges (*E*) of a polyhedron are related by the formula $F + V = E + 2$.

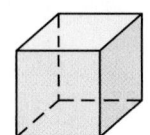

$F = 6, V = 8, E = 12$
$6 + 8 = 12 + 2$

EXAMPLE 2 **Use Euler's Theorem in a real-world situation**

HOUSE CONSTRUCTION Find the number of edges on the frame of the house.

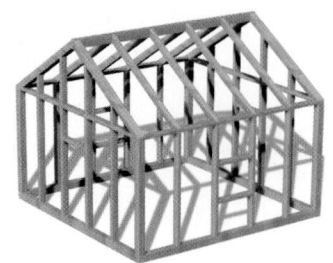

Solution

The frame has one face as its foundation, four that make up its walls, and two that make up its roof, for a total of 7 faces.

To find the number of vertices, notice that there are 5 vertices around each pentagonal wall, and there are no other vertices. So, the frame of the house has 10 vertices.

Use Euler's Theorem to find the number of edges.

$F + V = E + 2$ **Euler's Theorem**

$7 + 10 = E + 2$ **Substitute known values.**

$15 = E$ **Solve for E.**

▶ The frame of the house has 15 edges.

REGULAR POLYHEDRA A polyhedron is **regular** if all of its faces are congruent regular polygons. A polyhedron is **convex** if any two points on its surface can be connected by a segment that lies entirely inside or on the polyhedron. If this segment goes outside the polyhedron, then the polyhedron is nonconvex, or *concave*.

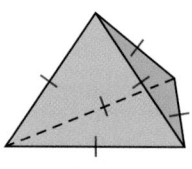

regular, convex

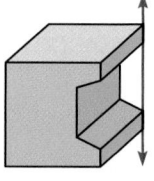

nonregular, concave

There are five regular polyhedra, called **Platonic solids** after the Greek philosopher Plato (c. 427 B.C.–347 B.C.). The five Platonic solids are shown.

Regular tetrahedron
4 faces

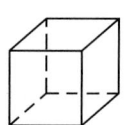 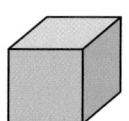

Cube
6 faces

 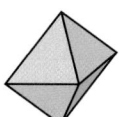

Regular octahedron
8 faces

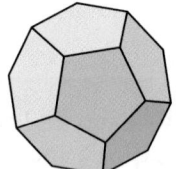

Regular dodecahedron
12 faces

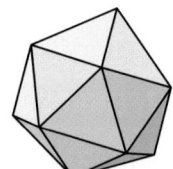

Regular icosahedron
20 faces

There are only five regular polyhedra because the sum of the measures of the angles that meet at a vertex of a convex polyhedron must be less than 360°. This means that the only possible combinations of regular polygons at a vertex that will form a polyhedron are 3, 4, or 5 triangles, 3 squares, and 3 pentagons.

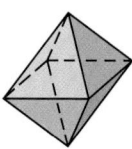

EXAMPLE 3   Use Euler's Theorem with Platonic solids

Find the number of faces, vertices, and edges of the regular octahedron. Check your answer using Euler's Theorem.

ANOTHER WAY

An octahedron has 8 faces, each of which has 3 vertices and 3 edges. Each vertex is shared by 4 faces; each edge is shared by 2 faces. They should only be counted once.

$V = \dfrac{8 \cdot 3}{4} = 6$

$E = \dfrac{8 \cdot 3}{2} = 12$

Solution

By counting on the diagram, the octahedron has 8 faces, 6 vertices, and 12 edges. Use Euler's Theorem to check.

$F + V = E + 2$ **Euler's Theorem**

$8 + 6 = 12 + 2$ **Substitute.**

$14 = 14$ ✓   **This is a true statement. So, the solution checks.**

CROSS SECTIONS Imagine a plane slicing through a solid. The intersection of the plane and the solid is called a **cross section**. For example, the diagram shows that an intersection of a plane and a triangular pyramid is a triangle.

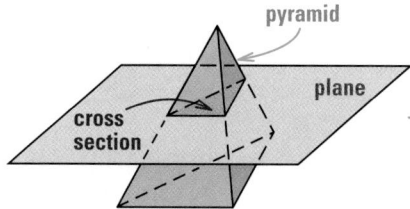

EXAMPLE 4   Describe cross sections

Describe the shape formed by the intersection of the plane and the cube.

a.
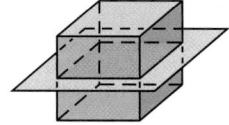

b.
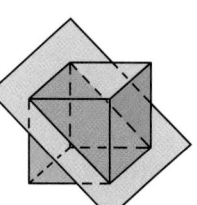

c.
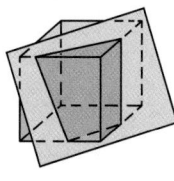

Solution

a. The cross section is a square.

b. The cross section is a rectangle.

c. The cross section is a trapezoid.

✓ **GUIDED PRACTICE**   for Examples 2, 3, and 4

4. Find the number of faces, vertices, and edges of the regular dodecahedron on page 796. Check your answer using Euler's Theorem.

Describe the shape formed by the intersection of the plane and the solid.

5.
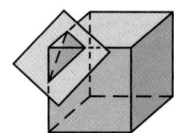

6.
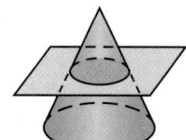

7.
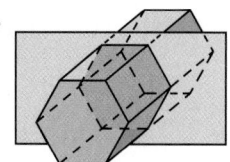

12.1 EXERCISES

SKILL PRACTICE

1. **VOCABULARY** Name the five Platonic solids and give the number of faces for each.

2. ★ **WRITING** State Euler's Theorem in words.

EXAMPLE 1
on p. 795
for Exs. 3–10

IDENTIFYING POLYHEDRA **Determine whether the solid is a polyhedron. If it is, name the polyhedron.** *Explain* **your reasoning.**

3.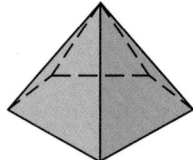

4.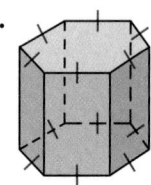

5.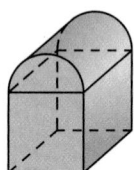

6. **ERROR ANALYSIS** *Describe* and correct the error in identifying the solid.

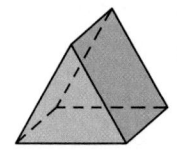

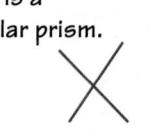

The solid is a rectangular prism.

SKETCHING POLYHEDRA **Sketch the polyhedron.**

7. Rectangular prism

8. Triangular prism

9. Square pyramid

10. Pentagonal pyramid

EXAMPLES 2 and 3
on pp. 796–797
for Exs. 11–24

APPLYING EULER'S THEOREM **Use Euler's Theorem to find the value of** *n.*

(11.) Faces: *n*
Vertices: 12
Edges: 18

12. Faces: 5
Vertices: *n*
Edges: 8

13. Faces: 10
Vertices: 16
Edges: *n*

14. Faces: *n*
Vertices: 12
Edges: 30

APPLYING EULER'S THEOREM **Find the number of faces, vertices, and edges of the polyhedron. Check your answer using Euler's Theorem.**

15.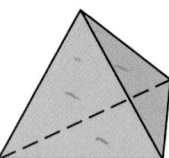

16.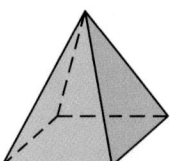

17.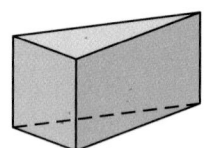

18.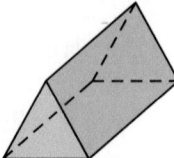

19.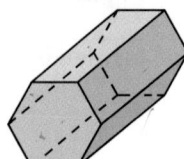

20.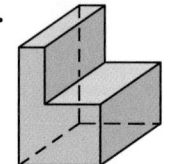

21. ★ **WRITING** *Explain* why a cube is also called a regular hexahedron.

PUZZLES Determine whether the solid puzzle is *convex* or *concave*.

22.

23.

24.

EXAMPLE 4
on p. 797
for Exs. 25–28

CROSS SECTIONS Draw and *describe* the cross section formed by the intersection of the plane and the solid.

(25.)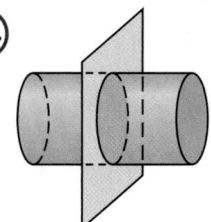

26.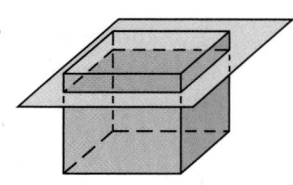

27.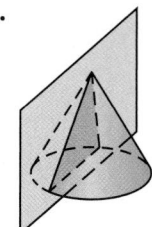

28. ★ **MULTIPLE CHOICE** What is the shape of the cross section formed by the plane parallel to the base that intersects the red line drawn on the square pyramid?

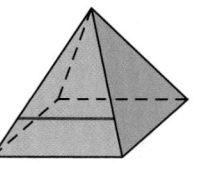

   (A) Square   **(B)** Triangle

   (C) Kite   **(D)** Trapezoid

29. **ERROR ANALYSIS** *Describe* and correct the error in determining that a tetrahedron has 4 faces, 4 edges, and 6 vertices.

30. ★ **MULTIPLE CHOICE** Which two solids have the same number of faces?

   (A) A triangular prism and a rectangular prism

   (B) A triangular pyramid and a rectangular prism

   (C) A triangular prism and a square pyramid

   (D) A triangular pyramid and a square pyramid

31. ★ **MULTIPLE CHOICE** How many faces, vertices, and edges does an octagonal prism have?

   (A) 8 faces, 6 vertices, and 12 edges

   (B) 8 faces, 12 vertices, and 18 edges

   (C) 10 faces, 12 vertices, and 20 edges

   (D) 10 faces, 16 vertices, and 24 edges

32. **EULER'S THEOREM** The solid shown has 32 faces and 90 edges. How many vertices does the solid have? *Explain* your reasoning.

33. **CHALLENGE** *Describe* how a plane can intersect a cube to form a hexagonal cross section.

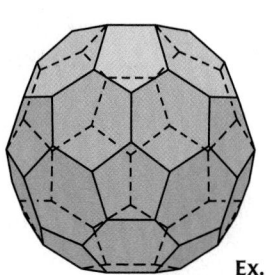

Ex. 32

EXAMPLE 2
on p. 796
for Exs. 34–35

34. MUSIC The speaker shown at the right has 7 faces. Two faces are pentagons and 5 faces are rectangles.

    a. Find the number of vertices.

    b. Use Euler's Theorem to determine how many edges the speaker has.

@HomeTutor for problem solving help at classzone.com

35. CRAFT BOXES The box shown at the right is a hexagonal prism. It has 8 faces. Two faces are hexagons and 6 faces are squares. Count the edges and vertices. Use Euler's Theorem to check your answer.

@HomeTutor for problem solving help at classzone.com

FOOD *Describe* the shape that is formed by the cut made in the food shown.

36. Watermelon

37. Bread

38. Cheese

39. ★ SHORT RESPONSE Name a polyhedron that has 4 vertices and 6 edges. Can you draw a polyhedron that has 4 vertices, 6 edges, and a different number of faces? *Explain* your reasoning.

40. MULTI-STEP PROBLEM The figure at the right shows a plane intersecting a cube through four of its vertices. An edge length of the cube is 6 inches.

    a. *Describe* the shape formed by the cross section.

    b. What is the perimeter of the cross section?

    c. What is the area of the cross section?

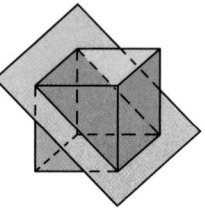

41. ★ EXTENDED RESPONSE Use the diagram of the square pyramid intersected by a plane.

    a. *Describe* the shape of the cross section shown.

    b. Can a plane intersect the pyramid at a point? If so, sketch the intersection.

    c. *Describe* the shape of the cross section when the pyramid is sliced by a plane parallel to its base.

    d. Is it possible to have a pentagon as a cross section of this pyramid? If so, draw the cross section.

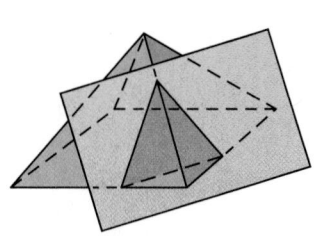

42. PLATONIC SOLIDS Make a table of the number of faces, vertices, and edges for the five Platonic solids. Use Euler's Theorem to check each answer.

○ = **WORKED-OUT SOLUTIONS**
on p. WS1

★ = **STANDARDIZED TEST PRACTICE**

REASONING Is it possible for a cross section of a cube to have the given shape? If yes, *describe* or sketch how the plane intersects the cube.

43. Circle

44. Pentagon

45. Rhombus

46. Isosceles triangle

47. Regular hexagon

48. Scalene triangle

49. CUBE *Explain* how the numbers of faces, vertices, and edges of a cube change when you cut off each feature.

    a. A corner   **b.** An edge   **c.** A face   **d.** 3 corners

50. TETRAHEDRON *Explain* how the numbers of faces, vertices, and edges of a regular tetrahedron change when you cut off each feature.

    a. A corner   **b.** An edge   **c.** A face   **d.** 2 edges

51. CHALLENGE The *angle defect D* at a vertex of a polyhedron is defined as follows:

$$D = 360° - \text{(sum of all angle measures at the vertex)}$$

Verify that for the figures with regular bases below, $DV = 720°$ where V is the number of vertices.

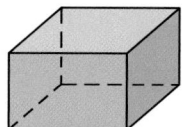 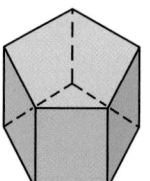 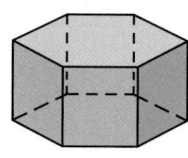

MIXED REVIEW

Find the value of *x*. *(p. 680)*

52.
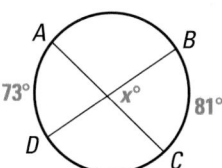

53.
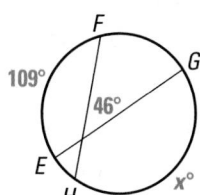

54.
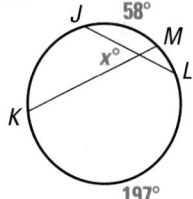

PREVIEW
Prepare for
Lesson 12.2 in
Exs. 55–60.

Use the given radius *r* or diameter *d* to find the circumference and area of the circle. Round your answers to two decimal places. *(p. 755)*

55. $r = 11$ cm   **56.** $d = 28$ in.   **57.** $d = 15$ ft

Find the perimeter and area of the regular polygon. Round your answers to two decimal places. *(p. 762)*

58.
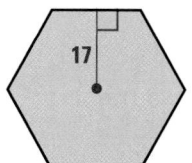

59.
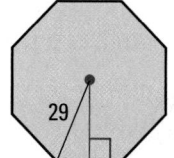

60.
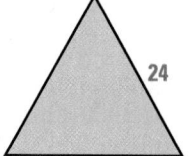

12.2 Investigate Surface Area

MATERIALS · graph paper · scissors · tape

QUESTION How can you find the surface area of a polyhedron?

A *net* is a pattern that can be folded to form a polyhedron. To find the *surface area* of a polyhedron, you can find the area of its net.

EXPLORE Create a polyhedron using a net

STEP 1 *Draw a net* Copy the net below on graph paper. Be sure to label the sections of the net.

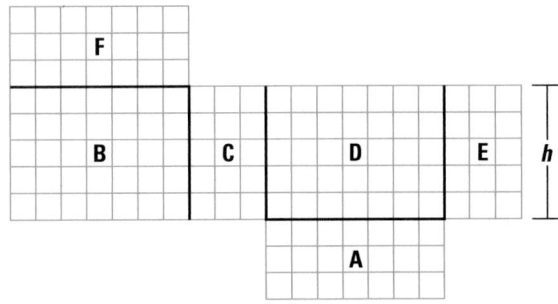

STEP 2 *Create a polyhedron* Cut out the net and fold it along the black lines to form a polyhedron. Tape the edges together. Describe the polyhedron. Is it regular? Is it convex?

STEP 3 *Find surface area* The *surface area* of a polyhedron is the sum of the areas of its faces. Find the surface area of the polyhedron you just made. (Each square on the graph paper measures 1 unit by 1 unit.)

DRAW CONCLUSIONS Use your observations to complete these exercises

1. Lay the net flat again and find the following measures.

   A: the area of Rectangle A

   P: the perimeter of Rectangle A

   h: the height of Rectangles B, C, D, and E

2. Use the values from Exercise 1 to find $2A + Ph$. *Compare* this value to the surface area you found in Step 3 above. What do you notice?

3. Make a conjecture about the surface area of a rectangular prism.

4. Use graph paper to draw the net of another rectangular prism. Fold the net to make sure that it forms a rectangular prism. Use your conjecture from Exercise 3 to calculate the surface area of the prism.

12.2 Surface Area of Prisms and Cylinders

Before	You found areas of polygons.
Now	You will find the surface areas of prisms and cylinders.
Why?	So you can find the surface area of a drum, as in Ex. 22.

Key Vocabulary
- **prism**
  lateral faces, lateral edges
- **surface area**
- **lateral area**
- **net**
- **right prism**
- **oblique prism**
- **cylinder**
- **right cylinder**

A **prism** is a polyhedron with two congruent faces, called *bases*, that lie in parallel planes. The other faces, called **lateral faces**, are parallelograms formed by connecting the corresponding vertices of the bases. The segments connecting these vertices are **lateral edges**. Prisms are classified by the shapes of their bases.

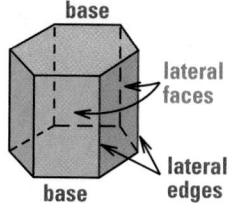

The **surface area** of a polyhedron is the sum of the areas of its faces. The **lateral area** of a polyhedron is the sum of the areas of its lateral faces.

Imagine that you cut some edges of a polyhedron and unfold it. The two-dimensional representation of the faces is called a **net**. As you saw in the Activity on page 802, the surface area of a prism is equal to the area of its net.

EXAMPLE 1 Use the net of a prism

Find the surface area of a rectangular prism with height 2 centimeters, length 5 centimeters, and width 6 centimeters.

Solution

STEP 1 **Sketch** the prism. Imagine unfolding it to make a net.

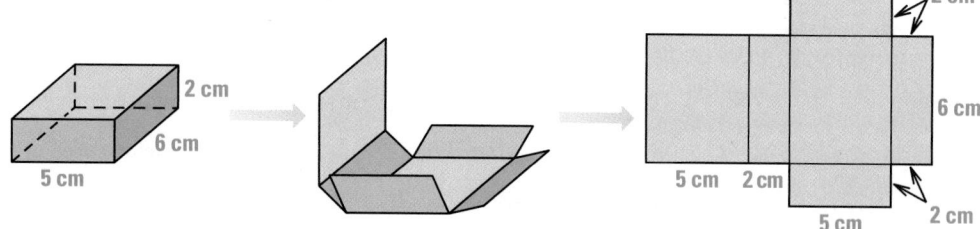

STEP 2 **Find** the areas of the rectangles that form the faces of the prism.

Congruent faces	Dimensions	Area of each face
Left and right faces	6 cm by 2 cm	$6 \cdot 2 = 12$ cm^2
Front and back faces	5 cm by 2 cm	$5 \cdot 2 = 10$ cm^2
Top and bottom faces	6 cm by 5 cm	$6 \cdot 5 = 30$ cm^2

STEP 3 **Add** the areas of all the faces to find the surface area.

▶ The surface area of the prism is $S = 2(12) + 2(10) + 2(30) = 104$ cm^2.

RIGHT PRISMS The height of a prism is the perpendicular distance between its bases. In a **right prism**, each lateral edge is perpendicular to both bases. A prism with lateral edges that are not perpendicular to the bases is an **oblique prism**.

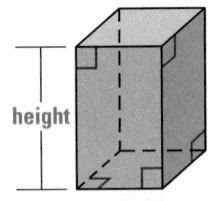

Right rectangular prism

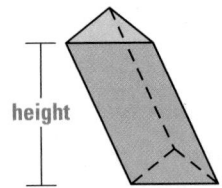

Oblique triangular prism

THEOREM 12.2 Surface Area of a Right Prism

The surface area S of a right prism is

$$S = 2B + Ph = aP + Ph,$$

where a is the apothem of the base, B is the area of a base, P is the perimeter of a base, and h is the height.

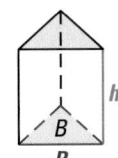

$S = 2B + Ph = aP + Ph$

EXAMPLE 2 Find the surface area of a right prism

Find the surface area of the right pentagonal prism.

Solution

STEP 1 **Find** the perimeter and area of a base of the prism.

Each base is a regular pentagon.

Perimeter $P = 5(7.05) = 35.25$

Apothem $a = \sqrt{6^2 - 3.525^2} \approx 4.86$

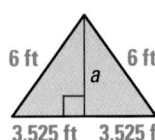

STEP 2 **Use** the formula for the surface area that uses the apothem.

$S = aP + Ph$ **Surface area of a right prism**

$\approx (4.86)(35.25) + (35.25)(9)$ **Substitute known values.**

≈ 488.57 **Simplify.**

▶ The surface area of the right pentagonal prism is about 488.57 square feet.

REVIEW APOTHEM
For help with finding the apothem, see p. 762.

✓ **GUIDED PRACTICE** | for Examples 1 and 2

1. Draw a net of a triangular prism.

2. Find the surface area of a right rectangular prism with height 7 inches, length 3 inches, and width 4 inches using (a) a net and (b) the formula for the surface area of a right prism.

CYLINDERS A **cylinder** is a solid with congruent circular bases that lie in parallel planes. The height of a cylinder is the perpendicular distance between its bases. The radius of a base is the *radius* of the cylinder. In a **right cylinder**, the segment joining the centers of the bases is perpendicular to the bases.

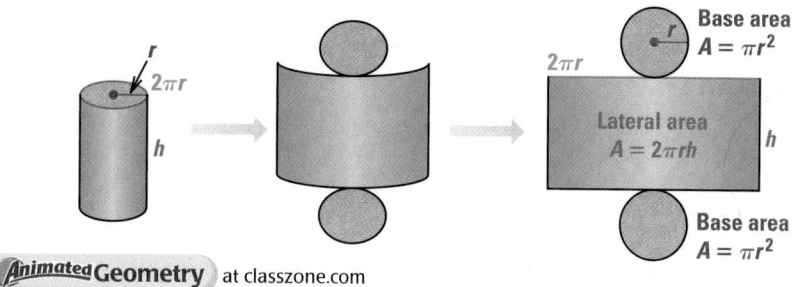

The lateral area of a cylinder is the area of its curved surface. It is equal to the product of the circumference and the height, or $2\pi rh$. The surface area of a cylinder is equal to the sum of the lateral area and the areas of the two bases.

Animated Geometry at classzone.com

THEOREM 12.3 Surface Area of a Right Cylinder

The surface area S of a right cylinder is

$$S = 2B + Ch = 2\pi r^2 + 2\pi rh,$$

where B is the area of a base, C is the circumference of a base, r is the radius of a base, and h is the height.

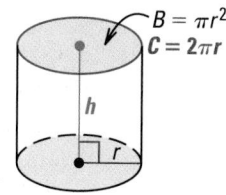

$$S = 2B + Ch = 2\pi r^2 + 2\pi rh$$

EXAMPLE 3   Find the surface area of a cylinder

COMPACT DISCS You are wrapping a stack of 20 compact discs using a shrink wrap. Each disc is cylindrical with height 1.2 millimeters and radius 60 millimeters. What is the minimum amount of shrink wrap needed to cover the stack of 20 discs?

Solution

The 20 discs are stacked, so the height of the stack will be $20(1.2) = 24$ mm. The radius is 60 millimeters. The minimum amount of shrink wrap needed will be equal to the surface area of the stack of discs.

$S = 2\pi r^2 + 2\pi rh$ **Surface area of a cylinder**

$\quad = 2\pi(60)^2 + 2\pi(60)(24)$ **Substitute known values.**

$\quad \approx 31,667$ **Use a calculator.**

▶ You will need at least 31,667 square millimeters, or about 317 square centimeters of shrink wrap.

EXAMPLE 4 Find the height of a cylinder

Find the height of the right cylinder shown, which has a surface area of 157.08 square meters.

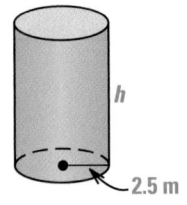

h

2.5 m

Solution

Substitute known values in the formula for the surface area of a right cylinder and solve for the height h.

$S = 2\pi r^2 + 2\pi rh$	**Surface area of a cylinder**
$157.08 = 2\pi(2.5)^2 + 2\pi(2.5)h$	**Substitute known values.**
$157.08 = 12.5\pi + 5\pi h$	**Simplify.**
$157.08 - 12.5\pi = 5\pi h$	**Subtract 12.5π from each side.**
$117.81 \approx 5\pi h$	**Simplify. Use a calculator.**
$7.5 \approx h$	**Divide each side by 5π.**

▶ The height of the cylinder is about 7.5 meters.

✔ **GUIDED PRACTICE**   for Examples 3 and 4

3. Find the surface area of a right cylinder with height 18 centimeters and radius 10 centimeters. Round your answer to two decimal places.

4. Find the radius of a right cylinder with height 5 feet and surface area 208π square feet.

12.2 **EXERCISES**

HOMEWORK KEY

○ = WORKED-OUT SOLUTIONS
on p. WS16 for Exs. 7, 9, and 23

★ = STANDARDIZED TEST PRACTICE
Exs. 2, 17, 24, 25, and 26

SKILL PRACTICE

1. VOCABULARY Sketch a triangular prism. Identify its *bases*, *lateral faces*, and *lateral edges*.

2. ★ WRITING *Explain* how the formula $S = 2B + Ph$ applies to finding the surface area of both a right prism and a right cylinder.

EXAMPLE 1
on p. 803
for Exs. 3–5

USING NETS **Find the surface area of the solid formed by the net. Round your answer to two decimal places.**

3.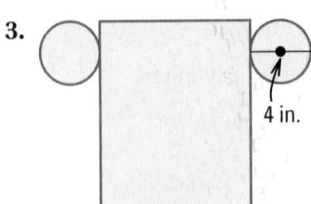

4 in.

10 in.

4.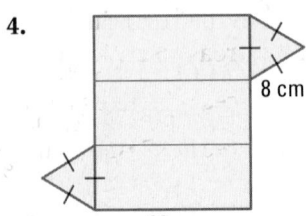

8 cm

20 cm

5.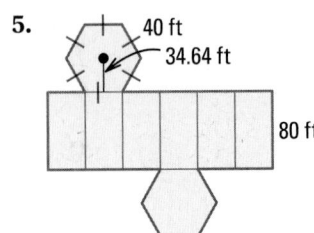

40 ft

34.64 ft

80 ft

EXAMPLE 2
on p. 804
for Exs. 6–8

SURFACE AREA OF A PRISM Find the surface area of the right prism. Round your answer to two decimal places.

6.

7.

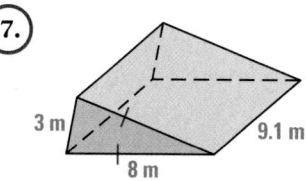

8.

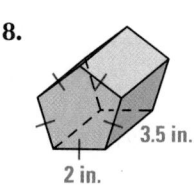

EXAMPLE 3
on p. 805
for Exs. 9–12

SURFACE AREA OF A CYLINDER Find the surface area of the right cylinder using the given radius r and height h. Round your answer to two decimal places.

9.

$r = 0.8$ in.
$h = 2$ in.

10.

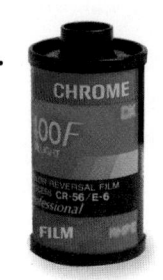

$r = 12$ mm
$h = 40$ mm

11.

$r = 8$ in.
$h = 8$ in.

12. **ERROR ANALYSIS** *Describe* and correct the error in finding the surface area of the right cylinder.

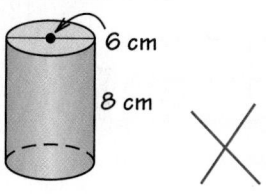

$$S = 2\pi(6^2) + 2\pi(6)(8)$$
$$= 2\pi(36) + 2\pi(48)$$
$$= 168\pi$$
$$\approx 528 \text{ cm}^2$$

6 cm

8 cm

EXAMPLE 4
on p. 806
for Exs. 13–15

ALGEBRA Solve for x given the surface area S of the right prism or right cylinder. Round your answer to two decimal places.

13. $S = 606 \text{ yd}^2$

15 yd

x

7 yd

14. $S = 1097 \text{ m}^2$

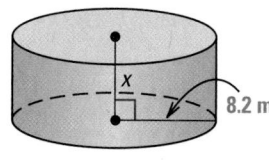

x

8.2 m

15. $S = 616 \text{ in.}^2$

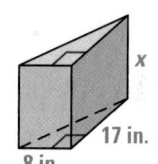

x

17 in.

8 in.

16. **SURFACE AREA OF A PRISM** A triangular prism with a right triangular base has leg length 9 units and hypotenuse length 15 units. The height of the prism is 8 units. Sketch the prism and find its surface area.

17. ★ **MULTIPLE CHOICE** The length of each side of a cube is multiplied by 3. What is the change in the surface area of the cube?

Ⓐ The surface area is 3 times the original surface area.

Ⓑ The surface area is 6 times the original surface area.

Ⓒ The surface area is 9 times the original surface area.

Ⓓ The surface area is 27 times the original surface area.

18. **SURFACE AREA OF A CYLINDER** The radius and height of a right cylinder are each divided by $\sqrt{5}$. What is the change in surface area of the cylinder?

19. SURFACE AREA OF A PRISM Find the surface area of a right hexagonal prism with all edges measuring 10 inches.

20. HEIGHT OF A CYLINDER Find the height of a cylinder with a surface area of 108π square meters. The radius of the cylinder is twice the height.

21. CHALLENGE The *diagonal* of a cube is a segment whose endpoints are vertices that are not on the same face. Find the surface area of a cube with diagonal length 8 units.

PROBLEM SOLVING

EXAMPLE 3
on p. 805
for Ex. 22

22. BASS DRUM A bass drum has a diameter of 20 inches and a depth of 8 inches. Find the surface area of the drum.

@*HomeTutor* for problem solving help at classzone.com

(23.) GIFT BOX An open gift box is shown at the right. When the gift box is closed, it has a length of 12 inches, a width of 6 inches, and a height of 6 inches.

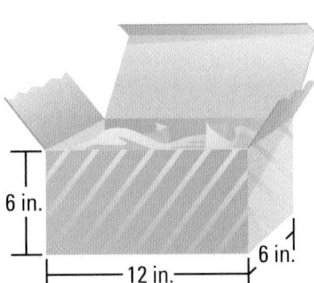

6 in.
12 in.
6 in.

a. What is the minimum amount of wrapping paper needed to cover the closed gift box?

b. Why is the area of the net of the box larger than the amount of paper found in part (a)?

c. When wrapping the box, why would you want more paper than the amount found in part (a)?

@*HomeTutor* for problem solving help at classzone.com

24. ★ EXTENDED RESPONSE A right cylinder has a radius of 4 feet and height of 10 feet.

a. Find the surface area of the cylinder.

b. Suppose you can either *double the radius* or *double the height*. Which do you think will create a greater surface area?

c. Check your answer in part (b) by calculating the new surface areas.

25. ★ MULTIPLE CHOICE Which three-dimensional figure does the net represent?

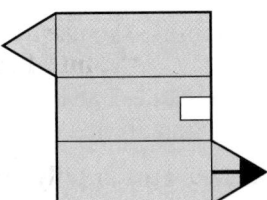

(A)

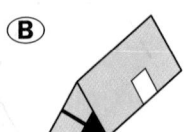
(B)

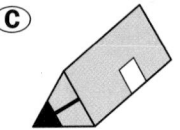
(C)

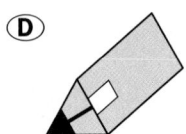
(D)

26. ★ **SHORT RESPONSE** A company makes two types of recycling bins. One type is a right rectangular prism with length 14 inches, width 12 inches, and height 36 inches. The other type is a right cylinder with radius 6 inches and height 36 inches. Both types of bins are missing a base, so the bins have one open end. Which bin requires more material to make? *Explain.*

27. **MULTI-STEP PROBLEM** Consider a cube that is built using 27 unit cubes as shown at the right.

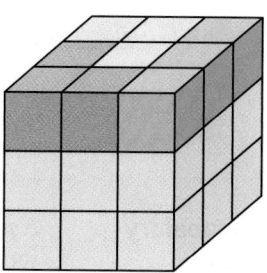

   a. Find the surface area of the solid formed when the red unit cubes are removed from the solid shown.

   b. Find the surface area of the solid formed when the blue unit cubes are removed from the solid shown.

   c. Why are your answers different in parts (a) and (b)?

28. **SURFACE AREA OF A RING** The ring shown is a right cylinder of radius r_1 with a cylindrical hole of radius r_2. The ring has height h.

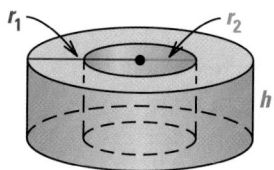

   a. Find the surface area of the ring if r_1 is 12 meters, r_2 is 6 meters, and h is 8 meters. Round your answer to two decimal places.

   b. Write a formula that can be used to find the surface area S of any cylindrical ring where $0 < r_2 < r_1$.

29. **DRAWING SOLIDS** A cube with edges 1 foot long has a cylindrical hole with diameter 4 inches drilled through one of its faces. The hole is drilled perpendicular to the face and goes completely through to the other side. Draw the figure and find its surface area.

30. **CHALLENGE** A cuboctahedron has 6 square faces and 8 equilateral triangle faces, as shown. A cuboctahedron can be made by slicing off the corners of a cube.

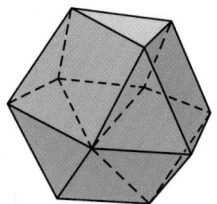

   a. Sketch a net for the cuboctahedron.

   b. Each edge of a cuboctahedron has a length of 5 millimeters. Find its surface area.

MIXED REVIEW

The sum of the measures of the interior angles of a convex polygon is given. Classify the polygon by the number of sides. *(p. 507)*

31. 1260°   **32.** 1080°   **33.** 720°   **34.** 1800°

PREVIEW
Prepare for
Lesson 12.3
in Exs. 35–37.

Find the area of the regular polygon. *(p. 762)*

35.   **36.**   **37.**

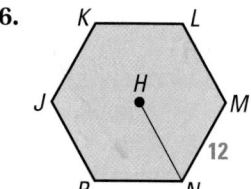

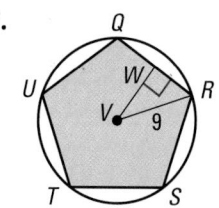

12.3 Surface Area of Pyramids and Cones

Before   You found surface areas of prisms and cylinders.

Now   You will find surface areas of pyramids and cones.

Why?   So you can find the surface area of a volcano, as in Ex. 33.

Key Vocabulary
- pyramid
- vertex of a pyramid
- regular pyramid
- slant height
- cone
- vertex of a cone
- right cone
- lateral surface

A **pyramid** is a polyhedron in which the base is a polygon and the lateral faces are triangles with a common vertex, called the **vertex of the pyramid**. The intersection of two lateral faces is a *lateral edge*. The intersection of the base and a lateral face is a *base edge*. The height of the pyramid is the perpendicular distance between the base and the vertex.

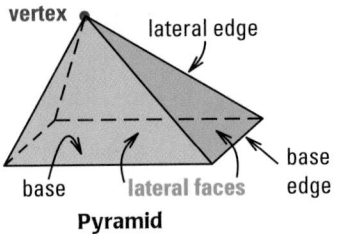
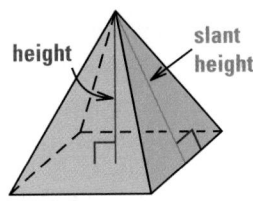

Pyramid   **Regular pyramid**

NAME PYRAMIDS
Pyramids are classified by the shapes of their bases.

A **regular pyramid** has a regular polygon for a base, and the segment joining the vertex and the center of the base is perpendicular to the base. The lateral faces of a regular pyramid are congruent isosceles triangles. The **slant height** of a regular pyramid is the height of a lateral face of the regular pyramid. A nonregular pyramid does not have a slant height.

EXAMPLE 1   **Find the area of a lateral face of a pyramid**

A regular square pyramid has a height of 15 centimeters and a base edge length of 16 centimeters. Find the area of each lateral face of the pyramid.

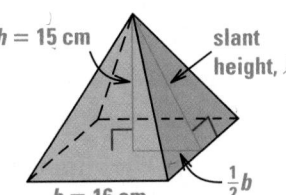

Solution

Use the Pythagorean Theorem to find the slant height ℓ.

$\ell^2 = h^2 + \left(\frac{1}{2}b\right)^2$ **Write formula.**

$\ell^2 = 15^2 + 8^2$ **Substitute for h and $\frac{1}{2}b$.**

$\ell^2 = 289$ **Simplify.**

$\ell = 17$ **Find the positive square root.**

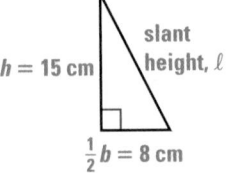

▶ The area of each triangular face is $A = \frac{1}{2}b\ell = \frac{1}{2}(16)(17) = 136$ square centimeters.

SURFACE AREA A regular hexagonal pyramid and its net are shown at the right. Let b represent the length of a base edge, and let ℓ represent the slant height of the pyramid.

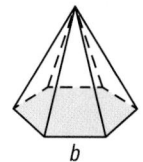

The area of each lateral face is $\frac{1}{2}b\ell$ and the perimeter of the base is $P = 6b$. So, the surface area S is as follows.

$S = $ (Area of base) $+ 6$(Area of lateral face)

$S = B + 6\left(\frac{1}{2}b\ell\right)$ **Substitute.**

$S = B + \frac{1}{2}(6b)\ell$ **Rewrite $6\left(\frac{1}{2}b\ell\right)$ as $\frac{1}{2}(6b)\ell$.**

$S = B + \frac{1}{2}P\ell$ **Substitute P for $6b$.**

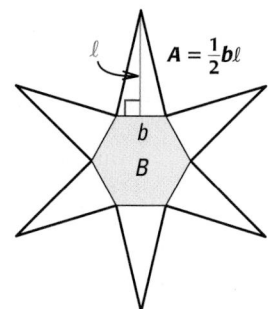

THEOREM   *For Your Notebook*

THEOREM 12.4   **Surface Area of a Regular Pyramid**

The surface area S of a regular pyramid is

$$S = B + \frac{1}{2}P\ell,$$

where B is the area of the base, P is the perimeter of the base, and ℓ is the slant height.

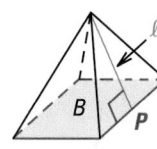

$S = B + \frac{1}{2}P\ell$

EXAMPLE 2   **Find the surface area of a pyramid**

Find the surface area of the regular hexagonal pyramid.

Solution

REVIEW AREA
For help with finding the area of regular polygons, see p. 762.

First, find the area of the base using the formula for the area of a regular polygon, $\frac{1}{2}aP$. The apothem a of the hexagon is $5\sqrt{3}$ feet and the perimeter P is $6 \cdot 10 = 60$ feet. So, the area of the base B is $\frac{1}{2}(5\sqrt{3})(60) = 150\sqrt{3}$ square feet. Then, find the surface area.

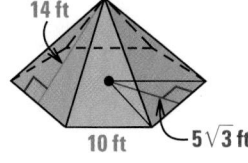

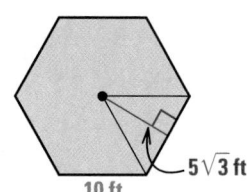

$S = B + \frac{1}{2}P\ell$ **Formula for surface area of regular pyramid**

$= 150\sqrt{3} + \frac{1}{2}(60)(14)$ **Substitute known values.**

$= 150\sqrt{3} + 420$ **Simplify.**

≈ 679.81 **Use a calculator.**

▶ The surface area of the regular hexagonal pyramid is about 679.81 ft^2.

1. Find the area of each lateral face of the regular pentagonal pyramid shown.

2. Find the surface area of the regular pentagonal pyramid shown.

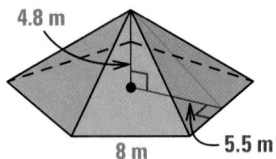

CONES A **cone** has a circular base and a **vertex** that is not in the same plane as the base. The radius of the base is the *radius* of the cone. The height is the perpendicular distance between the vertex and the base.

In a **right cone**, the segment joining the vertex and the center of the base is perpendicular to the base, and the slant height is the distance between the vertex and a point on the base edge.

The **lateral surface** of a cone consists of all segments that connect the vertex with points on the base edge.

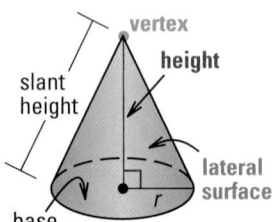

Right cone

SURFACE AREA When you cut along the slant height and base edge and lay a right cone flat, you get the net shown at the right.

The circular base has an area of πr^2 and the lateral surface is the sector of a circle. You can use a proportion to find the area of the sector, as shown below.

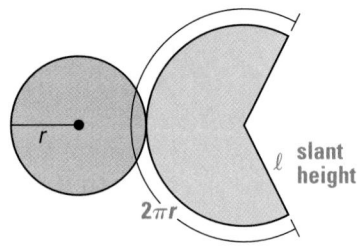

$$\frac{\text{Area of sector}}{\text{Area of circle}} = \frac{\text{Arc length}}{\text{Circumference of circle}}$$ Set up proportion.

$$\frac{\text{Area of sector}}{\pi \ell^2} = \frac{2\pi r}{2\pi \ell}$$ Substitute.

$$\text{Area of sector} = \pi \ell^2 \cdot \frac{2\pi r}{2\pi \ell}$$ Multiply each side by $\pi \ell^2$.

$$\text{Area of sector} = \pi r \ell$$ Simplify.

The surface area of a cone is the sum of the base area, πr^2, and the lateral area, $\pi r \ell$. Notice that the quantity $\pi r \ell$ can be written as $\frac{1}{2}(2\pi r)\ell$, or $\frac{1}{2}C\ell$.

THEOREM *For Your Notebook*

THEOREM 12.5 Surface Area of a Right Cone

The surface area S of a right cone is

$$S = B + \frac{1}{2}C\ell = \pi r^2 + \pi r \ell,$$

where B is the area of the base, C is the circumference of the base, r is the radius of the base, and ℓ is the slant height.

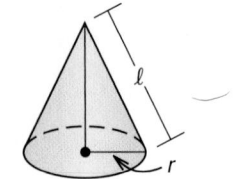

$S = B + \frac{1}{2}C\ell = \pi r^2 + \pi r\ell$

EXAMPLE 3 **Standardized Test Practice**

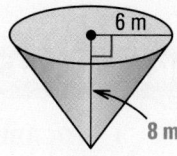

What is the surface area of the right cone?

(A) 72π m^2 (B) 96π m^2

(C) 132π m^2 (D) 136π m^2

Solution

To find the slant height ℓ of the right cone, use the Pythagorean Theorem.

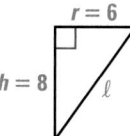

$\ell^2 = h^2 + r^2$ **Write formula.**

$\ell^2 = 8^2 + 6^2$ **Substitute.**

$\ell = 10$ **Find positive square root.**

Use the formula for the surface area of a right cone.

$S = \pi r^2 + \pi r\ell$ **Formula for surface area of a right cone**

$\quad = \pi(6^2) + \pi(6)(10)$ **Substitute.**

$\quad = 96\pi$ **Simplify.**

▶ The correct answer is B.   (A) (B) (C) (D)

ANOTHER WAY
You can use a Pythagorean triple to find ℓ.
$6 = 2 \cdot 3$ and $8 = 2 \cdot 4$,
so $\ell = 2 \cdot 5 = 10$.

EXAMPLE 4   **Find the lateral area of a cone**

TRAFFIC CONE The traffic cone can be approximated by a right cone with radius 5.7 inches and height 18 inches. Find the approximate lateral area of the traffic cone.

Solution

To find the slant height ℓ, use the Pythagorean Theorem.

$\ell^2 = 18^2 + (5.7)^2$, so $\ell \approx 18.9$ inches.

Find the lateral area.

Lateral area $= \pi r\ell$ **Write formula.**

$\qquad\qquad \approx \pi(5.7)(18.9)$ **Substitute known values.**

$\qquad\qquad = 338.4$ **Simplify and use a calculator.**

▶ The lateral area of the traffic cone is about 338.4 square inches.

 GUIDED PRACTICE   **for Examples 3 and 4**

3. Find the lateral area of the right cone shown.

4. Find the surface area of the right cone shown.

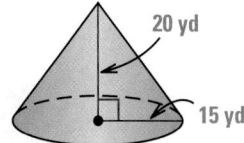

12.3 EXERCISES

SKILL PRACTICE

1. **VOCABULARY** Draw a regular square pyramid. Label its *height*, *slant height*, and *base*.

2. ★ **WRITING** *Compare* the height and slant height of a right cone.

EXAMPLE 1
on p. 810
for Exs. 3–5

AREA OF A LATERAL FACE **Find the area of each lateral face of the regular pyramid.**

3.
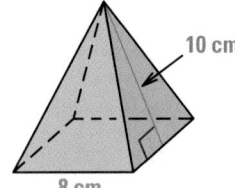
10 cm
8 cm

4.
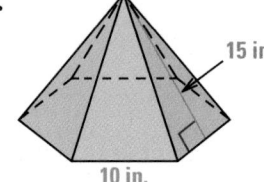
15 in.
10 in.

5.
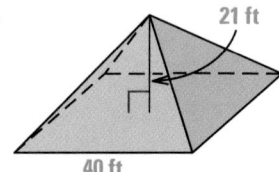
21 ft
40 ft

EXAMPLE 2
on p. 811
for Exs. 6–9

SURFACE AREA OF A PYRAMID **Find the surface area of the regular pyramid. Round your answer to two decimal places.**

6.
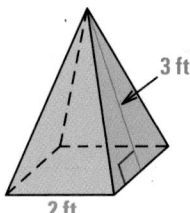
3 ft
2 ft

7.
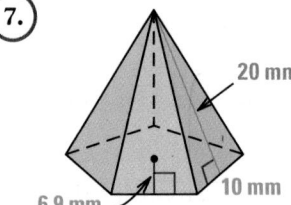
20 mm
10 mm
6.9 mm

8.
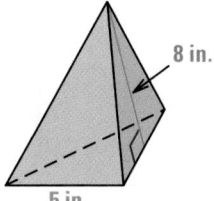
8 in.
5 in.

9. **ERROR ANALYSIS** *Describe* and correct the error in finding the surface area of the regular pyramid.

$$S = B + \frac{1}{2}P\ell$$
$$= 6^2 + \frac{1}{2}(24)(4)$$
$$= 84 \text{ ft}^2$$

4 ft
5 ft
6 ft

EXAMPLES 3 and 4
on p. 813
for Exs. 10–17

LATERAL AREA OF A CONE **Find the lateral area of the right cone. Round your answer to two decimal places.**

10.
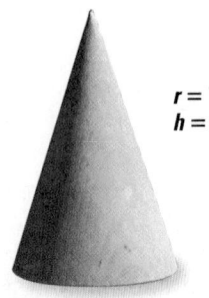
r = 7.5 cm
h = 25 cm

11.

r = 1 in.
h = 4 in.

12.

d = 7 in.
h = 1 ft

SURFACE AREA OF A CONE Find the surface area of the right cone.
Round your answer to two decimal places.

13.

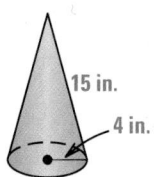

15 in.

4 in.

14.

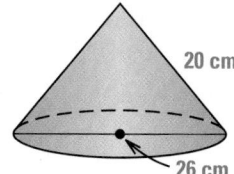

20 cm

26 cm

15.

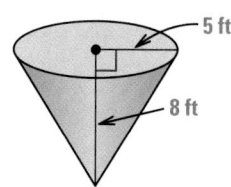

5 ft

8 ft

16. ERROR ANALYSIS *Describe* and correct the error in finding the surface area of the right cone.

$$S = \pi(r^2) + \pi r^2 \ell$$
$$= \pi(36) + \pi(36)(10)$$
$$= 396\pi \text{ cm}^2$$

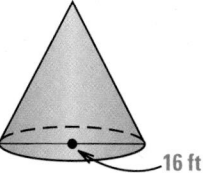

10 cm   8 cm

6 cm

17. ★ MULTIPLE CHOICE The surface area of the right cone is 200π square feet. What is the slant height of the cone?

Ⓐ 10.5 ft   Ⓑ 17 ft

Ⓒ 23 ft   Ⓓ 24 ft

16 ft

VISUAL REASONING **In Exercises 18–21, sketch the described solid and find its surface area. Round your answer to two decimal places.**

18. A right cone has a radius of 15 feet and a slant height of 20 feet.

19. A right cone has a diameter of 16 meters and a height of 30 meters.

20. A regular pyramid has a slant height of 24 inches. Its base is an equilateral triangle with a base edge length of 10 inches.

21. A regular pyramid has a hexagonal base with a base edge length of 6 centimeters and a slant height of 9 centimeters.

COMPOSITE SOLIDS **Find the surface area of the solid. The pyramids are regular and the cones are right. Round your answers to two decimal places, if necessary.**

22.

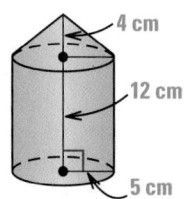

4 cm

12 cm

5 cm

23.

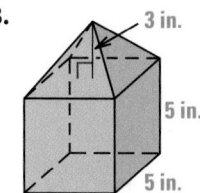

3 in.

5 in.

5 in.

24.

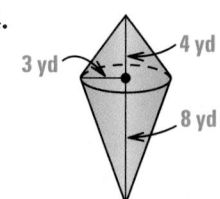

3 yd   4 yd

8 yd

25. TETRAHEDRON Find the surface area of a regular tetrahedron with edge length 4 centimeters.

26. CHALLENGE A right cone with a base of radius 4 inches and a regular pyramid with a square base both have a slant height of 5 inches. Both solids have the same surface area. Find the length of a base edge of the pyramid. Round your answer to the nearest hundredth of an inch.

EXAMPLE 2
on p. 811
for Ex. 27

27. CANDLES A candle is in the shape of a regular square pyramid with base edge length 6 inches. Its height is 4 inches. Find its surface area.

@HomeTutor for problem solving help at classzone.com

28. LAMPSHADE A glass lampshade is shaped like a regular square pyramid.

a. Approximate the lateral area of the lampshade shown.

b. *Explain* why your answer to part (a) is not the exact lateral area.

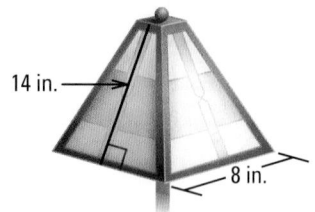

14 in.

8 in.

@HomeTutor for problem solving help at classzone.com

USING NETS **Name the figure that is represented by the net. Then find its surface area. Round your answer to two decimal places.**

29.

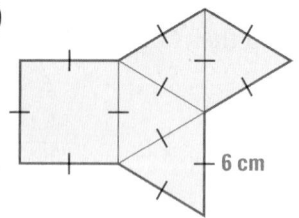

6 cm

30.

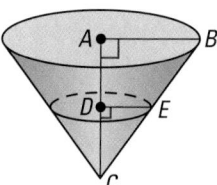

3 in.

120° 9 in.

31. ★ **SHORT RESPONSE** In the figure, $AC = 4$, $AB = 3$, and $DC = 2$.

a. Prove $\triangle ABC \sim \triangle DEC$.

b. Find BC, DE, and EC.

c. Find the surface areas of the larger cone and the smaller cone in terms of π. *Compare* the surface areas using a percent.

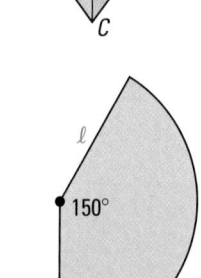

A B

D E

C

32. MULTI-STEP PROBLEM The sector shown can be rolled to form the lateral surface of a right cone. The lateral surface area of the cone is 20 square meters.

a. Write the formula for the area of a sector.

b. Use the formula in part (a) to find the slant height of the cone. *Explain* your reasoning.

c. Find the radius and height of the cone.

ℓ

150°

33. VOLCANOES Before 1980, Mount St. Helens was a conic volcano with a height from its base of about 1.08 miles and a base radius of about 3 miles. In 1980, the volcano erupted, reducing its height to about 0.83 mile.

Approximate the lateral area of the volcano after 1980. (*Hint:* The ratio of the radius of the destroyed cone-shaped top to its height is the same as the ratio of the radius of the original volcano to its height.)

Before

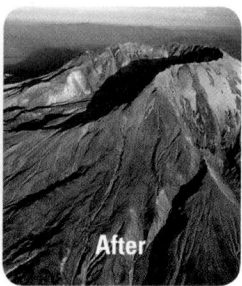

After

○ = **WORKED-OUT SOLUTIONS**
on p. WS1

★ = **STANDARDIZED TEST PRACTICE**

34. CHALLENGE An *Elizabethan collar* is used to prevent an animal from irritating a wound. The angle between the opening with a 16 inch diameter and the side of the collar is 53°. Find the surface area of the collar shown.

 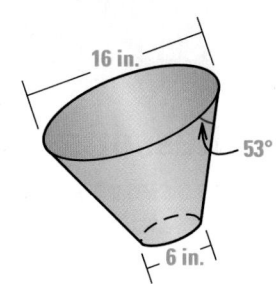

MIXED REVIEW

Find the value of *x*. *(p. 310)*

35.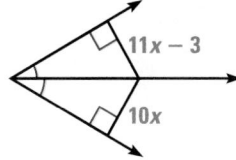

$11x - 3$

$10x$

36.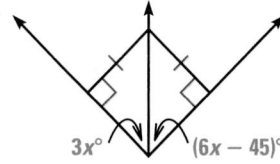

$3x°$ $(6x - 45)°$

PREVIEW
Prepare for
Lesson 12.4
in Exs. 37–39.

In Exercises 37–39, find the area of the polygon. *(pp. 720, 730)*

37.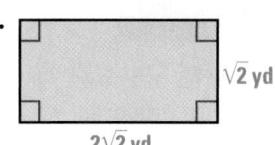

7 mi

38.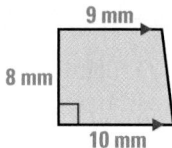

$\sqrt{2}$ yd

$2\sqrt{2}$ yd

39.

9 mm

8 mm

10 mm

QUIZ *for Lessons 12.1–12.3*

1. A polyhedron has 8 vertices and 12 edges. How many faces does the polyhedron have? *(p. 794)*

Solve for *x* given the surface area *S* of the right prism or right cylinder. Round your answer to two decimal places. *(p. 803)*

2. $S = 366 \text{ ft}^2$

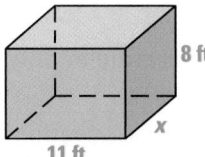

8 ft

x

11 ft

3. $S = 717 \text{ in.}^2$

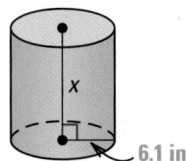

x

6.1 in.

4. $S = 567 \text{ m}^2$

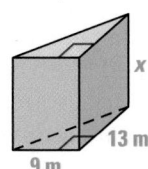

x

13 m

9 m

Find the surface area of the regular pyramid or right cone. Round your answer to two decimal places. *(p. 810)*

5.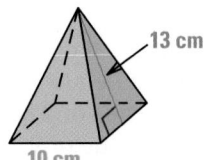

13 cm

10 cm

6.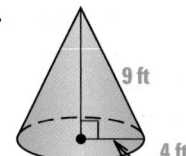

9 ft

4 ft

7.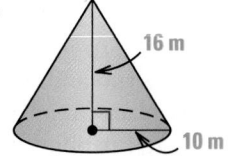

16 m

10 m

EXTRA PRACTICE for Lesson 12.3, p. 918   🔊 **ONLINE QUIZ** at classzone.com   **817**

Lessons 12.1–12.3

1. **SHORT RESPONSE** Using Euler's Theorem, *explain* why it is not possible for a polyhedron to have 6 vertices and 7 edges.

2. **SHORT RESPONSE** *Describe* two methods of finding the surface area of a rectangular solid.

3. **EXTENDED RESPONSE** Some pencils are made from slats of wood that are machined into right regular hexagonal prisms.

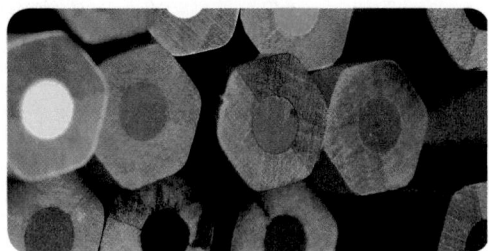

   a. The formula for the surface area of a new unsharpened pencil without an eraser is

   $$S = 3\sqrt{3}r^2 + 6rh.$$

   Tell what each variable in this formula represents.

   b. After a pencil is painted, a metal band that holds an eraser is wrapped around one end. Write a formula for the surface area of the visible portion of the pencil, shown below.

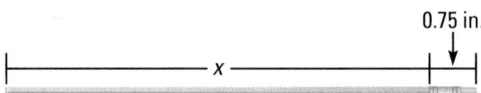

0.75 in.

   c. After a pencil is sharpened, the end is shaped like a cone. Write a formula to find the surface area of the visible portion of the pencil, shown below.

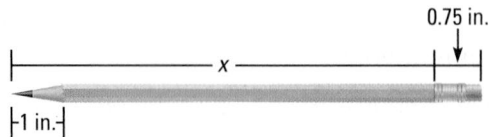

0.75 in.

1 in.

   d. Use your formulas from parts (b) and (c) to write a formula for the difference of the surface areas of the two pencils. Define any variables in your formula.

4. **GRIDDED ANSWER** The amount of paper needed for a soup can label is approximately equal to the lateral area of the can. Find the lateral area of the soup can in square inches. Round your answer to two decimal places.

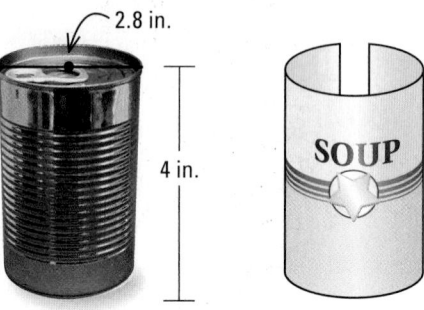

2.8 in.

4 in.

SOUP

5. **SHORT RESPONSE** If you know the diameter d and slant height ℓ of a right cone, how can you find the surface area of the cone?

6. **OPEN-ENDED** Identify an object in your school or home that is a rectangular prism. Measure its length, width, and height to the nearest quarter inch. Then approximate the surface area of the object.

7. **MULTI-STEP PROBLEM** The figure shows a plane intersecting a cube parallel to its base. The cube has a side length of 10 feet.

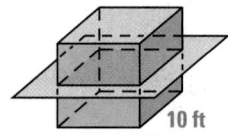

10 ft

   a. Describe the shape formed by the cross section.

   b. Find the perimeter and area of the cross section.

   c. When the cross section is cut along its diagonal, what kind of triangles are formed?

   d. Find the area of one of the triangles formed in part (c).

8. **SHORT RESPONSE** A cone has a base radius of $3x$ units and a height of $4x$ units. The surface area of the cone is 1944π square units. Find the value of x. *Explain* your steps.

 **Volume of Prisms and Cylinders**

Before	You found surface areas of prisms and cylinders.
Now	You will find volumes of prisms and cylinders.
Why	So you can determine volume of water in an aquarium, as in Ex. 33.

Key Vocabulary
• volume

The **volume** of a solid is the number of cubic units contained in its interior. Volume is measured in cubic units, such as cubic centimeters (cm³).

POSTULATES *For Your Notebook*

POSTULATE 27 Volume of a Cube Postulate

The volume of a cube is the cube of the length of its side.

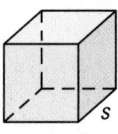

$V = s^3$

POSTULATE 28 Volume Congruence Postulate

If two polyhedra are congruent, then they have the same volume.

POSTULATE 29 Volume Addition Postulate

The volume of a solid is the sum of the volumes of all its nonoverlapping parts.

EXAMPLE 1 Find the number of unit cubes

3-D PUZZLE Find the volume of the puzzle piece in cubic units.

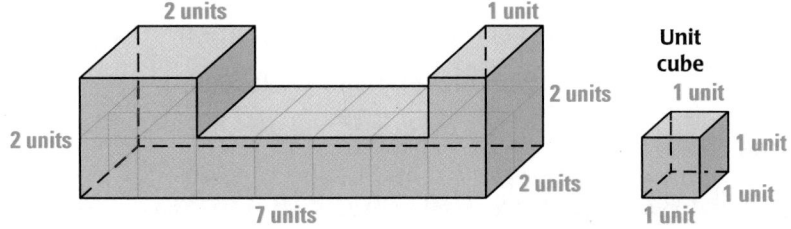

Solution

To find the volume, find the number of unit cubes it contains. Separate the piece into three rectangular boxes as follows:

The *base* is 7 units by 2 units. So, it contains 7 • 2, or 14 unit cubes.

The *upper left box* is 2 units by 2 units. So, it contains 2 • 2, or 4 unit cubes.

The *upper right box* is 1 unit by 2 units. So, it contains 1 • 2, or 2 unit cubes.

▶ By the Volume Addition Postulate, the total volume of the puzzle piece is 14 + 4 + 2 = 20 cubic units.

VOLUME FORMULAS The volume of any right prism or right cylinder can be found by multiplying the area of its base by its height.

> **THEOREMS** *For Your Notebook*
>
> **THEOREM 12.6 Volume of a Prism**
>
> The volume V of a prism is
>
> $$V = Bh,$$
>
> where B is the area of a base and h is the height.
>
>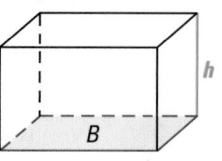
>
> **V = Bh**
>
> ---
>
> **THEOREM 12.7 Volume of a Cylinder**
>
> The volume V of a cylinder is
>
> $$V = Bh = \pi r^2 h,$$
>
> where B is the area of a base, h is the height, and r is the radius of a base.
>
>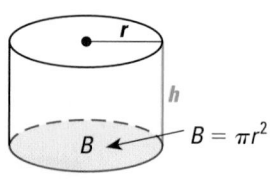
>
> $B = \pi r^2$
>
> **V = Bh = $\pi r^2 h$**

EXAMPLE 2 **Find volumes of prisms and cylinders**

Find the volume of the solid.

a. Right trapezoidal prism

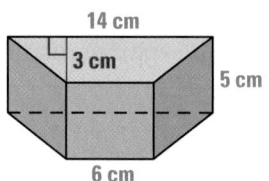

b. Right cylinder

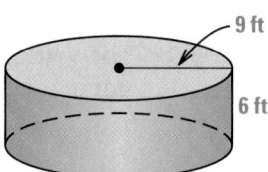

Solution

REVIEW AREA
For help with finding the area of a trapezoid, see p. 730.

a. The area of a base is $\frac{1}{2}(3)(6 + 14) = 30$ cm^2 and $h = 5$ cm.

$$V = Bh = 30(5) = 150 \text{ cm}^3$$

b. The area of the base is $\pi \cdot 9^2$, or 81π ft^2. Use $h = 6$ ft to find the volume.

$$V = Bh = 81\pi(6) = 486\pi \approx 1526.81 \text{ ft}^3$$

EXAMPLE 3 **Use volume of a prism**

(xy) ALGEBRA The volume of the cube is 90 cubic inches. Find the value of x.

Solution

A side length of the cube is x inches.

$V = x^3$	Formula for volume of a cube
$90 \text{ in.}^3 = x^3$	Substitute for V.
$4.48 \text{ in.} \approx x$	Find the cube root.

1. Find the volume of the puzzle piece shown in cubic units.

2. Find the volume of a square prism that has a base edge length of 5 feet and a height of 12 feet.

3. The volume of a right cylinder is 684π cubic inches and the height is 18 inches. Find the radius.

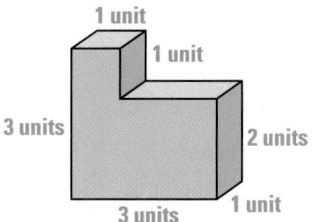

USING CAVALIERI'S PRINCIPLE Consider the solids below. All three have equal heights h and equal cross-sectional areas B. Mathematician Bonaventura Cavalieri (1598–1647) claimed that all three of the solids have the same volume. This principle is stated below.

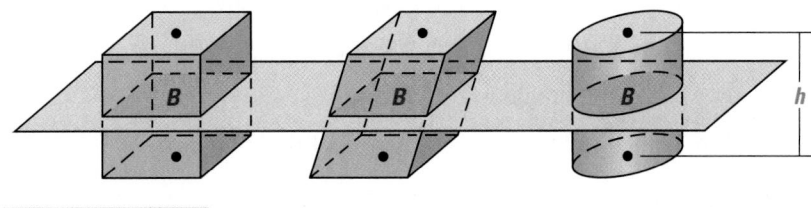

(Animated Geometry) at classzone.com

THEOREM   *For Your Notebook*

THEOREM 12.8 Cavalieri's Principle

If two solids have the same height and the same cross-sectional area at every level, then they have the same volume.

EXAMPLE 4 Find the volume of an oblique cylinder

Find the volume of the oblique cylinder.

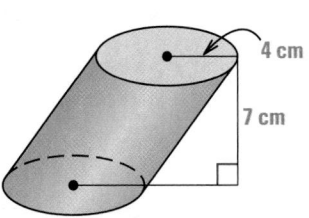

APPLY THEOREMS
Cavalieri's Principle tells you that the volume formulas on page 820 work for oblique prisms and cylinders.

Solution

Cavalieri's Principle allows you to use Theorem 12.7 to find the volume of the oblique cylinder.

$V = \pi r^2 h$ **Formula for volume of a cylinder**

$= \pi(4^2)(7)$ **Substitute known values.**

$= 112\pi$ **Simplify.**

≈ 351.86 **Use a calculator.**

▶ The volume of the oblique cylinder is about 351.86 cm³.

EXAMPLE 5   **Solve a real-world problem**

SCULPTURE The sculpture is made up of 13 beams. In centimeters, suppose the dimensions of each beam are 30 by 30 by 90. Find its volume.

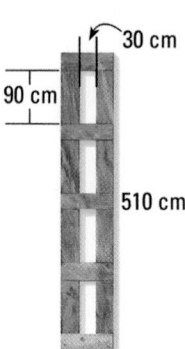

Romartyr Hamburg, 1989 © Carl Andre/ licensed by VAGA, NY

ANOTHER WAY
For alternative methods for solving the problem in Example 5, turn to page 826 for the **Problem Solving Workshop**.

Solution

The area of the base B can be found by subtracting the area of the small rectangles from the area of the large rectangle.

B = Area of large rectangle $-$ 4 $\cdot$ Area of small rectangle

$\quad = 90 \cdot 510 - 4(30 \cdot 90)$

$\quad = 35{,}100 \text{ cm}^2$

Use the formula for the volume of a prism.

$V = Bh$ **Formula for volume of a prism**

$\quad = 35{,}100(30)$ **Substitute.**

$\quad = 1{,}053{,}000 \text{ cm}^3$ **Simplify.**

▶ The volume of the sculpture is 1,053,000 cm³, or 1.053 m³.

✓ **GUIDED PRACTICE**   for Examples 4 and 5

4. Find the volume of the oblique prism shown below.

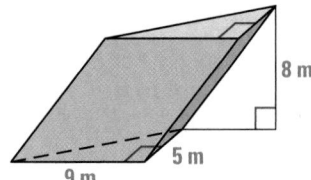

5. Find the volume of the solid shown below.

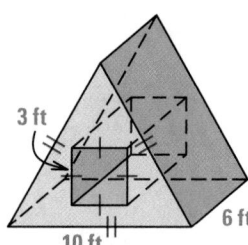

12.4 EXERCISES

HOMEWORK KEY

◯ = **WORKED-OUT SOLUTIONS**
on p. WS17 for Exs. 7, 11, and 29

★ = **STANDARDIZED TEST PRACTICE**
Exs. 2, 3, 21, and 33

SKILL PRACTICE

1. **VOCABULARY** In what type of units is the volume of a solid measured?

2. ★ **WRITING** Two solids have the same surface area. Do they have the same volume? *Explain* your reasoning.

EXAMPLE 1
on p. 819
for Exs. 3–6

3. ★ **MULTIPLE CHOICE** How many 3 inch cubes can fit completely in a box that is 15 inches long, 9 inches wide, and 3 inches tall?

    A 15   **B** 45   **C** 135   **D** 405

USING UNIT CUBES Find the volume of the solid by determining how many unit cubes are contained in the solid.

4.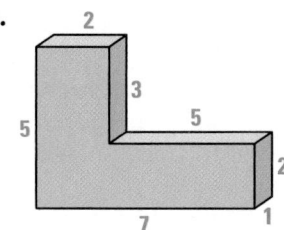

5.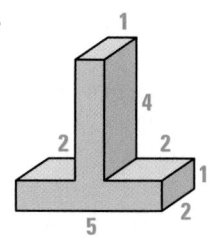

6.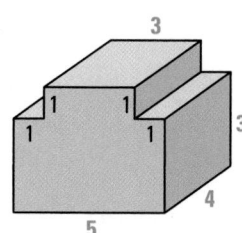

EXAMPLE 2
on p. 820
for Exs. 7–13

FINDING VOLUME Find the volume of the right prism or right cylinder. **Round your answer to two decimal places.**

(7.) 7 in. 10 in. 5 in.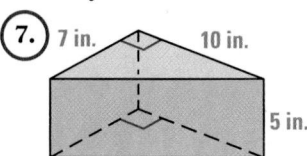

8. 1.5 m 2 m 4 m

9. 7.5 cm 18 cm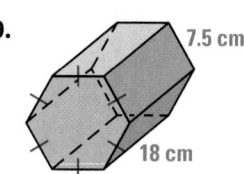

10. 7 ft 12 ft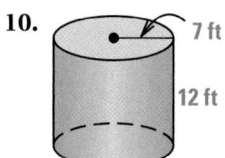

(11.) 10 in. 16 in.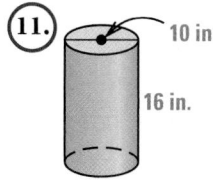

12. 26.8 cm 9.8 cm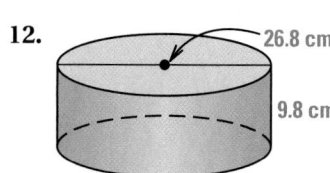

13. ERROR ANALYSIS *Describe* and correct the error in finding the volume of a right cylinder with radius 4 feet and height 3 feet.

$$V = 2\pi rh$$
$$= 2\pi(4)(3)$$
$$= 24\pi \text{ ft}^3$$

14. FINDING VOLUME Sketch a rectangular prism with height 3 feet, width 11 inches, and length 7 feet. Find its volume.

EXAMPLE 3
on p. 820
for Exs. 15–17

(xy) ALGEBRA Find the length x using the given volume V.

15. $V = 1000$ in.^{3}

x, x, x

16. $V = 45$ cm^3

x, 9 cm, 5 cm

17. $V = 128\pi$ in.^{3}

8 in., x

COMPOSITE SOLIDS Find the volume of the solid. **The prisms and cylinders are right. Round your answer to two decimal places, if necessary.**

18. 1 m 3 m 7 m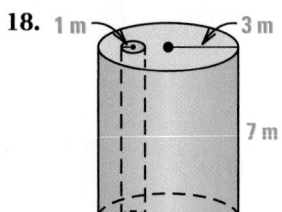

19. 1.8 ft 3 ft 9 ft 7.8 ft 12.4 ft

20. 4 in. 4 in. 4 in.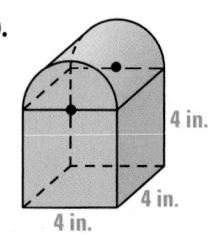

21. ★ **MULTIPLE CHOICE** What is the height of a cylinder with radius 4 feet and volume 64π cubic feet?

  (A) 4 feet   **(B)** 8 feet   **(C)** 16 feet   **(D)** 256 feet

22. **FINDING HEIGHT** The bases of a right prism are right triangles with side lengths of 3 inches, 4 inches, and 5 inches. The volume of the prism is 96 cubic inches. What is the height of the prism?

23. **FINDING DIAMETER** A cylinder has height 8 centimeters and volume 1005.5 cubic centimeters. What is the diameter of the cylinder?

EXAMPLE 4
on p. 821
for Exs. 24–26

VOLUME OF AN OBLIQUE SOLID Use Cavalieri's Principle to find the volume of the oblique prism or cylinder. Round your answer to two decimal places.

24.

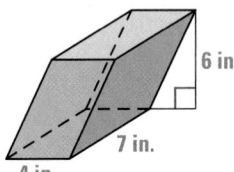

25.

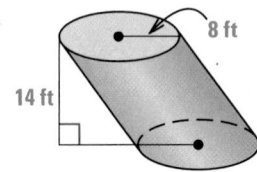

26.

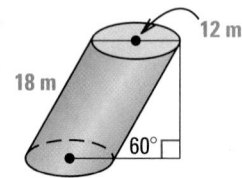

27. **CHALLENGE** The bases of a right prism are rhombuses with diagonals 12 meters and 16 meters long. The height of the prism is 8 meters. Find the lateral area, surface area, and volume of the prism.

PROBLEM SOLVING

EXAMPLE 5
on p. 822
for Exs. 28–30

28. **JEWELRY** The bead at the right is a rectangular prism of length 17 millimeters, width 9 millimeters, and height 5 millimeters. A 3 millimeter wide hole is drilled through the smallest face. Find the volume of the bead.

  @HomeTutor   for problem solving help at classzone.com

(29.) **MULTI-STEP PROBLEM** In the concrete block shown, the holes are 8 inches deep.

 a. Find the volume of the block using the Volume Addition Postulate.

 b. Find the volume of the block using the formula in Theorem 12.6.

 c. *Compare* your answers in parts (a) and (b).

  @HomeTutor   for problem solving help at classzone.com

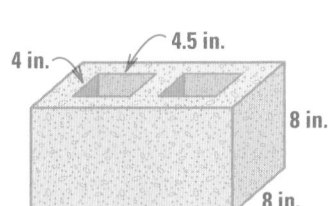

30. **OCEANOGRAPHY** The Blue Hole is a cylindrical trench located on Lighthouse Reef Atoll, an island off the coast of Central America. It is approximately 1000 feet wide and 400 feet deep.

 a. Find the volume of the Blue Hole.

 b. About how many gallons of water does the Blue Hole contain? ($1 \text{ ft}^3 = 7.48$ gallons)

  ◯ **= WORKED-OUT SOLUTIONS**
   on p. WS1

  ★ **= STANDARDIZED**
   TEST PRACTICE

31. ARCHITECTURE A cylindrical column in the building shown has circumference 10 feet and height 20 feet. Find its volume. Round your answer to two decimal places.

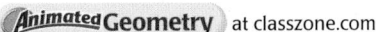 at classzone.com

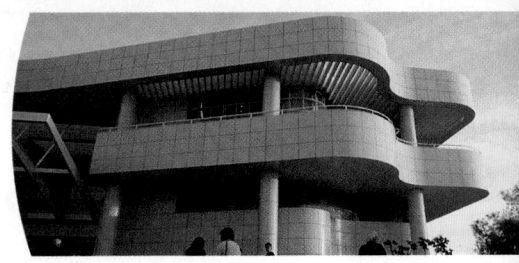

32. ROTATIONS A 3 inch by 5 inch index card is rotated around a horizontal line and a vertical line to produce two different solids, as shown. Which solid has a greater volume? *Explain* your reasoning.

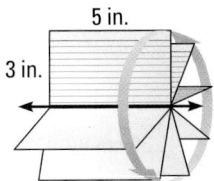

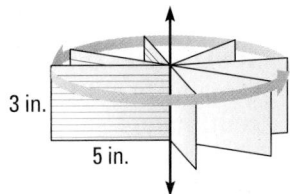

33. ★ EXTENDED RESPONSE An aquarium shaped like a rectangular prism has length 30 inches, width 10 inches, and height 20 inches.

    a. Calculate You fill the aquarium $\frac{3}{4}$ full with water. What is the volume of the water?

    b. Interpret When you submerge a rock in the aquarium, the water level rises 0.25 inch. Find the volume of the rock.

    c. Interpret How many rocks of the same size as the rock in part (b) can you place in the aquarium before water spills out?

34. CHALLENGE A barn is in the shape of a pentagonal prism with the dimensions shown. The volume of the barn is 9072 cubic feet. Find the dimensions of each half of the roof.

MIXED REVIEW

PREVIEW
Prepare for
Lesson 12.5 in
Exs. 35–40.

Find the value of *x*. Round your answer to two decimal places. *(pp. 466, 473)*

35.

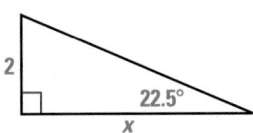

36.

37.

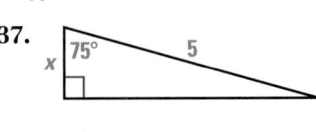

Find the area of the figure described. Round your answer to two decimal places. *(pp. 755, 762)*

38. A circle with radius 9.5 inches

39. An equilateral triangle with perimeter 78 meters and apothem 7.5 meters

40. A regular pentagon with radius 10.6 inches

EXTRA PRACTICE for Lesson 12.4, p. 919   **◉ ONLINE QUIZ** at classzone.com   **825**

Using ALTERNATIVE METHODS

Another Way to Solve Example 5, page 822

MULTIPLE REPRESENTATIONS In Lesson 12.4, you used volume postulates and theorems to find volumes of prisms and cylinders. Now, you will learn two different ways to solve Example 5 on page 822.

PROBLEM

SCULPTURE The sculpture is made up of 13 beams. In centimeters, suppose the dimensions of each beam are 30 by 30 by 90. Find its volume.

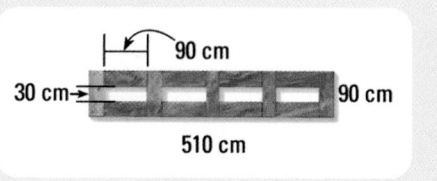

METHOD 1

Finding Volume by Subtracting Empty Spaces One alternative approach is to compute the volume of the prism formed if the holes in the sculpture were filled. Then, to get the correct volume, you must subtract the volume of the four holes.

STEP 1 **Read** the problem. In centimeters, each beam measures 30 by 30 by 90.

The dimensions of the entire sculpture are 30 by 90 by (4 • 90 + 5 • 30), or 30 by 90 by 510.

The dimensions of each hole are equal to the dimensions of one beam.

STEP 2 **Apply** the Volume Addition Postulate. The volume of the sculpture is equal to the volume of the larger prism minus 4 times the volume of a hole.

Volume *V* of sculpture = Volume of larger prism − Volume of 4 holes

$$= 30 \cdot 90 \cdot 510 - 4(30 \cdot 30 \cdot 90)$$

$$= 1,377,000 - 4 \cdot 81,000$$

$$= 1,377,000 - 324,000$$

$$= 1,053,000$$

▶ The volume of the sculpture is 1,053,000 cubic centimeters, or 1.053 cubic meters.

STEP 3 **Check** page 822 to verify your new answer, and confirm that it is the same.

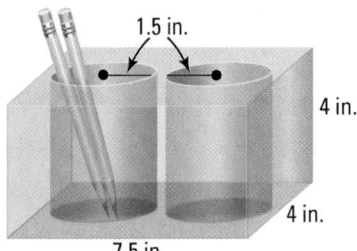

METHOD 2 **Finding Volume of Pieces** Another alternative approach is to use the dimensions of each beam.

> **STEP 1** **Look** at the sculpture. Notice that the sculpture consists of 13 beams, each with the same dimensions. Therefore, the volume of the sculpture will be 13 times the volume of one beam.

> **STEP 2** **Write** an expression for the volume of the sculpture and find the volume.

$$\text{Volume of sculpture} = 13(\text{Volume of one beam})$$
$$= 13(30 \cdot 30 \cdot 90)$$
$$= 13 \cdot 81{,}000$$
$$= 1{,}053{,}000$$

▶ The volume of the sculpture is 1,053,000 cm^3, or 1.053 m^3.

PRACTICE

1. **PENCIL HOLDER** The pencil holder has the dimensions shown.

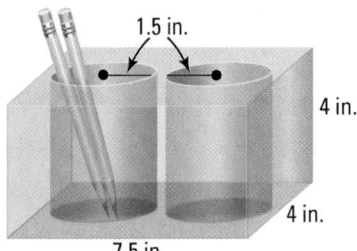

1.5 in.
4 in.
4 in.
7.5 in.

   a. Find its volume using the Volume Addition Postulate.

   b. Use its base area to find its volume.

2. **ERROR ANALYSIS** A student solving Exercise 1 claims that the surface area is found by subtracting four times the base area of the cylinders from the surface area of the rectangular prism. *Describe* and correct the student's error.

3. **REASONING** You drill a circular hole of radius r through the base of a cylinder of radius R. Assume the hole is drilled completely through to the other base. You want the volume of the hole to be half the volume of the cylinder. Express r as a function of R.

4. **FINDING VOLUME** Find the volume of the solid shown below. Assume the hole has square cross sections.

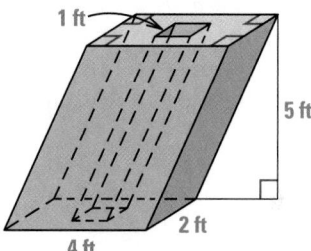

1 ft
5 ft
2 ft
4 ft

5. **FINDING VOLUME** Find the volume of the solid shown to the right.

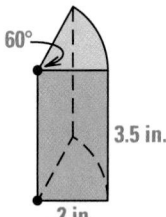

60°
3.5 in.
2 in.

6. **SURFACE AREA** Refer to the diagram of the sculpture on page 826.

   a. *Describe* a method to find the surface area of the sculpture.

   b. *Explain* why adding the individual surface areas of the beams will give an incorrect result for the total surface area.

12.5 Investigate the Volume of a Pyramid

MATERIALS · ruler · poster board · scissors · tape · uncooked rice

QUESTION How is the volume of a pyramid related to the volume of a prism with the same base and height?

EXPLORE Compare the volume of a prism and a pyramid using nets

STEP 1 *Draw nets* Use a ruler to draw the two nets shown below on poster board. (Use $1\frac{7}{16}$ inches to approximate $\sqrt{2}$ inches.)

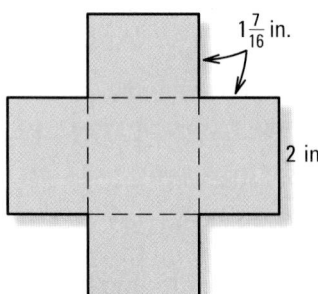

$1\frac{7}{16}$ in.

2 in.

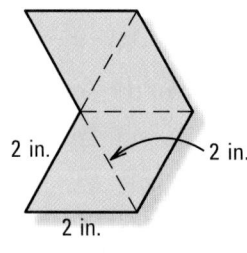

2 in.   2 in.

2 in.

STEP 2 *Create an open prism and an open pyramid* Cut out the nets. Fold along the dotted lines to form an open prism and an open pyramid, as shown below. Tape each solid to hold it in place, making sure that the edges do not overlap.

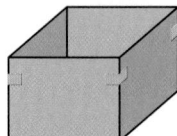

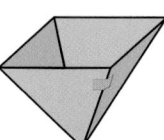

STEP 3 *Compare volumes* Fill the pyramid with uncooked rice and pour it into the prism. Repeat this as many times as needed to fill the prism. How many times did you fill the pyramid? What does this tell you about the volume of the solids?

DRAW CONCLUSIONS Use your observations to complete these exercises

1. *Compare* the area of the base of the pyramid to the area of the base of the prism. Placing the pyramid inside the prism will help. What do you notice?

2. *Compare* the heights of the solids. What do you notice?

3. Make a conjecture about the ratio of the volumes of the solids.

4. Use your conjecture to write a formula for the volume of a pyramid that uses the formula for the volume of a prism.

12.5 Volume of Pyramids and Cones

Before	You found surface areas of pyramids and cones.
Now	You will find volumes of pyramids and cones.
Why?	So you can find the edge length of a pyramid, as in Example 2.

Key Vocabulary
• **pyramid,** *p. 810*
• **cone,** *p. 812*
• **volume,** *p. 819*

Recall that the volume of a prism is Bh, where B is the area of a base and h is the height. In the figure at the right, you can see that the volume of a pyramid must be less than the volume of a prism with the same base area and height. As suggested by the Activity on page 828, the volume of a pyramid is one third the volume of a prism.

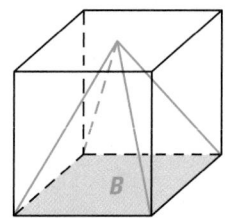

THEOREMS *For Your Notebook*

THEOREM 12.9 Volume of a Pyramid

The volume V of a pyramid is

$$V = \frac{1}{3}Bh,$$

where B is the area of the base and h is the height.

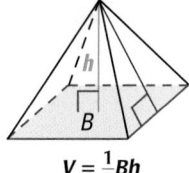
$V = \frac{1}{3}Bh$

THEOREM 12.10 Volume of a Cone

The volume V of a cone is

$$V = \frac{1}{3}Bh = \frac{1}{3}\pi r^2 h,$$

where B is the area of the base, h is the height, and r is the radius of the base.

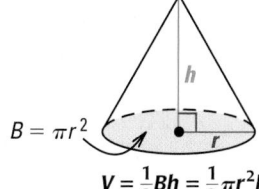
$B = \pi r^2$
$V = \frac{1}{3}Bh = \frac{1}{3}\pi r^2 h$

EXAMPLE 1 **Find the volume of a solid**

Find the volume of the solid.

APPLY FORMULAS
The formulas given in Theorems 12.9 and 12.10 apply to right and oblique pyramids and cones. This follows from Cavalieri's Principle, stated on page 821.

a.
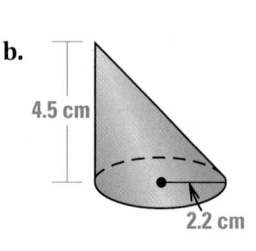
9 m
6 m
4 m

$V = \frac{1}{3}Bh$

$= \frac{1}{3}\left(\frac{1}{2} \cdot 4 \cdot 6\right)(9)$

$= 36 \text{ m}^3$

b.
4.5 cm
2.2 cm

$V = \frac{1}{3}Bh$

$= \frac{1}{3}(\pi r^2)h$

$= \frac{1}{3}(\pi \cdot 2.2^2)(4.5)$

$= 7.26\pi$

$\approx 22.81 \text{ cm}^3$

EXAMPLE 2 Use volume of a pyramid

Khafre's Pyramid, Egypt

ⓧⓨ ALGEBRA Originally, the pyramid had height 144 meters and volume 2,226,450 cubic meters. Find the side length of the square base.

Solution

$V = \frac{1}{3}Bh$	Write formula.
$2{,}226{,}450 = \frac{1}{3}(x^2)(144)$	Substitute.
$6{,}679{,}350 = 144x^2$	Multiply each side by 3.
$46{,}384 \approx x^2$	Divide each side by 144.
$215 \approx x$	Find the positive square root.

▶ Originally, the side length of the base was about 215 meters.

✓ **GUIDED PRACTICE** for Examples 1 and 2

Find the volume of the solid. Round your answer to two decimal places, if necessary.

1. Hexagonal pyramid

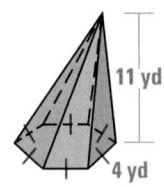

11 yd
4 yd

2. Right cone

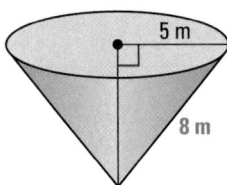

5 m
8 m

3. The volume of a right cone is 1350π cubic meters and the radius is 18 meters. Find the height of the cone.

EXAMPLE 3 Use trigonometry to find the volume of a cone

Find the volume of the right cone.

Solution

To find the radius r of the base, use trigonometry.

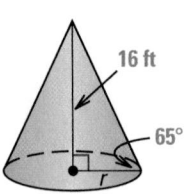

16 ft
65°
r

$\tan 65° = \dfrac{\text{opp.}}{\text{adj.}}$	Write ratio.
$\tan 65° = \dfrac{16}{r}$	Substitute.
$r = \dfrac{16}{\tan 65°} \approx 7.46$	Solve for r.

16 ft
65°
r

Use the formula for the volume of a cone.

$$V = \frac{1}{3}(\pi r^2)h \approx \frac{1}{3}\pi(7.46^2)(16) \approx 932.45 \text{ ft}^3$$

EXAMPLE 4 Find volume of a composite solid

Find the volume of the solid shown.

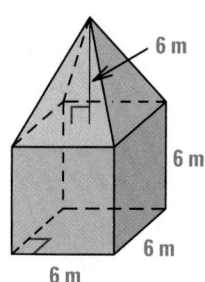

Solution

Volume of solid	=	Volume of cube	+	Volume of pyramid

$$= s^3 + \frac{1}{3}Bh \qquad \text{Write formulas.}$$

$$= 6^3 + \frac{1}{3}(6)^2 \cdot 6 \qquad \text{Substitute.}$$

$$= 216 + 72 \qquad \text{Simplify.}$$

$$= 288 \qquad \text{Add.}$$

▶ The volume of the solid is 288 cubic meters.

EXAMPLE 5 Solve a multi-step problem

SCIENCE You are using the funnel shown to measure the coarseness of a particular type of sand. It takes 2.8 seconds for the sand to empty out of the funnel. Find the flow rate of the sand in milliliters per second. (1 mL = 1 cm^3)

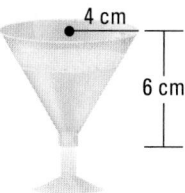

Solution

STEP 1 **Find** the volume of the funnel using the formula for the volume of a cone.

$$V = \frac{1}{3}(\pi r^2)h = \frac{1}{3}\pi(4^2)(6) \approx 101 \text{ cm}^3 = 101 \text{ mL}$$

STEP 2 **Divide** the volume of the funnel by the time it takes the sand to empty out of the funnel.

$$\frac{101 \text{ mL}}{2.8 \text{ s}} \approx 36.07 \text{ mL/s}$$

▶ The flow rate of the sand is about 36.07 milliliters per second.

✓ GUIDED PRACTICE for Examples 3, 4, and 5

4. Find the volume of the cone at the right. Round your answer to two decimal places.

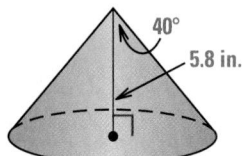

5. A right cylinder with radius 3 centimeters and height 10 centimeters has a right cone on top of it with the same base and height 5 centimeters. Find the volume of the solid. Round your answer to two decimal places.

6. **WHAT IF?** In Example 5, suppose a different type of sand is used that takes 3.2 seconds to empty out of the funnel. Find its flow rate.

12.5 EXERCISES

HOMEWORK KEY

○ = **WORKED-OUT SOLUTIONS**
on p. WS17 for Exs. 3, 17, and 33

★ = **STANDARDIZED TEST PRACTICE**
Exs. 2, 11, 18, and 35

◆ = **MULTIPLE REPRESENTATIONS**
Ex. 39

SKILL PRACTICE

1. **VOCABULARY** *Explain* the difference between a *triangular prism* and a *triangular pyramid*. Draw an example of each.

2. ★ **WRITING** *Compare* the volume of a square pyramid to the volume of a square prism with the same base and height as the pyramid.

EXAMPLE 1
on p. 829
for Exs. 3–11

VOLUME OF A SOLID Find the volume of the solid. Round your answer to two decimal places.

(3.)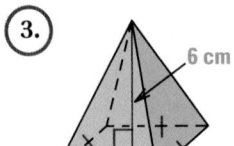
6 cm
5 cm

4.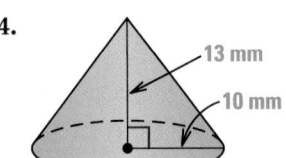
13 mm
10 mm

5.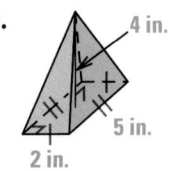
4 in.
5 in.
2 in.

6.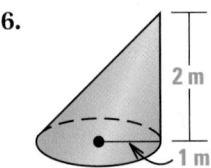
2 m
1 m

7.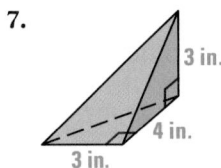
3 in.
4 in.
3 in.

8.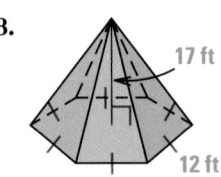
17 ft
12 ft

ERROR ANALYSIS *Describe* and correct the error in finding the volume of the right cone or pyramid.

9.
$$V = \frac{1}{3}\pi(9^2)(15)$$
$$= 405\pi$$
$$\approx 1272 \text{ ft}^3$$
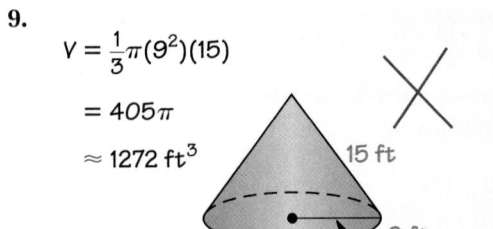
15 ft
9 ft

10.
$$V = \frac{1}{2}(49)(10)$$
$$= 245 \text{ ft}^3$$
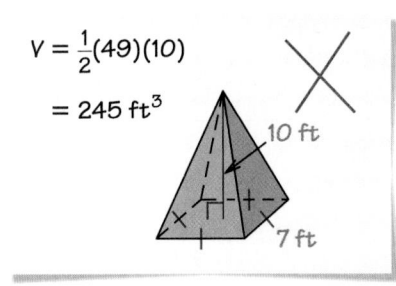
10 ft
7 ft

11. ★ **MULTIPLE CHOICE** The volume of a pyramid is 45 cubic feet and the height is 9 feet. What is the area of the base?

Ⓐ 3.87 ft²   Ⓑ 5 ft²   Ⓒ 10 ft²   Ⓓ 15 ft²

EXAMPLE 2
on p. 830
for Exs. 12–14

ALGEBRA Find the value of *x*.

12. Volume = 200 cm³
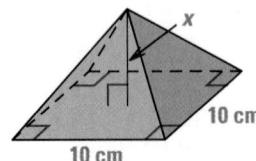
x
10 cm
10 cm

13. Volume = 216π in.³
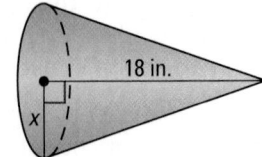
18 in.
x

14. Volume = 7√3 ft³
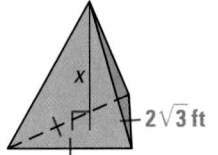
x
2√3 ft

EXAMPLE 3
on p. 830
for Exs. 15–19

VOLUME OF A CONE Find the volume of the right cone. Round your answer to two decimal places.

15.

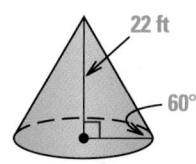

16.

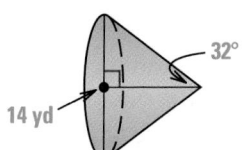

17.

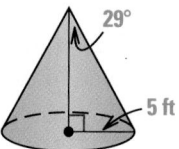

18. ★ **MULTIPLE CHOICE** What is the approximate volume of the cone?

(A) 47.23 ft³ (B) 236.15 ft³
(C) 269.92 ft³ (D) 354.21 ft³

19. HEIGHT OF A CONE A cone with a diameter of 8 centimeters has volume 143.6 cubic centimeters. Find the height of the cone. Round your answer to two decimal places.

EXAMPLE 4
on p. 831
for Exs. 20–25

COMPOSITE SOLIDS Find the volume of the solid. The prisms, pyramids, and cones are right. Round your answer to two decimal places.

20.

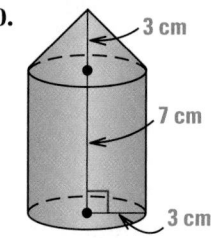

21.

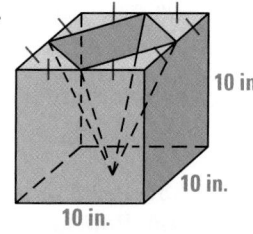

22.

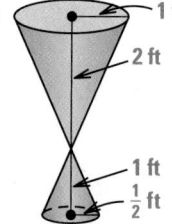

23.

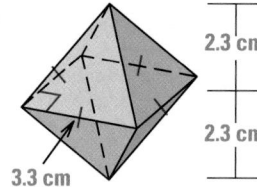

24.

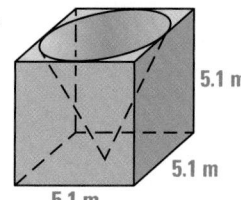

25.

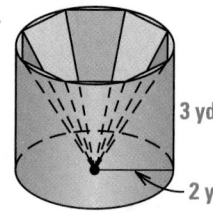

Animated Geometry at classzone.com

26. FINDING VOLUME The figure at the right is a cone that has been warped but whose cross sections still have the same area as a right cone with equal base area and height. Find the volume of this solid.

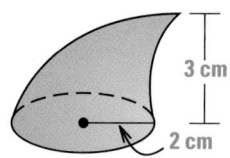

27. FINDING VOLUME Sketch a regular square pyramid with base edge length 5 meters inscribed in a cone with height 7 meters. Find the volume of the cone. *Explain* your reasoning.

28. CHALLENGE Find the volume of the regular hexagonal pyramid. Round your answer to the nearest hundredth of a cubic foot. In the diagram, m∠ABC = 35°.

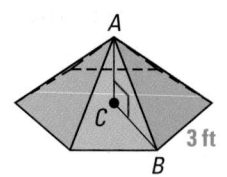

EXAMPLE 5
on p. 831
for Ex. 30

29. CAKE DECORATION A pastry bag filled with frosting has height 12 inches and radius 4 inches. A cake decorator can make 15 flowers using one bag of frosting.

   a. How much frosting is in the pastry bag? Round your answer to the nearest cubic inch.

   b. How many cubic inches of frosting are used to make each flower?

   @HomeTutor for problem solving help at classzone.com

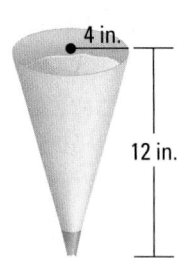

POPCORN A snack stand serves a small order of popcorn in a cone-shaped cup and a large order of popcorn in a cylindrical cup.

30. Find the volume of the small cup.

   @HomeTutor for problem solving help at classzone.com

31. How many small cups of popcorn do you have to buy to equal the amount of popcorn in a large container? Do not perform any calculations. *Explain.*

32. Which container gives you more popcorn for your money? *Explain.*

USING NETS In Exercises 33 and 34, use the net to sketch the solid. Then find the volume of the solid. Round your answer to two decimal places.

 33.

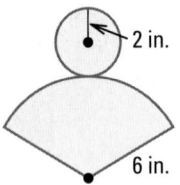

34.

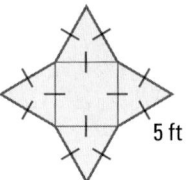

35. ★ EXTENDED RESPONSE A pyramid has height 10 feet and a square base with side length 7 feet.

   a. How does the volume of the pyramid change if the base stays the same and the height is doubled?

   b. How does the volume of the pyramid change if the height stays the same and the side length of the base is doubled?

   c. *Explain* why your answers to parts (a) and (b) are true for any height and side length.

36. AUTOMATIC FEEDER Assume the automatic pet feeder is a right cylinder on top of a right cone of the same radius. (1 cup = 14.4 in.^{3})

   a. Calculate the amount of food in cups that can be placed in the feeder.

   b. A cat eats one third of a cup of food, twice per day. How many days will the feeder have food without refilling it?

○ = **WORKED-OUT SOLUTIONS** on p. WS1   ★ = **STANDARDIZED TEST PRACTICE**   ◆ = **MULTIPLE REPRESENTATIONS**

37. NAUTICAL PRISMS The nautical deck prism shown is composed of the following three solids: a regular hexagonal prism with edge length 3.5 inches and height 1.5 inches, a regular hexagonal prism with edge length 3.25 inches and height 0.25 inch, and a regular hexagonal pyramid with edge length 3 inches and height 3 inches. Find the volume of the deck prism.

38. MULTI-STEP PROBLEM Calculus can be used to show that the average value of r^2 of a circular cross section of a cone is $\dfrac{r_b^2}{3}$, where r_b is the radius of the base.

  a. Find the average area of a circular cross section of a cone whose base has radius R.

  b. Show that the volume of the cone can be expressed as follows:
$$V_{\text{cone}} = (\text{Average area of a circular cross section}) \cdot (\text{Height of cone})$$

39. ◆ MULTIPLE REPRESENTATIONS Water flows into a reservoir shaped like a right cone at the rate of 1.8 cubic meters per minute. The height and diameter of the reservoir are equal.

  a. Using Algebra As the water flows into the reservoir, the relationship $h = 2r$ is always true. Using this fact, show that $V = \dfrac{\pi h^3}{12}$.

  b. Making a Table Make a table that gives the height h of the water after 1, 2, 3, 4, and 5 minutes.

  c. Drawing a Graph Make a graph of height versus time. Is there a linear relationship between the height of the water and time? *Explain.*

FRUSTUM A frustum of a cone is the part of the cone that lies between the base and a plane parallel to the base, as shown. Use the information to complete Exercises 40 and 41.

One method for calculating the volume of a frustum is to add the areas of the two bases to their geometric mean, then multiply the result by $\frac{1}{3}$ the height.

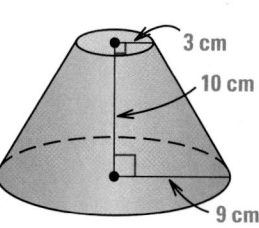

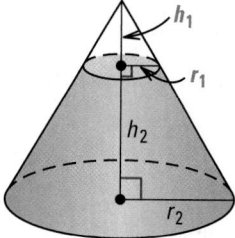

40. Use the measurements in the diagram at the left above to calculate the volume of the frustum.

41. Complete parts (a) and (b) below to write a formula for the volume of a frustum that has bases with radii r_1 and r_2 and a height h_2.

  a. Use similar triangles to find the value of h_1 in terms of h_2, r_1, and r_2.

  b. Write a formula in terms of h_2, r_1, and r_2 for
$V_{\text{frustum}} = (\text{Original volume}) - (\text{Removed volume})$.

  c. Show that your formula in part (b) is equivalent to the formula involving geometric mean described above.

42. CHALLENGE A square pyramid is inscribed in a right cylinder so that the base of the pyramid is on a base of the cylinder, and the vertex of the pyramid is on the other base of the cylinder. The cylinder has radius 6 feet and height 12 feet. Find the volume of the pyramid. Round your answer to two decimal places.

MIXED REVIEW

In Exercises 43–45, find the value of *x*. (p. 397)

43.
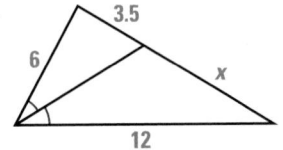

44.
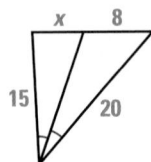

45.
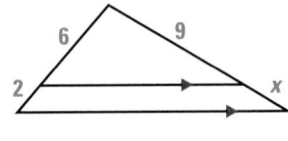

PREVIEW
Prepare for Lesson 12.6 in Exs. 46–52.

46. Copy the diagram at the right. Name a radius, diameter, and chord. (p. 651)

47. Name a minor arc of ⊙*F*. (p. 659)

48. Name a major arc of ⊙*F*. (p. 659)

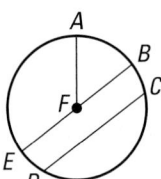

Find the area of the circle with the given radius *r*, diameter *d*, or circumference *C*. (p. 755)

49. $r = 3$ m   **50.** $d = 7$ mi   **51.** $r = 0.4$ cm   **52.** $C = 8\pi$ in.

QUIZ *for Lessons 12.4–12.5*

Find the volume of the figure. Round your answer to two decimal places, if necessary. (pp. 819, 829)

1.
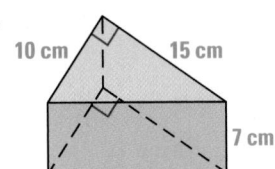

2.
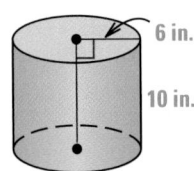

3.
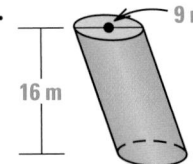

4.
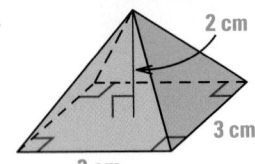

5.
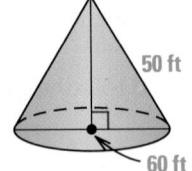

6.
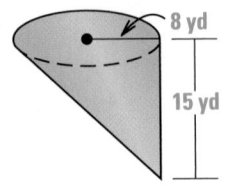

7. Suppose you fill up a cone-shaped cup with water. You then pour the water into a cylindrical cup with the same radius. Both cups have a height of 6 inches. Without doing any calculation, determine how high the water level will be in the cylindrical cup once all of the water is poured into it. *Explain* your reasoning. (p. 829)

12.5 Minimize Surface Area

MATERIALS · computer

QUESTION How can you find the minimum surface area of a solid with a given volume?

A manufacturer needs a cylindrical container with a volume of 72 cubic centimeters. You have been asked to find the dimensions of such a container so that it has a minimum surface area.

EXAMPLE Use a spreadsheet

STEP 1 *Make a table* Make a table with the four column headings shown in Step 4. The first column is for the given volume V. In cell A2, enter 72. In cell A3, enter the formula "=A2".

STEP 2 *Enter radius* The second column is for the radius r. Cell B2 stores the starting value for r. So, enter 2 into cell B2. In cell B3, use the formula "=B2 + 0.05" to increase r in increments of 0.05 centimeter.

STEP 3 *Enter formula for height* The third column is for the height. In cell C2, enter the formula "=A2/(PI()*B2^2)". *Note:* Your spreadsheet might use a different expression for π.

STEP 4 *Enter formula for surface area* The fourth column is for the surface area. In cell D2, enter the formula "=2*PI()*B2^2+2*PI()*B2*C2".

	A	B	C	D
1	Volume V	Radius r	Height$=V/(\pi r^2)$	Surface area $S=2\pi r^2+2\pi rh$
2	72.00	2.00	=A2/(PI()*B2^2)	=2*PI()*B2^2+2*PI()*B2*C2
3	=A2	=B2+0.05		

STEP 5 *Create more rows* Use the *Fill Down* feature to create more rows. Rows 3 and 4 of your spreadsheet should resemble the one below.

	A	B	C	D
...				
3	72.00	2.05	5.45	96.65
4	72.00	2.10	5.20	96.28

PRACTICE

1. From the data in your spreadsheet, which dimensions yield a minimum surface area for the given volume? *Explain* how you know.

2. **WHAT IF?** Find the dimensions that give the minimum surface area if the volume of a cylinder is instead 200π cubic centimeters.

12.6 Surface Area and Volume of Spheres

Before	You found surface areas and volumes of polyhedra.
Now	You will find surface areas and volumes of spheres.
Why?	So you can find the volume of a tennis ball, as in Ex. 33.

Key Vocabulary
- **sphere**
  center, radius, chord, diameter
- **great circle**
- **hemispheres**

A **sphere** is the set of all points in space equidistant from a given point. This point is called the **center** of the sphere. A **radius** of a sphere is a segment from the center to a point on the sphere. A **chord** of a sphere is a segment whose endpoints are on the sphere. A **diameter** of a sphere is a chord that contains the center.

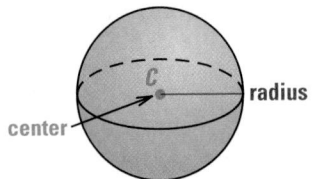

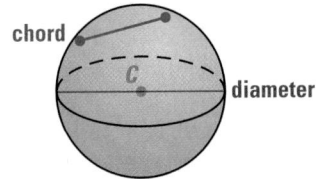

As with circles, the terms radius and diameter also represent distances, and the diameter is twice the radius.

THEOREM *For Your Notebook*

THEOREM 12.11 Surface Area of a Sphere

The surface area S of a sphere is

$$S = 4\pi r^2,$$

where r is the radius of the sphere.

$S = 4\pi r^2$

USE FORMULAS
If you understand how a formula is derived, then it will be easier for you to remember the formula.

SURFACE AREA FORMULA To understand how the formula for the surface area of a sphere is derived, think of a baseball. The surface area of a baseball is sewn from two congruent shapes, each of which resembles two joined circles, as shown.

So, the entire covering of the baseball consists of four circles, each with radius r. The area A of a circle with radius r is $A = \pi r^2$. So, the area of the covering can be approximated by $4\pi r^2$. This is the formula for the surface area of a sphere.

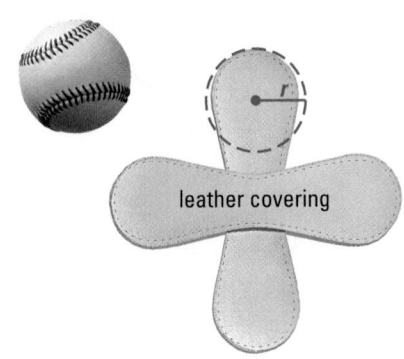

leather covering

EXAMPLE 1   Find the surface area of a sphere

Find the surface area of the sphere.

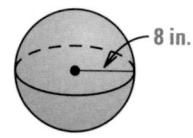

8 in.

Solution

$S = 4\pi r^2$ **Formula for surface area of a sphere**

$= 4\pi(8^2)$ **Substitute 8 for *r*.**

$= 256\pi$ **Simplify.**

≈ 804.25 **Use a calculator.**

▶ The surface area of the sphere is about 804.25 square inches.

EXAMPLE 2   Standardized Test Practice

The surface area of the sphere is 20.25π square centimeters. What is the diameter of the sphere?

  A 2.25 cm   **B** 4.5 cm

  C 5.5 cm   **D** 20.25 cm

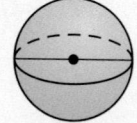

$S = 20.25\,\pi\,\text{cm}^2$

Solution

$S = 4\pi r^2$ **Formula for surface area of a sphere**

$20.25\pi = 4\pi r^2$ **Substitute 20.25π for *S*.**

$5.0625 = r^2$ **Divide each side by 4π.**

$2.25 = r$ **Find the positive square root.**

AVOID ERRORS
Be sure to multiply the value of *r* by 2 to find the diameter.

The diameter of the sphere is $2r = 2 \cdot 2.25 = 4.5$ centimeters.

▶ The correct answer is B.   **A** **B** **C** **D**

✓ **GUIDED PRACTICE**   for Examples 1 and 2

1. The diameter of a sphere is 40 feet. Find the surface area of the sphere.

2. The surface area of a sphere is 30π square meters. Find the radius of the sphere.

GREAT CIRCLES If a plane intersects a sphere, the intersection is either a single point or a circle. If the plane contains the center of the sphere, then the intersection is a **great circle** of the sphere. The circumference of a great circle is the circumference of the sphere. Every great circle of a sphere separates the sphere into two congruent halves called **hemispheres**.

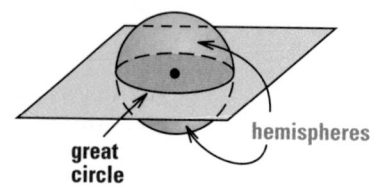

hemispheres

great circle

EXAMPLE 3 **Use the circumference of a sphere**

EXTREME SPORTS In a sport called *sphereing*, a person rolls down a hill inside an inflatable ball surrounded by another ball. The diameter of the outer ball is 12 feet. Find the surface area of the outer ball.

Solution

The diameter of the outer sphere is 12 feet, so the radius is $\frac{12}{2} = 6$ feet.

Use the formula for the surface area of a sphere.

$$S = 4\pi r^2 = 4\pi(6^2) = 144\pi$$

▶ The surface area of the outer ball is 144π, or about 452.39 square feet.

✓ **GUIDED PRACTICE** **for Example 3**

3. In Example 3, the circumference of the inner ball is 6π feet. Find the surface area of the inner ball. Round your answer to two decimal places.

VOLUME FORMULA Imagine that the interior of a sphere with radius r is approximated by n pyramids, each with a base area of B and a height of r. The volume of each pyramid is $\frac{1}{3}Br$ and the sum of the base areas is nB. The surface area of the sphere is approximately equal to nB, or $4\pi r^2$. So, you can approximate the volume V of the sphere as follows.

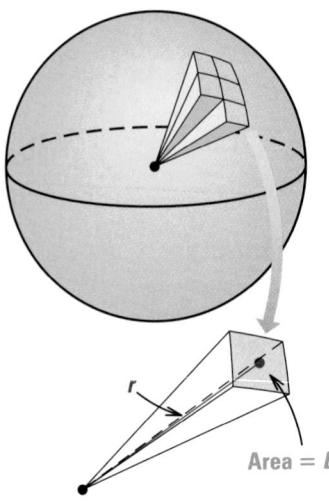

$V \approx n\left(\frac{1}{3}Br\right)$ **Each pyramid has a volume of $\frac{1}{3}Br$.**

$\approx \frac{1}{3}(nB)r$ **Regroup factors.**

$= \frac{1}{3}(4\pi r^2)r$ **Substitute $4\pi r^2$ for nB.**

$= \frac{4}{3}\pi r^3$ **Simplify.**

Area = B

THEOREM   *For Your Notebook*

THEOREM 12.12 **Volume of a Sphere**

The volume V of a sphere is

$$V = \frac{4}{3}\pi r^3,$$

where r is the radius of the sphere.

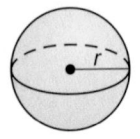

$V = \frac{4}{3}\pi r^3$

EXAMPLE 4　Find the volume of a sphere

The soccer ball has a diameter of 9 inches. Find its volume.

Solution

The diameter of the ball is 9 inches, so the radius is $\frac{9}{2}$ = 4.5 inches.

$V = \frac{4}{3}\pi r^3$　　　**Formula for volume of a sphere**

$\quad = \frac{4}{3}\pi(4.5)^3$　　**Substitute.**

$\quad = 121.5\pi$　　　**Simplify.**

$\quad \approx 381.70$　　　**Use a calculator.**

▶ The volume of the soccer ball is 121.5π, or about 381.70 cubic inches.

EXAMPLE 5　Find the volume of a composite solid

Find the volume of the composite solid.

Solution

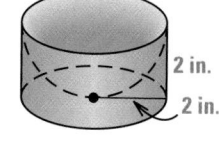

Volume of solid	=	Volume of cylinder	−	Volume of hemisphere

$= \pi r^2 h - \frac{1}{2}\left(\frac{4}{3}\pi r^3\right)$　　**Formulas for volume**

$= \pi(2)^2(2) - \frac{2}{3}\pi(2)^3$　　**Substitute.**

$= 8\pi - \frac{2}{3}(8\pi)$　　　**Multiply.**

$= \frac{24}{3}\pi - \frac{16}{3}\pi$　　　**Rewrite fractions using least common denominator.**

$= \frac{8}{3}\pi$　　　　**Simplify.**

▶ The volume of the solid is $\frac{8}{3}\pi$, or about 8.38 cubic inches.

Animated **Geometry**　at classzone.com

✓　**GUIDED PRACTICE**　for Examples 4 and 5

4. The radius of a sphere is 5 yards. Find the volume of the sphere. Round your answer to two decimal places.

5. A solid consists of a hemisphere of radius 1 meter on top of a cone with the same radius and height 5 meters. Find the volume of the solid. Round your answer to two decimal places.

12.6 EXERCISES

○ = **WORKED-OUT SOLUTIONS**
on p. WS18 for Exs. 3, 13, and 31

★ = **STANDARDIZED TEST PRACTICE**
Exs. 2, 6, 20, 28, 33, and 34

SKILL PRACTICE

1. **VOCABULARY** What are the formulas for finding the surface area of a sphere and the volume of a sphere?

2. ★ **WRITING** When a plane intersects a sphere, what point in the sphere must the plane contain for the intersection to be a great circle? *Explain.*

EXAMPLE 1
on p. 839
for Exs. 3–5

FINDING SURFACE AREA **Find the surface area of the sphere. Round your answer to two decimal places.**

3.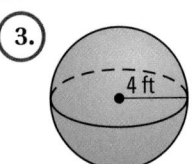
4 ft

4.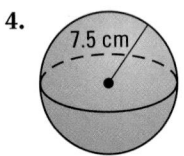
7.5 cm

5.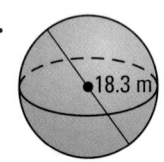
18.3 m

EXAMPLE 2
on p. 839
for Ex. 6

6. ★ **MULTIPLE CHOICE** What is the approximate radius of a sphere with surface area 32π square meters?

Ⓐ 2 meters Ⓑ 2.83 meters Ⓒ 4.90 meters Ⓓ 8 meters

EXAMPLE 3
on p. 840
for Exs. 7–11

USING A GREAT CIRCLE **In Exercises 7–9, use the sphere below. The center of the sphere is C and its circumference is 9.6π inches.**

7. Find the radius of the sphere.

8. Find the diameter of the sphere.

9. Find the surface area of one hemisphere.

10. **ERROR ANALYSIS** *Describe* and correct the error in finding the surface area of a hemisphere with radius 5 feet.

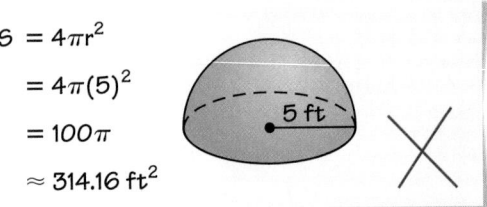

$$S = 4\pi r^2$$
$$= 4\pi(5)^2$$
$$= 100\pi$$
$$\approx 314.16 \text{ ft}^2$$

5 ft

11. **GREAT CIRCLE** The circumference of a great circle of a sphere is 48.4π centimeters. What is the surface area of the sphere?

EXAMPLE 4
on p. 841
for Exs. 12–15

FINDING VOLUME **Find the volume of the sphere using the given radius r or diameter d. Round your answer to two decimal places.**

12. $r = 6$ in.

13. $r = 40$ mm

14. $d = 5$ cm

15. ERROR ANALYSIS *Describe* and correct the error in finding the volume of a sphere with diameter 16 feet.

$$V = \frac{4}{3}\pi r^2$$

$$= \frac{4}{3}\pi(8)^2$$

$$= 85.33\pi \approx 268.08 \text{ ft}^2$$

USING VOLUME In Exercises 16–18, find the radius of a sphere with the given volume *V*. Round your answers to two decimal places.

16. $V = 1436.76 \text{ m}^3$ **17.** $V = 91.95 \text{ cm}^3$ **18.** $V = 20{,}814.37 \text{ in.}^3$

19. FINDING A DIAMETER The volume of a sphere is 36π cubic feet. What is the diameter of the sphere?

20. ★ MULTIPLE CHOICE Let *V* be the volume of a sphere, *S* be the surface area of the sphere, and *r* be the radius of the sphere. Which equation represents the relationship between these three measures?

A $V = \frac{rS}{3}$ **B** $V = \frac{r^2 S}{3}$ **C** $V = \frac{3}{2}rS$ **D** $V = \frac{3}{2}r^2 S$

EXAMPLE 5
on p. 841
for Exs. 21–23

COMPOSITE SOLIDS Find the surface area and the volume of the solid. The cylinders and cones are right. Round your answers to two decimal places.

21.
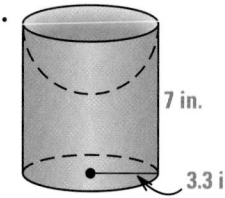
7 in.
3.3 in.

22.
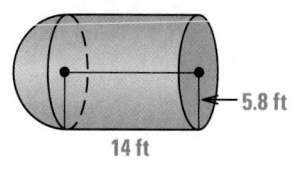
5.8 ft
14 ft

23.
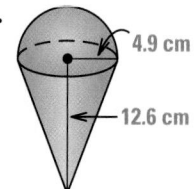
4.9 cm
12.6 cm

USING A TABLE Copy and complete the table below. Leave your answers in terms of π.

	Radius of sphere	Circumference of great circle	Surface area of sphere	Volume of sphere
24.	10 ft	?	?	?
25.	?	26π in.	?	?
26.	?	?	$2500\pi \text{ cm}^2$	?
27.	?	?	?	$12{,}348\pi \text{ m}^3$

28. ★ MULTIPLE CHOICE A sphere is inscribed in a cube with volume 64 cubic centimeters. What is the surface area of the sphere?

A $4\pi \text{ cm}^2$ **B** $\frac{32}{3}\pi \text{ cm}^2$ **C** $16\pi \text{ cm}^2$ **D** $64\pi \text{ cm}^2$

29. CHALLENGE The volume of a right cylinder is the same as the volume of a sphere. The radius of the sphere is 1 inch.

a. Give three possibilities for the dimensions of the cylinder.

b. Show that the surface area of the cylinder is sometimes greater than the surface area of the sphere.

EXAMPLE 5
on p. 841
for Ex. 30

30. GRAIN SILO A grain silo has the dimensions shown. The top of the silo is a hemispherical shape. Find the volume of the grain silo.

@**HomeTutor** for problem solving help at classzone.com

(31.) GEOGRAPHY The circumference of Earth is about 24,855 miles. Find the surface area of the Western Hemisphere of Earth.

@**HomeTutor** for problem solving help at classzone.com

32. MULTI-STEP PROBLEM A ball has volume 1427.54 cubic centimeters.

   a. Find the radius of the ball. Round your answer to two decimal places.

   b. Find the surface area of the ball. Round your answer to two decimal places.

33. ★ SHORT RESPONSE Tennis balls are stored in a cylindrical container with height 8.625 inches and radius 1.43 inches.

   a. The circumference of a tennis ball is 8 inches. Find the volume of a tennis ball.

   b. There are 3 tennis balls in the container. Find the amount of space within the cylinder not taken up by the tennis balls.

34. ★ EXTENDED RESPONSE A partially filled balloon has circumference 27π centimeters. Assume the balloon is a sphere.

   a. Calculate Find the volume of the balloon.

   b. Predict Suppose you double the radius by increasing the air in the balloon. *Explain* what you expect to happen to the volume.

   c. Justify Find the volume of the balloon with the radius doubled. Was your prediction from part (b) correct? What is the ratio of this volume to the original volume?

35. GEOGRAPHY The Torrid Zone on Earth is the area between the Tropic of Cancer and the Tropic of Capricorn, as shown. The distance between these two tropics is about 3250 miles. You can think of this distance as the height of a cylindrical belt around Earth at the equator, as shown.

   a. Estimate the surface area of the Torrid Zone and the surface area of Earth. (Earth's radius is about 3963 miles at the equator.)

   b. A meteorite is equally likely to hit anywhere on Earth. Estimate the probability that a meteorite will land in the Torrid Zone.

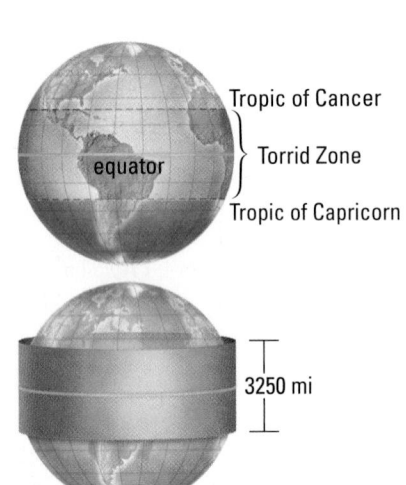

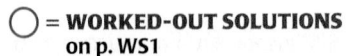

36. REASONING List the following three solids in order from least to greatest (a) surface area and (b) volume.

Solid I

Solid II

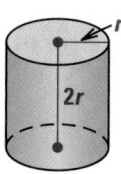

Solid III

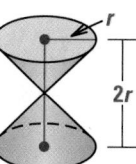

37. ROTATION A circle with diameter 18 inches is rotated about its diameter. Find the surface area and the volume of the solid formed.

38. TECHNOLOGY A cylinder with height $2x$ is inscribed in a sphere with radius 8 meters. The center of the sphere is the midpoint of the altitude that joins the centers of the bases of the cylinder.

   a. Show that the volume V of the cylinder is $2\pi x(64 - x^2)$.

   b. Use a graphing calculator to graph $V = 2\pi x(64 - x^2)$ for values of x between 0 and 8. Find the value of x that gives the maximum value of V.

   c. Use the value for x from part (b) to find the maximum volume of the cylinder.

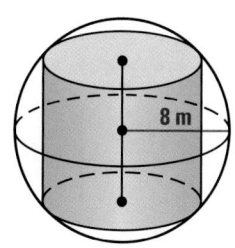

39. CHALLENGE A sphere with radius 2 centimeters is inscribed in a right cone with height 6 centimeters. Find the surface area and the volume of the cone.

MIXED REVIEW

PREVIEW
Prepare for
Lesson 12.7 in
Exs. 40–41.

In Exercises 40 and 41, the polygons are similar. Find the ratio (red to blue) of their areas. Find the unknown area. Round your answer to two decimal places. *(p. 737)*

40. Area of $\triangle ABC = 42$ ft^2
Area of $\triangle DEF = $ __?__

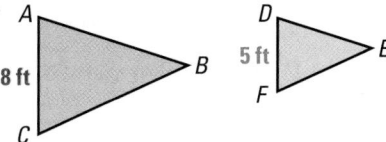

41. Area of $PQRS = 195$ cm^2
Area of $JKLM = $ __?__

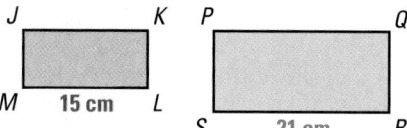

Find the probability that a randomly chosen point in the figure lies in the shaded region. *(p. 771)*

42.

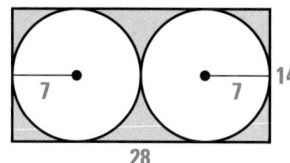

43.

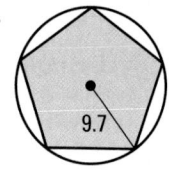

44. A cone is inscribed in a right cylinder with volume 330 cubic units. Find the volume of the cone. *(pp. 819, 829)*

EXTRA PRACTICE for Lesson 12.6, p. 919   **ONLINE QUIZ** at classzone.com   **845**

12.7 Investigate Similar Solids

MATERIALS · paper · pencil

QUESTION How are the surface areas and volumes of similar solids related?

EXPLORE Compare the surface areas and volumes of similar solids

The solids shown below are *similar.*

Pair 1 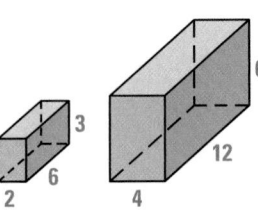 **Pair 2** 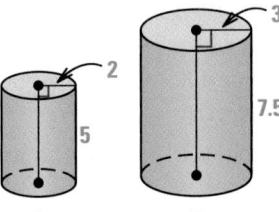 **Pair 3**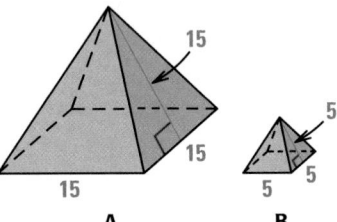

STEP 1 *Make a table* Copy and complete the table below.

	Scale factor of Solid A to Solid B	Surface area of Solid A, S_A	Surface area of Solid B, S_B	$\dfrac{S_A}{S_B}$
Pair 1	$\dfrac{1}{2}$	?	?	?
Pair 2	?	?	63π	?
Pair 3	?	?	?	$\dfrac{9}{1}$

STEP 2 *Insert columns* Insert columns for V_A, V_B, and $\dfrac{V_A}{V_B}$. Use the dimensions of the solids to find V_A, the volume of Solid A, and V_B, the volume of Solid B. Then find the ratio of these volumes.

STEP 3 *Compare ratios* Compare the ratios $\dfrac{S_A}{S_B}$ and $\dfrac{V_A}{V_B}$ to the scale factor.

DRAW CONCLUSIONS Use your observations to complete these exercises

1. Make a conjecture about how the surface areas and volumes of similar solids are related to the scale factor.

2. Use your conjecture to write a ratio of surface areas and volumes if the dimensions of two similar rectangular prisms are ℓ, w, h, and $k\ell$, kw, kh.

12.7 Explore Similar Solids

Before You used properties of similar polygons.

Now You will use properties of similar solids.

Why So you can determine a ratio of volumes, as in Ex. 26.

Key Vocabulary
• similar solids

Two solids of the same type with equal ratios of corresponding linear measures, such as heights or radii, are called **similar solids**. The common ratio is called the *scale factor* of one solid to the other solid. Any two cubes are similar, as well as any two spheres.

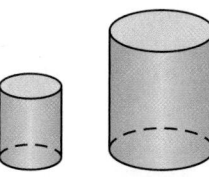

Similar cylinders

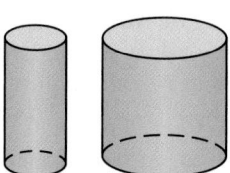

Nonsimilar cylinders

The green cylinders shown above are not similar. Their heights are equal, so they have a 1 : 1 ratio. The radii are different, however, so there is no common ratio.

EXAMPLE 1 Identify similar solids

Tell whether the given right rectangular prism is similar to the right rectangular prism shown at the right.

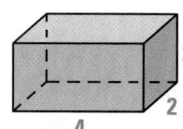

a.
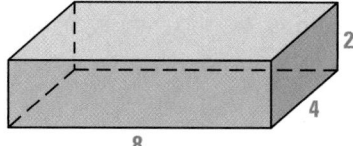

b.
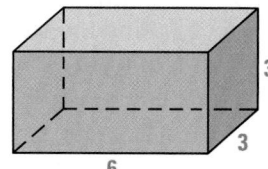

Solution

a. Lengths $\dfrac{4}{8} = \dfrac{1}{2}$ Widths $\dfrac{2}{4} = \dfrac{1}{2}$ Heights $\dfrac{2}{2} = \dfrac{1}{1}$

▶ The prisms are not similar because the ratios of corresponding linear measures are not all equal.

COMPARE RATIOS
To compare the ratios of corresponding side lengths, write the ratios as fractions in simplest form.

b. Lengths $\dfrac{4}{6} = \dfrac{2}{3}$ Widths $\dfrac{2}{3}$ Heights $\dfrac{2}{3}$

▶ The prisms are similar because the ratios of corresponding linear measures are all equal. The scale factor is 2 : 3.

Tell whether the pair of right solids is similar. *Explain* your reasoning.

1.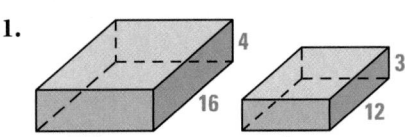

2.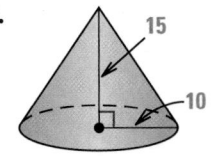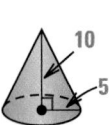

SIMILAR SOLIDS THEOREM The surface areas S and volumes V of the similar solids in Example 1, part (b), are as follows.

Prism	Dimensions	Surface area, $S = 2B + Ph$	Volume, $V = Bh$
Smaller	4 by 2 by 2	$S = 2(8) + 12(2) = 40$	$V = 8(2) = 16$
Larger	6 by 3 by 3	$S = 2(18) + 18(3) = 90$	$V = 18(3) = 54$

The ratio of side lengths is $2:3$. Notice that the ratio of surface areas is $40:90$, or $4:9$, which can be written as $2^2:3^2$, and the ratio of volumes is $16:54$, or $8:27$, which can be written as $2^3:3^3$. This leads to the following theorem.

THEOREM *For Your Notebook*

THEOREM 12.13 Similar Solids Theorem

If two similar solids have a scale factor of $a:b$, then corresponding areas have a ratio of $a^2:b^2$, and corresponding volumes have a ratio of $a^3:b^3$.

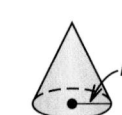 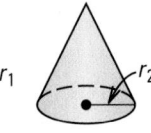

$$\frac{r_1}{r_2} = \frac{a}{b}, \quad \frac{S_1}{S_2} = \frac{a^2}{b^2}, \quad \frac{V_1}{V_2} = \frac{a^3}{b^3}$$

EXAMPLE 2 Use the scale factor of similar solids

PACKAGING The cans shown are similar with a scale factor of $87:100$. Find the surface area and volume of the larger can.

I  II

$S = 51.84$ in.^{2}
$V = 28.27$ in.^{3}

Solution

Use Theorem 12.13 to write and solve two proportions.

$$\frac{\text{Surface area of I}}{\text{Surface area of II}} = \frac{a^2}{b^2} \qquad \frac{\text{Volume of I}}{\text{Volume of II}} = \frac{a^3}{b^3}$$

$$\frac{51.84}{\text{Surface area of II}} = \frac{87^2}{100^2} \qquad \frac{28.27}{\text{Volume of II}} = \frac{87^3}{100^3}$$

$$\text{Surface area of II} \approx 68.49 \qquad \text{Volume of II} \approx 42.93$$

▶ The surface area of the larger can is about 68.49 square inches, and the volume of the larger can is about 42.93 cubic inches.

EXAMPLE 3 **Find the scale factor**

The pyramids are similar. Pyramid P
has a volume of 1000 cubic inches
and Pyramid Q has a volume of
216 cubic inches. Find the scale factor
of Pyramid P to Pyramid Q.

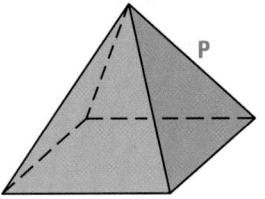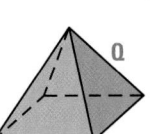

Solution

Use Theorem 12.13 to find the ratio of the two volumes.

$$\frac{a^3}{b^3} = \frac{1000}{216} \qquad \text{Write ratio of volumes.}$$

$$\frac{a}{b} = \frac{10}{6} \qquad \text{Find cube roots.}$$

$$\frac{a}{b} = \frac{5}{3} \qquad \text{Simplify.}$$

▶ The scale factor of Pyramid P to Pyramid Q is $5:3$.

EXAMPLE 4 **Compare similar solids**

CONSUMER ECONOMICS A store sells balls of yarn in two different sizes. The
diameter of the larger ball is twice the diameter of the smaller ball. If the balls
of yarn cost $7.50 and $1.50, respectively, which ball of yarn is the better buy?

Solution

STEP 1 **Compute** the ratio of volumes using the diameters.

$$\frac{\text{Volume of large ball}}{\text{Volume of small ball}} = \frac{2^3}{1^3} = \frac{8}{1}, \text{ or } 8:1$$

STEP 2 **Find** the ratio of costs.

$$\frac{\text{Price of large ball}}{\text{Price of small ball}} = \frac{\$7.50}{\$1.50} = \frac{5}{1}, \text{ or } 5:1$$

STEP 3 **Compare** the ratios in Steps 1 and 2.

If the ratios were the same, neither ball would be a better buy.
Comparing the smaller ball to the larger one, the price increase is
less than the volume increase. So, you get more yarn for your dollar
if you buy the larger ball of yarn.

▶ The larger ball of yarn is the better buy.

✓ **GUIDED PRACTICE** | for Examples 2, 3, and 4

3. Cube C has a surface area of 54 square units and Cube D has a surface
   area of 150 square units. Find the scale factor of C to D. Find the edge
   length of C, and use the scale factor to find the volume of D.

4. **WHAT IF?** In Example 4, calculate a new price for the larger ball of yarn
   so that neither ball would be a better buy than the other.

12.7 EXERCISES

HOMEWORK KEY

○ = **WORKED-OUT SOLUTIONS**
on p. WS18 for Exs. 3, 9, and 27

★ = **STANDARDIZED TEST PRACTICE**
Exs. 2, 7, 16, 28, 31, and 33

◆ = **MULTIPLE REPRESENTATIONS**
Ex. 34

SKILL PRACTICE

1. **VOCABULARY** What does it mean for two solids to be similar?

2. ★ **WRITING** How are the volumes of similar solids related?

EXAMPLE 1
on p. 847
for Exs. 3–7

IDENTIFYING SIMILAR SOLIDS **Tell whether the pair of right solids is similar.** *Explain* **your reasoning.**

(3.)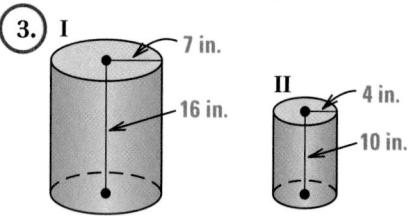

4.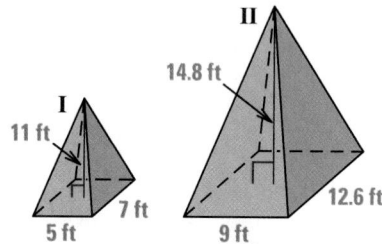

5.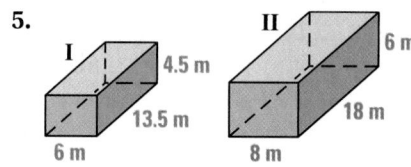

6.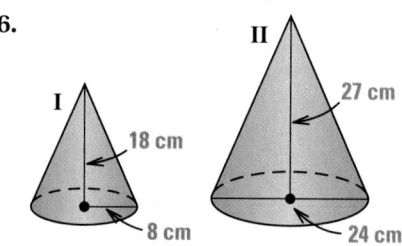

7. ★ **MULTIPLE CHOICE** Which set of dimensions corresponds to a triangular prism that is similar to the prism shown?

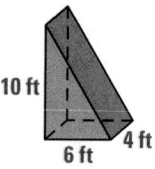

Ⓐ 2 feet by 1 foot by 5 feet   Ⓑ 4 feet by 2 feet by 8 feet

Ⓒ 9 feet by 6 feet by 20 feet   Ⓓ 15 feet by 10 feet by 25 feet

EXAMPLE 2
on p. 848
for Exs. 8–11

USING SCALE FACTOR **Solid A (shown) is similar to Solid B (not shown) with the given scale factor of A to B. Find the surface area and volume of Solid B.**

8. Scale factor of $1:2$

$S = 150\pi$ in.^{2}
$V = 250\pi$ in.^{3}

(9.) Scale factor of $3:1$

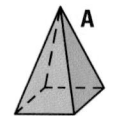

$S = 1500$ m^2
$V = 3434.6$ m^3

10. Scale factor of $5:2$

$S = 2356.2$ cm^2
$V = 7450.9$ cm^3

11. **ERROR ANALYSIS** The scale factor of two similar solids is $1:4$. The volume of the smaller Solid A is 500π. *Describe* and correct the error in writing an equation to find the volume of the larger Solid B.

$$\frac{500\pi}{\text{Volume of B}} = \frac{1^2}{4^2}$$

EXAMPLE 3
on p. 849
for Exs. 12–18

FINDING SCALE FACTOR In Exercises 12–15, Solid I is similar to Solid II. Find the scale factor of Solid I to Solid II.

12.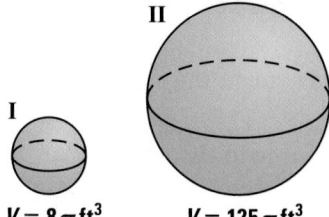

I $V = 8\pi$ ft³   II $V = 125\pi$ ft³

13.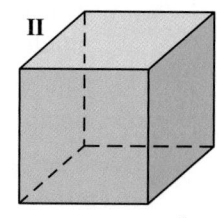

I $V = 27$ in.³   II $V = 729$ in.³

14.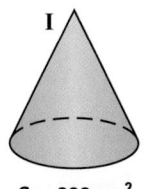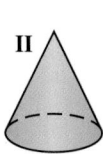

I $S = 288$ cm²   II $S = 128$ cm²

15.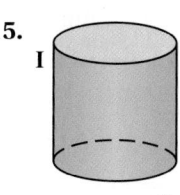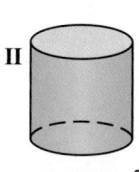

I $S = 192$ cm²   II $S = 108$ cm²

16. ★ **MULTIPLE CHOICE** The volumes of two similar cones are 8π and 27π. What is the ratio of the lateral areas of the cones?

Ⓐ $\frac{8}{27}$ Ⓑ $\frac{1}{3}$ Ⓒ $\frac{4}{9}$ Ⓓ $\frac{2}{3}$

17. **FINDING A RATIO** Two spheres have volumes of 2π cubic feet and 16π cubic feet. What is the ratio of the surface area of the smaller sphere to the surface area of the larger sphere?

18. **FINDING SURFACE AREA** Two similar cylinders have a scale factor of $2:3$. The smaller cylinder has a surface area of 78π square meters. Find the surface area of the larger cylinder.

COMPOSITE SOLIDS In Exercises 19–22, Solid I is similar to Solid II. Find the surface area and volume of Solid II.

19.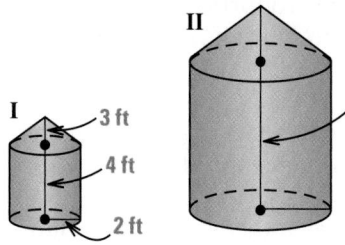

20.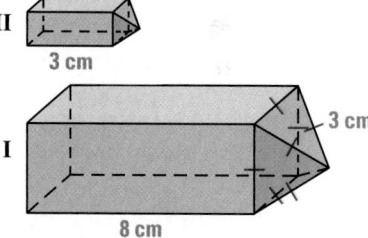

21.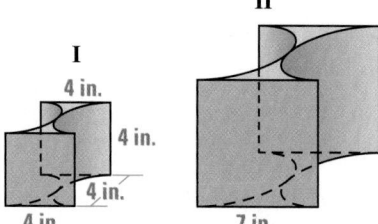

22.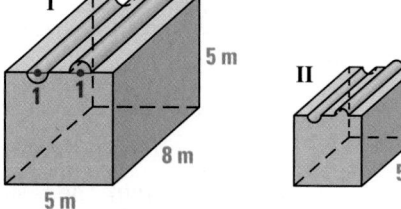

23. (xy) **ALGEBRA** Two similar cylinders have surface areas of 54π square feet and 384π square feet. The height of each cylinder is equal to its diameter. Find the radius and height of both cylinders.

24. CHALLENGE A plane parallel to the base of a cone divides the cone into two pieces with the dimensions shown. Find each ratio described.

  a. The area of the top shaded circle to the area of the bottom shaded circle

  b. The slant height of the top part of the cone to the slant height of the whole cone

  c. The lateral area of the top part of the cone to the lateral area of the whole cone

  d. The volume of the top part of the cone to the volume of the whole cone

  e. The volume of the top part of the cone to the volume of the bottom part

8 cm

2 cm

PROBLEM SOLVING

EXAMPLE 4
on p. 849
for Exs. 25–27

25. COFFEE MUGS The heights of two similar coffee mugs are 3.5 inches and 4 inches. The larger mug holds 12 fluid ounces. What is the capacity of the smaller mug?

@**HomeTutor** for problem solving help at classzone.com

26. ARCHITECTURE You have a pair of binoculars that is similar in shape to the structure on page 847. Your binoculars are 6 inches high, and the height of the structure is 45 feet. Find the ratio of the volume of your binoculars to the volume of the structure.

@**HomeTutor** for problem solving help at classzone.com

27. PARTY PLANNING Two similar punch bowls have a scale factor of 3 : 4. The amount of lemonade to be added is proportional to the volume. How much lemonade does the smaller bowl require if the larger bowl requires 64 fluid ounces?

28. ★ OPEN-ENDED MATH Using the scale factor 2 : 5, sketch a pair of solids in the correct proportions. Label the dimensions of the solids.

29. MULTI-STEP PROBLEM Two oranges are both spheres with diameters 3.2 inches and 4 inches. The skin on both oranges has an average thickness of $\frac{1}{8}$ inch.

  a. Find the volume of each unpeeled orange.

  b. *Compare* the ratio of the diameters to the ratio of the volumes.

  c. Find the diameter of each orange after being peeled.

  d. *Compare* the ratio of surface areas of the peeled oranges to the ratio of the volumes of the peeled oranges.

Animated Geometry at classzone.com

852

○ = WORKED-OUT SOLUTIONS
on p. WS1

★ = STANDARDIZED
TEST PRACTICE

◆◆ = MULTIPLE
REPRESENTATIONS

30. 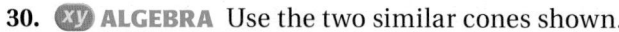 **ALGEBRA** Use the two similar cones shown.

    a. What is the scale factor of Cone I to Cone II? What should the ratio of the volume of Cone I to the volume of Cone II be?

    b. Write an expression for the volume of each solid.

    c. Write and simplify an expression for the ratio of the volume of Cone I to the volume of Cone II. Does your answer agree with your answer to part (a)? *Explain.*

31. ★ **EXTENDED RESPONSE** The scale factor of the model car at the right to the actual car is 1 : 18.

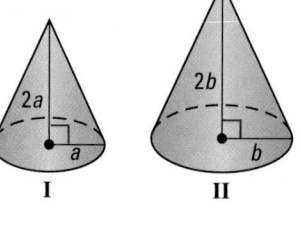

    a. The model has length 8 inches. What is the length of the actual car?

    b. Each tire of the model has a surface area of 12.1 square inches. What is the surface area of each tire of the actual car?

    c. The actual car's engine has volume 8748 cubic inches. Find the volume of the model car's engine.

32. **USING VOLUMES** Two similar cylinders have volumes 16π and 432π. The larger cylinder has lateral area 72π. Find the lateral area of the smaller cylinder.

33. ★ **SHORT RESPONSE** A snow figure is made using three balls of snow with diameters 25 centimeters, 35 centimeters, and 45 centimeters. The smallest weighs about 1.2 kilograms. Find the total weight of the snow used to make the snow figure. *Explain* your reasoning.

34. ◆ **MULTIPLE REPRESENTATIONS** A gas is enclosed in a cubical container with side length *s* in centimeters. Its temperature remains constant while the side length varies. By the *Ideal Gas Law*, the pressure *P* in atmospheres (atm) of the gas varies inversely with its volume.

    a. Writing an Equation Write an equation relating *P* and *s*. You will need to introduce a constant of variation *k*.

    b. Making a Table Copy and complete the table below for various side lengths. Express the pressure *P* in terms of the constant *k*.

Side length *s* (cm)	$\frac{1}{4}$	$\frac{1}{2}$	1	2	4
Pressure *P* (atm)	?	8*k*	*k*	?	?

    c. Drawing a Graph For this particular gas, $k = 1$. Use your table to sketch a graph of *P* versus *s*. Place *P* on the vertical axis and *s* on the horizontal axis. Does the graph show a linear relationship? *Explain.*

35. **CHALLENGE** A plane parallel to the base of a pyramid separates the pyramid into two pieces with equal volumes. The height of the pyramid is 12 feet. Find the height of the top piece.

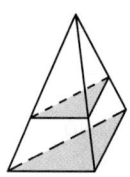

Determine whether the triangles are similar. If they are, write a similarity statement. *(p. 381)*

36. 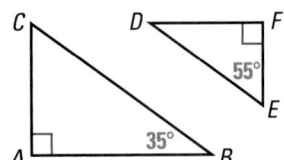   **37.** 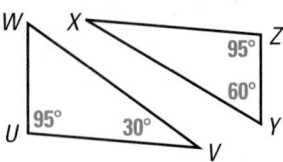   **38.**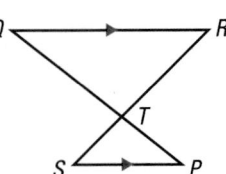

The sum of the measures of the interior angles of a convex polygon is given. Classify the polygon by the number of sides. *(p. 507)*

39. $900°$ **40.** $180°$ **41.** $540°$ **42.** $1080°$

Write a standard equation of the circle with the given center and radius. *(p. 699)*

43. Center $(2, 5)$, radius 4   **44.** Center $(-3, 2)$, radius 6

Sketch the described solid and find its surface area. Round your answer to two decimal places, if necessary. *(p. 803)*

45. Right rectangular prism with length 8 feet, width 6 feet, and height 3 feet

46. Right regular pentagonal prism with all edges measuring 12 millimeters

47. Right cylinder with radius 4 inches and height 4 inches

48. Right cylinder with diameter 9 centimeters and height 7 centimeters

QUIZ *for Lessons 12.6–12.7*

Find the surface area and volume of the sphere. Round your answers to two decimal places. *(p. 838)*

1. 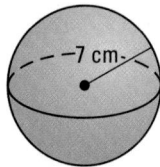   **2.** 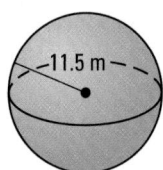   **3.**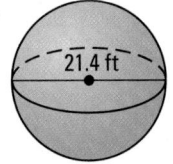

Solid A (shown) is similar to Solid B (not shown) with the given scale factor of A to B. Find the surface area S and volume V of Solid B. *(p. 847)*

4. Scale factor of $1:3$ **5.** Scale factor of $2:3$ **6.** Scale factor of $5:4$

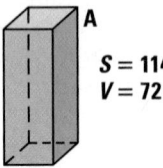
$S = 114$ in.^{2}
$V = 72$ in.^{3}

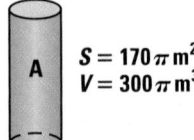
$S = 170\pi$ m^2
$V = 300\pi$ m^3

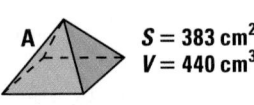
$S = 383$ cm^2
$V = 440$ cm^3

7. Two similar cones have volumes 729π cubic feet and 343π cubic feet. What is the scale factor of the larger cone to the smaller cone? *(p. 847)*

MIXED REVIEW *of Problem Solving*

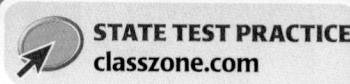

Lessons 12.4–12.7

1. **MULTI-STEP PROBLEM** You have a container in the shape of a right rectangular prism with inside dimensions of length 24 inches, width 16 inches, and height 20 inches.

   a. Find the volume of the inside of the container.

   b. You are going to fill the container with boxes of cookies that are congruent right rectangular prisms. Each box has length 8 inches, width 2 inches, and height 3 inches. Find the volume of one box of cookies.

   c. How many boxes of cookies will fit inside the cardboard container?

2. **SHORT RESPONSE** You have a cup in the shape of a cylinder with inside dimensions of diameter 2.5 inches and height 7 inches.

   a. Find the volume of the inside of the cup.

   b. You have an 18 ounce bottle of orange juice that you want to pour into the cup. Will all of the juice fit? *Explain* your reasoning. $(1 \text{ in.}^3 \approx 0.554 \text{ fluid ounces})$

3. **EXTENDED RESPONSE** You have a funnel with the dimensions shown.

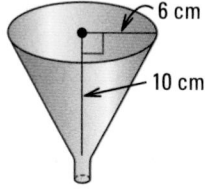

6 cm

10 cm

   a. Find the approximate volume of the funnel.

   b. You are going to use the funnel to put oil in a car. Oil flows out of the funnel at a rate of 45 milliliters per second. How long will it take to empty the funnel when it is full of oil? $(1 \text{ mL} = 1 \text{ cm}^3)$

   c. How long would it take to empty a funnel with radius 10 cm and height 6 cm?

   d. *Explain* why you can claim that the time calculated in part (c) is greater than the time calculated in part (b) without doing any calculations.

4. **EXTENDED RESPONSE** An official men's basketball has circumference 29.5 inches. An official women's basketball has circumference 28.5 inches.

   a. Find the surface area and volume of the men's basketball.

   b. Find the surface area and volume of the women's basketball using the formulas for surface area and volume of a sphere.

   c. Use your answers in part (a) and the Similar Solids Theorem to find the surface area and volume of the women's basketball. Do your results match your answers in part (b)?

5. **GRIDDED ANSWER** To accurately measure the radius of a spherical rock, you place the rock into a cylindrical glass containing water. When you do so, the water level rises $\frac{9}{64}$ inch. The radius of the glass is 2 inches. What is the radius of the rock?

6. **SHORT RESPONSE** Sketch a rectangular prism and label its dimensions. Change the dimensions of the prism so that its surface area increases and its volume decreases.

7. **SHORT RESPONSE** A hemisphere and a right cone have the same radius and the height of the cone is equal to the radius. *Compare* the volumes of the solids.

8. **SHORT RESPONSE** *Explain* why the height of a right cone is always less than its slant height. Include a diagram in your answer.

BIG IDEAS

For Your Notebook

Big Idea 1

Exploring Solids and Their Properties

Euler's Theorem is useful when finding the number of faces, edges, or vertices on a polyhedron, especially when one of those quantities is difficult to count by hand.

For example, suppose you want to find the number of edges on a regular icosahedron, which has 20 faces. You count 12 vertices on the solid. To calculate the number of edges, use Euler's Theorem:

$$F + V = E + 2 \qquad \text{Write Euler's Theorem.}$$

$$20 + 12 = E + 2 \qquad \text{Substitute known values.}$$

$$30 = E \qquad \text{Solve for } E.$$

Big Idea 2

Solving Problems Using Surface Area and Volume

Figure	Surface Area	Volume
Right prism	$S = 2B + Ph$	$V = Bh$
Right cylinder	$S = 2B + Ch$	$V = Bh$
Regular pyramid	$S = B + \frac{1}{2}P\ell$	$V = \frac{1}{3}Bh$
Right cone	$S = B + \frac{1}{2}C\ell$	$V = \frac{1}{3}Bh$
Sphere	$S = 4\pi r^2$	$V = \frac{4}{3}\pi r^3$

The volume formulas for prisms, cylinders, pyramids, and cones can be used for oblique solids.

While many of the above formulas can be written in terms of more detailed variables, it is more important to remember the more general formulas for a greater understanding of why they are true.

Big Idea 3

Connecting Similarity to Solids

The similarity concepts learned in Chapter 6 can be extended to 3-dimensional figures as well.

Suppose you have a right cylindrical can whose surface area and volume are known. You are then given a new can whose linear dimensions are k times the dimensions of the original can. If the surface area of the original can is S and the volume of the original can is V, then the surface area and volume of the new can can be expressed as k^2S and k^3V, respectively.

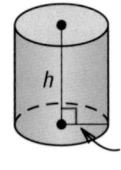
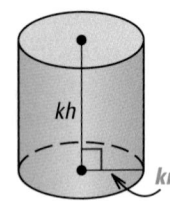

@*HomeTutor*
classzone.com
• Multi-Language Glossary
• Vocabulary practice

REVIEW KEY VOCABULARY

For a list of postulates and theorems, see pp. 926–931.

• polyhedron, *p. 794*
  face, edge, vertex, base
• regular polyhedron, *p. 796*
• convex polyhedron, *p. 796*
• Platonic solids, *p. 796*
• tetrahedron, *p. 796*
• cube, *p. 796*
• octahedron, *p. 796*
• dodecahedron, *p. 796*
• icosahedron, *p. 796*
• cross section, *p. 797*

• prism, *p. 803*
  lateral faces, lateral edges
• surface area, *p. 803*
• lateral area, *p. 803*
• net, *p. 803*
• right prism, *p. 804*
• oblique prism, *p. 804*
• cylinder, *p. 805*
• right cylinder, *p. 805*
• pyramid, *p. 810*
• vertex of a pyramid, *p. 810*
• regular pyramid, *p. 810*

• slant height, *p. 810*
• cone, *p. 812*
• vertex of a cone, *p. 812*
• right cone, *p. 812*
• lateral surface, *p. 812*
• volume, *p. 819*
• sphere, *p. 838*
  center, radius, chord, diameter
• great circle, *p. 839*
• hemisphere, *p. 839*
• similar solids, *p. 847*

VOCABULARY EXERCISES

1. Copy and complete: A __?__ is the set of all points in space equidistant from a given point.

2. **WRITING** Sketch a right rectangular prism and an oblique rectangular prism. *Compare* the prisms.

REVIEW EXAMPLES AND EXERCISES

Use the review examples and exercises below to check your understanding of the concepts you have learned in each lesson of Chapter 12.

12.1 Explore Solids
pp. 794–801

EXAMPLE

A polyhedron has 16 vertices and 24 edges. How many faces does the polyhedron have?

$F + V = E + 2$ **Euler's Theorem**

$F + 16 = 24 + 2$ **Substitute known values.**

$F = 10$ **Solve for F.**

▶ The polyhedron has 10 faces.

EXERCISES

EXAMPLES 2 and 3
on pp. 796–797 for Exs. 3–5

Use Euler's Theorem to find the value of *n*.

3. Faces: 20
   Vertices: *n*
   Edges: 30

4. Faces: *n*
   Vertices: 6
   Edges: 12

5. Faces: 14
   Vertices: 24
   Edges: *n*

12.2 Surface Area of Prisms and Cylinders

pp. 803–809

EXAMPLE

Find the surface area of the right cylinder.

$S = 2\pi r^2 + 2\pi rh$ **Write formula.**

$ = 2\pi(16)^2 + 2\pi(16)(25)$ **Substitute for *r* and *h*.**

$ = 1312\pi$ **Simplify.**

$ \approx 4121.77$ **Use a calculator.**

25 in.
16 in.

▸ The surface area of the cylinder is about 4121.77 square inches.

EXERCISES

EXAMPLES
2, 3, and 4
on pp. 804–806
for Exs. 6–9

Find the surface area of the right prism or right cylinder. Round your answer to two decimal places, if necessary.

6.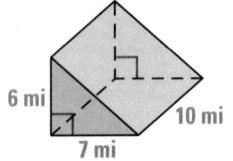

6 mi   10 mi   7 mi

7.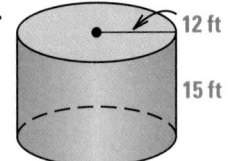

12 ft   15 ft

8.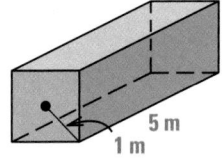

5 m   1 m

9. A cylinder has a surface area of 44π square meters and a radius of 2 meters. Find the height of the cylinder.

12.3 Surface Area of Pyramids and Cones

pp. 810–817

EXAMPLE

Find the lateral area of the right cone.

Lateral area $= \pi r \ell$ **Write formula.**

$\phantom{\text{Lateral area}} = \pi(6)(16)$ **Substitute for *r* and *l*.**

$\phantom{\text{Lateral area}} = 96\pi$ **Simplify.**

$\phantom{\text{Lateral area}} \approx 301.59$ **Use a calculator.**

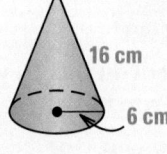

16 cm   6 cm

▸ The lateral area of the cone is about 301.59 square centimeters.

EXERCISES

EXAMPLES
1, 2, and 4
on pp. 810–813
for Exs. 10–12

10. Find the surface area of a right square pyramid with base edge length 2 feet and height 5 feet.

11. The surface area of a cone with height 15 centimeters is 500π square centimeters. Find the radius of the base of the cone. Round your answer to two decimal places.

12. Find the surface area of a right octagonal pyramid with height 2.5 yards, and its base has apothem length 1.5 yards.

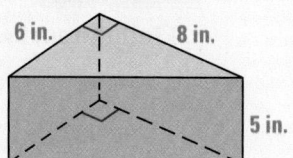
12.4 Volume of Prisms and Cylinders

pp. 819–825

EXAMPLE

Find the volume of the right triangular prism.

The area of the base is $B = \frac{1}{2}(6)(8) = 24$ square inches.
Use $h = 5$ to find the volume.

$V = Bh$ **Write formula.**

$\quad = 24(5)$ **Substitute for *B* and *h*.**

$\quad = 120$ **Simplify.**

▶ The volume of the prism is 120 cubic inches.

EXERCISES

**EXAMPLES
2 and 4**
on pp. 820–821
for Exs. 13–15

Find the volume of the right prism or oblique cylinder. Round your answer to two decimal places.

13.

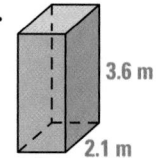

3.6 m
2.1 m
1.5 m

14.

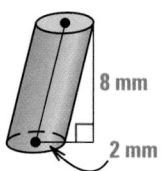

8 mm
2 mm

15.

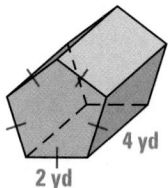

4 yd
2 yd

12.5 Volume of Pyramids and Cones

pp. 829–836

EXAMPLE

Find the volume of the right cone.

The area of the base is $B = \pi r^2 = \pi(11)^2 \approx 380.13$ cm².
Use $h = 20$ to find the volume.

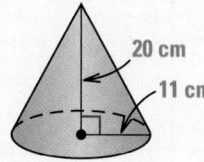

20 cm
11 cm

$V = \frac{1}{3}Bh$ **Write formula.**

$\quad \approx \frac{1}{3}(380.13)(20)$ **Substitute for *B* and *h*.**

$\quad \approx 2534.2$ **Simplify.**

▶ The volume of the cone is about 2534.2 cubic centimeters.

EXERCISES

**EXAMPLES
1 and 2**
on pp. 829–830
for Exs. 16–17

16. A cone with diameter 16 centimeters has height 15 centimeters. Find the volume of the cone. Round your answer to two decimal places.

17. The volume of a pyramid is 60 cubic inches and the height is 15 inches. Find the area of the base.

12.6 Surface Area and Volume of Spheres

pp. 838–845

pp. 838–845

EXAMPLE

Find the surface area of the sphere.

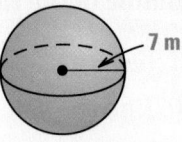

7 m

$S = 4\pi r^2$ **Write formula.**

$\quad = 4\pi(7)^2$ **Substitute 7 for *r*.**

$\quad = 196\pi$ **Simplify.**

▶ The surface area of the sphere is 196π, or about 615.75 square meters.

EXERCISES

EXAMPLES
1, 4, and 5
on pp. 839, 841
for Exs. 18–19

18. ASTRONOMY The shape of Pluto can be approximated as a sphere of diameter 2390 kilometers. Find the surface area and volume of Pluto.

19. A solid is composed of a cube with side length 6 meters and a hemisphere with diameter 6 meters. Find the volume of the solid. Round your answer to two decimal places.

12.7 Explore Similar Solids

pp. 847–854

pp. 847–854

EXAMPLE

The cones are similar with a scale factor of 1 : 2. Find the surface area and volume of Cone II given that the surface area of Cone I is 384π square inches and the volume of Cone I is 768π cubic inches.

I   II

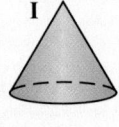
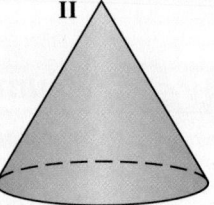

Use Theorem 12.13 to write and solve two proportions.

$$\frac{\text{Surface area of I}}{\text{Surface area of II}} = \frac{a^2}{b^2} \qquad\qquad \frac{\text{Volume of I}}{\text{Volume of II}} = \frac{a^3}{b^3}$$

$$\frac{384\pi}{\text{Surface area of II}} = \frac{1^2}{2^2} \qquad\qquad \frac{768\pi}{\text{Volume of II}} = \frac{1^3}{2^3}$$

$$\text{Surface area of II} = 1536\pi \text{ in.}^2 \qquad \text{Volume of II} = 6144\pi \text{ in.}^3$$

▶ The surface area of Cone II is 1536π, or about 4825.49 square inches, and the volume of Cone II is 6144π, or about 19,301.95 cubic inches.

EXERCISES

EXAMPLE 2
on p. 848
for Exs. 20–22

Solid A is similar to Solid B with the given scale factor of A to B. The surface area and volume of Solid A are given. Find the surface area and volume of Solid B.

20. Scale factor of 1 : 4
$S = 62 \text{ cm}^2$
$V = 30 \text{ cm}^3$

21. Scale factor of 1 : 3
$S = 112\pi \text{ m}^2$
$V = 160\pi \text{ m}^3$

22. Scale factor of 2 : 5
$S = 144\pi \text{ yd}^2$
$V = 288\pi \text{ yd}^3$

12 CHAPTER TEST

Find the number of faces, vertices, and edges of the polyhedron. Check your answer using Euler's Theorem.

1.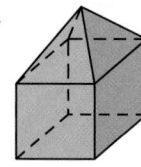

2.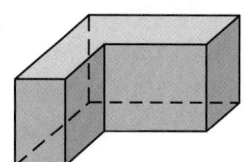

3.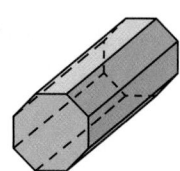

Find the surface area of the solid. The prisms, pyramids, cylinders, and cones are right. Round your answer to two decimal places, if necessary.

4.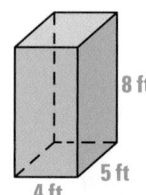
8 ft
5 ft
4 ft

5.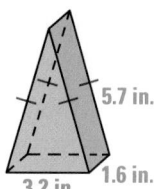
5.7 in.
1.6 in.
3.2 in.

6.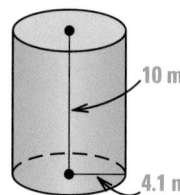
10 m
4.1 m

7.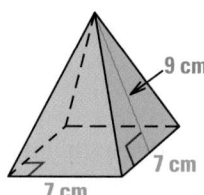
9 cm
7 cm
7 cm

8.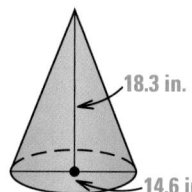
18.3 in.
14.6 in.

9.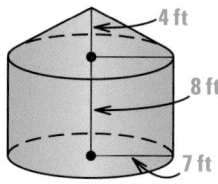
4 ft
8 ft
7 ft

Find the volume of the right prism or right cylinder. Round your answer to two decimal places, if necessary.

10.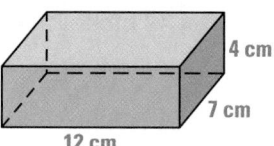
4 cm
7 cm
12 cm

11.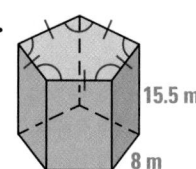
15.5 m
8 m

12.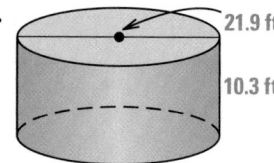
21.9 ft
10.3 ft

In Exercises 13–15, solve for x.

13. Volume = 324 in.^{3}

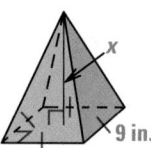
x
9 in.

14. Volume = $\dfrac{32\pi}{3}$ ft^3

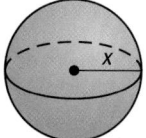
x

15. Volume = 180π cm^3

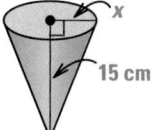
x
15 cm

16. MARBLES The diameter of the marble shown is 35 millimeters. Find the surface area and volume of the marble.

17. PACKAGING Two similar cylindrical cans have a scale factor of 2 : 3. The smaller can has surface area 308π square inches and volume 735π cubic inches. Find the surface area and volume of the larger can.

CONTEXT-BASED MULTIPLE CHOICE QUESTIONS

Some of the information you need to solve a context-based multiple choice question may appear in a table, a diagram, or a graph.

PROBLEM 1

One cubic foot of concrete weighs about 150 pounds. What is the approximate weight of the cylindrical section of concrete pipe shown?

(A) 145 lb   **(B)** 684 lb

(C) 2738 lb   **(D)** 5653 lb

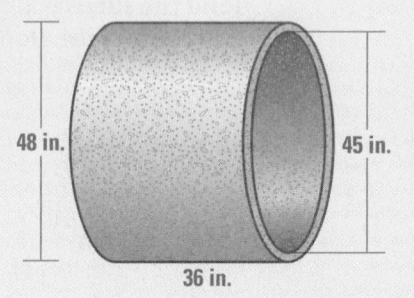

48 in.   45 in.

36 in.

Plan

INTERPRET THE DIAGRAM The pipe is a cylinder with length 36 inches and diameter 48 inches. The hollow center is also a cylinder with length 36 inches and diameter 45 inches. Find the volume of concrete used (in cubic feet). Then multiply by 150 pounds per cubic foot to find the weight of the concrete.

Solution

STEP 1
Find the volume of concrete used in the pipe.

Find the volume of a cylinder with diameter 48 inches and height 36 inches.

$$V = \pi r^2 h = \pi(24^2)(36) \approx 65{,}144 \text{ in.}^3$$

Find the volume of a cylinder with diameter 45 inches and height 36 inches.

$$V = \pi r^2 h = \pi(22.5^2)(36) \approx 57{,}256 \text{ in.}^3$$

To find the volume of concrete used in the pipe, subtract the smaller volume from the larger volume.

Volume of concrete used in pipe $\approx 65{,}144 - 57{,}256 = 7888 \text{ in.}^3$

STEP 2
Convert the volume to cubic feet.

Use unit analysis to convert 7888 cubic inches to cubic feet. There are 12 inches in 1 foot, so there are $12^3 = 1728$ cubic inches in 1 cubic foot.

$$7888 \text{ in.}^3 \cdot \frac{1 \text{ ft}^3}{1728 \text{ in.}^3} \approx 4.56 \text{ ft}^3$$

STEP 3
Find the weight of the pipe.

To find the weight of the pipe, multiply the volume of the concrete used in the pipe by the weight of one cubic foot of concrete.

$$\text{Weight of pipe} \approx 4.56 \text{ ft}^3 \cdot \frac{150 \text{ lb}}{1 \text{ ft}^3} = 684 \text{ lb}$$

The weight of the pipe is about 684 pounds.

The correct answer is B. **(A) (B) (C) (D)**

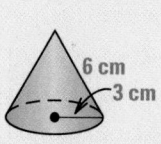
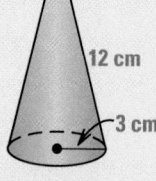

PROBLEM 2

What is the ratio of the surface area of Cone I to the surface area of Cone II?

(A) 1:2   **(B)** 1:4

(C) 3:5   **(D)** 3:8

Cone I

Cone II

6 cm
3 cm

12 cm
3 cm

Plan

INTERPRET THE DIAGRAM The diagram shows that the cones have the same radius, but different slant heights. Find and compare the surface areas.

Solution

STEP 1
Find the surface area of each cone.

Use the formula for the surface area of a cone.

Surface area of Cone I $= \pi r^2 + \pi r \ell = \pi(3^2) + \pi(3)(6) = 9\pi + 18\pi = 27\pi$

Surface area of Cone II $= \pi r^2 + \pi r \ell = \pi(3^2) + \pi(3)(12) = 9\pi + 36\pi = 45\pi$

STEP 2
Compare the surface areas.

Write a ratio.

$$\frac{\text{Surface area of Cone I}}{\text{Surface area of Cone II}} = \frac{27\pi}{45\pi} = \frac{3}{5}, \text{ or } 3:5$$

The correct answer is C. **(A) (B) (C) (D)**

PRACTICE

1. The amount a cannister can hold is proportional to its volume. The large cylindrical cannister in the table holds 2 kilograms of flour. About how many kilograms does the similar small cannister hold?

   (A) 0.5 kg   **(B)** 1 kg

   (C) 1.3 kg   **(D)** 1.6 kg

Size	Diameter
Small	24 cm
Medium	30 cm
Large	37.5 cm

2. The solid shown is made of a rectangular prism and a square pyramid. The height of the pyramid is one third the height of the prism. What is the volume of the solid?

   (A) $457\frac{1}{3}$ ft^3 **(B)** $6402\frac{2}{3}$ ft^3

   (C) 6860 ft^3 **(D)** 10,976 ft^3

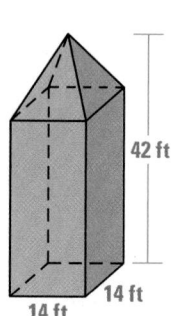

42 ft

14 ft
14 ft
14 ft

MULTIPLE CHOICE

In Exercises 1 and 2, use the diagram, which shows a bin for storing wood.

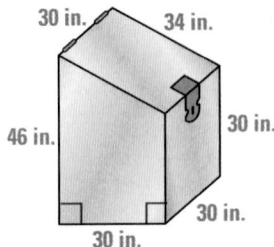

30 in.   34 in.
46 in.   30 in.
30 in.   30 in.
30 in.

1. The bin is a prism. What is the shape of the base of the prism?

   Ⓐ Triangle   Ⓑ Rectangle

   Ⓒ Square   Ⓓ Trapezoid

2. What is the surface area of the bin?

   Ⓐ 3060 in.^{2} Ⓑ 6480 in.^{2}

   Ⓒ 6960 in.^{2} Ⓓ 8760 in.^{2}

3. In the paperweight shown, a sphere with diameter 5 centimeters is embedded in a glass cube. What percent of the volume of the paperweight is taken up by the sphere?

   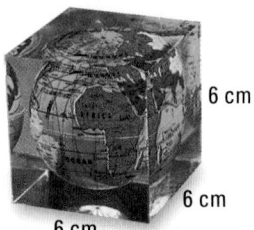

   6 cm
   6 cm
   6 cm

   Ⓐ About 30%   Ⓑ About 40%

   Ⓒ About 50%   Ⓓ About 60%

4. What is the volume of the solid formed when rectangle *JKLM* is rotated 360° about $\overline{KL}$?

   J   K
   1
   M   3   L

   Ⓐ π Ⓑ 3π

   Ⓒ 6π Ⓓ 9π

5. The skylight shown is made of four glass panes that are congruent isosceles triangles. One square foot of the glass used in the skylight weighs 3.25 pounds. What is the approximate total weight of the glass used in the four panes?

   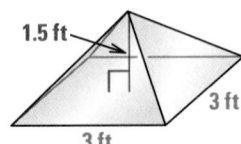

   1.5 ft
   3 ft
   3 ft

   Ⓐ 10 lb   Ⓑ 15 lb

   Ⓒ 29 lb   Ⓓ 41 lb

6. The volume of the right cone shown below is 16π cubic centimeters. What is the surface area of the cone?

   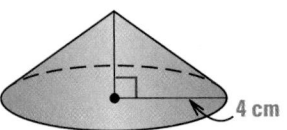

   4 cm

   Ⓐ 12π cm^2 Ⓑ 18π cm^2

   Ⓒ 36π cm^2 Ⓓ 72π cm^2

7. The shaded surface of the skateboard ramp shown is divided into a flat rectangular portion and a curved portion. The curved portion is one fourth of a cylinder with radius *r* feet and height *h* feet. Which equation can be used to find the area of the top surface of the ramp?

   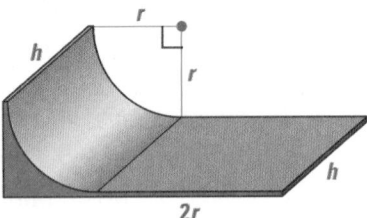

   r
   h
   r
   h
   2r

   Ⓐ $2rh + 2\pi r^2$ Ⓑ $2rh + 2\pi rh$

   Ⓒ $2rh + \frac{1}{4}\pi r^2$ Ⓓ $2rh + \frac{1}{2}\pi rh$

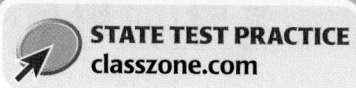
GRIDDED ANSWER

8. The scale factor of two similar triangular prisms is 3 : 5. The volume of the larger prism is 175 cubic inches. What is the volume (in cubic inches) of the smaller prism?

9. Two identical octagonal pyramids are joined together at their bases. The resulting polyhedron has 16 congruent triangular faces and 10 vertices. How many edges does it have?

10. The surface area of Sphere A is 27 square meters. The surface area of Sphere B is 48 square meters. What is the ratio of the diameter of Sphere A to the diameter of Sphere B, expressed as a decimal?

11. The volume of a square pyramid is 54 cubic meters. The height of the pyramid is 2 times the length of a side of its base. What is the height (in meters) of the pyramid? Round your answer to the nearest hundredth.

SHORT RESPONSE

12. Two cake layers are right cylinders, as shown. The top and sides of each layer will be frosted, including the portion of the top of the larger layer that is under the smaller layer. One can of frosting covers 100 square inches. How many cans do you need to frost the cake?

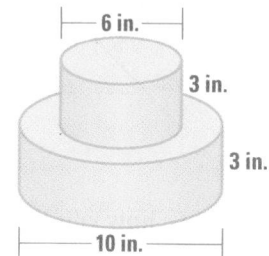

13. The height of Cylinder B is twice the height of Cylinder A. The diameter of Cylinder B is half the diameter of Cylinder A. Let r be the radius and let h be the height of Cylinder A. Write expressions for the radius and height of Cylinder B. Which cylinder has a greater volume? *Explain.*

EXTENDED RESPONSE

14. A cylindrical oil tank for home use has the dimensions shown.

   a. Find the volume of the tank to the nearest tenth of a cubic foot.

   b. Use the fact that 1 cubic foot = 7.48 gallons to find how many gallons of oil are needed to fill the tank.

   c. A homeowner uses about 1000 gallons of oil in a year. Assuming the tank is empty each time it is filled, how many times does the tank need to be filled during the year?

15. A manufacturer is deciding whether to package a product in a container shaped like a prism or one shaped like a cylinder. The manufacturer wants to use the least amount of material possible. The prism is 4 inches tall and has a square base with side length 3 inches. The height of the cylinder is 5 inches, and its radius is 1.6 inches.

   a. Find the surface area and volume of each container. If necessary, round to the nearest tenth.

   b. For each container, find the ratio of the volume to the surface area. *Explain* why the manufacturer should compare the ratios before making a decision.

Find the value of *x* that makes *m* ∥ *n*. *(p. 161)*

1.
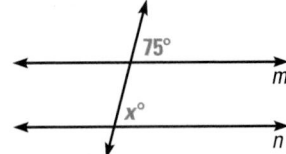

2.
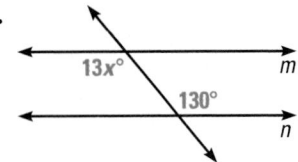

3.
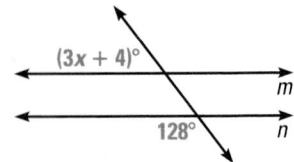

Find the value of the variable. *(p. 397)*

4.
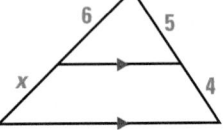

5.
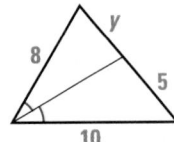

6.
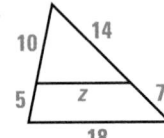

***Explain* how you know that the quadrilateral is a parallelogram.** *(p. 522)*

7.

8.

9.
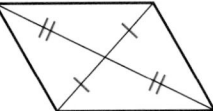

Find the value of the variable. *(pp. 651, 672, 689)*

10.
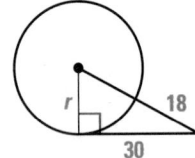

11.
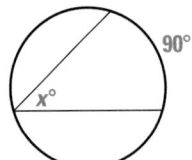

12.
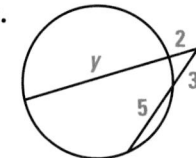

Find the area of the shaded region. *(p. 755)*

13.
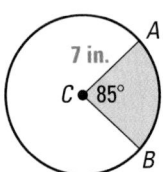

14.
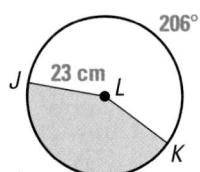

15.
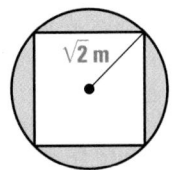

Find the surface area and volume of the right solid. Round your answer to two decimal places. *(pp. 803, 810, 819, 829)*

16.
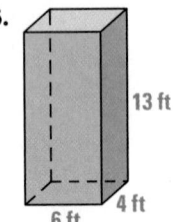

17.
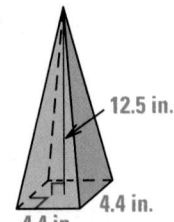

18.
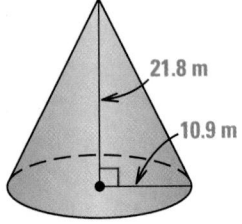

19. PHYSICS Find the coordinates of point *P* that will allow the triangular plate of uniform thickness to be balanced on a point. *(p. 319)*

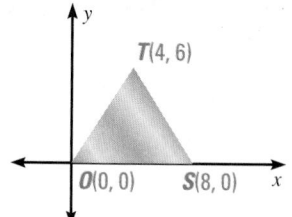

20. SYMMETRY Copy the figure on the right. Determine whether the figure has *line symmetry* and whether it has *rotational symmetry*. Identify all lines of symmetry and angles of rotation that map the figure onto itself. *(p. 619)*

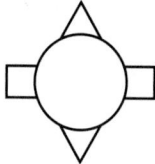

21. TWO-WAY RADIOS You and your friend want to test a pair of two-way radios. The radios are expected to transmit voices up to 6 miles. Your location is identified by the point $(-2, 4)$ on a coordinate plane where units are measured in miles. *(p. 699)*

a. Write an inequality that represents the area expected to be covered by the radios.

b. Determine whether your friend should be able to hear your voice when your friend is located at $(2, 0)$, $(3, 9)$, $(-6, -1)$, $(-6, 8)$, and $(-7, 5)$. *Explain* your reasoning.

22. COVERED BRIDGE A covered bridge has a roof with the dimensions shown. The top ridge of the roof is parallel to the base of the roof. The hidden back and left sides are the same as the front and right sides. Find the total area of the roof. *(pp. 720, 730)*

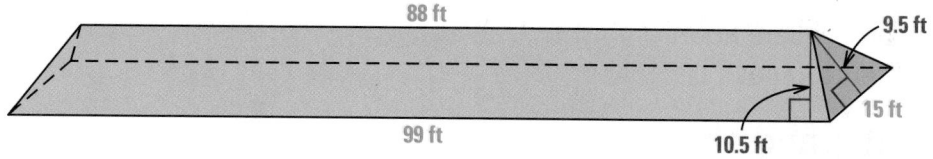

23. CANDLES The candle shown has diameter 2 inches and height 5.5 inches. *(pp. 803, 819)*

a. Find the surface area and volume of the candle. Round your answers to two decimal places.

b. The candle has a burning time of about 30 hours. Find the approximate volume of the candle after it has burned for 18 hours.

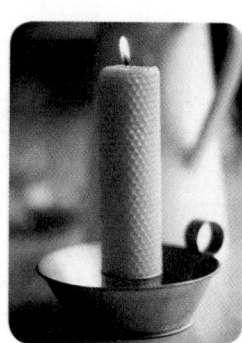

24. GEOGRAPHY The diameter of Earth is about 7920 miles. If approximately 70 percent of Earth's surface is covered by water, how many square miles of water are on Earth's surface? Round your answer to two decimal places. *(p. 838)*

Contents
of Student Resources

Skills Review Handbook

Operations with Rational Numbers

EXAMPLE Add or subtract: **a.** $-\dfrac{3}{4} + \dfrac{5}{8}$ **b.** $8.5 - (-1.4)$

a. Write the fractions with the same denominator, then add.

$$-\frac{3}{4} + \frac{5}{8} = -\frac{6}{8} + \frac{5}{8} = \frac{-6+5}{8} = \frac{-1}{8} = -\frac{1}{8}$$

b. To subtract a rational number, add its opposite.

$$8.5 - (-1.4) = 8.5 + 1.4 = 9.9 \qquad \textbf{The opposite of } -1.4 \textbf{ is 1.4, because } (-1.4) + (1.4) = 0.$$

The product or quotient of two numbers with the *same* sign is **positive**.

The product or quotient of two numbers with *different* signs is **negative**.

EXAMPLE Multiply: **a.** $4(5)$ **b.** $(-4)(-5)$ **c.** $4(-5)$

a. $4(5) = 20$ **b.** $(-4)(-5) = 20$ **c.** $4(-5) = -20$

EXAMPLE Divide $-\dfrac{1}{4} \div \dfrac{2}{5}$.

To divide by a fraction, multiply by its reciprocal.

$$-\frac{1}{4} \div \frac{2}{5} = -\frac{1}{4} \times \frac{5}{2} = -\frac{1 \times 5}{4 \times 2} = -\frac{5}{8} \qquad \textbf{The reciprocal of } \tfrac{2}{5} \textbf{ is } \tfrac{5}{2}, \textbf{ because } \tfrac{2}{5} \times \tfrac{5}{2} = 1.$$

PRACTICE

Add, subtract, multiply, or divide.

1. $4 - (-7)$ **2.** $-13 + 28$ **3.** $-5 \cdot 3$ **4.** $32 \div (-8)$

5. $(-2)(-3)(-4)$ **6.** $-8.1 + 4.5$ **7.** $(-2.7) \div (-9)$ **8.** $0.85 - 0.9$

9. $12.1 + (-0.5)$ **10.** $(-2.6) \cdot (-8.1)$ **11.** $-1.5 - 3.4$ **12.** $-3.6 \div 1.5$

13. $-3.1 \cdot 4.2$ **14.** $0.48 \div 4$ **15.** $-5.4 + (-3.8)$ **16.** $0.6 - 1.8$

17. $-\dfrac{5}{6} - \dfrac{1}{4}$ **18.** $-\dfrac{3}{4} \cdot \dfrac{7}{12}$ **19.** $\dfrac{4}{7} \div \dfrac{2}{3}$ **20.** $-\dfrac{11}{12} + \dfrac{7}{9}$

21. $-\dfrac{2}{3} + \left(-\dfrac{1}{4}\right)$ **22.** $\dfrac{5}{12} \div \dfrac{3}{8}$ **23.** $\dfrac{7}{9} - \left(-\dfrac{1}{6}\right)$ **24.** $\dfrac{5}{8} \cdot \dfrac{2}{11}$

Simplifying and Evaluating Expressions

To evaluate expressions involving more than one operation, mathematicians have agreed on the following set of rules, called the **order of operations**.

1. **Evaluate** expressions inside grouping symbols.

2. **Evaluate** powers.

3. **Multiply** and **divide** from left to right.

4. **Add** and **subtract** from left to right.

EXAMPLE Simplify: **a.** $10 + (1 - 5)^2 \div (-8)$ **b.** $3|-9 + 2| - 2 \cdot 6$

a. $10 + (1 - 5)^2 \div (-8)$

   $= 10 + (-4)^2 \div (-8)$ Subtract.

   $= 10 + 16 \div (-8)$ Evaluate powers.

   $= 10 + (-2)$ Divide.

   $= 8$ Add.

b. $3|-9 + 2| - 2 \cdot 6$

   $= 3|-7| - 2 \cdot 6$ Add.

   $= 3(7) - 2 \cdot 6$ Absolute value

   $= 21 - 12$ Multiply.

   $= 9$ Subtract.

To evaluate an algebraic expression, substitute values for the variables. Evaluate the resulting numerical expression using the order of operations.

EXAMPLE Evaluate the expression when $x = 4$ and $y = 9$.

a. $\dfrac{x^2 - 1}{x + 2} = \dfrac{4^2 - 1}{4 + 2} = \dfrac{16 - 1}{4 + 2} = \dfrac{15}{6} = \dfrac{5}{2} = 2\dfrac{1}{2}$

b. $[(2x + y) - 3x] \div 2 = (-x + y) \div 2 = (-4 + 9) \div 2 = 5 \div 2 = 2.5$

c. $2|x - 3y| = 2|4 - 3(9)| = 2|4 - 27| = 2|-23| = 2(23) = 46$

PRACTICE

Simplify the expression.

1. $5^2 - (-2)^3$

2. $-8 \cdot 3 - 12 \div 2$

3. $21|-7 + 4| - 4^3$

4. $24 \div (8 - |5 - 1|)$

5. $4(2 - 5)^2$

6. $4 + 21 \div 7 - 6^2$

7. $19.6 \div (2.8 \div 0.4)$

8. $20 - 4[2 + (10 - 3^2)]$

9. $\dfrac{6 + 3 \cdot 4}{2^2 - 7}$

10. $\dfrac{18 + |-2|}{(4 - 6)^2}$

11. $3(6x) + 7x$

12. $3|-5y + 4y|$

Evaluate the expression when $x = -3$ and $y = 5$.

13. $-4x^2$

14. $(-4x)^2$

15. $x(x + 8)$

16. $(11 - x) \div 2$

17. $3 \cdot |x - 2|$

18. $7x^2 - 2y$

19. $5 - |3x + y|$

20. $4x^3 + 3y$

21. $\dfrac{y^2 - 1}{5 - y^2}$

22. $|6y| - |x|$

23. $\dfrac{-6(2x + y)}{5 - x}$

24. $\dfrac{x - 7}{x + 7} + 1$

Properties of Exponents

An **exponent** tells you how many times to multiply a **base**. The expression 4^5 is called a **power** with base 4 and exponent 5.

$4^5 = 4 \times 4 \times 4 \times 4 \times 4 = 1024$

Product of Powers	Power of a Product	Power of a Power
$a^m \cdot a^n = a^{m+n}$ Add exponents.	$(a \cdot b)^m = a^m \cdot b^m$ Find the power of each factor.	$(a^m)^n = a^{mn}$ Multiply exponents.

Quotient of Powers	Power of a Quotient	Negative Exponent	Zero Exponent
$\dfrac{a^m}{a^n} = a^{m-n}, a \neq 0$ Subtract exponents.	$\left(\dfrac{a}{b}\right)^m = \dfrac{a^m}{b^m}, b \neq 0$ Find the power of the numerator and the power of the denominator.	$a^{-n} = \dfrac{1}{a^n}, a \neq 0$	$a^0 = 1, a \neq 0$

SKILLS REVIEW HANDBOOK

EXAMPLE **Simplify the expression. Use positive exponents.**

a. $x^2 \cdot x^5 = x^{2+5} = x^7$ **b.** $(2xy)^3 = 2^3 \cdot x^3 \cdot y^3 = 8x^3y^3$

c. $(y^4)^5 = y^{4 \cdot 5} = y^{20}$ **d.** $(-35)^0 = 1$

e. $\dfrac{m^9}{m^6} = m^{9-6} = m^3$ **f.** $\left(\dfrac{z}{4}\right)^3 = \dfrac{z^3}{4^3} = \dfrac{z^3}{64}$

g. $12^{-4} = \dfrac{1}{12^4} = \dfrac{1}{20{,}736}$ **h.** $\dfrac{20x^2y^{-4}z^5}{4x^4yz^3} = \dfrac{20}{4}x^{(2-4)}y^{(-4-1)}z^{(5-3)} = 5x^{-2}y^{-5}z^2 = \dfrac{5z^2}{x^2y^5}$

PRACTICE

Evaluate the power.

1. 5^2 **2.** $\left(-\dfrac{1}{2}\right)^3$ **3.** 4^{-2} **4.** 13^0

5. $5^3 \cdot 5^4$ **6.** $\left(\dfrac{3}{5}\right)^{-2}$ **7.** $(7^8)^4$ **8.** $\dfrac{4^6}{4^4}$

Simplify the expression. Write your answer using only positive exponents.

9. $a^5 \cdot a \cdot a^{-2}$ **10.** $3x^8 \cdot (2x)^3$ **11.** $5a^5 \cdot b^{-4}$ **12.** $(m^{-2})^{-3}$

13. $\left(\dfrac{3}{n}\right)^4$ **14.** $\left(\dfrac{x^5}{x^2}\right)^3$ **15.** $\dfrac{1}{m^{-2}}$ **16.** $\left(\dfrac{a^3}{3b}\right)^{-2}$

17. $(4 \cdot x^3 \cdot y)^2$ **18.** $(2n)^4 \cdot (3n)^2$ **19.** $(5a^3b^{-2}c)^{-1}$ **20.** $(r^2st^3)^0$

21. $\dfrac{16x^2y}{2xy}$ **22.** $\dfrac{(3r^{-3}s)^2}{10s}$ **23.** $\dfrac{3a^2b^0c}{21a^{-3}b^4c^2}$ **24.** $\left(\dfrac{6kn}{9k^2}\right)^2$

25. $6x^2 \cdot 5xy$ **26.** $2(r^{-4}s^2t)^{-3}$ **27.** $(5a^{-3}bc^4)^{-2} \cdot 15a^8$ **28.** $(3x^2y)^2 \cdot (-4xy^3)$

Using the Distributive Property

You can use the **Distributive Property** to simplify some expressions. Here are four forms of the Distributive Property.

$a(b + c) = ab + ac$ and $(b + c)a = ba + ca$ **Addition**

$a(b - c) = ab - ac$ and $(b - c)a = ba - ca$ **Subtraction**

EXAMPLE Write the expression without parentheses.

a. $x(x - 7) = x(x) - x(7)$
$= x^2 - 7x$

b. $(n + 5)(-3) = n(-3) + (5)(-3)$
$= -3n - 15$

Like terms are terms of an expression that have identical variable parts. You can use the Distributive Property to combine like terms and to simplify expressions that include adding, subtracting, factoring, and dividing polynomials.

EXAMPLE Simplify the expression.

a. $-2x^2 + 6x^2 = (-2 + 6)x^2 = 4x^2$

b. $9y - 4y + 8y = (9 - 4 + 8)y = 13y$

c. $5(x^2 - 3x) + (x + 2) = 5x^2 - 15x + x + 2 = 5x^2 + (-15 + 1)x + 2 = 5x^2 - 14x + 2$

d. $(3x^2 - 4x + 1) - (2x^2 - x - 7) = (3 - 2)x^2 + (-4 + 1)x + (1 + 7) = x^2 - 3x + 8$

e. $\dfrac{2x^2 - 4x}{2x} = \dfrac{2x(x - 2)}{2x} = \dfrac{\cancel{2x}(x - 2)}{\cancel{2x}} = x - 2$

PRACTICE

Use the Distributive Property to write an equivalent expression.

1. $3(x + 7)$
2. $-2(9a - 5)$
3. $(5n - 2)8$
4. $x(3x - 4)$

5. $-(x + 6)$
6. $(5b + c)(2a)$
7. $4(3x^2 - 2x + 4)$
8. $-5a(-a + 3b - 1)$

Simplify the expression.

9. $3x^2 - 9x^2 + x^2$
10. $4x - 7x + 12x$
11. $3n + 5 - n$
12. $-6r + 3s - 5r + 8$

13. $12h^2 + 5h^3 - 7h^2$
14. $6.5a + 2.4 - 5a$
15. $(x + 8) - (x - 2)$
16. $4.5(2r - 6) - 3r$

17. $\frac{1}{2}a + \frac{2}{5}a$
18. $\frac{1}{4}(x^2 - 4) + x$
19. $\dfrac{15n + 20}{5}$
20. $\dfrac{16r^3 - 12r^2}{2r}$

21. $(a^2 - 81) + (a^2 + 6a + 5)$
22. $(5a^2 + 3a - 2) - (2a^2 - a + 6)$

23. $2x + 3x(x - 4) + 5$
24. $3r(5r + 2) - 4(2r^2 - r + 3)$

25. $\dfrac{8a^3b + 4a^2b^2 - 2ab}{2ab}$
26. $\dfrac{7h^2 - 14h - 35 + 21h}{7}$

Binomial Products

To multiply two binomials, you can use the Distributive Property systematically. Multiply the *first* terms, the *outer* terms, the *inner* terms, and the *last* terms of the binomials. This method is called **FOIL** for the words **F**irst, **O**uter, **I**nner, and **L**ast.

For certain binomial products, you can also use a special product pattern.

$$(a + b)^2 = a^2 + 2ab + b^2 \qquad (a - b)^2 = a^2 - 2ab + b^2 \qquad (a - b)(a + b) = a^2 - b^2$$

EXAMPLE Find the product.

$$(x + 2)(3x - 4) = \underset{\text{First}}{x(3x)} + \underset{\text{Outer}}{x(-4)} + \underset{\text{Inner}}{2(3x)} + \underset{\text{Last}}{2(-4)}$$

$$= 3x^2 - 4x + 6x - 8$$

$$= 3x^2 + 2x - 8$$

a. $(x + 5)^2$

$$= x^2 + 2(x)(5) + 5^2$$

$$= x^2 + 10x + 25$$

b. $(y - 3)^2$

$$= y^2 - 2(y)(3) + 3^2$$

$$= y^2 - 6y + 9$$

c. $(z + 4)(z - 4)$

$$= z^2 - 4^2$$

$$= z^2 - 16$$

To simplify some expressions, multiply binomials first.

EXAMPLE Simplify the expression.

$$2(x + 1)(x + 6) - 4(x^2 - 5x + 4) = 2(x^2 + 7x + 6) - 4(x^2 - 5x + 4) \qquad \text{Multiply binomials.}$$

$$= 2x^2 + 14x + 12 - 4x^2 + 20x - 16 \qquad \text{Distributive Property}$$

$$= -2x^2 + 34x - 4 \qquad \text{Combine like terms.}$$

PRACTICE

Find the product.

1. $(a - 2)(a - 9)$ **2.** $(y - 4)^2$ **3.** $(t - 5)(t + 8)$ **4.** $(5n + 1)(n - 4)$

5. $(5a + 2)^2$ **6.** $(x - 10)(x + 10)$ **7.** $(c + 4)(4c - 3)$ **8.** $(n + 7)^2$

9. $(8 - z)^2$ **10.** $(a + 1)(a - 1)$ **11.** $(2x + 1)(x + 1)$ **12.** $(-7z + 6)(3z - 4)$

13. $(2x - 3)(2x + 3)$ **14.** $(5 + n)^2$ **15.** $(2d - 1)(3d + 2)$ **16.** $(a + 3)(a + 3)$

17. $(k - 1.2)^2$ **18.** $(6x - 5)(2x - 3)$ **19.** $(6 - z)(6 + z)$ **20.** $(4 - 5g)(3g + 2)$

Simplify the expression.

21. $3(y - 4)(y + 2) + (2y - 1)(y + 8)$ **22.** $4(t^2 + 3t - 4) + 2(t - 1)(t + 5)$

23. $2(x + 2)(x - 2) + (x - 3)(x + 3)$ **24.** $2(2c^2 + 3c - 1) + 7(c + 2)^2$

Radical Expressions

A **square root** of a number n is a number m such that $m^2 = n$. For example, $9^2 = 81$ and $(-9)^2 = 81$, so the square roots of 81 are 9 and -9.

Every positive number has two square roots, one positive and one negative. Negative numbers have no real square roots. The square root of zero is zero.

The radical symbol, $\sqrt{}$, represents a nonnegative square root: $\sqrt{81} = 9$. The opposite of a square root is negative: $-\sqrt{81} = -9$.

A **perfect square** is a number that is the square of an integer. So, 81 is a perfect square. A **radicand** is a number or expression inside a radical symbol.

Properties of Radicals	Simplest Form of a Radical Expression
For $a \geq 0$ and $b \geq 0$: $\sqrt{ab} = \sqrt{a} \cdot \sqrt{b}$ $\sqrt{\dfrac{a}{b}} = \dfrac{\sqrt{a}}{\sqrt{b}} = \dfrac{\sqrt{ab}}{b}$	• No perfect square factors other than 1 in the radicand • No fractions in the radicand • No radical signs in the denominator of a fraction

EXAMPLE Simplify the expression.

a. $\sqrt{9 + 36} = \sqrt{45} = \sqrt{9 \cdot 5} = \sqrt{9} \cdot \sqrt{5} = 3\sqrt{5}$

b. $\sqrt{50} - \sqrt{32} = \sqrt{25 \cdot 2} - \sqrt{16 \cdot 2} = 5\sqrt{2} - 4\sqrt{2} = (5 - 4)\sqrt{2} = 1\sqrt{2} = \sqrt{2}$

c. $\sqrt{18} \cdot \sqrt{72} = \sqrt{18 \cdot 72} = \sqrt{1296} = 36$ **d.** $\left(8\sqrt{3}\right)^2 = 8^2 \cdot \left(\sqrt{3}\right)^2 = 64 \cdot 3 = 192$

e. $\dfrac{6}{\sqrt{2}} = \dfrac{6}{\sqrt{2}} \cdot \dfrac{\sqrt{2}}{\sqrt{2}} = \dfrac{6 \cdot \sqrt{2}}{(\sqrt{2})^2} = \dfrac{6 \cdot \sqrt{2}}{2} = 3\sqrt{2}$ **f.** $\dfrac{\sqrt{20}}{\sqrt{500}} = \sqrt{\dfrac{20}{500}} = \sqrt{\dfrac{1}{25}} = \dfrac{1}{5}$

PRACTICE

Find all square roots of the number or write *no square roots*.

1. 100

2. 64

3. $\dfrac{1}{4}$

4. $\dfrac{9}{25}$

5. -16

6. 0

7. 0.81

8. 0.0016

Simplify the expression.

9. $\sqrt{121}$

10. $-\sqrt{169}$

11. $-\sqrt{99}$

12. $\sqrt{48}$

13. $\sqrt{16 + 4}$

14. $\sqrt{(-4)^2 + 6^2}$

15. $\sqrt{175} - \sqrt{28}$

16. $\sqrt{32} + \sqrt{162}$

17. $\sqrt{8} \cdot \sqrt{10}$

18. $4\sqrt{6} \cdot 2\sqrt{15}$

19. $\sqrt{210 \cdot 420}$

20. $\left(9\sqrt{3}\right)^2$

21. $\sqrt{137} \cdot \sqrt{137}$

22. $\sqrt{12} \cdot \sqrt{48}$

23. $5\sqrt{18} \cdot \sqrt{2}$

24. $3\sqrt{7} \cdot 5\sqrt{11}$

25. $\dfrac{\sqrt{192}}{\sqrt{3}}$

26. $\sqrt{\dfrac{2}{49}}$

27. $\dfrac{12}{\sqrt{6}}$

28. $\dfrac{2}{\sqrt{5}}$

Solving Linear Equations

To solve a linear equation, you isolate the variable.

Add the same number to each side of the equation.

Subtract the same number from each side of the equation.

Multiply each side of the equation by the same nonzero number.

Divide each side of the equation by the same nonzero number.

EXAMPLE Solve the equation: **a.** $3x - 5 = 13$ **b.** $2(y - 3) = y + 4$

a. $3x - 5 = 13$

$3x - 5 + 5 = 13 + 5$	Add 5.
$3x = 18$	Simplify.
$\dfrac{3x}{3} = \dfrac{18}{3}$	Divide by 3.
$x = 6$	Simplify.

b. $2(y - 3) = y + 4$

$2y - 6 = y + 4$	Distributive Property
$2y - y - 6 = y - y + 4$	Subtract y.
$y - 6 = 4$	Simplify.
$y - 6 + 6 = 4 + 6$	Add 6.
$y = 10$	Simplify.

CHECK
$3x - 5 = 13$
$3(6) - 5 \stackrel{?}{=} 13$
$13 = 13$ ✓

CHECK
$2(y - 3) = y + 4$
$2(10 - 3) \stackrel{?}{=} 10 + 4$
$14 = 14$ ✓

PRACTICE

Solve the equation.

1. $x - 8 = 23$

2. $n + 12 = 0$

3. $-18 = 3y$

4. $\dfrac{a}{6} = 7$

5. $\dfrac{2}{3}r = 26$

6. $-\dfrac{4}{5}t = -8$

7. $-4.8 = 1.5z$

8. $0 = -3x + 12$

9. $72 = 90 - x$

10. $7(y - 2) = 21$

11. $5 = 4k + 2 - k$

12. $4n + 1 = -2n + 8$

13. $2c + 3 = 4(c - 1)$

14. $9 - (3r - 1) = 12$

15. $12m + 3(2m + 6) = 0$

16. $\dfrac{6}{5}y - 2 = 10$

17. $\dfrac{w - 8}{3} = 4$

18. $-\dfrac{1}{4}(12 + h) = 7$

19. $2c - 8 = 24$

20. $2.8(5 - t) = 7$

21. $2 - c = -3(2c + 1)$

22. $-4k + 8 = 12 - 5k$

23. $3(z - 2) + 8 = 23$

24. $12 = 5(-3r + 2) - (r - 1)$

25. $12(z + 12) = 15^2$

26. $2 \cdot 3.14 \cdot r = 94.2$

27. $3.1(2f + 1.2) = 0.2(f - 6)$

28. $5(3t - 2) = -3(7 - t)$

29. $20a - 12(a - 3) = 4$

30. $5.5(h - 5.5) = 18.18$

31. $\dfrac{1}{2} \cdot b \cdot 8 = 10$

32. $\dfrac{4x + 12}{2} = 3x - 5$

33. $\dfrac{10 + 7y}{4} = \dfrac{5 - y}{3}$

34. $\dfrac{9 - 2x}{7} = x$

35. $\dfrac{23 - 11c}{7} = 5c$

36. $\dfrac{4n - 28}{3} = 2n$

Solving and Graphing Linear Inequalities

You can graph solutions to equations and inequalities on a number line.

Symbol	Meaning	Equation or Inequality	Graph
=	equals	$x = 3$	1 2 3 4 5
<	is less than	$x < 3$	1 2 3 4 5
≤	is less than or equal to	$x \le 3$	1 2 3 4 5
>	is greater than	$x > 3$	1 2 3 4 5
≥	is greater than or equal to	$x \ge 3$	1 2 3 4 5

You can use properties of inequalities to solve linear inequalities.

Add the same number to each side of the inequality.

Subtract the same number from each side of the inequality.

Multiply each side of the inequality by the same positive number.
If you multiply by a negative number, reverse the direction of the inequality symbol.

Divide each side of the inequality by the same positive number.
If you divide by a negative number, reverse the direction of the inequality symbol.

EXAMPLE   **Solve the inequality. Graph the solution.**

a. $2x + 1 \le 5$

$2x \le 4$ **Subtract 1 from each side.**

$x \le 2$ **Divide each side by 2.**

0 1 2 3 4 5

b. $-4y < 18$

$\dfrac{-4y}{-4} > \dfrac{18}{-4}$ **Divide by −4 and change < to >.**

$y > -4.5$ **Simplify.**

−6 −5 −4 −3 −2 −1

PRACTICE

Solve the inequality. Graph the solution.

1. $x - 2 < 5$

2. $16 < x + 5$

3. $10 - n \ge 6$

4. $2z \ge -9$

5. $8c + 24 < 0$

6. $6 \ge -3a$

7. $5a - 3 \ge -8$

8. $2n + 7 < 17$

9. $5 > 0.5y + 3$

10. $5 - 3x \le x + 13$

11. $5r + 2r \le 6r - 1$

12. $y - 3 \le 2y + 5$

13. $-2.4m \ge 3.6m - 12$

14. $-2(t - 6) > 7t - 6$

15. $4(8 - z) + 2 > 3z - 8$

16. $-\dfrac{3}{4}n > 3$

17. $\dfrac{c}{5} - 8 \le -6$

18. $\dfrac{n - 5}{2} \ge \dfrac{2n - 6}{3}$

Solving Formulas

A **formula** is an equation that relates two or more real-world quantities. You can rewrite a formula so that any one of the variables is a function of the other variable(s). In each case you isolate a variable on one side of the equation.

EXAMPLE Solve the formula for the indicated variable.

a. Solve $C = 2\pi r$ for r.

$$C = 2\pi r$$

$$\frac{C}{2\pi} = \frac{2\pi r}{2\pi} \qquad \text{Divide by } 2\pi.$$

$$\frac{C}{2\pi} = r \qquad \text{Simplify.}$$

$$r = \frac{C}{2\pi} \qquad \text{Rewrite.}$$

b. Solve $P = a + b + c$ for a.

$$P = a + b + c$$

$$P - b - c = a + b - b + c - c \qquad \text{Subtract.}$$

$$P - b - c = a \qquad \text{Simplify.}$$

$$a = P - b - c \qquad \text{Rewrite.}$$

EXAMPLE Rewrite the equation so that y is a function of x.

a. $2x + y = 3$

$$2x - 2x + y = 3 - 2x \qquad \text{Subtract } 2x.$$

$$y = 3 - 2x \qquad \text{Simplify.}$$

b. $\frac{1}{4}y = x$

$$4 \cdot \frac{1}{4}y = 4 \cdot x \qquad \text{Multiply by 4.}$$

$$y = 4x \qquad \text{Simplify.}$$

PRACTICE

Solve the formula for the indicated variable.

1. Solve $P = 4s$ for s.

2. Solve $d = rt$ for r.

3. Solve $V = \ell wh$ for ℓ.

4. Solve $V = \pi r^2 h$ for h.

5. Solve $A = \frac{1}{2}bh$ for b.

6. Solve $d = \frac{m}{v}$ for v.

7. Solve $P = 2(\ell + w)$ for w.

8. Solve $I = prt$ for r.

9. Solve $F = \frac{9}{5}C + 32$ for C.

10. Solve $A = \frac{1}{2}h(b_1 + b_2)$ for h.

11. Solve $S = 2\pi r^2 + 2\pi rh$ for h.

12. Solve $A = P(1 + r)^t$ for P.

Rewrite the equation so that y is a function of x.

13. $2x + y = 7$

14. $5x + 3y = 0$

15. $3x - y = -2$

16. $y + 1 = -2(x - 2)$

17. $\frac{4}{5}y = x$

18. $\frac{1}{4}x + 2y = 5$

19. $1.8x - 0.3y = 4.5$

20. $y - 4 = \frac{1}{3}(x + 6)$

Graphing Points and Lines

A **coordinate plane** is formed by the intersection of a horizontal number line called the **x-axis** and a vertical number line called the **y-axis**. The axes meet at a point called the **origin** and divide the coordinate plane into four **quadrants**, labeled I, II, III, and IV.

Each point in a coordinate plane is represented by an **ordered pair**. The first number is the **x-coordinate**, and the second number is the **y-coordinate**.

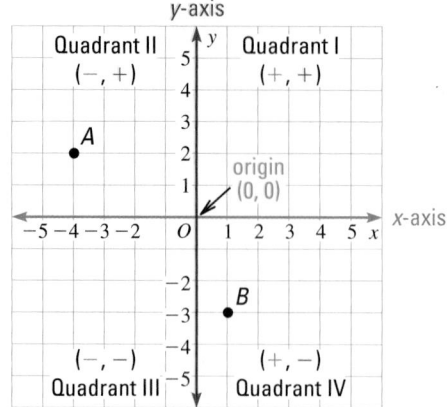

EXAMPLE   Give the coordinates of points *A* and *B* in the graph above.

Start at the origin. Count 4 units left and 2 units up. Point *A* is at $(-4, 2)$.
Start at the origin. Count 1 unit right and 3 units down. Point *B* is at $(1, -3)$.

A **solution** of an equation in x and y is an ordered pair (x, y) that makes the equation true. The graph of such an equation is the set of points in a coordinate plane that represent all the solutions. A **linear equation** has a line as its graph.

EXAMPLE   Graph the equation $y = 2x - 3$.

Make a table of values, graph each point, and draw the line.

x	$y = 2x - 3$	(x, y)	
0	$y = 2(0) - 3 = -3$	$(0, -3)$	→ 0 units right or left, 3 units down
1	$y = 2(1) - 3 = -1$	$(1, -1)$	→ 1 unit right, 1 unit down
2	$y = 2(2) - 3 = 1$	$(2, 1)$	→ 2 units right, 1 unit up

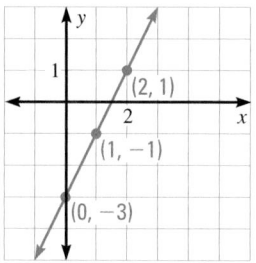

PRACTICE

Use the graph shown. Give the coordinates of the point.

1. *C*
2. *D*
3. *E*
4. *F*
5. *G*
6. *H*

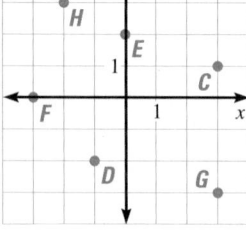

Plot the point in a coordinate plane.

7. $J(-3, 1)$
8. $K(2, -2)$
9. $L(0, -1)$
10. $M\left(\frac{3}{2}, 3\right)$
11. $N\left(-\frac{5}{2}, -\frac{1}{2}\right)$
12. $P(4.5, 0)$

Use a table of values to graph the equation.

13. $y = 3x - 2$
14. $y = -2x + 1$
15. $y = \frac{2}{3}x - 3$
16. $y = -\frac{1}{2}x$
17. $y = 1.5x - 2.5$
18. $y = 4 - 3x$
19. $4x + 2y = 0$
20. $2x - y = 3$

Slope and Intercepts of a Line

The **slope** of a nonvertical line is the ratio of the vertical change, called the **rise**, to the horizontal change, called the **run**. The table below shows some types of lines and slopes.

Rising Line	Falling Line	Horizontal Line	Vertical Line
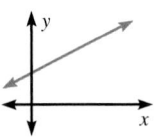	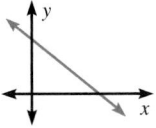	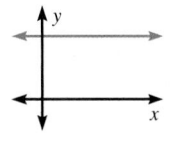	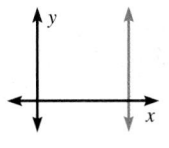
Positive Slope	Negative Slope	Zero Slope	Undefined Slope

EXAMPLE **Find the slope of the line.**

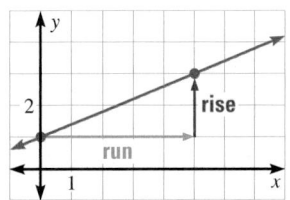

Use the graph of the line.

$$\text{Slope} = \frac{\text{rise}}{\text{run}} = \frac{2 \text{ units up}}{5 \text{ units right}} = \frac{2}{5}$$

An **x-intercept** is the x-coordinate of a point where a graph crosses the x-axis. A **y-intercept** is the y-coordinate of a point where a graph crosses the y-axis. The line graphed at the right has x-intercept 2 and y-intercept 3.

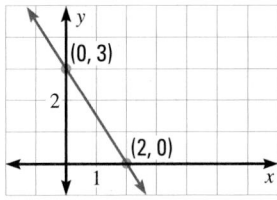

EXAMPLE **Find the x-intercept and the y-intercept of the graph of $x - 4y = 8$.**

To find the x-intercept, let $y = 0$.

$$x - 4(0) = 8$$
$$x = 8$$

The x-intercept is 8.

To find the y-intercept, let $x = 0$.

$$0 - 4y = 8$$
$$y = -2$$

The y-intercept is -2.

PRACTICE

Find the slope and intercept(s) of the line graphed.

1.	2.	3.	4.
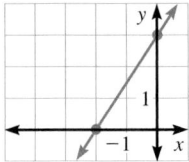	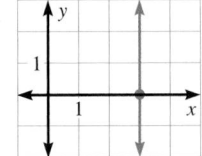	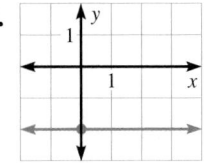	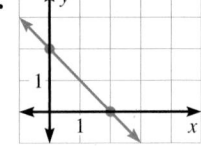

Find the intercepts of the line with the given equation.

5. $5x - y = 15$ **6.** $2x + 4y = 12$ **7.** $y = -x + 3$ **8.** $y = 3x - 2$

9. $-3x + y = -6$ **10.** $y = -2x - 7$ **11.** $y = 5x$ **12.** $9x - 3y = 15$

Systems of Linear Equations

A **system of linear equations** in two variables is shown at the right. A **solution** of such a system is an ordered pair (x, y) that satisfies both equations. A solution must lie on the graph of both equations.

$$x + 2y = 5 \quad \textbf{Equation 1}$$
$$x - y = -1 \quad \textbf{Equation 2}$$

EXAMPLE Use substitution to solve the linear system above.

Solve Equation 2 for x. $\quad x - y = -1$
$$x = y - 1 \quad \textbf{Revised Equation 2}$$

In Equation 1, substitute $y - 1$ for x. Solve for y. $\quad x + 2y = 5$
$$(y - 1) + 2y = 5$$
$$3y = 6$$
$$y = 2$$

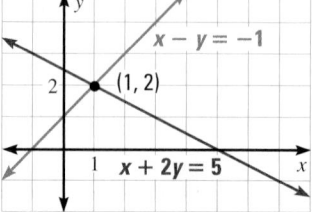

In Revised Equation 2, substitute 2 for y. $\quad x = y - 1 = 2 - 1 = 1$
Because $x = 1$ and $y = 2$, the solution (x, y) is $(1, 2)$.
The graph verifies that $(1, 2)$ is the point of intersection of the lines.

EXAMPLE Use elimination to solve the linear system above.

Multiply Equation 2 by 2, then add equations. $\quad x + 2y = 5 \quad\longrightarrow\quad x + 2y = 5$
$$x - y = -1 \quad\longrightarrow\quad \underline{2x - 2y = -2}$$
$$3x = 3$$
$$x = 1$$

Substitute 1 for x in Equation 2 and solve for y. $\quad 1 - y = -1$
$$2 = y$$

Because $x = 1$ and $y = 2$, the solution (x, y) is $(1, 2)$.
Substitute 1 for x and 2 for y in each original equation to check.

PRACTICE

Use substitution to solve the linear system. Check your solution.

1. $3x - 5y = 1$
$y = 2x - 3$

2. $7x + 4y = -13$
$x = -6y + 9$

3. $-4x + 3y = -19$
$2x + y = 7$

4. $x + y = -7$
$2x - 5y = 21$

5. $4x + 9y = -3$
$x + 2y = 0$

6. $0.5x + y = 5$
$1.5x - 2.5y = 4$

7. $2x + 4y = -18$
$3x - y = 1$

8. $4x + 7y = 3$
$6x + y = 14$

Use elimination to solve the linear system. Check your solution.

9. $3x - 6y = -3$
$12x + 6y = 48$

10. $12x + 20y = 56$
$-12x - 7y = -4$

11. $4x - y = 1$
$2x + 3y = -17$

12. $10x + 15y = 90$
$5x - 4y = -1$

13. $18x + 63y = -27$
$3x + 9y = -6$

14. $5x + 7y = 23$
$20x - 30y = 5$

15. $8x - 5y = 14$
$10x - 2y = 9$

16. $-5x + 8y = 4$
$6x - 5y = -14$

Linear Inequalities in Two Variables

A **linear inequality** in x and y can be written in one of the forms shown at the right. A **solution** of a linear inequality is an ordered pair (x, y) that satisfies the inequality. A **graph** of a linear inequality is the graph of all the solutions.

$ax + by < c$	$ax + by > c$
$ax + by \leq c$	$ax + by \geq c$

EXAMPLE   Graph the linear inequality $x + y < 4$.

Graph the corresponding equation $x + y = 4$. Use a dashed line to show that the points on the line are not solutions of the inequality.

Test a point on either side of the line to see if it is a solution.

Test $(3, 2)$ in $x + y < 4$:   Test $(0, 0)$ in $x + y < 4$:

$3 + 2 < 4$ ✗ $0 + 0 < 4$ ✓

So $(3, 2)$ is not a solution.   So $(0, 0)$ is a solution.

Shade the *half-plane* that includes a test point that is a solution.

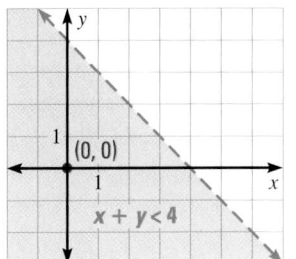

Two or more linear inequalities form a **system of linear inequalities**. A **solution** of such a system is an ordered pair (x, y) that satisfies all the inequalities in the system. A **graph** of the system shows all the solutions of the system.

EXAMPLE   Graph the system of linear inequalities $x \geq -2$ and $y \leq 3$.

Graph the linear inequality $x \geq -2$. Use a solid line for the graph of $x = 2$ to show that the points on the line are solutions of the inequality. Shade the half-plane to the right of the line.

Graph the linear inequality $y \leq 3$. Use a solid line for the graph of $y = 3$. Shade the half-plane below the line.

The intersection of the shaded half-planes is a graph of the system.

Check solution point $(0, 0)$ in both inequalities $x \geq -2$ and $y \leq 3$.

$0 \geq -2$ ✓   and $0 \leq 3$ ✓

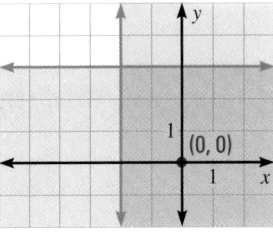

PRACTICE

Graph the linear inequality.

1. $x + y \geq 3$

2. $x - y < -2$

3. $y \leq -3x$

4. $x - 4y > 4$

5. $y > 1$

6. $x \leq 2$

7. $5x - y \geq 5$

8. $2x + 5y < 10$

Graph the system of linear inequalities.

9. $x > 1$
$\quad y > -2$

10. $x \leq 4$
$\quad\ x \geq -2$

11. $x - y \leq 1$
$\quad x + y < 5$

12. $y < x$
$\quad y \geq 3x$

13. $2x - y \leq 1$
$\quad\ 2x - y \geq -3$

14. $x \geq 0$
$\quad y \geq 0$
$\quad 4x + 3y < 12$

15. $y > -4$
$\quad y < -2$
$\quad x > -3$

16. $x + y \geq 0$
$\quad 4x - y \geq -5$
$\quad 7x + 2y \leq 10$

Quadratic Equations and Functions

A **quadratic equation** is an equation that can be written in the *standard form* $ax^2 + bx + c = 0$, where $a \neq 0$. A quadratic equation can have two solutions, one solution, or no real solutions. When $b = 0$, you can use square roots to solve the quadratic equation.

EXAMPLE Solve the quadratic equation.

a. $x^2 + 5 = 29$
$x^2 = 24$
$x = \pm\sqrt{24}$
$x = \pm 2\sqrt{6} \approx \pm 4.90$

Two solutions

b. $3x^2 - 4 = -4$
$3x^2 = 0$
$x^2 = 0$
$x = 0$

One solution

c. $-6x^2 + 3 = 21$
$-6x^2 = 18$
$x^2 = -3$

No real solution

A **quadratic function** is a function that can be written in the standard form $y = ax^2 + bx + c$, where $a \neq 0$.

The graph of a quadratic equation is a U-shaped curve called a **parabola**. The **vertex** is the lowest point of a parabola that opens upward ($a > 0$) or the highest point of a parabola that opens downward ($a < 0$). The vertical line passing through the vertex is the **axis of symmetry**.

To graph a quadratic function, you can make a table of values, plot the points, and draw the parabola. The x-intercepts of the graph (if any) are the real solutions of the corresponding quadratic equation.

EXAMPLE Graph the quadratic function. Label the vertex.

a. $y = x^2 - 4$

x	y
−2	0
−1	−3
0	−4
1	−3
2	0

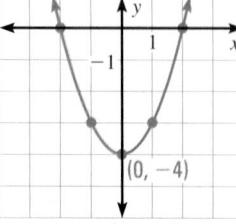

Two x-intercepts

b. $y = -x^2$

x	y
−2	−4
−1	−1
0	0
1	−1
2	−4

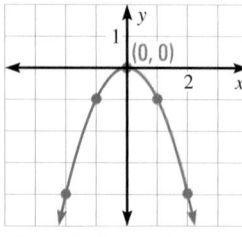

One x-intercept

c. $y = x^2 + 1$

x	y
−2	5
−1	2
0	1
1	2
2	5

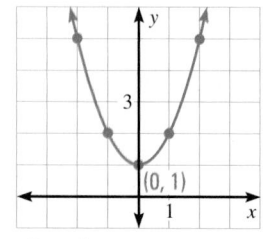

No x-intercepts

You can use the **quadratic formula** to solve any quadratic equation.

The solutions of the quadratic equation $ax^2 + bx + c = 0$ are

$$x = \frac{-b \pm \sqrt{b^2 - 4ac}}{2a} \text{ where } a \neq 0 \text{ and } b^2 - 4ac \geq 0.$$

EXAMPLE Use the quadratic formula to solve the equation $8x^2 + 6x = 1$.

Write the equation in standard form and identify a, b, and c.

The equation $8x^2 + 6x = 1$ is equivalent to $8x^2 + 6x - 1 = 0$. So, $a = 8$, $b = 6$, and $c = -1$.

Use the quadratic formula and simplify.

$$x = \frac{-b \pm \sqrt{b^2 - 4ac}}{2a} = \frac{-6 \pm \sqrt{6^2 - 4(8)(-1)}}{2(8)} = \frac{-6 \pm \sqrt{68}}{16} = \frac{-6 \pm 2\sqrt{17}}{16} = \frac{-3 \pm \sqrt{17}}{8}$$

▶ The solutions of the equation are $\dfrac{-3 + \sqrt{17}}{8} \approx 0.14$ and $\dfrac{-3 - \sqrt{17}}{8} \approx -0.89$.

Check the solutions in the original equation.

$$8(0.14)^2 + 6(0.14) \stackrel{?}{=} 1 \qquad 8(-0.89)^2 + 6(-0.89) \stackrel{?}{=} 1$$

$$0.9968 \approx 1 \checkmark \qquad\qquad 0.9968 \approx 1 \checkmark$$

PRACTICE

Solve the quadratic equation.

1. $x^2 = 144$

2. $x^2 + 7 = -5$

3. $x^2 - (x + 1)^2 = 5$

4. $x^2 - 18 = 0$

5. $8x^2 + 3 = 3$

6. $5x^2 - 2 = -12$

7. $(2x + 3)^2 - 4 = 4x^2 - 7$

8. $3x^2 + 2 = 14$

9. $1 - 4x^2 = 13$

10. $12 - 5x^2 = 12$

11. $15 - 9x^2 = 10$

12. $(x + 2)^2 + 2 = (x - 2)^2 + 8$

Graph the quadratic function. Label the vertex.

13. $y = x^2$

14. $y = x^2 - 3$

15. $y = -x^2 + 4$

16. $y = -2x^2$

17. $y = x^2 + 2$

18. $y = -x^2 - 1$

19. $y = \frac{1}{2}x^2$

20. $y = -\frac{1}{4}x^2$

21. $y = \frac{3}{4}x^2 - 2$

22. $y = 3x^2 + 1$

23. $y = (x - 1)^2$

24. $y = -(x + 2)^2$

Use the quadratic formula to solve the quadratic equation.

25. $x^2 + 6x + 5 = 0$

26. $x^2 - 4x - 2 = 0$

27. $x^2 + 6x = -9$

28. $2x = 8x^2 - 3$

29. $x^2 + 7x + 5 = 1$

30. $x^2 + 2x + 5 = 0$

31. $2x^2 + 8x - 3 = -11$

32. $x^2 + 5x = 6$

33. $5x^2 - 6 = 2x$

34. $3x^2 + 7x - 4 = 0$

35. $2x^2 - 3x = -4$

36. $4x + 4 = 3x^2$

37. $3x^2 - x = 5$

38. $(x + 4)(x - 4) = 8$

39. $(x + 2)(x - 2) = 1$

Functions

A function can be described by a table of values, a graph, an equation, or words.

EXAMPLE Graph the exponential functions $y = 2^x$ and $y = -2^x$.

For each function, make a table of values, plot the points, and draw a curve.

x	$y = 2^x$	(x, y)
−2	$2^{-2} = \frac{1}{4}$	$\left(-2, \frac{1}{4}\right)$
0	$2^0 = 1$	(0, 1)
1	$2^1 = 2$	(1, 2)
2	$2^2 = 4$	(2, 4)

x	$y = -2^x$	(x, y)
−2	$-2^{-2} = -\frac{1}{4}$	$\left(-2, -\frac{1}{4}\right)$
0	$-2^0 = -1$	(0, −1)
1	$-2^1 = -2$	(1, −2)
2	$-2^2 = -4$	(2, −4)

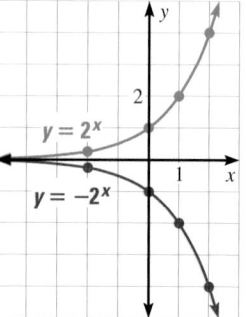

EXAMPLE The table shows Luke's earnings. Write an equation using his hourly pay rate. How much does Luke earn in 25 hours?

Hours worked	Earnings (dollars)
8	66
15	123.75
40	330

Use the values in the table to find Luke's hourly pay rate.

$66 \div 8 = 8.25$ $123.75 \div 15 = 8.25$ $330 \div 40 = 8.25$

Write an equation using words. Then use variables.

Earnings = Hourly pay rate • Hours worked

$$e = 8.25h \quad \text{Let } e \text{ be earnings and } h \text{ be hours worked.}$$
$$= 8.25(25) \quad \text{Substitute 25 for } h.$$
$$= 206.25 \quad \text{Multiply.}$$

▶ Luke earns $206.25 in 25 hours.

PRACTICE

Make a table of values and graph the function.

1. $y = 3^x$
2. $y = -3^x$
3. $y = (0.5)^x$
4. $y = -(0.5)^x$
5. $y = 2x$
6. $y = 2x^2$
7. $y = 2x^3$
8. $y = |2x|$

Write an equation for the function described by the table.

9.

x	1	2	3	4
y	1	4	9	16

10.

x	−2	−1	0	1
y	2	1	0	−1

11. Write an equation using Sue's hourly pay rate of $12. How much does Sue earn in 6 hours? How many hours must Sue work to earn $420?

Problem Solving with Percents

You can use equations to solve problems with percents. Replace words with symbols as shown in the table. To estimate with percents, use compatible numbers.

Words	*a* is *p* percent of *b*.
Symbols	$a = p \cdot b$

SKILLS REVIEW HANDBOOK

EXAMPLE **Use the percent equation to answer the question.**

a. What is 45% of 60?

$a = 0.45 \times 60$

$a = 27$

b. What percent of 28 is 7?

$7 = p \times 28$

$7 \div 28 = p$

$0.25 = p$

$25\% = p$

c. 30% of what number is 12?

$12 = 0.3 \times b$

$12 \div 0.3 = b$

$40 = b$

EXAMPLE **Solve the problem.**

a. Estimate 77% of 80.

$77\% \text{ of } 80 \approx 75\% \times 80$

$= \frac{3}{4} \times 80 = 60$

b. Find the percent of change from $25 to $36.

$\dfrac{\text{new} - \text{old}}{\text{old}} = \dfrac{36 - 25}{25}$

$= \dfrac{11}{25}$

$= 0.44 = 44\% \text{ increase}$

PRACTICE

1. A history test has 30 questions. How many questions must you answer correctly to earn a grade of 80%?

2. A class of 27 students has 15 girls. What percent of the class is boys?

3. Jill's goal is to practice her clarinet daily at least 80% of the time. She practiced 25 days in October. Did Jill meet her goal in October?

4. The price of a CD player is $98. About how much will the CD player cost with a 25% discount?

5. A jacket is on sale for $48. The original price was $60. What is the percent of discount?

6. A choir had 38 singers, then 5 more joined. What is the percent of increase?

7. A newspaper conducts a survey and finds that 475 of the residents who were surveyed want a new city park. The newspaper reports that 95% of those surveyed want a new park. How many residents were surveyed?

8. Ron received a raise at work. Instead of earning $8.75 per hour, he will earn $9.25. What is the percent of increase in Ron's hourly wage?

9. A school has 515 students. About 260 students ride the school bus. Estimate the percent of the school's students who ride the school bus.

Converting Measurements and Rates

The Table of Measures on page 921 gives many statements of equivalent measures. For each statement, you can write two different conversion factors.

Statement of Equivalent Measures	Conversion Factors
100 cm = 1 m	$\dfrac{100 \text{ cm}}{1 \text{ m}} = 1$ and $\dfrac{1 \text{ m}}{100 \text{ cm}} = 1$

To convert from one unit of measurement to another, multiply by a conversion factor. Use a conversion factor that allows you to divide out the original unit and keep the desired unit. You can also convert from one rate to another.

EXAMPLE Copy and complete: a. 5.4 m = __?__ cm   b. 9 ft² = __?__ in.²

a. $5.4 \text{ m} \times \dfrac{100 \text{ cm}}{1 \text{ m}} = 540 \text{ cm}$

b. 1 ft = 12 in., so 1 ft² = 12 · 12 = 144 in.²
Use the conversion factor $\dfrac{144 \text{ in.}^2}{1 \text{ ft}^2}$.

$9 \text{ ft}^2 \times \dfrac{144 \text{ in.}^2}{1 \text{ ft}^2} = 1296 \text{ in.}^2$

EXAMPLE Copy and complete: $425 \dfrac{\text{ft}}{\text{min}} = $ __?__ $\dfrac{\text{mi}}{\text{h}}$.

Use the conversion factors $\dfrac{60 \text{ min}}{1 \text{ h}}$ and $\dfrac{1 \text{ mi}}{5280 \text{ ft}}$.

$425 \dfrac{\text{ft}}{\text{min}} \times \dfrac{60 \text{ min}}{1 \text{ h}} \times \dfrac{1 \text{ mi}}{5280 \text{ ft}} \approx 4.8 \dfrac{\text{mi}}{\text{h}}$

PRACTICE

Copy and complete the statement.

1. 500 cm = __?__ m

2. 7 days = __?__ hours

3. 48 oz = __?__ lb

4. 14.8 kg = __?__ g

5. 3200 mL = __?__ L

6. 1200 sec = __?__ min

7. 10 gal = __?__ cups

8. 1 km = __?__ mm

9. 1 mi = __?__ in.

10. 90 ft² = __?__ yd²

11. 4 ft² = __?__ in.²

12. 12 cm² = __?__ mm²

13. 3 m³ = __?__ cm³

14. 2 yd³ = __?__ in.³

15. 6500 mm³ = __?__ cm³

16. $12 \dfrac{\text{mi}}{\text{min}} = $ __?__ $\dfrac{\text{mi}}{\text{h}}$

17. $17 \dfrac{\text{km}}{\text{sec}} = $ __?__ $\dfrac{\text{km}}{\text{min}}$

18. $0.9 \dfrac{\text{m}}{\text{min}} = $ __?__ $\dfrac{\text{mm}}{\text{min}}$

19. $58 \dfrac{\text{mi}}{\text{min}} = $ __?__ $\dfrac{\text{ft}}{\text{sec}}$

20. $82 \dfrac{\text{cm}}{\text{min}} = $ __?__ $\dfrac{\text{m}}{\text{h}}$

21. $60 \dfrac{\text{mi}}{\text{h}} = $ __?__ $\dfrac{\text{ft}}{\text{min}}$

22. $17 \dfrac{\text{km}}{\text{h}} = $ __?__ $\dfrac{\text{m}}{\text{sec}}$

23. $0.09 \dfrac{\text{m}^3}{\text{min}} = $ __?__ $\dfrac{\text{mm}^3}{\text{min}}$

24. $0.6 \dfrac{\text{km}^2}{\text{year}} = $ __?__ $\dfrac{\text{m}^2}{\text{month}}$

Mean, Median, and Mode

Three measures of *central tendency* are mean, median, and mode. One or more of these measures may be more representative of a given set of data than the others.

The **mean** of a data set is the sum of the values divided by the number of values. The mean is also called the *average*.	The **median** of a data set is the middle value when the values are written in numerical order. If a data set has an even number of values, the median is the mean of the two middle values.	The **mode** of a data set is the value that occurs most often. A data set can have no mode, one mode, or more than one mode.

EXAMPLE The website hits for one week are listed. Which measure of central tendency best represents the data? *Explain.*

Website Hits for One Week	
Day	**Number of hits**
Monday	88
Tuesday	95
Wednesday	87
Thursday	84
Friday	92
Saturday	95
Sunday	11

Mean Add the values. Then divide by the number of values.

$$88 + 95 + 87 + 84 + 92 + 95 + 11 = 552$$
$$\text{Mean} = 552 \div 7 \approx 79$$

Median Write the values in order from least to greatest. Then find the middle value(s).

11, 84, 87, **88**, 92, 95, 95
Median = 88

Mode Find the value that occurs most often.
Mode = 95

An *outlier* is a value that is much greater or lower than the other values in a data set. In the data set above, the outlier 11 causes the mean to be lower than the other six data values. So, the **mean** does not represent the data well. The **mode**, 95, does not represent the data well because it is the highest value. The **median**, 88, best represents the data because all but one value lie close to it.

PRACTICE

Tell which measure of central tendency best represents the given data. *Explain.*

1. Daily high temperatures (°F) for a week: 75, 74, 74, 70, 69, 68, 67

2. Movie ticket prices: $6.75, $7.50, $7.25, $6.75, $7, $7.50, $7.25, $6.75, $7

3. Number of eggs bought: 12, 12, 12, 6, 12, 18, 18, 12, 6, 12, 12, 12, 24, 18

4. Number of children in a family: 0, 0, 0, 1, 1, 1, 2, 2, 2, 2, 2, 2, 2, 3, 3, 4, 4, 5

5. Ages of employees: 36, 22, 30, 27, 41, 58, 33, 27, 62, 39, 21, 24, 22

6. Shoe sizes in a shipment: 5, $5\frac{1}{2}$, 6, $6\frac{1}{2}$, 7, $7\frac{1}{2}$, $7\frac{1}{2}$, 8, 8, 8, $8\frac{1}{2}$, 9, $9\frac{1}{2}$, 10

7. Test scores: 97%, 65%, 68%, 98%, 72%, 60%, 94%, 100%, 99%

8. Favorite of 3 colors: blue, yellow, red, yellow, red, red, blue, red, red, blue

Displaying Data

There are many ways to display data. An appropriate data display can help you analyze the data. The table summarizes how data are shown in some data displays.

Circle Graph	Bar Graph	Histogram	Line Graph	Stem-and-Leaf Plot	Box-and-Whisker Plot
Shows data as parts of a whole.	Compares data in distinct categories.	Compares data in intervals.	Shows how data change over time.	Shows data in numerical order.	Shows distribution of data in quartiles.

EXAMPLE The table shows bike sales at a shop. Display the data in two appropriate ways. *Describe* what each display shows about the data.

Season	Winter	Spring	Summer	Fall
Bikes sold	15	51	49	25

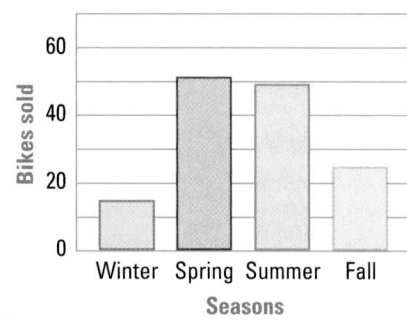

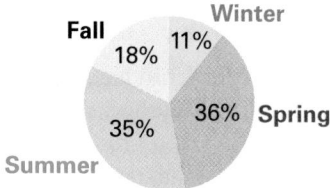

In the bar graph, the heights of the bars can be used to compare sales for the four seasons. Bikes sales were strongest in the spring and summer.

The circle graph shows the percent of annual sales for each season. Almost $\frac{3}{4}$ of the bikes were sold in the spring and summer.

EXAMPLE The test scores for a class were 82, 99, 68, 76, 84, 100, 85, 79, 92, 100, 82, 81, 60, 95, 98, 74, 95, 84, 88. Display the distribution of the scores.

Use a stem-and-leaf plot to organize the data. Identify the *lower* and *upper extremes*, the median, and the *lower* and *upper quartiles* (the medians of the lower and upper half of the ordered data set.)

6	0 8
7	4 6 9
8	1 2 2 4 4 5 8
9	2 5 5 8 9
10	0 0

Key: 7 | 4 = 74

Lower and upper extremes: 60 and 100

Median: 84

Lower and upper quartiles: 79 and 95

Then make a box-and-whisker plot. Draw a number line. Below it, plot the lower extreme (60), the lower quartile (79), the median (84), the upper quartile (95), and the upper extreme (100). Draw boxes and "whiskers," as shown.

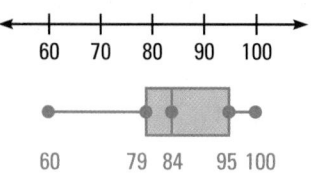

Name a data display that would be appropriate for the situation. (There may be more than one choice.) *Explain* **your reasoning.**

1. A store owner keeps track of how many cell phones are sold each week. The owner wants to see how sales change over a six-month period.

2. You measure the daily high temperature for 31 days in July. You want to see the distribution of the temperatures.

3. The ages of people in a survey are grouped into these intervals: 20–29, 30–39, 40–49, 50–59, 60–69, 70–79. You want to compare the numbers of people in the various groups.

Make a data display that can be used to answer the question. *Explain* **why you chose this display. Then answer the question.**

4. The table gives the number of gold medals won by U.S. athletes at five Summer Olympic games. *Question:* How has the number of medals won changed over time?

Year	1988	1992	1996	2000	2004
Number of gold medals	36	37	44	40	35

5. Students were surveyed about the amounts they spent at a mall one Saturday. These are the amounts (in dollars): 5, 70, 10, 40, 42, 45, 50, 4, 3, 10, 12, 15, 20, 5, 30, 35, 70, 80. *Question:* If the dollar amounts are grouped into intervals such as 0–9, 10–19, and so on, in which intervals do the greatest number of students fall?

Display the data in two appropriate ways. *Describe* **what each display shows about the data.**

6. During a game, a high school soccer team plays 2 forwards, 4 midfielders, 4 defenders, and 1 goalkeeper.

7. A high school has 131 students taking Geometry. The number of students in each class are: 18, 16, 17, 15, 16, 14, 17 and 18.

8. The table gives the number of calories in 8 different pieces of fresh fruit.

Fruit	Apple	Banana	Mango	Orange	Peach	Pear	Plum	Tangerine
Calories	117	100	85	65	35	60	40	35

The ages of actors in a community theater play are 18, 25, 19, 32, 26, 15, 33, 12, 36, 16, 18, 30, 25, 24, 32, 30, 13, 15, 37, 35, 72, 35. Use these data for Exercises 9–11.

9. Make a stem-and-leaf plot of the data. Identify the lower and upper extremes, the median, and the lower and upper quartiles of the data set.

10. Make a box-and-whisker plot of the data. About what percent of the actors are over 18? How does the box-and-whisker plot help you answer this question?

11. Suppose the two oldest actors drop out of the play. Draw a new box-and-whisker plot without the data values for those actors. How does the distribution of the data change? *Explain.*

Sampling and Surveys

A *survey* is a study of one or more characteristics of a group. A **population** is the group you want information about. A **sample** is part of the population. In a **random sample**, every member of a population has an equal chance of being selected for a survey. A random sample is most likely to represent the population. A sample that is not representative is a *biased sample*.

Using a biased sample may affect the results of a survey. In addition, survey results may be influenced by the use of *biased questions*. A biased question encourages a particular response.

EXAMPLE **Read the description of the survey. Identify any biased samples or questions.** *Explain.*

   a. A movie theater owner wants to know how often local residents go to the movies each month. The owner asks every tenth ticket buyer.

   ▶ The sample (every tenth ticket buyer) is unlikely to represent the population (local residents). It is biased because moviegoers are over-represented.

   b. The mayor's office asks a random sample of the city's residents the following question: Do you support the necessary budget cuts proposed by the mayor?

   ▶ The sample is random, so it is not biased. The question is biased because the word *necessary* suggests that people should support the budget cuts.

PRACTICE

Read the description of the survey. Identify any biased samples or questions. *Explain.*

   1. The coach of a high school soccer team wants to know whether students are more likely to come watch the team's games on Wednesdays or Thursdays. The team's first game is on a Friday. The coach asks all the students who come to watch which day they prefer.

   2. A town's recreation department wants to know whether to build a new skateboard park. The head of the department visits a local park and asks people at the park whether they would like to have a skateboard park built.

   3. A television producer wants to know whether people in a city would like to watch a one-hour local news program or a half-hour local news program. A television advertisement is run several times during the day asking viewers to e-mail their preference.

   4. The teachers at a music school want to know whether the students at the school practice regularly. Five of the ten teachers at the school ask their students the following question: How many hours do you spend practicing each day?

   5. A skating rink owner wants to know the ages of people who use the rink. Over a two-week period, the owner asks every tenth person who uses the rink his or her age.

   6. A cello teacher asks some of his students, "Do you practice every day?"

Counting Methods

To count the number of possibilities in a situation, you can make an organized list, draw a tree diagram, make a table, or use the counting principle.

The Counting Principle
If one event can occur in m ways, and for each of these ways a second event can occur in n ways, then the number of ways that the two events can occur together is $m \times n$.

The counting principle can be extended to three or more events.

EXAMPLE Use four different counting methods to find the number of possible salad specials.

Salad Special $5.95
Choose 1 salad and 1 dressing
Salad: Lettuce or Spinach
Dressing: Ranch, Blue cheese, or Italian

Method 1 Make an Organized List

Pair each salad with each dressing and list each possible special.

Lettuce salad with ranch

Lettuce salad with blue cheese

Lettuce salad with Italian

Spinach salad with ranch

Spinach salad with blue cheese

Spinach salad with Italian

Count the number of specials listed. There are 6 possible salad specials.

Method 2 Draw a Tree Diagram

Arrange the salads and dressings in a tree diagram.

Salad   **Dressing**

Lettuce — Ranch, Blue cheese, Italian

Spinach — Ranch, Blue cheese, Italian

Count the number of branches in the tree diagram. There are 6 possible salad specials.

Method 3 Make a Table

List the salads in the left column. List the dressings in the top row.

	Ranch	Blue cheese	Italian
Lettuce	Lettuce, Ranch	Lettuce, Blue cheese	Lettuce, Italian
Spinach	Spinach, Ranch	Spinach, Blue cheese	Spinach, Italian

Count the number of cells filled. There are 6 possible salad specials.

Method 4 Use the Counting Principle

There are 2 choices of salad, so $m = 2$. There are 3 choices of dressing, so $n = 3$. By the counting principle, the number of ways that the salad and dressing choices can be combined is $m \times n = 2 \times 3 = 6$.

There are 6 possible salad specials.

EXAMPLE Tyler must choose a 4-digit password for his bank account. Find the number of possible 4-digit passwords using four different digits.

Because there are many possible passwords, use the counting principle.

For one of the digits in the password, there are 10 choices: 0, 1, 2, 3, 4, 5, 6, 7, 8, and 9. Because one of these digits will be used for the first digit, there are only 9 choices for the next, 8 for the next after that, and so on.

$$\underset{\text{for first digit}}{10 \text{ choices}} \times \underset{\text{for second digit}}{9 \text{ choices}} \times \underset{\text{for third digit}}{8 \text{ choices}} \times \underset{\text{for fourth digit}}{7 \text{ choices}}$$

$10 \times 9 \times 8 \times 7 = 5040$

▶ There are 5040 possible 4-digit passwords using four different digits.

PRACTICE

Use one of the methods described in the Examples on pages 891 and 892 to solve each problem. *Explain* your reasoning.

1. Ann takes three pairs of shorts (red, blue, and green) and five T-shirts (black, white, yellow, orange, and brown) on a trip. Find the number of different shorts and T-shirt outfits Ann can wear while on the trip.

2. Art students can choose any two pieces of colored paper for a project. There are six colors available and students must choose two different colors. Find the number of different color combinations that can be chosen.

3. Steve must choose four characters for his computer password. Each character can be any letter from A through Z or any digit from 0 through 9. All letters and digits may be used more than once. Find the number of possible passwords.

4. A restaurant offers a pizza special, as shown at the right. Assuming that two different toppings are ordered, find the number of two-topping combinations that can be ordered.

Large Pizza Special	
Any 2 toppings for $12.49	
Pepperoni	Green Olive
Sausage	Green Pepper
Ground Beef	Red Onion
Black Olive	Mushroom

5. Each of the locker combinations at a gym uses three numbers from 0 through 49. Find the number of different locker combinations that are possible.

6. A movie theater sells three sizes of popcorn and six different soft drinks. Each soft drink can be bought in one of three sizes. Find the number of different popcorn and soft drink pairs that can be ordered.

7. A class has 28 students and elects two students to be class officers. One student will be president and one will be vice president. How many different pairs of class officers are possible?

8. Some students are auditioning for parts in the play *Our Town*. Twenty girls try out for the parts listed at the right. In how many different ways can 5 of the 20 girls be assigned these roles?

Parts in *Our Town*

Emily Webb
Mrs. Gibbs
Mrs. Webb
Mrs. Soames
Rebecca Gibbs

9. Bill, Allison, James, and Caroline are friends. In how many different ways can they stand in a row for a photo?

10. A cafeteria serves 4 kinds of sandwiches: cheese, veggie, peanut butter, and bologna. Students can choose any two sandwiches for lunch. How many different sandwich combinations are possible?

Probability

The **probability** of an event is a measure of the likelihood that the event will occur. An event that cannot occur has a probability of 0, and an event that is certain to occur has a probability of 1. Other probabilities lie between 0 and 1. You can write a probability as a decimal, a fraction, or a percent.

Probability of an Event
When all outcomes are equally likely, the probability of an event, P(event), is $\dfrac{\text{number of favorable outcomes}}{\text{number of possible outcomes}}$.

When you consider the probability of two events occurring, the events are called **compound events**. Compound events can be dependent or independent.

Two events are **independent events** if the occurrence of one event *does not* affect the occurrence of another.	Two events are **dependent events** if the occurrence of one event *does* affect the occurrence of another.
For two independent events A and B, $$P(A \text{ and } B) = P(A) \cdot P(B).$$	For two dependent events A and B, $$P(A \text{ and } B) = P(A) \cdot P(B \mid A),$$ where $P(B \mid A)$ is the probability of B given that A has occurred.

EXAMPLE   **A box holds 12 yellow marbles and 12 orange marbles. Without looking, you take a marble. Then you take another marble without replacing the first. Find the probability that both marbles are yellow.**

There are 24 marbles in the box when you take the first one, and only 23 when you take the second. So, the events are dependent.

$$P(A \text{ and } B) = P(A) \cdot P(B \mid A) = \frac{12}{24} \cdot \frac{11}{23} = \frac{11}{46} \approx 0.24, \text{ or } 24\%$$

PRACTICE

Identify the events as *independent* or *dependent*. Then answer the question.

1. There are 20 socks in your drawer, and 12 of them are white. You grab a sock without looking. Then you grab a second sock without putting the first one back. What is the probability that both socks are white?

2. You flip a coin two times. What is the probability that you get heads each time?

3. Your math, literature, Spanish, history, and science homework assignments are organized in five folders. You randomly choose one folder, finish your assignment, and then choose a new folder. What is the probability that you do your math homework first, and then history?

4. You roll a red number cube and a blue number cube. What is the probability that you roll an even number on the red cube and a number greater than 2 on the blue cube?

5. You flip a coin three times. What is the probability that you do not get heads on any of the flips?

Problem Solving Plan and Strategies

Here is a 4-step **problem solving plan** that you can use to solve problems.

STEP 1	Read and understand the problem.	Read the problem carefully. Organize the given information and decide what you need to find. Check for unnecessary or missing information. Supply missing facts, if needed.
STEP 2	Make a plan to solve the problem.	Choose a problem solving strategy. Choose the correct operations to use. Decide if you will use a tool such as a calculator, graph, or spreadsheet.
STEP 3	Carry out the plan to solve the problem.	Use the problem solving strategy and any tools you have chosen. Estimate before you calculate, if possible. Do any calculations that are needed. Answer the question that the problem asks.
STEP 4	Check to see if your answer is reasonable.	Reread the problem. See if your answer agrees with the given information and with any estimate you have made.

Here are some **problem solving strategies** that you can use to solve problems.

Strategy	When to use	How to use
Guess, check, and revise	Guess, check, and revise when you need a place to start or you want to see how the problem works.	Make a reasonable guess. Check to see if your guess solves the problem. If it does not, revise your guess and check again.
Draw a diagram or a graph	Draw a diagram or a graph when a problem involves any relationships that you can represent visually.	Draw a diagram or a graph that shows given information. See what your diagram reveals that can help you solve the problem.
Make a table or an organized list	Make a table or list when a problem requires you to record, generate, or organize information.	Make a table with columns, rows, and any given information. Generate a systematic list that can help you solve the problem.
Use an equation or a formula	Use an equation or a formula when you know a relationship between quantities.	Write an equation or formula that shows the relationship between known quantities. Solve the equation to solve the problem.
Use a proportion	Use a proportion when you know that two ratios are equal.	Write a proportion using the two equal ratios. Solve the proportion to solve the problem.
Look for a pattern	Look for a pattern when a problem includes numbers or diagrams that you need to analyze.	Look for a pattern in any given information. Organize, extend, or generalize the pattern to help you solve the problem.
Break a problem into parts	Break a problem into parts when a problem cannot be solved in one step but can be solved in parts.	Break the problem into parts and solve each part. Put the answers together to help you solve the original problem.
Solve a simpler or related problem	Solve a simpler or related problem when a problem seems difficult and can be made easier by using simpler numbers or conditions.	Think of a way to make the problem easier. Solve the simpler or related problem. Use what you learned to help you solve the original problem.
Work backward	Work backward when a problem gives you an end result and you need to find beginning conditions.	Work backward from the given information until you solve the problem. Work forward through the problem to check your answer.

EXAMPLE **A marching band receives a $2800 donation to buy new drums and piccolos. Each drum costs $350 and each piccolo costs $400. How many of each type of instrument can the band buy?**

STEP 1 **Choose** two strategies, *Use an Equation* and *Draw a Graph*.

STEP 2 **Write** an inequality. Let d = the number of drums and p = the number of piccolos.

Cost of drums	·	Number of drums	+	Cost of piccolos	·	Number of piccolos	≤	$2800

$$350d + 400p \leq 2800$$

STEP 3 **Graph** and shade the solution region of the inequality.

The band can buy only whole numbers of instruments. Also, you can assume that the band will buy at least one of each type of instrument. Mark each point in the solution region that has whole number coordinates greater than or equal to 1.

▶ The red points on the graph show 21 different ways that the band can buy drums and piccolos without spending more than $2800.

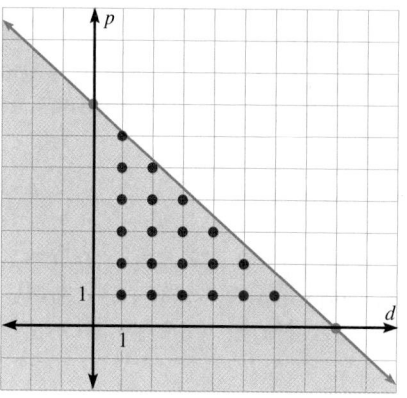

PRACTICE

1. A cell phone company offers a plan with an initial registration fee of $25 and a monthly fee of $15. How much will the plan cost for one year?

2. Rita wants to attend a swim camp that costs $220. She has $56 in a bank account. She also earns $25 each week walking dogs. Will Rita be able to make a full payment for the camp in 5 weeks? *Explain* your reasoning.

3. What is the 97th number in the pattern 4, 3, 2, 1, 4, 3, 2, 1, 4, 3, 2, 1, . . .?

4. Sam makes a down payment of $120 on a $360 bike. He will pay $30 each month until the balance is paid. How many monthly payments will he make?

5. Marie is buying tree seedlings for the school. She can spend no more than $310 on aspen and birch trees. She wants at least 20 trees in all and twice as many aspen trees as birch trees. Find three possible ways that Marie can buy the trees.

Tree Seedlings

Aspen	$10 each
Birch	$12 each

6. In how many different ways can you make 75¢ in change using quarters, dimes, and nickels?

7. Charlie is cutting a rectangular cake that is 9 inches by 13 inches into equal-sized rectangular pieces. Each piece of cake should be at least 2 inches on each side. What is the greatest number of pieces Charlie can cut?

8. Streamers cost $1.70 per roll and balloons cost $1.50 per bag. If the student council has $40 to spend for parent night and buys 10 rolls of streamers, how many bags of balloons can the student council buy?

Extra Practice

Chapter 1

1.1 **In Exercises 1–5, use the diagram.**

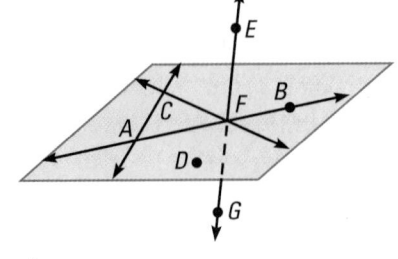

1. Name three points that are collinear. Then give a name for the line that contains the points.

2. Name the intersection of plane *ABC* and $\overleftrightarrow{EG}$.

3. Name two pairs of opposite rays.

4. Are points *A*, *C*, and *G* coplanar? *Explain.*

5. Name a line that intersects plane *AFD* at more than one point.

1.2 **In the diagram, *P*, *Q*, *R*, *S*, and *T* are collinear, *PT* = 54, *QT* = 42, *QS* = 31, and *RS* = 17. Find the indicated length.**

6. *PQ*	**7.** *PS*	**8.** *QR*
9. *PR*	**10.** *ST*	**11.** *RT*

$$\overset{P \quad\quad Q \quad\quad R \quad\quad\quad S \quad\quad T}{\longleftarrow\!\bullet\!\rule{1cm}{0.4pt}\!\bullet\!\rule{1cm}{0.4pt}\!\bullet\!\rule{1.3cm}{0.4pt}\!\bullet\!\rule{1cm}{0.4pt}\!\bullet\!\longrightarrow}$$

1.2 **Point *B* is between *A* and *C* on $\overline{AC}$. Use the given information to write an equation in terms of *x*. Solve the equation. Then find *AB* and *BC*, and determine whether $\overline{AB}$ and $\overline{BC}$ are congruent.**

12. $AB = x + 3$ $BC = 2x + 1$ $AC = 10$	**13.** $AB = 3x - 7$ $BC = 3x - 1$ $AC = 16$	**14.** $AB = 11x - 16$ $BC = 8x - 1$ $AC = 78$
15. $AB = 4x - 5$ $BC = 2x - 7$ $AC = 54$	**16.** $AB = 14x + 5$ $BC = 10x + 15$ $AC = 80$	**17.** $AB = 3x - 7$ $BC = 2x + 5$ $AC = 108$

1.3 **Find the coordinates of the midpoint of the segment with the given endpoints.**

18. $A(2, -4), B(7, 1)$	**19.** $C(-3, -2), D(-8, 4)$	**20.** $E(-2.3, -1.9), F(3.1, -9.7)$
21. $G(3, -7), H(-1, 9)$	**22.** $I(4, 3), J(2, 2)$	**23.** $K(1.7, -7.9), L(8.5, -8.2)$

1.3 **Find the length of the segment with given endpoint and midpoint *M*.**

24. $Z(0, 1)$ and $M(7, 1)$	**25.** $Y(4, 3)$ and $M(1, 7)$	**26.** $X(0, -1)$ and $M(12, 4)$
27. $W(5, 3)$ and $M(-10, -5)$	**28.** $V(-3, -4)$ and $M(9, 5)$	**29.** $U(3, 2)$ and $M(11, -4)$

1.4 **Use the given information to find the indicated angle measure.**

30. $m\angle QPS = \underline{\ ?\ }$

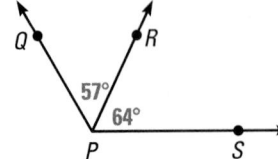

31. $m\angle LMN = \underline{\ ?\ }$

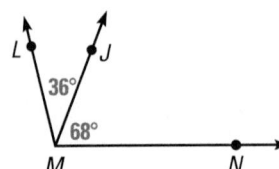

32. $m\angle XWZ = \underline{\ ?\ }$

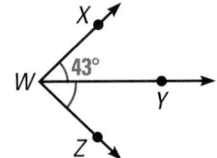

1.4 **33.** Given $m\angle ABC = 133°$, find $m\angle ABD$.

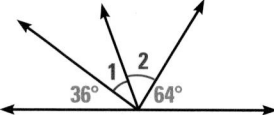

34. Given $m\angle GHK = 17°$, find $m\angle KHJ$.

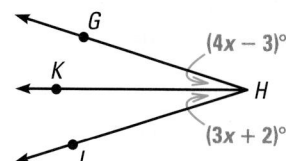

1.5 Tell whether $\angle 1$ and $\angle 2$ are *vertical angles*, *adjacent angles*, a *linear pair*, *complementary*, or *supplementary*. There may be more than one answer.

35.

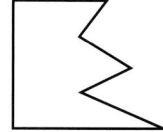

36.

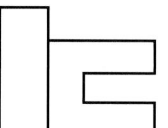

37.

1.5 Use the diagram.

38. Name two supplementary angles that are not a linear pair.

39. Name two vertical angles that are not complementary.

40. Name three pairs of complementary angles. Tell whether each pair contains vertical angles, adjacent angles, or neither.

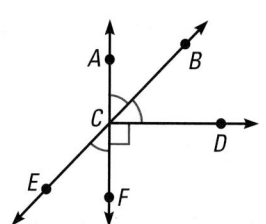

1.6 Tell whether the figure is a polygon. If it is not, *explain* why. If it is, tell whether it is *convex* or *concave*.

41.

42.

43.

44.

1.6 In Exercises 45 and 46, use the diagram.

45. Identify two different equilateral polygons in the diagram. Classify each by the number of sides.

46. Name one of each of the following figures as it appears in the five-pointed star diagram: triangle, quadrilateral, pentagon, hexagon, heptagon.

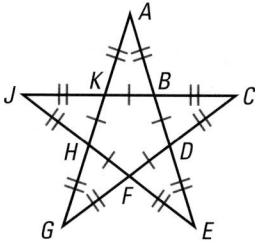

1.7 Use the information about the figure to find the indicated measure.

47. Area = 91 cm^2
Find the length ℓ.

48. Find the area of the triangle.

49. Area = 66 m^2
Find the height h.

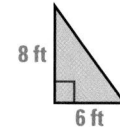

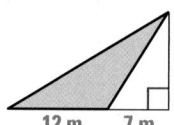

1.7 Find the perimeter and area of the triangle with the given vertices. Round to the nearest tenth.

50. $A(2, 1)$, $B(3, 6)$, $C(6, 1)$

51. $D(1, 1)$, $E(3, 1)$, $F(6, 5)$

Chapter 2

2.1 *Describe* the pattern in the numbers. Write the next number in the pattern.

1. 17, 23, 15, 21, 13, 19,… **2.** 1, 0.5, 0.25, 0.125, 0.0625,… **3.** 2, 3, 5, 7, 11, 13,…

4. 7.0, 7.5, 8.0, 8.5,… **5.** $1, \frac{1}{3}, \frac{1}{9}, \frac{1}{27},…$ **6.** 2, 2, 4, 6, 10, 16, 26,…

2.1 Show the conjecture is false by finding a counterexample.

7. The difference of any two numbers is a value that lies between those two numbers.

8. The value of $2x$ is always greater than the value of x.

9. If an angle A can be bisected, then angle A must be obtuse.

2.2 For the given statement, write the if-then form, the converse, the inverse, and the contrapositive.

10. Two lines that intersect form two pairs of vertical angles.

11. All squares are four-sided regular polygons.

2.2 Decide whether the statement is *true* or *false*. If false, provide a counterexample.

12. If a figure is a hexagon, then it is a regular polygon.

13. If two angles are complementary, then the sum of their measures is 90°.

2.3 Write the statement that follows from the pair of statements that are given.

14. If a triangle is equilateral, then it has congruent angles.
If a triangle has congruent angles, then it is regular.

15. If two coplanar lines are not parallel, then they intersect.
If two lines intersect, then they form congruent vertical angles.

2.3 Select the word(s) that make(s) the conclusion true.

16. John only does his math homework when he is in study hall. John is doing his math homework. So, John (*is, may be, is not*) in study hall.

17. May sometimes buys pretzels when she goes to the supermarket. May is at the supermarket. So, she (*will, might, will not*) buy pretzels.

2.4 Use the diagram to determine if the statement is *true* or *false*.

18. $\overleftrightarrow{SV} \perp$ plane Z

19. $\overleftrightarrow{XU}$ intersects plane Z at point Y.

20. $\overleftrightarrow{TW}$ lies in plane Z.

21. $\angle SYT$ and $\angle WYS$ are vertical angles.

22. $\angle SYT$ and $\angle TYV$ are complementary angles.

23. $\angle TYU$ and $\angle UYW$ are a linear pair.

24. $\angle UYV$ is acute.

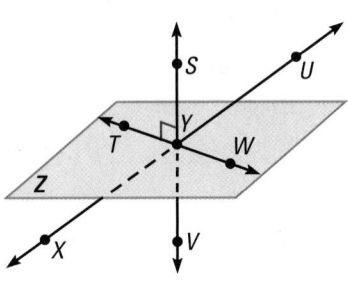

2.5 **Solve the equation. Write a reason for each step.**

25. $4x + 15 = 39$ **26.** $6x + 47 = 10x - 9$ **27.** $2(-7x + 3) = -50$

28. $54 + 9x = 3(7x + 6)$ **29.** $13(2x - 3) - 20x = 3$ **30.** $31 + 25x = 7x - 14 + 3x$

2.6 **Copy and complete the statement. Name the property illustrated.**

31. If $m\angle JKL = m\angle GHI$ and $m\angle GHI = m\angle ABC$, then __?__ = __?__.

32. If $m\angle MNO = m\angle PQR$, then $m\angle PQR =$ __?__

33. $m\angle XYZ =$ __?__

2.6 **34.** Copy and complete the proof.

GIVEN ▶ Point C is in the interior of $\angle ABD$.
               $\angle ABD$ is a right angle.

PROVE ▶ $\angle ABC$ and $\angle CBD$ are complementary.

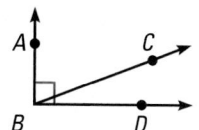

STATEMENTS	REASONS
1. $\angle ABD$ is a right angle.	1. Given
2. $m\angle ABD = 90°$	2. __?__
3. __?__	3. Given
4. $m\angle ABD = m\angle ABC + m\angle CBD$	4. __?__
5. __?__ $= m\angle ABC + m\angle CBD$	5. Substitution Property of Equality
6. __?__	6. Definition of complementary angles

2.6 **35.** Use the given information and the diagram to prove the statement.

GIVEN ▶ $\overline{XY} \cong \overline{YZ} \cong \overline{ZX}$

PROVE ▶ The perimeter of $\triangle XYZ$ is $3 \cdot XY$.

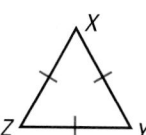

2.7 **Copy and complete the statement. $\angle AGD$ is a right angle and $\overleftrightarrow{AB}$, $\overleftrightarrow{CD}$, and $\overleftrightarrow{EF}$ intersect at point G.**

36. If $m\angle CGF = 158°$, then $m\angle EGD =$ __?__.

37. If $m\angle EGA = 67°$, then $m\angle FGD =$ __?__.

38. If $m\angle FGC = 149°$, then $m\angle EGA =$ __?__.

39. $m\angle DGB =$ __?__

40. $m\angle FGH =$ __?__

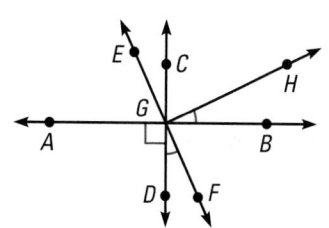

2.7 **41.** Write a two-column proof.

GIVEN ▶ $\angle UKV$ and $\angle VKW$ are complements.

PROVE ▶ $\angle YKZ$ and $\angle XKY$ are complements.

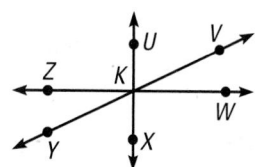

Chapter 3

3.1 **Classify the angle pair as *corresponding*, *alternate interior*, *alternate exterior*, or *consecutive interior* angles.**

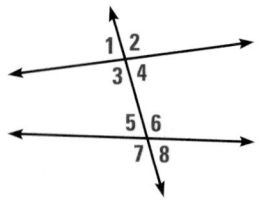

1. ∠6 and ∠2

2. ∠7 and ∠2

3. ∠5 and ∠3

4. ∠4 and ∠5

5. ∠1 and ∠5

6. ∠3 and ∠6

3.1 **Copy and complete the statement. List all possible correct answers.**

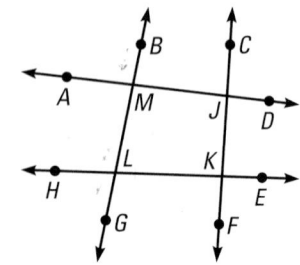

7. ∠*AMB* and __?__ are corresponding angles.

8. ∠*AML* and __?__ are alternate interior angles.

9. ∠*CJD* and __?__ are alternate exterior angles.

10. ∠*LMJ* and __?__ are consecutive interior angles.

11. __?__ is a transversal of $\overleftrightarrow{AD}$ and $\overleftrightarrow{HE}$.

3.2 **Find *m*∠1 and *m*∠2. *Explain* your reasoning.**

12.
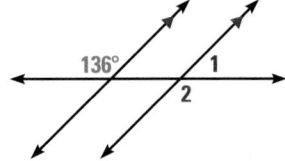

13.
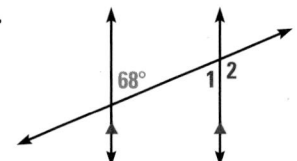

14.
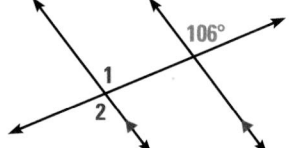

3.2 **Find the values of *x* and *y*.**

15.
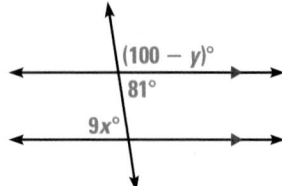

16.
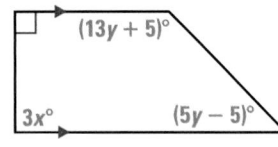

17.
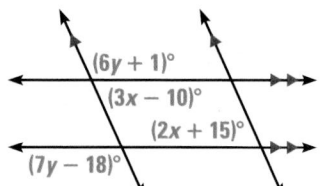

3.3 **Is there enough information to prove *m* ∥ *n*? If so, state the postulate or theorem you would use.**

18.
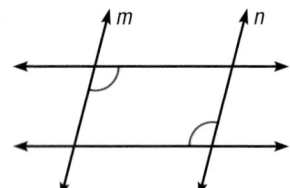

19.
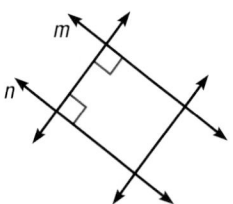

20.
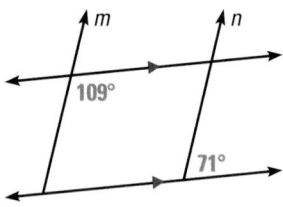

3.3 **Can you prove that lines *a* and *b* are parallel? If so, *explain* how.**

21.
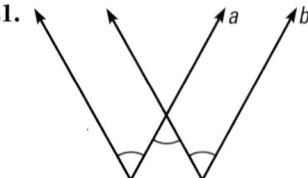

22.
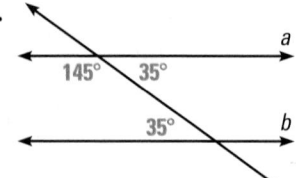

23.
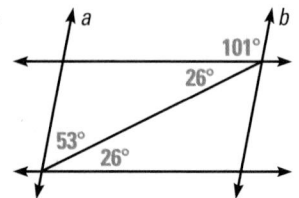

3.4 Tell whether the lines through the given points are *parallel*, *perpendicular*, or *neither*. *Justify* your answer.

24. Line 1: (7, 4), (10, 5)
Line 2: (2, 3), (8, 5)

25. Line 1: (−3, 1), (−2, 5)
Line 2: (−1, −3), (5, −2)

26. Line 1: (−6, 0), (8, 7)
Line 2: (1, 4), (2, 2)

3.4 Tell which line through the given points is steeper.

27. Line 1: (0, −6), (−4, −9)
Line 2: (−2, 5), (1, 9)

28. Line 1: (−1, −5), (−1, 3)
Line 2: (−3, 4), (−5, 4)

29. Line 1: (1, 1), (2, 6)
Line 2: (1, 1), (3, 10)

3.5 Write an equation of the line that passes through the given point *P* and has the given slope *m*.

30. $P(4, 7)$, $m = 2$

31. $P(-3, 0)$, $m = \frac{2}{3}$

32. $P(9, 4)$, $m = -\frac{1}{3}$

3.5 Write an equation of the line that passes through point *P* and is parallel to the line with the given equation.

33. $P(1, -2)$, $y = -2x - 6$

34. $P(6, 3)$, $y = -\frac{1}{3}x + 12$

35. $P(-7, 3)$, $y = x + 3$

36. $P(0, 3)$, $y = 4x - 2$

37. $P(-9, 4)$, $y = \frac{2}{5}x + 1$

38. $P(8, -3)$, $y = x - 5$

3.6 Find $m\angle ADB$.

39.

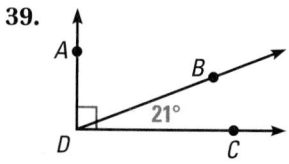

40.

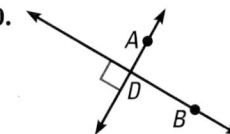

41.

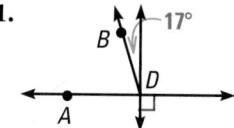

42.

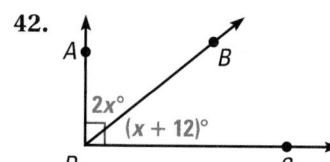

43.

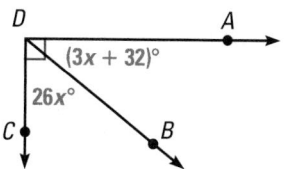

44.

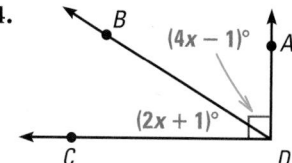

3.6 **45.** Copy and complete the proof.

GIVEN ▶ $\overrightarrow{BA} \perp \overrightarrow{BC}$,
$\overrightarrow{BD}$ bisects $\angle ABC$.

PROVE ▶ $m\angle ABD = 45°$

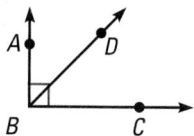

STATEMENTS	REASONS
1. $\overrightarrow{BA} \perp \overrightarrow{BC}$	1. _?_
2. _?_	2. Definition of perpendicular lines
3. $m\angle ABC = 90°$	3. _?_
4. _?_	4. Given
5. $m\angle ABD = m\angle DBC$	5. _?_
6. $m\angle ABC = $ _?_ + _?_	6. Angle Addition Postulate
7. $m\angle ABD + m\angle DBC = 90°$	7. _?_
8. $m\angle ABD + $ _?_ $= 90°$	8. Substitution Property of Equality
9. $2(m\angle ABD) = 90°$	9. _?_
10. $m\angle ABD = 45°$	10. _?_

Chapter 4

4.1 A triangle has the given vertices. Graph the triangle and classify it by its sides. Then determine if it is a right triangle.

1. $A(-1, -2), B(-1, 2), C(4, 2)$ **2.** $A(-1, -1), B(3, 1), C(2, -2)$ **3.** $A(-3, 4), B(2, 4), C(5, -2)$

4.1 Find the value of x. Then classify the triangle by its angles.

4.

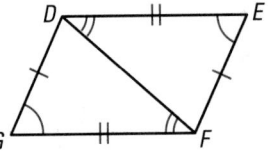

5.

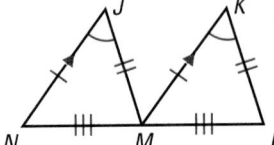

6.

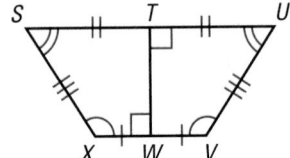

4.2 Write a congruence statement for any figures that can be proved congruent. *Explain* your reasoning.

7.

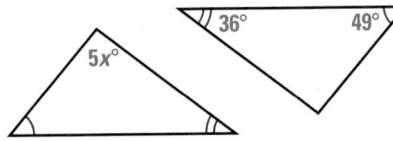

8.

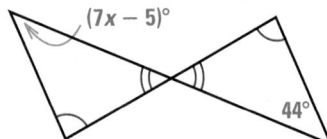

9.

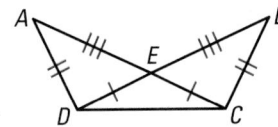

4.2 Find the value of x.

10.

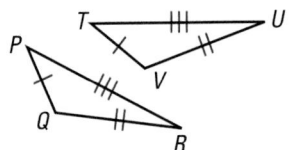

11.

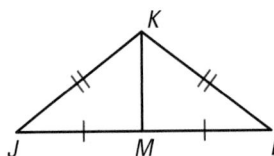

4.3 Decide whether the congruence statement is true. *Explain* your reasoning.

12. $\triangle PQR \cong \triangle TUV$

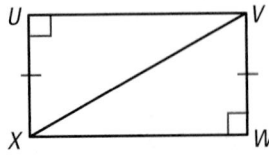

13. $\triangle JKM \cong \triangle LMK$

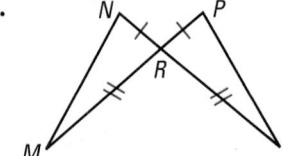

14. $\triangle ACD \cong \triangle BDC$

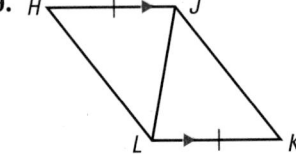

4.3 Use the given coordinates to determine if $\triangle ABC \cong \triangle PQR$.

15. $A(-2, 1), B(2, 6), C(6, 2), P(-1, -2), Q(3, 3), R(7, -1)$

16. $A(-4, 5), B(2, 6), C(-2, 3), P(2, 1), Q(8, 2), R(5, -1)$

4.4 Name the congruent triangles in the diagram. *Explain.*

17.

18.

19.

EXTRA PRACTICE

4.5 **Is it possible to prove that the triangles are congruent? If so, state the postulate or theorem you would use.**

20. △GHL, △JKL

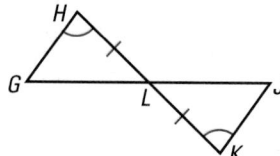

21. △MNQ, △PNQ

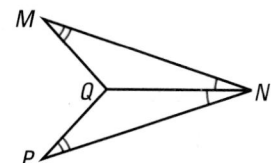

22. △STW, △UVW

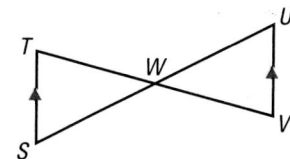

4.5 **Tell whether you can use the given information to determine whether △ABC ≅ △DEF. *Explain* your reasoning.**

23. $\angle A \cong \angle D$, $\overline{AB} \cong \overline{DE}$, $\angle B \cong \angle E$

24. $\overline{AB} \cong \overline{DE}$, $\overline{BC} \cong \overline{EF}$, $\angle A \cong \angle D$

4.6 **Use the information in the diagram to write a plan for proving that ∠1 ≅ ∠2.**

25.

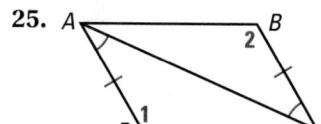

26.

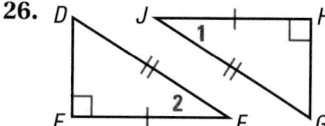

27.

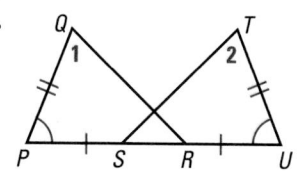

4.6 **Use the vertices of △ABC and △DEF to show that ∠A ≅ ∠D. *Explain*.**

28. $A(0, 8)$, $B(6, 0)$, $C(0, 0)$, $D(3, 10)$, $E(9, 2)$, $F(3, 2)$

29. $A(-3, -2)$, $B(-2, 3)$, $C(2, 2)$, $D(5, 1)$, $E(6, 6)$, $F(10, 5)$

4.7 **Find the value(s) of the variable(s).**

30.

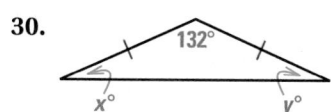

31.

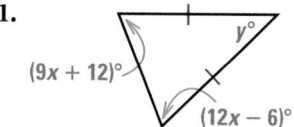

32.

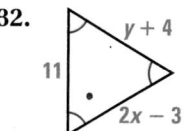

33.

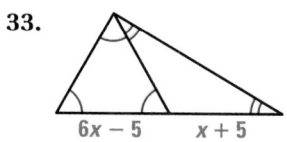

34.

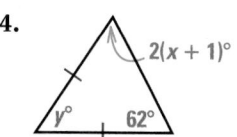

35.

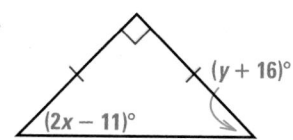

4.8 **Copy the figure and draw its image after the transformation.**

36. Reflection: in the *y*-axis

37. Reflection: in the *x*-axis

38. Translation: $(x, y) \rightarrow (x - 3, y + 7)$

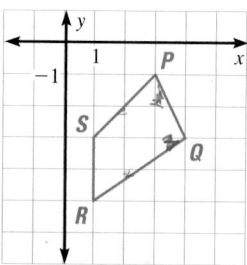

4.8 **Use the coordinates to graph $\overline{AB}$ and $\overline{CD}$. Tell whether $\overline{CD}$ is a rotation of $\overline{AB}$ about the origin. If so, give the angle and direction of rotation.**

39. $A(4, 2)$, $B(1, 1)$, $C(-4, -2)$, $D(-1, -1)$

40. $A(-1, 3)$, $B(0, 2)$, $C(-1, 2)$, $D(-3, 1)$

Chapter 5

5.1 Copy and complete the statement.

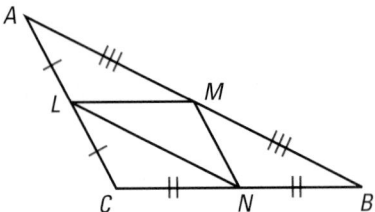

1. $\overline{LN} \parallel$ ___?___
2. $\overline{CB} \parallel$ ___?___
3. $\overline{MN} \parallel$ ___?___
4. $AM =$ ___?___ $=$ ___?___
5. $MN =$ ___?___ $=$ ___?___

5.1 Place the figure in a coordinate plane in a convenient way. Assign coordinates to each vertex.

6. Isosceles right triangle: leg length is 4 units
7. Scalene triangle: one side length is 6 units
8. Square: side length is 5 units
9. Right triangle: leg lengths are s and t

5.2 Find the length of $\overline{AB}$.

10.

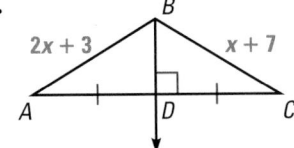

11.

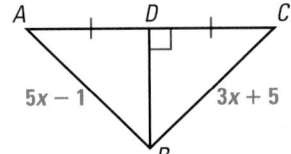

12.

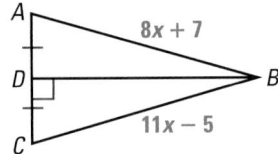

5.2 In Exercises 13–17, use the diagram. $\overrightarrow{LN}$ is the perpendicular bisector of $\overline{JK}$.

13. Find KN.
14. Find LJ.
15. Find KP.
16. Find JP.
17. Is P on $\overrightarrow{LN}$?

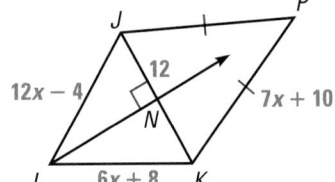

5.3 Use the information in the diagram to find the measure.

18. Find $m\angle ABC$.

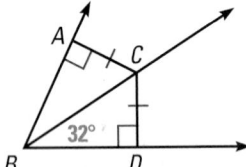

19. Find EH.

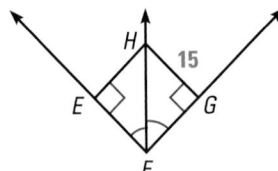

20. $m\angle JKL = 50°$. Find LM.

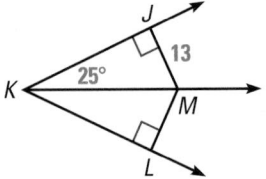

5.3 Can you find the value of x? *Explain.*

21.

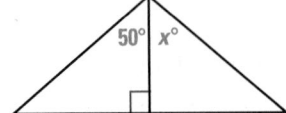

22.

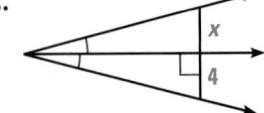

23.

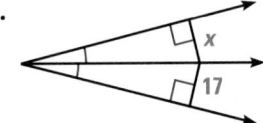

5.4 *P* is the centroid of △ *DEF*, *FP* = 14, *RE* = 24, and *PS* = 8.5. Find the length of the segment.

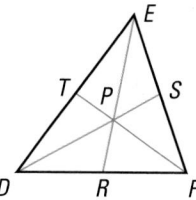

24. $\overline{TF}$

25. $\overline{DP}$

26. $\overline{DS}$

27. $\overline{PR}$

5.4 Use the diagram shown and the given information to decide whether $\overline{BD}$ is a *perpendicular bisector*, an *angle bisector*, a *median*, or an *altitude* of △ *ABC*.

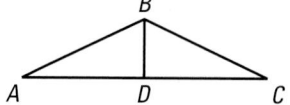

28. $\overline{BD} \perp \overline{AC}$

29. $\angle ABD \cong \angle CBD$

30. $\overline{AD} \cong \overline{CD}$

31. $\overline{BD} \perp \overline{AC}$ and $\overline{AD} \cong \overline{CD}$

32. △ *ABD* ≅ △ *CBD*

33. $\overline{BD} \perp \overline{AC}$ and $\overline{AB} \cong \overline{CB}$

5.5 List the sides and angles in order from smallest to largest.

34.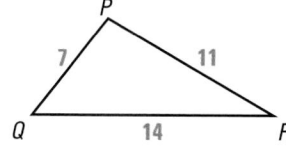

35.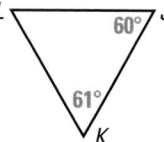

36.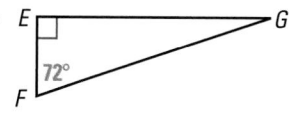

5.5 *Describe* the possible lengths of the third side of the triangle given the lengths of the other two sides.

37. 9 inches, 8 inches

38. 24 feet, 13 feet

39. 3 inches, 9 inches

40. 1 foot, 17 inches

41. 4 feet, 2 yards

42. 2 yards, 6 feet

5.6 Copy and complete with >, < or = . *Explain.*

43. *LN* __?__ *PR*

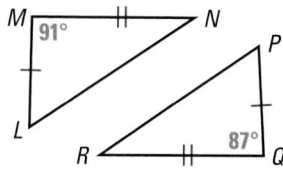

44. *VU* __?__ *ST*

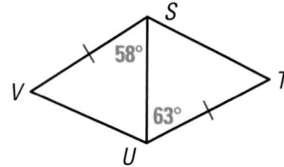

45. $m\angle WYX$ __?__ $m\angle WYZ$

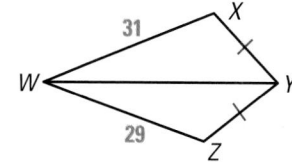

46. $m\angle 1$ __?__ $m\angle 2$

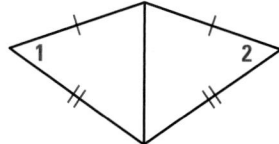

47. *JK* __?__ *MN*

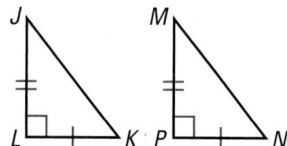

48. *BC* __?__ *DE*

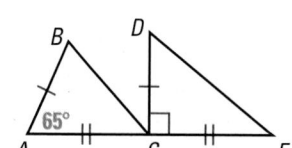

49. *GH* __?__ *QR*

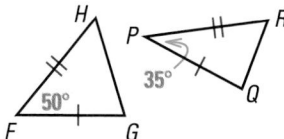

50. $m\angle 3$ __?__ $m\angle 4$

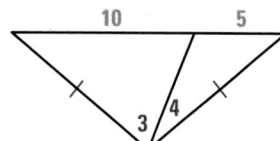

51. $m\angle 5$ __?__ $m\angle 6$

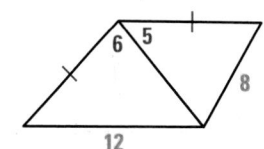

Extra Practice **905**

Chapter 6

6.1 The measures of the angles of a triangle are in the extended ratio given.
Find the measures of the angles of the triangle.

1. $1:3:5$ **2.** $1:5:6$ **3.** $2:3:5$ **4.** $5:6:9$

6.1 Solve the proportion.

5. $\dfrac{x}{14} = \dfrac{6}{21}$ **6.** $\dfrac{15}{y} = \dfrac{20}{4}$ **7.** $\dfrac{3}{2z+1} = \dfrac{1}{7}$ **8.** $\dfrac{a-3}{2} = \dfrac{2a-1}{6}$

9. $\dfrac{6}{3} = \dfrac{x+8}{-1}$ **10.** $\dfrac{x+6}{3} = \dfrac{x-5}{2}$ **11.** $\dfrac{x-2}{4} = \dfrac{x+10}{10}$ **12.** $\dfrac{12}{8} = \dfrac{5+t}{t-3}$

6.1 Find the geometric mean of the two numbers.

13. 4 and 9   **14.** 3 and 48   **15.** 9 and 16   **16.** 7 and 11

6.2 Copy and complete the statement.

17. If $\dfrac{7}{x} = \dfrac{9}{y}$, then $\dfrac{x}{7} = \dfrac{?}{?}$.   **18.** If $\dfrac{2}{8} = \dfrac{1}{x}$, then $\dfrac{8+2}{2} = \dfrac{?}{?}$.

6.2 Use the diagram and the given information to find the unknown length.

19. Given $\dfrac{NJ}{NK} = \dfrac{NL}{NM}$, find NK.   **20.** Given $\dfrac{CB}{DE} = \dfrac{BA}{EF}$, find CA.

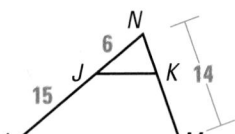   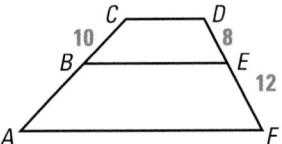

6.3 Determine whether the polygons are similar. If they are, write a similarity
statement and find the scale factor.

21. 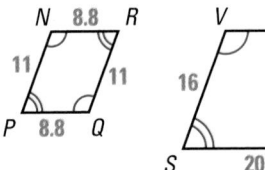   **22.**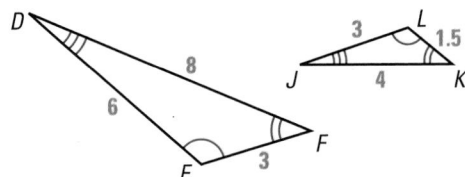

6.3 In the diagram, $\triangle PQR \sim \triangle LMN$.

23. Find the scale factor of $\triangle PQR$ to $\triangle LMN$.

24. Find the values of x, y, and z.

25. Find the perimeter of each triangle.

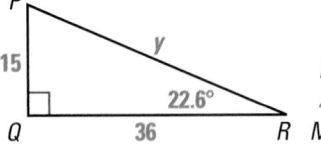

6.3 $\triangle ABC \sim \triangle DEF$. Identify the blue special segment and find the value of y.

26. 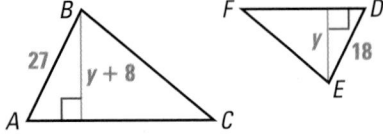   **27.** 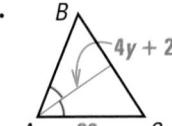   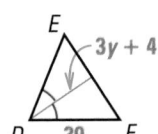

6.4 In Exercises 28–31, determine whether the triangles are similar. If they are, write a similarity statement. *Explain* your reasoning.

28.
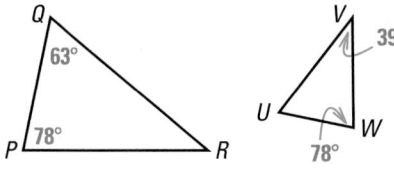

29.
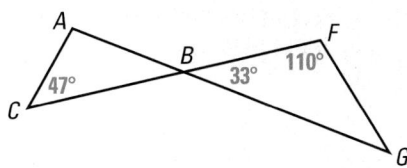

30.
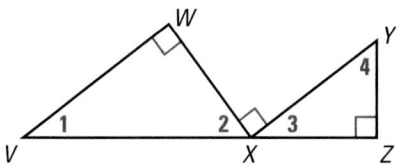

31.
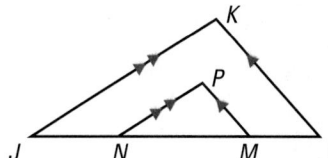

6.5 Show that the triangles are similar and write a similarity statement. *Explain* your reasoning.

32.
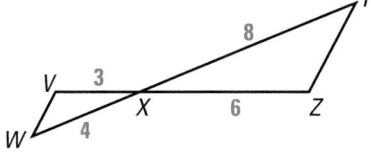

33.
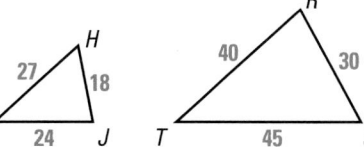

6.6 Use the diagram to find the value of each variable.

34.
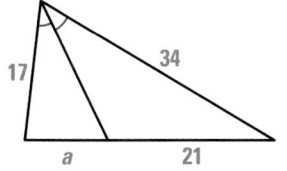

35.
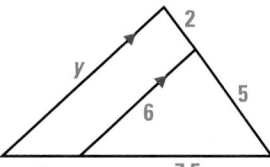

36.
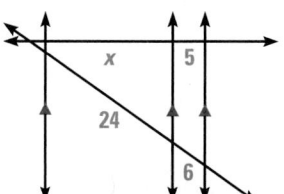

6.7 Draw a dilation of the polygon with the given vertices using the given scale factor of *k*.

37. $A(1, 1)$, $B(4, 1)$, $C(1, 2)$; $k = 3$

38. $A(2, 2)$, $B(-2, 2)$, $C(-1, -1)$, $D(2, -1)$; $k = 5$

39. $A(2, 2)$, $B(8, 2)$, $C(2, 6)$; $k = \dfrac{1}{2}$

40. $A(3, -6)$, $B(6, -6)$, $C(6, 9)$, $D(-3, 9)$; $k = \dfrac{1}{3}$

6.7 Determine whether the dilation from Figure A to Figure B is a *reduction* or an *enlargement*. Then find its scale factor.

41.
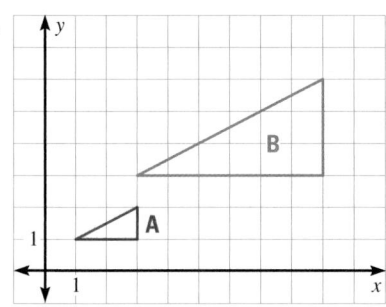

42.
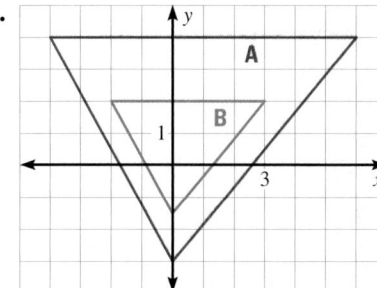

Chapter 7

7.1 Find the unknown side length of the right triangle using the Pythagorean Theorem or a Pythagorean triple.

1.
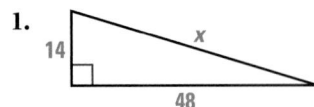

2.
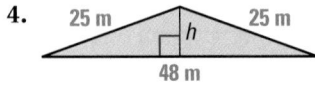

3.
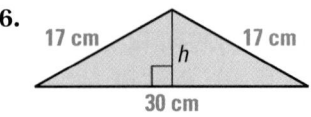

7.1 Find the area of the isosceles triangle.

4.
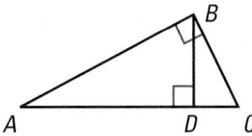

5.
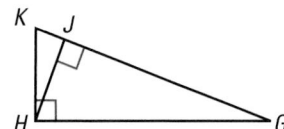

6.
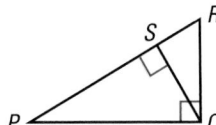

7.2 Tell whether the given side lengths of a triangle can represent a right triangle.

7. 24, 32, and 40

8. 21, 72, and 75

9. 11, 25, and 27

10. 7, 11, and 13

11. 17, 19, and $5\sqrt{26}$

12. 9, 10, and $\sqrt{181}$

7.2 Decide if the segment lengths form a triangle. If so, would the triangle be *acute*, *right*, or *obtuse*?

13. 14, 21, and 25

14. 32, 60, and 68

15. 11, 19, and 32

16. 3, 9, and $3\sqrt{11}$

17. 12, 15, and $3\sqrt{40}$

18. $4\sqrt{21}$, 25, and 31

7.3 Write a similarity statement for the three similar triangles in the diagram. Then complete the proportion.

19. $\dfrac{AB}{AD} = \dfrac{BC}{?}$

20. $\dfrac{KJ}{HJ} = \dfrac{?}{JG}$

21. $\dfrac{SR}{RQ} = \dfrac{RQ}{?}$

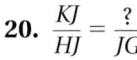

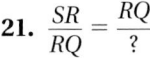

7.3 Find the value of the variable. Round decimal answers to the nearest tenth.

22.
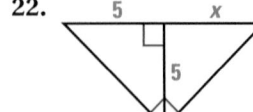

23.
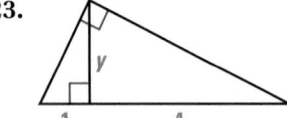

24.
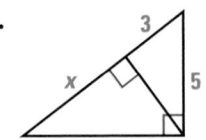

25.
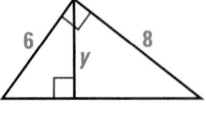

26.
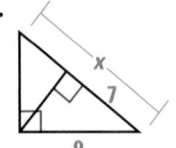

27.
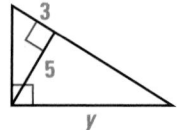

7.4 **Find the value of each variable. Write your answers in simplest radical form.**

28.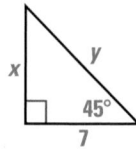

29.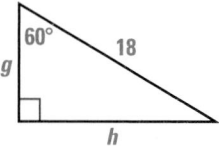

30.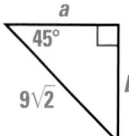

31.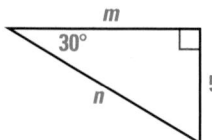

32.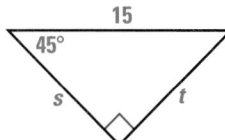

33.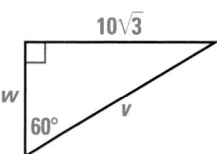

7.5 **Find tan *A* and tan *B*. Write each answer as a fraction and as a decimal rounded to four places.**

34.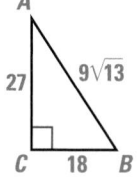

35.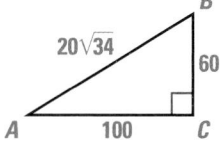

36.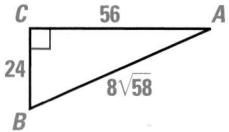

7.5 **Use a tangent ratio to find the value of *x*. Round to the nearest tenth. Check your solution using the tangent of the other acute angle.**

37.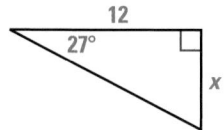

38.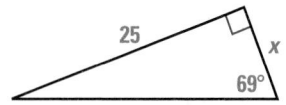

39.

7.6 **Use a sine or cosine ratio to find the value of each variable. Round decimals to the nearest tenth.**

40.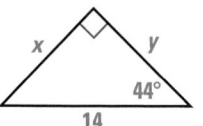

41.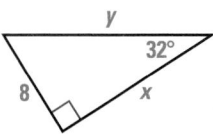

42.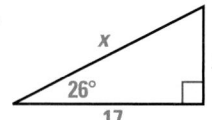

43.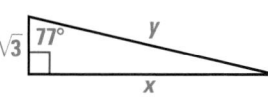

44.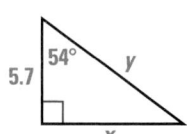

45.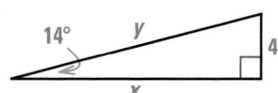

7.7 **Solve the right triangle. Round decimal answers to the nearest tenth.**

46.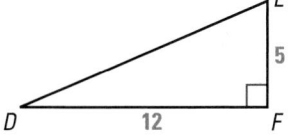

47.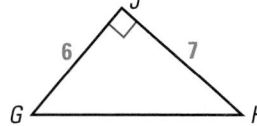

48.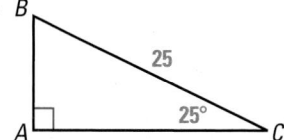

Chapter 8

8.1 **Find the value of *x*.**

1.
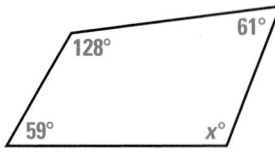

2.
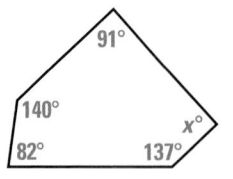

3.
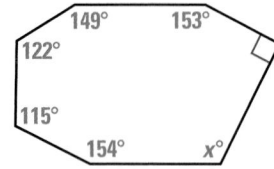

4.
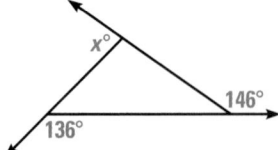

5.
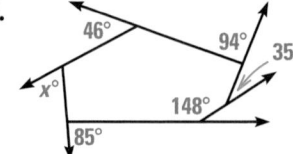

6.
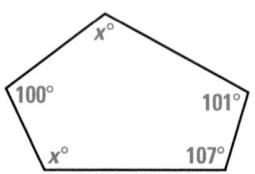

8.1 **Find the measure of an interior angle and an exterior angle of the indicated regular polygon.**

7. Regular hexagon

8. Regular 9-gon

9. Regular 17-gon

8.2 **Find the value of each variable in the parallelogram.**

10.
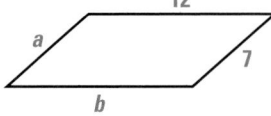

11.
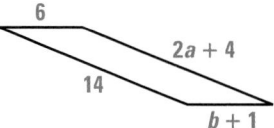

12.
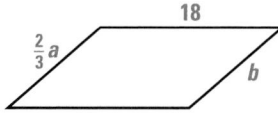

13.

14.
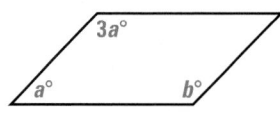

15.
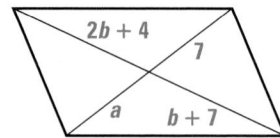

8.2 **Use the diagram to copy and complete the statement.**

16. $\angle WXV \cong$ __?__

17. $\angle ZWV \cong$ __?__

18. $\angle WVX \cong$ __?__

19. $WV =$ __?__

20. $WZ =$ __?__

21. $2 \cdot ZV =$ __?__

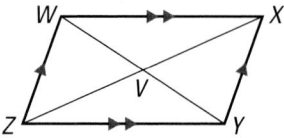

8.3 **The vertices of quadrilateral *ABCD* are given. Draw *ABCD* in a coordinate plane and show that it is a parallelogram.**

22. $A(5, 6)$, $B(7, 3)$, $C(5, -2)$, $D(3, 1)$

23. $A(-8, 2)$, $B(-6, 3)$, $C(-1, 2)$, $D(-3, 1)$

24. $A(-1, 11)$, $B(2, 14)$, $C(6, 11)$, $D(3, 8)$

25. $A(-1, -5)$, $B(4, -4)$, $C(6, -9)$, $D(1, -10)$

8.3 ***Describe* how to prove that quadrilateral *PQRS* is a parallelogram.**

26.
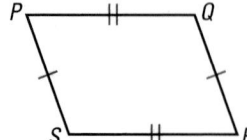

27.
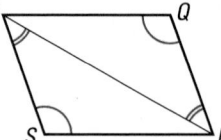

28.
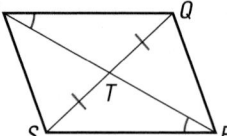

8.4 Classify the special quadrilateral. *Explain* your reasoning.

29.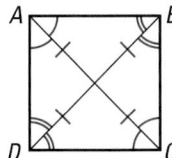

30.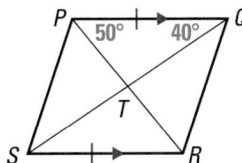

31.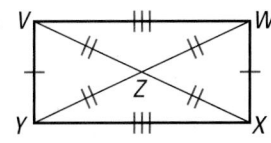

8.4 The diagonals of rhombus *LMNP* intersect at *Q*. Given that *LM* = 5 and *m∠QLM* = 30°, find the indicated measure.

32. *m∠LMQ*

33. *m∠LQM*

34. *MN*

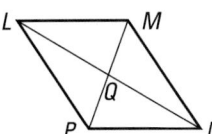

8.5 Find the value of *x*.

35.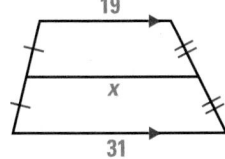

36.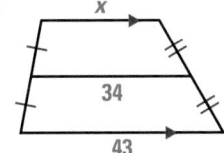

37.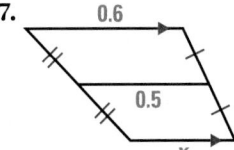

8.5 *RSTV* is a kite. Find *m∠V*.

38.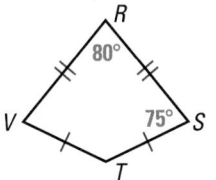

39.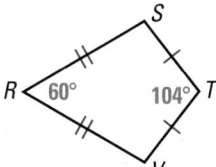

40.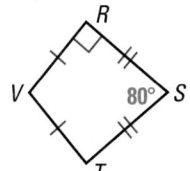

8.6 Give the most specific name for the quadrilateral. *Explain* your reasoning.

41.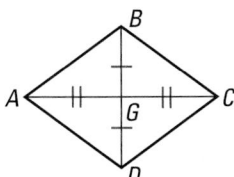

42.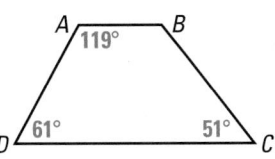

43.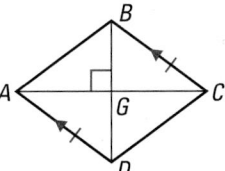

44.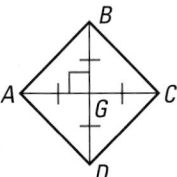

45.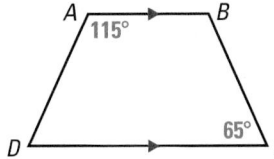

46.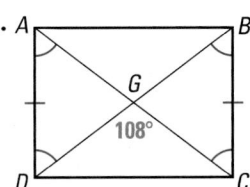

8.6 The vertices of quadrilateral *DEFG* are given. Give the most specific name for *DEFG*. *Justify* your answer.

47. *D*(6, 8), *E*(9, 12), *F*(12, 8), *G*(9, 6)

48. *D*(1, 2), *E*(4, 1), *F*(3, −2), *G*(0, −1)

49. *D*(10, 3), *E*(14, 4), *F*(20, 2), *G*(12, 0)

50. *D*(−2, 10), *E*(1, 13), *F*(5, 13), *G*(−2, 6)

Chapter 9

9.1 $\triangle A'B'C'$ is the image of $\triangle ABC$ after a translation. Write a rule for the translation. Then *verify* that the translation is an isometry.

1.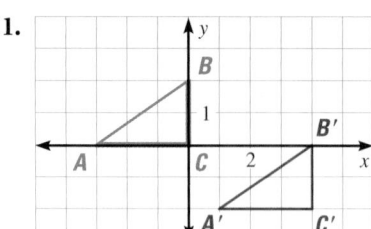

2.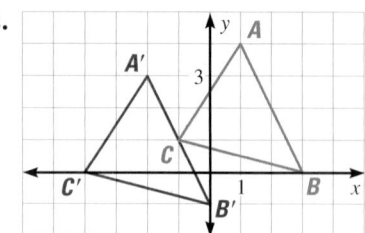

9.1 Use the point $P(7, -3)$. Find the component form of the vector that describes the translation to P'.

3. $P'(-3, 4)$ **4.** $P'(1, -1)$ **5.** $P'(3, 2)$ **6.** $P'(-8, -11)$

9.2 Add, subtract, or multiply.

7. $\begin{bmatrix} 2 \\ 7 \end{bmatrix} + \begin{bmatrix} 3 \\ 4 \end{bmatrix}$

8. $\begin{bmatrix} 5 & -3 \\ -9 & 4 \end{bmatrix} - \begin{bmatrix} 0 & 1 \\ 4 & -1 \end{bmatrix}$

9. $\begin{bmatrix} 7 & -3 \\ 5 & 9 \end{bmatrix}\begin{bmatrix} 2 & -1 \\ 6 & 8 \end{bmatrix}$

9.2 Find the image matrix that represents the translation of the polygon. Then graph the polygon and its image.

10. $\begin{bmatrix} 3 & -5 & 7 \\ -2 & -2 & 1 \end{bmatrix}$; 6 units left

11. $\begin{bmatrix} 1 & 9 & 4 & 3 \\ 5 & 6 & 4 & 2 \end{bmatrix}$; 1 unit right and 7 units down

12. $\begin{bmatrix} 7 & -3 & 0 \\ 6 & 8 & -4 \end{bmatrix}$; 3 units right and 4 units up

13. $\begin{bmatrix} 9 & 6 & 4 & 2 & 3 \\ -1 & -4 & -4 & -4 & 2 \end{bmatrix}$; 4 units left and 5 units up

9.3 Graph the reflection of the polygon in the given line.

14. y-axis

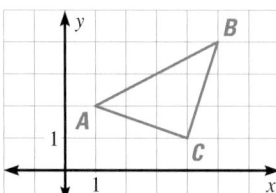

15. $x = 1$

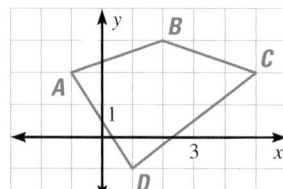

16. $y = x$

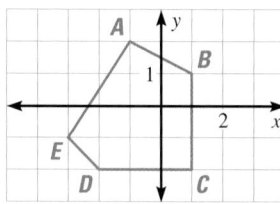

9.4 Rotate the figure the given number of degrees about the origin. List the coordinates of the vertices of the image.

17. $270°$

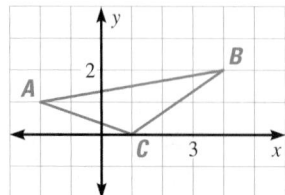

18. $180°$

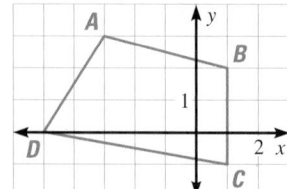

19. $90°$

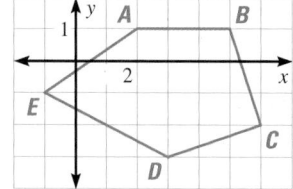

9.4 Find the image matrix that represents the rotation of the polygon about the origin. Then graph the polygon and its image.

        P Q R

20. $\begin{bmatrix} 1 & 2 & 4 \\ 4 & 1 & 3 \end{bmatrix}$; $180°$

        S T V

21. $\begin{bmatrix} 4 & 2 & 1 \\ 2 & -3 & 0 \end{bmatrix}$; $90°$

        A B C D

22. $\begin{bmatrix} 4 & -1 & -2 & 1 \\ 0 & -1 & -2 & -3 \end{bmatrix}$; $270°$

9.5 The vertices of $\triangle ABC$ are $A(1, 1)$, $B(4, 1)$, and $C(2, 4)$. Graph the image of $\triangle ABC$ after a composition of the transformations in the order they are listed.

23. Translation: $(x, y) \rightarrow (x - 2, y + 3)$
     Rotation: $270°$ about the origin

24. Reflection: in the line $x = 2$
     Translation: $(x, y) \rightarrow (x + 3, y)$

25. Rotation: $180°$ about the origin
     Reflection: in the line $y = -2$

26. Translation: $(x, y) \rightarrow (x - 4, y - 4)$
     Reflection: in the line $y = x$

9.5 Find the angle of rotation that maps A onto A''.

27.

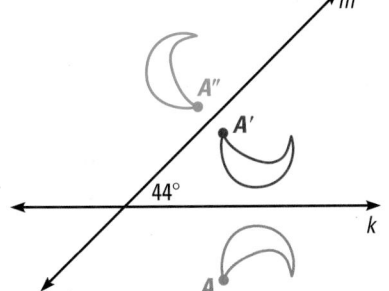

28.

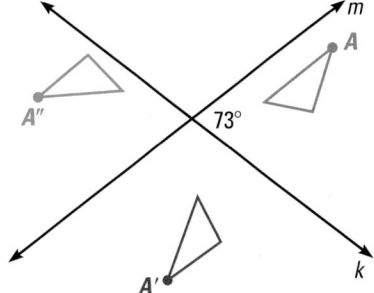

9.6 Determine whether the flag has *line symmetry* and whether it has *rotational symmetry*. Identify all lines of symmetry and angles of rotation that map the figure onto itself.

29.

30.

31.

9.7 Copy the diagram. Then draw the given dilation.

32. Center B; $k = 2$

33. Center E; $k = 3$

34. Center D; $k = \frac{1}{2}$

35. Center A; $k = \frac{2}{3}$

36. Center C; $k = \frac{3}{2}$

37. Center E; $k = \frac{1}{3}$

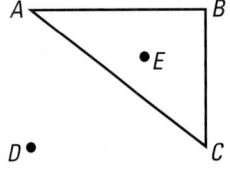

9.7 Find the image matrix that represents a dilation of a polygon centered at the origin with a given scale factor. Then graph the polygon and its image.

        G H J

38. $\begin{bmatrix} 1 & 3 & 4 \\ 4 & 2 & 4 \end{bmatrix}$; $k = 3$

        K L M N

39. $\begin{bmatrix} 2 & 4 & 6 & 5 \\ -2 & -2 & 0 & 4 \end{bmatrix}$; $k = \frac{1}{2}$

        P Q R

40. $\begin{bmatrix} -3 & -3 & -1 \\ -1 & -3 & -3 \end{bmatrix}$; $k = 4$

Chapter 10

10.1 Use the diagram to give an example of the term.

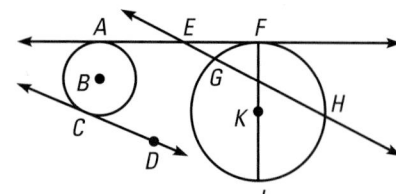

1. Radius
2. Common tangent
3. Tangent
4. Secant
5. Center
6. Point of tangency
7. Chord
8. Diameter

10.1 Find the value(s) of the variable. *P*, *Q*, and *R* are points of tangency.

9.
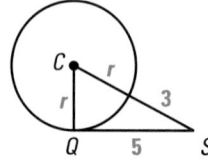

10.
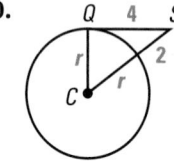

11.
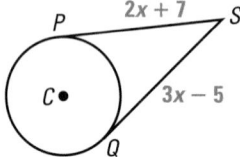

12.
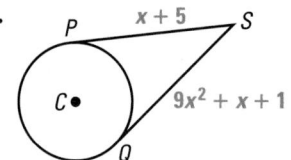

13.
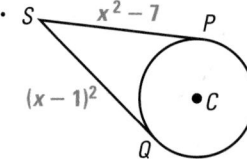

14.
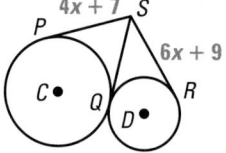

10.2 $\overline{AC}$ and $\overline{BD}$ are diameters of $\odot G$. Determine whether the arc is a *minor arc*, a *major arc*, or a *semicircle* of $\odot G$. Then find the measure of the arc.

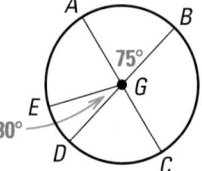

15. $\overset{\frown}{ED}$
16. $\overset{\frown}{EB}$
17. $\overset{\frown}{EC}$
18. $\overset{\frown}{BEC}$
19. $\overset{\frown}{BC}$
20. $\overset{\frown}{BCD}$

10.2 In $\odot C$, $m\overset{\frown}{AD} = 50°$, *B* bisects $\overset{\frown}{AD}$, and $\overline{AE}$ is a diameter. Find the measure of the arc.

21. $\overset{\frown}{AED}$
22. $\overset{\frown}{BD}$
23. $\overset{\frown}{DE}$
24. $\overset{\frown}{BAE}$

10.3 Find the measure of $\overset{\frown}{AB}$.

25.
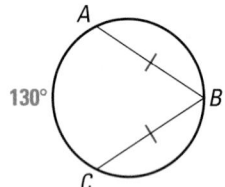

26.
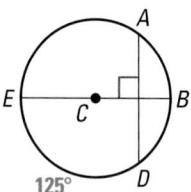

27.
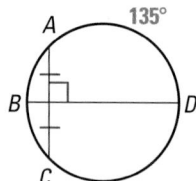

10.3 In Exercises 28–30, what can you conclude about the diagram shown? State theorems to justify your answer.

28.
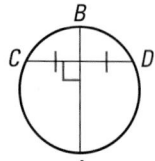

29.
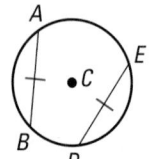

30.
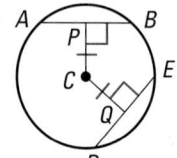

10.4 **Find the values of the variables.**

31.
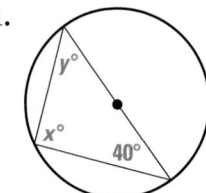

32.
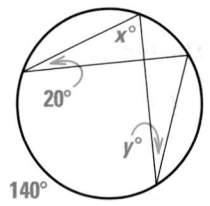

33.
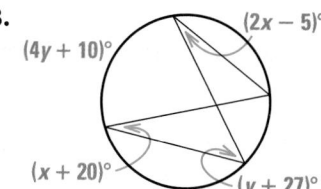

34.
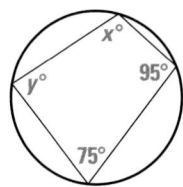

35.
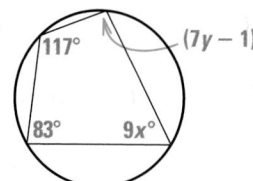

36.
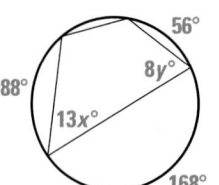

10.5 **Find the value of x.**

37.
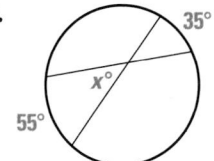

38.
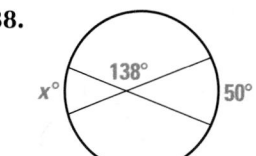

39.
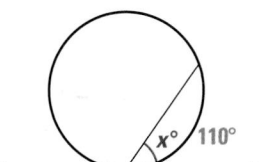

40.
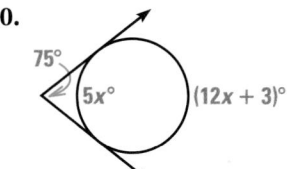

41.
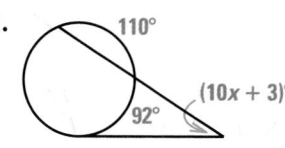

42.
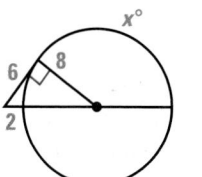

10.6 **Find the value of x.**

43.
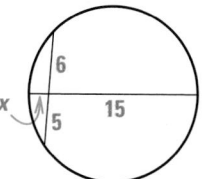

44.
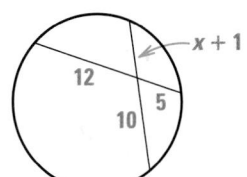

45.
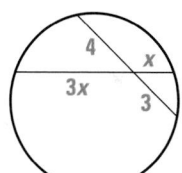

46.
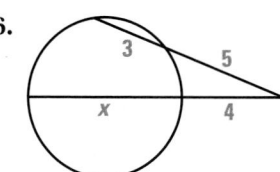

47.
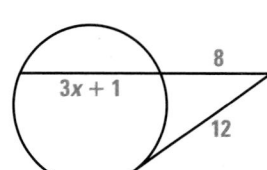

48.
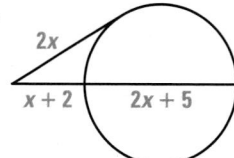

10.7 **Use the given information to write the standard equation for the circle.**

49. The center is $(0, -2)$, and the radius is 4 units.

50. The center is $(2, -3)$, and a point on the circle is $(7, -8)$.

51. The center is (m, n), and a point on the circle is $(m + h, n + k)$.

10.7 **Graph the equation.**

52. $x^2 + y^2 = 25$

53. $x^2 + (y - 5)^2 = 121$

54. $(x + 4)^2 + (y - 1)^2 = 49$

Chapter 11

11.1 Find the area of the polygon.

1.
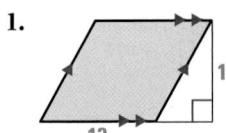
13, 11

2.
10
16

3.
7.5
15

4.
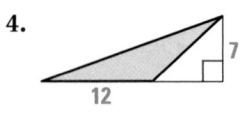
7
12

11.1 The lengths of the hypotenuse and one leg of a right triangle are given. Find the perimeter and area of the triangle.

5. Hypotenuse: 25 cm; leg: 20 cm

6. Hypotenuse: 51 ft; leg: 24 ft

11.1 Find the value of x.

7. $A = 22$ ft^2
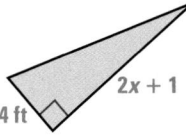
$2x + 1$
4 ft

8. $A = 14.3$ in.^{2}
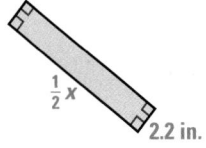
$\frac{1}{2}x$
2.2 in.

9. $A = 7.2$ m^2
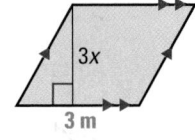
$3x$
3 m

10. $A = 276$ cm^2
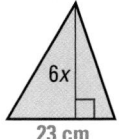
$6x$
23 cm

11.2 Find the area of the trapezoid.

11.
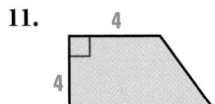
4
4
7

12.
12
10
21

13.
11
7
9

14.
18
9
6

11.2 Find the area of the rhombus or kite.

15.
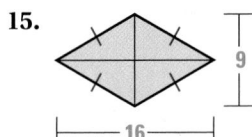
9
16

16.
11
11

17.
3
9

18.
2
4
2

11.3 The ratio of the areas of two similar figures is given. Write the ratio of the lengths of the corresponding sides.

19. Ratio of areas = 100:81

20. Ratio of areas = 25:100

21. Ratio of areas = 8:1

11.3 Use the given area to find ST.

22. $\triangle ABC \sim \triangle RST$
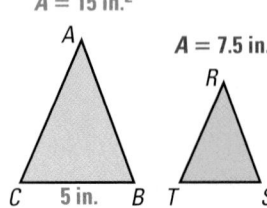
$A = 15$ in.^{2}
$A = 7.5$ in.^{2}
C 5 in. B T S

23. $DEFG \sim RSTU$
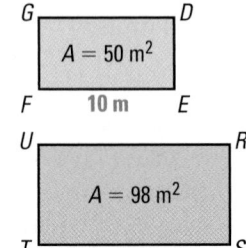
$A = 50$ m^2
10 m
$A = 98$ m^2

24. $HJKL \sim RSTU$
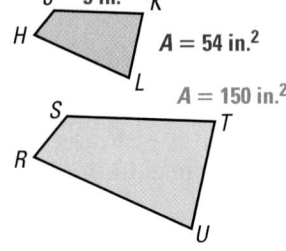
9 in.
$A = 54$ in.^{2}
$A = 150$ in.^{2}

11.4 Find the circumference of the red circle.

25.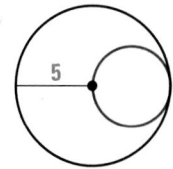

26.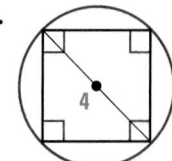

27.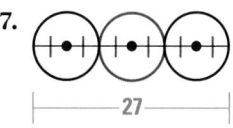

28.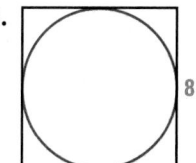

11.4 Find the length of $\overset{\frown}{AB}$.

29.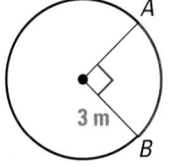

30.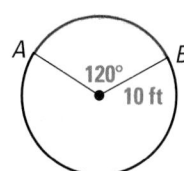

31.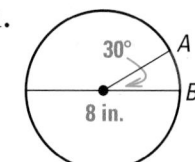

32.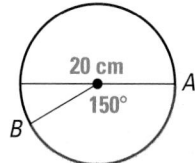

11.5 Find the exact area of a circle with the given radius r or diameter d. Then find the area to the nearest hundredth.

33. $r = 3$ in.

34. $r = 2.5$ cm

35. $d = 20$ ft

36. $d = 13$ m

11.5 Find the areas of the sectors formed by $\angle DFE$.

37.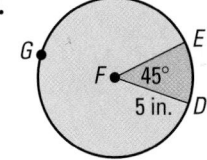

38.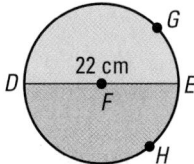

39.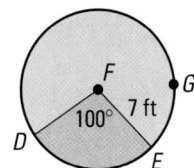

40.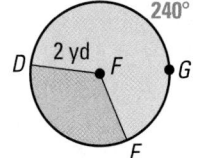

11.6 Find the measure of a central angle of a regular polygon with the given number of sides.

41. 8 sides

42. 12 sides

43. 20 sides

44. 25 sides

11.6 Find the perimeter and area of the regular polygon.

45.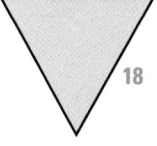

46.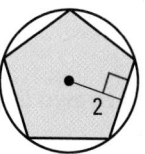

47.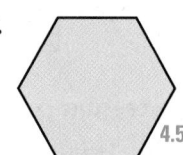

48.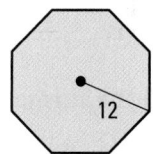

11.7 Find the probability that a randomly chosen point in the figure lies in the shaded region.

49.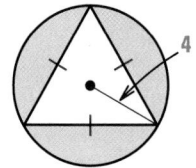

50.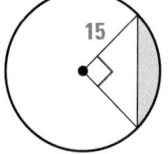

51.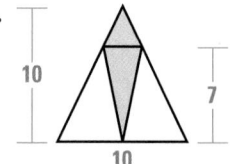

52.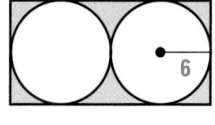

11.7 53. A local radio station plays your favorite song once every two hours. Your favorite song is 4.5 minutes long. If you randomly turn on the radio, what is the probability that your favorite song will be playing?

Chapter 12

12.1 **Determine whether the solid is a polyhedron. If it is, name the polyhedron.** *Explain* **your reasoning.**

1. 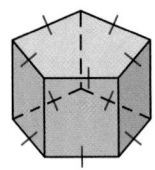 **2.** 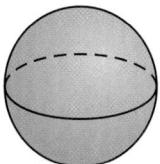 **3.** 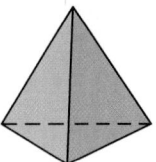 **4.**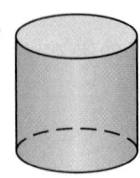

12.1 **5.** Determine the number of faces on a solid with six vertices and ten edges.

12.2 **Find the surface area of the right prism. Round to two decimal places.**

6. 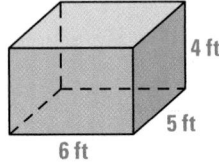 **7.** 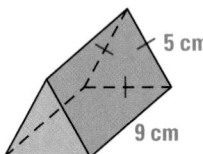 **8.**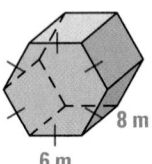

12.2 **Find the surface area of the right cylinder with the given radius *r* and height *h*. Round to two decimal places.**

9. $r = 2$ cm
$h = 11$ cm

10. $r = 1$ m
$h = 1$ m

11. $r = 22$ in.
$h = 9$ in.

12. $r = 17$ mm
$h = 5$ mm

12.2 **Solve for *x* given the surface area *S* of the right prism or right cylinder. Round to two decimal places.**

13. $S = 192$ in.^{2}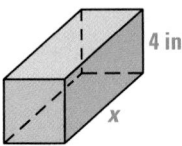

14. $S = 33.7$ m^2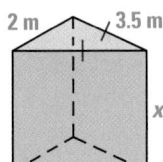

15. $S = 754$ ft^2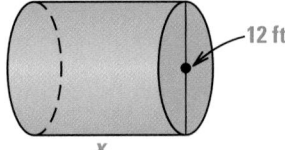

12.3 **Find the surface area of the regular pyramid. Round to two decimal places.**

16. 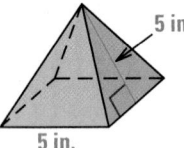 **17.** 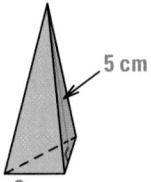 **18.**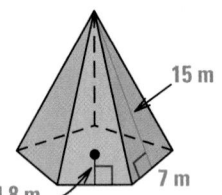

12.3 **Find the surface area of the right cone. Round to two decimal places.**

19. 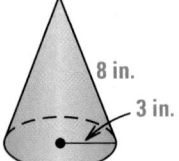 **20.** 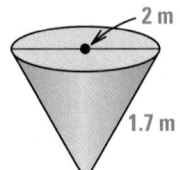 **21.**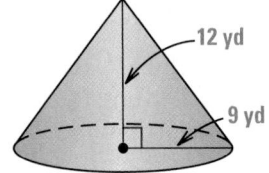

12.4 **Find the volume of the right prism or right cylinder. Round to two decimal places.**

22.

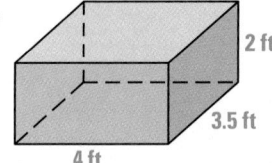

2 ft
3.5 ft
4 ft

23.

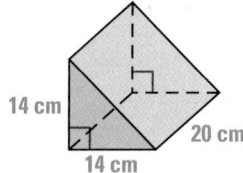

14 cm
20 cm
14 cm

24.

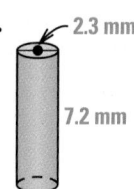

2.3 mm
7.2 mm

12.4 **Find the value of x. Round to two decimal places, if necessary.**

25. $V = 8 \text{ cm}^3$

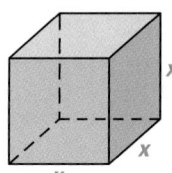

x
x
x

26. $V = 72 \text{ ft}^3$

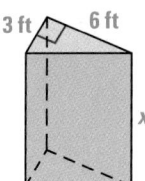

3 ft   6 ft
x

27. $V = 628 \text{ in.}^3$

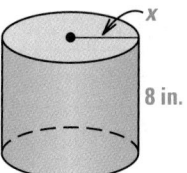

x
8 in.

12.5 **Find the volume of the solid. Round to two decimal places.**

28.

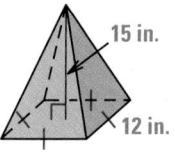

15 in.
12 in.

29.

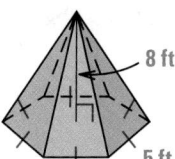

8 ft
5 ft

30.

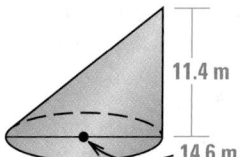

11.4 m
14.6 m

12.5 **Find the volume of the right cone. Round to two decimal places.**

31.

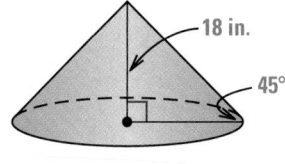

18 in.
45°

32.

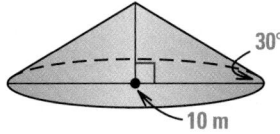

30°
10 m

33.

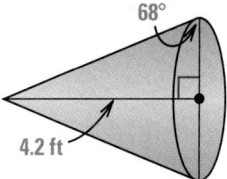

68°
4.2 ft

12.6 **Find the surface area and volume of a sphere with the given radius r or diameter d. Round to two decimal places.**

34. $r = 13 \text{ m}$ **35.** $r = 1.8 \text{ in.}$ **36.** $d = 28 \text{ yd}$ **37.** $d = 13.7 \text{ cm}$

38. $r = 20 \text{ in.}$ **39.** $r = 17.5 \text{ mm}$ **40.** $d = 15.2 \text{ m}$ **41.** $d = 23 \text{ ft}$

12.7 **Solid A (shown) is similar to Solid B (not shown) with the given scale factor of A to B. Find the surface area and volume of Solid B.**

42. Scale factor of $3:2$

$S = 324\pi \text{ in.}^2$
$V = 972\pi \text{ in.}^3$

43. Scale factor of $2:1$

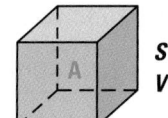

$S = 864 \text{ ft}^2$
$V = 1728 \text{ ft}^3$

44. Scale factor of $4:7$

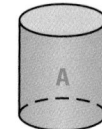

$S = 64\pi \text{ cm}^2$
$V = 64\pi \text{ cm}^3$

12.7 **45.** Two similar cylinders have volumes 12π cubic units and 324π cubic units. Find the scale factor of the smaller cylinder to the larger cylinder.

Tables

Symbols

Symbol	Meaning	Page
$-a$	opposite of a	**xxii**
$\overleftrightarrow{AB}$	line AB	**2**
$\overline{AB}$	segment AB	**3**
$\overrightarrow{AB}$	ray AB	**3**
$\cdot$	multiplication, times	**8**
AB	the length of AB	**9**
$|x|$	absolute value of x	**9**
x_1	x sub one	**9**
(x, y)	ordered pair	**11**
$=$	is equal to	**11**
$\cong$	is congruent to	**11**
$\sqrt{a}$	square root of a	**14**
$\angle ABC$	angle ABC	**24**
$m\angle A$	measure of angle A	**24**
$\circ$	degree(s)	**24**
$\llcorner$	right angle symbol	**25**
n-gon	polygon with n sides	**43**
π	pi; irrational number ≈ 3.14	**49**
$\approx$	is approximately equal to	**50**
$\ldots$	and so on	**72**
$\perp$	is perpendicular to	**81**
$\rightarrow$	implies	**94**
$\leftrightarrow$	if and only if	**94**
$\sim p$	negation of statement p	**94**
$\parallel$	is parallel to	**147**
m	slope	**171**
$\triangle ABC$	triangle ABC	**217**

Symbol	Meaning	Page
$\triangle$	triangles	**227**
$\angle$	angles	**250**
$\rightarrow$	maps to	**272**
$<$	is less than	**328**
$>$	is greater than	**328**
$\neq$	is not equal to	**337**
$\dfrac{a}{b}, a:b$	ratio of a to b	**356**
$\sim$	is similar to	**372**
$\stackrel{?}{=}$	is this statement true?	**389**
$\nparallel$	is not parallel to	**398**
$\tan$	tangent	**466**
$\sin$	sine	**473**
$\cos$	cosine	**473**
$\sin^{-1}$	inverse sine	**483**
$\cos^{-1}$	inverse cosine	**483**
$\tan^{-1}$	inverse tangent	**483**
$\square ABCD$	parallelogram $ABCD$	**515**
$\not\cong$	is not congruent to	**531**
A'	A prime	**572**
$\overrightarrow{AB}$	vector AB	**574**
$\langle a, b \rangle$	component form of a vector	**574**
A''	A double prime	**608**
$\odot P$	circle with center P	**651**
$m\overarc{AB}$	measure of minor arc AB	**659**
$m\overarc{ABC}$	measure of major arc ABC	**659**
$P(A)$	probability of event A	**771**

Measures

Time	
60 seconds (sec) = 1 minute (min) 60 minutes = 1 hour (h) 24 hours = 1 day 7 days = 1 week 4 weeks (approx.) = 1 month	$\left.\begin{array}{l}365 \text{ days}\\52 \text{ weeks (approx.)}\\12 \text{ months}\end{array}\right\} = 1 \text{ year}$ 10 years = 1 decade 100 years = 1 century

Metric	United States Customary
Length 10 millimeters (mm) = 1 centimeter (cm) $\left.\begin{array}{l}100 \text{ cm}\\1000 \text{ mm}\end{array}\right\} = 1 \text{ meter (m)}$ 1000 m = 1 kilometer (km)	**Length** 12 inches (in.) = 1 foot (ft) $\left.\begin{array}{l}36 \text{ in.}\\3 \text{ ft}\end{array}\right\} = 1 \text{ yard (yd)}$ $\left.\begin{array}{l}5280 \text{ ft}\\1760 \text{ yd}\end{array}\right\} = 1 \text{ mile (mi)}$
Area 100 square millimeters = 1 square centimeter (mm^2) (cm^2) $10{,}000 \text{ cm}^2 = 1 \text{ square meter (m}^2\text{)}$ $10{,}000 \text{ m}^2 = 1 \text{ hectare (ha)}$	**Area** 144 square inches ($in.^2$) = 1 square foot (ft^2) $9 \text{ ft}^2 = 1 \text{ square yard (yd}^2\text{)}$ $\left.\begin{array}{l}43{,}560 \text{ ft}^2\\4840 \text{ yd}^2\end{array}\right\} = 1 \text{ acre (A)}$
Volume 1000 cubic millimeters = 1 cubic centimeter (mm^3) (cm^3) $1{,}000{,}000 \text{ cm}^3 = 1 \text{ cubic meter (m}^3\text{)}$	**Volume** 1728 cubic inches ($in.^3$) = 1 cubic foot (ft^3) $27 \text{ ft}^3 = 1 \text{ cubic yard (yd}^3\text{)}$
Liquid Capacity $\left.\begin{array}{l}1000 \text{ milliliters (mL)}\\1000 \text{ cubic centimeters (cm}^3\text{)}\end{array}\right\} = 1 \text{ liter (L)}$ 1000 L = 1 kiloliter (kL)	**Liquid Capacity** 8 fluid ounces (fl oz) = 1 cup (c) 2 c = 1 pint (pt) 2 pt = 1 quart (qt) 4 qt = 1 gallon (gal)
Mass 1000 milligrams (mg) = 1 gram (g) 1000 g = 1 kilogram (kg) 1000 kg = 1 metric ton (t)	**Weight** 16 ounces (oz) = 1 pound (lb) 2000 lb = 1 ton
Temperature **Degrees Celsius (°C)** 0°C = freezing point of water 37°C = normal body temperature 100°C = boiling point of water	**Temperature** **Degrees Fahrenheit (°F)** 32°F = freezing point of water 98.6°F = normal body temperature 212°F = boiling point of water

Formulas

Angles

Sum of the measures of the interior angles of a triangle: $180°$ *(p. 218)*

Sum of the measures of the interior angles of a convex n-gon: $(n - 2) \cdot 180°$ *(p. 507)*

Exterior angle of a triangle:
$m\angle 1 = m\angle A + m\angle B$ *(p. 219)*

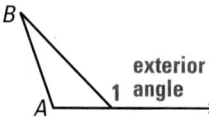

Sum of the measures of the exterior angles of a convex polygon: $360°$ *(p. 509)*

Right Triangles

Pythagorean Theorem:
$c^2 = a^2 + b^2$ *(p. 433)*

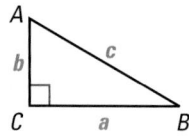

Trigonometric ratios:

$\sin A = \dfrac{BC}{AB}$ *(p. 473)* $\sin^{-1} \dfrac{BC}{AB} = m\angle A$ *(p. 483)*

$\cos A = \dfrac{AC}{AB}$ *(p. 473)* $\cos^{-1} \dfrac{AC}{AB} = m\angle A$ *(p. 483)*

$\tan A = \dfrac{BC}{AC}$ *(p. 466)* $\tan^{-1} \dfrac{BC}{AC} = m\angle A$ *(p. 483)*

$45°$-$45°$-$90°$ triangle *(p. 457)* $30°$-$60°$-$90°$ triangle *(p. 459)*

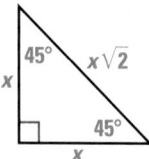 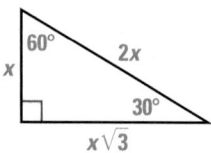

Ratio of sides:
$1 : 1 : \sqrt{2}$

Ratio of sides:
$1 : \sqrt{3} : 2$

$\triangle ABC \sim \triangle ACD \sim \triangle CBD$ *(p. 449)*

$\dfrac{BD}{CD} = \dfrac{CD}{AD}, \dfrac{AB}{CB} = \dfrac{CB}{DB}, \dfrac{AB}{AC} = \dfrac{AC}{AD}$ *(p. 451)*

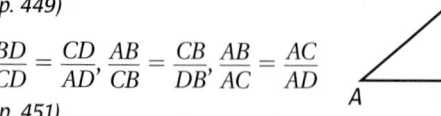

$\dfrac{BD}{CD} = \dfrac{CD}{AD}$, and $CD = \sqrt{AD \cdot DB}$ *(pp. 359, 452)*

Circles

Angle and segments formed by two chords:
$m\angle 1 = \frac{1}{2}(m\overset{\frown}{CD} + m\overset{\frown}{AB})$ *(p. 681)*

$EA \cdot EC = EB \cdot ED$ *(p. 689)*

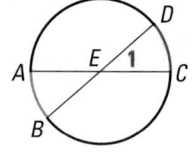

Angle and segments formed by a tangent and a secant:
$m\angle 2 = \frac{1}{2}(m\overset{\frown}{BC} - m\overset{\frown}{AB})$ *(p. 681)*

$EB^2 = EA \cdot EC$ *(p. 691)*

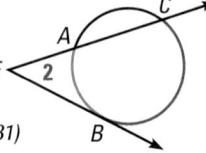

Angle and segments formed by two tangents:
$m\angle 3 = \frac{1}{2}(m\overset{\frown}{AQB} - m\overset{\frown}{AB})$ *(p. 681)*

$EA = EB$ *(p. 654)*

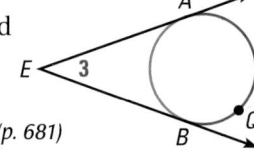

Angle and segments formed by two secants:
$m\angle 4 = \frac{1}{2}(m\overset{\frown}{CD} - m\overset{\frown}{AB})$ *(p. 681)*

$EA \cdot EC = EB \cdot ED$ *(p. 690)*

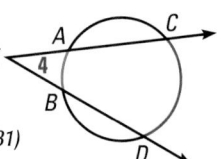

Coordinate Geometry

Given: points $A(x_1, y_1)$ and $B(x_2, y_2)$

Midpoint of $\overline{AB} = \left(\dfrac{x_1 + x_2}{2}, \dfrac{y_1 + y_2}{2} \right)$ *(p. 16)*

$AB = \sqrt{(x_2 - x_1)^2 + (y_2 - y_1)^2}$ *(p. 17)*

Slope of $\overleftrightarrow{AB} = \dfrac{\text{rise}}{\text{run}} = \dfrac{y_2 - y_1}{x_2 - x_1}$ *(p. 171)*

Slope-intercept form of a linear equation with slope m and y-intercept b: $y = mx + b$ *(p. 180)*

Standard equation of a circle with center (h, k) and radius r: $(x - h)^2 + (y - k)^2 = r^2$ *(p. 699)*

Taxicab distance $AB = \left| x_2 - x_1 \right| + \left| y_2 - y_1 \right|$ *(p. 198)*

Perimeter

P = perimeter, C = circumference, s = side, ℓ = length, w = width, a, b, c = lengths of the sides of a triangle, d = diameter, r = radius

Polygon:	P = sum of side lengths	(p. 49)
Square:	$P = 4s$	(p. 49)
Rectangle:	$P = 2\ell + 2w$	(p. 49)
Triangle:	$P = a + b + c$	(p. 49)
Regular n-gon:	$P = ns$	(pp. 49, 765)
Circle:	$C = \pi d = 2\pi r$	(p. 49)

Arc length of $\overset{\frown}{AB} = \dfrac{m\overset{\frown}{AB}}{360°} \cdot 2\pi r$ (p. 747)

Area

A = area, s = side, b = base, h = height, ℓ = length, w = width, d = diagonal, a = apothem, P = perimeter, r = radius

Square:	$A = s^2$	(pp. 49, 720)
Rectangle:	$A = lw$	(pp. 49, 720)
Triangle:	$A = \frac{1}{2}bh$	(pp. 49, 721)
Parallelogram:	$A = bh$	(p. 721)
Trapezoid:	$A = \frac{1}{2}h(b_1 + b_2)$	(p. 730)
Rhombus:	$A = \frac{1}{2}d_1 d_2$	(p. 731)
Kite:	$A = \frac{1}{2}d_1 d_2$	(p. 731)
Equilateral triangle:	$A = \frac{1}{4}\sqrt{3}s^2$	(pp. 726, 766)
Regular polygon:	$A = \frac{1}{2}aP$	(p. 763)
Circle:	$A = \pi r^2$	(pp. 49, 755)
Area of a sector:	$A = \dfrac{m\overset{\frown}{AB}}{360°} \cdot \pi r^2$	(p. 756)

Surface Area

B = area of a base, P = perimeter, C = circumference, h = height, r = radius, ℓ = slant height

Right prism:	$S = 2B + Ph$	(p. 804)
Right cylinder:	$S = 2B + Ch$	
	$= 2\pi r^2 + 2\pi rh$	(p. 805)
Regular pyramid:	$S = B + \frac{1}{2}P\ell$	(p. 811)
Right cone:	$S = B + \frac{1}{2}C\ell$	
	$= \pi r^2 + \pi r\ell$	(p. 812)
Sphere:	$S = 4\pi r^2$	(p. 838)

Volume

V = volume, B = area of a base, h = height, r = radius, s = side length

Cube:	$V = s^3$	(p. 819)
Prism:	$V = Bh$	(p. 820)
Cylinder:	$V = Bh = \pi r^2 h$	(p. 820)
Pyramid:	$V = \frac{1}{3}Bh$	(p. 829)
Cone:	$V = \frac{1}{3}Bh = \frac{1}{3}\pi r^2 h$	(p. 829)
Sphere:	$V = \frac{4}{3}\pi r^3$	(p. 840)

Miscellaneous

Geometric mean of a and b: $\sqrt{a \cdot b}$ (p. 359)

Euler's Theorem for Polyhedra, F = faces, V = vertices, E = edges: $F + V = E + 2$ (p. 795)

Given: similar polygons or similar solids with a scale factor of $a : b$

Ratio of perimeters = $a : b$	(p. 374)
Ratio of areas = $a^2 : b^2$	(p. 737)
Ratio of volumes = $a^3 : b^3$	(p. 848)

Given a quadratic equation $ax^2 + bx + c = 0$, the solutions are given by the formula:

$$x = \frac{-b \pm \sqrt{b^2 - 4ac}}{2a}$$ (pp. 641, 883)

Squares and Square Roots

No.	Square	Sq. Root	No.	Square	Sq. Root	No.	Square	Sq. Root
1	1	1.000	51	2601	7.141	101	10,201	10.050
2	4	1.414	52	2704	7.211	102	10,404	10.100
3	9	1.732	53	2809	7.280	103	10,609	10.149
4	16	2.000	54	2916	7.348	104	10,816	10.198
5	25	2.236	55	3025	7.416	105	11,025	10.247
6	36	2.449	56	3136	7.483	106	11,236	10.296
7	49	2.646	57	3249	7.550	107	11,449	10.344
8	64	2.828	58	3364	7.616	108	11,664	10.392
9	81	3.000	59	3481	7.681	109	11,881	10.440
10	100	3.162	60	3600	7.746	110	12,100	10.488
11	121	3.317	61	3721	7.810	111	12,321	10.536
12	144	3.464	62	3844	7.874	112	12,544	10.583
13	169	3.606	63	3969	7.937	113	12,769	10.630
14	196	3.742	64	4096	8.000	114	12,996	10.677
15	225	3.873	65	4225	8.062	115	13,225	10.724
16	256	4.000	66	4356	8.124	116	13,456	10.770
17	289	4.123	67	4489	8.185	117	13,689	10.817
18	324	4.243	68	4624	8.246	118	13,924	10.863
19	361	4.359	69	4761	8.307	119	14,161	10.909
20	400	4.472	70	4900	8.367	120	14,400	10.954
21	441	4.583	71	5041	8.426	121	14,641	11.000
22	484	4.690	72	5184	8.485	122	14,884	11.045
23	529	4.796	73	5329	8.544	123	15,129	11.091
24	576	4.899	74	5476	8.602	124	15,376	11.136
25	625	5.000	75	5625	8.660	125	15,625	11.180
26	676	5.099	76	5776	8.718	126	15,876	11.225
27	729	5.196	77	5929	8.775	127	16,129	11.269
28	784	5.292	78	6084	8.832	128	16,384	11.314
29	841	5.385	79	6241	8.888	129	16,641	11.358
30	900	5.477	80	6400	8.944	130	16,900	11.402
31	961	5.568	81	6561	9.000	131	17,161	11.446
32	1024	5.657	82	6724	9.055	132	17,424	11.489
33	1089	5.745	83	6889	9.110	133	17,689	11.533
34	1156	5.831	84	7056	9.165	134	17,956	11.576
35	1225	5.916	85	7225	9.220	135	18,225	11.619
36	1296	6.000	86	7396	9.274	136	18,496	11.662
37	1369	6.083	87	7569	9.327	137	18,769	11.705
38	1444	6.164	88	7744	9.381	138	19,044	11.747
39	1521	6.245	89	7921	9.434	139	19,321	11.790
40	1600	6.325	90	8100	9.487	140	19,600	11.832
41	1681	6.403	91	8281	9.539	141	19,881	11.874
42	1764	6.481	92	8464	9.592	142	20,164	11.916
43	1849	6.557	93	8649	9.644	143	20,449	11.958
44	1936	6.633	94	8836	9.695	144	20,736	12.000
45	2025	6.708	95	9025	9.747	145	21,025	12.042
46	2116	6.782	96	9216	9.798	146	21,316	12.083
47	2209	6.856	97	9409	9.849	147	21,609	12.124
48	2304	6.928	98	9604	9.899	148	21,904	12.166
49	2401	7.000	99	9801	9.950	149	22,201	12.207
50	2500	7.071	100	10,000	10.000	150	22,500	12.247

TABLES

Trigonometric Ratios

Angle	Sine	Cosine	Tangent
1°	.0175	.9998	.0175
2°	.0349	.9994	.0349
3°	.0523	.9986	.0524
4°	.0698	.9976	.0699
5°	.0872	.9962	.0875
6°	.1045	.9945	.1051
7°	.1219	.9925	.1228
8°	.1392	.9903	.1405
9°	.1564	.9877	.1584
10°	.1736	.9848	.1763
11°	.1908	.9816	.1944
12°	.2079	.9781	.2126
13°	.2250	.9744	.2309
14°	.2419	.9703	.2493
15°	.2588	.9659	.2679
16°	.2756	.9613	.2867
17°	.2924	.9563	.3057
18°	.3090	.9511	.3249
19°	.3256	.9455	.3443
20°	.3420	.9397	.3640
21°	.3584	.9336	.3839
22°	.3746	.9272	.4040
23°	.3907	.9205	.4245
24°	.4067	.9135	.4452
25°	.4226	.9063	.4663
26°	.4384	.8988	.4877
27°	.4540	.8910	.5095
28°	.4695	.8829	.5317
29°	.4848	.8746	.5543
30°	.5000	.8660	.5774
31°	.5150	.8572	.6009
32°	.5299	.8480	.6249
33°	.5446	.8387	.6494
34°	.5592	.8290	.6745
35°	.5736	.8192	.7002
36°	.5878	.8090	.7265
37°	.6018	.7986	.7536
38°	.6157	.7880	.7813
39°	.6293	.7771	.8098
40°	.6428	.7660	.8391
41°	.6561	.7547	.8693
42°	.6691	.7431	.9004
43°	.6820	.7314	.9325
44°	.6947	.7193	.9657
45°	.7071	.7071	1.0000

Angle	Sine	Cosine	Tangent
46°	.7193	.6947	1.0355
47°	.7314	.6820	1.0724
48°	.7431	.6691	1.1106
49°	.7547	.6561	1.1504
50°	.7660	.6428	1.1918
51°	.7771	.6293	1.2349
52°	.7880	.6157	1.2799
53°	.7986	.6018	1.3270
54°	.8090	.5878	1.3764
55°	.8192	.5736	1.4281
56°	.8290	.5592	1.4826
57°	.8387	.5446	1.5399
58°	.8480	.5299	1.6003
59°	.8572	.5150	1.6643
60°	.8660	.5000	1.7321
61°	.8746	.4848	1.8040
62°	.8829	.4695	1.8807
63°	.8910	.4540	1.9626
64°	.8988	.4384	2.0503
65°	.9063	.4226	2.1445
66°	.9135	.4067	2.2460
67°	.9205	.3907	2.3559
68°	.9272	.3746	2.4751
69°	.9336	.3584	2.6051
70°	.9397	.3420	2.7475
71°	.9455	.3256	2.9042
72°	.9511	.3090	0.0777
73°	.9563	.2924	3.2709
74°	.9613	.2756	3.4874
75°	.9659	.2588	3.7321
76°	.9703	.2419	4.0108
77°	.9744	.2250	4.3315
78°	.9781	.2079	4.7046
79°	.9816	.1908	5.1446
80°	.9848	.1736	5.6713
81°	.9877	.1564	6.3138
82°	.9903	.1392	7.1154
83°	.9925	.1219	8.1443
84°	.9945	.1045	9.5144
85°	.9962	.0872	11.4301
86°	.9976	.0698	14.3007
87°	.9986	.0523	19.0811
88°	.9994	.0349	28.6363
89°	.9998	.0175	52.2900

Postulates

1 Ruler Postulate The points on a line can be matched one to one with the real numbers. The real number that corresponds to a point is the coordinate of the point. The distance between points A and B, written as AB, is the absolute value of the difference between the coordinates of A and B. *(p. 9)*

2 Segment Addition Postulate If B is between A and C, then $AB + BC = AC$. If $AB + BC = AC$, then B is between A and C. *(p. 10)*

3 Protractor Postulate Consider $\overrightarrow{OB}$ and a point A on one side of $\overrightarrow{OB}$. The rays of the form $\overrightarrow{OA}$ can be matched one to one with the real numbers from 0 to 180. The measure of $\angle AOB$ is equal to the absolute value of the difference between the real numbers for $\overrightarrow{OA}$ and $\overrightarrow{OB}$. *(p. 24)*

4 Angle Addition Postulate If P is in the interior of $\angle RST$, then $m\angle RST = m\angle RSP + m\angle PST$. *(p. 25*)

5 Through any two points there exists exactly one line. *(p. 96)*

6 A line contains at least two points. *(p. 96)*

7 If two lines intersect, then their intersection is exactly one point. *(p. 96)*

8 Through any three noncollinear points there exists exactly one plane. *(p. 96)*

9 A plane contains at least three noncollinear points. *(p. 96)*

10 If two points lie in a plane, then the line containing them lies in the plane. *(p. 96)*

11 If two planes intersect, then their intersection is a line. *(p. 96)*

12 Linear Pair Postulate If two angles form a linear pair, then they are supplementary. *(p. 126)*

13 Parallel Postulate If there is a line and a point not on the line, then there is exactly one line through the point parallel to the given line. *(p. 148)*

14 Perpendicular Postulate If there is a line and a point not on the line, then there is exactly one line through the point perpendicular to the given line. *(p. 148)*

15 Corresponding Angles Postulate If two parallel lines are cut by a transversal, then the pairs of corresponding angles are congruent. *(p. 154)*

16 Corresponding Angles Converse If two lines are cut by a transversal so the corresponding angles are congruent, then the lines are parallel. *(p. 161)*

17 Slopes of Parallel Lines In a coordinate plane, two nonvertical lines are parallel if and only if they have the same slope. Any two vertical lines are parallel. *(p. 172)*

18 Slopes of Perpendicular Lines In a coordinate plane, two nonvertical lines are perpendicular if and only if the product of their slopes is -1. Horizontal lines are perpendicular to vertical lines. *(p. 172)*

19 Side-Side-Side (SSS) Congruence Postulate If three sides of one triangle are congruent to three sides of a second triangle, then the two triangles are congruent. *(p. 234)*

20 Side-Angle-Side (SAS) Congruence Postulate If two sides and the included angle of one triangle are congruent to two sides and the included angle of a second triangle, then the two triangles are congruent. *(p. 240)*

21 Angle-Side-Angle (ASA) Congruence Postulate If two angles and the included side of one triangle are congruent to two angles and the included side of a second triangle, then the two triangles are congruent. *(p. 249)*

22 Angle-Angle (AA) Similarity Postulate If two angles of one triangle are congruent to two angles of another triangle, then the two triangles are similar. *(p. 381)*

23 Arc Addition Postulate The measure of an arc formed by two adjacent arcs is the sum of the measures of the two arcs. *(p. 660)*

24 Area of a Square Postulate The area of a square is the square of the length of its side, or $A = s^2$. *(p. 720)*

25 Area Congruence Postulate If two polygons are congruent, then they have the same area. *(p. 720)*

26 Area Addition Postulate The area of a region is the sum of the areas of its nonoverlapping parts. *(p. 720)*

27 Volume of a Cube The volume of a cube is the cube of the length of its side, or $V = s^3$. *(p. 819)*

28 Volume Congruence Postulate If two polyhedra are congruent, then they have the same volume. *(p. 819)*

29 Volume Addition Postulate The volume of a solid is the sum of the volumes of all its nonoverlapping parts. *(p. 819)*

Theorems

2.1 Properties of Segment Congruence
Segment congruence is reflexive, symmetric, and transitive.

Reflexive: For any segment AB, $\overline{AB} \cong \overline{AB}$.

Symmetric: If $\overline{AB} \cong \overline{CD}$, then $\overline{CD} \cong \overline{AB}$.

Transitive: If $\overline{AB} \cong \overline{CD}$ and $\overline{CD} \cong \overline{EF}$, then $\overline{AB} \cong \overline{EF}$. *(p. 113)*

2.2 Properties of Angles Congruence
Angle congruence is reflexive, symmetric, and transitive.

Reflexive: For any angle A, $\angle A \cong \angle A$.

Symmetric: If $\angle A \cong \angle B$, then $\angle B \cong \angle A$.

Transitive: If $\angle A \cong \angle B$ and $\angle B \cong \angle C$, then $\angle A \cong \angle C$. *(p. 113)*

2.3 Right Angles Congruence Theorem All right angles are congruent. *(p. 124)*

2.4 Congruent Supplements Theorem If two angles are supplementary to the same angle (or to congruent angles), then the two angles are congruent. *(p. 125)*

2.5 Congruent Complements Theorem If two angles are complementary to the same angle (or to congruent angles), then the two angles are congruent. *(p. 125)*

2.6 Vertical Angles Congruence Theorem
Vertical angles are congruent. *(p. 126)*

3.1 Alternate Interior Angles Theorem If two parallel lines are cut by a transversal, then the pairs of alternate interior angles are congruent. *(p. 155)*

3.2 Alternate Exterior Angles Theorem If two parallel lines are cut by a transversal, then the pairs of alternate exterior angles are congruent. *(p. 155)*

3.3 Consecutive Interior Angles Theorem If two parallel lines are cut by a transversal, then the pairs of consecutive interior angles are supplementary. *(p. 155)*

3.4 Alternate Interior Angles Converse If two lines are cut by a transversal so the alternate interior angles are congruent, then the lines are parallel. *(p. 162)*

3.5 Alternate Exterior Angles Converse If two lines are cut by a transversal so the alternate exterior angles are congruent, then the lines are parallel. *(p. 162)*

3.6 Consecutive Interior Angles Converse If two lines are cut by a transversal so the consecutive interior angles are supplementary, then the lines are parallel. *(p. 162)*

3.7 Transitive Property of Parallel Lines If two lines are parallel to the same line, then they are parallel to each other. *(p. 164)*

3.8 If two lines intersect to form a linear pair of congruent angles, then the lines are perpendicular. *(p. 190)*

3.9 If two lines are perpendicular, then they intersect to form four right angles. *(p. 190)*

3.10 If two sides of two adjacent acute angles are perpendicular, then the angles are complementary. *(p. 191)*

3.11 Perpendicular Transversal Theorem If a transversal is perpendicular to one of two parallel lines, then it is perpendicular to the other. *(p. 192)*

3.12 Lines Perpendicular to a Transversal Theorem In a plane, if two lines are perpendicular to the same line, then they are parallel to each other. *(p. 192)*

4.1 Triangle Sum Theorem The sum of the measures of the interior angles of a triangle is $180°$. *(p. 218)*

Corollary The acute angles of a right triangle are complementary. *(p. 220)*

4.2 Exterior Angle Theorem The measure of an exterior angle of a triangle is equal to the sum of the measures of the two nonadjacent interior angles. *(p. 219)*

4.3 Third Angles Theorem If two angles of one triangle are congruent to two angles of another triangle, then the third angles are also congruent. *(p. 227)*

4.4 Properties of Triangle Congruence
Triangle congruence is reflexive, symmetric, and transitive.

Reflexive: For any $\triangle ABC$, $\triangle ABC \cong \triangle ABC$.

Symmetric: If $\triangle ABC \cong \triangle DEF$, then $\triangle DEF \cong \triangle ABC$.

Transitive: If $\triangle ABC \cong \triangle DEF$ and $\triangle DEF \cong \triangle JKL$, then $\triangle ABC \cong \triangle JKL$. *(p. 228)*

4.5 Hypotenuse-Leg (HL) Congruence Theorem If the hypotenuse and a leg of a right triangle are congruent to the hypotenuse and a leg of a second right triangle, then the two triangles are congruent. *(p. 241)*

4.6 Angle-Angle-Side (AAS) Congruence Theorem If two angles and a non-included side of one triangle are congruent to two angles and the corresponding non-included side of a second triangle, then the two triangles are congruent. *(p. 249)*

4.7 Base Angles Theorem If two sides of a triangle are congruent, then the angles opposite them are congruent. *(p. 264)*

Corollary If a triangle is equilateral, then it is equiangular. *(p. 265)*

4.8 Converse of the Base Angles Theorem If two angles of a triangle are congruent, then the sides opposite them are congruent. *(p. 264)*

Corollary If a triangle is equiangular, then it is equilateral. *(p. 265)*

5.1 Midsegment Theorem The segment connecting the midpoints of two sides of a triangle is parallel to the third side and is half as long as that side. *(p. 295)*

5.2 Perpendicular Bisector Theorem If a point is on a perpendicular bisector of a segment, then it is equidistant from the endpoints of the segment. *(p. 303)*

5.3 Converse of the Perpendicular Bisector Theorem If a point is equidistant from the endpoints of a segment, then it is on the perpendicular bisector of the segment. *(p. 303)*

5.4 Concurrency of Perpendicular Bisectors Theorem The perpendicular bisectors of a triangle intersect at a point that is equidistant from the vertices of the triangle. *(p. 305)*

5.5 Angle Bisector Theorem If a point is on the bisector of an angle, then it is equidistant from the two sides of the angle. *(p. 310)*

5.6 Converse of the Angle Bisector Theorem If a point is in the interior of an angle and is equidistant from the sides of the angle, then it lies on the bisector of the angle. *(p. 310)*

5.7 Concurrency of Angle Bisectors of a Triangle The angle bisectors of a triangle intersect at a point that is equidistant from the sides of the triangle. *(p. 312)*

5.8 Concurrency of Medians of a Triangle The medians of a triangle intersect at a point that is two thirds of the distance from each vertex to the midpoint of the opposite side. *(p. 319)*

5.9 Concurrency of Altitudes of a Triangle The lines containing the altitudes of a triangle are concurrent. *(p. 320)*

5.10 If one side of a triangle is longer than another side, then the angle opposite the longer side is larger than the angle opposite the shorter side. *(p. 328)*

5.11 If one angle of a triangle is larger than another angle, then the side opposite the larger angle is longer than the side opposite the smaller angle. *(p. 328)*

5.12 Triangle Inequality Theorem The sum of the lengths of any two sides of a triangle is greater than the length of the third side. *(p. 330)*

5.13 Hinge Theorem If two sides of one triangle are congruent to two sides of another triangle, and the included angle of the first is larger than the included angle of the second, then the third side of the first is longer than the third side of the second. *(p. 335)*

5.14 Converse of the Hinge Theorem If two sides of one triangle are congruent to two sides of another triangle, and the third side of the first is longer than the third side of the second, then the included angle of the first is larger than the included angle of the second. *(p. 335)*

6.1 If two polygons are similar, then the ratio of their perimeters is equal to the ratios of their corresponding side lengths. *(p. 374)*

6.2 Side-Side-Side (SSS) Similarity Theorem If the corresponding side lengths of two triangles are proportional, then the triangles are similar. *(p. 388)*

6.3 Side-Angle-Side (SAS) Similarity Theorem If an angle of one triangle is congruent to an angle of a second triangle and the lengths of the sides including these angles are proportional, then the triangles are similar. *(p. 390)*

6.4 Triangle Proportionality Theorem If a line parallel to one side of a triangle intersects the other two sides, then it divides the two sides proportionally. *(p. 397)*

6.5 Converse of the Triangle Proportionality Theorem If a line divides two sides of a triangle proportionally, then it is parallel to the third side. *(p. 397)*

6.6 If three parallel lines intersect two transversals, then they divide the transversals proportionally. *(p. 398)*

6.7 If a ray bisects an angle of a triangle, then it divides the opposite side into segments whose lengths are proportional to the lengths of the other two sides. *(p. 398)*

7.1 **Pythagorean Theorem** In a right triangle, the square of the length of the hypotenuse is equal to the sum of the squares of the lengths of the legs. *(p. 433)*

7.2 **Converse of the Pythagorean Theorem** If the square of the length of the longest side of a triangle is equal to the sum of the squares of the lengths of the other two sides, then the triangle is a right triangle. *(p. 441)*

7.3 If the square of the length of the longest side of a triangle is less than the sum of the squares of the lengths of the other two sides, then the triangle is an acute triangle. *(p. 442)*

7.4 If the square of the length of the longest side of a triangle is greater than the sum of the squares of the lengths of the other two sides, then the triangle is an obtuse triangle. *(p. 442)*

7.5 If the altitude is drawn to the hypotenuse of a right triangle, then the two triangles formed are similar to the original triangle and to each other. *(p. 449)*

7.6 **Geometric Mean (Altitude) Theorem** In a right triangle, the altitude from the right angle to the hypotenuse divides the hypotenuse into two segments. The length of the altitude is the geometric mean of the lengths of the two segments. *(p. 452)*

7.7 **Geometric Mean (Leg) Theorem** In a right triangle, the altitude from the right angle to the hypotenuse divides the hypotenuse into two segments. The length of each leg of the right triangle is the geometric mean of the lengths of hypotenuse and the segment of the hypotenuse that is adjacent to the leg. *(p. 452)*

7.8 **45°-45°-90° Triangle Theorem** In a 45°-45°-90° triangle, the hypotenuse is $\sqrt{2}$ times as long as each leg. *(p. 457)*

7.9 **30°-60°-90° Triangle Theorem** In a 30°-60°-90° triangle, the hypotenuse is twice as long as the shorter leg, and the longer leg is $\sqrt{3}$ times as long as the shorter leg. *(p. 459)*

8.1 **Polygon Interior Angles Theorem** The sum of the measures of the interior angles of a convex n-gon is $(n - 2) \cdot 180°$. *(p. 507)*

Corollary The sum of the measures of the interior angles of a quadrilateral is 360°. *(p. 507)*

8.2 **Polygon Exterior Angles Theorem** The sum of the measures of the exterior angles of a convex polygon, one angle at each vertex, is 360°. *(p. 509)*

8.3 If a quadrilateral is a parallelogram, then its opposite sides are congruent. *(p. 515)*

8.4 If a quadrilateral is a parallelogram, then its opposite angles are congruent. *(p. 515)*

8.5 If a quadrilateral is a parallelogram, then its consecutive angles are supplementary. *(p. 516)*

8.6 If a quadrilateral is a parallelogram, then its diagonals bisect each other. *(p. 517)*

8.7 If both pairs of opposite sides of a quadrilateral are congruent, then the quadrilateral is a parallelogram. *(p. 522)*

8.8 If both pairs of opposite angles of a quadrilateral are congruent, then the quadrilateral is a parallelogram. *(p. 522)*

8.9 If one pair of opposite sides of a quadrilateral are congruent and parallel, then the quadrilateral is a parallelogram. *(p. 523)*

8.10 If the diagonals of a quadrilateral bisect each other, then the quadrilateral is a parallelogram. *(p. 523)*

Rhombus Corollary A quadrilateral is a rhombus if and only if it has four congruent sides. *(p. 533)*

Rectangle Corollary A quadrilateral is a rectangle if and only if it has four right angles. *(p. 533)*

Square Corollary A quadrilateral is a square if and only if it is a rhombus and a rectangle. *(p. 533)*

8.11 A parallelogram is a rhombus if and only if its diagonals are perpendicular. *(p. 535)*

8.12 A parallelogram is a rhombus if and only if each diagonal bisects a pair of opposite angles. *(p. 535)*

8.13 A parallelogram is a rectangle if and only if its diagonals are congruent. *(p. 535)*

8.14 If a trapezoid is isosceles, then both pairs of base angles are congruent. *(p. 543)*

8.15 If a trapezoid has a pair of congruent base angles, then it is an isosceles trapezoid. *(p. 543)*

8.16 A trapezoid is isosceles if and only if its diagonals are congruent. *(p. 543)*

8.17 Midsegment Theorem for Trapezoids The midsegment of a trapezoid is parallel to each base and its length is one half the sum of the lengths of the bases. *(p. 544)*

8.18 If a quadrilateral is a kite, then its diagonals are perpendicular. *(p. 545)*

8.19 If a quadrilateral is a kite, then exactly one pair of opposite angles are congruent. *(p. 545)*

9.1 Translation Theorem A translation is an isometry. *(p. 573)*

9.2 Reflection Theorem A reflection is an isometry. *(p. 591)*

9.3 Rotation Theorem A rotation is an isometry. *(p. 601)*

9.4 Composition Theorem The composition of two (or more) isometries is an isometry. *(p. 609)*

9.5 Reflections in Parallel Lines If lines k and m are parallel, then a reflection in line k followed by a reflection in line m is the same as a translation. If P'' is the image of P, then:

(1) $\overline{PP'}$ is perpendicular to k and m, and
(2) $PP'' = 2d$, where d is the distance between k and m. *(p. 609)*

9.6 Reflections in Intersecting Lines If lines k and m intersect at point P, then a reflection in k followed by a reflection in m is the same as a rotation about point P. The angle of rotation is $2x°$, where $x°$ is the measure of the acute or right angle formed by k and m. *(p. 610)*

10.1 In a plane, a line is tangent to a circle if and only if the line is perpendicular to a radius of the circle at its endpoint on the circle. *(p. 653)*

10.2 Tangent segments from a common external point are congruent. *(p. 654)*

10.3 In the same circle, or in congruent circles, two minor arcs are congruent if and only if their corresponding chords are congruent. *(p. 664)*

10.4 If one chord is a perpendicular bisector of another chord, then the first chord is a diameter. *(p. 665)*

10.5 If a diameter of a circle is perpendicular to a chord, then the diameter bisects the chord and its arc. *(p. 665)*

10.6 In the same circle, or in congruent circles, two chords are congruent if and only if they are equidistant from the center. *(p. 666)*

10.7 Measure of an Inscribed Angle Theorem The measure of an inscribed angle is one half the measure of its intercepted arc. *(p. 672)*

10.8 If two inscribed angles of a circle intercept the same arc, then the angles are congruent. *(p. 673)*

10.9 If a right triangle is inscribed in a circle, then the hypotenuse is a diameter of the circle. Conversely, if one side of an inscribed triangle is a diameter of the circle, then the triangle is a right triangle and the angle opposite the diameter is the right angle. *(p. 674)*

10.10 A quadrilateral can be inscribed in a circle if and only if its opposite angles are supplementary. *(p. 675)*

10.11 If a tangent and a chord intersect at a point on a circle, then the measure of each angle formed is one half the measure of its intercepted arc. *(p. 680)*

10.12 Angles Inside the Circle If two chords intersect inside a circle, then the measure of each angle is one half the sum of the measures of the arcs intercepted by the angle and its vertical angle. *(p. 681)*

10.13 Angles Outside the Circle If a tangent and a secant, two tangents, or two secants intersect outside a circle, then the measure of the angle formed is one half the difference of the measures of the intercepted arcs. *(p. 681)*

10.14 Segments of Chords Theorem If two chords intersect in the interior of a circle, then the product of the lengths of the segments of one chord is equal to the product of the lengths of the segments of the other chord. *(p. 689)*

10.15 Segments of Secants Theorem If two secant segments share the same endpoint outside a circle, then the product of the lengths of one secant segment and its external segment equals the product of the lengths of the other secant segment and its external segment. *(p. 690)*

10.16 Segments of Secants and Tangents Theorem If a secant segment and a tangent segment share an endpoint outside a circle, then the product of the lengths of the secant segment and its external segment equals the square of the length of the tangent segment. *(p. 691)*

11.1 Area of a Rectangle The area of a rectangle is the product of its base and height. $A = bh$ *(p. 720)*

11.2 Area of a Parallelogram The area of a parallelogram is the product of a base and its corresponding height. $A = bh$ *(p. 721)*

11.3 Area of a Triangle The area of a triangle is one half the product of a base and its corresponding height. $A = \frac{1}{2}bh$ *(p. 721)*

11.4 Area of a Trapezoid The area of a trapezoid is one half the product of the height and the sum of the lengths of the bases. $A = \frac{1}{2}h(b_1 + b_2)$ *(p. 730)*

11.5 Area of a Rhombus The area of a rhombus is one half the product of the lengths of its diagonals. $A = \frac{1}{2}d_1d_2$ *(p. 731)*

11.6 Area of a Kite The area of a kite is one half the product of the lengths of its diagonals. $A = \frac{1}{2}d_1d_2$ *(p. 731)*

11.7 Areas of Similar Polygons If two polygons are similar with the lengths of corresponding sides in the ratio of $a : b$, then the ratio of their areas is $a^2 : b^2$. *(p. 737)*

11.8 Circumference of a Circle The circumference C of a circle is $C = \pi d$ or $C = 2\pi r$, where d is the diameter of the circle and r is the radius of the circle. *(p. 746)*

Arc Length Corollary In a circle, the ratio of the length of a given arc to the circumference is equal to the ratio of the measure of the arc to 360°.

$$\frac{\text{Arc length of } \overset{\frown}{AB}}{2\pi r} = \frac{m\overset{\frown}{AB}}{360°}, \text{ or}$$

$$\text{Arc length of } \overset{\frown}{AB} = \frac{m\overset{\frown}{AB}}{360°} \cdot 2\pi r \text{ *(p. 747)*}$$

11.9 Area of a Circle The area of a circle is π times the square of the radius. $A = \pi r^2$ *(p. 755)*

11.10 Area of a Sector The ratio of the area A of a sector of a circle to the area of the whole circle (πr^2) is equal to the ratio of the measure of the intercepted arc to 360°.

$$\frac{A}{\pi r^2} = \frac{m\overset{\frown}{AB}}{360°}, \text{ or } A = \frac{m\overset{\frown}{AB}}{360°} \cdot \pi r^2 \text{ *(p. 756)*}$$

11.11 Area of a Regular Polygon The area of a regular n-gon with side length s is half the product of the apothem a and the perimeter P, so $A = \frac{1}{2}aP$, or $A = \frac{1}{2}a \cdot ns$. *(p. 763)*

12.1 Euler's Theorem The number of faces (F), vertices (V), and edges (E) of a polyhedron are related by the formula $F + V = E + 2$. *(p. 795)*

12.2 Surface Area of a Right Prism The surface area S of a right prism is $S = 2B + Ph = aP + Ph$, where a is the apothem of the base, B is the area of a base, P is the perimeter of a base, and h is the height. *(p. 804)*

12.3 Surface Area of a Right Cylinder The surface area S of a right cylinder is $S = 2B + Ch = 2\pi r^2 + 2\pi rh$, where B is the area of a base, C is the circumference of a base, r is the radius of a base, and h is the height. *(p. 805)*

12.4 Surface Area of a Regular Pyramid The surface area S of a regular pyramid is $S = B + \frac{1}{2}P\ell$, where B is the area of the base, P is the perimeter of the base, and ℓ is the slant height. *(p. 811)*

12.5 Surface Area of a Right Cone The surface area S of a right cone is $S = B + \frac{1}{2}C\ell = \pi r^2 + \pi r\ell$, where B is the area of the base, C is the circumference of the base, r is the radius of the base, and ℓ is the slant height. *(p. 812)*

12.6 Volume of a Prism The volume V of a prism is $V = Bh$, where B is the area of a base and h is the height. *(p. 820)*

12.7 Volume of a Cylinder The volume V of a cylinder is $V = Bh = \pi r^2 h$, where B is the area of a base, h is the height, and r is the radius of a base. *(p. 820)*

12.8 Cavalieri's Principle If two solids have the same height and the same cross-sectional area at every level, then they have the same volume. *(p. 821)*

12.9 Volume of a Pyramid The volume V of a pyramid is $V = \frac{1}{3}Bh$, where B is the area of the base and h is the height. *(p. 829)*

12.10 Volume of a Cone The volume V of a cone is $V = \frac{1}{3}Bh = \frac{1}{3}\pi r^2 h$, where B is the area of the base, h is the height, and r is the radius of the base. *(p. 829)*

12.11 Surface Area of a Sphere The surface area S of a sphere with radius r is $S = 4\pi r^2$. *(p. 838)*

12.12 Volume of a Sphere The volume V of a sphere with radius r is $V = \frac{4}{3}\pi r^3$. *(p. 840)*

12.13 Similar Solids Theorem If two similar solids have a scale factor of $a : b$, then corresponding areas have a ratio of $a^2 : b^2$, and corresponding volumes have a ratio of $a^3 : b^3$. *(p. 848)*

Additional Proofs

Proof of Theorem 4.5
Hypotenuse-Leg (HL) Congruence Theorem

THEOREM 4.5
PAGE 241

If the hypotenuse and a leg of a right triangle are congruent to the hypotenuse and a leg of a second right triangle, then the two triangles are congruent.

GIVEN ▶ In $\triangle ABC$, $\angle C$ is a right angle.
In $\triangle DEF$, $\angle F$ is a right angle.
$\overline{AB} \cong \overline{DE}$, $\overline{AC} \cong \overline{DF}$

PROVE ▶ $\triangle ABC \cong \triangle DEF$

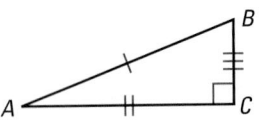

Plan for Proof Construct $\triangle DGF$ with $\overline{GF} \cong \overline{BC}$, as shown. Prove that $\triangle ABC \cong \triangle DGF$. Then use the fact that corresponding parts of congruent triangles are congruent to show that $\triangle DGF \cong \triangle DEF$. By the Transitive Property of Congruence, you can show that $\triangle ABC \cong \triangle DEF$.

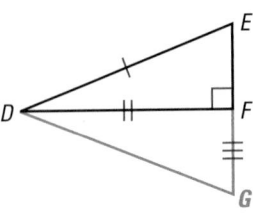

STATEMENTS	REASONS
1. $\angle C$ is a right angle. $\angle DFE$ is a right angle.	1. Given
2. $\overline{DF} \perp \overline{EG}$	2. Definition of perpendicular lines
3. $\angle DFG$ is a right angle.	3. If 2 lines are $\perp$, then they form 4 rt. $\angle$s.
4. $\angle C \cong \angle DFG$	4. Right Angles Congruence Theorem
5. $\overline{AC} \cong \overline{DF}$	5. Given
6. $\overline{BC} \cong \overline{GF}$	6. Given by construction
7. $\triangle ABC \cong \triangle DGF$	7. SAS Congruence Postulate
8. $\overline{DG} \cong \overline{AB}$	8. Corresp. parts of $\cong$ $\triangle$s are $\cong$.
9. $\overline{AB} \cong \overline{DE}$	9. Given
10. $\overline{DG} \cong \overline{DE}$	10. Transitive Property of Congruence
11. $\angle E \cong \angle G$	11. If 2 sides of a $\triangle$ are $\cong$, then the $\angle$s opposite them are $\cong$.
12. $\angle DFG \cong \angle DFE$	12. Right Angles Congruence Theorem
13. $\triangle DGF \cong \triangle DEF$	13. AAS Congruence Theorem
14. $\triangle ABC \cong \triangle DEF$	14. Transitive Property of $\cong$ $\triangle$s

Proof of Theorem 5.4
Concurrency of Perpendicular Bisectors of a Triangle

THEOREM 5.4
PAGE 305
....
The perpendicular bisectors of a triangle intersect at a point that is equidistant from the vertices of the triangle.

GIVEN ▶ △*ABC*; the ⊥ bisectors of $\overline{AB}$, $\overline{BC}$, and $\overline{AC}$

PROVE ▶ The ⊥ bisectors intersect in a point; that point is equidistant from *A*, *B*, and *C*.

Plan for Proof Show that *P*, the point of intersection of the perpendicular bisectors of $\overline{AB}$ and $\overline{BC}$, also lies on the perpendicular bisector of $\overline{AC}$. Then show that *P* is equidistant from the vertices of the triangle, *A*, *B*, and *C*.

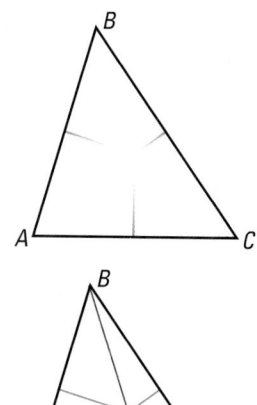

STATEMENTS	REASONS
1. △*ABC*; the ⊥ bisectors of $\overline{AB}$, $\overline{BC}$, and $\overline{AC}$	**1.** Given
2. The perpendicular bisectors of $\overline{AB}$ and $\overline{BC}$ intersect at some point *P*.	**2.** *ABC* is a triangle, so its sides $\overline{AB}$ and $\overline{BC}$ cannot be parallel; therefore, segments perpendicular to those sides cannot be parallel. So, the perpendicular bisectors must intersect in some point. Call it *P*.
3. Draw $\overline{PA}$, $\overline{PB}$, and $\overline{PC}$.	**3.** Through any two points there is exactly one line.
4. *PA* = *PB*, *PB* = *PC*	**4.** In a plane, if a point is on the perpendicular bisector of a segment, then it is equidistant from the endpoints of the segment. (Theorem 5.2)
5. *PA* = *PC*	**5.** Substitution Property of Equality
6. *P* is on the perpendicular bisector of $\overline{AC}$.	**6.** In a plane, if a point is equidistant from the endpoints of a segment, then it is on the perpendicular bisector of the segment. (Theorem 5.3)
7. *PA* = *PB* = *PC*, so *P* is equidistant from the vertices of the triangle.	**7.** From the results of Steps 4 and 5 and the definition of equidistant

Proof of Theorem 5.8
Concurrency of Medians of a Triangle

THEOREM 5.8
PAGE 319
The medians of a triangle intersect at a point that is two thirds of the distance from each vertex to the midpoint of the opposite side.

GIVEN ▶ $\triangle OBC$; medians $\overline{OM}$, $\overline{BN}$, and $\overline{CQ}$

PROVE ▶ The medians intersect in a point P; that point is two thirds of the distance from vertices O, B, and C to midpoints M, N, and Q.

Plan for Proof The medians $\overline{OM}$ and $\overline{BN}$ intersect at some point P. Show that point P lies on $\overleftrightarrow{CQ}$. Then show that $OP = \frac{2}{3}OM$, $BP = \frac{2}{3}BN$, and $CP = \frac{2}{3}CQ$.

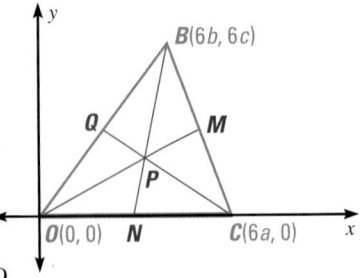

STEP 1 **Find** the equations of the lines containing the medians $\overline{OM}$, $\overline{BN}$, and $\overline{CQ}$.

By the *Midpoint Formula*,

the coordinates of M are $\left(\dfrac{6b + 6a}{2}, \dfrac{6c + 0}{2}\right) = (3b + 3a, 3c)$;

the coordinates of N are $\left(\dfrac{0 + 6a}{2}, \dfrac{0 + 0}{2}\right) = (3a, 0)$;

the coordinates of Q are $\left(\dfrac{6b + 0}{2}, \dfrac{6c + 0}{2}\right) = (3b, 3c)$.

By the *slope formula*,

slope of $\overline{OM} = \dfrac{3c - 0}{(3b + 3a) - 0} = \dfrac{3c}{3b + 3a} = \dfrac{c}{b + a}$;

slope of $\overline{BN} = \dfrac{6c - 0}{6b - 3a} = \dfrac{6c}{6b - 3a} = \dfrac{2c}{2b - a}$;

slope of $\overline{CQ} = \dfrac{0 - 3c}{6a - 3b} = \dfrac{-3c}{6a - 3b} = \dfrac{-c}{2a - b} = \dfrac{c}{b - 2a}$.

Using the *point-slope form of an equation of a line*,

the equation of $\overleftrightarrow{OM}$ is $y - 0 = \dfrac{c}{b + a}(x - 0)$, or $y = \dfrac{c}{b + a}x$;

the equation of $\overleftrightarrow{BN}$ is $y - 0 = \dfrac{2c}{2b - a}(x - 3a)$, or $y = \dfrac{2c}{2b - a}(x - 3a)$;

the equation of $\overleftrightarrow{CQ}$ is $y - 0 = \dfrac{c}{b - 2a}(x - 6a)$, or $y = \dfrac{c}{b - 2a}(x - 6a)$.

STEP 2 **Find** the coordinates of the point P where two medians (say, $\overline{OM}$ and $\overline{BN}$) intersect. Using the substitution method, set the values of y in the equations of $\overleftrightarrow{OM}$ and $\overleftrightarrow{BN}$ equal to each other:

$$\frac{c}{b + a}x = \frac{2c}{2b - a}(x - 3a)$$

$$cx(2b - a) = 2c(x - 3a)(b + a)$$

$$2cxb - cxa = 2cxb + 2cxa - 6cab - 6ca^2$$

$$-3cxa = -6cab - 6ca^2$$

$$x = 2b + 2a$$

Substituting to find y, $y = \dfrac{c}{b + a}x = \dfrac{c}{b + a}(2b + 2a) = 2c$.

So, the coordinates of P are $(2b + 2a, 2c)$.

WRITE PROOFS
Because you want to prove something involving the fraction $\frac{2}{3}$, it is convenient to position the vertices at points whose coordinates are multiples of both 2 and 3.

STEP 3 **Show** that P is on $\overleftrightarrow{CQ}$.

Substituting the x-coordinate for P into the equation of $\overleftrightarrow{CQ}$,
$y = \dfrac{c}{b - 2a}([2b + 2a] - 6a) = \dfrac{c}{b - 2a}(2b - 4a) = 2c$.
So, $P(2b + 2a, 2c)$ is on $\overleftrightarrow{CQ}$ and the three medians intersect at the same point.

STEP 4 **Find** the distances OM, OP, BN, BP, CQ, and CP.
Use the *Distance Formula*.

$$OM = \sqrt{((3b + 3a) - 0)^2 + (3c - 0)^2} = \sqrt{(3(b + a))^2 + (3c)^2} =$$
$$\sqrt{9((b + a)^2 + c^2)} = 3\sqrt{(b + a)^2 + c^2}$$

$$OP = \sqrt{((2b + 2a) - 0)^2 + (2c - 0)^2} = \sqrt{(2(b + a))^2 + (2c)^2} =$$
$$\sqrt{4((b + a)^2 + c^2)} = 2\sqrt{(b + a)^2 + c^2}$$

$$BN = \sqrt{(3a - 6b)^2 + (0 - 6c)^2} = \sqrt{(3a - 6b)^2 + (-6c)^2} =$$
$$\sqrt{(3(a - 2b))^2 + (3(-2c))^2} = \sqrt{9(a - 2b)^2 + 9(4c^2)} =$$
$$\sqrt{9((a - 2b)^2 + 4c^2)} = 3\sqrt{(a - 2b)^2 + 4c^2}$$

$$BP = \sqrt{((2b + 2a) - 6b)^2 + (2c - 6c)^2} = \sqrt{(2a - 4b)^2 + (-4c)^2} =$$
$$\sqrt{(2(a - 2b))^2 + (2(-2c))^2} = \sqrt{4(a - 2b)^2 + 4(4c^2)} =$$
$$\sqrt{4((a - 2b)^2 + 4c^2)} = 2\sqrt{(a - 2b)^2 + 4c^2}$$

$$CQ = \sqrt{(6a - 3b)^2 + (0 - 3c)^2} = \sqrt{(3(2a - b))^2 + (-3c)^2} =$$
$$\sqrt{9((2a - b)^2 + c^2)} = 3\sqrt{(2a - b)^2 + c^2}$$

$$CP = \sqrt{(6a - (2b + 2a))^2 + (0 - 2c)^2} = \sqrt{(4a - 2b)^2 + (-2c)^2} =$$
$$\sqrt{(2(2a - b))^2 + 4c^2} = \sqrt{4((2a - b)^2 + c^2)} =$$
$$2\sqrt{(2a - b)^2 + c^2}$$

STEP 5 **Multiply** OM, BN, and CQ by $\frac{2}{3}$.

$$\frac{2}{3}OM = \frac{2}{3}\left(3\sqrt{(b + a)^2 + c^2}\right)$$
$$= 2\sqrt{(b + a)^2 + c^2}$$

$$\frac{2}{3}BN = \frac{2}{3}\left(3\sqrt{(a - 2b)^2 + 4c^2}\right)$$
$$= 2\sqrt{(a - 2b)^2 + 4c^2}$$

$$\frac{2}{3}CQ = \frac{2}{3}\left(3\sqrt{(2a - b)^2 + c^2}\right)$$
$$= 2\sqrt{(2a - b)^2 + c^2}$$

Thus, $OP = \frac{2}{3}OM$, $BP = \frac{2}{3}BN$, and $CP = \frac{2}{3}CQ$.

Proof of Theorem 5.9
Concurrency of Altitudes of a Triangle

THEOREM 5.9
PAGE 320
The lines containing the altitudes of a triangle are concurrent.

GIVEN ▶ $\triangle OGH$

PROVE ▶ The altitudes to the sides of $\triangle OGH$ all intersect at J.

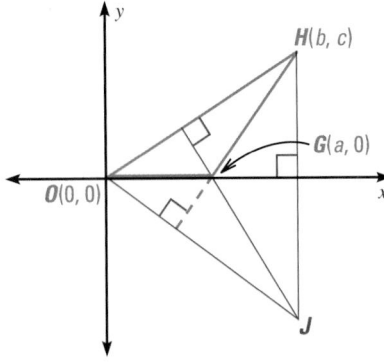

Plan for Proof Find the equations of the lines containing the altitudes of $\triangle OGH$. Find the intersection point of two of these lines. Show that the intersection point is also on the line containing the third altitude.

STEP 1 **Find** the slopes of the lines containing the sides $\overline{OH}$, $\overline{GH}$, and $\overline{OG}$.

Slope of $\overleftrightarrow{OH} = \dfrac{c}{b}$ Slope of $\overleftrightarrow{GH} = \dfrac{c}{b-a}$ Slope of $\overleftrightarrow{OG} = 0$

STEP 2 **Use** the *Slopes of Perpendicular Lines Postulate* to find the slopes of the lines containing the altitudes.

Slope of line containing altitude to $\overline{OH} = \dfrac{-b}{c}$

Slope of line containing altitude to $\overline{GH} = \dfrac{-(b-a)}{c} = \dfrac{a-b}{c}$

The line containing the altitude to $\overline{OG}$ has an undefined slope.

> **WRITE PROOFS**
> Choose a general triangle, with one vertex at the origin and one side along an axis. In the proof shown, the triangle is obtuse.

STEP 3 **Use** the *point-slope form of an equation of a line* to write equations for the lines containing the altitudes.

An equation of the line containing the altitude to $\overline{OH}$ is
$$y - 0 = \dfrac{-b}{c}(x - a), \text{ or } y = \dfrac{-b}{c}x + \dfrac{ab}{c}.$$

An equation of the line containing the altitude to $\overline{GH}$ is
$$y - 0 = \dfrac{a-b}{c}(x - 0), \text{ or } y = \dfrac{a-b}{c}x.$$

An equation of the vertical line containing the altitude to $\overline{OG}$ is $x = b$.

STEP 4 **Find** the coordinates of the point J where the lines containing two of the altitudes intersect. Using substitution, set the values of y in two of the above equations equal to each other, then solve for x:

$$\dfrac{-b}{c}x + \dfrac{ab}{c} = \dfrac{a-b}{c}x$$

$$\dfrac{ab}{c} = \dfrac{a-b}{c}x + \dfrac{b}{c}x$$

$$\dfrac{ab}{c} = \dfrac{a}{c}x$$

$$x = b$$

Next, substitute to find y: $y = \dfrac{-b}{c}x + \dfrac{ab}{c} = \dfrac{-b}{c}(b) + \dfrac{ab}{c} = \dfrac{ab - b^2}{c}$.

So, the coordinates of J are $\left(b, \dfrac{ab - b^2}{c}\right)$.

STEP 5 **Show** that J is on the line that contains the altitude to side $\overline{OG}$. J is on the vertical line with equation $x = b$ because its x-coordinate is b. Thus, the lines containing the altitudes of $\triangle OGH$ are concurrent.

Proof of Theorem 8.17
Midsegment Theorem for Trapezoids

THEOREM 8.17
PAGE 544
....
The midsegment of a
trapezoid is parallel
to each base and its
length is one half the
sum of the lengths of
the bases.

GIVEN ▶ Trapezoid $ABCD$ with midsegment $\overline{MN}$

PROVE ▶ $\overline{MN} \parallel \overline{AB}$, $\overline{MN} \parallel \overline{DC}$,

$MN = \frac{1}{2}(AB + DC)$

Plan for Proof Draw $\overline{AN}$, then extend $\overline{AN}$ and $\overline{DC}$ so that they intersect at point G. Then prove that $\triangle ANB \cong \triangle GNC$, and use the fact that $\overline{MN}$ is a midsegment of $\triangle ADG$ to prove that

$MN = \frac{1}{2}(AB + DC)$.

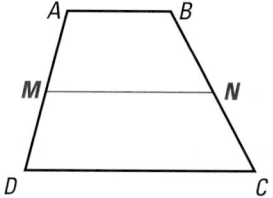

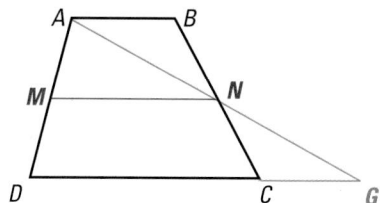

STATEMENTS	REASONS
1. $ABCD$ is a trapezoid with midsegment $\overline{MN}$.	1. Given
2. Draw $\overline{AN}$, then extend $\overline{AN}$ and $\overline{DC}$ so that they intersect at point G.	2. Through any two points there is exactly one line.
3. N is the midpoint of $\overline{BC}$.	3. Definition of midsegment of a trapezoid
4. $\overline{BN} \cong \overline{NC}$	4. Definition of midpoint
5. $\overline{AB} \parallel \overline{DC}$	5. Definition of trapezoid
6. $\angle ABN \cong \angle GCN$	6. Alternate Interior $\angle$s Theorem
7. $\angle ANB \cong \angle GNC$	7. Vertical angles are congruent.
8. $\triangle ANB \cong \triangle GNC$	8. ASA Congruence Postulate
9. $\overline{AN} \cong \overline{GN}$	9. Corresp. parts of $\cong$ $\triangle$s are $\cong$.
10. N is the midpoint of $\overline{AG}$.	10. Definition of midpoint
11. $\overline{MN}$ is a midsegment of $\triangle AGD$.	11. Definition of midsegment of a $\triangle$
12. $\overline{MN} \parallel \overline{DG}$ (so $\overline{MN} \parallel \overline{DC}$)	12. Midsegment of a $\triangle$ Theorem
13. $\overline{MN} \parallel \overline{AB}$	13. Two lines $\parallel$ to the same line are $\parallel$.
14. $MN = \frac{1}{2}DG$	14. Midsegment of a $\triangle$ Theorem
15. $DG = DC + CG$	15. Segment Addition Postulate
16. $\overline{CG} \cong \overline{AB}$	16. Corresp. parts of $\cong$ $\triangle$s are $\cong$.
17. $CG = AB$	17. Definition of congruent segments
18. $DG = DC + AB$	18. Substitution Property of Equality
19. $MN = \frac{1}{2}(DC + AB)$	19. Substitution Property of Equality

ADDITIONAL PROOFS

Proof of Theorem 10.10
A Theorem about Inscribed Quadrilaterals

**THEOREM 10.10
PAGE 675**
A quadrilateral can be inscribed in a circle if and only if its opposite angles are supplementary.

STEP 1 **Prove** that if a quadrilateral is inscribed in a circle, then its opposite angles are supplementary.

GIVEN ▶ *DEFG* is inscribed in ⊙*C*.

PROVE ▶ ∠*D* and ∠*F* are supplementary,
∠*E* and ∠*G* are supplementary.

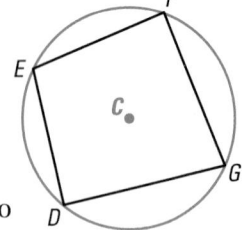

Paragraph Proof Arcs $\widehat{EFG}$ and $\widehat{GDE}$ together make a circle, so $m\widehat{EFG} + m\widehat{GDE} = 360°$ by the Arc Addition Postulate. ∠*D* is inscribed in $\widehat{EFG}$ and ∠*F* is inscribed in $\widehat{GDE}$, so the angle measures are half the arc measures. Using the Substitution and Distributive Properties, the sum of the measures of the opposite angles is

$$m\angle D + m\angle F = \tfrac{1}{2}m\widehat{EFG} + \tfrac{1}{2}m\widehat{GDE} = \tfrac{1}{2}(m\widehat{EFG} + m\widehat{GDE}) = \tfrac{1}{2}(360°) = 180°.$$

So, ∠*D* and ∠*F* are supplementary by definition. Similarly, ∠*E* and ∠*G* are inscribed in $\widehat{FGD}$ and $\widehat{DEF}$ and $m\angle E + m\angle G = 180°$. Then ∠*E* and ∠*G* are supplementary by definition.

STEP 2 **Prove** that if the opposite angles of a quadrilateral are supplementary, then the quadrilateral can be inscribed in a circle.

GIVEN ▶ ∠*E* and ∠*G* are supplementary (or ∠*D* and ∠*F* are supplementary).

PROVE ▶ *DEFG* is inscribed in ⊙*C*.

Plan for Proof Draw the circle that passes through *D*, *E*, and *F*. Use an *indirect proof* to show that the circle also passes through *G*. Begin by assuming that *G* does not lie on ⊙*C*.

Case 1 *G lies inside ⊙C.* Let *H* be the intersection of $\overrightarrow{DG}$ and ⊙*C*. Then *DEFH* is inscribed in ⊙*C* and ∠*E* is supplementary to ∠*DHF* (by proof above). Then ∠*DGF* ≅ ∠*DHF* by the given information and the Congruent Supplements Theorem. This implies that $\overline{FG} \parallel \overline{FH}$, which is a contradiction.

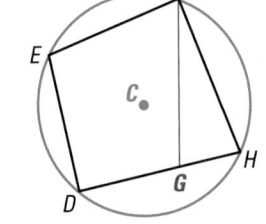

Case 2 *G lies outside ⊙C.* Let *H* be the intersection of $\overrightarrow{DG}$ and ⊙*C*. Then *DEFH* is inscribed in ⊙*C* and ∠*E* is supplementary to ∠*DHF* (by proof above). Then ∠*DGF* ≅ ∠*DHF* by the given information and the Congruent Supplements Theorem. This implies that $\overline{FG} \parallel \overline{FH}$, which is a contradiction.

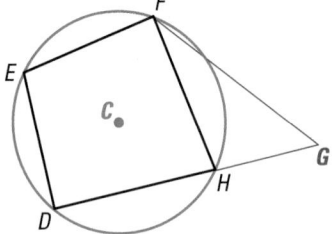

Because the original assumption leads to a contradiction in both cases, *G* lies on ⊙*C* and *DEFG* is inscribed in ⊙*C*.

acute angle (p. 25) An angle with measure between 0° and 90°.

ángulo agudo (pág. 25) Ángulo que mide más de 0° y menos de 90°.

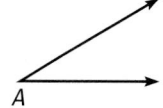

---

acute triangle (p. 217) A triangle with three acute angles.

triángulo acutángulo (pág. 217) Triángulo que tiene los tres ángulos agudos.

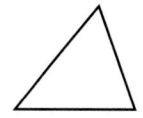

---

adjacent angles (p. 35) Two angles that share a common vertex and side, but have no common interior points.

ángulos adyacentes (pág. 35) Dos ángulos que comparten un vértice y un lado comunes, pero que no tienen puntos interiores comunes.

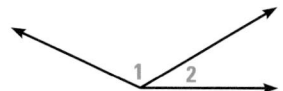

∠1 and ∠2 are adjacent angles.
∠1 y ∠2 son ángulos adyacentes.

---

alternate exterior angles (p. 149) Two angles that are formed by two lines and a transversal and lie outside the two lines and on opposite sides of the transversal.

ángulos externos alternos (pág. 149) Dos ángulos formados por dos rectas y una transversal y que se encuentran en el exterior de las dos rectas en lados opuestos de la transversal.

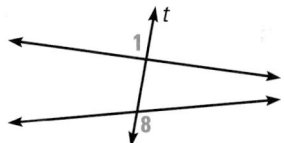

∠1 and ∠8 are alternate exterior angles.
∠1 y ∠8 son ángulos externos alternos.

---

alternate interior angles (p. 149) Two angles that are formed by two lines and a transversal and lie between the two lines and on opposite sides of the transversal.

ángulos internos alternos (pág. 149) Dos ángulos formados por dos rectas y una transversal y que se encuentran entre las dos rectas en lados opuestos de la transversal.

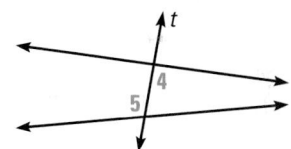

∠4 and ∠5 are alternate interior angles.
∠4 y ∠5 son ángulos internos alternos.

---

altitude of a triangle (p. 320) The perpendicular segment from one vertex of the triangle to the opposite side or to the line that contains the opposite side.

altura de un triángulo (pág. 320) El segmento perpendicular que va desde uno de los vértices del triángulo hasta el lado opuesto o hasta la recta que contiene el lado opuesto.

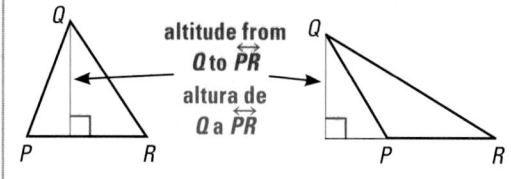

angle (p. 24) Consists of two different rays with the same endpoint. The rays are the sides of the angle, and the endpoint is the vertex of the angle.

ángulo (pág. 24) Formado por dos rayos diferentes con el mismo extremo. Los rayos son los lados del ángulo, y el extremo es el vértice del ángulo.

∠*A*, ∠*BAC*, or ∠*CAB*
∠*A*, ∠*BAC* o ∠*CAB*

angle bisector (p. 28) A ray that divides an angle into two angles that are congruent.

bisectriz de un ángulo (pág. 28) Rayo que divide a un ángulo en dos ángulos congruentes.

$\overrightarrow{YW}$ bisects ∠*XYZ*.
$\overrightarrow{YW}$ biseca a ∠*XYZ*.

angle of depression (p. 475) When you look down at an object, the angle that your line of sight makes with a line drawn horizontally.

ángulo de depresión (pág. 475) Cuando observas un objeto que está situado abajo, es el ángulo que forman tu línea de visión y una línea horizontal.

angle of depression
ángulo de depresión

angle of elevation
ángulo de elevación

angle of elevation (p. 475) When you look up at an object, the angle that your line of sight makes with a line drawn horizontally.

ángulo de elevación (pág. 475) Cuando observas un objeto que está situado arriba, es el ángulo que forman tu línea de visión y una línea horizontal.

See **angle of depression.**

Ver ángulo de depresión.

angle of rotation (p. 598) The angle formed by rays drawn from the center of rotation to a point and its image. *See also* rotation.

ángulo de rotación (pág. 598) El ángulo formado por los rayos trazados desde el centro de rotación hasta un punto y su imagen. *Ver también* rotación.

See **rotation.**

Ver rotación.

apothem of a polygon (p. 762) The distance from the center to any side of the polygon.

apotema de un polígono (pág. 762) La distancia del centro a cualquier lado del polígono.

apothem
apotema

arc length (p. 747) A portion of the circumference of a circle.

longitud de arco (pág. 747) Porción de la circunferencia de un círculo.

Arc length of $\overset{\frown}{AB} = \dfrac{m\overset{\frown}{AB}}{360°} \cdot 2\pi r$

Longitud de arco de $\overset{\frown}{AB} = \dfrac{m\overset{\frown}{AB}}{360°} \cdot 2\pi r$

axiom (p. 9) *See* postulate.

axioma (pág. 9) *Ver* postulado.

See postulate.

Ver postulado.

B

base angles of a trapezoid (p. 542) Either pair of angles whose common side is a base of a trapezoid.

ángulos básicos de un trapecio (pág. 542) Cualquier par de ángulos cuyo lado común es una base del trapecio.

∠*A* and ∠*D* are a pair of base angles.
∠*B* and ∠*C* are another pair.

∠*A* y ∠*D* son un par de ángulos básicos.
∠*B* y ∠*C* son otro par.

base angles of an isosceles triangle (p. 264) The two angles that are adjacent to the base of an isosceles triangle.

ángulos básicos de un triángulo isósceles (pág. 264) Los dos ángulos adyacentes a la base de un triángulo isósceles.

See vertex angle of an isosceles triangle.

Ver ángulo del vértice de un triángulo isósceles.

base of a parallelogram (p. 720) Either pair of parallel sides of a parallelogram.

base de un paralelogramo (pág. 720) Uno de los pares de lados paralelos de un paralelogramo.

base of a prism (p. 794) *See* prism.

base de un prisma (pág. 794) *Ver* prisma.

See prism.

Ver prisma.

base of a pyramid (p. 794) *See* pyramid.

base de una pirámide (pág. 794) *Ver* pirámide.

See pyramid.

Ver pirámide.

base of an isosceles triangle (p. 264) The noncongruent side of an isosceles triangle that has only two congruent sides.

base de un triángulo isósceles (pág. 264) El lado no congruente de un triángulo isósceles que tiene sólo dos lados congruentes.

See isosceles triangle.

Ver triángulo isósceles.

bases of a trapezoid (p. 542) The parallel sides of a trapezoid.

bases de un trapecio (pág. 542) Los lados paralelos de un trapecio.

See trapezoid.

Ver trapecio.

between (p. 10) When three points lie on a line, you can say that one point is *between* the other two.

entre (pág. 10) Cuando tres puntos están en una recta, se puede decir que un punto está *entre* los otros dos.

Point **B** is between points **A** and **C**.
El punto **B** está entre los puntos **A** y **C**.

---

biconditional statement (p. 82) A statement that contains the phrase "if and only if."

enunciado bicondicional (pág. 82) Enunciado que contiene la frase "si y sólo si".

Two lines are perpendicular if and only if they intersect to form a right angle.

Dos rectas son perpendiculares si y sólo si se cortan para formar un ángulo recto.

C

center of a circle (p. 651) *See* circle.

centro de un círculo (pág. 651) *Ver* círculo.

See circle.

Ver círculo.

---

center of a polygon (p. 762) The center of a polygon's circumscribed circle.

centro de un polígono (pág. 762) El centro del círculo circunscrito de un polígono.

---

center of a sphere (p. 838) *See* sphere.

centro de una esfera (pág. 838) *Ver* esfera.

See sphere.

Ver esfera.

---

center of dilation (p. 409) In a dilation, the fixed point about which the figure is enlarged or reduced.

centro de dilatación (pág. 409) En una dilatación, el punto fijo en torno al cual la figura se amplía o se reduce.

See dilation.

Ver dilatación.

---

center of rotation (p. 598) *See* rotation.

centro de rotación (pág. 598) *Ver* rotación.

See rotation.

Ver rotación.

---

center of symmetry (p. 620) *See* rotational symmetry.

centro de simetría (pág. 620) *Ver* simetría rotacional.

See rotational symmetry.

Ver simetría rotacional.

---

central angle of a circle (p. 659) An angle whose vertex is the center of the circle.

ángulo central de un círculo (pág. 659) Ángulo cuyo vértice es el centro del círculo.

∠**PCQ** is a central angle of ⊙**C**.
∠**PCQ** es un ángulo central de ⊙**C**.

central angle of a regular polygon (p. 762) An angle formed by two radii drawn to consecutive vertices of the polygon.

ángulo central de un polígono regular (pág. 762) Ángulo formado por dos radios trazados hasta los vértices consecutivos del polígono.

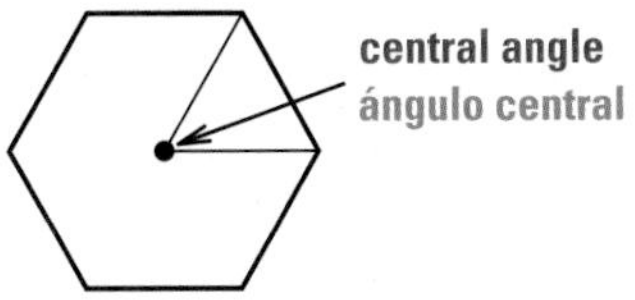

central angle
ángulo central

centroid of a triangle (p. 319) The point of concurrency of the three medians of the triangle.

baricentro de un triángulo (pág. 319) El punto de concurrencia de las tres medianas del triángulo.

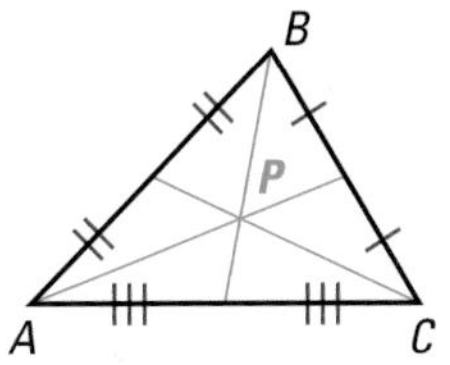

P is the centroid of △*ABC*.
P es el baricentro de △*ABC*.

chord of a circle (p. 651) A segment whose endpoints are on a circle.

cuerda de un círculo (pág. 651) Segmento cuyos extremos están en un círculo.

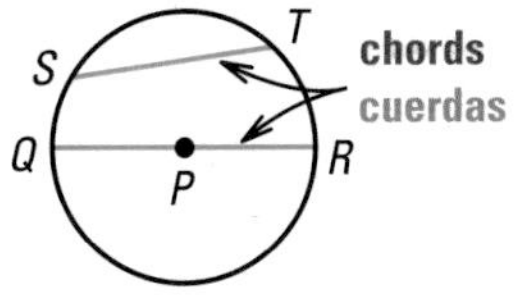

chords
cuerdas

chord of a sphere (p. 838) A segment whose endpoints are on a sphere.

cuerda de una esfera (pág. 838) Segmento cuyos extremos están en una esfera.

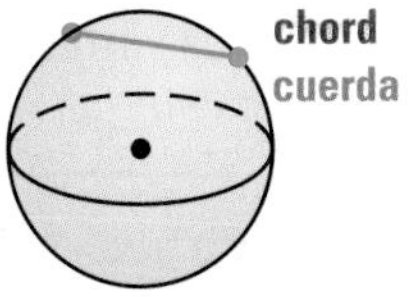

chord
cuerda

circle (p. 651) The set of all points in a plane that are equidistant from a given point called the center of the circle.

círculo (pág. 651) El conjunto de todos los puntos de un plano que son equidistantes de un punto dado, llamado centro del círculo.

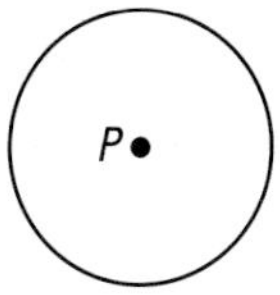

Circle with center *P*, or ⊙*P*
Círculo con centro *P*, o ⊙*P*

circumcenter of a triangle (p. 306) The point of concurrency of the three perpendicular bisectors of the triangle.

circuncentro de un triángulo (pág. 306) El punto de concurrencia de las tres mediatrices del triángulo.

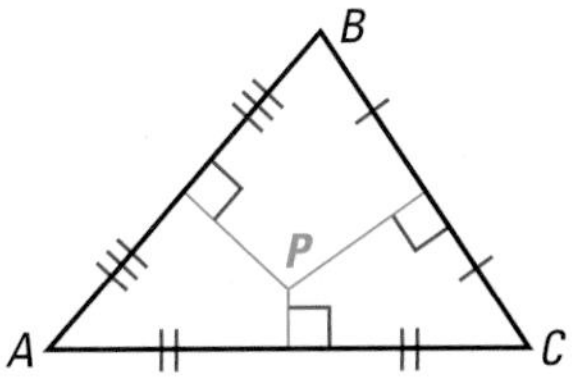

P is the circumcenter of △*ABC*.
P es el circuncentro de △*ABC*.

circumference (p. 746) The distance around a circle.

circunferencia (pág. 746) La distancia por el contorno de un círculo.

circumscribed circle (p. 674) The circle that contains the vertices of an inscribed polygon.

círculo circunscrito (pág. 674) El círculo que contiene los vértices de un polígono inscrito.

circumscribed circles
círculos circunscritos

collinear points (p. 2) Points that lie on the same line.

puntos colineales (pág. 2) Puntos situados sobre la misma recta.

A, *B*, and *C* are collinear.
A, *B* y *C* son colineales.

complementary angles (p. 35) Two angles whose measures have the sum 90°. The sum of the measures of an angle and its *complement* is 90°.

ángulos complementarios (pág. 35) Dos ángulos cuyas medidas suman 90°. La suma de las medidas de un ángulo y de su *complemento* es 90°.

component form of a vector (p. 574) The form of a vector that combines the horizontal and vertical components of the vector.

forma de componentes de un vector (pág. 574) La forma de un vector que combina los componentes horizontal y vertical del vector.

The component form of $\overrightarrow{PQ}$ is $\langle 4, 2 \rangle$.
La forma de componentes de $\overrightarrow{PQ}$ es $\langle 4, 2 \rangle$.

composition of transformations (p. 609) The result when two or more transformations are combined to produce a single transformation.

composición de transformaciones (pág. 609) El resultado de combinar dos o más transformaciones para producir una sola transformación.

A glide reflection is an example of a composition of transformations.

La reflexión con desplazamiento y traslación es un ejemplo de composición de transformaciones.

concave polygon (p. 42) A polygon that is not convex. *See also* convex polygon.

polígono cóncavo (pág. 42) Polígono que no es convexo. *Ver también* polígono convexo.

interior
interior

conclusion (p. 79) The "then" part of a conditional statement. **conclusión** (pág. 79) La parte de "entonces" de un enunciado condicional.	*See* conditional statement. *Ver* enunciado condicional.
concurrent (p. 305) Three or more lines, rays, or segments that intersect in the same point. **concurrentes** (pág. 305) Tres o más rectas, rayos o segmentos que se cortan en el mismo punto.	*See* point of concurrency. *Ver* punto de concurrencia.
conditional statement (p. 79) A type of logical statement that has two parts, a hypothesis and a conclusion. **enunciado condicional** (pág. 79) Tipo de enunciado lógico que tiene dos partes, una hipótesis y una conclusión.	conditional statement If $m\angle A = 90°$, then $\angle A$ is a right angle. Hypothesis Conclusion enunciado condicional Si $m\angle A = 90°$, entonces $\angle A$ es un ángulo recto. Hipótesis Conclusión
cone (p. 812) A solid that has one circular base and a vertex that is not in the same plane as the base. **cono** (pág. 812) Sólido que tiene una base circular y cuyo vértice no está en el mismo plano que la base.	vertex vértice height altura h base base r
congruence transformation (p. 272) A transformation that preserves length and angle measure. Also called *isometry*. **transformación de congruencia** (pág. 272) Transformación que conserva la longitud y la medida de los ángulos. También se llama *isometría*.	Translations, reflections, and rotations are three types of congruence transformations. Las traslaciones, las reflexiones y las rotaciones son tres tipos de transformaciones de congruencia.
congruent angles (p. 26) Angles that have the same measure. **ángulos congruentes** (pág. 26) Ángulos que tienen la misma medida.	A B $\angle A \cong \angle B$
congruent arcs (p. 660) Two arcs that have the same measure and are arcs of the same circle or of congruent circles. **arcos congruentes** (pág. 660) Dos arcos que tienen la misma medida y son arcos del mismo círculo o de círculos congruentes.	D E $80°$ $80°$ C F $\overset{\frown}{CD} \cong \overset{\frown}{EF}$

congruent circles (p. 660) Two circles that have the same radius.

círculos congruentes (pág. 660) Dos círculos que tienen el mismo radio.

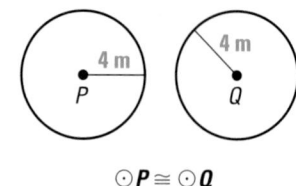

$\odot P \cong \odot Q$

congruent figures (p. 225) Two geometric figures that have exactly the same size and shape. When two figures are congruent, all pairs of corresponding sides and corresponding angles are congruent.

figuras congruentes (pág. 225) Dos figuras geométricas de igual tamaño y forma. Cuando dos figuras son congruentes, todos los pares de lados correspondientes y de ángulos correspondientes son congruentes.

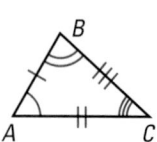

$\triangle ABC \cong \triangle FED$
$\angle A \cong \angle F, \angle B \cong \angle E,$
$\angle C \cong \angle D$
$\overline{AB} \cong \overline{FE}, \overline{BC} \cong \overline{ED},$
$\overline{AC} \cong \overline{FD}$

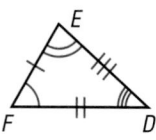

congruent segments (p. 11) Line segments that have the same length.

segmentos congruentes (pág. 11) Segmentos de recta que tienen la misma longitud.

$\overline{AB} \cong \overline{CD}$

conjecture (p. 73) An unproven statement that is based on observations.

conjetura (pág. 73) Enunciado sin demostrar que se basa en observaciones.

Conjecture: All prime numbers are odd.

Conjetura: Todos los números primos son impares.

consecutive interior angles (p. 149) Two angles that are formed by two lines and a transversal and lie between the two lines and on the same side of the transversal. Also called *same-side interior angles.*

ángulos internos consecutivos (pág. 149 Dos ángulos formados por dos rectas y una transversal y que se encuentran entre las dos rectas en el mismo lado de la transversal. También se llaman *ángulos internos colaterales.*

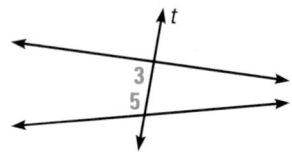

∠3 and ∠5 are consecutive interior angles.
∠3 y ∠5 son ángulos internos consecutivos.

construction (p. 33) A geometric drawing that uses a limited set of tools, usually a compass and straightedge.

construcción (pág. 33) Dibujo geométrico que requiere una serie limitada de instrumentos, que por lo general son un compás y una regla.

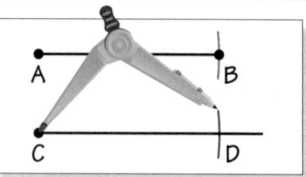

contrapositive (p. 80) The equivalent statement formed by negating the hypothesis and conclusion of the converse of a conditional statement. **contrapositivo** (pág. 80) El enunciado equivalente formado al negar la hipótesis y la conclusión del recíproco de un enunciado condicional.	**Statement:** If $m\angle A = 90°$, then $\angle A$ is right. **Contrapositive:** If $\angle A$ is not right, then $m\angle A \neq 90°$. **Enunciado:** Si $m\angle A = 90°$, entonces $\angle A$ es recto. **Contrapositivo:** Si $\angle A$ no es recto, entonces $m\angle A \neq 90°$.
converse (p. 80) The statement formed by exchanging the hypothesis and conclusion of a conditional statement. **recíproco** (pág. 80) El enunciado formado al intercambiar la hipótesis y la conclusión de un enunciado condicional.	**Statement:** If $m\angle A = 90°$, then $\angle A$ is right. **Converse:** If $\angle A$ is right, then $m\angle A = 90°$. **Enunciado:** Si $m\angle A = 90°$, entonces $\angle A$ es recto. **Recíproco:** Si $\angle A$ es recto, entonces $m\angle A = 90°$.
convex polygon (p. 42) A polygon such that no line containing a side of the polygon contains a point in the interior of the polygon. A polygon that is not convex is nonconvex or concave. **polígono convexo** (pág. 42) Polígono tal que ninguna recta que contiene un lado del polígono contiene un punto del interior del polígono. Un polígono que no es convexo se conoce como no convexo o cóncavo.	 interior interior
convex polyhedron (p. 796) A polyhedron is convex if any two points on its surface can be connected by a segment that lies entirely inside or on the polyhedron. If this segment goes outside the polyhedron, then the polyhedron is nonconvex or concave. **poliedro convexo** (pág. 796) Un poliedro es convexo si dos puntos cualesquiera de su superficie pueden unirse mediante un segmento situado totalmente sobre el poliedro o en su interior. Si el segmento se extiende al exterior del poliedro, entonces es un poliedro cóncavo o no convexo.	 **convex** **concave** convexo cóncavo
coordinate (p. 9) The real number that corresponds to a point on a line. **coordenada** (pág. 9) El número real que corresponde a un punto de una recta.	 **coordinates of points** coordenadas de puntos
coordinate proof (p. 296) A type of proof that involves placing geometric figures in a coordinate plane. **prueba de coordenadas** (pág. 296) Tipo de prueba en la que se colocan figuras geométricas en un plano de coordenadas.	*See* **Example 5 on page 297.** *Ver* **el ejemplo 5 de la página 297.**

coplanar points (p. 2) Points that lie in the same plane. **puntos coplanarios** (pág. 2) Puntos situados sobre el mismo plano.	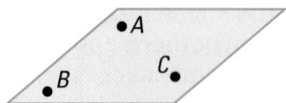 **A, B**, and **C** are coplanar. **A, B** y **C** son coplanarios.
corollary to a theorem (p. 220) A statement that can be proved easily using the theorem. **corolario de un teorema** (pág. 220) Enunciado que puede demostrarse fácilmente usando el teorema.	The Corollary to the Triangle Sum Theorem states that the acute angles of a right triangle are complementary. El corolario del teorema de la suma de los ángulos del triángulo establece que los ángulos agudos de un triángulo rectángulo son complementarios.
corresponding angles (p. 149) Two angles that are formed by two lines and a transversal and occupy corresponding positions. **ángulos correspondientes** (pág. 149) Dos ángulos formados por dos rectas y una transversal y que ocupan posiciones correspondientes.	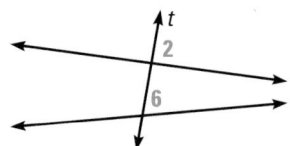 ∠**2** and ∠**6** are corresponding angles. ∠**2** y ∠**6** son ángulos correspondientes.
corresponding parts (p. 225) A pair of sides or angles that have the same relative position in two congruent or similar figures. **partes correspondientes** (pág. 225) Un par de lados o ángulos que tienen la misma posición relativa en dos figuras congruentes o semejantes.	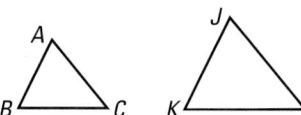 ∠**A** and ∠**J** are corresponding angles. $\overline{AB}$ and $\overline{JK}$ are corresponding sides. ∠**A** y ∠**J** son ángulos correspondientes. $\overline{AB}$ y $\overline{JK}$ son lados correspondientes.
cosine (p. 473) A trigonometric ratio, abbreviated as *cos*. For a right triangle *ABC*, the cosine of the acute angle *A* is $\cos A = \dfrac{\text{length of leg adjacent to } \angle A}{\text{length of hypotenuse}} = \dfrac{AC}{AB}.$ **coseno** (pág. 473) Razón trigonométrica, abreviada *cos*. Para un triángulo rectángulo *ABC*, el coseno del ángulo agudo *A* es $\cos A = \dfrac{\text{longitud del cateto adyacente a } \angle A}{\text{longitud de la hipotenusa}} = \dfrac{AC}{AB}.$	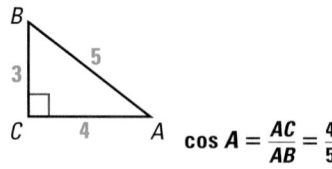 $\cos A = \dfrac{AC}{AB} = \dfrac{4}{5}$

counterexample (p. 74) A specific case that shows a conjecture is false.

contraejemplo (pág. 74) Caso específico que muestra la falsedad de una conjetura.

Conjecture: All prime numbers are odd.
Counterexample: 2, a prime number that is not odd

Conjetura: Todos los números primos son impares.
Contraejemplo: 2, un número primo que no es impar

---

cross section (p. 797) The intersection of a plane and a solid.

sección transversal (pág. 797) La intersección de un plano y un sólido.

plane
plano

cross section
sección transversal

---

cube (p. 796) A polyhedron with six congruent square faces.

cubo (pág. 796) Poliedro con seis caras cuadradas congruentes.

---

cylinder (p. 805) A solid with congruent circular bases that lie in parallel planes.

cilindro (pág. 805) Sólido con bases circulares congruentes que se encuentran en planos paralelos.

base
base

base
base

D

decagon (p. 43) A polygon with ten sides.

decágono (pág. 43) Polígono con diez lados.

---

deductive reasoning (p. 87) A process that uses facts, definitions, accepted properties, and the laws of logic to form a logical argument.

razonamiento deductivo (pág. 87) Proceso que usa datos, definiciones, propiedades aceptadas y las leyes de la lógica para formar un argumento lógico.

You use deductive reasoning in writing geometric proofs.

Puedes usar el razonamiento deductivo para escribir pruebas geométricas.

---

defined terms (p. 3) Terms that can be described using known words.

términos definidos (pág. 3) Términos que pueden describirse con palabras conocidas.

Line segment and *ray* are two defined terms.

Segmento de recta y *rayo* son dos términos definidos.

diagonal of a polygon (p. 507) A segment that joins two nonconsecutive vertices of a polygon.

diagonal de un polígono (pág. 507) Segmento que une dos vértices no consecutivos de un polígono.

diameter of a circle (p. 651) A chord that passes through the center of a circle. The distance across a circle through its center.

diámetro de un círculo (pág. 651) Cuerda que pasa por el centro de un círculo. La distancia de un punto a otro de un círculo pasando por el centro.

diameter of a sphere (p. 838) A chord that contains the center of a sphere. The distance across a sphere through its center.

diámetro de una esfera (pág. 838) Cuerda que contiene el centro de una esfera. La distancia de un punto a otro de una esfera pasando por el centro.

dilation (pp. 409, 626) A transformation that stretches or shrinks a figure to create a similar figure.

dilatación (págs. 409, 626) Transformación que expande o contrae una figura para crear una figura semejante.

Scale factor of dilation is $\frac{XY}{AB}$.

El factor de escala de la dilatación es $\frac{XY}{AB}$.

center of dilation
centro de dilatación

dimensions of a matrix (p. 580) The numbers of rows and columns in the matrix. If a matrix has m rows and n columns, the dimensions of the matrix are $m \times n$.

dimensiones de una matriz (pág. 580) El número de filas y columnas que hay en una matriz. Si la matriz tiene m filas y n columnas, sus dimensiones son $m \times n$.

The dimensions of a matrix with 3 rows and 4 columns is 3×4 ("3 by 4").

Las dimensiones de una matriz con 3 filas y 4 columnas son 3×4 ("3 por 4").

distance between two points on a line (p. 9) The absolute value of the difference of the coordinates of the points. The distance between points A and B, written as AB, is also called the length of $\overline{AB}$.

distancia entre dos puntos de una recta (pág. 9) El valor absoluto de la diferencia entre las coordenadas de los puntos. La distancia entre los puntos A y B, escrita AB, también se llama longitud de $\overline{AB}$.

distance from a point to a line (p. 192) The length of the perpendicular segment from the point to the line.

distancia de un punto a una recta (pág. 192) La longitud del segmento perpendicular del punto a la recta.

The distance from *Q* to *m* is *QP*.
La distancia de *Q* a *m* es *QP*.

dodecagon (p. 43) A polygon with twelve sides.

dodecágono (pág. 43) Polígono con doce lados.

dodecahedron (p. 796) A polyhedron with twelve faces.

dodecaedro (pág. 796) Poliedro con doce caras.

E

edge of a polyhedron (p. 794) A line segment formed by the intersection of two faces of a polyhedron.

arista de un poliedro (pág. 794) Segmento de recta formado por la intersección de dos caras de un poliedro.

edge
arista

element of a matrix (p. 580) A number in a matrix. Also called *entry*.

elemento de una matriz (pág. 580) Número de una matriz. También se llama *entrada*.

See matrix.

Ver matriz.

endpoints (p. 3) *See* line segment.

extremos (pág. 3) *Ver* segmento de recta.

See line segment.

Ver segmento de recta.

enlargement (p. 409) A dilation with a scale factor greater than 1.

ampliación (pág. 409) Dilatación con un factor de escala mayor que 1.

A dilation with a scale factor of 2 is an enlargement.

Una dilatación con un factor de escala de 2 es una ampliación.

equiangular polygon (p. 43) A polygon with all of its interior angles congruent.

polígono equiángulo (pág. 43) Polígono que tiene todos los ángulos interiores congruentes.

equiangular triangle (p. 217) A triangle with three congruent angles.

triángulo equiángulo (pág. 217) Triángulo que tiene los tres ángulos congruentes.

equidistant (p. 303) The same distance from one figure as from another figure.

equidistante (pág. 303) Situado a igual distancia de dos figuras.

X is equidistant from *Y* and *Z*.
X es equidistante de *Y* y *Z*.

equilateral polygon (p. 43) A polygon with all of its sides congruent.

polígono equilátero (pág. 43) Polígono que tiene todos los lados congruentes.

equilateral triangle (p. 217) A triangle with three congruent sides.

triángulo equilátero (pág. 217) Triángulo que tiene los tres lados congruentes.

equivalent statements (p. 80) Two statements that are both true or both false.

enunciados equivalentes (pág. 80) Dos enunciados que son ambos verdaderos o ambos falsos.

A conditional statement and its contrapositive are equivalent statements.

Un enunciado condicional y su contrapositivo son enunciados equivalentes.

exterior angles of a triangle (p. 218) When the sides of a triangle are extended, the angles that are adjacent to the interior angles.

ángulos exteriores de un triángulo (pág. 218) Los ángulos adyacentes a los ángulos interiores al prolongar los lados del triángulo.

external segment (p. 690) The part of a secant segment that is outside the circle.

segmento externo (pág. 690) La parte de un segmento secante que está en el exterior del círculo.

external segment
segmento externo

extremes of a proportion (p. 358) The first and last terms of a proportion. *See also* proportion.

extremos de una proporción (pág. 358) Los términos primero y último de una proporción. *Ver también* proporción.

The extremes of $\frac{a}{b} = \frac{c}{d}$ are a and d.

Los extremos de $\frac{a}{b} = \frac{c}{d}$ son a y d.

face of a polyhedron (p. 794) *See* polyhedron.

cara de un poliedro (pág. 794) *Ver* poliedro.

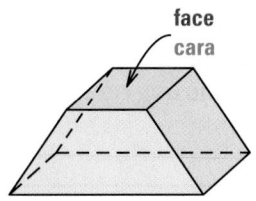

face
cara

---

flow proof (p. 250) A type of proof that uses arrows to show the flow of a logical argument.

prueba de flujo (pág. 250) Tipo de prueba que usa flechas para indicar el flujo de un argumento lógico.

See Example 2 on page 250.

Ver el ejemplo 2 de la página 250.

---

fractal (p. 406) An object that is self-similar. *See* self-similar.

fractal (pág. 406) Objeto autosemejante. *Ver* autosemejante.

---

geometric mean (p. 359) For two positive numbers a and b, the positive number x that satisfies $\frac{a}{x} = \frac{x}{b}$. So, $x^2 = ab$ and $x = \sqrt{ab}$.

media geométrica (pág. 359) Para dos números positivos a y b, el número positivo x que satisface $\frac{a}{x} = \frac{x}{b}$. Así pues, $x^2 = ab$ y $x = \sqrt{ab}$.

The geometric mean of 4 and 16 is $\sqrt{4 \cdot 16}$, or 8.

La media geométrica de 4 y 16 es $\sqrt{4 \cdot 16}$, ó 8.

---

geometric probability (p. 771) A probability that involves a geometric measure such as length or area.

probabilidad geométrica (pág. 771) Probabilidad relacionada con una medida geométrica, como la longitud o el área.

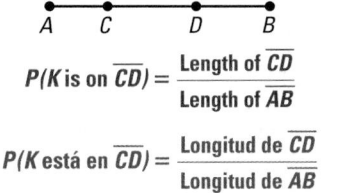

$$P(K \text{ is on } \overline{CD}) = \frac{\text{Length of } \overline{CD}}{\text{Length of } \overline{AB}}$$

$$P(K \text{ está en } \overline{CD}) = \frac{\text{Longitud de } \overline{CD}}{\text{Longitud de } \overline{AB}}$$

---

glide reflection (p. 608) A transformation in which every point P is mapped to a point P'' by the following steps. (1) A translation maps P to P'. (2) A reflection in a line k parallel to the direction of the translation maps P' to P''.

reflexión con desplazamiento y traslación (pág. 608) Transformación en la que cada punto P se hace corresponder con un punto P'' siguiendo estos pasos. (1) Al realizar una traslación, se hace corresponder P con P'. (2) Al realizar una reflexión sobre una recta k paralela a la dirección de la traslación, se hace corresponder P' con P''.

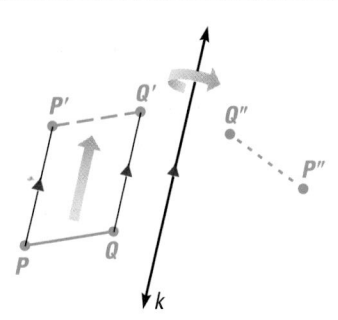

ENGLISH-SPANISH GLOSSARY

great circle (pp. 753, 839) The intersection of a sphere and a plane that contains the center of the sphere.

círculo máximo (págs. 753, 839) La intersección de una esfera y un plano que contiene el centro de la esfera.

great circle
círculo máximo

---

greatest possible error (p. 727) The maximum amount that a measured length can differ from an actual length.

máximo error posible (pág. 727) La cantidad máxima que una longitud medida puede diferir de una longitud real.

If the unit of measure is $\frac{1}{8}$ inch, the greatest possible error is $\frac{1}{16}$ inch.

Si la unidad de medida es $\frac{1}{8}$ pulgada, el máximo error posible es $\frac{1}{16}$ pulgada.

H

height of a parallelogram (p. 720) The perpendicular distance between the bases of a parallelogram.

altura de un paralelogramo (pág. 720) La distancia perpendicular entre las bases de un paralelogramo.

height
altura

---

height of a trapezoid (p. 730) The perpendicular distance between the bases of a trapezoid.

altura de un trapecio (pág. 730) La distancia perpendicular entre las bases de un trapecio.

base
base

height
altura

base
base

---

hemisphere (p. 839) Half of a sphere, formed when a great circle separates a sphere into two congruent halves.

hemisferio (pág. 839) Media esfera, formada cuando un círculo máximo divide a una esfera en dos mitades congruentes.

hemispheres
hemisferios

---

heptagon (p. 43) Polygon with seven sides.

heptágono (pág. 43) Polígono con siete lados.

---

hexagon (p. 43) Polygon with six sides.

hexágono (pág. 43) Polígono con seis lados.

---

horizontal component of a vector (p. 574) The horizontal change from the initial point to the terminal point of a vector.

componente horizontal de un vector (pág. 574) El cambio horizontal desde el punto inicial al punto final del vector.

See component form of a vector.

Ver forma de componentes de un vector.

hypotenuse (p. 241) In a right triangle, the side opposite the right angle.

hipotenusa (pág. 241) En un triángulo rectángulo, el lado opuesto al ángulo recto.

hypotenuse
hipotenusa

---

hypothesis (p. 79) The "if" part of a conditional statement.

hipótesis (pág. 79) La parte de "si" de un enunciado condicional.

See conditional statement.

Ver enunciado condicional.

I

icosahedron (p. 796) A polyhedron with twenty faces.

icosaedro (pág. 796) Poliedro con veinte caras.

---

if-then form (p. 79) The form of a conditional statement that uses the words "if" and "then." The "if" part contains the hypothesis and the "then" part contains the conclusion.

forma de "si..., entonces..." (pág. 79) La forma de un enunciado condicional que usa las palabras "si" y "entonces". La parte de "si" contiene la hipótesis, y la parte de "entonces" contiene la conclusión.

See conditional statement.

Ver enunciado condicional.

---

image (pp. 272, 572) The new figure that is produced in a transformation. *See also* preimage.

imagen (págs. 272, 572) La nueva figura que resulta tras una transformación. *Ver también* preimagen.

$\triangle P'Q'R'$ is the image of $\triangle PQR$ after a translation.
$\triangle P'Q'R'$ es la imagen de $\triangle PQR$ tras una traslación.

---

incenter of a triangle (p. 312) The point of concurrency of the three angle bisectors of the triangle.

incentro de un triángulo (pág. 312) El punto de concurrencia de las tres bisectrices de los ángulos del triángulo.

P is the incenter of $\triangle ABC$.
P es el incentro de $\triangle ABC$.

indirect proof (p. 337) A proof in which you prove that a statement is true by first assuming that its opposite is true. If this assumption leads to an impossibility, then you have proved that the original statement is true.	*See* Example 4 on page 338.
prueba indirecta (pág. 337) Prueba en la que, para demostrar que un enunciado es verdadero, primero se supone que su opuesto es verdadero. Si esta suposición lleva a una imposibilidad, entonces se habrá demostrado que el enunciado original es verdadero.	*Ver* el ejemplo 4 de la página 338.
inductive reasoning (p. 73) A process that includes looking for patterns and making conjectures.	**Given the number pattern 1, 5, 9, 13, …, you can use inductive reasoning to determine that the next number in the pattern is 17.**
razonamiento inductivo (pág. 73) Proceso en el que se buscan patrones y se hacen conjeturas.	**Dado el patrón numérico 1, 5, 9, 13, …, puedes utilizar el razonamiento inductivo para determinar que el número siguiente del patrón es 17.**
initial point of a vector (p. 574) The starting point of a vector.	*See* vector.
punto inicial de un vector (pág. 574) El punto de partida del vector.	*Ver* vector.
inscribed angle (p. 672) An angle whose vertex is on a circle and whose sides contain chords of the circle. **ángulo inscrito** (pág. 672) Ángulo cuyo vértice está en un círculo y cuyos lados contienen cuerdas del círculo.	inscribed angle / ángulo inscrito — intercepted arc / arco interceptado
inscribed polygon (p. 674) A polygon whose vertices all lie on a circle. **polígono inscrito** (pág. 674) Polígono que tiene todos los vértices en un círculo.	inscribed triangle / triángulo inscrito — inscribed quadrilateral / cuadrilátero inscrito
intercepted arc (p. 672) The arc that lies in the interior of an inscribed angle and has endpoints on the angle.	*See* inscribed angle.
arco interceptado (pág. 672) El arco situado en el interior de un ángulo inscrito y que tiene los extremos en el ángulo.	*Ver* ángulo inscrito.

interior angles of a triangle (p. 218) When the sides of a triangle are extended, the three original angles of the triangle.

ángulos interiores de un triángulo (pág. 218) Los tres ángulos originales de un triangulo al prolongar los lados del triángulo.

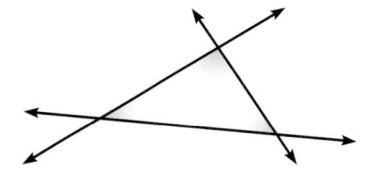

intersection (p. 4) The set of points that two or more geometric figures have in common.

intersección (pág. 4) El conjunto de puntos que dos o más figuras geométricas tienen en común.

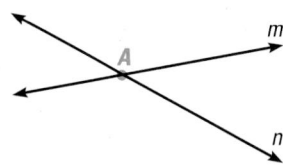

The intersection of lines *m* and *n* is point *A*.

La intersección de las rectas *m* y *n* es el punto *A*.

inverse (p. 80) The statement formed by negating the hypothesis and conclusion of a conditional statement.

inverso (pág. 80) El enunciado formado al negar la hipótesis y la conclusión de un enunciado condicional.

Statement: If $m\angle A = 90°$, then $\angle A$ is right.
Inverse: If $m\angle A \neq 90°$, then $\angle A$ is not right.

Enunciado: Si $m\angle A = 90°$, entonces $\angle A$ es recto.
Inverso: Si $m\angle A \neq 90°$, entonces $\angle A$ no es recto.

inverse cosine (p. 483) An inverse trigonometric ratio, abbreviated as cos^{-1}. For acute angle A, if $\cos A = z$, then $\cos^{-1} z = m\angle A$.

coseno inverso (pág. 483) Razón trigonométrica inversa, abreviada cos^{-1}. Para el ángulo agudo A, si $\cos A = z$, entonces $\cos^{-1} z = m\angle A$.

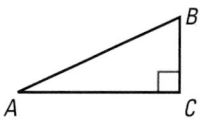

$$\cos^{-1}\frac{AC}{AB} = m\angle A$$

inverse sine (p. 483) An inverse trigonometric ratio, abbreviated as sin^{-1}. For acute angle A, if $\sin A = y$, then $\sin^{-1} y = m\angle A$.

seno inverso (pág. 483) Razón trigonométrica inversa, abreviada sen^{-1}. Para el ángulo agudo A, si $sen\ A = y$, entonces $sen^{-1} y = m\angle A$.

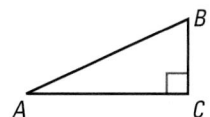

$$\sin^{-1}\frac{BC}{AB} = m\angle A$$
$$sen^{-1}\frac{BC}{AB} = m\angle A$$

inverse tangent (p. 483) An inverse trigonometric ratio, abbreviated as tan^{-1}. For acute angle A, if $\tan A = x$, then $\tan^{-1} x = m\angle A$.

tangente inversa (pág. 483) Razón trigonométrica inversa, abreviada tan^{-1}. Para el ángulo agudo A, si $\tan A = x$, entonces $\tan^{-1} x = m\angle A$.

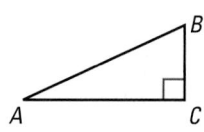

$$\tan^{-1}\frac{BC}{AC} = m\angle A$$

isometric drawing (p. 550) A technical drawing that looks three-dimensional and can be created on a grid of dots using three axes that intersect to form 120° angles.

dibujo isométrico (pág. 550) Dibujo técnico de aspecto tridimensional; puede crearse en una cuadrícula de puntos usando tres ejes que al cortarse forman ángulos de 120°.

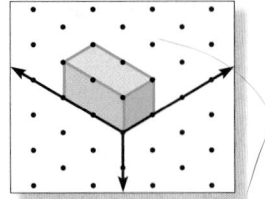

isometry (p. 573) A transformation that preserves length and angle measure. Also called *congruence transformation*.

isometría (pág. 573) Transformación que conserva la longitud y la medida de los ángulos. También se llama *transformación de congruencia*.

Translations, reflections, and rotations are three types of isometries.

Las traslaciones, las reflexiones y las rotaciones son tres tipos de isometrías.

isosceles trapezoid (p. 543) A trapezoid with congruent legs.

trapecio isósceles (pág. 543) Trapecio que tiene los catetos congruentes.

isosceles triangle (p. 217) A triangle with at least two congruent sides.

triángulo isósceles (pág. 217) Triángulo que tiene al menos dos lados congruentes.

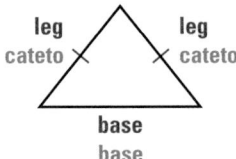

iteration (p. 406) A repetition of a sequence of steps.

iteración (pág. 406) Repetición de una secuencia de pasos.

Fractals are created using iterations.

Los fractales se crean usando iteraciones.

kite (p. 545) A quadrilateral that has two pairs of consecutive congruent sides, but in which opposite sides are not congruent.

cometa (pág. 545) Cuadrilátero que tiene dos pares de lados congruentes consecutivos pero cuyos lados opuestos no son congruentes.

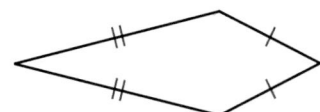

lateral area (p. 803) The sum of the areas of the lateral faces of a polyhedron or other solid with one or two bases.

área lateral (pág. 803) La suma de las áreas de las caras laterales de un poliedro o de otro sólido con una o dos bases.

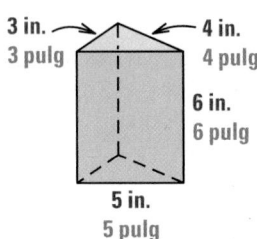

3 in.
3 pulg
4 in.
4 pulg
6 in.
6 pulg
5 in.
5 pulg

Lateral area = 5(6) + 4(6) + 3(6) = 72 in.^{2}

Área lateral = 5(6) + 4(6) + 3(6) = 72 pulg^2

lateral edges of a prism (p. 803) The segments connecting the corresponding vertices of the bases of a prism.

aristas laterales de un prisma (pág. 803) Los segmentos que unen los vértices correspondientes de las bases de un prisma.

---

lateral faces of a prism (p. 803) The faces of a prism that are parallelograms formed by connecting the corresponding vertices of the bases of the prism.

caras laterales de un prisma (pág. 803) Las caras de un prisma que son paralelogramos formados al unir los vértices correspondientes de las bases del prisma.

See lateral edges of a prism.

Ver aristas laterales de un prisma.

---

lateral surface of a cone (p. 812) Consists of all segments that connect the vertex with points on the edge of the base.

superficie lateral de un cono (pág. 812) Todos los segmentos que unen el vértice con los puntos de la arista de la base.

---

legs of a right triangle (p. 241) In a right triangle, the sides adjacent to the right angle.

catetos de un triángulo rectángulo (pág. 241) En un triángulo rectángulo, los lados adyacentes al ángulo recto.

---

legs of a trapezoid (p. 542) The nonparallel sides of a trapezoid.

catetos de un trapecio (pág. 542) Los lados no paralelos de un trapecio.

See trapezoid.

Ver trapecio.

---

legs of an isosceles triangle (p. 264) The two congruent sides of an isosceles triangle that has only two congruent sides.

catetos de un triángulo isósceles (pág. 264) Los dos lados congruentes de un triángulo isósceles que tiene sólo dos lados congruentes.

See isosceles triangle.

Ver triángulo isósceles.

line (p. 2) A line has one dimension. It is usually represented by a straight line with two arrowheads to indicate that the line extends without end in two directions. In this book, lines are always straight lines. *See also* undefined term.

recta (pág. 2) Una recta tiene una dimensión. Normalmente se representa por una línea recta con dos puntas de flecha para así indicar que la recta se prolonga sin fin en dos direcciones. En este texto las líneas son siempre líneas rectas. *Ver también* término indefinido.

line ℓ, $\overleftrightarrow{AB}$, or $\overleftrightarrow{BA}$
recta ℓ, $\overleftrightarrow{AB}$ o $\overleftrightarrow{BA}$

---

line of reflection (p. 589) *See* reflection.

eje de reflexión (pág. 589) *Ver* reflexión.

See reflection.

Ver reflexión.

---

line of symmetry (p. 619) *See* line symmetry.

eje de simetría (pág. 619) *Ver* simetría lineal.

See line symmetry.

Ver simetría lineal.

---

line perpendicular to a plane (p. 98) A line that intersects the plane in a point and is perpendicular to every line in the plane that intersects it at that point.

recta perpendicular a un plano (pág. 98) Recta que corta al plano en un punto y es perpendicular a cada recta del plano que la corta en ese punto.

Line *n* is perpendicular to plane *P*.

La recta *n* es perpendicular al plano *P*.

---

line segment (p. 3) Part of a line that consists of two points, called endpoints, and all points on the line that are between the endpoints. Also called *segment*.

segmento de recta (pág. 3) Parte de una recta que consta de dos puntos, llamados extremos, y de todos los puntos de la recta situados entre los extremos. También se llama *segmento*.

$\overline{AB}$ with endpoints *A* and *B*
$\overline{AB}$ con extremos *A* y *B*

---

line symmetry (p. 619) A figure in the plane has line symmetry if the figure can be mapped onto itself by a reflection in a line. This line of reflection is a line of symmetry.

simetría lineal (pág. 619) Una figura del plano tiene simetría lineal si se corresponde a sí misma al realizar una reflexión sobre una recta. Este eje de reflexión es un eje de simetría.

Two lines of symmetry
Dos ejes de simetría

linear pair (p. 37) Two adjacent angles whose noncommon sides are opposite rays.

par lineal (pág. 37) Dos ángulos adyacentes cuyos lados no comunes son rayos opuestos.

∠3 and ∠4 are a linear pair.

∠3 y ∠4 son un par lineal.

---

locus in a plane (p. 697) The set of all points in a plane that satisfy a given condition or set of given conditions. Plural is *loci*.

lugar geométrico de un plano (pág. 697) El conjunto de todos los puntos de un plano que satisfacen una condición dada o un conjunto de condiciones dadas.

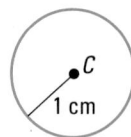

⊙ *C* is the locus of points that are 1 centimeter from point *C*.

⊙ *C* es el lugar geométrico de los puntos situados a 1 centímetro del punto *C*.

---

major arc (p. 659) Part of a circle that measures between 180° and 360°.

arco mayor (pág. 659) Parte de un círculo que mide entre 180° y 360°.

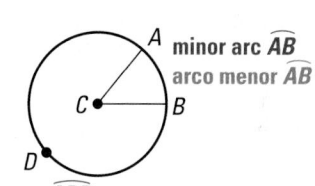

minor arc $\overset{\frown}{AB}$
arco menor $\overset{\frown}{AB}$

major arc $\overset{\frown}{ADB}$
arco mayor $\overset{\frown}{ADB}$

---

matrix (p. 580) A rectangular arrangement of numbers in rows and columns. Plural is *matrices*.

matriz (pág. 580) Disposición rectangular de números colocados en filas y columnas. El plural es *matrices*.

column
columna

$$\text{row} \atop \text{fila} \begin{bmatrix} 5 & 4 & 4 & 9 \\ -3 & 5 & 2 & 6 \\ 3 & -7 & 8 & 7 \end{bmatrix}$$

The element in the second row and third column is 2.

El elemento situado en la segunda fila y la tercera columna es 2.

---

means of a proportion (p. 358) The middle terms of a proportion. *See also* proportion.

medios de una proporción (pág. 358) Los términos centrales de una proporción. *Ver también* proporción.

The means of $\frac{a}{b} = \frac{c}{d}$ are b and c.

Los medios de $\frac{a}{b} = \frac{c}{d}$ son b y c.

---

measure of a major arc (p. 659) The difference between 360° and the measure of the related minor arc.

medida de un arco mayor (pág. 659) La diferencia entre 360° y la medida del arco menor relacionado.

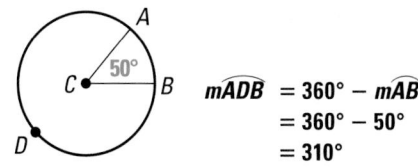

$m\overset{\frown}{ADB} = 360° - m\overset{\frown}{AB}$
$= 360° - 50°$
$= 310°$

measure of a minor arc (p. 659) The measure of the arc's central angle.

medida de un arco menor (pág. 659) La medida del ángulo central del arco.

See **measure of a major arc.**

Ver **medida de un arco mayor.**

---

measure of an angle (p. 24) Consider $\overleftrightarrow{OB}$ and a point A on one side of $\overleftrightarrow{OB}$. The rays of the form $\overrightarrow{OA}$ can be matched one to one with the real numbers from 0 to 180. The measure of $\angle AOB$ is equal to the absolute value of the difference between the real numbers for $\overrightarrow{OA}$ and $\overrightarrow{OB}$.

medida de un ángulo (pág. 24) Considera $\overleftrightarrow{OB}$ y un punto A situado sobre un lado de $\overleftrightarrow{OB}$. Los rayos de la forma $\overrightarrow{OA}$ pueden hacerse corresponder de uno en uno con los números reales de 0 a 180. La medida de $\angle AOB$ es igual al valor absoluto de la diferencia entre los números reales correspondientes a $\overrightarrow{OA}$ y a $\overrightarrow{OB}$.

$m\angle AOB = 140°$

---

median of a triangle (p. 319) A segment from one vertex of the triangle to the midpoint of the opposite side.

mediana de un triángulo (pág. 319) Segmento que va desde uno de los vértices del triángulo hasta el punto medio del lado opuesto.

$\overline{BD}$ is a median of $\triangle ABC$.

$\overline{BD}$ es una mediana de $\triangle ABC$.

---

midpoint (p. 15) A point that divides, or bisects, a segment into two congruent segments.

punto medio (pág. 15) Punto que divide, o biseca, a un segmento separándolo en dos segmentos congruentes.

M is the midpoint of $\overline{AB}$.

M es el punto medio de $\overline{AB}$.

---

midsegment of a trapezoid (p. 544) A segment that connects the midpoints of the legs of a trapezoid.

paralela media de un trapecio (pág. 544) Segmento que une los puntos medios de los catetos del trapecio.

---

midsegment of a triangle (p. 295) A segment that connects the midpoints of two sides of the triangle.

paralela media de un triángulo (pág. 295) Segmento que une los puntos medios de dos lados del triángulo.

The midsegments of $\triangle ABC$ are $\overline{MP}$, $\overline{MN}$, and $\overline{NP}$.

Las paralelas medias de $\triangle ABC$ son $\overline{MP}$, $\overline{MN}$ y $\overline{NP}$.

---

minor arc (p. 659) Part of a circle that measures less than 180°.

arco menor (pág. 659) Parte de un círculo que mide menos de 180°.

See **major arc.**

Ver **arco mayor.**

negation (p. 79) The opposite of a statement. The symbol for negation is ~.

negación (pág. 79) El opuesto de un enunciado. El símbolo de la negación es ~.

Statement: The ball is red.
Negation: The ball is not red.

Enunciado: La pelota es roja.
Negación: La pelota no es roja.

---

net (p. 803) The two-dimensional representation of the faces of a polyhedron.

patrón (pág. 803) La representación bidimensional de las caras de un poliedro.

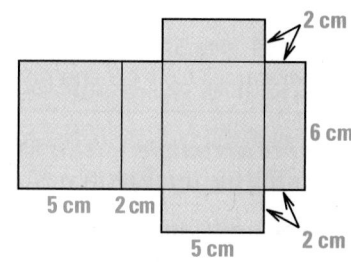

***n*-gon** (p. 43) A polygon with *n* sides.

***n*-gono** (pág. 43) Polígono con *n* lados.

A polygon with 14 sides is a 14-gon.

Un polígono con 14 lados es un 14-gono.

---

nonagon (p. 43) A polygon with nine sides.

nonágono (pág. 43) Polígono con nueve lados.

---

oblique prism (p. 804) A prism with lateral edges that are not perpendicular to the bases.

prisma oblicuo (pág. 804) Prisma con aristas laterales que no son perpendiculares a las bases.

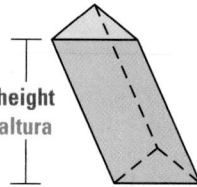

height
altura

---

obtuse angle (p. 25) An angle with measure between 90° and 180°.

ángulo obtuso (pág. 25) Ángulo que mide más de 90° y menos de 180°.

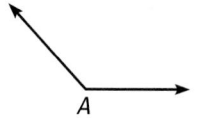

A

---

obtuse triangle (p. 217) A triangle with one obtuse angle.

triángulo obtusángulo (pág. 217) Triángulo que tiene un ángulo obtuso.

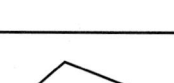

---

octagon (p. 43) A polygon with eight sides.

octágono (pág. 43) Polígono con ocho lados.

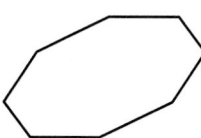

octahedron (p. 796) A polyhedron with eight faces.

octaedro (pág. 796) Poliedro con ocho caras.

opposite rays (p. 3) If point C lies on $\overleftrightarrow{AB}$ between A and B, then $\overrightarrow{CA}$ and $\overrightarrow{CB}$ are opposite rays.

rayos opuestos (pag. 3) Si el punto C se encuentra sobre $\overleftrightarrow{AB}$ entre A y B, entonces $\overrightarrow{CA}$ y $\overrightarrow{CB}$ son rayos opuestos.

$\overrightarrow{CA}$ and $\overrightarrow{CB}$ are opposite rays.
$\overrightarrow{CA}$ y $\overrightarrow{CB}$ son rayos opuestos.

orthocenter of a triangle (p. 321) The point at which the lines containing the three altitudes of the triangle intersect.

ortocentro de un triángulo (pág. 321) El punto donde se cortan las rectas que contienen las tres alturas del triángulo.

P is the orthocenter of $\triangle ABC$.
P es el ortocentro de $\triangle ABC$.

orthographic projection (p. 551) A technical drawing that is a two-dimensional drawing of the front, top, and side views of an object.

proyección ortográfica (pág. 551) Dibujo técnico bidimensional de las vistas delantera, superior y lateral de un objeto.

| front | top | side |
| delantera | superior | lateral |

P

paragraph proof (p. 163) A type of proof written in paragraph form.

prueba en forma de párrafo (pág. 163) Tipo de prueba escrita en forma de párrafo.

See Example 4 on page 163.

Ver el ejemplo 4 de la página 163.

parallel lines (p. 147) Two lines that do not intersect and are coplanar.

rectas paralelas (pág. 147) Dos rectas que no se cortan y que son coplanarias.

$\ell \parallel m$

parallel planes (p. 147) Two planes that do not intersect.

planos paralelos (pág. 147) Dos planos que no se cortan.

$S \parallel T$

parallelogram (p. 515) A quadrilateral with both pairs of opposite sides parallel.

paralelogramo (pág. 515) Cuadrilátero que tiene ambos pares de lados opuestos paralelos.

▱*PQRS*

pentagon (p. 43) A polygon with five sides.

pentágono (pág. 43) Polígono con cinco lados.

perpendicular bisector (p. 303) A segment, ray, line, or plane that is perpendicular to a segment at its midpoint.

mediatriz (pág. 303) Segmento, rayo, recta o plano que es perpendicular a un segmento en su punto medio.

perpendicular lines (p. 81) Two lines that intersect to form a right angle.

rectas perpendiculares (pág. 81) Dos rectas que se cortan para formar un ángulo recto.

plane (p. 2) A plane has two dimensions. It is usually represented by a shape that looks like a floor or a wall. You must imagine that the plane extends without end, even though the drawing of a plane appears to have edges. *See also* undefined term.

plano (pág. 2) Un plano tiene dos dimensiones. Normalmente se representa por una figura que parece un suelo o una pared. Hay que imaginar que el plano se prolonga sin fin, aunque dibujado parezca tener bordes. *Ver también* término indefinido.

plane *M* or plane *ABC*

plano *M* o plano *ABC*

Platonic solids (p. 796) Five regular polyhedra, named after the Greek mathematician and philosopher Plato.

sólidos platónicos (pág. 796) Cinco poliedros regulares, que llevan el nombre del matemático y filósofo griego Platón.

The Platonic solids include a regular tetrahedron, a cube, a regular octahedron, a regular dodecahedron, and a regular icosahedron.

Los sólidos platónicos son el tetraedro regular, el cubo, el octaedro regular, el dodecaedro regular y el icosaedro regular.

point (p. 2) A point has no dimension. It is usually represented by a dot. *See also* undefined term.

punto (pág. 2) Un punto no tiene dimensiones. Normalmente se representa por un pequeño punto. *Ver también* término indefinido.

point *A*

punto *A*

point of concurrency (p. 305) The point of intersection of concurrent lines, rays, or segments.

punto de concurrencia (pág. 305) El punto de intersección de rectas, rayos o segmentos concurrentes.

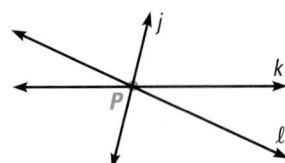

P is the point of concurrency for lines *j*, *k*, and ℓ.

P es el punto de concurrencia de las rectas *j*, *k* y ℓ.

---

polygon (p. 42) A closed plane figure with the following properties. (1) It is formed by three or more line segments called sides. (2) Each side intersects exactly two sides, one at each endpoint, so that no two sides with a common endpoint are collinear.

polígono (pág. 42) Figura plana cerrada que tiene las siguientes propiedades. (1) Está formada por tres o más segmentos de recta, llamados lados. (2) Cada lado corta a sólo dos lados, uno en cada extremo, de modo que en ningún caso son colineales dos lados que tienen un extremo común.

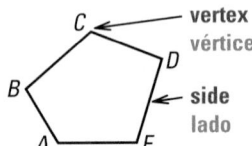

Polygon *ABCDE*

Polígono *ABCDE*

---

polyhedron (p. 794) A solid that is bounded by polygons, called faces, that enclose a single region of space. Plural is *polyhedra* or *polyhedrons*.

poliedro (pág. 794) Sólido limitado por polígonos, llamados caras, que rodean una sola región del espacio.

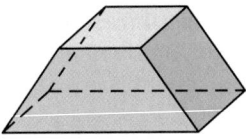

---

postulate (p. 9) A rule that is accepted without proof. Also called *axiom*.

postulado (pág. 9) Regla aceptada sin necesidad de pruebas. También se llama *axioma*.

The Segment Addition Postulate states that if *B* is between *A* and *C*, then $AB + BC = AC$.

El postulado de la suma de segmentos establece que si *B* está entre *A* y *C*, entonces $AB + BC = AC$.

---

preimage (p. 572) The original figure in a transformation. *See also* image.

preimagen (pág. 572) La figura original en una transformación. *Ver también* imagen.

See image.

Ver imagen.

---

prism (p. 803) A polyhedron with two congruent faces, called bases, that lie in parallel planes.

prisma (pág. 803) Poliedro con dos caras congruentes, llamadas bases, que se encuentran en planos paralelos.

base

base

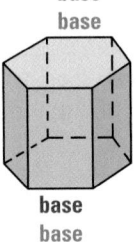

base

base

probability (p. 771) A number from 0 to 1 that measures the likelihood that an event will occur. It can be expressed as a fraction, decimal, or percent.

probabilidad (pág. 771) Número comprendido entre 0 y 1 que mide la posibilidad de que ocurra un suceso. Este número puede expresarse en forma de fracción, decimal o porcentaje.

See geometric probability.

Ver probabilidad geométrica.

---

proof (p. 112) A logical argument that shows a statement is true.

prueba (pág. 112) Argumento lógico que muestra que un enunciado es verdadero.

See two-column proof, paragraph proof, *and* flow proof.

Ver prueba de dos columnas, prueba en forma de párrafo *y* prueba de flujo.

---

proportion (p. 358) An equation that states that two ratios are equal.

proporción (pág. 358) Ecuación que establece la igualdad entre dos razones.

$\frac{2}{3} = \frac{4}{6}$ and $\frac{5}{7} = \frac{15}{x}$ are proportions.

$\frac{2}{3} = \frac{4}{6}$ y $\frac{5}{7} = \frac{15}{x}$ son proporciones.

---

pyramid (p. 810) A polyhedron in which the base is a polygon and the lateral faces are triangles with a common vertex, called the vertex of the pyramid.

pirámide (pág. 810) Poliedro que tiene por base un polígono y cuyas caras laterales son triángulos que tienen un vértice común, llamado vértice de la pirámide.

vertex / vértice · lateral edge / arista lateral · base / base · lateral faces / caras laterales · base edge / arista base

---

Pythagorean triple (p. 435) A set of three positive integers a, b, and c that satisfy the equation $c^2 = a^2 + b^2$.

terna pitagórica (pág. 435) Conjunto de tres números enteros positivos a, b y c que satisfacen la ecuación $c^2 = a^2 + b^2$.

Common Pythagorean triples:

3, 4, 5
5, 12, 13
8, 15, 17
7, 24, 25

Algunas ternas pitagóricas comunes son:

3, 4, 5
5, 12, 13
8, 15, 17
7, 24, 25

Q

quadrilateral (p. 43) A polygon with four sides.

cuadrilátero (pág. 43) Polígono con cuatro lados.

radius of a circle (p. 651) A segment whose endpoints are the center of the circle and a point on the circle. The distance from the center of a circle to any point on the circle. Plural is *radii*.

radio de un círculo (pág. 651) Un segmento cuyos extremos son el centro del círculo y un punto del círculo. La distancia desde el centro de un círculo a cualquier punto del círculo.

radius of a polygon (p. 762) The radius of a polygon's circumscribed circle.

radio de un polígono (pág. 762) El radio del círculo circunscrito de un poligono.

radius of a sphere (p. 838) A segment from the center of a sphere to a point on the sphere. The distance from the center of a sphere to any point on the sphere.

radio de una esfera (pág. 838) Segmento que va desde el centro de una esfera hasta un punto de la esfera. La distancia desde el centro de una esfera a cualquier punto de la esfera.

ratio of *a* to *b* (p. 356) A comparison of two numbers using division. The ratio of *a* to *b*, where $b \neq 0$, can be written as *a* to *b*, as $a : b$, or as $\frac{a}{b}$.

razón de *a* a *b* (pág. 356) Comparación entre dos números usando la división. La razón de *a* a *b*, donde $b \neq 0$, puede escribirse *a* a *b*, $a : b$ o $\frac{a}{b}$.

The ratio of 3 feet to 7 feet can be written as 3 to 7, $\frac{3}{7}$, or $3 : 7$.

La razón de 3 pies a 7 pies puede escribirse 3 a 7, $\frac{3}{7}$ ó $3 : 7$.

ray (p. 3) Part of a line that consists of a point called an endpoint and all points on the line that extend in one direction.

rayo (pág. 3) Parte de una recta que consta de un punto, llamado extremo, y de todos los puntos de la recta que se prolongan en una dirección.

$\overrightarrow{AB}$ with endpoint *A*
$\overrightarrow{AB}$ con extremo *A*

rectangle (p. 533) A parallelogram with four right angles.

rectángulo (pág. 533) Paralelogramo que tiene los cuatro ángulos rectos.

reduction (p. 409) A dilation with a scale factor between 0 and 1.

reducción (pág. 409) Dilatación con un factor de escala entre 0 y 1.

A dilation with a scale factor of $\frac{1}{2}$ is a reduction.

Una dilatación con un factor de escala de $\frac{1}{2}$ es una reducción.

reflection (pp. 272, 589) A transformation that uses a line of reflection to create a mirror image of the original figure.

reflexión (págs. 272, 589) Transformación que usa un eje de reflexión para crear una imagen especular de la figura original.

line of reflection
eje de reflexión

regular polygon (p. 43) A polygon that has all sides and all angles congruent.

polígono regular (pág. 43) Polígono que tiene todos los lados y todos los ángulos congruentes.

regular polyhedron (p. 796) A convex polyhedron in which all of the faces are congruent regular polygons.

poliedro regular (pág. 796) Poliedro convexo en el que todas las caras son polígonos regulares congruentes.

regular pyramid (p. 810) A pyramid that has a regular polygon for a base and in which the segment joining the vertex and the center of the base is perpendicular to the base.

pirámide regular (pág. 810) Pirámide que tiene por base un polígono regular y en la que el segmento que une el vértice y el centro de la base es perpendicular a la base.

height
altura

slant height
apotema lateral

relative error (p. 727) The ratio of the greatest possible error to the measured length.

error relativo (pág. 727) La razón entre el máximo error posible y la longitud medida.

If the greatest possible error of a measure is 0.5 inch and the measured length of an object is 8 inches, then the relative error is $\frac{0.5}{8} = 0.0625 = 6.25\%$.

Si el máximo error posible de una medida es 0.5 pulgada y la longitud medida de un objeto es de 8 pulgadas, entonces el error relativo es $\frac{0.5}{8} = 0.0625 = 6.25\%$.

rhombus (p. 533) A parallelogram with four congruent sides.

rombo (pág. 533) Paralelogramo que tiene los cuatro lados congruentes.

right angle (p. 25) An angle with measure equal to 90°.

ángulo recto (pág. 25) Ángulo que mide 90°.

right cone (p. 812) A cone in which the segment joining the vertex and the center of the base is perpendicular to the base. The slant height is the distance between the vertex and a point on the base edge.

cono recto (pág. 812) Cono en el que el segmento que une el vértice y el centro de la base es perpendicular a la base. El apotema lateral es la distancia entre el vértice y un punto de la arista de la base.

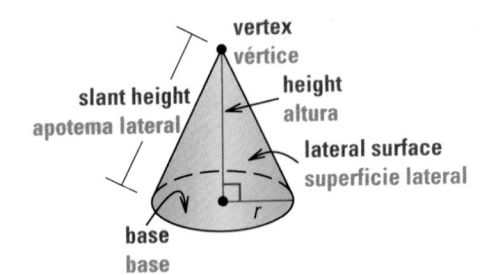

right cylinder (p. 805) A cylinder in which the segment joining the centers of the bases is perpendicular to the bases.

cilindro recto (pág. 805) Cilindro en el que el segmento que une los centros de las bases es perpendicular a las bases.

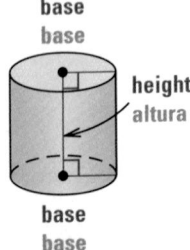

right prism (p. 804) A prism in which each lateral edge is perpendicular to both bases.

prisma recto (pág. 804) Prisma en el que cada arista lateral es perpendicular a ambas bases.

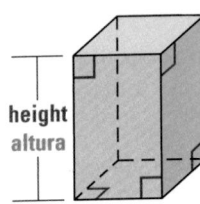

right triangle (pp. 217, 241) A triangle with one right angle.

triángulo rectángulo (págs. 217, 241) Triángulo que tiene un ángulo recto.

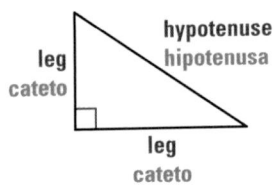

rotation (pp. 272, 598) A transformation in which a figure is turned about a fixed point called the center of rotation.

rotación (págs. 272, 598) Transformación en la que una figura gira en torno a un punto fijo, llamado centro de rotación.

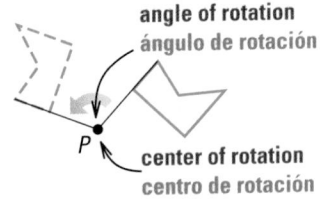

rotational symmetry (p. 620) A figure in the plane has rotational symmetry if the figure can be mapped onto itself by a rotation of 180° or less about the center of the figure. This point is the center of symmetry.

simetría rotacional (pág. 620) Una figura del plano tiene simetría rotacional si se corresponde a sí misma al realizar una rotación de 180° ó menos en torno al centro de la figura. Este punto es el centro de simetría.

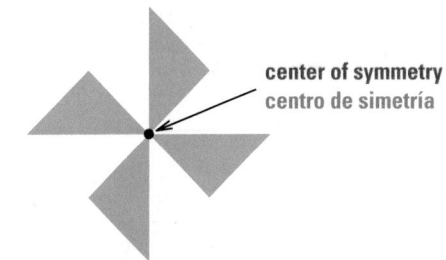

center of symmetry
centro de simetría

Rotations of 90° and 180° map the figure onto itself.
Al realizar rotaciones de 90° y 180°, la figura se corresponde.

 S

scalar multiplication (p. 627) The process of multiplying each element of a matrix by a real number, or scalar.

multiplicación escalar (pág. 627) El proceso de multiplicar cada elemento de una matriz por un número real, o escalar.

$$3\begin{bmatrix} 5 & -2 & 1 \\ 0 & 2 & -3 \end{bmatrix} = \begin{bmatrix} 15 & -6 & 3 \\ 0 & 6 & -9 \end{bmatrix}$$

scale (p. 365) A ratio that describes how the dimensions in a scale drawing are related to the actual dimensions of the object.

escala (pág. 365) Razón que describe qué relación hay entre las dimensiones de un dibujo a escala y las dimensiones reales del objeto.

The scale 1 in. : 12 ft on a floor plan means that 1 inch in the floor plan represents an actual distance of 12 feet.

La escala 1 pulg : 12 pies de un plano significa que 1 pulgada del plano representa una distancia real de 12 pies.

scale drawing (p. 365) A drawing that is the same shape as the object it represents.

dibujo a escala (pág. 365) Dibujo que tiene la misma forma que el objeto que representa.

A floor plan of a house is a scale drawing.

El plano de una casa es un dibujo a escala.

scale factor of a dilation (p. 409) In a dilation, the ratio of a side length of the image to the corresponding side length of the original figure.

factor de escala de una dilatación (pág. 409) En una dilatación, la razón entre una longitud de lado de la imagen y la longitud de lado correspondiente de la figura original.

See dilation.

Ver dilatación.

scale factor of two similar polygons (p. 373) The ratio of the lengths of two corresponding sides of two similar polygons.

factor de escala entre dos polígonos semejantes (pág. 373) La razón entre las longitudes de dos lados correspondientes de dos polígonos semejantes.

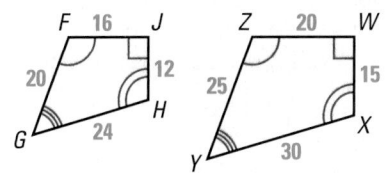

The scale factor of *ZYXW* to *FGHJ* is $\frac{5}{4}$.

El factor de escala entre *ZYXW* y *FGHJ* es $\frac{5}{4}$.

scalene triangle (p. 217) A triangle with no congruent sides.

triángulo escaleno (pág. 217) Triángulo que no tiene lados congruentes.

secant line (p. 651) A line that intersects a circle in two points.

recta secante (pág. 651) Recta que corta a un círculo en dos puntos.

Line *m* is a secant.

La recta *m* es una secante.

secant segment (p. 690) A segment that contains a chord of a circle and has exactly one endpoint outside the circle.

segmento secante (pág. 690) Segmento que contiene una cuerda de un círculo y tiene sólo un extremo en el exterior del círculo.

secant segment
segmento secante

sector of a circle (p. 756) The region bounded by two radii of the circle and their intercepted arc.

sector de un círculo (pág. 756) La región limitada por dos radios del círculo y su arco interceptado.

sector *APB*

segment (p. 3) *See* line segment.

segmento (pág. 3) *Ver* segmento de recta.

See line segment.

Ver segmento de recta.

segment bisector (p. 15) A point, ray, line, segment, or plane that intersects a segment at its midpoint.

bisectriz de un segmento (pág. 15) Punto, rayo, recta, segmento o plano que corta a un segmento en su punto medio.

$\overleftrightarrow{CD}$ is a segment bisector of $\overline{AB}$.

$\overleftrightarrow{CD}$ es una bisectriz del segmento $\overline{AB}$.

segments of a chord (p. 689) When two chords intersect in the interior of a circle, each chord is divided into two segments called segments of the chord.

segmentos de una cuerda (pág. 689) Cuando dos cuerdas se cortan en el interior de un círculo, cada cuerda se divide en dos segmentos, llamados segmentos de la cuerda.

$\overline{EA}$ and $\overline{EB}$ are segments of chord $\overline{AB}$. $\overline{DE}$ and $\overline{EC}$ are segments of chord $\overline{DC}$.

$\overline{EA}$ y $\overline{EB}$ son segmentos de la cuerda $\overline{AB}$. $\overline{DE}$ y $\overline{EC}$ son segmentos de la cuerda $\overline{DC}$.

self-similar (p. 406) An object such that one part of the object can be enlarged to look like the whole object.	*See* fractal.
autosemejante (pág. 406) Objeto tal que una parte de él puede ampliarse de modo que parece el objeto entero.	*Ver* fractal.
semicircle (p. 659) An arc with endpoints that are the endpoints of a diameter of a circle. The measure of a semicircle is 180°. **semicírculo** (pág. 659) Arco cuyos extremos son los extremos de un diámetro de un círculo. Un semicírculo mide 180°.	 $\overparen{QSR}$ is a semicircle. $\overparen{QSR}$ es un semicírculo.
side of a polygon (p. 42) Each line segment that forms a polygon. *See also* polygon.	*See* polygon.
lado de un polígono (pág. 42) Cada segmento de recta que forma un polígono. *Ver también* polígono.	*Ver* polígono.
sides of an angle (p. 24) *See* angle.	*See* angle.
lados de un ángulo (pág. 24) *Ver* ángulo.	*Ver* ángulo.
similar polygons (p. 372) Two polygons such that their corresponding angles are congruent and the lengths of corresponding sides are proportional. **polígonos semejantes** (pág. 372) Dos polígonos tales que los ángulos correspondientes son congruentes y las longitudes de los lados correspondientes son proporcionales.	 **ABCD ~ EFGH**
similar solids (p. 847) Two solids of the same type with equal ratios of corresponding linear measures, such as heights or radii. **sólidos semejantes** (pág. 847) Dos sólidos del mismo tipo y con razones iguales de medidas lineales correspondientes, como las alturas o los radios.	
sine (p. 473) A trigonometric ratio, abbreviated as *sin*. For a right triangle ABC, the sine of the acute angle A is $$\sin A = \frac{\text{length of leg opposite } \angle A}{\text{length of hypotenuse}} = \frac{BC}{AB}.$$ **seno** (pág. 473) Razón trigonométrica, abreviada *sen*. Para un triángulo rectángulo ABC, el seno del ángulo agudo A es $$\text{sen } A = \frac{\text{longitud del cateto opuesto a } \angle A}{\text{longitud de la hipotenusa}} = \frac{BC}{AB}.$$	 $\sin A = \dfrac{BC}{AB} = \dfrac{3}{5}$ $\text{sen } A = \dfrac{BC}{AB} = \dfrac{3}{5}$

skew lines (p. 147) Lines that do not intersect and are not coplanar.

rectas alabeadas (pág. 147) Rectas que no se cortan y que no son coplanarias.

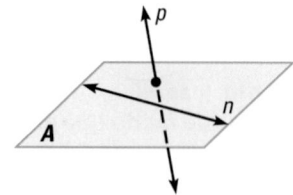

Lines *n* and *p* are skew lines.

Las rectas *n* y *p* son rectas alabeadas.

---

slant height of a regular pyramid (p. 810) The height of a lateral face of the regular pyramid.

apotema lateral de una pirámide regular (pág. 810) La altura de una cara lateral de la pirámide regular.

See regular pyramid.

Ver pirámide regular.

---

slope of a line (p. 171) The slope *m* of a nonvertical line is the ratio of the vertical change (the *rise*) to horizontal change (the *run*) between any two points on the line: $m = \dfrac{y_2 - y_1}{x_2 - x_1}$.

pendiente de una recta (pág. 171) La pendiente *m* de una recta no vertical es la razón entre el cambio vertical (la *distancia vertical*) y el cambio horizontal (la *distancia horizontal*) entre dos puntos cualesquiera de la recta: $m = \dfrac{y_2 - y_1}{x_2 - x_1}$.

---

slope-intercept form (p. 180) A linear equation written in the form $y = mx + b$ where *m* is the slope and *b* is the *y*-intercept of the equation's graph.

forma pendiente-intercepto (pág. 180) Ecuación lineal escrita en la forma $y = mx + b$, donde *m* es la pendiente y *b* es el intercepto en *y* de la gráfica de la ecuación.

The equation $y = 3x + 4$ is in slope-intercept form. The slope of the line is 3, and the *y*-intercept is 4.

La ecuación $y = 3x + 4$ está en la forma pendiente-intercepto. La pendiente de la recta es 3, y el intercepto en *y* es 4.

---

solve a right triangle (p. 483) To find the measures of all of the sides and angles of a right triangle.

resolver un triángulo rectángulo (pág. 483) Hallar las medidas de todos los lados y todos los ángulos de un triángulo rectángulo.

You can solve a right triangle if you know either of the following:
- Two side lengths
- One side length and the measure of one acute angle

Puedes resolver un triángulo rectángulo conociendo uno de estos grupos:
- Las longitudes de dos lados
- La longitud de un lado y la medida de un ángulo agudo

sphere (p. 838) The set of all points in space equidistant from a given point called the center of the sphere.

esfera (pág. 838) El conjunto de todos los puntos del espacio que son equidistantes de un punto dado, llamado centro de la esfera.

square (p. 533) A parallelogram with four congruent sides and four right angles.

cuadrado (pág. 533) Paralelogramo que tiene los cuatro lados congruentes y los cuatro ángulos rectos.

standard equation of a circle (p. 699) The standard equation of a circle with center (h, k) and radius r is $(x - h)^2 + (y - k)^2 = r^2$.

ecuación general de un círculo (pág. 699) La ecuación general de un círculo con centro (h, k) y radio r es $(x - h)^2 + (y - k)^2 = r^2$.

The standard equation of a circle with center $(2, 3)$ and radius 4 is $(x - 2)^2 + (y - 3)^2 = 16$.

La ecuación general de un círculo con centro $(2, 3)$ y radio 4 es $(x - 2)^2 + (y - 3)^2 = 16$.

standard form of a linear equation (p. 182) A linear equation written in the form $Ax + By = C$, where A, B, and C are real numbers and A and B are not both zero.

forma general de una ecuación lineal (pág. 182) Ecuación lineal escrita en la forma $Ax + By = C$, donde A, B y C son números reales y A y B no son ambos cero.

The equation $2x + 3y = 12$ is in standard form.

La ecuación $2x + 3y = 12$ está en la forma general.

straight angle (p. 25) An angle with measure equal to 180°.

ángulo llano (pág. 25) Ángulo que mide 180°.

supplementary angles (p. 35) Two angles whose measures have the sum 180°. The sum of the measures of an angle and its *supplement* is 180°.

ángulos suplementarios (pág. 35) Dos ángulos cuyas medidas suman 180°. La suma de las medidas de un ángulo y de su *suplemento* es 180°.

surface area (p. 803) The sum of the areas of the faces of a polyhedron or other solid.

área superficial (pág. 803) La suma de las áreas de las caras de un poliedro o de otro sólido.

$S = 2(3)(4) + 2(4)(6) + 2(3)(6) = 108 \text{ ft}^2$
$S = 2(3)(4) + 2(4)(6) + 2(3)(6) = 108 \text{ pies}^2$

tangent (p. 466) A trigonometric ratio, abbreviated as *tan*. For a right triangle *ABC*, the tangent of the acute angle *A* is

$\tan A = \dfrac{\text{length of leg opposite } \angle A}{\text{length of leg adjacent to } \angle A} = \dfrac{BC}{AC}.$

tangente (pág. 466) Razón trigonométrica, abreviada *tan*. Para un triángulo rectángulo *ABC*, la tangente del ángulo agudo *A* es $\tan A = \dfrac{\text{longitud del cateto opuesto a } \angle A}{\text{longitud del cateto adyacente a } \angle A} = \dfrac{BC}{AC}.$

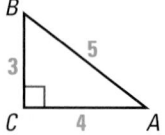

$\tan A = \dfrac{BC}{AC} = \dfrac{3}{4}$

tangent line (p. 651) A line in the plane of a circle that intersects the circle in exactly one point, the point of tangency.

recta tangente (pág. 651) Recta del plano de un círculo que corta al círculo en sólo un punto, el punto de tangencia.

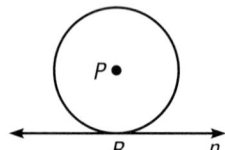

Line *n* is a tangent. *R* is the point of tangency.

La recta *n* es una tangente. *R* es el punto de tangencia.

taxicab geometry (p. 198) A non-Euclidean geometry in which all lines are horizontal or vertical.

geometría de taxis (pág. 198) Geometría no euclidiana en la que todas las rectas son horizontales o verticales.

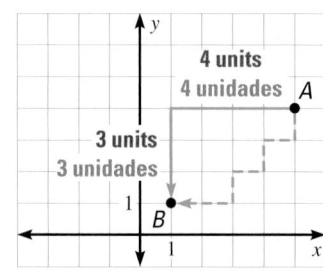

In taxicab geometry, the distance between *A* and *B* is 7 units.

En la geometría de taxis, la distancia entre *A* y *B* es de 7 unidades.

terminal point of a vector (p. 574) The ending point of a vector.

punto final de un vector (pág. 574) El punto donde termina el vector.

See vector.

Ver vector.

tessellation (p. 616) A collection of figures that cover a plane with no gaps or overlaps.

teselación (pág. 616) Colección de figuras que recubren un plano sin sobreponerse y sin huecos.

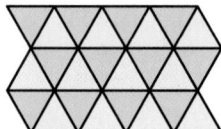

tetrahedron (p. 796) A polyhedron with four faces.

tetraedro (pág. 796) Poliedro con cuatro caras.

theorem (p. 113) A true statement that follows as a result of other true statements.	**Vertical angles are congruent.**
teorema (pág. 113) Enunciado verdadero que surge como resultado de otros enunciados verdaderos.	**Los ángulos opuestos por el vértice son congruentes.**
transformation (p. 272) An operation that moves or changes a geometric figure in some way to produce a new figure.	**Four basic transformations are translations, reflections, rotations, and dilations.**
transformación (pág. 272) Operación que desplaza o cambia de alguna manera una figura geométrica para crear una nueva figura.	**Cuatro transformaciones básicas son las traslaciones, las reflexiones, las rotaciones y las dilataciones.**
translation (pp. 272, 572) A transformation that moves every point of a figure the same distance in the same direction.	
traslación (págs. 272, 572) Transformación que desplaza cada punto de una figura la misma distancia en la misma dirección.	
transversal (p. 149) A line that intersects two or more coplanar lines at different points.	
transversal (pág. 149) Recta que corta a dos o más rectas coplanarias en distintos puntos.	transversal *t*
trapezoid (p. 542) A quadrilateral with exactly one pair of parallel sides, called bases. The nonparallel sides are legs.	
trapecio (pág. 542) Cuadrilátero que tiene sólo un par de lados paralelos, llamados bases. Los lados no paralelos son catetos.	
triangle (pp. 43, 217) A polygon with three sides.	
triángulo (págs. 43, 217) Polígono con tres lados.	△*ABC*

trigonometric ratio (p. 466) A ratio of the lengths of two sides in a right triangle. *See also* sine, cosine, *and* tangent.

razón trigonométrica (pág. 466) Razón entre las longitudes de dos lados de un triángulo rectángulo. *Ver también* seno, coseno *y* tangente.

Three common trigonometric ratios are sine, cosine, and tangent.

Tres razones trigonométricas comunes son el seno, el coseno y la tangente.

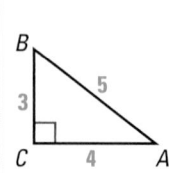

$$\tan A = \frac{BC}{AC} = \frac{3}{4}$$
$$\sin A = \frac{BC}{AB} = \frac{3}{5}$$
$$\cos A = \frac{AC}{AB} = \frac{4}{5}$$

$$\tan A = \frac{BC}{AC} = \frac{3}{4}$$
$$\text{sen } A = \frac{BC}{AB} = \frac{3}{5}$$
$$\cos A = \frac{AC}{AB} = \frac{4}{5}$$

---

truth table (p. 95) A table that shows the truth values for a hypothesis, a conclusion, and a conditional statement using the hypothesis and conclusion.

tabla de verdad (pág. 95) Tabla que muestra los valores de verdad de una hipótesis, de una conclusión y de un enunciado condicional usando la hipótesis y la conclusión.

Truth Table		
p	q	$p \to q$
T	T	T
T	F	F
F	T	T
F	F	T

Tabla de verdad		
p	q	$p \to q$
V	V	V
V	F	F
F	V	V
F	F	V

---

truth value of a statement (p. 95) The truth or falsity of the statement.

valor de verdad de un enunciado (pág. 95) La verdad o falsedad de un enunciado.

See **truth table.**

Ver **tabla de verdad.**

---

two-column proof (p. 112) A type of proof written as numbered statements and corresponding reasons that show an argument in a logical order.

prueba de dos columnas (pág. 112) Tipo de prueba en la que se escriben enunciados numerados y razones correspondientes que muestran un argumento siguiendo un orden lógico.

See **Example 1 on page 112.**

Ver **el ejemplo 1 de la página 112.**

---

undefined term (p. 2) A word that does not have a formal definition, but there is agreement about what the word means.

término indefinido (pág. 2) Palabra que no tiene una definición establecida, pero cuyo significado se acepta comúnmente.

Point, *line*, and *plane* are undefined terms.

Punto, *recta* y *plano* son términos indefinidos.

unit of measure (p. 727) The quantity or increment to which something is measured.

unidad de medida (pág. 727) La cantidad o el incremento con que algo se mide.

If a segment is measured using a ruler marked in eighths of an inch, the unit of measure is $\frac{1}{8}$ inch.

Si un segmento se mide con una regla que lleva señalados los octavos de pulgada, la unidad de medida es $\frac{1}{8}$ pulgada.

V

vector (p. 574) A quantity that has both direction and magnitude, and is represented in the coordinate plane by an arrow drawn from one point to another.

vector (pág. 574) Cantidad que tiene tanto dirección como magnitud y es representada en el plano de coordenadas por una flecha dibujada de un punto a otro.

$\overrightarrow{FG}$ with initial point *F* and terminal point *G*.
$\overrightarrow{FG}$ con punto inicial *F* y punto final *G*.

---

vertex angle of an isosceles triangle (p. 264) The angle formed by the legs of an isosceles triangle.

ángulo del vértice de un triángulo isósceles (pág. 264) El ángulo formado por los catetos de un triángulo isósceles.

vertex angle
ángulo del vértice

base angles
ángulos básicos

---

vertex of a cone (p. 812) *See* cone.

vértice de un cono (pág. 812) *Ver* cono.

See cone.

Ver cono.

---

vertex of a polygon (p. 42) Each endpoint of a side of a polygon. Plural is *vertices*. *See also* polygon.

vértice de un polígono (pág. 42) Cada extremo de un lado de un polígono. *Ver también* polígono.

See polygon.

Ver polígono.

---

vertex of a polyhedron (p. 794) A point where three or more edges of a polyhedron meet.

vértice de un poliedro (pág. 794) Punto donde confluyen tres o más aristas de un poliedro.

vertex
vértice

---

vertex of a pyramid (p. 810) *See* pyramid.

vértice de una pirámide (pág. 810) *Ver* pirámide.

See pyramid.

Ver pirámide.

---

vertex of an angle (p. 24) *See* angle.

vértice de un ángulo (pág. 24) *Ver* ángulo.

See angle.

Ver ángulo.

vertical angles (p. 37) Two angles whose sides form two pairs of opposite rays.

ángulos opuestos por el vértice (pág. 37) Dos ángulos cuyos lados forman dos pares de rayos opuestos.

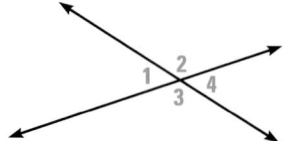

∠1 and ∠4 are vertical angles.
∠2 and ∠3 are vertical angles.

∠1 y ∠4 son ángulos opuestos por el vértice.
∠2 y ∠3 son ángulos opuestos por el vértice.

vertical component of a vector (p. 574) The vertical change from the initial point to the terminal point of a vector.

componente vertical de un vector (pág. 574) El cambio vertical entre el punto inicial y el punto final del vector.

See component form of a vector.

Ver forma de componentes de un vector.

volume of a solid (p. 819) The number of cubic units contained in the interior of a solid.

volumen de un sólido (pág. 819) El número de unidades cúbicas contenidas en el interior de un sólido.

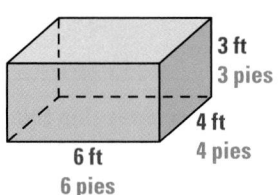

3 ft
3 pies
4 ft
4 pies
6 ft
6 pies

Volume = 3(4)(6) = 72 ft³
Volumen = 3(4)(6) = 72 pies³

Index

A

Absolute value, 287, 870
Accuracy, of measurements, 727–728
ACT, *See* Standardized Test
  Preparation
Activities
  angle sums
    in polygons, 506
    in triangles, 216
  angles
    inscribed, 671
    intersecting lines and, 122–123,
      153, 154
    similar triangles and, 381
  area
    perimeter and, 48
    of trapezoids and kites, 729
  congruent figures, 233
  constructions
    bisect an angle, 34
    bisect a segment, 33
    copy an angle, 34
    copy a segment, 33
    copy a triangle, 235
    dilations, 408, 625
  drawing and interpreting lines, 146
  folding
    an angle bisector, 27
    perpendicular bisectors of a
      triangle, 304
    perpendicular lines, 190
    a segment bisector, 15
    solids, 792–793
  geometric probability, 770
  intersecting medians, 318
  parallel lines and angles, 153, 154
  parallelograms, 514
  proportionality, 396
  puzzles
    logic, 86
    number, 104
  Pythagorean Theorem, 432
    converse of, 440
  right triangle ratio, 466
  segments
    length of, 688
    midsegment of a trapezoid, 541
    tangent, 650
    in triangles, 294
  similar polygons, 371
  similar right triangles, 448
  similar solids, 846
  slopes, 179

  spreadsheet
    minimize surface area, 837
    perimeter and area of polygons,
      769
  surface area, 802
  transformations, 154, 271, 408, 588,
    607, 625, 633
  volume of a pyramid, 828
Acute angle, 25
Acute triangle, 217
Addition
  matrix, 581, 584, 637
  order of operations and, 870
  rational number, 869
  real number, 105
Addition Property, 105
Adjacent angles, 35
Adjacent arcs, 660
Adjacent sides, 241, 466, 467
Algebra, *See also* Algebra Review;
    Skills Review Handbook
  examples, *Throughout. See for
    example* 16, 26, 37, 44, 89, 155,
    161, 266, 303, 311, 330, 357,
    358
  exercises, *Throughout. See for
    example* 29, 54, 84, 91, 158,
    186, 229, 268, 323, 339, 363,
    385
  properties from, 105–111, 136
  skills check, xxii, 70, 144, 214, 292,
    354, 430, 504, 570, 648, 718,
    790
Algebra Review, *See also* Skills Review
    Handbook
  algebraic models, 65, 207, 785
  equations
    absolute value, 287
    linear, 65
    quadratic, 423, 499, 641
  expressions
    radical, 139
    rational, 139
  factor binomials and trinomials,
    713
  graphing
    exponential functions, 565
    inequalities, 207, 287
    nonlinear functions, 565
    quadratic functions, 499, 565
  inequalities, 207, 287
  multiply binomials, 641
  the quadratic formula, 641

  radicals, 139, 423
    properties of, 457
  ratios and percent of change, 349
Algorithm
  for bisecting an angle, 34, 261
  for bisecting a segment, 33
  for constructing inscribed angles
    of a circle, 671
  for constructing a parallel to a line,
    152
  for constructing a parallelogram,
    514
  for constructing a perpendicular to
    a line, 195
  for creating a tessellation, 617
  for dividing a segment into equal
    parts, 401
  for drawing a dilation, 408, 625, 627
  for finding a locus, 697
  for rotating a figure, 598
  for solving a problem, 894
Alternate exterior angles, 149–152,
    155, 157–160
Alternate Exterior Angles Theorem,
    155
  converse, 162
Alternate interior angles, 149–152,
    153, 155–160
Alternate Interior Angles Theorem,
    155
  converse, 162, 163
Alternative method, *See* Another
    Way; Problem Solving
    Workshop
Altitude
  of a cone, 812
  of a cylinder, 805
  of a prism, 804
  of a pyramid, 810
  of a triangle, 320
    right, 448–456
Angle(s), 24, 59
  acute, 25
  adjacent, 35
  alternate exterior, 149–152, 155,
    157–160
  alternate interior, 149–152, 153,
    155–160
  bisector, 28
    construction, 27, 34
  central, 659, 762
  classifying, 25, 29, 62
  classifying triangles by, 217–218,
    221, 281

INDEX

Credits

Photographs

Cover Jerry Dodrill/Outdoor Collection/Aurora Photos; **v** *top* Meridian Creative Group; *top center* Robert C. Jenks, Jenks Studio; *bottom center* McDougal Littell; *bottom* Jerry Head Jr.; **viii** Greg Epperson/Index Stock Imagery; **ix** Chris Mellor/Getty Index Stock Imagery; **xii** Johannes Kroemer/Photonica/Getty Images; **xiii** Photowood/Corbis; **xiv** Steve Dunwell/Getty Images; **xv** Philip Gould/Corbis; **xvi** Veer; **xvii** Grant Faint/Getty Images; **xviii** Patrick Schneider/The Charlotte Observer/AP/Wide World Photos; **xix** Wes Thompson/Corbis; **1−2** Brian Bailey/Getty Images; **2** William Sallaz/Duomo/Corbis; **7** *center left* Robert Landau/Corbis; *center right* Daisuke Morita/Getty Images; *bottom* Davis Barber/PhotoEdit; *center* LUCKYLOOK/DanitaDelimont.com; **9** Ronan Coyne; **13** Buddy Mays/Corbis; **14** Doug Pensinger/Getty Images; **15** Brett Froomer/Getty Images; **21** *top* John Greim/Index Stock Imagery; *center* William R. Curtsinger/National Geographic Society; **24** Southern Stock/Getty Images; **27** Timothy Fadek/Polaris Images; **30** Collier Campbell Lifeworks/Corbis; **31** *top* "Bird in Flight" by Starr Kempf/Starr Enterprises. Photo by: Llewellyn Falco; *bottom* Robert Llewellyn/Corbis; **35** Jeff Greenberg/The Image Works; **40** Mark Duncan/AP/Wide World Photos; **42** Nancy Crane; **44** Ryan McVay/Getty Images; **46** *center left* S Meltzer/PhotoLink/Getty Images; *center right, left* PhotoDisc/Getty Images; *right* Thinkstock/PunchStock; **49** Hubble Heritage Team/AP/Wide World Photos; **51** Dennis MacDonald/AGE Fotostock; **53** *center left* Samba Photo/Photonica/Getty Images; *left* foodfolio/Alamy; *center right* School Division/Houghton Mifflin; *right* Burke/Triolo/Brand X Pictures/PictureQuest; *bee* Photospin Power Photos/Bugs & Buttterflies, Volume 8; **54** Will & Deni McIntyre/Stone/Getty Images; **55** *center right* Scott Ols/Getty Images; *bottom* NASA/AP/Wide World Photos; **70−71** Philip Rostron/Masterfile; **72** *top* Allsport Concepts/Mike Powell/Getty Images; **74** *both* Royalty-Free/Corbis; **78** PhotoDisc/Getty Images; **79** Martha Granger/Edge Productions/McDougal Littell; **80** Gerard Lacz/Animals Animals - Earth Scenes; **84** Jim Sugar/Corbis; **87** George H. H. Huey/Corbis; **89** Thomas Schmitt/Getty Images; **90** *left* Katrina Wittkamp/Getty Images; *right* William Whitehurst/Corbis; **91** Royalty-Free/Corbis; **92** *center right* Custom Medical Stock Photo; *center left* Kaj R. Svensson/Science Photo Library; *right* Michael Barnett/Science Photo Library; *left* Kaj R. Svensson/Science Photo Library; **96** Bernd Obermann/Corbis; **101** *top center* Caron Philippe/Sygma/Corbis; *top right* Jay Penni Photography/McDougal Littell; *top left* Bob Daemmrich/The Image Works; **105** Bob Thomas/Getty Images; **112** John Sohm/Alamy; **117** Charles D. Winters/Photo Researchers, Inc.; **119** Sculpture: "Adam" by Alexander Liberman. Photo Credit: Omni Photo Communications Inc./Index Stock Imagery; **124** Image du Sud/eStock Photo; **128** Image Farm/PictureQuest; **130** *bottom* Barbara Van Zanten/Lonely Planet Images; *top* Jay Penni Photography/McDougal Littell; **144−145** John Angerson/Alamy; **147** Gary Rhijnsburger/Masterfile; **148** Corbis/PictureQuest; **150** Michael Newman/PhotoEdit; **151** Mike Powell/Getty Images; **152** Paul Rocheleau Photography; **154** Gareth McCormack/Lonely Planet Images; **157** Paul Eekhoff/Masterfile; **159** *both* Copyright 2005 Parallax, Inc. Toddler is a registered trademark of Parallax, Inc. All rights reserved.; **161** Digital Vision/Getty Images; **164** Ryan McVay/Getty Images; **167** *bottom* Peter Sterling/Getty Images; *top* Erin Hogan/Getty Images; **168** C-Squared Studios/Getty Images; **170** *center left* Bruno Morandi/Getty Images; *bottom right* Paul A. Souders/Corbis; **171** SHOGORO/Photonica/Getty Images; **174** Courtesy of Cedar Point Amusement Park/Resort; **177** Bruce Leighty/Index Stock Imagery; **180** Lori Adamski Peek/Getty Images; **183** Bill Aron/PhotoEdit; **186** David R. Frazier PhotoLibrary, Inc/Alamy; **190** *First Aid Folly with waterwheel.* Parc de la Vilette, Paris, 1986, by Bernard Tschumi. Photo credit: Art on File/Corbis; **190**; **193** Sculpture: Lucas Samaras, "Chair Transformation #20B", 1996. Patinated bronze. 11'9"x7'2"x2'2-3/4" National Gallery of Art, Washington D.C. © Lucas Samaras, courtesy PaceWildenstein, New York. Photo credit: Ventura/FOLIO, Inc.; **195** *center* Jeffrey Becorn/Lonely Planet Images; *left* Ned Friary/Lonely Planet Images; *right* Image Source/ImageState; **196** Stephen Wilkes/Getty Images; **200** Dennis MacDonald/Alamy; **213** *right* plainpicture/Alamy; *left* Royalty-Free/Corbis; *center* Tom Benoit/SuperStock; **214−215** Bill Ross/Corbis; **217** *top* Nancy Sheehan/PhotoEdit; *bottom* Royalty-Free/Corbis; **220** Nicolas Sapieha/Corbis; **223** MedioImages/SuperStock; **225** Image Source/Alamy; **230** *top* Collier Campbell Lifeworks/Corbis; *center right* Tony Freeman/PhotoEdit; **234** Mark Downey/Getty Images; **240** Ron Watts/Corbis; **242** Terry W. Eggers/Corbis; **245** *right* Jeremy Woodhouse/Masterfile; *left* Photowood Inc./Corbis; **248** *top left* Comstock; *top right* William Harrigan/Lonely Planet Images; **249** ShotFile/Alamy; **250** *right* Richard Cummins/Lonely Planet Images; *center* SuperStock; *left* Doug Houghton/Alamy; **254** *bottom* Michael Melford/Getty Images; **256** *top* Douglas C Pizac, Staff/AP/Wide World Photos; *center* Max Earey/Alamy; **257** Richard Hamilton Smith/Corbis; **261** Buddy Mays/Corbis; **262** *top center* Scott Gilchrist/Masterfile; *top right* Ron Watts/Corbis; *top left* Royalty-Free/Corbis; **264** Morton Beebe/Corbis; **266** Jeff Baker/Getty Images; **268** *left* Bob Elsdale/Getty Images; *center* Royalty-Free/Corbis; *right* Radlund & Associates/PictureQuest; **269** *top right* JupiterImages/Comstock; *center right* Digital Vision/Getty Images; **272** *top* Michael Newman/PhotoEdit; *bottom* Digital Vision/Getty Images; **280** *center right* Jay Penni Photography/McDougal Littell; *bottom right* Michael Matisse/Getty Images; **286** Peter Christopher/Masterfile; **292−293** Johannes Kroemer/Photonica/Getty Images; **295** Bob Elsdale/Getty Images; **296** Alfred Pasieka/Science Photo Library; **300** *bottom* Graham Henderson/Elizabeth Whiting and Associates/Corbis; **303** Alex Wong/Getty Images; **306** *left* Dennis Hallinan/Alamy; *center* Royalty Free/PictureQuest; *right* Fernando Bueno/Getty Images; **310** Tracy Frankel/Getty Images; **317** Martin Llado/Lonely Planet Images; **318** *all* Jay Penni Photography/McDougal Littell; **319** Sculpture: Big Crinkley, Estate of Alexander Calder/Artists Rights Society (ARS), New York. Photo Credit: Owaki-Kulla/Corbis; **322** *left* Phil Jason/Getty Images; *center* Adrienne Cleveland, www.naturalsights.com; *right* Chris Daniels/Corbis; **324** Lawrence Lawry/Getty Images; **328** James Randklev/Corbis; **333** Jay Penni Photography/McDougal Littell; **335** Marc Romanelli/Getty Images; **340** Robert Brenner/PhotoEdit; **342** *top* DK Limited/Corbis; *bottom* Dorling Kindersley/Getty Images; **352** oote boe/Alamy; **354−355** age fotostock/SuperStock; **356** Karl Maslowski/Photo Researchers, Inc.; **357** Jeff Greenberg/The Image Works; **359** Mike Powell/Getty Images; **362** Stockdisc/Getty Images; **364** The Longaberger Company Home Office, Newark, Ohio; **366** Joseph Sohm/ChromoSohm, Inc./Corbis; **368** The Longaberger Company Home Office, Newark, Ohio; **369** *bottom* Erick Fowke/PhotoEdit; **369** *top* SciMat/Photo Researchers, Inc.; **371** *both* Barry Winiker/Index Stock Imagery; **372** Detlev Van Ravenswaay/Science Photo Library; **380** Royalty-Free/Corbis; **381** Steve Fitchett/Getty Images; **386** Hubert Stadler/Corbis; **388** Matthias Kulka/Corbis; **397** Premium Stock/Corbis; **406** Stephen Johnson/Corbis; **409** Tom Stewart/Corbis; **410** *both* Sean Justice/Getty Images; **414** Bonnie Kamin/PhotoEdit; **416** Main Street America/PhotoDisc/Veer;

Illustrations and Maps

Argosy **1, 71, 145, 199, 215, 290** *top right*, **290** *top left*, **293, 355, 386** *top center*, **426, 431, 463** *top left*, **503** *bottom right*, **503** *center right*, **505, 523, 532** *center left*, **566, 567, 571, 578** *center*, **579, 613, 620, 624** *top right*, **640, 644, 647** *bottom*, **649, 682, 685** *center right*, **694** *center right*, **716, 717, 719, 730, 732, 735, 742, 761, 788** *center right*, **791, 800** *center*, **808, 816, 818** *left*, **831, 834** *top*, **838, 844** *center right*, **855** *right*; Kenneth Batelman **226, 300, 315** *bottom right*, **386** *center right*, **394** *center right*, **417, 424, 475** *center*, **685** *top right*, **706** *right*, **749**; Steve Cowden **6, 21, 36, 39, 41, 58** *bottom*, **77, 101, 115, 156**; Stephen Durke **187, 223, 308** *top center*, **308** *bottom right*, **317** *top right*, **319, 320, 335, 335, 340, 342** *center right*, **383, 390, 416** *left*, **439, 450, 479** *bottom right*, **479** *center right*, **485, 488** *top*, **575, 578** *center right*, **596** *center*, **657** *center*, **674, 687** *top left*, **774, 834** *center right*; John Francis **336, 393, 475** *top*, **520** *center*, **539, 614, 623, 624** *center right*, **631, 760, 778** *bottom left*, **778** *top right*, **822,**
826; Patrick Gnan/Deborah Wolfe, Ltd. **10** *bottom right*, **31, 110, 119, 167, 238** *bottom right*, **248** *bottom right*, **254, 254, 305, 334, 339, 352** *center right*, **403** *both*, **422, 445, 471, 474, 488** *center*, **536, 663** *center right*, **665, 670, 686, 698, 745** *left*, **751, 763, 776, 796, 825**; Chris Lyons **238** *top*, **333** *center*, **512** *center*, **526, 543, 591, 595, 597**; Steve McEntee **159** *top*, **196, 261, 262, 311, 317, 452, 482, 596** *center right*, **752, 752** *top right*; Sarah Buss/McDougal Littell **578** *top right*; Karen Minot **91, 168, 333** *center right*, **369, 703, 738, 754, 844** *bottom right*; Paul Mirocha **298, 834** *bottom right*; Laurie O'Keefe **363, 694** *top right*, **773, 778** *bottom right*, **817**; Jun Park **848**; David Puckett **329, 329**; Tony Randazzo/American Artists **706** *left*, **726, 767**; Mark Schroeder **365, 520** *top*, **528, 548, 663** *top right*, **669** *center*, **669** *bottom*, **692, 827, 853**; Dan Stuckenschneider **151, 162, 170** *top left*, **170** *center right*, **176, 177, 278** *center*, **315** *center right*, **316, 324** *top right*, **438, 455, 463** *top right*; Robert Ulrich **510**; Carol Zuber-Mallison **32** *top*, **159** *bottom*, **213, 695**. All other illustrations © McDougal Littell/Houghton Mifflin Company.

Worked-Out Solutions

This section of the book provides step-by-step solutions to exercises with circled exercise numbers. These solutions provide models that can help guide your work with the homework exercises.

The separate **Selected Answers** section follows this section. It provides numerous answers that you can use to check your own answers.

Chapter 1

Lesson 1.1 (pp. 5–8)

15.
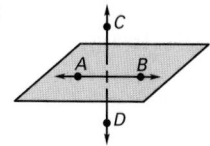

19. Plane PQS and plane HGS intersect at $\overleftrightarrow{RS}$.

43. A 4-legged table may rock from side to side because four points are not necessarily coplanar. A 3-legged table would not rock because three points determine a unique plane.

Lesson 1.2 (pp. 12–14)

13.
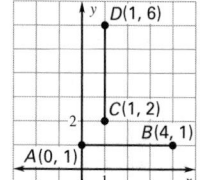
$AB = \left|4 - 0\right| = 4$
$CD = \left|6 - 2\right| = 4$
So, $\overline{AB} \cong \overline{CD}$.

17. $JL = \left|1 - (-6)\right| = \left|1 + 6\right| = 7$

33. **a.** $AC = AB + BC = 1282 + 601 = 1883$ mi

 b. $d = rt \rightarrow 2000 = r(40) \rightarrow r \approx 50$ mi/h

Lesson 1.3 (pp. 19–22)

15. $SM = MU$

 $x + 15 = 4x - 45 \rightarrow x = 20$

 $SU = SM + MU = x + 15 + 4x - 45 = 70$

35. Length: $\left|3 - (-4)\right| = 7$ units

 Coordinate of midpoint: $\dfrac{x_1 + x_2}{2} = \dfrac{-4 + 3}{2}$
 $= -\dfrac{1}{2}$

49.
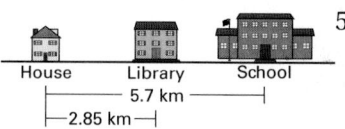 $5.7 \div 2 = 2.85$ km

Lesson 1.4 (pp. 28–32)

15. Another name for $\angle ACB$ is $\angle BCA$. The angle is a right angle because it is labeled with a red square.

23. $m\angle ADC = m\angle ADB + m\angle CDB$
 $= 21° + 44° = 65°$

53. **a.** $m\angle DEF = m\angle ABC = 112°$

 b. $m\angle ABG = \dfrac{1}{2} \cdot m\angle ABC = \dfrac{1}{2}(112°) = 56°$

 c. $m\angle CBG = \dfrac{1}{2} \cdot m\angle ABC = \dfrac{1}{2}(112°) = 56°$

 d. $m\angle DEG = \dfrac{1}{2} \cdot m\angle DEF = \dfrac{1}{2}(112°) = 56°$

Lesson 1.5 (pp. 38–41)

9. $m\angle 1 + m\angle 2 = 90° \rightarrow 21° + m\angle 2 = 90° \rightarrow$
 $m\angle 2 = 69°$

21. $\angle 1$ and $\angle 2$ are a linear pair.

47. Neither, because the sum of their measures is greater than 180°.

Lesson 1.6 (pp. 44–47)

13. The polygon is a quadrilateral because it has 4 sides. It is equiangular but not equilateral, so it is not regular.

19. A decagon is sometimes regular, because all of its sides and all of its angles can be congruent, but they don't have to be.

33. The polygon has 3 sides, so it is a triangle. It appears to be regular.

Lesson 1.7 (pp. 52–56)

7. $P = a + b + c = 30 + 72 + 78 = 180$ yd

$A = \frac{1}{2}bh = \frac{1}{2}(72)(30) = 1080$ yd^2

21. $13 \, ft^2 \cdot \dfrac{1 \text{ yd}^2}{9 \, ft^2} \approx 1.44$ yd^2

41. $A = \ell w = 45(30) = 1350$

$P = 2\ell + 2w = 2(45) + 2(30) = 150$

You need to cover 1350 square yards with grass seed, and you need

$150 \, \text{yd} \cdot \dfrac{3 \text{ ft}}{1 \, \text{yd}} = 450$ feet of fencing.

Chapter 2

Lesson 2.1 (pp. 75–78)

7. 3,   12,   48,   192, . . .
     ×4   ×4   ×4   ×4

Each number in the pattern is four times the previous number. The next number is 768.

15. Counterexample:
$(2 + 5)^2 = 7^2 = 49 \neq 2^2 + 5^2 = 4 + 25 = 29$

33. *Sample answer:* Conjecture: In 2004, more than 7 trillion e-mail messages will be sent. The number of e-mail messages has increased each year for 7 years prior to 2004. If this pattern continues, the total will exceed 7 trillion in 2004.

Lesson 2.2 (pp. 82–85)

11. False; a polygon could have 5 sides without being a regular pentagon.

Counterexample:

17. False; it is not marked that $\overleftrightarrow{PQ}$ and $\overleftrightarrow{ST}$ intersect at a right angle, so you do not know that they are perpendicular.

33. You can show that the statement is false by finding a counterexample: swimming is a sport, but the participants do not wear helmets.

Lesson 2.3 (pp. 90–93)

7. If a rectangle has four equal side lengths, then it is a regular polygon.

17. If the bakery's revenue is greater than its costs, you will get a raise.

21. Deductive reasoning; the conclusion is reached by using laws of logic and the facts about school rules and what you did that day.

Lesson 2.4 (pp. 99–102)

7. Line p intersects line q at point H.

13. False. *Sample answer:* Consider any pair of opposite sides of a prism, which do not intersect.

31. Postulate 7: If two lines intersect, then their intersection is exactly one point.

Lesson 2.5 (pp. 108–111)

9.

$3(2x + 11) = 9$	Given
$6x + 33 = 9$	Distributive Property
$6x = -24$	Subtraction Property of Equality
$x = -4$	Division Property of Equality

21. If $AB = 20$, then $AB + CD = 20 + CD$.

31.

$P = 2\ell + 2w$	Given
$P - 2w = 2\ell$	Subtraction Property of Equality
$\dfrac{P}{2} - w = \ell$	Division Property of Equality

When $P = 55$ and $w = 11$:

$\ell = \dfrac{55}{2} - 11 = 16.5$ meters

Lesson 2.6 (pp. 116–119)

7. If $\angle F \cong \angle J$ and $\angle J \cong \angle L$, then $\angle F \cong \angle L$.

15.

Cottage   Snack   Bike   Arcade   Kite
          shop   rentals   shop

21.

Statements	Reasons
1. $\overrightarrow{TV}$ bisects $\angle UTW$.	1. Given
2. $\angle 1 \cong \angle 2$	2. Definition of angle bisector
3. $\angle 2 \cong \angle 3$	3. Given
4. $\angle 1 \cong \angle 3$	4. Transitive Property of Angle Congruence

Lesson 2.7 (pp. 127–131)

5. $\angle FGH \cong \angle WXZ$; $\angle WXZ$ is a right angle because $58° + 32° = 90°$, so they are congruent by the Right Angles Congruence Theorem.

13. Using the Vertical Angles Congruence Theorem:

$4x = 6x - 26 \rightarrow x = 13$

$6y + 8 = 7y - 12 \rightarrow y = 20$

39.

Statements	Reasons
1. $\overline{JK} \perp \overline{JM}$, $\overline{KL} \perp \overline{ML}$, $\angle J \cong \angle M$, $\angle K \cong \angle L$	1. Given
2. $\angle J$ is a right angle; $\angle L$ is a right angle.	2. Definition of perpendicular lines
3. $\angle M$ is a right angle; $\angle K$ is a right angle.	3. Right Angles Congruence Theorem
4. $\overline{JM} \perp \overline{ML}$, $\overline{JK} \perp \overline{KL}$	4. Definition of perpendicular lines

Chapter 3

Lesson 3.1 (pp. 150–152)

11. The pairs of corresponding angles are $\angle 1$ and $\angle 5$, $\angle 2$ and $\angle 6$, $\angle 3$ and $\angle 7$, and $\angle 4$ and $\angle 8$.

25. If two lines are not coplanar, then they never intersect.

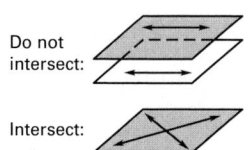

35. The arm is skew to a telephone pole.

Lesson 3.2 (pp. 157–160)

5. If $m\angle 7 = 110°$, then $m\angle 2 = 110°$, by the Alternate Exterior Angles Theorem.

9. Corresponding Angles Postulate

39. a. yes; $\angle 1$ and $\angle 5$, $\angle 2$ and $\angle 6$; yes; $\angle 1$ and $\angle 2$, $\angle 1$ and $\angle 6$, $\angle 2$ and $\angle 5$, $\angle 5$ and $\angle 6$

b. Because the bars are parallel, corresponding angles between the bars and the foot are congruent. Because the body and the foot are parallel, the bars act as transversals, and so the alternate interior angles are congruent. (See diagram.) This forces the foot to stay parallel with the floor.

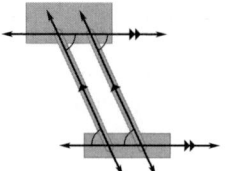

Lesson 3.3 (pp. 165–169)

11. Yes; Alternate Exterior Angles Converse

29. Because the alternate interior angles are congruent, you know that the top of the picnic table is parallel to the ground.

37. It is given that $\angle 3$ and $\angle 5$ are supplementary. $\angle 3$ is supplementary to $\angle 4$ because they form a straight angle. $\angle 4 \cong \angle 5$ by the Congruent Supplements Theorem. Therefore, $m \parallel n$ by the Alternate Interior Angles Converse.

Lesson 3.4 (pp. 175–178)

7. $m = \dfrac{y_2 - y_1}{x_2 - x_1} = \dfrac{6 - 5}{5 - 3} = \dfrac{1}{2}$

13. Line 1: $m_1 = \dfrac{y_2 - y_1}{x_2 - x_1} = \dfrac{4 - 0}{7 - 1} = \dfrac{2}{3}$

Line 2: $m_2 = \dfrac{y_2 - y_1}{x_2 - x_1} = \dfrac{6 - 0}{3 - 7} = -\dfrac{3}{2}$

Because $m_1 \cdot m_2 = \dfrac{2}{3} \cdot \left(-\dfrac{3}{2}\right) = -1$, the lines are perpendicular.

35.

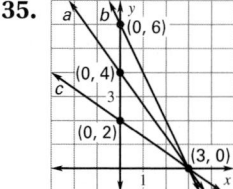

Line b is the most steep because the absolute value of its slope is the greatest. Line c is the least steep because the absolute value of its slope is the least.

Lesson 3.5 (pp. 184–187)

17. $P(5, 4)$, $m = 4$

$y = mx + b \rightarrow 4 = 4(5) + b \rightarrow b = -16$

An equation of the line is $y = 4x - 16$.

23. The slope of a line parallel to $y = -2x + 3$ is $m = -2$.

$y = mx + b \rightarrow -1 = -2(0) + b \rightarrow b = -1$

An equation of the line is $y = -2x - 1$.

61. x = days since age 14; y = weight (in kg)

$y = 2.1x + 2000$

The slope, 2.1, represents the rate of weight gain, in kilograms per day. The y-intercept, 2000, represents the weight, in kilograms, at age 14.

Lesson 3.6 (pp. 194–197)

19. Line f is parallel to line g because they are both perpendicular to line d.

23. Slope of parallel lines: $m = \dfrac{4 - 0}{1 - 0} = 4$

A perpendicular segment joining the two lines has endpoints $(0, 0)$ and $(4, -1)$, since its slope is $-\dfrac{1}{4}$.

Distance from $(4, -1)$ to $(0, 0)$:

$d = \sqrt{(4 - 0)^2 + (-1 - 0)^2} \approx 4.1$

29. Jump to point C, because the shortest distance is the length of the perpendicular segment.

Chapter 4

Lesson 4.1 (pp. 221–224)

9. The triangle has 3 congruent sides and 3 congruent angles, so it is an equiangular equilateral triangle.

15. $x° + 3x° + 60° = 180° \rightarrow x = 30$

$3x° = 3(30)° = 90°$

Because the triangle has a right angle, it is a right triangle.

41.

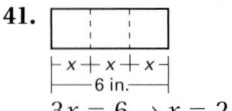

$3x = 6 \rightarrow x = 2$

Each side of the triangle is 2 inches.

The measure of each angle is $180° \div 3 = 60°$.

Lesson 4.2 (pp. 228–231)

9. $\triangle LNM \cong \triangle ZYX$

15. By the Triangle Sum Theorem,
$m\angle M = 180° - 90° - 70° = 20°$.
By the Third Angles Theorem,
$x° = m\angle M = 20°$, so $x = 20$.

25. The length, height, and depth have to be the same.

Lesson 4.3 (pp. 236–239)

7. True; $\overline{DE} \cong \overline{DG}$, $\overline{EF} \cong \overline{GF}$, and $\overline{FD} \cong \overline{FD}$ by the Reflexive Property.

So, $\triangle DEF \cong \triangle DGF$ by the SSS Congruence Postulate.

9. $AB = 6$, $BC = 8$,

$CA = \sqrt{(-2 - 4)^2 + (-2 - 6)^2} = 10$

$DE = 6$, $EF = 8$,

$FD = \sqrt{(5 - 13)^2 + (7 - 1)^2} = 10$

By the SSS Congruence Postulate, $\triangle ABC \cong \triangle DEF$.

25. Because $\overline{WY} \cong \overline{VY}$ and $\overline{YZ} \cong \overline{YX}$, then $\overline{WZ} \cong \overline{VX}$. By the Reflexive Property, $\overline{WV} \cong \overline{VW}$. It is given that $\overline{WX} \cong \overline{VZ}$. So, by the SSS Congruence Postulate, $\triangle VWX \cong \triangle WVZ$.

Lesson 4.4 (pp. 243–246)

13. There is enough information given, since $\overline{GH} \cong \overline{EF}$, $\angle GHF \cong \angle EFH$, and $\overline{HF} \cong \overline{FH}$.

19.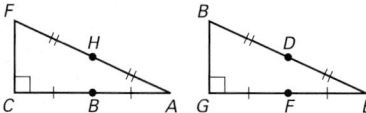

Because $\overline{FH} \cong \overline{HA} \cong \overline{BD} \cong \overline{DE}$, then $\overline{FA} \cong \overline{BE}$. Because $\overline{CB} \cong \overline{BA} \cong \overline{GF} \cong \overline{FE}$, then $\overline{CA} \cong \overline{GE}$. Also, $\triangle ACF$ and $\triangle EGB$ are right triangles. So, $\triangle ACF \cong \triangle EGB$ by the Hypotenuse-Leg Congruence Theorem.

31. SAS Congruence Postulate

Lesson 4.5 (pp. 252–255)

5. Yes; ASA Congruence Postulate

9. $\angle F \cong \angle L$

27. AAS Congruence Theorem

Lesson 4.6 (pp. 259–263)

19. Show $\triangle KNP \cong \triangle MNP$ by SSS. Now $\angle KPL \cong \angle MPL$ and $\overline{PL} \cong \overline{PL}$ leads to $\triangle LKP \cong \triangle LMP$ by SAS, which gives you $\angle 1 \cong \angle 2$.

23.

Statements	Reasons
1. $\angle X \cong \angle Z$, $\angle U \cong \angle T$, $\overline{ZY} \cong \overline{XY}$	1. Given
2. $\triangle TYZ \cong \triangle UYX$	2. AAS Congruence Postulate
3. $\angle VYX \cong \angle Z + \angle T$, $\angle WYZ \cong \angle X + \angle U$	3. Exterior Angle Theorem
4. $\angle VYX \cong \angle Z + \angle T$, $\angle WYZ \cong \angle Z + \angle T$	4. Substitution
5. $\angle VYX \cong \angle WYZ$	5. Transitive Property of Congruence

31. A; Once you show that $\angle XWZ \cong \angle YZW$ by the Alternate Interior Angles Theorem, $\overline{WZ} \cong \overline{ZW}$ by the Reflexive Property, and $\angle Y \cong \angle X$ by the Right Angles Congruence Theorem, you can show that $\triangle WYZ \cong \triangle ZXW$ by the AAS Congruence Theorem. This means that $\overline{WY} \cong \overline{ZX}$.

Lesson 4.7 (pp. 267–270)

5. If $\angle D \cong \angle CED$, then $\overline{CE} \cong \overline{CD}$ by the Converse of Base Angles Theorem.

17. $9y° = x°$ by the Base Angles Theorem and $9y° + x° = 90°$ by the Corollary to the Triangle Sum Theorem. So, $9y° + x° = 90° \rightarrow 9y° + 9y° = 90 \rightarrow 18y° = 90 \rightarrow y = 5$ and $x° = 9y° \rightarrow x = 9(5) = 45$.

41. a.

Statements	Reasons
1. $\angle BAC \cong \angle BCA \cong \angle DCE \cong \angle DEC$	1. Given
2. $\overline{BA} \cong \overline{BC} \cong \overline{DC} \cong \overline{DE}$	2. Converse of Base Angles Theorem
3. $\angle CBD \cong \angle CDB$	3. Base Angles Theorem
4. $\angle BCA \cong \angle CBD$	4. Alternate Interior Angles Theorem
5. $\angle CDB \cong \angle BAC$	5. Substitution
6. $\triangle ABC \cong \triangle BCD$	6. AAS Congruence Postulate

b. $\triangle ABC, \triangle CDE, \triangle EFG, \triangle BCD, \triangle DEF$

c. $\angle CDE, \angle EFG, \angle BCD, \angle DEF$

Lesson 4.8 (pp. 276–279)

11. $(x, y) \rightarrow (x + 4, y + 1)$

$A(-3, 1) \rightarrow (1, 2)$

$B(2, 3) \rightarrow (6, 4)$

$C(3, 0) \rightarrow (7, 1)$

$D(-1, -1) \rightarrow (3, 0)$

23.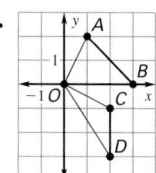

$m\angle AOC > m\angle BOD$

This is not a rotation.

39. From A to B, use a 90° clockwise rotation. From A to C, use a 90° counterclockwise rotation.

Chapter 5

Lesson 5.1 (pp. 298–301)

9. $\overline{YJ} \cong \overline{JX} \cong \overline{LK}$

21.

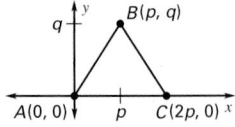

$AB = \sqrt{(p-0)^2 + (q-0)^2} = \sqrt{p^2 + q^2}$

$BC = \sqrt{(2p-p)^2 + (0-q)^2} = \sqrt{p^2 + q^2}$

$AC = 2p$

$m_{AB} = \dfrac{q-0}{p-0} = \dfrac{q}{p}$

$m_{BC} = \dfrac{0-q}{2p-p} = -\dfrac{q}{p}$

$m_{AC} = \dfrac{0-0}{2p-0} = 0$

$M_{AB}\left(\dfrac{0+p}{2}, \dfrac{0+q}{2}\right) = \left(\dfrac{p}{2}, \dfrac{q}{2}\right)$

$M_{BC}\left(\dfrac{p+2p}{2}, \dfrac{q+0}{2}\right) = \left(\dfrac{3p}{2}, \dfrac{q}{2}\right)$

$M_{AC}\left(\dfrac{0+2p}{2}, \dfrac{0+0}{2}\right) = (p, 0)$

$\triangle ABC$ is not a right triangle because no two sides are perpendicular since their slopes are not negative reciprocals. $\triangle ABC$ is isosceles because $AB = BC$.

37. $W\left(\dfrac{0+6}{2}, \dfrac{0+6}{2}\right) = W(3, 3)$

$V\left(\dfrac{6+8}{2}, \dfrac{6+0}{2}\right) = V(7, 3)$

$m_{WV} = \dfrac{3-3}{7-3} = 0 = m_{OH} = \dfrac{0-0}{8-0} = 0 \to$

$\overline{WV} \| \overline{OH}$

$WV = |7-3| = 4,\ OH = |8-0| = 8 \to$

$WV = \dfrac{1}{2}OH$

Lesson 5.2 (pp. 306–309)

15. Because $LK = LM$, L lies on the perpendicular bisector of $\overline{KM}$ by the Converse of the Perpendicular Bisector Theorem.

17. By Theorem 5.4, $GA = GB = GC = 11$.

25. Connect the three houses with line segments. Fold your house to Mike's house, Mike's house to Ken's house, and Ken's house to your house. The folded lines are the perpendicular bisectors. You should meet where they intersect.

Lesson 5.3 (pp. 313–316)

7. Not enough information is given.

15. No, because you do not know that the blue line segments are perpendicular to the sides of the angle.

29. Build the fountain where the angle bisectors meet at the incenter, which is equidistant from the 3 sides.

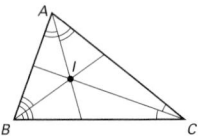

Lesson 5.4 (pp. 322–325)

5. $AG = \dfrac{2}{3}AE \to AG = \dfrac{2}{3}(15) \to AG = 10$

21. Because $\triangle XYW \cong \triangle ZYW$, $\overline{YW}$ is a perpendicular bisector, an angle bisector, a median, and an altitude.

39. Base of red triangle $= \dfrac{1}{2}(9) = 4.5$

Height of red triangle $= 3$

Area of red triangle $= \dfrac{1}{2}(4.5)(3) = 6.75 \text{ in.}^2$

The altitude was used.

Lesson 5.5 (pp. 331–334)

9. $\overline{KL}, \overline{JL}, \overline{JK}$, and $\angle J, \angle K, \angle L$ by Theorem 5.10.

17. No, because $3 + 6 \not> 9$.

39. a. Using the Triangle Inequality Theorem:

$x + 489 > 565 \qquad x < 565 + 489$

$\qquad x > 76 \qquad\qquad x < 1054$

A value of $x = 1080$ does not satisfy $76 < x < 1054$.

b. No, $x = 40$ does not satisfy $x > 76$.

c. $x > 76;\ x < 1054$

d. Because $m\angle 2 < m\angle 1$, $x < 489$. Because $m\angle 2 < m\angle 3$, $x < 565$. Since $x < 489$ and $x < 565$, the distance is less than 489 kilometers.

Lesson 5.6 (pp. 338–341)

5. $TR < UR$ by the Hinge Theorem, because $\angle TQR < \angle USR$.

7. $m\angle 1 = m\angle 2$ because both triangles are congruent using the SSS Congruence Postulate.

23. E, A, D, B, C

Chapter 6

Lesson 6.1 (pp. 360–363)

5. $\dfrac{6\ \text{L}}{10\ \text{mL}} = \dfrac{6\ \cancel{L}}{10\ \cancel{mL}} \cdot \dfrac{1000\ \cancel{mL}}{1\ \cancel{L}} = \dfrac{6000}{10} = \dfrac{600}{1}$

27. $\dfrac{1}{c+5} = \dfrac{3}{24} \rightarrow 24 = 3(c+5) \rightarrow c = 3$

59. Total amount of trail mix $= 36\left(\dfrac{1}{2}\right) = 18$ cups.

$5x + 1x + 4x = 18 \rightarrow x = \dfrac{9}{5}$ cups

Peanuts: $5\left(\dfrac{9}{5}\right) = 9$ cups

Chocolate chips: $1\left(\dfrac{9}{5}\right) = \dfrac{9}{5} = 1\dfrac{4}{5}$ cups

Raisins: $4\left(\dfrac{9}{5}\right) = \dfrac{36}{5} = 7\dfrac{1}{5}$ cups

Lesson 6.2 (pp. 367–370)

11. $\dfrac{CB}{BA} = \dfrac{DE}{EF} \rightarrow \dfrac{6}{x} = \dfrac{4}{7} \rightarrow 6(7) = 4x \rightarrow 10.5 = x$

So, $BA = 10.5$.

13. $\dfrac{1\ \text{inch}}{50\ \text{yards}} = \dfrac{2\ \text{inches}}{x\ \text{yards}} \rightarrow x = 2(50) = 100$ yards

25. $\dfrac{1\ \text{inch}}{3.2\ \text{miles}} \approx \dfrac{2.5\ \text{inches}}{x\ \text{miles}} \rightarrow x \approx 3.2(2.5) = 8$ miles

Lesson 6.3 (pp. 376–379)

3. $\angle A \cong \angle L$, $\angle B \cong \angle M$, and $\angle C \cong \angle N$

$\dfrac{AB}{LM} = \dfrac{BC}{MN} = \dfrac{CA}{NL}$

7. $\dfrac{RS}{WX} = \dfrac{64}{32} = 2$ $\qquad \dfrac{ST}{XY} = \dfrac{48}{24} = 2$

$\dfrac{TU}{YZ} = \dfrac{64}{32} = 2$ $\qquad \dfrac{UR}{ZW} = \dfrac{48}{24} = 2$

The ratios are equal, so the corresponding side lengths are proportional, and the polygons are similar. So, $RSTU \sim WXYZ$, and the scale factor is 2.

31. $\dfrac{9\ \text{ft long}}{78\ \text{ft long}} = \dfrac{3}{26}$ $\qquad \dfrac{5\ \text{ft wide}}{36\ \text{ft wide}} = \dfrac{5}{36}$

The ratios are not equal, so the corresponding side lengths are not proportional, and the surfaces are not similar.

Lesson 6.4 (pp. 384–387)

9. Yes; $\angle H \cong \angle J$, and $m\angle F = 42°$ by the Triangle Sum Theorem, so $\angle F \cong \angle K$. So, $\triangle GFH \sim \triangle LKJ$ by the AA Similarity Postulate.

13. By the Triangular Sum Theorem, $m\angle YZX = 50°$ and $m\angle U = 45°$. So, $\triangle XYZ \sim \triangle UYW$ by the AA Similarity Postulate.

33. All angles of any two equilateral triangles are congruent, so the triangles are similar by the AA Similarity Postulate

Lesson 6.5 (pp. 391–395)

3. $\dfrac{AB}{DE} = \dfrac{15}{10} = \dfrac{3}{2}$ $\quad \dfrac{BC}{EF} = \dfrac{18}{12} = \dfrac{3}{2}$ $\quad \dfrac{AC}{DF} = \dfrac{12}{8} = \dfrac{3}{2}$

Because $\dfrac{AB}{DE} = \dfrac{BC}{EF} = \dfrac{AC}{DF}$, $\triangle ABC \sim \triangle DEF$.

The scale factor of $\triangle ABC$ to $\triangle DEF$ is $\dfrac{3}{2}$.

7. Yes, because $\dfrac{DE}{WY} = \dfrac{9}{6} = \dfrac{3}{2} = \dfrac{FD}{XW} = \dfrac{15}{10} = \dfrac{3}{2}$, and $\angle D \cong \angle W$. $\triangle DEF \sim \triangle WYX$, and the scale factor of $\triangle WYX$ to $\triangle DEF$ is $\dfrac{2}{3}$.

31. To use the SAS Similarity Theorem, you need $\angle CBD \cong \angle CAE$.

Lesson 6.6 (pp. 400–403)

5. Yes, by Theorem 6.5 because

$$\frac{LK}{KJ} = \frac{8}{5} = \frac{LM}{MN} = \frac{12}{7.5} = \frac{8}{5}.$$

9. $\frac{15}{x} = \frac{21}{14} \rightarrow 21x = 210 \rightarrow x = 10$

21. Let x = the distance along University Avenue from 12th Street to Washington Street.

$$\frac{200}{400} = \frac{x}{700} \rightarrow 400x = 140{,}000 \rightarrow x = 350 \text{ yards}$$

Lesson 6.7 (pp. 412–415)

5. $(x, y) \rightarrow (1.5x, 1.5y)$

$A(1, 1) \rightarrow L(1.5, 1.5)$

$B(6, 1) \rightarrow M(9, 1.5)$

$C(6, 3) \rightarrow N(9, 4.5)$

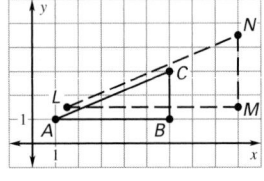

11. The dilation is an enlargement.

A: (2, 0), (1, 2), and (3, 2)

B: (6, 0), (3, 6), and (9, 6)

For each vertex (x, y) of Figure A, the corresponding vertex of Figure B is $(3x, 3y)$. The scale factor is 3.

27. The scale factor is $\frac{15 \text{ ft}}{6 \text{ ft}} = \frac{5}{2}$, or 2.5.

Chapter 7

Lesson 7.1 (pp. 436–439)

9. $13.4^2 = 9.8^2 + x^2$

$179.56 = 96.04 + x^2$

$83.52 = x^2 \rightarrow 9.139 \approx x$

x is about 9.1 inches.

11.

$8^2 + h^2 = 17^2$

$h^2 = 225$

$h = 15$

Area $= \frac{1}{2} bh = \frac{1}{2}(16)(15) = 120 \text{ m}^2$

33. *Sample answer:* The longest side of the triangle is opposite the largest angle, which in a right triangle is the right angle.

Lesson 7.2 (pp. 444–447)

7. $(\sqrt{26})^2 \stackrel{?}{=} 5^2 + 1^2 \rightarrow 26 \stackrel{?}{=} 25 + 1 \rightarrow 26 = 26 \checkmark$

The triangle is a right triangle.

17. $24 + 30 = 54 \qquad 30 + 6\sqrt{43} \approx 69.3$

$54 > 6\sqrt{43} \qquad 69.3 > 24$

$6\sqrt{43} + 24 \approx 63.3$

$63.3 > 30$

The segment lengths form a triangle.

Because $(6\sqrt{43})^2 > 24^2 + 30^2$, the segment lengths form an obtuse triangle.

37. a. Let $x = BC$.

$12^2 + x^2 = 13^2 \rightarrow x^2 = 25 \rightarrow x = 5 = BC$

b. Because $5^2 = 3^2 + 4^2$, $\triangle ABC$ is a right triangle.

c. *Sample answer:*

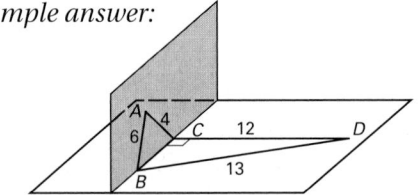

Lesson 7.3 (pp. 453–456)

5. $\frac{107.5}{76} = \frac{76}{h} \rightarrow 107.5h = 5776 \rightarrow h \approx 53.7 \text{ ft}$

15. $\frac{z}{27} = \frac{27}{16} \rightarrow 16z = 729 \rightarrow z \approx 45.6$

29. Let c represent the hypotenuse of the large triangle.

$1.5^2 + 1.5^2 = c^2 \rightarrow 4.5 = c^2 \rightarrow \sqrt{4.5} = c$

$\frac{x}{1.5} = \frac{1.5}{\sqrt{4.5}} \rightarrow \sqrt{4.5}x = 2.25 \rightarrow x \approx 1.1 \text{ ft}$

Lesson 7.4 (pp. 461–464)

5. hypotenuse $=$ leg $\cdot \sqrt{2} \rightarrow 3\sqrt{2} = x \cdot \sqrt{2} \rightarrow 3 = x$

9. $3\sqrt{3} = x\sqrt{3} \rightarrow x = 3$

$y = 2x = 2(3) = 6$

27. $11 = 2 \cdot h \rightarrow h = 5.5 \text{ feet}$

Lesson 7.5 (pp. 469–472)

5. $\tan A = \dfrac{\text{opp. }\angle A}{\text{adj. to }\angle A} = \dfrac{48}{20} = \dfrac{12}{5} = 2.4000$

$\tan B = \dfrac{\text{opp. }\angle B}{\text{adj. to }\angle B} = \dfrac{20}{48} = \dfrac{5}{12} \approx 0.4167$

7. $\tan 27° = \dfrac{\text{opp.}}{\text{adj.}} = \dfrac{x}{15} \rightarrow x \approx 7.6$

31.

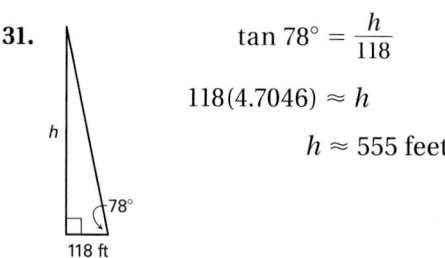

$\tan 78° = \dfrac{h}{118}$

$118(4.7046) \approx h$

$h \approx 555 \text{ feet}$

Lesson 7.6 (pp. 477–480)

5. $\sin D = \dfrac{\text{opp. }\angle D}{\text{hyp.}} = \dfrac{28}{53} \approx 0.5283$

$\sin E = \dfrac{\text{opp. }\angle E}{\text{hyp.}} = \dfrac{45}{53} \approx 0.8491$

9. $\cos X = \dfrac{\text{adj. to }\angle X}{\text{hyp.}} = \dfrac{13}{26} = \dfrac{1}{2} = 0.5$

$\cos Y = \dfrac{\text{adj. to }\angle Y}{\text{hyp.}} = \dfrac{13\sqrt{3}}{26} = \dfrac{\sqrt{3}}{2} \approx 0.8660$

33.

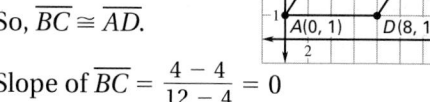

$\sin 31° = \dfrac{19}{y} \rightarrow y = \dfrac{19}{\sin 31°} \rightarrow y \approx 36.9 \text{ ft}$

Lesson 7.7 (pp. 485–489)

5. $\tan A = \dfrac{14}{4} = \dfrac{7}{2} = 3.5$

$m\angle A = \tan^{-1} 3.5 \approx 74.1°$

13. $9^2 + 12^2 = (AC)^2 \rightarrow 225 = (AC)^2 \rightarrow 15 = AC$

$\tan A = \dfrac{9}{12} = 0.75$

$m\angle A = \tan^{-1} 0.75 \approx 36.9°$

$180° \approx 90° + 36.9° + m\angle C \rightarrow m\angle C \approx 53.1°$

The side lengths are 9 units, 12 units, and 15 units. The angle measures are 90°, about 36.9°, and about 53.1°.

35. The angle of depression is 90° minus the measure of the angle you can find:

$90 - \tan^{-1}\left(\dfrac{7}{12}\right) \approx 90 - \tan^{-1} 0.5833 \approx$

$90 - 30.3° = 59.7°$.

Chapter 8

Lesson 8.1 (pp. 510–513)

9. $(n - 2) \cdot 180° = 1980° \rightarrow n - 2 = 11 \rightarrow n = 13$

The polygon is a 13-gon.

11. Pentagon; $(5 - 2) \cdot 180° = 540°$

$x° + 86° + 140° + 138° + 59° = 540° \rightarrow x = 117$

29. Hexagon; $(6 - 2) \cdot 180° = 720°$

Lesson 8.2 (pp. 518–521)

9. $m\angle A + m\angle B = 180°$

$51° + m\angle B = 180°$

$m\angle B = 129°$

13. $b - 1 = 9 \rightarrow b = 10$ and $5a = 15 \rightarrow a = 3$

39. a. $PQRS$ is a parallelogram, so $\overline{PQ} \cong \overline{RS}$.

$RS = PQ = 3$ inches

b. $PQRS$ is a parallelogram, so $\angle Q \cong \angle S$.

$m\angle S = m\angle Q = 70°$

c. The sum of the measures of the interior angles always is 360°. As $m\angle Q$ increases so does $m\angle S$, therefore $m\angle P$ must decrease to maintain the sum of 360°. As $m\angle Q$ decreases $m\angle P$ increases, moving Q farther away from S.

Lesson 8.3 (pp. 526–529)

5. Theorem 8.7, because both pairs of opposite sides are congruent.

11. $BC = 12 - 4 = 8$;

$AD = 8 - 0 = 8$

So, $\overline{BC} \cong \overline{AD}$.

Slope of $\overline{BC} = \dfrac{4 - 4}{12 - 4} = 0$

Slope of $\overline{AD} = \dfrac{1 - 1}{8 - 0} = 0$

Slopes are equal, so $\overline{BC} \parallel \overline{AD}$.

$\overline{BC} \cong \overline{AD}$ and $\overline{BC} \parallel \overline{AD}$, so $ABCD$ is a parallelogram.

31. a. *Quadrilateral EFJK:*

Because $\overline{EG} \cong \overline{KH}$, and F and J are midpoints of $\overline{EG}$ and $\overline{KH}$, then $\overline{EF} \cong \overline{FG} \cong \overline{KJ} \cong \overline{JH}$. Because $\overline{EF} \cong \overline{KJ}$ and $\overline{EK} \cong \overline{FJ}$, *EFJK* is a parallelogram.

Quadrilateral FGHJ:

Because $\overline{FG} \cong \overline{JH}$ and $\overline{FJ} \cong \overline{GH}$, *FGHJ* is a parallelogram.

Quadrilateral EGHK:

Because $\overline{EG} \cong \overline{KH}$ and $\overline{EK} \cong \overline{GH}$, *EGHK* is a parallelogram.

b. Although the angles may change, $\overline{EG}$ is always congruent to $\overline{KH}$ and $\overline{EK}$ is always congruent to $\overline{GH}$. So, *EGHK* is always a parallelogram. Therefore $\overline{EG}$ is always parallel to $\overline{KH}$.

Lesson 8.4 (pp. 537–540)

7. 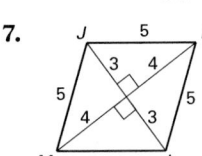 The diagonals are congruent if the rhombus is a square. Or, you can sketch a rhombus that has the diagonals shown. So, the statement is sometimes true.

15. The quadrilateral is a square because it is a parallelogram with four congruent sides and four congruent angles, which must be right angles.

55. Use the tape measure to measure the diagonals. If they are congruent, the region is a square.

Lesson 8.5 (pp. 546–549)

11. Because $\angle E$ and $\angle H$ are right angles, $\overline{EF} \parallel \overline{HG}$. $\overline{EH}$ is not parallel to $\overline{FG}$, so *EFGH* is a trapezoid.

19. By Theorem 8.19, because $\overline{EF} \cong \overline{EH}$, then $\angle F \cong \angle H$.

$$m\angle G + m\angle E + m\angle F + m\angle H = 360°$$
$$m\angle G + 60° + 110° + 110° = 360°$$
$$m\angle G = 80°$$

35.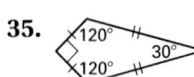

Lesson 8.6 (pp. 554–557)

3.

Property	▱	Rectangle	Rhombus	Square	Kite	Trapezoid
All sides are ≅.			X	X		

15. Trapezoid; it has exactly one pair of parallel sides ($\overline{PS}$ and $\overline{QR}$).

33. A trapezoid is outlined. The figure has only one pair of parallel sides. Since the non-parallel sides are not congruent, the figure is not an isosceles trapezoid.

Chapter 9

Lesson 9.1 (pp. 576–579)

7. $(x, y) \rightarrow (x + 4, y + 6)$

$P(-2, 3) \rightarrow P'(2, 9)$

$Q(1, 2) \rightarrow Q'(5, 8)$

$R(3, -1) \rightarrow R'(7, 5)$

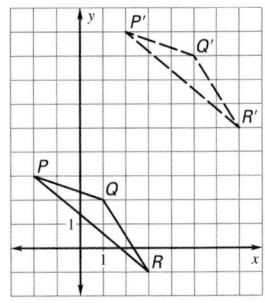

11. A rule is $(x, y) \rightarrow (x - 5, y + 2)$.

$AC = A'C' = 4$

$AB = \sqrt{(4 - 1)^2 + (1 + 1)^2} = \sqrt{13}$

$A'B' = \sqrt{(-1 + 4)^2 + (3 - 1)^2} = \sqrt{13}$

$BC = \sqrt{(5 - 4)^2 + (-1 - 1)^2} = \sqrt{5}$

$B'C' = \sqrt{(0 + 1)^2 + (1 - 3)^2} = \sqrt{5}$

By the SSS Congruence Postulate, $\triangle ABC \cong \triangle A'B'C'$, so the translation is an isometry.

35. From cabin to ski lodge:

$\langle 1 - 0, 2 - 0 \rangle = \langle 1, 2 \rangle$

Lesson 9.2 (pp. 584–587)

13.
$$\begin{bmatrix} 0 & 0 & 0 \\ 4 & 4 & 4 \end{bmatrix} + \begin{matrix} A & B & C \\ \begin{bmatrix} -2 & 2 & 1 \\ 4 & 1 & -3 \end{bmatrix} \end{matrix} = \begin{matrix} A' & B' & C' \\ \begin{bmatrix} -2 & 2 & 1 \\ 8 & 5 & 1 \end{bmatrix} \end{matrix}$$

Translation   Polygon   Image
matrix   matrix   matrix

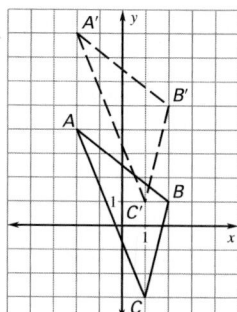

19.
$$\begin{bmatrix} 1.2 & 3 \end{bmatrix} \begin{bmatrix} -2 \\ -1.5 \end{bmatrix} = \begin{bmatrix} 1.2(-2) + 3(-1.5) \end{bmatrix}$$
$$= \begin{bmatrix} -6.9 \end{bmatrix}$$

31. Equipment matrix: Cost matrix:

	Mice	CDs	Keyboards
Lab 1	25	10	18
Lab 2	15	20	12

	Dollars
Mice	10
CDs	32
Keyboards	15

Total cost:

$$\begin{bmatrix} 25 & 10 & 18 \\ 15 & 20 & 12 \end{bmatrix} \begin{bmatrix} 10 \\ 32 \\ 15 \end{bmatrix} = \begin{bmatrix} 840 \\ 970 \end{bmatrix}$$

Lab 1: $840; Lab 2: $970

Lesson 9.3 (pp. 593–596)

5.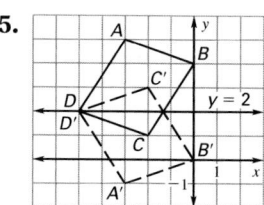

13.
$$\begin{bmatrix} 1 & 0 \\ 0 & -1 \end{bmatrix} \begin{matrix} A & B & C \\ \begin{bmatrix} -2 & 3 & 4 \\ 5 & -3 & 6 \end{bmatrix} \end{matrix} = \begin{matrix} A' & B' & C' \\ \begin{bmatrix} -2 & 3 & 4 \\ -5 & 3 & -6 \end{bmatrix} \end{matrix}$$

Reflection   Polygon   Image
matrix   matrix   matrix

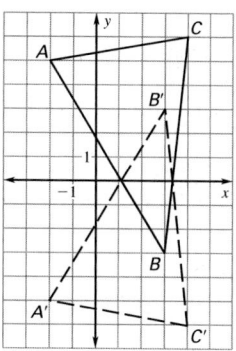

33. Case 1

Lesson 9.4 (pp. 602–605)

13. $(a, b) \rightarrow (-a, -b)$

$J(1, 4) \rightarrow J'(-1, -4)$

$K(5, 5) \rightarrow K'(-5, -5)$

$L(7, 2) \rightarrow L'(-7, -2)$

$M(2, 2) \rightarrow M'(-2, -2)$

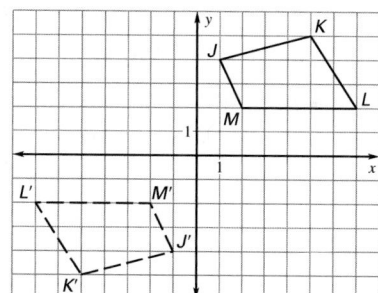

15.
$$\begin{bmatrix} 0 & -1 \\ 1 & 0 \end{bmatrix} \begin{matrix} A & B & C \\ \begin{bmatrix} 1 & 5 & 4 \\ 4 & 6 & 3 \end{bmatrix} \end{matrix} = \begin{matrix} A' & B' & C' \\ \begin{bmatrix} -4 & -6 & -3 \\ 1 & 5 & 4 \end{bmatrix} \end{matrix}$$

Rotation   Polygon   Image
matrix   matrix   matrix

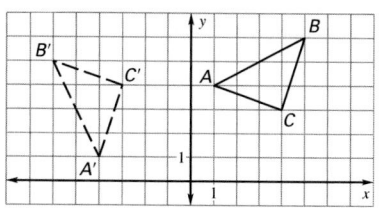

29. Rotation of 270°, because it would take three of the four 90° rotations for the blade to reach its original starting point.

Lesson 9.5 (pp. 611–615)

7.

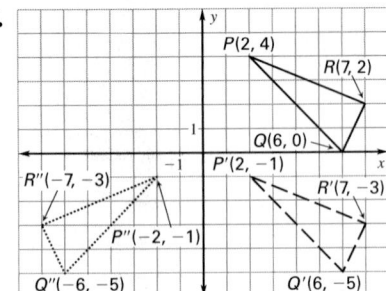

17. *Sample answer:* $\overrightarrow{CC'} \parallel \overrightarrow{BB''}$ and $\overrightarrow{AA'} \parallel \overrightarrow{BB''}$

27.

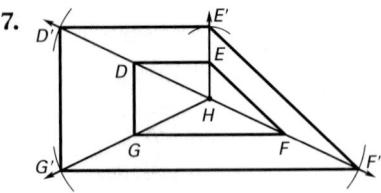

Translate 9 inches to the right, reflect in the *x*-axis.

Lesson 9.6 (pp. 621–624)

7. Yes; a rotation of 72° or 144° about the center maps the figure onto itself.

13. C; there are no lines of symmetry, but a rotation of 90° maps the figure onto itself.

31. There are 8 lines of symmetry, so $n = 8$.

$$n(m\angle 1) = 180°$$
$$8(m\angle 1) = 180°$$
$$m\angle 1 = 22.5°$$

The angle between the mirrors is 22.5°.

Lesson 9.7 (pp. 629–632)

7.

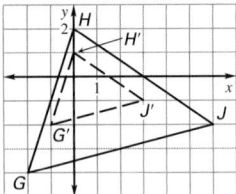

19. $\dfrac{1}{2} \begin{bmatrix} G & H & J \\ -2 & 0 & 6 \\ -4 & 2 & -2 \end{bmatrix} = \begin{bmatrix} G' & H' & J' \\ -1 & 0 & 3 \\ -2 & 1 & -1 \end{bmatrix}$

Scale   Polygon   Image
factor   matrix   matrix

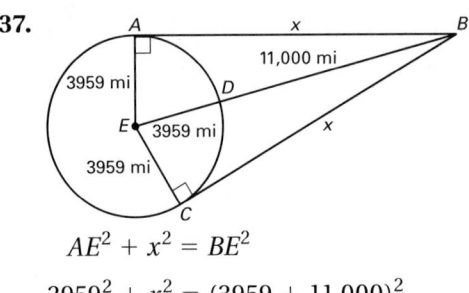

35. $k = 20$; $20 = \dfrac{x}{47} \to x = 940$

The length of the dragonfly seen through the magnifying glass is 940 mm, or 94 cm.

Chapter 10

Lesson 10.1 (pp. 655–658)

7. $\overleftrightarrow{AE}$ is a tangent line because it intersects the circle in exactly one point.

19. No; because $9^2 + 15^2 \neq 18^2$, $\triangle ABC$ is not a right triangle and $\overline{AB}$ is not perpendicular to $\overline{BC}$.

37.

$$AE^2 + x^2 = BE^2$$
$$3959^2 + x^2 = (3959 + 11{,}000)^2$$
$$x^2 = 208{,}098{,}000$$
$$x \approx 14{,}426$$

The length of $\overline{BA}$ and of $\overline{BC}$ is about 14,426 miles.

Lesson 10.2 (pp. 661–663)

5. $\overset{\frown}{DB}$ is a minor arc.

$$m\overset{\frown}{DB} = 180° - m\overset{\frown}{DE} = 180° - 45° = 135°$$

13. No; $\overset{\frown}{LP}$ and $\overset{\frown}{MN}$ have the same measure, but are arcs of circles that are not congruent.

23. The measure of each arc is $360° \div 20 = 18°$.

Lesson 10.3 (pp. 667–670)

7. Because $\overline{LN}$ is a diameter and $\overline{LN} \perp \overline{PM}$, $\overline{LN}$ bisects $\overline{PM}$.

So, $2x + 9 = 5x - 6 \rightarrow x = 5$.

9. Because $\overline{AB}$ and $\overline{CD}$ are equidistant from the center, $\overline{AB} \cong \overline{CD}$.

So, $18 = 5x - 7 \rightarrow x = 5$.

25. $\overline{AB}$ and $\overline{BC}$ must be congruent in order for $\overparen{AB}$ and $\overparen{BC}$ to be congruent.

Lesson 10.4 (pp. 676–679)

11. $\angle JMK$ and $\angle JLK$ intercept the same arc, so $\angle JMK \cong \angle JLK$. Also, $\angle MKL$ and $\angle MJL$ intercept the same arc, so $\angle MKL \cong \angle MJL$.

13. $x° + 80° = 180° \rightarrow x = 100$

$y° + 95° = 180° \rightarrow y = 85$

29. If a right triangle is inscribed in a circle, its hypotenuse is a diameter of the circle, so the length of the hypotenuse is twice the radius.

Lesson 10.5 (pp. 683–686)

3. $m\overparen{AB} = 2(65°) = 130°$

9. $180° - x° = \frac{1}{2}(30° + (2x - 30)°)$

$180° - x° = \frac{1}{2}(2x°)$

$180° = 2x°$

$90 = x$

23. Let D and E represent the points shown in the diagram. Because $\overline{CE}$ is a diameter, $m\overparen{CDE} = 180°$.

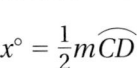

$x° = \frac{1}{2}m\overparen{CD}$

$x° = \frac{1}{2}(m\overparen{CDE} - m\overparen{DE})$

$x° = \frac{1}{2}(180° - 80°)$

$x = 50$

Lesson 10.6 (pp. 692–695)

3. $12x = 10(6)$

$x = 5$

9. $x^2 = 9(9 + 7)$

$x^2 = 144$

$x = 12$

21. Given: Chords $\overline{AB}$ and $\overline{CD}$ intersect in the interior of the circle.

Prove: $EA \cdot EB = EC \cdot ED$

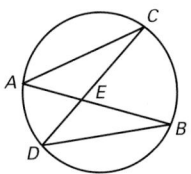

Statements	Reasons
1. $m\angle AEC \cong m\angle DEB$	1. Vertical Angles Theorem
2. $m\angle CAB \cong m\angle CDB$	2. Theorem 10.8
3. $\triangle AEC \sim \triangle DEB$	3. AA Similarity Postulate
4. $\dfrac{EA}{ED} = \dfrac{EC}{EB}$	4. Definition of similarity
5. $EA \cdot EB = ED \cdot EC$	5. Cross Products Property

Lesson 10.7 (pp. 702–705)

7. Center $(50, 50)$; radius 10

$(x - h)^2 + (y - k)^2 = r^2$

$(x - 50)^2 + (y - 50)^2 = 10^2$

$(x - 50)^2 + (y - 50)^2 = 100$

17. $r = \sqrt{(0 - 0)^2 + (6 - 0)^2} = 6$

$(h, k) = (0, 0)$

$(x - h)^2 + (y - k)^2 = r^2$

$(x - 0)^2 + (y - 0)^2 = 6^2$

$x^2 + y^2 = 36$

37. Outside edge: $(h, k) = (0, 0)$; $r = 2.4$

$(x - 0)^2 + (y - 0)^2 = 2.4^2$

$x^2 + y^2 = 5.76$

Edge of hole: $(h, k) = (0, 0)$; $r = 0.3$

$(x - 0)^2 + (y - 0)^2 = 0.3^2$

$x^2 + y^2 = 0.09$

Chapter 11

Lesson 11.1 (pp. 723–726)

7. $30^2 = b^2 + 18^2 \rightarrow b^2 = 576 \rightarrow b = 24$

$A = \frac{1}{2}bh = \frac{1}{2}(24)(18) = 216$ square units

23. Area = Area of Parallelogram

+ Area of left triangle

+ Area of right triangle

$= (18)(13) + \frac{1}{2}(9)(13) + \frac{1}{2}(11)(13)$

$= 234 + 58.5 + 71.5$

$= 364 \text{ cm}^2$

37. Triangular plot: $A = \frac{1}{2}bh = \frac{1}{2}(24)(25) = 300 \text{ yd}^2$

$300 \text{ yd}^2 \cdot \frac{1 \text{ min}}{10 \text{ yd}^2} = 30 \text{ min}$

It takes you 30 minutes to mow the triangular plot.

Rectangular plot: $A = bh = 24(36) = 864 \text{ yd}^2$

$864 \text{ yd}^2 \cdot \frac{1 \text{ min}}{10 \text{ yd}^2} = 86.4 \text{ min}$

It takes you 86.4 minutes to mow the rectangular plot.

Lesson 11.2 (pp. 733–736)

9. $A = \frac{1}{2}d_1d_2 = \frac{1}{2}(18)(21) = 189$ square units

17. $A = \frac{1}{2}h(b_1 + b_2)$

$300 = \frac{1}{2}(20)[x + 10]$

$300 = 10x + 100$

$200 = 10x$

$20 = x$

$x = 20 \text{ m}$

35. $A = \frac{1}{2}d_1d_2 = \frac{1}{2}(5)(8) = 20$ square millimeters

Sample answer:

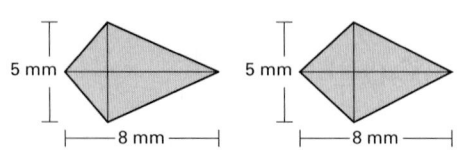

Lesson 11.3 (pp. 740–743)

7. The ratio of the lengths of corresponding sides is $\frac{7}{9}$, or 7 : 9.

The ratio of perimeters is 7 : 9.

The ratio of areas is $\frac{7^2}{9^2} = \frac{49}{81}$, or 49 : 81.

$\dfrac{\text{Red area}}{\text{Blue area}} = \dfrac{49}{81}$

$\dfrac{\text{Red area}}{210} = \dfrac{49}{81}$

$\text{Red area} = \dfrac{10{,}290}{81} \approx 127$ square inches

17.

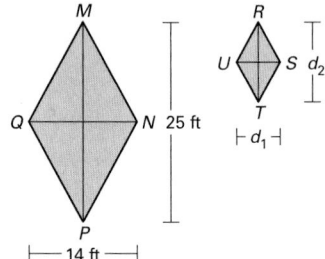

Area of $MNPQ = \frac{1}{2}(14)(25) = 175 \text{ ft}^2$

Area of $RSTU = 28 \text{ ft}^2$

Ratio of areas $= \dfrac{175 \text{ ft}^2}{28 \text{ ft}^2} = \dfrac{25}{4} = \dfrac{5^2}{2^2}$

Ratio of corresponding lengths $= \dfrac{5}{2}$

$\dfrac{14}{d_1} = \dfrac{5}{2} \rightarrow d_1 = 5.6 \text{ ft}; \quad \dfrac{25}{d_2} = \dfrac{5}{2} \rightarrow d_2 = 10 \text{ ft}$

The lengths of the diagonals of $RSTU$ are 5.6 feet and 10 feet.

27.

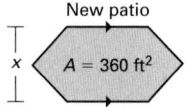

Ratio of areas $= \dfrac{360 \text{ ft}^2}{250 \text{ ft}^2} = \dfrac{36}{25} = \dfrac{6^2}{5^2}$

Ratio of corresponding lengths $= \dfrac{6}{5}$

Let x represent the distance between the long parallel sides of the new patio.

$\dfrac{x}{12.5} = \dfrac{6}{5} \rightarrow x = 15 \text{ feet}$

Lesson 11.4 (pp. 749–752)

23. $\dfrac{\text{Arc length of } \overset{\frown}{LM}}{2\pi r} = \dfrac{m\,\overset{\frown}{LM}}{360°}$

$$\dfrac{38.95}{2\pi r} = \dfrac{260°}{360°}$$

$$r = \dfrac{38.95(360°)}{2\pi(260°)}$$

$$r = \dfrac{7011}{260\pi} \approx 8.58$$

25. $\boxed{\text{Perimeter}} = 2 \cdot \boxed{\begin{array}{c}\text{Length of}\\\text{each straight}\\\text{section}\end{array}} + 2 \cdot \boxed{\begin{array}{c}\text{Length of}\\\text{each quarter}\\\text{circle}\end{array}}$

$$= 2(6) + 2 \cdot \left(\dfrac{90°}{360°} \cdot 2\pi(3)\right)$$

$$= 12 + 3\pi$$

$$\approx 21.42 \text{ units}$$

35. The length 21 feet 8 inches represents the circumference of the trunk. They can substitute $21\dfrac{8}{12} = \dfrac{65}{3}$ for C in the equation $C = \pi d$ and solve for d.

$$\dfrac{65}{3} = \pi d \rightarrow d \approx 7 \text{ feet}$$

Lesson 11.5 (pp. 758–761)

7. $A = \pi r^2$

$$154 = \pi r^2$$

$$\dfrac{154}{\pi} = r^2$$

$$7 \approx r$$

The radius is about 7 meters.

17. $\boxed{\begin{array}{c}\text{Shaded}\\\text{area}\end{array}} = \boxed{\begin{array}{c}\text{Area of}\\\text{rectangle}\end{array}} - 2 \cdot \boxed{\begin{array}{c}\text{Area of}\\\text{semicircle}\end{array}}$

$$= 6(6) - 2 \cdot \left(\dfrac{180°}{360°}\right)\!(\pi \cdot 3^2)$$

$$= 36 - 9\pi$$

$$\approx 7.7$$

The shaded area is about 7.73 square meters.

39. a. A circle graph is appropriate because the data values add up to 100%.

b. Bus: central angle $= 0.65(360°) = 234°$

Walk: central angle $= 0.25(360°) = 90°$

Other: central angle $= 0.10(360°) = 36°$

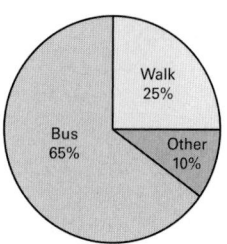

c. *Sample answer:* Use $r \approx 2$ in.

Area of "bus" sector $= \dfrac{234°}{360°} \cdot \left(\pi \cdot 2^2\right)$

$$\approx 8.2 \text{ in.}^2$$

Area of "walk" sector $= \dfrac{90°}{360°} \cdot \left(\pi \cdot 2^2\right)$

$$\approx 3.1 \text{ in.}^2$$

Area of "other" sector $= \dfrac{36°}{360°} \cdot \left(\pi \cdot 2^2\right)$

$$\approx 1.3 \text{ in.}^2$$

Lesson 11.6 (pp. 765–768)

7. $\dfrac{360°}{18} = 20°$

21. $P = 7s = 7(9) = 63$ units

$$m\angle DEF = \dfrac{360°}{7}$$

$$m\angle DEG = \dfrac{1}{2}\left(\dfrac{360}{7}\right)° = \left(\dfrac{180}{7}\right)°$$

$$\tan\!\left(\dfrac{180}{7}\right)° = \dfrac{4.5}{a}$$

$$a = \dfrac{4.5}{\tan\!\left(\dfrac{180}{7}\right)°}$$

$$A = \dfrac{1}{2}aP$$

$$= \dfrac{1}{2}\left(\dfrac{4.5}{\tan\!\left(\dfrac{180}{7}\right)°}\right)\!(63) \approx 294.3 \text{ square units.}$$

37. Apothem = $a = 0.2 + 1 = 1.2$ centimeters

$$\theta = \frac{1}{2}\left(\frac{360°}{8}\right) = 22.5°$$

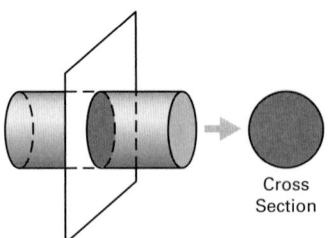

$$\frac{x}{a} = \tan \theta$$

$$\frac{x}{1.2} = \tan 22.5°$$

$$x = 1.2 \tan 22.5°$$

$$s = 2x = 2.4 \tan 22.5°$$

Area of octagon $= \frac{1}{2}a \cdot ns$

$$= \frac{1}{2}(1.2)(8)(2.4 \tan 22.5°)$$

$$\approx 4.8 \text{ square centimeters}$$

Area of silver border

= Area of octagon − Area of circle

$$= \frac{1}{2}a \cdot ns - \pi r^2$$

$$\approx 4.77 - \pi(1^2)$$

$$\approx 1.6 \text{ square centimeters}$$

Lesson 11.7 (pp. 774–777)

3. $P(K \text{ is on } \overline{AD}) = \frac{AD}{AE} = \frac{|3 - (-12)|}{|12 - (-12)|} = \frac{5}{8}$,
0.625, or 62.5%

9. $P(\text{Point lies in shading}) = \dfrac{\text{Area of shaded region}}{\text{Area of large triangle}}$

$$= \frac{\frac{1}{2}(6)(7)}{\frac{1}{2}(12)(14)} = \frac{1}{4},$$

0.25, or 25%

33. $P(\text{You miss call}) = \dfrac{\text{Time from 7:00–7:10}}{\text{Time from 7:00–8:00}}$

$$= \frac{10 \text{ min}}{60 \text{ min}} = \frac{1}{6} \approx 0.167$$

The probability that you missed your friend's call is about 16.7%.

Chapter 12

Lesson 12.1 (pp. 798–801)

11. $F + V = E + 2$

$$n + 12 = 18 + 2$$

$$n = 8$$

25. The cross section is a circle.

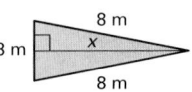

Cross Section

35. There are 6 vertices around each hexagonal face, and there are no other vertices. Each hexagonal face has 6 edges, and there are 6 additional edges between the square faces. So, there are $2(6) = 12$ vertices and $2(6) + 6 = 18$ edges.

Check:

$$F + V = E + 2$$

$$8 + 12 \overset{?}{=} 18 + 2$$

$$20 = 20 \checkmark$$

Lesson 12.2 (pp. 806–809)

7. Base of prism:

$$x^2 + 1.5^2 = 8^2$$

$$x = \sqrt{61.75} \text{ meters}$$

Area of base $= B = \frac{1}{2}(3)\left(\sqrt{61.75}\right)$

$$S = 2B + Ph$$

$$\approx 2\left(\frac{1}{2} \cdot 3\sqrt{61.75}\right) + (8 + 8 + 3)(9.1)$$

$$\approx 196.47 \text{ square meters}$$

9. $S = 2\pi r^2 + 2\pi rh$

$$= 2\pi(0.8)^2 + 2\pi(0.8)(2)$$

$$\approx 14.07 \text{ square inches}$$

23. a. $S = 2(6 \cdot 6) + 2(6 \cdot 12) + 2(6 \cdot 12) = 360$

The minimum amount of wrapping paper needed is 360 square inches.

b. The area of the net of the box is larger because there are flaps that fold over and overlap.

c. You would want more than 360 square inches of wrapping paper so that you could wrap the paper around the box and fold it down to fit; this causes sections of paper to overlap.

Lesson 12.3 (pp. 814–817)

7. Area of base $= \frac{1}{2}aP$

$$= \frac{1}{2}(6.9)(5 \cdot 10)$$

$$= 172.5$$

$$S = B + \frac{1}{2}P\ell$$

$$= 172.5 + \frac{1}{2}(50)(20)$$

$$= 672.5 \text{ square millimeters}$$

11. $\ell^2 = 4^2 + 1^2 \rightarrow \ell = \sqrt{17}$ inches

Lateral area $= \pi r \ell$

$$= \pi(1)(\sqrt{17})$$

$$\approx 12.95 \text{ square inches}$$

29. The net represents a regular square pyramid.

Area of one triangle $= \frac{1}{2}bh = \frac{1}{2}(6)(3\sqrt{3})$

$$= 9\sqrt{3}$$

Surface area = area of square + 4(area of triangle)

$$= 6^2 + 4 \cdot 9\sqrt{3}$$

$$= 36 + 36\sqrt{3} \approx 98.35 \text{ cm}^2$$

Lesson 12.4 (pp. 822–825)

7. Area of base $= \frac{1}{2}(7)(10) = 35 \text{ in.}^2$

Volume $= Bh = 35(5) = 175 \text{ in.}^3$

11. Volume $= \pi r^2 h$

$$= \pi(5^2)(16) \approx 1256.64 \text{ in.}^3$$

29. a. Visualize the concrete block broken into five parts:

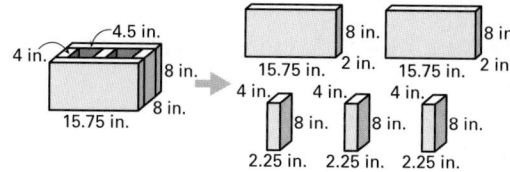

Total volume $= 2(15.75 \cdot 2 \cdot 8)$

$$+ 3(2.25 \cdot 4 \cdot 8) = 720 \text{ in.}^3$$

b. Volume of block = Volume of large prism

$$- \text{ Volume of holes}$$

$$= (15.75 \cdot 8)(8) - 2(4 \cdot 4.5)(8) = 720 \text{ in.}^3$$

c. The volumes found in parts (a) and (b) are equal.

Lesson 12.5 (pp. 832–836)

3. Area of base $= 5^2 = 25 \text{ cm}^2$

$$V = \frac{1}{3}Bh$$

$$= \frac{1}{3}(25)(6)$$

$$= 50 \text{ cm}^3$$

17.

$\sin 54° = \dfrac{h}{15}$

$$h = 15 \sin 54°$$

$$\cos 54° = \frac{r}{15}$$

$$r = 15 \cos 54°$$

$$V = \frac{1}{3}\pi r^2 h$$

$$= \frac{1}{3}\pi(15 \cos 54°)^2 (15 \sin 54°)$$

$$\approx 987.86 \text{ cm}^3$$

33.

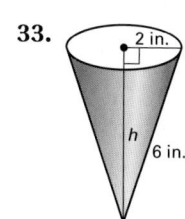

$h^2 + 2^2 = 6^2$

$$h = 4\sqrt{2} \text{ in.}$$

$$V = \frac{1}{3}\pi r^2 h$$

$$= \frac{1}{3}\pi(2^2)(4\sqrt{2})$$

$$\approx 23.70 \text{ in.}^3$$

Lesson 12.6 (pp. 842–845)

3. $S = 4\pi r^2 = 4\pi(4^2) \approx 201.06 \text{ ft}^2$

13. $V = \frac{4}{3}\pi r^3 = \frac{4}{3}\pi(40^3) \approx 268{,}082.57 \text{ mm}^3$

31.
$$C = 2\pi r$$
$$24{,}855 = 2\pi r$$
$$r = \frac{24{,}855}{2\pi}$$

Surface area of Western Hemisphere

$$= \frac{1}{2}(4\pi r^2) = \frac{1}{2}(4\pi)\left(\frac{24{,}855}{2\pi}\right)^2 \approx 98{,}321{,}312 \text{ mi}^2$$

Lesson 12.7 (pp. 850–854)

3. Radii: $\frac{7}{4}$ Heights: $\frac{16}{10} = \frac{8}{5}$

The cylinders are not similar because the ratios of corresponding linear measures are not equal.

9. $\dfrac{\text{Surface area of } A}{\text{Surface area of } B} = \dfrac{3^2}{1^2}$

$\dfrac{1500}{\text{Surface area of } B} = \dfrac{9}{1}$

Surface area of $B \approx 166.67 \text{ m}^2$

$\dfrac{\text{Volume of } A}{\text{Volume of } B} = \dfrac{3^3}{1^3}$

$\dfrac{3434.6}{\text{Volume of } B} = \dfrac{27}{1}$

Volume of $B \approx 127.21 \text{ m}^3$

27. Let x represent the amount to be added to the smaller bowl and y represent the amount to be added to the larger bowl.

$$\frac{x}{y} = \frac{3^3}{4^3}$$

$$\frac{x}{64} = \frac{27}{64}$$

$$x = 27$$

The smaller bowl needs 27 fluid ounces to be added.

Chapter 1

1.1 Skill Practice (pp. 5–7) **1. a.** point Q **b.** line segment MN **c.** ray ST **d.** line FG **3.** $\overleftrightarrow{QW}$, line g **5.** *Sample answer:* points R, Q, S; point T **7.** Yes; through any three points not on the same line, there is exactly one plane. **9.** $\overrightarrow{VY}$, $\overrightarrow{VX}$, $\overrightarrow{VZ}$, $\overrightarrow{VW}$ **11.** $\overrightarrow{WX}$

15. *Sample:*

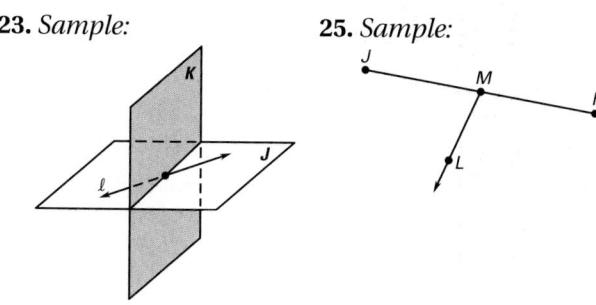

17. point R
19. $\overleftrightarrow{RS}$
21. yes; yes

23. *Sample:*   **25.** *Sample:*

27. on the line **29.** not on the line **31.** on the line
33.

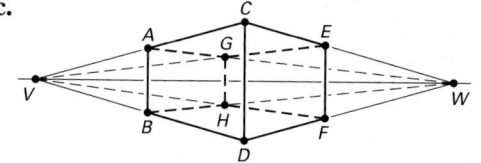

ray
35. segment

1.1 Problem Solving (pp. 7–8) **41.** intersection of a line and a plane **43.** Four points are not necessarily coplanar; no; three points determine a unique plane.
45. a–c.

1.2 Skill Practice (pp. 12–13) **1.** $\overline{MN}$ means segment MN while MN is the length of $\overline{MN}$. **3.** 2.1 cm
5. 3.5 cm **7.** 44 **9.** 23 **11.** 13 **13.** congruent
15. not congruent **17.** 7 **19.** 9 **21.** 10 **23.** 20 **25.** 30
29. $(3x - 16) + (4x - 8) = 60$; 12; 20, 40

1.2 Problem Solving (pp. 13–14)
33. a. 1883 mi **b.** about 50 mi/h
35. a. *Sample:* **b.** 21 ft

1.3 Skill Practice (pp. 19–20) **1.** Distance Formula
3. $10\frac{1}{4}$ in. **5.** 26 cm **7.** $4\frac{3}{4}$ in. **9.** $2\frac{3}{8}$ in. **11.** 10 **13.** 1
15. 70 **17.** (5, 5) **19.** (1, 4) **21.** $\left(1\frac{1}{2}, -1\right)$ **23.** $\left(\frac{m}{2}, \frac{n}{2}\right)$; when x_2 and y_2 are replaced by zero in the Midpoint Formula and x_1 and y_1 are replaced by m and n the result is $\left(\frac{m}{2}, \frac{n}{2}\right)$. **25.** $(-3, 10)$ **27.** (4, 8) **29.** $(-18, 22)$
31. 4.5 **33.** 5.7 **35.** 7; $-\frac{1}{2}$ **37.** 40; 5 **39.** 9; $-3\frac{1}{2}$
43. $AB = 3\sqrt{5}$, $CD = 2\sqrt{10}$; not congruent
45. $JK = 8\sqrt{2}$, $LM = \sqrt{130}$; not congruent

1.3 Problem Solving (pp. 21–22)
49. House   Library   School   2.85 km

5.7 km

51. objects B and D; objects A and C **53. a.** 191 yd
b. 40 yd **c.** About 1.5 min; find the total distance, about 230 yards, and divide by 150 yards per minute.

1.4 Skill Practice (pp. 28–31)
1. *Sample:*

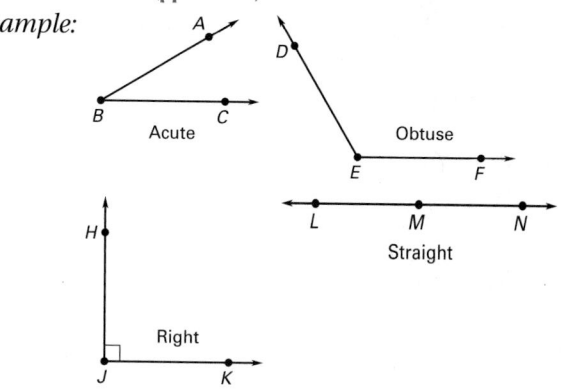

3. $\angle ABC$, $\angle B$, $\angle CBA$; B, $\overrightarrow{BA}$, $\overrightarrow{BC}$ **5.** $\angle MTP$, $\angle T$, $\angle PTM$; T, $\overrightarrow{TM}$, $\overrightarrow{TP}$ **7.** straight **9.** right **11.** 90°; right
13. 135°; obtuse **15–19.** Sample answers are given.
15. $\angle BCA$; right **17.** $\angle DFB$; straight **19.** $\angle CDB$; acute
23. 65° **25.** 55° **29.** $m\angle XWY = 104°$, $m\angle ZWY = 52°$

31. $m \angle XWZ = 35.5°$, $m \angle YWZ = 35.5°$ **33.** $38°$
35. $142°$ **37.** $53°$

39. If a ray bisects $\angle AGC$, then its endpoint must be point G. *Sample:*

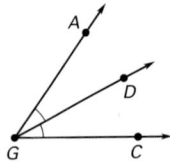

41. $80°$ **43.** $75°$; both angle measures are $5°$ less.

45.

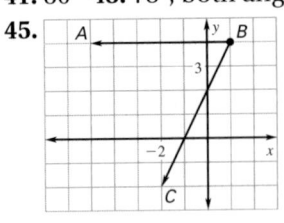

Acute.
Sample answer: $(-2, 0)$

47.

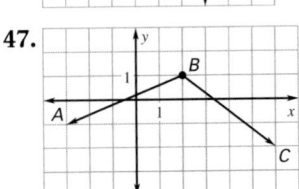

Obtuse.
Sample answer: $(2, 0)$

1.4 Problem Solving (pp. 31–32) **51.** $32°$ **53. a.** $112°$
b. $56°$ **c.** $56°$ **d.** $56°$ **55.** *Sample answer:* acute: $\angle ABG$, obtuse: $\angle ABC$, right: $\angle DGE$, straight: $\angle DGF$
57. about $140°$ **59.** about $62°$ **61.** about $107°$

1.5 Skill Practice (pp. 38–40)

1.

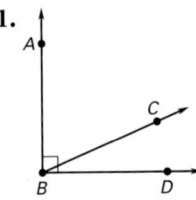

No. *Sample answer:* Any two angles whose angle measures add up to $90°$ are complementary, but they do not have to have a common vertex and side.

3. adjacent **5.** adjacent **7.** $\angle GLH$ and $\angle HLJ$, $\angle GLJ$ and $\angle JLK$ **9.** $69°$ **11.** $85°$ **13.** $25°$ **15.** $153°$ **17.** $135°$, $45°$
19. $54°$, $36°$ **21.** linear pair **23.** vertical angles
25. linear pair **27.** neither **29.** The angles are complementary so they should be equal to $90°$; $x + 3x = 90°$, $4x = 90$, $x = 22.5$. **31.** 10, 35 **33.** 55, 30
35. Never; a straight angle is $180°$, and it is not possible to have a complement of an angle that is $180°$.
37. Always; the sum of complementary angles is $90°$, so each angle must be less than $90°$, making them acute. **39.** $71°$, $19°$ **41.** $68°$, $22°$ **43.** $58°$, $122°$

1.5 Problem Solving (pp. 40–41) **47.** neither
49–51. Sample answers are given. **49.** $\angle FGB$, $\angle BGC$
51. $\angle AGE$, $\angle EGD$ **53.** *Sample answer:* Subtract $90°$ from $m \angle FGB$. **55. a.** $y_1 = 90 - x$, $0 < x < 90$; $y_2 = 180 - x$, $0 < x < 180$; the measure of the complement must be less than $90°$ and the measure of its supplement must be less than $180°$.

55. b.

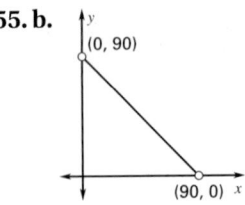 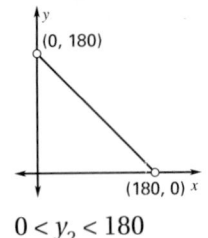

$0 < y_1 < 90$ $0 < y_2 < 180$

1.6 Skill Practice (pp. 44–46) **1.** An n-gon is a polygon with n sides. **3.** polygon; concave **5.** polygon; convex **9.** Pentagon; regular; it has 5 congruent sides and angles. **11.** Triangle; none of these; the sides and/or the angles are not all congruent. **13.** Quadrilateral; equiangular; it has 4 congruent angles.
15. 8 in. **17.** 3 ft **19.** sometimes **21.** never **23.** never
25. *Sample:*   **27.** *Sample:*

29. 1

1.6 Problem Solving (pp. 46–47) **33.** triangle; regular
35. octagon; regular **39.** 105 mm; each side of the button is 15 millimeters long, so the perimeter of the button is $15(7) = 105$ millimeters. **41. a.** 3 **b.** 5
c. 6 **d.** 8

1.7 Skill Practice (pp. 52–54) **1.** *Sample answer:* The diameter is twice the radius. **3.** $(52)(9)$ must be divided by 2; $\dfrac{52(9)}{2} = 234$ ft^2. **5.** 22.4 m, 29.4 m^2
7. 180 yd, 1080 yd^2 **9.** 36 cm, 36 cm^2 **11.** 84.8 cm, 572.3 cm^2 **13.** 76.0 cm, 459.7 cm^2
15.   59.3 cm, 280.4 cm^2

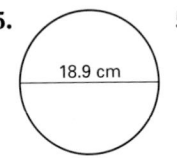

18.9 cm

17. 12.4 **21.** 1.44 **23.** 8,000,000 **25.** 3,456 **27.** 14.5 m
29. 4.5 in. **31.** 6 in., 3 in. **33.** Octagon; dodecagon; the square has 4 sides, so a polygon with the same side length and twice the perimeter would have to have $2(4) = 8$ sides, an octagon; a polygon with the same side length and three times the perimeter would have to have $4(3) = 12$ sides, a dodecagon. **35.** $\sqrt{346}$ in.
37. $5\sqrt{42}$ km

1.7 Problem Solving (pp. 54–56) **41.** 1350 yd^2; 450 ft
43. a. 15 in. **b.** 6 in.; the spoke is 21 inches long from the center to the tip, and it is 15 inches from the center to the outer edge, so $21 - 15 = 6$ inches is the length of the handle.

45. a. 106.4 m² **b.** 380 rows, 175 columns. *Sample answer:* The panel is 1520 centimeters high and each module is 4 centimeters so there are 1520 ÷ 4 = 380 rows; the panel is 700 centimeters wide and each module is 4 centimeters therefore there are 700 ÷ 4 = 175 columns.

1.7 Problem Solving Workshop (p. 57)
1. 2.4 h **3.** $26,730

Chapter Review (pp. 60–63) **1.** endpoints **3.** midpoint
5. *Sample answer:* points P, Y, Z **7.** $\overrightarrow{YZ}, \overrightarrow{YX}$ **9.** 1.2
11. 7 **13.** 16 **15.** 8.6; (3.5, 3.5) **17.** 16.4; (5, −0.5)
19. 5 **21.** 162°; obtuse **23.** 7° **25.** 88° **27.** 124° **29.** 168°
31. 92°, 88°; obtuse **33.** Quadrilateral; equiangular; it has four congruent angles but its four sides are not all congruent. **35.** 21 **37.** 14 in., 11.3 in.² **39.** 5 m

Algebra Review (p. 65) **1.** 6 **3.** −2 **5.** $1\frac{1}{2}$ **7.** 4 **9.** −11
11. 17 people

Chapter 2

2.1 Skill Practice (pp. 75–76) **1.** *Sample answer:* A guess based on observation

3.
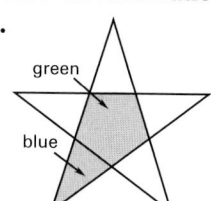
green
blue

7. The numbers are 4 times the previous number; 768. **9.** The rate of decrease is increasing by 1; −6. **11.** The numbers are increasing by successive multiples of 3; 25. **13.** even

15. *Sample answer:* $(3 + 4)^2 = 7^2 = 49 \neq 3^2 + 4^2 = 9 + 16 = 25$ **17.** *Sample answer:* $3 \cdot 6 = 18$ **19.** To be true, a conjecture must be true for all cases. **21.** $y = 2x$
23. Previous numerator becomes the next denominator while the numerator is one more than the denominator; $\frac{6}{5}$.

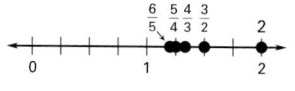

25. 0.25 is being added to each number; 1.45.

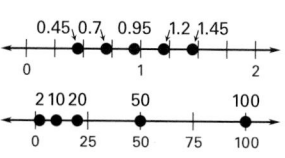

27. Multiply the first number by 10 to get the second number, take half of the second number to get the third number, and repeat the pattern; 500.
29. $r > 1; 0 < r < 1$; raising numbers greater than one by successive natural numbers increases the result while raising a number between 0 and 1 by successive natural numbers decreases the result.

2.1 Problem Solving (pp. 77–78) **33.** *Sample answer:* The number of e-mail messages will increase in 2004; the number of e-mail messages has increased for the past 7 years.

35. a.

x	y
−3	−5
0	1
5	11
7	15
12	25
15	31

b.
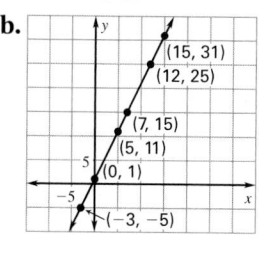
(15, 31)
(12, 25)
(7, 15)
(5, 11)
(0, 1)
(−3, −5)

c. Double the value of x and add 1 to the result, $y = 2x + 1$. **37. a.** sum, two **b.** 144, 233, 377 **c.** *Sample answer:* spiral patterns on the head of a sunflower

2.2 Skill Practice (pp. 82–84) **1.** converse **3.** If $x = 6$, then $x^2 = 36$. **5.** If a person is registered to vote, then they are allowed to vote. **7.** If two angles are complementary, then they add to 90°; if two angles add to 90°, then they are complementary; if two angles are not complementary, then they do not add to 90°; if two angles do not add to 90°, then they are not complementary. **9.** If $x = 2$, then $3x + 10 = 16$; if $3x + 10 = 16$, then $x = 2$; if $x \neq 2$, then $3x + 10 \neq 16$; if $3x + 10 \neq 16$, then $x \neq 2$.
11. False. *Sample:*

13. False. *Sample answer:* $m \angle ABC = 60°$, $m \angle GEF = 120°$ **15.** False. *Sample answer:* 2
17. False; there is no indication of a right angle in the diagram. **19.** An angle is obtuse if and only if its measure is between 90° and 180°. **21.** Points are coplanar if and only if they lie in the same plane. **23.** good definition **27.** If $-x > -6$, then $x < 6$; true. **29.** *Sample answer:* If the dog sits, she gets a treat.

2.2 Problem Solving (pp. 84–85) **31.** true **33.** Find a counterexample. *Sample answer:* Tennis is a sport, but the participants do not wear helmets. **35.** *Sample answer:* If a student is a member of the jazz band, then the student is a member of the band but not the chorus. **37.** no

2.3 Skill Practice (pp. 90–91) **1.** Detachment
3. *Sample answer:* The door to this room is closed.
5. $-15 < -12$ **7.** If a rectangle has four equal side lengths, then it is a regular polygon. **9.** If you play the clarinet, then you are a musician. **11.** The sum is even; the sum of two even integers is even; $2n$ and $2m$ are even, $2n + 2m = 2(n + m)$, $2(n + m)$ is even.

13. Linear pairs are not the only pairs of angles that are supplementary; angles C and D are supplementary, the sum of their measures is 180°.

2.3 Problem Solving (pp. 91–93) **17.** You will get a raise if the revenue is greater than its costs. **19.** is **21.** Deductive; laws of logic were used to reach the conclusion. **23.** $2n + (2n + 1) = (2n + 2n) + 1 = 4n + 1$, which is odd because $4n$ is even. **25.** True; since the game is not sold out, Arlo goes and buys a hot dog. **27.** False; Mia will buy popcorn.

Extension (p. 95) **1.** $\sim q \rightarrow \sim p$ **3.** Polygon $ABCDE$ is not equiangular and equilateral. **5.** Polygon $ABCDE$ is equiangular and equilateral if and only if it is a regular polygon. **7.** No; it is false when the hypothesis is true while the conclusion is false.

2.4 Skill Practice (pp. 99–100) **1.** line perpendicular to a plane **3.** Postulate 5 **5. a.** If three points are not collinear, then there exists exactly one plane that contains all three points. **b.** If there exists exactly one plane that contains three points, then the three points are noncollinear; if three points are collinear, then there does not exist exactly one plane that contains all three; if there is not exactly one plane containing three points, then the three points are collinear. **c.** contrapositive **7.** *Sample answer:* Lines p and q intersecting in point H

9. *Sample:*

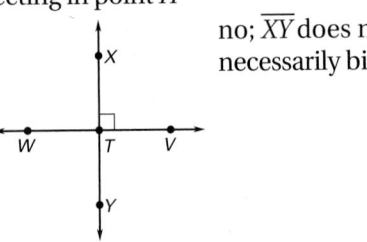

no; $\overline{XY}$ does not necessarily bisect $\overline{WV}$.

11. False. *Sample answer:* Consider a highway with two houses on the right side and one house on the left. **13.** False. *Sample answer:* Consider any pair of opposite sides of a rectangular prism. **15.** false **17.** false **19.** true **21.** true **23.** false

25. *Sample:*

Highway   City B m Postulate 5
City A

Sample:

Lincoln Way n Postulate 7
Pine Street m
P

Sample:

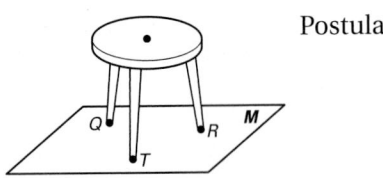

Postulate 8

27. *Sample answer:* Postulate 9 guarantees three noncollinear points in a plane while Postulate 5 guarantees that through any two there exists exactly one line, therefore there exists at least one line in the plane.

2.4 Problem Solving (pp. 101–102) **31.** Postulate 7 **33.** *Sample answer:* A stoplight with a red, yellow, and green light. **35.** *Sample answer:* Through point Z and point U there exists $\overleftrightarrow{ZU}$. **37.** *Sample answer:* The floor is a plane containing points W, X, and Y.

39. a. *Sample:*

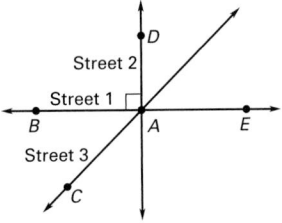

b. Building A **c.** right angle **d.** No; since $\angle CAE$ is obtuse, Building E must be on the east side of Building A. **e.** Street 1

41. They must be collinear. *Sample:*

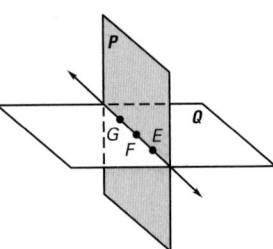

They must be noncollinear. *Sample:*

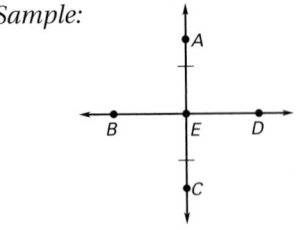

43. *Sample:*

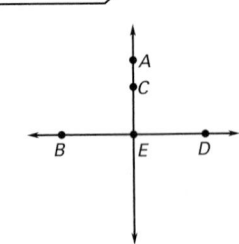

2.5 Skill Practice (pp. 108–109) **1.** Reflexive Property of Equality for Angle Measure **3.** Subtraction Property of Equality, Addition Property of Equality, Division Property of Equality

7.
$4x + 9 = 16 - 3x$	Given
$7x + 9 = 16$	Addition Property of Equality
$7x = 7$	Subtraction Property of Equality
$x = 1$	Division Property of Equality

9.
$3(2x + 11) = 9$	Given
$6x + 33 = 9$	Distributive Property
$6x = -24$	Subtraction Property of Equality
$x = -4$	Division Property of Equality

11.
$44 - 2(3x + 4) = -18x$	Given
$44 - 6x - 8 = -18x$	Distributive Property
$36 - 6x = -18x$	Simplify.
$36 = -12x$	Addition Property of Equality
$-3 = x$	Division Property of Equality

13.
$2x - 15 - x = 21 + 10x$	Given
$x - 15 = 21 + 10x$	Simplify.
$-15 = 21 + 9x$	Subtraction Property of Equality
$-36 = 9x$	Subtraction Property of Equality
$-4 = x$	Division Property of Equality

15.
$5x + y = 18$	Given
$y = 18 - 5x$	Subtraction Property of Equality

17.
$12 - 3y = 30x$	Given
$-3y = 30x - 12$	Subtraction Property of Equality
$y = \dfrac{30x - 12}{-3}$	Division Property of Equality
$y = -10x + 4$	Simplify.

19.
$2y + 0.5x = 16$	Given
$2y = -0.5x + 16$	Subtraction Property of Equality
$y = \dfrac{-0.5x + 16}{2}$	Division Property of Equality
$y = -0.25x + 8$	Simplify.

21. $20 + CD$ **23.** AB, CD **25.** $m\angle 1 = m\angle 3$ **27.** *Sample answer:* Look in the mirror and see your reflection; 12 in. = 1 ft, so 1 ft = 12 in.; 10 pennies = 1 dime and 1 dime = 2 nickels, so 10 pennies = 2 nickels.

29.
$AD = CB$	Given
$DC = BA$	Given
$AC = AC$	Reflexive Property of Equality
$AD + DC = CB + DC$	Addition Property of Equality
$AD + DC = CB + BA$	Substitution
$AD + DC + AC =$ $CB + BA + AC$	Addition Property of Equality

2.5 Problem Solving (pp. 110–111)

31.
$P = 2\ell + 2w$	Given
$P - 2w = 2\ell$	Subtraction Property of Equality
$\dfrac{P - 2w}{2} = \ell$	Division Property of Equality

length: 16.5 m

33. Row 1: Marked in diagram; Row 2: Substitute $m\angle GHF$ for 90°; Row 3: Angle Addition Postulate; Row 4: Substitution Property of Equality; Row 5: $m\angle 1 + m\angle 2 = m\angle 3 + m\angle 1$; Substitution Property of Equality; Row 6: Subtract $m\angle 1$ from both sides. **35.** 116°

2.6 Skill Practice (pp. 116–117) **1.** A theorem is a statement that can be proven; a postulate is a rule that is accepted without proof. **3.** 3. Substitution; 4. $AC = 11$ **5.** $\overline{SE}$ **7.** $\angle J$, $\angle L$ **9.** Reflexive Property of Congruence **11.** Reflexive Property of Equality **13.** The reason is the Transitive Property of Congruence, not the Reflexive Property of Congruence.

15.
Cottage   Snack   Bike   Arcade   Kite
          Shop   Rentals   Shop

17. Because $\overline{QR}$ and $\overline{RS}$ are both congruent to $\overline{PQ}$, $\overline{QR} \cong \overline{RS}$ by the Transitive Property. Using the given segment lengths, $2x + 5 = 10 - 3x$. Using properties of algebra, this is equivalent to $5x + 5 = 10$, $5x = 5$, and $x = 1$. **19.** A proof is deductive reasoning because it uses facts, definitions, accepted properties, and laws of logic.

2.6 Problem Solving (pp. 118–119) **21.** 2. Definition of angle bisector; 4. Transitive Property of Congruence

23.
Statements	Reasons
1. $2AB = AC$	1. Given
2. $AC = AB + BC$	2. Segment Addition Postulate
3. $2AB = AB + BC$	3. Transitive Property of Segment Equality
4. $AB = BC$	4. Subtraction Property of Equality

25.
Statements	Reasons
1. A is an angle.	1. Given
2. $m\angle A = m\angle A$	2. Reflexive Property of Equality
3. $\angle A \cong \angle A$	3. Definition of congruent angles

27. Equiangular; the Transitive Property of Congruent Angles implies $\angle 1 \cong \angle 3$, so all angle measures are the same.

29. a.

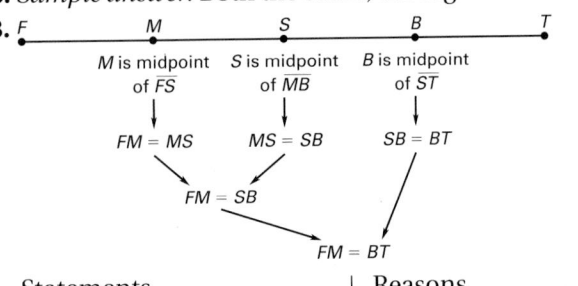

Restaurant · Shoe store · Movie theater · Cafe · Florist · Dry cleaners

(R S M C F D)

b. Given: $\overline{RS} \cong \overline{CF}$, $\overline{SM} \cong \overline{MC} \cong \overline{FD}$, Prove: $\overline{RM} \cong \overline{CD}$

c.

Statements	Reasons
1. $\overline{RS} \cong \overline{CF}$, $\overline{SM} \cong \overline{MC} \cong \overline{FD}$	1. Given
2. $RS + SM = RM$	2. Segment Addition Postulate
3. $CF + FD = CD$	3. Segment Addition Postulate
4. $CF + FD = RM$	4. Substitution Property of Equality
5. $RM = CD$	5. Transitive Property of Equality
6. $\overline{RM} \cong \overline{CD}$	6. Definition of congruent segments

2.6 Problem Solving Workshop (p. 121) **1. a.** *Sample answer:* The logic used is similar; one uses segment length and the other uses segment congruence.
b. *Sample answer:* Both the same; the logic is similar.

3.

F ——— M ——— S ——— B ——— T

M is midpoint of $\overline{FS}$ → FM = MS
S is midpoint of $\overline{MB}$ → MS = SB
B is midpoint of $\overline{ST}$ → SB = BT

FM = MS, MS = SB → FM = SB
FM = SB, SB = BT → FM = BT

Statements	Reasons
1. M is halfway between F and S; S is halfway between M and B; B is halfway between S and T.	1. Given
2. M is the midpoint of $\overline{FS}$; S is the midpoint of $\overline{MB}$; B is the midpoint of $\overline{ST}$.	2. Definition of midpoint
3. FM = MS, MS = SB, SB = BT	3. Definition of midpoint
4. FM = SB	4. Transitive Property of Equality
5. FM = BT	5. Transitive Property of Equality

5. a. *Sample answer:* The proof on page 114 is angle congruence, while this one is segment congruence.
b. *Sample answer:* If $\overline{FG} \cong \overline{DE}$ is the second statement, the reason would have to be Symmetric Property of Segment Congruence and that is what

is being proven and you cannot use a property that you are proving as a reason in the proof.

2.7 Skill Practice (pp. 127–129) **1.** vertical **3.** $\angle MSN$ and $\angle PSQ$, $\angle NSP$ and $\angle QSR$, $\angle MSP$ and $\angle PSR$; indicated in diagram, Congruent Complements Theorem, Right Angles Congruence Theorem **5.** $\angle FGH$ and $\angle WXZ$; Right Angles Congruence Theorem **7.** Yes; perpendicular lines form right angles, and all right angles are congruent. **9.** 168°, 12°, 12° **11.** 118°, 118°, 62° **13.** $x = 13$, $y = 20$ **15.** *Sample answer:* It was assumed that $\angle 1$ and $\angle 3$, and $\angle 2$ and $\angle 4$ are linear pairs, but they are not; $\angle 1$ and $\angle 4$, and $\angle 2$ and $\angle 3$ are not vertical angles and are not congruent. **17.** 30° **19.** 27° **21.** 58° **23.** true **25.** false **27.** true **29.** 140°, 40°, 140°, 40° **31.** $\angle FGH$ and $\angle EGH$; Definition of angle bisector **33.** *Sample answer:* $\angle CEB$ and $\angle DEB$; Right Angles Congruence Theorem

2.7 Problem Solving (pp. 129–131)
37. 1. Given; 2. Definition of complementary angles; 3. $m\angle 1 + m\angle 2 = m\angle 1 + m\angle 3$; 4. $m\angle 2 = m\angle 3$; 5. Definition of congruent angles

39.

Statements	Reasons
1. $\overline{JK} \perp \overline{JM}$, $\overline{KL} \perp \overline{ML}$, $\angle J \cong \angle M$, $\angle K \cong \angle L$	1. Given
2. $\angle J$ and $\angle L$ are right angles.	2. Definition of perpendicular lines
3. $\angle M$ and $\angle K$ are right angles.	3. Right Angles Congruence Theorem
4. $\overline{JM} \perp \overline{ML}$ and $\overline{JK} \perp \overline{KL}$	4. Definition of perpendicular lines

41.

Statements	Reasons
1. $\angle 1$ and $\angle 2$ are complementary; $\angle 3$ and $\angle 4$ are complementary; $\angle 1 \cong \angle 4$.	1. Given
2. $m\angle 1 + m\angle 2 = 90°$, $m\angle 3 + m\angle 4 = 90°$	2. Definition of complementary angles
3. $m\angle 1 = m\angle 4$	3. Definition of congruent angles
4. $m\angle 1 + m\angle 2 = m\angle 3 + m\angle 4$	4. Transitive Property of Equality
5. $m\angle 1 + m\angle 2 = m\angle 3 + m\angle 1$	5. Substitution
6. $m\angle 2 = m\angle 3$	6. Subtraction Property of Equality
7. $\angle 2 \cong \angle 3$	7. Definition of congruent angles

43.

Statements	Reasons
1. $\angle QRS$ and $\angle PSR$ are supplementary.	1. Given
2. $\angle QRS$ and $\angle QRL$ are a linear pair.	2. Definition of linear pair
3. $\angle QRS$ and $\angle QRL$ are supplementary.	3. Linear pair Postulate
4. $\angle QRL$ and $\angle PSR$ are supplementary.	4. Congruent Supplements Theorem

45. a.

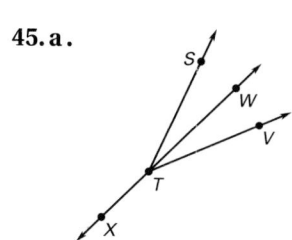

b. Given: $\angle STV$ is bisected by $\overrightarrow{TW}$, and $\overrightarrow{TX}$ and $\overrightarrow{TW}$ are opposite rays
Prove: $\angle STX \cong \angle VTX$

c.

Statements	Reasons
1. $\angle STV$ is bisected by $\overrightarrow{TW}$; $\overrightarrow{TX}$ and $\overrightarrow{TW}$ are opposite rays.	1. Given
2. $\angle STW \cong \angle VTW$	2. Definition of angle bisector
3. $\angle VTW$ and $\angle VTX$ are a linear pair; $\angle STW$ and $\angle STX$ are a linear pair.	3. Definition of linear pair
4. $\angle VTW$ and $\angle VTX$ are supplementary; $\angle STW$ and $\angle STX$ are supplementary.	4. Linear pair Postulate
5. $\angle STX \cong \angle VTX$	5. Congruent Supplements Theorem

Chapter Review (pp. 134–137) **1.** theorem
3. $m\angle A = m\angle C$ **5.** *Sample answer:* $\dfrac{-10}{-2} = 5$
7. Yes. *Sample answer:* This is the definition for complementary angles. **9.** $\angle B$ measures $90°$.
11. The sum of two odd integers is even. *Sample answer:* $7 + 1 = 8$; $2n + 1$ and $2m + 1$ are odd, but their sum $(2n + 1) + (2m + 1) = 2m + 2n + 2 = 2(m + n + 1)$ is even.
15.

$15x + 22 = 7x + 62$	Given
$8x + 22 = 62$	Subtraction Property of Equality
$8x = 40$	Subtraction Property of Equality
$x = 5$	Division Property of Equality

17.

$5x + 2(2x - 23) = -154$	Given
$5x + 4x - 46 = -154$	Distributive Property
$9x - 46 = -154$	Simplify.
$9x = -108$	Addition Property of Equality
$x = -12$	Division Property of Equality

19. Reflexive Property of Congruence
21.

Statements	Reasons
1. $\angle A \cong \angle B$, $\angle B \cong \angle C$	1. Given
2. $m\angle A = m\angle B$, $m\angle B = m\angle C$	2. Definition of congruent angles
3. $m\angle A = m\angle C$	3. Transitive Property of Equality
4. $\angle A \cong \angle C$	4. Definition of congruent angles

23. $123°, 57°, 123°$

Algebra Review (p. 139) **1.** $\dfrac{x^2}{4}$ **3.** $m + 7$ **5.** $\dfrac{k + 3}{-2k + 3}$
7. 2 **9.** $\dfrac{x - 2}{2x - 1}$ **11.** $-6\sqrt{5}$ **13.** $-2\sqrt{2} + 2\sqrt{6}$ **15.** $20\sqrt{2}$
17. $100\sqrt{2}$ **19.** 25 **21.** a **23.** $\sqrt{13}$

Chapter 3

3.1 Skill Practice (pp. 150–151) **1.** transversal **3.** $\overleftrightarrow{AB}$
5. $\overleftrightarrow{BF}$ **7.** $\overleftrightarrow{MK}, \overleftrightarrow{LS}$ **9.** No. *Sample answer:* The lines intersect. **11.** $\angle 1$ and $\angle 5$, $\angle 3$ and $\angle 7$, $\angle 2$ and $\angle 6$, $\angle 4$ and $\angle 8$ **13.** $\angle 1$ and $\angle 8$, $\angle 2$ and $\angle 7$ **15.** $\angle 1$ and $\angle 8$ are not in corresponding positions. $\angle 1$ and $\angle 8$ are alternate exterior angles.
17. 1 line

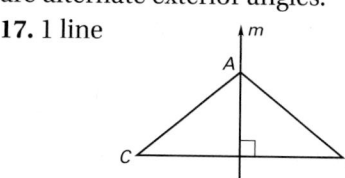

19. consecutive interior
21. alternate exterior
23. corresponding

25. never

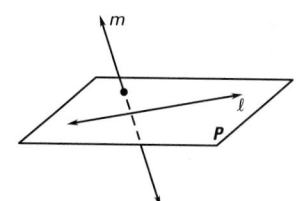

27. sometimes

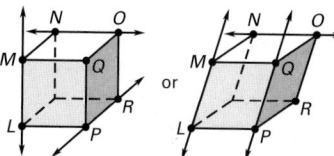

29. $\angle CFJ, \angle HJG$ **31.** $\angle DFC, \angle CJH$

3.1 Problem Solving (pp. 151–152) **35.** skew **39.** The adjacent interior angles are supplementary thus the measure of the other two angles must be 90°. **41.** false

3.2 Skill Practice (pp. 157–158)

1. *Sample:*

5. 110°; Alternate Exterior Angles Theorem **7.** 63°; Consecutive Interior Angles Theorem

9. Corresponding Angles Postulate **11.** Alternate Interior Angles Theorem **13.** Alternate Exterior Angles Theorem **15.** Alternate Exterior Angles Theorem **17.** $m\angle 1 = 150°$, Corresponding Angles Postulate; $m\angle 2 = 150°$, Vertical Angles Congruence Theorem **19.** $m\angle 1 = 122°$, $m\angle 2 = 58°$; Alternate Interior Angles Theorem, Consecutive Interior Angles Theorem **21.** *Sample answer:* $\angle 1 \cong \angle 4$ by the Alternate Exterior Angles Theorem; $\angle 1 \cong \angle 2 \cong \angle 3 \cong \angle 4$ by Vertical Angles Congruence Theorem, Alternate Interior Angles Theorem, and the Transitive Property of Angle Congruence. **23.** $m\angle 1 = 90°$, supplementary to the right angle by the Consecutive Interior Angles Theorem; $m\angle 3 = 65°$, it forms a linear pair with the angle measuring 115°; $m\angle 2 = 115°$, supplementary to $\angle 3$ by the Consecutive Interior Angles Theorem **25.** *Sample answer:* $\angle BAC$ and $\angle DCA$, $\angle ABD$ and $\angle CDB$ **27.** 45, 85 **29.** 65, 60 **31.** 13, 12

3.2 Problem Solving (pp. 159–160)

37.

Statements	Reasons
1. $p \parallel q$	1. Given
2. $\angle 1 \cong \angle 3$	2. Corresponding Angles Postulate
3. $\angle 3 \cong \angle 2$	3. Vertical Angles Congruence Theorem
4. $\angle 1 \cong \angle 2$	4. Transitive Property of Angle Congruence

39. a. yes; $\angle 1$ and $\angle 5$, $\angle 2$ and $\angle 6$; yes; $\angle 1$ and $\angle 2$, $\angle 1$ and $\angle 6$, $\angle 2$ and $\angle 5$, $\angle 5$ and $\angle 6$. **b.** *Sample answer:* The transversal stays parallel to the floor.

41.

Statements	Reasons
1. $n \parallel p$	1. Given
2. $\angle 1 \cong \angle 3$	2. Alternate Interior Angles Postulate
3. $m\angle 1 = m\angle 3$	3. Definition of congruent angles
4. $m\angle 2 + m\angle 3 = 180°$	4. Definition of supplementary angles
5. $m\angle 2 + m\angle 1 = 180°$	5. Substitution
6. $\angle 1$ and $\angle 2$ are supplementary.	6. Definition of supplementary angles.

3.3 Skill Practice (pp. 165–167)

1. *Sample:* $\angle 1$ and $\angle 8$, $\angle 2$ and $\angle 7$

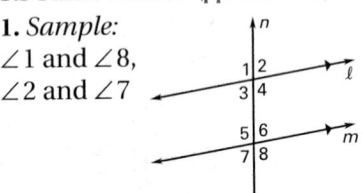

3. 40 **5.** 15 **7.** 60 **9.** The student believes that $x = y$ but there is no indication that they are equal.

11. yes; Alternate Exterior Angles Converse **13.** yes; Corresponding Angles Converse **15.** yes; Alternate Exterior Angles Converse **17. a.** $m\angle DCG = 115°$, $m\angle CGH = 65°$ **b.** They are consecutive interior angles and they are supplementary. **c.** yes; Consecutive Interior Angles Converse **19.** yes; Consecutive Interior Angles Converse **21.** no **25.** *Sample answer:* $\angle 1 \cong \angle 4$ therefore $\angle 4$ and $\angle 7$ are supplementary. Lines j and k are parallel by the Consecutive Interior Angles Converse. **27. a.** 1 line **b.** an infinite number of lines **c.** 1 plane

3.3 Problem Solving (pp. 167–169) **29.** Alternate Interior Angles Converse **31.** Substitution, Definition of supplementary angles, Consecutive Interior Angles Converse **33.** Yes. *Sample answer:* E 20th is parallel to E 19th by the Corresponding Angles Converse. E 19th is parallel to E 18th by the Alternate Exterior Angles Converse. E 18th is parallel to E 17th by the Alternate Interior Angles Converse. They are all parallel by the Transitive Property of Parallel Lines.

35.

Statements	Reasons
1. $a \parallel b$, $\angle 2 \cong \angle 3$	1. Given
2. $\angle 2$ and $\angle 4$ are supplementary.	2. Consecutive Interior Angles Theorem
3. $\angle 3$ and $\angle 4$ are supplementary.	3. Substitution
4. $c \parallel d$	4. Consecutive Interior Angles Converse

37. You are given that $\angle 3$ and $\angle 5$ are supplementary. By the Linear Pair Postulate, $\angle 5$ and $\angle 6$ are also supplementary. So $\angle 3 \cong \angle 6$ by the Congruent Supplements Theorem. By the converse of the Alternate Interior Angles Theorem, $m \parallel n$.

39. a. *Sample answer:* Corresponding Angles Converse **b.** Slide the triangle along a fixed horizontal line and use the edge that forms the 90° angle to draw vertical lines. **40–44.** Sample answers are given. **41.** Corresponding Angles Converse **43.** Vertical Angles Congruence Theorem followed by the Corresponding Angles Converse

3.4 Skill Practice (pp. 175–176) **1.** The slope of a nonvertical line is the ratio of vertical change (rise) to horizontal change (run) between any two points on the line. **7.** $\frac{1}{2}$ **9.** 0 **11.** Slope was computed using $\frac{\text{run}}{\text{rise}}$, it should be $\frac{\text{rise}}{\text{run}}$; $m = \frac{3}{4}$. **13.** Perpendicular; the product of their slopes is -1. **15.** Perpendicular; the product of their slopes is -1.

17.
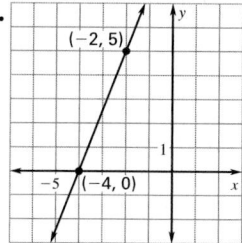
19. line 2 **21.** line 1

23. -2
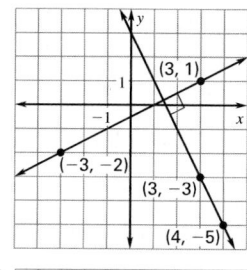

25. 7
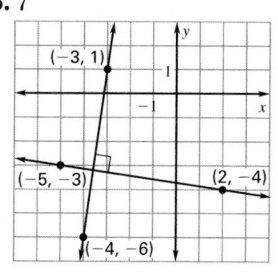

27.
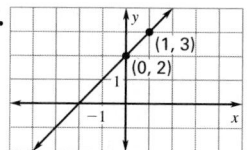

29.
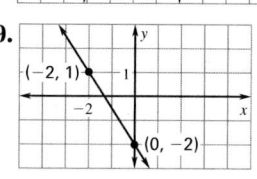

3.4 Problem Solving (pp. 176–178) **33.** $\frac{2}{3}$

35. line b; line c. Sample:
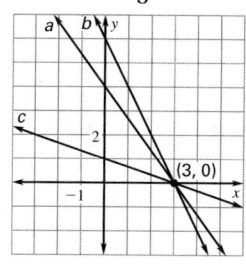

37. a.

Horizontal Distance (ft)	50	100	150	200	250	300	350
Height (ft)	29	58	87	116	145	174	203
Horizontal Distance (ft)	400	450	500	550	600	650	700
Height (ft)	232	261	290	319	348	377	406

406 ft

b. $\frac{29}{50}$ **c.** $\frac{144}{271}$; Duquesne
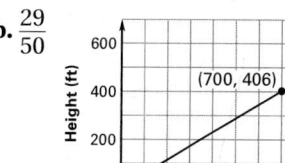

39. \$1150 per year **41. a.** 1985 to 1990. *Sample answer:* about 2 million people per year **b.** 1995 to 2000. *Sample answer:* about 3 million people per year **c.** *Sample answer:* There was moderate but steady increase in attendance for the NFL over the time period of 1985–2000.

3.5 Skill Practice (pp. 184–186) **1.** The point of intersection on the y-axis when graphing a line.
3. $y = \frac{4}{3}x - 4$ **5.** $y = -\frac{3}{2}x - \frac{1}{2}$ **7.** $y = \frac{3}{2}x - \frac{3}{2}$
11. $y = 3x + 2$ **13.** $y = -\frac{5}{2}x$ **15.** $y = -\frac{11}{5}x - 12$
17. $y = 4x - 16$ **19.** $y = -\frac{2}{3}x - \frac{22}{3}$ **21.** $y = 7$
23. $y = -2x - 1$ **25.** $y = \frac{1}{5}x + \frac{37}{5}$ **27.** $y = -\frac{5}{2}x - 4$
31. $y = -\frac{3}{7}x + \frac{4}{7}$ **33.** $y = \frac{1}{2}x + 2$ **35.** $y = -\frac{5}{3}x - \frac{40}{3}$

37.
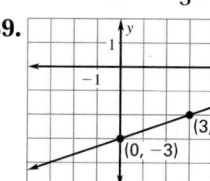
39.

45. To find the x-intercept, let $y = 0$, $5x - 3(0) = -15$, $x = -3$, $(-3, 0)$. To find the y-intercept, let $x = 0$, $5(0) - 3y = -15$, $y = 5$, $(0, 5)$. **47.** $y = 0.5x + 7$ and $-x + 2y = -5$ **49.** 4, 4; $y = -x + 4$ **51.** -20, 10; $y = \frac{1}{2}x + 10$

53. 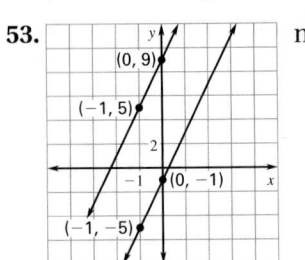 none

55. 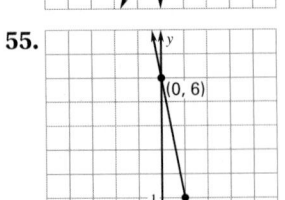 infinitely many

57. 4

3.5 Problem Solving (pp. 186–187) **61.** $y = 2.1x + 2000$; slope: gain in weight per day, y-intercept: starting weight before the growth spurt **63.** $2x + 3y = 24$; A: cost of a small slice, B: cost of a large slice, C: amount of money you can spend **65. a.** $2b + c = 13$, $5b + 2c = 27.50$

b. 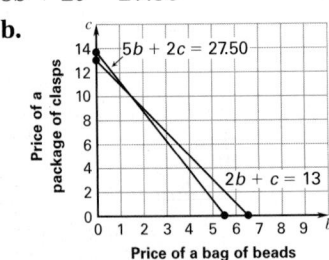 **c.** The intersection represents the price of one bag of beads and the price of one package of clasps.

3.5 Problem Solving Workshop (p. 189) **1.** 27 h **3.** 115 buttons **5.** *Sample answer:* In each case an equation modeling the situation was solved.

3.6 Skill Practice (pp. 194–195) **1.** $\overline{AB}$; it's $\perp$ to the parallel lines. **3.** If two sides of two adjacent acute angles are perpendicular, then the angles are complementary. **5.** 25° **7.** 52° **9.** Since the two angles labeled $x°$ form a linear pair of congruent angles, $t \perp n$; since the two lines are perpendicular to the same line, they are parallel to each other. **11.** *Sample answer:* Draw a line. Construct a second line perpendicular to the first line. Construct a third line perpendicular to the second line. **13.** There is no information to indicate that $y \parallel z$ or $y \perp x$. **15.** 13 **17.** 33 **19.** Lines f and g; they are perpendicular to line d. **23.** 4.1 **27.** 2.5

3.6 Problem Solving (pp. 196–197) **29.** Point C; the shortest distance is the length of the perpendicular segment. **31.** Linear Pair Postulate; $m\angle 1 + m\angle 2 = 180°$; Definition of congruent angles; Division Property of Equality; $\angle 1$ is a right angle; Definition of perpendicular lines

33. 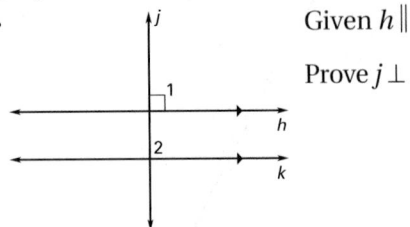 Given $h \parallel k, j \perp h$

Prove $j \perp k$

Statements	Reasons
1. $h \parallel k, j \perp h$	1. Given
2. $\angle 1 \cong \angle 2$	2. Corresponding Angles Postulate
3. $\angle 1$ is a right angle.	3. $\perp$ lines intersect to form 4 right angles.
4. $m\angle 1 = 90°$	4. Definition of right angle
5. $m\angle 1 = m\angle 2$	5. Definition of congruent angles
6. $m\angle 2 = 90°$	6. Substitution
7. $\angle 2$ is a right angle.	7. Definition of right angle
8. $j \perp k$	8. Definition of perpendicular lines

Extension (p. 199) **1.** 6 **3.** 16 **5.** 2

7. 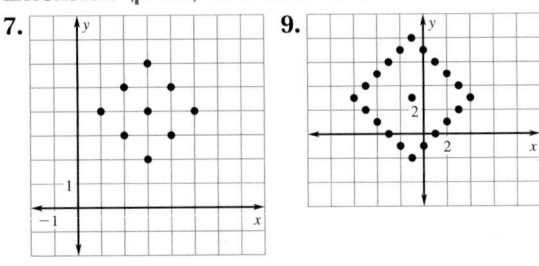 **9.**

11. $(1, 0)$ **13.** $(10, 4)$

Chapter Review (pp. 202–205) **1.** skew lines **3.** $\angle 5$ **5.** $\angle 6$ **7.** standard form **9.** $\overleftrightarrow{NR}$ **11.** $\overleftrightarrow{JN}$ **13.** $m\angle 1 = 54°$, vertical angles; $m\angle 2 = 54°$, corresponding angles **15.** $m\angle 1 = 135°$, corresponding angles; $m\angle 2 = 45°$, supplementary angles **17.** 13, 132 **19.** 35°. *Sample answer:* $\angle 2$ and $\angle 3$ are complementary, so $m\angle 2 = 90° - 55° = 35°$. $m\angle 1 = m\angle 2$ because $\angle 1$ and $\angle 2$ are corresponding angles for two parallel lines cut by a transversal. **21.** 133 **23.** perpendicular **25. a.** $y = 6x - 19$ **b.** $y = -\frac{1}{6}x - \frac{1}{2}$ **27.** 3.2

Algebra Review (p. 207)

1.
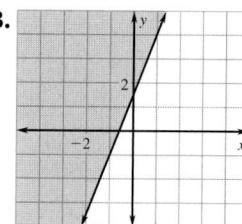

3.

5.
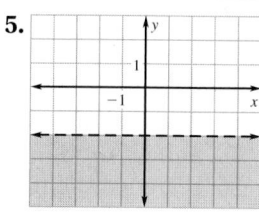

7.

9. 6 mo **11.** after 100 min

Cumulative Review (pp. 212–213) **1.** 28, 56 **3.** acute
5. acute **7.** 40 in., 84 in.^{2} **9.** 15.2 yd, 14.44 yd^2

11. Each number is being multiplied by $\frac{1}{4}$; $\frac{1}{2}$. **13.** $x < 7$

15. The musician is playing a stringed instrument.

17.

Equation	Reason
$-4(x + 3) = -28$	Given
$x + 3 = 7$	Division Property of Equality
$x = 4$	Subtraction Property of Equality

19. 29 **21.** $x = 9$, $y = 31$ **23.** $x = 101$, $y = 79$ **25.** 0
27. 2 **29. a.** $y = -x + 10$ **b.** $y = x + 14$ **31.** Yes; if two
lines intersect to form a linear pair of congruent
angles, then the lines are perpendicular. **33.** *Sample
answer:* parallel and perpendicular lines **35.** 89 mi
37. If you want the lowest television prices, then
come see Matt's TV Warehouse; you want the
lowest television prices; come see Matt's TV
Warehouse. **39.** Yes. *Sample answer:* Transitive
Property of Congruence of Segments

Chapter 4

4.1 Skill Practice (pp. 221–222) **1.** C **3.** F **5.** B
7. No; in a right triangle, the other two angles are
complementary so they are both less than 90°.
9. equilateral, equiangular

11.
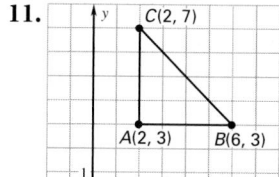
isosceles; right triangle

13.
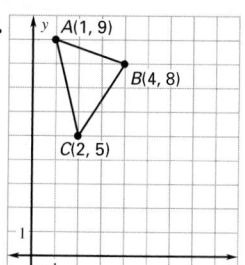
scalene; not a right triangle

15. 30; right **17.** 92° **19.** 158° **21.** 50° **23.** 50°
25. 40° **27.** $m \angle P = 45°$, $m \angle Q = 90°$, $m \angle R = 45°$
29. Isosceles does not guarantee the third side is
congruent to the two congruent sides; so if $\triangle ABC$ is
equilateral, then it is isosceles as well. **33.** 118, 96
35. 26, 64 **37.** 35, 37

4.1 Problem Solving (pp. 223–224) **41.** 2 in.; 60°; in
an equilateral triangle all sides have the same
length $\left(\frac{6}{3}\right)$. In an equiangular triangle the angles
always measure 60°. **45.** 115° **47.** 65°
49. a. $2\sqrt{2x} + 5\sqrt{2x} + 2\sqrt{2x} = 180$ **b.** 40°, 100°, 40°
c. obtuse **51.** *Sample answer:* They both reasoned
correctly but their initial plan was incorrect. The
measure of the exterior angle should be 150°.

4.2 Skill Practice (pp. 228–229)

1.
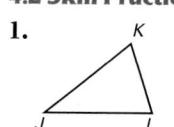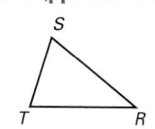
$\overline{JK} \cong \overline{RS}$, $\overline{KL} \cong \overline{ST}$,
$\overline{JL} \cong \overline{RT}$, $\angle J \cong \angle R$,
$\angle K \cong \angle S$, $\angle L \cong \angle T$

3. $\angle A$ and $\angle D$, $\angle C$ and $\angle F$, $\angle B$ and $\angle E$, $\overline{AB}$ and $\overline{DE}$,
$\overline{AC}$ and $\overline{DF}$, $\overline{BC}$ and $\overline{EF}$. *Sample answer:* $\triangle CAB \cong$
$\triangle FDE$. **5.** 124° **7.** 8 **9.** $\triangle ZYX$ **11.** $\triangle XYZ \cong \triangle ZWX$;
all corresponding sides and angles are congruent.
13. $\triangle BAG \cong \triangle CDF$; all corresponding sides and
angles are congruent. **15.** 20 **17.** Student still needs
to show that corresponding sides are congruent.
19. 3, 1

4.2 Problem Solving (pp. 230–231) **23.** Transitive
Property of Congruent Triangles **25.** length, width,
and depth

27.
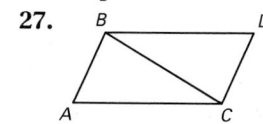
Yes; alternate interior
angles are congruent.

29. no
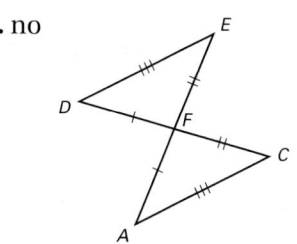

31. a. Corresponding parts of congruent figures are congruent. **b.** They are supplementary to two congruent angles and therefore are congruent. **c.** *Sample answer:* All right angles are congruent. **d.** Yes; all corresponding parts of both triangles are congruent.

4.2 Problem Solving Workshop (p. 232)

1. a.

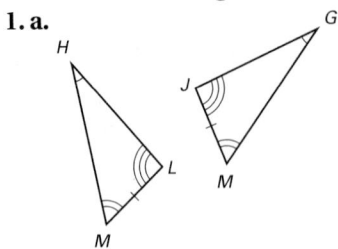

b.

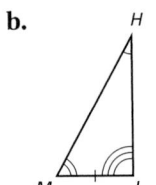
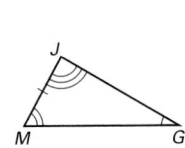

4.3 Skill Practice (pp. 236–237) **1.** corresponding angles **3.** corresponding sides **5.** not true; $\triangle RST \cong \triangle PQT$ **7.** true; SSS **9.** congruent **11.** congruent **13.** Stable; the figure has diagonal support with fixed side lengths. **15.** Stable; the figure has diagonal support with fixed side lengths. **19.** Not congruent; the congruence statement should read $\triangle ABC \cong \triangle FED$.

4.3 Problem Solving (pp. 238–239) **23.** Gate 1. *Sample answer:* Gate 1 has a diagonal support that forms two triangles with fixed side lengths, and these triangles cannot change shape. Gate 2 is not stable because that gate is a quadrilateral which can take many different shapes.

25.

Statements	Reasons
1. $\overline{WX} \cong \overline{VZ}, \overline{WY} \cong \overline{VY},$ $\overline{YZ} \cong \overline{YX}$	1. Given
2. $\overline{WV} \cong \overline{VW}$	2. Reflexive Property of Congruence
3. $WY = VY, YZ = YX$	3. Definition of congruent segments
4. $WY + YZ = VY + YZ$	4. Addition Property of Equality
5. $WY + YZ = VY + YX$	5. Substitution Property of Equality
6. $WZ = VX$	6. Segment Addition Postulate
7. $\overline{WZ} \cong \overline{VX}$	7. Definition of congruent segments
8. $\triangle VWX \cong \triangle WVZ$	8. SSS

27.

Statements	Reasons
1. $\overline{FM} \cong \overline{FN}, \overline{DM} \cong \overline{HN},$ $\overline{EF} \cong \overline{GF}, \overline{DE} \cong \overline{HG}$	1. Given
2. $MN = NM$	2. Reflexive Property of Equality
3. $FM = FN, DM = HN,$ $EF = GF$	3. Definition of congruent segments
4. $EF + FN = GF + FN,$ $DM + MN = HN + MN$	4. Addition Property of Equality
5. $EF + FN = GF + FM,$ $DM + MN = HN + NM$	5. Substitution Property of Equality
6. $EN = GM, DN = HM$	6. Segment Addition Postulate
7. $\overline{EN} \cong \overline{GM}, \overline{DN} \cong \overline{HM}$	7. Definition of congruent segments
8. $\triangle DEN \cong \triangle HGM$	8. SSS

29. Only one triangle can be created from three fixed sides.

4.4 Skill Practice (pp. 243–244) **1.** included **3.** $\angle XYW$ **5.** $\angle ZWY$ **7.** $\angle XYZ$ **9.** not enough **11.** not enough **13.** enough **17.** *Sample answer:* $\triangle STU, \triangle RVU$; they are congruent by SAS.

19.

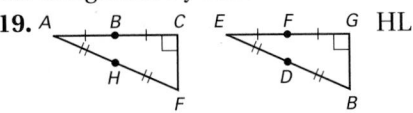

HL

21. SAS **23.** Yes; they are congruent by the SAS Congruence Postulate. **25.** $\overline{AC} \cong \overline{DF}$ **27.** $\overline{BC} \cong \overline{EF}$ **29.** Because $\overline{RM} \perp \overline{PQ}, \angle RMQ$ and $\angle RMP$ are right angles and thus are congruent. $\overline{QM} \cong \overline{MP}$ and $\overline{MR} \cong \overline{MR}$. It follows that $\triangle RMP \cong \triangle RMQ$ by SAS.

4.4 Problem Solving (pp. 245–246) **31.** SAS **33.** Two sides and the included angle of one sail need to be congruent to two sides and the included angle of the second sail; the two sails need to be right triangles with congruent hypotenuses and one pair of congruent legs.

35.

Statements	Reasons
1. $\overline{PQ}$ bisects $\angle SPT,$ $\overline{SP} \cong \overline{TP}$	1. Given
2. $\angle SPQ \cong \angle TPQ$	2. Definition of angle bisector
3. $\overline{PQ} \cong \overline{PQ}$	3. Reflexive Property of Congruence
4. $\triangle SPQ \cong \triangle TPQ$	4. SAS

37.

Statements	Reasons
1. $\overline{JM} \cong \overline{LM}$	1. Given
2. $\angle KJM$ and $\angle KLM$ are right angles.	2. Given
3. $\triangle JKM$ and $\triangle LKM$ are right triangles.	3. Definition of right triangle
4. $\overline{KM} \cong \overline{KM}$	4. Reflexive Property of Congruence
5. $\triangle JKM \cong \triangle LKM$	5. HL

4.5 Skill Practice (pp. 252–253) **1.** *Sample answer:* A flow proof shows the flow of a logical argument. **3.** yes; AAS **5.** yes; ASA **9.** $\angle F$, $\angle L$ **11.** $\angle AFE \cong \angle DFB$ by the Vertical Angles Congruence Theorem. **13.** $\angle EDA \cong \angle DCB$ by the Corresponding Angles Postulate. **15.** No; there is no AAA postulate or theorem. **17.** No; the segments that are congruent are not corresponding sides.

19. yes; the SAS Congruence Postulate **21. a.** $\overline{BC}$ and $\overline{AD}$ are parallel with $\overline{AC}$ being a transversal. The Alternate Interior Angles Theorem applies. **b.** $\overline{AB}$ and $\overline{CD}$ are parallel with $\overline{AC}$ being a transversal. The Alternate Interior Angles Theorem applies. **c.** Using parts 21a, 21b, and the fact that $\overline{AC} \cong \overline{CA}$, they are congruent by ASA.

4.5 Problem Solving (pp. 254–255) **23.** Two pairs of angles and an included pair of sides are congruent. The triangles are congruent by ASA.

25.

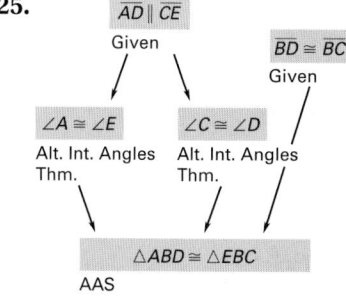

27. AAS

29. Since all right angles are congruent the two triangles are congruent by either AAS, if the side is not included, or ASA if it is the included side.

31.

Statements	Reasons
1. $\overline{AK} \cong \overline{CJ}$, $\angle BJK \cong \angle BKJ$, $\angle A \cong \angle C$	1. Given
2. $\triangle ABK \cong \triangle CBJ$	2. ASA

33.

$\boxed{\begin{array}{c}\triangle NKM \cong \angle LMK \\ \angle L \cong \angle N\end{array}}$ Given $\longrightarrow$ $\boxed{\triangle NMK \cong \triangle LKM}$ AAS

$\boxed{\overline{KM} \cong \overline{MK}}$ Reflexive Prop. of Congruence

4.6 Skill Practice (pp. 259–260) **1.** congruent **3.** $\triangle CBA$, $\triangle CBD$; SSS **5.** $\triangle JKM$, $\triangle LKM$; HL **7.** $\triangle JNH$, $\triangle KLG$; AAS **9.** The angle is not the included angle; the triangles cannot be said to be congruent. **11.** Show $\triangle NML \cong \triangle PQL$ by AAS since $\angle NLM \cong \angle PLQ$ by the Vertical Angles Congruence Theorem. Then $\overline{LM} \cong \overline{LQ}$ because corresponding parts of congruent triangles are congruent. **13.** 20, 120, ± 6 **15.** Show $\triangle KFG \cong \triangle HGF$ by AAS, which gives you $\overline{HG} \cong \overline{KF}$. This along with $\angle FJK \cong \angle GJH$ by vertical angles gives you $\triangle FJK \cong \triangle GJH$, therefore $\angle 1 \cong \angle 2$. **17.** Show $\triangle STR \cong \triangle QTP$ by ASA using the givens and vertical angles STR and QTP. Since $\overline{PT} \cong \overline{RT}$ and using vertical angles PTS and RTQ, by SAS, $\triangle PTS \cong \triangle RTQ$ which gives you $\angle 1 \cong \angle 2$. **19.** Show $\triangle KNP \cong \triangle MNP$ by SSS. Now $\angle KPL \cong \angle MPL$ and $\overline{PL} \cong \overline{PL}$ leads to $\triangle LKP \cong \triangle LMP$ by SAS, which gives you $\angle 1 \cong \angle 2$. **21.** The triangles are congruent by SSS.

23.

Statements	Reasons
1. $\angle T \cong \angle U$, $\angle Z \cong \angle X$, $\overline{YZ} \cong \overline{YX}$	1. Given
2. $\triangle TYZ \cong \triangle UYX$	2. AAS
3. $\angle TYZ \cong \angle UYX$	3. Corr. parts of $\cong \triangle$ are $\cong$.
4. $m\angle TYZ = m\angle UYX$	4. Definition of congruent angles
5. $m\angle TYW + m\angle WYZ = m\angle TYZ$, $m\angle TYW + m\angle VYX = m\angle UYX$	5. Angle Addition Postulate
6. $m\angle TYW + m\angle WYZ = m\angle TYW + m\angle VYX$	6. Transitive Property of Equality
7. $m\angle WYZ = m\angle VYX$	7. Subtraction Property of Equality
8. $\angle WYZ \cong \angle VYX$	8. Definition of congruent angles

4.6 Problem Solving (pp. 261–263)

29.

Statements	Reasons
1. $\overline{PQ} \parallel \overline{VS}$, $\overline{QU} \parallel \overline{ST}$, $\overline{PQ} \cong \overline{VS}$	1. Given
2. $\angle QPU \cong \angle SVT$, $\angle QUP \cong \angle STV$	2. Corresponding Angles Postulate
3. $\triangle PQU \cong \triangle VST$	3. AAS
4. $\angle Q \cong \angle S$	4. Corr. parts of $\cong \triangle$ are $\cong$.

33. No; the given angle is not an included angle.
35. Yes; $\angle BDA \cong \angle BDC$, $\overline{AD} \cong \overline{CD}$ and $\overline{BD} \cong \overline{BD}$. By SAS, $\triangle ABD \cong \triangle CBD$. Corr. parts of $\cong \triangle$ are $\cong$, so $\overline{AB} \cong \overline{BC}$.

37.

Statements	Reasons
1. $\overline{MN} \cong \overline{KN}$, $\angle PMN \cong \angle NKL$	1. Given
2. $\angle MNP \cong \angle KNL$	2. Vertical Angles Congruence Theorem
3. $\triangle PMN \cong \triangle LKN$	3. ASA
4. $\overline{MP} \cong \overline{KL}$, $\angle MPJ \cong \angle KLQ$	4. Corr. parts of $\cong$ △ are $\cong$.
5. $\overline{MJ} \perp \overline{PN}$, $\overline{KQ} \perp \overline{LN}$	5. Given in diagram
6. $\angle KQL$ and $\angle MJP$ are right angles.	6. Theorem 3.9
7. $\angle KQL \cong \angle MJP$	7. Right Angles Congruence Theorem
8. $\triangle MJP \cong \triangle KQL$	8. AAS
9. $\angle 1 \cong \angle 2$	9. Corr. parts of $\cong$ △ are $\cong$.

4.7 Skill Practice (pp. 267–268) **1.** The angle formed by the legs is the vertex angle. **3.** *A, D*; Base Angles Theorem **5.** $\overline{CD}, \overline{CE}$; Converse of Base Angles Theorem **7.** 12 **9.** 60° **11.** 20 **13.** 8 **15.** 39, 39 **17.** 45, 5 **21.** There is not enough information to find *x* or *y*. We need to know the measure of one of the vertex angles. **23.** 16 ft **25.** 39 in. **27.** possible **29.** possible **31.** $\triangle ABD \cong \triangle CBD$ by SAS making $\overline{BA} \cong \overline{BC}$ because corresponding parts of congruent triangles are congruent. **33.** 60, 120; solve the system $x + y = 180$ and $180 + 2x - y = 180$. **35.** 50°, 50°, 80°; 65°, 65°, 50°; there are two distinct exterior angles. If the angle is supplementary to the base angle, the base angle measures 50°. If the angle is supplementary to the vertex angle, then the base angles measure 65°.

4.7 Problem Solving (pp. 269–270)

39.
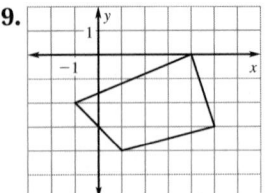
5 cm, 5 cm, 60°, 60°, 60°, 5 cm

41. a. $\angle A$, $\angle ACB$, $\angle CBD$, and $\angle CDB$ are congruent and $\overline{BC} \cong \overline{CB}$ making $\triangle ABC \cong \triangle BCD$ by AAS. **b.** $\triangle ABC$, $\triangle BCD$, $\triangle CDE$, $\triangle DEF$, $\triangle EFG$ **c.** $\angle BCD$, $\angle CDE$, $\angle DEF$, $\angle EFG$

43. 90°, 45°, 45°

47. No; $m\angle 1 = 50°$, so $m\angle 2 = 50°$ and it corresponds to the angle measuring 45°; therefore, *p* is not parallel to *q*. **49.** *Sample answer:* Choose point $P(x, y) \neq (2, 2)$ and set $PT = PU$. Solve the equation $\sqrt{x^2 + (y - 4)^2} = \sqrt{(x - 4)^2 + y^2}$ and get $y = x$. The point $(2, 2)$ is excluded because it is a point on $\overleftrightarrow{TU}$.

4.8 Skill Practice (pp. 276–277) **1.** Subtract one from each *x*-coordinate and add 4 to each *y*-coordinate. **3.** translation **5.** reflection **7.** no

9.
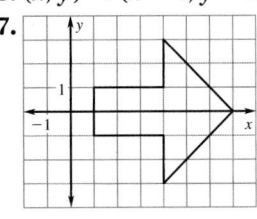

11.

13. $(x, y) \to (x - 4, y - 2)$ **15.** $(x, y) \to (x + 2, y - 1)$

17.

19.

21.
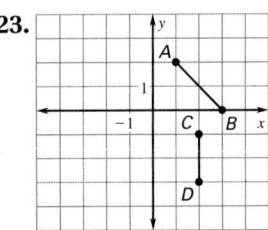
not a rotation

23.
not a rotation

25. Yes; take any point or any line segment and rotate 360°.
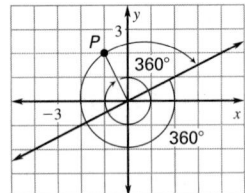

27. $(3, 4)$ **29.** $(2, 3)$ **31.** $(13, -5)$ **33.** $\overline{UV}$ **35.** $\triangle DST$

4.8 Problem Solving (pp. 278–279) **39.** 90° clockwise, 90° counterclockwise **41. a.** $(x, y) \rightarrow (x - 1, y + 2)$ **b.** $(x, y) \rightarrow (x + 2, y - 1)$ **c.** No; the translation needed does not match a knight's move.

Chapter Review (pp. 282–285) **1.** equiangular **3.** An isosceles triangle has at least two congruent sides, while a scalene triangle has no congruent sides. **5.** $\angle P$ and $\angle L$, $\angle Q$ and $\angle M$, $\angle R$ and $\angle N$; $\overline{PQ}$ and $\overline{LM}$, $\overline{QR}$ and $\overline{MN}$, $\overline{RP}$ and $\overline{NL}$ **7.** 120° **9.** 60° **11.** 60° **13.** 18 **15.** true; SSS **17.** true; SAS **19.** $\angle F$, $\angle J$ **21.** Show $\triangle ACD$ and $\triangle BED$ are congruent by AAS, which makes $\overline{AD}$ congruent to $\overline{BD}$. $\triangle ABD$ is then an isosceles triangle, which makes $\angle 1$ and $\angle 2$ congruent. **23.** Show $\triangle QVS$ congruent to $\triangle QVT$ by SSS, which gives us $\angle QSV$ congruent to $\angle QTV$. Using vertical angles and the Transitive Property you get $\angle 1$ congruent to $\angle 2$. **25.** 20

27. 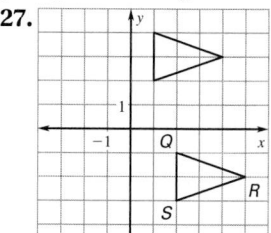 **29.**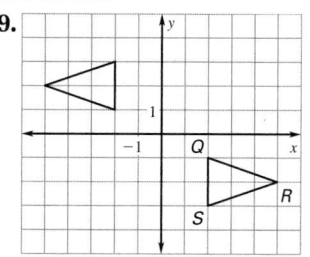

Algebra Review (p. 287)

1. $x > 2$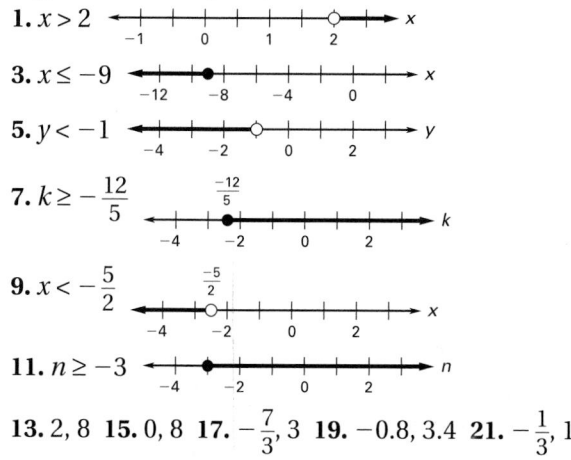

3. $x \le -9$

5. $y < -1$

7. $k \ge -\dfrac{12}{5}$

9. $x < -\dfrac{5}{2}$

11. $n \ge -3$

13. 2, 8 **15.** 0, 8 **17.** $-\dfrac{7}{3}$, 3 **19.** -0.8, 3.4 **21.** $-\dfrac{1}{3}$, 1 **23.** -5, 14 **25.** $-\dfrac{6}{5}$, 2 **27.** $\dfrac{7}{3}$, 5

Chapter 5

5.1 Skill Practice (pp. 298–299) **1.** midsegment **3.** 13 **5.** 6 **7.** $\overline{XZ}$ **9.** $\overline{JX}$, $\overline{KL}$ **11.** $\overline{YL}$, $\overline{LZ}$ **13.** $(0, 0)$, $(7, 0)$, $(0, 7)$ **15.** *Sample answer:* $(0, 0)$, $(2m, 0)$, (a, b) **17.** $(0, 0)$, $(s, 0)$, (s, s), $(0, s)$ **19.** *Sample answer:* $(0, 0)$, $(r, 0)$, $(0, s)$

21.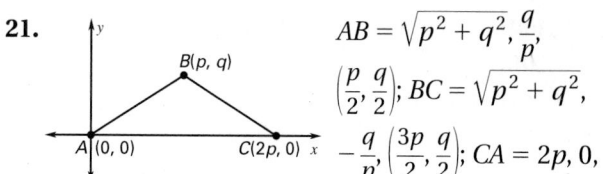

$AB = \sqrt{p^2 + q^2}$, $\dfrac{q}{p}$, $\left(\dfrac{p}{2}, \dfrac{q}{2}\right)$; $BC = \sqrt{p^2 + q^2}$, $-\dfrac{q}{p}$, $\left(\dfrac{3p}{2}, \dfrac{q}{2}\right)$; $CA = 2p$, 0, $(p, 0)$; no; yes; it's not a right triangle because none of the slopes are negative reciprocals, and it is isosceles because two of the sides have the same length.

23.

$AB = m$, 0, $\left(\dfrac{m}{2}, n\right)$, $BC = n$, undefined, $\left(m, \dfrac{n}{2}\right)$, $CA = \sqrt{m^2 + n^2}$, $-\dfrac{n}{m}$, $\left(\dfrac{m}{2}, \dfrac{n}{2}\right)$; yes; no; one side is vertical and one side is horizontal thus the triangle is a right triangle. It is not isosceles since none of the sides have the same length.

25. 13 **27.** You don't know that $\overline{DE}$ and $\overline{BC}$ are parallel. **29.** $(0, k)$. *Sample answer:* Since $\triangle OPQ$ and $\triangle RSQ$ are right triangles with $\overline{OP} \cong \overline{RS}$ and $\overline{PQ} \cong \overline{SQ}$, the triangles are congruent by SAS. **33.** $GE = \dfrac{1}{2}DB$, $EF = \dfrac{1}{2}BC$, area of $\triangle EFG = \dfrac{1}{2}\left[\dfrac{1}{2}DB\left(\dfrac{1}{2}BC\right)\right] = \dfrac{1}{8}(DB)(BC)$, area of $\triangle BCD = \dfrac{1}{2}(DB)(BC)$.

5.1 Problem Solving (pp. 300–301) **35.** 10 ft **37.** The coordinates of W are $(3, 3)$ and the coordinates of V are $(7, 3)$. The slope of $\overline{WV}$ is 0 and the slope of $\overline{OH}$ is 0 making $\overline{WV} \parallel \overline{OH}$. $WV = 4$ and $OH = 8$ thus $WV = \dfrac{1}{2}OH$. **39.** 16. *Sample answer:* DE is half the length of $\overline{FG}$ which makes $FG = 8$. FG is half the length of $\overline{AC}$ which makes $AC = 16$. **41.** *Sample answer:* You already know the coordinates of D are (q, r) and can show the coordinates of F are $(p, 0)$ since $\left(\dfrac{2p + 0}{2}, \dfrac{0 + 0}{2}\right) = (p, 0)$. The slope of $\overline{DF}$ is $\dfrac{r - 0}{q - p} = \dfrac{r}{q - p}$ and the slope of $\overline{BC}$ is $\dfrac{2r - 0}{2q - 2p} = \dfrac{r}{q - p}$ making them parallel. $DF = \sqrt{(q - p)^2 + r^2}$ and $BC = \sqrt{(2q - 2p)^2 + (2r)^2} = 2\sqrt{(q - p)^2 + r^2}$ making $DF = \dfrac{1}{2}BC$. **43. a.** $\dfrac{1}{2}$ **b.** $\dfrac{5}{4}$ **c.** $\dfrac{19}{8}$ **45.** *Sample answer:* $\triangle ABD$ and $\triangle CBD$ are congruent right isosceles triangles with $A(0, p)$, $B(0, 0)$, $C(p, 0)$ and $D\left(\dfrac{p}{2}, \dfrac{p}{2}\right)$.

$AB = p$, $BC = p$, and $\overline{AB}$ is a vertical line and $\overline{BC}$ is a horizontal line, so $\overline{AB} \perp \overline{BC}$. By definition, $\triangle ABC$ is a right isosceles triangle.

5.1 Problem Solving Workshop (p. 302) **1.** The slopes of $\overline{AC}$ and $\overline{BC}$ are negative reciprocals of each other, so $\overline{AC} \perp \overline{BC}$ making $\angle C$ a right angle; $AC = h\sqrt{2}$ and $BC = h\sqrt{2}$ making $\triangle ABC$ isosceles.

3. a.

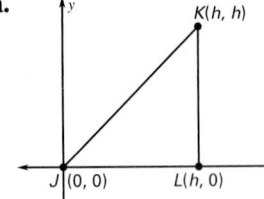

$JL = LK = h$ and $\overline{JL}$ is a horizontal line and $\overline{LK}$ is a vertical line, so $\overline{JL} \perp \overline{LK}$; $h\sqrt{2}$, $\left(\dfrac{h}{2}, \dfrac{h}{2}\right)$.

b.

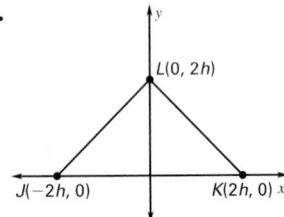

$JL = LK = 2h\sqrt{2}$ and the slope of $\overline{JL} = 1$ and the slope of $\overline{LK} = -1$, so $\overline{JL} \perp \overline{LK}$; $4h$, $(0, 0)$.

5. *Sample answer: PQRS with P(0, 0), Q(0, m), R(n, m),* and *S(n, 0). PR = QS = $\sqrt{m^2 + n^2}$ making $\overline{PR} \cong \overline{QS}$.*

5.2 Skill Practice (pp. 306–307) **1.** circumcenter **3.** 15 **5.** 55 **7.** yes **11.** 35 **13.** 50 **15.** Yes; the Converse of the Perpendicular Bisector Theorem guarantees L is on $\overleftrightarrow{JP}$. **17.** 11

19. *Sample:*

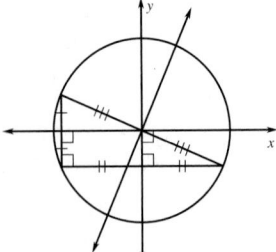

21. Always; congruent sides are created.

5.2 Problem Solving (pp. 308–309) **25.** Theorem 5.4 shows you that you can find a point equidistant from three points by using the perpendicular bisectors of the sides of the triangle formed by the three points.

27.

Statements	Reasons
1. $CA = CB$	1. Given
2. Draw $\overleftrightarrow{PC} \perp \overline{AB}$ through point C.	2. Perpendicular Postulate
3. $\overline{CA} \cong \overline{CB}$	3. Definition of congruent segments
4. $\overline{CP} \cong \overline{CP}$	4. Reflexive Property of Segment Congruence
5. $\angle CPA$ and $\angle CPB$ are right angles.	5. Definition of $\perp$ lines
6. $\triangle CPA$ and $\triangle CPB$ are right triangles.	6. Definition of right triangle
7. $\triangle CPA \cong \triangle CPB$	7. HL
8. $\overline{PA} \cong \overline{PB}$	8. Corr. parts of $\cong$ $\triangle$ are $\cong$.
9. P is the midpoint of $\overline{AB}$.	9. Definition of midpoint
10. C is on the perpendicular bisector of $\overline{AB}$.	10. Definition of perpendicular bisector

5.3 Skill Practice (pp. 313–314) **1.** bisector **3.** 20° **5.** 9 **7.** No; you don't know that $\angle BAD \cong \angle CAD$. **9.** No; you don't know that $\overline{HG} \cong \overline{HF}$, $\overline{HF} \perp \overrightarrow{EF}$, or $\overline{HG} \perp \overrightarrow{EG}$. **11.** No; you don't know that $\overline{HF} \perp \overrightarrow{EF}$, or $\overline{HG} \perp \overrightarrow{EG}$. **13.** 4 **15.** No; the segments with length x and 3 are not perpendicular to their respective rays. **17.** Yes; $x = 7$ using the Angle Bisector Theorem. **19.** 9 **21.** GD is not the perpendicular distance from G to $\overline{CE}$. The same is true about GF; the distance from G to each side of the triangle is the same. **25.** 0.5

5.3 Problem Solving (pp. 315–316) **29.** at the incenter of the pond

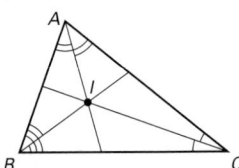

31. a. Equilateral; 3; the angle bisector would also be the perpendicular bisector. **b.** Scalene; 6; each angle bisector would be different than the corresponding perpendicular bisector. **33.** perpendicular bisectors; (10, 10); 100 yd; about 628 yd

35.

Statements	Reasons
1. $\angle BAC$ with D interior, $\overrightarrow{DB} \perp \overrightarrow{AB}$, $\overrightarrow{DC} \perp \overrightarrow{AC}$, $DB = DC$	1. Given
2. $\angle ABD$ and $\angle ACD$ are right angles.	2. Definition of perpendicular
3. $\triangle ABD$ and $\triangle ACD$ are right triangles.	3. Definition of right triangle
4. $\overline{DB} \cong \overline{DC}$	4. Definition of congruent segments
5. $\overline{AD} \cong \overline{AD}$	5. Reflexive Property of Segment Congruence
6. $\triangle ABD \cong \triangle ACD$	6. HL
7. $\angle BAD \cong \angle CAD$	7. Corr. parts of $\cong$ △ are $\cong$.
8. $\overrightarrow{AD}$ bisects $\angle BAC$.	8. Definition of angle bisector

37. a. Use the Concurrency of Angle Bisectors of a Triangle Theorem; if you move the circle to any other spot it will extend into the walkway.

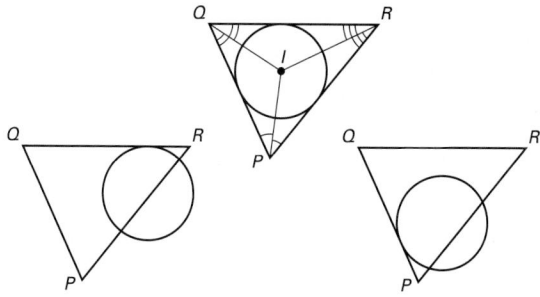

b. Yes; the incenter will allow the largest tent possible.

5.4 Skill Practice (pp. 322–323) **1.** circumcenter: when it is an acute triangle, when it is a right triangle, when it is an obtuse triangle; incenter: always, never, never; centroid: always, never, never; orthocenter: when it is an acute triangle, when it is a right triangle, when it is an obtuse triangle **3.** 12 **5.** 10 **9.** (3, 2)

11.

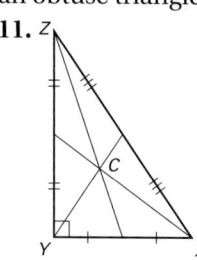

13. no; no; yes **15.** no; yes; no
17. altitude **19.** median
21. perpendicular bisector, angle bisector, median, altitude
23. 6, 22°; $\triangle ABD \cong \triangle CBD$ by HL, use Corr. parts of $\cong$ △ are $\cong$.
25. 3 **27.** $\frac{3}{2}$

29.

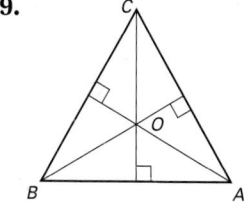

31.

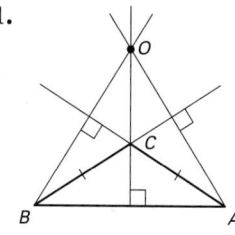

33. $\frac{5}{2}$ **35.** 4

5.4 Problem Solving (pp. 324–325) **37.** B; it is the centroid of the triangle. **39.** 6.75 in.^{2}; altitude (0, 2)

41.

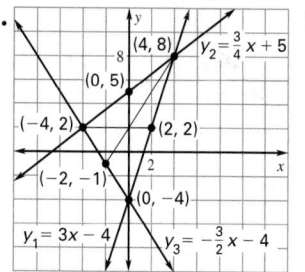

43. b. Their areas are the same. **c.** They weigh the same; it means the weight of $\triangle ABC$ is evenly distributed around its centroid.

5.5 Skill Practice (pp. 331–332) **1.** $\angle A$, $\overline{BC}$; $\angle B$, $\overline{CA}$; $\angle C$, $\overline{AB}$ **3.** *Sample answer:* The longest side is opposite the largest angle. The shortest side is opposite the smallest angle. **5.** *Sample answer:* The longest side is opposite the obtuse angle and the two angles with the same measure are opposite the sides with the same length. **7.** $\overline{XY}$, $\overline{YZ}$, $\overline{ZX}$; $\angle Z$, $\angle X$, $\angle Y$ **9.** $\overline{KL}$, $\overline{JL}$, $\overline{JK}$; $\angle J$, $\angle K$, $\angle L$ **11.** $\overline{DF}$, $\overline{FG}$, $\overline{GD}$; $\angle G$, $\angle D$, $\angle F$

13. **15.**

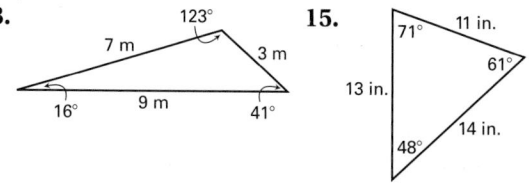

17. No; $3 + 6$ is not greater than 9. **19.** yes
21. 7 in. $< x <$ 17 in. **23.** 6 ft $< x <$ 30 ft
25. 16 in. $< x <$ 64 in. **27.** $\angle A$ and $\angle B$ are the nonadjacent interior angles to $\angle 1$ thus by the Exterior Angle Theorem $m\angle 1 = m\angle A + m\angle B$, which guarantees $m\angle 1 > m\angle A$ and $m\angle 1 > m\angle B$. **29.** The longest side is not opposite the largest angle. **31.** yes; $\angle Q$, $\angle P$, $\angle R$ **33.** $2 < x < 15$
35. $\angle WXY$, $\angle Z$, $\angle ZXY$, $\angle WYX$ and $\angle ZYX$, $\angle W$; $\angle ZYX$ is the largest angle in $\triangle ZYX$ and $\angle WYX$ is the middle sized angle in $\triangle WXY$ making $\angle W$ the largest angle. $m\angle WXY + m\angle W = m\angle Z + m\angle ZXY$ making $\angle WXY$ the smallest.

5.5 Problem Solving (pp. 333–334) **37.** $m\angle P < m\angle Q$, $m\angle P < m\angle R$; $m\angle Q = m\angle R$ **39. a.** The sum of the other two side lengths is less than 1080. **b.** No; the sum of the distance from Granite Peak to Fort Peck Lake and Granite Peak to Glacier National Park must be more than 565. **c.** $d > 76$ km, $d < 1054$ km **d.** The distance is less than 489 kilometers.
41. *Sample:*

8 cm / 8 cm	9 cm / 9 cm	7 cm \ 7 cm	10 cm / 10 cm
8 cm	6 cm	10 cm	4 cm
acute	acute	obtuse	acute

43. *Sample answer:* 3, 4, 17; 2, 5, 17; 4, 4, 16
45. $1\frac{1}{4}$ mi $\le d \le 2\frac{3}{4}$ mi; if the locations are collinear then the distance could be $1\frac{1}{4}$ miles or $2\frac{3}{4}$ miles. If the locations are not collinear then the distance must be between $1\frac{1}{4}$ miles and $2\frac{3}{4}$ miles because of the Triangle Inequality Theorem.

5.6 Skill Practice (pp. 338–339) **1.** You temporarily assume that the desired conclusion is false and this leads to a logical contradiction. **3.** > **5.** < **7.** =
11. Suppose xy is even. **13.** $\angle A$ could be a right angle or a straight angle. **15.** The Hinge Theorem is about triangles not quadrilaterals. **17.** $x > \frac{1}{2}$ **19.** Using the Converse of the Hinge Theorem, $\angle NRQ > \angle NRP$. Since $\angle NRQ$ and $\angle NRP$ are a linear pair, $\angle NRQ$ must be obtuse and $\angle NRP$ must be acute.
5.6 Problem Solving (pp. 340–341) **23.** E, A, D, B, C
25. a. It gets larger; it gets smaller. **b.** KM **c.** *Sample answer:* Since $NL = NK = NM$ and as $m\angle LNK$ increases KL increases and $m\angle KNM$ decreases as KM decreases, you have two pairs of congruent sides with $m\angle LNK$ eventually larger than $m\angle KNM$. The Hinge Theorem guarantees KL will eventually be larger than KM. **27.** Prove: If x is divisible by 4, then x is even. Proof: Since x is divisible by 4, $x = 4a$. When you factor out a 2, you get $x = 2(2a)$ which is in the form $2n$, which implies x is an even number; your temporary assumption in the indirect proof is the same as the hypothesis in the direct proof.

Chapter Review (pp. 344–347) **1.** midpoint **3.** B **5.** C
7. 45 **9.** BA and BC, DA and DC **11.** 25 **13.** 15
15. $(-2, 4)$ **17.** 3.5 **19.** 4 in. $< \ell <$ 12 in.
21. 8 ft $< \ell <$ 32 ft **23.** $\overline{LM}$, $\overline{MN}$, $\overline{LN}$; $\angle N$, $\angle L$, $\angle M$
25. > **27.** C, B, A, D

Algebra Review (p. 349) **1. a.** $\frac{3}{1}$ **b.** $\frac{1}{4}$ **3.** $\frac{5}{4}$
5. 9% decrease **7.** 12.5% increase **9.** 0.25% decrease **11.** 84%; 37.8 h **13.** 107.5%; 86 people

Chapter 6
6.1 Skill Practice (pp. 360–361) **1.** means: n and p, extremes: m and q **3.** 4 : 1 **5.** 600 : 1 **7.** $\frac{7}{1}$ **9.** $\frac{24}{5}$
11. $\frac{5\ \text{in.}}{15\ \text{in.}}; \frac{1}{3}$ **13.** $\frac{320\ \text{cm}}{1000\ \text{cm}}; \frac{8}{25}$ **15.** $\frac{5}{2}$ **17.** $\frac{4}{3}$ **19.** 8, 28
21. 20°, 70°, 90° **23.** 4 **25.** 42 **27.** 3 **29.** 3 **31.** 6 **33.** 16
35. $5\sqrt{2}$ **37.** The unit conversion should be $\frac{1\ \text{ft}}{12\ \text{in.}}$; $\frac{8\ \text{in.}}{3\ \text{ft}} \cdot \frac{1\ \text{ft}}{12\ \text{in.}} = \frac{8}{36} = \frac{2}{9}$. **39.** $\frac{12}{5}$ **41.** $\frac{4}{3}$ **43.** $\frac{7}{11}$ **45.** ± 6
47. Obtuse; since the angles are supplementary, $x + 4x = 180$. Find $x = 36$, so the measure of the interior angle is 144°. **49.** 9 **51.** 5 **53.** 72 in., 60 in.
55. 45, 30

6.1 Problem Solving (pp. 362–363) **57.** 18 ft, 15 ft, 270 ft^2; 270 tiles; $534.60 **59.** 9 cups, 1.8 cups, 7.2 cups **61.** about 189 hits **63.** All three ratios reduce to 4 : 3. **65.** 600 Canadian dollars **67.** $\frac{a}{b} = \frac{c}{d}$, $b \ne 0$, $d \ne 0$; $\frac{a}{b} \cdot bd = \frac{c}{d} \cdot bd$; $ad = cb$; $ad = bc$

6.2 Skill Practice (pp. 367–368) **1.** scale drawing
3. $\frac{x}{y}$ **5.** $\frac{y + 15}{15}$ **7.** true **9.** true **11.** 10.5 **13.** about 100 yd
15. 4 should have been added to numerator of the the second fraction instead of 3; $\frac{a + 3}{3} = \frac{c + 4}{4}$. **17.** $\frac{49}{3}$

6.2 Problem Solving (pp. 368–370) **23.** 1 in. : $\frac{1}{3}$ mi
25. about 8 mi **27.** about 0.022 mm **29.** 48 ft
31.
$$\frac{a}{b} = \frac{c}{d}$$
$$\frac{a}{b} \cdot bd = \frac{c}{d} \cdot bd$$
$$ad = cb$$
$$ad \cdot \frac{1}{ac} = cb \cdot \frac{1}{ac}$$
$$\frac{d}{c} = \frac{b}{a}$$

33.
$$\frac{a}{b} = \frac{c}{d}$$
$$\frac{a}{b} + 1 = \frac{c}{d} + 1$$
$$\frac{a}{b} + \frac{b}{b} = \frac{c}{d} + \frac{d}{d}$$
$$\frac{a + b}{b} = \frac{c + d}{d}$$

35.
$$\frac{a + c}{b + d} = \frac{a - c}{b - d}$$
$$(a + c)(b - d) = (a - c)(b + d)$$
$$ab - ad + bc - cd = ab + ad - bc - cd$$
$$-ad + bc = ad - bc$$
$$-2ad = -2bc$$
$$ad = bc$$
$$\frac{a}{b} = \frac{c}{d}$$

pro...

$\dfrac{AB}{LM}$ ...

$\angle$ ...

R... ...ger

t... ...ld have
...ays

...$\dfrac{}{3}$ in. **23.** $\dfrac{11}{5}$

...responding

...No; the lengths
..., 5.6, 2.1

...$\dfrac{10}{7}x$; $\dfrac{10}{7}$; they are

...e.

...rger and smaller image
...*answer:* Let $\ell = 8$, $w = 8$,
...$\dfrac{2}{3}$, $\dfrac{\ell}{\ell + a} = \dfrac{8}{12} = \dfrac{2}{3}$. **37. a.** They
...**b.** $\angle BOA \cong \angle DOC$ by the
...rem. $\angle OBA \cong \angle ODC$ by the
...ngles Theorem. $\angle BAO \cong \angle DCO$
by the Alternate Interior Angles Theorem. **c.** $(-3, 0)$,
$(0, 4)$, $(6, 0)$, $(0, -8)$; $AO = 3$, $OB = 4$, $BA = 5$,
$CO = 6$, $OD = 8$, $DC = 10$ **d.** Since corresponding
angles are congruent and the ratios of corresponding
sides are all the same the triangles are similar.

6.4 Skill Practice (pp. 384–385) **1.** similar **3.** $\triangle FED$
5. 15, y **7.** 20 **9.** similar; $\triangle FGH \sim \triangle KLJ$
11. not similar **13.** similar; $\triangle YZX \sim \triangle YWU$
15. The AA Similarity Postulate is for triangles,
not quadrilaterals. **17.** 5 should be replaced by 9,
which is the length of the corresponding side of
the larger triangle. *Sample answer:* $\dfrac{4}{9} = \dfrac{6}{x}$.
19. *Sample:*

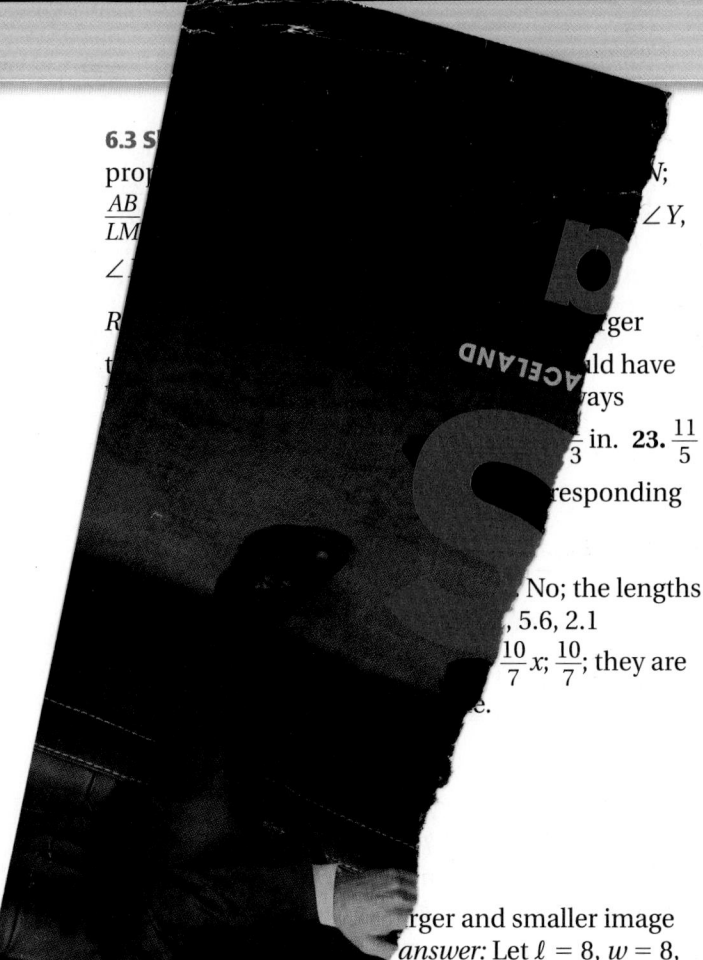

21. (10, 0) **23.** (24, 0)

25. a.

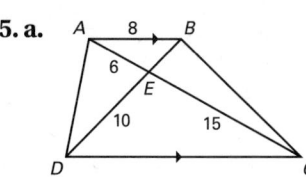

b. *Sample answer:*
$\angle ABE$ and $\angle CDE$,
$\angle BAE$ and $\angle DCE$
c. $\triangle ABE$ and $\triangle CDE$,
$\triangle ABE \sim \triangle CDE$
d. 4, 20

27. Yes; either $m \angle X$ or $m \angle Y$ could be 90°, and the
other angles could be the same. **29.** No; since
$m \angle J + m \angle K = 85°$ then $m \angle L = 95°$. Since $m \angle Y + m \angle Z = 80°$ then $m \angle X = 100°$ and thus neither $\angle Y$
nor $\angle Z$ can measure 95°.

6.4 Problem Solving (pp. 386–387) **31.** about 30.8 in.
33. The measure of all
angles in an equilateral
triangle is 60°. *Sample:*

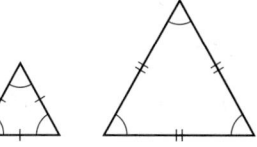

35.

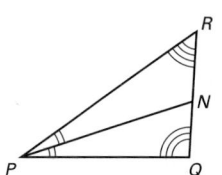

Since $\triangle STU \sim \triangle PQR$ you know that $\angle T \cong \angle Q$ and
$\angle UST \cong \angle RPQ$. Since $\overline{SV}$ bisects $\angle TSU$ and $\overline{PN}$
bisects $\angle QPR$ you know that $\angle USV \cong \angle VST$ and
$\angle RPN \cong \angle NPQ$ by definition of angle bisector.
You know that $m \angle USV + m \angle VST = m \angle UST$
and $m \angle RPN + m \angle NPQ = m \angle RPQ$, therefore,
$2m \angle VST = 2m \angle NPQ$ using the Substitution
Property of Equality. You now have $\angle VST \cong \angle NPQ$,
which makes $\triangle VST \sim \triangle NPQ$ using the AA
Similarity Postulate. From this you know that
$\dfrac{SV}{PN} = \dfrac{ST}{PQ}$.
37. a. *Sample:*

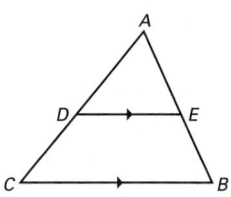

b. $m \angle ADE = m \angle ACB$ and $m \angle AED = m \angle ABC$
c. $\triangle ADE \sim \triangle ACB$ **d.** *Sample answer:* $\dfrac{AD}{AC} = \dfrac{AE}{AB} = \dfrac{DE}{CB} = \dfrac{1}{2}$ **e.** The measures of the angles change, but
the equalities remain the same. The lengths of the
sides change, but they remain proportional; yes;
the triangles remain similar by the AA Similarity
Postulate.

6.5 Skill Practice (pp. 391–393) **1.** $\frac{AC}{PX} = \frac{CB}{XQ} = \frac{AB}{PQ}$
3. $\frac{18}{12} = \frac{15}{10} = \frac{12}{8}; \frac{3}{2}$ **5.** $\triangle RST$ **7.** similar;
$\triangle FDE \sim \triangle XWY; 2:3$
9. 3

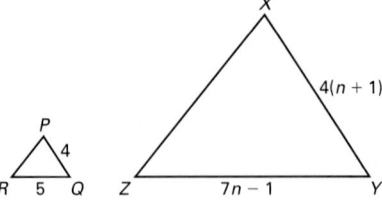

11. $\triangle ABC \sim \triangle DEC; \angle ACB \cong \angle DCE$ by the Vertical
Angles Congruence Theorem and $\frac{AC}{DC} = \frac{BC}{EC} = \frac{3}{2}$.
The triangles are similar using the SAS Similarity
Theorem. **13.** *Sample answer:* The triangle
correspondence is not listed in the correct order;
$\triangle ABC \sim \triangle RQP$.

15.

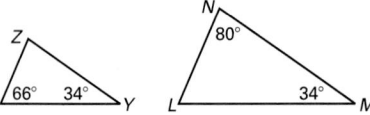

They are similar by the AA Similarity Postulate.

17.

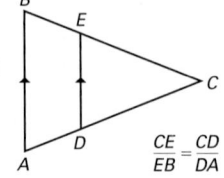

They are not similar since the ratio of
corresponding sides is not constant.

19. 45° **21.** 24 **23.** $16\sqrt{2}$

6.5 Problem Solving (pp. 393–395) **29.** The triangle
whose sides measure 4 inches, 4 inches, and 7 inches
is similar to the triangle whose sides measure 3 inches,
3 inches, and 5.25 inches. **31.** $\angle CBD \cong \angle CAE$
33. a. AA Similarity Postulate **b.** 75 ft **c.** 66 ft
35. *Sample answer:* Given that D and E are midpoints
of $\overline{AB}$ and $\overline{BC}$ respectively the Midsegment Theorem
guarantees that $\overline{AC} \parallel \overline{DE}$. By the Corresponding
Angles Postulate $\angle A \cong \angle BDE$ and so $\angle BDE$ is a
right angle. Reasoning similarly $\overline{AB} \parallel \overline{EF}$.
By the Alternate Interior Angles Congruence
Theorem $\angle BDE \cong \angle DEF$. This makes $\angle DEF$ a
right angle that measures 90°.

6.6 Skill Practice (pp. 400–401)
1. If a line parallel to one side
of a triangle intersects the
other two sides then it divides
the two sides proportionally.

$\frac{CE}{EB} = \frac{CD}{DA}$

3. 9 **5.** Parallel; $\frac{8}{5} = \frac{12}{7.5}$ so the Converse of the Triangle
Proportionality Theorem applies. **7.** Parallel; $\frac{20}{18} = \frac{25}{22.5}$
so the Converse of the Triangle Proportionality
Theorem applies. **9.** 10 **11.** 1 **15.** 9 **17.** $a = 9$, $b = 4$,
$c = 3$, $d = 2$
19. a–b. See figure in part (c).
c.

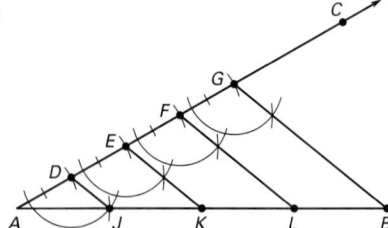

Theorem 6.6 guarantees that parallel lines divide
transversals proportionally. Since $\frac{AD}{DE} = \frac{DE}{EF} = \frac{EF}{FG} = 1$ implies $\frac{AJ}{JK} = \frac{JK}{KL} = \frac{KL}{LB} = 1$ which means $AJ = JK = KL = LB$.

6.6 Problem Solving (pp. 402–403) **21.** 350 yd
23. Since $k_1 \parallel k_2 \parallel k_3$, $\angle FDA \cong \angle CAD$ and $\angle CDA \cong \angle FAD$ by the Alternate Interior Angles Congruence
Theorem. $\triangle ACD \sim \triangle DFA$ by the AA Similarity
Postulate. Let point G be at the intersection of $\overline{AD}$
and $\overline{BE}$. Using the Triangle Proportionality Theorem
$\frac{CB}{BA} = \frac{DG}{GA}$ and $\frac{DE}{EF} = \frac{DG}{GA}$. Using the Transitive Property
of Equality $\frac{CB}{BA} = \frac{DE}{EF}$.

25.

In an isosceles triangle, the legs
are congruent, so the ratio of
their lengths is $1:1$. By Theorem
6.7, this ratio is equal to the ratio
of the lengths of the segments
created by the ray, so it is also $1:1$.

27. Since $\overline{XW} \parallel \overline{AZ}$, $\angle XZA \cong \angle WXZ$ using the
Alternate Interior Angles Congruence Theorem.
This makes $\triangle AXZ$ isosceles because it is shown that
$\angle A \cong \angle WXZ$ and by the Converse of the Base Angles
Theorem, $AX = XZ$. Since $\overline{XW} \parallel \overline{AZ}$ using the Triangle
Proportionality Theorem you get
$\frac{YW}{WZ} = \frac{XY}{AX}$. Substituting you get $\frac{YW}{WX} = \frac{XY}{XZ}$.

6.6 Problem Solving Workshop (p. 405)
1. a. 270 yd **b.** 67.5 yd **3.** 4.5 mi/h **5.** 5.25, 7.5

Extension (p. 407) **1.** $3:1$. *Sample answer:* It's one
unit longer; each of the three edges went from
measuring one unit to four edges each measuring
$\frac{1}{3}$ of a unit.

3. a.

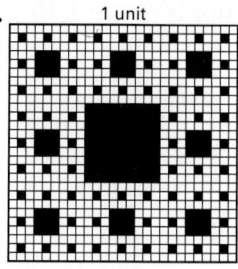

1 unit

1 unit

b. *Sample answer:* The upper left square is simply a smaller version of the whole square.

c.

Stage	Number of colored squares	Area of 1 colored square	Total Area
0	0	0	0
1	1	$\frac{1}{9}$	$\frac{1}{9}$
2	8	$\frac{1}{81}$	$\frac{17}{81}$
3	64	$\frac{1}{729}$	$\frac{217}{729}$

6.7 Skill Practice (pp. 412–413) **1.** similar

3. 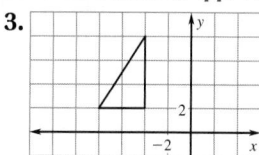 **5.**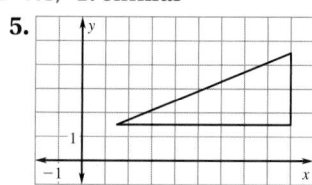

9. reduction; $\frac{1}{2}$ **11.** enlargement; 3 **15.** The figures are not similar. **17.** reflection **19.** 2; $m = 4$, $n = 5$

6.7 Problem Solving (pp. 414–415)

25. 24 ft by 12 ft **27.** $\frac{5}{2}$

29. a. 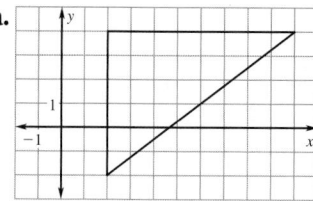 **b.** $\frac{2}{3}$; they are the same. **c.** $\frac{4}{9}$; it's the square of the scale factor.

31. Perspective drawings use converging lines to give the illusion that an object is three dimensional. Since the back of the drawing is similar to the front, a dilation can be used to create this illusion with the vanishing point as the center of dilation.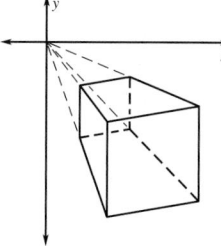

33. The slope of $\overline{PQ}$ is $\frac{d - b}{c - a}$ and the slope of $\overline{XY}$ is $\frac{kd - kb}{kc - ka} = \frac{k(d - b)}{k(c - a)} = \frac{d - b}{c - a}$. Since the slopes are the same, the lines are parallel.

Chapter Review (pp. 418–421) **1.** dilation **3.** In a ratio two numbers are compared. In a proportion

two ratios are set equal to one another. *Sample answer:* $\frac{2}{4}$, $\frac{6}{10} = \frac{3}{5}$ **5.** 45°, 45°, 90° **7.** $\frac{20}{3}$ **9.** similar; $ABCD \sim EFGH$, $\frac{4}{3}$ **11.** 68 in. **13.** By the Triangle Sum Theorem $m\angle D = 60°$ so $\angle A \cong \angle D$. $\angle C \cong \angle F$ by the Right Angles Congruence Theorem. So, $\triangle ABC \sim \triangle DEF$ by the AA Similarity Postulate.

15. Since $\frac{4}{8} = \frac{3.5}{7}$ and the included angle, $\angle C$, is congruent to itself, $\triangle BCD \sim \triangle ACE$ by the SAS Similarity Theorem. **17.** not parallel

19. 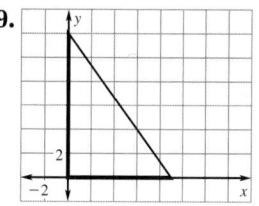 **21.**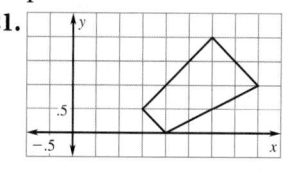

Algebra Review (p. 423) **1.** ± 10 **3.** $\pm\sqrt{17}$ **5.** $\pm\sqrt{10}$ **7.** $\pm 2\sqrt{5}$ **9.** $\pm 3\sqrt{2}$ **11.** $\frac{\sqrt{15}}{5}$ **13.** $\frac{\sqrt{21}}{2}$ **15.** $\frac{1}{10}$ **17.** $\frac{\sqrt{2}}{2}$

Cumulative Review (pp. 428–429) **1. a.** 33° **b.** 123° **3. a.** 2° **b.** 92°

5.

$3x - 19 = 47$	Given
$3x = 66$	Addition Property of Equality
$x = 22$	Division Property of Equality

7.

$-5(x + 2) = 25$	Given
$x + 2 = -5$	Division Property of Equality
$x = -7$	Subtraction Property of Equality

9. Alternate Interior Angles Theorem **11.** Corresponding Angles Postulate **13.** Linear Pair Postulate **15.** 78°, 78°, 24°; acute **17.** congruent; $\triangle ABC \cong \triangle CDA$, SSS Congruence Postulate **19.** not congruent **21.** 8 **23.** similar; $\triangle FCD \sim \triangle FHG$, SAS Similarity Theorem **25.** not similar **27. a.** $y = 59x + 250$ **b.** The slope is the monthly membership and the y-intercept is the initial cost to join the club. **c.** $958 **29.** *Sample answer:* Since $\overline{BC} \parallel \overline{AD}$, you know that $\angle CBD \cong \angle ADB$ by the Alternate Interior Angles Theorem. $\overline{BD} \cong \overline{BD}$ by the Reflexive Property of Segment Congruence and with $\overline{BC} \cong \overline{AD}$ given, then $\triangle BCD \cong \triangle DAB$ by the SAS Congruence Theorem. **31.** 43 mi < d < 397 mi

Chapter 7

7.1 Skill Practice (pp. 436–438) **1.** Pythagorean triple **3.** 130 **5.** 58 **7.** In Step 2, the Distributive Property was used incorrectly; $x^2 = 49 + 576$, $x^2 = 625$, $x = 25$.

9. about 9.1 in. **11.** 120 m² **13.** 48 cm² **15.** 40
19. 15, leg **21.** 52, hypotenuse **23.** 21, leg **25.** $11\sqrt{2}$

7.1 Problem Solving (pp. 438–439) **31.** about 127.3 ft
33. *Sample answer:* The longest side of the triangle is opposite the largest angle, which in a right triangle is the right angle.

35. a–b.

BC	AC	CE	AC + CE
10	60.8	114.0	174.8
20	63.2	104.4	167.6
30	67.1	94.9	162
40	72.1	85.4	157.6
50	78.1	76.2	154.3
60	84.9	67.1	152
70	92.2	58.3	150.5
80	100	50	150
90	108.2	42.4	150.6
100	116.6	36.1	152.7
110	125.3	31.6	156.9
120	134.2	30	164.2

150 ft

c.

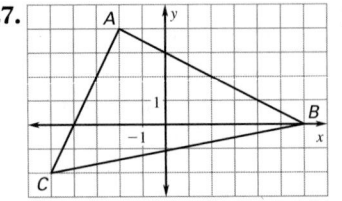

7.2 Skill Practice (pp. 444–445) **1.** hypotenuse **3.** right triangle **5.** not a right triangle **7.** right triangle **9.** right triangle **11.** right triangle **13.** right triangle **15.** yes; acute **17.** yes; obtuse **19.** yes; right **21.** no **23.** yes; obtuse

27.

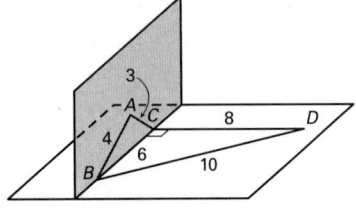

right

29. right **31.** < **33.** $12 < x < 16$

7.2 Problem Solving (pp. 445–447) **35.** Measure diagonally across the painting and it should be about 12.8 inches. **37. a.** 5 **b.** $3^2 + 4^2 = 5^2$ therefore $\triangle ABC$ is a right triangle.
c. *Sample:*

39. a. yes; $12^2 + 16^2 = 20^2$ **b.** no; $9^2 + 12^2 \neq 18^2$
c. No; if the car was not in an accident, the angles should form a right triangle.
41. Given: In $\triangle ABC$, $c^2 > a^2 + b^2$, where c is the length of the longest side. Prove: $\triangle ABC$ is obtuse.

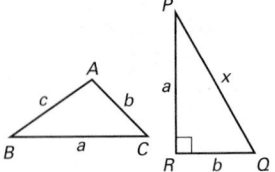

Statements	Reasons
1. In $\triangle ABC$, $c^2 > a^2 + b^2$ where c is the length of the longest side. In $\triangle PQR$, $\angle R$ is a right angle.	1. Given
2. $a^2 + b^2 = x^2$	2. Pythagorean Theorem
3. $c^2 > x^2$	3. Substitution
4. $c > x$	4. A property of square roots
5. $m\angle R = 90°$	5. Definition of a right angle
6. $m\angle C > m\angle R$	6. Converse of the Hinge Theorem
7. $m\angle C > 90°$	7. Substitution Property
8. $\angle C$ is an obtuse angle.	8. Definition of an obtuse angle
9. $\triangle ABC$ is an obtuse triangle.	9. Definition of an obtuse triangle

43. $\triangle ABC \sim \triangle DEC$, $\angle BAC$ is 90°, so $\angle EDC$ must also be 90°.

7.3 Skill Practice (pp. 453–454) **1.** similar **3.** $\triangle FHG \sim \triangle HEG \sim \triangle FEH$ **5.** about 53.7 ft **7.** about 6.7 ft **9.** $\triangle QSR \sim \triangle STR \sim \triangle QTS$; RQ **11.** *Sample answer:* The proportion must compare corresponding parts, $\dfrac{v}{z} = \dfrac{z}{w + v}$ **13.** about 6.7 **15.** about 45.6 **17.** about 6.3 **21.** 3 **23.** $x = 9$, $y = 15$, $z = 20$ **25.** right triangle; about 6.7 **27.** 25, 12

7.3 Problem Solving (pp. 455–456) **29.** about 1.1 ft **31.** 15 ft; no, but the values are slightly off because the measurements are not exact.
33. a. $\overline{FH}$, $\overline{GF}$, $\overline{EF}$; each segment has a vertex as an endpoint and is perpendicular to the opposite side.
b. $\sqrt{35}$ **c.** about 35.5

37.

Statements	Reasons
1. $\triangle ABC$ is a right triangle; $\overline{CD}$ is the altitude to $\overline{AB}$.	1. Given
2. $\triangle ABC \sim \triangle CBD$	2. Theorem 7.5
3. $\dfrac{AB}{CB} = \dfrac{CB}{DB}$	3. Definition of similar figures
4. $\triangle ABC \sim \triangle ACD$	4. Theorem 7.5
5. $\dfrac{AB}{AC} = \dfrac{AC}{AD}$	5. Definition of similar figures

7.4 Skill Practice (pp. 461–462) **1.** an isosceles right triangle **3.** $7\sqrt{2}$ **5.** 3 **7.** 2; 4 in. **9.** $x = 3, y = 6$

11.

a	7	11	$5\sqrt{2}$	6	$\sqrt{5}$
b	7	11	$5\sqrt{2}$	6	$\sqrt{5}$
c	$7\sqrt{2}$	$11\sqrt{2}$	10	$6\sqrt{2}$	$\sqrt{10}$

13. $x = \dfrac{15}{2}\sqrt{3}, y = \dfrac{15}{2}$ **15.** $p = 12, q = 12\sqrt{3}$
17. $t = 4\sqrt{2}, u = 7$ **21.** The hypotenuse of a $45°$-$45°$-$90°$ triangle should be $x\sqrt{2}$; if $x = \sqrt{5}$, then the hypotenuse is $\sqrt{10}$. **23.** $f = \dfrac{20\sqrt{3}}{3}, g = \dfrac{10\sqrt{3}}{3}$
25. $x = 4, y = \dfrac{4\sqrt{3}}{3}$

7.4 Problem Solving (pp. 463–464) **27.** 5.5 ft **29.** *Sample answer:* Method 1. Use the Angle-Angle Similarity postulate, because by definition of an isosceles triangle, the base angles must be the same and in a right isosceles triangle, the angles are 45°. Method 2. Use the Side-Angle-Side Similarity Theorem, because the right angle is always congruent to another right angle and the ratio of sides of an isosceles triangle will always be the same. **31.** $10\sqrt{3}$ in. **33. a.** $45°$-$45°$-$90°$ for all triangles **b.** $\dfrac{3\sqrt{2}}{2}$ in. $\times \dfrac{3\sqrt{2}}{2}$ in. **c.** 1.5 in. $\times$ 1.5 in.

7.5 Skill Practice (pp. 469–470) **1.** the opposite leg, the adjacent leg **3.** $\dfrac{24}{7}$ or 3.4286, $\dfrac{7}{24}$ or 0.2917 **5.** $\dfrac{12}{5}$ or 2.400, $\dfrac{5}{12}$ or 0.4167 **7.** 7.6 **9.** 6; 6; they are the same. **11.** 6.9282; $4\sqrt{3}$; they are the same. **13.** Tangent is the ratio of the opposite and the adjacent side, not adjacent to hypotenuse; $\dfrac{80}{18}$. **15.** You need to know: that the triangle is a right triangle, which angle you will be applying the ratio to, and the lengths of the opposite side and the adjacent side to the angle. **19.** 15.5 **21.** 77.4 **23.** 60.6 **25.** 27.6 **27.** 60; 54.0 **29.** 82; 154.2

7.5 Problem Solving (pp. 471–472) **31.** 555 ft
33. about 33.4 ft **35.** $\tan A = \dfrac{a}{b}$, $\tan B = \dfrac{b}{a}$; the tangent of one acute angle is the reciprocal of the other acute angle; complementary. **37. a.** 29 ft
b. 3 ramps and 2 landings;

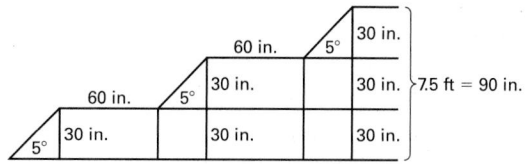

c. 96 ft

7.6 Skill Practice (pp. 477–478) **1.** the opposite leg, the hypotenuse **3.** $\dfrac{4}{5}$ or 0.8, $\dfrac{3}{5}$ or 0.6 **5.** $\dfrac{28}{53}$ or 0.5283, $\dfrac{45}{53}$ or 0.8491 **7.** $\dfrac{3}{5}$ or 0.6, $\dfrac{4}{5}$ or 0.8 **9.** $\dfrac{1}{2}$ or 0.5, $\dfrac{\sqrt{3}}{2}$ or 0.8660 **11.** $a = 14.9, b = 11.1$ **13.** $s = 17.7, r = 19.0$ **15.** $m = 6.7, n = 10.4$ **17.** The triangle must be a right triangle, and you need either an acute angle measure and the length of one side or the lengths of two sides of the triangle. **19.** 3.0 **21.** 20.2
23. 12; $\dfrac{2\sqrt{2}}{2}$ or 0.9428, $\dfrac{1}{3}$ or 0.3333 **25.** 3; $\dfrac{\sqrt{5}}{5}$ or 0.4472, $\dfrac{2\sqrt{5}}{5}$ or 0.8944 **27.** 33; $\dfrac{56}{65}$ or 0.8615, $\dfrac{33}{65}$ or 0.5077
31. about 18 cm

7.6 Problem Solving (pp. 479–480) **33.** about 36.9 ft
35. a.

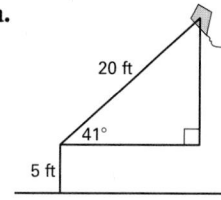

b. About 18.1 ft; the height that the spool is off the ground has to be added.

37. Both; since different angles are used in each ratio, both the sine and cosine relationships can be used to correctly answer the question.

39. a.

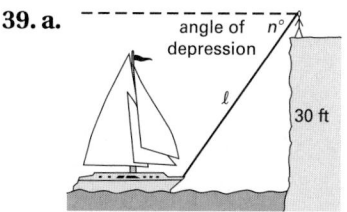

b.

n°	40°	50°	60°	70°	80°
ℓ (ft)	46.7	39.2	34.6	31.9	30.5

c.

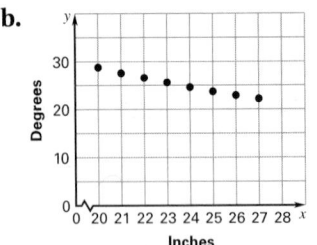

d. *Sample answer:* 60 ft

7.6 Problem Solving Workshop (p. 482) **1.** about 8.8 ft, about 18 ft **3.** $\cos 34° = \frac{x}{17}$, $\tan 34° = \frac{9.5}{x}$, $x^2 + 9.5^2 = 17^2$ **5.** The cosine ratio is the adjacent side over the hypotenuse, not opposite over adjacent; $\cos A = \frac{7}{25}$.

7.7 Skill Practice (pp. 485–487) **1.** angles, sides **3.** 33.7°; $\tan^{-1} 12/7 \approx 59.7°$ **5.** 74.1° **7.** 53.1° **11.** $N = 25°$, $NP \approx 21.4$, $NQ \approx 23.7$ **13.** $A \approx 36.9°$, $B \approx 53.1°$, $AC = 15$ **15.** $G \approx 29°$, $J \approx 61°$, $HJ = 7.7$ **17.** $D \approx 29.7°$, $E \approx 60.3°$, $ED \approx 5.4$ **19.** Since an angle was given, the $\sin^{-1}$ should not have been used; $\sin 36° = \frac{7}{WX}$.

21. 30° **23.** 70.7° **25.** 45° **27.** 11° **31.** 45°; 60°

7.7 Problem Solving (pp. 487–489) **35.** about 59.7°; $\tan^{-1} \frac{12}{7} \approx 59.7°$ **37.** $\tan^{-1} \frac{BC}{AC}$. *Sample answer:* The information needed to determine the measure of A is given. If you use the tangent ratio, this will make the answer more accurate since no rounding has occurred.

39. a.

x (in.)	20	21	22	23
y (°)	28.8°	27.6°	26.6°	25.6°

x (in.)	24	25	26	27
y (°)	24.6°	23.7°	22.9°	22.2°

b.

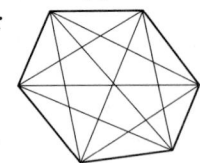

c. *Sample answer:* The longer the rack, the closer to 20° the angle gets.

41. a. 38.4 ft **b.** about 71.2 ft **c.** about 48.7 ft **d.** About 57.4°, about 38.0°; neither; the sides are not the same, so the triangles are not congruent, and the angles are not the same, so the triangles are not similar. **e.** I used tangent because the height and the distance along the ground form a tangent relationship for the angle of elevation.

Extension (p. 491) **1.** $C = 66°$, $a \approx 4.4$, $c \approx 8.3$ **3.** $B \approx 81.8°$, $C \approx 47.2°$, $b \approx 22.9$ **5.** $A \approx 58.1°$, $B \approx 85.6°$, $C \approx 36.2°$ **7.** about 10 blocks

Chapter Review (pp. 494–497) **1.** $a^2 + b^2 = c^2$ **3.** *Sample answer:* The difference is your perspective on the situation. The angle of depression is the measure from your line of sight down, and the angle of elevation is the measure from your line of sight up, but if you construct the parallel lines in any situation, the angles are alternate interior angles and are congruent by Theorem 3.1. **5.** $2\sqrt{34}$ **7.** acute **9.** right **11.** right **13.** 13.5 **15.** $2\sqrt{10}$ **17.** 9 **19.** $6\sqrt{2}$ **21.** $16\sqrt{3}$ **23.** about 5.7 ft **25.** 9.3 **27.** $\frac{3}{5} = 0.6$, $\frac{4}{5} = 0.8$ **29.** $\frac{55}{73} \approx 0.7534$, $\frac{48}{73} \approx 0.6575$ **31.** $L = 53°$, $ML \approx 4.5$, $NL \approx 7.5$ **33.** 50°, 40°, 50°; about 6.4, about 13.1, about 8.4

Algebra Review (p. 499)

1.

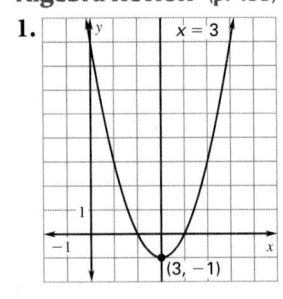

3.

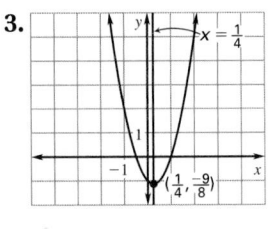

5.

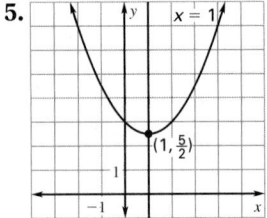

7. $-2, 3$ **9.** no solution **11.** no solution **13.** 0, 8 **15.** 2, 4 **17.** -5

Chapter 8

8.1 Skill Practice (pp. 510–511)

1. *Sample:*

3. 1260° **5.** 2520° **7.** quadrilateral **9.** 13-gon **11.** 117 **13.** $28\frac{1}{3}$ **15.** 66

17. The student thinks that because an octagon has 8 exterior angles while a hexagon has only 6 exterior angles, the sum of the measures of the 8 angles must be greater than the sum of the measures of the 6 angles. The sum of the measures of the exterior angles of any convex n-gon is always 360°. **19.** 108°, 72° **21.** 176°, 4° **23.** The interior angle measures are the same in both pentagons and the ratios of corresponding sides would be the same. **25.** 40

8.1 Problem Solving (pp. 512–513) **29.** 720° **31.** 144°; 36°
33. In a pentagon, draw all the diagonals from one vertex. Observe that the polygon is divided up into three triangles. Since the sum of the measures of the interior angles of each triangle is 180°, the sum of the measures of the interior angles of the pentagon is $(5 - 2) \cdot 180° = 3 \cdot 180° = 540°$.
35. *Sample answer:* In a convex *n*-gon, the sum of the measures of the *n* interior angles is $(n - 2) \cdot 180°$ by the Polygon Interior Angles Theorem. Since each of the *n* interior angles forms a linear pair with its corresponding exterior angle, you know that the sum of the measures of the interior and exterior angles is $180°n$. Subtracting the sum of the interior angle measures from the sum of the measures of the linear pairs $(180°n - (n - 2) \cdot 180°)$, you get 360°.
37. a.

Polygon	Number of sides	Number of triangles	Sum of measures of interior angles
Quadrilateral	4	2	$2 \cdot 180° = 360°$
Pentagon	5	3	$3 \cdot 180° = 540°$
Hexagon	6	4	$4 \cdot 180° = 720°$
Heptagon	7	5	$5 \cdot 180° = 900°$

b. $s(n) = (n - 2) \cdot 180°$; the table shows that the number of triangles is two less than the number of sides.

8.2 Skill Practice (pp. 518–519) **1.** A parallelogram is a quadrilateral with both pairs of opposite sides parallel; opposite sides are congruent, opposite angles are congruent, consecutive angles are supplementary, and the diagonals bisect each other.
3. $x = 9$, $y = 15$ **5.** $a = 55$ **7.** $d = 126$, $z = 28$ **9.** 129°
11. 61° **13.** $a = 3$, $b = 10$ **15.** $x = 4$, $y = 4$ **17.** $\overline{BC}$; opposite sides of a parallelogram are congruent.
19. $\angle DAC$; alternate interior angles are congruent.
21. 47°; consecutive angles of a parallelogram are supplementary and alternate interior angles are congruent. **23.** 120°; $\angle EJF$ and $\angle FJG$ are a linear pair. **25.** 35°; Triangle Sum Theorem **27.** 130°; sum of the measures of $\angle HGE$ and $\angle EGF$. **31.** 26°, 154°
33. 20, 60°; $UV = TS = QR$ using the fact that opposite sides are congruent and the Transitive Property of Equality. $\angle TUS \cong \angle VSU$ by the Alternate Interior Angles Congruence Theorem and $m\angle TSU = 60°$ by the Triangle Sum Theorem.
35. *Sample answer:* In a parallelogram, opposite angles are congruent. $\angle A$ and $\angle C$ are opposite angles but not congruent.

8.2 Problem Solving (pp. 520–521) **39. a.** 3 in. **b.** 70°
c. It decreases; it gets longer; the sum of the measures of the interior angles always is 360°. As $m\angle Q$ increases so does $m\angle S$ therefore $m\angle P$ must decrease to maintain the sum of 360°. As $m\angle Q$ decreases $m\angle P$ increases moving Q farther away from S.
41. *Sample:*

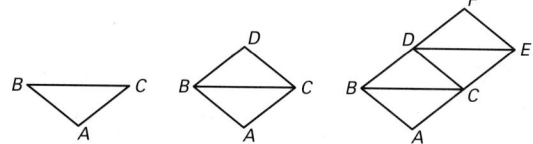

Since $\triangle ABC \cong \triangle DCB$ you know $\angle ACB \cong \angle DBC$ and $\angle ABC \cong \angle DCB$. By the Alternate Interior Angles Converse, $\overline{BD} \parallel \overline{AC}$ and $\overline{AB} \parallel \overline{CD}$ thus making $ABDC$ a parallelogram; if two more triangles are positioned the same as the first, you can line up the pair of congruent sides and form a larger parallelogram since corresponding angles are congruent and the ratios of the lengths of corresponding sides are equal, $\square ABCD \sim \square ABFE$ by definition. **43.** *Sample answer:* Given that $PQRS$ is a parallelogram you know that $\overline{QR} \parallel \overline{PS}$ with $\overline{QP}$ a transversal. By definition and the fact that $\angle Q$ and $\angle P$ are consecutive interior angles, they are supplementary by the Consecutive Interior Angles Theorem. $x° + y° = 180°$ by definition of supplementary angles.

8.3 Skill Practice (pp. 526–527) **1.** The definition of a parallelogram is that it is a quadrilateral with opposite pairs of parallel sides. Since $\overline{AB}$, $\overline{CD}$ and $\overline{AD}$, $\overline{BC}$ are opposite pairs of parallel sides the quadrilateral $ABCD$ is a parallelogram. **3.** The congruent sides must be opposite one another. **5.** Theorem 8.7
7. Since both pairs of opposite sides of $JKLM$ always remain congruent, $JKLM$ is always a parallelogram and $\overline{JK}$ remains parallel to $\overline{ML}$. **9.** 8

11.

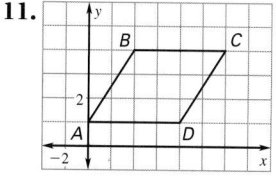

Sample answer:
$AB = CD = 5$ and
$BC = DA = 8$

13.

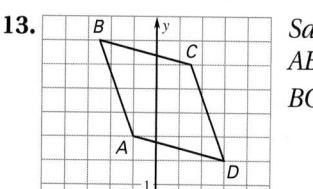

Sample answer:
$AB = CD = 5$ and
$BC = DA = \sqrt{65}$

15. *Sample answer:* Show $\triangle ADB \cong \triangle CBD$ by the SAS Congruence Postulate. This makes $\overline{AD} \cong \overline{CB}$ and $\overline{BA} \cong \overline{CD}$ because corresponding parts of congruent triangles are congruent. **17.** *Sample answer:* Show $\overline{AB} \parallel \overline{DC}$ by the Alternate Interior Angles Converse, and show $\overline{AD} \parallel \overline{BC}$ by the Corresponding Angles Converse. **19.** 114 **21.** 50

23. *PQRS* is a parallelogram if and only if $\angle P \cong \angle R$ and $\angle Q \cong \angle S$. **25.** $(-3, 2)$; since $\overline{DA}$ must be parallel and congruent to $\overline{BC}$, use the slope and length of $\overline{BC}$ to find point *D* by starting at point *A*. **27.** $(-5, -3)$; since $\overline{DA}$ must be parallel and congruent to $\overline{BC}$, use the slope and length of $\overline{BC}$ to find point *D* by starting at point *A*.

29. *Sample answer:* Draw a line passing through points *A* and *B*. At points *A* and *B* construct $\overrightarrow{AP}$ and $\overrightarrow{BQ}$ such that the angle each ray makes with the line is the same. Mark off congruent segments starting at *A* and *B* along $\overrightarrow{AP}$ and $\overrightarrow{BQ}$ respectively. Draw the line segment joining these two endpoints.

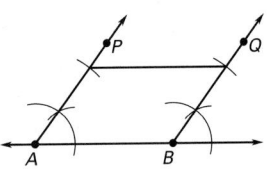

8.3 Problem Solving (pp. 528–529) **31. a.** *EFJK, FGHJ, EGHK*; in each case opposite pairs of sides are congruent. **b.** Since *EGHK* is a parallelogram, opposite sides are parallel. **33.** Alternate Interior Angles Congruence Theorem, Reflexive Property of Segment Congruence, Given, SAS, Corr. Parts of $\cong \triangle$ are $\cong$, Theorem 8.7

35.

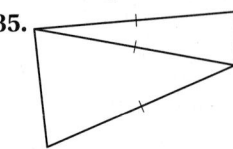

The opposite sides that are not marked in the given diagram are not necessarily the same length.

37. In a quadrilateral, if consecutive angles are supplementary, then the quadrilateral is a parallelogram; in *ABCD* you are given $\angle A$ and $\angle B$, $\angle C$ and $\angle B$ are supplementary which gives you $m\angle A = m\angle C$. Also $\angle B$ and $\angle C$, $\angle C$ and $\angle D$ are supplementary, which gives you $m\angle B = m\angle D$. So *ABCD* is a parallelogram by Theorem 8.8.

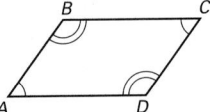

39. It is given that $\overline{KP} \cong \overline{MP}$ and $\overline{JP} \cong \overline{LP}$ by definition of segment bisector. $\angle KPL \cong \angle MPJ$ and $\angle KPJ \cong \angle MPL$ since they are vertical angles. $\triangle KPL \cong \triangle MPJ$ and $\triangle KPJ \cong \triangle MPL$ by the SAS Congruence Postulate. Because corresponding parts of congruent triangles are congruent, $\overline{KJ} \cong \overline{ML}$

and $\overline{JM} \cong \overline{LK}$. By Theorem 8.7, *JKLM* is a parallelogram.
41. *Sample answer:* Consider the diagram.

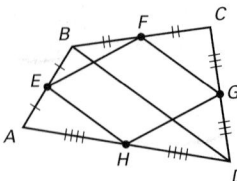

$\overline{FG}$ is the midsegment of $\triangle CBD$ and therefore is parallel to $\overline{BD}$ and half of its length. $\overline{EH}$ is the midsegment of $\triangle ABD$ and therefore is parallel to $\overline{BD}$ and half of its length. This makes $\overline{EH}$ and $\overline{FG}$ both parallel and congruent. By Theorem 8.9, *EFGH* is a parallelogram.

8.3 Problem Solving Workshop (p. 531) **1.** The slope of $\overline{AB}$ and $\overline{CD}$ is $\frac{2}{5}$ and the slope of $\overline{BC}$ and $\overline{DA}$ is -1. *ABCD* is a parallelogram by definition. **3.** No; the slope of the line segment joining Newton to Packard is $\frac{1}{3}$ while the slope of the line segment joining Riverdale to Quarry is $\frac{2}{7}$. **5.** $\overline{PQ}$ and $\overline{QR}$ are not opposite sides. $\overline{PQ}$ and $\overline{RS}$ are opposite sides, so they should be parallel and congruent. The slope of $\overline{PQ} = \frac{4-2}{3-2} = \frac{2}{1}$. The slope of $\overline{RS} = \frac{5-3}{6-5} = \frac{2}{1}$. They are parallel. $PQ = \sqrt{(3-2)^2 + (4-2)^2} = \sqrt{5}$; $RS = \sqrt{(6-5)^2 + (5-3)^2} = \sqrt{5}$; $\overline{PQ}$ and $\overline{RS}$ are parallel and congruent, so *PQRS* is a parallelogram.

8.4 Skill Practice (pp. 537–539) **1.** square

3. Sometimes; *JKLM* would need to be a square. **5.** Always; in a rhombus all four sides are congruent. **7.** Sometimes; diagonals are congruent if the rhombus is a square. **9.** Always; in a rectangle all interior angles measure 90°. **11.** Sometimes; adjacent sides are congruent if the rectangle is a square. **13.** Sometimes; diagonals are perpendicular if the rectangle is a square. **15.** Square; the quadrilateral has four congruent sides and angles. **17.** Rhombus. *Sample answer:* The fourth angle measure is 40°, meaning that both pairs of opposite sides are parallel. So the figure is a parallelogram with two consecutive sides congruent. But this is only possible if the remaining two sides are also congruent, so the quadrilateral is a rhombus. **19.** rectangle, square **21.** rhombus, square **23.** parallelogram, rectangle, rhombus, square **25.** $7x - 4$ is not necessarily equal to $3x + 14$;

$(7x - 4) + (3x + 4) = 90$, $x = 9$. **27.** Rectangle; *JKLM* is a quadrilateral with four right angles; $x = 10$, $y = 15$. **29.** Parallelogram; *EFGH* is a quadrilateral with opposite pairs of sides congruent; $x = 13$, $y = 2$. **33.** 90° **35.** 16 **37.** 12 **39.** 112° **41.** 5 **43.** about 5.6 **45.** 45° **47.** 1 **49.** $\sqrt{2}$

51. 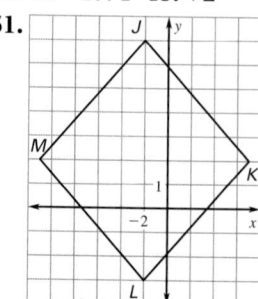 Rhombus; four congruent sides and opposite sides are parallel; $4\sqrt{106}$.

8.4 Problem Solving (pp. 539–540) **55.** Measure the diagonals. If they are the same it is a square. **57.** If a quadrilateral is a rhombus, then it has four congruent sides; if a quadrilateral has four congruent sides, then it is a rhombus; the conditional statement is true since a quadrilateral is a parallelogram and a rhombus is a parallelogram with four congruent sides; the converse is true since a quadrilateral with four congruent sides is also a parallelogram with four congruent sides making it a rhombus. **59.** If a quadrilateral is a square, then it is a rhombus and a rectangle; if a quadrilateral is a rhombus and a rectangle, then it is a square; the conditional statement is true since a square is a parallelogram with four right angles and four congruent sides; the converse is true since a rhombus has four congruent sides and the rectangle has four right angles and thus a square follows. **61.** Since *WXYZ* is a rhombus the diagonals are perpendicular, making $\triangle WVX$, $\triangle WVZ$, $\triangle YVX$, and $\triangle YVZ$ right triangles. Since *WXYZ* is a rhombus $\overline{WX} \cong \overline{XY} \cong \overline{YZ} \cong \overline{ZW}$. Using Theorem 8.11 $\overline{WV} \cong \overline{YV}$ and $\overline{ZV} \cong \overline{XV}$. Now $\triangle WVX \cong \triangle WVZ \cong \triangle YVX \cong \triangle YVZ$. Using corresponding parts of congruent triangles are congruent, you now know $\angle WVZ \cong \angle WVX$ and $\angle YVZ \cong \angle YVX$ which implies $\overline{WY}$ bisects $\angle ZWX$ and $\angle XYZ$. Similarly $\angle VZW \cong \angle VZY$ and $\angle VXW \cong \angle VXY$. This implies $\overline{ZX}$ bisects $\angle WZY$ and $\angle YXW$. **63.** *Sample answer:* Let rectangle *ABCD* have vertices $(0, 0)$, $(a, 0)$, (a, b), and $(0, b)$ respectively. The diagonal $\overline{AC}$ has a length of $\sqrt{a^2 + b^2}$ and diagonal $\overline{BD}$ has a length of $\sqrt{a^2 + b^2}$. $AC = BD = \sqrt{a^2 + b^2}$.

8.5 Skill Practice (pp. 546–547)
1. 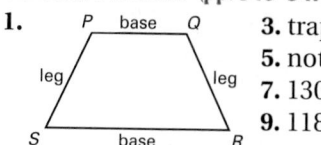 **3.** trapezoid **5.** not a trapezoid **7.** 130°, 50°, 150° **9.** 118°, 62°, 62°

11. Trapezoid; $\overline{EF} \parallel \overline{HG}$ since they are both perpendicular to $\overline{EH}$. **13.** 14 **15.** 66.5 **17.** Only one pair of opposite angles in a kite is congruent. In this case $m\angle B = m\angle D = 120°$; $m\angle A + m\angle B + m\angle C + m\angle D = 360°$, $m\angle A + 120° + 50° + 120° = 360°$, so $m\angle A = 70°$. **19.** 80° **21.** $WX = XY = 3\sqrt{2}$, $YZ = ZW = \sqrt{34}$ **23.** $XY = YZ = 5\sqrt{5}$, $WX = WZ = \sqrt{461}$ **25.** 2 **27.** 2.3
29. 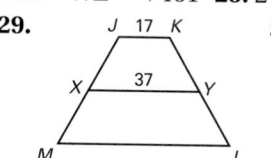 57

33. A kite or a general quadrilateral are the only quadrilaterals where a point on a line containing one of its sides can be found inside the figure.

8.5 Problem Solving (pp. 548–549)
35. *Sample:*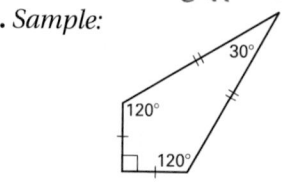

37. Since $\overline{BC} \parallel \overline{AE}$ and $\overline{AB} \parallel \overline{EC}$, *ABCE* is a parallelogram which makes $\overline{AB} \cong \overline{EC}$. Using the Transitive Property of Segment Congruence, $\overline{CE} \cong \overline{CD}$ making $\triangle ECD$ isosceles. Since $\triangle ECD$ is isosceles $\angle D \cong \angle CED$. $\angle A \cong \angle CED$ using the Corresponding Angles Congruence Postulate, therefore $\angle A \cong \angle D$ using the Transitive Property of Angle Congruence. $\angle CED$ and $\angle CEA$ form a linear pair and therefore are supplementary. $\angle A$ and $\angle ABC$, $\angle CEA$ and $\angle ECB$ are supplementary since they are consecutive pairs of angles in a parallelogram. Using the Congruent Supplements Theorem $\angle B \cong \angle C (\angle ECB)$. **39.** Given *JKLM* is an isosceles trapezoid with $\overline{KL} \parallel \overline{JM}$ and $\overline{JK} \cong \overline{LM}$. Since pairs of base angles are congruent in an isosceles trapezoid $\angle JKL \cong \angle MLK$. Using the Reflexive Property of Segment Congruence $\overline{KL} \cong \overline{KL}$. $\triangle JKL \cong \triangle MLK$ using the SAS Congruence Postulate. Using corresponding parts of congruent triangles are congruent, $\overline{JL} \cong \overline{KM}$.

41. Given *ABCD* is a kite with $\overline{AB} \cong \overline{CB}$ and $\overline{AD} \cong \overline{CD}$. By the Reflexive Property of Segment Congruence, $\overline{BD} \cong \overline{BD}$ and $\overline{ED} \cong \overline{ED}$. By the SSS Congruence Postulate, $\triangle BAD \cong \triangle BCD$. Since corresponding parts of congruent triangles are congruent, $\angle CDE \cong \angle ADE$. By the SAS Congruence Postulate, $\triangle CDE \cong \triangle ADE$. Since corresponding parts of congruent triangles are congruent, $\angle CED \cong \angle AED$. Since $\angle CED$ and $\angle AED$ are congruent and form a linear pair, they are right angles. This makes $\overline{AC} \perp \overline{BD}$.

Extension (p. 551)

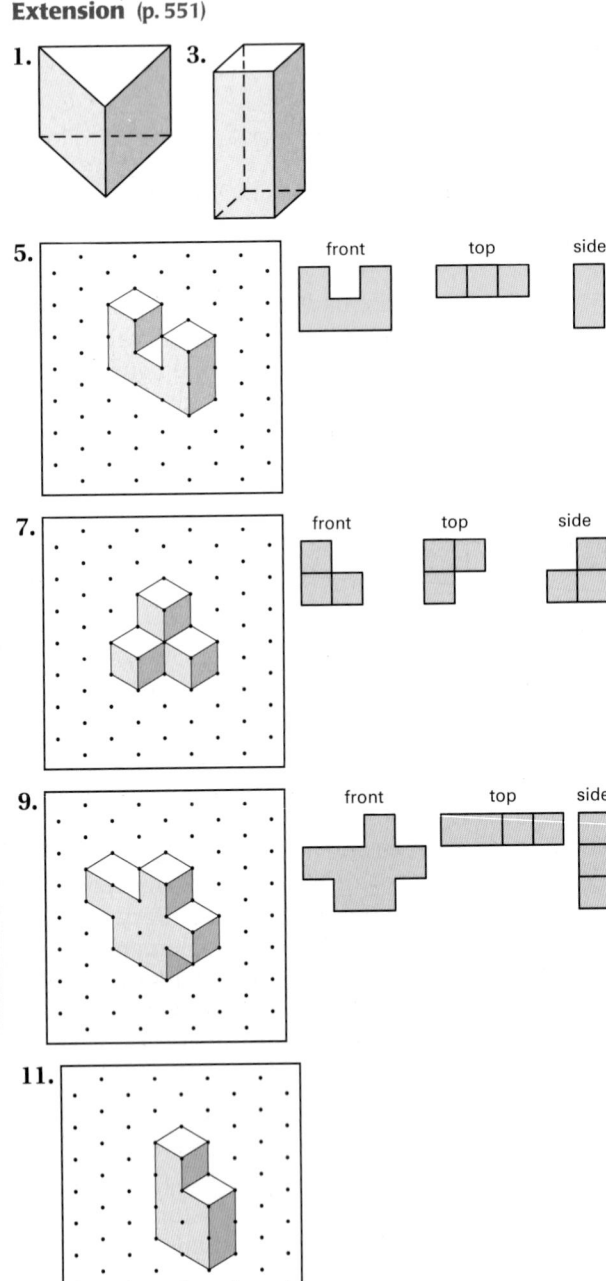

8.6 Skill Practice (pp. 554–555) **1.** isosceles trapezoid

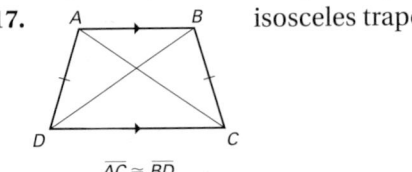

	Property	Parallelogram	Rectangle	Rhombus	Square	Kite	Trapezoid
3.	All sides are ≅.			✗	✗		
5.	Both pair of opp. sides are ∥.	✗	✗	✗	✗		
7.	All ∠ are ≅.		✗		✗		
9.	Diagonals are ⊥.			✗	✗	✗	
11.	Diagonals bisect each other.	✗	✗	✗	✗		

15. Trapezoid; there is one pair of parallel sides.
17. isosceles trapezoid

$\overline{AC} \cong \overline{BD}$

19. No; $m\angle F = 109°$ which is not equal to $m\angle E$.
21. Kite; it has two pair of consecutive congruent sides. **23.** Rectangle; opposite sides are parallel with four right angles. **25. a.** rhombus, square, kite **b.** Parallelogram, rectangle, trapezoid; two consecutive pairs of sides are always congruent and one pair of opposite angles remain congruent. **27.** *Sample answer:* $m\angle B = 60°$ or $m\angle C = 120°$; then $\overline{AB} \parallel \overline{DC}$ and the base angles would be congruent. **29.** No; if $m\angle JKL = m\angle KJM = 90°$, *JKLM* would be a rectangle. **31.** Yes; *JKLM* has one pair of non-congruent parallel sides with congruent diagonals.

8.6 Problem Solving (pp. 556–557) **33.** trapezoid **35.** parallelogram **37.** Consecutive interior angles are supplementary making each interior angle 90°. **39. a.** Using the definition of a regular hexagon, $\overline{UV} \cong \overline{VQ} \cong \overline{RS} \cong \overline{ST}$ and $\angle V \cong \angle S$. So, $\triangle QVU$ and $\triangle RST$ are isosceles. Using the SAS Congruence Postulate, $\triangle QVU \cong \triangle RST$. **b.** By the definition of a regular hexagon, $\overline{QR} \cong \overline{UT}$. Since corresponding parts of congruent triangles are congruent, $\overline{QU} \cong \overline{RT}$. **c.** Since $\angle Q \cong \angle R \cong \angle T \cong \angle U$ and $\angle VUQ \cong \angle VQU \cong \angle STR \cong \angle SRT$, you know that $\angle UQR \cong \angle QRT \cong \angle RTU \cong \angle TUQ$ by the Angle Addition Postulate; 90°. **d.** Rectangle; there are 4 right angles and opposite sides are congruent.
Chapter Review (pp. 560–563) **1.** midsegment
3. Prove the trapezoid has a pair of congruent base angles or the diagonals are congruent. **5.** A
7. 24-gon; 165° **9.** 82

11. 40°; the sum of the measures of the exterior angles is always 360°, and there are nine congruent external angles in a nonagon. **13.** $c = 6$, $d = 10$

15.

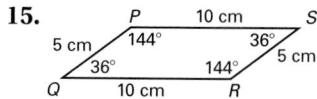

17. 100°, 80°; solve $5x + 4x = 180$ for x. **19.** 3
21. rectangle; 9, 5 **23.** 79°, 101°, 101° **25.** Rhombus; since all four sides are congruent, it is a rhombus. There are no known right angles. **27.** Parallelogram; since opposite pairs of sides are congruent, it is a parallelogram. There are no known right angles.

Algebra Review (p. 565)

1.
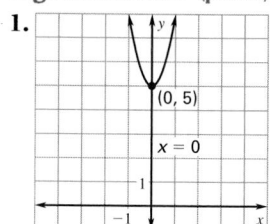

3.
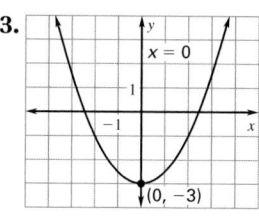

5.
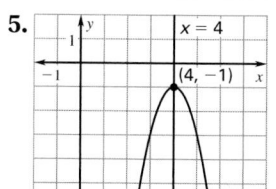

7.
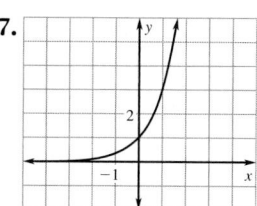

9.
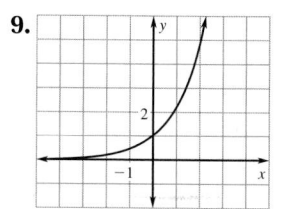

11.
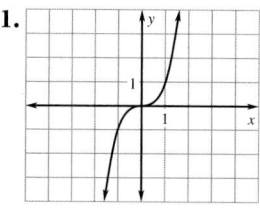

13.
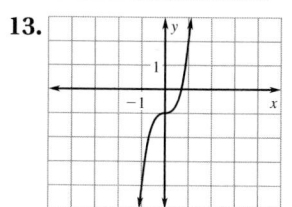

15.
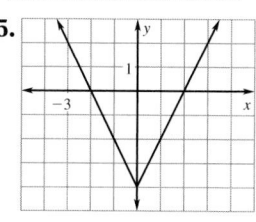

Chapter 9

9.1 Skill Practice (pp. 576–577) **1.** vector, direction
3. $A'(-6, 10)$ **5.** $C(5, -14)$

7.
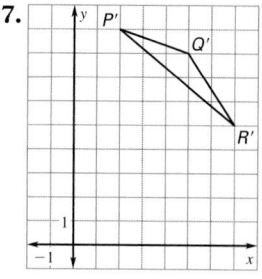

9.
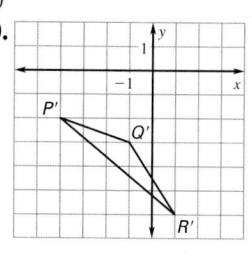

11. $(x, y) \rightarrow (x - 5, y + 2)$; $AB = A'B' = \sqrt{13}$, $AC = A'C' = 4$, and $BC = B'C' = \sqrt{5}$. $\triangle ABC \cong \triangle A'B'C'$ using the SSS Congruence Postulate.

13. The image should be 1 unit to the left instead of right and 2 units down instead of up.

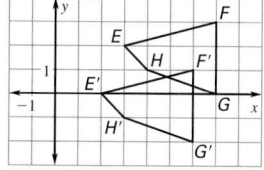

15. $\overrightarrow{CD}$, $\langle 7, -3 \rangle$ **17.** $\overrightarrow{JP}$, $\langle 0, 4 \rangle$ **19.** $\langle -1, 2 \rangle$ **21.** $\langle 0, -11 \rangle$
23. The vertical component is the distance from the ground up to the plane entrance.
25. $D'(7, 4)$, $E'(11, 2)$, $F'(9, -1)$

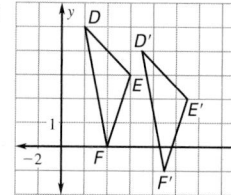

27. $D'(0, 1)$, $E'(4, -1)$, $F'(2, -4)$

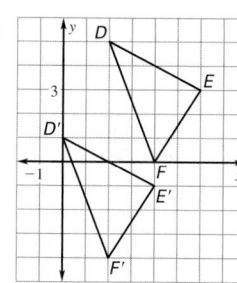

29. $a = 35$, $b = 14$, $c = 5$ **31. a.** $Q'(-1, -5)$, $R'(-1, 2)$, $S'(2, 2)$, $T'(2, -5)$; 21, 21 **b.** The areas are the same; the area of an image and its preimage under a translation are the same.

9.1 Problem Solving (pp. 578–579) **33.** $(x, y) \rightarrow (x + 6, y)$, $(x, y) \rightarrow (x, y - 4)$, $(x, y) \rightarrow (x + 3, y - 4)$, $(x, y) \rightarrow (x + 6, y - 4)$ **35.** $\langle 1, 2 \rangle$ **37.** $\langle -4, -2 \rangle$ **39.** $\langle 3, 1 \rangle$
41. $\langle 22, 5 \rangle$; about 22.6 km **43. a.** 5 squares to the right followed by 4 squares down. **b.** $2\sqrt{41}$ mm **c.** about 0.523 mm/sec **45. a.** The graph is 4 units lower. **b.** The graph is 4 units to the right.

9.2 Skill Practice (pp. 584–585) **1.** elements

$$\begin{array}{c} \ \ B\ \ \ C\ \ \ D \\ \end{array}$$
3. $\begin{bmatrix} -1 & 2 & 6 \\ -2 & 2 & 1 \end{bmatrix}$ **5.** $\begin{array}{cccc} B & C & D & E \\ \begin{bmatrix} 2 & 6 & 5 & -1 \\ 2 & 1 & -1 & -2 \end{bmatrix} \end{array}$ **7.** $\begin{bmatrix} 12 & 7 \end{bmatrix}$

9. $\begin{bmatrix} 16 & 9 \\ 0 & 0 \\ -5 & -3 \end{bmatrix}$ **11.** $\begin{bmatrix} -13 & -4 \\ -12 & 16 \end{bmatrix}$

13. $\begin{array}{ccc} A' & B' & C' \\ \begin{bmatrix} -2 & 2 & 1 \\ 8 & 5 & 1 \end{bmatrix} \end{array}$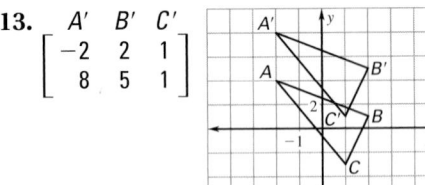

15. $\begin{array}{cccc} L' & M' & N' & P' \\ \begin{bmatrix} 6 & 4 & 6 & 7 \\ 1 & 5 & 5 & 1 \end{bmatrix} \end{array}$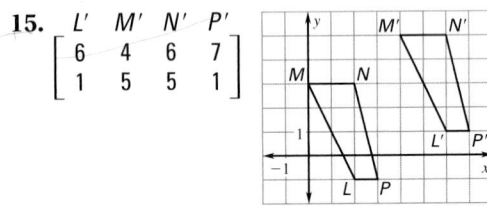

19. $\begin{bmatrix} -6.9 \end{bmatrix}$ **21.** $\begin{bmatrix} -4 & 15.2 \\ -32.3 & -43.4 \end{bmatrix}$ **23.** $\begin{bmatrix} 38 \\ 36 \end{bmatrix}$

25. *Sample answer:* $\begin{bmatrix} -2 & 1 \\ 0 & 4 \end{bmatrix}, \begin{bmatrix} 1 & 1 \\ 2 & 1 \end{bmatrix}; \begin{bmatrix} 0 & -1 \\ 8 & 4 \end{bmatrix}$

27. $\begin{array}{cccc} A & B & C & D \\ \begin{bmatrix} -7 & 0 & 0 & -7 \\ 3 & 3 & -1 & -1 \end{bmatrix} \end{array}$ **29.** $a = 8, b = -20, c = 20,$
$m = 21, n = -1, v = -7, w = 12$; the sum of the
corresponding elements on the left equals the
corresponding elements on the right; $(21, -1)$,
$(20, -9)$, $(-8, 13)$.

9.2 Problem Solving (pp. 586–587) **31.** Lab 1: $840,
Lab 2: $970 **33. a.** $AB = BA$ **b.** $\begin{bmatrix} -3 & 15 \\ -14 & 30 \end{bmatrix}, \begin{bmatrix} 25 & -7 \\ 10 & 2 \end{bmatrix},$
$AB \neq BA$ **c.** Matrix multiplication is not commutative.
35. $\begin{bmatrix} 2 & 36 \\ 16 & 68 \end{bmatrix}, \begin{bmatrix} 2 & 36 \\ 16 & 68 \end{bmatrix}$; the Distributive Property
holds for matrices.

9.3 Skill Practice (pp. 593–594) **1.** a line which acts like
a mirror to reflect an image across the line

3. 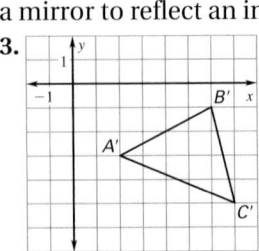 **5.**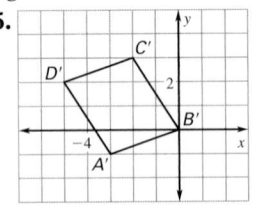

13.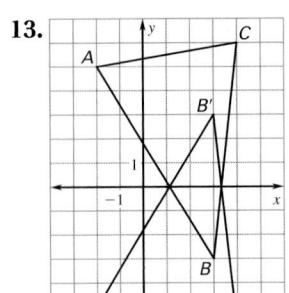

15. $\begin{array}{ccc} A & B & C \\ \begin{bmatrix} 1 & 4 & 3 \\ 2 & 2 & -2 \end{bmatrix} \end{array}; \begin{array}{ccc} A' & B' & C' \\ \begin{bmatrix} -1 & -4 & -3 \\ 2 & 2 & -2 \end{bmatrix} \end{array}$

17. $\begin{array}{ccc} A & B & C \\ \begin{bmatrix} -4 & 3 & 2 \\ -2 & 1 & -3 \end{bmatrix} \end{array}; \begin{array}{ccc} A' & B' & C' \\ \begin{bmatrix} 4 & -3 & -2 \\ -2 & 1 & -3 \end{bmatrix} \end{array}$

19. $(5, 0)$ **21.** $(-4, 0)$

23. 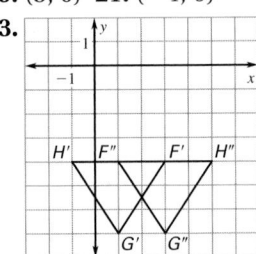 **25.** The order is reversed.
27. $y = -3x - 4$

29.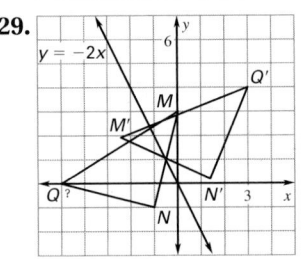

9.3 Problem Solving (pp. 595–596) **31.** Case 4 **33.** Case 1

35. a.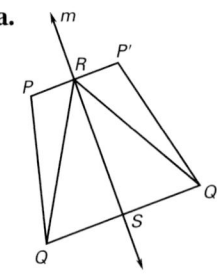

Given: a reflection in m
maps P to P' and Q to Q'.
Using the definition of a
line of reflection, $\overline{QS} \cong \overline{Q'S}$
and $\angle QSR \cong \angle Q'SR$. By the
Reflexive Property
of Segment Congruence,
$\overline{RS} \cong \overline{RS}$. By the SAS
Congruence Postulate,
$\triangle RSQ \cong \triangle RSQ'$.

b. Because corresponding parts of congruent triangles are congruent, $\overline{RQ} \cong \overline{RQ'}$. By the definition of a line of reflection $\overline{PR} \cong \overline{P'R}$. Since $\overline{PP'}$ and $\overline{QQ'}$ are both perpendicular to m, they are parallel. By the Alternate Interior Angles Theorem, $\angle SQ'R \cong \angle P'RQ'$ and $\angle SQR \cong \angle PRQ$. Because corresponding parts of congruent triangles are congruent, $\angle SQ'R \cong \angle SQR$. By the Transitive Property of Angle Congruence, $\angle P'RQ' \cong \angle PRQ$. $\triangle PRQ \cong \triangle P'RQ'$ by the SAS Congruence Postulate. Because corresponding parts of congruent triangles are congruent, $\overline{PQ} \cong \overline{P'Q'}$ which implies $PQ = P'Q'$. **37.** Given: a reflection in m maps P to P' and Q to Q'. Also, P lies on m, and $\overline{PQ}$ is not perpendicular to m. Draw $\overline{Q'Q}$ intersecting m at point R. Using the definition of a line of reflection, m is the perpendicular bisector of $\overline{Q'Q}$, which implies $\overline{Q'R} \cong \overline{QR}$, $\angle Q'RP' \cong \angle QRP$, and P and P' are the same point. By the Reflexive Property of Segment Congruence, $\overline{RP} \cong \overline{RP}$. By the SAS Congruence Postulate, $\triangle Q'RP' \cong \triangle QRP$. Because corresponding parts of congruent triangles are congruent, $\overline{Q'P'} \cong \overline{QP}$ which implies $Q'P' = QP$. **39. a.** $(3, 5)$ **b.** $(0, 6); (-1, 4)$ **c.** In each case point C bisects each line segment.

9.4 Skill Practice (pp. 602–603) **1.** a point which a figure is turned about during a rotation transformation **3.** Reflection; the horses are reflected across the edge of the stream which acts like a line of symmetry. **5.** Translation; the train moves horizontally from right to left. **7.** A

9.
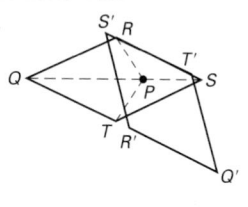

11.
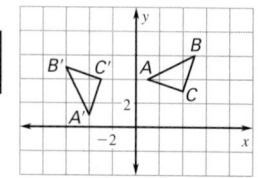

13. $J'(-1, -4)$, $K'(-5, -5)$, $L'(-7, -2)$, $M'(-2, -2)$

15.
$$\begin{array}{ccc} A' & B' & C' \\ \left[\begin{array}{ccc} -4 & -6 & -3 \\ 1 & 5 & 4 \end{array}\right] \end{array}$$
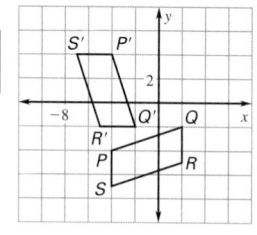

17.
$$\begin{array}{cccc} P' & Q' & R' & S' \\ \left[\begin{array}{cccc} -4 & -2 & -5 & -7 \\ 4 & -2 & -2 & 4 \end{array}\right] \end{array}$$

19. The rotation matrix should be first;
$$\left[\begin{array}{cc} 0 & 1 \\ -1 & 0 \end{array}\right]\left[\begin{array}{cc} -1 & 2 \\ 1 & 3 \end{array}\right].$$ **25.** $(-3, 2, 0)$

9.4 Problem Solving (pp. 604–605) **29.** 270°; the line segment joining A' to the center of rotation is perpendicular to the line segment joining A to the center of rotation. **31.** 120°; the line segment joining A' to the center of rotation is rotated $\frac{1}{3}$ of a circle from the line segment joining A to the center of rotation. **33.** a rotation about a point, Angle Addition Postulate, Transitive, Subtraction, $\triangle RPQ \cong \triangle R'PQ'$, Corr. Parts of $\cong \triangle$ are $\cong$, definition of segment congruence **35.** Given: a rotation about P maps Q to Q' and R to R'. P and R are the same point. Using the definition of rotation about a point P, $PQ = PQ'$ and P, R, and R' are the same point. Substituting R for P on the left and R' for P on the right side, you get $RQ = R'Q'$.

37. a.
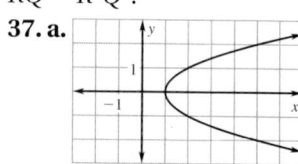
b. 270°
c. No; the image does not pass the vertical line test.

39.
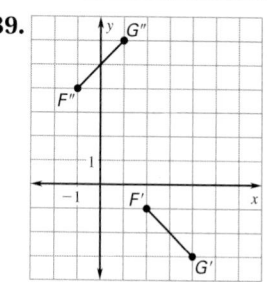

9.4 Problem Solving Workshop (p. 606)

1.
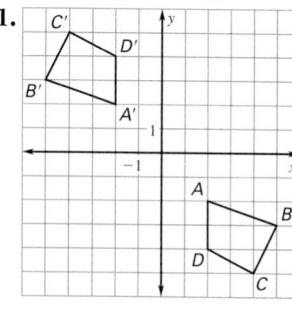
3. Since they are rotating in opposite directions they will each place you at 90° below your reference line.
5. The x-coordinate is now -4; the y-coordinate is now 3.

9.5 Skill Practice (pp. 611–613) **1.** parallel

3.
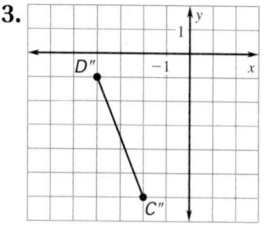

5.

7.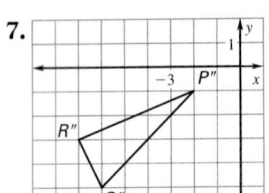

9.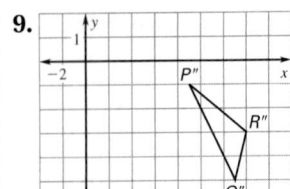

11. 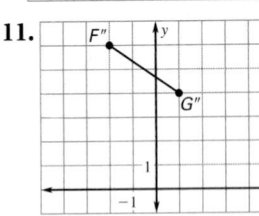 yes
13. $(x, y) \rightarrow (x + 5, y + 1)$
followed by a rotation
of 180° about the origin.
15. $\triangle A''B''C''$
17. *Sample answer:* $\overline{AA'}$, $\overline{AA''}$

19. yes; definition of reflection of a point over a line
21. 30°
23.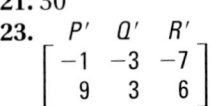

$$\begin{array}{ccc} P' & Q' & R' \\ \begin{bmatrix} -1 & -3 & -7 \\ 9 & 3 & 6 \end{bmatrix} \end{array}$$

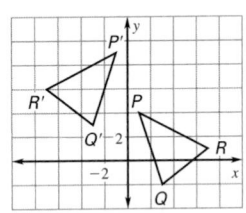

9.5 Problem Solving (pp. 613–615) **27.** *Sample answer:*
$(x, y) \rightarrow (x + 9, y)$, reflected over a horizontal line
that separates the left and right prints **31.** reflection
33. translation **35.** Use the Rotation Theorem
followed by the Reflection Theorem. **37.** Given a
reflection in ℓ maps $\overline{JK}$ to $\overline{J'K'}$, a reflection in m
maps $\overline{J'K'}$ to $\overline{J''K''}$, $\ell \parallel m$ and the distance between
ℓ and m is d. Using the definition of reflection ℓ
is the perpendicular bisector of $\overline{KK'}$ and m is
perpendicular bisector of $\overline{K'K''}$. Using the Segment
Addition Postulate, $KK' + K'K'' = KK''$. It follows
that $\overline{KK'}$ is perpendicular to ℓ and m. Using the
definition of reflection the distance from K to ℓ
is the same as the distance from ℓ to K' and the
distance from K' to m is the same as the distance
from m to K''. Since the distance from ℓ to K' plus
the distance from K' to m is d, it follows that
$K'K'' = 2d$. **39. a.** translation and a rotation **b.** One
transformation is not followed by the second. They
are done simultaneously.

Extension (pp. 617–618) **1.** yes; regular **3.** yes; not
regular **5. a.** 360°; the sum of the angle measures at
any vertex is 360°. **b.** The sum of the measures of
the interior angles is 360°.

7. *Sample:*

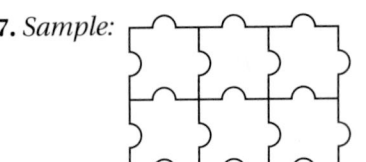

9. a. **b.** **c.**

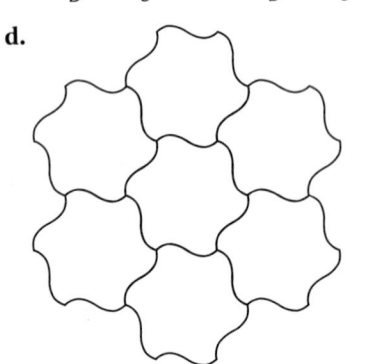

d.

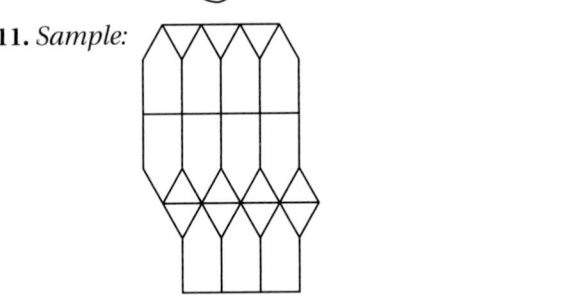

11. *Sample:*

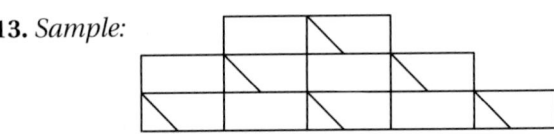

13. *Sample:*

15. translation **17.** rotations

9.6 Skill Practice (pp. 621–623) **1.** If a figure has
rotational symmetry it is the point about which the
figure is rotated. **3.** 1 **5.** 1 **7.** yes; 72° or 144° about
the center **9.** no **11.** Line symmetry, rotational
symmetry; there are four lines of symmetry, two
passing through the outer opposite pairs of leaves
and two passing through the inner opposite pairs
of leaves; 90° or 180° about the center. **15.** There
is no rotational symmetry; the figure has 1 line of
symmetry but no rotational symmetry.

17. *Sample:*

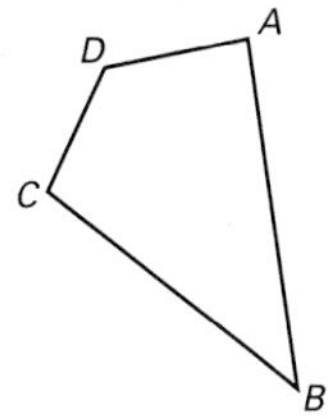

19. *Sample:*

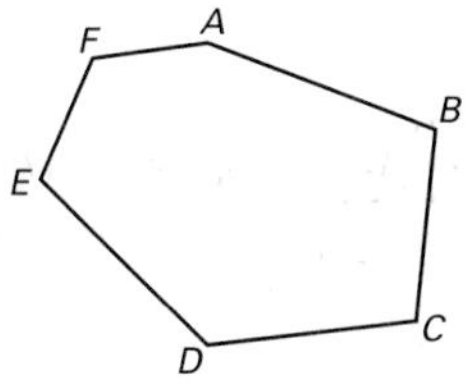

21. *Sample:*

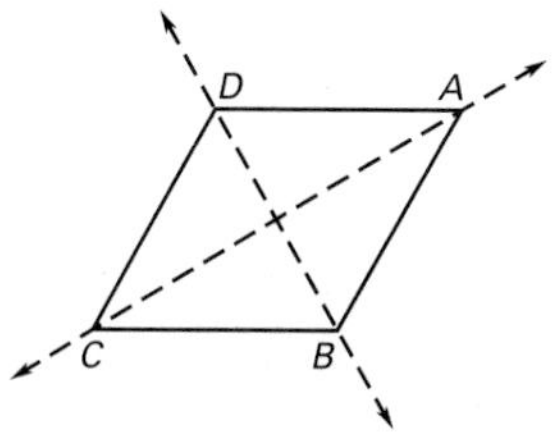

23. No; what's on the left and right of the first line would have to be the same as what's on the left and right of the second line which is not possible. **25.** 9

9.6 Problem Solving (pp. 623–624) **27.** no line symmetry, rotational symmetry of 180° about the center of the letter *O*. **29.** It has a line of symmetry passing horizontally through the center of each *O*, no rotational symmetry. **31.** 22.5° **33.** 15° **35. a.** line symmetry and rotational symmetry **b.** planes, *z*-axis

9.7 Skill Practice (pp. 629–630) **1.** a real number
3. $\frac{7}{3}$; enlargement; 8 **5.** $\frac{3}{2}$; enlargement; 10

7.

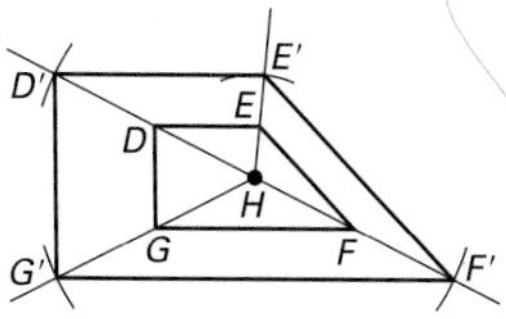

9.

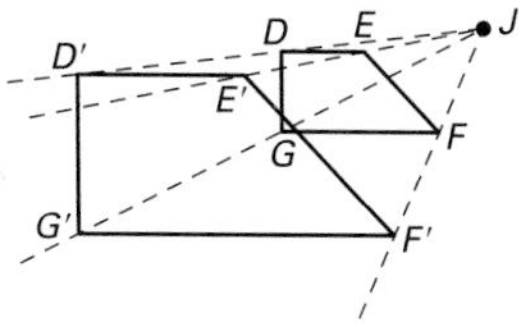

15. $\begin{bmatrix} 12 & 28 & 16 \\ 0 & 36 & -4 \end{bmatrix}$ **17.** $\begin{bmatrix} 0 & 27 & 18 \\ -9 & 63 & 0 \end{bmatrix}$

19. $\begin{array}{ccc} G' & H' & J' \end{array}$ $\begin{bmatrix} -1 & 0 & 3 \\ -2 & 1 & -1 \end{bmatrix}$

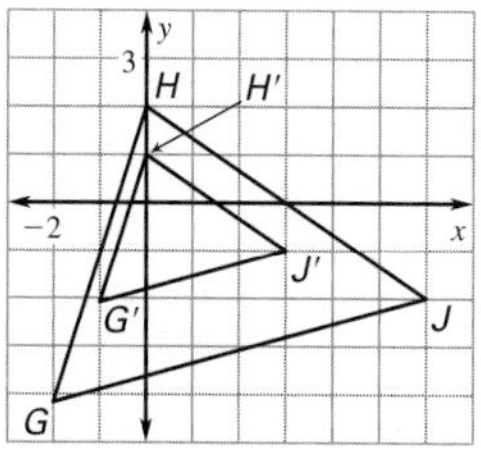

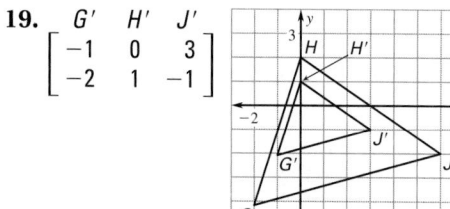

21.

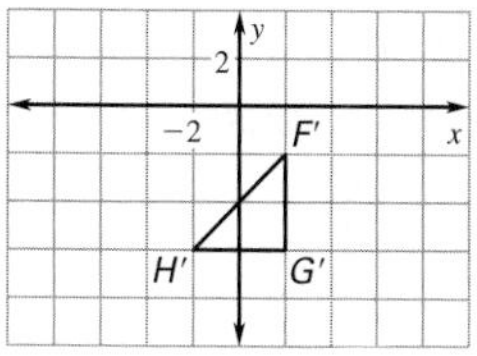

23.

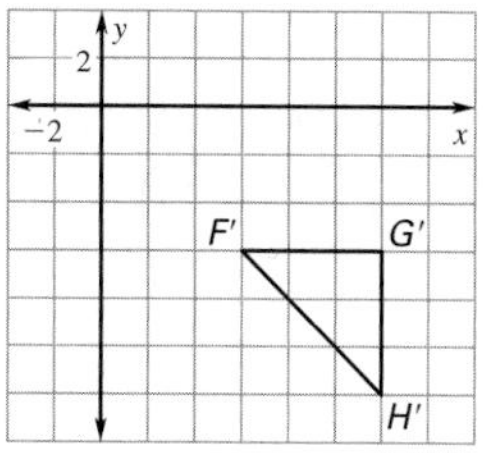

27. *Sample:*

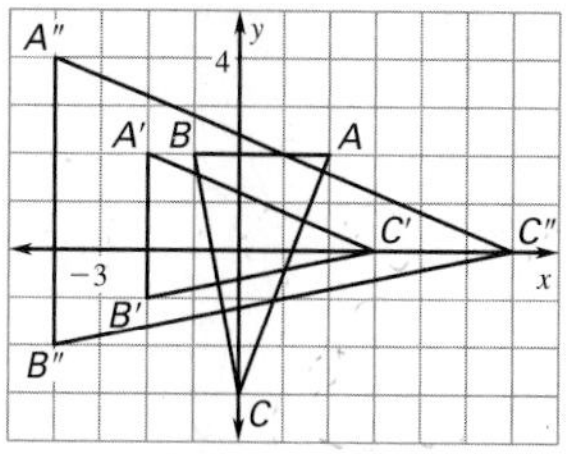

No; the result is the same.

31. No; the ratio of the lengths of corresponding sides is not the same.

9.7 Problem Solving (pp. 631–632) **33.** 300 mm **35.** 940 mm **37. a.** $\frac{6}{1}$ **b.** 8.75 in.

39. a. $\begin{array}{c} \begin{array}{ccc} F & G & H \end{array} \\ \begin{bmatrix} 0 & 4 & -2 \\ 2 & 2 & -2 \end{bmatrix} \end{array}$; $\begin{array}{c} \begin{array}{ccc} F' & G' & H' \end{array} \\ \begin{bmatrix} 0 & -8 & 4 \\ -4 & -4 & 4 \end{bmatrix} \end{array}$

b.

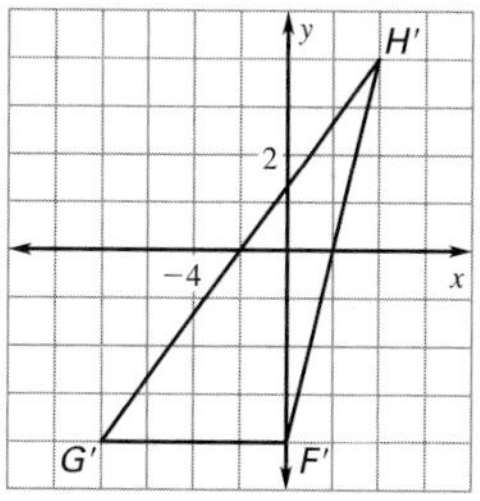

c. $\begin{array}{c} \begin{array}{ccc} F'' & G'' & H'' \end{array} \\ \begin{bmatrix} 0 & -2 & 1 \\ -1 & -1 & 1 \end{bmatrix} \end{array}$

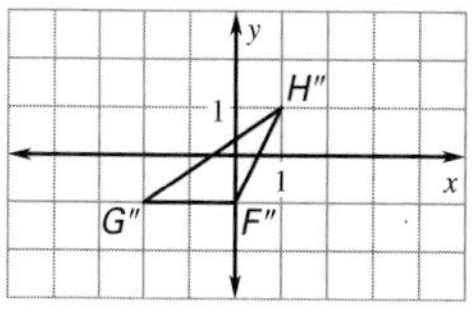

d. A reflection in both the *x*-axis and *y*-axis occurs as well as dilation. **41.** It's the center point of the dilation.

Chapter Review (pp. 636–639) **1.** isometry
3. Count the number of rows, *n*, and the number of columns, *m*. The dimensions are $n \times m$.
Sample answer: $\begin{bmatrix} 2 & 0 & 3 \\ -1 & 4 & 7 \end{bmatrix}$ is 2×3. **5.** A

7.

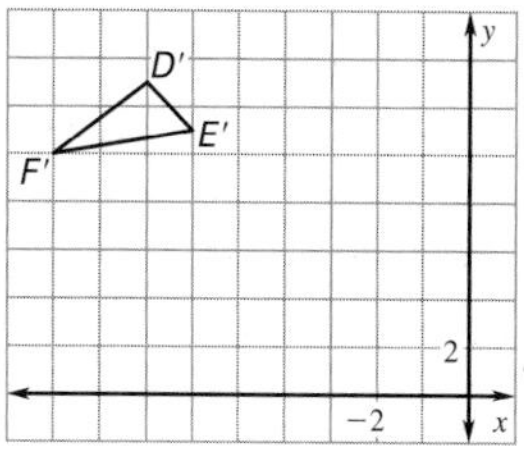

SELECTED ANSWERS

9.
$$\begin{array}{c} D' E' F' G' \\ \begin{bmatrix} -2 & 3 & 4 & -1 \\ 1 & 4 & 2 & -3 \end{bmatrix} \end{array}$$
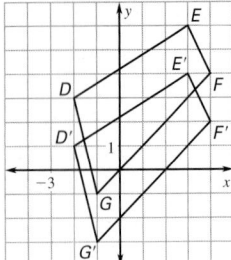

11.
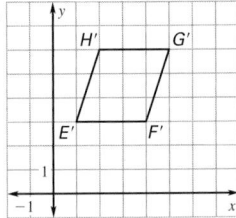

13.
$$\begin{array}{c} Q' R' S' \\ \begin{bmatrix} -3 & -4 & -1 \\ 0 & -5 & 2 \end{bmatrix} \end{array}$$
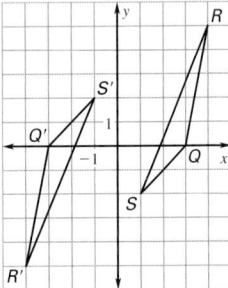

15.
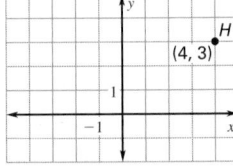

17. line symmetry, no rotational symmetry; one
19. line symmetry, rotational symmetry; two, 180° about the center

21.
$$\begin{array}{c} L' M' N' \\ \begin{bmatrix} -3 & 3 & 6 \\ -6 & 9 & 12 \end{bmatrix} \end{array}$$
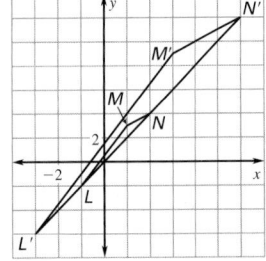

Algebra Review (p. 641) **1.** $x^2 + x - 6$ **3.** $x^2 - 16$
5. $49x^2 + 84x + 36$ **7.** $4x^2 - 1$ **9.** $2x^2 + 3xy + y^2$
11. 3, 4 **13.** $-2, -\frac{1}{4}$ **15.** $\frac{-1 \pm \sqrt{29}}{2}$ **17.** $\frac{-11 \pm \sqrt{105}}{2}$

Cumulative Review (pp. 646–647) **1.** neither **3.** $x = 4$
5. $y = \frac{1}{2}x - 2$ **7.** $\overline{QP} \cong \overline{SR}$ **9.** altitude **11.** median
13. triangle; right **15.** not a triangle **17.** triangle; right
19. Rectangle; the diagonals are congruent and they bisect each other; 5, 3.

21.
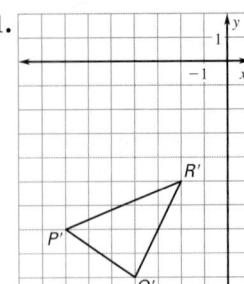

23. $\angle 4, \angle 5, \angle 8$
25. 132°
27. about 135 mi
29. about $7.69
31. translation and rotation

Chapter 10

10.1 Skill Practice (pp. 655–657) **1.** diameter **3.** G **5.** C
7. F **9.** B **11.** $\overline{AB}$ is not a secant it is a chord; the length of chord $\overline{AB}$ is 6. **13.** 6, 12

15. 4
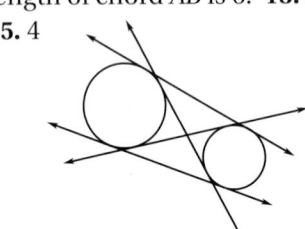

17. 1
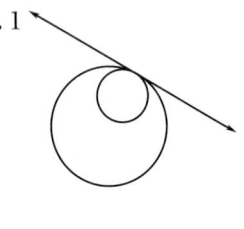

19. not tangent; $9^2 + 15^2 \neq 18^2$ **21.** 10 **23.** 10.5
25. ± 2 **27.** external **31.** They will be parallel if they are tangent to opposite endpoints of the same diameter; lines perpendicular to the same line are parallel. **33.** No; no; no matter what the distance the external point is from the circle there will always be two tangents.

10.1 Problem Solving (pp. 657–658) **35.** radial spokes
37. 14,426 mi **39. a.** Since R is exterior to $\odot Q$, $QR > QP$.
b. Since $\overline{QR}$ is perpendicular to line m it must be the shortest distance from Q to line m, thus $QR < QP$.
c. It was assumed $\overline{QP}$ was not perpendicular to line m but $\overline{QR}$ was perpendicular to line m. Since R is outside of $\odot Q$ you know that $QR > QP$, but Exercise 39b tells you that $QR < QP$ which is a contradiction. Therefore, line m is perpendicular to $\overline{QP}$.
41. Given $\overline{SR}$ and $\overline{ST}$ are tangent to $\odot P$. Construct $\overline{PR}$, $\overline{PT}$, and $\overline{PS}$. Since $\overline{PR}$ and $\overline{PT}$ are radii of $\odot P$, $\overline{PR} \cong \overline{PT}$. With $\overline{PS} \cong \overline{PS}$, using the HL Congruence Theorem $\triangle RSP \cong \triangle TSP$. Using corresponding parts of congruent triangles are congruent, $\overline{SR} \cong \overline{ST}$.

10.2 Skill Practice (pp. 661–662) **1.** congruent
3. minor arc; 70° **5.** minor arc; 135° **7.** minor arc; 115°
9. major arc; 245° **13.** Not congruent; they are arcs of circles that are not congruent. **15.** You can tell that the circles are congruent since they have the same radius $\overline{CD}$. **19.** *Sample answer:* 175°, 185°

10.2 Problem Solving (p. 663) **23.** 18°

10.3 Skill Practice (pp. 667–668) **1.** *Sample answer:* Point *Y* bisects $\widehat{XZ}$ if $\widehat{XY} \cong \widehat{YZ}$. **3.** 75° **5.** 8 **7.** 5; use Theorem 10.5 and solve $5x - 6 = 2x + 9$. **9.** 5; use Theorem 10.6 and solve $18 = 5x - 7$. **11.** $\frac{7}{3}$; use Theorem 10.6 and solve $4x + 1 = x + 8$.

13. $\overline{JH}$ bisects $\overline{FG}$ and $\widehat{FG}$; Theorem 10.5. **17.** You don't know that $\overline{AC} \perp \overline{DB}$ therefore you can't show $\widehat{BC} \cong \widehat{CD}$.

19. Diameter; the two triangles are congruent by the SAS Congruence Postulate which makes $\overline{AB}$ the perpendicular bisector of $\overline{CD}$. Use Theorem 10.4. **21.** Using the facts that $\triangle APB$ is equilateral which makes it equiangular and that $m\widehat{AC} = 30°$, you can conclude that $m\angle APD = m\angle BPD = 30°$. You now know that $m\widehat{BC} = 30°$ which makes $\overline{AC} \cong \overline{BC}$. $\triangle APD \cong \triangle BPD$ by the SAS Congruence Postulate since $\overline{BP} \cong \overline{AP}$ and $\overline{PD} \cong \overline{PD}$. Because corresponding parts of congruent triangles are congruent, $\overline{AD} \cong \overline{BD}$. Along with $\overline{DC} \cong \overline{DC}$ you have $\triangle ADC \cong \triangle BDC$ by the SSS Congruence Postulate. **23.** From the diagram, $m\widehat{AC} = m\widehat{CB}$ and $m\widehat{AB} = x°$, so you know that $m\widehat{AC} + m\widehat{CB} + x° = 360°$. Replacing $m\widehat{CB}$ by $m\widehat{AC}$ and solving for $m\widehat{AC}$ you get $m\widehat{AC} = \dfrac{360° - x°}{2}$. This along with the fact that all arcs have integral measure implies that *x* is even.

10.3 Problem Solving (pp. 669–670) **25.** $\overline{AB}$ should be congruent to $\overline{BC}$. **27.** Given $\overline{AB} \cong \overline{CD}$. Since $\overline{PA}$, $\overline{PB}$, $\overline{PC}$, and $\overline{PD}$ are radii of $\odot P$, they are congruent. By the SSS Congruence Postulate, $\triangle PCD \cong \triangle PAB$. Because corresponding parts of congruent triangles are congruent, $\angle CPD \cong \angle APB$. With $m\angle CPD = m\angle APB$ and the fact they are both central angles, you now have $m\widehat{CD} = m\widehat{AB}$ which leads to $\widehat{CD} \cong \widehat{AB}$.

29. a. longer chord
b. The length of a chord in a circle increases as the distance from the center of the circle to the chord decreases.

c. Given radius *r* and real numbers *a* and *b* such that $r > a > b > 0$. Let *a* be the distance from one chord to the center of the circle and *b* be the distance from a second chord to the center of the circle. By the Pythagorean Theorem, the length of the chord *a* units away from the center is $2\sqrt{r^2 - a^2}$ and the length of the chord *b* units away from the center is $2\sqrt{r^2 - b^2}$. Using properties of

real numbers, $\sqrt{r^2 - b^2} > \sqrt{r^2 - a^2}$. **31.** Given: $\overline{QS}$ is perpendicular bisector of $\overline{RT}$ in $\odot L$. Suppose center *L* is not on $\overline{QS}$. Since $\overline{LT}$ and $\overline{LR}$ are radii of the circle they are congruent. With $\overline{PL} \cong \overline{PL}$, $\triangle RLP \cong \triangle TLP$ by the SSS Congruence Postulate. $\angle RPL$ and $\angle TPL$ are congruent and they form a linear pair. This makes them right angles and leads to $\overline{PL}$ being perpendicular to $\overline{RT}$. By the Perpendicular Postulate, *L* must be on $\overline{QS}$ and thus $\overline{QS}$ must be a diameter.

10.4 Skill Practice (pp. 676–677) **1.** inscribed **3.** 42° **5.** 10° **7.** 120° **9.** The measure of the arcs add up to 370°; change the measure of $\angle Q$ to 40° or change the measure of $\widehat{QS}$ to 90°. **11.** $\angle JMK$, $\angle JLK$ and $\angle LKM$, $\angle LJM$ **13.** $x = 100$, $y = 85$ **15.** $a = 20$, $b = 22$ **17. a.** 36°; 180° **b.** about 25.7°; 180° **c.** 20°; 180° **19.** 90° **21.** Yes; opposite angles are 90° and thus are supplementary. **23.** No; opposite angles are not supplementary. **25.** Yes; opposite angles are supplementary.

10.4 Problem Solving (pp. 677–679)
27.

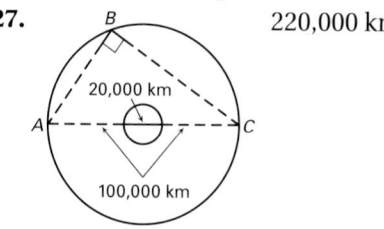

220,000 km

29. Double the length of the radius. **31.** Given $\angle B$ inscribed in $\odot Q$. Let $m\angle B = x°$. Point *Q* lies on $\overline{BC}$. Since all radii of a circle are congruent, $\overline{AQ} \cong \overline{BQ}$. Using the Base Angles Theorem, $\angle B \cong \angle A$ which implies $m\angle A = x°$. Using the Exterior Angles Theorem, $m\angle AQC = 2x°$ which implies $m\widehat{AC} = 2x°$. Solving for *x*, you get $\frac{1}{2} m\widehat{AC} = x°$. Substituting you get $\frac{1}{2} m\widehat{AC} = m\angle B$. **33.** Given: $\angle ABC$ is inscribed in $\odot Q$. Point *Q* is in the exterior of $\angle ABC$; Prove: $m\angle ABC = \frac{1}{2} m\widehat{AC}$; construct the diameter $\overline{BD}$ of $\odot Q$ and show $m\angle ABD = \frac{1}{2} m\widehat{AD}$ and $m\angle CBD = \frac{1}{2} m\widehat{CD}$. Use the Arc Addition Postulate and the Angle Addition Postulate to show $m\angle ABD - m\angle CBD = m\angle ABC$. Then use substitution to show $2m\angle ABC = m\widehat{AC}$.

35. Case 1: Given: $\odot D$ with inscribed $\triangle ABC$ where $\overline{AC}$ is a diameter of $\odot D$; Prove: $\triangle ABC$ is a right triangle; let E be a point on $\overset{\frown}{AC}$. Show that $m\overset{\frown}{AEC} = 180°$ and then that $m\angle B = 90°$. Case 2: Given: $\odot D$ with inscribed $\triangle ABC$ with $\angle B$ a right angle; Prove: $\overline{AC}$ is a diameter of $\odot D$; using the Measure of an Inscribed Angle Theorem, show that $m\overset{\frown}{AC} = 180°$. **39.** yes

10.5 Skill Practice (pp. 683–684) **1.** outside **3.** 130°
5. 130° **7.** 115 **9.** 90 **11.** 56 **15.** $m\angle LPJ \le 90°$; if $\overrightarrow{PL}$ is perpendicular to $\overline{KJ}$ at K, then $m\angle LPJ = 90°$, otherwise it would measure less than 90°.
17. 120°, 100°, 140°

19. a.

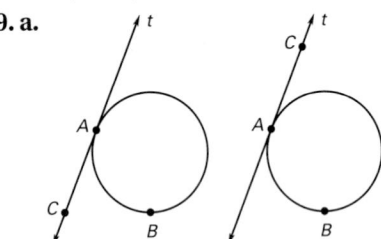

b. $m\overset{\frown}{AB} = 2m\angle BAC$, $m\overset{\frown}{AB} = 2(180 - m\angle BAC)$
c. when $\overline{AB}$ is perpendicular to line t at point A

10.5 Problem Solving (pp. 685–686) **23.** 50° **25.** about 2.8° **27.** Given $\overleftrightarrow{CA}$ tangent to $\odot Q$ at A and diameter $\overline{AB}$. Using Theorem 10.1, $\overline{AB}$ is perpendicular to $\overleftrightarrow{CA}$. It follows that $m\angle CAB = 90°$. This is half of 180°, which is $m\overset{\frown}{AB}$; Case 1: the center of the circle is interior to $\angle CAB$, Case 2: the center of the circle is exterior to $\angle CAB$.

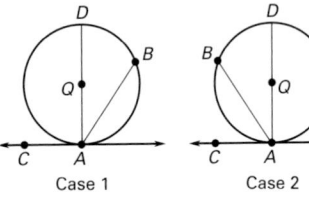
Case 1   Case 2

Construct diameter $\overline{AD}$. Case 1: Let B be a point on the right semicircle. Use Theorem 10.1 to show $m\angle CAB = 90°$. Use the Angle Addition Postulate and the Arc Addition Postulate to show that $m\angle CAD = \frac{1}{2}m\overset{\frown}{AB}$. Case 2: Let B be a point on the left semicircle. Prove similarly to Case 1.

10.6 Skill Practice (pp. 692–693) **1.** external segment
3. 5 **5.** 4 **7.** 6 **9.** 12 **11.** 4 **13.** 5 **15.** 1 **17.** 18

10.6 Problem Solving (pp. 694–695)

21.

Statements	Reasons
1. Two intersecting chords in the same circle.	1. Given
2. Draw $\overline{AC}$ and $\overline{BD}$.	2. Two points determine a line.
3. $\angle ACD \cong \angle ABD$, $\angle CAB \cong \angle CDB$	3. Theorem 10.8
4. $\triangle AEC \sim \triangle DEB$	4. AA Similarity Postulate
5. $\frac{EA}{ED} = \frac{EC}{EB}$	5. If two triangles are similar, then the ratios of corresponding sides are equal.
6. $EA \cdot EB = EC \cdot ED$	6. Cross Products Property

23. Given: EA is a tangent segment to circle P, ED is a secant segment of circle P, and ED is a diameter of circle P. Prove: $EA^2 = EC \cdot ED$

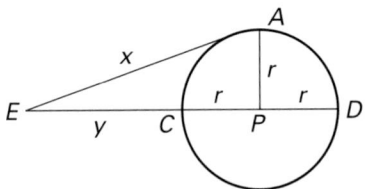

By Theorem 10.1, $EA \perp AP$, so $\triangle EAP$ is a right triangle. By the Pythagorean Theorem, $(y + r)^2 = x^2 + r^2$. So, $y^2 + 2yr + r^2 = x^2 + r^2$. By the Subtraction Property of Equality, $y^2 + 2yr = x^2$. Factoring, this is $y(y + 2r) = x^2$, or $EC \cdot ED = EA^2$.

25. Given $\overline{EB}$ and $\overline{ED}$ are secant segments. Draw $\overline{AD}$ and $\overline{BC}$. Using the Measure of an Inscribed Angle Theorem, $m\angle B = \frac{1}{2}m\overset{\frown}{AC}$ and $m\angle D = \frac{1}{2}m\overset{\frown}{AC}$ which implies $\angle B \cong \angle D$. Using the Reflexive Property of Angle Congruence, $\angle E \cong \angle E$. Using the AA Similarity Postulate, $\triangle BCE \sim \triangle DAE$. Using corresponding sides of similar triangles are proportional, $\frac{EA}{EC} = \frac{ED}{EB}$. Cross multiplying you get $EA \cdot EB = EC \cdot ED$. **27. a.** 60° **b.** Using the Vertical Angles Theorem, $\angle ACB \cong \angle FCE$. Since $m\angle CAB = 60°$ and $m\angle EFD = 60°$, then $\angle CAB \cong \angle EFD$. Using the AA Similarity Postulate, $\triangle ABC \sim \triangle FEC$. **c.** $\frac{y}{3} = \frac{x + 10}{6}$; $y = \frac{x + 10}{2}$ **d.** $y^2 = x(x + 16)$
e. 2, 6 **f.** Since $\frac{CE}{CB} = \frac{2}{1}$, let $CE = 2x$ and $CB = x$. Using Theorem 10.14, $2x^2 = 60$ which implies $x = \sqrt{30}$ which implies $CE = 2\sqrt{30}$.

10.6 Problem Solving Workshop (p. 696) **1.** $2\sqrt{13}$ **3.** $\frac{24}{5}$

Extension (p. 698)

1.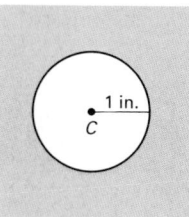

3.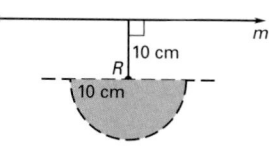

5. The locus of points consists of two points on line ℓ each 3 centimeters away from P.

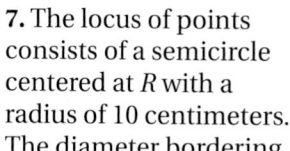

7. The locus of points consists of a semicircle centered at R with a radius of 10 centimeters. The diameter bordering the semicircle is 10 centimeters from line k and parallel to line k.

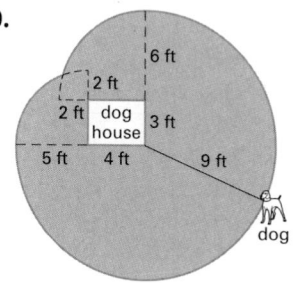

9.

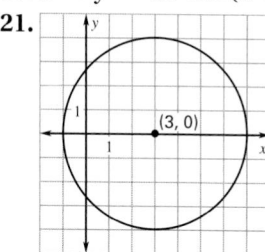

10.7 Skill Practice (pp. 702–703) **1.** center, radius
3. $x^2 + y^2 = 4$ **5.** $x^2 + y^2 = 400$
7. $(x - 50)^2 + (y - 50)^2 = 100$ **9.** $x^2 + y^2 = 49$
11. $(x - 7)^2 + (y + 6)^2 = 64$ **13.** $(x - 3)^2 + (y + 5)^2 = 49$
15. If (h, k) is the center of a circle with a radius r, the equation of the circle should be $(x - h)^2 + (y - k)^2 = r^2$; $(x + 3)^2 + (y + 5)^2 = 9$.
17. $x^2 + y^2 = 36$ **19.** $(x + 3)^2 + (y - 5)^2 = 25$

21. 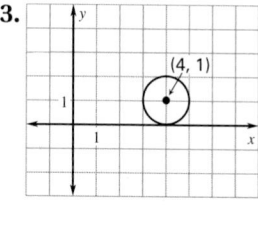 **23.**

27. circle; $x^2 + (y - 3)^2 = 4$ **29.** circle; $x^2 + (y + 2)^2 = 17$ **31.** secant **33.** secant

10.7 Problem Solving (pp. 703–705) **37.** $x^2 + y^2 = 5.76$, $x^2 + y^2 = 0.09$ **39.** $(x - 3)^2 + y^2 = 49$ **41.** The height (or width) always remains the same as the figure is

rolled on its edge. **43. a.** $(1, 9), 5$
b. $(x - 1)^2 + (y - 9)^2 = 169$

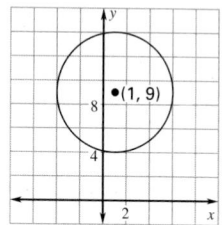

Chapter Review (pp. 708–711) **1.** diameter **3.** The measure of the central angle and the corresponding minor arc are the same. The measure of the major arc is 360° minus the measure of the minor arc.
5. C **7.** 2 **9.** 12 **11.** 60° **13.** 80° **15.** 65° **17.** $c = 28$
19. $q = 100, r = 20$ **21.** 16 **23.** $10\frac{2}{3}$ ft
25. $(x - 8)^2 + (y - 6)^2 = 36$ **27.** $x^2 + y^2 = 81$
29. $(x - 6)^2 + (y - 21)^2 = 16$
31. $(x - 10)^2 + (y - 7)^2 = 12.25$

Algebra Review (p. 713) **1.** $6x^2(3x^2 + 1)$ **3.** $3r(3r - 5s)$
5. $2t(4t^3 + 3t - 5)$ **7.** $y^3(5y^3 - 4y^2 + 2)$
9. $3x^2y(2x + 5y^2)$ **11.** $(y - 3)(y + 2)$ **13.** $(z - 4)^2$
15. $(5b - 1)(b - 3)$ **17.** $(5r - 9)(5r + 9)$
19. $(x + 3)(x + 7)$ **21.** $(y + 3)(y - 2)$ **23.** $(x - 7)(x + 7)$

Chapter 11

11.1 Skill Practice (pp. 723–724) **1.** bases, height
3. 28 units² **5.** 225 units² **7.** 216 units²
9. $A = 10(16) = 160$ units² or $A = 8(20) = 160$ units²; the results are the same. **11.** 7 is not the base of the parallelogram; $A = bh = 3(4) = 12$ units². **13.** 80 ft, 240 ft² **15.** 70 cm, 210 cm² **17.** 23 ft **19.** 4 ft, 2 ft

21.

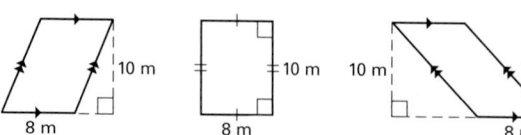

23. 364 cm² **25.** 625 in.² **27.** 52 in.²
29. 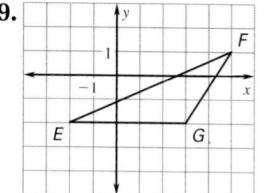 7.5 units²

11.1 Problem Solving (pp. 725–726) **37.** 30 min; 86.4 min **39.** No; 2 inch square; the area of a square is side length squared, so $2^2 = 4$. **41.** 23 cm × 34 cm; 611 cm², 171 cm² **43.** Opposite pairs of sides are congruent making *XYZW* a parallelogram. The area of the parallelogram is *bh*, and since the parallelogram is made of two congruent triangles, the area of one triangle, △*XYW*, is $\frac{1}{2}bh$. **45.** The height is not necessarily a side length of the parallelogram; yes; no; if the base and height represent a rectangle, then the perimeter is 20 ft, the greatest possible perimeter cannot be determined from the given data.

Extension (p. 728) **1.** Precision depends on the greatest possible error while accuracy depends on the relative error. *Sample answer:* Consider a target, if you are consistently hitting the same area, that is precision, if you hit the bull's eye, that is accuracy. **3.** 1 m; 0.5 m **5.** $\frac{1}{16}$ yd; $\frac{1}{32}$ yd **7.** about 1.8% **9.** about 0.04% **11.** This measurement is more accurate if you are measuring large items, if you are measuring small items, this would not be very accurate. **13.** 18.65 ft is more precise; 18.65 ft is more accurate. **15.** 35 in. is more precise; they are about the same accuracy.

11.2 Skill Practice (pp. 733–734) **1.** height **3.** 95 units² **5.** 31 units² **7.** 1500 units² **9.** 189 units² **11.** 360 units² **13.** 13 is not the height of the trapezoid; $A = \frac{1}{2}(12)(14 + 19)$, $A = 198$ cm². **17.** 20 m **19.** 10.5 units² **21.** 10 units² **23.** 5 cm and 13 cm **25.** 168 units² **27.** 67 units² **29.** 42 units² **31.**

7 · · · 6 · 15 · 38 units, 66 units²

11.2 Problem Solving (pp. 735–736) **35.** 20 mm²;

37. a. right triangle and trapezoid **b.** 103,968 ft²; 11,552 yd² **39.** If the kite in the activity were a rhombus, the results would be the same.

41. $A_{\triangle PSR} = \frac{1}{2}\left(\frac{1}{2}d_1\right)d_2$ and $A_{\triangle PQR} = \frac{1}{2}\left(\frac{1}{2}d_1\right)d_2$, so

$A_{\triangle PSR} = \frac{1}{4}d_1d_2$ and $A_{\triangle PQR} = \frac{1}{4}d_1d_2$;

$A_{PQRS} = A_{\triangle PQR} + A_{\triangle PSR}$

$A_{PQRS} = \frac{1}{4}d_1d_2 + \frac{1}{4}d_1d_2 = \frac{1}{2}d_1d_2$

11.3 Skill Practice (pp. 740–741)

1. 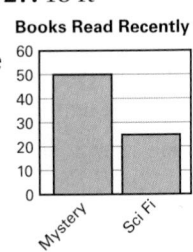 △*ABC* ~ △*DEF* tells you that the sides in the same position are proportional. *AB* and *DE* are corresponding side lengths because the sides are both the hypotenuse of their respective triangle and are listed in the same order in the similarity statement. **3.** 6 : 11, 36 : 121 **5.** 1 : 3, 1 : 9; 18 ft² **7.** 7 : 9, 49 : 81; about 127 in.² **9.** 7 : 4 **11.** 11 : 12 **13.** 8 cm **15.** The ratio of areas is 1 : 4, so the ratio of side lengths is 1 : 2; *ZY* = 2(12) = 24. **17.** 175 ft²; 10 ft, 5.6 ft **19.** Never; doubling the side length of a square always quadruples the area. **21.** The triangles are similar since the ratio of sides is 3 : 4. So, the ratio of areas must be 9 : 16. Use this ratio with the area of △*ABC* to find the area of △*DEF*. **23.** AA Similarity Postulate; $\frac{10}{35} = \frac{2}{7}$ is the ratio of side lengths, so the ratio of areas is 4 : 49.

11.3 Problem Solving (pp. 742–743) **27.** 15 ft **31.** There were twice as many mysteries read, but the area of the mystery bar is 4 times the area of the science fiction bar, giving the impression that 4 times as many mysteries were read.

Books Read Recently

60
50
40
30
20
10
0
Mystery · Sci Fi

33. a. △*ACD* ~ △*AEB*, △*BCF* ~ △*DEF*; AA Similarity Postulate **b.** *Sample answer:* 100 : 81 **c.** $\frac{10}{9} = \frac{20}{10 + x}$, $180 = 100 + 10x$, $x = 8$ OR $20(9) = (10 + x)(10)$, $180 = 100 + 10x$, $x = 8$

11.3 Problem Solving Workshop (p. 744) **1.** 18 in. **3.** $s\sqrt{2}$

11.4 Skill Practice (pp. 749–751) **1.** arc length of $\overparen{AB}$, 360° **3.** about 37.70 in. **5.** about 10.03 ft **7.** 14 m **9.** about 31.42 units **11.** about 4.19 m **13.** about 3.14 ft **15.** 300° **17.** 150° **19.** about 20.94 ft **21.** about 50° **23.** about 8.58 units **25.** about 21.42 units **27.** 6π **29.** $r = \frac{C}{2\pi}$; $d = \frac{C}{\pi}$; $r = 13$, $d = 26$ **31. a.** twice as large **b.** twice as large

11.4 Problem Solving (pp. 751–752) **35.** 21 feet 8 inches represents the circumference of the tree, so if you divide by π, you will get the diameter; about 7 ft. **37.** about 2187 in. **39.** 7.2°; 28,750 mi

Extension (p. 754) **1.** Equator and longitude lines; latitude lines; the equator and lines of longitude have the center of Earth as the center. Lines of latitude do not have the center of Earth as the center. **3.** If two lines intersect then their intersection is exactly 2 points. **5.** 4π, 12π

11.5 Skill Practice (pp. 758–759) **1.** sector **3.** 25π in.^{2}; 78.54 in.^{2} **5.** 132.25π cm^2; 415.48 cm^2 **7.** about 7 m **9.** 52 cm **11.** about 52.36 in.^{2} **13.** about 937.31 m^2 **15.** about 66.04 cm^2 **17.** about 7.73 m^2 **21.** about 57.23 in. **23.** about 66.24 in. **25.** about 27.44 in. **27.** about 33.51 ft^2 **29.** about 1361.88 cm^2 **31.** about 7.63 m **33.** For any two circles the ratio of their circumferences is equal to the ratio of their corresponding radii; for any two circles, if the length of their radii is in the ratio of $a:b$, then the ratio of their areas is $a^2:b^2$; all circles are similar, so you do not need to include similarity in the hypothesis.

35.

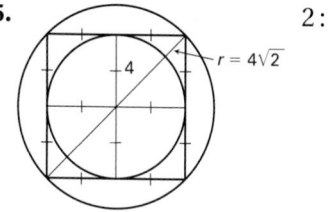

2:1

11.5 Problem Solving (pp. 760–761)
37. about 314.16 mi^2 **39. a.** The data is in percentages.
b. bus: 234°, walk: 90°, other: 36°

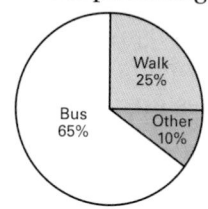

c. bus: $\frac{13}{20}\pi r^2$, walk: $\frac{1}{4}\pi r^2$, other: $\frac{1}{10}\pi r^2$ **41. a.** old: about 399 mm^2, new: 733 mm^2; about 84%
b. *Sample answer:* No, the increase in overall area of the "a" is about 30%, which is much less than the percent increase in the interior area.

11.6 Skill Practice (pp. 765–766) **1.** F **3.** 6.8 **5.** Divide 360° by the number of sides of the polygon. **7.** 20°
9. 51.4° **11.** 22.5° **13.** 135° **15.** about 289.24 units^2
17. 7.5 is not the measure of a side length, it is the measure of the base of the triangle, it needs to be doubled to become the measure of the side length; $A = \frac{1}{2}a \cdot ns$, $A = \frac{1}{2}(13)(6)(15) = 585$ units^2. **19.** about 122.5 units, about 1131.8 units^2 **21.** 63 units, about 294.3 units^2 **23.** apothem, side length; special right triangles or trigonometry; about 392 units^2
25. side length; Pythagorean Theorem or trigonometry; about 204.9 units^2 **27.** about 79.6 units^2 **29.** about 1.4 units^2 **31.** True; since the radius

is the same, the circle around the n-gons is the same but more and more of the circle is covered as the value of n increases. **33.** False; the radius can be equal to the side length as it is in a hexagon.

11.6 Problem Solving (pp. 767–768) **37.** 1.2 cm, about 4.8 cm^2; about 1.6 cm^2 **39.** 15.5 in.^{2}; 43.0 in.^{2}
41. $\frac{360}{6} = 60$, so the central angle is 60°. All of the triangles are of the same side length, r, and therefore all six triangles have a vertex on the center with central angle 60° and side lengths r.
43. Because P is both the incenter and circumcenter of $\triangle ABC$ and letting E be the midpoint of $\overline{AB}$, you can show that $\overline{BD}$ and $\overline{CE}$ are both medians of $\triangle ABC$ and they intersect at P. By the Concurrency of Medians of a Triangle Theorem, $BP = \frac{2}{3}BD$ and $CP = \frac{2}{3}CE$. Using algebra, show that $2PD = CP$.
45. a. About 141.4 cm^2; square: about 225 cm^2, pentagon: about 247.7 cm^2, hexagon: about 259.9 cm^2, decagon: about 277 cm^2; the area is getting larger with each larger polygon. **b.** about 286.22 cm^2, 286.41 cm^2
c.

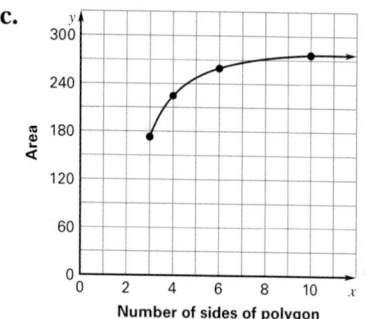

circle; about 286.5 cm^2

11.7 Skill Practice (pp. 774–775) **1.** 0, 1 **3.** $\frac{5}{8}$, 0.625, 62.5%
5. $\frac{3}{8}$, 0.375, 37.5% **7.** $AD + DE = AE$, so $\frac{5}{8} + \frac{3}{8} = 1$
9. $\frac{1}{4}$ or 25% **11.** There is more than a semicircle in the rectangle, so you need to take the area of the rectangle minus the sum of the area of the semicircle and the area of a small rectangle located under the semicircle that has dimensions of 10×2; $\frac{10(7) - \left(\frac{1}{2}\pi(5)^2 + 10(2)\right)}{7(10)} = \frac{70 - (12.5\pi + 20)}{70} \approx 0.153$ or about 15.3%. **13.** $\frac{63}{128}$ or about 49.2% **15.** The two triangles are similar by the AA Similarity Postulate and the ratio of sides is the same; 7:14 or 1:2, so the ratio of the areas is 1:4. **17.** $\frac{2}{7}$ **19.** 1 **21.** $\frac{1}{9}$ or 11.1%; find the area of the whole figure, $\frac{1}{2}(14)(12) = 84$

which is the denominator of the fraction. The top triangle is similar to the whole figure by the AA Similarity Postulate, so use proportions to find the base of the small triangle to be $4\frac{2}{3}$. Since the height of the small triangle is 4, the area is $9\frac{1}{3}$, which is the numerator of the fraction. **25.** about 82.7% **27.** 100%, 50%

11.7 Problem Solving (pp. 776–777) **31. a.** $\frac{2}{5}$ or 40%
b. $\frac{3}{5}$ or 60% **33.** $\frac{1}{6}$ or about 16.7%

35. The probability stays the same; the sector takes up the same percent of the area of the circle regardless of the length of the radius. *Sample answer:* Let the central angle be 90° and the radius be 2 units. The probability for that sector is $\dfrac{\frac{4\pi}{4}}{4\pi} = \dfrac{1}{4}$. Let the radius be doubled. The probability is $\dfrac{\frac{16\pi}{4}}{16\pi} = \dfrac{1}{4}$. **37. a.** $\frac{1}{81}$ or about 1.2% **b.** about 2.4% **c.** about 45.4%

Chapter Review (pp. 780–783) **1.** two radii of a circle and their intercepted arc **3.** $\overline{XZ}$ **5.** 60 units^2
7. 448 units^2

9. 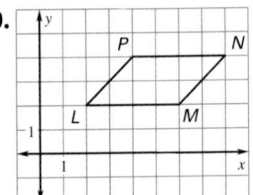 8 units^2

11. 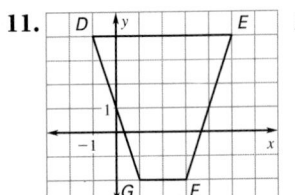 24 units^2

13. 10 : 13, 100 : 169, 152.1 cm^2 **15.** about 30 ft
17. about 26.09 in. **19.** about 17.72 in.^{2} **21.** about 39.8 in., about 119.3 in.^{2} **23.** $\frac{4}{7}$ or about 57.1%
25. about 76.1%

Algebra Review (p. 785) **1.** $d = \left(\dfrac{14.25}{1.5}\right)(2)$; 19 mi
3. $29.50 + 0.25m = 32.75$; 13 min
5. $18,000(1 - 0.1)^5 = A$; \$10,628.82
7. $0 = -16t^2 + 47t + 6$; about 3.06 sec

Chapter 12

12.1 Skill Practice (pp. 798–799) **1.** tetrahedron, 4 faces; hexahedron or cube, 6 faces; octahedron, 8 faces;

dodecahedron, 12 faces; icosahedron, 20 faces
3. Polyhedron; pentagonal pyramid; the solid is formed by polygons and the base is a pentagon.
5. Not a polyhedron; the solid is not formed by polygons.

7. 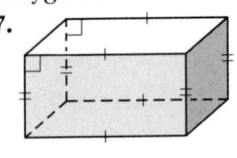 **9.**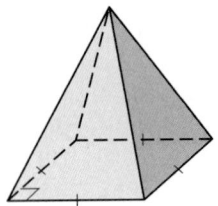

11. 8 **13.** 24 **15.** 4, 4, 6 **17.** 5, 6, 9 **19.** 8, 12, 18
21. A cube has six faces, and "hexa" means six.
23. concave

25. 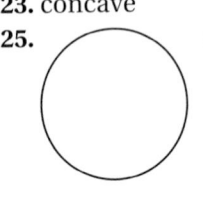 circle **27.** 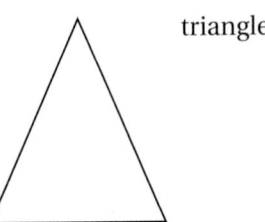 triangle

29. The concepts of edge and vertex are confused; the number of vertices is 4, and the number of edges is 6.

12.1 Problem Solving (pp. 800–801) **35.** 18, 12
37. square **39.** Tetrahedron; no; you cannot have a different number of faces because of Euler's Theorem. **41. a.** trapezoid
b. Yes. *Sample:* 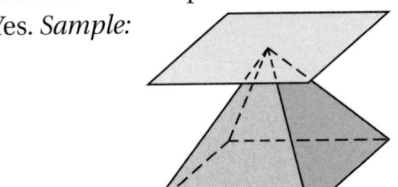 **c.** square

d. Yes. *Sample:* 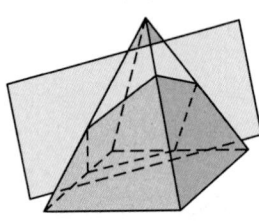 **43.** no
45. Yes, but only if the rhombus is a square; *Sample answer:*
The plane intersects the cube parallel to a base so it forms a square, which is a rhombus.

47. Yes. *Sample:*

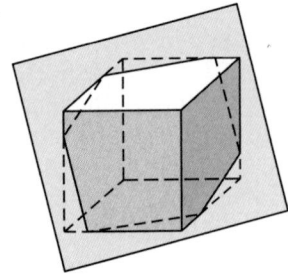

49. a. It will increase the number of faces by 1, the number of vertices by 2, and the number of edges by 3. **b.** It will increase the number of faces by 1, the number of vertices by 2, and the number of edges by 3. **c.** It will not change the number of faces, vertices, or edges. **d.** It will increase the number of faces by 3, the number of vertices by 6, and the number of edges by 9.

12.2 Skill Practice (pp. 806–808)
1.

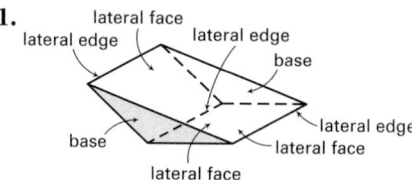

3. 150.80 in.^{2} **5.** 27,513.6 ft^2 **7.** 196.47 m^2 **9.** 14.07 in.^{2} **11.** 804.25 in.^{2} **13.** 9 yd **15.** 10.96 in. **19.** 1119.62 in.^{2}

12.2 Problem Solving (pp. 808–809) **23. a.** 360 in.^{2} **b.** There is overlap in some of the sides of the box. **c.** *Sample answer:* It is easier to wrap a present if you have some overlap of wrapping paper. **27. a.** 54 units^2 **b.** 52 units^2 **c.** When the red cubes are removed, inner faces of the cubes remaining replace the area of the red cubes that are lost. When the blue cubes are removed, there are still 2 faces of the blue cubes whose area is not replaced by inner faces of the remaining cubes. Therefore, the area of the solid after removing blue cubes is 2 units^2 less than the solid after removing red cubes.

29. 989.66 in.^{2}

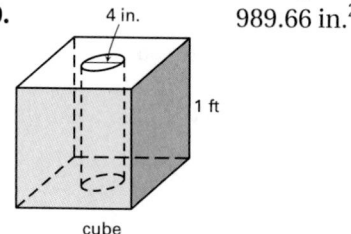

12.3 Skill Practice (pp. 814–815)
1.

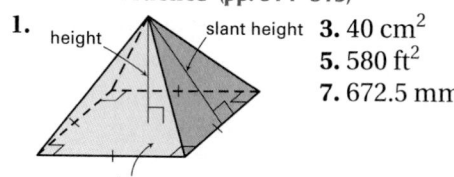

3. 40 cm^2
5. 580 ft^2
7. 672.5 mm^2

9. The height of the pyramid is used rather than the slant height; $S = 6^2 + \frac{1}{2}(24)(5) = 96$ ft^2. **11.** 12.95 in.^{2} **13.** 238.76 in.^{2} **15.** 226.73 ft^2

19. 981.39 m^2

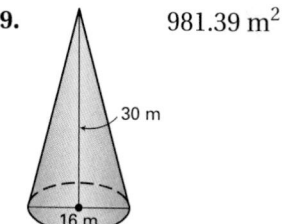

21. 255.53 cm^2

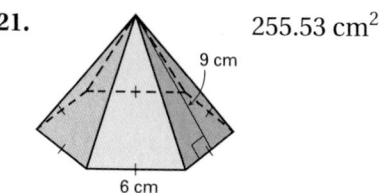

23. 164.05 in.^{2}
25. 27.71 cm^2

12.3 Problem Solving (pp. 816–817) **27.** 96 in.^{2}
29. square pyramid; 98.35 cm^2
31. a. Given: $\overline{AB} \perp \overline{AC}$; $\overline{DE} \perp \overline{DC}$
Prove: $\triangle ABC \sim \triangle DEC$

Statements	Reasons
1. $\overline{AB} \perp \overline{AC}$; $\overline{DE} \perp \overline{DC}$	1. Given
2. $\angle BAC$ and $\angle EDC$ are right angles.	2. Definition of perpendicular
3. $\angle BAC \cong \angle EDC$	3. Right angles are congruent.
4. $\angle ACB \cong \angle DCE$	4. Reflexive Property
5. $\triangle ABC \sim \triangle DEC$	5. AA Similarity Postulate

b. 5, $\frac{3}{2}$, $\frac{5}{2}$ **c.** larger cone: 24π units^2, smaller cone: 6π units^2; the small cone has 25% of the surface area of the large cone. **33.** about 28.44 mi^2

12.4 Skill Practice (pp. 822–824) **1.** cubic units **5.** 18 units^3 **7.** 175 in.^{3} **9.** 2630.55 cm^3 **11.** 1256.64 in.^{3} **13.** The area of a circle (the base) is πr^2, not $2\pi r$; $V = \pi r^2 h = \pi(4^2)(3) = 48\pi$ ft^3. **15.** 10 in. **17.** 8 in. **19.** 821.88 ft^3 **23.** 12.65 cm **25.** 2814.87 ft^3

12.4 Problem Solving (pp. 824–825) **29. a.** 720 in.^{3} **b.** 720 in.^{3} **c.** They are the same. **31.** 159.15 ft^3 **33. a.** 4500 in.^{3} **b.** 75 in.^{3} **c.** 20 rocks

12.4 Problem Solving Workshop (p. 827)
1. a. about 63.45 in.^{3} **b.** about 63.45 in.^{3}
3. $r = \frac{R\sqrt{2}}{2}$ **5.** about 7.33 in.^{3}

12.5 Skill Practice (pp. 832–833) **1.** A triangular prism is a solid with two bases that are triangles and parallelograms for the lateral faces, while a triangular pyramid is a solid with a triangle for a base and triangles for lateral faces.

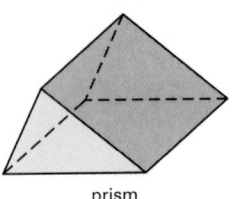
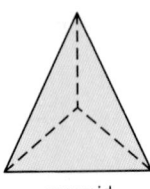

prism   pyramid

3. 50 cm^3 **5.** 13.33 in.^{3} **7.** 6 in.^{3} **9.** The slant height is used in the volume formula instead of the height; $V = \frac{1}{3}\pi(9^2)(12) = 324\pi \approx 1018$ ft^3. **13.** 6 in.
15. 3716.85 ft^3 **17.** 987.86 cm^3 **19.** 8.57 cm
21. 833.33 in.^{3} **23.** 16.70 cm^3 **25.** 26.39 yd^3
27.

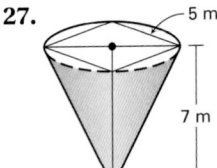

about 91.63 m^3

12.5 Problem Solving (pp. 834–836) **29. a.** 201 in.^{3}
b. 13.4 in.^{3} **31.** 3; since the cone and cylinder have the same radius and height, the volume of the cone will be $\frac{1}{3}$ the volume of the cylinder.
33.   23.70 in.^{3}

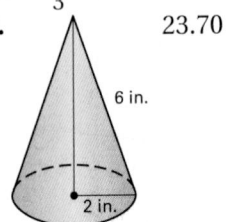

35. a. The volume doubles. **b.** The volume is multiplied by 4. **c.** If you replace the height h by $2h$ in the volume formula, it will multiply the volume by 2. If you replace the side length s by $2s$ in the volume formula, it will multiply the volume by 4 because $(2s)^2 = 4s^2$. **37.** about 78 in.^{3}
39. a. $V_{cone} = \frac{1}{3}Bh = \frac{1}{3}\pi r^2 \cdot h = \frac{\pi\left(\frac{1}{2}h\right)^2 \cdot h}{3} = \frac{\pi h^3}{12}$, where B is the area of the base of the cone, r is the radius, and h is the height
b.

Time (min)	Height h (m)
1	1.90
2	2.40
3	2.74
4	3.02
5	3.25

c.

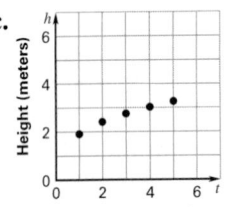

No; the points of the graph do not lie in a straight line.

41. a. $h_1 = \dfrac{r_1 h_2}{r_2 - r_1}$ **b.** $V = \dfrac{\pi r_2{}^2(h_1 + h_2)}{3} - \dfrac{\pi r_1{}^2 h_1}{3} = $

$\dfrac{\pi r_2{}^2\left(\frac{r_1 h_2}{r_2 - r_1} + h_2\right)}{3} - \dfrac{\pi r_1{}^2\left(\frac{r_1 h_2}{r_2 - r_1}\right)}{3}$

12.6 Skill Practice (pp. 842–843) **1.** $S = 4\pi r^2$, $V = \frac{4}{3}\pi r^3$, where r is the radius of the sphere **3.** 201.06 ft^2
5. 1052.09 m^2 **7.** 4.8 in. **9.** about 144.76 in.^{2}
11. about 7359.37 cm^2 **13.** 268,082.57 mm^3
15. The radius should be cubed; $V = \frac{4}{3}\pi r^3 = \frac{4}{3}\pi(8)^3 \approx$ 682.67$\pi \approx$ 2144.66 ft^3. **17.** 2.80 cm **19.** 6 ft
21. 247.78 in.^{2}, 164.22 in.^{3} **23.** 358.97 cm^2, 563.21 cm^3
25. 13 in.; 676π in.^{2}; $\frac{8788}{3}\pi$ in.^{3} **27.** 21 m; 42π m; 1764π m^2

12.6 Problem Solving (pp. 844–845) **31.** about 98,321,312 mi^2 **33. a.** 8.65 in.^{3} **b.** 29.47 in.^{3}
35. a. about 80,925,856 mi^2, about 197,359,488 mi^2
b. about 41% **37.** 324π in.^{2}, 972π in.^{3}

12.7 Skill Practice (pp. 850–852) **1.** They are the same type of solid and corresponding linear measures have the same ratio. **3.** Not similar; the corresponding dimensions are not in the same ratio. **5.** Similar; each corresponding ratio is 3:4. **9.** about 166.67 m^2, about 127.21 m^3 **11.** The volumes are related by the third power; $\dfrac{500\pi}{\text{Volume of B}} = \dfrac{1^3}{4^3}$. **13.** 1:3 **15.** 4:3
17. 1:4 **19.** about 341.94 ft^2, about 502.65 ft^3
21. about 272.97 in.^{2}, about 73.61 in.^{3} **23.** $r = 3$ ft, $h = 6$ ft; $r = 8$ ft, $h = 16$ ft

12.7 Problem Solving (pp. 852–853) **25.** about 8.04 fl oz
27. 27 fl oz **29. a.** large orange: about 33.51 in.^{3}, small orange: about 17.16 in.^{3} **b.** The ratio of the volumes is the cube of the ratio of diameters.
c. large orange: 3.75 in., small orange: 2.95 in.
d. The ratio of surface area multiplied by the ratio of the corresponding diameters equals the ratio of the volumes. **31. a.** 144 in. **b.** 3920.4 in.^{2} **c.** 1.5 in.^{3}
33. About 11.5 kg; the ratio of the small snowball to the medium snowball is 5:7, so the ratio of their volumes is $5^3:7^3$. Solve $\dfrac{5^3}{7^3} = \dfrac{1.2}{x}$ to find the weight of the middle ball. Similarly, find the weight of the large ball.

Chapter Review (pp. 857–860) **1.** sphere **3.** 12 **5.** 36
7. 2035.75 ft² **9.** 9 m **11.** 14.29 cm **13.** 11.34 m³
15. 27.53 yd³ **17.** 12 in.² **19.** 272.55 m³ **21.** 1008π m²;
4320π m³

Cumulative Review (pp. 866–867) **1.** 75 **3.** 16 **5.** 4
7. Both pairs of opposite angles are congruent.
9. The diagonals bisect each other. **11.** 45 **13.** about
36.35 in.² **15.** about 2.28 m² **17.** 131.05 in.², 80.67 in.³
19. (4, 2) **21. a.** $(x + 2)^2 + (y - 4)^2 \leq 36$ **b.** (2, 0): yes,
because it is a solution of the inequality; (3, 9): no,
because it is not a solution of the inequality; $(-6, -1)$:
no, because it is not a solution of the inequality;
$(-6, 8)$: yes, because it is a solution of the inequality;
$(-7, 5)$: yes, because it is a solution of the inequality.
23. a. 40.84 in.², 17.28 in.³ **b.** about 6.91 in.³

Skills Review Handbook

Operations with Rational Numbers (p. 869) **1.** 11
3. -15 **5.** -24 **7.** 0.3 **9.** 11.6 **11.** -4.9 **13.** -13.02
15. 29.2 **17.** $-\frac{13}{12}$ **19.** $\frac{6}{7}$ **21.** $-\frac{11}{12}$ **23.** $\frac{17}{18}$

Simplifying and Evaluating Expressions (p. 870) **1.** 33
3. -1 **5.** 36 **7.** 2.8 **9.** -6 **11.** $25x$ **13.** -36 **15.** -15
17. 15 **19.** 1 **21.** $-\frac{6}{5}$ **23.** $\frac{3}{4}$

Properties of Exponents (p. 871) **1.** 25 **3.** $\frac{1}{16}$ **5.** 78,125
7. 7^{32} **9.** a^4 **11.** $\frac{5a^5}{b^4}$ **13.** $\frac{81}{n^4}$ **15.** m^2 **17.** $16x^6y^2$
19. $\frac{b^2}{5a^3c}$ **21.** $8x$ **23.** $\frac{a^5}{7b^4c}$ **25.** $30x^3y$ **27.** $\frac{3a^{14}}{5b^2c^8}$

Using the Distributive Property (p. 872) **1.** $3x + 21$
3. $40n - 16$ **5.** $-x - 6$ **7.** $12x^2 - 8x + 16$ **9.** $-5x^2$
11. $2n + 5$ **13.** $5h^3 + 5h^2$ **15.** 10 **17.** $\frac{9}{10}a$ **19.** $3n + 4$
21. $2a^2 + 6a - 76$ **23.** $3x^2 - 10x + 5$ **25.** $4a^2 + 2ab - 1$

Binomial Products (p. 873) **1.** $a^2 - 11a + 18$
3. $t^2 + 3t - 40$ **5.** $25a^2 + 20a + 4$ **7.** $4c^2 + 13c - 12$
9. $z^2 - 16z + 64$ **11.** $2x^2 + 3x + 1$ **13.** $4x^2 - 9$
15. $6d^2 + d - 2$ **17.** $k^2 - 2.4k + 1.44$ **19.** $-z^2 + 36$
21. $5y^2 + 9y - 32$ **23.** $3x^2 - 17$

Radical Expressions (p. 874) **1.** ± 10 **3.** $\pm\frac{1}{2}$
5. no square roots **7.** ± 0.9 **9.** 11 **11.** $-3\sqrt{11}$
13. $2\sqrt{5}$ **15.** $3\sqrt{7}$ **17.** $4\sqrt{5}$ **19.** $210\sqrt{2}$ **21.** 137
23. 30 **25.** 8 **27.** $2\sqrt{6}$

Solving Linear Equations (p. 875) **1.** 31 **3.** -6 **5.** 39
7. -3.2 **9.** 18 **11.** 1 **13.** $\frac{7}{2}$ **15.** -1 **17.** 20 **19.** 16
21. -1 **23.** 7 **25.** 6.75 **27.** -0.82 **29.** -4 **31.** $\frac{5}{2}$

33. $-\frac{2}{5}$ **35.** $\frac{1}{2}$

Solving and Graphing Linear Inequalities (p. 876)
1. $x < 7$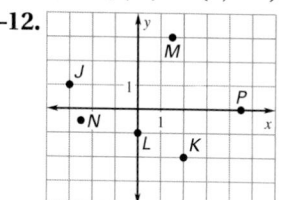
3. $n \leq 4$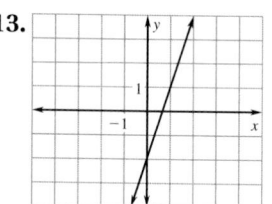

Solving Formulas (p. 877) **1.** $s = \frac{P}{4}$ **3.** $\ell = \frac{V}{wh}$ **5.** $b = \frac{2A}{h}$
7. $w = \frac{P}{2} - \ell$ **9.** $C = \frac{5}{9}(F - 32)$ **11.** $h = \frac{S - 2\pi r^2}{2\pi r}$
13. $y = -2x + 7$ **15.** $y = 3x + 2$ **17.** $y = \frac{5}{4}x$
19. $y = 62 - 15$

Graphing Points and Lines (p. 878)
1. (3, 1) **3.** (0, 2) **5.** (3, -3)
7–12. 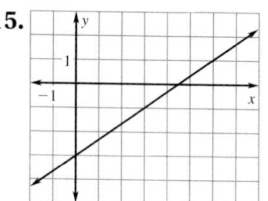 **13.**

15.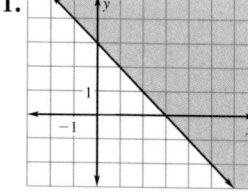

Slope and Intercepts of a Line (p. 879)
1. $\frac{3}{2}$, x-intercept -2, y-intercept 3 **3.** 0, no x-intercept,
y-intercept -2 **5.** x-intercept 3, y-intercept -15
7. x-intercept 3, y-intercept 3 **9.** x-intercept 2,
y-intercept -6 **11.** x-intercept 0, y-intercept 0

Systems of Linear Equations (p. 880) **1.** (2, 1) **3.** (4, -1)
5. (6, -3) **7.** (-1, -4) **9.** (3, 2) **11.** (-1, -5) **13.** (-5, 1)
15. (0.5, -2)

Linear Inequalities (p. 881)
1. 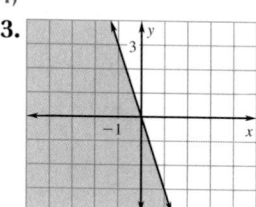 **3.**

9. 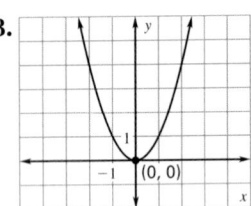 **11.**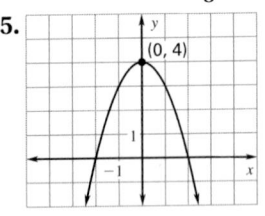

Quadratic Equations and Functions (p. 883)
1. ± 12
3. -3 **5.** 0 **7.** -1 **9.** no real solutions **11.** $\pm\dfrac{\sqrt{5}}{3}$

13. 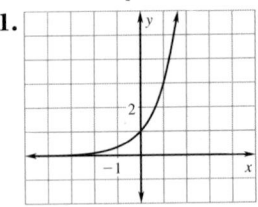 **15.**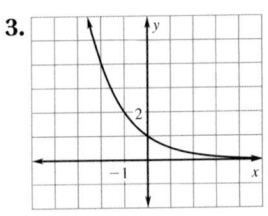

25. $-5, -1$ **27.** -3 **29.** $\dfrac{-7 \pm \sqrt{33}}{2}$ **31.** -2 **33.** $\dfrac{1 \pm \sqrt{31}}{5}$

35. no real solutions **37.** $\dfrac{1 \pm \sqrt{61}}{6}$ **39.** $\pm\sqrt{5}$

Functions (p. 884)
1. 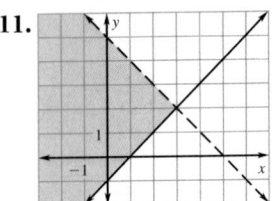 **3.** (graph)

9. $y = x^2$ **11.** $y = 12x$; $72; 35$ h

Problem Solving with Percents (p. 885)
1. 24 questions
3. yes **5.** 20% **7.** 500 residents **9.** about 50%

Converting Measurements and Rates (p. 886)
1. 5 **3.** 3
5. 3.2 **7.** 160 **9.** 63,360 **11.** 576 **13.** 3,000,000 **15.** 6.5
17. 1020 **19.** 5104 **21.** 5280 **23.** 90,000,000

Mean, Median, and Mode (p. 887)
1. The mean or the median best represent the given data because all of the values are close to these measures. **3.** The median or the mode best represent the data because all of the values are close to these measures.
5. Median; the mean is too high and the mode is too low. **7.** Mean; there is no mode and the median is too high.

Displaying Data (p. 889)
1. Line graph; this type of graph shows change over time and this is what the storeowner wants to evaluate. **3.** Histogram; this displays data in intervals.

5.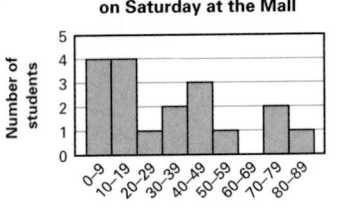

The data is put into intervals; $0–$19 and 10–19.

7.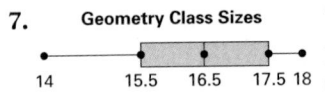

The box-and-whisker plot shows how the class sizes relate to each other.

Geometry Class Sizes (circle graph)
- 17 students 26%
- 16 students 24.4%
- 18 students 27.4%
- 14 students 10.7%
- 15 students 11.5%

The circle graph shows how each class size contributes to the total number of students enrolled in Geometry.

9.
```
Stem | Leaves
  1  | 2 3 5 5 6 8 8 9
  2  | 4 5 5 6
  3  | 0 0 2 2 3 5 5 6 7
  4  |
  5  |
  6  |
  7  | 2
Key: 1|2 = 12
```
12, 72, 25.5, 18, 33

11.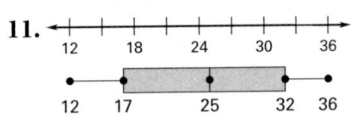

The data is more closely related to the mean and median in the new box-and-whisker plot than before dropping the two highest ages.

Sampling and Surveys (p. 890)
1. Biased sample; the sample is unlikely to represent the entire population of students because only students at a soccer game are asked which day they prefer. **3.** Biased sample; the sample is biased because only people with e-mail can respond. **5.** The sample and the question are random.

Counting Methods (p. 892)
1. 15 outfits **3.** 1,679,616 passwords **5.** 125,000 combinations **7.** 756 pairs
9. 24 ways

Probability (p. 893)
1. dependent; $\dfrac{33}{95} \approx 0.347$ or about 34.7% **3.** dependent; $\dfrac{1}{20} = 0.05$ or 5%
5. dependent; $\dfrac{1}{8} = 0.125$ or 12.5%

Problem Solving Plan and Strategies (p. 895)
1. $205 **3.** 4 **5.** 14 aspen and 7 birch, 16 aspen and 8 birch, or 18 aspen and 9 birch **7.** 24 pieces

Extra Practice

Chapter 1 (pp. 896–897) **1.** *Sample answer: A, F, B;* $\overleftrightarrow{AB}$
3. *Sample answer:* $\overrightarrow{FA}$, $\overrightarrow{FB}$ **5.** *Sample answer:* $\overleftrightarrow{AB}$
7. 43 **9.** 26 **11.** 28 **13.** $(3x - 7) + (3x - 1) = 16$;
$x = 4$; $AB = 5$, $BC = 11$; not congruent
15. $(4x - 5) + (2x - 7) = 54$; $x = 11$; $AB = 39$, $BC = 15$;
not congruent **17.** $(3x - 7) + (2x + 5) = 108$; $x = 22$;
$AB = 59$, $BC = 49$; not congruent **19.** $\left(-4\frac{1}{2}, 1\right)$
21. $(1, 1)$ **23.** $(5.1, -8.05)$ **25.** 10 **27.** 34 **29.** 20
31. 104° **33.** 88° **35.** adjacent angles **37.** vertical
angles, supplementary **39.** *Sample answer:* $\angle ACE$,
$\angle BCF$ **41.** polygon; concave **43.** Not a polygon;
part of the figure is not a line segment. **45.** *DFHKB*,
pentagon; *ABCDEFGHJK*, decagon **47.** 13 cm
49. 11 m **51.** about 13.4 units, 4 units²

Chapter 2 (pp. 898–899) **1.** Add 6 for the next number,
then subtract 8 for the next number; 11. **3.** no pattern
5. Each number is $\frac{1}{3}$ of the previous number; $\frac{1}{81}$.
7. *Sample answer:* $-8 - (-5) = -3$ **9.** *Sample
answer:* $m\angle A = 90°$ **11.** If-then form: if a figure
is a square, then it is a four-sided regular polygon;
Converse: if a figure is a four-sided regular polygon,
then it is a square; Inverse: if a figure is not a
square, then it is not a four-sided regular polygon;
Contrapositive: if a figure is not a four-sided
regular polygon, then it is not a square. **13.** true
15. If two coplanar lines are not parallel, then they
form congruent vertical angles. **17.** might **19.** true
21. false **23.** true
25. $4x + 15 = 39$ Write original equation.
     $4x = 24$ Subtraction Property of Equality
      $x = 6$ Division Property of Equality
27. $2(-7x + 3) = -50$ Write original equation.
     $-14x + 6 = -50$ Distributive Property
     $-14x = -56$ Subtraction Property of Equality
      $x = 4$ Division Property of Equality
29. $13(2x - 3) - 20x = 3$ Write original equation.
     $26x - 39 - 20x = 3$ Distributive Property
     $6x - 39 = 3$ Simplify.
     $6x = 42$ Addition Property of Equality
      $x = 7$ Division Property of Equality
31. $m\angle JKL$, $m\angle ABC$; Transitive Property of Equality
33. $m\angle XYZ$; Reflexive Property of Equality

21.

Statements	Reasons
1. $\overline{XY} \cong \overline{YZ} \cong \overline{ZX}$	1. Given
2. $XY = YZ = ZX$	2. Definition of congruence for segments
3. Perimeter of $\triangle XYZ = XY + YZ + ZX$	3. Perimeter formula
4. Perimeter of $\triangle XYZ = XY + XY + XY$	4. Substitution
5. Perimeter of $\triangle XYZ = 3 \cdot XY$	5. Simplify.

37. 23° **39.** 90°
41.

Statements	Reasons
1. $\angle UKV$ and $\angle VKW$ are complements.	1. Given
2. $m\angle UKV + m\angle VKW = 90°$	2. Definition of complementary angles
3. $\angle UKV \cong \angle XKY$, $\angle VKW \cong \angle YKZ$	3. Vertical angles are congruent.
4. $m\angle UKV = m\angle XKY$, $m\angle VKW = m\angle YKZ$	4. Definition of angle congruence
5. $m\angle YKZ + m\angle XKY = 90°$	5. Substitution
6. $\angle YKZ$ and $\angle XKY$ are complements.	6. Definition of complementary angles

Chapter 3 (pp. 900–901) **1.** corresponding
3. consecutive interior **5.** corresponding
7. $\angle HLM$ and $\angle MJC$ **9.** $\angle FKL$ and $\angle AML$
11. $\overleftrightarrow{BG}$ and $\overleftrightarrow{CF}$ **13.** 68°, 112°; $m\angle 1 = 68°$ because if
two parallel lines are cut by a transversal, then the
alternate interior angles are congruent, $m\angle 2 = 112°$
because it is a linear pair with $\angle 1$. **15.** 9, 1
17. 25, 19 **19.** Yes; if two lines are cut by a transversal
so that a pair of consecutive interior angles are
supplementary, then the lines are parallel.
21. Yes; if two lines are cut by a transversal so that
alternate interior angles are congruent, then the
lines are parallel. **23.** Yes; if two lines are cut by a
transversal so that a pair of consecutive interior
angles are supplementary, then the lines are parallel.
25. Neither; the slopes are not equal and they are not
opposite reciprocals. **27.** Line 2 **29.** Line 1
31. $y = \frac{2}{3}x + 2$ **33.** $y = -2x$ **35.** $y = x + 10$
37. $y = \frac{2}{5}x + \frac{38}{5}$ **39.** 69° **41.** 73° **43.** 38°
45. 1. Given; 2. $\angle ABC$ is a right angle.; 3. Definition
of right angle; 4. $\overrightarrow{BD}$ bisects $\angle ABC$.; 5. Definition of
angle bisector; 6. $m\angle ABD$, $m\angle DBC$; 7. Substitution
Property of Equality; 8. $m\angle ABD$; 9. Simplify; 10.
Division Property of Equality

Chapter 4 (pp. 902–903)

1. 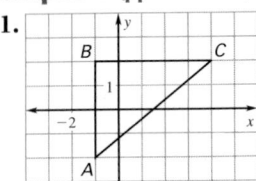 scalene; right triangle

3. 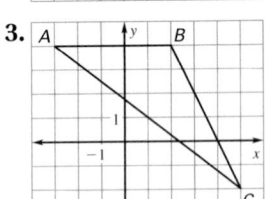 scalene; not a right triangle

5. 58; acute **7.** $\triangle DFG \cong \triangle FDE$; SAS Congruence Postulate or ASA Congruence Postulate
9. $STWX \cong UTWV$; all pairs of corresponding angles and sides are congruent. **11.** 7 **13.** No; a true congruence statement would be $\triangle JKM \cong \triangle LKM$.
15. congruent **17.** $\triangle XUV \cong \triangle VWX$; since $\overline{XV} \cong \overline{XV}$, with the givens you can use the HL Congruence Theorem. **19.** $\triangle HJL \cong \triangle KLJ$; use alternate interior angles to get $\angle HJL \cong \angle JLK$. Since $\overline{JL} \cong \overline{JL}$, with the given you can use the SAS Congruence Postulate.
21. yes; AAS Congruence Theorem **23.** Yes; use the ASA Congruence Postulate. **25.** State the givens from the diagram, and state that $\overline{AC} \cong \overline{AC}$ by the Reflexive Property of Congruence. Then use the SAS Congruence Postulate to prove $\triangle ABC \cong \triangle CDA$, and state $\angle 1 \cong \angle 2$ because corresponding parts of congruent triangles are congruent.
27. State the givens from the diagram and state that $\overline{SR} \cong \overline{SR}$ by the Reflexive Property of Congruence. Then use the Segment Addition Postulate to show that $\overline{PR} \cong \overline{US}$. Use the SAS Congruence Postulate to prove $\triangle QPR \cong \triangle TUS$, and state $\angle 1 \cong \angle 2$ because corresponding parts of congruent triangles are congruent. **29.** $AB = DE = \sqrt{26}$; $AC = DF = \sqrt{41}$; $BC = EF = \sqrt{17}$; $\triangle ABC \cong \triangle DEF$ by the SSS Congruence Postulate, and $\angle A \cong \angle D$ because corresponding parts of congruent triangles are congruent. **31.** $x = 6, y = 48$ **33.** $x = 2$
35. $x = 28, y = 29$

37.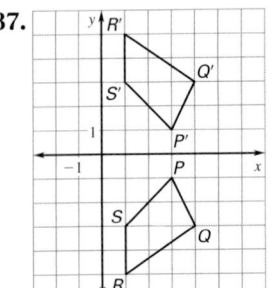

39. 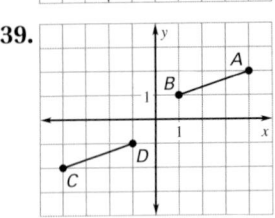 yes; 180°

Chapter 5 (pp. 904–905) **1.** $\overline{AB}$ **3.** $\overline{AC}$ **5.** LC, AL

7. *Sample answer:* 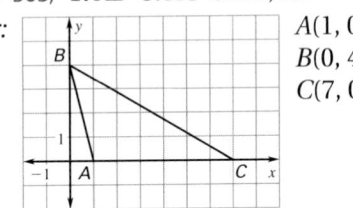 $A(1, 0)$, $B(0, 4)$, $C(7, 0)$

9. 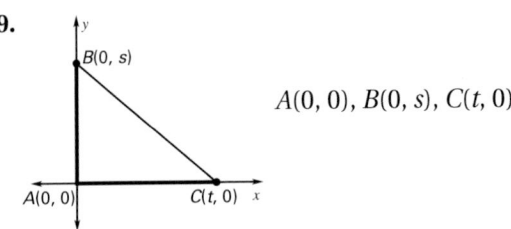 $A(0, 0), B(0, s), C(t, 0)$

11. 14 **13.** 12 **15.** 24 **17.** yes **19.** 15 **21.** No; there is not enough information. **23.** Yes; $x = 17$ by the Angle Bisector Theorem. **25.** 17 **27.** 8 **29.** angle bisector
31. perpendicular bisector **33.** perpendicular bisector and angle bisector **35.** $\overline{JK}, \overline{LK}, \overline{JL}, \angle L, \angle J, \angle K$
37. 1 in. $< \ell < 17$ in. **39.** 6 in. $< \ell < 12$ in.
41. 2 ft $< \ell < 10$ ft **43.** $>$ **45.** $>$ **47.** $=$ **49.** $>$ **51.** $<$

Chapter 6 (pp. 906–907) **1.** 20°, 60°, 100° **3.** 36°, 54°, 90°
5. 4 **7.** 10 **9.** -10 **11.** 10 **13.** 6 **15.** 12 **17.** $\dfrac{y}{9}$ **19.** 4
21. similar; $RQPN \sim STUV$, 11 : 20 **23.** 3 : 1
25. $\triangle PQR$: 90, $\triangle LMN$: 30 **27.** angle bisector, 7
29. not similar **31.** Similar; $\triangle JKL \sim \triangle NPM$; since $\overline{JK} \parallel \overline{NP}$ and $\overline{KL} \parallel \overline{PM}$, $\angle J \cong \angle PNM$ and $\angle L \cong \angle PMN$ by the Corresponding Angles Postulate. Then the triangles are similar by the AA Similarity Postulate.
33. Since $\dfrac{KH}{TS} = \dfrac{KJ}{TR} = \dfrac{HJ}{SR} = \dfrac{3}{5}$, $\triangle KHJ \sim \triangle TSR$ by the SSS Similarity Theorem. **35.** $x = 3, y = 8.4$

37. 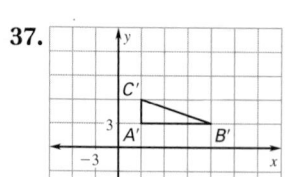 **39.**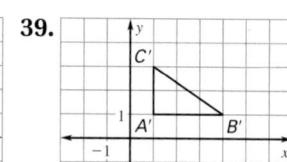

41. enlargement; $1:3$

Chapter 7 (pp. 908–909) **1.** 50 **3.** 60 **5.** 240 ft² **7.** right triangle **9.** not a right triangle **11.** right triangle **13.** triangle; acute **15.** not a triangle **17.** triangle; acute **19.** $\triangle ADB \sim \triangle BDC \sim \triangle ABC$; DB **21.** $\triangle PSQ \sim \triangle QSR \sim \triangle PQR$; RP **23.** 2 **25.** 4.8 **27.** 9.7 **29.** $g = 9$, $h = 9\sqrt{3}$ **31.** $m = 5\sqrt{3}$, $n = 10$ **33.** $v = 20$, $w = 10$ **35.** $\frac{3}{5}$, 0.6; $\frac{5}{3}$, 1.6667 **37.** 6.1 **39.** 16.5 **41.** $x = 12.8$, $y = 15.1$ **43.** $x = 7.5$, $y = 7.7$ **45.** $x = 16.0$, $y = 16.5$ **47.** $GH = 9.2$, $m\angle G = 49.4°$, $m\angle H = 40.6°$

Chapter 8 (pp. 910–911) **1.** 112 **3.** 117 **5.** 68 **7.** 120°, 60° **9.** about 158.8°, about 21.2° **11.** $a = 5$, $b = 5$ **13.** $a = 117°$, $b = 63°$ **15.** $a = 7$, $b = 3$ **17.** $\angle XYV$ **19.** YV **21.** ZX

23. 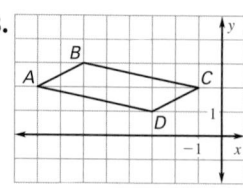 $\overline{AB} \parallel \overline{DC}, \overline{AD} \parallel \overline{BC}$

25. 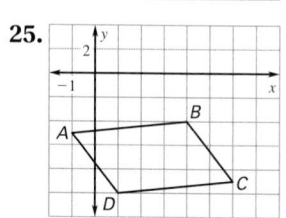 $\overline{AB} \parallel \overline{DC}, \overline{AD} \parallel \overline{BC}$

27. Show $\angle QPR \cong \angle SRP$ making $\angle SPQ \cong \angle QRS$. You now have opposite pairs of angles congruent which makes the quadrilateral a parallelogram. **29.** Square; since the quadrilateral is both a rectangle and rhombus it is a square. **31.** Rectangle; since the quadrilateral is a parallelogram with congruent diagonals it is a rectangle. **33.** 90° **35.** 25 **37.** 0.4 **39.** 98° **41.** Parallelogram; the diagonals bisect one another. **43.** Rhombus; it is a parallelogram with perpendicular diagonals. **45.** Isosceles trapezoid; it has one pair of parallel opposite sides and congruent base angles. **47.** Kite; it has consecutive pairs of congruent sides and perpendicular diagonals. **49.** Trapezoid; it has one pair of parallel sides.

Chapter 9 (pp. 912–913) **1.** $(x, y) \rightarrow (x + 4, y - 2)$; $AB = A'B', BC = B'C', AC = A'C'$ **3.** $\langle -10, 7 \rangle$

5. $\langle -4, 5 \rangle$ **7.** $\begin{bmatrix} 5 \\ 11 \end{bmatrix}$ **9.** $\begin{bmatrix} -4 & -31 \\ 64 & 67 \end{bmatrix}$

11. $\begin{bmatrix} 2 & 10 & 5 & 4 \\ -2 & -1 & -3 & -5 \end{bmatrix}$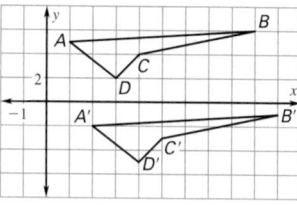

13. $\begin{bmatrix} 5 & 2 & 0 & -2 & -1 \\ 4 & 1 & 1 & 1 & 7 \end{bmatrix}$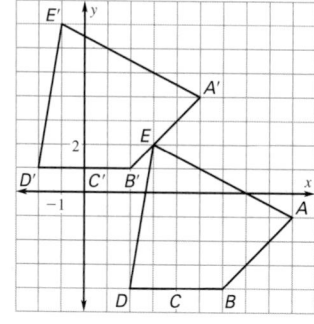

15. 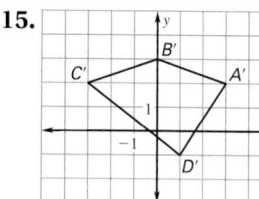 **17.** $A'(1, 2)$, $B'(2, -4)$, $C'(0, -1)$ **19.** $A'(-1, 2)$, $B'(-1, 5)$, $C'(2, 6)$, $D'(3, 3)$, $E'(1, -1)$

21. $\begin{matrix} S' & T' & V' \\ \begin{bmatrix} -2 & 3 & 0 \\ 4 & 2 & 1 \end{bmatrix} \end{matrix}$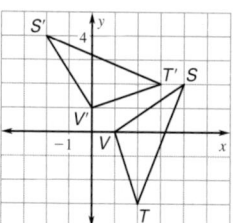

23. 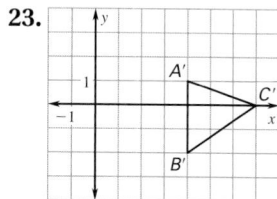 **25.**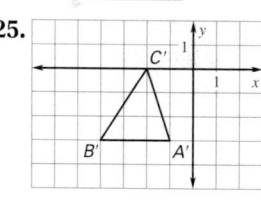

27. 88° **29.** Line symmetry, rotational symmetry; the flag has two lines of symmetry, one line passing horizontally through the center of the circle and the other passing vertically through the center of the circle; it has rotational symmetry of 180°. **31.** Line symmetry, no rotational symmetry; the flag has one line of symmetry passing vertically through the center of the rectangle; it does not have rotational symmetry.

33.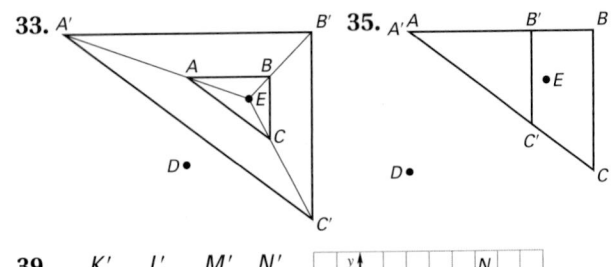

35.

39.
$$\begin{array}{cccc} K' & L' & M' & N' \\ \begin{bmatrix} 1 & 2 & 3 & \frac{5}{2} \\ -1 & -1 & 0 & 2 \end{bmatrix} \end{array}$$

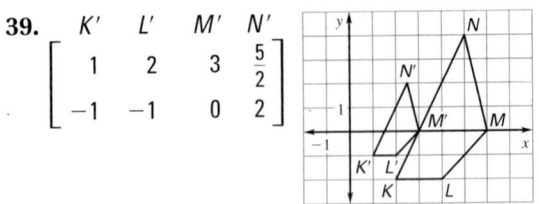

Chapter 10 (pp. 914–915) **1.** *Sample answer:* $\overline{KF}$
3. *Sample answer:* $\overleftrightarrow{CD}$ **5.** *Sample answer:* K **7.** $\overline{GH}$
9. $\frac{8}{3}$ **11.** 12 **13.** 4 **15.** minor arc; 30° **17.** minor arc;
105° **19.** minor arc; 105° **21.** 310° **23.** 130° **25.** 115°
27. 45° **29.** $\overarc{AB} \cong \overarc{DE}$ using Theorem 10.3. **31.** $x = 90°$,
$y = 50°$ **33.** $x = 25, y = 22$ **35.** $x = 7, y = 14$ **37.** 45
39. 55 **41.** 3 **43.** 2 **45.** 2 **47.** 3 **49.** $x^2 + (y + 2)^2 = 16$
51. $(x - m)^2 + (y - n)^2 = h^2 + k^2$

53.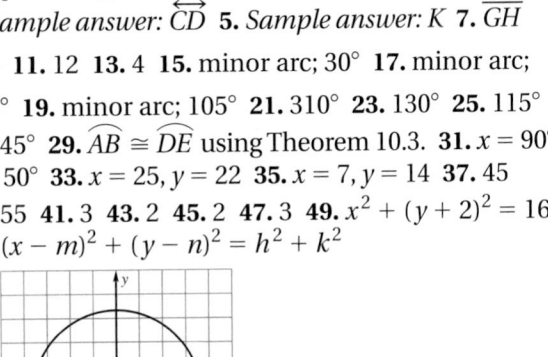

Chapter 11 (pp. 916–917) **1.** 143 units^2 **3.** 56.25 units^2
5. 60 cm, 150 cm^2 **7.** 5 **9.** 0.8 **11.** 22 units^2
13. 70 units^2 **15.** 72 units^2 **17.** 13.5 units^2 **19.** 10 : 9
21. $2\sqrt{2}$: 1 **23.** 14 m **25.** about 15.71 units **27.** about
28.27 units **29.** about 4.71 m **31.** about 2.09 in.
33. 9π in.^{2}; 28.27 in.^{2} **35.** 100π ft^2; 314.16 ft^2
37. about 9.82 in.^{2}; about 68.72 in.^{2} **39.** about 42.76 ft^2;
about 111.18 ft^2 **41.** 45° **43.** 18° **45.** 54 units,
$81\sqrt{3}$ units^2 **47.** 27 units, about 52.61 units^2
49. about 58.7% **51.** 30% **53.** 3.75%

Chapter 12 (pp. 918–919) **1.** Polyhedron; pentagonal
prism; it is a solid bounded by polygons.
3. Polyhedron; triangular pyramid; it is a solid
bounded by polygons. **5.** 6 faces **7.** 156.65 cm^2
9. 163.36 cm^2 **11.** 4285.13 in.^{2} **13.** 10 in. **15.** 14 ft
17. 16.73 cm^2 **19.** 103.67 in.^{2} **21.** 678.58 yd^2
23. 1960 cm^3 **25.** 2 cm **27.** 5.00 in. **29.** 173.21 ft^3
31. 6107.26 in.^{3} **33.** 12.66 ft^3 **35.** 40.72 in.^{2}, 24.43 in.^{3}
37. 589.65 cm^2, 1346.36 cm^3 **39.** 3848.45 mm^2,
22,449.30 mm^3 **41.** 1661.90 ft^2, 6370.63 ft^3
43. 216 ft^2, 216 ft^3 **45.** 1 : 3